BARRON'S

PROFILES OF AMERICAN COLLEGES

NORTHEAST

19TH EDITION

Regional Edition

Compiled and Edited by the College
Division of Barron's Educational Series, Inc.

All inquiries should be addressed to:
Barron's Educational Series, Inc.
250 Wireless Boulevard
Hauppauge, New York 11788
www.barronseduc.com

ISBN-13: 978-0-7641-4486-8
ISBN-10: 0-7641-4486-3

International Standard Serial No. 1075-8275

PRINTED IN THE UNITED STATES OF AMERICA
9 8 7 6 5 4 3 2 1

CONTENTS

PREFACE

The first edition of *Profiles of American Colleges*, published in 1964, was included in *Outstanding Reference books*, 1964, compiled by the Reference Services Division of the American Library Association. Revised editions have appeared regularly since then; each not only has updated facts contained in earlier editions but also has included new kinds of information. *Profiles* has become the standard college directory used by students, parents, and guidance counselors.

The newly revised Northeast edition anticipates the needs and concerns of college-bound students in the 21st century. This is a time when career choice is increasingly dictated by the demands of the job market, and students are selecting colleges with occupational goals in mind. The occupation-oriented categories of programs of study, including listings of the strongest and most popular, will help students find colleges with a program in their desired major. Students will also be able to gauge the success of each school's recent graduates by comparing percentages of graduates who found jobs or went on to graduate school within six months of graduation.

In addition, the profiles in this edition cover numerous other areas of importance. A detailed admissions section lists requirements and other factors colleges use in arriving at admissions decisions. The financial-aid information in the profiles and the article on financial aid will be especially important to many because of ever-increasing tuition costs at many schools. Statistics on financial aid awards and debt will be especially relevant.

As in the past, Barron's *Profiles of American Colleges Northeast Edition* is the most comprehensive, easy-to-use regional guide available. All four-year institutions that offer bachelor's degrees are described if they are fully accredited or are recognized candidates for accreditation. The comprehensive, readable capsule and detailed essay on each school give an easy-to-absorb, complete picture of the colleges that interest the reader. College-locator maps help pinpoint the geographic area of schools in each state.

The capsule of each profile lists important information for quick reference: address and phone and fax numbers; enrollment; calendar; fall application deadline; size and salary level of the faculty; percentage of faculty members who hold doctorates; student/faculty ratio; tuition and fees; room and board costs; the number of students who applied to the freshman class, were accepted, and enrolled; the median SAT and/or ACT scores for 2007–2008; and finally, the College Admissions Selector Rating for the school. The information in the essay portion of each profile ranges from available housing and the financial aid climate to admissions requirements and the success of graduates. There are 21 categories of information under eight main headings: Student Life, Programs of Study, Admissions, Financial Aid, International Students, Computers, Graduates, and web site and Admissions Contact. The Admissions Contact section also gives e-mail address and DVD availability.

Several other features in this edition will be especially helpful to parents and students alike: two self-help questionnaires aimed at helping students set priorities and an article giving advice on surviving the freshman year. There is more information on tutoring and remedial math, reading, and writing programs. Information about faculty, size of classes, and whether graduate students teach any introductory courses are also part of this edition. The College Admissions Selector, Barron's rating of colleges and universities by degree of admissions competitiveness, will help students assess their chances of being accepted by various schools.

We are confident that all of these features make this new Northeast edition of *Profiles* the best guide available to the college-bound student.

A Word of Thanks

To all the college admissions officers, to participating high school advisers, to the students, parents, and other supporters of Barron's *Profiles of American Colleges*, we offer our sincere thanks.

Grateful acknowledgment is made to the late Gloria M. Barron, who inspired the editors and production personnel to create a book that would offer every possible assistance in selecting the best college.

We acknowledge with thanks the demanding editing tasks performed by Editor Darrell Buono and Editorial Assistant Lena Perfetto, along with the database designers and our hard-working editing and data entry staff.

CONTRIBUTORS

Steven R. Antonoff, Ph.D.
Educational Consultant
Antonoff Associates, Inc.
Denver, Colorado

Barbara J. Aronson
Career Center Coordinator
Miramonte High School
Orinda, California

Anthony F. Capraro, III, Ph.D.
President, Teach Inc.
College Counseling
Larchmont, New York

Marguerite J. Dennis
Vice President for
Enrollment and International
Programs
Suffolk University
Boston, Massachusetts

Benjamin W. Griffith
Former Dean of the
Graduate School
West Georgia College
Carrolton, Georgia

Sheldon Halpern
Former Dean
Enrollment Management
Caldwell College
Caldwell, New Jersey

Ira Wolf, Ph.D.
President, PowerPrep, Inc.
Roslyn Heights, New York

---

*SAT is a registered trademark owned by the College Entrance Examination Board. No endorsement of this product is implied or given.

You have in your hands a book that will give you answers to your questions about the qualities and features of more than 1650 colleges. But before you start reading the descriptions and getting the answers, you need to know what questions to ask about finding the college that is right for you. Although you need to ask questions about "getting in" i.e., exploring colleges in terms of ease of admission for you, most of your questions should focus on the more significant issue of "fitting in." Fitting in means finding a college where you will be comfortable; where you are compatible with your peers, and where the overall atmosphere encourages your growth as a student and as a person.

This article is designed to help you assess some values and attitudes that will help you determine where you will fit in. It will enable you to ask the right questions. Not all colleges are for everyone; careful thinking about your interests, ideals, and values will lead you to find the college that is right for you. Colleges are not "good" or "bad" in a generic sense; they are either good or bad matches for you.

The two assessments that follow will be helpful in thinking about yourself as a future college student; they should help you make the right college choice.

THE COLLEGE PLANNING VALUES ASSESSMENT

Students have different reasons for going to college. Eleven reasons or values are found to be most important to students as they think about college. Knowing about your values is the important first step in identifying the colleges where you will fit in and be happy.

To complete the assessment, read through the list of ten values—A through K. Think about the outcomes you hope college will produce for you. Each student will rank them differently; hence, there are no "right" answers. Whereas several, or even most, of these values may be significant for you in one way or another, the goal is to decide which three are the most important. After you read each of the values, go back and circle the THREE most important ones on the basis of the following question:

What do you want college to do for you?
—— A. To provide me with a place to learn and study.
—— B. To provide me with opportunities to interact with teachers inside and outside the classroom.
—— C. To provide me with lots of fun experiences.
—— D. To prepare me to make a lot of money.
—— E. To provide me with recognition for accomplishments.
—— F. To get politically involved and/or to use much of my college years to help those who are disadvantaged.
—— G. To help me prepare for a career.
—— H. To enable me to be more independent.
—— I. To provide opportunities for me to grow religiously or spiritually.
—— J. To provide me with a variety of new experiences.
—— K. To enable me to receive a degree from a prestigious school.

What do your college planning values say about you?

If **A** was among the top three priorities on your list, you will want to explore the academic character of the colleges you are considering. Although all colleges are, by definition, intellectual centers, some put more priority on challenging students and pushing them to their limits. Reading about the academic features of the colleges you are considering will be important. (In the college Profiles, pay attention to the *special* section to learn about these features.) Your high ranking of this value says that you will be able to take advantage of intellectual opportunities at college. You may want to select a college where your SAT scores are similar to or slightly above the ranges of other admitted students—at those colleges you will be able to shine academically. You may desire to take an active part in

classroom discussions and will want a college where the student faculty ratio is low.

If **B** was among your top three priorities, you feel challenged and stimulated by academics and classroom learning. You will want to find a college where your mind will be stretched. You will want to choose a college where you can explore a range of new academic subjects. A liberal arts and sciences college may give you an enriching breadth of academic offerings. You will want to look for a college where academic clubs are popular and where you have a good chance of knowing professors and sharing ideas with them. Access to faculty is important to you and you will want to look at the student faculty ratio in colleges you consider. Also note the ratio of undergraduate students to graduate students. Primarily undergraduate institutions will be the colleges that may best be able to meet your needs, because you will be the focus of teachers' attention. Teachers at such colleges place their priority on teaching and are not distracted by the needs of graduate students or by pressure to balance teaching and student time with research and writing.

If **C** was circled, you derive satisfaction from social opportunities. You will want a college where the academic demands will not diminish your ability to socialize. You likely will want a good balance between the social and academic sides of campus life. You will want to explore the percentage of students who get involved in intramural sports, clubs, or fraternities and sororities. (This information is listed in each college profile.) Look at your college choices on the basis of school spirit and sporting events offered. The profiles list popular campus events—see if they sound exciting to you. Also look at the percentage of students who stay on campus over the weekend. You will also want a college where it is easy to make friends. Both small and larger colleges would be appropriate for you. Although a larger college would expose you to more students and a larger quantity of potential friends, studies show that students at smaller colleges become more involved in activities and build deep friendships more quickly. Look for supportiveness and camaraderie in the student body.

If **D** is circled, you will want to consider earning potential, advancement opportunities, and the future market for the careers you consider. You will want to consider this value in your career planning. Remember, however, that there is no sure road to riches! You not only must pick a career direction carefully, but must choose a college where the potential for academic success—good grades—is high. The name of a particular college is less important than good grades or contributions to campus life when securing a good job or being admitted to graduate school. Even if you find that a particular career has tremendous earning potential, those earnings may come to only those who are most successful in the profession. Look at average salaries, but also consider your interests, values, and personality before making your final career choice. Be sure to take advantage of hands-on learning opportunities. Perhaps, for example, there are internships that meet your needs. Also, finding good, career-focused summer jobs can be helpful.

If **E** is high on your list, you take pleasure in being known for your success in an area of interest. For instance, you might feel good about being recognized or known in school as a good student, a top athlete, or a leader in a club. No doubt this type of recognition contributes to your confidence. You might look for colleges where you will be able to acquire or continue to receive this recognition. Often, recognition is easier to achieve at smaller colleges where you would not be competing against large numbers of students hoping to achieve the same recognition. You will also want to choose colleges where it is easy to get involved and where the activities offered are appealing to you. You may want to consider the benefits of being a "big fish in a small pond."

If **F** is important, that value will no doubt guide your vocational or avocational pursuits. You may find yourself choosing a career in which this value can be fulfilled, or you may seek opportunities on a college campus where you can be of service to others. You will want to choose a college where community service is valued. Look at the *activities* section and note whether community service-related involvements are available. Colleges vary a great deal in terms of political awareness. At some colleges, students are attuned to national and international events, often express feelings about current issues and policies, and in general, show interest in political affairs. Students at other colleges show little or no interest in these matters and find other ways to interact with peers.

If **G** was circled, you may know what career you want to pursue or you may be concerned but uncertain about your career decision. If you have tentatively selected a career, you will want to choose a college where you can take courses leading to the attainment of a degree in your chosen field. Explore the *programs of study* section in the profiles to determine whether a college you are considering offers the course work you desire. You will want to make a note of the most popular majors and the strongest majors as they are listed. If you don't yet know what career would suit you, remember, that for most careers, a broad, solid liberal arts foundation is considered good preparation. You will want to look at opportunities for internships and take advantage of the career planning and placement office at your chosen college. Finding a career that will be fulfilling is one of the most important choices you will make in your life. Your selection of a college will be your first step toward achieving your career goal.

If **H** is circled, it suggests that personal autonomy is important to you. College is, in general, a time for independence, and students are often anxious to make their own decisions without parental involvement. If you feel you can handle lots of independence, you will want to look for colleges where there is some freedom in choosing courses and where students are given responsibility for their own lives. Colleges vary in terms of these factors. Note particularly the *required* section under *programs of study*, which tells you the courses that must be fulfilled by all students. Be certain that you will not be stifled by too many rules and regulations. You may also want to look for colleges where the personal development of students receives high priority. A priority on independence also suggests that you will be comfortable being away from home and on your own.

If **I** is one of your top three choices, you will want to look first at the religious affiliation of each of your college options. There are two ways to consider religious life on college campuses. First is the question of how religion affects the day-to-day life of the college. For example, are biblical references made in class? Are religious convocations mandatory? Second is the question of whether there is a religious heritage at the college. Many hundreds of colleges have historical relationships with a religious denomination, but this tie does not affect the rules or the general life of the students. (For example, the college may have a certain number of religion classes required to graduate, but these classes are typically broad-based and not doctrinal.) You may want a college that has a relationship with your particular religious group. Or you may desire a large number of students who belong to the same denomination as you do. The profiles will also give you the percentage of students who are members of the major religious denominations. As you explore colleges, you will also want to see if the college has a commitment to the values and ideals held by you or your family.

If **J** is appealing, you like newness and will likely be stimulated by new experiences and new activities. You are in for a treat at most colleges. New experiences are the "stuff" of which college life is made. You may see college-going as an adventure and will want to pick colleges where you can meet your need for stimulation and excitement. Because you value newness, you should not hesitate to attend college in a different part of the country or to experience an environment or a climate that is quite different from your high school. You will also want to look for evidence of diversity in the student body. As you read the descriptions, look for colleges with lots of new opportunities for growth and for personal expansion.

If **K** is appealing, be cautious. Students who are overly concerned about this value might find college planning traumatic, and even painful, because of the admission

selectivity of "name brand" colleges. Even though it is perfectly acceptable for students to be attuned to the overall excellence of a college, academic quality and prestige are not the same thing. Some colleges are well-known because of, say, a fine football team or because of academic excellence in a subject like psychology or physics. Although it is appropriate to look for a strong faculty and a highly regarded college, you want a college that will give you the greatest chance of academic success. It is success in college, not just academic reputation or prestige, that will lead to admission into graduate school or a broad selection of jobs.

Now that you've read about your top three values, answer the following question on a separate sheet of paper: In your own words, what do your top three values say about what you are looking for in a college? Then, share that information with your college adviser as he or she assists you in finding colleges that are right for you.

SELF-KNOWLEDGE QUESTIONNAIRE

The following seven items—A–G—will help you in thinking about yourself as a college student and the ease with which you will likely proceed through the college selection process. Read each statement and determine whether it is true or not true of you. After each question, you will see numbers ranging from 1 to 5. Circle 1 if the statement is very true of you. Circle 5 if the statement is not true of you. Use 2, 3, or 4 to reflect varying levels of preference. Be realistic and honest.

A. My academic abilities for college (such as reading, writing, and note taking) are good.
Very true of me   1   2   3   4   5   Not true of me
Academic abilities such as reading speed and comprehension, writing, note taking, calculating, speaking, and listening are important for college students. You will be called upon to use such skills in your college classes. If you are confident about your academic skills, you can approach picking a college with the ease of knowing that you will be able to master the academic rigors of college life. If you circled 3, 4, or 5 you will want to work on these skills in your remaining days in high school. You will want to choose colleges where you can work to strengthen these skills. Some colleges provide a learning skills center in which you are able to get help if you are having difficulty writing a paper or understanding the content of a class. If you are less than confident, you might look to colleges where you will not be intimidated by the skills of the other students.

B. My study skills and time management are good.
Very true of me   1   2   3   4   5   Not true of me
Study skills and time management are two of the most important qualities for an efficient and productive college student. Successful college students are average or above in organizing themselves for studying, scheduling, and using study time productively, and differentiating important content of a lecture or a book from supplementary information. In addition, they complete assignments on time and don't get flustered if they have several papers or a couple of tests due on the same day. If you circled 3, 4, or 5, it is important to work on improving these skills during your remaining high school days. You might consider the following:
- Seek help from your parents, a teacher, a counselor, or a learning specialist in becoming more organized.
- Try keeping a calendar. Anticipate each step necessary in preparing for every test and every paper.
- Be responsible for your own appointments.
- Check to see if a study skills course is offered at a local community college or university. Or consider reading a book on study skills.

C. I am motivated to succeed in college.
Very true of me   1   2   3   4   5   Not true of me
Motivation is definitely the most important skill you bring to college. Those students who want to succeed do succeed! Studies show that it is motivation, not your SAT scores, that determines academic success in college. And motivation means knowing not only that you want to go to college, but

that you also want to be a student. Some students want to go to college for the fun aspects, but forget that college is primarily an academic experience. So if you circled 1 or 2, great, you're off to a good start. If you circled 3, 4, or 5, it may be an appropriate time to consider your wants and needs in a college. What sort of college would help motivate you? Would a college with a balance between academics and social life be appealing? Would you be more motivated if you were near a large and interesting city? Would nice weather be a distraction rather than an energizer? Is a trade or technical school best for you? Have you considered taking some time off between high school and college? Considering such questions is important, and the time to do that exploration is now.

D. I am a good decision maker.

Very true of me   1   2   3   4   5   Not true of me

Decisions, decisions, decisions. The college selection process is full of decisions! What colleges will I initially consider? To which colleges will I apply for admission? What college will I eventually attend? You will be facing these decisions in the upcoming months. If you circled 1 or 2, you are on your way. If you circled 3, 4, or 5, think about an important decision you made recently. Why didn't it go well? If you can analyze your decision-making weakness in that situation, it may help to avoid any potential pitfalls in your college decision-making. The following suggestions will help you improve your ability to make the right college choice:

- Clearly articulate what you're looking for in a college. Write down those features that will make a college right for you.
- Involve lots of people and resources in your search for a college. Your parents, counselors, and friends can help you.
- List and compare pros and cons of alternative colleges. Every college has both.
- Evaluate each college on the basis of the criteria you set for yourself.

Remember, you're looking for a college where you will get in and fit in.

E. I'm a good information gatherer; for example, I am usually able to find books, articles, and so on to help me do a research paper for, say, a history class.

Very true of me   1   2   3   4   5   Not true of me

Finding a college requires you to be a good researcher. There is so much information about colleges to sort through and analyze. If you feel you can do good research, fine, you're on your way. If you circled 3, 4, or 5, the following ideas may be helpful:

- Start with this book and look for colleges that are consistent with what you want. Remember that your primary concern is where you will fit in. Use your college-going values and your responses in this questionnaire to guide your thinking about colleges that will match you.
- Work closely with your college counselor, and seek impressions from students and others with reliable and up-to-date information about colleges of interest. You will make a better decision with credible and extensive input.
- Look for differences in features that are important to you. Is ease of making friends important to you? What about balance between academics and social life? Do you want teachers to know you?

F. I feel I adapt to new situations easily.

Very true of me   1   2   3   4   5   Not true of me

Everyone goes through changes in life. Some move through transition periods with great ease, others find them more difficult. You may have experienced the changes that come after a change of schools (even from middle school to high school), the illness or death of a relative, or the divorce of your parents. If you circled 1 or 2, you are not likely to be intimidated by a college in another part of the country or a college very different from your high school. If you circled 3, 4, or 5, you may want to carefully look at colleges that are a bit closer to home or colleges where the same values, perceptions, and attitudes exist as were true in your high school. Almost everyone has fear and apprehension about leaving for college. But if that fear is significant, you will want to choose a college where you will feel comfortable. Visits to college campuses may be particularly significant in feeling good about potential choices.

G. It is easy for me to meet people and establish friendships.

Very true of me   1   2   3   4   5   Not true of me

Identifying and nurturing friendships is an important skill for college adjustment. If you circled 3, 4, or 5, you will want to look carefully at colleges where there are few cliques, where there is an atmosphere of sharing, and where students report that it is relatively easy to integrate into the campus environment. Your choice of a college is a quest for a good social fit. Your thorough review of the profiles and even visits to college campuses will be helpful in assuring your ability to fit in and be comfortable.

FINAL THOUGHTS

If you took time to carefully consider the issues raised in both the Values Assessment and the Self-Knowledge Questionnaire, you should have gained new insights and perspectives about yourself. You will want to share these results with your parents and with your guidance counselor. Elicit their help in getting more insight as to how they see you as a prospective college student. Finally, two suggestions:

- As you research colleges, consider what you have learned about yourself. You want a college that is a good match with your values and interests.
- Spend time on your college search. It will take many hours of organized planning and investigation. But the time spent will result in a better choice and a greater likelihood that you will spend four productive and exciting years in college.

Good luck. There are lots of colleges out there that want you. Let your knowledge of yourself and your objective analysis of potential college options guide you to college environments where you will be able to shine. Success in college is in your hands. Make the most of the opportunity.

Steven R. Antonoff, Ph.D., Certified Educational Planner
Educational Consultant
Antonoff Associates, Inc.
Denver, Colorado

When it's right, something inside you will ignite a singularly focused pursuit and you'll find it difficult to look anywhere else.

Sarah Caldwell, Bryn Mawr, Class of 2008

Start your college search positively. Start with the knowledge that there are many schools out there that want you. Start with the idea that there are many good college choices for every student. Too often these days, articles on college admission make students and their parents apprehensive. You can have choices. You can get financial aid. You can have a happy, successful college career.

When you begin to think about college, you are embarking on a major research project. You have many choices available to you in order to get the best possible education for which you are qualified. This article is intended to help you think of some of the important variables in your college search.

Let us help make the book work for you!

THE CURRENT ADMISSION SCENE

Today there are approximately 2,000 four-year colleges and universities, as well as an additional 300 nontraditional, four-year institutions. Most existing institutions have grown larger, and many have expanded their programs, offering master's and doctoral degrees as well as bachelor's.

Total graduate and undergraduate students has also grown, from under 4 million in 1960 to more than 16 million today. In fact, between 2000 and 2013 total enrollment at U.S. colleges and universities is expected to rise 19 percent, to 18.2 million students. Almost 40 percent are part-time students, including many working adults. Part-time enrollments are mostly concentrated in the two-year colleges, which enroll about a third of all students.

What does this all mean to you? There is good news and bad news. The good news is that most of the colleges you will read about in this book are colleges you can get into! In other words, the vast majority of colleges in the U.S. admit more than 70 percent of those who apply. Many hundreds admit all of those who apply. So, on one level, you shouldn't worry that you won't be able to get a college education. The bad news is for the student with extremely high grades who seeks admission to the 50 or so most competitive colleges in the country. These "brand name" colleges have many times more candidates than they admit. Even incredibly qualified students are sometimes denied admission.

The key to good college planning is, as mentioned above, research. Find out about what makes one college different from another. Find out what students say about their experiences. Rely on many sources of information—many people, many books, many web sites, and so on. There are lots of people and materials available to help you. This book is one of them. Let the information be your guide. But also let your instincts and your sense of what's best for you play a part. The higher education opportunities in the U.S. are unlimited. The opportunity to let education help pave the way to achieving your dreams is a worthy goal of your college search.

MAKING A SHORT LIST

You have probably already started a list of colleges you know about from friends or relatives who have attended them, from recommendations by counselors or teachers, or by their academic or social reputations. This list will grow as you read the Profiles, receive college mailings, and attend college fairs. If you are interested in preparing for a very specific career, such as engineering, agriculture, nursing, or architecture, you should add only institutions that offer that program. If you want to study business, teacher education, or the arts and sciences, almost every college can provide a suitable major. Either way, your list will soon include dozens of institutions. Most students apply to between four and seven colleges. To narrow your list, you should keep the following process in mind:

- As you explore, be attuned to the admission requirements. You will want to have colleges on your list that span the admission selectivity continuum—from "reach" colleges (those where your grades, test scores, etc., suggest less chance of admission) to "safety" schools (those where your credentials are a bit better than the average student admitted), eliminating colleges at which you clearly would not qualify for admission.
- You also will want to keep an eye on cost. You want to consider colleges that are generally in line with your family's ability to finance your education. Be very cautious as you do this. Literally millions of dollars are available each year for students. There is both "need-based" aid (aid based on your family's ability to pay) and "merit-based" aid (aid based on such things as grades, test scores, and leadership ability).
- Screen the list according to your preferences, such as size, academic competitiveness, religious focus, and location.
- Make quality judgments, using published information and campus visits, to decide which colleges can give you the best quality and value.

The following sections are organized around the factors most important in researching a college. Discussion of admission competitiveness and cost comes first. After that, a wide range of factors important to consider as you evaluate colleges is examined. These include size, housing, the faculty, academic programs, internships, accreditation, libraries and computer technology, and religious/racial considerations. The final two sections are a discussion of campus visits and, finally, a checklist of 25 important questions to ask about each of the colleges you are exploring.

In the end, you must allow yourself to be a good decision maker. You will have to make some quality judgments. It is not as difficult as you may think. You have to be willing to read the information in this book and the literature that the schools make available, to visit a few campuses, and to ask plenty of questions. Usually you can ask questions of the admissions office by regular mail, e-mail, or in person during a campus visit. Because colleges sincerely are interested in helping you make the right choice, they generally will welcome your questions and answer them politely and honestly. In addition, your high school counselor is a key person who can offer advice and guidance. Finally, there are many resources available, in printed form and on the web, to help you.

SELECTION FACTORS

Admissions Competitiveness

The first question most students ask about a college is, "How hard is it to get in?" It should certainly not be the last question. Admissions competitiveness is not the only, or even the most important, measurement of institutional quality. It makes sense to avoid wasting time, money, and useless disappointment applying to institutions for which you clearly are not qualified. Nevertheless, there are many colleges for which you are qualified, and you can make a good choice from among them. The most prestigious institutions are rarely affected by market conditions. Most of the better known private and public colleges and universities have raised their admission standards in recent years. But there remain hundreds of fine public and private colleges, with good local reputations, that will welcome your application.

Use the College Admissions Selector to compare your qualifications to the admissions competitiveness of the institutions of your list. Make sure you read the descriptions of standards very carefully. Even if you meet the stated qualifications for *Most Competitive* or *Highly Competitive* institutions, you cannot assume that you will be offered admission. These colleges receive applications from many more students than they can enroll and reject far more than they accept. When considering colleges rated *Very Competitive* or *Competitive*, remember that the median test scores identify the middle of the most recent freshman class;

half of the admitted students had scores lower than the median, and half were above. Students of average ability are admissible to most of the colleges and universities rated as *Competitive* and to virtually all of those rated as *Less Competitive*.

Cost

The basic cost of the most expensive colleges and universities can exceed $40,000 a year. This is widely publicized and very frightening, especially to your parents. But you don't have to spend that much for a good education. Private colleges charge an average of nearly $30,000 a year for tuition and room and board. Public institutions generally cost an average of $14,000 a year for in-state residents. Because many states have been cutting budgets in recent years, tuition at public institutions is now rising faster than at private ones. If you can commute to school from home, you can save about $6000 to $7000 in room and board, but should add the cost of transportation. The least expensive option is to attend a local community college for two years, at about $1500 a year, and then transfer to a four-year institution to complete your bachelor's degree. Depending on what you may qualify for in financial aid, and what your family is willing to sacrifice, you may have more choices than you think.

Size

Only one-fifth of American colleges and universities have enrollments of 5000 or more, but they account for more than half the ten million plus students who are pursuing bachelor's degrees. The rest are spread out among more than 1000 smaller schools. There are advantages and disadvantages that go with size.

At a college of 5000 or fewer students, you will get to know the campus quickly. You will not have to compete with many other students when registering for courses or for use of the library or other facilities. You can get to know your professors personally and become familiar with most of your fellow students. On the other hand, the school may not have as many majors and it may have less emphasis on spectator sports. Students at small schools are not able to be as "anonymous" as those at larger schools.

As colleges and universities enroll more students, they offer more courses and activities. Within a large campus community, you can probably find others who share your special interests and form a circle of good friends. But you may also find the facilities more crowded, classes closed out, and competition very stiff for athletic teams or musical groups.

Many of the largest institutions are universities offering medical, law, or other doctoral programs as well as bachelor's and master's degrees. Many colleges that do not offer these programs call themselves universities; and a few universities, Dartmouth among them, continue to call themselves colleges. Don't go by the name, but by the academic program. Universities emphasize research. University faculty need specialized laboratory equipment, computers, library material, and technical assistance for their research. Colleges tend to emphasize teaching.

Because research is very expensive, universities usually charge higher tuition than colleges, even to their undergraduate students. In effect, undergraduates at universities subsidize the high cost of graduate programs. Freshmen and sophomores usually receive some instruction from graduate student assistants and fellows, who are paid to be apprentice faculty members.

Of course, many larger private universities, and many public ones, have fine reputations. They have larger and more up-to-date libraries, laboratories, computers, and other special resources than colleges. They attract students from many states and countries and provide a rich social and cultural environment.

Housing

Deciding whether you will stay in a residence hall or at home is more than a matter of finances or how close to the college you live. You should be aware that students who live on campus, especially during the freshman year, are more likely to pass their courses and graduate than students who commute from home. Campus residents spend more time with faculty members, have more opportunity to use the library and laboratories, and are linked to other students who help one another with their studies. Residence hall life usually helps students mature faster as they participate in social and organizational activities.

If you commute to school, you can get maximum benefits from your college experience by spending time on campus between and after classes. If you need a part-time job, get employment in the college library, offices, or dining halls. Use the library to do homework in an environment that may be less distracting than home. If possible, have some dinners on campus, to make friends with other students and participate in evening social and cultural events. Get involved in campus activities, participating in athletics, working on the newspaper, attending a meeting, or rehearsing a play.

You will have a choice of food plans. Most meal plans include a certain number of meals per week. Other plans allow you to prepay a fixed dollar amount and purchase food by the item rather than by the meal. Choose a meal plan that fits your own eating habits. Most colleges today offer a tremendous variety of food and are accommodating to most diets and preferences.

Many students live off campus after their freshman or sophomore year, either by choice or because the school does not have room for them on campus. Schools try to provide listings of available off-campus rooms and apartments that meet good standards for safety and cleanliness. Many colleges also offer health care and food services to students who live off campus.

It is usually more expensive to live in an apartment than in a residence hall, especially if you plan to prepare your own meals. But that option is appealing to some students, particularly those in their junior or senior years.

The Faculty

The most important resources of any college or university are its professors. Admissions brochures usually point out the strengths of the faculty, but provide little detail. You should direct your questions about the faculty and other academic matters to the specific department or to the office that coordinates academic advising. Recruiting brochures also emphasize faculty research, because the prestige of professors depends largely on the books and articles they have published. Good researchers may or may not make good teachers. Ask how often the best researchers teach undergraduate courses, and whether they instruct small as well as large classes. For example, a Nobel prize chemist may lecture to 500 students at a time but never show up in the laboratories where graduate assistants actually teach individual students.

Also ask about class size, because this determines the amount of individual attention students get from professors. Student/faculty ratios, which usually range from 10 to 20 students per professor, don't really tell you much. Every school offers a mixture of large and small classes. Ask admission officers for the average size of a freshman class. You will want to look for such factors as those that follow:

- Science and technology courses should enroll only 25 to 30 students in each laboratory session, but may combine a number of laboratory classes for large weekly lectures.
- Skill development courses such as speech, foreign language, English composition, and fine and performing arts should have classes of 25 or fewer. Mathematics and computer science require considerable graded homework, and classes should be no larger than 35.
- Most other courses in humanities, social sciences, and professional areas are taught by classroom lectures and discussion. Classes should average 35 to 45 in introductory courses such as general psychology or American government. They should be smaller in advanced or specialized courses, such as Shakespeare or tax accounting.
- Many introductory courses, especially at universities, are taught in lecture classes of 100 or more. This is acceptable, if those courses also include small weekly discussion

groups for individual instruction. Sometimes these discussion groups are taught by graduate student assistants rather than regular professors. Although graduate assistants lack teaching experience, they are very often highly capable. You should ask whether the teaching done by graduate assistants is closely supervised by regular faculty members.

Academic Programs

Even colleges and universities that boast fine and well qualified faculties can be short of professors in certain programs. Some schools depend on instruction by part-time faculty members or fill in with available teachers from other specializations. Many international students are enrolled in technical doctoral programs, so you may find yourself being taught mathematics or engineering by a teaching assistant who is not a native English speaker. If you are interested in these subjects, check to see whether full-time faculty members teach the majority of the courses.

Other programs may have sufficient faculty but too few student majors. Majors such as physics and philosophy, for example, often have many students in required introductory courses, but few taking the major. Because of small enrollments, these departments may not be able to offer their advanced and specialized courses on a regular basis.

Academic departments give strength to the program by bringing together faculty members who share a common area of study and make sure their students get the classes they need. Some programs, usually called interdisciplinary, are taught by groups of faculty members from several departments. These programs generally have the word studies in their titles; for example, Middle-Eastern Studies, Communication Studies, Women's Studies, or Ethnic Studies. If you are enrolled in one of these programs, be sure to ask about the student advising. (Sometimes, advising suffers if faculty members are primarily loyal to their own department.)

Internships

Internships are available at many colleges. They provide an opportunity to experience work in your major and learn from experienced people in your field. Many students have received job offers after participating in an internship program during the school year or during summer vacation. These internships can make a big difference as you enter the job market.

Accreditation

General standards of academic quality are established by associations of colleges and universities through a process called voluntary accreditation. The criteria include: standards for admission of students; faculty qualifications; content of courses; grading standards; professional success of alumni; adequacy of libraries, laboratories, computers, and other support facilities; administrative systems and policy decision making; and financial support.

Six regional associations (New England, Middle States, Southern, North Central, Northwest, and Western) evaluate and accredit colleges as total institutions. Bible colleges have their own accrediting association. Other organizations evaluate and accredit specific programs, primarily in technical fields, like engineering and architecture; or those that require licensing, such as teaching and health care.

Libraries and Computer Technology

Most people judge libraries by the size of the collection, the bigger the better. Collection size is important, but only in relation to the variety and level of programs offered. A small liberal arts college can support its baccalaureate programs with a collection of 200,000 to 400,000 volumes. A university with many professional schools and doctoral programs may require over 2 million. Many books and journals are available through various methods of information technology, computer storage, and the Internet.

The main stacks should be open to students, with the possible exception of rare books, bound journals, and other special items. Open stacks encourage browsing and save students from waiting on line while a library assistant fetches a few books at a time. Instead, assistants constantly should be picking up unused materials from reading desks or carts and putting them back on the shelves.

Good circulation policies encourage students to check materials out for short periods and to return them promptly. One week or less loans are appropriate for books regularly used in courses, and four week loans should be the maximum for other materials. A recall system should be available to get back borrowed material when it is needed. Journals, reference material, or books placed on reserve for assigned reading should be used within the library while it is open, and circulated overnight only at closing time.

Using a computer is integral to university study. Some institutions require students to have personal computers. Colleges often offer the best price for new computers. You may want to check out the options on campus before you purchase a computer elsewhere. Many residence hall rooms are wired for computers and direct connections are linked to the main campus system. More and more campuses have wireless capability.

Religious/Ethnic Considerations

For some students, the religious life of the campus is important as college choices are reviewed. Religious life can vary from being pervasive to being absent. Most colleges are independent of religious influence. Some are historically affiliated with a religious group, yet religious matters are not part of student life. Other schools exist, in part, to educate students in the doctrine and the practices of their own religious perspective. Information you find on these pages will give you answers to some of your initial questions about religious life at particular schools.

If connecting with and learning from members of your racial/ethnic heritage is important, you will find many colleges and universities from which to choose. Again, this guide provides information about the diversity of the campus and the composition of students who are white, African-American, Hispanic, Asian-American, Latino, and so forth.

GETTING THE MOST FROM YOUR CAMPUS VISIT

It is best not to eliminate any options without at least visiting a few campuses of different types to judge their feeling and style first hand.

To learn everything important about a college, you need more than the standard presentation and tour given to visiting students and parents. Plan your visit for a weekday during the school term. This will let you see how classes are taught and how students live. It also is the best time to meet faculty and staff members. If the college does not schedule group presentations or tours at the time you want, call the office of admissions to arrange for an individual tour and interview. (This is more likely at a small college.) At the same time, ask the admissions office to make appointments with people you want to meet.

To find out about a specific academic program, ask to meet the department chairperson or a professor. If you are interested in athletics, religion, or music, arrange to meet with the coach, the chaplain, or the conductor of the orchestra. Your parents will also want to talk to a financial aid counselor about scholarships, grants, and loans. The office of academic affairs can help with your questions about courses or the faculty. The office of student affairs is in charge of residence halls, health services, and extracurricular activities. Each of these areas has a dean or vice president and a number of assistants, so you should be able to get your questions answered even if you go in without an appointment.

Take advantage of a group presentation and tour if one is scheduled on the day of your visit. Much of what you learn may be familiar, but other students and parents will ask about some of the same things you want to know. Student tour guides are also good sources of information. They love to talk about their own courses, professors, and campus experiences.

Finally, explore the campus on your own. Check the condition of the buildings and the grounds. If they appear well maintained, the college probably has good overall management. If they look run down, the college may have financial problems that also make it scrimp on the book budget or laboratory supplies. Visit a service office, such as the registrar, career planning, or academic advising. Observe whether they treat students courteously and seem genuinely interested in helping them. Look at bulletin boards for signs of campus activities.

And, perhaps most importantly, talk to some of the students who are already enrolled at the college. They will usually speak frankly about weekend activities, whether they find it easy to talk to professors out of class, and how much drinking or drug abuse there is on campus. Most importantly, meeting other students will help you discover how friendly the campus is and whether the college will suit you socially and intellectually.

More than buildings and courses of study, a college is a community of people. Only during a campus visit can you experience the human environment in which you will live and work during four critical years.

25 CRITICAL QUESTIONS

The following questions form a checklist to evaluate each college or university you are considering. Use the profiles, material from the colleges, and your own inquiries and observations to get the answers.

1. Do I have a reasonable chance of being admitted?
2. Can my family manage the costs?
3. Is the overall size of the school right for my personality?
4. Is the location right? (Consider such specifics as region, distance from a major city, distance from home, and weather.)
5. Are class sizes right for my learning style and my need for involvement in class?
6. Will I be comfortable with the setting of the campus?
7. Are the housing and food services suitable?
8. Does the college offer the program I want to study? (Or, often more importantly, does the college offer people and classes that will help me decide what I want to study?)
9. Will the college push me academically, but not shove me?
10. Do the best professors teach undergraduate courses?
11. Can I change majors easily, if I need to?
12. Do students say the majority of classes are taught by fun, stimulating, interesting professors?
13. Is the library collection adequate and accessible?
14. Are computer facilities readily available and are campus networking opportunities up-to-date?
15. Is the connection to the Internet adequate?
16. Are there resources for career development?
17. Do the people in the financial aid, housing, and other service offices seem attentive and genuinely interested in helping students?
18. Will I find activities that meet my interests?
19. Does the campus seem well maintained and managed?
20. Will the college meet my religious and/or ethnic needs?

And, finally, the five most critical questions:

21. Is there a good chance I will be academically successful there?
22. Will I be happy as a student there?
23. Do I seem compatible with the student population? Do they seem to enjoy what I enjoy?
24. Does the student life seem in sync with my personality and my goals? Is the student life what I'm looking for in a college?
25. Does the college "feel" right for me?

Steven R. Antonoff
Sheldon Halpern
Barbara Aronson

High scores mean different things to different schools, but they can make or break your chances.
Raymond A. Lutzky, Rensselaer Polytechnic Institute, Class of 2002

COLLEGE ENTRANCE EXAMINATIONS

By providing you with exactly the same information about each of the colleges in which you are interested, the book you are now reading, *Profiles of American Colleges*, will help you narrow down the list of colleges to which you will apply. Of course, your final decision will be influenced by many other factors, many of which are far more important: actual visits to the colleges; virtual visits on the Internet; viewings of videotapes; advice from guidance counselors, parents, teachers, and friends.

In much the same way, by providing college admissions officers with the same information about thousands of applicants, the results of college entrance exams can help them narrow down the list of students they are considering accepting. The results of these exams help admissions officers compare students with widely differing backgrounds. Students from different high schools in different states who earn the same grade in their biology classes, B+ say, have used different textbooks, have performed different labs, have taken different tests, and in general often exhibit great disparity in their level of mastery of the subject; indeed, even within the same school, a grade of B+ from one teacher might not represent the same level of accomplishment as a B+ from another teacher. However, a grade of 650 on the Biology SAT Subject Test, or a 4 on the Biology AP test means the same thing whether it was earned by a student from a rural community in Idaho, an inner-city school in New York, or a private prep school in Massachusetts. Because students all across the country take the same standardized test on the same day, colleges can give greater credence to the results of those tests, than they can to the results of final exams from different schools.

KINDS OF COLLEGE ENTRANCE EXAMINATIONS

Although some students who go from high school to two-year community colleges do not take any college entrance tests, most do, and virtually all students who are applying to four-year colleges will take some of the following exams:
- PSAT/NMSQT or the Preliminary SAT/National Merit Scholarship Qualifying Test.
- SAT Reasoning Test.
- SAT Subject Tests.
- Advanced Placement (AP) Examinations.
- The ACT Assessment.

The PSAT/NMSQT

The PSAT/NMSQT measures verbal and mathematical reasoning necessary for success in college. It is a standardized test taken by students in high schools throughout the country in October of their junior year. The test consists of five sections: two 25-minute critical reading sections, two 25-minute math sections, and one 30-minute writing section.

This Preliminary SAT is also the qualifying test for the scholarship competition conducted by the National Merit Scholarship Corporation, an independent, nonprofit organization supported by grants from over 600 corporations, private foundations, colleges, and universities. All students whose scores are in the top 5% of students taking the exam that year receive National Merit Letters of Commendation. In addition, students whose scores are in the top 1% of those taking the exam that year become National Merit Semifinalists. Those who advance to finalist standing by meeting additional requirements compete for one-time National Merit $2000 Scholarships and renewable four-year Merit Scholarships, which may be worth as much as $2000 a year or more for four years.

In addition, this test is used by the National Achievement Scholarship Program for outstanding African-American students. Top-scoring African-American students in each of the regional selection units established for the competition continue in the competition for nonrenewable National Achievement $2000 Scholarships and for four-year Achievement Scholarships sponsored by more than 175 organizations.

Test-Taking Strategies for the PSAT/NMSQT

1. Know what to expect. Each critical reading section has sentence completion questions and reading comprehension questions. A few of the reading questions are based on short passages (often a single paragraph), whereas most are based on longer passages (typically four to seven paragraphs). The first math section has 20 multiple-choice questions; the second math section has 8 quantitative comparison questions and 10 questions for which no choices are provided and whose answers must be entered in a special grid. Calculators may be used on any question in the math sections. The writing skills section, which does *not* have an essay, has three types of multiple-choice questions that test your knowledge of standard written English (grammar and usage).

2. On average, wild guessing has no effect on your score. Educated guessing, on the other hand, can improve your score dramatically. On all multiple-choice questions, try to eliminate as many obviously incorrect answer choices as possible, and then guess from among the choices still remaining.

3. Expect easy questions at the beginning of each set of the same question type. Within each set (except for the reading comprehension questions), the questions progress from easy to difficult. In other words, the first sentence completion questions in a set will be easier than the last sentence completion questions in that set; the first grid-in questions will be easier than the last ones.

4. Take advantage of the easy questions to boost your score. Remember: each question is worth the same number of points. Whether it is easy or difficult, whether it takes you ten seconds or two minutes to answer, you get the same number of points for each question you answer correctly. Your job is to answer as many questions as you can without rushing so fast that you make careless errors. Take enough time to get those easy questions right!

The SAT

The SAT is a reasoning test consisting of three parts—critical reading, mathematical reasoning, and writing. It is designed to measure your ability to do college work. Part of the test deals with verbal skills with an emphasis on critical reading, including a double passage with different points of view. The critical reading sections measure the extent of your vocabulary, your ability to interpret and create ideas, and your ability to reason logically and draw conclusions correctly. The mathematics part measures your ability to reason with numbers and mathematical concepts. It tests your ability to handle general number concepts rather than specific achievement in mathematics. Calculators are permitted on each math section.

The writing part consists of a short essay and multiple-choice questions that test your knowledge of standard written English (grammar and usage).

The SAT is given on seven Saturdays during the year—once each in January, March, May, June, October, November, and December. Applicants may request, for religious reasons, to take the test on the Sunday following the regularly scheduled date.

You can register online at *www.collegeboard.org* or by mail by using the registration form available at your school.

On each part of the SAT—critical reading, math, and writing—you will receive a scaled score between 200 and 800. On each part the national mean is approximately 500.

Test-Taking Strategies for the SAT

1. Pace yourself properly. It is much better to slow down and avoid careless errors than it is to speed up in an effort to answer all the questions. You can earn an above-average score (over 1000) by correctly answering fewer than half of the questions on the test and omitting the rest. Even scores of 1300 can be achieved by omitting more than 20% of the questions.

2. Read carefully. Make sure you are answering the question asked, not a similar one you once encountered. Underline key words (e.g., NOT and EXCEPT) to make sure you do not answer the opposite of the question asked.

3. Learn the directions for each type of question before taking the test. During the test, do not waste even one second reading the directions or looking at the sample questions.

4. Always answer the easy questions first (the ones at the beginning of each section). Do not panic if you can't answer a question. Do not spend too much time on any one question. If you are truly stuck, make an educated guess if possible (see below), and move on. Remember that each question is worth the same one point, and the next few questions may be much easier for you.

5. On average, wild guessing does not affect your score—it is unlikely to help, but it is equally unlikely to hurt you. The choice is yours. However, educated guessing—when you can eliminate one or more of the answer choices—can significantly increase your score! In particular, don't omit critical reading questions if you have read the passage; you can always eliminate some of the choices. Most math questions contain at least one or two choices that are absurd (for example, negative choices when you know that the answer must be positive); eliminate them and guess.

SAT Subject Tests

These tests are one-hour multiple-choice question tests. You may take one, two, or three tests on any one test date. Some colleges do not require SAT Subject Tests. Of those that do, some colleges require specific subject tests, whereas others allow applicants to choose the ones they wish to present with the admission application. Those colleges that do require these tests may use them to determine acceptance or placement in college courses. The tests in foreign language are used not only for placement, but also for possible exemption from a foreign language requirement. If the college of your choice does not require these tests, but you would like to demonstrate proficiency in a particular field, take the test anyway and have your scores sent. Tests are given in writing, literature, history, mathematics, sciences, and several foreign languages.

Advanced Placement (AP) Examinations

The College Board also conducts Advanced Placement tests, given to high school students who have completed advanced or honors courses and wish to get college credit. Many secondary schools offer college-level courses in calculus, statistics, art, psychology, European history, American history, Latin, Spanish, French, German, biology, chemistry, and physics. As a result of scores obtained on these tests, colleges grant credit or use the results for placement in advanced college courses.

The ACT Assessment

The registration form for the ACT includes a detailed questionnaire that takes about one hour to complete. As a result of the answers to those questions about your high school courses, personal interests, and career plans, plus the scores on your ACT, an ACT Assessment Student Report is produced. This is made available to you, your high school, and to any college or scholarship source that you request. Decisions regarding college acceptance and award of scholarships are the result. This information is kept confidential and is released only according to your written instructions. (To obtain an ACT application form, write or call ACT Registration, P.O. Box 414, Iowa City, Iowa 52243, telephone (319) 337-1270.) For more information, consult the ACT web site at *www.actstudent.org*.

The ACT measures knowledge, understanding, and skills acquired in the educational process. The test is made up of four distinct sections: English, mathematics, reading, and science reasoning.

In addition, you may register to take an optional fifth section: a 30-minute writing test. Some colleges require their applicants to take the writing test, but most do not. Check with the colleges to which you will be applying to know whether you need to take the writing part of the ACT.

On the ACT, you should answer all questions, because your score is based on the number of questions you answer correctly. There is no penalty for wrong answers. For each of the four tests the total number of correct responses yields a raw score. A table is used to convert the raw scores to *scaled scores*. The highest possible scaled score for each test is 36. The average of the four scaled scores yields the *composite score*.

The ACT English Test is a 75-question, 45-minute test that measures punctuation, grammar, usage, and sentence structure. The test consists of five passages, each accompanied by multiple-choice test items.

Test-Taking Strategies for the ACT English Test

1. Pace yourself. You have 45 minutes to complete 75 questions.

2. Read the sentences immediately before and after the one containing an underlined portion.

The ACT Mathematics Test has 60 questions to answer in 60 minutes. The test emphasizes quantitative reasoning rather than memorized formulas. Five content areas are included in the mathematics test. About 14 questions deal with pre-algebra topics, such as operations with whole numbers, decimals, fractions, and integers, and about 10 questions deal with elementary algebra. Usually 18 questions are based on intermediate algebra and coordinate geometry. About 14 questions are based on plane geometry and usually four items are based on right triangle trigonometry and basic trigonometric identities.

Test-Taking Strategies for the ACT Mathematics Test

1. Spend an average of one minute on each question, less on the easy questions, more on the difficult ones.

2. Be sure to answer each question even if you have to guess.

3. Make sure your answers are reasonable.

The ACT Reading Test is a 40-question, 35-minute test that measures reading comprehension. Three scores are reported for this test: a total score, a subscore based on the 20 items in the social studies and natural sciences sections, and a subscore on the 20 items in the prose fiction and humanities sections.

Test-Taking Strategies for the ACT Reading Test

1. Read each passage carefully. Underline important ideas in the passage.

2. Pace yourself. You have 40 questions to answer in 35 minutes.

3. Refer to the passage and in particular to your underlined sections when answering the questions.

The ACT Science Reasoning Test presents seven sets of scientific information in three different formats: data representations (graphs, tables, and other schematic forms); research summaries (description of experiments); and conflicting viewpoints. The 40 questions are to be answered in 35 minutes. The content of the test is drawn from biology, chemistry, physics, geology, astronomy, and meteorology. Background knowledge at the level of a high school general science course is all that is needed to answer these questions. The test emphasizes scientific reasoning skills rather than recall of scientific content, skill in mathematics, or reading ability.

Test-Taking Strategies for the ACT Science Reasoning Test

1. Read the scientific material before you begin answering a question. Read tables and text carefully, underlining important ideas.
2. Look for flaws in the experiments and devise ways of improving the experiments.
3. When you are asked to compare viewpoints, make notes in the margin of the printed material summarizing each viewpoint.

A FINAL WORD

Don't take any examination without preparation, even though you will find descriptions of these tests that say they test skills developed over years of study both in and out of school. Don't walk in cold, even though you believe that you meet all the qualities colleges are looking for.

Although the College Board suggests no special preparation, it does distribute to applicants the booklet, "Taking the SAT Reasoning Test." It also makes available other publications containing former test questions along with advice on how to cope with the questions. Evidently, all candidates need some form of preparation.

The American College Testing Program furnishes the booklet, "Preparing for the ACT Assessment." This gives specific information about the test, test questions, and strategies for taking each of the four parts. It also describes what to expect on the test day and gives practice with typical questions.

Barron's Educational Series publishes books to help you prepare for these tests. They are available at all bookstores and in many libraries. You should be sure to use them before taking any of these tests.

Although no high school student takes all of the college-entrance exams described above, virtually all students planning to attend a four-year college take at least one of them—the SAT or ACT. Prepare conscientiously for each exam that you take and you will provide the colleges to which you are applying with valuable information about your abilities. Good luck!

Ira K. Wolf
President
PowerPrep, Inc.

It's important to be organized. While the admissions process can be daunting, if you use your time well, it doesn't have to take over your life.

Kristi Johnson, Bucknell University, Class of 2003

The college admission process—getting in—begins the minute you start making your first choices in course selection and in cocurricular activities in junior high school, middle school, and high school. These initial and ongoing decisions are crucial to your future well-being. They lay the groundwork for the curriculum you will follow throughout your high school career: they are not easily reversed. These are the decisions that will allow you to market yourself to the colleges of your choice.

STUDENTS TAKE NOTE!

There is a myth prevalent among college-bound students throughout the country that the best way to gain entrance to the selective colleges is to be well rounded. This term usually refers to students who have earned good grades in high school (B+ or better) and participated in a wide range of cocurricular activities.

However, most admission officers at the selective colleges prefer applications from candidates they term angular—students who have demonstrated solid academic achievement in and out of school *and* who have developed one or two particularly strong cocurricular skills, interests, and activities. These angular students are very different in character from the well-rounded students who are very good at everything, yet excel at little, if anything.

William Fitzsimmons, Dean of Admission at Harvard, says that Harvard is looking for a well-rounded class, which means Harvard is most interested in admitting angular students—students who have excelled at something. He cautions, though, that "…It is a mistake to denigrate or underestimate that persuasive power of high grades, rank, triple 800s on the SAT, 36 on the ACT, and equally impressive SAT Subject Test scores. The selective colleges take many of these academically high profile applicants. But the numbers game alone often won't get you in! It would be fairly simple for Harvard to enroll an entire freshman class with a superior academic profile and little depth of quality in areas that make up the personality of the class. We just would not do that!"

Dean Fitzsimmons is saying that the majority of the successful applicants to selective colleges must have some major commitment(s) combined with excellent academic qualities. A strong impact results from quality involvements rather than a proliferation of joinings and transient interests. Essentially, the angular applicant is a committed individual, while the well-rounded candidate is merely involved.

STUDENTS AND PARENTS TAKE AN EARLY, ACTIVE ROLE

Students and parents must make time to ensure an early, active role in the college admissions process. Each year, starting in the seventh grade, students and parents should take the time to sit down with the student's guidance counselor and talk meaningfully about the following:

- selection and level of courses, projecting through the senior year of high school;
- cocurricular activities available, such as drama, music, athletics, academic clubs, community activities, student government, and other special interest groups; and
- summer study, work, or recreation.

Why is this important to getting in? As sure as taxes and death, there is going to come a time in your senior year when you, the college-bound student, will be asked to choose colleges, complete the college application, write your college essay(s), and have an interview—either on the college campus, or in your hometown.

You must create the personal marketing, which will take place during the application process in your senior year, long before your senior year starts. By the time you reach that long-awaited dream of being a senior, you and you alone have created the person you must market to the colleges of your choice. You must understand that the person you have created is the only person you have to market. There is no Madison Avenue glitz involved in this marketing process! You don't create a pseudo marketing campaign that shows you jumping off a bridge with a bungee cord tied to your sneakers. Admission counselors can tell the difference between a real marketing effort and a pseudo marketing campaign.

THE APPLICATION FORM

Today colleges are offering their application on hard copy, computer disk, E-mail, or through on-line services of the Internet. Each application form differs from college to college, with the exception of those colleges that use the common application. When you start to work, be sure to note all deadlines, follow all directions, be complete, be neat, fill out the geographical data with accurate facts, and type it all (unless you print exceptionally well). Always review the entire application before you start to fill it out, and complete the entire application before you start the next one. Remember the application is *you* to the admissions committee member reading it. Even though "a book should not be judged by its cover," appearances do influence opinions.

It is best to work through a rough draft of the application before you actually work on the application copy to be submitted. Remember to make a copy of all parts of the finished application in the event that yours gets lost and a replacement must be sent.

You are responsible for giving the Secondary School Report, found in each application, directly to your high school guidance counselor. Your counselor is responsible for sending official copies of grades, rank in class (if any), the school's profile, and a written recommendation regarding you. It also is your responsibility to call or fill out the appropriate forms for either the SAT and/or SAT Subject Tests or the ACT, to send the appropriate test information directly to each college to which you have applied, even if your scores are on your high school transcript. Your college file will not be considered complete, and will not be sent to the admission committee for a decision, without these official scores. Additionally, many colleges want recommendations from one or two teachers. Choose wisely and allow each teacher plenty of time. Request letters from teachers who know you best. If English is your interest, be sure to choose an English teacher. If you are fluent in Spanish and have future interest in Spanish at college, ask the Spanish teacher. Remember, though you have many interests and have participated in many activities—you are developing an admissions package as part of your marketing of yourself. Emphasize your strengths and show how they are integrated into your activities and achievements.

Cocurricular activities usually are athletic or nonathletic. If you have won athletic awards, note them. If you have had the starring role in the spring musical for the last two years, say so. If you are an editor on the school newspaper, specify this. Admissions people view your activities with special interest. They realize how very time consuming these activities can be and how they sometimes bring very few accolades. List these activities in the order of importance to you. If you do not believe that the application allows you the opportunity to show your depth of commitment to one or two cocurricular areas, you may add an addendum. Use the KISS (Keep It Short and Simple) method. This is an addendum, not an essay, letter, or dissertation. Be honest!

Some applications have mini essays. When space is provided, be sure you are concise, clear, and grammatically correct. Here, less is more. Your ability to organize your thoughts and present them concisely is being tested. You will receive your chance to impress each college with your prose in the long essay segment of the application. Some colleges have as many as four long essays, whereas some require none. In addition to the short and long essay questions, some colleges ask the student for a graded paper signed by the teacher.

Some colleges encourage you to support your application with additional materials. If you are given this option, consider what will strengthen your application: musical tapes, art and/or photography portfolios, published writings, an exceptional graded term paper, all the additional opportunities for the college to get to know you better and for you to increase your image as an angular candidate. Such additions help the admissions committee to get a better handle on who you are in relation to other applicants. Be sure your presentation is clear and as professional as possible. These additions are not going to be evaluated by the admissions committee. Your material will be directed to the appropriate department for evaluation and an evaluative note will be sent back to the admissions committee. It is this note that will become part of your admissions package, the same way an athletic coach evaluates potential student/athletes.

Proofread all parts of the application. Be sure you, the student, place your signature where it is required. If you are not sending your application on-line, then place everything, including the registration fee check, in a large manila envelope and give it to your college guidance counselor. After adding the completed Secondary School Report to the application, your guidance counselor will mail it. Your job is now finished and the waiting begins!

E-Mail, On-line Services through the College or the Internet

We have joined the 21st century with E-mail and on-line services of the Internet offering college applications. This movement promises to be the wave of the future. Certainly ecologically correct, by producing as close to a paperless process as possible, this method is still in cyberspace. Be sure you know what you are doing when you use any of these methods. It is seriously suggested that you take the time to call the college shortly after sending this type of application, to ensure that your application is on file. If you have an addendum or two, you may want to speak to an admission clerk to make sure each addendum has reached the office of admission in the format you desired. If it were my application and I chose any of these methods, I'd still send my musical tape, the slides for my art portfolio, and such, by certified or registered mail. Clarity is so important to the professionals who will be evaluating these addenda for your college admission process!

PC- and Mac-Based Computer Disk Applications

Since the emergence of on-line applications, fewer colleges have a computer disk application. If you wish to apply this way, make sure that your target college has authorized the disk: there are a number of organizations selling computer disk applications without the consent of the college. Make sure the service to which you have subscribed allows you to print a hard copy of the application, even if they want you to send the disk back to the service or to the college. Do yourself a favor and print an extra copy of the application for your personal college file—it is very easy for the post office or college to lose your information. It is also wise, if you have to send the disk with the application, to write, "DO NOT SCAN" on the envelope. It is highly probable that the information on the disk will be lost if it is passed through a scanning machine.

The Common Application

About 200 colleges in the United States have agreed that students may apply to their colleges by completing one common application. Some of the colleges using the common application also have their own application. Students applying to a college that allows an applicant a choice of using either the college's own application or the common application, obviously face a choice. The use of the common application substantially reduces the time spent composing different essay answers and neatly typing separate application forms. If you are one of those who must make a choice between the common application and the application of the college, you should understand that each college using the common application (either as its only application or as an alternative application) has the right to ask for a supplement. If you choose the common application, be very sure to read

the pages surrounding the common application carefully. Each college has a paragraph in which they discuss their deadlines, requirements for admission, and specify if they require supplemental information. The supplemental information can range from an additional essay or two, to additional information about your cocurricular activities.

All the colleges participating in the common application have each member of their admission staff sign a statement that they will NOT discriminate in the admissions process among students who submit the common application versus students who submit the college's application. However, there are counselors who believe that when there is a choice, the applicant has a better chance of conveying information by using the college's application; there is a vast difference in format between the two applications, even if the college requires a supplement. Check with your guidance counselor if you are unsure regarding your choice of format. To access the common application online, go to:

www.commonapp.org

College Web Sites

Most colleges today have their own web site. Here you will find a wealth of information. Some colleges have even put their viewbook, course curriculum guide, a campus tour, as well as their application, on their site. Visit each college's web page—the addresses are in the Admissions Contact section of the college Profiles in this book. You'll be a much better informed consumer.

THE INTERVIEW

The interview is a contrived situation that few people enjoy, of which many people misunderstand the value, and about which everyone is apprehensive. However, no information from a college catalog, no friend's friend, no high school guidance counselor's comments, and no parental remembrances from bygone days can surpass the value of your college campus visit and interview. This first hand opportunity to assess your future alma mater will confirm or contradict other impressions and help you make a sound college acceptance.

Many colleges will recommend or request a personal interview. It is best to travel to the campus to meet with a member of the admissions staff if you can; however, if you can't, many colleges will arrange to have one of their representatives, usually an alumnus, interview you in your hometown.

Even though the thought of an interview might give you enough butterflies to lift you to the top of your high school's flagpole, here are some tips that might make it a little easier.

1. **Go prepared.** Read the college's catalog and this book's Profile ahead of time so you won't ask "How many books are in your library?" or "How many students do you have?" Ask intelligent questions that introduce a topic of conversation that you want the interviewer to know about you. The key is to distinguish yourself in a positive way from thousands of other applicants. Forge the final steps in the marketing process you have been building since your first choices in the college admission process back in junior high school. The interview is your chance to enhance those decisions.

2. **Nervousness** is absolutely and entirely normal. The best way to handle it is to admit it, out loud, to the interviewer. Richard Shaw, Dean of Admission at Yale University, sometimes relates this true story to his apprehensive applicants. One extremely agitated young applicant sat opposite him for her interview with her legs crossed, wearing loafers on her feet. She swung her top leg back and forth to some inaudible rhythm. The loafer on her top foot flew off her foot, hit him in the head, ricocheted to the desk lamp and broke it. She looked at him in terror, but when their glances met, they both dissolved in

laughter. The moral of the story—the person on the other side of the desk is also a human being and wants to put you at ease. So admit to your anxiety, and don't swing your foot if you're wearing loafers! (And by the way, she was admitted.)

3. **Be yourself.** Nobody's perfect, and everyone knows nobody's perfect, so admit to a flaw or two before the interviewer goes hunting for them. The truly impressive candidate will convey a thorough knowledge of self.

4. **Interview the interviewer.** Don't passively sit there and allow the interviewer to ask all the questions and direct the conversation. Participate in this responsibility by assuming an active role. A thoughtful questioner will accomplish three important tasks in a successful interview:

   demonstrate interest, initiative, and maturity for taking partial responsibility for the content of the conversation; **guide the conversation** to areas where he/she feels most secure and accomplished; and **obtain answers.** Use your genuine feelings to react to the answers you hear. If you are delighted to learn of a certain program or activity, show it. If you are curious, ask more questions. If you are disappointed by something you learn, try to find a path to a positive answer. Then consider yourself lucky that you discovered this particular inadequacy in time.

5. **Parents** do belong in your college decision process as your advisers! Often it is they who spend the megabucks for your next four years. They can provide psychological support and a stabilizing influence for sensible, rational decisions. However, they do NOT belong in your interview session. In essence, the sage senior will find constructive ways to include parents in the decision-making process as catalysts, without letting them take over (as many are apt to do) the interview process. You may want your parents to meet and speak briefly to your interviewer prior to your interview and that is fine, but parents may not accompany you into the interview session! Arrange with your parents to meet somewhere out of the interview building after your interview is over. You do not want the interviewer inviting your parents back to the interview room. As intelligent as parents may be, they do not perceive the answers to questions the same way you do. The worst scenario I can imagine is the interviewer asking your parents some of the same questions that were asked you, and that is highly likely. Parents just answer questions differently than teenagers. At best, the scenario creates a long, long ride home, and when you get home you can't punish your parents by taking the car keys away from them, or grounding them for a week. At worst, the scenario has caused a blight in your admissions file. This is your time! Keep it that way!

6. **Practice makes perfect.** Begin your interviews at colleges that are low on your list of preferred choices, and leave your first-choice colleges until last. If you are shy, you will have a chance to practice vocalizing what your usually silent inner voice tells you. Others will have the opportunity to commit their inevitable first blunders where they won't count as much.

7. **Departing impressions.** There is a remarkable tendency for the student to base final college preferences on the quality of the interview only, or on the personal reaction to the interviewer as the personification of the entire institution. Do not do yourself the disservice of letting it influence an otherwise rational selection, one based on institutional programs, students, services, and environment. After the last good-bye and thank you has been smiled, and you exhale deeply on your way out the door, go ahead and congratulate yourself. If you used the interview properly, you will know whether or not you wish to attend that college and why.

8. **Send a thank-you note** to your interviewer. A short and simple handwritten or typed note will do—and if you forgot to mention something important about yourself at the interview, here's your chance.

WRITING THE COLLEGE ESSAY

Do the colleges read the essays you write on their applications? You bet your diploma they do. Here is your chance to strut your stuff, stand up, be counted, and stylize your way into the hearts of the decision makers.

Write it, edit it, review it. Rewrite it. Try to show why you are unique and how the college will benefit having you in its student body. This is not a routine homework assignment, but a college level essay that will be carefully examined for spelling, grammar, content, and style of a high school senior. As strenuous an effort as it may be, completing the essay gives the admissions committee a chance to know the real you, a three-dimensional human being with passions, preferences, strengths, weaknesses, imagination, energy, and ambition. Your ability to market yourself will help the deans and directors of admission remember your application from among the sea of thousands that flood their offices each year.

First, maximize your strengths—use your essays to say what you want to say. The answer to a specific question on the college's part still provides an opening for you to furnish background information about yourself, your interests, ambitions, and insights. For example, the essay that asks you to name your favorite book and the reason for your selection could be answered with the title of a Dr. Seuss book because you are considering a career as an elementary school teacher. If you are interested in business, read about a famous businessman you admire and then discuss your interest in business.

Whatever the essay questions are, autobiographical or otherwise, select the person or issue that puts you in the position to discuss the subject in which you are the most well versed. In essence, all of your essay responses are autobiographical in the sense that they will illustrate something important about yourself, your values, and the kind of person you are (or hope to become). If personal values are important to you, and they should be, then here is your opportunity to stress their importance.

Because many colleges will ask for more than one essay, make sure that the *sum* of the essays in any one college application covers your best points. Do not repeat your answers, even if the questions sound alike. Cover the most important academic and cocurricular activities (most important meaning the one in which you excelled and/or in which you spent the most quality time).

If you are fortunate to have a cooperative English teacher, you might request a critique of your first draft, but be sure to allow enough time for a careful evaluation and your revision.

Write the essays yourself—no substitutes or stand-ins. College admission professionals can discern mature adult prose from student prose.

PARTING WORDS

You may wish to ask yourself the following questions to help you decide which is your Paradise College. Most of this information is in the individual college Profiles in this book.

1. **Caliber of School Programs** Is the college known for its English department or chemistry department? What are its strengths?

2. **Selectivity of Admissions** Is the college Most Competitive, Highly Competitive, Very Competitive, Competitive, Less Competitive or Noncompetitive? Check the Selector Ratings.

3. **Chances of Admission** Be realistic. What are your chances of getting in? How far can you reach? Listen when you are given advice!

4. **Location of the School**   Is the school near home, one hour away, 300 miles away, or across the United States?

5. **Rural, Suburban, Urban Campus**   Is the school in the city or in a rural area?

6. **Size of the School**   Can you spend four years at a small liberal arts college of 800 undergraduates? Do you need the larger atmosphere of a university? Do not equate size with social life!

7. **State College vs. Private College**   Is the college a large state university with most of the student population from the state where it's located? Is it one of the public "Ivies"? Will you be a minority in the state school?

8. **Geographical Diversity**   Is the college a regional one attracting students from the same state or region? Or is it a college, regardless of its size, which attracts students from all over the United States, or the world at large?

9. **Cost of College**   What is the tuition? What are the living costs? What travel costs are there from home to campus? Are there hidden costs?

10. **Financial Aid**   With a great percentage of undergraduates at many private colleges on financial aid of some type, where do you fit? What monies are available for the students at the schools of your choice? Is the college need blind in its admission program?

11. **Living Conditions**   Is housing on campus guaranteed for all four years? Are the dorms coed? Are there single-sex dorms? Are alternatives in housing available?

12. **Socialization**   Is it a grind school—all work, work, work? Is it fraternity- and sorority-oriented? What are the on-campus facilities for socialization?

13. **Safety on Campus**   Are the dorms secure and locked? What's the safety system on the campus?

14. **Core Curriculum—Distribution Credits**   Does the college require (for graduation) a specific number of credits in different academic disciplines? For example, does the student have to take six credits in philosophy before graduating? Is a self-designed curriculum possible?

15. **Sophomore Standing**   Does the college accept AP credits? Does it offer advanced standing for an AP course, or just a credit toward graduation?

16. **Junior Year Abroad**   Are there opportunities to study in Italy, Japan, or Australia, for example, while you are an undergraduate?

17. **Internships**   Are there opportunities for hands-on experience while in college? Which departments have formal internship opportunities?

18. **Graduate School After College**   What percentage of its graduates go on to graduate school immediately upon graduation, or within five years? What is the record of those who successfully get into the law, medical, or business school of their choice?

19. **Placement After Graduation**   Is there an office for job placement after college? Is there an alumni network that helps in job placement?

20. **Weekend College**   Do the students remain on campus on weekends, or is it a suitcase college?

21. **Minorities**   What percentage of the students are minorities? Reflect on the racial, ethnic, and religious minority roles in the college you are considering. How would you feel being Jewish at a Roman Catholic college for example—or Catholic at a Jewish college?

22. **Sports Facilities**   Is there a swimming pool? Are there horse stables? Is there an ice hockey rink on campus?

23. **Library Facilities**   How many books are in the library? Is it computerized? Is the campus library tied into a larger network?

24. **Athletic Programs**   Is the ice hockey team a varsity sport? Does the lacrosse team play Division I or III? Is basketball strong? Do they have a women's squash team?

25. **Honors Programs**   Are honors programs available? What are they? Who is eligible?

26. **Student Body**   Are the students politically active? Are they professional in orientation?

27. **Faculty**   Are all classes taught by full professors? Or are TAs (teaching assistants) the norm?

28. **Computer Labs**   Are computers required of incoming freshmen? What are the facilities on campus? Can you have your own PC in your room?

29. **Campus Visits**   If possible, make a visit to the campus. Spend some time talking to students for a feel of the campus.

30. **Special Talents**   Recognize your special talents and discover where they fit best. Often, a special talent becomes a scale-tipper in the admissions process.

31. **Special Family Circumstances**   Talk with your parents about their expectations. Discuss your needs as well as their thoughts.

32. **Legacy**   Does your family have a history at a specific school? Are you interested in continuing the tradition?

33. **Note Well—Final List**   Be sure the final list is a realistic one. It should include "reaches," "targets," and "safeties." No matter which one admits you—it must fit!

Finding and applying to the best colleges for you is not supposed to be easy, but it can be fun. Parents, guidance counselors, and teachers are there to help you, so don't struggle alone. Keep your sense of humor and a smile on your face as you go about researching, exploring, and discovering your ideal college.

Last but not least is The Parent Credo: The right college is the one where your child will fit in scholastically and socially. Be realistic in your aspirations and support the child's choice!

Anthony F. Capraro, III, Ph.D.
President, Teach Inc.
College Counseling
Purchase, New York

Sometimes getting more aid is a matter of simply asking for it.
Raymond A. Lutzky, Rensselaer Polytechnic Institute, Class
of 2002

Postsecondary education is a major American industry. A greater proportion of students pursue postsecondary education in the United States than in any other industrialized country. Annually, more than 13 million students study at over 8000 institutions of higher learning. The diversity of our system of higher education is admired by educators and students throughout the world. There is no reason to believe that this system will change in the future. However, college costs and the resources available to parents and students to meet those costs have changed.

Unfortunately, many high school students and their parents believe either that there is no financial aid available or that they will not qualify for any type of financial assistance from any source. Neither assumption is correct. College costs have increased and will continue to increase. Federal allocations, for some financial aid programs, have decreased. But this decline has been met with generous increases in financial aid from state and school sources.

American students and their parents should realize that they must assume the primary role in planning to meet their future college costs and that the family financial planning process must begin much earlier than has been the case.

COLLEGE COSTS

- Nearly all parents believe college costs are too expensive.
- Currently, the average cost of education, including tuition and fees for one year at a public college would have been about $21,000 and for a private college and university, the cost could have exceeded $34,000.
- While college costs will increase each year, it is important to remember that currently a majority of all college students attend schools with tuition costs below $5,000.

STUDENT FINANCIAL AID

- In 2010, the total amount of financial aid available from federal, state, and institutional sources to postsecondary students is approximately $170 billion.
- A majority of all students enrolled in higher education receive some type of financial assistance.
- Federal student aid remains the largest source of funding.
- Not long ago the majority of federal financial assistance was grants. Today, a greater amount of financial aid is from loan money.

TIMETABLE FOR APPLYING FOR FINANCIAL AID

Sophomore Year of High School

Most families wait until a child has been accepted into a college or university to begin planning on how the family will meet those college costs. However, a family's college financial planning should begin much earlier.

Students, as early as the sophomore year of high school, should begin a systematic search for colleges that offer courses of study that are of interest. There are many computer programs that can be helpful in this process. These programs can match a student's interest with colleges fitting the profile. Considering that half of all students who enter college either drop out or transfer to another school, this type of early selection analysis can be invaluable.

After selecting certain schools for further consideration, you should write to the school and request a viewbook, catalog, and financial aid brochure. After receiving this information, you and your family should compare the schools. Your comparison should include academic considerations as well as financial. Don't rule out a school because you think you can't afford it. Remember the financial aid programs at that school may be more generous than at a lower-priced school. If possible, visit the college and speak with both an admission and financial aid counselor. If it is not possible to visit all the schools, call the schools and obtain answers to your questions about admission, financial aid, and placement after graduation.

Junior Year of High School

The comparative analysis of colleges and universities that you began in your sophomore year should continue in your junior year. By the completion of your junior year, you and your parents should have some idea of what it will cost to attend and the financial aid policies of each of the schools you are considering.

Some colleges and universities offer prospective applicants an early estimate of their financial aid award. This estimate is based upon information supplied by the family and can provide assistance in planning a family's budget. Remember that for most families, financial aid from federal, state, and school sources will probably not meet the total cost of attendance.

Families should remember that college costs can be met over the course of the academic year. It is not necessary to have all of the money needed to attend school available at the beginning of the academic year. Student and family savings, as well as student employment throughout the year, can be used to meet college costs.

Senior Year of High School

January

By January of your senior year of high school you should know which colleges and universities you want to receive your financial aid application forms. Be certain that you have completed not only the federal financial aid application form, but also any necessary state or school forms. Read carefully all of the instructions. Application methods and deadline dates may differ from one college to another. Submit an application clean of erasures or notations in the margins, and sign all of the application forms.

February

You will receive a report from the service agency you selected containing information on your family's expected contribution and your eligibility for financial aid. You and your parents should discuss the results of the financial aid application with regard to family contribution, educational costs, and how those costs can be met.

March

Beginning in March, most colleges begin to make financial aid decisions. If your application is complete, your chances of receiving an award letter early are greater than if additional information is required.

The financial aid award letter you receive from your school serves as your official document indicating the amount of financial aid you will receive for the year. You must sign and return a copy of the award letter to your school if you agree to accept their offer of financial aid.

If your family's financial circumstances change and you need additional funding, you should make an appointment to speak with your school's financial aid director or counselor. College financial aid personnel are permitted to exercise professional judgment and make adjustments to a student's financial need. Your letter of appeal should state explicitly how much money you need and why you need it.

TIPS ON APPLYING FOR FINANCIAL AID

1. Families can no longer wait until a child is accepted into college before deciding how they will finance that education. Earlier college financial planning is necessary.

2. Families should assume a much more active role in locating the resources necessary to fund future college costs.

3. Families should assume that college costs will continue to increase.

4. Families should assume that in the future the federal government will not substantially increase financial aid allocations.

5. Families should obtain information on a wide range of colleges including the many excellent low-cost schools.

6. Families should seek information about all of the funding sources available at each school they are considering.

7. Families should seek the advice and expertise of financial experts for college financing strategies. College financial planning should specify the amount of money a family should invest or save each month in order to meet future college bills.

8. Families should investigate all of the legitimate ways of reducing their income and assets before filing for financial aid.

9. Families should know how financial aid is awarded and the financial aid policies and programs of each school they are considering.

10. Families should realize that although the job of financing a college education rests primarily with them, they probably will not be able to save the entire cost of their child's college education. They probably will be eligible to receive some type of financial aid from some source and they will have to borrow a portion of their child's college education costs.

11. Families should be advised that the federal government frequently changes the rules and regulations governing financial aid eligibility. Check with your high school guidance counselor or college financial aid administrator for the latest program qualifications.

12. Part-time employment during the school year and full-time employment during the summer should be a part of every family's financing plan.

13. Families should investigate all colleges and universities that offer three-year graduation options.

14. Not every student can afford to live on campus. Commuting to college is one way to reduce college costs.

15. It is important to find out a school's policy on awarding financial aid on the basis of need and merit.

16. Check with the financial aid office on the availability of loan forgiveness programs.

17. Find out if the aid awarded in the first year will be awarded in subsequent years if the family income does not change.

18. Find out the statistics on graduating seniors: how many were employed or accepted to graduate schools at the time of graduation.

19. Plan for the future. What was the average debt of graduating students in each of the schools you applied to?

20. Going to college should be a family decision. All family members should be aware of the financial implications of attendance, not just for the first year, but for all four years.

Marguerite J. Dennis
Vice President for Enrollment
and International Programs
Suffolk University
Boston, Massachusetts

The greatest advice I ever received was keep an open mind and stick it out.

Sarah Caldwell, Bryn Mawr, Class of 2008

COLLEGE: IT'S DIFFERENT

In college you are likely to hear fellow students say, "I don't know what that prof *wants*, and she won't *tell* me." "I wrote about three papers in high school, and now they want one every week." Though these students may be exaggerating a bit, college *is* different, both in the quality and the amount of work expected. Sometimes in high school the basic concepts of a course are reduced to a set of facts on a study sheet, handed to students to be reviewed and learned for a test.

In college, it is the concepts and ideas that are most important. These can only be grasped through a real understanding of the facts as they interrelate and form larger patterns. Writing papers and answering essay questions on tests can demonstrate a genuine understanding of the concepts, and this is why they are so important to college instructors. Learning to deal with ideas in this way can be a long-term asset, developing your independence, intellectual interests, and self-awareness.

Don't be discouraged; you are not alone. Most of your fellow students are having equally difficult times adjusting to a new learning method. Persist, and you will improve, leading to a lifetime habit of critical thinking and problem solving that can benefit you in many important ways.

College is also different outside of classes. Now that you have the freedom to choose how to spend time and what types of relationships to make, you have a bewildering number of possibilities.

MAKING A GOOD IMPRESSION

Here you are, plopped down in a strange place, feeling a bit like Dorothy transported to Oz. Your first goal is to make a good impression, showing your best self to those who will be important in your life for the next four years and even longer.

Impressing Faculty Members Favorably

Faculty members come in all ranks, from the graduate assistant, who teaches part-time while pursuing a degree, to a lofty full professor, who teaches primarily graduate students. Though different in rank and seniority, they respond to their students in roughly the same ways. They are, after all, people, with families and relationships much like your own. To have a good working relationship with them, try the following suggestions:

- **Make up your own mind about your instructors.** Listening to other students talk about teachers can be confusing. If you listen long enough, you will hear arguments for and against each of them. Don't allow hearsay to affect your own personal opinion.

- **Get to know your instructors firsthand.** Set up a meeting during regular office hours. Don't try to settle important issues in the few moments before and after class.

- **Approach a discussion of grades carefully.** If you honestly believe that you have been graded too low, schedule a conference. Do not attack your instructor's integrity or judgment. Instead, say that you had expected your work to result in a better grade and would like to know ways to improve. Be serious about overcoming faults.

- **Don't make excuses.** Instructors have heard them all and can rarely be fooled. Accept responsibility for your mistakes, and learn from them.

- **Pay attention in class.** Conversing and daydreaming can insult your instructor and inhibit the learning process.

- **Arrive ahead of time for class.** You will be more relaxed, and you can use these moments to review notes or talk with classmates. You also demonstrate to your instructor a commitment to the class.

- **Participate in class discussions.** Ask questions and give answers to the instructor's questions. Nothing pleases an instructor more than an intelligent question that proves you are interested and prepared.

- **Learn from criticism.** It is an instructor's job to correct your errors in thinking. Don't take in-class criticism personally.

Impressing Fellow Students Favorably

Relationships with other students can be complex, but there are some basic suggestions that may make life easier in the residence halls and classrooms:

- **Don't get into the habit of bragging.** Frequent references to your wealth, your outstanding friends, your social status, or your family's successes are offensive to others.

- **Don't pry.** When your fellow students share their feelings and problems, listen carefully and avoid any tendency to intrude or ask embarrassing questions.

- **Don't borrow.** Borrowing a book, a basketball, or a few bucks may seem like a small thing to you, but some people who have trouble saying no may resent your request.

- **Divide chores.** Do your part; agree on a fair division of work in a lab project or a household task.

- **Support others.** Respect your friends' study time and the "Do not disturb" signs on their doors. Helping them to reach their goals will help you as well.

- **Allow others to be upset.** Sometimes, turning someone's anger into a joke, minimizing their difficulties, or belittling their frustration is your worst response. Support them by letting them release their emotions.

- **Don't preach.** Share your opinions when asked for, but don't try to reform the world around you.

- **Tell the truth.** Your reputation is your most important asset. When you make an agreement, keep it.

MANAGING YOUR TIME

Everyone, no matter how prominent or how insignificant, has 168 hours a week to spend. In this one asset we are all equal. There are students on every college campus, however, who seem to accomplish all their goals and still find time for play and socializing. There are others who seem to be alternating between frantic dashes and dull idleness, accomplishing very little. To the first group, college is a happy, fulfilling experience; to the latter, it is maddeningly frustrating. The first group has gained control of time, the second is controlled by that elusive and precious commodity.

- **Know where your time goes.** Unfortunately, we cannot store up time as we do money, to be used when the need is greatest. We use it as it comes, and it is amazing how it sometimes comes slowly (as in the last five minutes of a Friday afternoon class) or quickly (as in the last hour before a final exam). The first step in controlling time is to determine exactly how you use it. For a while, at least, you should carefully record how much time you spend in class, going to and from class, studying, sleeping, eating, listening to music, watching television, and running errands. You need to know what happens to your 168 hours. Only then can you make sensible decisions about managing them.

- **Make a weekly schedule.** You can schedule your routine for the week, using the time plan forms available at most college bookstores or by making your own forms.

- **First schedule the inflexible blocks of time.** Your class periods, transportation time, sleeping, and eating will form relatively routine patterns throughout the week.

Trying to shave minutes off these important activities is often a mistake.

- **Plan your study time.** It is preferable, though not always possible, to set your study hours at the same time every weekday. Try to make your study time *prime time*, when your body and mind are ready for a peak performance.

- **Plan time for fun.** No one should plan to spend four years of college as a working robot. Fun and recreation are important, but they can be enjoyed in short periods just as well as long. For example, jogging with friends for 30 minutes can clear the mind, tone up the muscles, and give you those all-important social contacts. Parties and group activities can be scheduled for weekends.

- **Be reasonable in your time allotments.** As you progress through your freshman year, you will learn more precisely how much time is required to write a paper or complete a book report. Until then, schedule some extra minutes for these tasks. You are being unfair to yourself by planning one hour for a job that requires two.

- **Allow flexibility.** The unexpected is to be expected. There will be interruptions to your routine and errands that must be run at certain times. Allow for these unforeseen circumstances.

STUDYING EFFECTIVELY

Your most important activity in college is studying. Efficient study skills separate the inept student (who may spend just as many hours studying as an "A" student) from the excellent student, who thinks while studying and who uses common sense strategies to discover the important core of courses. The following suggested game plan for good study has worked in the past; it can work for you.

- **Make a commitment.** It is universally recommended that you spend two hours studying for every hour in class. At the beginning of your college career, be determined to do just that. It doesn't get easy until you make up your mind to do it.

- **Do the tough jobs first.** If certain courses are boring or particularly difficult, study them first. Don't read the interesting, enjoyable materials first, saving the toughies for the last sleepy twinges of your weary brain.

- **Study in short sessions.** Three two-hour sessions, separated from each other by a different activity, are much better than a long six-hour session.

- **Use your bits of time.** Use those minutes when you're waiting for a bus, a return call, laundry to wash, or a friend to arrive. Some of the best students I know carry 3×5 cards filled with definitions, formulas, or equations and learn during brief waiting periods. Most chief executives form the habit early of using bits of time wisely.

Digesting a Textbook

1. **Preview chapters.** Before you read a chapter in your textbook, preview it. Quickly examine the introductory paragraphs, headings, tables, illustrations, and other features of the chapter. The purpose is to discover the major topics. Then you can read with increased comprehension because you know where the author is leading.

2. **Underline the important points as you read.** Underlining should never be overdone; it can leave your textbook almost completely marked and less legible to read. Only the major ideas and concepts should be highlighted.

3. **Seven categories of information are commonly found in textbooks.** Be particularly alert when you see the following; get your marking pen ready.
   Definitions of terms.
   Types or *categories* of items.
   Methods of accomplishing certain tasks.
   Sequences of events or stages in a process.

Reasons or *causes*.
Results or *effects*.
Contrasts or *comparisons* between items.

4. **Repeat information you need to learn.** When the object is to learn information, nothing is so effective as reciting the material, either silently or aloud.

5. **Don't read all material the same way.** Decide what you need to learn from the material and read accordingly. You read a work of fiction to learn the characters and the narrative; a poem, to learn an idea, an emotion, or a theme; a work of history, to learn the interrelationships of events. Do not read every sentence with the same speed and concentration; learn when to skim rapidly along. Remember, your study time is limited and the trick is to discriminate between the most important and the least important. No one can learn *everything* equally well.

6. **The five-minute golden secret.** As soon as possible after class is over—preferably at your desk in the classroom—skim through the chapter that has just been covered, marking the points primarily discussed. Copy what was written on the board. Now you know what the professor thinks is important!

TAKING TESTS SKILLFULLY

Try to predict the test questions. At some college libraries, copies of old examinations are made available to students. If you can legally find out your professor's previous test methods do so.

Ask your professor to describe the format of the upcoming test: multiple-choice? true-false? essay questions? problems? Adjust your study to the format described.

Listen for clues in the professor's lecture. Sometimes the questions posed in class have a way of reappearing on tests. If a statement is repeated several times or recurs in a subsequent lecture, note it as important.

As you review for the test, devise questions based on the material, and answer them. If you are part of a study group, have members ask questions of the others.

Common Sense Tactics

Arrive on the scene early; relax by breathing deeply. If the instructor gives instructions while distributing the test, listen very carefully.

- **Scan the whole test first.** Notice the point value for each section and budget your time accordingly.

- **Read the directions carefully** and then reread them. Don't lose points because you misread the directions.

- **Answer the short, easy questions first.** A bit of early success stimulates the mind and builds your confidence.

- **Leave space between answers.** You may think of a brilliant comment to add later.

- **Your first instinct is often the best** in answering true-false and multiple-choice questions. Look for qualifiers such as *never, all, often,* or *seldom* in true-false statements. Usually a qualifier that is absolute (*never, all,* or *none*) will indicate a false statement. Work fast on short-answer questions: they seldom count many points.

- **Open-book tests are no picnic.** Don't think that less study is required for an open-book test. They are often the most difficult of all examinations. If the material is unfamiliar, you won't have time to locate it and learn it during the test period.

Important Essay Strategies

- **Read the question carefully** and find out exactly what is asked for. If you are asked to contrast the French Revolution with the American Revolution and you spend your time describing each, without any contrasting references, your grade will be lowered.

- **Know the definitions of key words** used in essay questions:
  analyze: discuss the component parts.
  compare: examine for similarities.
  criticize: give a judgment or evaluation.
  define: state precise meaning of terms.

  describe: give a detailed picture of qualities and characteristics.
  discuss: give the pros and cons: debate them, and come to a conclusion.
  enumerate: briefly mention a number of ideas, things, or events.
  evaluate: give an opinion, with supporting evidence.
  illustrate: give examples (illustrations) relating to a general statement.
  interpret: usually means to state in other words, to explain, make clear.
  outline: another way of asking for brief listings of principal ideas or characteristics. Normally the sentence or topic outline format is not required.
  prove: give evidence and facts to support the premise stated in the test.
  summarize: give an abbreviated account, with your conclusions.
- **Write a short outline** before you begin your essay. This organizes your thinking, making you less likely to leave out major topics.
- **Get to the point immediately.** Don't get bogged down in a lengthy introduction.
- **Read your essay over** before you hand it in. Words can be left out or misspelled. Remember that essay answers are graded somewhat subjectively, and papers that are correctly and neatly written make a better impression.
- **Learn from your test paper** when it is returned. Students who look at a test grade and discard the paper are throwing away a valuable tool. Analyze your mistakes honestly; look for clues for improvement in the professor's comments.

WRITING A TERM PAPER

Doing convincing library research and writing a term paper with correct footnotes and bibliography is a complicated procedure. Most first-year English composition courses include this process. Good students will work hard to master this skill because they know that research papers are integral parts of undergraduate and graduate courses.

Many students make the mistake of waiting until near the deadline to begin a term paper. At the busy end of the term, with final exams approaching, they embark on the uncertain time span of research and writing. Begin your term paper early, when the library staff is unhurried and ready to help and when you are under less pressure. It will pay dividends.

REGULATING YOUR RELATIONSHIPS

Find your special friends who believe in your definition of success. In a fast-paced environment like college, it is important to spend most of your time with people who share your ideas toward learning, where you can be yourself, without defensiveness. To find your kind of friends, first ask yourself: What is success? Is it a secure position and a comfortable home? A life of serving others? A position of power with a commodious executive suite? A challenging job that allows you to be creative? When you have answered honestly, you will have a set of long-range personal goals, and you can begin looking for kindred souls to walk with you on the road to success.

There will be, of course, some persons around you who are determined not to succeed, who for some reason program their lives for failure. Many college freshmen never receive a college degree; some may start college with no intention of passing courses. Their goal is to spend one hectic term as a party animal. If you intend to succeed at college, spending time among this type will be a considerable handicap. Consider making friends who will be around longer than the first year.

If possible, steer clear of highly emotional relationships during your first year of college. You don't have time for a broken heart, and relationships that begin with a rush often end that way.

MAINTAINING YOUR HEALTH

Poor health can threaten your success in the first year of college as nothing else can. No matter how busy you are, you must not forget your body and its needs: proper food, sufficient sleep, and healthy exercise. Many students, faced with the stress of college life, find themselves overmunching junk foods and gaining weight. Guard against this. Drugs and alcohol threaten the health and the success of many college students.

A FINAL WORD

So there it is. If you have read this far, you probably have a serious interest in succeeding in your first year of college. You probably have also realized that these suggestions, even if they sound a bit preachy, are practical and workable. They are based on many years of observing college students.

Benjamin W. Griffith
Former Dean, Graduate School
West Georgia College
Carrollton, Georgia

COLLEGE ADMISSIONS SELECTOR

This index groups all the colleges listed in this book according to degree of admissions competitiveness. The *Selector* is not a rating of colleges by academic standards or quality of education; it is rather an attempt to describe, in general terms, the situation a prospective student will meet when applying for admission.

THE CRITERIA USED

The factors used in determining the category for each college were: median entrance examination scores for the 2009–2010 freshman class (the SAT score used was derived by averaging the median critical reading, math, and writing scores; the ACT score used was the median composite score); percentages of 2009–2010 freshmen scoring 500 and above and 600 and above on the critical reading, math, and writing sections of the SAT; percentages of 2009–2010 freshmen scoring 21 and above and 27 and above on the ACT; percentage of 2009–2010 freshmen who ranked in the upper fifth and the upper two-fifths of their high school graduating classes; minimum class rank and grade point average required for admission (if any); and percentage of applicants to the 2009–2010 freshman class who were accepted. The *Selector* cannot and does not take into account all the other factors that each college considers when making admissions decisions. Colleges place varying degrees of emphasis on the factors that comprise each of these categories.

USING THE SELECTOR

To use the *Selector* effectively, the prospective student's records should be compared realistically with the freshmen enrolled by the colleges in each category, as shown by the SAT or ACT scores, the quality of high school record emphasized by the colleges in each category, and the kinds of risks that the applicant wishes to take.

The student should also be aware of what importance a particular school places on various nonacademic factors; when available, this information is presented in the profile of the school. If a student has unusual qualifications that may compensate for exam scores or high school record, the student should examine admissions policies of the colleges in the next higher category than the one that encompasses his or her score and consider those colleges that give major consideration to factors other than exam scores and high school grades. The "safety" college should usually be chosen from the next lower category, where the student can be reasonably sure that his or her scores and high school record will fall above the median scores and records of the freshmen enrolled in the college.

The listing within each category is alphabetical and not in any qualitative order. State-supported institutions have been classified according to the requirements for state residents, but standards for admission of out-of-state students are usually higher. Colleges that are experimenting with the admission of students of higher potential but lower achievement may appear in a less competitive category because of this fact.

A WORD OF CAUTION

The *Selector* is intended primarily for preliminary screening, to eliminate the majority of colleges that are not suitable for a particular student. Be sure to examine the admissions policies spelled out in the *Admissions* section of each profile. And remember that many colleges have to reject *qualified* students; the *Selector* will tell you what your chances are, not which college will accept you.

MOST COMPETITIVE

Even superior students will encounter a great deal of competition for admission to the colleges in this category. In general, these colleges require high school rank in the top 10% to 20% and grade averages of A to B+. Median freshman test scores at these colleges are generally between 655 and 800 on the SAT and 29 and above on the ACT. In addition, many of these colleges admit only a small percentage of those who apply—usually fewer than one third.

Amherst College, MA
Bates College, ME
Boston College, MA
Bowdoin College, ME
Brandeis University, MA
Brown University, RI
Bryn Mawr College, PA
Bucknell University, PA
Carnegie Mellon University, PA
Colby College, ME
Colgate University, NY
College of New Jersey, NJ
College of the Holy Cross, MA
Columbia University, NY
Columbia University/Barnard College, NY
Columbia University/School of General Studies, NY
Connecticut College, CT
Cooper Union for the Advancement of Science and Art, NY
Cornell University, NY
Dartmouth College, NH
Franklin and Marshall College, PA
George Washington University, DC
Georgetown University, DC
Hamilton College, NY
Harvard University/Harvard College, MA

Haverford College, PA
Johns Hopkins University, MD
Lafayette College, PA
Lehigh University, PA
Massachusetts Institute of Technology, MA
Middlebury College, VT
New York University, NY
Princeton University, NJ
Rensselaer Polytechnic Institute, NY
Smith College, MA
State University of New York/College at Geneseo, NY
Swarthmore College, PA
Tufts University, MA
United States Military Academy, NY
United States Naval Academy, MD
University of Pennsylvania, PA
University of Rochester, NY
Vassar College, NY
Villanova University, PA
Webb Institute, NY
Wellesley College, MA
Wesleyan University, CT
Williams College, MA
Yale University, CT

HIGHLY COMPETITIVE

Colleges in this group generally look for students with grade averages of B+ to B and accept most of their students from the top 20% to 35% of the high school class. Median freshman test scores at these colleges generally range from 620 to 654 on the SAT and 27 or 28 on the ACT. These schools generally accept between one third and one half of their applicants.

To provide for finer distinctions within this admissions category, a plus (+) symbol has been placed before some entries. These are colleges with median freshman scores of 645 or more on the SAT or 28 or more on the ACT (depending on which test the college prefers), and colleges that accept fewer than one quarter of their applicants.

Allegheny College, PA
+American University, DC
Babson College, MA
+Bennington College, VT
Bentley University, MA
+Boston University, MA
Bryant University, RI
Clark University, MA
+Dickinson College, PA
Emerson College, MA
Eugene Lang College New School for Liberal Arts, NY
Fordham University, NY
Gettysburg College, PA
+Grove City College, PA
Hampshire College, MA
Juniata College, PA
+Mount Holyoke College, MA
Muhlenberg College, PA
Northeastern University, MA
Providence College, RI
Ramapo College of New Jersey, NJ
Rutgers, The State University of New Jersey/New Brunswick/Piscataway Campus, NJ
Saint John's College, MD

Saint Lawrence University, NY
Saint Mary's College of Maryland, MD
Sarah Lawrence College, NY
+State University of New York at Binghamton /Binghamton University, NY
State University of New York/College of Environmental Science and Forestry, NY
State University of New York/University at Stony Brook, NY
Stevens Institute of Technology, NJ
Stonehill College, MA
Syracuse University, NY
Trinity College, CT
+Union College, NY
United States Coast Guard Academy, CT
United States Merchant Marine Academy, NY
University of Connecticut, CT
University of Maryland/College Park, MD
University of Pittsburgh at Pittsburgh, PA
+Wheaton College, MA
+Worcester Polytechnic Institute, MA

VERY COMPETITIVE

The colleges in this category generally admit students whose averages are no less than B- and who rank in the top 35% to 50% of their graduating class. They generally report median freshman test scores in the 573 to 619 range on the SAT and from 24 to 26 on the ACT. These schools generally accept between one half and three quarters of their applicants.

The plus (+) has been placed before colleges with median freshman scores of 610 or above on the SAT or 26 or better on the ACT (depending on which test the college prefers), and colleges that accept fewer than one third of their applicants.

Alfred University, NY
+Bard College, NY
Canisius College, NY
Catholic University of America, DC
Champlain College, VT
City University of New York/Baruch College, NY
City University of New York/Hunter College, NY
Clarkson University, NY
College of New Rochelle, NY
College of the Atlantic, ME
Drew University/College of Liberal Arts, NJ
Drexel University, PA
Duquesne University, PA
Elizabethtown College, PA
Elms College, MA
Fairfield University, CT
+Gordon College, MA
+Goucher College, MD
Hellenic College/Holy Cross Greek Orthodox School of Theology, MA
Hobart and William Smith Colleges, NY
+Hofstra University, NY
Hood College, MD
+Houghton College, NY
Iona College, NY
Ithaca College, NY
Le Moyne College, NY
Loyola University in Maryland, MD

Manhattan College, NY
Manhattanville College, NY
Marlboro College, VT
Marymount Manhattan College, NY
McDaniel College, MD
Messiah College, PA
Metropolitan College of New York, NY
Monmouth University, NJ
Moravian College, PA
Nazareth College of Rochester, NY
New Jersey Institute of Technology, NJ
New York Institute of Technology, NY
Pace University, NY
Penn State University/University Park Campus, PA
Polytechnic Institute of New York University, NY
Quinnipiac University, CT
Richard Stockton College of New Jersey, NJ
Rochester Institute of Technology, NY
Rowan University, NJ
Rutgers, The State University of New Jersey/Camden Campus, NJ
Rutgers, The State University of New Jersey/Newark Campus, NJ
Saint Joseph's University, PA
Saint Michael's College, VT
Saint Vincent College, PA
Salve Regina University, RI
Siena College, NY

Simmons College, MA
+Simon's Rock College of Bard, MA
State University of New York at Fredonia, NY
State University of New York at Oswego, NY
State University of New York/College at Brockport, NY
State University of New York/College at Oneonta, NY
State University of New York/University at Albany, NY
Susquehanna University, PA
Temple University, PA
Towson University, MD
+University at Buffalo/State University of New York, NY
University of Delaware, DE

University of Maryland/Baltimore County, MD
University of Massachusetts Amherst, MA
University of New Hampshire, NH
University of Scranton, PA
University of the Sciences in Philadelphia, PA
University of Vermont, VT
+Ursinus College, PA
Wagner College, NY
Washington and Jefferson College, PA
Washington College, MD
Wells College, NY
Yeshiva University, NY

COMPETITIVE

This category is a very broad one, covering colleges that generally have median freshman test scores between 500 and 572 on the SAT and between 21 and 23 on the ACT. Some of these colleges require that students have high school averages of B- or better, although others state a minimum of C+ or C. Generally, these colleges prefer students in the top 50% to 65% of the graduating class and accept between 75% and 85% of their applicants.

Colleges with a plus (+) are those with median freshman SAT scores of 563 or more or median freshman ACT scores of 24 or more (depending on which test the college prefers), and those that admit fewer than half of their applicants.

Adelphi University, NY
Albertus Magnus College, CT
Albright College, PA
Alvernia College, PA
+Arcadia University, PA
Assumption College, MA
Bay Path College, MA
Bloomfield College, NJ
Bloomsburg University of Pennsylvania, PA
Boricua College, NY
Bowie State University, MD
Bridgewater State College, MA
Bryn Athyn College of the New Church, PA
Cabrini College, PA
California University of Pennsylvania, PA
Capitol College, MD
Carlow University, PA
Castleton State College, VT
Cazenovia College, NY
+Cedar Crest College, PA
Central Connecticut State University, CT
Chatham University, PA
+City University of New York/Brooklyn College, NY
City University of New York/City College, NY
City University of New York/John Jay College of Criminal
    Justice, NY
City University of New York/Queens College, NY
Clarion University of Pennsylvania, PA
Colby-Sawyer College, NH
College of Mount Saint Vincent, NY
College of Notre Dame of Maryland, MD
College of Saint Rose, NY
+Columbia Union College, MD
Concordia College-New York, NY
Coppin State University, MD
Curry College, MA
Daemen College, NY
Daniel Webster College, NH
De Sales University, PA
Delaware Valley College, PA
Dominican College, NY
D'Youville College, NY
East Stroudsburg University of Pennsylvania, PA
Eastern Connecticut State University, CT
Eastern Nazarene College, MA
Eastern University, PA
Edinboro University of Pennsylvania, PA
+Elmira College, NY
Emmanuel College, MA
Endicott College, MA
Fairleigh Dickinson University/College at Florham, NJ
Fairleigh Dickinson University/Metropolitan Campus, NJ
Farmingdale State College, NY

Fashion Institute of Technology/State University of New York,
    NY
Felician College, NJ
Fitchburg State College, MA
Framingham State College, MA
Franklin Pierce University, NH
Frostburg State University, MD
Gannon University, PA
Geneva College, PA
Goddard College, VT
Goldey-Beacom College, DE
Gwynedd-Mercy College, PA
+Hartwick College, NY
Hilbert College, NY
Holy Family University, PA
Howard University, DC
Immaculata University, PA
Indiana University of Pennsylvania, PA
Johnson and Wales University/Providence Campus, RI
Johnson State College, VT
Kean University, NJ
Keene State College, NH
Keuka College, NY
King's College, PA
Kutztown University of Pennsylvania, PA
La Roche College, PA
La Salle University, PA
Lasell College, MA
Lebanon Valley College, PA
Lesley University, MA
+Lincoln University, PA
Long Island University/Brooklyn Campus, NY
Long Island University/C.W. Post Campus, NY
Lycoming College, PA
Lyndon State College, VT
Maine Maritime Academy, ME
Mansfield University, PA
Marist College, NY
Marywood University, PA
Massachusetts College of Liberal Arts, MA
Massachusetts Maritime Academy, MA
Mercyhurst College, PA
Merrimack College, MA
Millersville University of Pennsylvania, PA
Misericordia University, PA
Mitchell College, CT
Molloy College, NY
Monroe College, NY
Montclair State University, NJ
Morgan State University, MD
Mount Saint Mary College, NY
Mount Saint Mary's University, MD
+New Jersey City University, NJ

Newbury College, MA
Niagara University, NY
Norwich University, VT
Nyack College, NY
Penn State Erie/The Behrend College, PA
Penn State University/Altoona, PA
Philadelphia University, PA
Plymouth State University, NH
Point Park University, PA
Post University, CT
Rider University, NJ
Rivier College, NH
+Roberts Wesleyan College, NY
Roger Williams University, RI
Rosemont College, PA
Russell Sage College, NY
Sacred Heart University, CT
Saint Anselm College, NH
Saint Bonaventure University, NY
Saint John Fisher College, NY
Saint John's University, NY
Saint Joseph's College of Maine, ME
Saint Joseph's College, New York, Brooklyn Campus, NY
Saint Joseph's College, New York, Suffolk Campus, NY
Saint Thomas Aquinas College, NY
Salisbury University, MD
Seton Hall University, NJ
Seton Hill University, PA
Shippensburg University of Pennsylvania, PA
Southern Connecticut State University, CT
Southern New Hampshire University, NH
Springfield College, MA
State University of New York at Potsdam, NY
+State University of New York/College at Buffalo, NY
State University of New York/College at Cortland, NY
State University of New York/College at Old Westbury, NY
State University of New York/College at Plattsburgh, NY
State University of New York/College at Purchase, NY
State University of New York/College of Agriculture and Technology at Cobleskill, NY
State University of New York/College of Technology at Alfred, NY

State University of New York/Institute of Technology, NY
State University of New York/Maritime College, NY
State University of New York/University at New Paltz, NY
Sterling College, VT
Stevenson University, MD
Suffolk University, MA
Thomas More College of Liberal Arts, NH
Touro College, NY
Trinity Washington University, DC
University of Hartford, CT
University of Maine, ME
University of Maine at Augusta, ME
University of Maine at Farmington, ME
University of Maine at Machias, ME
University of Maryland/Eastern Shore, MD
University of Massachusetts Boston, MA
University of Massachusetts Dartmouth, MA
University of Massachusetts Lowell, MA
University of New England, ME
University of New Haven, CT
+University of Pittsburgh at Bradford, PA
University of Pittsburgh at Greensburg, PA
University of Rhode Island, RI
University of Southern Maine, ME
Utica College, NY
Vermont Technical College, VT
Waynesburg University, PA
Wentworth Institute of Technology, MA
Wesley College, DE
West Chester University of Pennsylvania, PA
Western Connecticut State University, CT
Western New England College, MA
Westfield State College, MA
+Westminster College, PA
Wheelock College, MA
Widener University, PA
Wilkes University, PA
William Paterson University of New Jersey, NJ
Wilson College, PA
Worcester State College, MA
York College of Pennsylvania, PA

LESS COMPETITIVE

Included in this category are colleges with median freshman test scores generally below 500 on the SAT and below 21 on the ACT; some colleges that require entrance examinations but do not report median scores; and colleges that admit students with averages generally below C who rank in the top 65% of the graduating class. These colleges usually admit 85% or more of their applicants.

American International College, MA
Anna Maria College, MA
Atlantic Union College, MA
Becker College, MA
Berkeley College/New Jersey, NJ
Berkeley College/New York City, NY
Berkeley College/Westchester Campus, NY
Caldwell College, NJ
Centenary College, NJ
Chestnut Hill College, PA
Cheyney University of Pennsylvania, PA
City University of New York/Herbert H. Lehman College, NY
College of Saint Elizabeth, NJ
College of Saint Joseph, VT
Delaware State University, DE
DeVry College of Technology/North Brunswick, NJ
DeVry Institute of Technology/New York, NY
DeVry University/Fort Washington, PA
Dowling College, NY
Georgian Court University, NJ
Green Mountain College, VT
Husson University, ME
Keystone College, PA
LIM College, NY
Lock Haven University of Pennsylvania, PA
Medaille College, NY
Mount Aloysius College, PA

Mount Ida College, MA
Neumann College, PA
New England College, NH
Nichols College, MA
Philadelphia Biblical University, PA
Pine Manor College, MA
Regis College, MA
Rhode Island College, RI
Robert Morris University, PA
Saint Francis College, NY
Saint Francis University, PA
Saint Joseph College, CT
Saint Peter's College, NJ
Salem State College, MA
Slippery Rock University of Pennsylvania, PA
Sojourner-Douglass College, MD
Southern Vermont College, VT
Thiel College, PA
Thomas College, ME
Unity College, ME
University of Bridgeport, CT
University of Maine at Fort Kent, ME
University of Maine at Presque Isle, ME
University of Pittsburgh at Johnstown, PA
University of the District of Columbia, DC
Woodbury Institute of Champlain College in Burlington, VT

NONCOMPETITIVE

The colleges in this category generally only require evidence of graduation from an accredited high school (although they may also require completion of a certain number of high school units). Some require that entrance examinations be taken for placement purposes only, or only by graduates of unaccredited high schools or only by out-of-state students. In some cases, insufficient capacity may compel a college in this category to limit the number of students that are accepted; generally, however, if a college accepts 98% or more of its applicants, it automatically falls in this category. Colleges are also rated Noncompetitive if they admit all state residents, but have some requirements for nonresidents.

City University of New York/College of Staten Island, NY
City University of New York/Medgar Evers College, NY
City University of New York/New York City College of
   Technology, NY
City University of New York/York College, NY

Hesser College, NH
Mercy College, NY
Peirce College, PA
Pennsylvania College of Technology, PA
Wilmington College, DE

SPECIAL

Listed here are colleges whose programs of study are specialized; professional schools of art, music, nursing, and other disciplines. In general, the admissions requirements are not based primarily on academic criteria, but on evidence of talent or special interest in the field. Many other colleges and universities offer special-interest programs *in addition* to regular academic curricula, but such institutions have been given a regular competitive rating based on academic criteria. Schools oriented toward working adults have also been assigned this rating.

Albany College of Pharmacy and Health Sciences, NY
Art Institute of Boston at Lesley University, MA
Benjamin Franklin Institute of Technology, MA
Berklee College of Music, MA
Boston Architectural College, MA
Boston Conservatory, MA
Burlington College, VT
Cambridge College, MA
Charter Oak State College, CT
College of New Rochelle - School of New Resources, NY
Corcoran College of Art and Design, DC
Curtis Institute of Music, PA
Eastman School of Music, NY
Excelsior College, NY
Five Towns College, NY
Franklin W. Olin College of Engineering, MA
Gallaudet University, DC
Granite State College, NH
Juilliard School, NY

Maine College of Art, ME
Manhattan School of Music, NY
Mannes College New School for Music, NY
Maryland Institute College of Art, MD
Massachusetts College of Art and Design, MA
Massachusetts College of Pharmacy and Health Sciences, MA
Montserrat College of Art, MA
Moore College of Art and Design, PA
New England Conservatory of Music, MA
Parsons New School for Design, NY
Pratt Institute, NY
Rhode Island School of Design, RI
School of Visual Arts, NY
State University of New York/Empire State College, NY
Thomas Edison State College, NJ
University of Maryland/University College, MD
University of the Arts, PA
Vaughn College of Aeronautics and Technology, NY
Westminster Choir College, NJ

THE BASICS

More than 460 colleges in 11 states and the District of Columbia are described in the profiles that follow.

The Choice of Schools

Colleges and universities in this country may achieve recognition from a number of professional organizations, but we have based our choice of U.S. colleges on accreditation from one of the U.S. regional accrediting associations.

Accreditation amounts to a stamp of approval given to a college. The accreditation process evaluates institutions and programs to determine whether they meet established standards of educational quality. The regional associations listed below supervise an aspect of the accrediting procedure—the study of a detailed report submitted by the institution applying for accreditation, and then an inspection visit by members of the accrediting agency. The six agencies are associated with the Commission on Recognition of Postsecondary Accreditation (CORPA). They include:

Middle States Association of Colleges and Schools
New England Association of Schools and Colleges
North Central Association of Colleges and Schools
Northwest Commission on Colleges and Universities
Southern Association of Colleges and Schools
Western Association of Schools and Colleges

Getting accreditation for the first time can take a school several years. To acknowledge that schools have begun this process, the agencies accord them candidate status. Most candidates eventually are awarded full accreditation.

The schools included in this book are fully accredited by the Middle States Association or the New England Association, or are candidates for that status. If the latter is the case, it is indicated below the address of the school.

Four-Year Colleges Only

This book presents Profiles for all northeast region accredited four-year colleges that grant bachelor's degrees and admit freshmen with no previous college experience. Most of these colleges also accept transfer students. Profiles of upper-division schools, which offer only the junior or senior year of undergraduate study, are not included, nor are junior or community colleges.

Consistent Entries

Each Profile is organized in the same way. Every Profile begins with a capsule and is followed by separate sections covering the campus environment, student life, programs of study, admissions, financial aid, information for international students, computers, graduates, and the admissions contact. These categories are always introduced in the same sequence, so you can find data and compare specific points easily. The following commentary will help you evaluate and interpret the information given for each college.

Data Collection

Barron's *Profiles of American Colleges,* from which the information in this book was extracted, was first published in 1964. Since then, it has been revised almost every year; comprehensive revisions are undertaken every two years. Such frequent updating is necessary because so much information about colleges—particularly enrollment figures, costs, programs of study, and admissions standards—changes rapidly.

The facts included in this edition were gathered in the fall of 2009 and apply to the 2009–2010 academic year. Figures on tuition and room-and-board costs generally change soon after the book is published. For the most up-to-date information on such items, you should always check with the colleges. Other information—such as the basic nature of the school, its campus, and the educational goals of its students—changes less rapidly. A few new programs of study might be added or new services made available, but the basic educational offerings generally will remain constant.

THE CAPSULE

The capsule of each Profile provides basic information about the college at a glance. An explanation of the standard capsule is shown in the accompanying box.

All toll-free phone numbers are presumed to be out-of-state or both in-state and out-of-state, unless noted.

A former name is given if the name has been changed since the previous edition of *Profiles.* To use the map code to the right of the college name, turn to the appropriate college-locator map at the beginning of each chapter. Wherever "n/av" is used in the capsule, it means the information was not available. The abbreviation "n/app" means not applicable.

Full-time, Part-time, Graduate

Enrollment figures are the clearest indication of the size of a college, and show whether or not it is coeducational and what the male-female ratio is. Graduate enrollment is presented to give a better idea of the size of the entire student body; some schools have far more graduate students enrolled than undergraduates.

Year

Some of the more innovative college calendars include the 4-1-4, 3-2-3, 3-3-1, and 1-3-1-4-3 terms. College administrators some-

---

COMPLETE NAME OF SCHOOL
(Former Name, if any)
City, State, Zip Code
(Accreditation Status, if a candidate)

MAP CODE

Fax and Phone Numbers

Full-time: Full-time undergraduate enrollment
Part-time: Part-time undergraduate enrollment
Graduate: Graduate enrollment
Year: Type of calendar, whether there is a summer session
Application Deadline: Fall admission deadline

Freshman Class: Number of students who applied, number accepted, number enrolled
SAT: Median Critical Reading, Median Math, Median Writing (abbreviated CR/M/W)

Faculty: Number of full-time faculty; AAUP category of school, salary-level symbol
Ph.D.s: Percentage of faculty holding Ph.D.
Student/Faculty: Full-time student/full-time faculty ratio
Tuition: Yearly tuition and fees (out-of-state if different)
Room & Board: Yearly room-and-board costs

ACT: Median ACT

ADMISSIONS SELECTOR RATING

times utilize various intersessions or interims—special short terms—for projects, independent study, short courses, or travel programs. The early semester calendar, which allows students to finish spring semesters earlier than those of the traditional semester calendar, gives students a head start on finding summer jobs. A modified semester (4-1-4) system provides a January or winter term, approximately four weeks long, for special projects that usually earn the same credit as one semester-long course. The trimester calendar divides the year into three equal parts; students may attend college during all three but generally take a vacation during any one. The quarter calendar divides the year into four equal parts; students usually attend for three quarters each year. The capsule also indicates schools that offer a summer session.

Application Deadline

Indicated here is the deadline for applications for admission to the fall semester. If there are no specific deadlines, it will say "open." Application deadlines for admission to other semesters are, where available, given in the admissions section of the profile.

Faculty

The first number given refers to the number of full-time faculty members at the college or university.

The Roman numeral and symbol that follow represent the salary level of faculty at the entire organization as compared with faculty salaries nationally. This information is based on the salary report* published by the American Association of University Professors (AAUP). The Roman numeral refers to the AAUP category to which the particular college or university is assigned. (This allows for comparison of faculty salaries at the same types of schools.) Category I includes "institutions that offer the doctorate degree, and that conferred in the most recent three years an annual average of fifteen or more earned doctorates covering a minimum of three nonrelated disciplines." Category IIA includes "institutions awarding degrees above the baccalaureate, but not included in Category I." Category IIB includes "institutions awarding only the baccalaureate or equivalent degree." Category III includes "institutions with academic ranks, mostly two-year institutions." Category IV includes "institutions without academic ranks." (With the exception of a few liberal arts colleges, this category includes mostly two-year institutions.)

The symbol that follows the Roman numeral indicates into which percentile range the average salary of professors, associate professors, assistant professors, and instructors at the school falls, as compared with other schools in the same AAUP category. The symbols used in this book represent the following:

++$	95th percentile and above
+$	80th–94.9th percentile
av$	60th–79.9th percentile
–$	40th–59.9th percentile
––$	39.9th percentile and below

If the school is not a member of AAUP, nothing will appear.

Ph.D.s

The figure here indicates the percentage of full-time faculty who have Ph.D.s or the highest terminal degree in their field.

Student/Faculty

Student/faculty ratios may be deceptive because the faculties of many large universities include scholars and scientists who do little or no teaching. Nearly every college has some large lecture classes, usually in required or popular subjects, and many small classes in advanced or specialized fields. Here, the ratio reflects full-time students and full-time faculty, and some colleges utilize the services of a large part-time faculty. Additionally, some institutions factor in an FTE component in determining this ratio.

*Source: Annual Report on the Economic Status of the Profession published in the March-April 2009 issue of *Academe: Bulletin of the AAUP*, 1012 Fourteenth St. N.W., Suite 500, Washington, D.C. 20005.

We do not, and thus the Student/Faculty ratio that we report may differ somewhat from what the college reports. In general, a student/faculty ratio of 10 to 1 is very good.

If the faculty and student body are both mostly part-time, the entry will say "n/app."

Tuition

It is important to remember that tuition costs change continually and that in many cases, these changes are substantial. Particularly heavy increases have occurred recently and will continue to occur. On the other hand, some smaller colleges are being encouraged to lower tuitions, in order to make higher education more affordable. Students are therefore urged to contact individual colleges for the most current tuition figures.

The figure given here includes tuition and student fees for the school's standard academic year. If costs differ for state residents and out-of-state residents, the figure for nonresidents is given in parentheses. Where tuition costs are listed per credit hour (p/c), per course (p/course), or per unit (p/unit), student fees are not included. In some university systems, tuition is the same for all schools. However, student fees, and therefore the total tuition figure, may vary from school to school.

Room and Board

It is suggested that students check with individual schools for the most current room-and-board figures because, like tuition figures, they increase continually. The room-and-board figures given here represent the annual cost of a double room and all meals. The word "none" indicates that the college does not charge for room and board; "n/app" indicates that room and board are not provided.

Freshman Class

The numbers apply to the number of students who applied, were accepted, and enrolled in the 2009–2010 freshman class or in a recent class.

SAT, ACT

Whenever available, the median SAT scores—Critical Reading, Math, and Writing—and the median ACT composite score for the 2009–2010 freshman class are given. If the school has not reported median SAT or ACT scores, the capsule indicates whether the SAT or ACT is required. Note: Test scores are reported for mainstream students.

Admissions Selector Rating

The College Admissions Selector Rating indicates the degree of competitiveness of admission to the college.

THE GENERAL DESCRIPTION

The Introductory Paragraph

This paragraph indicates, in general, what types of programs the college offers, when it was founded, whether it is public or private, and its religious affiliation. Baccalaureate program accreditation and information on the size of the school's library collection are also provided.

In evaluating the size of the collection, keep in mind the difference between college and university libraries: A university's graduate and professional schools require many specialized books that would be of no value to an undergraduate. For a university, a ratio of one undergraduate to 500 books generally means an outstanding library, one to 200 an adequate library, one to 100 an inferior library. For a college, a ratio of one to 400 is outstanding, one to 300 superior, one to 200 adequate, one to 50 inferior.

These figures are somewhat arbitrary, because a large university with many professional schools or campuses requires more books than a smaller university. Furthermore, a recently founded college would be expected to have fewer books than an older school, since it has not inherited from the past what might be a great quantity of outdated and useless books. Most libraries can make up for deficiencies through interlibrary loans.

The ratio of students to the number of subscriptions to periodicals is less meaningful, and again, a university requires more periodicals than a college. But for a university, subscription to more than 15,000 periodicals is outstanding, and 6000 is generally more than adequate. For a college, 1500 subscriptions is exceptional, 700 very good, and 400 adequate. Subscription to fewer than 200 periodicals generally implies an inferior library with a very tight budget. Microform items are assuming greater importance within a library's holdings, and this information is included when available. Services of a Learning Resource Center and special facilities, such as a museum, radio or TV station, and Internet access are also described in this paragraph.

This paragraph also provides information on the campus: its size, the type of area in which it is located, and its proximity to a large city.

At most institutions, the existence of classrooms, administrative offices, and dining facilities may be taken for granted, and they generally are not mentioned in the entries unless they have been recently constructed or are considered exceptional.

Student Life

This section, with subdivisions that detail housing, campus activities, sports, facilities for disabled students, services offered to students, and campus safety concentrates on the everyday life of students.

The introductory paragraph, which includes various characteristics of the student body, gives an idea of the mix of attitudes and backgrounds. It includes, where available, percentages of students from out-of-state and from private or public high schools. It also indicates what percentage of the students belong to minority groups and what percentages are Protestant, Catholic, and Jewish. Finally, it tells the average age of all enrolled freshmen and of all undergraduates, and gives data on the freshman dropout rate and the percentage of freshmen who remain to graduate.

Housing. Availability of on-campus housing is described here. If you plan to live on campus, note the type, quantity, and capacity of the dormitory accommodations. Some colleges provide dormitory rooms for freshmen, but require upperclass students to make their own arrangements to live in fraternity or sorority houses, off-campus apartments, or rented rooms in private houses. Some small colleges require all students who do not live with parents or other relatives to live on campus. And some colleges have no residence halls.

This paragraph tells whether special housing is available and whether campus housing is single-sex or coed. It gives the percentage of those who live on campus and those who remain on campus on weekends. Finally, it states if alcohol is not permitted on campus and whether students may keep cars on campus.

Activities. Campus organizations play a vital part in students' social lives. This subsection lists types of activities, including student government, special interest or academic clubs, fraternities and sororities, and cultural and popular campus events sponsored at the college.

Sports. Sports are important on campus, so we indicate the extent of the athletic program by giving the number of intercollegiate and intramural sports offered for men and for women. We have also included the athletic and recreation facilities and campus stadium seating capacity.

Disabled Students. The colleges' own estimates of how accessible their campuses are to the physically disabled are provided. This information should be considered along with the specific kinds of special facilities available. If a Profile does not include a subsection on the disabled, the college did not provide the information.

Services. Services that may be available to students—free or for a fee—include counseling, tutoring, remedial instruction, and reader service for the blind.

Safety. This section lists the safety and security measures that are in place on the campus. These vary among schools, but may include 24-hour foot and vehicle patrol, self-defense education, security escort services, shuttle buses, informal discussions, pamphlets/posters/films, emergency telephones, and lighted pathways/sidewalks.

Programs of Study

Listed here are the bachelor's degrees granted, strongest and most popular majors, and whether associate, master's, and doctoral degrees are awarded. Major areas of study have been included under broader general areas (shown in capital letters in the profiles) for quicker reference; however, the general areas do not necessarily correspond to the academic divisions of the college or university but are more career-oriented.

Required. Wherever possible, information on specific required courses and distribution requirements is supplied, in addition to the number of credits or hours required for graduation. If the college requires students to maintain a certain grade point average (GPA) or pass comprehensive exams to graduate, that also is given.

Special. Special programs are described here. Students at almost every college now have the opportunity to study abroad, either through their college or through other institutions. Internships with businesses, schools, hospitals, and public agencies permit students to gain work experience as they learn. The pass/fail grading option, now quite prevalent, allows students to take courses in unfamiliar areas without threatening their academic average. Many schools offer students the opportunity to earn a combined B.A.-B.S. degree, pursue a general studies (no major) degree, or design their own major. Frequently students may take advantage of a cooperative program offered by two or more universities. Such a program might be referred to, for instance, as a 3-2 engineering program; a student in this program would spend three years at one institution and two at another. The number of national honor societies represented on campus is included. Schools also may conduct honors programs for qualified students, either university-wide or in specific major fields, and these also are listed.

Faculty/Classroom. The percentage of male and female faculty is mentioned here if provided by the college, along with the percentage of introductory courses taught by graduate students (if any). The average class size in an introductory lecture, laboratory, and regular class offering may also be indicated.

Admissions

The admissions section gives detailed information on standards so you can evaluate your chances for acceptance. Where the SAT or ACT scores of the 2009–2010 freshman class are broken down, you may compare your own scores. Because the role of standardized tests in the admissions process has been subject to criticism, more colleges are considering other factors such as recommendations from high school officials, leadership record, special talents, extracurricular activities, and advanced placement or honors courses completed. A few schools may consider education of parents, ability to pay for college, and relationship to alumni. Some give preference to state residents; others seek a geographically diverse student body.

If a college indicates that it follows an open admissions policy, it is noncompetitive and generally accepts all applicants who meet certain basic requirements, such as graduation from an accredited high school. If a college has rolling admissions, it decides on each application as soon as possible if the applicant's file is complete and does not specify a notification deadline. As a general rule, it is best to submit applications as early as possible.

Some colleges offer special admissions programs for nontraditional applicants. Early admissions programs allow students to begin college either during the summer before their freshman year or during what would have been their last year of high school; in the latter case, a high school diploma is not required.

These programs are designed for students who are emotionally and educationally prepared for college at an earlier age than usual.

Deferred admissions plans permit students to spend a year at another activity, such as working or traveling, before beginning college. Students who take advantage of this option can relax during the year off, because they already have been accepted at a college and have a space reserved. During the year off from study, many students become clearer about their educational goals, and they perform better when they do begin study.

Early decision plans allow students to be notified by their first-choice school during the first term of the senior year. This plan may eliminate the anxiety of deciding whether or not to send a deposit to a second-choice college that offers admission before the first-choice college responds.

Requirements. This subsection specifies the minimum high school class rank and GPA, if any, required by the college for freshman applicants. It indicates what standardized tests (if any) are required, specifically the SAT or ACT, or for Puerto Rican schools, the CEEB (the Spanish-language version of the SAT). Additional requirements are given such as whether an essay, interview, or audition is necessary, and if AP*/CLEP credit is given. If a college accepts applications on computer disk or on-line, those facts are so noted and described. Other factors used by the school in the admissions decision are also listed.

Procedure. This subsection indicates when you should take entrance exams, the application deadlines for various sessions, the application fee, and when students are notified of the admissions decision. Some schools note that their application deadlines are open; this can mean either that they will consider applications until a class is filled, or that applications are considered right up until registration for the term in which the student wishes to enroll. If a waiting list is an active part of the admissions procedure, the college may indicate the number of applicants placed on that list and the number of wait-listed applicants accepted.

Transfer. Nearly every college admits some transfer students. These students may have earned associate degrees at two-year colleges and want to continue their education at a four-year college or wish to attend a different school. One important thing to consider when transferring is how many credits earned at one school will be accepted at another, so entire semesters won't be spent making up lost work. Because most schools require students to spend a specified number of hours in residence to earn a degree, it is best not to wait too long to transfer if you decide to do so.

Visiting. Some colleges hold special orientation programs for prospective students to give them a better idea of what the school is like. Many also will provide guides for informal visits, often allowing students to spend a night in the residence halls. You should make arrangements with the college before visiting.

Financial Aid

This paragraph in each Profile describes the availability of financial aid. It includes the percentage of freshmen and continuing students who receive aid, the average freshman award, and average and maximum amounts for various types of need-based and non-need-based financial aid. Aid application deadlines and required forms are also indicated.

International Students

This section begins by telling how many of the school's students come from outside the United States. It tells which English proficiency exam, if any, applicants must take. Any necessary college entrance exams, including SAT Subject Tests, are listed, as are any minimum scores required on those exams.

Computers

This section details the scope of computerized facilities that are available for academic use. Limitations (if any) on student use of computer facilities are outlined. It also gives information on the required or recommended ownership of a PC.

Graduates

This section gives the number of graduates in the 2008–2009 class, the most popular majors and percentage of graduates earning degrees in those fields, and the percentages of graduates in the 2008 class who enrolled in graduate school or found employment within 6 months of graduation.

Admissions Contact

This is the name or title of the person to whom all correspondence regarding your application should be sent. Internet addresses are included here, along with the availability of a video of the campus.

DEGREES

A.A.—Associate of Arts
A.A.S.—Associate of Applied Science
A.B. or B.A.—Bachelor of Arts
A.B.J.—Bachelor of Arts in Journalism
A.S.—Associate of Science

B.A.—Bachelor of Arts
B.A.A.—Bachelor of Applied Arts
B.A.A.S. or B.Applied A.S.—Bachelor of Applied Arts and Sciences
B.Ac. or B.Acc.—Bachelor of Accountancy
B.A.C.—Bachelor of Science in Air Commerce
B.A.C.V.I.—Bachelor of Arts in Computer and Video Imaging
B.A.E. or B.A.Ed.—Bachelor of Arts in Education
B.A.G.E.—Bachelor of Arts in General Education
B.Agri.—Bachelor of Agriculture
B.A.G.S.—Bachelor of Arts in General Studies
B.A.J.S.—Bachelor of Arts in Judaic Studies
B.A.M.—Bachelor of Arts in Music
B.Applied Sc.—Bachelor of Applied Science
B.A.R.—Bachelor of Religion
B.Arch.—Bachelor of Architecture
B.Arch.Hist.—Bachelor of Architectural History
B.Arch.Tech.—Bachelor of Architectural Technology
B.Ar.Sc.—Baccalaurium Artium et Scientiae (honors college degree) (Bachelor of Arts & Sciences)
B.Art.Ed.—Bachelor of Art Education
B.A.S.—Bachelor of Applied Science
B.A.S.—Bachelor of Arts and Sciences
B.A.Sec.Ed.—Bachelor of Arts in Secondary Ed.
B.A.S.W.—B.A. in Social Work
B.A.T.—Bachelor of Arts in Teaching
B.B. or B.Bus.—Bachelor of Business
B.B.A.—Bachelor of Business Administration
B.B.E.—Bachelor of Business Education
B.C. or B.Com. or B.Comm.—Bachelor of Commerce
B.C.A.—Bachelor of Creative Arts
B.C.E.—Bachelor of Civil Engineering
B.C.E.—Bachelor of Computer Engineering
B.Ch. or B.Chem.—Bachelor of Chemistry
B.Ch.E.—Bachelor of Chemical Engineering
B.C.J.—Bachelor of Criminal Justice
B.C.M.—Bachelor of Christian Ministries
B.Church Mus.—Bachelor of Church Music
B.C.S.—Bachelor of College Studies
B.E.—Bachelor of English
B.E. or B.Ed.—Bachelor of Education
B.E.—Bachelor of Engineering
B.E.D.—Bachelor of Environmental Design
B.E.E.—Bachelor of Electrical Engineering
B.En. or B.Eng.—Bachelor of Engineering
B.E.S. or B.Eng.Sc.—Bachelor of Engineering Science
B.E.T.—Bachelor of Engineering Technology
B.F.A.—Bachelor of Fine Arts
B.G.S.—Bachelor of General Studies
B.G.S.—Bachelor of Geological Sciences
B.H.E.—Bachelor of Health Education
B.H.P.E.—Bachelor of Health and Physical Education
B.H.S.—Bachelor of Health Science
B.I.D.—Bachelor of Industrial Design
B.I.M.—Bachelor of Industrial Management
B.Ind.Tech.—Bachelor of Industrial Technology
B.Int.Arch.—Bachelor of Interior Architecture
B.Int.Design—Bachelor of Interior Design
B.I.S.—Bachelor of Industrial Safety
B.I.S.—Bachelor of Interdisciplinary Studies
B.J.—Bachelor of Journalism
B.J.S.—Bachelor of Judaic Studies
B.L.A. or B.Lib.Arts—Bachelor of Liberal Arts
B.L.A. or B.Land.Arch.—Bachelor in Landscape Architecture
B.L.I.—Bachelor of Literary Interpretation
B.L.S.—Bachelor of Liberal Studies
B.M. or B.Mus. or Mus.Bac.—Bachelor of Music
B.M.E.—Bachelor of Mechanical Engineering

B.M.E. or B.M.Ed. or B.Mus.Ed.—Bachelor of Music Education
B.Med.Lab.Sc.—Bachelor of Medical Laboratory Science
B.Min—Bachelor of Ministry
B.M.P. or B.Mu.—Bachelor of Music in Performance
B.Mus.A.—Bachelor of Applied Music
B.M.T.—Bachelor of Music Therapy
B.O.T.—Bachelor of Occupational Therapy
B.P.A.—Bachelor of Public Administration
B.P.E.—Bachelor of Physical Education
B.Perf.Arts—Bachelor of Performing Arts
B.Ph.—Bachelor of Philosophy
B.Pharm.—Bachelor of Pharmacy
B.Phys.Hlth.Ed.—Bachelor of Physical Health Education
B.P.S.—Bachelor of Professional Studies
B.P.T.—Bachelor of Physical Therapy
B.R.E.—Bachelor of Religious Education
B.R.T.—Bachelor of Respiratory Therapy
B.S. or B.Sc. or S.B.—Bachelor of Science
B.S.A. or B.S.Ag. or B.S.Agr.—Bachelor of Science in Agriculture
B.Sacred Mus.—Bachelor of Sacred Music
B.Sacred Theol.—Bachelor of Sacred Theology
B.S.A.E.—Bachelor of Science in Agricultural Engineering
B.S.A.E. or B.S.Art Ed.—Bachelor of Science in Art Education
B.S.Ag.E.—Bachelor of Science in Agricultural Engineering
B.S.A.S.—Bachelor of Science in Administrative Sciences
B.S.A.T.—Bachelor of Science in Athletic Training
B.S.B.—Bachelor of Science (business)
B.S.B.A. or B.S.Bus. Adm.—Bachelor of Science in Business Administration
B.S.Bus.—Bachelor of Science in Business
B.S.Bus.Ed.—Bachelor of Science in Business Education
B.S.C.—Bachelor of Science in Commerce
B.S.C.E. or B.S.C.I.E.—Bachelor of Science in Civil Engineering
B.S.C.E.T—B.S. in Computer Engineering Technology
B.S.Ch. or B.S.Chem. or B.S. in Ch.—Bachelor of Science in Chemistry
B.S.C.H.—Bachelor of Science in Community Health
B.S.Ch.E.—Bachelor of Science in Chemical Engineering
B.S.C.I.S.—Bachelor of Science in Computer Information Sciences
B.S.C.J.—Bachelor of Science in Criminal Justice
B.S.C.L.S.—Bachelor of Science in Clinical Laboratory Science
B.S.Comp.Eng.—Bachelor of Science in Computer Engineering
B.S.Comp.Sci. or B.S.C.S.—Bachelor of Science in Computer Science
B.S.Comp.Soft—Bachelor of Science in Computer Software
B.S.Comp.Tech.—Bachelor of Science in Computer Technology
B.Sc.(P.T.)—Bachelor of Science in Physical Therapy
B.S.C.S.T.—Bachelor of Science in Computer Science Technology
B.S.D.H.—Bachelor of Science in Dental Hygiene
B.S.Die—Bachelor of Science in Dietetics
B.S.E. or B.S.Ed. or B.S.Educ.—Bachelor of Science in Education
B.S.E. or B.S in E. or B.S. in Eng.—Bachelor of Science in Engineering
B.S.E.E.—Bachelor of Science in Electrical Engineering
B.S.E.E.T.—Bachelor of Science in Electrical Engineering Technology
B.S.E.H.—Bachelor of Science in Environmental Health
B.S.Elect.T.—Bachelor of Science in Electronics Technology
B.S.El.Ed. or B.S. in Elem. Ed.—Bachelor of Science in Elementary Education
B.S.E.P.H.—Bachelor of Science in Environmental and Public Health
B.S.E.S.—Bachelor of Science in Engineering Science
B.S.E.S.—Bachelor of Science in Environmental Studies
B.S.E.T.—Bachelor of Science in Engineering Technology
B.S.F.—Bachelor of Science in Forestry
B.S.F.R.—Bachelor of Science in Forestry Resources
B.S.F.W.—Bachelor of Science in Fisheries and Wildlife

B.S.G.—Bachelor of Science in Geology
B.S.G.—Bachelor of Science in Gerontology
B.S.G.E.—Bachelor of Science in Geological Engineering
B.S.G.S.—Bachelor of Science in General Studies
B.S.H.C.A.—Bachelor of Science in Health Care Administration
B.S.H.E.—Bachelor of Science in Home Economics
B.S.H.F.—Bachelor of Science in Health Fitness
B.S.H.M.S.—Bachelor of Science in Health Management Systems
B.S.H.S.—Bachelor of Science in Health Sciences
B.S.H.S.—Bachelor of Science in Human Services
B.S.I.A.—Bachelor of Science in Industrial Arts
B.S.I.E.—Bachelor of Science in Industrial Engineering
B.S.I.M.—Bachelor of Science in Industrial Management
B.S. in Biomed.Eng.—Bachelor of Science in Biomedical Engineering
B.S. in C.D.—Bachelor of Science in Communication Disorders
B.S.Ind.Ed.—Bachelor of Science in Industrial Education
B.S.Ind.Tech.—Bachelor of Science in Industrial Technology
B.S. in Sec.Ed.—Bachelor of Science in Secondary Education
B.S.I.S.—Bachelor of Science in Interdisciplinary Studies
B.S.I.T.—Bachelor of Science in Industrial Technology
B.S.J.—Bachelor of Science in Journalism
B.S.L.E.—Bachelor of Science in Law Enforcement
B.S.M.—Bachelor of Science in Management
B.S.M.—Bachelor of Science in Music
B.S.M.E.—Bachelor of Science in Mechanical Engineering
B.S.Med.Tech. or B.S.M.T.—Bachelor of Science in Medical Technology
B.S.Met.E.—Bachelor of Science in Metallurgical Engineering
B.S.M.R.A.—Bachelor of Science in Medical Records Administration
B.S.M.T.—Bachelor of Science in Medical Technology
B.S.M.T.—Bachelor of Science in Music Therapy
B.S.Mt.E.—Bachelor of Science in Materials Engineering
B.S.Mus.Ed.—Bachelor of Science in Music Education
B.S.N.—Bachelor of Science in Nursing
B.S.Nuc.T.—Bachelor of Science in Nuclear Technology
B.S.O.A.—Bachelor of Science in Office Administration
B.S.O.E.—Bachelor of Science in Occupational Education
B.S.O.T.—Bachelor of Science in Occupational Therapy
B.S.P. or B.S.Pharm—Bachelor of Science in Pharmacy
B.S.P.A.—Bachelor of Science in Public Administration
B.S.Pcs.—Bachelor of Science in Physics
B.S.P.E.—Bachelor of Science in Physical Education
B.S.P.T.—Bachelor of Science in Physical Therapy
B.S.Rad.Tech.—Bachelor of Science in Radiation Technology
B.S.R.C.—Bachelor of Science in Respiratory Care
B.S.R.S.—Bachelor of Science in Radiological Science
B.S.R.T.T.—Bachelor of Science in Radiation Therapy Technology
B.S.S.—Bachelor of Science in Surveying
B.S.S.—Bachelor of Special Studies
B.S.S.A.—Bachelor of Science in Systems Analysis
B.S.Soc. Work or B.S.S.W.—Bachelor of Science in Social Work
B.S.Sp.—Bachelor of Science in Speech
B.S.S.T.—Bachelor of Science in Surveying and Topography
B.S.T. or B.S.Tech.—Bachelor of Science in Technology
B.S.S.W.E.—Bachelor of Science in Software Engineering
B.S.V.T.E.—Bachelor of Science in Vocational Technical Education
B.S.W.—Bachelor of Social Work
B.T. or B.Tech.—Bachelor of Technology
B.Th.—Bachelor of Theology
B.T.S.—Bachelor of Technical Studies
B.U.S.—Bachelor of Urban Studies
B.V.M.—Bachelor of Veterinarian Medicine
B.Voc.Arts or B.V.A.—Bachelor of Vocational Arts
B.V.E.D. or B.Voc.Ed.—Bachelor of Vocational Education

D.D.S.—Doctor of Dental Surgery

Ed.S.—Education Specialist

J.D.—Doctor of Jurisprudence

LL.B.—Bachelor of Laws

M.A.—Master of Arts
M.A.Ed.—Master of Arts in Education
M.A.T.—Master of Arts in Teaching
M.B.A.—Master of Business Administration
M.D.—Doctor of Medicine
M.F.A.—Master of Fine Arts
M.P.A.—Master of Public Administration
M.S.—Master of Science
Mus.B. or Mus.Bac.—Bachelor of Music

Ph.D.—Doctor of Philosophy

R.N.—Registered Nurse

S.B. or B.S. or B.Sc.—Bachelor of Science

OTHER ABBREVIATIONS

AABC—Accrediting Association of Bible Colleges
AACN—American Association of Colleges of Nursing
AACSB—American Assembly of Collegiate Schools of Business
AAFCS—American Association of Family and Consumer Sciences
AALE—American Academy for Liberal Education
AALS—Association of American Law Schools
AAMFT—American Association for Marriage and Family Therapy
ABA—American Bar Association
ABET—Accreditation Board for Engineering and Technology
ABFSE—American Board of Funeral Service Education
ABHES—Accrediting Bureau of Health Education Schools
ACBSP—Association of Collegiate Business Schools and Programs
ACCE—American Council for Construction Education
ACE HSA—Accrediting Commission on Education for Health Services Administration
ACE JMC—American Council on Education in Journalism and Mass Communication
ACOTE—American Council for Occupational Therapy Education
ACPE—Association for Clinical Pastoral Education, Inc.
ACPE—American Council on Pharmaceutical Education
ACS—American Chemical Society
ACT—American College Testing Program
ADA—American Dietetic Association
ADA—American Dental Association
ADDA—American Design Drafting Association
AFSA—Application for Federal Student Aid
AHEA—American Home Economics Association
AHIMA—American Health Information Management Association
ALA—American Library Association
ALIGU—American Language Institute of Georgetown University
AMAC AHEA—American Medical Association Committee on Allied Health Education and Accreditation
AOA—American Osteopathic Association
AOA—American Optometric Association
AOTA—American Occupational Therapy Association
AP—Advanced Placement
APA—American Podiatry Association
APA—American Psychological Association
APET—Asset Placement Evaluation Test
APIEL—Advance Placement International English Language Exam

APTA—American Physical Therapy Association
ASHA—American School Health Association
ASLA—American Society of Landscape Architects
ASLHA—American Speech-Language-Hearing Association
ATSUSC—Association of Theological Schools in the United States and Canada
AUCC—Association of Universities and Colleges of Canada
AVMA—American Veterinary Medical Association

BEOG—Basic Educational Opportunity Grant (now Pell Grant)

CAA—Council on Aviation Accreditation
CAADE—California Association for Alcohol/Drug Educators
CAAHEP—Commission on Accreditation of Allied Health Education Programs
CAAP—College Achievement Admission Program
CACREP—Council for Accreditation of Counseling and Related Educational Programs
CADE—Commission on Accreditation for Dietetics Education
CAPTE—Commission on Accreditation in Physical Therapy Education
CAS—Certificate of Advanced Study
CCE—Council on Chiropractic Education
CCNE—Commission on Collegiate Nursing Education
CCTE—California Commission on Teacher Credentialing
CDN—Canadian
CED—Council for Education of the Deaf
CEEB—College Entrance Examination Board
CELT—Comprehensive English Language Test
CEPH—Council on Education for Public Health
CLAST—College Level Academic Skills Test
CLEP—College-Level Examination Program
COE—Council on Occupational Education
CRDA—Candidates Reply Date Agreement
CRE—Council on Rehabilitation Education
CSAB—Computing Science Accreditation Board
CSS—College Scholarship Service
CSS/Profile—College Scholarship Service Financial Aid Profile
CSWE—Council on Social Work Education
CWS—College Work-Study

EESL—Examination of English as a Second Language
ELPT—English Language Proficiency Test (SAT II)
ELS/ALA—English Language Services/American Language Academy
EMH—Educable Mentally Handicapped
EOP—Equal Opportunity Program
ESL—English as a Second Language
ETS—Educational Testing Service

FAFSA—Free Application for Federal Student Aid
FET—Full-time equivalent
FFS—Family Financial Statement
FIDER—Foundation for Interior Design Education Research
FISL—Federally Insured Student Loan
FTE—Full-Time Equivalent

GED—General Educational Development (high school equivalency examination)
GPA—Grade Point Average
GRE—Graduate Record Examination
GSLP—Guaranteed Student Loan Program
G-STEP—Georgia State Test for English Proficiency

HEOP—Higher Equal Opportunity Program
HPER—Health, Physical Education, and Recreation

IACBE—International Assembly for Collegiate Business Education
IAME—International Association for Management Education

IB—International Baccalaureate
IELTS—International English Language Testing System
JRCERT—Joint Review Committee on Education in Radiologic Technology
JRCNMT—Joint Review Committee on Educational Programs in Nuclear Medicine Technology

LCME—Liaison Committee on Medical Education

MAPS—Multiple Assessment Program/Services
MELAB—Michigan English Language Assessment Battery
MUSIC—Multi User System for Interactive Computing

NAAB—National Architectural Accrediting Board
NAACLS—National Accrediting Agency for Clinical Laboratory Educators
NAIT—National Association of Industrial Technology
NAPNES—National Association for Practical Nurse Education and Service
NASAD—National Association of Schools of Art and Design
NASD—National Association of Schools of Dance
NASDTEC—National Association of State Development Teacher Education
NASM—National Association of Schools of Music
NASPAA—National Association of Schools of Public Affairs and Administration
NASPE—National Association of Sport and Physical Education
NAST—National Association of Schools of Theatre
NCATE—National Council for Accreditation of Teacher Education
NCCAA—National Christian College Athletic Association
NCOPE—National Commission on Orthotic and Prosthetic Education
NDEA—National Defense Education Act
NLN—National League for Nursing
NRPA—National Recreation and Park Association

PCS—Parents' Confidential Statement
PAIR—PHEAA Aid Information Request
PEP—Proficiency Examination Program
PHEAA—Pennsylvania Higher Education Assistance Agency
PSAT/NMSQT—Preliminary Scholastic Aptitude Test/National Merit Scholarship Qualifying Test

ROTC—Reserve Officers Training Corps
RSE—Regents Scholarship Examination (New York State)

SAAC—Student Aid Application for California
SACU—Service for Admission to College and University (Canada)
SAF—Society of American Foresters
SAM—Single Application Method
SAR—Student Aid Report
SAT—Scholastic Assessment Testing (formerly ATP–Admissions Testing Program)
SCAT—Scholastic College Aptitude Test
SCS—Students' Confidential Statement
SEOG—Supplementary Educational Opportunity Grant
SOA—Society of Actuaries

TAP—Tuition Assistance Program (New York State)
TDD—Telecommunication Device for the Deaf
TEAC—Teacher Education Accreditation Council
TOEFL—Test of English as a Foreign Language
TTY—Talking Typewriter

UAP—Undergraduate Assessment Program
UP—Undergraduate Program (area tests)

VFAF—Virginia Financial Assistance Form

WPCT—Washington Pre-College Test

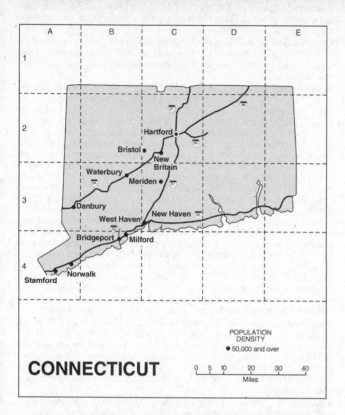

POPULATION DENSITY

● 50,000 and over

CONNECTICUT

0 5 10 20 30 40
Miles

ALBERTUS MAGNUS COLLEGE

C-3

New Haven, CT 06511-1189

(203) 773-8501
(800) 578-9160; (203) 773-9539

Full-time: 477 men, 1028 women	**Faculty:** 46; IIB, av$
Part-time: 32 men, 76 women	**Ph.D.s:** 92%
Graduate: 148 men, 262 women	**Student/Faculty:** 37 to 1
Year: semesters, summer session	**Tuition:** $23,126
Application Deadline: open	**Room & Board:** $9914
Freshman Class: 534 applied, 431 accepted, 107 enrolled	
SAT CR/M/W: 466/451/462	**COMPETITIVE**

Albertus Magnus College, founded in 1925, is a private college affiliated with the Roman Catholic Church and sponsored by the Dominican Sisters of Peace. The college offers undergraduate and graduate degrees in the liberal arts and sciences and in business. There are 3 undergraduate schools and 3 graduate schools. The library contains 125,000 volumes, 7,500 microform items, and 2,000 audio/video tapes/CDs/DVDs, and subscribes to 780 periodicals including electronic. Computerized library services include interlibrary loans, database searching, and Internet access. Special learning facilities include a learning resource center, art gallery, a theater, an academic skill center, and computer centers. The 55-acre campus is in a suburban area 80 miles from New York City. Including any residence halls, there are 17 buildings.

Student Life: 95% of undergraduates are from Connecticut. Others are from 6 states, and 3 foreign countries. 85% are from public schools. 49% are white; 29% African American; 11% Hispanic. 55% are Catholic; 18% claim no religious affiliation; 17% Protestant. The average age of freshmen is 18; all undergraduates, 22. 24% do not continue beyond their first year; 74% remain to graduate.

Housing: 320 students can be accommodated in college housing, which includes single-sex and coed dorms. Residence halls are mainly old mansions that have been converted into student housing. Each building houses 15 to 65 students. On-campus housing is guaranteed for all 4 years. 55% of students live on campus; of those, 70% remain on campus on weekends. All students may keep cars.

Activities: There are no fraternities or sororities. There are 20 groups on campus, including art, computers, dance, drama, ethnic, honors, international, literary magazine, musical theater, photography, political, professional, religious, social, social service, and student government. Popular campus events include Fall Candlelight Ceremony, Christmas events, and Laurel Day.

Sports: There are 7 intercollegiate sports for men and 7 for women. Facilities include an Olympic-size pool, a gym, indoor and outdoor tracks, racquetball and volleyball courts, weight and dance rooms, 4 tennis courts, a game room, and soccer and softball fields.

Disabled Students: All of the campus is accessible. Facilities include wheelchair ramps, elevators, special parking, specially equipped restrooms, special class scheduling, lowered drinking fountains, and lowered telephones.

Services: Counseling and information services are available, as is tutoring in every subject. There is remedial math, reading, and writing.

Campus Safety and Security: Measures include 24-hour foot and vehicle patrol, emergency notification system, and security escort services. There are shuttle buses, emergency telephones, and lighted pathways/sidewalks.

Programs of Study: Albertus Magnus confers B.A., B.S., and B.F.A. degrees. Associate and master's degrees are also awarded. Bachelor's degrees are awarded in BIOLOGICAL SCIENCE (biology/biological science), BUSINESS (accounting, business administration and management, and management information systems), COMMUNICATIONS AND THE ARTS (communications, dramatic arts, English, and fine arts), COMPUTER AND PHYSICAL SCIENCE (mathematics), EDUCATION (education), HEALTH PROFESSIONS (art therapy, predentistry, premedicine, and preveterinary science), SOCIAL SCIENCE (criminology, history, human services, humanities, industrial and organizational psychology, liberal arts/general studies, philosophy, political science/government, prelaw, psychology, religion, sociology, and urban studies). Liberal arts, business, and computer technology are the strongest academically. Business management, sociology/criminal justice, and psychology are the largest.

Required: To graduate, all students must complete at least 120 credit hours, including 60 outside the major and at least 30 in the major. General education requirements, including 6 credits each in English and humanities, and 3 each in fine arts, math, science, and senior humanities, must be fulfilled. Distribution requirements include 3 credits each of history, social science, philosophy, religion, and literature. Service learning or career explorations are also required. A minimum 2.0 GPA is required.

Special: The college offers junior-and senior-year internships allowing up to 12 credits, study abroad, a Washington semester, work-study programs, and accelerated degree programs in business and information technology, psychology, criminal justice, communications, English, humanities, and general studies. Also available are dual and student-designed majors, nondegree study, pass/fail options, independent study, and preprofessional programs. Students may take accelerated degree programs in the evening or take weekend courses. The college also offers a teacher certification program, including placement for the student teaching. There are 5 national honor societies, a freshman honors program, and 12 departmental honors programs.

Faculty/Classroom: 54% of faculty are male; 46% are female. All teach and do research. No introductory courses are taught by graduate students. The average class size in an introductory lecture, 20, in a laboratory, 10, and in a regular course, 15.

Admissions: 81% of the 2009-2010 applicants were accepted. The SAT scores for the 2009-2010 freshman class were: Critical Reading--43% below 500, 41% between 500 and 599, 14% between 600 and 700, and 2% above 700; Math--53% below 500, 30% between 500 and 599, 15% between 600 and 700, and 1% above 700; Writing--48% below 500, 36% between 500 and 599, 15% between 600 and 700, and 1% above 700. 23% of the current freshmen were in the top fifth of their class; 45% were in the top two fifths. 4 freshmen graduated first in their class.

Requirements: The SAT is required, with a satisfactory score. Applicants must be graduates of an accredited secondary school or have a GED certificate and have completed 16 academic credits, including 4 years of English, 2 or 3 years each of foreign language, math, and science, 2 years of history, and 1 year of social studies. High school transcripts, rank, and 2 letters of recommendation are required. An interview is recommended. Albertus Magnus requires applicants to be in the upper 50% of their class. A GPA of 2.5 is required. AP and CLEP credits are accepted. Important factors in the admissions decision are advanced placement or honors courses, recommendations by school officials, and leadership record.

Procedure: Freshmen are admitted to all sessions. Entrance exams should be taken between April of the junior year and November of the senior year. There are deferred admissions and rolling admissions plans. Application deadlines are open. Application fee is $35. Notifications are sent December 15. Applications are accepted on-line.

Transfer: 29 transfer students enrolled in a recent year. Transfer students must present a minimum 2.0 overall GPA and a 2.0 GPA for all transferable, compatible course work. 30 of 120 credits required for the bachelor's degree must be completed at Albertus Magnus.

Visiting: There are regularly scheduled orientations for prospective students, consisting of registration, a general introduction, a financial aid/

major introduction, lunch, a campus tour, and an interview. There are guides for informal visits; visitors may sit in on classes and stay overnight. To schedule a visit, contact the Admissions Office.

Financial Aid: In a recent year, 50% of all full-time freshmen and 66% of continuing full-time students received some form of financial aid. 34% of all full-time freshmen and 57% of continuing full-time students received need-based aid. The average freshman award was $12,992. Need-based scholarships or need-based grants averaged $9,860 ($14,000 maximum); need-based self-help aid (loans and jobs) averaged $4,123 ($8,940 maximum); and other non-need based awards and non-need based scholarships averaged $8,529 ($20,166 maximum). 8% of undergraduate students worked part-time. Average annual earnings from campus work were $1688. The average financial indebtedness of the 2009 graduate was $16,039. The FAFSA and the college's own financial statement are required. Check with the school for current application deadlines.

International Students: The school actively recruits these students. They must take the TOEFL.from need-based self-help aid (loans and jobs); and $8,529 ($20,166 maximum) from other non-need-based awards and non-need-based scholarships.

Computers: Wireless access is available in residence hall rooms, library, cyber-café, several stations throughout the academic buildings besides the labs and classrooms when not being used for class. All students may access the system 24/7. There are no time limits and no fees. It is strongly recommended that all students have a personal computer.

Graduates: From July 1, 2008 to June 30, 2009, 372 bachelor's degrees were awarded. The most popular majors were management (62%), sociology (13%), and psychology (7%). 28 companies recruited on campus in 2008-2009. In an average class, 64% graduate in 4 years or less, 73% graduate in 5 years or less, and 74% graduate in 6 years or less. Of the 2008 graduating class, 25% were enrolled in graduate school within 6 months of graduation, and 70% were employed.

Admissions Contact: Richard Lolatte, Dean of Admissions and Financial Aid. E-Mail: *admissions@albertus.edu* Web: *www.albertus.edu*

CENTRAL CONNECTICUT STATE UNIVERSITY   C-2

New Britain, CT 06050

(860) 832-2278
(888) 733-2278; (860) 832-2522

Full-time: 4022 men, 3837 women	**Faculty:** 433; IIA, +$
Part-time: 1099 men, 1031 women	**Ph.D.s:** 82%
Graduate: 852 men, 1620 women	**Student/Faculty:** 18 to 1
Year: semesters, summer session	**Tuition:** $7394 ($16,988)
Application Deadline: May 1	**Room & Board:** $9280
Freshman Class: 6759 applied, 3687 accepted, 1281 enrolled	
SAT CR/M/W: 500/510/510	**COMPETITIVE**

Central Connecticut State University, founded in 1849, offers degree programs in liberal arts, engineering technology, business, and education. It is part of the Connecticut State University system. There are 4 undergraduate schools and one graduate school. In addition to regional accreditation, CCSU has baccalaureate program accreditation with ABET, CSAB, CSWE, NCATE, and NLN. The library contains 711,328 volumes, 554,684 microform items, and 8,903 audio/video tapes/CDs/DVDs, and subscribes to 2,623 periodicals including electronic. Computerized library services include interlibrary loans, database searching, Internet access, and laptop Internet portals. Special learning facilities include a learning resource center, art gallery, planetarium, radio station, TV station, and writing and math centers. The 294-acre campus is in a suburban area 10 miles west of Hartford. Including any residence halls, there are 39 buildings.

Student Life: 95% of undergraduates are from Connecticut. Others are from 33 states, 45 foreign countries, and Canada. 75% are white. The average age of freshmen is 18; all undergraduates, 21. 21% do not continue beyond their first year.

Housing: 2100 students can be accommodated in college housing, which includes single-sex and coed dorms. On-campus housing is guaranteed for all 4 years. 72% of students commute. All students may keep cars.

Activities: 1% of men belong to 2 national fraternities; 1% of women belong to 1 national sorority. There are 100 groups on campus, including art, band, cheerleading, choir, chorale, chorus, computers, dance, drama, ethnic, gay, honors, international, jazz band, literary magazine, marching band, newspaper, orchestra, pep band, photography, political, professional, radio and TV, religious, social, social service, student government, and symphony. Popular campus events include Winter and Spring Weekends, First Week, and Vance Lectures.

Sports: There are 7 intercollegiate sports for men and 8 for women. Facilities include a 3,800-seat gym, 8 tennis courts, a 6,000-seat football stadium, a 37,000-square-foot air-supported recreation facility, a natatorium, weight training rooms, and softball, baseball, touch football, and soccer fields.

Disabled Students: 90% of the campus is accessible. Facilities include wheelchair ramps, elevators, special parking, specially equipped restrooms, special class scheduling, lowered drinking fountains, lowered

telephones, and personal care attendants who serve as roommates for physically disabled resident students.

Services: Counseling and information services are available, as is tutoring in some subjects. There is a reader service for the blind, and remedial math, reading, and writing.

Campus Safety and Security: Measures include 24-hour foot and vehicle patrol, self-defense education, and security escort services. There are shuttle buses, emergency telephones, and lighted pathways/sidewalks.

Programs of Study: CCSU confers B.A., B.S., B.F.A., and B.S.N. degrees. Master's and doctoral degrees are also awarded. Bachelor's degrees are awarded in BIOLOGICAL SCIENCE (biology/biological science), BUSINESS (accounting, banking and finance, business administration and management, hospitality management services, international business management, management information systems, marketing/retailing/merchandising, and office supervision and management), COMMUNICATIONS AND THE ARTS (art, communications, dramatic arts, English, French, German, graphic design, Italian, music, and Spanish), COMPUTER AND PHYSICAL SCIENCE (chemistry, computer science, earth science, mathematics, physical sciences, and physics), EDUCATION (art education, athletic training, elementary education, music education, physical education, technical education, and vocational education), ENGINEERING AND ENVIRONMENTAL DESIGN (civil engineering technology, construction technology, electrical/electronics engineering technology, industrial engineering technology, manufacturing technology, and mechanical engineering technology), HEALTH PROFESSIONS (nursing), SOCIAL SCIENCE (anthropology, criminology, economics, geography, history, international studies, philosophy, political science/government, psychology, social work, and sociology). Elementary education, psychology, and criminology are the largest.

Required: To graduate, all students must complete at least 122 to 130 credit hours, depending on the major, with a minimum GPA of 2.0. General education requirements total 44 to 46 credits in arts and humanities, sciences, math, communications, and fitness/wellness studies. Students must also demonstrate foreign language proficiency, complete 6 credits in courses with a global context, and satisfy a First-Year Experience requirement.

Special: The university offers co-op programs and cross-registration with several other Connecticut educational institutions, study abroad in more than 45 countries, internships in most departments, work-study programs, dual majors, and student-designed majors. There are 7 national honor societies, a freshman honors program, and 1 departmental honors program.

Faculty/Classroom: 57% of faculty are male; 43% are female. All teach undergraduates. No introductory courses are taught by graduate students. The average class size in an introductory lecture is 35; in a laboratory is 20; and in a regular course is 25.

Admissions: 55% of the 2009-2010 applicants were accepted. The SAT scores for the 2009-2010 freshman class were: Critical Reading--46% below 500, 44% between 500 and 599, and 10% between 600 and 700; Math--38% below 500, 48% between 500 and 599, and 12% between 600 and 700; Writing--43% below 500, 47% between 500 and 599, and 10% between 600 and 700.

Requirements: The SAT is required. The ACT Optional Writing test is also required. In addition, applicants must be graduates of an accredited secondary school or have earned a GED. An interview is recommended. CCSU also recommends that applicants have 14 academic credits: 4 in English, 3 each in math and a foreign language, and 2 each in science and social sciences, including 1 in U.S. history. AP and CLEP credits are accepted. Important factors in the admissions decision are extracurricular activities record, recommendations by school officials, and advanced placement or honors courses.

Procedure: Freshmen are admitted fall and spring. Entrance exams should be taken in May of the junior year or November of the senior year. There are deferred admissions and rolling admissions plans. Applications should be filed by May 1 for fall entry and November 1 for spring entry, along with a $50 fee. Notifications are sent December 1. Applications are accepted on-line.

Transfer: 779 transfer students enrolled in 2008-2009. Applicants must have a minimum of 12 transferable credits and a GPA of 2.0, and must submit official transcripts from previous schools attended. 45 of 122 credits required for the bachelor's degree must be completed at CCSU.

Visiting: There are regularly scheduled orientations for prospective students, including a fall open house in October and daily and select Saturday visits throughout the fall and spring. There are guides for informal visits and visitors may sit in on classes. To schedule a visit, contact the Admissions Office.

Financial Aid: In 2009-2010, 70% of all full-time freshmen and 62% of continuing full-time students received some form of financial aid. 51% of all full-time freshmen and 47% of continuing full-time students received need-based aid. The average freshman award was $3,200, with $1,846 ($7,180 maximum) from need-based scholarships or need-based grants; $2,824 ($3,848 maximum) from need-based self-help aid (loans and jobs); $9,273 ($26,200 maximum) from non-need-based athletic scholarships; and $1,895 ($7,400 maximum) from other non-need-based awards and non-need-based scholarships. 40% of undergraduate students work part-time. Average annual earnings from campus work are $1000. The average financial indebtedness of the 2009 graduate was $19,205. CCSU is a member of CSS. The FAFSA and federal income tax returns are required. The priority date for freshman financial aid applications for fall entry is March 1. The deadline for filing freshman financial aid applications for fall entry is September 1.

International Students: There are 125 international students enrolled. The school actively recruits these students. They must take the TOEFL with a minimum score of 500 on the paper-based TOEFL (PBT).

Computers: All students may access the system. 8:30 A.M. to 12 P.M., Monday to Thursday; 8:30 A.M. to 6 P.M., Friday; 9 A.M. to 6 P.M., Saturday; and 1 P.M. to 10 P.M., Sunday. There are no time limits and no fees.

Graduates: From July 1, 2008 to June 30, 2009, 1660 bachelor's degrees were awarded. The most popular majors were psychology (9%), accounting (7%), and criminology (6%). In an average class, 14% graduate in 4 years or less, 41% graduate in 5 years or less, and 49% graduate in 6 years or less.

Admissions Contact: Larry Hall, Director of Recruitment and Admissions. E-Mail: *admissions@ccsu.edu* Web: *www.ccsu.edu*

CHARTER OAK STATE COLLEGE   C-2

New Britain, CT 06053-2142	(860) 832-3800; (860) 832-3999
Full-time: 45 men, 123 women	Faculty: n/av
Part-time: 733 men, 1178 women	Ph.D.s: 50%
Graduate: none	Student/Faculty: n/av
Year: see profile, summer session	Tuition: $5825 ($7840)
Application Deadline: open	Room & Board: n/app
Freshman Class: n/av	
SAT or ACT: not required	SPECIAL

Charter Oak State College, founded in 1973, is a public liberal arts institution offering degree programs for adult students who cannot complete a college degree by conventional means because of family, job, or financial considerations. Credits may be earned by transfer, testing, portfolio review, contract learning, or by taking Charter Oak's online and video courses. Computerized library services include interlibrary loans and database searching. Special learning facilities include a learning resource center. The offices are in a suburban area 7 miles south of Hartford. There are 2 buildings.

Student Life: 69% of undergraduates are from Connecticut. Others are from 46 states, 3 foreign countries, and Canada. 74% are white; 14% African American. The average age of all undergraduates is 39.

Housing: There are no residence halls. All students commute.

Activities: There are no fraternities or sororities.

Sports: There is no sports program at Charter Oak.

Disabled Students: All of the campus is accessible. Facilities include wheelchair ramps, elevators, special parking, specially equipped restrooms, and lowered drinking fountains. The program is a distance-learning one that does not require students to come to the facility. They can obtain services by phone, fax, and e-mail.

Services: Counseling and information services are available, as is tutoring in some subjects, including writing, math, psychology, sciences, and accounting. Tutoring is available on-line.

Programs of Study: Charter Oak confers B.A. and B.S. degrees. Associate degrees are also awarded. Bachelor's degrees are awarded in SOCIAL SCIENCE (liberal arts/general studies).

Required: All baccalaureate students must complete 120 total credits, at least 60 of which must be in liberal arts for the B.S. and 90 for the B.A.; 36 credits must be in the field of concentration. Students must maintain a 2.0 GPA and complete an academic autobiography as part of a comprehensive exam.

Special: Student-designed concentrations and accelerated degree programs are available in all majors. A B.A.-B.S. degree is possible. There is 1 national honor society.

Faculty/Classroom: 50% of faculty are male; 50% are female. All teach undergraduates.

Requirements: Charter Oak State College requires applicants to have earned at least 9 college credits. AP and CLEP credits are accepted.

Procedure: Freshmen are admitted to all sessions. There is a rolling admissions plan. Application deadlines are open. The application fee is $75. Applications are accepted on-line.

Transfer: Most students who enroll in Charter Oak State College have attended college previously.

Visiting: There are regularly scheduled orientations for prospective students..

Financial Aid: The FAFSA and the college's own financial statement are required. Check with the school for current application deadlines.

Computers: There are no time limits and no fees.

Graduates: In a recent year, 560 bachelor's degrees were awarded.

Admissions Contact: Lori Gagne Pendleton, Director of Admissions. E-Mail: *info@charteroak.edu* Web: *www.charteroak.edu*

CONNECTICUT COLLEGE   E-3

New London, CT 06320-4196	(860) 439-2200; (860) 439-4301
Full-time: 710 men, 1129 women	Faculty: 177; IIB, +$
Part-time: 38 men, 29 women	Ph.D.s: 91%
Graduate: no men, 5 women	Student/Faculty: 9 to 1
Year: varies	Tuition: $
Application Deadline: January 1	Room & Board: $8780
Freshman Class: 4733 applied, 1732 accepted, 503 enrolled	
SAT CR/M/W: 660/650/660	ACT: 27 MOST COMPETITIVE

Connecticut College, founded in 1911, is a private institution offering degree programs in the liberal arts and sciences. There are no undergraduate schools and one graduate school. The 2 libraries contain 616,590 volumes, 151,979 microform items, and 98,432 audio/video tapes/CDs/DVDs, and subscribe to 5,599 periodicals including electronic. Computerized library services include interlibrary loans, database searching, Internet access, and laptop Internet portals. Special learning facilities include an art gallery, radio station, an observatory, and an arboretum. The 750-acre campus is in a small town midway between Boston and New York City. Including any residence halls, there are 51 buildings.

Student Life: 85% of undergraduates are from out of state, mostly the Northeast. Students are from 42 states, 46 foreign countries, and Canada. 50% are from public schools. 75% are white. 27% are Protestant; 26% Catholic; 17% claim no religious affiliation; 14% Jewish. The average age of freshmen is 18; all undergraduates, 20. 10% do not continue beyond their first year; 85% remain to graduate.

Housing: 1750 students can be accommodated in college housing, which includes coed dorms and on-campus apartments. In addition, there are language houses and special-interest houses. On-campus housing is guaranteed for all 4 years and is available on a lottery system for upperclassmen. 99% of students live on campus. All students may keep cars.

Activities: There are no fraternities or sororities. There are 55 groups on campus, including a cappella, art, band, chess, choir, chorale, chorus, communications, computers, dance, drama, environmental, ethnic, film, gay, honors, international, jazz band, literary magazine, newspaper, opera, orchestra, photography, political, professional, radio and TV, religious, social, social service, student government, and symphony. Popular campus events include Eclipse Weekend, Harvestfest, and Floralia.

Sports: There are 12 intercollegiate sports for men and 14 for women, and 12 intramural sports for men and 10 for women. Facilities include an 800-seat gym, playing fields, an ice rink, a boathouse, a weight training room, an indoor pool, a dance studio, 12 tennis courts, and courts for squash, racquetball, badminton, basketball, and volleyball. There is also a track and field facility with an all-weather, 8-lane, 400-meter track, facilities for all field events, and a game field.

Disabled Students: The campus is accessible. Facilities include wheelchair ramps, elevators, special parking, specially equipped restrooms, special class scheduling, lowered drinking fountains, and lowered telephones.

Services: Counseling and information services are available, as is tutoring in some subjects, math, writing, and biological sciences.

Campus Safety and Security: Measures include 24-hour foot and vehicle patrol, emergency notification system, and security escort services. There are shuttle buses, emergency telephones, lighted pathways/sidewalks, and controlled access to dorms/residences.

Programs of Study: Connecticut College confers B.A. degrees. Master's degrees are also awarded. Bachelor's degrees are awarded in BIOLOGICAL SCIENCE (biochemistry, biology/biological science, botany, and neurosciences), COMMUNICATIONS AND THE ARTS (art, art history and appreciation, Chinese, classics, dance, dramatic arts, English, film arts, French, German, Japanese, music, and music technology), COMPUTER AND PHYSICAL SCIENCE (astrophysics, chemistry, mathematics, and physics), ENGINEERING AND ENVIRONMENTAL DESIGN (architecture and environmental science), SOCIAL SCIENCE (African studies, American studies, anthropology, East Asian studies, economics, gender studies, Hispanic American studies, history, human development, international relations, Italian studies, Latin American studies, philosophy, political science/government, psychology, religion, Russian and Slavic studies, sociology, and urban studies). Economics, English, and government are the largest.

Required: To graduate, students must complete at least 128 credit hours with a minimum GPA of 2.0. Distribution requirements cover 7 courses from 7 academic areas, plus a foreign language and 2 writing-intensive courses.

Special: Cross-registration with 12 area colleges, internships in government, human services, and other fields, a Washington semester at American University, dual majors, student-designed majors, a 3-2 engineering degree with Washington University in St. Louis and Boston University, non-degree study, and satisfactory/unsatisfactory options are available. One third of the junior class studies abroad. An international studies certificate program is available, which combines competency in a foreign language, an internship, and study abroad. There are also certificate programs in museum studies, community action and public policy, conservation biology and environmental studies, arts and technology, and teaching. There are 5 national honor societies, including Phi Beta Kappa, and a freshman honors program.

Faculty/Classroom: 52% of faculty are male; 48% are female. All teach undergraduates, all do research, and all teach and do research. No introductory courses are taught by graduate students. The average class size in an introductory lecture is 23; in a laboratory is 13; and in a regular course is 18.

Admissions: 37% of the 2009-2010 applicants were accepted. The SAT scores for the 2009-2010 freshman class were: Critical Reading--2% below 500, 17% between 500 and 599, 49% between 600 and 700, and 32% above 700; Math--1% below 500, 17% between 500 and 599, 61% between 600 and 700, and 21% above 700; Writing--3% below 500, 10% between 500 and 599, 54% between 600 and 700, and 33% above 700.

Requirements: In addition, the submission of standardized tests are optional, although students whose primary language is not English are required to submit the TOEFL or its equivalent. In addition, applicants must be graduates of an accredited secondary school. An essay is required and an interview is recommended. AP credits are accepted.

Procedure: Freshmen are admitted fall and spring. Entrance exams should be taken by January of the senior year. There is a early decision, and deferred admissions plans. Early decision applications should be filed by November 15, regular application January 1 for fall entry and December 1 for spring entry, along with a $60 fee. Notification of early decision is sent December 15, regular decision, April 1. Applications are accepted on-line. 367 applicants were on a recent waiting list, 49 were accepted.

Transfer: 18 transfer students enrolled in 2008-2009. Applicants must have a minimum college GPA of 3.0 and be in good standing at the previous school attended. SAT or ACT scores are required and an interview is recommended. 64 of 128 credits required for the bachelor's degree must be completed at Connecticut College.

Visiting: There are regularly scheduled orientations for prospective students, visits include an introduction to the college, student perspectives, academic programs, a luncheon for parents and students, tours, and a reception. There are guides for informal visits, visitors may sit in on classes, and stay overnight. To schedule a visit, contact the Admissions Office at admission@conncoll.edu.

Financial Aid: In 2009-2010, 40% of continuing full-time students received some form of financial aid. 45% of continuing full-time students received need-based aid. The average freshmen award was $31,457. The average financial indebtedness of the 2009 graduate was $22,038. Connecticut College is a member of CSS. The CSS/Profile and FAFSA, and parent and student tax forms, including noncustodial parent's statement are required. The deadline for filing freshman financial aid applications for fall entry is January 15.

International Students: There are 90 international students enrolled. The school actively recruits these students. They must take the TOEFL with a minimum score of 600 on the paper-based TOEFL (PBT) or 100 on the Internet-based version (iBT), APIEL, IELTS, MELAB, ELPT or equivalent.

Computers: Wireless access is available. The campus has 84 wireless access points in academic buildings and all residence halls, with 3100 network drops. The college owns and supports about 1600 computers, some for faculty/staff, others in student labs. All students may access the system 24 hours a day. There are no time limits and no fees. It is strongly recommended that all students have a personal computer.

Graduates: From July 1, 2008 to June 30, 2009, 437 bachelor's degrees were awarded. The most popular majors were economics (15%), government (9%), and English (8%). In an average class, 83% graduate in 4 years or less, 85% graduate in 5 years or less, and 85% graduate in 6 years or less. Of the 2008 graduating class, 25% were enrolled in graduate school within 6 months of graduation, and 75% were employed.

Admissions Contact: Martha Merrill, Dean of Admissions. E-Mail: *admission@conncoll.edu* Web: *www.conncoll.edu*

CONNECTICUT STATE UNIVERSITY SYSTEM

The Connecticut State University System, established in 1983. It is governed by a board of trustees, whose chief administrator is chancellor. The primary goal of the system is teaching. The main priorities are access, with emphasis on a multi-cultural experience; quality, within a context of curriculum diversity and a range of delivery systems; and public service, including linkages with schools, state government, and private enterprise. With more than 36,000 students and 180,000 alumni, CSUS is the largest public university system in Connecticut, with baccalaureate, graduate and professional degrees. Profiles of the 4-year campuses are included in this section.

EASTERN CONNECTICUT STATE UNIVERSITY   D-2

Willimantic, CT 06226   (860) 465-5286; (860) 465-4382

Full-time: 2038 men, 2288 women	Faculty: 198; IIA, av$
Part-time: 381 men, 535 women	Ph.D.s: 97%
Graduate: 98 men, 234 women	Student/Faculty: 22 to 1
Year: semesters, summer session	Tuition: $7983 ($17,675)
Application Deadline: May 1	Room & Board: $9580
Freshman Class: 3785 applied, 2355 accepted, 981 enrolled	
SAT CR/M/W: 513/518/515	ACT: required COMPETITIVE

Eastern Connecticut State University, founded in 1889, is the state's public liberal arts university. There are 3 undergraduate schools and 1 graduate school. The library contains 374,501 volumes, 862,959 microform items, and 7577 audio/video tapes/CDs/DVDs, and subscribes to 3845 periodicals including electronic. Computerized library services include interlibrary loans, database searching, Internet access, and laptop Internet portals. Special learning facilities include a learning resource center, art gallery, planetarium, radio station, TV station, arboretum, and child and family development center. The 182-acre campus is in a suburban area 29 miles east of Hartford and 90 miles southwest of Boston. Including any residence halls, there are 55 buildings.

Student Life: 92% of undergraduates are from Connecticut. Others are from 22 states, 34 foreign countries, and Canada. 74% are white. The average age of freshmen is 18; all undergraduates, 22. 22% do not continue beyond their first year; 50% remain to graduate.

Housing: 2670 students can be accommodated in college housing, which includes coed dorms and on-campus apartments. In addition, there are special-interest houses. On-campus housing is guaranteed for the freshman year only, is available on a first-come, first-served basis, and is available on a lottery system for upperclassmen. Priority is given to out-of-town students. 53% of students live on campus; of those, 55% remain on campus on weekends. Alcohol is not permitted. Upperclassmen may keep cars.

Activities: There are no fraternities or sororities. There are 67 groups on campus, including art, band, cheerleading, chess, choir, chorale, chorus, computers, dance, drama, drill team, environmental, ethnic, gay, honors, international, jazz band, literary magazine, musical theater, newspaper, orchestra, photography, political, professional, radio and TV, religious, social, social service, and student government. Popular campus events include Open Rec Night, Springfest, and University Hour.

Sports: There are 7 intercollegiate sports for men and 10 for women, and 20 intramural sports for men and 20 for women. Facilities include a student center with theaters, café, billiards, fitness center, a 2800-seat field house, a 6-lane swimming pool, soccer field, baseball complex, softball stadium, 400-meter 8-lane track, field hockey field, intramural field, tennis, basketball, racquetball, and squash courts, weight room, matted rooms for yoga and martial arts, and trails in an arboretum.

Disabled Students: 93% of the campus is accessible. Facilities include wheelchair ramps, elevators, special parking, specially equipped restrooms, special class scheduling, lowered drinking fountains, lowered telephones, and special housing.

Services: Counseling and information services are available, as is tutoring in most subjects. There is a reader service for the blind, and remedial math, reading, and writing.

Campus Safety and Security: Measures include 24-hour foot and vehicle patrol, self-defense education, and security escort services. There are shuttle buses, emergency telephones, and lighted pathways/sidewalks.

Programs of Study: Eastern confers B.A., B.S., and B.G.S. degrees. Associate and master's degrees are also awarded. Bachelor's degrees are awarded in BIOLOGICAL SCIENCE (biochemistry and biology/biological science), BUSINESS (accounting, business administration and management, recreation and leisure services, and sports management), COMMUNICATIONS AND THE ARTS (communications, English, fine arts, performing arts, Spanish, studio art, and visual and performing arts), COMPUTER AND PHYSICAL SCIENCE (computer science, information sciences and systems, and mathematics), EDUCATION (early childhood education, elementary education, and physical education), ENGINEERING AND ENVIRONMENTAL DESIGN (environmental science), SOCIAL SCIENCE (American studies, economics, history, liberal arts/general studies, political science/government, psychology, social science, social work, and sociology). Biology, math, and English are the strongest academically. Business administration, psychology, and social sciences are the largest.

Required: To graduate, students must complete 120 credit hours, including 30 to 48 hours in the major, with a GPA of 2.0. General education requirements include 12 credits in interdisciplinary studies, 9 in social sciences, 7 in natural sciences, and 3 each in math, fine arts, literature, writing, health and phys ed, and computer literacy.

Special: Eastern offers co-op programs in all majors, cross-registration with the University of Connecticut, internships, study abroad in 22 countries, a Washington semester, work-study programs, accelerated degree programs, dual majors, a general studies degree, nondegree study, pass/fail options, and credit for military experience. In addition to the B.S./

certification programs for early childhood and elementary education, teacher certification is available for middle school and secondary education studies. There are 5 national honor societies, a freshman honors program, and 4 departmental honors programs.

Faculty/Classroom: 56% of faculty are male; 44% are female. All teach undergraduates. No introductory courses are taught by graduate students. The average class size in a laboratory is 16 and in a regular course, 23.

Admissions: 62% of the 2009-2010 applicants were accepted. The SAT scores for the 2009-2010 freshman class were: Critical Reading--40% below 500, 49% between 500 and 599, and 11% between 600 and 700; Math--37% below 500, 50% between 500 and 599, 12% between 600 and 700, and 1% above 700. 25% of the current freshmen were in the top fifth of their class; 60% were in the top two fifths.

Requirements: The SAT or ACT is required. In addition, applicants must be graduates of an accredited secondary school or have a GED. They should have completed 13 high school academic credits, including 4 years of English, 3 of math, and 2 each of foreign language, social studies, and science (including 1 of lab science). An interview is recommended. AP and CLEP credits are accepted. Important factors in the admissions decision are recommendations by school officials, advanced placement or honors courses, and leadership record.

Procedure: Freshmen are admitted fall and spring. Entrance exams should be taken in November or December of the senior year. There are deferred admissions and rolling admissions plans. Applications should be filed by May 1 for fall entry, along with a $50 fee. Notification is sent on a rolling basis. 188 applicants were on the 2009 waiting list; 61 were admitted.

Transfer: 388 transfer students enrolled in 2008-2009. Official college and high school transcripts are required. 30 of 120 credits required for the bachelor's degree must be completed at Eastern.

Visiting: There are regularly scheduled orientations for prospective students, including small group discussions, a tour of the campus, and a personal interview. There are guides for informal visits and visitors may sit in on classes. To schedule a visit, contact the Office of Admissions.

Financial Aid: Eastern is a member of CSS. The FAFSA is required. The deadline for filing freshman financial aid applications for fall entry is March 15.

International Students: There are 105 international students enrolled. The school actively recruits these students. They must take the TOEFL. They must also take the SAT or ACT.

Computers: Wireless access is available. All students may access the system. There are no time limits and no fees.

Graduates: In a recent year, 840 bachelor's degrees were awarded. The most popular majors were business (15%), psychology (13%), and social sciences (13%). 210 companies recruited on campus in a recent year. In an average class, 1% graduate in 3 years or less, 25% graduate in 4 years or less, 38% graduate in 5 years or less, and 42% graduate in 6 years or less. Of a recent graduating class, 35% were enrolled in graduate school within 6 months of graduation, and 95% were employed.

Admissions Contact: Kim Crone, Director of Admissions and Enrollment Management. A campus DVD is available.
E-mail: *admissions@easternct.edu* Web: *www.easternct.edu*

FAIRFIELD UNIVERSITY

FAIRFIELD UNIVERSITY		B-4
Fairfield, CT 06824-5195		(203) 254-4100; (203) 254-4199
Full-time: 1395 men, 1935 women	**Faculty:** 229; IIA, +$	
Part-time: 263 men, 302 women	**Ph.D.s:** 93%	
Graduate: 403 men, 828 women	**Student/Faculty:** 14 to 1	
Year: semesters, summer session	**Tuition:** $37,490	
Application Deadline: January 15	**Room & Board:** $11,270	
Freshman Class: 8316 applied, 5376 accepted, 849 enrolled		
SAT CR/M/W: 570/570/580	**ACT:** 25	**VERY COMPETITIVE**

Fairfield University, founded by the Jesuits in 1942, is a private, Roman Catholic Jesuit institution. There are 5 undergraduate schools and 5 graduate schools. In addition to regional accreditation, Fairfield has baccalaureate program accreditation with AACSB, ABET, and NLN. The library contains 394,588 volumes, 881,677 microform items, and 12,788 audio/video tapes/CDs/DVDs, and subscribes to 34,405 periodicals including electronic. Computerized library services include interlibrary loans, database searching, Internet access, and laptop Internet portals. Special learning facilities include an art gallery, radio station, TV station, media center, 750-seat concert hall/theater, a rehearsal and improvisation theater, language learning lab, Business Education Simulation Training (BEST) classroom, and SIM/simulated hospital environment and human patient simulators in the nursing facility. The 200-acre campus is in a suburban, residential community 60 miles northeast of New York City. Including any residence halls, there are 42 buildings.

Student Life: 74% of undergraduates are from out of state, mostly the Northeast. Students are from 33 states, 39 foreign countries, and Canada. 55% are from public schools. 83% are white. 71% are Catholic; 12%

Protestant. The average age of freshmen is 18; all undergraduates, 20. 12% do not continue beyond their first year; 85% remain to graduate.

Housing: 2500 students can be accommodated in college housing, which includes coed dorms and on-campus apartments. In addition, there are special-interest houses and a substance-free floor. On-campus housing is guaranteed for all 4 years. 76% of students live on campus; of those, 90% remain on campus on weekends. Upperclassmen may keep cars.

Activities: There are no fraternities or sororities. There are 110 groups on campus, including art, band, cheerleading, chorale, computers, dance, debate, drama, environmental, ethnic, film, gay, honors, international, jazz band, literary magazine, newspaper, orchestra, pep band, photography, political, professional, radio and TV, religious, social, social service, student government, and yearbook. Popular campus events include Hunger Clean-up, Noche Caliente, and Annual Midnight Breakfast.

Sports: There are 9 intercollegiate sports for men and 11 for women, and 18 intramural sports for men and 18 for women. Facilities include a gym, a 25-meter swimming pool, weight rooms, indoor and outdoor tennis courts, racquetball and volleyball courts, indoor and outdoor tracks, a sauna, a whirlpool, and fitness equipment.

Disabled Students: All of the campus is accessible. Facilities include wheelchair ramps, elevators, special parking, specially equipped restrooms, special class scheduling, lowered drinking fountains, lowered telephones, and special housing. Accommodations for seeing-eye dogs and a library computer station for physically challenged students are also available.

Services: Counseling and information services are available, as is tutoring in every subject. There is a reader service for the blind.

Campus Safety and Security: Measures include 24-hour foot and vehicle patrol, emergency notification system, self-defense education, and security escort services. There are shuttle buses, emergency telephones, lighted pathways/sidewalks, EMT security officers, bike patrol, closed circuit television system, crime prevention seminars, and information via campus television network.

Programs of Study: Fairfield confers B.A. and B.S. degrees. Associate and master's degrees are also awarded. Bachelor's degrees are awarded in BIOLOGICAL SCIENCE (biochemistry and biology/biological science), BUSINESS (accounting, banking and finance, business administration and management, international business management, management information systems, and marketing/retailing/merchandising), COMMUNICATIONS AND THE ARTS (art history and appreciation, communications, dramatic arts, English, fine arts, French, German, Italian, music, Spanish, studio art, and visual and performing arts), COMPUTER AND PHYSICAL SCIENCE (chemistry, computer science, information sciences and systems, mathematics, physics, and software engineering), ENGINEERING AND ENVIRONMENTAL DESIGN (computer engineering, electrical/electronics engineering, and mechanical engineering), HEALTH PROFESSIONS (nursing), SOCIAL SCIENCE (American studies, economics, history, international studies, philosophy, political science/government, psychology, religion, and sociology). Finance, marketing, and nursing are the strongest academically. Finance, communications, and biology are the largest.

Required: To graduate, students must complete 120 credits, 60 of them in general education core requirements, with a minimum GPA of 2.0. Distribution requirements include 15 credits in philosophy, religious studies, and ethics, 15 credits in English and fine arts, 12 credits in math and natural sciences, 12 credits in history and social sciences, and 6 credits in foreign languages. First-year students are required to take a course in multiculturalism.

Special: Fairfield administers its own study abroad program in several countries and has affiliations with 17 programs, a Washington semester, a federal work-study program, B.A.-B.S. degrees in economics, international studies, and psychology, student-designed majors, and dual majors in all subjects. A 3-2 engineering degree is offered with the University of Connecticut, Rensselaer Polytechnic Institute, Columbia University, and Stevens Institute of Technology. A general studies degree and credit for life and work experience are available through Continuing Studies at University College. Internships, both credit and noncredit, are offered at area corporations, publications, banks, and other organizations. Interdisciplinary minors include women's studies, marine science, Black studies, environmental studies, jazz, classical performance, Italian studies, Russian and Eastern European studies, Catholic and Judaic studies, applied ethics, Asian studies, Irish studies, Latin American and Caribbean studies, and peace and justice. There are 18 national honor societies, including Phi Beta Kappa, a freshman honors program, and 1 departmental honors program.

Faculty/Classroom: 53% of faculty are male; 47% are female. 91% teach undergraduates, all do research, and 91% do both. No introductory courses are taught by graduate students. The average class size in a regular course is 23.

Admissions: 65% of the 2009-2010 applicants were accepted. The SAT scores for the 2009-2010 freshman class were: Critical Reading--16% below 500, 49% between 500 and 599, 28% between 600 and 700, and 2% above 700; Math--12% below 500, 42% between 500 and

599, 36% between 600 and 700, and 4% above 700; Writing--12% below 500, 40% between 500 and 599, 37% between 600 and 700, and 6% above 700. The ACT scores were 12% below 21, 19% between 21 and 23, 43% between 24 and 26, 16% between 27 and 28, and 11% above 28. 71% of the current freshmen were in the top fifth of their class; 92% were in the top two fifths.

Requirements: Fairfield has test optional admission. Students who choose to apply without test scores must submit a second essay and are encouraged to complete an on-campus interview. A B average is required. Students should have completed 15 academic credits, including 4 credits of English, 3 to 4 credits each of history, math, and lab science, and 2 to 4 credits of a foreign language. The school recommends SAT Subject tests in language and math, and, for nursing and science majors, in the sciences. A GPA of 3.0 is required. AP and CLEP credits are accepted. Important factors in the admissions decision are advanced placement or honors courses, leadership record, and evidence of special talent.

Procedure: Freshmen are admitted in the fall. Entrance exams should be taken in the spring of the junior year or fall of the senior year. There are early admissions and deferred admissions plans. Applications should be filed by January 15 for fall entry. The fall 2009 application fee was $60. Notifications are sent April 1. 1196 applicants were on the 2009 waiting list; 91 were admitted. Applications are accepted on-line.

Transfer: 37 transfer students enrolled in 2008-2009. The SAT and a college GPA of 2.5 are required (2.8 in business), as are high school and college transcripts, an essay/personal statement, and a report of good standing from the previous college. 60 of 120 credits required for the bachelor's degree must be completed at Fairfield.

Visiting: There are regularly scheduled orientations for prospective students, including information sessions and tours offered weekdays and some weekends. Individualized class visits are available. There are guides for informal visits, visitors may sit in on classes, and stay overnight. To schedule a visit, contact the Admissions Office at (203) 254-4100.

Financial Aid: In 2009-2010, 70% of all full-time freshmen and 68% of continuing full-time students received some form of financial aid. 50% of all full-time freshmen and 50% of continuing full-time students received need-based aid. The average freshman award was $29,123, with $24,000 ($43,200 maximum) from need-based scholarships or need-based grants; $5,392 ($7,000 maximum) from need-based self-help aid (loans and jobs); $20,286 ($51,040 maximum) from non-need-based athletic scholarships; and $17,000 ($20,000 maximum) from other non-need-based awards and non-need-based scholarships. 11% of undergraduate students work part-time. Average annual earnings from campus work are $1109. The average financial indebtedness of the 2009 graduate was $35,161. Fairfield is a member of CSS. The CSS/Profile and FAFSA, parent and student federal tax returns, and all schedules and W-2 forms are required. The deadline for filing freshman financial aid applications for fall entry is February 15.

International Students: There are 43 international students enrolled. The school actively recruits these students. They must take the TOEFL with a minimum score of 550 on the paper-based TOEFL (PBT) or 80 on the Internet-based version (iBT). They must take the TOEFL or the SAT or ACT.

Computers: Wireless access is available. Students have access to grades and scheduling on the Internet. All students may access the system daily until midnight. There are no time limits and no fees. It is strongly recommended that all students have a personal computer.

Graduates: From July 1, 2008 to June 30, 2009, 935 bachelor's degrees were awarded. The most popular majors were finance (12%), nursing (9%), and biology (5%). 147 companies recruited on campus in 2008-2009. In an average class, 78% graduate in 4 years or less and 85% graduate in 6 years or less. Of the 2008 graduating class, 21% were enrolled in graduate school within 6 months of graduation, and 72% were employed.

Admissions Contact: Karen Pellegrino, Director. A campus DVD is available. E-Mail: *admis@fairfield.edu* Web: *www.fairfield.edu*

MITCHELL COLLEGE

New London, CT 06320

E-3

(800) 443-2811
(800) 443-2811; (860) 444-1209

Full-time: 375 men, 380 women	Faculty: n/av
Part-time: 65 men, 85 women	Ph.D.s: 36%
Graduate: none	Student/Faculty: n/av
Year: semesters, summer session	Tuition: $22,000
Application Deadline: see profile	Room & Board: $10,000
Freshman Class: n/av	COMPETITIVE

Mitchell College, founded in 1938, is a private institution offering associate and bachelor degree programs in the liberal arts and professional areas. Figures in the above capsule are approximate. The library contains 73,590 volumes, 38,928 microform items, and 572 audio/video tapes/CDs/DVDs, and subscribes to 90 periodicals including electronic. Computerized library services include interlibrary loans, database search-

ing, Internet access, and laptop Internet portals. Special learning facilities include a learning resource center. The 68-acre campus is in a suburban area on the shore of the Thames River where it meets Long Island Sound. Including any residence halls, there are 26 buildings.

Student Life: 54% of undergraduates are from Connecticut. Others are from 17 states, and 5 foreign countries. 50% are from public schools. 72% are white; 12% African American. 44% are Catholic; 31% claim no religious affiliation; 16% Protestant. The average age of freshmen is 18; all undergraduates, 20. 35% do not continue beyond their first year; 65% remain to graduate.

Housing: 450 students can be accommodated in college housing, which includes single-sex and coed dorms. On-campus housing is guaranteed for all 4 years. 85% of students live on campus; of those, 68% remain on campus on weekends. Alcohol is not permitted. All students may keep cars.

Activities: There are no fraternities or sororities. There are 35 groups on campus, including art, cheerleading, choir, chorus, computers, dance, drama, ethnic, gay, honors, international, newspaper, professional, religious, social, social service, student government, and yearbook.

Sports: There are 8 intercollegiate sports for men and 7 for women, and 15 intramural sports for men and 15 for women. Facilities include a basketball court, a fitness center, 2 beaches, natural and groomed trails, woods, tennis courts, and athletic fields for all varsity teams.

Disabled Students: 50% of the campus is accessible. Facilities include wheelchair ramps, elevators, special parking, specially equipped restrooms, and special class scheduling.

Services: Counseling and information services are available, as is tutoring in most subjects. There is a reader service for the blind.

Campus Safety and Security: Measures include 24-hour foot and vehicle patrol, emergency notification system, and security escort services. There are shuttle buses, emergency telephones, and lighted pathways/sidewalks.

Programs of Study: Mitchell confers B.A. and B.S. degrees. Associates degrees are also awarded. Bachelor's degrees are awarded in AGRICULTURE (environmental studies), BUSINESS (business administration and management, hospitality management services, and sports management), COMMUNICATIONS AND THE ARTS (communications), EDUCATION (early childhood education), SOCIAL SCIENCE (criminal justice, human development, liberal arts/general studies, and psychology). Early childhood education is the strongest academically. Business administration and liberal and professional studies are the largest.

Required: To graduate, students must complete 120 credits with a minimum GPA of 2.0 (2.67 for early childhood education). A first-year seminar and a course in computer systems is required. A capstone is required in human development.

Special: Numerous internships are available through department heads. Work-study programs and B.A.-B.S. degrees are available. Student-designed majors are possible in liberal and professional studies. There are 3 national honor societies, including Phi Beta Kappa, and 1 departmental honors programs.

Faculty/Classroom: 45% of faculty are male; 44% are female. All teach undergraduates. No introductory courses are taught by graduate students. The average class size in an introductory lecture is 12; in a laboratory, 10; and in a regular course, 12.

Requirements: The GED is accepted. A recommendation and a personal statement are required. A GPA of 2.0 is required. AP and CLEP credits are accepted. Important factors in the admissions decision are personality/intangible qualities, recommendations by school officials, and extracurricular activities record.

Procedure: Freshmen are admitted fall and spring. Entrance exams should be taken during summer orientation. There are early decision, deferred admissions and rolling admissions plans. Check with the school for current application deadlines. Notification is sent on a rolling basis. Applications are accepted on-line.

Transfer: 45 transfer students enrolled in a recent year. Applicants must submit college transcripts and a letter of good standing, in addition to fulfilling regular application requirements. 30 of 120 credits required for the bachelor's degree must be completed at Mitchell.

Visiting: There are regularly scheduled orientations for prospective students, including a student-guided tour and an interview with an admissions counselor. There are guides for informal visits and visitors may sit in on classes. To schedule a visit, contact the Admissions Office.

Financial Aid: The FAFSA is required. Check with the school for current application deadlines.

International Students: There were 12 international students enrolled in a recent year. The school actively recruits these students. They must take the TOEFL with a minimum score of 500 on the paper-based TOEFL (PBT) or take the APIEL.

Computers: Wireless access is available. All students may access the system at all times. There are no time limits and no fees. It is strongly recommended that all students have a personal computer.

Graduates: In a recent year, 113 bachelor's degrees were awarded. 30 companies recruited on campus in a recent year. In an average class, 60% graduate in 4 years or less.

Admissions Contact: Kimberly S. Hodges, Director of Admissions. A campus DVD is available. E-Mail: hodges_k@mitchell.edu Web: www.mitchell.edu

POST UNIVERSITY B-3
Waterbury, CT 06723-2540
(203) 596-4520
(800) 345-2562; (203) 756-5810

Full-time: 300 men, 375 women	Faculty: n/av
Part-time: 150 men, 300 women	Ph.D.s: 61%
Graduate: none	Student/Faculty: n/av
Year: semesters, summer session	Tuition: $22,500
Application Deadline: open	Room & Board: $7375
Freshman Class: n/av	
SAT or ACT: recommended	COMPETITIVE

Post University, founded in 1890, is a private institution offering liberal arts and business programs. Figures in the above capsule are approximate. There are 2 undergraduate schools. The library contains 85,000 volumes, 75,158 microform items, and 1027 audio/video tapes/CDs/DVDs, and subscribes to 427 periodicals including electronic. Computerized library services include interlibrary loans and database searching. Special learning facilities include a learning resource center and a tutorial center. The 70-acre campus is in an urban area 1 mile west of Waterbury. Including any residence halls, there are 13 buildings.

Student Life: 83% of undergraduates are from Connecticut. Others are from 12 states, 20 foreign countries, and Canada. 75% are from public schools. 63% are white; 17% African American. The average age of freshmen is 19; all undergraduates, 26. 23% do not continue beyond their first year; 39% remain to graduate.

Housing: 424 students can be accommodated in college housing, which includes coed dorms and off-campus apartments. On-campus housing is guaranteed for all 4 years. 58% of students live on campus; of those, 60% remain on campus on weekends. All students may keep cars.

Activities: There are no fraternities or sororities. There are 30 groups on campus, including cheerleading, chorale, chorus, computers, drama, ethnic, gay, honors, international, literary magazine, musical theater, social, social service, student government, and yearbook. Popular campus events include dances, concerts, and international food festivals.

Sports: There are 5 intercollegiate sports for men and 5 for women, and 4 intramural sports for men and 4 for women. Facilities include a soccer field, a fitness center, a weight room, a racquetball court, a swimming pool, and tennis courts.

Disabled Students: 70% of the campus is accessible. Facilities include wheelchair ramps, elevators, special parking, specially equipped restrooms, and special class scheduling.

Services: Counseling and information services are available, as is tutoring in most subjects. There is a reader service for the blind and remedial math, reading, and writing.

Campus Safety and Security: Measures include 24-hour foot and vehicle patrol, self-defense education, and security escort services. There are shuttle buses and lighted pathways/sidewalks.

Programs of Study: TPU confers B.A. and B.S. degrees. Associates degrees are also awarded. Bachelor's degrees are awarded in BUSINESS (accounting, banking and finance, business administration and management, management science, and marketing/retailing/merchandising), COMMUNICATIONS AND THE ARTS (English), SOCIAL SCIENCE (criminal justice, history, liberal arts/general studies, psychology, and sociology). Biology is the strongest academically. Management and general studies are the largest.

Required: To graduate, all students must maintain a minimum GPA of 2.0, earn a total of 120 credits, including at least 33 in the major, and take a computer course.

Special: Co-op programs in all majors, cross-registration with Naugatuck Valley Community College, study abroad in England, the Netherlands, and Japan, internships with area businesses, general studies degrees, accelerated degree programs, B.A.-B.S. degrees, and credit for life experience are available. There are 2 national honor societies and 1 departmental honors program.

Faculty/Classroom: 57% of faculty are male; 43% are female. All teach undergraduates. The average class size in an introductory lecture is 20; in a laboratory, 15; and in a regular course, 35.

Requirements: The SAT or ACT is recommended. In addition, applicants must be graduates of an accredited secondary school, with 4 years of English and at least 16 total academic credits. The GED is accepted. A GPA of 2.0 is required. AP and CLEP credits are accepted. Important factors in the admissions decision are personality/intangible qualities, extracurricular activities record, and recommendations by school officials.

Procedure: Freshmen are admitted to all sessions. There are early decision, early admissions, deferred admissions, and rolling admissions plans. Check with the school for current application deadlines. The application fee is $40. Notification is sent on a rolling basis. Applications are accepted on-line.

Transfer: Applicants must have a minimum college GPA of 2.0, submit an official college transcript, and have an interview. The SAT is recommended. 30 of 120 credits required for the bachelor's degree must be completed at TPU.

Visiting: There are regularly scheduled orientations for prospective students, including tours, interviews with admissions counselors, and meetings with faculty and students. There are guides for informal visits, and visitors may sit in on classes and stay overnight. To schedule a visit, contact the Admissions Office at (203) 596-4620.

Financial Aid: The FAFSA, the college's own financial statement, and parent and student federal tax returns are required. Check with the school for current application deadlines.

International Students: There were 65 international students enrolled in a recent year. The school actively recruits these students. They must take the TOEFL.

Computers: All students may access the system. There are no time limits and no fees. It is strongly recommended that all students have a personal computer.

Admissions Contact: Jay Murray, Director of Admissions. A campus DVD is available. E-Mail: admissions@post.edu Web: www.post.edu

QUINNIPIAC UNIVERSITY C-3
Hamden, CT 06518
(203) 582-8600
(800) 462-1944; (203) 582-8906

Full-time: 2168 men, 3518 women	Faculty: IIA, ++$
Part-time: 112 men, 173 women	Ph.D.s: 86%
Graduate: 658 men, 1129 women	Student/Faculty: n/av
Year: semesters, summer session	Tuition: $32,400
Application Deadline: February 1	Room & Board: $12,380
Freshman Class: 13850 applied, 9619 accepted, 1587 enrolled	
SAT CR/M/W: 560/580/570	ACT: 25 VERY COMPETITIVE

Quinnipiac University, founded in 1929, is a private institution offering undergraduate and graduate degrees in health sciences, business, communications, liberal arts, education, and law. There are 4 undergraduate schools and 5 graduate schools. In addition to regional accreditation, Quinnipiac has baccalaureate program accreditation with AACSB, ABET, APTA, CAHEA, NCATE, and NLN. The 2 libraries contain 4,875 volumes, 9,100 microform items, and 1,890 audio/video tapes/CDs/DVDs, and subscribe to 4,000 periodicals including electronic. Computerized library services include interlibrary loans, database searching, Internet access, and laptop Internet portals. Special learning facilities include a learning resource center, art gallery, radio station, TV station, and an exhibit on the Irish famine. The 600-acre campus is in a suburban area 8 miles north of New Haven and 35 miles south of Hartford. Including any residence halls, there are 54 buildings.

Student Life: 74% of undergraduates are from out of state, mostly the Middle Atlantic. Students are from 28 states, 12 foreign countries, and Canada. 75% are from public schools. 88% are white. 58% are Catholic; 20% Protestant; 12% claim no religious affiliation. The average age of freshmen is 19; all undergraduates, 21. 9% do not continue beyond their first year; 74% remain to graduate.

Housing: 4200 students can be accommodated in college housing, which includes coed dorms, on-campus apartments, and off-campus apartments. In addition, there is wellness housing. 80% of students live on campus; of those, 75% remain on campus on weekends. Upperclassmen may keep cars.

Activities: 5% of men belong to 2 local and 2 national fraternities; 6% of women belong to 2 local and 2 national sororities. There are 85 groups on campus, including cheerleading, choir, chorale, dance, drama, environmental, ethnic, film, gay, honors, international, literary magazine, newspaper, pep band, political, professional, radio and TV, religious, social, social service, student government, and yearbook. Popular campus events include Siblings Weekend, Parents Weekend, and holiday party.

Sports: There are 7 intercollegiate sports for men and 12 for women, and 6 intramural sports for men and 6 for women. Facilities include a sports center with twin arenas, each seating more than 3000 for ice hockey and basketball, more than 20 acres of playing fields, and a recreation center with a weight training room, a steam room, a large multipurpose room for indoor tennis, basketball, volleyball, and aerobics, and a suspended indoor track.

Disabled Students: All of the campus is accessible. Facilities include wheelchair ramps, elevators, special parking, specially equipped restrooms, special class scheduling, lowered drinking fountains, lowered telephones, and special housing.

Services: Counseling and information services are available, as is tutoring in most subjects, including all freshman-level courses and others by request. Special workshops on work study skills, library resources, and time management are available.

Campus Safety and Security: Measures include 24-hour foot and vehicle patrol, emergency notification system, self-defense education, and security escort services. There are shuttle buses, emergency telephones, lighted pathways/sidewalks, perimeter security in the form of contract security officers at all entrances, and vehicle and occupant check-in identification.

Programs of Study: Quinnipiac confers B.A., B.S. degrees. Master's and doctoral degrees are also awarded. Bachelor's degrees are awarded in BIOLOGICAL SCIENCE (biochemistry, biology/biological science, biotechnology, and microbiology), BUSINESS (accounting, banking and finance, business administration and management, business economics, entrepreneurial studies, international business management, management science, and marketing/retailing/merchandising), COMMUNICATIONS AND THE ARTS (advertising, communications, dramatic arts, English, journalism, public relations, and Spanish), COMPUTER AND PHYSICAL SCIENCE (chemistry, computer science, digital arts/technology, and mathematics), HEALTH PROFESSIONS (health science, nursing, occupational therapy, predentistry, premedicine, and radiological science), SOCIAL SCIENCE (criminal justice, economics, gerontology, history, liberal arts/general studies, paralegal studies, political science/government, prelaw, psychobiology, psychology, social science, and sociology). Psychology, physical therapy, and nursing are the strongest academically. Communications, physical therapy, and management are the largest.

Required: All students must complete 46 semester hours of the core curriculum, which includes a series of 3 seminars that explore community as it relates to the individual and the world, plus English, math, fine arts, social sciences, humanities and science. To graduate, students must maintain a GPA of 2.0 over 120 total semester hours.

Special: Internships in all majors, study abroad in more than 25 countries, a Washington semester with American University, work-study programs, dual and student-designed majors, B.A.-B.S. degrees, credit for life experience, and nondegree study are available. A 6 1/2-year freshman entry-level doctorate in physical therapy and a 5 1/2 year freshman entry-level master's in occupational therapy are offered, as well as a 6-year BS in Health Sciences/MHS in a physician assistant master's program, and a 5-year master of arts in education for those interested in teaching at the elementary, or high school level. There are 20 national honor societies, a freshman honors program, and 20 departmental honors programs.

Faculty/Classroom: 58% of faculty are male; 42% are female. 85% teach undergraduates, 58% do research, and 58% do both. No introductory courses are taught by graduate students. The average class size in an introductory lecture, 24, in a laboratory, 15, and in a regular course, 22.

Admissions: 69% of the 2009-2010 applicants were accepted. 55% of the current freshmen were in the top fifth of their class; 90% were in the top two fifths. 45 freshmen graduated first in their class.

Requirements: The SAT or ACT is required. The ACT Optional Writing test is also required. A satisfactory score on the SAT (critical reading plus math) or 23 composite on the ACT is recommended. The scores are used for admission and scholarship purposes. All students must have completed 16 academic credits, including 4 in English, 3 in math, 2 each in science and social studies, and 5 in electives. The GED is accepted. An interview is recommended, and an essay and at least one letter of recommendation are required. For majors in the health sciences, 4 years each of math and science are required. Quinnipiac requires applicants to be in the upper 40% of their class. A GPA of 2.8 is required. AP and CLEP credits are accepted. Important factors in the admissions decision are advanced placement or honors courses, extracurricular activities record, and personality/intangible qualities.

Procedure: Freshmen are admitted fall and spring. Entrance exams should be taken in the junior year and early in the senior year. There are deferred admissions and rolling admissions plans. Applications should be filed by February 1 for fall entry and December 15 for spring entry, along with a $45 fee. Nursing, physical therapy, and physician assistant should file applications by November 1 for fall entry. Notifications are sent December 15. 1750 applicants were on the 2009 waiting list; 250 were admitted. Applications are accepted on-line.

Transfer: 178 transfer students enrolled in 2008-2009. Transfer students must have a minimum college GPA of 2.5 (some programs require a minimum of 3.0) and must submit SAT scores and high school or college transcripts if they have not received an associate degree prior to enrollment. An interview is recommended. 45 of 120 credits required for the bachelor's degree must be completed at Quinnipiac.

Visiting: There are regularly scheduled orientations for prospective students, consisting of interviews, a group information session, student-guided tours, financial aid sessions, an opportunity to speak with faculty, and open houses. Visitors may sit in on classes and stay overnight. To schedule a visit, contact the Admissions Office at admissions@quinnipiac.edu.

Financial Aid: In 2009-2010, 74% of all full-time freshmen and 72% of continuing full-time students received some form of financial aid. 55% of all full-time freshmen and 55% of continuing full-time students received need-based aid. The average freshman award was $17,115. Need-based scholarships or need-based grants averaged $14,162. 28% of undergraduate students work part-time. Average annual earnings from campus work are $2100. The average financial indebtedness of the 2009 graduate was $37,000. Quinnipiac is a member of CSS. The FAF-SA is required. The priority date for freshman financial aid applications for fall entry is March 1.

International Students: There are 78 international students enrolled. The school actively recruits these students. They must take the TOEFL with a minimum score of 550 on the paper-based TOEFL (PBT) or 75 on the Internet-based version (iBT). They must also take the SAT or ACT.

Computers: Wireless access is available. All students must purchase a university-recommended laptop when they enter Quinnipiac for classroom and residence hall use. All students may access the system 24 hours a day. There are no time limits and no fees. The current vendor is Dell.

Graduates: From July 1, 2008 to June 30, 2009, 1330 bachelor's degrees were awarded. The most popular majors were mass communications (11%), nursing (10%), and physical therapy (9%). 250 companies recruited on campus in 2008-2009. In an average class, 64% graduate in 4 years or less, 68% graduate in 5 years or less, and 70% graduate in 6 years or less. Of the 2008 graduating class, 22% were enrolled in graduate school within 6 months of graduation, and 72% were employed.

Admissions Contact: Joan Isaac Mohr, Dean of Admissions. E-Mail: *admissions@quinnipiac.edu* Web: *www.quinnipiac.edu*

SACRED HEART UNIVERSITY   B-4
Fairfield, CT 06825   (203) 371-7881; (203) 365-7607

Full-time: 1452 men, 2082 women	**Faculty:** 182; IIA, -$
Part-time: 202 men, 456 women	**Ph.D.s:** 80%
Graduate: 573 men, 1258 women	**Student/Faculty:** 17 to 1
Year: semesters, summer session	**Tuition:** $30,298
Application Deadline: rolling	**Room & Board:** $11,684
Freshman Class: 7343 applied, 4864 accepted, 909 enrolled	
SAT CR/M: not required	**ACT:** not required **COMPETITIVE**

Sacred Heart University, founded in 1963, is a private Catholic institution that offers majors within health sciences, liberal arts and sciences, business, education, and information technology. There are 4 undergraduate schools and 3 graduate schools. In addition to regional accreditation, SHU has baccalaureate program accreditation with AACSB, APTA, CSWE, and NLN. The 2 libraries contain 148,803 volumes, 226,110 microform items, and 2,161 audio/video tapes/CDs/DVDs, and subscribe to 67,240 periodicals including electronic. Computerized library services include interlibrary loans, database searching, and Internet access. Special learning facilities include a learning resource center, art gallery, radio station, TV station, and a center for performing arts. The 67-acre campus is in a suburban area in southwestern Connecticut, 55 miles northeast of New York City. Including any residence halls, there are 23 buildings.

Student Life: 68% of undergraduates are from out of state, mostly the Northeast. Students are from 33 states, 35 foreign countries, and Canada. 70% are from public schools. 85% are white. 67% are Catholic; 15% Protestant. The average age of freshmen is 18; all undergraduates, 20. 18% do not continue beyond their first year; 66% remain to graduate.

Housing: 2500 students can be accommodated in college housing, which includes coed dorms, on-campus apartments, off-campus apartments, and honors floors, wellness floors, and special academic major floors. On-campus housing is guaranteed for all 4 years. 60% of students live on campus; of those, 75% remain on campus on weekends. Alcohol is not permitted. Upperclassmen may keep cars.

Activities: 11% of men belong to 1 local fraternity and 3 national fraternities. 10% of women belong to 4 national sororities. 85 groups exist on campus, including art, band, cheerleading, choir, chorale, chorus, communications, computers, dance, debate, drama, drill team, environmental, ethnic, film, gay, honors, international, jazz band, literary magazine, marching band, musical theater, newspaper, orchestra, pep band, photography, political, professional, radio and TV, religious, social, social service, student government, and yearbook. Popular campus events include Student Affairs Lecture Series, Multicultural Lunch Series, and Fear No People Series.

Sports: There are 14 intercollegiate sports for men and 17 for women, and 25 intramural sports for men and 27 for women. Facilities include a health and recreation center with 4 multipurpose athletic courts, seating for 2,200, and a fitness center. There is a field turf football field, an all-weather track, 6 championship tennis courts, and a softball field.

Disabled Students: 90% of the campus is accessible. Facilities include wheelchair ramps, elevators, special parking, specially equipped rest rooms, special class scheduling, lowered drinking fountains, and lowered telephones.

Services: Counseling and information services are available, as is tutoring in every subject. There is a reader service for the blind, and remedial math, reading, and writing.

Campus Safety and Security: Measures include 24-hour foot and vehicle patrol, emergency notification system, self-defense education, and security escort services. There are shuttle buses, emergency telephones, and lighted pathways/sidewalks. All campus-owned residence halls have sprinklers and alarms and are designated nonsmoking.

Programs of Study: SHU confers B.A., B.S., and B.S.W. degrees. Associates, master's, and doctoral degrees are also awarded. Bachelor's degrees are awarded in BIOLOGICAL SCIENCE (biology/biological science), BUSINESS (accounting, banking and finance, business administration and management, business economics, marketing management, and sports management), COMMUNICATIONS AND THE ARTS (art, communications, communications technology, English, graphic design, media arts, and Spanish), COMPUTER AND PHYSICAL SCIENCE (chemistry, computer science, information sciences and systems, and mathematics), EDUCATION (athletic training, business education, education, elementary education, English education, foreign languages education, mathematics education, middle school education, science education, social science education, and social studies education), HEALTH PROFESSIONS (exercise science, nursing, occupational therapy, physical therapy, predentistry, premedicine, preosteopathy, prepharmacy, prephysical therapy, and preveterinary science), SOCIAL SCIENCE (criminal justice, history, liberal arts/general studies, philosophy, political science/government, prelaw, psychology, religion, social work, and sociology). Health sciences, business/ finance, and biology are the strongest academically. Psychology, business, and media studies/communiications are the largest.

Required: All students must complete 120 credit hours, including 30 to 58 in the major, while maintaining a minimum 2.0 GPA. Distribution requirements include a 22-credit required core consisting of composition, oral communication, college math, information literacy, literature and civilizations, social or natural sciences, and religious studies or philosophy and a 33- to 35-credit elective core consisting of 9 credits of arts and humanities, 9 credits of social science, 9 credits of philosophy and religious studies, and 6-8 credits of math and natural sciences; B.S. candidates fulfill the maximum math and science requirement; B.A. candidates fulfill the maximum foreign language requirement (6 credits of the same modern foreign language).

Special: SHU offers co-op programs in all majors, paid and unpaid internships at local, regional, and national organizations, including Fortune 500 and 1000 companies, hospitals, media outlets, social service agencies, and schools. Study abroad opportunities exist worldwide and year-round, and on-campus employment is available through the University's work-study program. There are 14 national honor societies, a freshman honors program, and 1 departmental honors program.

Faculty/Classroom: 52% of faculty are male; 49% are female. 92% teach undergraduates, 80% do research, and 80% do both. No introductory courses are taught by graduate students. The average class size in an introductory lecture is 20; in a laboratory is 10; and in a regular course is 22.

Admissions: 66% of the 2009-2010 applicants were accepted. 44% of the current freshmen were in the top fifth of their class; 73% were in the top two fifths. 5 freshmen graduated first in their class.

Requirements: A completed application, essay, and 1 letter of recommendation are required. An interview is required for early decision candidates and recommended for all other candidates. Required are 4 years of English and 3 years of math, science, history, and language, with 4 years preferred. AP and CLEP credits are accepted. Important factors in the admissions decision are advanced placement or honors courses, leadership record, and recommendations by school officials.

Procedure: Freshmen are admitted fall and spring. Entrance exams should be taken in May of the junior year and/or November of the senior year. There are early decision, deferred admissions and rolling admissions plans. Early decision applications should be filed by November 15; check with the school for other current application deadlines. The application fee is $50. Notification of early decision is sent December 15, regular decision, February 1. Applications are accepted on-line.

Transfer: 159 transfer students enrolled in 2008-2009. A minimum GPA of 2.7 is required. 30 of 120 credits required for the bachelor's degree must be completed at SHU.

Visiting: There are regularly scheduled orientations for prospective students, including Monday-Friday tours and interviews, weekend tours, information sessions, and open house programs during the academic year and summer. There are guides for informal visits, visitors may sit in on classes, and stay overnight. To schedule a visit, contact the Office of Undergraduate Admissions at (203) 371-7881.

Financial Aid: In 2009-2010, 93% of all full-time freshmen and 89% of continuing full-time students received some form of financial aid. 70% of all full-time freshmen and 68% of continuing full-time students received need-based aid. The average freshmen award was $19,074, with $15,411 ($20,448 maximum) from need-based scholarships or need-based grants; $4,434 ($7,500 maximum) from need-based self-help aid (loans and jobs); $16,844 ($46,159 maximum) from non-need-based athletic scholarships; and $6,470 ($16,000 maximum) from other non-need-based awards and non-need-based scholarships. 38% of undergraduate students work part-time. Average annual earnings from campus work are $1665. The average financial indebtedness of the 2009 graduate was $18,819. SHU is a member of CSS. The CSS/Profile and FAFSA are required. The priority date for freshman financial aid applications for fall entry is February 15.

International Students: There are 54 international students enrolled. The school actively recruits these students. They must take the TOEFL with a minimum score of 550 on the paper-based TOEFL (PBT) or 70 on the Internet-based version (iBT). They must also take the SAT or ACT.

Computers: The entire campus, including all dorms and all outside areas, is located within the university's wireless footprint. Each full-time student is required to have a laptop computer upon arrival at the University. An on-campus facility services the computers. All students may access the system 24 hours a day. There are no time limits and no fees.

Graduates: From July 1, 2008 to June 30, 2009, 868 bachelor's degrees were awarded. The most popular majors were business/finance (31%), psychology (16%), and health sciences (15%). 110 companies recruited on campus in 2008-2009. In an average class, 1% graduate in 3 years or less, 56% graduate in 4 years or less, 64% graduate in 5 years or less, and 66% graduate in 6 years or less. Of the 2008 graduating class, 43% were enrolled in graduate school within 6 months of graduation, and 49% were employed.

Admissions Contact: Karen N. Guastelle, Dean of Undergraduate Admissions. E-Mail: *enroll@sacredheart.edu* Web: *www.sacredheart.edu*

SAINT JOSEPH COLLEGE   C-2

West Hartford, CT 06117	**(860) 231-5216; (866) 442-8752**
Full-time: 1 man, 767 women	**Faculty:** IIA, -$
Part-time: 6 men, 189 women	**Ph.D.s:** 78%
Graduate: 133 men, 839 women	**Student/Faculty:** n/av
Year: semesters, summer session	**Tuition:** $27,202
Application Deadline: open	**Room & Board:** $12,437
Freshman Class: 1150 applied, 961 accepted, 184 enrolled	
SAT CR/M: 480/480	**LESS COMPETITIVE**

Saint Joseph College founded in 1932 and affiliated with the Catholic Church, is a private institution consisting of an undergraduate women's college, the Prime Time Program (a coed degree-completion program for adults), and coed graduate programs. There is 1 graduate school. In addition to regional accreditation, SJC has baccalaureate program accreditation with ADA and CSWE. Computerized library services include interlibrary loans, database searching, and Internet access. Special learning facilities include a learning resource center and art gallery. The 84-acre campus is in a suburban area 3 miles west of Hartford. Including any residence halls, there are 16 buildings.

Student Life: 93% of undergraduates are from Connecticut. 68% are white. The average age of freshmen is 18; all undergraduates, 24. 25% do not continue beyond their first year; 46% remain to graduate.

Housing: College-sponsored housing includes single-sex dorms. 60% of students commute. Alcohol is not permitted. All students may keep cars.

Activities: There are no fraternities or sororities. Groups on campus include art, choir, chorale, chorus, dance, drama, ethnic, honors, international, literary magazine, musical theater, political, professional, religious, social, social service, and student government.

Sports: Facilities include indoor and outdoor tracks, a gym, an exercise room, tennis courts, a dance studio, a pool, and a softball diamond.

Disabled Students: Facilities include wheelchair ramps, elevators, special parking, specially equipped rest rooms, special class scheduling, lowered drinking fountains, lowered telephones and other needs are met on a case-by-case basis.

Services: Counseling and information services are available, as is tutoring in most subjects. There is remedial math, reading, and writing.

Campus Safety and Security: Measures include 24-hour foot and vehicle patrol, emergency notification system, and security escort services. There are shuttle buses, emergency telephones, and lighted pathways/sidewalks.

Programs of Study: SJC confers B.A., B.S. degrees. Master's degrees are also awarded. Bachelor's degrees are awarded in BIOLOGICAL SCIENCE (biochemistry, biology/biological science, and nutrition), BUSINESS (accounting and management science), COMMUNICATIONS AND THE ARTS (art history and appreciation, English, and Spanish), COMPUTER AND PHYSICAL SCIENCE (chemistry and mathematics), EDUCATION (special education), HEALTH PROFESSIONS (nursing), SOCIAL SCIENCE (American studies, child psychology/development, family/consumer studies, history, international studies, liberal arts/general studies, philosophy, psychology, religion, social work, sociology, and women's studies).

Required: All students must maintain a minimum GPA of 2.0 and take 120 total credit hours, including a minimum of 30 in the major.

Special: The college offers cross-registration through the Greater Hartford consortium, internships, study abroad, work study, double majors, and student-designed majors. There is a freshman honors program.

Faculty/Classroom: No introductory courses are taught by graduate students.

Admissions: 84% of the 2009-2010 applicants were accepted. The SAT scores for the 2009-2010 freshman class were: Critical Reading-- 60% below 500, 32% between 500 and 599, 7% between 600 and 700, and 1% above 700; Math--55% below 500, 39% between 500 and 599,

4% between 600 and 700, and 2% above 700. 38% of the current freshmen were in the top fifth of their class; 69% were in the top two fifths.

Requirements: The SAT is required. AP and CLEP credits are accepted.

Procedure: Freshmen are admitted fall and spring. There are deferred admissions and rolling admissions plans. Application deadlines are open. Application fee is $50. Applications are accepted on-line.

Transfer: 45 of 120 credits required for the bachelor's degree must be completed at SJC.

Visiting: There are regularly scheduled orientations for prospective students. There are guides for informal visits; visitors may sit in on classes and stay overnight. To schedule a visit, contact Nancy Wunderly, Director of Admissions at (866) 442-8752.

Financial Aid: SJC is a member of CSS. The FAFSA is required. The priority date for freshman financial aid applications for fall entry is February 15.

International Students: They must take the TOEFL with a minimum score of 530 on the paper-based TOEFL (PBT). They must also take the SAT.

Computers: Wireless access is available. All students may access the system any time. There are no time limits and no fees.

Graduates: From July 1, 2008 to June 30, 2009, 228 bachelor's degrees were awarded. The most popular majors were nursing (21%), psychology (12%), and social work (10%). In an average class, 46% graduate in 6 years or less.

Admissions Contact: Nancy Wunderly, Director of Admissions. A campus DVD is available. E-Mail: *admissions@sjc.edu* Web: *www.sjc.edu*

SOUTHERN CONNECTICUT STATE UNIVERSITY   C-3

New Haven, CT 06515	(203) 392-5644; (203) 392-5727
Full-time: 6010 men and women	Faculty: IIA, av$
Part-time: 900 men, 1200 women	Ph.D.s: 90%
Graduate: 1015 men, 2930 women	Student/Faculty: n/av
Year: semesters, summer session	Tuition: $7500 ($16,500)
Application Deadline: open	Room & Board: $9000
Freshman Class: n/av	
SAT: required	COMPETITIVE

Southern Connecticut State University, founded in 1893, provides undergraduate and graduate liberal arts programs in the arts, business, education, professional studies, and the sciences. It is part of the Connecticut State University system. Figures in the above capsule are approximate. There are 5 undergraduate schools and 6 graduate schools. In addition to regional accreditation, SCSU has baccalaureate program accreditation with CSWE and NLN. The library contains 495,660 volumes, 753,033 microform items, and 4689 audio/video tapes/CDs/DVDs, and subscribes to 3549 periodicals including electronic. Computerized library services include interlibrary loans and database searching. Special learning facilities include a learning resource center, art gallery, planetarium, radio station, and TV station. The 168-acre campus is in an urban area 35 miles south of Hartford and 90 miles from New York City. Including any residence halls, there are 28 buildings.

Student Life: 92% of undergraduates are from Connecticut. Others are from 20 states, 36 foreign countries, and Canada. 90% are from public schools. 77% are white. 64% are Catholic; 18% Protestant. The average age of freshmen is 19; all undergraduates, 22. 25% do not continue beyond their first year; 48% remain to graduate.

Housing: 2100 students can be accommodated in college housing, which includes single-sex dorms and on-campus apartments. On-campus housing is guaranteed for all 4 years. 72% of students commute. Upperclassmen may keep cars.

Activities: 1% of men belong to 3 local and 3 national fraternities; 1% of women belong to 1 local and 2 national sororities. There are 70 groups on campus, including art, band, cheerleading, choir, chorale, chorus, computers, dance, drama, drill team, ethnic, gay, honors, international, jazz band, literary magazine, marching band, musical theater, newspaper, pep band, photography, political, professional, radio and TV, religious, social, social service, student government, and yearbook. Popular campus events include Springfest, Parents Day, and Octoberfest.

Sports: There are 9 intercollegiate sports for men and 8 for women. Facilities include a 6000-seat artificial-surface playing complex for football, soccer, field hockey, and track; a field house and gym facilities for basketball, gymnastics, badminton, tennis, track and field, volleyball, and indoor baseball; and an 8-lane swimming pool.

Disabled Students: 80% of the campus is accessible. Facilities include wheelchair ramps, elevators, special parking, specially equipped restrooms, special class scheduling, lowered drinking fountains, lowered telephones, and special computer facilities.

Services: Counseling and information services are available, as is tutoring in every subject. There is a reader service for the blind and remedial math, reading, and writing.

Campus Safety and Security: Measures include 24-hour foot and vehicle patrol, self-defense education, and security escort services. There are shuttle buses, emergency telephones, and lighted pathways/sidewalks. Campus security is provided by a campus-based police force.

Programs of Study: SCSU confers B.A., B.S., B.S.Bus.Adm., and B.S.Ed. degrees. Associates and master's degrees are also awarded. Bachelor's degrees are awarded in BIOLOGICAL SCIENCE (biochemistry and biology/biological science), BUSINESS (accounting, banking and finance, business administration and management, business economics, marketing/retailing/merchandising, and recreation and leisure services), COMMUNICATIONS AND THE ARTS (art history and appreciation, communications, dramatic arts, English, fine arts, French, German, Italian, journalism, Spanish, and studio art), COMPUTER AND PHYSICAL SCIENCE (chemistry, computer science, earth science, mathematics, and physics), EDUCATION (art education, early childhood education, elementary education, foreign languages education, health education, library science, physical education, science education, secondary education, and special education), HEALTH PROFESSIONS (nursing and public health), SOCIAL SCIENCE (economics, geography, history, philosophy, political science/government, psychology, social work, and sociology). Psychology, communications, and elementary education are the largest.

Required: All students must complete distribution requirements that include 6 credits each in English composition and speech, natural sciences, and social sciences, 3 credits each in American politics, fine arts, foreign languages, math, literature, philosophy, and Western civilization, and 1 credit each in phys ed and health. Students must take 122 total credits, with a minimum of 30 hours in the major field, and maintain a minimum overall GPA of 2.0.

Special: SCSU offer co-op programs in all academic majors, internships in many departments, study abroad in a variety of countries, a combined B.A.-B.S. degree, dual majors, a general studies degree, student-designed majors in liberal studies, and pass/fail options. There are 2 national honor societies, a freshman honors program, and 1 departmental honors program.

Faculty/Classroom: 61% of faculty are male; 39% are female. 96% teach undergraduates. No introductory courses are taught by graduate students. The average class size in an introductory lecture is 30; in a laboratory, 25; and in a regular course, 22.

Requirements: The SAT is required. In addition, applicants should be in the upper 50% of their high school class and should graduate with 4 years in English, 3 in math, and 2 each in natural sciences and social sciences, including American history. The GED is accepted. 2 years of foreign language are recommended. An essay is required, as is a GPA of 2.5. AP and CLEP credits are accepted. Important factors in the admissions decision are advanced placement or honors courses, recommendations by school officials, and leadership record.

Procedure: Freshmen are admitted fall and spring. There are early decision, early admissions and rolling admissions plans. Application deadlines are open. The application fee is $50.

Transfer: Transfer applicants must have a minimum of 6 college credits with a grade of C or better and an overall GPA of 2.0. The SAT is required for applicants with fewer than 24 college credits. 30 of 122 credits required for the bachelor's degree must be completed at SCSU.

Visiting: There are regularly scheduled orientations for prospective students. Visitors may sit in on classes. To schedule a visit, contact the Admissions Office.

Financial Aid: SCSU is a member of CSS. The FAFSA and the college's own financial statement are required. Check with the school for current application deadlines.

International Students: There were 60 international students enrolled in a recent year. They must take the TOEFL. They must also take the SAT or ACT, scoring 900 on the SAT.

Computers: All students may access the system 17 hours a day. There are no time limits and no fees.

Admissions Contact: Linda Benichak, Assistant Director of Admissions. Web: *www.southernct.edu*

TRINITY COLLEGE   C-2

Hartford, CT 06106	(860) 297-2180; (860) 297-2287
Full-time: 1000 men, 1000 women	Faculty: IIB, +$
Part-time: 80 men, 110 women	Ph.D.s: 90%
Graduate: 100 men, 80 women	Student/Faculty: n/av
Year: semesters	Tuition: $37,000
Application Deadline: see profile	Room & Board: $9500
Freshman Class: n/av	
SAT or ACT: required	HIGHLY COMPETITIVE

Founded in 1823, Trinity College in Hartford is an independent, nonsectarian liberal arts college. Figures in the above capsule are approxiamte. There is 1 graduate school. In addition to regional accreditation, Trinity has baccalaureate program accreditation with ABET. The library contains 992,817 volumes, 399,394 microform items, and 225,477 audio/video tapes/CDs/DVDs, and subscribes to 2438 periodicals including electronic. Computerized library services include interlibrary loans, database searching, and Internet access. Special learning facilities include an art gallery and Connecticut Public Television and Radio. The 100-acre campus is in an urban area southwest of downtown Hartford. Including any residence halls, there are 78 buildings.

Student Life: 79% of undergraduates are from out of state, mostly the Northeast. Students are from 44 states, 28 foreign countries, and Canada. 43% are from public schools. 79% are white. 32% are Protestant; 28% Catholic; 25% claim no religious affiliation. The average age of freshmen is 18; all undergraduates, 20. 8% do not continue beyond their first year; 84% remain to graduate.

Housing: 1861 students can be accommodated in college housing, which includes coed dorms and on-campus apartments. In addition, there are special-interest houses and fraternity houses. On-campus housing is guaranteed for all 4 years. 93% of students live on campus; of those, 70% remain on campus on weekends. Upperclassmen may keep cars.

Activities: 20% of men belong to 3 local and 4 national fraternities. There are no sororities. There are 112 groups on campus, including art, bagpipe, band, cheerleading, chess, choir, chorale, chorus, dance, debate, drama, ethnic, film, gay, honors, international, jazz band, literary magazine, musical theater, newspaper, pep band, photography, political, professional, radio and TV, religious, social, social service, student government, and yearbook. Popular campus events include Human Rights Lecture Series, Black History Month, and Latino Heritage Week.

Sports: There are 15 intercollegiate sports for men and 13 for women, and 14 intramural sports for men and 14 for women. Facilities include a pool, outdoor and indoor tracks, playing fields, a weight room, a fitness center, and tennis, squash, and basketball courts.

Disabled Students: 60% of the campus is accessible. Facilities include wheelchair ramps, elevators, special parking, specially equipped restrooms, special class scheduling, lowered drinking fountains, and lowered telephones.

Services: Counseling and information services are available, as is tutoring in every subject. There is a reader service for the blind. The writing center offers instruction in all forms of writing, and the math center provides individual tutoring on topics related to math and other courses involving quantitative reasoning.

Campus Safety and Security: Measures include 24-hour foot and vehicle patrol, self-defense education, and security escort services. There are shuttle buses, emergency telephones, and lighted pathways/sidewalks.

Programs of Study: Trinity confers B.A. and B.S. degrees. Master's degrees are also awarded. Bachelor's degrees are awarded in BIOLOGICAL SCIENCE (biochemistry, biology/biological science, and neurosciences), COMMUNICATIONS AND THE ARTS (art history and appreciation, classics, comparative literature, dance, dramatic arts, English, fine arts, French, German, Italian, modern language, music, Russian, Spanish, studio art, and theater management), COMPUTER AND PHYSICAL SCIENCE (chemistry, computer science, mathematics, and physics), EDUCATION (education), ENGINEERING AND ENVIRONMENTAL DESIGN (engineering and environmental science), SOCIAL SCIENCE (American studies, anthropology, classical/ancient civilization, economics, history, interdisciplinary studies, international studies, Judaic studies, philosophy, political science/government, psychology, public affairs, religion, sociology, and women's studies). Political science, economics, and English are the largest.

Required: All students must complete 36 course credits, including 10 to 15 in the major and 1 from each of 5 distribution areas: arts, humanities, natural sciences, numerical and symbolic reasoning, and social sciences. Students must maintain at least a C average overall.

Special: Trinity offers special freshman programs for exceptional students, including interdisciplinary programs in the sciences and the humanities. There is an intensive study program under which students can devote a semester to 1 subject. Cross-registration through such programs as the Hartford Consortium and the Twelve-College Exchange Program, hundreds of internships (some with Connecticut Public Radio and TV on campus), study abroad in Rome, South Africa, Trinidad, Russia, Nepal, and other countries, a Washington semester, dual majors in all disciplines, student-designed majors, nondegree study, and pass/fail options also are offered. A 5-year advanced degree in electrical or mechanical engineering with Rensselaer Polytechnic Institute is available. There are 4 national honor societies, including Phi Beta Kappa.

Faculty/Classroom: 60% of faculty are male; 40% are female. All teach and do research. No introductory courses are taught by graduate students. The average class size in an introductory lecture is 21; in a laboratory, 15; and in a regular course, 13.

Requirements: The SAT or ACT is required. Trinity strongly emphasizes individual character and personal qualities in admission. Consequently, an interview and essay are recommended. The college requires 4 years of English, 2 years each in foreign language and algebra, and 1 year each in geometry, history, and lab science. AP credits are accepted. Important factors in the admissions decision are advanced placement or honors courses, extracurricular activities record, and evidence of special talent.

Procedure: Freshmen are admitted fall. Entrance exams should be taken in the fall of the senior year. There are early decision and deferred admissions plan. Check with the school for current application deadlines. The application fee is $50. Applications are accepted on-line. A waiting list is maintained.

Transfer: Transfer applicants must take the SAT or ACT. A minimum college GPA of 3.0 is recommended. 18 of 36 credits required for the bachelor's degree must be completed at Trinity.

Visiting: There are regularly scheduled orientations for prospective students. There are guides for informal visits, and visitors may sit in on classes and stay overnight. To schedule a visit, contact the Admissions Office.

Financial Aid: Trinity is a member of CSS. The CSS/Profile and FAFSA are required. Check with the school for current application deadlines.

International Students: The school actively recruits these students. They must take the TOEFL. They must also take the SAT or ACT.

Computers: All students may access the system 24 hours a day. There are no time limits and no fees. It is strongly recommended that all students have a personal computer.

Admissions Contact: Larry R. Dow, Dean of Admissions/Financial Aid. E-Mail: *admissions.office@trincoll.edu* Web: *www.trincoll.edu*

UNITED STATES COAST GUARD ACADEMY   E-3
New London, CT 06320-8103
(860) 444-8500
(800) 883-8724; (860) 701-6700

Full-time: 990 men and women	**Faculty:** n/av
Part-time: none	**Ph.D.s:** 30%
Graduate: none	**Student/Faculty:** n/av
Year: semesters, summer session	**Tuition:** see profile
Application Deadline: see profile	**Room & Board:** see profile
Freshman Class: n/av	
SAT or ACT: required	**HIGHLY COMPETITIVE**

The U.S. Coast Guard Academy, founded in 1876, is an Armed Forces Service Academy for men and women. Appointments are made solely on the basis of an annual nationwide competition. Except for an entrance fee of $3,000, the federal government covers all cadet expenses by providing a yearly allowance of $11,150. Figures in the above capsule are approximate. In addition to regional accreditation, USCGA has baccalaureate program accreditation with ABET. The library contains 150,000 volumes, 60,000 microform items, and 1500 audio/video tapes/CDs/DVDs, and subscribes to 850 periodicals including electronic. Computerized library services include interlibrary loans and database searching. The 110-acre campus is in a suburban area 45 miles southeast of Hartford. Including any residence halls, there are 25 buildings.

Student Life: 93% of undergraduates are from out of state, mostly the Northeast. Students are from 50 states and 14 foreign countries. 79% are white. 33% are Catholic; 30% claim no religious affiliation; 29% Protestant. The average age of freshmen is 18; all undergraduates, 21. 21% do not continue beyond their first year; 67% remain to graduate.

Housing: 1000 students can be accommodated in college housing, which includes coed dorms. On-campus housing is guaranteed for all 4 years. Alcohol is not permitted. Upperclassmen may keep cars.

Activities: There are no fraternities or sororities. Groups on campus include bagpipe, band, cheerleading, choir, chorale, chorus, dance, debate, drama, drill team, drum and bugle corps, ethnic, international, jazz band, marching band, musical theater, newspaper, pep band, political, professional, religious, social, social service, student government, and yearbook. Popular campus events include Parents Weekend, Coast Guard Day, and Hispanic Heritage and Black History months.

Sports: There are 13 intercollegiate sports for men and 11 for women, and 13 intramural sports for men and 13 for women. Facilities include a field house with 3 basketball courts, a 6-lane swimming pool, 5 racquetball courts, and facilities for track meets, tennis matches, and baseball and softball games; an additional athletic facility with wrestling and weight rooms, basketball courts, gymnastics areas, a swimming pool, and saunas; a 4500-seat stadium; and practice and playing fields, outdoor tennis courts, and rowing and seamanship-sailing centers.

Disabled Students: 24% of the campus is accessible. Facilities include wheelchair ramps, elevators, special parking, and specially equipped restrooms.

Services: Counseling and information services are available, as is tutoring in every subject.

Campus Safety and Security: Measures include 24-hour foot and vehicle patrol and self-defense education. There are lighted pathways/sidewalks.

Programs of Study: USCGA confers B.S. degrees. Bachelor's degrees are awarded in BIOLOGICAL SCIENCE (marine science), BUSINESS (management science and operations research), ENGINEERING AND ENVIRONMENTAL DESIGN (civil engineering, electrical/electronics engineering, mechanical engineering, and naval architecture and marine engineering), SOCIAL SCIENCE (political science/government). Political science/government is the largest.

Required: To graduate, cadets must pass at least 37 courses, of which 25 are core; accumulate a minimum of 126 credit hours, with at least 90 credits of C or better, exclusive of phys ed; complete the academic requirements for one of the approved majors and attain a minimum GPA of 2.0 in all required upper-division courses in the major; successfully complete all professional development and phys ed requirements; and maintain a high sense of integrity.

Special: Cross-registration with Connecticut College, summer cruises to foreign ports, 6-week internships with various government agencies and some engineering and science organizations, and a 1-semester exchange program with the 3 other military academies are available. All graduates are commissioned in the U.S. Coast Guard. There are 2 national honor societies, a freshman honors program, and 3 departmental honors programs.

Faculty/Classroom: 90% of faculty are male; 10% are female. The average class size in an introductory lecture is 28; in a laboratory, 18; and in a regular course, 20.

Requirements: The SAT or ACT is required. The ACT Optional Writing test is also required. In addition, applicants must have reached the age of 17 but not the age of 23 by July 1 of the year of admission, be citizens of the United States, and be single at the time of appointment and remain single while attending the academy. Required secondary school courses include 4 years each of English and math.

Procedure: Freshmen are admitted fall. Entrance exams should be taken by January 31. There are early admissions and rolling admissions plans. Check with the school for current application deadlines. Notification is sent on a rolling basis. Applications are accepted on-line. A waiting list is maintained.

Transfer: All transfer students must meet the same standards as incoming freshmen and must begin as freshmen no matter how many semesters or years of college they have completed.

Visiting: There are regularly scheduled orientations for prospective students, including an admissions briefing and tour of the academy every Monday, Wednesday, and Friday. To schedule a visit, contact Admissions Receptionist.

International Students: They must take the TOEFL. They must also take the SAT or ACT.

Computers: All students may access the system 24 hours a day. There are no time limits and no fees. All students are required to have a personal computer.

Admissions Contact: Stephan Finton, Director of Admissions. A campus DVD is available. E-Mail: *admissions@.uscga.edu*
Web: *www.uscga.edu*

UNIVERSITY OF BRIDGEPORT   B-4

Bridgeport, CT 06604

(203) 576-4552
(800) EXCEL-UB; (203) 576-4941

Full-time: 581 men, 923 women	**Faculty:** 80; IIA, -$
Part-time: 148 men, 596 women	**Ph.D.s:** 89%
Graduate: 1473 men, 1382 women	**Student/Faculty:** 18 to 1
Year: semesters, summer session	**Tuition:** $25,465
Application Deadline: April 1	**Room & Board:** $11,080
Freshman Class: 8165 applied, 4510 accepted, 440 enrolled	
SAT CR/M/W: 440/440/440	**ACT:** 18 **LESS COMPETITIVE**

The University of Bridgeport, founded in 1927, is a private, independent, nonsectarian university offering programs in the arts, humanities, social sciences, business, engineering and design, natural sciences, human services, dental hygiene, chiropractic and naturopathic medicine, and teacher preparation. There are 7 undergraduate schools and 9 graduate schools. In addition to regional accreditation, UB has baccalaureate program accreditation with ABET, ADA, and NASAD. The library contains 275,000 volumes, 1,000,000 microform items, and 5,000 audio/video tapes/CDs/DVDs, and subscribes to 1,700 periodicals including electronic. Computerized library services include interlibrary loans and database searching. Special learning facilities include a learning resource center and art gallery. The 86-acre campus is in an urban area 60 miles northeast of New York City. Including any residence halls, there are 30 buildings.

Student Life: 58% of undergraduates are from Connecticut. Others are from 40 states, 52 foreign countries, and Canada. 89% are from public schools. 37% are African American; 27% white; 15% Hispanic; 11% foreign nationals. 69% claim no religious affiliation; 14% Catholic. The average age of freshmen is 19; all undergraduates, 26. 48% do not continue beyond their first year; 43% remain to graduate.

Housing: 1179 students can be accommodated in college housing, which includes coed dorms. In addition, there are special-interest houses, and alcohol- and tobacco-free buildings. On-campus housing is guaranteed for all 4 years. 53% of students commute. All students may keep cars.

Activities: 1% of men belong to 2 local fraternities; 2% of women belong to 1 local sorority. There are 52 groups on campus, including art, cheerleading, choir, chorale, computers, debate, ethnic, gay, honors, international, literary magazine, newspaper, photography, political, profes-

sional, radio and TV, religious, social, social service, and student government. Popular campus events include International Festival, Winter Prelude, and Wisteria Ball.

Sports: There are 5 intercollegiate sports for men and 8 for women, and 8 intramural sports for men and 8 for women. Facilities include a gym, athletic fields, tennis and racquetball courts, and a recreation center with an indoor pool.

Disabled Students: 80% of the campus is accessible. Facilities include wheelchair ramps, elevators, special parking, specially equipped rest rooms, and special class scheduling.

Services: Counseling and information services are available, as is tutoring in every subject. There is a reader service for the blind, and remedial math, reading, and writing.

Campus Safety and Security: Measures include 24-hour foot and vehicle patrol, emergency notification system, and security escort services. There are shuttle buses, emergency telephones, lighted pathways/sidewalks, controlled access to dorms/residences, and campus security systems.

Programs of Study: UB confers B.A., B.F.A., B.M., and B.S. degrees. Associates, master's, and doctoral degrees are also awarded. Bachelor's degrees are awarded in BIOLOGICAL SCIENCE (biology/biological science), BUSINESS (accounting, banking and finance, business administration and management, fashion merchandising, international business management, international economics, management information systems, management science, and marketing/retailing/merchandising), COMMUNICATIONS AND THE ARTS (communications, English, graphic design, illustration, industrial design, journalism, literature, and music), COMPUTER AND PHYSICAL SCIENCE (computer science and mathematics), ENGINEERING AND ENVIRONMENTAL DESIGN (computer engineering and interior design), HEALTH PROFESSIONS (dental hygiene, medical technology, predentistry, and premedicine), SOCIAL SCIENCE (criminal justice, human development, human services, interdisciplinary studies, international studies, prelaw, psychology, religion, and social science). Computer science/engineering, business, and dental hygiene are the strongest academically. Dental hygiene, psychology, and computer science/engineering are the largest.

Required: All students are required to complete at least 120 credit hours, including at least 30 in the major field. A minimum GPA of 2.0 is necessary. Distribution requirements cover 33 core credits and are composed of skills, heritage, and capstone sections, including 3 hours each in English composition and quantitative skills, and 24 semester hours consisting of 6 hours each in humanities, natural science, and social science, and 3 each in integrated studies and fine arts.

Special: UB offers co-op programs with several local institutions, cross-registration with Sacred Heart and Fairfield Universities, internships in many degree programs, study abroad in England, Switzerland, or Spain, a Washington semester, and work-study programs. In addition, a general studies accelerated degree program, dual majors, student-designed majors, and B.A.-B.S. degrees are available. Credit for life experience, non-degree study, and pass/fail options are offered. There are 11 national honor societies and 1 departmental honors program.

Faculty/Classroom: 63% of faculty are male; 37% are female. All teach and do research. No introductory courses are taught by graduate students. The average class size in an introductory lecture is 17; in a laboratory is 10; and in a regular course is 16.

Admissions: 55% of the 2009-2010 applicants were accepted. The SAT scores for the 2009-2010 freshman class were: Critical Reading--78% below 500, 20% between 500 and 599, and 2% between 600 and 700; Math--73% below 500, 23% between 500 and 599, and 4% between 600 and 700; Writing--81% below 500, 16% between 500 and 599, and 3% between 600 and 700. 20% of the current freshmen were in the top fifth of their class; 52% were in the top two fifths. 1 freshman graduated first in the class.

Requirements: The SAT or ACT is required. In addition, applicants are required to have 16 academic credits or Carnegie units, including 4 units of English, 3 of math, 2 in social studies, 2 in a lab science, and 5 electives. A portfolio is required for B.F.A. students and an audition for B.M. candidates. UB requires applicants to be in the upper 40% of their class. A GPA of 2.0 is required. AP and CLEP credits are accepted. Important factors in the admissions decision are advanced placement or honors courses, extracurricular activities record, and recommendations by school officials.

Procedure: Freshmen are admitted in the fall and spring. Entrance exams should be taken during the senior year. There are early decision, early admissions, deferred admissions, and rolling admissions plans. Applications should be filed by April 1 for fall entry and December 1 for spring entry. The fall 2008 application fee was $25. Applications are accepted on-line.

Transfer: 170 transfer students enrolled in 2008-2009. Transfer applicants need a minimum GPA of 2.5 and at least 12 earned credit hours. The SAT or ACT and an interview are recommended. 30 of 120 credits required for the bachelor's degree must be completed at UB.

Visiting: There are regularly scheduled orientations for prospective students. There are guides for informal visits, and visitors may sit in on classes and stay overnight. To schedule a visit, contact the Admissions Office at admit@bridgeport.edu.

Financial Aid: In 2009-2010, 97% of all full-time freshmen and 97% of continuing full-time students received some form of financial aid. UB is a member of CSS. The FAFSA and the college's own financial statement are required. The deadline for filing freshman financial aid applications for fall entry is April 15.

International Students: There are 253 international students enrolled. The school actively recruits these students. They must take the TOEFL with a minimum score of 500 on the paper-based TOEFL (PBT) or 61 on the Internet-based version(iBT). They must also take the SAT or ACT.

Computers: Wireless access is available. All dorm rooms have access to the Internet. PCs are located in the library and various labs. All students may access the system 8 A.M. to 11 P.M. daily. UBnet is available 24 hours a day from dorm rooms or dial-ups. There are no time limits and no fees.

Graduates: From July 1, 2008 to June 30, 2009, 270 bachelor's degrees were awarded. The most popular majors were general studies (20%), business administration (13%), and dental hygiene (13%). In an average class, 30% graduate in 4 years or less, 40% graduate in 5 years or less, and 43% graduate in 6 years or less. Of the 2008 graduating class, 10% were enrolled in graduate school within 6 months of graduation, and 60% were employed.

Admissions Contact: Bryan Gross, Dean of Admissions. A campus DVD is available. E-Mail: *admit@bridgeport.edu*
Web: *www.bridgeport.edu*

UNIVERSITY OF CONNECTICUT — D-2

Storrs, CT 06269-3088　　(860) 486-3137; (860) 486-1476

Full-time: 8170 men, 8166 women	**Faculty:** 1003; I, av$
Part-time: 390 men, 282 women	**Ph.D.s:** 94%
Graduate: 3851 men, 4170 women	**Student/Faculty:** 16 to 1
Year: semesters, summer session	**Tuition:** $10,416 ($26,880)
Application Deadline: February 1	**Room & Board:** $10,782
Freshman Class: 21,999 applied, 10,931 accepted, 3221 enrolled	
SAT CR/M/W: 600/630/600	**ACT:** 27 **HIGHLY COMPETITIVE**

The University of Connecticut, founded in 1881, is a public, land-grant, sea-grant, multicampus research institution offering degree programs in liberal arts and sciences and professional studies. There are 9 undergraduate schools and 5 graduate schools. In addition to regional accreditation, UConn has baccalaureate program accreditation with AACSB, ABET, ACPE, ADA, APTA, ASLA, CSAB, NASAD, NASM, NCATE, and NLN. The library contains 2.3 million volumes, 2.6 million microform items, and 5067 audio/video tapes/CDs/DVDs, and subscribes to 35,263 periodicals including electronic. Computerized library services include interlibrary loans, database searching, and Internet access. Special learning facilities include a learning resource center, art gallery, natural history museum, planetarium, radio station, and TV station. The 4108-acre campus is in a rural area 25 miles east of Hartford. Including any residence halls, there are 350 buildings.

Student Life: 77% of undergraduates are from Connecticut. Others are from 46 states, 58 foreign countries, and Canada. 87% are from public schools. 72% are white. The average age of freshmen is 18; all undergraduates, 20. 8% do not continue beyond their first year; 78% remain to graduate.

Housing: 11,858 students can be accommodated in college housing, which includes single-sex and coed dorms, on-campus apartments, off-campus apartments, and married student housing. In addition, there are honors houses, language houses, special-interest houses, fraternity houses, sorority houses, and older-student, freshman-year experience, and global housing, plus "women in math, science, and engineering" and other learning communities. On-campus housing is guaranteed for the freshman year only. 73% of students live on campus; of those, 70% remain on campus on weekends. Upperclassmen may keep cars.

Activities: 8% of men belong to 18 national fraternities; 10% of women belong to 9 national sororities. There are 350 groups on campus, including art, band, cheerleading, chess, choir, chorale, chorus, computers, dance, debate, drama, drill team, environmental, ethnic, film, gay, honors, international, jazz band, literary magazine, marching band, musical theater, newspaper, opera, orchestra, pep band, photography, political, professional, radio and TV, religious, social, social service, student government, symphony, and yearbook. Popular campus events include Spring Weekend, campus clean-up day, and Winter Weekend.

Sports: There are 11 intercollegiate sports for men and 13 for women, and 29 intramural sports for men and 28 for women. Facilities include a sports center, a field house, a 16,000-seat football stadium, a 10,000-seat basketball stadium, and a student, faculty, and staff workout center.

Disabled Students: 80% of the campus is accessible. Facilities include wheelchair ramps, elevators, special parking, specially equipped restrooms, special class scheduling, lowered drinking fountains, lowered telephones, special housing, a tactile map, and 4 specially equipped transportation vans.

Services: Counseling and information services are available, as is tutoring in most subjects. There is a reader service for the blind. Also available are a Braille printer, a Kurzweil reading machine and Mac computer with voice synthesizer, a machine to enlarge printed material, a talking calculator, and a TDD.

Campus Safety and Security: Measures include 24-hour foot and vehicle patrol, emergency notification system, self-defense education, and security escort services. There are shuttle buses, emergency telephones, and lighted pathways/sidewalks.

Programs of Study: UConn confers B.A., B.S., B.F.A., B.G.S., B.Mus., B.S.E., B.S.N., and B.S.Pharm. degrees. Associate, master's, and doctoral degrees are also awarded. Bachelor's degrees are awarded in AGRICULTURE (agricultural economics, agriculture, agronomy, animal science, horticulture, and natural resource management), BIOLOGICAL SCIENCE (biology/biological science, biophysics, evolutionary biology, genetics, marine science, molecular biology, nutrition, and physiology), BUSINESS (accounting, banking and finance, business administration and management, insurance and risk management, management information systems, marketing/retailing/merchandising, and real estate), COMMUNICATIONS AND THE ARTS (art, art history and appreciation, classics, communications, dramatic arts, English, French, German, journalism, linguistics, music, Spanish, theater design, and visual and performing arts), COMPUTER AND PHYSICAL SCIENCE (chemistry, computer science, geology, mathematics, physics, and statistics), EDUCATION (agricultural education, athletic training, education, elementary education, English education, foreign languages education, mathematics education, music education, recreation education, science education, social studies education, and special education), ENGINEERING AND ENVIRONMENTAL DESIGN (biomedical engineering, chemical engineering, civil engineering, computer engineering, electrical/electronics engineering, environmental engineering, environmental science, landscape architecture/design, manufacturing engineering, materials engineering, and mechanical engineering), HEALTH PROFESSIONS (cytotechnology, exercise science, health care administration, medical laboratory technology, nursing, pharmacy, and physical therapy), SOCIAL SCIENCE (anthropology, dietetics, economics, geography, history, human development, Italian studies, Latin American studies, Middle Eastern studies, philosophy, political science/government, psychology, sociology, urban studies, and women's studies). Biological sciences, psychology, and political science are the largest.

Required: To graduate, students must complete 120 credits with a GPA of 2.0. There are general education requirements in foreign language, expository writing, math, literature and the arts, culture and modern society, philosophical and ethical analysis, social scientific and comparative analysis, and science and technology. Students must complete a course that provides hands-on experience in a major computer application.

Special: UConn offers co-op programs in most majors, internships, more than 200 study-abroad programs in 65 countries, dual majors, general studies degrees, student-designed majors, work-study programs, nondegree study, and pass/fail options. There are 31 national honor societies, including Phi Beta Kappa, a freshman honors program, and 8 departmental honors programs.

Faculty/Classroom: 64% of faculty are male; 36% are female. 76% teach undergraduates. Graduate students teach 33% of introductory courses. The average class size in an introductory lecture is 48; in a laboratory, 20; and in a regular course, 38.

Admissions: 50% of the 2009-2010 applicants were accepted. The SAT scores for the 2009-2010 freshman class were: Critical Reading--5% below 500, 43% between 500 and 599, 45% between 600 and 700, and 7% above 700; Math--3% below 500, 29% between 500 and 599, 56% between 600 and 700, and 12% above 700; Writing--5% below 500, 38% between 500 and 599, 49% between 600 and 700, and 8% above 700. The ACT scores were 3% below 21, 11% between 21 and 23, 35% between 24 and 26, 25% between 27 and 28, and 26% above 28. 73% of the current freshmen were in the top fifth of their class; 96% were in the top two fifths. 49 freshmen graduated first in their class.

Requirements: The SAT or ACT is required. In addition, applicants must be graduates of an approved secondary school and should rank in the upper range of their class. The GED is accepted. Students must complete 16 high school academic units, including 4 years of English, 3 of math, 2 each of foreign language, science, and social studies, and 3 of electives. An essay is required. An audition is required for music and theater students and a portfolio for art students. AP credits are accepted. Important factors in the admissions decision are advanced placement or honors courses, evidence of special talent, and leadership record.

Procedure: Freshmen are admitted fall and spring. Entrance exams should be taken in the spring of the junior year or fall of the senior year. There are early action, deferred admissions, and rolling admissions plans. Early action applications should be filed by December 1; regular applications by February 1 for fall entry and October 15 for spring entry, along with a $70 fee. Notifications for early action are sent December through February; regular decision, late March through mid-April. 1668 applicants were on the 2009 waiting list; 434 were admitted. Applications are accepted on-line.

Transfer: 780 transfer students enrolled in 2008-2009. Applicants should have a minimum GPA of 2.7 and submit official transcripts from all colleges previously attended, the high school transcript, and SAT or ACT scores as needed. An associate degree or a minimum of 54 credit hours is recommended. 30 of 120 credits required for the bachelor's degree must be completed at UConn.

Visiting: There are regularly scheduled orientations for prospective students, including daily tours and information sessions. Visitors may sit in on classes. To schedule a visit, contact the Lodewick Visitors Center at (860) 486-4900.

Financial Aid: 49% of undergraduate students work part-time. Average annual earnings from campus work are $2050. The FAFSA is required. The priority date for freshman financial aid applications for fall entry is March 1.

International Students: There are 147 international students enrolled. The school actively recruits these students. They must take the TOEFL with a minimum score of 550 on the paper-based TOEFL (PBT) or 79 on the Internet-based version (iBT) or the IELTS, scoring 6.5. They must also take the SAT or ACT.

Computers: All students may access the system 24 hours weekdays and 8 A.M. to 12 P.M. weekends. There are no time limits and no fees.

Graduates: From July 1, 2008 to June 30, 2009, 4610 bachelor's degrees were awarded. The most popular majors were psychology (7%), political science (6%), and English (5%). 200 companies recruited on campus in 2008-2009. In an average class, 68% graduate in 4 years or less, 78% graduate in 5 years or less, and 79% graduate in 6 years or less. Of the 2008 graduating class, 34% were enrolled in graduate school within 6 months of graduation, and 85% were employed.

Admissions Contact: Brian Usher, Interim Director of Admissions. E-mail: *beahusky@uconnvm.uconn.edu* Web: *www.uconn.edu*

UNIVERSITY OF HARTFORD   C-2

West Hartford, CT 06117   **(860) 243-4296**
                                  (800) 947-4303; (860) 768-4961

Full-time: 2277 men, 2420 women	Faculty: 345; IIA, av$
Part-time: 321 men, 498 women	Ph.D.s: 85%
Graduate: 682 men, 1014 women	Student/Faculty: 11 to 1
Year: semesters, summer session	Tuition: $28,890
Application Deadline: open	Room & Board: $11,762
Freshman Class: 11,900 applied, 8250 accepted, 1394 enrolled	
SAT CR/M: 523/535	ACT: 22	COMPETITIVE

The University of Hartford, founded in 1877, is an independent, nonsectarian institution offering extensive undergraduate and graduate programs ranging from liberal arts to business. There are 7 undergraduate schools and 6 graduate schools. In addition to regional accreditation, the university has baccalaureate program accreditation with AACSB, ABET, APTA, CAHEA, NASAD, NASM, NCATE, and NLN. The 3 libraries contain 627,287 volumes, 49,278 microform items, and 3,885 audio/video tapes/CDs/DVDs. Computerized library services include interlibrary loans, database searching, Internet access, and laptop Internet portals. Special learning facilities include a learning resource center, art gallery, radio station, TV station, and the Museum of American Political Life. The 320-acre campus is in a suburban area 4 miles northwest of Hartford. Including any residence halls, there are 32 buildings.

Student Life: 58% of undergraduates are from out of state, mostly the Northeast. Students are from 49 states, 44 foreign countries, and Canada. 89% are from public schools. 60% are white; 11% African American. 89% claim no religious affiliation. The average age of freshmen is 18; all undergraduates, 22. 27% do not continue beyond their first year; 54% remain to graduate.

Housing: 3784 students can be accommodated in college housing, which includes coed dorms and on-campus apartments. In addition, there are honors houses, special-interest houses, the Residential College for the Arts, and the International Residential College. On-campus housing is guaranteed for all 4 years. 60% of students live on campus; of those, 85% remain on campus on weekends. All students may keep cars.

Activities: 17% of men belong to 7 national fraternities; 21% of women belong to 7 national sororities. There are 45 groups on campus, including art, band, cheerleading, choir, chorale, chorus, computers, drama, ethnic, gay, honors, international, jazz band, literary magazine, musical theater, newspaper, opera, orchestra, pep band, political, professional, radio and TV, religious, social, social service, student government, and symphony. Popular campus events include Welcome Weekend, Spring Weekend, and Winter Carnival.

Sports: There are 9 intercollegiate sports for men and 9 for women, and 15 intramural sports for men and 15 for women. Facilities include playing fields, a 25-meter outdoor pool, tennis courts, golf practice cages, a fitness trail, and a sports center with a 4,600-seat multipurpose court, an 8-lane swimming pool, a weight room, racquetball courts, a squash court, and saunas.

Disabled Students: Facilities include wheelchair ramps, elevators, special parking, specially equipped restrooms, lowered drinking fountains, lowered telephones, and special housing.

Services: Counseling and information services are available, as is tutoring in most subjects. There is a reader service for the blind, and remedial math, reading, and writing. The health education office offers peer counseling and workshops on health-related topics. Professional counseling is available.

Campus Safety and Security: Measures include 24-hour foot and vehicle patrol, emergency notification system, self-defense education, and security escort services. There are shuttle buses, emergency telephones, lighted pathways/sidewalks, and a bicycle patrol.

Programs of Study: The university confers B.A., B.F.A., B.Mus., B.S., B.S.A.E.T., B.S.B.A., B.S.C.E., B.S.Comp.E., B.S.Ed., B.S.E.E.,B.S.M.E. degrees. Associate, master's, and doctoral degrees are also awarded. Bachelor's degrees are awarded in BIOLOGICAL SCIENCE (biology/biological science), BUSINESS (accounting, banking and finance, business administration and management, entrepreneurial studies, insurance, management information systems, management science, and marketing/retailing/merchandising), COMMUNICATIONS AND THE ARTS (art history and appreciation, audio technology, ceramic art and design, communications, dance, design, dramatic arts, drawing, English, film arts, illustration, jazz, languages, media arts, music, music business management, music history and appreciation, music performance, music technology, music theory and composition, musical theater, painting, performing arts, photography, printmaking, sculpture, technical and business writing, theater management, video, and visual and performing arts), COMPUTER AND PHYSICAL SCIENCE (chemistry, computer science, information sciences and systems, mathematics, physics, and radiological technology), EDUCATION (early childhood education, elementary education, music education, secondary education, and special education), ENGINEERING AND ENVIRONMENTAL DESIGN (architectural engineering, biomedical engineering, chemical engineering technology, civil engineering, computer engineering, electrical/electronics engineering, electrical/electronics engineering technology, engineering, engineering technology, mechanical engineering, and mechanical engineering technology), HEALTH PROFESSIONS (health science, medical laboratory technology, nursing, occupational therapy, physical therapy, predentistry, premedicine, and preoptometry), SOCIAL SCIENCE (criminal justice, economics, history, human services, interdisciplinary studies, international studies, Judaic studies, law, philosophy, political science/government, psychology, and sociology). Accounting, management, and engineering are the strongest academically. Communication, psychology, and architectural engineering are the largest.

Required: To graduate, students must complete at least 120 credit hours, fulfill the university's core curriculum requirements, and maintain an overall GPA of 2.0. Specific core and course requirements vary with the major.

Special: Cross-registration with the Greater Hartford Consortium, internships in all majors, study abroad, a Washington semester, work-study programs, credit for life experience, nondegree study, and pass/fail options are available. In addition, students may pursue accelerated degrees, B.A.-B.S. degrees, dual majors, or their own individually designed majors. There are interdisciplinary majors in acoustics and music and in experimental studio combining performing, literary, and visual arts. Also available are preprofessional programs in biology/preoptometry with the New England College of Optometry, predentistry with the New York University School of Dentistry, prechiropractic with the New York Chiropractic College, preosteopathic with the University of New England College of Osteopathic Medicine, and prepodiatry with the New York College of Podiatric Medicine. There are 19 national honor societies, a freshman honors program, and 7 departmental honors programs.

Faculty/Classroom: 56% of faculty are male; 44% are female. All teach undergraduates, and 97% do research. No introductory courses are taught by graduate students. The average class size in an introductory lecture is 43; in a laboratory is 21; and in a regular course is 24.

Admissions: 69% of the 2009-2010 applicants were accepted. The SAT scores for the 2009-2010 freshman class were: Critical Reading--49% below 500, 39% between 500 and 599, 11% between 600 and 700, and 1% above 700; Math--45% below 500, 38% between 500 and 599, 15% between 600 and 700, and 2% above 700. The ACT scores were 40% below 21, 36% between 21 and 23, 15% between 24 and 26, 6% between 27 and 28, and 3% above 28. 14% of the current freshmen were in the top fifth of their class; 28% were in the top two fifths.

Requirements: The SAT is required. In addition, applicants should have 16 academic high school credits and 16 Carnegie units, including 4 units in English, 3 in math (3.5 for B.S. candidates), and 2 each in foreign language, science, and social studies. A portfolio and an audition are required for B.F.A. and B.Mus. candidates, respectively. A personal statement is required, and an interview is recommended for all students. AP and CLEP credits are accepted. Important factors in the admissions decision are advanced placement or honors courses, recommendations by school officials, and leadership record.

Procedure: Freshmen are admitted fall and spring. Entrance exams should be taken in the spring of the junior year or the fall of the senior year. There are deferred admissions and rolling admissions plans. Application deadlines are open. The fall 2009 application fee was $35. Notification is sent on a rolling basis. Applications are accepted on-line.

Transfer: 267 transfer students enrolled in 2008-2009. Transfer students must have a minimum college GPA of 2.25, with 2.5 recommended, and must submit SAT or ACT scores if they have fewer than 30 transferable college-level credits. An interview is also recommended. 30 of 120 credits required for the bachelor's degree must be completed at the university.

Visiting: There are regularly scheduled orientations for prospective students. There are guides for informal visits, visitors may sit in on classes, and stay overnight. To schedule a visit, contact the Office of Admissions.

Financial Aid: In 2009-2010, 97% of all full-time freshmen and 95% of continuing full-time students received some form of financial aid. 71% of all full-time freshmen and 78% of continuing full-time students received need-based aid. The average freshman award was $19,964. 22% of undergraduate students work part-time. Average annual earnings from campus work are $3200. The average financial indebtedness of the 2009 graduate was $34,385. The FAFSA is required. The priority date for freshman financial aid applications for fall entry is February 1.

International Students: There are 179 international students enrolled. The school actively recruits these students. They must take the TOEFL with a minimum score of 550 on the paper-based TOEFL (PBT). The SAT or the ACT is recommended.

Computers: Wireless access is available. There is access at the main library and PC connections in each dorm room. All students may access the system. There are no time limits and no fees. It is strongly recommended that all students have a personal computer.

Graduates: From July 1, 2008 to June 30, 2009, 964 bachelor's degrees were awarded. The most popular majors were communications (7%), psychology (6%), and economics and finance (4%). 185 companies recruited on campus in 2008-2009. In an average class, 51% graduate in 4 years or less, 58% graduate in 5 years or less, and 63% graduate in 6 years or less. Of the 2008 graduating class, 30% were enrolled in graduate school within 6 months of graduation, and 83% were employed.

Admissions Contact: Richard A. Zeiser, Dean of Admissions. E-Mail: *admission@hartford.edu* Web: *www.hartford.edu*

UNIVERSITY OF NEW HAVEN	C-3
West Haven, CT 06516	**(203) 932-7319**
	(800) DIAL-UNH; (203) 931-6093
Full-time: 1752 men, 1786 women	Faculty: n/av
Part-time: 219 men, 215 women	Ph.D.s: 90%
Graduate: 811 men, 920 women	Student/Faculty: n/av
Year: 4-1-4, summer session	Tuition: $29,470
Application Deadline: open	Room & Board: $12,372
Freshman Class: 6105 applied, 3753 accepted, 1252 enrolled	
SAT CR/M/W: n/av	ACT: n/av COMPETITIVE

The University of New Haven, founded in 1920, is a private institution offering undergraduate programs in arts and sciences, business, engineering, public safety, and professional studies. There are 5 undergraduate schools and 1 graduate school. In addition to regional accreditation, UNH has baccalaureate program accreditation with ABET and ADA. The library contains 383,969 volumes, 511,144 microform items, and 1066 audio/video tapes/CDs/DVDs, and subscribes to 1321 periodicals including electronic. Computerized library services include interlibrary loans, database searching, and Internet access. Special learning facilities include a learning resource center, art gallery, radio station, TV station, Institute of Forensic Science, crime scene training and technology center, nutrition lab, dental center, finance and technology center, communication studios, and music and sound recording facilities. The 84-acre campus is in a suburban area. Including any residence halls, there are 34 buildings.

Student Life: 52% of undergraduates are from Connecticut. Others are from 37 states, 25 foreign countries, and Canada. 60% are from public schools. 56% are white; 9% African American. The average age of freshmen is 18; all undergraduates, 20.

Housing: 1800 students can be accommodated in college housing, which includes coed dorms, on-campus apartments, and off-campus apartments. In addition, there is theme housing. On-campus housing is available on a first-come, first-served basis and is available on a lottery system for upperclassmen. 62% of students commute. Upperclassmen may keep cars.

Activities: 5% of men belong to 2 local and 3 national fraternities; 8% of women belong to 3 local and 3 national sororities. There are 60 groups on campus, including cheerleading, chorus, computers, criminal justice, dance, debate, drama, ethnic, film, fire science, forensics, gay, honors, international, jazz band, literary magazine, music and entertainment industry, newspaper, pep band, photography, political, professional, radio, religious, social, social service, and student government. Popular campus events include Family Day, Snow Ball Formal, and Spring Weekend.

Sports: There are 9 intercollegiate sports for men and 10 for women, and 15 intramural sports for men and 15 for women. Facilities include baseball, softball, and intramural playing fields, tennis courts, a gym with basketball courts, a weight training room, and a racquetball court, a 5600-square-foot recreation center, and a stadium for football, soccer, and lacrosse.

Disabled Students: 90% of the campus is accessible. Facilities include wheelchair ramps, elevators, special parking, specially equipped restrooms, special class scheduling, lowered drinking fountains, lowered telephones, and special door handles.

Services: Counseling and information services are available, as is tutoring in every subject. There is remedial math, reading, and writing. There are support services for students with disabilities and a center for learning resources.

Campus Safety and Security: Measures include 24-hour foot and vehicle patrol, emergency notification system, self-defense education, and security escort services. There are shuttle buses, emergency telephones, lighted pathways/sidewalks, controlled access to dorms/residences, and required programs during orientation for new students.

Programs of Study: UNH confers B.A. and B.S. degrees. Associate and master's degrees are also awarded. Bachelor's degrees are awarded in BIOLOGICAL SCIENCE (biochemistry, biology/biological science, biotechnology, marine biology, and nutrition), BUSINESS (accounting, banking and finance, business administration and management, hospitality management services, hotel/motel and restaurant management, marketing/retailing/merchandising, sports management, and tourism), COMMUNICATIONS AND THE ARTS (art, audio technology, broadcasting, communications, communications technology, creative writing, design, English, graphic design, journalism, literature, multimedia, music, music business management, music performance, music technology, music theory and composition, visual and performing arts, and visual design), COMPUTER AND PHYSICAL SCIENCE (applied mathematics, chemistry, computer management, computer mathematics, computer programming, computer science, mathematics, and natural sciences), EDUCATION (education, elementary education, English education, mathematics education, science education, and secondary education), ENGINEERING AND ENVIRONMENTAL DESIGN (chemical engineering, civil engineering, computer engineering, electrical/electronics engineering, engineering, environmental science, fire protection engineering, interior design, mechanical engineering, and systems engineering), HEALTH PROFESSIONS (dental hygiene, predentistry, premedicine, and preveterinary science), SOCIAL SCIENCE (behavioral science, clinical psychology, community psychology, corrections, counseling/psychology, criminal justice, criminology, dietetics, family and community services, family/juvenile justice, fire control and safety technology, fire protection, fire science, fire services administration, forensic studies, history, international public service, international relations, international studies, law enforcement and corrections, liberal arts/general studies, political science/government, psychology, public administration, and public affairs). Forensic science, engineering, and dental hygiene are the strongest academically. Criminal justice, forensic science, and music and sound recording are the largest.

Required: To graduate, all students must maintain a GPA of 2.0, pass a writing proficiency exam, and complete a total of 120 to 132 credits, depending on the major. Students must complete the Freshman Experience Seminar and take at least 40 credits from the university core curriculum, including a total of 28 in lab science, social sciences, history, literature or philosophy, and art, music, or theater, 9 in communication skills, and 3 each in quantitative skills, computers, and scientific methodology.

Special: UNH offers co-op programs in most majors, internships, work-study programs, student-designed majors in the School of Professional Studies, interdisciplinary majors including biomedical computing, B.A.-B.S. degrees, 5-year B.S.-M.S. programs in environmental science and in education, and nondegree study. Study-abroad programs are available. There are 5 national honor societies and a freshman honors program.

Faculty/Classroom: 72% of faculty are male; 28% are female. 90% teach undergraduates. No introductory courses are taught by graduate students. The average class size in an introductory lecture is 20; in a laboratory, 15; and in a regular course, 21.

Admissions: 61% of the 2009-2010 applicants were accepted. 45% of the current freshmen were in the top fifth of their class; 75% were in the top two fifths. 9 freshmen graduated first in their class in a recent year.

Requirements: The SAT or ACT is required. In addition, applicants should be graduates of an accredited secondary school. The GED is accepted. An interview is recommended. A letter of recommendation is required along with a personal essay. A GPA of 2.3 is required. AP and CLEP credits are accepted. Important factors in the admissions decision are advanced placement or honors courses, extracurricular activities record, and recommendations by school officials.

Procedure: Freshmen are admitted fall and spring. Entrance exams should be taken in the fall or winter of the senior year. There is an early action plan and a rolling admissions plan. Early action applications should be filed by November 15; regular application deadlines are open. Application fee is $75. Notification of early action is sent December 17;

regular decision, within 2 to 4 weeks of completed application. 59 applicants were on the 2009 waiting list; none were admitted. Applications are accepted on-line.

Transfer: 229 transfer students enrolled in 2008-2009. Applicants should have a minimum college GPA of 2.3 and should submit all official transcripts. An interview is recommended, and the SAT is required for students with fewer than 24 college credits. 30 of 120 to 132 credits required for the bachelor's degree must be completed at UNH.

Visiting: There are regularly scheduled orientations for prospective students, including daily information sessions, Open Houses, Accepted Student Days, Charger Days, and Summer Preview Days. There are guides for informal visits, and visitors may sit in on classes and stay overnight. To schedule a visit, contact the Office of Undergraduate Admissions.

Financial Aid: In 2009-2010, an estimated 83% of all full-time freshmen and 78% of continuing full-time students received some form of financial aid. An estimated 83% of all full-time freshmen and at least 77% of continuing full-time students received need-based aid. The estimated average freshman award was $20,193. Need-based scholarships or need-based grants averaged an estimated $17,221; need-based self-help aid (loans and jobs) averaged $3515; non-need-based athletic scholarships averaged $14,827; and other non-need-based awards and non-need-based scholarships averaged $10,430. 15% of undergraduate students work part-time. Average annual earnings from campus work are $882. The estimated average financial indebtedness of the 2009 graduate was $18,883. UNH is a member of CSS. The FAFSA and copies of the student's and parents' 1040 tax forms and W-2 forms are required. The deadline for filing freshman financial aid applications for fall entry is March 1.

International Students: There were 55 international students enrolled in a recent year. The school actively recruits these students. They must take the TOEFL with a minimum score of 68 on the Internet-based version (iBT). English-speaking students may submit the SAT or ACT scores instead.

Computers: Wireless access is available. Students can access the network through several computer stations throughout campus, computer labs, and the library. Each dorm room has a plug-per-pillow program, and wireless access is available in the library and campus center. All students may access the system 24 hours a day. There are no time limits and no fees. It is strongly recommended that all students have a personal computer. Students in the departments of music, graphic design, and interior design may be required to have a personal computer.

Graduates: From July 1, 2008 to June 30, 2009, 539 bachelor's degrees were awarded. The most popular majors were security and protective services (42%), business/marketing (15%), and visual and performing arts (11%). In an average class, 40% graduate in 6 years or less. Of the 2008 graduating class, 5% were enrolled in graduate school within 6 months of graduation, and 94% were employed.

Admissions Contact: Kevin J. Phillips, Director of Undergraduate Admissions. E-mail: *adminfo@newhaven.edu* Web: *www.newhaven.edu*

WESLEYAN UNIVERSITY   C-3
Middletown, CT 06459-4890   (860) 685-3000; (860) 685-3001

Full-time: 1376 men, 1398 women	**Faculty:** 330; IIA, ++$
Part-time: 3 men, 10 women	**Ph.D.s:** 94%
Graduate: 178 men, 183 women	**Student/Faculty:** 9 to 1
Year: semesters	**Tuition:** $51,132
Application Deadline: January 1	**Room & Board:** $11,040
Freshman Class: 10068 applied, 2218 accepted, 745 enrolled	
SAT CR/M/W: 700/700/700	**ACT:** 32 **MOST COMPETITIVE**

Wesleyan University, founded in 1831, is a private institution offering programs in the liberal arts and sciences. There are no undergraduate schools and one graduate school. The 3 libraries contain 1.7 million volumes, 369,640 microform items, and 60,605 audio/video tapes/CDs/DVDs, and subscribe to 10,489 periodicals including electronic. Computerized library services include interlibrary loans, database searching, Internet access, and laptop Internet portals. Special learning facilities include a learning resource center, art gallery, radio station, and an observatory. The 340-acre campus is in a suburban area 15 miles south of Hartford, CN and 2 hours from both Boston and New York City. Including any residence halls, there are 316 buildings.

Student Life: 93% of undergraduates are from out of state, mostly the Northeast. Students are from 48 states, 53 foreign countries, and Canada. 56% are from public schools. 58% are white. The average age of freshmen is 19; all undergraduates, 20. 5% do not continue beyond their first year; 93% remain to graduate.

Housing: 2778 students can be accommodated in college housing, which includes single-sex and coed dorms, on-campus apartments, off-campus apartments, and married student housing. In addition, there are language houses, special-interest houses, and fraternity houses. On-campus housing is guaranteed for all 4 years. 98% of students live on campus; of those, 99% remain on campus on weekends. All students may keep cars.

Activities: 4% of men belong to 8 local fraternities. There are 278 groups on campus, including art, band, cheerleading, chess, choir, cho-

rale, chorus, computers, dance, debate, drama, environmental, ethnic, film, gay, honors, international, jazz band, literary magazine, musical theater, newspaper, opera, orchestra, pep band, photography, political, professional, radio and TV, religious, social, social service, student government, symphony, and yearbook. Popular campus events include Fall Ball and Spring Fling.

Sports: There are 15 intercollegiate sports for men and 14 for women, and 13 intramural sports for men and 13 for women. Facilities include a 5000-seat stadium, a 3000-seat gym, a 50-meter Olympic-size pool, a 400-meter outdoor track, a 200-meter indoor track, a hockey arena, a strength and fitness center, 16 tennis courts, 8 squash courts, 4 soccer fields, 2 football practice fields, 2 rugby pitches, a boathouse, and field hockey, ultimate Frisbee, and baseball, softball and multi-purpose artificial turf fields.

Disabled Students: 52% of the campus is accessible. Facilities include wheelchair ramps, elevators, special parking, specially equipped restrooms, special class scheduling, lowered drinking fountains, lowered telephones, and special housing.

Services: Counseling and information services are available, as is tutoring in most subjects. Peer advisor assistance in time management and academic skills development, writing tutors, math tutoring, quantitative skills and quantitative analysis, as well as supplemental instruction in biology and chemistry are available for students.

Campus Safety and Security: Measures include 24-hour foot and vehicle patrol, emergency notification system, self-defense education, and security escort services. There are shuttle buses, emergency telephones, and lighted pathways/sidewalks.

Programs of Study: Wesleyan confers B.A. degrees. Master's and doctoral degrees are also awarded. Bachelor's degrees are awarded in AGRICULTURE (environmental studies), BIOLOGICAL SCIENCE (biochemistry, biology/biological science, molecular biology, and neurosciences), COMMUNICATIONS AND THE ARTS (art history and appreciation, classics, dance, dramatic arts, English, film arts, Italian, music, romance languages and literature, Russian, Spanish, and studio art), COMPUTER AND PHYSICAL SCIENCE (astronomy, chemistry, computer science, earth science, mathematics, physics, and science technology), SOCIAL SCIENCE (African American studies, American studies, anthropology, archeology, classical/ancient civilization, East Asian studies, economics, French studies, gender studies, German area studies, history, Iberian studies, Latin American studies, medieval studies, philosophy, political science/government, psychology, religion, Russian and Slavic studies, and sociology). Sciences, economics, and history are the strongest academically. English, government, and psychology are the largest.

Required: To graduate, all students must complete 128 credit hours. All students are expected, but not required to take courses each in humanities and arts, social and behavioral sciences, and natural science and math. A minimum academic average of 74 must be maintained, with at least 6 semesters of full-time residency.

Special: Wesleyan offers exchange programs with 11 northeastern colleges, cross-registration with 2 area colleges, study abroad in 42 countries on 6 continents, internships, a Washington semester, dual and student-designed majors, and pass/fail options. 3-2 engineering programs with Cal Tech and Columbia University are also available. There are 2 national honor societies, including Phi Beta Kappa, and 40 departmental honors programs.

Faculty/Classroom: 58% of faculty are male; 42% are female. All teach and do research. No introductory courses are taught by graduate students. The average class size in an introductory lecture is 25; in a laboratory is 26; and in a regular course is 18.

Admissions: 22% of the 2009-2010 applicants were accepted. The SAT scores for the 2009-2010 freshman class were: Critical Reading--1% below 500, 13% between 500 and 599, 34% between 600 and 700, and 52% above 700; Math--1% below 500, 10% between 500 and 599, 37% between 600 and 700, and 52% above 700; Writing--1% below 500, 10% between 500 and 599, 36% between 600 and 700, and 53% above 700. The ACT scores were % below 21, 2% between 21 and 23, 7% between 24 and 26, 13% between 27 and 28, and 78% above 28. 86% of the current freshmen were in the top fifth of their class.

Requirements: The SAT or ACT is required. In addition, applicants must submit the common application, transcript, recommendations, and either the ACT or SAT and 2 subject tests. Students should have a minimum of 20 academic credits, including 4 years each of English, foreign language, math, science, and social studies. AP credits are accepted. Important factors in the admissions decision are advanced placement or honors courses, recommendations by school officials, and leadership record.

Procedure: Freshmen are admitted fall. Entrance exams should be taken in the spring of the junior year or the fall of the senior year. There are early decision and deferred admissions plans. Early decision applications should be filed by November 15; regular decision, January 1 for fall entry, along with a $55 fee. Notification of early decision is sent December 15; regular decision, April 1. Applications are accepted on-line. 600 applicants were on a recent waiting list, 40 were accepted.

Transfer: 56 transfer students enrolled in 2008-2009. Applicants need a strong academic record and either SAT or ACT scores. An interview is recommended. 64 of 128 credits required for the bachelor's degree must be completed at Wesleyan.

Visiting: There are regularly scheduled orientations for prospective students, Student visits include hour-long campus tours and group information sessions. There are guides for informal visits, visitors may sit in on classes, and stay overnight. To schedule a visit, contact the Admissions Office at (860) 685-3000.

Financial Aid: In 2009-2010, 47% of all full-time freshmen and 46% of continuing full-time students received some form of financial aid. 47% of all full-time freshmen and 46% of continuing full-time students received need-based aid. The average freshmen award was $38,050. 75% of undergraduate students work part-time. Average annual earnings from campus work are $1431. The average financial indebtedness of the 2009 graduate was $19,769. Wesleyan is a member of CSS. The CSS/Profile and FAFSA are required. The deadline for filing freshman financial aid applications for fall entry is February 1.

International Students: The school actively recruits these students. They must take the TOEFL with a minimum score of 600 on the paper-based TOEFL (PBT) or 100 on the Internet-based version (iBT), or take the IELTS. They must also take the SAT or ACT.

Computers: Wireless access is available. Dorms and residence halls are connected to the campus network backbone. Students living in wood frame houses around campus are connected to the Internet through Comcast Cable modem. The campus has 290 wireless access points and provides close to 100% wireless coverage on campus. Each of the wood frame houses also has a wireless router. The campus network is connected to the Internet through the Connecticut Education Network. All students may access the system. There are no time limits and no fees. It is strongly recommended that all students have a personal computer.

Graduates: From July 1, 2008 to June 30, 2009, 735 bachelor's degrees were awarded. The most popular majors were psychology (8%), English (7%), and government (7%). 54 companies recruited on campus in 2008-2009. In an average class, 88% graduate in 4 years or less, 91% graduate in 5 years or less, and 93% graduate in 6 years or less. Of the 2008 graduating class, 17% were enrolled in graduate school within 6 months of graduation, and 42% were employed.

Admissions Contact: Nancy Hargrave-Meislahn, Dean of Admissions and Financial Aid. E-Mail: *www.wesleyan.edu*
Web: *www.wesleyan.edu/admission*

WESTERN CONNECTICUT STATE UNIVERSITY
A-3
Danbury, CT 06810-6855

(203) 837-9000
(877) 837-9278; (203) 837-8338

Full-time: 2177 men, 2599 women	**Faculty:** 221; IIA, +$
Part-time: 515 men, 598 women	**Ph.D.s:** 85%
Graduate: 230 men, 518 women	**Student/Faculty:** 22 to 1
Year: semesters, summer session	**Tuition:** $7462 ($17,154)
Application Deadline: May 1	**Room & Board:** $9517
Freshman Class: 4175 applied, 2596 accepted, 1008 enrolled	
SAT CR/M/W: 500/490/490	**COMPETITIVE**

Western Connecticut State University, founded in 1903, is a public institution offering programs in business, arts and sciences, professional studies, and visual and performing arts. It is part of the Connecticut State University system. There are 4 undergraduate schools and 1 graduate school. In addition to regional accreditation, West Conn has baccalaureate program accreditation with CSWE and NASM. The 2 libraries contain 215,096 volumes, 513,783 microform items, and 13,100 audio/video tapes/CDs/DVDs, and subscribe to 1010 periodicals including electronic. Computerized library services include interlibrary loans, database searching, Internet access, and laptop Internet portals. Special learning facilities include a learning resource center, art gallery, radio station, observatory, electron microscope, and photography studio. The 398-acre campus is in a suburban area 65 miles north of New York City. Including any residence halls, there are 25 buildings.

Student Life: 90% of undergraduates are from Connecticut. Others are from 24 states, 39 foreign countries, and Canada. 95% are from public schools. 76% are white. The average age of freshmen is 20; all undergraduates, 24. 30% do not continue beyond their first year; 40% remain to graduate.

Housing: 1679 students can be accommodated in college housing, which includes single-sex and coed dorms and on-campus apartments. On-campus housing is available on a first-come, first-served basis. 71% of students commute. All students may keep cars.

Activities: 4% of men belong to 3 national fraternities; 4% of women belong to 4 national sororities. There are 50 groups on campus, including art, band, cheerleading, chess, choir, chorale, chorus, computers, dance, debate, drama, environmental, ethnic, film, gay, honors, international, jazz band, literary magazine, musical theater, newspaper, opera, orchestra, photography, political, professional, radio and TV, religious, social, social service, and student government. Popular campus events include West Fest, Midnight Breakfast, and Student Leadership Banquet.

Sports: There are 6 intercollegiate sports for men and 7 for women, and 2 intramural sports for men. Facilities include 2 gyms, a weight training area, 4 tennis courts, 5 playing fields, an indoor swimming pool, and a field house with an indoor running track.

Disabled Students: All of the campus is accessible. Facilities include wheelchair ramps, elevators, special parking, specially equipped restrooms, special class scheduling, lowered drinking fountains, and lowered telephones.

Services: Counseling and information services are available, as is tutoring in every subject. There is a reader service for the blind and remedial math, reading, and writing. There is a computer science clinic, a math clinic, and a writing lab.

Campus Safety and Security: Measures include 24-hour foot and vehicle patrol, emergency notification system, and security escort services. There are shuttle buses, emergency telephones, lighted pathways/sidewalks, and controlled access to dorms/residences.

Programs of Study: West Conn confers B.A., B.S., B.B.A., and B.Mus. degrees. Associate, master's, and doctoral degrees are also awarded. Bachelor's degrees are awarded in BIOLOGICAL SCIENCE (biology/biological science), BUSINESS (accounting, banking and finance, business administration and management, management information systems, and marketing management), COMMUNICATIONS AND THE ARTS (art, communications, dramatic arts, English, illustration, music, music performance, photography, Spanish, and studio art), COMPUTER AND PHYSICAL SCIENCE (atmospheric sciences and meteorology, chemistry, computer science, earth science, and mathematics), EDUCATION (elementary education, health education, music education, and secondary education), ENGINEERING AND ENVIRONMENTAL DESIGN (environmental science), HEALTH PROFESSIONS (community health work, health care administration, medical laboratory technology, and nursing), SOCIAL SCIENCE (American studies, anthropology, criminal justice, economics, history, law enforcement and corrections, liberal arts/general studies, paralegal studies, political science/government, psychology, social science, social work, and sociology). Education, business, and justice and law administration are the largest.

Required: To graduate, students must complete 122 credit hours, with a minimum GPA of 2.0 or higher for some programs. All students must also fulfill the general education distribution requirements, including phys ed, and the foreign language requirement. In addition, at least 30 credits and at least half of the major requirements must be completed at WestConn.

Special: The university offers co-op programs with local corporations and the New England Regional Student Program. Student-designed majors, dual majors, study abroad, and pass/fail options are available. Non-degree study is offered at the University Center for Adult Education. There are 11 national honor societies, a freshman honors program, and 2 departmental honors programs.

Faculty/Classroom: 55% of faculty are male; 45% are female. All teach undergraduates, 25% do research, and 25% do both. No introductory courses are taught by graduate students. The average class size in an introductory lecture is 33; in a laboratory, 18; and in a regular course, 19.

Admissions: 62% of the 2009-2010 applicants were accepted. The SAT scores for the 2009-2010 freshman class were: Critical Reading--49% below 500, 40% between 500 and 599, 10% between 600 and 700; and 1% above 700; Math--52% below 500, 37% between 500 and 599, 10% between 600 and 700, and 1% above 700; Writing--52% below 500, 38% between 500 and 599, 9% between 600 and 700; and 1% above 700. 19% of the current freshmen were in the top fifth of their class; 44% were in the top two fifths.

Requirements: The SAT is required; the ACT is accepted in lieu of SAT scores. Applicants must be graduates of an accredited secondary school. The GED is accepted. Students should have completed 13 high school academic credits, including 4 in English, 3 in math, 2 to 3 in foreign language, 2 in science, and 1 each in history and social studies. Additional credits in art, music, and computer science are highly recommended. An essay and an interview are recommended. A GPA of 2.7 is required. AP and CLEP credits are accepted. Important factors in the admissions decision are advanced placement or honors courses, evidence of special talent, and recommendations by school officials.

Procedure: Freshmen are admitted fall and spring. Entrance exams should be taken by December of the senior year. There are early admissions, deferred admissions, and rolling admissions plans. Applications should be filed by May 1 for fall entry, along with a $50 fee. Notification is sent December 15. Applications are accepted on-line.

Transfer: 454 transfer students enrolled in 2008-2009. Transfers must have a minimum of 12 college credits. Applicants must have a cumulative GPA of 2.0 for all college course work. A higher GPA is required for some programs. 30 of 122 credits required for the bachelor's degree must be completed at West Conn.

Visiting: There are regularly scheduled orientations for prospective students, including campus tours on weekdays when classes are in session. There is an open house on a Sunday in early November. There are guides for informal visits and visitors may sit in on classes. To schedule a visit, contact the Office of Admissions at (203) 837-9000.

Financial Aid: West Conn is a member of CSS. The FAFSA and the college's own financial statement are required. The deadline for filing freshman financial aid applications for fall entry is April 15.

International Students: They must take the TOEFL, scoring 550 on the paper-based version or 79 on the Internet-based version. They must also take the SAT.

Computers: There are a total of 1021 wired computers available to all students (70 in the library, 656 in classrooms, 231 in computer labs, and 64 elsewhere). The wireless network accommodates 5000 simultaneous users. All students may access the system at any time. There are no time limits and no fees.

Graduates: From July 1, 2008 to June 30, 2009, 807 bachelor's degrees were awarded. The most popular majors were management (10%), justice and law administration (9%), and psychology (8%).

Admissions Contact: Steven Goetsch, Director of Admissions. E-mail: *admissions@wcsu.edu* Web: *www.wcsu.ctstate.edu*

YALE UNIVERSITY   C-3

New Haven, CT 06520-8234   (203) 432-9316; (203) 432-9392

Full-time: 5250 men and women	**Faculty:** I, ++$
Part-time: 15 men, 15 women	**Ph.D.s:** 85%
Graduate: 2320 men, 2440 women	**Student/Faculty:** n/av
Year: semesters, summer session	**Tuition:** $35,000
Application Deadline: see profile	**Room & Board:** $10,000
Freshman Class: n/av	
SAT or ACT: required	**MOST COMPETITIVE**

Yale University, founded in 1701, is a private liberal arts institution. Figures in the above capsule are approximate. There are 11 graduate schools. In addition to regional accreditation, Yale has baccalaureate program accreditation with AACSB, ABET, CAHEA, NAAB, NASM, NLN, and SAF. The 43 libraries contain 10.9 million volumes, 6.5 million microform items, and 15,554 audio/video tapes/CDs/DVDs, and subscribe to 69,664 periodicals including electronic. Computerized library services include interlibrary loans and database searching. Special learning facilities include an art gallery, natural history museum, planetarium, radio station, Beinecke Rare Books and Manuscript Library, Marsh Botanical Gardens and Yale Natural Preserves, and several research centers. The 200-acre campus is in an urban area 75 miles northeast of New York City. Including any residence halls, there are 200 buildings.

Student Life: 91% of undergraduates are from out of state, mostly the Middle Atlantic. Students are from 49 states, 74 foreign countries, and Canada. 60% are from public schools. 51% are white; 14% Asian American. The average age of freshmen is 18; all undergraduates, 20. 2% do not continue beyond their first year; 96% remain to graduate.

Housing: 4690 students can be accommodated in college housing, which includes coed dorms and on-campus apartments. Students are ramdomly assigned to one of 12 residential colleges where they live, eat, socialize, and pursue varius academic and extracurricular activities. On-campus housing is guaranteed for the freshman year only and is available on a lottery system for upperclassmen. 87% of students live on campus. All students may keep cars.

Activities: There are 300 groups on campus, including art, band, cheerleading, chess, choir, chorale, chorus, computers, dance, debate, drama, ethnic, film, gay, honors, international, jazz band, literary magazine, marching band, musical theater, newspaper, opera, orchestra, pep band, photography, political, professional, radio and TV, religious, social, social service, student government, symphony, and yearbook. Popular campus events include Communiversity Day, fall and spring concerts, and the East/West Film Festival.

Sports: There are 16 intercollegiate sports for men and 18 for women, and 25 intramural sports for men and 21 for women. Facilities include the 71,000-seat Yale Bowl, a sports complex, a gym, a swimming pool, a skating rink, a sailing center, an equestrian center, and golf courses.

Disabled Students: Facilities include wheelchair ramps, elevators, special parking, specially equipped restrooms, special class scheduling, lowered drinking fountains, lowered telephones, and a door-to-door lift-van service.

Services: Counseling and information services are available, as is tutoring in every subject. There is a reader service for the blind.

Campus Safety and Security: Measures include 24-hour foot and vehicle patrol, self-defense education, and security escort services. There are shuttle buses, emergency telephones, and lighted pathways/sidewalks.

Programs of Study: Yale confers B.A., B.S., and B.L.S. degrees. Master's and doctoral degrees are also awarded. Bachelor's degrees are awarded in BIOLOGICAL SCIENCE (biochemistry, biology/biological science, and biophysics), COMMUNICATIONS AND THE ARTS (art, art history and appreciation, Chinese, classics, dramatic arts, English, film arts, French, German, Italian, Japanese, linguistics, literature, music, Portuguese, Russian, Spanish, and theater management), COMPUTER AND PHYSICAL SCIENCE (applied mathematics, astronomy, chemistry, computer science, geology, mathematics, and physics), ENGINEERING AND ENVIRONMENTAL DESIGN (architecture, biomedical engineering, chemical engineering, electrical/electronics engineering, engineering, engineering and applied science, and mechanical engineering), SOCIAL SCIENCE (African American studies, American studies, anthropology, archeology, classical/ancient civilization, East Asian studies, Eastern European studies, economics, ethics, politics, and social policy, ethnic studies, German area studies, history, history of science, humanities, Judaic studies, Latin American studies, Near Eastern studies, philosophy, political science/government, psychology, religion, sociology, and women's studies). History, political science, and economics are the largest.

Required: To graduate, students must complete 36 semester courses, including at least 3 courses in each of 4 distributional groups and at least 12 courses from outside the distributional group that includes their major. Foreign language proficiency must be demonstrated.

Special: The university offers study abroad in several countries, including England, Russia, Germany, and Japan, and cooperates with other study-abroad opportunities. It also offers an accelerated degree program, B.A.-B.S. degrees, dual majors, and student-designed majors. Directed Studies, a special freshman program in the humanities, affords outstanding students the opportunity to survey the Western cultural tradition. Programs in the residential colleges allow students with special interests to pursue them in a more informal atmosphere. There is a Phi Beta Kappa honors program.

Faculty/Classroom: 66% of faculty are male; 34% are female. No introductory courses are taught by graduate students.

Requirements: The SAT or ACT is required. The ACT Optional Writing test is also required. Only those applicants submitting SAT scores must also take any 3 SAT Subject tests. Most successful applicants rank in the top 10% of their high school class. All students must have completed a rigorous high school program encompassing all academic disciplines. 2 essays are required, and an interview is recommended. AP credits are accepted. Important factors in the admissions decision are advanced placement or honors courses, leadership record, and extracurricular activities record.

Procedure: Freshmen are admitted fall. Entrance exams should be taken at any time up to and including the January test date in the year of application. There are early decision and deferred admissions plan. Check with the school for current application deadlines. The fall 2009 application fee was $75. Applications are accepted on-line. A waiting list is maintained.

Transfer: Applicants must take either the SAT or the ACT and have 1 full year of credit. An essay and 3 letters of recommendation are required. 18 of 36 credits required for the bachelor's degree must be completed at Yale.

Visiting: There are regularly scheduled orientations for prospective students. There are guides for informal visits, and visitors may sit in on classes and stay overnight. To schedule a visit, contact the Admissions Office.

Financial Aid: Yale is a member of CSS. The CSS/Profile, FAFSA, and student and parent tax returns, as well as the CSS Divorced/Separated Parents Statement and Business/Farm Supplement, if applicable, are required. Check with the school for current application deadlines.

International Students: There were 463 international students enrolled in a recent year. The school actively recruits these students. They must take the TOEFL, the SAT and 2 SAT Subject tests, or the ACT.

Computers: All students may access the system 24 hours a day. There are no time limits and no fees. It is strongly recommended that all students have a personal computer.

Graduates: In a recent year, 1339 bachelor's degrees were awarded.

Admissions Contact: Director of Admissions. E-Mail: *student.questions@yale.edu* Web: *www.yale.edu*

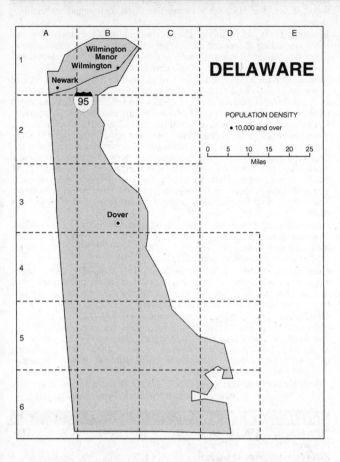

DELAWARE

POPULATION DENSITY

• 10,000 and over

0 5 10 15 20 25
Miles

DELAWARE STATE UNIVERSITY — B-3
Dover, DE 19901 — (302) 739-4917

Full-time: 975 men, 1305 women   **Faculty:** n/av
Part-time: 245 men, 405 women   **Ph.D.s:** 74%
Graduate: 85 men, 175 women   **Student/Faculty:** n/av
Year: semesters, summer session   **Tuition:** $6200 ($13,100)
Application Deadline: see profile   **Room & Board:** $8500
Freshman Class: n/av
SAT or ACT: required   **LESS COMPETITIVE**

Delaware State University, founded in 1891, is a publicly assisted institution offering programs in agricultural and technical fields, business, engineering, liberal and fine arts, health science, professional training, and teacher preparation. Figures in the above capsule are approximate. There are 4 undergraduate schools and 1 graduate school. In addition to regional accreditation, DSU has baccalaureate program accreditation with ACBSP and NCATE. The library contains 201,550 volumes, 76,096 microform items, and 13,652 audio/video tapes/CDs/DVDs, and subscribes to 3058 periodicals including electronic. Computerized library services include interlibrary loans and database searching. Special learning facilities include a learning resource center, art gallery, planetarium, and radio station. The 400-acre campus is in a suburban area 45 miles south of Wilmington. Including any residence halls, there are 31 buildings.

Student Life: 56% of undergraduates are from Delaware. Others are from 29 states, 40 foreign countries, and Canada. 90% are from public schools. 64% are African American; 32% white. 18% claim no religious affiliation The average age of freshmen is 18; all undergraduates, 21. 32% do not continue beyond their first year; 28% remain to graduate.

Housing: 1334 students can be accommodated in college housing, which includes single-sex dorms. In addition, there are honors houses and an honors dorm. On-campus housing is available on a first-come, first-served basis. 54% of students commute. Alcohol is not permitted. All students may keep cars.

Activities: 50% of men belong to 4 national fraternities; 50% of women belong to 4 national sororities. There are 53 groups on campus, including cheerleading, choir, drama, ethnic, honors, international, jazz band, marching band, newspaper, pep band, radio and TV, religious, social service, student government, and yearbook. Popular campus events include Parents Day, Annual Career Fair, and Annual Pride Day.

Sports: There are 8 intercollegiate sports for men and 7 for women, and 20 intramural sports for men and 20 for women. Facilities include an indoor swimming pool, a dance studio, racquetball and handball courts, 2 gyms, a football stadium, a baseball field, an outdoor track, and tennis courts.

Disabled Students: Facilities include wheelchair ramps, elevators, special parking, and specially equipped restrooms. The Office of Disabilities Services provides assistance to students with all types of disabilities.

Services: Counseling and information services are available, as is tutoring in every subject. There is remedial math, reading, and writing. A university tutoring program is available with a tutoring lab and tutorial service available in residence halls. A supplemental instruction program is available for challenging courses.

Campus Safety and Security: Measures include 24-hour foot and vehicle patrol. There are shuttle buses, emergency telephones, and lighted pathways/sidewalks.

Programs of Study: DSU confers B.A., B.S., B.S.W., and B.Tech. degrees. Master's degrees are also awarded. Bachelor's degrees are awarded in AGRICULTURE (agricultural business management, fish and game management, and natural resource management), BIOLOGICAL SCIENCE (biology/biological science and botany), BUSINESS (accounting, business administration and management, fashion merchandising, hotel/motel and restaurant management, and marketing/retailing/merchandising), COMMUNICATIONS AND THE ARTS (English, French, journalism, music, and Spanish), COMPUTER AND PHYSICAL SCIENCE (chemistry, computer science, mathematics, and physics), EDUCATION (agricultural education, art education, business education, early childhood education, elementary education, health education, home economics education, music education, physical education, science education, and special education), ENGINEERING AND ENVIRONMENTAL DESIGN (chemical engineering, civil engineering, electrical/electronics engineering, and mechanical engineering), HEALTH PROFESSIONS (community health work, environmental health science, and nursing), SOCIAL SCIENCE (economics, history, parks and recreation management, political science/government, psychology, social work, and sociology). Education is the strongest academically. Business administration, education, and English and mass communications are the largest.

Required: 52 hours of general education requirements must be completed, distributed as follows: 16 hours of core courses, 3 hours of arts and humanities, 6 hours of foreign languages, 6 hours of literature, 6 hours of math, 6 hours of natural sciences, and a minimum 3-hour Senior Capstone Experience course. A total of 121 credit hours and a minimum GPA of 2.0 are required.

Special: The university offers accelerated degrees, combined B.A.-B.S. degrees, student-designed majors, and a 3-2 engineering program with the University of Delaware. Work-study is available on campus. There are assisted internships in airway science and nursing and co-op programs in business, education, home economics, social work, and agriculture. There are 6 national honor societies, including Phi Beta Kappa, and a freshman honors program.

Faculty/Classroom: 61% of faculty are male; 39% are female. No introductory courses are taught by graduate students. The average class size in a regular course is 16.

Requirements: The SAT or ACT is required. In addition, applicants should graduate from an accredited secondary school or have a GED. 16 academic credits are required, including 4 units of English and 3 of math, of which 2 must be in algebra and 1 must be in geometry, 3 of science courses with a lab, 2 of history and/or social studies, and 4 of electives, including foreign language or computer science courses. A GPA of 2.0 is required. CLEP credits are accepted. Important factors in the admissions decision are extracurricular activities record, advanced placement or honors courses, and recommendations by school officials.

Procedure: Freshmen are admitted fall and spring. Entrance exams should be taken in December or January of the senior year. There are early admissions and rolling admissions plans. Check with the school for current application deadlines. The application fee is $25.

Transfer: Applicants must submit a statement of honorable withdrawal and high school and college transcripts. 30 of 121 credits required for the bachelor's degree must be completed at DSU.

Visiting: There are regularly scheduled orientations for prospective students, including a High School Day Program. There are guides for informal visits. To schedule a visit, contact the Admissions Office.

Financial Aid: DSU is a member of CSS. The CSS/Profile and FFS are required. Check with the school for current application deadlines.

International Students: They must take the TOEFL. They must also take the SAT or ACT.

Computers: All students may access the system 24 hours a day. There are no time limits and no fees.

Admissions Contact: Admissions Office. E-Mail: admissions@desu.edu Web: www.desu.edu

GOLDEY-BEACOM COLLEGE   B-1
Wilmington, DE 19808

(302) 225-6248
(800) 833-4877; (302) 996-5408

Full-time: 225 men, 262 women	**Faculty:** 20
Part-time: 85 men, 139 women	**Ph.D.s:** 100%
Graduate: 333 men, 210 women	**Student/Faculty:** 24
Year: semesters, summer session	**Tuition:** $17,880
Application Deadline: open	**Room & Board:** $4782
Freshman Class: n/av	
SAT CR/M: 450/450	**COMPETITIVE**

Goldey-Beacom College, founded in 1886, is a private college offering programs in psychology, economics, computer information systems, and other areas of business. There is 1 graduate school. In addition to regional accreditation, Goldey-Beacom has baccalaureate program accreditation with ACBSP. The library contains 90,000 volumes, 27,283 microform items, and 693 audio/video tapes/CDs/DVDs, and subscribes to 1000 periodicals including electronic. Computerized library services include interlibrary loans, database searching, Internet access, and laptop Internet portals. Special learning facilities include a learning resource center. The 24-acre campus is in a suburban area 10 miles west of Wilmington. Including any residence halls, there are 6 buildings.
Student Life: 60% of undergraduates are from Delaware. Others are from 19 states, 50 foreign countries, and Canada. 75% are from public schools. 46% are white; 29% Asian American; 15% African American. The average age of freshmen is 19; all undergraduates, 21. 8% do not continue beyond their first year; 62% remain to graduate.
Housing: 271 students can be accommodated in college housing, which includes coed on-campus apartments. In addition, there are special-interest houses. On-campus housing is guaranteed for all 4 years. 79% of students commute. All students may keep cars.
Activities: 10% of men belong to 1 national fraternity; 10% of women belong to 1 national sorority. There are 11 groups on campus, including cheerleading, chorus, computers, drama, ethnic, honors, international, literary magazine, newspaper, professional, religious, social service, and student government. Popular campus events include Spring Fest, Karaoke Night, and Casino Night.
Sports: There are 4 intercollegiate sports for men and 6 for women. Facilities include soccer and softball fields, tennis and handball courts, a gym with basketball and volleyball courts, and a fitness center available to all students and staff.
Disabled Students: All of the campus is accessible. Facilities include wheelchair ramps, elevators, special parking, specially equipped restrooms, lowered drinking fountains, and lowered telephones.
Services: Counseling and information services are available, as is tutoring in most subjects. There is a reader service for the blind, remedial math, reading, and writing, and computer-based tutorials.
Campus Safety and Security: Measures include 24-hour foot and vehicle patrol, emergency notification system, and self-defense education. There are lighted pathways/sidewalks and security from 6 P.M. to 6 A.M. on campus.
Programs of Study: Goldey-Beacom confers B.A. and B.S. degrees. Associates and master's degrees are also awarded. Bachelor's degrees are awarded in BUSINESS (accounting, banking and finance, business administration and management, human resources, international business management, management information systems, marketing management, and sports management), COMPUTER AND PHYSICAL SCIENCE (information sciences and systems), SOCIAL SCIENCE (economics and psychology). Accounting, economics, and finance are the strongest academically. Accounting and management are the largest.
Required: To graduate, students must complete a minimum of 136 credit hours with an overall GPA of 2.5. Students must also fulfill the college's core requirements in English, math, and computer science.
Special: Co-op programs in all majors, an accelerated degree program, a 5-year B.S/M.B.A degree, dual majors, internships, and work-study programs are available. There is 1 national honor society, a freshman honors program, and 3 departmental honors programs.
Faculty/Classroom: 63% of faculty are male; 37% are female. All teach undergraduates. No introductory courses are taught by graduate students. The average class size in an introductory lecture is 35 and in a regular course is 25.
Admissions: The SAT scores for the 2009-2010 freshman class were: Critical Reading--75% below 500, 21% between 500 and 599, and 3% between 600 and 700; Math--68% below 500, 28% between 500 and 599, and 3% between 600 and 700.
Requirements: The SAT is required. In addition, applicants must be high school graduates or have a GED and submit their official high school transcripts. A GPA of 2.0 is required. AP and CLEP credits are accepted. Important factors in the admissions decision are leadership record, evidence of special talent, and recommendations by school officials.
Procedure: Freshmen are admitted to all sessions. There are early admissions, deferred admissions, and rolling admissions plans. Application deadlines are open. Applications are accepted on-line.

Transfer: 66 transfer students enrolled in a recent year. Transfer applicants must submit high school and college transcripts. 65 of 136 credits required for the bachelor's degree must be completed at Goldey-Beacom.
Visiting: There are regularly scheduled orientations for prospective students, including a meeting with a representative and a campus tour. There are guides for informal visits, and visitors may sit in on classes and stay overnight. To schedule a visit, contact the Admissions Office.
Financial Aid: In 2009-2010,66% of all full-time freshmen and 84% of continuing full-time students received some form of financial aid. 99% of all full-time freshmen and 97% of continuing full-time students received need-based aid. The average freshman award was $9584. Need-based scholarships or need-based grants averaged $8205 ($10,000 maximum); need-based self-help aid (loans and jobs) averaged $4422 ($6700 maximum); and other non-need-based awards and non-need-based scholarships averaged $8940 ($10,000 maximum). 10% of undergraduate students work part-time. Average annual earnings from campus work are $1200. The average financial indebtedness of a recent graduate was $17,125. Goldey-Beacom is a member of CSS. The FAFSA is required. The priority date for freshman financial aid applications for fall entry is APril 1.
International Students: There are 62 international students enrolled. The school actively recruits these students. They must take the TOEFL with a minimum score of 475 on the paper-based TOEFL (PBT) or 60 on the Internet-based version (iBT).
Computers: Wireless access is available. The computing center has a 1:8 ratio of computers to students. In addition, students have access to the campus-wide GBC wireless network. All students may access the system. There are no time limits and no fees.
Graduates: From July 1, 2008 to June 30, 2009, 148 bachelor's degrees were awarded. The most popular majors were accounting (25%), management (22%), and human resource management (11%). In an average class, 54% graduate in 6 years or less. Of the 2008 graduating class, 45% were enrolled in graduate school within 6 months of graduation and 90% were employed.
Admissions Contact: Larry Eby, Director of Admissions. A campus DVD is available. E-mail: *admissions@gbc.edu* Web: *www.gbc.edu*

UNIVERSITY OF DELAWARE   A-1
Newark, DE 19716-6210

(302) 831-8123; (302) 831-6905

Full-time: 6363 men, 8679 women	**Faculty:** 1165; I, av$
Part-time: 313 men, 402 women	**Ph.D.s:** 85%
Graduate: 1745 men, 1889 women	**Student/Faculty:** 12 to 1
Year: 4-1-4, summer session	**Tuition:** $9486 ($23,186)
Application Deadline: January 15	**Room & Board:** $9,066
Freshman Class: 23005 applied, 14109 accepted, 4223 enrolled	
SAT CR/M/W: 580/600/580	**ACT:** required
	VERY COMPETITIVE

The University of Delaware, founded in 1743 and chartered in 1833, is a state-assisted, Land-Grant, Sea-Grant, Space-Grant, Carnegie Research University offering programs in agriculture and natural resources, arts and sciences, business and economics, engineering, health sciences, and education and public policy. There are 7 undergraduate schools and 7 graduate schools. In addition to regional accreditation, Delaware has baccalaureate program accreditation with AACSB, ABET, ADA, APTA, CAHEA, NASM, NCATE, and NLN. The 5 libraries contain 2.8 million volumes, 3.4 million microform items, 600,000 audio/video tapes/CDs/DVDs, and subscribe to 30,000 periodicals including electronic. Computerized library services include interlibrary loans, database searching, Internet access, and laptop Internet portals. Special learning facilities include a learning resource center, art gallery, radio station, TV station, a preschool lab, development ice skating science center, computer-controlled greenhouse, nursing practice labs, physical therapy clinic, 400-acre agricultural research complex, exercise physiology biomechanics labs, foreign language media center, and composite materials center. The 969-acre campus is in a small town 12 miles southwest of Wilmington, DE. Including any residence halls, there are 347 buildings.
Student Life: 64% of undergraduates are from out of state, mostly the Middle Atlantic. Students are from 47 states, 77 foreign countries, and Canada. 79% are white. 36% are Catholic; 26% claim no religious affiliation. The average age of freshmen is 18; all undergraduates, 20. 10% do not continue beyond their first year; 80% remain to graduate.
Housing: 7214 students can be accommodated in college housing, which includes single-sex and coed dorms, on-campus apartments, and married student housing. In addition, there are honors houses, special-interest houses, fraternity houses, sorority houses, alcohol/smoke-free residence halls, and suites. On-campus housing is guaranteed for all 4 years. 54% of students commute. All students may keep cars.
Activities: 10% of men belong to 20 national fraternities; 14% of women belong to 15 national sororities. There are 310 groups on campus, including art, band, cheerleading, chess, choir, chorale, chorus, computers, dance, debate, drama, drill team, drum and bugle corps, environmental, ethnic, film, gay, honors, international, jazz band, literary

magazine, marching band, musical theater, newspaper, opera, orchestra, pep band, political, professional, radio and TV, religious, social service, student government, and symphony. Popular campus events include Greek Week, Convocation, and Commencement.

Sports: There are 11 intercollegiate sports for men and 12 for women, and 32 intramural sports for men and 32 for women. Facilities include a 23,000-seat football stadium, 3 multipurpose gyms, 6 outdoor multipurpose fields, 8 outdoor basketball courts, 1 squash court, 15 racquetball courts, 21 outdoor tennis courts, indoor and outdoor pools, a universal weight room, a 5,000-seat basketball arena, a rock-climbing wall, a high-ropes challenge course, 4 student fitness centers, a strength and conditioning room with free weights, outdoor and indoor tracks, softball, baseball, lacrosse, and soccer fields, 2 ice arenas, and an outdoor hockey rink.

Disabled Students: 95% of the campus is accessible. Facilities include wheelchair ramps, elevators, special parking, specially equipped rest rooms, special class scheduling, lowered drinking fountains, lowered telephones, and special housing.

Services: Counseling and information services are available, as is tutoring in every subject. There is a reader service for the blind, and remedial math, reading, and writing. There is also a writing center, a math center, an academic services center for assistance with academic self-management development, critical thinking, and problem solving, as well as individual assistance for learning-disabled students.

Campus Safety and Security: Measures include 24-hour foot and vehicle patrol, emergency notification system, self-defense education, and security escort services. There are shuttle buses, emergency telephones, lighted pathways/sidewalks, access controls for dorms/residences, ongoing student-awareness programs in the residence halls, community policing, and keycard access to residence halls.

Programs of Study: Delaware confers B.A., B.S., B.A.E.S., B.A. Liberal Studies, B.C.E., B.Ch.E., B.C.P.E., B.E.E., B.En. E., B.F.A., B.M.E., B.Mus., B.R.N., B.S.Ed., and B.S.N. degrees. Associates, master's, and doctoral degrees are also awarded. Bachelor's degrees are awarded in AGRICULTURE (agricultural business management, agricultural economics, agriculture, animal science, natural resource management, plant science, soil science, and wildlife management), BIOLOGICAL SCIENCE (biochemistry, biology/biological science, biotechnology, entomology, nutrition, and plant pathology), BUSINESS (accounting, banking and finance, business administration and management, hotel/motel and restaurant management, management information systems, management science, marketing/retailing/merchandising, operations management, organizational leadership and management, and sports management), COMMUNICATIONS AND THE ARTS (apparel design, applied music, art, art history and appreciation, communications, comparative literature, English, fine arts, historic preservation, Italian, journalism, languages, music, music theory and composition, theater management, and visual design), COMPUTER AND PHYSICAL SCIENCE (astronomy, chemistry, computer science, geology, information sciences and systems, mathematics, physics, and statistics), EDUCATION (athletic training, early childhood education, education, elementary education, English education, foreign languages education, mathematics education, music education, physical education, psychology education, science education, secondary education, and special education), ENGINEERING AND ENVIRONMENTAL DESIGN (bioengineering, chemical engineering, civil engineering, computer engineering, electrical/electronics engineering, engineering, engineering technology, environmental engineering, environmental science, landscape architecture/design, and mechanical engineering), HEALTH PROFESSIONS (health, health science, medical laboratory technology, and nursing), SOCIAL SCIENCE (anthropology, criminal justice, dietetics, East Asian studies, economics, European studies, family and community services, fashion design and technology, food production/management/services, food science, geography, history, human development, human services, interdisciplinary studies, international relations, Latin American studies, liberal arts/general studies, philosophy, political science/government, psychology, sociology, and women's studies). Biological sciences, psychology, and nursing. are the largest.

Required: For graduation, students must complete at least 120 credits with a minimum GPA of 2.0. All students must take freshman English and 3 credits of course work with multicultural, ethnic, and/or gender-related content. Most majors require more than 120 credits. Most degree programs require that half of the courses be in the major field of study. Students must also have 1 incoming semester of First Year Experience (FYE) and 3 credits of Discovery Learning Experience (DLE).

Special: Students may participate in cooperative programs, internships, study abroad in 55 countries, a Washington semester, and work-study programs. The university offers accelerated degree programs, B.A.and B.S. degrees, dual majors, minors, student-designed majors (Bachelor of Arts in Liberal Studies), and pass/fail options. There are 4-1 degree programs in engineering, and hotel and restaurant management. Non-degree study is available through the Division of Continuing Education. There is an extensive undergraduate research program. Students may earn an enriched degree through the University Honors Program. There

are 35 national honor societies, including Phi Beta Kappa, and a freshman honors program.

Faculty/Classroom: 60% of faculty are male; 40% are female. All teach undergraduates. No introductory courses are taught by graduate students. The average class size in a laboratory is 18 and in a regular course is 35.

Admissions: 61% of the 2009-2010 applicants were accepted.

Requirements: The SAT or ACT is required. The ACT Optional Writing test is also required. In addition, applicants should be graduates of an accredited secondary school. The GED is accepted. Students should have completed a minimum of 18 high school academic units, including 4 units of English, 3 units of math, 3 units of science with 2 lab units, 2 units each of foreign language, history, and social studies, and 2 units of academic course electives. SAT Subject Tests are recommended, especially for honors program applicants. A writing sample and at least 1 letter of recommendation are required for all. AP credits are accepted. Important factors in the admissions decision are advanced placement or honors courses, recommendations by school officials, and personality/intangible qualities.

Procedure: Freshmen are admitted fall and spring. Entrance exams should be taken by their junior year or the beginning of the senior year. There are early admissions and deferred admissions plans. Applications should be filed by January 15 for fall entry and December 15 for spring entry, along with a $75 fee. Notifications are sent in mid-March. Applications are accepted on-line. 1488 applicants were on a recent waiting list, 288 were accepted.

Transfer: 431 transfer students enrolled in 2008-2009. Applicants for transfer should have completed at least 24 credits with a minimum GPA of 2.5 for most majors. Some majors require a GPA of 3.0 or better and/or specific course work. All transfer students must submit high school and college transcripts, an essay, and a statement of good standing from their prior institution. In some cases, an interview and standardized test scores are required. 30 of 120 credits required for the bachelor's degree must be completed at Delaware.

Visiting: There are regularly scheduled orientations for prospective students, Student visits consist of a 40-minute admissions information session and a 90-minute walking tour of campus. There are guides for informal visits and visitors may sit in on classes. To schedule a visit, contact the Admissions Office at (302) 831-8123.

Financial Aid: In 2009-2010, 36% of all full-time freshmen and 34% of continuing full-time students received some form of financial aid. 26% of all full-time freshmen and 24% of continuing full-time students received need-based aid. The average freshman award was $9,706. The average financial indebtedness of the 2009 graduate was $17,200. The FAFSA is required. The priority date for freshman financial aid applications for fall entry is February 1. The deadline for filing freshman financial aid applications for fall entry is March 15.

International Students: There are 299 international students enrolled. The school actively recruits these students. They must take the TOEFL with a minimum score of 550 on the paper-based TOEFL (PBT) or 80 on the Internet-based version (iBT), or take the IELTS. The SAT is recommended.

Computers: Wireless access is available. All students may access the system. 24 hours a day. There are no time limits and no fees.

Graduates: From July 1, 2008 to June 30, 2009, 3569 bachelor's degrees were awarded. The most popular majors were finance (7%), nursing (5%), and english (5%). 491 companies recruited on campus in 2008-2009. In an average class, 67% graduate in 4 years or less, 78% graduate in 5 years or less, and 80% graduate in 6 years or less. Of the 2008 graduating class, 15% were enrolled in graduate school within 6 months of graduation, and 75% were employed.

Admissions Contact: Lou Hirsh, Director of Admissions. E-Mail: *admissions@udel.edu* Web: *http://admissions.udel.edu/*

WESLEY COLLEGE	B-3
Dover, DE 19901-3875	**(302) 736-2400**
	(800) 937-5398; (302) 736-2301

Full-time: 700 men, 650 women	Faculty: n/av
Part-time: 150 men, 200 women	Ph.D.s: 75%
Graduate: 20 men, 105 women	Student/Faculty: n/av
Year: semesters, summer session	Tuition: $18,000
Application Deadline: open	Room & Board: $7000
Freshman Class: n/av	
SAT: required	**COMPETITIVE**

Wesley College, founded in 1873, is a private liberal arts institution affiliated with the United Methodist Church. Figures in the above capsule are approximate. There are 4 graduate schools. In addition to regional accreditation, Wesley has baccalaureate program accreditation with NLN. The library contains 100,842 volumes, 172,548 microform items, and 940 audio/video tapes/CDs/DVDs, and subscribes to 232 periodicals including electronic. Computerized library services include interlibrary loans, database searching, and Internet access. Special learning facilities include a learning resource center. The 26-acre campus is in a small town 75 miles south of Philadelphia. Including any residence halls, there are 20 buildings.

Student Life: 60% of undergraduates are from out of state, mostly the Middle Atlantic. Students are from 18 states and 9 foreign countries. 85% are from public schools. 78% are white; 17% African American. 61% are Protestant; 35% Catholic. The average age of freshmen is 18; all undergraduates, 20. 23% do not continue beyond their first year; 53% remain to graduate.

Housing: 778 students can be accommodated in college housing, which includes single-sex and coed dorms and on-campus apartments. In addition, there are honors houses. On-campus housing is guaranteed for all 4 years. 62% of students live on campus; of those, 30% remain on campus on weekends. Alcohol is not permitted. All students may keep cars.

Activities: 15% of men belong to 3 national fraternities; 15% of women belong to 3 local sororities. There are 30 groups on campus, including band, cheerleading, choir, chorale, chorus, drama, ethnic, honors, international, jazz band, literary magazine, newspaper, photography, political, professional, religious, social, social service, student government, and yearbook. Popular campus events include Family Day, International Fair, and Spring Fling.

Sports: There are 8 intercollegiate sports for men and 8 for women, and 4 intramural sports for men and 4 for women. Facilities include a swimming pool, tennis courts, a football stadium, athletic fields, a gym, a game room, and an exercise room.

Disabled Students: 65% of the campus is accessible. Facilities include wheelchair ramps, elevators, special parking, specially equipped restrooms, special class scheduling, and lowered drinking fountains.

Services: Counseling and information services are available, as is tutoring in every subject. There is remedial math, reading, and writing.

Campus Safety and Security: Measures include 24-hour foot and vehicle patrol and security escort services. There are emergency telephones and lighted pathways/sidewalks.

Programs of Study: Wesley confers B.A. and B.S. degrees. Associates and master's degrees are also awarded. Bachelor's degrees are awarded in BIOLOGICAL SCIENCE (biology/biological science), BUSINESS (accounting, business administration and management, management science, and marketing/retailing/merchandising), COMMUNICATIONS AND THE ARTS (communications and English), EDUCATION (elementary education, English education, physical education, secondary education, and social studies education), ENGINEERING AND ENVIRONMENTAL DESIGN (environmental science), HEALTH PROFESSIONS (medical laboratory technology and nursing), SOCIAL SCIENCE (American studies, history, liberal arts/general studies, paralegal studies, political science/government, and psychology). Education, psychology, and business are the strongest academically and have the largest enrollments.

Required: For graduation, students must complete 124 credit hours, with at least 15 hours in the major and a minimum GPA of 2.0. 50 hours of core courses including English, religion, science, math, American culture, non-American culture, and phys ed are required.

Special: Wesley offers internships in business and industry, environmental science, medical technology, and government agencies. Study abroad in 5 countries, work-study programs, dual majors, pass/fail options, and credit for life, military, and work experience are available. There are 2 national honor societies and 1 departmental honors program.

Faculty/Classroom: 58% of faculty are male; 42% are female. All teach undergraduates, 3% do research, and 3% do both. No introductory courses are taught by graduate students. The average class size in an introductory lecture is 20; in a laboratory, 12; and in a regular course, 20.

Requirements: The SAT is required. In addition, applicants must be graduates of an accredited secondary school; the GED is accepted. Students should have completed 12 academic credits or 16 Carnegie units, including 4 units of English and 2 units each of math, history, science, and social studies. An interview is recommended. A GPA of 2.2 is required. AP and CLEP credits are accepted. Important factors in the admissions decision are recommendations by school officials, extracurricular activities record, and leadership record.

Procedure: Freshmen are admitted fall and winter. Entrance exams should be taken in the junior year. There are early decision, deferred admissions and rolling admissions plans. Application deadlines are open. The fall 2009 application fee was $20. Applications are accepted on-line. A waiting list is maintained.

Transfer: 30 transfer students enrolled in a recent year. Applicants must have a minimum GPA of 2.0 and a minimum composite SAT score of 800. 36 of 124 credits required for the bachelor's degree must be completed at Wesley.

Visiting: There are regularly scheduled orientations for prospective students. There are guides for informal visits, and visitors may sit in on classes and stay overnight. To schedule a visit, contact the Office of Admissions.

Financial Aid: The FAFSA, SFS, and the college's own financial statement are required. Check with the school for current application deadlines.

International Students: The school actively recruits these students. They must take the TOEFL. They must also take the SAT.

Computers: All students may access the system 24 hours a day, 7 days a week. There are no time limits and no fees. It is strongly recommended that all students have a personal computer.

Admissions Contact: Arthur Jacobs, Director of Admissions. A campus DVD is available. E-Mail: *jacobsar@wesley.edu* Web: *www.wesley.edu*

WILMINGTON COLLEGE　　B-1

New Castle, DE 19720	(302) 328-9407; (302) 328-5902
Full-time: 725 men, 1300 women	**Faculty:** 41; IIA, -$
Part-time: 570 men, 1395 women	**Ph.D.s:** 55%
Graduate: 730 men, 1725 women	**Student/Faculty:** 49 to 1
Year: semesters, summer session	**Tuition:** $6000
Application Deadline:	
Freshman Class: n/av	NONCOMPETITIVE

Wilmington College, founded in 1967, is a private, liberal arts commuter college offering admission to students from varied academic backgrounds. There are 6 undergraduate schools and 7 graduate schools. In addition to regional accreditation, Wilmington has baccalaureate program accreditation with NASDTEC and NLN. The library contains 191,885 volumes, 93,545 microform items, and 2,611 audio/video tapes/CDs/DVDs, and subscribes to 468 periodicals including electronic. Computerized library services include interlibrary loans, database searching, and Internet access. Special learning facilities include a learning resource center, radio station, and TV station. The 18-acre campus is in an urban area 7 miles south of Wilmington. Including any residence halls, there are 18 buildings.

Student Life: 87% of undergraduates are from Delaware. Others are from 12 states, 5 foreign countries, and Canada. 85% are from public schools. 45% are white; 12% African American. The average age of freshmen is 27; all undergraduates, 30. 8% do not continue beyond their first year; 76% remain to graduate.

Housing: There are no residence halls. All students commute.

Activities: There are no fraternities or sororities. There are 11 groups on campus, including behavioral science division club, criminal justice club, cheerleading, film, honors, International Reading Association, newspaper, photography, radio and TV, student government, and yearbook.

Sports: There are 4 intercollegiate sports for men and 5 for women. Facilities include a 1000-seat gym and a recreation room.

Disabled Students: All of the campus is accessible. Facilities include wheelchair ramps, elevators, special parking, specially equipped restrooms, lowered drinking fountains, and lowered telephones.

Services: Counseling and information services are available, as is tutoring in some subjects, math and English. There is remedial math and reading. Staff members also are available to assist students with study skills such as test taking, reading, concentration development, and time management.

Campus Safety and Security: Measures include 24-hour foot and vehicle patrol and security escort services. There are emergency telephones and lighted pathways/sidewalks.

Programs of Study: Wilmington confers B.A., B.S., and B.S.N. degrees. Associate, master's, and doctoral degrees are also awarded. Bachelor's degrees are awarded in BUSINESS (accounting, banking and finance, business administration and management, personnel management, and sports management), COMMUNICATIONS AND THE ARTS (communications technology, media arts, multimedia, and video), EDUCATION (early childhood education and elementary education), ENGINEERING AND ENVIRONMENTAL DESIGN (aeronautical science and aviation administration/management), HEALTH PROFESSIONS (nursing), SOCIAL SCIENCE (behavioral science and criminal justice). Nursing and elementary education is the strongest academically. Business, nursing, and elementary education are the largest.

Required: To graduate, students must complete a total of 120 hours with a minimum GPA of 2.0. 54 hours are required in the major. The 36-hour general studies core requirement includes 12 hours of social science, 9 each of English and humanities, and 3 each of math and science. At least 45 credit hours of upper-division course work are required, as is demonstrated competence in verbal and written communication and computational skills. At least 3 credits must be taken in computer operations. Nursing students must also submit official transcripts verifying graduation from a diploma or associate degree nursing program. Candidates for the B.S.N. degree must possess an R.N. license.

Special: The school offers practicums for education students, co-op programs, work-study programs with area employers, internships, a general studies degree, an accelerated degree program, dual majors, pass/fail options, credit for life experience, and by-challenge exam. There are 1 national honor society and 2 departmental honors programs.

Faculty/Classroom: 70% of faculty are male; 30% are female. 66% teach undergraduates. No introductory courses are taught by graduate students. The average class size in an introductory lecture is 25; in a laboratory is 10; and in a regular course is 17.

Requirements: In addition, Graduation from an accredited secondary school or satisfactory scores on the GED are required for admission. An interview may be required of some students, and an essay is recommended. A GPA of 2.0 is required. AP and CLEP credits are accepted.

Procedure: Freshmen are admitted to all sessions. There are deferred admissions and rolling admissions plans. Application deadlines are open. Application fee is $25.

Transfer: 2736 transfer students enrolled in 2008-2009. Applicants must have a 2.0 GPA; those with a lower GPA must have an interview. Some applicants may be required to submit SAT I or ACT scores. Those with fewer than 15 semester credits must submit high school transcripts. No more than 75 semester credits will be accepted for transfer credit. 45 of 120 credits required for the bachelor's degree must be completed at Wilmington.

Visiting: There are guides for informal visits and visitors may sit in on classes. To schedule a visit, contact the Admissions Office.

Financial Aid: In 2009-2010, 33% of all full-time freshmen and % of continuing full-time students received some form of financial aid. 10% of all full-time freshmen and % of continuing full-time students received need-based aid. The average freshman award was $5,034.. The FAFSA is required. The deadline for filing freshman financial aid applications for fall entry is August 15.

International Students: There are 40 international students enrolled. They must take the TOEFL, or they may submit a transcript of successful completion of at least 12 credit hours from a U.S. institution of higher education.

Computers: Only students matriculated in communications technology majors may access the system during designated class/lab time may access the system. There are no time limits and no fees.

Graduates: 128 companies recruited on campus in 2008-2009.

Admissions Contact: Andrey Mattern, Manager of Admissions. E-Mail: *apara@wilmcoll.edu* Web: *www.wimington.edu*

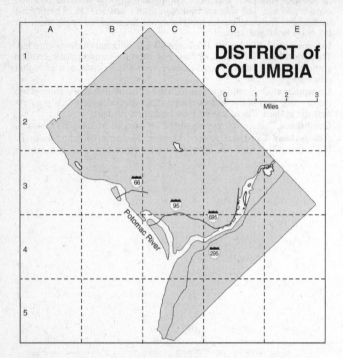

DISTRICT of COLUMBIA

0   1   2   3
Miles

AMERICAN UNIVERSITY   A-2
Washington, DC 20016-8001   (202) 885-6000; (202) 885-1025
Full-time: 2204 men, 3581 women   **Faculty:** 578; I, av$
Part-time: 110 men, 151 women   **Ph.D.s:** 94%
Graduate: 2015 men, 2143 women   **Student/Faculty:** 14 to 1
Year: semesters, summer session   **Tuition:** $34,973
Application Deadline: January 15   **Room & Board:** $12,930
Freshman Class: 14969 applied, 7978 accepted, 1641 enrolled
SAT CR/M: 640/620   **ACT:** 28
                                        HIGHLY COMPETITIVE+

American University, founded in 1893, is a private liberal arts institution affiliated with the United Methodist Church. There are 5 undergraduate schools and 6 graduate schools. In addition to regional accreditation, AU has baccalaureate program accreditation with AACSB, ACEJMC, NAS-DTEC, NASM, and NCATE. The library contains 1.0 million volumes, 1.1 million microform items, and 60,870 audio/video tapes/CDs/DVDs, and subscribes to 23,955 periodicals including electronic. Computerized library services include interlibrary loans, database searching, Internet access, and laptop Internet portals. Special learning facilities include a learning resource center, art gallery, radio station, TV station, state-of-the-art language resource center, multimedia design and development labs, science and computer science labs, and buildings for art and the performing arts. The 84-acre campus is in an urban area 5 miles northwest of downtown Washington D.C. Including any residence halls, there are 41 buildings.

Student Life: 89% of undergraduates are from out of state, mostly the Middle Atlantic. Students are from 50 states, 81 foreign countries, and Canada. 62% are white. The average age of freshmen is 18; all undergraduates, 20. 12% do not continue beyond their first year; 74% remain to graduate.

Housing: College-sponsored housing includes single-sex and coed dorms and on-campus apartments. In addition, there are honors houses, special-interest houses, an international-intercultural hall, honors floors, and special-interest floors, including a community service floor. All dorms are smoke-free. On-campus housing is guaranteed for the freshman year only and is available on a first-come, first-served basis. Alcohol is not permitted. Upperclassmen may keep cars.

Activities: 14% of men belong to 11 national fraternities. There are 12 national sororities. There are 207 groups on campus, including art, band, cheerleading, chess, choir, chorale, chorus, computers, dance, debate, drama, environmental, ethnic, film, gay, honors, international, jazz band, literary magazine, musical theater, newspaper, orchestra, pep band, political, professional, radio and TV, religious, social, social service, student government, symphony, and yearbook. Popular campus events include Family Weekend, Founders Day Ball, and Campus Beautification Day.

Sports: There are 7 intercollegiate sports for men and 9 for women. Facilities include a 6000-seat gym, 2 swimming pools, hockey and soccer fields, a softball diamond, an all-purpose field, cardiovascular and strength training equipment, weight rooms, courts for tennis, basketball, and volleyball, an aerobics studio, an indoor jogging track, and an outdoor 6-lane tartan track.

Disabled Students: 95% of the campus is accessible. Facilities include wheelchair ramps, elevators, special parking, specially equipped rest rooms, special class scheduling, lowered drinking fountains, lowered telephones, special housing, and a university shuttle equipped to accommodate students in wheelchairs.

Services: Counseling and information services are available, as is tutoring in every subject. There is a reader service for the blind and remedial math, reading, and writing. A math and statistics tutoring lab, a writing center, and a foreign language resource center are available.

Campus Safety and Security: Measures include 24-hour foot and vehicle patrol, emergency notification system, self-defense education, and security escort services. There are shuttle buses, emergency telephones, lighted pathways/sidewalks, controlled access to dorms/residences, safety orientation programs, alarms, closed-circuit cameras, and posted crime alerts.

Programs of Study: AU confers B.A., B.F.A., B.S., and B.S.B.A. degrees. Associates, master's, and doctoral degrees are also awarded. Bachelor's degrees are awarded in AGRICULTURE (environmental studies), BIOLOGICAL SCIENCE (biochemistry, biology/biological science, and marine science), BUSINESS (business administration and management and international business management), COMMUNICATIONS AND THE ARTS (Arabic, art history and appreciation, audio technology, communications, dramatic arts, film arts, fine arts, graphic design, journalism, literature, multimedia, music, musical theater, performing arts, public relations, and studio art), COMPUTER AND PHYSICAL SCIENCE (applied mathematics, chemistry, computer science, mathematics, physics, and statistics), EDUCATION (elementary education, foreign languages education, and secondary education), ENGINEERING AND ENVIRONMENTAL DESIGN (environmental science), HEALTH PROFESSIONS (health science), SOCIAL SCIENCE (American studies, anthropology, area studies, criminal justice, economics, French studies, gender studies, German area studies, history, interdisciplinary studies, international studies, Judaic studies, Latin American studies, law, philosophy, political science/government, psychology, Russian and Slavic studies, sociology, Spanish studies, and women's studies). International studies, business administration, and political science are the strongest academically and the largest.

Required: To graduate, students must complete 120 credit hours with a minimum GPA of 2.0. In addition, students must complete 30 credit hours of general education requirements in 5 curricular areas and fulfill the school's competency requirements in English composition and math by either passing an exam or taking a course in each area. Many majors require internships, selecting a minor, or senior seminars.

Special: AU offers co-op programs and internships in all majors, study abroad in more than 40 countries, and a Washington semester program. Work-study is available on campus and with local community service agencies. Dual majors, interdisciplinary programs, student-designed majors, 3-2 engineering degrees, and B.A.-B.S. degrees are also available. Combined bachelor's/master's programs are available in most majors. Cross-registration may be arranged through the Consortium of Universities of the Washington Metropolitan Area. Credit for life experience, non-degree study, and pass/fail options are available. There are preprofessional programs in dentistry, engineering, law, medicine, optometry, osteopathy, pharmacy, and veterinary medicine. There are 12 national honor societies, including Phi Beta Kappa, and a freshman honors program.

Faculty/Classroom: 54% of faculty are male; 46% are female. No introductory courses are taught by graduate students.

Admissions: 53% of the 2009-2010 applicants were accepted. The SAT scores for the 2009-2010 freshman class were: Critical Reading--4% below 500, 25% between 500 and 599, 46% between 600 and 700, and 25% above 700; Math--6% below 500, 30% between 500 and 599, 48% between 600 and 700, and 17% above 700. The ACT scores were 1% below 21, 8% between 21 and 23, 29% between 24 and 26, 23% between 27 and 28, and 40% above 28. 71% of the current freshmen were in the top fifth of their class; 95% were in the top two fifths.

Requirements: The SAT or ACT is required. The ACT Optional Writing test is also required. In addition, students must have graduated from an accredited secondary school with at least 16 Carnegie units, including at least 4 units in English, 3 units in college preparatory math (including the equivalent of 2 units in algebra), 2 units in social sciences, and 2 units in foreign language(s). Applicants who have satisfactory scores on the GED may also apply. All students must submit an essay and 2 letters of recommendation. Interviews are recommended. AP and CLEP credits are accepted. Important factors in the admissions decision are advanced placement or honors courses, recommendations by school officials, and extracurricular activities record.

Procedure: Freshmen are admitted to all sessions. Entrance exams should be taken in the spring of the junior year or the fall of the senior year. There are early decision and deferred admissions plans. Early decision applications should be filed by November 15; regular applications, by January 15 for fall entry, December 1 for spring entry, and April 1 for summer entry, along with a $60 fee. Notification of early decision is sent December 31; regular decision, April 1. Applications are accepted online. 1225 applicants were on a recent waiting list.

Transfer: 372 transfer students enrolled in 2008-2009. Transfer applicants who wish to be considered competitive candidates should have a cumulative GPA of at least 2.5 from all schools attended. All applicants with a cumulative GPA of 2.0 or above will be considered. 45 of 120 credits required for the bachelor's degree must be completed at AU.

Visiting: There are regularly scheduled orientations for prospective students, including student-led daily tours and information sessions, open houses, and overnight programs. There are guides for informal visits and visitors may sit in on classes. To schedule a visit, contact the Admissions Office.

Financial Aid: In 2009-2010, 83% of all full-time freshmen and 78% of continuing full-time students received some form of financial aid. The average freshmen award was $29,771. 7% of undergraduate students work part-time. The average financial indebtedness of the 2009 graduate was $20,444. The FAFSA and the college's own financial statement are required. The deadline for filing freshman financial aid applications for fall entry is February 15.

International Students: The school actively recruits these students. They must take the TOEFL, with a minimum score of 550 on the paper-based TOEFL (PBT) or 80 on the Internet-based version (iBT), the college's own test, the SAT with a score of 530 or higher on the critical reading section, or the IELTS with a score of 6.5 or higher.

Computers: Wireless access is available. Computing resources are delivered via a fiber optic network as well as a wireless network. Wireless access for laptop computers and other devices is available everywhere on campus with appropriate hardware. AU is a T-Mobile HotSpot, which provides high-speed Wi-Fi wireless Internet access in public on campus locations such as residence halls, classrooms, the library, and the quad. In addition, there are more than 20 computer labs with approximately 700 computers available. All students may access the system. There are no time limits and no fees. It is strongly recommended that all students have a personal computer.

Graduates: From July 1, 2008 to June 30, 2009, 1482 bachelor's degrees were awarded. The most popular majors were international studies (24%), business administration (16%), and political science (11%). In an average class, 3% graduate in 3 years or less, 74% graduate in 4 years or less, 76% graduate in 5 years or less, and 76% graduate in 6 years or less.

Admissions Contact: Greg Grauman, Acting Director of Admissions. E-Mail: *admissions@american.edu* Web: *www.american.edu*

CATHOLIC UNIVERSITY OF AMERICA C-2
Washington, DC 20064

	(202) 319-5305
	(800) 673-2772; (202) 319-6171
Full-time: 1250 men, 1550 women	**Faculty:** I, -$
Part-time: 85 men, 175 women	**Ph.D.s:** 98%
Graduate: 1500 men, 1595 women	**Student/Faculty:** n/av
Year: semesters, summer session	**Tuition:** $28,000
Application Deadline: see profile	**Room & Board:** $10,000
Freshman Class: n/av	
SAT or ACT: required	**VERY COMPETITIVE**

Catholic University of America, founded in 1887 and affiliated with the Roman Catholic Church, offers undergraduate programs in arts and sciences, engineering, architecture, nursing, philosophy, and music and through the Metropolitan College. Figures in the above capsule are approximate. There are 7 undergraduate schools and 11 graduate schools. In addition to regional accreditation, CUA has baccalaureate program accreditation with ABET, ACPE, CSWE, NAAB, NASM, NCATE, and NLN. The 3 libraries contain 1.6 million volumes, 1.2 million microform items, and 40,697 audio/video tapes/CDs/DVDs, and subscribe to 10,448 periodicals including electronic. Computerized library services include interlibrary loans, database searching, Internet access, and laptop Internet portals. Special learning facilities include a learning resource center, art gallery, radio station, archeology lab, rare book collection, and electronic/computer classrooms. The 193-acre campus is in an urban area in Washington, D.C. Including any residence halls, there are 52 buildings.

Student Life: 93% of undergraduates are from out of state, mostly the Middle Atlantic. Students are from 50 states, 34 foreign countries, and Canada. 67% are white. 88% are Catholic. The average age of freshmen is 18; all undergraduates, 22. 18% do not continue beyond their first year; 73% remain to graduate.

Housing: 2101 students can be accommodated in college housing, which includes single-sex and coed dorms and on-campus apartments. In addition, there are honors houses, special-interest houses, a freshman residential college, and a residential college for upperclassmen. On-campus housing is available on a first-come, first-served basis and is available on a lottery system for upperclassmen. 95% of students live on campus. Upperclassmen may keep cars.

Activities: 1% of men belong to 2 national fraternities; there is 1 local and 1 national sorority. There are 128 groups on campus, including art, cheerleading, choir, chorale, chorus, computers, dance, debate, drama, ethnic, film, gay, honors, international, jazz band, literary magazine, musical theater, newspaper, opera, orchestra, pep band, political, professional, radio and TV, religious, social, social service, student government, symphony, and yearbook. Popular campus events include Family Weekend, Beaux Arts Ball, and Mistletoe Ball.

Sports: There are 10 intercollegiate sports for men and 11 for women, and 9 intramural sports for men and 9 for women. Facilities include an athletic center that houses 4 basketball and 5 handball/racquetball courts, a 6-lane, 25-meter swimming pool, a tennis plaza, a weight training room, an aerobics room, men's and women's saunas, adjoining playing fields, 2 dance studios, an indoor jogging track, and 3 volleyball courts.

Disabled Students: 78% of the campus is accessible. Facilities include wheelchair ramps, elevators, special parking, specially equipped restrooms, special class scheduling, lowered drinking fountains, lowered telephones, and special housing.

Services: Counseling and information services are available, as is tutoring in most subjects. There is a reader service for the blind and remedial math, reading, and writing. Taped books/scanned books, assistive technology, including reading software and screen readers, test accommodations, and sign language interpreters are available.

Campus Safety and Security: Measures include 24-hour foot and vehicle patrol, self-defense education, and security escort services. There are shuttle buses, emergency telephones, lighted pathways/sidewalks, fixed security posts, emergency whistles, watch captains in every building, and an access control system.

Programs of Study: CUA confers B.A., B.S., B.A.G.S., B. Arch, B.B.E., B.C.E., B.E.E., B.M., B.M.E., B. S. Arch, and B.S.N., degrees. Master's and doctoral degrees are also awarded. Bachelor's degrees are awarded in BIOLOGICAL SCIENCE (biochemistry and biology/biological science), BUSINESS (accounting, banking and finance, business administration and management, international economics, and management science), COMMUNICATIONS AND THE ARTS (art, art history and appreciation, classics, communications, dramatic arts, English, French, German, Latin, music, music history and appreciation, music performance, music theory and composition, musical theater, painting, piano/organ, sculpture, Spanish, and voice), COMPUTER AND PHYSICAL SCIENCE (chemistry, computer science, elementary particle physics, mathematics, and physics), EDUCATION (art education, drama education, early childhood education, education, elementary education, English education, mathematics education, music education, and secondary education), ENGINEERING AND ENVIRONMENTAL DESIGN (architecture, biomedical engineering, civil engineering, electrical/electronics engineering, engineering, environmental science, and mechanical engineering), HEALTH PROFESSIONS (medical laboratory technology and nursing), SOCIAL SCIENCE (anthropology, economics, history, liberal arts/general studies, medieval studies, philosophy, political science/government, psychology, religion, social work, and sociology). Politics is the strongest academically. Architecture is the largest.

Required: To graduate, students must complete 120 credit hours, including 36 to 42 hours in the major, with a minimum GPA of 2.0. Courses must meet distribution requirements in theology and religious studies, philosophy, English composition, humanities, language and literature, math and natural sciences, and social and behavioral sciences. A comprehensive exam is required in most majors.

Special: Cross-registration is available with the Consortium of Universities of the Washington Metropolitan Area. Opportunities are also provided for internships, accelerated degree programs, dual majors, B.A.-B.S. degrees, work study, pass/fail options, and study abroad in 13 countries. There are 15 national honor societies, including Phi Beta Kappa, and a freshman honors program.

Faculty/Classroom: 62% of faculty are male; 38% are female. 68% teach undergraduates, and all do research. Graduate students teach 20% of introductory courses. The average class size in an introductory lecture is 21; in a laboratory, 20; and in a regular course, 19.

Requirements: The SAT or ACT is required. In addition, applicants must be graduates of an accredited secondary school. Students should present 17 academic credits, including 4 each in English and social studies, 3 each in math and science, 2 in foreign languages, and 1 in fine arts or humanities. An essay is required. An audition is required for music applicants, and a portfolio for architecture applicants is recommended. A GPA of 3.0 is required. AP credits are accepted. Important factors in the admissions decision are extracurricular activities record, leadership record, and advanced placement or honors courses.

Procedure: Freshmen are admitted fall and spring. Entrance exams should be taken by February of the senior year of high school. There is early decision and deferred admissions plans. Check with the school for current application deadlines. The fall 2009 application fee was $55. Applications are accepted on-line.

Transfer: Applicants must submit a high school transcript, SAT or ACT scores, and a college transcript. A letter of recommendation and an essay are required. Terms of admission are finalized by the dean of the appropriate school. 30 of 120 credits required for the bachelor's degree must be completed at CUA.

Visiting: There are regularly scheduled orientations for prospective students, including an information session with an admissions counselor and a guided campus tour. There are guides for informal visits, and visitors may sit in on classes and stay overnight. To schedule a visit, contact the Admissions Office.

Financial Aid: CUA is a member of CSS. The FAFSA is required. Check with the school for current application deadlines.

International Students: There were 66 international students enrolled in a recent year. The school actively recruits these students. They must take the TOEFL.

Computers: Wireless access is available. There are 500 PCs located around campus for student use. All students may access the system 24 hours a day, 7 days a week. There are no time limits and no fees. It is strongly recommended that all students have a personal computer. A Dell or Gateway is recommended.

Admissions Contact: Christine Mica, Dean of University Admissions. A campus DVD is available. E-Mail: *cua-admissions@cua.edu* Web: *www.cua.edu*

CORCORAN COLLEGE OF ART AND DESIGN — C-3
Corcoran School of Art and Design

Washington, DC 20006

(202) 639-1814
(888) CORCORAN; (202) 639-1830

Full-time: 120 men, 220 women	**Faculty:** n/av
Part-time: 20 men, 35 women	**Ph.Ds:** n/av
Graduate: 15 men, 65 women	**Student/Faculty:** n/av
Year: semesters, summer session	**Tuition:** $25,000
Application Deadline: open	**Room & Board:** $10,500
Freshman Class: n/av	
SAT or ACT: required	SPECIAL

Established in 1890, Corcoran College of Art and Design is a private professional art college offering undergraduate programs in fine art, design, and photography. Figures in the above capsule are approximate. There is 1 graduate school. In addition to regional accreditation, Corcoran has baccalaureate program accreditation with NASAD. The library contains 19,000 volumes and subscribes to 130 periodicals including electronic. Computerized library services include interlibrary loans, Internet access, and laptop Internet portals. Special learning facilities include a learning resource center and art gallery. The 7-acre campus is in an urban area in Washington, D.C. Including any residence halls, there are 3 buildings.

Student Life: 73% of undergraduates are from out of state, mostly the Middle Atlantic. Students are from 24 states, 32 foreign countries, and Canada. 75% are from public schools. 64% are white; 21% foreign nationals. The average age of freshmen is 18; all undergraduates, 22. 3% do not continue beyond their first year; 60% remain to graduate.

Housing: 110 students can be accommodated in college housing, which includes coed off-campus apartments. On-campus housing is guaranteed for the freshman year only and is available on a first-come, first-served basis. 73% of students commute. Alcohol is not permitted. No one may keep cars.

Activities: There are no fraternities or sororities. There are 4 groups on campus, including art, literary magazine, newspaper, and student government. Popular campus events include New York trip, Off-the-Walls Art Sale, and juried art exhibits.

Sports: There is no sports program at Corcoran.

Disabled Students: 70% of the campus is accessible. Facilities include wheelchair ramps, elevators, special parking, specially equipped restrooms, lowered drinking fountains, and lowered telephones.

Services: Counseling and information services are available, as is tutoring in most subjects, including art history, writing, humanities, and general academic subjects. There is remedial writing.

Campus Safety and Security: Measures include 24-hour foot and vehicle patrol. There are lighted pathways/sidewalks.

Programs of Study: Corcoran confers B.F.A. degrees. Associates and master's degrees are also awarded. Bachelor's degrees are awarded in COMMUNICATIONS AND THE ARTS (fine arts, graphic design, and photography), EDUCATION (art education). Fine arts is the largest.

Required: Students must complete 126 credits, with 65 to 70 in the major and 23 in the core curriculum, and must maintain a minimum GPA of 2.0. Course distribution involves the disciplines of art history, humanities, liberal arts, and writing. Required curricula include courses in draw-

ing, design, idea resources, and media. Seniors must present thesis exhibitions.

Special: Cooperative programs are permitted with the ACE and AICA art college consortiums. Opportunities are provided for internships in graphic design and photography, credit by exam, work-study programs with the Corcoran Gallery of Art, and nondegree study. A B.F.A.-M.A.T. degree is offered.

Faculty/Classroom: 45% of faculty are male; 55% are female. All teach undergraduates. No introductory courses are taught by graduate students. The average class size in an introductory lecture is 23; in a laboratory, 10; and in a regular course, 10.

Requirements: The SAT or ACT is required. In addition, applicants must have graduated from an approved secondary school; the GED is accepted. A portfolio is required, and an interview is recommended. A GPA of 2.5 is required. AP and CLEP credits are accepted. Important factors in the admissions decision are evidence of special talent, personality/intangible qualities, and advanced placement or honors courses.

Procedure: Freshmen are admitted fall and spring. Entrance exams should be taken prior to January 30 of the senior year. There are deferred admissions and rolling admissions plans. Application deadlines are open. The fall 2009 application fee was $40. Applications are accepted on-line.

Transfer: A review of studio art transcripts is considered for the level of entry of transfer students. A portfolio review is the final determining factor. 48 of 126 credits required for the bachelor's degree must be completed at Corcoran.

Visiting: There are regularly scheduled orientations for prospective students, including an introduction to staff, faculty, and the city and an overview of activities and housing. There are guides for informal visits and visitors may sit in on classes. To schedule a visit, contact the Admissions Department.

Financial Aid: Corcoran is a member of CSS. The FAFSA and the college's own financial statement are required. Check with the school for current application deadlines.

International Students: The school actively recruits these students. They must take the TOEFL. They must also take the SAT or ACT.

Computers: Wireless access is available. All students may access the system. There are no fees. Students enrolled in Graphic Design (sophomore year) must have a personal computer.

Admissions Contact: Director of Admissions. E-Mail: *admissions@corcoran.org* Web: *www.corcoran.edu*

GALLAUDET UNIVERSITY — C-3

Washington, DC 20002-3695

(202) 651-5750
(800) 995-0550; (202) 651-5744

Full-time: 485 men, 575 women	**Faculty:** IIA, ++$
Part-time: 105 men, 105 women	**Ph.Ds:** 66%
Graduate: 100 men, 335 women	**Student/Faculty:** n/av
Year: semesters, summer session	**Tuition:** $12,000
Application Deadline: open	**Room & Board:** $10,000
Freshman Class: n/av	
SAT or ACT: recommended	SPECIAL

Gallaudet University, founded in 1864 as a university designed exclusively for deaf and hard-of-hearing students, offers programs in liberal and fine arts, teacher preparation, and professional training. Figures in the above capsule are approximate. There are 4 undergraduate schools and 4 graduate schools. In addition to regional accreditation, Gallaudet has baccalaureate program accreditation with CSWE and NCATE. The library contains 215,500 volumes, 371,000 microform items, and 4530 audio/video tapes/CDs/DVDs, and subscribes to 1415 periodicals including electronic. Computerized library services include interlibrary loans and database searching. Special learning facilities include a learning resource center, TV station, child development center, national and international centers on deafness, and research institute on deafness. The 99-acre campus is in an urban area in Washington, D.C. Including any residence halls, there are 30 buildings.

Student Life: 95% of undergraduates are from out of state, mostly the Northeast. Students are from 50 states and Canada. 74% are white; 14% foreign nationals.

Housing: College-sponsored housing includes single-sex and coed dorms. On-campus housing is guaranteed for the freshman year only and is available on a first-come, first-served basis. 51% of students live on campus; of those, 51% remain on campus on weekends. Alcohol is not permitted. All students may keep cars.

Activities: 15% of men belong to 1 local and 3 national fraternities; 20% of women belong to 2 local and 3 national sororities. There are 32 groups on campus, including art, cheerleading, computers, dance, drama, ethnic, gay, honors, international, literary magazine, newspaper, political, religious, social, social service, student government, and yearbook. Popular campus events include rock festival, drama productions, and lecture series.

Sports: There are 9 intercollegiate sports for men and 8 for women, and 12 intramural sports for men and 12 for women. Facilities include a field house, a gym, a swimming pool, tennis and racquetball courts, weight training rooms, playing fields, and bowling alleys.

Disabled Students: Facilities include wheelchair ramps, elevators, special parking, specially equipped restrooms, special class scheduling, lowered drinking fountains, lowered telephones, and phones with TTY. Sign language skills are required of all faculty and professional staff.

Services: Counseling and information services are available, as is tutoring in every subject, throughout the tutorial, English, and writing centers. There is remedial math, reading, and writing. An information-on-deafness center is also available.

Campus Safety and Security: Measures include 24-hour foot and vehicle patrol and security escort services. There are shuttle buses and lighted pathways/sidewalks.

Programs of Study: Gallaudet confers B.A. and B.S. degrees. Associate, master's, and doctoral degrees are also awarded. Bachelor's degrees are awarded in BIOLOGICAL SCIENCE (biology/biological science), BUSINESS (accounting, business administration and management, entrepreneurial studies, management science, and recreation and leisure services), COMMUNICATIONS AND THE ARTS (apparel design, art history and appreciation, communications, dramatic arts, English, French, German, graphic design, media arts, Russian, Spanish, and studio art), COMPUTER AND PHYSICAL SCIENCE (chemical technology, chemistry, computer science, mathematics, and physics), EDUCATION (art education, early childhood education, elementary education, home economics education, physical education, and secondary education), ENGINEERING AND ENVIRONMENTAL DESIGN (engineering technology), HEALTH PROFESSIONS (recreation therapy), SOCIAL SCIENCE (child care/child and family studies, economics, family/consumer studies, history, interpreter for the deaf, parks and recreation management, philosophy, political science/government, psychology, religion, and social work).

Required: The core curriculum requires 12 hours each of social science and English, 9 of literature and humanities, 8 of lab science, 5 of communication arts, 4 of phys ed, and 3 of philosophy, plus demonstrated proficiency in a foreign language. A total of 124 credits, with 30 to 60 in the major, and a minimum 2.0 GPA are required for graduation.

Special: Gallaudet offers co-op programs, cross-registration with the Consortium of Universities of the Washington Metropolitan Area, and a 3-2 engineering degree with George Washington University. Internships, study abroad, dual majors, work-study programs, and B.A.-B.S. degrees are available. There is a Phi Beta Kappa honors program and a freshman honors program.

Faculty/Classroom: No introductory courses are taught by graduate students.

Requirements: Applicants must submit a recent audiogram. SAT or ACT scores may be submitted. High school transcripts, letters of recommendation, and writing samples are required. The GED is accepted. AP and CLEP credits are accepted. Important factors in the admissions decision are advanced placement or honors courses, recommendations by school officials, and leadership record.

Procedure: Freshmen are admitted fall and spring. Entrance exams should be taken in October or November of the senior year. There are deferred admissions and rolling admissions plans. Application deadlines are open. The fall 2009 application fee was $35.

Transfer: Deaf and hard-of-hearing transfer applicants must submit a recent audiogram, official college transcripts from all schools attended, and at least 2 letters of recommendation. Students should have completed 12 or more credit hours with at least a 2.0 GPA; those who do not meet these requirements must submit recent SAT or ACT scores and a final high school transcript.

Visiting: There are regularly scheduled orientations for prospective students, including a tour of campus, classroom observations, and interviews with selected offices and programs. There are guides for informal visits and visitors may sit in on classes. To schedule a visit, contact the Gallaudet University Visitor's Center at (202) 651-5050.

Financial Aid: The FAFSA and the college's own financial statement are required. Check with the school for current application deadlines.

International Students: They must take the SAT or ACT and the college's own entrance exam.

Computers: All students may access the system 24 hours a day. There are no time limits and no fees.

Admissions Contact: Charity Reedy-Hines, Director of Admissions. E-Mail: *admission@gallua.gallaudet.edu* Web: *www.gallaudet.edu*

GEORGE WASHINGTON UNIVERSITY — B-3
Washington, DC 20052

(202) 994-6040
(800) 447-3765; (202) 994-0325

Full-time: 4240 men, 5515 women	Faculty: I, +$
Part-time: 505 men, 520 women	Ph.D.s: n/av
Graduate: 6120 men, 7230 women	Student/Faculty: n/av
Year: semesters, summer session	Tuition: $39,500
Application Deadline: see profile	Room & Board: $11,500
Freshman Class: n/av	
SAT or ACT: required	**MOST COMPETITIVE**

George Washington University, founded in 1821, is a private institution providing degree programs in arts and sciences, business, engineering, international affairs, health sciences, education, law, and public health. Figures in the above capsule are approximate. There are 7 undergraduate schools and 9 graduate schools. In addition to regional accreditation, GW has baccalaureate program accreditation with AACSB, ABET, CAHEA, CSAB, NASAD, NASM, and NCATE. Computerized library services include interlibrary loans and database searching. Special learning facilities include a learning resource center, art gallery, radio station, and TV station. The 37-acre campus is in an urban area 3 blocks west of the White House. Including any residence halls, there are 123 buildings.

Student Life: 98% of undergraduates are from out of state, mostly the Middle Atlantic. Students are from 50 states, 137 foreign countries, and Canada. 70% are from public schools. 65% are white. The average age of freshmen is 19; all undergraduates, 20. 9% do not continue beyond their first year; 78% remain to graduate.

Housing: 7015 students can be accommodated in college housing, which includes coed dorms and on-campus apartments. In addition, there are special-interest houses, fraternity houses, sorority houses, and sorority floors. On-campus housing is available on a lottery system for upperclassmen. 67% of students live on campus. All students may keep cars.

Activities: 16% of men belong to 11 national fraternities; 13% of women belong to 7 national sororities. There are 257 groups on campus, including art, band, cheerleading, chess, choir, chorale, chorus, computers, dance, debate, drama, ethnic, film, folk life, forensics, gay, geology, honors, international, jazz band, literary magazine, marching band, musical theater, newspaper, opera, orchestra, pep band, photography, political, professional, radio and TV, religious, social, social service, and student government. Popular campus events include a yearly benefit auction, Spring Fling, and Fall Fest.

Sports: There are 9 intercollegiate sports for men and 8 for women, and 16 intramural sports for men and 16 for women. Facilities include a 5000-seat gym with 2 auxiliary gyms, an AAU swimming pool, weight rooms, a jogging track, squash and racquetball courts, and soccer and baseball fields.

Disabled Students: 95% of the campus is accessible. Facilities include wheelchair ramps, elevators, special parking, specially equipped restrooms, special class scheduling, lowered drinking fountains, and lowered telephones.

Services: Counseling and information services are available, as is tutoring in every subject. There is a reader service for the blind.

Campus Safety and Security: Measures include 24-hour foot and vehicle patrol, self-defense education, and security escort services. There are emergency telephones, lighted pathways/sidewalks, and a bike patrol.

Programs of Study: GW confers B.A., B.S., B.Accy., B.B.A., B.Mus., B.S.C.E., B.S.C.Eng., B.S.C.S., B.S.E.E., B.S.H.S., B.S.M.E., and B.S.S.A. degrees. Associates, master's, and doctoral degrees are also awarded. Bachelor's degrees are awarded in BIOLOGICAL SCIENCE (biology/biological science), BUSINESS (accounting, banking and finance, business administration and management, business economics, human resources, international business management, marketing management, and tourism), COMMUNICATIONS AND THE ARTS (art history and appreciation, broadcasting, Chinese, classics, communications, dance, dramatic arts, English, fine arts, French, German, Japanese, journalism, literature, multimedia, music, music performance, public relations, Russian, and Spanish), COMPUTER AND PHYSICAL SCIENCE (applied mathematics, chemistry, computer science, geology, information sciences and systems, mathematics, physics, statistics, and systems analysis), ENGINEERING AND ENVIRONMENTAL DESIGN (civil engineering, computer engineering, electrical/electronics engineering, engineering, environmental science, and mechanical engineering), HEALTH PROFESSIONS (clinical science, emergency medical technologies, medical laboratory technology, nuclear medical technology, physician's assistant, premedicine, radiological science, and speech pathology/audiology), SOCIAL SCIENCE (American studies, anthropology, archeology, criminal justice, East Asian studies, economics, European studies, geography, history, human services, humanities, interdisciplinary studies, international relations, Judaic studies, Latin American studies, liberal arts/general studies, Middle Eastern studies, philosophy, physical fitness/movement, political science/government, psychology, religion, and sociology). Political communication, international affairs, and biological sciences are the strongest academically. Psychology, political science, and international affairs are the largest.

Required: Students must complete 120 semester hours with a minimum GPA of 2.0 for most majors. Arts and sciences majors must meet general curriculum requirements that include literacy, quantitative and logical reasoning, natural sciences, social and behavioral sciences, creative and performing arts, literature, Western civilization, and foreign languages or culture. Other specific course requirements vary with the different divisions of the university.

Special: Cross-registration is available through the Consortium of Colleges and Universities. There are co-op programs in education, business, engineering, arts and sciences, and international affairs and internships in the Washington metropolitan area. Study abroad in locations throughout the world, work-study programs, dual majors, student-designed majors, and a 3-2 engineering degree program with 8 colleges are also available. Nondegree study, a general studies degree, credit by exam, and pass/fail options are possible. There are 12 national honor societies, including Phi Beta Kappa, a freshman honors program, and 21 departmental honors programs.

Faculty/Classroom: 61% of faculty are male; 39% are female. No introductory courses are taught by graduate students.

Requirements: The SAT or ACT is required. In addition, students must have successfully completed a strong academic program in high school. SAT: Subject tests are strongly recommended. An essay, 1 teacher recommendation, and 1 counselor recommendation are required. An interview is encouraged. AP and CLEP credits are accepted. Important factors in the admissions decision are advanced placement or honors courses, recommendations by school officials, and leadership record.

Procedure: Freshmen are admitted to all sessions. Entrance exams should be taken in the junior year or the fall semester of the senior year. There are early decision and deferred admissions plans. Check with the school for current application deadlines. The fall 2009 application fee was $60. Applications are accepted on-line. A waiting list is maintained.

Transfer: In addition to a record of high grades and exam scores, applicants must submit official transcripts of all postsecondary work. Minimum GPA requirements vary from 2.5 to 3.0, depending on the major. The SAT or ACT is required, and an interview is encouraged. 30 of 120 credits required for the bachelor's degree must be completed at GW.

Visiting: There are regularly scheduled orientations for prospective students, including group information sessions and campus tours. Class visitation, lunch with current students, and other activities can be arranged, if requested in advance. There are guides for informal visits, and visitors may sit in on classes and stay overnight. To schedule a visit, contact the University Visitor Center at (202) 994-6602.

Financial Aid: GW is a member of CSS. The CSS/Profile and FAFSA are required. Check with the school for current application deadlines.

International Students: The school actively recruits these students. They must take the TOEFL and the college's own test. They must also take the SAT or ACT.

Computers: All students may access the system at any time. There are no time limits and no fees. It is strongly recommended that all students have a personal computer. A IBM, Mac, Dell, or Compaq is recommended.

Admissions Contact: Kathryn M. Napper, Executive Dean for Undergraduate Admissions. E-Mail: gwadm@gwu.edu Web: www.gwu.edu

GEORGETOWN UNIVERSITY	B-3
Washington, DC 20057	(202) 687-3600; (202) 687-5084
Full-time: 3202 men, 3913 women	**Faculty:** I, +$
Part-time: 135 men, 183 women	**Ph.D.s:** 74%
Graduate: 4647 men, 4357 women	**Student/Faculty:** 11 to 1
Year: semesters, summer session	**Tuition:** $39,036
Application Deadline: January 10	**Room & Board:** $8745
Freshman Class: 18619 applied, 3683 accepted, 1558 enrolled	
SAT or ACT: required	MOST COMPETITIVE

Georgetown University, founded in 1789, is a private institution affiliated with the Roman Catholic Church and offers programs in arts and sciences, business administration, foreign service, languages and linguistics, and nursing. There are 4 undergraduate schools and 3 graduate schools. In addition to regional accreditation, Georgetown has baccalaureate program accreditation with AACSB. The 6 libraries contain 3.0 million volumes, 4.0 million microform items, and 54,513 audio/video tapes/CDs/DVDs, and subscribe to 61,257 periodicals including electronic. Computerized library services include interlibrary loans, database searching, Internet access, and laptop Internet portals. Special learning facilities include a learning resource center, art gallery, planetarium, radio station, and TV station. The 104-acre campus is in an urban area 1.5 miles northwest of downtown Washington D.C. Including any residence halls, there are 64 buildings.

Student Life: 99% of undergraduates are from out of state, mostly the Middle Atlantic. Students are from 50 states, 86 foreign countries, and Canada. 46% are from public schools. 63% are white. 48% are Catholic; 25% Protestant; 15% Hindu, Buddhist, Islamic, unspecified; 12% claim

no religious affiliation. The average age of freshmen is 18; all undergraduates, 20. 4% do not continue beyond their first year; 94% remain to graduate.

Housing: 5053 students can be accommodated in college housing, which includes coed dorms and on-campus apartments. Special interest floors are available in some residence halls. On-campus housing is available on a lottery system for upperclassmen. 70% of students live on campus. No one may keep cars.

Activities: There are no fraternities or sororities. There are 171 groups on campus, including art, band, cheerleading, chess, choir, chorale, chorus, computers, dance, debate, drama, ethnic, film, gay, honors, international, jazz band, literary magazine, musical threater, newspaper, orchestra, pep band, photography, political, professional, radio and TV, religious, social, social service, student government, and symphony. Popular campus events include GU Day and Career Week.

Sports: There are 11 intercollegiate sports for men and 12 for women. Facilities include a 5,000-seat gym for basketball and volleyball, along with sports medicine and training room facilities, a 2,500-seat multi-sport field for football and lacrosse, and a 4-level sports and recreation facility that houses a swimming pool, basketball courts, aerobics rooms, a weight area, cardiovascular equipment, a wellness center, locker rooms, and racquetball courts.

Disabled Students: 94% of the campus is accessible. Facilities include wheelchair ramps, elevators, special parking, specially equipped rest rooms, special class scheduling, lowered drinking fountains, lowered telephones, special housing, a special map of the campus with accessibility routes, a tactile map of the campus for visually disabled students, and a paratransit vehicle for mobility on the main campus.

Services: Counseling and information services are available, as is tutoring in some subjects, accounting, finance, biological sciences, math, Spanish, French, and Arabic. There is a reader service for the blind.

Campus Safety and Security: Measures include 24-hour foot and vehicle patrol and security escort services. There are shuttle buses, emergency telephones, lighted pathways/sidewalks, laptop computer registration, bicycle registration, and off-campus security assesments.

Programs of Study: Georgetown confers A.B., B.S., B.A.L.S., B.S.B.A., B.S.F.S., and B.S.N. degrees. Master's and doctoral degrees are also awarded. Bachelor's degrees are awarded in BIOLOGICAL SCIENCE (biochemistry and biology/biological science), BUSINESS (accounting, banking and finance, business administration and management, international business management, and marketing/retailing/merchandising), COMMUNICATIONS AND THE ARTS (Arabic, Chinese, classics, comparative literature, English, fine arts, French, German, Italian, Japanese, linguistics, Portuguese, Russian, and Spanish), COMPUTER AND PHYSICAL SCIENCE (chemistry, computer science, mathematics, and physics), HEALTH PROFESSIONS (health and nursing), SOCIAL SCIENCE (American studies, anthropology, economics, history, interdisciplinary studies, international relations, philosophy, political science/government, psychology, religion, and sociology). International affairs, government, and international politics are the largest.

Required: Students must complete 120 credits and maintain a minimum GPA of 2.0. A core of liberal arts courses is required, consisting of 2 courses each in philosophy and theology. Additional requirements are specific to undergraduate school as well as major concentration.

Special: Cross-registration is available with a consortium of universities in the Washington metropolitian area. Opportunities are provided for internships, study abroad in 30 countries, work-study programs, student-designed majors, and dual majors. A liberal studies degree, B.A. and B.S. degrees, non-degree study, credit by examination, and pass/fail options are also offered. There is a chapter of Phi Beta Kappa and a freshman honors program.

Faculty/Classroom: 62% of faculty are male; 38% are female. All teach and do research. No introductory courses are taught by graduate students.

Admissions: 20% of the 2009-2010 applicants were accepted. The SAT scores for the 2009-2010 freshman class were: Critical Reading--1% below 500, 10% between 500 and 599, 43% between 600 and 700, and 46% above 700; Math--1% below 500, 8% between 500 and 599, 42% between 600 and 700, and 50% above 700. The ACT scores were 1% below 21, 10% between 21 and 23, 10% between 24 and 26, 16% between 27 and 28, and 63% above 28.

Requirements: The SAT or ACT is required. In addition, graduation from an accredited secondary school is required, including 4 years of English, a minimum of 2 each of a foreign language, math, and social studies, and 1 of natural science. An additional 2 years each of math and science is required for students intending to major in math, science, nursing, or business. SAT subject tests are strongly recommended. AP credits are accepted. Important factors in the admissions decision are evidence of special talent and leadership record.

Procedure: Freshmen are admitted in the fall. Entrance exams should be taken in the junior year and again at the beginning of the senior year. There is a deferred admissions plan. Applications should be filed by January 10 for fall entry, along with a $65 fee. Notifications are sent April 1. 2425 applicants were on a recent waiting list, 158 were accepted.

Transfer: 227 transfer students enrolled in 2008-2009. Transfer students must have successfully completed a minimum of 12 credit hours with a minimum GPA of 3.0. Either the SAT or the ACT is required. An interview is recommended. Transfers must complete their last 2 years at Georgetown. 60 of 120 credits required for the bachelor's degree must be completed at Georgetown.

Visiting: There are regularly scheduled orientations for prospective students throughout the year, including a question and answer period led by an admissions officer, followed by a campus tour led by a student guide. There are guides for informal visits and visitors may sit in on classes. To schedule a visit, contact the Office of Undergraduate Admissions at (202) 687-3600.

Financial Aid: Average annual earnings from campus work are $3000. The average financial indebtedness of the 2009 graduate was $27,117. Georgetown is a member of CSS. The CSS/Profile and FAFSA, and non-custodial profile, business/farm supplement, and tax returns are required. The deadline for filing freshman financial aid applications for fall entry is February 1.

International Students: The school actively recruits these students. They must take the TOEFL. They must also take the SAT or ACT.

Computers: There is a campuswide wired network in all of the dorms. One network jack per dorm resident in the room is guaranteed. The campus wireless network is available in all identified common areas of the university where individuals congregate and work collaboratively, and in select locations to facilitate teaching, research, and learning. There are 11 computer labs and print stations across campus open to students, containing a variety of Windows and Apple computers. All students may access the system. There are no time limits and no fees.

Graduates: From July 1, 2008 to June 30, 2009, 2201 bachelor's degrees were awarded. The most popular majors were international relations (14%), finance (11%), and political science/government (9%). In an average class, 1% graduate in 3 years or less, 88% graduate in 4 years or less, 92% graduate in 5 years or less, and 94% graduate in 6 years or less.

Admissions Contact: Charles A. Deacon, Dean of Admissions.
Web: *www.georgetown.edu*

HOWARD UNIVERSITY
Washington, DC 20059

C-3

(202) 806-2763
(800) 822-6363; (202) 806-2740

Full-time: 2230 men, 4550 women	Faculty: I, --$
Part-time: 150 men, 255 women	Ph.D.s: 78%
Graduate: 1460 men, 2410 women	Student/Faculty: n/av
Year: semesters, summer session	Tuition: $13,500
Application Deadline: see profile	Room & Board: $7000
Freshman Class: n/av	
SAT or ACT: required	COMPETITIVE

Howard University, founded in 1867, is a private, nonsectarian institution and the largest predominantly black university in the United States. Figures in the above capsule are approximate. There are 6 undergraduate schools and 11 graduate schools. In addition to regional accreditation, Howard has baccalaureate program accreditation with AACSB, ABET, ACEJMC, ACPE, ADA, AHEA, APTA, ASLA, CAHEA, CSAB, CSWE, NAAB, NASAD, NASDTEC, NASM, NCATE, and NLN. The 8 libraries contain 2.2 million volumes and 3.4 million microform items, and subscribe to 26,280 periodicals including electronic. Computerized library services include interlibrary loans, database searching, Internet access, and laptop Internet portals. Special learning facilities include a learning resource center, art gallery, radio station, TV station, and history and culture research centers. The 256-acre campus is in an urban area in Washington, D.C., and Silver Spring and Beltsville, Maryland. Including any residence halls, there are 116 buildings.

Student Life: 86% of undergraduates are from out of state, mostly the Middle Atlantic. Students are from 50 states, 61 foreign countries, and Canada. 78% are from public schools. 86% are African American. The average age of freshmen is 18; all undergraduates, 21. 11% do not continue beyond their first year; 63% remain to graduate.

Housing: 4748 students can be accommodated in college housing, which includes coed dorms, on-campus apartments, off-campus apartments, and married student housing. On-campus housing is guaranteed for the freshman year only, is available on a first-come, first-served basis, and is available on a lottery system for upperclassmen. Priority is given to out-of-town students. 55% of students commute. All students may keep cars.

Activities: There are 4 national fraternities; 1% of women belong to 4 national sororities. There are 150 groups on campus, including art, bagpipe, band, cheerleading, chess, choir, chorale, chorus, computers, dance, debate, drama, drill team, drum and bugle corps, film, gay, honors, international, jazz band, literary magazine, marching band, musical theater, newspaper, orchestra, pep band, political, professional, radio and TV, religious, social, social service, student government, and yearbook. Popular campus events include Spring Festival, Opening Convocation, and Charter Day.

Sports: There are 15 intercollegiate sports for men and 15 for women, and 5 intramural sports for men and 5 for women. Facilities include a sports center, a gym, and practice fields.

Disabled Students: All of the campus is accessible. Facilities include wheelchair ramps, elevators, special parking, specially equipped restrooms, special class scheduling, lowered drinking fountains, and lowered telephones.

Services: Counseling and information services are available, as is tutoring in most subjects. There is a reader service for the blind and remedial math, reading, and writing.

Campus Safety and Security: Measures include 24-hour foot and vehicle patrol and security escort services. There are shuttle buses, emergency telephones, and lighted pathways/sidewalks.

Programs of Study: Howard confers B.A., B.S., B.Arch., B.B.A., B.F.A., B.M., B.M.E., B.S.C.E., B.S.C.L.S., B.S.Ch.E., B.S. Comp.Eng., B.S. Comp. Sci., B.S.E.E., B.S.M.E., B.S.N., B.S.N.S., B.S.O.T., B.S.P.T., B.S. in P.A., and B.S. in R.T.T. degrees. Master's and doctoral degrees are also awarded. Bachelor's degrees are awarded in BIOLOGICAL SCIENCE (biology/biological science, microbiology, and zoology), BUSINESS (accounting, banking and finance, business administration and management, hospitality management services, insurance, international business management, and marketing/retailing/merchandising), COMMUNICATIONS AND THE ARTS (art history and appreciation, classics, communications, dance, design, dramatic arts, English, French, German, Greek, jazz, journalism, music, music business management, music history and appreciation, musical theater, photography, printmaking, Russian, and Spanish), COMPUTER AND PHYSICAL SCIENCE (chemistry, computer science, information sciences and systems, mathematics, and physics), EDUCATION (art education, early childhood education, elementary education, health education, music education, physical education, recreation education, and secondary education), ENGINEERING AND ENVIRONMENTAL DESIGN (architecture, chemical engineering, civil engineering, electrical/electronics engineering, and mechanical engineering), HEALTH PROFESSIONS (medical laboratory technology, music therapy, nursing, occupational therapy, pharmacy, physical therapy, physician's assistant, predentistry, premedicine, radiograph medical technology, and speech pathology/audiology), SOCIAL SCIENCE (African studies, African American studies, anthropology, criminal justice, dietetics, economics, history, philosophy, political science/government, psychology, and sociology). Psychology, business, and engineering are the strongest academically. Accounting, finance, and electrical engineering are the largest.

Required: To graduate, students must complete 121 to 171 credit hours, including 21 to 78 in a major and 12 to 39 in a minor, with a minimum GPA of 2.0. General requirements include 4 courses in phys ed, 2 in freshman English, 1 in writing, and 1 in Afro-American studies; 1 year of college-level math; demonstrated proficiency in a foreign language; and successful completion of a comprehensive exam in the major.

Special: Cross-registration is available with the Consortium of Universities in the Washington Metropolitan Area. Opportunities are also provided for internships, work-study, co-op programs, study abroad in 5 countries in Europe and Africa, B.A.-B.S. degrees in engineering and business, student-designed majors, pass/fail options, and accelerated degree programs in medicine and dentistry. There are 15 national honor societies, including Phi Beta Kappa, a freshman honors program, and 15 departmental honors programs.

Faculty/Classroom: 68% of faculty are male; 32% are female. No introductory courses are taught by graduate students. The average class size in an introductory lecture is 40; in a laboratory, 20; and in a regular course, 20.

Requirements: The SAT or ACT is required. In addition, graduation from an accredited secondary school is required. The GED is accepted. Students must have a minimum of 14 academic credits, including 4 in English and 2 each in foreign language, math, science, history, and social studies. Students must submit letters of recommendation from 2 high school teachers and 1 high school counselor. Other requirements vary by college. Engineering majors must take the SAT: Subject test in math I. Art majors must submit a portfolio. A GPA of 2.0 is required. AP credits are accepted. Important factors in the admissions decision are advanced placement or honors courses, recommendations by school officials, and personality/intangible qualities.

Procedure: Freshmen are admitted fall, spring, and summer. Entrance exams should be taken in the fall of the senior year. There are early admissions, deferred admissions, and rolling admissions plans. Check with the school for current application deadlines. The fall 2009 application fee was $45. Notification is sent on a rolling basis.

Transfer: All applicants must submit 2 official transcripts from each college or university attended. Students transferring to the School of Business must have successfully completed 18 semester hours or 23 quarter hours of courses, with a minimum GPA of 2.5. For many other majors, the requirement is 12 semester hours or 18 quarter hours, with a minimum GPA of 2.0. Applicants to the College of Arts and Sciences need 3 credits each in English composition and college-level algebra. 30 of

121 credits required for the bachelor's degree must be completed at Howard.

Visiting: There are regularly scheduled orientations for prospective students, including an admissions interview, classroom and dorm visits, and visits to other university facilities. There are guides for informal visits, and visitors may sit in on classes and stay overnight. To schedule a visit, contact the Office of Enrollment Management/Recruitment at (202) 806-2900.

Financial Aid: Howard is a member of CSS. The FAFSA is required. Check with the school for current application deadlines.

International Students: They must take the TOEFL. They must also take the SAT or ACT.

Computers: All students may access the system. Facilities are open 24 hours a day. There are no time limits and no fees. It is strongly recommended that all students have a personal computer.

Admissions Contact: Office of Enrollment Management/Admissions. A campus DVD is available. E-Mail: *admission@howard.edu* Web: *www.howard.edu*

TRINITY WASHINGTON UNIVERSITY   C-2

Washington, DC 20017

(202) 884-9400
(800) 492-6882; (202) 884-9403

Full-time: 17 men, 841 women	Faculty: 48; IIB, --$
Part-time: 45 men, 488 women	Ph.D.s: 98%
Graduate: 107 men, 515 women	Student/Faculty: 18 to 1
Year: semesters	Tuition: $19,959
Application Deadline: open	Room & Board: $8850
Freshman Class: n/av	
SAT or ACT: recommended	COMPETITIVE

Trinity Washington University, founded in 1897, is a private, women's liberal arts college in the nation's capital. The school year consists of traditional semesters plus 1-week courses during January and May. The School of Professional Studies and School of Education are both co-ed and offer adult students bachelor's and master's degrees with evening and weekend classes. There are 2 undergraduate schools and 2 graduate schools. In addition to regional accreditation, Trinity has baccalaureate program accreditation with NASDTEC and NCATE. The library contains 215,338 volumes, 6826 microform items, and 13,797 audio/video tapes/CDs/DVDs, and subscribes to 509 periodicals including electronic. Computerized library services include interlibrary loans and database searching. Special learning facilities include a learning resource center, art gallery, a computer center, a writing center, and a career and counseling center. The 26-acre campus is in an urban area 2 1/2 miles north of the U.S. Capitol. Including any residence halls, there are 7 buildings.

Student Life: 50% of undergraduates are from out of state, mostly the Middle Atlantic. Students are from 21 states and 2 foreign countries. 60% are from public schools. 68% are African American. 52% claim no religious affiliation; 35% Protestant; 12% Catholic. The average age of freshmen is 18; all undergraduates, 22. 30% do not continue beyond their first year; 50% remain to graduate.

Housing: 275 students can be accommodated in college housing, which includes single-sex dorms. On-campus housing is guaranteed for all 4 years. 80% of students commute. Alcohol is not permitted. All students may keep cars.

Activities: There are no sororities. There are 23 groups on campus, including choir, chorale, computers, dance, drama, ethnic, Future Female Attorneys of America, gay, honors, international, literary magazine, newspaper, photography, political, professional, psychology, religious, social, social service, and student government. Popular campus events include Founders Day, Class Days, and Junior Ring Day.

Sports: There are 7 intercollegiate sports for women. Facilities include 2 athletic fields for soccer and field hockey, a fitness center, 6 tennis courts, an outdoor sand volleyball court, and a state-of-the-art sports center with pool, weight room, and basketball court.

Disabled Students: 80% of the campus is accessible. Facilities include wheelchair ramps, elevators, special parking, specially equipped restrooms, and lowered telephones.

Services: Counseling and information services are available, as is tutoring in every subject. There is a reader service for the blind and signing for hearing-impaired students.

Campus Safety and Security: Measures include 24-hour foot and vehicle patrol, self-defense education, and security escort services. There are shuttle buses, emergency telephones, and lighted pathways/sidewalks.

Programs of Study: Trinity confers B.A. and B.S. degrees. Associate and master's degrees are also awarded. Bachelor's degrees are awarded in BIOLOGICAL SCIENCE (biochemistry and biology/biological science), BUSINESS (business administration and management and business economics), COMMUNICATIONS AND THE ARTS (communications, English, languages, and Spanish), COMPUTER AND PHYSICAL SCIENCE (chemistry, computer science, mathematics, and physical sciences), EDUCATION (elementary education), ENGINEERING AND ENVIRONMENTAL DESIGN (engineering and environmental science),

HEALTH PROFESSIONS (nursing), SOCIAL SCIENCE (criminal justice, economics, history, human services, international studies, political science/government, psychology, and sociology). English, history, and political science are the strongest academically. Psychology, business administration, and criminal justice are the largest.

Required: To graduate, students must complete a total of 128 credit hours with a minimum GPA of 2.0. Between 42 and 50 hours are required in the major. All students must take the courses required in the general education curriculum and must complete a senior seminar.

Special: Cross-registration is offered through the Consortium of Universities of the Washington Metropolitan Area. Trinity offers internships in all majors and minors, as well as work-study programs. Students may study in France, Italy, and various other countries by arrangement with their faculty adviser. B.A.-B.S. degrees, a 5-year accelerated degree in teaching, dual and student-designed majors, a general studies degree, credit for life experience, nondegree study, and pass/fail options are also available. There are 2 national honor societies, including Phi Beta Kappa, and a freshman honors program.

Faculty/Classroom: 35% of faculty are male; 65% are female. 72% teach undergraduates. No introductory courses are taught by graduate students. The average class size in an introductory lecture is 16; in a laboratory, 16; and in a regular course, 13.

Requirements: The SAT or ACT is recommended. In addition, graduation from an accredited secondary school or satisfactory scores on the GED are required for admission. A total of 16 academic credits is required, including 4 years of English and 3 to 4 years each of a foreign language, history, math, and science. AP exams, an interview, and an essay or graded writing sample are required. A GPA of 2.0 is required. AP and CLEP credits are accepted. Important factors in the admissions decision are leadership record, extracurricular activities record, and recommendations by school officials.

Procedure: Freshmen are admitted fall and spring. Entrance exams should be taken in the junior year. There are deferred admissions and rolling admissions plans. Application deadlines are open. Application fee is $40. Applications are accepted on-line.

Transfer: 58 transfer students enrolled in 2008-2009. Transfer applicants must have a GPA of 2.5. An interview is recommended, and an essay is required. 45 of 128 credits required for the bachelor's degree must be completed at Trinity.

Visiting: There are regularly scheduled orientations for prospective students, consisting of a full-day program, including an overview of the college, the curriculum, and financing. There are guides for informal visits, and visitors may sit in on classes and stay overnight. To schedule a visit, contact the Office of Admissions.

Financial Aid: In 2009-2010, 98% of all full-time freshmen and 95% of continuing full-time students received some form of financial aid. 83% of all full-time freshmen and 82% of continuing full-time students received need-based aid. The average freshman award was $23,280. Need-based scholarships or need-based grants averaged $14,000; need-based self-help aid (loans and jobs) averaged $7000; and other non-need-based awards and non-need-based scholarships averaged $2280. 7% of undergraduate students work part-time. Average annual earnings from campus work are $1400. The average financial indebtedness of the 2009 graduate was $17,000. Trinity is a member of CSS. The FAFSA is required. The priority date for freshman financial aid applications for fall entry is March 1.

International Students: There are 2 international students enrolled. The school actively recruits these students. They must take the TOEFL with a minimum score of 543 on the paper-based TOEFL (PBT) or 76 on the Internet-based version (iBT).

Computers: Wireless access is available. All students may access the system. There are no time limits and no fees. It is strongly recommended that all students have a personal computer.

Graduates: From July 1, 2008 to June 30, 2009, 130 bachelor's degrees were awarded. The most popular majors were psychology (36%), business administration (15%), and English (10%).

Admissions Contact: Kelly Gosnell, Vice President of Admissions. E-mail: *admissions@trinitydc.edu* Web: *www.trinitydc.edu*

UNIVERSITY OF THE DISTRICT OF COLUMBIA   C-2

Washington, DC 20008

(202) 274-6069; (202) 274-6341

Full-time: 790 men, 1115 women	Faculty: IIA, av$
Part-time: 1060 men, 2050 women	Ph.D.s: 52%
Graduate: 85 men, 155 women	Student/Faculty: n/av
Year: semesters, summer session	Tuition: $2500 ($5000)
Application Deadline: open	Room & Board: n/app
Freshman Class: n/av	
ACT: required	LESS COMPETITIVE

The University of the District of Columbia, founded in 1977, is a publicly funded, land-grant commuter institution offering programs in liberal arts, business, education, and technical fields. Figures in the above capsule are approximate. There are 5 undergraduate schools and 1 graduate school. In addition to regional accreditation, UDC has baccalaureate program accreditation with ABET, CAHEA, CSWE, NASDTEC, NASM, and NLN. The 4 libraries contain 470,330 volumes, 623,991 microform items, and 21,207 audio/video tapes/CDs/DVDs, and subscribe to 2787 periodicals including electronic. Computerized library services include database searching. Special learning facilities include a learning resource center, art gallery, radio station, TV station, and early childhood learning center. The 22-acre campus is in a suburban area in northwest Washington, D.C. There are 26 buildings.

Student Life: 87% of undergraduates are from District of Columbia. Others are from 49 states and 55 foreign countries. 85% are from public schools. 72% are African American. The average age of freshmen is 18; all undergraduates, 27. 35% do not continue beyond their first year; 65% remain to graduate.

Housing: There are no residence halls. All students commute.

Activities: 2% of men belong to 7 national fraternities; 2% of women belong to 5 national sororities. There are 139 groups on campus, including art, band, cheerleading, chess, choir, chorale, computers, dance, drama, drum and bugle corps, ethnic, film, honors, international, jazz band, marching band, newspaper, orchestra, pep band, photography, political, professional, radio and TV, religious, social, social service, student government, and yearbook. Popular campus events include the Cross-Cultural Extended Family Program and International Multicultural Recognition Day.

Sports: There are 6 intercollegiate sports for men and 6 for women, and 8 intramural sports for men and 6 for women. Facilities include a 3000-seat gym, a swimming pool, a weight room, and racquetball and tennis courts.

Disabled Students: All of the campus is accessible. Facilities include wheelchair ramps, elevators, special parking, specially equipped restrooms, lowered drinking fountains, and lowered telephones.

Services: Counseling and information services are available, as is tutoring in every subject. There is a reader service for the blind and remedial math and reading.

Campus Safety and Security: Measures include 24-hour foot and vehicle patrol. There are emergency telephones and lighted pathways/sidewalks.

Programs of Study: UDC confers B.A. and B.S. degrees. Associates and master's degrees are also awarded. Bachelor's degrees are awarded in BIOLOGICAL SCIENCE (biology/biological science), BUSINESS (accounting, banking and finance, business administration and management, marketing/retailing/merchandising, and office supervision and management), COMMUNICATIONS AND THE ARTS (dramatic arts, English, fine arts, French, media arts, music, and Spanish), COMPUTER AND PHYSICAL SCIENCE (chemistry, computer science, mathematics, and physics), EDUCATION (early childhood education, elementary education, health education, and physical education), ENGINEERING AND ENVIRONMENTAL DESIGN (architecture, aviation administration/management, civil engineering, construction engineering, electrical/ electronics engineering, electromechanical technology, environmental science, and mechanical engineering), HEALTH PROFESSIONS (nursing and speech pathology/audiology), SOCIAL SCIENCE (criminal justice, economics, fire science, food science, geography, history, philosophy, political science/government, psychology, public administration, social work, sociology, and urban studies). Business is the strongest academically. Fine arts is the largest.

Required: To graduate, students must complete 120 to 130 semester hours with a minimum GPA of 2.0. All students must take 6 hours each of English composition, literature and advanced writing, foreign language, social science, math, and natural sciences; 4 of personal and community health; and 3 each of philosophy and fine arts.

Special: Cross-registration may be arranged through the Consortium of Universities of the Washington Metropolitan Area. Co-op programs with the federal government, internships, study abroad in 4 countries, work-study programs, and B.A.-B.S. degrees in administration of justice, chemistry, and physics are offered. Nondegree study and credit for life experience are also available. There are 4 national honor societies and a freshman honors program.

Faculty/Classroom: 66% of faculty are male; 34% are female. 89% teach undergraduates, 3% do research, and 20% do both. No introductory courses are taught by graduate students. The average class size in an introductory lecture is 23; in a laboratory, 23; and in a regular course, 23.

Requirements: The ACT is required. In addition, a high school diploma or GED is required for admission, along with an interview. High school courses must include 4 years of English and 2 each of foreign language, social science, lab science, and math (algebra and geometry). AP and CLEP credits are accepted. Important factors in the admissions decision are ability to finance college education, advanced placement or honors courses, and recommendations by school officials.

Procedure: Freshmen are admitted to all sessions. Application deadlines are open. The application fee is $35. Notification is sent on a rolling basis.

Transfer: Applicants must have a minimum GPA of 2.0. Those with fewer than 30 hours of college credit must submit a high school transcript along with college records. 30 of 120 credits required for the bachelor's degree must be completed at UDC.

Visiting: There are guides for informal visits and visitors may sit in on classes. To schedule a visit, contact the Office of Student Recruitment at (202) 282-3350.

Financial Aid: UDC is a member of CSS. The CSS/Profile and FFS are required. Check with the school for current application deadlines.

International Students: They must take the TOEFL or the university's own English, math, and reading tests.

Computers: All students may access the system 24 hours a day. There are no time limits and no fees.

Admissions Contact: LaVerne Hill-Flanagan, Director of Recruitment and Admissions. E-Mail: *lflanagan@udc.edu* Web: *www.udc.edu*

MAINE

POPULATION DENSITY

● 10,000 and over

0 20 40 60 80
Miles

BATES COLLEGE
Lewiston, ME 04240   B-5

Full-time: 800 men, 860 women
Part-time: none
Graduate: none
Year: 4-1-4
Application Deadline: January 1
Freshman Class: n/av
SAT or ACT: not required

(207) 786-6330; (207) 786-6484
Faculty: 179; IIB, ++$
Ph.D.s: 100%
Student/Faculty: n/av
Tuition: $51,300
Room & Board: see profile

MOST COMPETITIVE

Bates College, founded in 1855, is a small, private, liberal arts institution dedicated to the principle of active agreement, offering undergraduate programs in humanities, social sciences, and natural sciences. Students are charged a comprehensive fee of $51,300 annually, which includes tuition, room and board, and required fees. Some figures in the above capsule and in this profile are approximate. The library contains 620,000 volumes, 290,000 microform items, and 35,000 audio/video tapes/CDs/DVDs, and subscribes to 27,000 periodicals including electronic. Computerized library services include interlibrary loans, database searching, and Internet access. Special learning facilities include a learning resource center, art gallery, planetarium, radio station, TV station, a 654-acre mountain conservation area, an observatory, a language resource center, and the Edmund S. Muskie archives. The 109-acre campus is in a small town 35 miles north of Portland. Including any residence halls, there are 79 buildings.

Student Life: 90% of undergraduates are from out of state, mostly the Northeast. Students are from 46 states, 70 foreign countries, and Canada. 54% are from public schools. 81% are white. The average age of freshmen is 18; all undergraduates, 20. 7% do not continue beyond their first year; 89% remain to graduate.

Housing: 1592 students can be accommodated in college housing, which includes single-sex and coed dorms. In addition, there are special-interest houses, chemical-free housing, and quiet/study housing. On-campus housing is guaranteed for all 4 years. 92% of students live on campus; of those, 95% remain on campus on weekends. All students may keep cars.

Activities: There are no fraternities or sororities. There are 112 groups on campus, including art, chess, choir, chorale, chorus, computers, dance, debate, drama, environmental, ethnic, film, gay, honors, international, jazz band, literary magazine, musical theater, newspaper, orchestra, outdoor recreation, pep band, photography, political, professional, radio and TV, religious, social, social service, student government, symphony, and yearbook. Popular campus events include Winter Carnival, international dinners, and ocean clambakes.

Sports: There are 15 intercollegiate sports for men and 16 for women, and 8 intramural sports for men and 8 for women. Facilities include a

pool, a field house, indoor and outdoor tracks, indoor and outdoor tennis courts, 3 basketball courts, 3 volleyball courts, dance and fencing space, squash and racquetball courts, training rooms, a rock-climbing wall, a boathouse, a winter sports arena, a weight room, and football, soccer, baseball, softball, and lacrosse fields.

Disabled Students: 60% of the campus is accessible. Facilities include wheelchair ramps, elevators, special parking, specially equipped rest rooms, special class scheduling, and lowered telephones.

Services: Counseling and information services are available, as is tutoring in every subject. There is a reader service for the blind, and remedial math and writing.

Campus Safety and Security: Measures include 24-hour foot and vehicle patrol, emergency notification system, self-defense education, and security escort services. There are shuttle buses, emergency telephones, lighted pathways/sidewalks, electronic access control in residence halls and all major buildings on campus, and an automated 911 telephone system.

Programs of Study: Bates confers B.A. and B.S. degrees. Bachelor's degrees are awarded in AGRICULTURE (environmental studies), BIOLOGICAL SCIENCE (biochemistry, biology/biological science, and neurosciences), COMMUNICATIONS AND THE ARTS (art, Chinese, dramatic arts, English, French, German, Japanese, music, Russian, Spanish, and speech/debate/rhetoric), COMPUTER AND PHYSICAL SCIENCE (chemistry, geology, mathematics, and physics), ENGINEERING AND ENVIRONMENTAL DESIGN (engineering), SOCIAL SCIENCE (African American studies, American studies, anthropology, classical/ancient civilization, East Asian studies, economics, gender studies, history, interdisciplinary studies, medieval studies, philosophy, political science/government, psychology, religion, sociology, and women's studies). Psychology, political science, and economics are the largest.

Required: Requirements for graduation include 2 four-course concentrations, 3 writing attentive courses, and 3 courses focused on scientific reasoning, laboratory experience, and quantitative literacy. The total number of hours in the major varies by department, but students should take at least 32 courses, plus 2 short terms, and maintain a minimum GPA of 2.0. A senior thesis is required.

Special: Co-op programs in engineering, internships, research apprenticeships, work-study programs, study abroad, and a Washington semester are possible. Dual, student-designed, and interdisciplinary majors, and a 3-2 engineering degree with Columbia University, Dartmouth College, Case Western Reserve University, Rensselaer Polytechnic Institute, and Washington University in St. Louis are available. Students in any major may graduate in 3 years, and a B.A.-B.S. is possible in all majors. Students may also participate in the Williams-Mystic Seaport program in marine biology and maritime history, and exchanges with Spelman College, Morehouse College, Washington and Lee University, and McGill University are possible. There are 2 national honor societies, including Phi Beta Kappa, and 100 departmental honors programs.

Faculty/Classroom: 52% of faculty are male; 48% are female. All teach and do research. The average class size in an introductory lecture is 30; in a laboratory, 17; and in a regular course, 21.

Admissions: 30% of a recent year's applicants were accepted. 81% of a recent year's freshmen were in the top fifth of their class; 98% were in the top two fifths.

Requirements: Candidates for admission should have completed at least 4 years of English, 3 each of math, social science, and a foreign language, and 2 of lab science. Essays are required, and an interview on or off campus is strongly recommended. The submission of test scores is optional. AP credits are accepted. Important factors in the admissions decision are advanced placement or honors courses, evidence of special talent, and leadership record.

Procedure: Freshmen are admitted fall and winter. There are early decision and deferred admissions plans. Early decision applications should be filed by November 15; regular applications, by January 1 for fall entry, along with a $60 fee. Notification of early decision is sent December 20; regular decision, March 31. 180 early decision candidates were accepted for a recent class. A waiting list is maintained. Applications are accepted on-line.

Transfer: 14 transfer students enrolled in a recent year. More weight is given to the student's college record than to high school credentials. Applicants must submit official college and final high school transcripts, a statement of good standing, 3 letters of recommendation, and an essay. An interview is strongly recommended. 16 of 32 courses required for the bachelor's degree must be completed at Bates.

Visiting: There are guides for informal visits, and visitors may sit in on classes and stay overnight. To schedule a visit, contact the Admissions Office.

Financial Aid: In a recent year, 41% of all full-time freshmen and 43% of continuing full-time students received some form of financial aid, including need-based aid. The average freshman award was $27,686. 50% of undergraduate students work part-time. Average annual earnings from campus work are $1600. The average financial indebtedness of a recent year's graduate was $13,947. Bates is a member of CSS. The CSS/Profile, FAFSA, and parent and student tax returns and W-2 forms are required. Check with the school for current application deadlines.

International Students: There were 88 international students enrolled in a recent year. The school actively recruits these students. They must take an English proficiency exam; the TOEFL is preferred.

Computers: Wireless access is available. There are 100 MB network connections in residence halls for each student, network access in every classroom and wireless in some, plus 400 open ports on campus. More than 400 college-owned computers are available for student use. All students may access the system. There are no time limits and no fees.

Graduates: In a recent year, 464 bachelor's degrees were awarded. The most popular majors were politics (12%), psychology (11%), and economics (10%). In an average class, 1% graduate in 3 years or less, 86% graduate in 4 years or less, 89% graduate in 5 years or less, and 89% graduate in 6 years or less. Of a recent year's graduating class, 13% were enrolled in graduate school within 6 months of graduation, and 70% were employed.

Admissions Contact: Dean of Admissions.
E-mail: *admissions@bates.edu* Web: *www.bates.edu*

BOWDOIN COLLEGE
B-5

Brunswick, ME 04011 — (207) 725-3100; (207) 725-3101

Full-time: 867 men, 904 women	Faculty: 177; IIB, ++$
Part-time: 4 men, 2 women	Ph.D.s: 98%
Graduate: none	Student/Faculty: 9 to 1
Year: semesters	Tuition: $40,020
Application Deadline: January 1	Room & Board: $10,880
Freshman Class: 5940 applied, 1153 accepted, 494 enrolled	
SAT CR/M/W: 710/710/710	ACT: 32 MOST COMPETITIVE

Bowdoin College, established in 1794, is a private liberal arts institution.. The 5 libraries contain 1 million volumes, 122,698 microform items, and 29,499 audio/video tapes/CDs/DVDs, and subscribe to 15,307 periodicals including electronic. Computerized library services include interlibrary loans, database searching, Internet access, and laptop Internet portals. Special learning facilities include a learning resource center, art gallery, radio station, TV station, a museum of art, arctic museum, language media center, women's resource center, electronic classroom, coastal studies center, African American center, the craft center ceramics studio and photography darkroom, scientific station, located in the Bay of Fundy, educational research and development program, theaters, music hall, community service resource center, environmental studies center, and visual arts center. The 205-acre campus is in a small town 25 miles northeast of Portland. Including any residence halls, there are 116 buildings.

Student Life: 88% of undergraduates are from out of state, mostly the Northeast. Students are from 50 states, 38 foreign countries, and Canada. 55% are from public schools. 66% are white; 11% Asian American. 39% claim no religious affiliation; 27% Protestant; 19% Catholic. The average age of freshmen is 18; all undergraduates, 20. 4% do not continue beyond their first year; 92% remain to graduate.

Housing: 1711 students can be accommodated in college housing, which includes coed dorms, on-campus apartments, and off-campus apartments. In addition, there are special-interest houses, All first-year students participate in the new College House System; their residence hall is associated with 1 of 8 campus houses. All upper class students are also eligible to participate. On-campus housing is available on a lottery system for upperclassmen. 94% of students live on campus; of those, 99% remain on campus on weekends. All students may keep cars.

Activities: There are no fraternities or sororities. There are 109 groups on campus, including art, band, cheerleading, choir, chorale, chorus, club sports, computers, dance, debate, drama, environmental, equestrian, ethnic, film, gay, honors, improvisational comedy, international, jazz band, literary magazine, musical theater, newspaper, orchestra, organic garden, outing, peer counseling and advising, photography, political, professional, radio and TV, religious, social, social service, science, student government, symphony, women's and yearbook. Popular campus events include Sara and James Bowdoin Day, Common Good Day, and Asian Week.

Sports: There are 13 intercollegiate sports for men and 15 for women, and 15 intramural sports for men and 12 for women. Facilities include an ice arena, a field house, a swimming pool, 2 gyms, indoor and outdoor track facilities, tennis and squash courts, a climbing wall, a boathouse, outdoor leadership center, and cross-country ski trails. There are also weight and aerobics rooms and 60 acres of playing fields for football, baseball, softball, lacrosse, field hockey, and soccer.

Disabled Students: 70% of the campus is accessible. Facilities include wheelchair ramps, elevators, special parking, specially equipped restrooms, special class scheduling, lowered drinking fountains, lowered telephones, and special housing. All new buildings and renovations to old buildings are built to ADA compliance standards.

Services: Counseling and information services are available, as is tutoring in most subjects. There is a reader service for the blind. A counselor is available to assist students with accommodations as needed. Tutoring is available through the Quantitative Skills Program and the Writing Project.

Campus Safety and Security: Measures include 24-hour foot and vehicle patrol, emergency notification system, self-defense education, and security escort services. There are shuttle buses, emergency telephones, lighted pathways/sidewalks, and emergency warning whistles. Residences are locked 24 hours a day, and a staffed communications center is available around the clock.

Programs of Study: Bowdoin confers A.B. degrees. Bachelor's degrees are awarded in BIOLOGICAL SCIENCE (biochemistry, biology/biological science, and neurosciences), COMMUNICATIONS AND THE ARTS (art history and appreciation, classics, dramatic arts, English, French, German, music, romance languages and literature, Russian, Spanish, and visual and performing arts), COMPUTER AND PHYSICAL SCIENCE (chemical physics, chemistry, computer science, geochemistry, geology, geophysics and seismology, mathematics, and physics), ENGINEERING AND ENVIRONMENTAL DESIGN (environmental science), SOCIAL SCIENCE (African studies, anthropology, archeology, Asian/Oriental studies, classical/ancient civilization, Eastern European studies, economics, history, interdisciplinary studies, Latin American studies, philosophy, political science/government, psychology, religion, sociology, and women's studies). Biology, economics, government and legal studies are the strongest academically and the largest.

Required: Degree requirements include 32 courses, with a first-year seminar, at least 1 course in natural sciences and math, social and behavioral sciences and humanities, 1 course in each of the 5 distribution areas, and completion of major requirements.

Special: A.B. offers degrees in 43 majors, with single, coordinate, double and self-designed major options, and Plus (+) and minus (-) grading system, with credit/D/fail option. Dean's list, Latin Honors and departmental honors are awarded. First-year seminars, intermediate and advanced independent study, student research and close work with faculty advisors is strongly emphasized. Study abroad during the junior year is encouraged. Academic support programs include the Baldwin Program, the Quantitative Skills Program, and the Engineering, Legal Studies, Health Professions Advising and Teacher Certification. There is 1 national honor society, including Phi Beta Kappa, and all departments have honors programs.

Faculty/Classroom: 51% of faculty are male; 49% are female. All teach and do research. No introductory courses are taught by graduate students. The average class size in an introductory lecture, 28, in a laboratory, 13, and in a regular course, 16.

Admissions: 19% of the 2009-2010 applicants were accepted. The SAT scores for the 2009-2010 freshman class were: Critical Reading-- 9% between 500 and 599, 34% between 600 and 700, and 57% above 700; Math-- 7% between 500 and 599, 35% between 600 and 700, and 58% above 700; Writing-- 8% between 500 and 599, 36% between 600 and 700, and 56% above 700. The ACT scores were % below 21, 3% between 21 and 23, 7% between 24 and 26, 9% between 27 and 28, and 81% above 28. 93% of the current freshmen were in the top fifth of their class; 98% were in the top two fifths. There were 39 National Merit finalists. 55 freshmen graduated first in their class.

Requirements: There are no specific academic requirements, but typical applicants for admission will have 4 years each of English, social studies, foreign language, and math, 3 1/2 years of science, and 1 course each in art, music, and history. A high school record, 2 teacher recommendations, and an essay are required. AP credits are accepted.

Procedure: Freshmen are admitted in the fall. Entrance exams should be taken by the late summer before the freshman year. There are early decision and deferred admissions plans. Early decision applications should be filed by November 15; regular applications, by January 1 for fall entry, along with a $60 fee. Notification of early decision is sent December 15; regular decision, April 5. Applications are accepted on-line. A waiting list is maintained.

Transfer: 3 transfer students enrolled in 2008-2009. College grades of B or better are required to transfer. Applicants should submit high school and college transcripts, a dean's or adviser's statement from the most recent college attended, and 2 recommendations from recent professors. 16 of 32 credits required for the bachelor's degree must be completed at Bowdoin.

Visiting: There are regularly scheduled orientations for prospective students, in which students should be prepared to talk informally about their academic record, interests, and talents. There are guides for informal visits; visitors may sit in on classes and stay overnight. To schedule a visit, contact the Admissions Office at admissions@bowdoin.edu.

Financial Aid: In 2009-2010, 44% of all full-time freshmen and 44% of continuing full-time students received some form of financial aid. 40% of all full-time freshmen and 40% of continuing full-time students received need-based aid. The average freshmen award was $36,316, with $35,492 ($53,800 maximum) from need-based scholarships or need-based grants; $1,724 ($2,000 maximum) from need-based self-help aid (loans and jobs); and $1,000 ($2,000 maximum) from other non-need-based awards and non-need-based scholarships. 51% of undergraduate students work part-time. Average annual earnings from campus work are

$1525. The average financial indebtedness of the 2009 graduate was $18,135. Bowdoin is a member of CSS. The CSS/Profile and FAFSA, and Noncustodial PROFILE and Business/Farm Supplement are required. The deadline for filing freshman financial aid applications for fall entry is February 15.

International Students: There are 62 international students enrolled. The school actively recruits these students. They must take the TOEFL with a minimum score of 600 on the paper-based TOEFL (PBT) or 100 on the Internet-based version (iBT). SAT scores are not required for admission but must be submitted at matriculation for counseling and placement.

Computers: Wireless access is available. Computer equipment and network and Internet access are available to all students in computer labs (150 stations), all residence halls, the library (250 stations), the student center and classrooms (500 stations). Students have access to the wireless network, available in all libraries, some classrooms, computer labs and some residence halls. Students may check out laptops and wireless cards. All students may access the system 24 hours a day. There are no time limits and no fees. It is strongly recommended that all students have a personal computer.

Graduates: In a recent year, 452 bachelor's degrees were awarded. The most popular majors were government and legal studies (16%), economics (15%), and history (11%). 350 companies recruited on campus in 2008-2009. In an average class, 87% graduate in 4 years or less, 91% graduate in 5 years or less, and 92% graduate in 6 years or less. Of the 2008 graduating class, 13% were enrolled in graduate school within 6 months of graduation, and 71% were employed.

Admissions Contact: Scott A. Meiklejohn, Interim Dean of Admissions/Student Aid. A campus DVD is available. E-Mail: *admissions@bowdoin.edu* Web: *www.bowdoin.edu/admissions/*

COLBY COLLEGE
B-4

Waterville, ME 04901-8841

(207) 859-4800
(800) 723-3032; (207) 859-4828

Full-time: 800 men, 1000 women	**Faculty:** 160; IIB, ++$
Part-time: none	**Ph.D.s:** 96%
Graduate: none	**Student/Faculty:** n/av
Year: 4-1-4	**Tuition:** $51,990
Application Deadline: January 1	**Room & Board:** see profile
Freshman Class: n/av	
SAT or ACT: required	**MOST COMPETITIVE**

Colby College, founded in 1813, is a private liberal arts college. Students are charged a comprehensive fee of $51,990 annually, which includes tuition, room and board, and required fees. Some of the figures in the above capsule and in this profile are approximate. In addition to regional accreditation, Colby has baccalaureate program accreditation with ACS. The 3 libraries contain 1.0 million volumes, 402,000 microform items, and 22,779 audio/video tapes/CDs/DVDs, and subscribe to 17,840 periodicals including electronic. Computerized library services include interlibrary loans, database searching, Internet access, and laptop Internet portals. Special learning facilities include a learning resource center, art gallery, radio station, observatory, astronomy classroom, arboretum, state wildlife management area, and electronic-research classroom. The 714-acre campus is in a small town 75 miles north of Portland. Including any residence halls, there are 60 buildings.

Student Life: 90% of undergraduates are from out of state, mostly the Northeast. Students are from 43 states, 62 foreign countries, and Canada. 55% are from public schools. 75% are white. The average age of freshmen is 18; all undergraduates, 20. 7% do not continue beyond their first year; 89% remain to graduate.

Housing: 1742 students can be accommodated in college housing, which includes coed dorms and on-campus apartments. In addition, there are special-interest houses, substance-free halls, quiet residence halls, and apartments for seniors. On-campus housing is guaranteed for all 4 years. 95% of students live on campus. All students may keep cars.

Activities: There are no fraternities or sororities. There are 98 groups on campus, including art, band, cheerleading, choir, chorale, chorus, coed woodsmen's team, communications, computers, dance, debate, drama, environmental, ethnic, film, gay, honors, human rights, international, jazz band, literary magazine, musical theater, newspaper, orchestra, outdoor, photography, political, professional, radio and TV, religious, social, social service, student government, symphony, women's, and yearbook. Popular campus events include Winter Carnival, Foss Arts Festival, and International Extravaganza.

Sports: There are 16 intercollegiate sports for men and 17 for women, and 8 intramural sports for men and 8 for women. Facilities include an athletic center with fitness, weight training, and exercise areas; a gym with badminton, volleyball, and basketball courts; a hockey and skating rink; a field house for track and field, climbing wall, soccer, baseball, softball, tennis, lacrosse, and golf; a swimming pool and saunas; and squash and handball courts. There are also outdoor playing fields, tennis courts, an all-weather track, cross-country skiing, and running trails.

Disabled Students: 90% of the campus is accessible. Facilities include wheelchair ramps, elevators, special parking, specially equipped rest rooms, special class scheduling, lowered drinking fountains, and lowered telephones.

Services: Counseling and information services are available, as is tutoring in every subject. There is a reader service for the blind. There is also a writing center and a support program for learning-disabled students.

Campus Safety and Security: Measures include 24-hour foot and vehicle patrol, emergency notification system, self-defense education, and security escort services. There are shuttle buses, emergency telephones, lighted pathways/sidewalks, keycard-controlled access to dorms, a women's safety program, a property identification program, party monitors (security officers), a student emergency response team, and courtesy rides.

Programs of Study: Colby confers B.A. degrees. Bachelor's degrees are awarded in BIOLOGICAL SCIENCE (biochemistry, biology/biological science, and neurosciences), COMMUNICATIONS AND THE ARTS (art history and appreciation, classics, creative writing, English, Germanic languages and literature, music, performing arts, Russian languages and literature, Spanish, and studio art), COMPUTER AND PHYSICAL SCIENCE (applied mathematics, chemistry, computer science, geology, geoscience, mathematics, physics, and science technology), ENGINEERING AND ENVIRONMENTAL DESIGN (environmental science), SOCIAL SCIENCE (African American studies, American studies, anthropology, classical/ancient civilization, East Asian studies, economics, French studies, history, international studies, Latin American studies, philosophy, political science/government, psychology, religion, sociology, and women's studies). Chemistry, economics, and biology are the strongest academically. Biology, economics, and government are the largest.

Required: To graduate, all students must take English composition and fulfill a 3-semester foreign language requirement. They must also take 2 courses in the natural sciences and 1 course each in the arts, historical studies, literature, quantitative reasoning, the social sciences, and human or cultural diversity, and meet Colby's wellness requirement by attending 8 lectures. Students must complete a total of 128 credit hours, including 3 January term courses, and maintain a GPA of 2.0.

Special: Colby offers study abroad in numerous countries. Colby also offers Washington semester programs through American University and the Washington Center, on-campus work-study, exchange programs with various colleges and universities, a 3-2 engineering degree with Dartmouth College, and maritime and oceanographic studies programs. Dual and student-designed majors are possible. There are 9 national honor societies, including Phi Beta Kappa, and 26 departmental honors programs.

Faculty/Classroom: 52% of faculty are male; 48% are female. All teach and do research. The average class size in a regular course is 17.

Admissions: 32% of a recent year's applicants were accepted. 81% of a recent year's freshmen were in the top fifth of their class; 96% were in the top two fifths. 19 freshmen graduated first in their class in a recent year.

Requirements: The SAT or ACT is required. In addition, candidates should be high school graduates with a recommended academic program of 4 years of English, 3 each of foreign language and math, and 2 each of science (including lab work), social studies/history, and other college preparatory courses. AP credits are accepted. Important factors in the admissions decision are advanced placement or honors courses, recommendations by school officials, and extracurricular activities record.

Procedure: Freshmen are admitted fall and spring. Entrance exams should be taken by January of the senior year. There are early decision and deferred admissions plan. Early decision applications should be filed by November 15; regular applications, by January 1 for fall entry, along with a $65 fee. Notification of early decision is sent December 15; regular decision, April 1. 192 early decision candidates were accepted for a recent class. 396 applicants were on a recent year's waiting list; 4 were admitted. Applications are accepted on-line.

Transfer: 9 transfer students enrolled in a recent year. Applicants must have a minimum GPA of 3.0 and, as a rule, have earned enough credit hours to qualify for at least sophomore standing. They must be in good academic and social standing and should submit references from a faculty member and a dean of their current school. If the SAT or ACT has been taken, the results may be submitted as well. 64 of 128 credits required for the bachelor's degree must be completed at Colby.

Visiting: There are regularly scheduled orientations for prospective students, including panel discussions, tours, class visits, complimentary meals, interviews, and information sessions. There are guides for informal visits, and visitors may sit in on classes and stay overnight. To schedule a visit, contact the Overnight Host Hotline at (207) 859-4829.

Financial Aid: In a recent year, 39% of all full-time freshmen and 38% of continuing full-time students received some form of financial aid, including need-based aid. The average freshmen award was $29,231. Need-based scholarships or need-based grants averaged $28,134; need-based self-help aid (loans and jobs) averaged $13,531. 67% of undergraduate students work part-time. Average annual earnings from campus work are $1290. The average financial indebtedness of a recent year's graduate was $19,222. Colby is a member of CSS. The CSS/Profile, FAFSA, and the college's own financial statement are required. Check with the school for current application deadlines.

International Students: There were 208 international students enrolled in a recent year. The school actively recruits these students. They must take the TOEFL. They must also take the SAT or ACT.

Computers: Wireless access is available in all dorm rooms and in many public locations. More than 350 public/student lab computers with Internet access are available. A computer loaner pool is available only to faculty and staff. All students may access the system 24 hours a day. There are no time limits and no fees. It is strongly recommended that all students have a personal computer.

Graduates: In a recent year, 484 bachelor's degrees were awarded. The most popular majors were English (14%), economics (12%), and biology (12%). In an average class, 84% graduate in 4 years or less, 87% graduate in 5 years or less, and 88% graduate in 6 years or less. 113 companies recruited on campus in a recent year. Of a recent year's graduating class, 21% were enrolled in graduate school within 6 months of graduation, and 79% were employed.

Admissions Contact: Dean of Admissions and Financial Aid.
E-mail: *admissions@colby.edu* Web: *www.colby.edu*

COLLEGE OF THE ATLANTIC   D-5
Bar Harbor, ME 04609

| | (207) 288-5015 |
| | (800) 528-0025; (207) 288-4126 |

Full-time: 101 men, 220 women	Faculty: 25
Part-time: 7 men, 17 women	Ph.D.s: 90%
Graduate: 2 men, 3 women	Student/Faculty: 11 to 1
Year: varies	Tuition: $33,060
Application Deadline: February 15	Room & Board: $8490
Freshman Class: 307 applied, 244 accepted, 76 enrolled	
SAT CR/M/W: 642/565/622	ACT: 25 VERY COMPETITIVE

College of the Atlantic, founded in 1969, is a private liberal arts college dedicated to the study of human ecology. The library contains 40,500 volumes, 274 microform items, and subscribes to 600 periodicals including electronic. Computerized library services include interlibrary loans, database searching, Internet access, and laptop Internet portals. Special learning facilities include a learning resource center, art gallery, natural history museum, writing center, taxidermy lab, photography lab, sculpture and painting studio, ceramics studio, marine mammal research center, 2 greenhouses, 80-acre organic farm (12 miles off campus), and 2 offshore research centers. The 35-acre campus is in a small town 45 miles southeast of Bangor, along the Atlantic Ocean shoreline. Including any residence halls, there are 15 buildings.

Student Life: 81% of undergraduates are from out of state, mostly the Northeast. Students are from 36 states, 32 foreign countries, and Canada. 68% are from public schools. The average age of freshmen is 19; all undergraduates, 21. 6% do not continue beyond their first year; 68% remain to graduate.

Housing: 150 students can be accommodated in college housing, which includes coed dorms and substance-free houses. On-campus housing is guaranteed for the freshman year only, is available on a first-come, first-served basis, and is available on a lottery system for upperclassmen. Priority is given to out-of-town students. 56% of students commute. Alcohol is not permitted. All students may keep cars.

Activities: There are no fraternities or sororities. There are 20 groups on campus, including art, chess, chorus, computers, dance, debate, drama, environmental, film, gay, international, jazz band, literary magazine, musical theater, newspaper, orchestra, photography, political, social, social service, student government, and yearbook. Popular campus events include the annual Bar Island swim, Winter Carnival, and Earth Day celebration and activities.

Sports: There is no sports program at COA. All students are members of the local YMCA and may use its pool, Nautilus equipment, and volleyball and basketball facilities, as well as nearby tennis courts. Acadia National Park offers seasonal outdoor activities. The college has camping and outdoor equipment and canoes, sea kayaks, and sailboats for student use and offers a sailing class, sea kayaking class, and wilderness first responder class. There are yoga and martial arts classes on campus. SCUBA instruction is offered using the Y facilities.

Disabled Students: 80% of the campus is accessible. Facilities include wheelchair ramps, elevators, special parking, specially equipped restrooms, lowered drinking fountains, lowered telephones, and specially equipped residence hall rooms.

Services: Counseling and information services are available, as is tutoring in writing, math, language, photography, and computer use. There is remedial math and writing.

Campus Safety and Security: Measures include 24-hour foot and vehicle patrol and security escort services. There are shuttle buses, emergency telephones, and lighted pathways/sidewalks.

Programs of Study: COA confers B.A. degrees. Master's degrees are also awarded. Bachelor's degrees are awarded in SOCIAL SCIENCE (human ecology).

Required: All students major in human ecology. Each student designs his or her program. They must complete a total of 36 COA credits, including 2 interdisciplinary core courses and 2 courses each in environmental science, human studies, and arts and design. Also required are a 3-credit internship, a human ecology essay, participation in a 3-credit senior project, and community service.

Special: Students may cross-register with the University of Maine and other local nautical schools. Eco League exchanges are available with Alaska Pacific University, and Green Mountain, Antioch, Northland, and Prescott colleges. COA offers study abroad programs in Mexico, the Czech Republic, France, and Guatemala. A 10-week internship is a requirement of graduation, and students are assisted in finding internships in the US and abroad in an area of interest. All students design their own path to completion of their B.A. in human ecology.

Faculty/Classroom: 64% of faculty are male; 36% are female. All teach undergraduates, 80% do research, and 80% do both. No introductory courses are taught by graduate students. The average class size in an introductory lecture is 16; in a laboratory is 17; and in a regular course is 14.

Admissions: 79% of the 2009-2010 applicants were accepted. The SAT scores for the 2009-2010 freshman class were: Critical Reading--3% below 500, 14% between 500 and 599, 63% between 600 and 700, and 20% above 700; Math--20% below 500, 46% between 500 and 599, 34% between 600 and 700, and % above 700; Writing--5% below 500, 23% between 500 and 599, 61% between 600 and 700, and 11% above 700. The ACT scores were 10% below 21, 20% between 21 and 23, 40% between 24 and 26, 10% between 27 and 28, and 20% above 28. 54% of the current freshmen were in the top fifth of their class; 83% were in the top two fifths. 1 freshman graduated first in the class.

Requirements: In addition, Candidates for admission must be high school graduates who have completed 4 years of English, 3 to 4 of math, 2 to 3 of science, 2 of a foreign language, and 1 of history. AP and CLEP credits are accepted. Important factors in the admissions decision are personality/intangible qualities, extracurricular activities record, and advanced placement or honors courses.

Procedure: Freshmen are admitted fall, winter, and spring. Entrance exams should be taken in the junior or senior year. There are early decision and deferred admissions plans. Early decision applications should be filed by December 1; regular applications, by February 15 for fall entry; November 15 for winter entry; and February 15 for spring entry, along with a $45 fee. Notification of early decision is sent December 15; regular decision, April 1. 28 early decision candidates were accepted for the 2009-2010 class. 12 applicants were on the 2009 waiting list; 1 was admitted. Applications are accepted on-line.

Transfer: 28 transfer students enrolled in 2008-2009. 18 of 36 credits required for the bachelor's degree must be completed at COA.

Visiting: There are regularly scheduled orientations for prospective students, including an annual fall tour for high school seniors on Columbus Day. Students attend classes, stay in student housing, and are invited to join outings at Acadia National Park. There are guides for informal visits, visitors may sit in on classes, and stay overnight. To schedule a visit, contact Donna McFarland at (800) 528-0025.

Financial Aid: In 2009-2010, 89% of all full-time freshmen and 85% of continuing full-time students received some form of financial aid. 88% of all full-time freshmen and 83% of continuing full-time students received need-based aid. The average freshman award was $32,034. Need-based scholarships or need-based grants averaged $30,543 ($43,230 maximum); and need-based self-help aid (loans and jobs) averaged $5,134 ($7,701 maximum). 78% of undergraduate students work part-time. Average annual earnings from campus work are $1800. The average financial indebtedness of the 2009 graduate was $23,760. COA is a member of CSS. The FAFSA and the college's own financial statement are required. The deadline for filing freshman financial aid applications for fall entry is February 15.

International Students: There are 49 international students enrolled. The school actively recruits these students. They must take the TOEFL with a minimum score of 550 on the paper-based TOEFL (PBT) or 82 on the Internet-based version (iBT), or submit SAT scores or the IB English exam score.

Computers: 16 public computers (13 PCs and 3 Macs) are available for use in various areas. In addition, 4 notebook computers are available for use within the library. All computers are connected to the campus network and have access to e-mail and Internet. Most campus locations (dorms, classrooms and public spaces) have wireless access and all dormitory rooms have wired access to the campus network. In addition, 11 library study carrels are equipped with network connections for notebook computers. All students may access the system 24 hours a day. There are no time limits and no fees. It is strongly recommended that all students have a personal computer.

Graduates: From July 1, 2008 to June 30, 2009, 56 bachelor's degrees were awarded. 10 companies recruited on campus in 2008-2009. In an average class, 3% graduate in 3 years or less, 48% graduate in 4 years or less, 62% graduate in 5 years or less, and 63% graduate in 6 years or less. Of the 2008 graduating class, 21% were enrolled in graduate school within 6 months of graduation, and 90% were employed.

Admissions Contact: Sarah G. Baker, Dean. E-Mail: *inquiry@coa.edu* Web: *www.coa.edu*

HUSSON UNIVERSITY C-4
Husson College

| Bangor, ME 04401-2999 | (207) 941-7067 |
| | (800) 448-7766; (207) 941-7935 |

Full-time: 834 men, 1069 women	Faculty: 101
Part-time: 185 men, 383 women	Ph.D.s: 68%
Graduate: 163 men, 342 women	Student/Faculty: 19 to 1
Year: semesters, summer session	Tuition: $12,990
Application Deadline: open	Room & Board: $6994
Freshman Class: 1953 applied, 1538 accepted, 753 enrolled	
SAT CR/M/W: 462/465/446	ACT: 20 LESS COMPETITIVE

Husson University, previously known as Husson College, was founded in 1898 and is a private institution offering business, health careers, teaching, pharmacy, law and legal studies, and other professional training. There are 6 undergraduate schools and 2 graduate schools. The library contains 40,814 volumes, 14,148 microform items, and 405 audio/video tapes/CDs/DVDs, and subscribes to 27,881 periodicals including electronic. Computerized library services include interlibrary loans, database searching, and Internet access. Special learning facilities include a learning resource center, art gallery, and radio station. The 200-acre campus is in an urban area in the city of Bangor. Including any residence halls, there are 8 buildings.

Student Life: 79% of undergraduates are from Maine. Others are from 37 states, 25 foreign countries, and Canada. 87% are from public schools. 93% are white. The average age of freshmen is 18; all undergraduates, 21. 28% do not continue beyond their first year.

Housing: 1011 students can be accommodated in college housing, which includes coed dorms. On-campus housing is guaranteed for all 4 years. 53% of students live on campus; of those, 45% remain on campus on weekends. All students may keep cars.

Activities: 1% of men belong to 1 national fraternity; 1% of women belong to 3 local sororities. There are 33 groups on campus, including cheerleading, choir, computers, drama, ethnic, international, literary magazine, newspaper, pep band, professional, radio and TV, religious, social, social service, and student government. Popular campus events include Spring Fling, Winter Carnival, and Greek Alumni Weekend.

Sports: There are 57 intercollegiate sports for men and 69 for women, and 8 intramural sports for men and 8 for women. Facilities include a gym, an Olympic-size swimming pool, weight training and mat rooms, a health and fitness center, basketball and tennis courts, a baseball complex, and a turf soccer field.

Disabled Students: 80% of the campus is accessible. Facilities include wheelchair ramps, elevators, special parking, specially equipped restrooms, lowered drinking fountains, and lowered telephones.

Services: Counseling and information services are available, as is tutoring in most subjects. There is remedial math and writing.

Campus Safety and Security: Measures include 24-hour foot and vehicle patrol, security escort services, and lighted pathways/sidewalks.

Programs of Study: Husson confers B.S. degrees. Associate, master's, and doctoral degrees are also awarded. Bachelor's degrees are awarded in BIOLOGICAL SCIENCE (biology/biological science), BUSINESS (accounting, banking and finance, business administration and management, business systems analysis, hospitality management services, marketing/retailing/merchandising, and sports management), COMMUNICATIONS AND THE ARTS (English), COMPUTER AND PHYSICAL SCIENCE (chemistry and computer programming), EDUCATION (elementary education, English education, physical education, and science education), HEALTH PROFESSIONS (health, nursing, and pre-pharmacy), SOCIAL SCIENCE (criminal justice, paralegal studies, and psychology). Accounting, nursing, and physical therapy are the strongest academically. Business administration is the largest.

Required: Requirements for graduation vary by program, but a total of 120 credit hours with a minimum GPA of 2.0 is necessary.

Special: Experiential learning is part of the core curriculum in all majors. Internships are incorporated in accounting, sports management, hospitality management, nursing, physical therapy, occupational therapy, international business, and family business. Co-op programs, externships, and clinicals are included in the curriculum in all other majors. Students can go a fifth year and obtain a master's in business in accounting, business administration, or CIS, and in phys ed with a concentration in sports management. An accelerated degree program, dual majors, and student-designed majors are also available.

Faculty/Classroom: 53% of faculty are male; 47% are female. All teach undergraduates. No introductory courses are taught by graduate students. The average class size in an introductory lecture is 20; in a laboratory, 16; and in a regular course, 19.

Admissions: 79% of the 2009-2010 applicants were accepted. The SAT scores for the 2009-2010 freshman class were: Critical Reading--67% below 500, 29% between 500 and 599, and 4% between 600 and 700; Math--67% below 500, 29% between 500 and 599, and 4% between 600 and 700; Writing--72% below 500, 24% between 500 and 599, and 4% between 600 and 700. The ACT scores were 58% below 21, 27% between 21 and 23, and 15% between 24 and 26. 24% of the current freshmen were in the top fifth of their class; 49% were in the top two fifths. 4 freshmen graduated first in their class.

Requirements: The SAT is required. In addition, applicants must be graduates of an accredited secondary school or have earned a GED. A recommendation from a high school counselor is required. Husson requires applicants to be in the upper 50% of their class. A GPA of 2.0 is required. AP and CLEP credits are accepted. Important factors in the admissions decision are advanced placement or honors courses, recommendations by school officials, and leadership record.

Procedure: Freshmen are admitted to all sessions. Entrance exams should be taken prior to enrollment. There are deferred admissions and rolling admissions plans. Application deadlines are open. Application fee is $25. Notification is sent on a rolling basis. 39 applicants were on the 2009 waiting list; 11 were admitted. Applications are accepted on-line.

Transfer: 151 transfer students enrolled in 2008-2009. Applicants must have a 2.0 GPA. Courses with a C grade or better transfer. 30 of 120 credits required for the bachelor's degree must be completed at Husson.

Visiting: There are regularly scheduled orientations for prospective students, including an interview and campus tour. There are guides for informal visits; visitors may sit in on classes and stay overnight. To schedule a visit, contact the Admissions Office.

Financial Aid: In 2009-2010, 98% of all full-time freshmen and 75% of continuing full-time students received some form of financial aid. 83% of all full-time freshmen and 69% of continuing full-time students received need-based aid. Need-basd scholarships or need-based grants averaged $9119 ($13,900 maximum), and need-based self-help aid (loans and jobs) averaged $3994 ($8250 maximum). 80% of undergraduate students work part-time. The average financial indebtedness of the 2009 graduate was $32,041. Husson is a member of CSS. The FAFSA is required. The deadline for filing freshman financial aid applications for fall entry is open.

International Students: There are 25 international students enrolled. They must take the TOEFL with a minimum score of 500 on the paper-based TOEFL (PBT) or 80 on the Internet-based version (iBT). They must also take the SAT or ACT. Students who score unsatisfactorily on the TOEFL may be accepted conditionally.

Computers: Wireless access is available. Students have access in their dorm rooms, the library, and various labs, which have 100 PCs available for student use. There is wireless access in the academic buildings and residence halls. All students may access the system 24 hours a day. There are no time limits and no fees.

Graduates: From July 1, 2008 to June 30, 2009, 381 bachelor's degrees were awarded. The most popular majors were business administration (30%), accounting (19%), and nursing (13%). 30 companies recruited on campus in 2008-2009. In an average class, 62% graduate in 4 years or less, 43% graduate in 5 years or less, and 45% graduate in 6 years or less. Of the 2008 graduating class, 4% were enrolled in graduate school within 6 months of graduation.

Admissions Contact: Carlena Bean, Director. A campus DVD is available. E-mail: *admit@husson.edu* Web: *www.husson.edu*

MAINE COLLEGE OF ART B-6
Portland, ME 04101

| Portland, ME 04101 | (207) 775-5157, ext. 254 |
| | (800) 639-4808; (207) 772-5069 |

Full-time: 100 men, 220 women	Faculty: n/av
Part-time: 20 men, 30 women	Ph.D.s: n/av
Graduate: 20 men, 20 women	Student/Faculty: n/av
Year: semesters	Tuition: $28,280
Application Deadline: open	Room & Board: $9676
Freshman Class: n/av	
SAT or ACT: required	SPECIAL

Maine College of Art, established in 1882, is a private, independent visual art college. There is 1 graduate school. Some figures in the above capsule and in this profile are approximate. In addition to regional accreditation, MECA has baccalaureate program accreditation with NASAD. The library contains 18,500 volumes and 150 audio/video tapes/CDs/DVDs, and subscribes to 100 periodicals including electronic. Computerized library services include interlibrary loans and database searching. Special learning facilities include an art gallery. The campus is in an urban area 100 miles north of Boston in downtown Portland. Including any residence halls, there are 6 buildings.

Student Life: 65% of undergraduates are from out of state, mostly the Northeast. Students are from 29 states and 6 foreign countries. 94% are white. The average age of freshmen is 20; all undergraduates, 22. 30% do not continue beyond their first year.

Housing: 100 students can be accommodated in college housing, which includes coed dorms and on-campus apartments. On-campus housing is available on a first-come, first-served basis. 75% of students commute. Alcohol is not permitted. All students may keep cars.

Activities: There are no fraternities or sororities. There are 10 groups on campus, including art, computers, dance, drama, gay, international, newspaper, photography, social, and student government. Popular campus events include an annual art sale, art auction, and Earth Day celebration.

Sports: There is no sports program at MECA.

Disabled Students: 65% of the campus is accessible. Facilities include wheelchair ramps, elevators, specially equipped restrooms, and lowered drinking fountains.

Services: Counseling and information services are available, as is tutoring in every subject. There is remedial math, reading, and writing. Academic support for writing papers, study skills, and time management is available, as is help for students with learning disabilities.

Campus Safety and Security: Measures include self-defense education. There are emergency telephones and safety training by local police.

Programs of Study: MECA confers B.F.A. degrees. Master's degrees are also awarded. Bachelor's degrees are awarded in COMMUNICATIONS AND THE ARTS (graphic design, media arts, metal/jewelry, painting, photography, printmaking, and sculpture), ENGINEERING AND ENVIRONMENTAL DESIGN (ceramic science). Painting, photography, and ceramics are the largest.

Required: All students must take 2 years of studio foundation courses and 2 years in the studio major, as well as 5 semesters of art history, 3 of humanities or social science, 2 each of English composition, natural science, and Western civilization, and 1 of critical issues. 129 total credit hours are necessary, with 36 in the major. Students must maintain a minimum GPA of 2.0. A senior thesis is required.

Special: Cross-registration with Bowdoin College, the Greater Portland Alliance of Colleges and Universities, and AICAD Mobility is available, as are internships utilizing professional artists and design and photography studios. An internship coordinator supervises the formal program for elective credit. There are also Art in Service internships. The continuing studies program provides for nondegree study. Minors in art history, drawing, and illustration are also offered, as are dual and student-designed majors.

Faculty/Classroom: 50% of faculty are male; 50% are female. All teach undergraduates. No introductory courses are taught by graduate students. The average class size in an introductory lecture is 136; in a laboratory, 18; and in a regular course, 20.

Requirements: The SAT or ACT is required. In addition, it is recommended that candidates for admission complete 4 years of English, 3 years each of art and math, and 2 years each of foreign language, science, and social studies. AP credits are accepted. Important factors in the admissions decision are personality/intangible qualities, advanced placement or honors courses, and evidence of special talent.

Procedure: Freshmen are admitted fall and spring. Entrance exams should be taken in the fall of the senior year. There are deferred admissions and rolling admissions plans. Application deadlines are open. Application fee is $40.

Transfer: Transfers must submit an official copy of their college transcripts. 65 of 129 credits required for the bachelor's degree must be completed at MECA.

Visiting: There are regularly scheduled orientations for prospective students, including a tour, a portfolio review, a faculty-student panel, and opportunities to observe classes and meet with an admissions counselor or other staff. There are guides for informal visits, and visitors may sit in on classes. To schedule a visit, contact the Admissions Office.

Financial Aid: MECA is a member of CSS. The FAFSA is required. Check with the school for current application deadlines.

International Students: The school actively recruits these students. They must take the TOEFL. They must also take the SAT or ACT.

Computers: All students may access the system. Time is scheduled around classroom use. There are no time limits and no fees.

Admissions Contact: Dean of Admissions. A campus DVD is available. E-mail: *admissions@meca.edu* Web: *www.meca.edu*

MAINE MARITIME ACADEMY　　　　C-5
Castine, ME 04420

(207) 326-2215
(800) 227-8465; (207) 326-2515

Full-time: 745 men, 171 women	Faculty: 70
Part-time: 4 men, 2 women	Ph.D.s: 40%
Graduate: 8 men, 9 women	Student/Faculty: 13 to 1
Year: semesters	Tuition: $10,105 ($17,805)
Application Deadline: July 1	Room & Board: $8450
Freshman Class: n/av	
SAT or ACT: required	COMPETITIVE

Maine Maritime Academy, founded in 1941, is a public institution offering degree programs in ocean and marine-oriented studies with emphasis on engineering, transportation, business management, and ocean sciences, to prepare graduates for private and public sector careers and the uniformed services of the United States. The academic calendar consists of 2 semesters plus a 2- to 3- month annual training cruise for the USCG Unlimited license majors and summer internships for others. There are 4 undergraduate schools and 1 graduate school. In addition to regional accreditation, MMA has baccalaureate program accreditation with ABET. The library contains 88,490 volumes, 5000 microform items, and 808 audio/video tapes/CDs/DVDs, and subscribes to 1311 periodicals including electronic. Computerized library services include interlibrary loans, database searching, Internet access, and laptop Internet portals. Special learning facilities include a natural history museum, planetarium, more than 60 vessels, bridge, radar, power plant, and cargo system simulators, and multiple sophisticated training vessels. The 50-acre campus is in a small town 38 miles south of Bangor on the east coast of Penobscot Bay. Including any residence halls, there are 14 buildings.

Student Life: 69% of undergraduates are from Maine. Others are from 40 states, 7 foreign countries, and Canada. 90% are from public schools. 98% are white. The average age of freshmen is 19; all undergraduates, 24. 12% do not continue beyond their first year; 75% remain to graduate.

Housing: 625 students can be accommodated in college housing, which includes single-sex and coed dorms and on-campus apartments. In addition, there is graduate housing. On-campus housing is guaranteed for all 4 years. 85% of students live on campus; of those, 40% remain on campus on weekends. Alcohol is not permitted. All students may keep cars.

Activities: 10% of men belong to 1 national fraternity. There are 30 groups on campus, including amateur radio, bagpipe, billiards, band, chess, chorale, drama, drill team, engineering, environmental, ethnic, hockey, international, marshal arts, newspaper, outing, pep band, photography, professional, rugby, sailing, scuba, social, social service, student government, and yearbook. Popular campus events include GSA Weekend, BSA Klondike Derby, and Veterans Day.

Sports: There are 6 intercollegiate sports for men and 6 for women, and 10 intramural sports for men and 10 for women. Facilities include 2 weight rooms, Olympic pool, field house with 3 climbing walls, gym, racquetball/squash courts, aerobics room, weight/workout room on training ship, and synthetic multisport athletic field.

Disabled Students: All of the campus is accessible. Facilities include wheelchair ramps, elevators, special parking, specially equipped restrooms, and special housing.

Services: Counseling and information services are available, as is tutoring in most subjects. There is a reader service for the blind and remedial math, reading, and writing.

Campus Safety and Security: Measures include 24-hour foot and vehicle patrol and self-defense education. There are lighted pathways/sidewalks, controlled access to dorms/residences, on-campus medical and counseling services, and locked dorms.

Programs of Study: MMA confers B.S. degrees. Associate and master's degrees are also awarded. Bachelor's degrees are awarded in BUSINESS (international business management), COMPUTER AND PHYSICAL SCIENCE (oceanography), ENGINEERING AND ENVIRONMENTAL DESIGN (engineering, engineering technology, marine engineering, maritime science, and transportation technology). Marine systems engineering is the strongest academically. Marine transportation and marine engineering degree programs are the largest.

Required: A minimum GPA of 2.0 in an average of 140 total credit hours is required for graduation. The GPA in the major must be at least 2.25. A senior thesis is required for some majors and a comprehensive exam is required for USCG license candidates.

Special: The 2-month freshman and junior year training cruises give students practical experience aboard the academy's 500-foot ship. Cadet shipping co-ops on assigned merchant ships for 65 to 90 days. Co-op programs and internships for all programs are offered, as is study abroad through special agreements with other maritime colleges worldwide. Dual and student-designed majors are possible.

Faculty/Classroom: 75% of faculty are male; 25% are female. All teach undergraduates. No introductory courses are taught by graduate students. The average class size in an introductory lecture is 30; in a laboratory, 8 to 15; and in a regular course, 25.

Requirements: The SAT or ACT is required. In addition, candidates for admission must have completed 4 years of English, 3 years of math, and 2 years of lab science. Courses must include algebra I, algebra II, trigonometry, geometry, and either chemistry or physics with a lab. A GPA of 2.0 is required. AP and CLEP credits are accepted. Important factors in the admissions decision are advanced placement or honors courses, evidence of special talent, and leadership record.

Procedure: Freshmen are admitted fall and spring. Entrance exams should be taken as early as possible in the senior year. There are early decision, deferred admissions and rolling admissions plans. Early decision applications should be filed December 20; regular applications, by July 1 for fall entry and November 1 for spring entry. The fall 2009 application fee was $15. Applications are accepted on-line.

Transfer: 16 transfer students enrolled in a recent year. Applicants must have a minimum 2.0 GPA in previous college work and meet the same prerequisites as entering freshmen.

Visiting: There are regularly scheduled orientations for prospective students, consisting of 3 open houses per year; campus visits are available weekdays throughout the year. There are guides for informal visits; visitors may sit in on classes and stay overnight. To schedule a visit, contact the Admissions Office at (207) 326-2206.

Financial Aid: In 2009-2010, 60% of all full-time freshmen and 82% of all full-time continuing students received some form of financial aid. 54% of full-time freshmen and 74% of full-time continuing students received need-based aid. Need-based scholarships or need-based grants averaged $2047 ($5350 maximum); need-based self-help (loans and jobs) averaged $2212 ($4000 maxiumu). 45% of students work on campus. The average earnings from campus work are $704. The FAFSA, student and parent tax returns, and a verification worksheet is required. The deadline for filing freshmen financial aid applications for fall entry is April 15.

Computers: All students may access the system. There are no time limits. The fee is $100. All students are required to have a personal computer.

Graduates: From July 1, 2008, to June 30, 2009, 160 bachelor's degrees were awarded. The most popular majors were marine engineering (30%), marine transportation (30%), and power engineering (15%).

Admissions Contact: Jeff Wright, Director of Admissions. A campus DVD is available. E-mail: *jeff.wright@mma.edu*
Web: *www.mainemaritime.edu*

SAINT JOSEPH'S COLLEGE OF MAINE A-6

Standish, ME 04084-5263

(207) 893-7746
(800) 338-7057; (207) 893-7862

Full-time: 300 men, 600 women	**Faculty:** n/av
Part-time: 10 men, 20 women	**Ph.Ds:** n/av
Graduate: none	**Student/Faculty:** n/av
Year: semesters, summer session	**Tuition:** $26,050
Application Deadline: open	**Room & Board:** $10,350
Freshman Class: n/av	
SAT or ACT: required	**COMPETITIVE**

Saint Joseph's College of Maine, founded in 1912, is a private, Roman Catholic institution offering liberal arts and preprofessional programs. Some figures in the above capsule and in this profile are approximate. The library contains 98,626 volumes, 29,010 microform items, and 1000 audio/video tapes/CDs/DVDs, and subscribes to 11,461 periodicals including electronic. Computerized library services include interlibrary loans, database searching, and Internet access. Special learning facilities include a learning resource center, radio station, and telescope observatory. The 350-acre campus is in a rural area 18 miles west of Portland. Including any residence halls, there are 20 buildings.

Student Life: 60% of undergraduates are from Maine. Others are from 15 states, 3 foreign countries, and Canada. 82% are white. The average age of freshmen is 18; all undergraduates, 20. 18% do not continue beyond their first year; 59% remain to graduate.

Housing: 829 students can be accommodated in college housing, which includes single-sex and coed dorms and substance-free housing. On-campus housing is guaranteed for all 4 years. 83% of students live on campus; of those, 65% remain on campus on weekends. All students may keep cars.

Activities: There are no fraternities or sororities. There are 28 groups on campus, including campus activities board, campus ministry, cheerleading, choir, chorale, computers, dance, drama, ethnic, Habitat for Humanity, high adventure club, honors, international, literary magazine, musical theater, newspaper, pep band, photography, political, professional, radio and TV, religious, social, social service, student government, and yearbook. Popular campus events include Family Weekend, Christmas Benefit Concert, and Spring Fling.

Sports: There are 5 intercollegiate sports for men and 6 for women, and 12 intramural sports for men and 12 for women. Facilities include a multipurpose facility housing a gym, a workout room with free weights, Nautilus and other weight-training equipment, a cardiovascular workout room, dance aerobics rooms, a climbing wall, a 25-meter pool, saunas, and an elevated jogging track. There are also soccer and field hockey fields, a private beach on a lake, lighted athletic fields for baseball and softball, cross-country running and ski trails, and a low ropes course.

Disabled Students: 75% of the campus is accessible. Facilities include wheelchair ramps, elevators, special parking, specially equipped rest rooms, special class scheduling, and lowered drinking fountains.

Services: Counseling and information services are available, as is tutoring in every subject. There is a reader service for the blind.

Campus Safety and Security: Measures include 24-hour foot and vehicle patrol, self-defense education, and security escort services. There are emergency telephones, lighted pathways/sidewalks, and round-the-clock security officers.

Programs of Study: Saint Joseph's College of Maine confers B.A., B.S., B.S.B.A., and B.S.N. degrees. Associate degrees are also awarded. Bachelor's degrees are awarded in BIOLOGICAL SCIENCE (biology/biological science), BUSINESS (business administration and manage-

ment), COMMUNICATIONS AND THE ARTS (communications and English), COMPUTER AND PHYSICAL SCIENCE (chemistry and mathematics), EDUCATION (elementary education and physical education), ENGINEERING AND ENVIRONMENTAL DESIGN (environmental science), HEALTH PROFESSIONS (nursing and prepharmacy), SOCIAL SCIENCE (criminal justice, history, philosophy, psychology, sociology, and theological studies). Business, nursing, and biology are the strongest academically. Elementary education, business, and nursing are the largest.

Required: To graduate, students must complete 128 credit hours with a minimum GPA of 2.0, including 8 hours of English, history, theology, and a foreign language, 4 each of science and math, and 8 of electives.

Special: Saint Joseph's offers internships, cross-registration with 4 southern Maine colleges, study abroad in 5 countries, a semester at sea, dual majors, work-study programs, and non-degree study. There are 2 national honor societies, a freshman honors program, and 6 departmental honors programs.

Faculty/Classroom: 48% of faculty are male; 52% are female. The average class size in an introductory lecture is 25; in a laboratory, 12; and in a regular course, 18.

Requirements: The SAT or ACT is required. In addition, candidates for admission must be high school graduates who have completed a college preparatory curriculum with a recommended 4 units in English, 3 to 4 in math, 2 in foreign language, and 1 to 3 each in history, science, and social studies. A GPA of 2.0 is required. AP and CLEP credits are accepted. Important factors in the admissions decision are advanced placement or honors courses, recommendations by school officials, and extracurricular activities record.

Procedure: Freshmen are admitted fall and spring. Entrance exams should be taken by January of the senior year. There are early admissions, deferred admissions, and rolling admissions plans. Application deadlines are open. Check with the school for current application deadlines and fee. Applications are accepted on-line. 45 applicants were on a recent waiting list, 25 were accepted.

Transfer: Transfer students should have a minimum GPA of 2.0. 32 of 128 credits required for the bachelor's degree must be completed at Saint Joseph's College of Maine.

Visiting: There are regularly scheduled orientations for prospective students, including Application and Acceptance Day programs, visits on 5 fall Saturdays, and summer visits. There are guides for informal visits, and visitors may sit in on classes and stay overnight. To schedule a visit, contact the Office of Admission.

Financial Aid: Saint Joseph's College of Maine is a member of CSS. The FAFSA and the college's own financial statement are required. Check with the school for current application deadlines.

International Students: For non-English speaking students, the TOEFL is required. English-speaking international students must take the SAT or ACT.

Computers: Wireless access is available. All students may access the system 24 hours a day in all labs and until 10 P.M. in the library. There are no time limits and no fees. It is strongly recommended that all students have a personal computer.

Admissions Contact: Dean of Admissions.
E-mail: *admission@sjcme.edu* Web: *www.sjcme.edu*

THOMAS COLLEGE B-4

Waterville, ME 04901 (207) 877-0101; (207) 877-0114

Full-time: 350 men, 290 women	**Faculty:** IIB, --$
Part-time: 40 men, 90 women	**Ph.Ds:** n/av
Graduate: 80 men, 140 women	**Student/Faculty:** n/av
Year: semesters, summer session	**Tuition:** $22,130
Application Deadline: open	**Room & Board:** $8380
Freshman Class: n/av	**LESS COMPETITIVE**

Thomas College, founded in 1894, is a private institution offering undergraduate programs in liberal arts and business. Some figures in the above capsule and in this profile are approximate. There is 1 graduate school. The library contains 21,938 volumes and 770 audio/video tapes/CDs/DVDs and subscribes to 18,430 periodicals including electronic. Computerized library services include interlibrary loans, database searching, Internet access, and laptop Internet portals. Special learning facilities include a learning resource center and an art gallery. The 70-acre campus is in a rural area 75 miles north of Portland. Including any residence halls, there are 11 buildings.

Student Life: 80% of undergraduates are from Maine. Others are from 10 states. 85% are from public schools. 96% are white. The average age of freshmen is 18; all undergraduates, 21. 37% do not continue beyond their first year; 25% remain to graduate.

Housing: 375 students can be accommodated in college housing, which includes coed dorms and off-campus apartments. On-campus housing is guaranteed for the freshman year only, is available on a first-come, first-served basis, and is available on a lottery system for upperclassmen. 54% of students live on campus; of those, 60% remain on campus on weekends. All students may keep cars.

Activities: There is 1 national fraternity, 2 local sororities, and 1 national sorority. There are 30 groups on campus, including art, chorale, computers, drama, honors, international, newspaper, professional, religious, social, social service, student government, and yearbook. Popular campus events include Winter Carnival, Spring Fling, and Welcome Week.

Sports: There are 6 intercollegiate sports for men and 6 for women, and 6 intramural sports for men and 6 for women. Facilities include a gym, a basketball court, a weight, fitness, and aerobics room, soccer and softball fields, a training area, a baseball field, a field hockey field, an intramural field, and cross-country skiing and snowshoe trails. Facilities for swimming, indoor tennis, racquetball, and hockey are available locally.

Disabled Students: 80% of the campus is accessible. Facilities include wheelchair ramps, special parking, specially equipped restrooms, and special class scheduling.

Services: Counseling and information services are available, as is tutoring in most subjects. There is remedial math, reading, and writing.

Campus Safety and Security: Measures include 24-hour foot and vehicle patrol. There are lighted pathways/sidewalks.

Programs of Study: Thomas confers B.S. degrees. Associate and master's degrees are also awarded. Bachelor's degrees are awarded in BUSINESS (accounting, business administration and management, business economics, management information systems, management science, marketing management, and sports management), COMMUNICATIONS AND THE ARTS (communications), COMPUTER AND PHYSICAL SCIENCE (information sciences and systems), EDUCATION (business education and elementary education), SOCIAL SCIENCE (criminal justice, international studies, and psychology). Accounting and management information systems are the strongest academically. Accounting, management, and computer information systems are the largest.

Required: To graduate, students must achieve a minimum GPA of 2.0, fulfill all course requirements, and complete a minimum of 120 total credit hours of study including 30 hours in the major.

Special: Students may cross-register with Colby College and Kennebec Valley Community College. There are co-op programs and internships available in most majors. The college also offers study in Canada through the New England/Quebec Exchange and in France and Australia. 5-year degrees are offered in most majors where a B.S. is available. There are 2 national honor societies.

Faculty/Classroom: 60% of faculty are male; 40% are female. All teach undergraduates. No introductory courses are taught by graduate students. The average class size in an introductory lecture is 22; in a regular course, 14.

Requirements: The SAT or ACT is required. In addition, candidates for admission must be high school graduates with an academic program that includes 4 years of English, 3 each of math and sciences, 2 each of social studies and foreign language, and 2 other. A letter of recommendation from a secondary school counselor is required. An interview is highly recommended. Thomas requires applicants to be in the upper 46% of their class. A GPA of 2.0 is required. AP and CLEP credits are accepted. Important factors in the admissions decision are advanced placement or honors courses, recommendations by school officials, and personality/intangible qualities.

Procedure: Freshmen are admitted to all sessions. Entrance exams should be taken by the fall of the senior year. There are deferred admissions and rolling admissions plans. Application deadlines are open. Application fee is $50. Applications are accepted on-line.

Transfer: Applicants should have a minimum college GPA of 2.0. The school recommends the SAT as well as an interview. Official transcripts from all previously attended postsecondary institutions are required. 60 of 120 credits required for the bachelor's degree must be completed at Thomas.

Visiting: There are regularly scheduled orientations for prospective students, including 3 to 4 open houses and 1 new student orientation/preregistration. There are guides for informal visits, and visitors may sit in on classes. To schedule a visit, contact the Admissions Office.

Financial Aid: In a recent year, 96% of all full-time freshmen and 87% of continuing full-time students received some form of financial aid. 86% of all full-time freshmen and 79% of continuing full-time students received need-based aid. The average freshman award was $17,077. All undergraduate students work part-time. Average annual earnings from campus work are $2200. The average financial indebtedness of a recent year's graduate was $38,734. The FAFSA is required. Check with the school for current application deadlines.

International Students: The school actively recruits these students. They must take the TOEFL. They must also take the SAT.

Computers: Wireless access is available. Campuswide network ports and wireless access points along with more than 130 workstations in various computer labs and clusters provide students 24/7 access. There are no time limits and no fees. It is strongly recommended that all students have a personal computer.

Graduates: In a recent year, 108 bachelor's degrees were awarded. The most popular majors were business/marketing (50%), computer information sciences (16%), and security and protective services (14%). In an average class, 49% graduate in 5 years or less and 52% graduate in

6 years or less. 60 companies recruited on campus in a recent year. Of a recent year's graduating class, 11% were enrolled in graduate school within 6 months of graduation, and 91% were employed.

Admissions Contact: Director of Admissions.
E-mail: *admiss@thomas.edu* Web: *www.thomas.edu*

UNITY COLLEGE   C-4
Unity, ME 04988-0532   (207) 948-3131
                                        (800) 624-1024; (207) 948-6277

Full-time: 300 men, 200 women	**Faculty:** n/av
Part-time: 10 men and women	**Ph.D.s:** n/av
Graduate: none	**Student/Faculty:** n/av
Year: semesters, summer session	**Tuition:** $22,500
Application Deadline: open	**Room & Board:** $8220
Freshman Class: n/av	
SAT or ACT: recommended	**LESS COMPETITIVE**

Unity College, founded in 1965, is a private, independent institution offering undergraduate programs in environmental science, natural resource management, and wilderness-based outdoor recreation. Some figures in the above capsule and in this profile are approximate. In addition to regional accreditation, Unity has baccalaureate program accreditation with SAF. The library contains 46,000 volumes and 750 audio/video tapes/CDs/DVDs, and subscribes to 651 periodicals including electronic. Computerized library services include interlibrary loans and database searching. Special learning facilities include a learning resource center and art gallery. The 205-acre campus is in a rural area 18 miles east of Waterville. Including any residence halls, there are 18 buildings.

Student Life: 67% of undergraduates are from out of state, mostly the Northeast. Students are from 30 states and 1 foreign country. 97% are from public schools. 98% are white. 57% are Catholic; 30% Protestant. The average age of freshmen is 18; all undergraduates, 20. 35% do not continue beyond their first year; 47% remain to graduate.

Housing: 335 students can be accommodated in college housing, which includes single-sex and coed dorms and on-campus apartments. On-campus housing is guaranteed for all 4 years. 90% of students live on campus; of those, 68% remain on campus on weekends. All students may keep cars.

Activities: There are no fraternities or sororities. There are 36 groups on campus, including art, drama, environmental, literary magazine, newspaper, outdoor, photography, student government, and yearbook. Popular campus events include Regional Woodsman's Meet in October.

Sports: There are 3 intercollegiate sports for men and 2 for women, and 10 intramural sports for men and 8 for women. Facilities include a gym, a weight-training room, playing fields, a nature trail, and game rooms.

Disabled Students: 80% of the campus is accessible. Facilities include wheelchair ramps, special parking, and special class scheduling.

Services: Counseling and information services are available, as is tutoring in every subject. There is remedial math, reading, and writing. A full-time learning disability specialist is on staff.

Campus Safety and Security: Measures include 24-hour foot and vehicle patrol. There are emergency telephones.

Programs of Study: Unity confers B.A. and B.S. degrees. Associate degrees are also awarded. Bachelor's degrees are awarded in AGRICULTURE (conservation and regulation and fishing and fisheries), BIOLOGICAL SCIENCE (ecology, environmental biology, and wildlife biology), EDUCATION (environmental education), ENGINEERING AND ENVIRONMENTAL DESIGN (environmental science), HEALTH PROFESSIONS (environmental health science), SOCIAL SCIENCE (human ecology, interdisciplinary studies, and parks and recreation management). Aquaculture, fisheries, and ecology are the strongest academically. Conservation wildlife law enforcement, wilderness-based recreation, and wildlife are the largest.

Required: General education requirements include 38 credits in English composition, oral communication, math, computer science, life science, physical science, and electives, as well as 9 credits in a specialization outside the major field. Students must complete at least 120 credit hours with a minimum GPA of 2.0. An internship, thesis, or seminar is required in all bachelor's degree programs.

Special: The college offers co-op programs, credit-bearing internships, study abroad, a Washington semester, work-study programs, accelerated degree programs, dual and student-designed majors, and credit for life experience. A mentor program, in which a faculty member assists a student with research, is available to those students who earn a minimum GPA of 3.33 in their first 30 credit hours. There is 1 national honor society and a freshman honors program.

Faculty/Classroom: 68% of faculty are male; 32% are female.

Requirements: Applicants must be graduates of an accredited secondary school with a minimum GPA of 2.0. The GED is accepted. SAT or ACT scores, though not required, should be submitted, if available, for placement purposes. An essay is required, and an interview is recommended. AP and CLEP credits are accepted. Important factors in the admissions decision are advanced placement or honors courses, recommendations by alumni, and leadership record.

Procedure: Freshmen are admitted fall and spring. Entrance exams should be taken in the junior or senior year. There are deferred admissions and rolling admissions plans. Application deadlines are open. Check with the school for the current application fee. Notification is sent on a rolling basis. A waiting list is maintained.

Transfer: Applicants must present a minimum college GPA of 2.0 and are encouraged to submit SAT or ACT scores. 30 of 120 credits required for the bachelor's degree must be completed at Unity.

Visiting: There are regularly scheduled orientations for prospective students. There are guides for informal visits, and visitors may sit in on classes and stay overnight. To schedule a visit, contact the Admissions Office.

Financial Aid: The CSS/Profile, FAFSA, and the college's own financial statement are required. Check with the school for current application deadlines.

International Students: The school actively recruits these students. They must take the TOEFL.

Computers: All students may access the system. There are no time limits and no fees.

Admissions Contact: Dean of Enrollment and Retention Services/ Registrar. E-mail: *admissions@unity.edu* Web: *www.unity.edu*

UNIVERSITY OF MAINE SYSTEM

The University of Maine System, established in 1968, is a private system in Maine. It is governed by a board of trustees, whose chief administrator is chancellor. The primary goal of the system is teaching, research, and public service. The main priorities are to strengthen human services through programs in education, health, and social services; to provide international exchange and foreign language programs; and to conduct science and technology education and basic and applied research. Profiles of the 4-year campuses are included in this section.

UNIVERSITY OF MAINE
C-4

Orono, ME 04473-9966

(207) 581-1561
(877) 486-2364; (207) 581-1213

Full-time: 4166 men, 3790 women	**Faculty:** I, --$
Part-time: 390 men, 413 women	**Ph.D.s:** 84%
Graduate: 1035 men, 696 women	**Student/Faculty:** n/av
Year: semesters, summer session	**Tuition:** $9626 ($24,776)
Application Deadline: open	**Room & Board:** $8348
Freshman Class: 6958 applied, 5387 accepted, 1914 enrolled	
SAT CR/M/W: 480/480/470	**ACT:** required **COMPETITIVE**

The University of Maine, established in 1865, is a publicly funded, landgrant institution in the University of Maine system. The university offers degree programs in the arts and sciences, business, public policy, health fields, engineering, education, forestry, and agriculture. There are 6 undergraduate schools and 1 graduate school. In addition to regional accreditation, Umaine has baccalaureate program accreditation with AACSB, ABET, ADA, AHEA, CSAB, CSWE, NASM, NCATE, NLN, and SAF. The library contains 1.1 million volumes, 1.6 million microform items, and 26,647 audio/video tapes/CDs/DVDs, and subscribes to 12,412 periodicals including electronic. Computerized library services include interlibrary loans, database searching, Internet access, and laptop Internet portals. Special learning facilities include an art gallery, natural history museum, planetarium, radio station, a concert hall and other music facilities, 2 theaters, a digital media lab, an anthropology museum, and a laboratory for surface science and technology. The 3300-acre campus is in a small town 8 miles north of Bangor. Including any residence halls, there are 205 buildings.

Student Life: 84% of undergraduates are from Maine. Others are from 48 states, 65 foreign countries, and Canada. 81% are white. The average age of freshmen is 18; all undergraduates, 22. 21% do not continue beyond their first year; 59% remain to graduate.

Housing: 3800 students can be accommodated in college housing, which includes coed dorms, on-campus apartments, off-campus apartments, and married student housing. In addition, there are honors houses, language houses, special-interest houses, substance-free housing, quiet sections, graduate family, and first-year residential experience. On-campus housing is guaranteed for the freshman year only, is available on a first-come, and first-served basis. 60% of students commute. All students may keep cars.

Activities: There is 1 local and 12 national fraternities; and 6 national sororities. There are 226 groups on campus, including art, band, cheerleading, chess, choir, chorale, chorus, computers, dance, debate, drama, drill team, environmental, ethnic, film, forensics, gay, honors, international, jazz band, literary magazine, marching band, musical theater, newspaper, opera, orchestra, pep band, photography, political, professional, radio and TV, religious, social, social service, student government, symphony, and yearbook. Popular campus events include Maine Day, Family and Friends Weekend, and International Week.

Sports: There are 7 intercollegiate sports for men and 8 for women, and 35 intramural sports for men and 35 for women. Facilities include a sports arena for hockey and basketball, a field house, an indoor climbing center, a student recreation center, a swimming pool, a weight room, an indoor track, a dance studio, basketball, volleyball, badminton, squash, tennis, and racquetball courts, and baseball, softball, soccer, field hockey, and football fields.

Disabled Students: 90% of the campus is accessible. Facilities include wheelchair ramps, elevators, special parking, specially equipped restrooms, special class scheduling, lowered drinking fountains, lowered telephones, and a transport van.

Services: Counseling and information services are available, as is tutoring in some subjects, 100- and 200-level courses. There is a reader service for the blind. Developmental courses are offered in remedial math, reading and writing.

Campus Safety and Security: Measures include 24-hour foot and vehicle patrol, emergency notification system, self-defense education, and security escort services. There are emergency telephones and lighted pathways/sidewalks.

Programs of Study: Umaine confers B.A., B.S., B.F.A., B.M.E., and B.U.S. degrees. Master's and doctoral degrees are also awarded. Bachelor's degrees are awarded in AGRICULTURE (agriculture, animal science, fishing and fisheries, forest engineering, forestry and related sciences, horticulture, natural resource management, wildlife management, and wood science), BIOLOGICAL SCIENCE (biochemistry, biology/biological science, biotechnology, botany, cell biology, marine biology, marine science, microbiology, molecular biology, nutrition, and zoology), BUSINESS (business administration and management and business economics), COMMUNICATIONS AND THE ARTS (art, communications, dramatic arts, English, French, German, journalism, Latin, media arts, modern language, music, music performance, romance languages and literature, Spanish, speech/debate/rhetoric, and studio art), COMPUTER AND PHYSICAL SCIENCE (chemistry, computer science, earth science, mathematics, and physics), EDUCATION (art education, elementary education, health education, music education, physical education, recreation education, and secondary education), ENGINEERING AND ENVIRONMENTAL DESIGN (bioengineering, chemical engineering, civil engineering, computer engineering, construction technology, electrical/electronics engineering, electrical/electronics engineering technology, engineering physics, environmental science, mechanical engineering, mechanical engineering technology, paper and pulp science, and surveying engineering), HEALTH PROFESSIONS (clinical science, medical laboratory technology, nursing, and speech pathology/audiology), SOCIAL SCIENCE (anthropology, child care/child and family studies, economics, food science, history, interdisciplinary studies, international studies, parks and recreation management, philosophy, political science/government, psychology, public administration, social work, sociology, and women's studies): Education, engineering, and biological science are the largest.

Required: To graduate, students must complete a minimum of 120 credit hours, including a minimum of 48 in the major, with a minimum GPA of 2.0. 40 credits in approved courses must be taken. General education requirements include 18 credits in human values and social context, 6 credits in math/statistics/computer science, 2 courses in science, and at least 1 course in ethics. English composition is required. Students must demonstrate writing competency and complete a capstone.

Special: Cross-registration through the National Student Exchange and at other University of Maine campuses, internships at the upper level, a Washington semester, work-study programs both on- and off-campus, dual majors, a general studies degree, and pass/fail options are available. Students may study abroad in more than 40 countries. Cooperative programs are available in most majors, and accelerated degrees may be arranged. There are 43 national honor societies, including Phi Beta Kappa, and a freshman honors program.

Faculty/Classroom: 59% of faculty are male; 41% are female. Graduate students teach 6% of introductory courses. The average class size in an introductory lecture, 24, in a laboratory, 16, and in a regular course, 21.

Admissions: 77% of the 2009-2010 applicants were accepted. The SAT scores for the 2009-2010 freshman class were: Critical Reading-- 35% below 500, 43% between 500 and 599, 18% between 600 and 700, and 4% above 700; Math--30% below 500, 44% between 500 and 599, 22% between 600 and 700, and 4% above 700; Writing--36% below 500, 46% between 500 and 599, 17% between 600 and 700, and 1% above 700. 43% of the current freshmen were in the top fifth of their class; 74% were in the top two fifths. There were 3 National Merit finalists. 33 freshmen graduated first in their class.

Requirements: The SAT or ACT is required. The GED is accepted. The number of academic or Carnegie credits required varies according to the program. The required secondary school courses also vary with each program but should include 4 credits of English, 3 of math, 2 of lab science, 2 of social studies, 2 in a foreign language, and 3 of electives. Guidance counselor recommendation is required for high school students. An essay is required. An audition is required for music majors. A GPA of 2.0 is required. AP and CLEP credits are accepted. Important factors in the admissions decision are advanced placement or honors courses, recommendations by school officials, and evidence of special talent.

Procedure: Freshmen are admitted fall and spring. Entrance exams should be taken by January of the senior year. There are deferred admissions and rolling admissions plans. Application deadlines are open. The fall 2008 application fee was $40. Notifications are sent February 1. Applications are accepted on-line.

Transfer: 477 transfer students enrolled in 2008-2009. Applicants must submit transcripts of all college and high school records. A minimum GPA of 2.0 is required. Some majors specify a higher cumulative GPA. 30 of 120 credits required for the bachelor's degree must be completed at Umaine.

Visiting: There are regularly scheduled orientations for prospective students, including an opening welcome, campus tours, registration, department tours, a student panel, admissions, financial aid and student life sessions, a performing arts presentation, and music auditions. There are guides for informal visits and visitors may sit in on classes. To schedule a visit, contact the Visitors' Center at (207) 581-3740.

Financial Aid: In a recent year, 82% of all full-time freshmen and 83% of continuing full-time students received some form of financial aid. 61% of all full-time freshmen and 58% of continuing full-time students received need-based aid. The average freshmen award was $9,667. 60% of undergraduate students worked part-time. Average annual earnings from campus work were $2000. The average financial indebtedness of the 2009 graduate was $17,235. The FAFSA is required. Check with the school for current application deadlines.

International Students: There are 139 international students enrolled. The school actively recruits these students. They must take the TOEFL with a minimum score of 530 on the paper-based TOEFL (PBT) or 71 on the Internet-based version (iBT). They must also take the SAT or ACT.

Computers: All dorms have wired connectivity. All academic buildings and some administrative buildings have wireless access. Public and private PC clusters are set up throughout campus with the largest clusters in the library and the student union. There are approximately 500 PCs and Macs available. All students may access the system 24 hours a day. There are no time limits and no fees. It is strongly recommended that all students have a personal computer. Students enrolled in The College of Education must have a personal computer. A Apple iBook is recommended.

Graduates: From July 1, 2008 to June 30, 2009, 1681 bachelor's degrees were awarded. The most popular majors were business (13%), education (12%), and engineering (8%). 269 companies recruited on campus in 2008-2009. In an average class, 32% graduate in 4 years or less, 52% graduate in 5 years or less, and 59% graduate in 6 years or less. Of the 2008 graduating class, 19% were enrolled in graduate school within 6 months of graduation, and 80% were employed.

Admissions Contact: Sharon M. Oliver, Director of Admissions. A campus DVD is available. E-Mail: *um-admit@maine.edu* Web: *www.umaine.edu*

UNIVERSITY OF MAINE AT AUGUSTA B-5

Augusta, ME 04430   (207) 621-3465; (207) 621-3333

Full-time: 540 men, 1159 women	**Faculty:** 104; IIB, -$
Part-time: 818 men, 2537 women	**Ph.D.s:** 54%
Graduate: none	**Student/Faculty:** 15 to 1
Year: semesters, summer session	**Tuition:** $6855 ($15,375)
Application Deadline: June 15	**Room & Board:** n/app
Freshman Class: 3215 applied, 2444 accepted, 1411 enrolled	

COMPETITIVE

The University of Maine at Augusta, founded in 1965, offers both associate and baccalaureate degrees and is part of the University of Maine System. There are 3 undergraduate schools. In addition to regional accreditation, UMA has baccalaureate program accreditation with ADA and NLN. The 2 libraries contain 93,897 volumes, 4676 microform items, and 4783 audio/video tapes/CDs/DVDs, and subscribe to 493 periodicals including electronic. Computerized library services include interlibrary loans, database searching, Internet access, and laptop Internet portals. Special learning facilities include a learning resource center, art gallery, and interactive television system. The 159-acre campus is in a small town 50 miles north of Portland. There are 15 buildings.

Student Life: 97% of undergraduates are from Maine. Others are from 35 states, 3 foreign countries, and Canada. 99% are from public schools. 73% are white. The average age of freshmen is 27; all undergraduates, 32. 46% do not continue beyond their first year; 30% remain to graduate.

Housing: There are no residence halls. All students commute.

Activities: There are no fraternities or sororities. There are 17 groups on campus, including art, gay, honors, international, jazz band, newspaper, pep band, professional, religious, social, social service, and student government. Popular campus events include Mile of Art, Jazz Week, and Plunkett Poetry Festival.

Sports: There are 2 intercollegiate sports for men and 3 for women, and 4 intramural sports for men and 4 for women. Facilities include the UMA Community Outdoor Leisure Center, which is also open to the public. Facilities provide for seasonal activities and feature a running and cross-country skiing trail, tennis courts, a soccer field, and a softball field. Indoor facilities include a small gym, a racquetball court, and a small fitness center.

Disabled Students: 95% of the campus is accessible. Facilities include wheelchair ramps, elevators, special parking, specially equipped rest rooms, special class scheduling, lowered drinking fountains, and lowered telephones.

Services: Counseling and information services are available, as is tutoring in some subjects and developmental and introductory level courses. There is remedial math and writing. There are workshops on a variety of student success skills, such as effective learning and reducing test anxiety.

Campus Safety and Security: Measures include emergency notification system and security escort services. There are emergency telephones and lighted pathways/sidewalks.

Programs of Study: UMA confers B.A., B.A.S., B. Mus., and B.S. degrees. Associates degrees are also awarded. Bachelor's degrees are awarded in BIOLOGICAL SCIENCE (biology/biological science), BUSINESS (accounting and business administration and management), COMMUNICATIONS AND THE ARTS (art, English, and jazz), COMPUTER AND PHYSICAL SCIENCE (applied science and information sciences and systems), EDUCATION (library science), ENGINEERING AND ENVIRONMENTAL DESIGN (architecture), HEALTH PROFESSIONS (dental hygiene, mental health/human services, and nursing), SOCIAL SCIENCE (interdisciplinary studies, law enforcement and corrections, liberal arts/general studies, public administration, and social science). Mental health and human services are the largest.

Required: All students must complete at least 120 hours, including 30 to 40 in the major, with a minimum GPA of 2.0. All degree programs require courses in communications, humanities, college writing, and fine arts. 6 credits of writing-intensive course work is required.

Special: Work-study and internship programs with local employers, study abroad in Germany, and a student-designed interdisciplinary studies major are available. Cross-registration is offered with University of Maine System campuses. There is 1 national honor society.

Faculty/Classroom: 43% of faculty are male; 47% are female. All teach undergraduates. The average class size in an introductory lecture is 20, in a laboratory, 16, and in a regular course, 18.

Admissions: 76% of the 2009-2010 applicants were accepted. 12% of the current freshmen were in the top fifth of their class; 63% were in the top two fifths.

Requirements: Students are encouraged to submit SAT scores for placement only. Applicants should have a high school diploma or the GED. Recommended secondary preparation varies according to the degree program. Applicants for the B.Mus. program must audition. UMA requires applicants to be in the upper 25% of their class. A GPA of 2.0 is required. AP and CLEP credits are accepted.

Procedure: Freshmen are admitted fall, spring, and summer. There are deferred admissions and rolling admissions plans. Applications should be filed by June 15 for fall entry and October 15 for spring entry, along with a $40 fee. Notification is sent on a rolling basis. Applications are accepted on-line.

Transfer: High school/college transcripts and a statement of good standing from prior institutions are required. Standardized test scores are required for some students, and an interview is recommended. 30 of 120 credits required for the bachelor's degree must be completed at UMA.

Visiting: There are regularly scheduled orientations for prospective students during the month before the beginning of a semester. There are guides for informal visits and visitors may sit in on classes. To schedule a visit, contact the Admissions Office at umaar@maine.edu.

Financial Aid: In 2009-2010, 90% of all full-time freshmen and 99% of continuing full-time students received some form of financial aid. 84% of all full-time freshmen and 90% of continuing full-time students received need-based aid. The average freshmen award was $7998, with $4513 ($6640 maximum) from need-based scholarships or need-based grants; $3463 ($7500 maximum) from need-based self-help aid (loans and jobs); and $3892 ($2600 maximum) from other non-need-based awards and non-need-based scholarships. 5% of undergraduate students work part-time. Average annual earnings from campus work are $1757. The average financial indebtedness of the 2009 graduate was $15,152. The FAFSA is required. The priority date for freshman financial aid applications for fall entry is March 1.

International Students: There were 42 international students enrolled in a recent year. They must take the TOEFL with a minimum score of 500 on the paper-based TOEFL (PBT).

Computers: Wireless access is available anywhere on campus and in all PC classrooms and student labs. All students may access the system. There are no time limits and no fees.

Graduates: From July 1, 2008 to June 30, 2009, 244 bachelor's degrees were awarded. The most popular majors were mental health/

human services (32%), business administration (15%), and liberal studies (14%). 10 companies recruited on campus in 2008-2009.

Admissions Contact: Jonathan Henry, Dean of Enrollment Services. E-Mail: *jhenry@maine.edu* Web: *www.uma.edu*

UNIVERSITY OF MAINE AT FARMINGTON   B-4

Farmington, ME 04938-1990   **(207) 778-7050; (207) 778-8182**

Full-time: 680 men, 1400 women	Faculty: 128; IIB, -$
Part-time: 70 men, 170 women	Ph.D.s: 89%
Graduate: none	Student/Faculty: n/av
Year: semesters, summer session	Tuition: $8676 ($17,092)
Application Deadline: open	Room & Board: $7552
Freshman Class: n/av	
SAT or ACT: not required	**COMPETITIVE**

The University of Maine at Farmington, founded in 1863 and part of the University of Maine System, is a public liberal arts institution offering programs in arts and sciences, teacher education, and human services. Some figures in the above capsule and in this profile are approximate. There are 2 undergraduate schools. In addition to regional accreditation, UMF has baccalaureate program accreditation with NCATE. The library contains 100,464 volumes, 89,997 microform items, and 7857 audio/video tapes/CDs/DVDs, and subscribes to 1768 periodicals including electronic. Computerized library services include interlibrary loans, database searching, and Internet access. Special learning facilities include a learning resource center, art gallery, radio station, an instructional media center, archeology research center, 20-workstation electronic classroom, observatory, on-site nursery, school teaching lab, on-site day care teaching lab, and multimedia graphic lab. The 55-acre campus is in a small town 38 miles northwest of Augusta and 80 miles north of Portland. Including any residence halls, there are 35 buildings.

Student Life: 83% of undergraduates are from Maine. Others are from 29 states, 7 foreign countries, and Canada. 88% are from public schools. 95% are white. The average age of freshmen is 19; all undergraduates, 22. 25% do not continue beyond their first year; 61% remain to graduate.

Housing: 1100 students can be accommodated in college housing, which includes single-sex and coed dorms and on-campus apartments. In addition, there are special-interest houses, an international guest house, a wellness floor, and scholar areas. On-campus housing is guaranteed for all 4 years. 60% of students commute. All students may keep cars.

Activities: There are no fraternities or sororities. There are 53 groups on campus, including chamber choir, club sports, commuter, environmental, history, cheerleading, choir, chorus, communications, computers, dance, drama, film, gay, honors, international, language, literary magazine, musical theater, newspaper, orchestra, pep band, photography, political, professional, radio and TV, religious, social, social service, student government, and yearbook. Popular campus events include Parents and Alumni weekends, Winter Carnival Weekend, and Student Symposium Day.

Sports: There are 5 intercollegiate sports for men and 6 for women, and 12 intramural sports for men and 12 for women. Facilities include a 500-seat gym, baseball, softball, and soccer fields, a field house with an indoor jogging track, 4 multipurpose courts, a swimming pool, and a weight-training center. A ski area, mountain climbing, canoeing, fishing, white-water rafting, and mountain biking opportunities are nearby.

Disabled Students: 80% of the campus is accessible. Facilities include wheelchair ramps, elevators, special parking, specially equipped restrooms, special class scheduling, lowered drinking fountains, and lowered telephones.

Services: Counseling and information services are available, as is tutoring in every subject. There is a reader service for the blind, and remedial math, reading, and writing.

Campus Safety and Security: Measures include 24-hour foot and vehicle patrol, self-defense education, and security escort services. There are emergency telephones, lighted pathways/sidewalks, safety whistles, an anonymous tip line, and property identification.

Programs of Study: UMF confers B.A., B.S., B.F.A., and B.G.S. degrees. Bachelor's degrees are awarded in BIOLOGICAL SCIENCE (biology/biological science), BUSINESS (business economics), COMMUNICATIONS AND THE ARTS (art, creative writing, English, language arts, music, and visual and performing arts), COMPUTER AND PHYSICAL SCIENCE (computer science, geochemistry, geology, and mathematics), EDUCATION (early childhood education, elementary education, health education, secondary education, and special education), ENGINEERING AND ENVIRONMENTAL DESIGN (environmental science), HEALTH PROFESSIONS (community health work and rehabilitation therapy), SOCIAL SCIENCE (geography, history, interdisciplinary studies, international studies, liberal arts/general studies, philosophy, political science/government, psychology, sociology, and women's studies). Education, environmental science, and creative writing are the strongest academically. Elementary education, psychology, and interdisciplinary studies are the largest.

Required: All students must maintain a minimum GPA of 2.0 while earning 120 semester hours, including 30 in their majors. Core requirements include 9 hours each in social and behavioral sciences and the humanities, 8 in natural science, 4 in English composition, 3 each in math, health, and phys ed, and a foreign language.

Special: Study abroad in 4 countries, as well as numerous opportunities through the National Student Exchange program, work-study with UMF, and student-designed majors are available. Study abroad is possible through other universities as well. Internships are required in rehabilitation and health and are available in all disciplines. Student teaching is required of all education majors. Also possible is interdisciplinary field study in many disciplines, a ski industry certificate, nondegree study, and pass/fail options. There are 2 national honor societies, a freshman honors program, and 10 departmental honors programs.

Faculty/Classroom: 46% of faculty are male; 54% are female. All teach, and 80% do research. The average class size in an introductory lecture is 30; in a laboratory, 20; and in a regular course, 19.

Admissions: 71% of a recent year's applicants were accepted. 25% of a recent year's freshmen were in the top fifth of their class; 54% were in the top two fifths. 3 freshmen graduated first in their class in a recent year.

Requirements: Applicants are required to have 16 to 19 college preparatory courses, including 4 in English, 3 to 5 in math, 3 electives, 2 to 3 in lab science, and 2 each in social science and foreign language. An essay and a counselor recommendation are required, and an interview is recommended. The GED is accepted for older, highly motivated students. UMF requires applicants to be in the upper 50% of their class. AP credits are accepted. Important factors in the admissions decision are advanced placement or honors courses, recommendations by school officials, and leadership record.

Procedure: Freshmen are admitted fall and spring. There are deferred admissions and rolling admissions plans. Application deadlines are open. Check with the school for current application fees. Notification is sent on a rolling basis. Applications are accepted on-line.

Transfer: 94 transfer students enrolled in a recent year. Applicants must have a minimum GPA of 2.0 (2.5 for some majors). 30 of 120 credits required for the bachelor's degree must be completed at UMF.

Visiting: There are regularly scheduled orientations for prospective students, including sessions on financial aid, majors, student life, the admissions process, and special opportunities such as study abroad, and tours of the campus. There are guides for informal visits, and visitors may sit in on classes. To schedule a visit, contact the Admissions Office.

Financial Aid: In a recent year, 92% of all full-time freshmen and 85% of continuing full-time students received some form of financial aid. 82% of all full-time freshmen and 67% of continuing full-time students received need-based aid. The average freshman award was $8497. 39% of undergraduate students work part-time. Average annual earnings from campus work are $1658. The average financial indebtedness of a recent year's graduate was $19,424. UMF is a member of CSS. The FAFSA is required. Check with the school for current application deadlines.

International Students: There were 6 international students enrolled in a recent year. The school actively recruits these students. They must take the TOEFL.

Computers: Wireless access is available. All residence halls have Ethernet hook-ups for each resident, free Internet, and e-mail. 128 stations in the computer center are available 24/7. 50 other stations are available in labs and library during regular hours. All students may access the system. There are no time limits and no fees.

Graduates: In a recent year, 475 bachelor's degrees were awarded. The most popular majors were education (41%), interdisciplinary (31%), and English (12%). In an average class, 33% graduate in 4 years or less, 52% graduate in 5 years or less, and 61% graduate in 6 years or less. 35 companies recruited on campus in a recent year. Of a recent year's graduating class, 19% were enrolled in graduate school within 6 months of graduation, and 90% were employed.

Admissions Contact: Director of Admissions. E-mail: *umfadmit@maine.edu* Web: *www.umf.maine.edu*

UNIVERSITY OF MAINE AT FORT KENT   D-1

Fort Kent, ME 04743   **(207) 834-7600 ext. 7602**
(888) TRY-UMFK; (207) 834-7609

Full-time: 243 men, 334 women	Faculty: 39; IIB, --$
Part-time: 134 men, 415 women	Ph.D.s: 80%
Graduate: none	Student/Faculty: 15 to 1
Year: semesters, summer session	Tuition: $6803 ($15,953)
Application Deadline: open	Room & Board: $7080
Freshman Class: 770 applied, 603 accepted, 364 enrolled	
SAT CR/M/W: 470/460/460	**ACT: 18 LESS COMPETITIVE**

The University of Maine at Fort Kent, founded in 1878, is a publicly funded liberal arts institution within the University of Maine system. There are 7 undergraduate schools and 2 graduate schools. In addition to regional accreditation, UMFK has baccalaureate program accreditation with NLN and SAF. The library contains 67,137 volumes and 1300 audio/video tapes/CDs/DVDs, and subscribes to 333 periodicals including electronic. Computerized library services include interlibrary loans, database searching, and Internet access. Special learning facilities include a learning resource center, radio station, greenhouse, and biological park. The 52-acre campus is in a small town 200 miles north of Bangor. Including any residence halls, there are 16 buildings.

Student Life: 83% of undergraduates are from Maine. Others are from 20 states, 9 foreign countries, and Canada. 98% are from public schools. 71% are white; 26% foreign nationals. The average age of freshmen is 22; all undergraduates, 26. 23% do not continue beyond their first year; 40% remain to graduate.

Housing: 300 students can be accommodated in college housing, which includes coed dorms. On-campus housing is guaranteed for all 4 years. 80% of students commute. Alcohol is not permitted. All students may keep cars.

Activities: 2% of men belong to 1 national fraternity; 1% of women belong to 1 national sorority. There are 15 groups on campus, including cheerleading, chorale, chorus, computers, dance, drama, environmental, international, literary magazine, literature, musical theater, newspaper, outing, professional, radio and TV, religious, and student government. Popular campus events include French Heritage Festival, Spring Meltdown, and Winter Carnival.

Sports: There are 6 intercollegiate sports for men and 6 for women, and 10 intramural sports for men and 10 for women. Facilities include an 11,500-square-foot gym, racquetball courts, a soccer field, a weight room, a cardiovascular room, intramural fields, and game rooms in the residence halls.

Disabled Students: 80% of the campus is accessible. Facilities include wheelchair ramps, elevators, special parking, specially equipped restrooms, special class scheduling, lowered drinking fountains, lowered telephones, and special housing.

Services: Counseling and information services are available, as is tutoring in every subject. There is a reader service for the blind and remedial math, reading, and writing.

Campus Safety and Security: There are lighted pathways/sidewalks and night watchmen on duty from 11 P.M. to 7 A.M.

Programs of Study: UMFK confers B.A., B.S., B.S.E.S, B.S.N., and B.U.S. degrees. Associates degrees are also awarded. Bachelor's degrees are awarded in BIOLOGICAL SCIENCE (biology/biological science), BUSINESS (business administration and management), COMMUNICATIONS AND THE ARTS (English and French), COMPUTER AND PHYSICAL SCIENCE (computer science), EDUCATION (elementary education), ENGINEERING AND ENVIRONMENTAL DESIGN (environmental science), HEALTH PROFESSIONS (nursing), SOCIAL SCIENCE (behavioral science, liberal arts/general studies, safety management, and social science). Environmental studies, nursing, and biology are the strongest academically. Education, nursing, and behavioral science are the largest.

Required: A minimum GPA of 2.0 and a total of 120 credit hours (2.5 GPA and 127 credit hours for nursing, 128 credit hours for business management) are required for graduation. Curricula and distribution requirements vary by major.

Special: Internships are required for business majors, nursing (clinicals), social sciences, public safety administration, and education (student teaching). A general studies degree, a B.A.-B.S. degree in bilingual-bicultural studies, credit for life experience, nondegree study, and an accelerated nursing program are available. Students may cross-register with the College Universitaire St. Louis Maillet in New Brunswick. Study abroad may be arranged in Canada, France, and Mexico through the University of Maine at Farmington. Interactive TV courses broadcast from other universities are available on campus. There is 1 national honor society.

Faculty/Classroom: 53% of faculty are male; 47% are female. All teach undergraduates. The average class size in an introductory lecture is 24; in a laboratory, 14; and in a regular course, 18.

Admissions: 78% of the 2009-2010 applicants were accepted. The SAT scores for the 2009-2010 freshman class were: Critical Reading--73% below 500, 23% between 500 and 599, and 4% between 600 and 700; Math--78% below 500, 20% between 500 and 599, and 2% between 600 and 700; Writing--78% below 500, 18% between 500 and 599, and 4% between 600 and 700. The ACT scores were 100% below 21. 20% of the current freshmen were in the top fifth of their class; 54% were in the top two fifths.

Requirements: The ACT Optional Writing test is required. The SAT is recommended. In addition, applicants should be graduates of an accredited secondary school. The GED is accepted. Required secondary school courses include 4 years of English and 2 each of social studies, math, and lab science. A foreign language is suggested. An essay and an interview are recommended. A GPA of 2.0 is required. AP and CLEP credits are accepted. Important factors in the admissions decision are recommendations by school officials, advanced placement or honors courses, and evidence of special talent.

Procedure: Freshmen are admitted fall and spring. Entrance exams should be taken before March of the senior year. There are early deci-

sion, early admissions, deferred admissions, and rolling admissions plans. Application deadlines are open. The application fee is $40. Notification is sent on a rolling basis. Applications are accepted on-line.

Transfer: 238 transfer students enrolled in 2008-2009. Applicants must submit transcripts from each college and secondary school attended. The SAT and an interview are recommended. 30 of 120 credits required for the bachelor's degree must be completed at UMFK.

Visiting: There are regularly scheduled orientations for prospective students, including placement testing, meetings with advisers, campus tours, and get-aquainted activities. There are guides for informal visits, and visitors may sit in on classes and stay overnight. To schedule a visit, contact the Admissions Office.

Financial Aid: In 2009-2010, 82% of all full-time freshmen and 80% of continuing full-time students received need-based aid. 75% of undergraduate students work part-time. Average annual earnings from campus work are $1500. The FAFSA and income tax forms is required. The deadline for filing freshman financial aid applications for fall entry is March 1.

International Students: There are 132 international students enrolled. The school actively recruits these students. They must take the TOEFL with a minimum score of 500 on the paper-based TOEFL (PBT). The SAT scores may be submitted in place of the TOEFL.

Computers: Wireless access is available. All students may access the system from 8 A.M. to 11 P.M. in the library and computer centers and 24 hours a day in the dorms. There are no time limits. The fee is $5.

Graduates: From July 1, 2008 to June 30, 2009, 212 bachelor's degrees were awarded. The most popular majors were education (62%), nursing (23%), and business (8%). 2 companies recruited on campus in 2008-2009. In an average class, 25% graduate in 4 years or less, 18% graduate in 5 years or less, and 3% graduate in 6 years or less. Of the 2008 graduating class, 5% were enrolled in graduate school within 6 months of graduation and 90% were employed.

Admissions Contact: Jill Cairns, Director of Admissions. A campus DVD is available. E-Mail: *Jillb@maine.edu* Web: *www.umfk.maine.edu*

UNIVERSITY OF MAINE AT MACHIAS   E-4

Machias, ME 04654
(207) 255-1318
(888) 468-6866; (207) 255-1363

Full-time: 200 men, 300 women	**Faculty:** IIB, -$
Part-time: 200 men, 500 women	**Ph.D.s:** n/av
Graduate: none	**Student/Faculty:** n/av
Year: semesters, summer session	**Tuition:** $6775 ($17,515)
Application Deadline: open	**Room & Board:** $6936
Freshman Class: n/av	
SAT or ACT: required	**COMPETITIVE**

The University of Maine at Machias, founded in 1909, is a publicly funded liberal arts institution in the University of Maine system. Some figures in the above capsule and in this profile are approximate. In addition to regional accreditation, UMM has baccalaureate program accreditation with NRPA. The library contains 82,000 volumes, 5000 microform items, and 3000 audio/video tapes/CDs/DVDs, and subscribes to 320 periodicals including electronic. Computerized library services include interlibrary loans, database searching, and Internet access. Special learning facilities include a learning resource center, art gallery, radio station, and aquariums for marine and aquaculture studies. The 42-acre campus is in a rural area 85 miles east of Bangor. Including any residence halls, there are 8 buildings.

Student Life: 82% of undergraduates are from Maine. Others are from 26 states, 16 foreign countries, and Canada. 98% are from public schools. 90% are white. The average age of freshmen is 20; all undergraduates, 29. 28% do not continue beyond their first year; 45% remain to graduate.

Housing: 353 students can be accommodated in college housing, which includes single-sex and coed dorms. On-campus housing is guaranteed for all 4 years. 76% of students commute. All students may keep cars.

Activities: 7% of men belong to 2 local and 2 national fraternities; 3% of women belong to 1 local sorority and 3 national sororities. There are 34 groups on campus, including art, cheerleading, chorale, chorus, communications, computers, dance, drama, gay, honors, international, literary magazine, musical theater, outing club, pep band, photography, pop band, professional, radio and TV, religious, social service, and student government. Popular campus events include Winter Carnival, Spring Weekend, and Family Weekend.

Sports: There are 3 intercollegiate sports for men and 4 for women, and 10 intramural sports for men and 10 for women. Facilities include 2 gyms, weight/exercise rooms, handball/racquetball courts, a pool, and a 64-acre recreational center with a lodge and cabins on the lake.

Disabled Students: 85% of the campus is accessible. Facilities include wheelchair ramps, elevators, special parking, specially equipped restrooms, lowered drinking fountains, and automatic doors.

Services: Counseling and information services are available, as is tutoring in every subject. There is remedial math, reading, and writing. The

Student Resource Coordinator provides one-on-one services, including learning strategies, study skills, and assistance with papers and learning styles.

Campus Safety and Security: Measures include self-defense education and security escort services. There are lighted pathways/sidewalks, a keyless entry system for residence halls, and a security patrol from 5 P.M. to 5 A.M. daily.

Programs of Study: UMM confers B.A., B.S., and B.C.S. degrees. Bachelor's degrees are awarded in BIOLOGICAL SCIENCE (biology/biological science and marine biology), BUSINESS (accounting, business administration and management, marketing/retailing/merchandising, and recreation and leisure services), COMMUNICATIONS AND THE ARTS (English and fine arts), EDUCATION (business education and elementary education), ENGINEERING AND ENVIRONMENTAL DESIGN (environmental science), SOCIAL SCIENCE (behavioral science, history, human services, and liberal arts/general studies). Elementary education, marine biology, and environmental studies are the strongest academically. Elementary education, business administration, and behavioral science are the largest.

Required: To graduate, students must complete a minimum of 120 credit hours with a GPA of 2.0. The core curriculum consists of 40 to 43 hours in the areas of communication skills, science and math, humans in social context, fine arts, historical and cultural perspectives, and lifetime fitness.

Special: Co-op programs in all majors except education, cross-registration, internships, work-study programs, a B.A.-B.S. degree, study abroad in England and Wales, and a student-designed concentration in environmental science are available. UMM also offers a Bachelor of College Studies program, credit for prior learning, nondegree study, and a pass/fail option in certain courses. There is a freshman honors program.

Faculty/Classroom: 54% of faculty are male; 46% are female. The average class size in an introductory lecture is 21; in a laboratory, 16; and in a regular course, 17.

Requirements: The SAT or ACT is required. In addition, all candidates must be graduates of an accredited secondary school, although the GED is accepted. UMM recommends that students place in the top half of their graduating class and that composite SAT or ACT scores be satisfactory. UMM also recommends completion of 4 units of English, 3 of math, 2 each of lab science, social science/history, and fine arts or foreign language, and 3 of electives. An essay is required, and an interview is strongly recommended. A GPA of 2.0 is required. AP and CLEP credits are accepted. Important factors in the admissions decision are extracurricular activities record, leadership record, and recommendations by school officials.

Procedure: Freshmen are admitted fall, spring, and summer. There are early admissions, deferred admissions, and rolling admissions plans. Application deadlines are open. Application fee is $40. Notification is sent on a rolling basis. Applications are accepted on-line.

Transfer: A minimum college GPA of 2.0 and evidence of good standing are required of transfer applicants. 30 of 120 credits required for the bachelor's degree must be completed at UMM.

Visiting: There are regularly scheduled orientations for prospective students, consisting of traditional orientations prior to the fall and spring semesters, which include programming to guide students in all aspects of starting college—academic, student services and activities, and administrative. UMM also offers 2 summer student orientations, which include aspects of the fall orientations plus a parent orientation. There are guides for informal visits, and visitors may sit in on classes. To schedule a visit, contact the Admissions Office.

Financial Aid: The FAFSA is required. Check with the school for current application deadlines.

International Students: The school actively recruits these students. They must take the TOEFL. They must also take the SAT or ACT.

Computers: All students may access the system 24 hours a day, 7 days a week in dorms and the 24-hour room. Other computer labs are open during library hours. There is no set limit, but students must yield a machine for academic priorities. There are no fees.

Admissions Contact: Admissions Counselor. A campus DVD is available. E-mail: *ummadmissions@maine.edu* Web: *www.umm.maine.edu*

UNIVERSITY OF MAINE AT PRESQUE ISLE — D-2

Presque Isle, ME 04769-2888	(207) 768-9453; (207) 768-9777
Full-time: 400 men, 700 women	Faculty: IIB, -$
Part-time: 100 men, 300 women	Ph.Ds: n/av
Graduate: none	Student/Faculty: n/av
Year: semesters, summer session	Tuition: $6030 ($15,180)
Application Deadline: open	Room & Board: $6462
Freshman Class: n/av	
SAT or ACT: not required	LESS COMPETITIVE

The University of Maine at Presque Isle, founded in 1903, is a public institution within the University of Maine system offering liberal arts, teacher education, and professional programs leading to postsecondary certificates and associate and bachelor's degrees. Some of the figures in the above capsule and in this profile are approximate. There are 2 undergraduate schools. In addition to regional accreditation, UM-Presque Isle has baccalaureate program accreditation with CSWE. The library contains 75,000 volumes, 750,000 microform items, and 1400 audio/video tapes/CDs/DVDs, and subscribes to 2000 periodicals including electronic. Computerized library services include interlibrary loans, database searching, and Internet access. Special learning facilities include a learning resource center, art gallery, natural history museum, radio station, and a theater. The 150-acre campus is in a rural area 150 miles north of Bangor. Including any residence halls, there are 11 buildings.

Student Life: 73% of undergraduates are from Maine. Others are from 14 states, 5 foreign countries, and Canada. 67% are white. The average age of freshmen is 20; all undergraduates, 26. 45% do not continue beyond their first year; 28% remain to graduate.

Housing: 359 students can be accommodated in college housing, which includes coed dorms, off-campus apartments, and married student housing. On-campus housing is guaranteed for all 4 years. 78% of students commute. All students may keep cars.

Activities: 2% of men belong to 1 national fraternity; 1% of women belong to 1 national sorority. There are 25 groups on campus, including band, chess, chorale, communications, debate, drama, ethnic, gay, honors, international, newspaper, professional, radio and TV, religious, social, social service, and student government. Popular campus events include Spring Ball, Winter Blast, and Spring Fest.

Sports: There are 6 intercollegiate sports for men and 6 for women, and 15 intramural sports for men and 15 for women. Facilities include a building that houses a swimming pool, a gym, a track, a fitness room, and a climbing wall. Another multifunctional structure houses a gym, a weight room, phys ed labs, a sports medicine facility, the Athletic Hall of Fame, and an auditorium. A large playing field contains baseball, soccer, and tennis courts. There are also hiking trails, a bike path, and a ropes course. The campus also hosts a club ice hockey team.

Disabled Students: All of the campus is accessible. Facilities include wheelchair ramps, elevators, special parking, specially equipped restrooms, special class scheduling, lowered drinking fountains, and lowered telephones.

Services: Counseling and information services are available, as is tutoring in most subjects. There is remedial math, reading, and writing.

Campus Safety and Security: Measures include security escort services. There are lighted pathways/sidewalks.

Programs of Study: UM-Presque Isle confers B.A., B.S., B.A.A.E., B.F.A., B.L.S., and B.S.W. degrees. Associate degrees are also awarded. Bachelor's degrees are awarded in BIOLOGICAL SCIENCE (biology/biological science), BUSINESS (accounting, business administration and management, and recreation and leisure services), COMMUNICATIONS AND THE ARTS (art and English), EDUCATION (elementary education, health education, physical education, and secondary education), ENGINEERING AND ENVIRONMENTAL DESIGN (environmental science), SOCIAL SCIENCE (behavioral science, criminal justice, international studies, liberal arts/general studies, and social work). Education, social work, and criminal justice are the largest.

Required: Core requirements for the B.A. degrees include 18 credits in humanities, 12 in social science, 11 in math/science, and 4 in phys ed/health. The student must complete a minimum number of credits, which varies according to major, with a cumulative GPA of 2.0 in 120 to 128 credit hours. Requirements for the B.S. and other degrees vary considerably with each major.

Special: The university participates in transfer programs in agriculture, nutrition science, and animal and veterinary science. There is a nursing program with the University of Maine at Fort Kent. There are study-abroad programs in France, Ireland, and Canada (other countries are available) and internships in many majors. UM-Presque Isle offers work-study programs, dual and student-designed majors, a B.A.-B.S. degree, and nondegree study. Students can apply for credit by exam and credit for life, military, and work experience. A credit/no credit option is available. There is 1 national honor society, a freshman honors program, and 5 departmental honors programs.

Faculty/Classroom: 56% of faculty are male; 44% are female. The average class size in an introductory lecture is 20; in a laboratory, 12; and in a regular course, 15.

Requirements: Applicants should have completed 16 academic credits at an accredited secondary school, including 4 in English, 3 each in math and social studies, and 2 each in science with a lab, foreign language, and electives. A GED certificate may be substituted. The university recommends an essay and an interview for all candidates. Art majors must submit a portfolio. AP and CLEP credits are accepted. Important factors in the admissions decision are advanced placement or honors courses, recommendations by school officials, and extracurricular activities record.

Procedure: Freshmen are admitted fall, spring, and summer. Entrance exams should be taken by January 1. There are early decision, deferred admissions and rolling admissions plans. Application deadlines are open. Application fee is $40. Applications are accepted on-line.

Transfer: Applicants must have a 2.0 GPA from a regionally accredited two- or four-year college. Applicants must submit official transcripts from all colleges attended, along with an official transcript from the high school from which they graduated. 30 of 120 credits required for the bachelor's degree must be completed at UM-Presque Isle.

Visiting: There are regularly scheduled orientations for prospective students, including advisement, a campus tour, and meetings with faculty and coaches. There are guides for informal visits, and visitors may sit in on classes and stay overnight.

Financial Aid: The FAFSA is required. Check with the school for current application deadlines.

International Students: The school actively recruits these students. They must take the TOEFL.

Computers: Wireless access is available. Wireless can be accessed everywhere inside except for the dorms. The university owns 500 PCs, which can all access the Internet. All students may access the system. There are no time limits. The fee is nominal.

Admissions Contact: Director of Enrollment Management and University Relations. A campus DVD is available.
E-mail: *adventure@umpi.maine.edu* Web: *www.umpi.maine.edu*

UNIVERSITY OF NEW ENGLAND — A-6

Biddeford, ME 04005   (207) 283-0171; (207) 286-3678

Full-time: 2000 men and women	Faculty: IIA, -$
Part-time: 350 men and women	Ph.D.s: n/av
Graduate: 2000 men and women	Student/Faculty: n/av
Year: semesters, summer session	Tuition: $28,300
Application Deadline: February 15	Room & Board: $11,410
Freshman Class: n/av	
SAT or ACT: required	COMPETITIVE

University of New England, founded in 1831, offers undergraduate degrees in the health sciences, natural sciences, social sciences, liberal arts, education, and business administration; graduate degrees in professional and occupational programs; teacher education, doctor of osteopathic medicine, and continuing education. Some figures in the above capsule and in this profile are approximate. There are 2 undergraduate schools and 8 graduate schools. In addition to regional accreditation, UNE has baccalaureate program accreditation with ADA, AOA, APTA, CAAHEP, CSWE, and NLN. The 2 libraries contain 143,278 volumes, 6371 microform items, and 10,532 audio/video tapes/CDs/DVDs, and subscribe to 25,063 periodicals including electronic. Computerized library services include interlibrary loans, database searching, Internet access, and laptop Internet portals. Special learning facilities include a learning resource center and art gallery. The 623-acre campus is in a rural area. Including any residence halls, there are 47 buildings.

Student Life: 59% of undergraduates are from out of state, mostly the Northeast. Students are from 33 states, 4 foreign countries, and Canada. 96% are white.

Housing: 1071 students can be accommodated in college housing, which includes single-sex and coed dorms. On-campus housing is guaranteed for the freshman year only. 65% of students live on campus. Upperclassmen may keep cars.

Activities: There are no fraternities or sororities. There are 44 groups on campus, including communications, environmental, gay, honors, international, literary magazine, newspaper, professional, religious, sailing, social, social service, student government, and yearbook. Popular campus events include welcome week, family and friends weekend, and full leadership retreat.

Sports: There are 5 intercollegiate sports for men and 8 for women, and 17 intramural sports for men and 17 for women. Facilities include a 1500-seat gym, a fitness center, a pool, racquetball courts, soccer and softball fields, outdoor volleyball facilities, and a multipurpose recreational field.

Disabled Students: 85% of the campus is accessible. Facilities include wheelchair ramps, elevators, special parking, specially equipped restrooms, special class scheduling, lowered drinking fountains, lowered telephones, and stair climbers.

Services: Counseling and information services are available, as is tutoring in most subjects. There is a reader service for the blind, and remedial math, reading, and writing.

Campus Safety and Security: Measures include 24-hour foot and vehicle patrol, self-defense education, and security escort services. There are emergency telephones and lighted pathways/sidewalks. A safe-ride program provides drivers for students.

Programs of Study: UNE confers B.A., B.S., and B.S.N. degrees. Associate, master's, and doctoral degrees are also awarded. Bachelor's degrees are awarded in AGRICULTURE (environmental studies), BIOLOGICAL SCIENCE (biochemistry, biology/biological science, marine biology, and marine science), BUSINESS (business administration and management and sports management), COMMUNICATIONS AND THE ARTS (communications and English), COMPUTER AND PHYSICAL SCIENCE (chemistry and mathematics), EDUCATION (art education, athletic training, education, and elementary education), ENGINEERING AND ENVIRONMENTAL DESIGN (environmental science), HEALTH PROFESSIONS (biomedical science, dental hygiene, health care admin-

istration, health science, nursing, and preventive/wellness health care), SOCIAL SCIENCE (American studies, history, liberal arts/general studies, political science/government, psychobiology, psychology, and sociology). Medical biology, marine biology, and athletic training are the largest.

Required: A total of at least 120 credits with a minimum GPA of 2.0 is required for graduation. Students must take 43 credits in a liberal arts core curriculum of humanities, sciences, and social sciences. Most majors require 1-semester internships. Courses in English composition, human traditions, environmental studies, lab science, creative arts, and math are required.

Special: UNE offers cross-registration with the Greater Portland Alliance of Colleges and Universities, internships in all majors, work-study programs, study abroad, dual majors in all departments, a 3-4 medical program, and a 3-2 pre-physician assistant program. There are 2 national honor societies.

Faculty/Classroom: 50% of faculty are male; 50% are female. The average class size in an introductory lecture is 25; in a laboratory, 18; and in a regular course, 22.

Requirements: The SAT or ACT is required. In addition, applicants should be high school graduates with 4 years of English, 3 each of math and science, and 2 each of history and social studies. The GED is accepted. A personal interview is recommended. AP and CLEP credits are accepted. Important factors in the admissions decision are advanced placement or honors courses, recommendations by school officials, and leadership record.

Procedure: Freshmen are admitted fall and spring. Entrance exams should be taken in the spring of the junior year or fall of the senior year. There are deferred admissions and rolling admissions plans. Priority decision applications should be filed by December 1; regular decision, by February 15. Application fee is $40. Notification of priority decision is sent by December 31; regular decision, on a rolling basis. Applications are accepted on-line.

Transfer: Transfer applicants should present a GPA of at least 2.5 in college work. An interview is recommended. 30 of 120 credits required for the bachelor's degree must be completed at UNE.

Visiting: There are regularly scheduled orientations for prospective students, including a tour and information session, and an interview if the student has formally applied. There are guides for informal visits, and visitors may sit in on classes. To schedule a visit, contact the Admissions Office.

Financial Aid: The FAFSA is required. Check with the school for current application deadlines.

International Students: They must take the TOEFL.

Computers: Wireless access is available. All students may access the system. There are no time limits and no fees.

Admissions Contact: Associate Dean of Admissions.
E-mail: *admissions@une.edu* Web: *www.une.edu*

UNIVERSITY OF SOUTHERN MAINE — B-6

Gorham, ME 04038-1088   (207) 780-5670
(800) 800-4876; (207) 780-5640

Full-time: 2166 men, 2665 women	Faculty: n/av
Part-time: 1128 men, 1659 women	Ph.D.s: 74%
Graduate: 686 men, 1351 women	Student/Faculty: n/av
Year: semesters, summer session	Room & Board: $8762
Application Deadline: February 15	
Freshman Class: 3676 applied, 3819 accepted, 924 enrolled	
SAT CR/M/W: 500/500/490	ACT: 21 COMPETITIVE

The University of Southern Maine, founded in 1878, is a publicly funded, multi-campus, comprehensive, residential, liberal arts institution serving the University of Maine system. There are 5 undergraduate schools and 8 graduate schools. In addition to regional accreditation, USM has baccalaureate program accreditation with AACSB, ABET, CSAB, CSWE, NASM, NCATE, NLN, and NRPA. The 3 libraries contain 455,129 volumes, 731,755 microform items, and 5,288 audio/video tapes/CDs/DVDs, and subscribe to 3,249 periodicals including electronic. Computerized library services include interlibrary loans and database searching. Special learning facilities include a learning resource center, art gallery, planetarium, radio station, TV station, and cartography collections. The 144-acre campus is in an urban area 110 miles north of Boston, MA. Including any residence halls, there are 66 buildings.

Student Life: 90% of undergraduates are from Maine. Students are from 35 states, 27 foreign countries, and Canada. 97% are white. The average age of freshmen is 19; all undergraduates, 25.

Housing: 1835 students can be accommodated in college housing, which includes coed dorms, on-campus apartments, and married student housing. In addition, there are honors houses, special-interest houses, a fine arts house. On-campus housing is guaranteed for all 4 years. 81% of students commute. All students may keep cars.

Activities: 2% of men belong to 1 local and 3 national fraternities; 2% of women belong to 2 local and 2 national sororities. There are 100 groups on campus, including ski, commuter, environmental, art, band, cheerleading, chess, choir, chorale, chorus, computers, dance, drama, ethnic, gay, honors, international, jazz band, literary magazine, musical theater, opera, orchestra, outing, photography, political, professional, religious, social, social service, and student government. Popular campus events include Winter Weekend, Spring Fling, and comedy nights.

Sports: There are 12 intercollegiate sports for men and 13 for women, and 14 intramural sports for men and 14 for women. Facilities include gyms, tennis courts, athletic fields, racquetball and squash courts, cross-country ski trails, two weight-training and fitness facilities, an ice arena, a field house, and an indoor track.

Disabled Students: All of the campus is accessible. Facilities include wheelchair ramps, elevators, special parking, specially equipped restrooms, special class scheduling, lowered drinking fountains, and lowered telephones.

Services: Counseling and information services are available, as is tutoring in most subjects. There is a reader service for the blind, and remedial math, reading, and writing.

Campus Safety and Security: Measures include 24-hour foot and vehicle patrol, self-defense education, and security escort services. There are shuttle buses, emergency telephones, lighted pathways/sidewalks, and preventive programs within residence halls.

Programs of Study: USM confers B.A., B.S., B.F.A., and B.M. degrees. Associate, master's, and doctoral degrees are also awarded. Bachelor's degrees are awarded in BIOLOGICAL SCIENCE (biology/biological science), BUSINESS (accounting and business administration and management), COMMUNICATIONS AND THE ARTS (communications, dramatic arts, English, fine arts, French, music, and music performance), COMPUTER AND PHYSICAL SCIENCE (chemistry, computer science, geology, geoscience, mathematics, and physics), EDUCATION (music education and technical education), ENGINEERING AND ENVIRONMENTAL DESIGN (electrical/electronics engineering, environmental science, and industrial engineering technology), HEALTH PROFESSIONS (environmental health science, health science, nursing, recreation therapy, and sports medicine), SOCIAL SCIENCE (anthropology, economics, geography, history, philosophy, political science/government, psychology, social work, sociology, and women's studies). Electrical engineering, computer science, and nursing are the strongest academically. Business administration, nursing, and psychology are the largest.

Required: A total of 120 hours, of which 36 to 94 are in the major, and a minimum GPA of 2.0 are required for graduation. All students must fulfill the distribution requirements of the 3-part core curriculum: basic competence, methods of inquiry/ways of knowing, and interdisciplinary studies.

Special: Cross-registration within the University of Maine system and 4 Greater Portland colleges, a Washington semester, and study abroad in more than 12 countries are offered. Internships, co-op and work-study programs, a B.A.-B.S. degree, dual and student-designed majors, a 2-2 engineering program with the University of Maine, credit for life experience, nondegree study, and pass/fail options are also available. There is a January intersession. There are 2 national honor societies, a freshman honors program, and 1 departmental honors program.

Faculty/Classroom: 53% of faculty are male; 47% are female. 80% teach undergraduates, all do research, and 80% do both. No introductory courses are taught by graduate students. The average class size in an introductory lecture is 50; in a laboratory is 20; and in a regular course is 22.

Admissions: 104% of the 2009-2010 applicants were accepted. The SAT scores for the 2009-2010 freshman class were: Critical Reading--47% below 500, 39% between 500 and 599, 12% between 600 and 700, and 2% above 700; Math--50% below 500, 40% between 500 and 599, 9% between 600 and 700, and 1% above 700; Writing--51% below 500, 37% between 500 and 599, 11% between 600 and 700, and 1% above 700. The ACT scores were 45% below 21, 32% between 21 and 23, 15% between 24 and 26, 3% between 27 and 28, and 5% above 28. 22% of the current freshmen were in the top fifth of their class; 51% were in the top two fifths.

Requirements: The SAT or ACT is required. In addition, applicants must be graduates of an accredited secondary school. The GED is accepted. Either 41 academic credits or 20 1/2 Carnegie units are required. Secondary school courses should include 4 years of English, 3 of math, 2 each of a foreign language and lab science, and 1 each of history and social studies. An essay is required, as are auditions for music applicants and interviews for applicants to the School of Applied Science. Guidance counselor recommendations are required for those students applying during their senior year. A GPA of 2.0 is required. AP and CLEP credits are accepted. Important factors in the admissions decision are advanced placement or honors courses, recommendations by school officials, and extracurricular activities record.

Procedure: Freshmen are admitted fall and spring. Entrance exams should be taken by May of the junior year or January of the senior year. There are deferred admissions and rolling admissions plans. Applications should be filed by February 15 for fall entry; December 1 for spring entry. The fall 2009 application fee was $40. Applications are accepted online.

Transfer: 848 transfer students enrolled in 2008-2009. Applicants must have a minimum GPA of 2.0 or 2.75 for those from non-regionally accredited institutions. Students who have been out of high school for less than 3 years must submit SAT scores. 30 of 120 credits required for the bachelor's degree must be completed at USM.

Visiting: There are regularly scheduled orientations for prospective students, including regularly scheduled campus tours and group information sessions, as well as special events such as fall open houses. Interviews are also available on request. There are guides for informal visits and visitors may sit in on classes. To schedule a visit, contact the Office of Admission.

Financial Aid: The FAFSA is required. The priority date for freshman financial aid applications for fall entry is February 15. The deadline for filing freshman financial aid applications for fall entry is February 15.

International Students: They must take the TOEFL.

Computers: Wireless access is available. There are approximately 485 PCs available. All students may access the system 16 hours per day. There are no time limits and no fees.

Graduates: From July 1, 2008 to June 30, 2009, 1101 bachelor's degrees were awarded. The most popular majors were Health Professions (20%), Social Sciences (19%), and Business (13%).

Admissions Contact: Scott Steinberg, Dean of Undergraduate Admission. E-Mail: usmadm@maine.maine.edu Web: www.usm.maine.edu

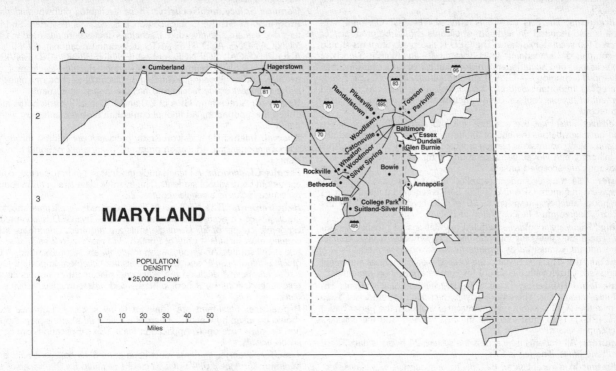

MARYLAND

POPULATION
DENSITY
• 25,000 and over

0 10 20 30 40 50
Miles

BOWIE STATE UNIVERSITY   D-3

Bowie, MD 20715   (301) 860-3427; (301) 860-3438

Full-time: 1300 men, 1200 women   **Faculty:** 158; IIA, av$
Part-time: 200 men, 400 women   **Ph.D:s:** 60%
Graduate: 300 men, 900 women   **Student/Faculty:** n/av
Year: semesters, summer session   **Tuition:** $6040 ($16,479)
Application Deadline: April 1   **Room & Board:** $6879
Freshman Class: n/av
SAT or ACT: required   **COMPETITIVE**

Bowie State University, founded in 1865, is a historically black, publicly supported, comprehensive liberal arts institution within the University System of Maryland. Some figures in the above capsule and in this profile are approximate. There are 4 undergraduate schools and 1 graduate school. In addition to regional accreditation, BSU has baccalaureate program accreditation with ACBSP, CSAB, NCATE, and NLN. The library contains 245,336 volumes, 428,296 microform items, and 6164 audio/video tapes/CDs/DVDs, and subscribes to 748 periodicals including electronic. Computerized library services include interlibrary loans, database searching, Internet access, and laptop Internet portals. Special learning facilities include a learning resource center, art gallery, radio station, TV station, media center, and satellite operations and control center. The 295-acre campus is in a suburban area 18 miles north of Washington, D.C. Including any residence halls, there are 22 buildings.

Student Life: 90% of undergraduates are from Maryland. Others are from 27 states, 19 foreign countries, and Canada. 95% are from public schools. 88% are African American. The average age of freshmen is 18; all undergraduates, 24. 25% do not continue beyond their first year; 75% remain to graduate.

Housing: 1400 students can be accommodated in college housing, which includes single-sex and coed dorms and off-campus apartments. In addition, there are honors houses. On-campus housing is available on a first-come, first-served basis. 75% of students commute. Alcohol is not permitted. Upperclassmen may keep cars.

Activities: 2% of men belong to 5 national fraternities; 1% of women belong to 4 national sororities. There are 50 groups on campus, including art, band, cheerleading, choir, chorale, communications, commuter club, computers, dance, drama, drill team, honors, international, jazz band, literary magazine, marching band, musical theater, NAACP, newspaper, pep band, political, professional, radio and TV, religious, social, social service, student government, Urban League, and yearbook. Popular campus events include Black History Month Convocation, Parents/Founders Day, and Honors Convocation.

Sports: There are 5 intercollegiate sports for men and 8 for women, and 10 intramural sports for men and 10 for women. Facilities include an athletic complex with a basketball arena, an Olympic-size pool, 8 handball/racquetball courts, a wrestling room, weight-training rooms, a dance studio, a gymnastics room, a 4500-seat football/soccer stadium, a baseball diamond, 6 outdoor tennis courts, 4 outdoor basketball courts, a track-and-field facility with a walking/jogging lane, and a practice football field.

Disabled Students: All of the campus is accessible. Facilities include wheelchair ramps, elevators, special parking, specially equipped restrooms, lowered drinking fountains, lowered telephones, and special housing.

Services: Counseling and information services are available, as is tutoring in most subjects. There is a reader service for the blind, and remedial math, reading, and writing.

Campus Safety and Security: Measures include 24-hour foot and vehicle patrol, emergency notification system, self-defense education, and security escort services. There are shuttle buses, emergency telephones, lighted pathways/sidewalks, and the Bowie State University Electronic Emergency System (BEES), designed as a volunteer service that communicates campus disruptions (in real time) to multiple electronic devices provided by the student. Such events (like inclement weather) are also communicated through land-based devices and the university switchboard.

Programs of Study: BSU confers B.A. and B.S. degrees. Master's and doctoral degrees are also awarded. Bachelor's degrees are awarded in BIOLOGICAL SCIENCE (biology/biological science), BUSINESS (business administration and management), COMMUNICATIONS AND THE ARTS (English and fine arts), COMPUTER AND PHYSICAL SCIENCE (computer science and mathematics), EDUCATION (early childhood education, elementary education, and science education), ENGINEERING AND ENVIRONMENTAL DESIGN (computer technology), HEALTH PROFESSIONS (nursing), SOCIAL SCIENCE (criminal justice, history, interdisciplinary studies, psychology, social work, and sociology). Business administration, computer science, and elementary education are the largest.

Required: A total of 120 credit hours with a minimum GPA of 2.0 is required for graduation. The number of hours that must be taken in a student's major varies. General education requirements include 12 credits in social science, 9 in arts and humanities, 7 to 8 in sciences, 6 in English composition, and 3 each in math, computer literacy, health and wellness, and freshman seminar.

Special: BSU offers cooperative programs, internships in communications and practice teaching, work-study programs, B.A.-B.S. degrees, dual majors, credit for life experience, and a 3-2 engineering degree with Morgan State University, Howard University, University of Maryland Baltimore County, the George Washington University, and University of Maryland College Park. Dual-degree programs in engineering and mathematics are available. Cross-registration is offered with other members of the University System of Maryland. There are 16 national honor societies and a freshman honors program.

Faculty/Classroom: 54% of faculty are male; 46% are female. No introductory courses are taught by graduate students. The average class size in an introductory lecture is 50; in a laboratory, 7; and in a regular course, 19.

Requirements: The SAT or ACT is required. The ACT Optional Writing test is also required. In addition, applicants should be graduates of an accredited secondary school. The GED is accepted. Students should have completed 15 academic units, including 4 in English, 3 each of math, sciences, and social science/history, and 2 of a foreign language or advanced technology. A GPA of 2.0 is required. AP and CLEP credits are accepted. Important factors in the admissions decision are advanced placement or honors courses, extracurricular activities record, and leadership record.

Procedure: Freshmen are admitted fall and spring. Entrance exams should be taken before the end of January. There are deferred admissions and rolling admissions plans. Applications should be filed by April 1 for fall entry and November 1 for spring entry, along with a $40 fee. Applications are accepted on-line.

Transfer: 434 transfer students enrolled in a recent year. Applicants must have a minimum GPA of 2.0. The SAT is required if fewer than 24 credit hours are being transferred. 30 of 120 credits required for the bachelor's degree must be completed at BSU.

Visiting: There are regularly scheduled orientations for prospective students. There are guides for informal visits. To schedule a visit, contact Undergraduate Admissions at ugradadmissions@bowiestate.edu.

Financial Aid: The FAFSA and the college's own financial statement are required. Check with the school for current application deadlines.

International Students: There were 180 international students enrolled in a recent year. The school actively recruits these students. They must take the TOEFL with a minimum score of 500 on the paper-based TOEFL (PBT). They must also take the SAT or ACT and the college's own entrance exam.

Computers: All students may access the system 24 hours a day. There are no time limits. The fee is $75.

Graduates: In a recent year, 621 bachelor's degrees were awarded. The most popular majors were business administration (18%), communication media (13%), and sociology (12%). In an average class, 38% graduate in 6 years or less. 255 companies recruited on campus in a recent year.

Admissions Contact: Director of Admissions.
E-mail: *ugradadmissions@bowiestate.edu* Web: *www.bowiestate.edu*

CAPITOL COLLEGE · D-3
Laurel, MD 20708

(301) 369-2800
(800) 950-1992; (301) 953-1442

Full-time: 100 men, 40 women	**Faculty:** n/av
Part-time: 130 men, 30 women	**Ph.D.s:** n/av
Graduate: 340 men, 130 women	**Student/Faculty:** n/av
Year: semesters, summer session	**Tuition:** $19,890
Application Deadline: open	**Room & Board:** $4000
Freshman Class: n/av	
SAT or ACT: required	**COMPETITIVE**

Capitol College was founded in 1927 as the Capitol Radio Engineering Institute, a correspondence school. Today it is a private college offering undergraduate programs in engineering and computer technology, as well as graduate programs in management and electronic commerce. Some of the figures in the above capsule and in this profile are approximate. There is 1 graduate school. In addition to regional accreditation, Capitol has baccalaureate program accreditation with ABET. The library contains 10,000 volumes and subscribes to 100 periodicals including electronic. Computerized library services include interlibrary loans and database searching. Special learning facilities include a learning resource center and state-of-the-art labs. The 52-acre campus is in a rural area 19 miles north of Washington, D.C. Including any residence halls, there are 9 buildings.

Student Life: 72% of undergraduates are from Maryland. Others are from 16 states and 21 foreign countries. 43% are white; 39% African American. The average age of freshmen is 23; all undergraduates, 28. 41% do not continue beyond their first year.

Housing: 100 students can be accommodated in college housing, which includes coed on-campus apartments. On-campus housing is available on a first-come, first-served basis. Priority is given to out-of-town students. 87% of students commute. All students may keep cars.

Activities: There are no fraternities or sororities. There are 17 groups on campus, including chess, computers, literary magazine, newspaper, professional, and student government. Popular campus events include Octoberfest and Spring Bash.

Sports: Facilities include an off-campus gym, a basketball court, a student center, and an athletic field.

Disabled Students: All of the campus is accessible. Facilities include wheelchair ramps, elevators, special parking, specially equipped restrooms, and lowered drinking fountains.

Services: Counseling and information services are available, as is tutoring in most subjects, including math, electronics, English, and developmental English.

Campus Safety and Security: There are lighted pathways/sidewalks.

Programs of Study: Capitol confers B.S. degrees. Associate and master's degrees are also awarded. Bachelor's degrees are awarded in COMMUNICATIONS AND THE ARTS (telecommunications), COMPUTER AND PHYSICAL SCIENCE (optics), ENGINEERING AND ENVIRONMENTAL DESIGN (computer engineering, electrical/electronics engineering, and engineering technology). Electrical/electronics engineering is the strongest academically and has the largest enrollment.

Required: A minimum GPA of 2.0 and 130 to 137 credit hours are required for graduation. Additional curriculum requirements vary with the major.

Special: Internships and work-study programs are offered through the school's cooperative education program. There are 2 national honor societies.

Faculty/Classroom: All teach undergraduates. No introductory courses are taught by graduate students. The average class size in an introductory lecture is 20; in a regular course, 22.

Requirements: The SAT or ACT is required. Applicants should be graduates of an accredited secondary school. The GED is accepted. 20 academic credits or 20 Carnegie units are required. Secondary school courses must include 4 units of English, 3 of math, and 2 each of science and social studies. An essay and an interview are recommended. A GPA of 2.8 is required. AP and CLEP credits are accepted. Important factors in the admissions decision are advanced placement or honors courses, recommendations by school officials, and extracurricular activities record.

Procedure: Freshmen are admitted to all sessions. Entrance exams should be taken by March 1. There is a rolling admissions plan. Application deadlines are open. Application fee is $25. Applications are accepted on-line.

Transfer: Transfer students must have earned 15 college credits and a minimum GPA of 2.0. 40 of 130 credits required for the bachelor's degree must be completed at Capitol.

Visiting: There are regularly scheduled orientations for prospective students. There are guides for informal visits, and visitors may sit in on classes and stay overnight. To schedule a visit, contact the Admissions Office.

Financial Aid: Capitol is a member of CSS. The CSS/Profile is required. Check with the school for current application deadlines.

International Students: The school actively recruits these students. They must take the TOEFL.

Computers: All students may access the system. There are no time limits and no fees.

Admissions Contact: Director of Admissions.
E-mail: *admissions@capitol-college.edu* Web: *www.capitol-college.edu*

COLLEGE OF NOTRE DAME OF MARYLAND · D-2
Baltimore, MD 21210

(410) 532-5330
(800) 435-0200; (410) 532-6287

Full-time: 650 women	**Faculty:** IIB, av$
Part-time: 100 men, 900 women	**Ph.D.s:** n/av
Graduate: 300 men, 1200 women	**Student/Faculty:** n/av
Year: 4-1-4, summer session	**Tuition:** $27,275
Application Deadline: open	**Room & Board:** $9100
Freshman Class: n/av	
SAT or ACT: required	**COMPETITIVE**

The College of Notre Dame of Maryland, founded in 1873, is a private liberal arts institution primarily for women and affiliated with the Catholic Church. Some figures in the above capsule and in this profile are approximate. There is 1 graduate school. In addition to regional accreditation, Notre Dame has baccalaureate program accreditation with NLN. The library contains 290,000 volumes, 378,138 microform items, and 24,000 audio/video tapes/CDs/DVDs, and subscribes to 2000 periodicals including electronic. Computerized library services include database searching. Special learning facilities include a learning resource center, art gallery, planetarium, radio station, TV station, graphic arts studio, roof-top greenhouse, and cultural center. The 58-acre campus is in a suburban area 10 miles north of Baltimore. Including any residence halls, there are 11 buildings.

Student Life: 70% of undergraduates are from Maryland. Others are from 21 states.

Housing: 450 students can be accommodated in college housing, which includes single-sex dorms. On-campus housing is guaranteed for all 4 years. 65% of students live on campus; of those, 60% remain on campus on weekends. Alcohol is not permitted. All students may keep cars.

Activities: There are no fraternities or sororities. There are 24 groups on campus, including art, choir, dance, drama, ethnic, honors, international, literary magazine, newspaper, political, professional, radio and

TV, religious, social, social service, student government, and yearbook. Popular campus events include Honors Convocation, Antostal Day, and Multicultural Awareness Week.

Sports: Facilities include a sports/activities complex that houses racquetball courts, a dance studio, a fitness center, an indoor walking track, a game room, an activities resource center, and a basketball court.

Disabled Students: 98% of the campus is accessible. Facilities include wheelchair ramps, elevators, special parking, specially equipped restrooms, and lowered drinking fountains.

Services: Counseling and information services are available, as is tutoring in most subjects.

Campus Safety and Security: Measures include 24-hour foot and vehicle patrol, self-defense education, and security escort services. There are lighted pathways/sidewalks.

Programs of Study: Notre Dame confers B.A. and B.S. degrees. Master's degrees are also awarded. Bachelor's degrees are awarded in BIOLOGICAL SCIENCE (biology/biological science), BUSINESS (accounting, banking and finance, business administration and management, international business management, and marketing/retailing/merchandising), COMMUNICATIONS AND THE ARTS (art history and appreciation, classics, communications, English, graphic design, modern language, music, photography, and studio art), COMPUTER AND PHYSICAL SCIENCE (chemistry, computer science, information sciences and systems, mathematics, and physics), EDUCATION (art education, early childhood education, elementary education, foreign languages education, music education, science education, secondary education, and special education), ENGINEERING AND ENVIRONMENTAL DESIGN (preengineering), HEALTH PROFESSIONS (nursing, predentistry, premedicine, and prepharmacy), SOCIAL SCIENCE (economics, history, interdisciplinary studies, international relations, liberal arts/general studies, political science/government, prelaw, psychology, and religion). Business, education, and communication arts are the strongest academically.

Required: To graduate, students must complete a total of 128 credit hours with a minimum GPA of 2.0 (2.5 in many majors). All students must fulfill the distribution requirements in the general education core, the major, and electives, and must demonstrate proficiency in writing, public speaking, computer literacy, and library research. In most majors, a minimum of 42 hours is required. All students must take a speech course and 2 courses in phys ed, and some majors require senior practicums.

Special: The college offers cross-registration with Johns Hopkins, Towson State, and Morgan State Universities; Coppin State, Goucher, and Loyola Colleges; and the Maryland Institute College of Art. Study abroad, internships, dual bachelor's degrees in nursing and engineering, 3-2 engineering degrees with Johns Hopkins University and the University of Maryland, and pass/fail options are available. Notre Dame's Weekend College offers bachelor's degree programs for employed adults. There are 8 national honor societies, a freshman honors program, and 4 departmental honors programs.

Faculty/Classroom: 30% of faculty are male; 70% are female. All teach undergraduates. No introductory courses are taught by graduate students. The average class size in an introductory lecture is 30; in a laboratory, 20; and in a regular course, 20.

Requirements: The SAT or ACT is required. In addition, applicants should be graduates of an accredited secondary school. 18 academic credits are required, including 4 units of English, 3 each of math and a foreign language, and 2 each of history and science, plus 4 electives. An essay is required, and an interview is recommended. A GPA of 2.5 is required. AP credits are accepted. Important factors in the admissions decision are recommendations by school officials, advanced placement or honors courses, and leadership record.

Procedure: Freshmen are admitted fall and spring. Entrance exams should be taken no later than January of the senior year. There are early decision, early admissions, deferred admissions, and rolling admissions plans. Application deadlines are open. Notification is sent on a rolling basis. Applications are accepted on-line.

Transfer: Notre Dame requires a minimum GPA of 2.5 for transfer students but recommends a GPA of 3.0. Students must also submit a letter of recommendation and an essay. 60 of 128 credits required for the bachelor's degree must be completed at Notre Dame.

Visiting: There are regularly scheduled orientations for prospective students, consisting of programs in June and January, each of which includes a stay in the dorm, registration, and advisement. There are guides for informal visits, and visitors may sit in on classes. To schedule a visit, contact the Office of Admissions.

Financial Aid: Notre Dame is a member of CSS. The CSS/Profile and FAFSA are required. Check with the school for current application deadlines.

International Students: The school actively recruits these students. They must take the TOEFL.

Computers: All students may access the system 7 days a week. There are no time limits and no fees.

Admissions Contact: Director of Admissions.
E-mail: admiss@ndm.edu Web: www.ndm.edu

COLUMBIA UNION COLLEGE D-3
Takoma Park, MD 20912

(301) 891-4080
(800) 835-4212; (301) 891-4230

Full-time: 270 men, 430 women	**Faculty:** 50
Part-time: 110 men, 190 women	**Ph.D.s:** 48%
Graduate: 30 men, 50 women	**Student/Faculty:** 14 to 1
Year: semesters, summer session	**Tuition:** $19,480
Application Deadline: see profile	**Room & Board:** $7200
Freshman Class: n/av	
SAT or ACT: required	**COMPETITIVE+**

Washington Adventist University, formerly Columbia Union College and founded in 1904, is a Christ-centered institution offering degree programs in liberal arts, sciences, and selected professional fields. Some figures in the above capsule and in this profile are approximate. There is 1 graduate school. In addition to regional accreditation, WAU has baccalaureate program accreditation with CAHEA and NLN. The library contains 142,903 volumes and 7500 audio/video tapes/CDs/DVDs, and subscribes to 9000 periodicals including electronic. Computerized library services include interlibrary loans, database searching, and Internet access. Special learning facilities include a learning resource center and radio station. The 19-acre campus is in a suburban area 7 miles north of Washington, D.C. Including any residence halls, there are 17 buildings.

Student Life: 61% of undergraduates are from Maryland. Others are from 37 states, 22 foreign countries, and Canada. 50% are African American; 14% white. The average age of freshmen is 19; all undergraduates, 27.

Housing: 440 students can be accommodated in college housing, which includes single-sex dorms and married student housing. On-campus housing is guaranteed for all 4 years. 60% of students live on campus; of those, 70% remain on campus on weekends. Alcohol is not permitted. All students may keep cars.

Activities: There are no fraternities or sororities. There are 22 groups on campus, including band, choir, chorale, chorus, debate, drill team, ethnic, fitness, honors, international, musical theater, newspaper, orchestra, political, radio and TV, religious, running, social, social service, student government, volleyball, and yearbook. Popular campus events include Student Missions Week, Spirit Week, and Service Day.

Sports: There are 5 intercollegiate sports for men and 5 for women, and 5 intramural sports for men and 4 for women. Facilities include a gym, racquetball and tennis courts, a sports field, a weight room, and a student lounge with Ping-Pong and pool/billiards tables and table games.

Disabled Students: 30% of the campus is accessible. Facilities include wheelchair ramps, elevators, special parking, specially equipped restrooms, and lowered telephones.

Services: Counseling and information services are available, as is tutoring in some subjects, including all English, math, accounting, chemistry, biology, psychology, Spanish, and history courses, and other courses as needed. There is a reader service for the blind, and remedial math and writing.

Campus Safety and Security: Measures include 24-hour foot and vehicle patrol, emergency notification system, and security escort services. There are lighted pathways/sidewalks.

Programs of Study: WAU confers B.A., B.S., and B.M. degrees. Associate and master's degrees are also awarded. Bachelor's degrees are awarded in BIOLOGICAL SCIENCE (biochemistry and biology/biological science), BUSINESS (accounting, business administration and management, and organizational leadership and management), COMMUNICATIONS AND THE ARTS (communications, English, journalism, music, and music performance), COMPUTER AND PHYSICAL SCIENCE (chemistry, computer science, information sciences and systems, and mathematics), EDUCATION (elementary education, English education, mathematics education, music education, and physical education), HEALTH PROFESSIONS (exercise science, health care administration, nursing, predentistry, and respiratory therapy), SOCIAL SCIENCE (counseling/psychology, history, liberal arts/general studies, philosophy and religion, political science/government, prelaw, psychology, religion, and theological studies). Nursing, health care, administration, and business administration are the largest.

Required: To graduate, students must earn 120 to 128 credit hours, including 36 upper division, with a minimum GPA of 2.0 overall and 2.5 in the major. Students must take 12 hours of religion, 9 of social sciences, 8 of physical sciences, natural sciences, and math, 6 of humanities and practical and applied arts, and 3 of phys ed and health. Courses in English, communication, and computer science are also required.

Special: WAU offers co-op programs in business, communication, computer science, English, biochemistry, and math, internships in counseling psychology, history and political science, and through a Washington D.C. Experience, work-study programs, a general studies degree, credit for life experience, nondegree study, and pass/fail options. Dual majors are available in engineering/chemistry and math, and a 3-2 engineering degree is offered with the University of Maryland. The School of Graduate and Professional Studies provides evening degree completion and an external (correspondence) degree. There are 6 national honor societies and a freshman honors program.

Faculty/Classroom: 56% of faculty are male; 44% are female. All teach undergraduates, and 10% both teach and do research. No introductory courses are taught by graduate students.

Admissions: 49% of a recent year's applicants were accepted.

Requirements: The SAT or ACT is required. In addition, applicants must be graduates of an accredited secondary school. The GED is accepted. 21 Carnegie units are required, including 4 years of high school English and 2 years each of history, math, and lab science. An essay is recommended. A GPA of 2.5 is required. Applicants with a GPA of 2.0 to 2.5 can be enrolled in an enrichment program, given they have satisfactory scores on the ACT or SAT. Applicants with a GPA of 3.25 or higher can be enrolled without standardized test scores. AP and CLEP credits are accepted. Important factors in the admissions decision are advanced placement or honors courses, leadership record, and recommendations by school officials.

Procedure: Freshmen are admitted to all sessions. Entrance exams should be taken in the fall semester of the senior year.. There are early admissions, deferred admissions, and rolling admissions plans. Check with the school for current application deadlines and fee. Applications are accepted on-line.

Transfer: 69 transfer students enrolled in a recent year. Transfer students must have at least 12 hours of college credit and a minimum GPA of 2.0. 30 of 120 to 128 credits required for the bachelor's degree must be completed at WAU.

Visiting: There are regularly scheduled orientations for prospective students. There are guides for informal visits, and visitors may sit in on classes and stay overnight. To schedule a visit, contact the Office of Enrollment Services.

Financial Aid: In a recent year, about 95% of all full-time freshmen and 90% of continuing full-time students received some form of financial aid. The FAFSA is required. Check with the school for current application deadlines.

International Students: There were 36 international students enrolled in a recent year. They must take the TOEFL or MELAB and also take the SAT or ACT.

Computers: Wireless access is available. All students may access the system. There are no time limits. The fee is $575. It is strongly recommended that all students have a personal computer.

Graduates: In a recent year, 255 bachelor's degrees were awarded.

Admissions Contact: Director of Admissions.
E-mail: *enroll@wau.edu* Web: *www.wau.edu*

COPPIN STATE UNIVERSITY
Coppin State College
D-2

Baltimore, MD 21216

(410) 951-3600
(800) 635-3674; (410) 523-7351

Full-time: 555 men, 1935 women	**Faculty:** 143; IIA, -$
Part-time: 140 men, 620 women	**Ph.D.s:** 55%
Graduate: 175 men, 520 women	**Student/Faculty:** 17 to 1
Year: semesters, summer session	**Tuition:** $5441 ($14,136)
Application Deadline: June 15	**Room & Board:** $7722
Freshman Class: 5593 applied, 1988 accepted, 632 enrolled	
SAT or ACT: required	**COMPETITIVE**

Coppin State University, founded in 1900 and part of the University System of Maryland, offers undergraduate programs in liberal arts, teacher education, and nursing. Enrollment figures in the above capsule are approximate. There are 5 undergraduate schools and 1 graduate school. In addition to regional accreditation, Coppin has baccalaureate program accreditation with NCATE and NLN. The library contains 200,000 volumes and 233,000 microform items, and subscribes to 715 periodicals including electronic. Computerized library services include interlibrary loans, database searching, and Internet access. Special learning facilities include a learning resource center and art gallery. The 65-acre campus is in an urban area in Baltimore. Including any residence halls, there are 13 buildings.

Student Life: 90% of undergraduates are from Maryland. Others are from 10 states, 5 foreign countries, and Canada. 90% are from public schools. 86% are African American. The average age of freshmen is 19; all undergraduates, 23.

Housing: 600 students can be accommodated in college housing, which includes coed dorms. The housing office maintains lists of community housing available. On-campus housing is available on a first-come, first-served basis. 79% of students commute. Alcohol is not permitted. Upperclassmen may keep cars.

Activities: 20% of men belong to 5 national fraternities; 27% of women belong to 4 national sororities. There are 35 groups on campus, including art, cheerleading, choir, chorus, computers, dance, drama, ethnic, film, honors, international, marching band, musical theater, newspaper, political, professional, religious, social, social service, and student government. Popular campus events include the Lyceum Series, the Honors Program, and Black History Month.

Sports: There are 7 intercollegiate sports for men and 7 for women, and 5 intramural sports for men and 5 for women. Facilities include a 4000-seat gym, an Olympic-sized indoor swimming pool, handball and racquetball courts, a soccer field, a dance studio, a weight room, an outdoor track, a softball field, and tennis courts.

Disabled Students: 95% of the campus is accessible. Facilities include wheelchair ramps, elevators, special parking, specially equipped restrooms, lowered drinking fountains, lowered telephones, and individual attention for students requiring specialized materials, equipment, or instructional-style accommodation.

Services: Counseling and information services are available, as is tutoring in every subject. There is remedial math, reading, and writing.

Campus Safety and Security: Measures include 24-hour foot and vehicle patrol, emergency notification system, and security escort services. There are shuttle buses, emergency telephones, and lighted pathways/sidewalks.

Programs of Study: Coppin confers B.A., B.S., and B.S.N. degrees. Master's degrees are also awarded. Bachelor's degrees are awarded in BIOLOGICAL SCIENCE (biology/biological science), BUSINESS (business administration and management, management science, and sports management), COMMUNICATIONS AND THE ARTS (English), COMPUTER AND PHYSICAL SCIENCE (chemistry, computer science, and mathematics), EDUCATION (elementary education and special education), HEALTH PROFESSIONS (health, nursing, and rehabilitation therapy), SOCIAL SCIENCE (criminal justice, history, interdisciplinary studies, international studies, liberal arts/general studies, political science/government, psychology, social science, social work, and urban studies). Management science, education, and nursing are the strongest academically and the largest.

Required: To graduate, all students must have a minimum 2.0 GPA and complete a minimum of 120 credit hours (varies by program of study), with 36 to 40 hours in the major. Students must complete about 50 hours of liberal arts courses in English, math, speech, history, health, physical education, natural and social sciences, and philosophy. All seniors must take a standardized exit exam relevant to their major.

Special: Internships are available in management science, as are B.A.-B.S. degrees in all majors. Student-designed majors are possible with approval. There are 3 national honor societies, including Phi Beta Kappa, and a freshman honors program.

Faculty/Classroom: 55% of faculty are male; 45% are female. No introductory courses are taught by graduate students. The average class size in a regular course is 25.

Admissions: 36% of the 2009-2010 applicants were accepted.

Requirements: The SAT or ACT is required. In addition, applicants must be graduates of an accredited secondary school with a minimum GPA of 2.0 or have a GED certificate. Students must have completed 4 courses in English, 2 courses each in history, math, science, and social studies, and 1 course in foreign language. Up to 15% of a freshman class may be admitted conditionally without these requirements, and those students who graduated high school more than 5 years ago will be reviewed individually. A GPA of 2.5 is required. AP and CLEP credits are accepted. Important factors in the admissions decision are advanced placement or honors courses, extracurricular activities record, and evidence of special talent.

Procedure: Freshmen are admitted to all sessions. There is a rolling admissions plan. Applications should be filed by June 15 for fall entry; December 15 for spring entry. The fall 2009 application fee was $35. Applications are accepted on-line.

Transfer: Transfer students must have a minimum 2.0 GPA and be in good academic standing at their former institutions. Applicants with fewer than 25 credits must meet freshman requirements. 30 of 120 credits required for the bachelor's degree must be completed at Coppin.

Visiting: There are regularly scheduled orientations for prospective students, consisting of open houses. There are guides for informal visits and visitors may sit in on classes, with prior notice. To schedule a visit, contact Admissions.

Financial Aid: Coppin is a member of CSS. The FAFSA and the college's own financial statement are required. The priority date for freshman financial aid applications for fall entry is March 1.

International Students: They must take the TOEFL with a minimum score of 500 on the paper-based TOEFL (PBT). They must also take the SAT or ACT.

Computers: Wireless access is available. More than 700 workstations are available for student use throughout the campus. All students may access the system. There are no time limits and no fees.

Graduates: In a recent year, 484 bachelor's degrees were awarded. The most popular majors were nursing (16%), criminal justice (12%), and applied psychology (10%).

Admissions Contact: Michelle Gross, Director of Admissions. E-Mail: *admissions@coppin.edu* Web: *www.coppin.edu/*

FROSTBURG STATE UNIVERSITY — B-1

Frostburg, MD 21532 (301) 687-4201; (301) 687-7074

Full-time: 2100 men, 2000 women	**Faculty:** 233; IIA, av$
Part-time: 120 men, 120 women	**Ph.D.s:** 85%
Graduate: 230 men, 430 women	**Student/Faculty:** n/av
Year: semesters, summer session	**Tuition:** $6684 ($16,880)
Application Deadline: open	**Room & Board:** $7034
Freshman Class: n/av	
SAT or ACT: required	**COMPETITIVE**

Frostburg State University, founded in 1898, is a part of the University System of Maryland. The university offers programs through the colleges of liberal arts and sciences, business, and education. Some figures in the above capsule and in this profile are approximate. There are 3 undergraduate schools and 3 graduate schools. In addition to regional accreditation, FSU has baccalaureate program accreditation with AACSB, CSWE, NCATE, and NRPA. The library contains 356,200 volumes, 300,203 microform items, and 71,985 audio/video tapes/CDs/DVDs, and subscribes to 3390 periodicals including electronic. Computerized library services include interlibrary loans, database searching, Internet access, and laptop Internet portals. Special learning facilities include a learning resource center, art gallery, planetarium, radio station, TV station, environmental lab, distance education labs, and exploratorium. The 260-acre campus is in a small town about 150 miles west of Baltimore and northwest of Washington, D.C. Including any residence halls, there are 32 buildings.

Student Life: 91% of undergraduates are from Maryland. Others are from 27 states, 20 foreign countries, and Canada. 76% are white; 17% African American. The average age of freshmen is 18; all undergraduates, 21. 32% do not continue beyond their first year; 51% remain to graduate.

Housing: 1700 students can be accommodated in college housing, which includes single-sex and coed dorms. In addition, there are honors houses, special-interest houses, and international houses. On-campus housing is guaranteed for all 4 years. 65% of students commute. All students may keep cars.

Activities: 10% of men belong to 5 national fraternities; 10% of women belong to 5 national sororities. There are 150 groups on campus, including art, band, cheerleading, choir, chorale, chorus, communications, computers, dance, drama, drill team, ethnic, gay, honors, international, jazz band, literary magazine, marching band, musical theater, newspaper, orchestra, pep band, photography, political, professional, radio and TV, religious, social, social service, student government, and symphony. Popular campus events include Parents Weekend, cultural events series, and Welcome Week.

Sports: There are 9 intercollegiate sports for men and 10 for women, and 5 intramural sports for men and 4 for women. Facilities include a game room, a 3600-seat main arena, a practice gym, 5 athletic fields, 2 intramural fields, an indoor swimming pool, a dance studio, a wellness room, 6 lighted tennis courts, weight rooms, a dance lab, a football stadium, an 8-lane, 400-meter track, training rooms, team rooms, and baseball, racquetball, squash, and archery rooms.

Disabled Students: All of the campus is accessible. Facilities include wheelchair ramps, elevators, special parking, specially equipped restrooms, special class scheduling, lowered drinking fountains, lowered telephones, and special housing.

Services: Counseling and information services are available, as is tutoring in every subject. There is a reader service for the blind, and remedial math, reading, and writing.

Campus Safety and Security: Measures include 24-hour foot and vehicle patrol, emergency notification system, self-defense education, and security escort services. There are shuttle buses, emergency telephones, lighted pathways/sidewalks, and a bicycle patrol.

Programs of Study: FSU confers B.A., B.S., B.F.A., B.T.P., and B.U.R. degrees. Master's degrees are also awarded. Bachelor's degrees are awarded in AGRICULTURE (fish and game management and wildlife management), BIOLOGICAL SCIENCE (biology/biological science), BUSINESS (accounting, business administration and management, and recreation and leisure services), COMMUNICATIONS AND THE ARTS (communications, design, dramatic arts, English, languages, and music), COMPUTER AND PHYSICAL SCIENCE (chemistry, computer science, mathematics, physics, and science), EDUCATION (early childhood education, elementary education, middle school education, and physical education), ENGINEERING AND ENVIRONMENTAL DESIGN (environmental science), SOCIAL SCIENCE (criminal justice, economics, ethnic studies, geography, history, international studies, law enforcement and corrections, liberal arts/general studies, philosophy, political science/government, psychology, social science, social work, and sociology). Business, education, and the natural sciences are the strongest academically. Education, business, and computer science are the largest.

Required: A minimum GPA of 2.0 and 120 credit hours are required to graduate. All students must complete 7 to 14 credits in natural science, 6 to 9 credits in humanities and social sciences, and 3 to 6 credits in creative and performing arts. Courses in computer science, speech and composition, personalized health fitness, and math are also required.

Special: FSU offers co-op programs in applied physics, electrical engineering, and mechanical engineering with the University of Maryland, internships through individual departments, study abroad in Ireland, England, Germany, Denmark, and Ecuador through the International Student Exchange Program, work-study and accelerated degree programs, B.A.-B.S. degrees in all majors, and a dual major in engineering. The 3-2 engineering degree is coordinated with the University of Maryland at College Park. Cross-registration, nondegree study, and pass/fail options are also available. Distance learning and an advanced degree program are available. There are 18 national honor societies, a freshman honors program, and 15 departmental honors programs.

Faculty/Classroom: 58% of faculty are male; 42% are female. All teach undergraduates. No introductory courses are taught by graduate students. The average class size in an introductory lecture is 25; in a laboratory, 15; and in a regular course, 20.

Admissions: 63% of a recent year's applicants were accepted. 25% of a recent year's freshmen were in the top fifth of their class; 56% were in the top two fifths.

Requirements: The SAT or ACT is required. In addition, applicants must be graduates of an accredited secondary school or have the GED. Secondary preparation should include 4 units of English, 3 each of math and social studies, and 2 of a foreign language and science. An interview is recommended. A GPA of 2.0 is required. AP and CLEP credits are accepted. Important factors in the admissions decision are recommendations by school officials, extracurricular activities record, and advanced placement or honors courses.

Procedure: Freshmen are admitted to all sessions. Entrance exams should be taken in the junior or senior year. There are early decision and rolling admissions plans. Application deadlines are open. Application fee is $30. Applications are accepted on-line.

Transfer: 356 transfer students enrolled in a recent year. Transfer students with 12 to 23 credits must have a minimum GPA of 2.5 and provide an official high school transcript and SAT scores. Students with 24 or more credits must have a minimum GPA of 2.0. 30 of 120 credits required for the bachelor's degree must be completed at FSU.

Visiting: There are regularly scheduled orientations for prospective students, including tours Monday through Friday at 11 A.M. and noon. There are guides for informal visits, and visitors may sit in on classes. To schedule a visit, contact the Office of Admissions.

Financial Aid: The FAFSA and the college's own financial statement are required. Check with the school for current application deadlines.

International Students: There were 20 international students enrolled in a recent year. The school actively recruits these students. They must take the TOEFL with a minimum score of 550 on the paper-based TOEFL (PBT) or 79 on the Internet-based version (iBT). They must also take the SAT or ACT, scoring 850 on the SAT (Critical Reading and Math).

Computers: Wireless access is available. All students may access the system 8 A.M. to midnight. There are no time limits and no fees. It is strongly recommended that all students have a personal computer.

Graduates: In a recent year, 796 bachelor's degrees were awarded. The most popular majors were business administration (14%), education (10%), and psychology (9%). In an average class, 25% graduate in 4 years or less, 48% graduate in 5 years or less, and 51% graduate in 6 years or less. 61 companies recruited on campus in a recent year.

Admissions Contact: Director of Admissions.
E-mail: *fsuadmissions@frostburg.edu* Web: *www.frostburg.edu*

GOUCHER COLLEGE — D-2

Baltimore, MD 21204 (410) 337-6100
(800) 468-2437; (410) 337-6354

Full-time: 455 men, 991 women	**Faculty:** 129; IIB, av$
Part-time: 15 men, 20 women	**Ph.D.s:** n/av
Graduate: 164 men, 634 women	**Student/Faculty:** 10 to 1
Year: semesters	**Tuition:** $33,785
Application Deadline: February 1	**Room & Board:** $10,006
Freshman Class: 3651 applied, 2664 accepted, 400 enrolled	
SAT CR/M/W: 620/570/600	**ACT:** 26 **VERY COMPETITIVE+**

Goucher College, founded in 1885, is an independent, coeducational institution offering programs based on the interdisciplinary traditions of the liberal arts with an international perspective. The college offers 30 majors, many minors, and emphasizes international and intercultural awareness throughout the curriculum. There is 1 one graduate school. In addition to regional accreditation, Goucher has baccalaureate program accreditation with NCATE. The library contains 280,000 volumes, 22,268 microform items, and 45,660 audio/video tapes/CDs/DVDs, and subscribes to 25,200 periodicals including electronic. Computerized library services include interlibrary loans, database searching, and Internet access. Special learning facilities include a learning resource center, art gallery, radio station, TV station, TV studio, theater, technology/learning center, international technology and media center, and centers for writing, math, and politics. The 287-acre campus is in a suburban area 8 miles north of Baltimore. Including any residence halls, there are 20 buildings.

Student Life: 72% of undergraduates are from out of state, mostly the Middle Atlantic. Students are from 43 states, 24 foreign countries, and Canada. 64% are from public schools. 66% are white. The average age of freshmen is 18; all undergraduates, 20. 25% do not continue beyond their first year; 75% remain to graduate.

Housing: 1217 students can be accommodated in college housing, which includes single-sex and coed dorms, on-campus apartments, and off-campus apartments. In addition, there are language houses, special-interest houses, and quiet, medical needs, and substance-free housing. 82% of students live on campus; of those, 77% remain on campus on weekends. All students may keep cars.

Activities: There are no fraternities or sororities. There are 60 groups on campus, including art, chorale, chorus, computers, dance, drama, environmental, ethnic, film, gay, honors, international, jazz band, literary magazine, martial arts, newspaper, orchestra, political, professional, radio and TV, religious, social, social service, student government, and symphony. Popular campus events include Get into Goucher Day, Spring Gala, and Blind Date Ball.

Sports: There are 8 intercollegiate sports for men and 11 for women, and 6 intramural sports for men and 6 for women. Facilities include 2 gyms, an indoor swimming pool, a weight room, a training room, a cardio fitness center, racquetball, squash, and tennis courts, indoor outdoor equestrian facilities, an outdoor track, an outdoor volleyball court, an outdoor basketball court, and a disc golf course.

Disabled Students: 90% of the campus is accessible. Facilities include wheelchair ramps, elevators, special parking, specially equipped rest rooms, special class scheduling, special housing, and an auditorium loop for the hearing impaired.

Services: Counseling and information services are available, as is tutoring in most subjects. There is a reader service for the blind. Many academic support options are available through the college's Academic Center for Excellence (ACE).

Campus Safety and Security: Measures include 24-hour foot and vehicle patrol, emergency notification system, self-defense education, and security escort services. There are shuttle buses, emergency telephones, lighted pathways/sidewalks, controlled access to dorms/residences, and an officer-manned gatehouse during evening and overnight hours.

Programs of Study: Goucher confers B.A. degrees. Master's degrees are also awarded. Bachelor's degrees are awarded in BIOLOGICAL SCIENCE (biology/biological science), BUSINESS (international business management), COMMUNICATIONS AND THE ARTS (art, communications, dance, English, French, music, Russian, Spanish, and theater management), COMPUTER AND PHYSICAL SCIENCE (chemistry, computer science, mathematics, and physics), EDUCATION (elementary education and special education), SOCIAL SCIENCE (American studies, anthropology, economics, history, interdisciplinary studies, international relations, peace studies, philosophy, political science/government, psychology, religion, sociology, and women's studies). Biology, chemistry, and history are the strongest academically. Communication, psychology, and English are the largest.

Required: To graduate, all students must complete 120 hours, with a minimum GPA of 2.0. The number of hours in the major varies, with a minimum of 3.0. Requirements include 1 lab-related course in the natural sciences, 1 course each in the humanities, social sciences, math, and the arts, and the first-year colloquium course for freshmen. Students are also required to demonstrate proficiency in computers, writing, and a foreign language. Other requirements include a 4-class distribution requirement in phys ed, a transitions course, and at least 1 study abroad experience, for which students receive a voucher of $1200 or more.

Special: Goucher offers internships, study abroad in 27 countries, and other off-campus experiences. The college also collaborates with many of the 22 other colleges in the Baltimore Collegetown Network (www.colltown.org). Students may cross-register with Johns Hopkins, Towson University, College of Notre Dame, Peabody Institute, Villa Julie College, Coppin State College, University of Maryland Baltimore, University of Maryland Baltimore County, Loyola College, and Maryland Institute College of Art. An advanced degree program with the Monterey Institute for International Studies, and a 3-2 engineering degree with Johns Hopkins University are offered. Dual majors are an option, and student-designed majors and pass/no pass options are also available. There is 1 national honor society, including Phi Beta Kappa.

Faculty/Classroom: 37% of faculty are male; 63% are female. All teach undergraduates. No introductory courses are taught by graduate students.

Admissions: 73% of the 2009-2010 applicants were accepted. The SAT scores for the 2009-2010 freshman class were: Critical Reading--11% below 500, 34% between 500 and 599, 39% between 600 and 700, and 16% above 700; Math--21% below 500, 42% between 500 and 599, 31% between 600 and 700, and 6% above 700; Writing--14% below 500, 35% between 500 and 599, 38% between 600 and 700, and 13% above 700.

Requirements: Applicants should be graduates of an accredited high school or have earned the GED. Secondary preparation should include at least 16 academic units, preferably 4 in English, 3 in math (algebra I and II and geometry) and social studies, and 2 each in the same foreign language, lab science, and electives. A personal essay is required, and an interview is recommended. Prospective arts majors are urged to seek an audition or submit a portfolio. AP credits are accepted. Important factors in the admissions decision are extracurricular activities record, recommendations by school officials, and advanced placement or honors courses.

Procedure: Freshmen are admitted fall and spring. Entrance exams should be taken in spring of the junior year or fall of the senior year. There is a deferred admissions plan. Applications should be filed by February 1 for fall entry and December 1 for spring entry, along with a $55 fee. Notifications are sent April 1. Applications are accepted on-line. 192 applicants were on a recent waiting list, 23 were accepted.

Transfer: 35 transfer students enrolled in 2008-2009. Applicants must present a GPA of at least 2.5 in 30 hours of college work. An interview, a personal essay, and recommendations from college teachers or counselors are also required, as is a graded paper. 60 of 120 credits required for the bachelor's degree must be completed at Goucher.

Visiting: There are regularly scheduled orientations for prospective students, including an academic presentation, student panel, discussions, a campus tour, an interview, and an opportunity to sit in on classes and to meet with faculty, coaches, and other staff. There are guides for informal visits; visitors may sit in on classes and stay overnight. To schedule a visit, contact the Office of Admissions at admissions@goucher.edu.

Financial Aid: In 2009-2010, 82% of all full-time freshmen and 83% of continuing full-time students received some form of financial aid. 74% of all full-time freshmen and 62% of continuing full-time students received need-based aid. Need-based scholarships or need-based grants averaged $3,816; need-based self-help aid (loans and jobs) averaged $3,994 and other non-need based awards and non-need based scholarships averaged $13,046. 46% of undergraduate students work part-time. Average annual earnings from campus work are $1300. The average financial indebtedness of the 2009 graduate was $14,783. Goucher is a member of CSS. The CSS/Profile, FAFSA, and the college's own financial statement are required. The deadline for filing freshman financial aid applications for fall entry is February 15.

International Students: There are 36 international students enrolled. The school actively recruits these students. They must take the TOEFL with a minimum score of 550 on the paper-based TOEFL (PBT) or 79 on the Internet-based version (iBT). They must also take the SAT or ACT.

Computers: Wireless access is available. Goucher has 193 public computer workstations, some of which are located within 24-hour computer labs. There are wireless network Internet capabilities in most locations throughout the campus. All students may access the system. Some facilities are available around the clock. There are no time limits and no fees.

Graduates: From July 1, 2008 to June 30, 2009, 309 bachelor's degrees were awarded. The most popular majors were visual and performing arts (17%), psychology (13%), and social sciences (12%). In an average class, 1% graduate in 3 years or less, 56% graduate in 4 years or less, 62% graduate in 5 years or less, and 63% graduate in 6 years or less. Of the 2008 graduating class, 26% were enrolled in graduate school within 6 months of graduation, and 90% were employed.

Admissions Contact: Carlton E. Surbeck, Director of Admissions. A campus DVD is available. E-Mail: admissions@goucher.edu Web: www.goucher.edu

HOOD COLLEGE   C-2
Frederick, MD 21701-8575   (301) 696-3400
(800) 922-1599; (301) 696-3819

Full-time: 400 men, 859 women	**Faculty:** 80; IIA, --$
Part-time: 54 men, 119 women	**Ph.D.s:** 98%
Graduate: 319 men, 742 women	**Student/Faculty:** 15 to 1
Year: semesters, summer session	**Tuition:** $28,170
Application Deadline: February 15	**Room & Board:** $9,440
Freshman Class: 1622 applied, 1166 accepted, 251 enrolled	
SAT CR/M/W: 551/535/542	**ACT:** 23 **VERY COMPETITIVE**

Hood College, founded in 1893, is an independent, comprehensive college that offers an integration of the liberal arts and professional preparation, as well as undergraduate majors in the natural sciences. There are no undergraduate schools and one graduate school. In addition to regional accreditation, Hood has baccalaureate program accreditation with CSWE. The library contains 208,950 volumes, 743,691 microform items, 5,696 audio/video tapes/CDs/DVDs, and subscribes to 339 periodicals including electronic. Computerized library services include interlibrary loans, database searching, Internet access, and laptop Internet portals. Special learning facilities include a learning resource center, art gallery, radio station, aquatic center, a child development lab, an observatory, and information technology center. The 50-acre campus is in a suburban area 45 miles northwest of Washington, D.C. and 45 miles west of Baltimore. Including any residence halls, there are 31 buildings.

Student Life: 81% of undergraduates are from Maryland. Others are from 26 states, and 30 foreign countries. 78% are from public schools. 72% are white; 11% African American. 28% are Protestant; 24% Christian; 21% Catholic. The average age of freshmen is 18; all undergraduates, 22. 15% do not continue beyond their first year; 69% remain to graduate.

Housing: 749 students can be accommodated in college housing, which includes single-sex and coed dorms and off-campus apartments. In addition, there are language houses, special-interest floors in the residence halls include a living/learning floor and a community service floor. On-campus housing is guaranteed for the freshman year only and is available on a lottery system for upperclassmen. 54% of students live on campus; of those, 60% remain on campus on weekends. All students may keep cars.

Activities: There are no fraternities or sororities. There are 40 groups on campus, including art, band, cheerleading, choir, chorale, chorus, computers, dance, drama, environmental, ethnic, gay, honors, international, literary magazine, musical theater, newspaper, orchestra, political, professional, radio and TV, religious, social, social service, and student government. Popular campus events include Ring Formal, Liberation of the Black Mind Weekend, and Crab Fest.

Sports: There are 7 intercollegiate sports for men and 10 for women, and 1 intramural sports for men and 1 for women. Facilities include an basketball and volleyball courts, a weight room, an aerobics room, indoor and outdoor swimming pools, a 1-mile par course, a softball diamond, 6 tennis courts, an outdoor volleyball court, and 3 multiuse fields (field hockey, soccer, and lacrosse).

Disabled Students: 30% of the campus is accessible. Facilities include wheelchair ramps, elevators, special parking, specially equipped rest rooms, and special class scheduling.

Services: Counseling and information services are available, as is tutoring in some subjects, readers for the blind and interpreters for the hearing impaired. There is a reader service for the blind, and remedial math and writing. There are also services for students with learning disabilities, a language lab, and courses in time management and study skills.

Campus Safety and Security: Measures include 24-hour foot and vehicle patrol, self-defense education, and security escort services. There are emergency telephones, lighted pathways/sidewalks, an electronic access control system with 24-hour monitoring in all residence halls.

Programs of Study: Hood confers B.A. and B.S. degrees. Master's degrees are also awarded. Bachelor's degrees are awarded in BIOLOGICAL SCIENCE (biochemistry and biology/biological science), BUSINESS (business administration and management and management science), COMMUNICATIONS AND THE ARTS (art, communications, English, French, German, music, and Spanish), COMPUTER AND PHYSICAL SCIENCE (chemistry, computer science, and mathematics), EDUCATION (early childhood education, elementary education, English education, foreign languages education, mathematics education, science education, secondary education, and special education), ENGINEERING AND ENVIRONMENTAL DESIGN (environmental science), SOCIAL SCIENCE (archeology, economics, history, Latin American studies, law, philosophy, political science/government, psychology, religion, social work, and sociology). Biology, art, and archaeology are the strongest academically. Management, psychology, and biology are the largest.

Required: To graduate, students must complete a total of 124 credit hours, with a minimum GPA of 2.0, and a 2.0 GPA in the major. 24 to 52 credits are required in a student's major. All students must complete 42 to 48 credits in the core curriculum, which includes English, math, and language courses, courses in methods of inquiry, and interdisciplinary courses in Western civilization, non-Western civilization and society, science, and technology. Phys ed courses are also required. Enrollment in the final 30 credits must be on the Hood Campus as a degree candidate.

Special: The college offers a Washington semester with American University, dual majors, student-designed majors, a B.A.-B.S. degree in engineering/math, credit for life experience, nondegree study, an accelerated degree program, pass/fail options, and cross-registration with area colleges and the Duke University Marine Sciences Education Consortium. Internships of up to 15 credits are available in all majors at more than 100 sites throughout the United States and abroad. Students may study abroad in the Dominican Republic, Japan, Spain, France, and other countries. There is a 4-year honors program featuring 1 interdisciplinary course per semester and special co-curricular activities. There are 14 national honor societies, a freshman honors program, and 14 departmental honors programs.

Faculty/Classroom: 47% of faculty are male; 53% are female. All teach and do research. No introductory courses are taught by graduate students. The average class size in an introductory lecture is 17; in a laboratory is 14; and in a regular course is 17.

Admissions: 72% of the 2009-2010 applicants were accepted. The SAT scores for the 2009-2010 freshman class were: Critical Reading--29% below 500, 41% between 500 and 599, 22% between 600 and 700, and 8 above 700; Math--38% below 500, 39% between 500 and 599, 20% between 600 and 700, and 3 above 700; Writing--30% below

500, 44% between 500 and 599, 23% between 600 and 700, and 3 above 700. The ACT scores were 29% below 21, 33% between 21 and 23, 19% between 24 and 26, 6% between 27 and 28, and 13% above 28. 41% of the current freshmen were in the top fifth of their class; 71% were in the top two fifths. 3 freshmen graduated first in their class.

Requirements: The SAT or ACT is required. In addition, applicants should be graduates of an accredited secondary school. The GED is accepted. Hood recommends the completion of at least 16 academic credits in high school, including courses in English, social sciences, natural sciences, foreign languages, and math. A GPA of 2.5 is required. AP and CLEP credits are accepted. Important factors in the admissions decision are advanced placement or honors courses, leadership record, and extracurricular activities record.

Procedure: Freshmen are admitted fall and spring. Entrance exams should be taken in spring of the junior year or fall of the senior year. There are early admissions, deferred admissions, and rolling admissions plans. Applications should be filed by February 15 for fall entry and December 31 for spring entry. The fall 2008 application fee was $35. Applications are accepted on-line.

Transfer: 189 transfer students enrolled in 2008-2009. Applicants must have at least 12 college credits and a minimum GPA of 2.5. A total of 70 credits may be transferred. 30 of 124 credits required for the bachelor's degree must be completed at Hood.

Visiting: There are regularly scheduled orientations for prospective students, including tours and meetings with faculty, students, and administrators; and admissions interviews. There are guides for informal visits, visitors may sit in on classes, and stay overnight. To schedule a visit, contact the Admissions Office at 800-922-1599.

Financial Aid: In 2009-2010, 98% of all full-time freshmen and 99% of continuing full-time students received some form of financial aid. 76% of all full-time freshmen and 81% of continuing full-time students received need-based aid. The average freshmen award was $25,347, with $20,993 ($27,910 maximum) from need-based scholarships or need-based grants; $3,673 ($10,300 maximum) from need-based self-help aid (loans and jobs); and $21,810 ($28,170 maximum) from other non-need-based awards and non-need-based scholarships. 18% of undergraduate students work part-time. Average annual earnings from campus work are $1700. The average financial indebtedness of the 2009 graduate was $17,382. Hood is a member of CSS. The FAFSA is required. The priority date for freshman financial aid applications for fall entry is February 15.

International Students: There are 42 international students enrolled. The school actively recruits these students. They must take the TOEFL with a minimum score of 550 on the paper-based TOEFL (PBT) or 79 on the Internet-based version (iBT). They must also take the SAT or ACT. SAT scores may be substituted for the TOEFL.

Computers: Wireless access is available. The campus Whitaker Center, the library, and residence halls are wireless. There are 2 labs and 5 simple machines for students to access in those locations, plus 4 to 5 per residence halls. There are more than 150 computers in labs available for student use. All students may access the system. 24 hours per day, 7 days a week. There are no time limits and no fees. It is strongly recommended that all students have a personal computer. A Pentium 4 class machine with WinXP Pro, 256 MB memory is recommended.

Graduates: From July 1, 2008 to June 30, 2009, 349 bachelor's degrees were awarded. The most popular majors were psychology (14%), education (13%), and management (10%). 76 companies recruited on campus in 2008-2009. In an average class, 1% graduate in 3 years or less, 64% graduate in 4 years or less, 69% graduate in 5 years or less, and 70% graduate in 6 years or less. Of the 2008 graduating class, 40% were enrolled in graduate school within 6 months of graduation, and 65% were employed.

Admissions Contact: Kathleen Bands, Vice President for Enrollment Management. A campus DVD is available. E-Mail: *admissions@hood.edu* Web: *www.hood.edu*

JOHNS HOPKINS UNIVERSITY D-2

Baltimore, MD 21218   (410) 516-8341; (410) 516-6025

Full-time: 2400 men, 2200 women	Faculty: 447
Part-time: 25 men, 5 women	Ph.D.s: 92%
Graduate: 1000 men, 600 women	Student/Faculty: n/av
Year: 4-1-4, summer session	Tuition: $39,150
Application Deadline: January 1	Room & Board: $12,040
Freshman Class: 16,123 applied, 4318 accepted	
SAT or ACT: required	MOST COMPETITIVE

The Johns Hopkins University, founded in 1876, is a private multicampus institution offering undergraduate degrees at the Homewood campus through the Zanvyl Krieger School of Arts and Sciences, the Whiting School of Engineering, and the Peabody Institute (music). Some figures in the above capsule and in this profile are approximate. There are 5 undergraduate schools and 8 graduate schools. In addition to regional accreditation, Johns Hopkins has baccalaureate program accreditation with ABET. The 4 libraries contain 2.6 million volumes, 4.1 million microform items, and 9707 audio/video tapes/CDs/DVDs, and subscribe to 30,120 periodicals including electronic. Computerized library services include interlibrary loans, database searching, Internet access, and laptop Internet portals. Special learning facilities include an art gallery, radio station, and Space Telescope Science Institute. The 140-acre campus is in a suburban area in a residential setting in northern Baltimore. Including any residence halls, there are 40 buildings.

Student Life: 85% of undergraduates are from out of state, mostly the Middle Atlantic. Students are from 50 states, 49 foreign countries, and Canada. 60% are from public schools. 46% are white; 24% Asian American. The average age of freshmen is 18; all undergraduates, 20. 3% do not continue beyond their first year; 93% remain to graduate.

Housing: 2700 students can be accommodated in college housing, which includes single-sex and coed dorms, on-campus apartments, and off-campus apartments. In addition, there are special-interest houses and non-university-sponsored fraternity and sorority houses. On-campus housing is available on a lottery system for upperclassmen. 61% of students live on campus. Upperclassmen may keep cars.

Activities: 24% of men belong to 11 national fraternities; 23% of women belong to 7 national sororities. There are 250 groups on campus, including art, band, cheerleading, chess, choir, chorale, chorus, computers, dance, debate, drama, ethnic, film, forensics, gay, honors, international, jazz band, literary magazine, marching band, musical theater, newspaper, opera, orchestra, pep band, photography, political, professional, radio and TV, religious, social, social service, student government, symphony, and volunteer organizations. Popular campus events include Culturefest, Fall Fest, and Spring Fair.

Sports: There are 14 intercollegiate sports for men and 12 for women, and 20 intramural sports for men and 20 for women. Facilities include a recreation center with a swimming pool and diving pool, wrestling and fencing rooms, a varsity weight room, a fitness center, saunas, a climbing wall, an indoor jogging track, and courts for basketball, badminton, squash, volleyball, and handball. There is also a 4000-seat stadium, outdoor playing fields, and tennis courts.

Disabled Students: Facilities include wheelchair ramps, elevators, special parking, specially equipped restrooms, special class scheduling, lowered drinking fountains, and lowered telephones. JHU works with all individuals to ensure access to all programs. Also, existing housing is accommodated as needed.

Services: Counseling and information services are available, as is tutoring in most subjects. There is a reader service for the blind.

Campus Safety and Security: Measures include 24-hour foot and vehicle patrol, emergency notification system, self-defense education, and security escort services. There are shuttle buses, emergency telephones, and lighted pathways/sidewalks.

Programs of Study: Johns Hopkins confers B.A. and B.S. degrees. Master's and doctoral degrees are also awarded. Bachelor's degrees are awarded in BIOLOGICAL SCIENCE (biology/biological science, biophysics, cell biology, molecular biology, and neurosciences), COMMUNICATIONS AND THE ARTS (art history and appreciation, classics, creative writing, English, French, German, Italian, media arts, romance languages and literature, and Spanish), COMPUTER AND PHYSICAL SCIENCE (applied mathematics, chemistry, computer science, earth science, mathematics, natural sciences, and physics), ENGINEERING AND ENVIRONMENTAL DESIGN (biomedical engineering, chemical engineering, civil engineering, computer engineering, electrical/electronics engineering, engineering, engineering mechanics, environmental engineering, environmental science, materials engineering, materials science, and mechanical engineering), SOCIAL SCIENCE (African studies, anthropology, cognitive science, East Asian studies, economics, history, history of science, humanities, interdisciplinary studies, international studies, Latin American studies, Near Eastern studies, philosophy, political science/government, psychology, social science, and sociology). International studies, public health studies, and biomedical engineering are the largest.

Required: Although there is no required core curriculum, all students must take 40 hours in the major and 30 hours outside their major field. The B.A. requires a total of 120 hours; the B.S. in engineering requires 120 to 128 hours, depending on the major. A GPA of at least 2.0 is required for graduation. All students must take at least 4 courses (2 for engineers) with a writing-intensive component to graduate.

Special: Internships, dual majors in music and arts and sciences/engineering, cross-registration with Baltimore-area colleges and Johns Hopkins divisions, a cooperative double degree with Peabody Conservatory of Music, a student-designed semester at the Johns Hopkins School of International Studies in Washington, D.C., and various multidisciplinary programs are offered. Students may enroll at Johns Hopkins in Bologna, Italy, or Nanjing, China, or arrange programs in Europe, South America, the Far East, or Australia. Students may earn combined B.A.-B.S. degrees in physics, computer science, applied math, and statistics. There are 4 national honor societies, including Phi Beta Kappa, and 25 departmental honors programs.

Faculty/Classroom: 72% of faculty are male; 28% are female. No introductory courses are taught by graduate students.

Admissions: 24% of a recent year's applicants were accepted. 92% of a recent year's freshmen were in the top fifth of their class; 98% were in the top two fifths. 81 freshmen graduated first in their class in a recent year.

Requirements: The SAT or ACT with Writing is required. For those submitting SAT scores, Johns Hopkins recommends that applicants also submit 3 SAT Subject Tests. In addition, applicants should be graduates of an accredited secondary school or have the GED. The university recommends that secondary preparation include 4 years each of English and math, 2 (prefer 3) of social science or history and lab science, and 3 to 4 of a foreign language (2 for engineering majors). 2 personal essays are required, and an interview is recommended. AP credits are accepted. Important factors in the admissions decision are advanced placement or honors courses, extracurricular activities record, and personality/intangible qualities.

Procedure: Freshmen are admitted fall. Entrance exams should be taken by December for regular decision, or November for early decision. There are early decision and deferred admissions plans. Early decision applications should be filed by November 1; regular applications by January 1 for fall entry, along with a $70 fee. Notification for early decision is sent December 15; regular decision, April 1. Applications are accepted on-line.

Transfer: 36 transfer students enrolled in a recent year. Applicants should have sophomore or junior standing and at least a B average in previous college work. Applications must include a written essay and at least 1 letter of recommendation. High school records are also required. 60 of 120 credits required for the bachelor's degree must be completed at Johns Hopkins.

Visiting: There are regularly scheduled orientations for prospective students, including scheduled open house programs, campus tours and group information sessions offered weekday mornings and afternoons, and individual day visits with a current student. A schedule of events and a virtual tour are available at *http://apply.jhu.edu/visit/tour.html*. There are guides for informal visits, and visitors may sit in on classes and stay overnight. To schedule a visit, contact the Office of Undergraduate Admissions at (410) 516-8171.

Financial Aid: Johns Hopkins is a member of CSS. The CSS/Profile and FAFSA are required. The deadline for filing freshman financial aid applications for fall entry is March 1.

International Students: There were 290 international students enrolled in a recent year. The school actively recruits these students. They must take the TOEFL with a minimum score of 600 on the paper-based TOEFL (PBT). They must also take the SAT or ACT.

Computers: Wireless access is available. All students may access the system 24 hours a day, 7 days a week. There are no time limits and no fees.

Graduates: In a recent year, 1004 bachelor's degrees were awarded. The most popular majors were biomedical engineering (11%), international studies (10%), and public health studies (9%). In an average class, 3% graduate in 3 years or less, 83% graduate in 4 years or less, 91% graduate in 5 years or less, and 92% graduate in 6 years or less. 224 companies recruited on campus in a recent year. Of a recent year's graduating class, 38% were enrolled in graduate school within 6 months of graduation, and 47% were employed.

Admissions Contact: Director of Undergraduate Admissions. E-mail: *gotojhu@jhu.edu* Web: *www.jhu.edu*

LOYOLA UNIVERSITY IN MARYLAND   D-2
Loyola College in Maryland

Baltimore, MD 21210   (410) 617-5012
                                      (800) 221-9107; (410) 617-2176

Full-time: 1507 men, 2212 women	**Faculty:** 331; IIA, +$
Part-time: 17 men, 21 women	**Ph.D.s:** 79%
Graduate: 830 men, 1391 women	**Student/Faculty:** 11 to 1
Year: semesters, summer session	**Tuition:** $37,775
Application Deadline: January 15	**Room & Board:** $10,200
Freshman Class: 9117 applied, 6008 accepted, 968 enrolled	
SAT or ACT: required	**VERY COMPETITIVE**

Loyola University, formerly Loyola College, founded in 1852, is a private liberal arts college affiliated with the Roman Catholic Church and the Jesuit tradition. It offers degree programs in arts and sciences, business, and management. There are 2 undergraduate schools and 2 graduate schools. In addition to regional accreditation, Loyola College has baccalaureate program accreditation with AACSB, ABET, CSAB, NASDTEC, and NCATE. The library contains 437,571 volumes, 338,337 microform items, and 39,422 audio/video tapes/CDs/DVDs, and subscribes to 14,901 periodicals including electronic. Computerized library services include interlibrary loans and database searching. Special learning facilities include an art gallery and radio station. The 89-acre campus is in an urban area 3 miles from downtown Baltimore. Including any residence halls, there are 29 buildings.

Student Life: 82% of undergraduates are from out of state, mostly the Middle Atlantic. Students are from 38 states, 15 foreign countries, and

Canada. 85% are white. 78% are Catholic. The average age of freshmen is 18; all undergraduates, 20. 11% do not continue beyond their first year; 86% remain to graduate.

Housing: 2798 students can be accommodated in college housing, which includes coed dorms and on-campus apartments. In addition, there are honors houses and special-interest houses. On-campus housing is guaranteed for the freshman year only, is available on a first-come, and first-served basis. 84% of students live on campus. Alcohol is not permitted. Upperclassmen may keep cars.

Activities: There are no fraternities or sororities. There are 101 groups on campus, including art, band, cheerleading, chess, choir, chorale, chorus, computers, dance, drama, ethnic, honors, international, jazz band, literary magazine, musical theater, newspaper, orchestra, pep band, photography, political, professional, radio, religious, social, social service, student government, and symphony.

Sports: There are 7 intercollegiate sports for men and 8 for women, and 15 intramural sports for men. Facilities include a pool, a sauna, a weight room, racquetball, tennis, and squash courts, a 3000-seat arena, a 2000-seat multipurpose outdoor facility, and a fitness center.

Disabled Students: 99% of the campus is accessible. Facilities include wheelchair ramps, elevators, special parking, specially equipped restrooms, special class scheduling, lowered drinking fountains, and lowered telephones.

Services: Counseling and information services are available, as is tutoring in most subjects. There is a reader service for the blind and remedial math.

Campus Safety and Security: Measures include 24-hour foot and vehicle patrol, self-defense education, and security escort services. There are shuttle buses, emergency telephones, and lighted pathways/sidewalks.

Programs of Study: Loyola College confers B.A., B.S., B.B.A., B.S.E.E., and B.S.E.S. degrees. Master's and doctoral degrees are also awarded. Bachelor's degrees are awarded in BIOLOGICAL SCIENCE (biology/biological science), BUSINESS (accounting and business administration and management), COMMUNICATIONS AND THE ARTS (communications, creative writing, English, fine arts, French, German, Latin, and Spanish), COMPUTER AND PHYSICAL SCIENCE (chemistry, computer science, mathematics, and physics), EDUCATION (elementary education), ENGINEERING AND ENVIRONMENTAL DESIGN (electrical/electronics engineering and engineering), HEALTH PROFESSIONS (speech pathology/audiology), SOCIAL SCIENCE (classical/ancient civilization, economics, history, philosophy, political science/government, psychology, sociology, and theological studies). General business, psychology, and communication are the largest.

Required: All students must complete 120 hours, including 36 in the major, with at least a 2.0 GPA. The required core curriculum includes 2 courses each in history, language (at the second-year level), literature, philosophy, social sciences, and theology; 1 course each in composition, ethics, fine arts, math, humanities, and natural sciences; and 1 additional course in math, natural science, or computer science.

Special: Loyola offers cross-registration with Johns Hopkins, Towson, and Morgan State Universities, Goucher College, the College of Notre Dame, Maryland Art Institute, and Peabody Conservatory. Credit-bearing internships are available in most majors and study abroad is possible in 36 countries. Work-study programs and dual majors are also offered. There are 23 national honor societies, including Phi Beta Kappa, a freshman honors program, and 1 departmental honors program.

Faculty/Classroom: 54% of faculty are male; 46% are female. 90% teach undergraduates, 98% do research, and 87% do both. No introductory courses are taught by graduate students. The average class size in an introductory lecture, 25, in a laboratory, 16, and in a regular course, 21.

Admissions: 66% of the 2009-2010 applicants were accepted. 65% of the current freshmen were in the top fifth of their class; 92% were in the top two fifths. 10 freshmen graduated first in their class.

Requirements: The SAT or ACT is required. In addition, applicants should have graduated from an accredited secondary school or have earned the GED. Secondary preparation should include 4 years of English, 4 each of math, foreign language, natural science, and classical or modern foreign language, and 2 to 3 of history. A personal essay is required; an interview is recommended. AP and CLEP credits are accepted. Important factors in the admissions decision are advanced placement or honors courses, recommendations by school officials, and extracurricular activities record.

Procedure: Freshmen are admitted fall, spring, and summer. Entrance exams should be taken by December of the senior year. There is a deferred admissions plan. Early action applications should be filed by November 15; regular applications, by January 15 for fall entry; and December 15 for spring entry, along with a $50 fee. Notification of early action is sent November 15; regular decision, April 1. 1079 applicants were on the 2009 waiting list; 917 were admitted. Applications are accepted on-line.

Transfer: 31 transfer students enrolled in 2008-2009. Transfer applicants should have at least a 2.5 GPA in previous college work and

should submit SAT scores. Other factors considered include types of college courses taken and the secondary school record. 60 of 120 credits required for the bachelor's degree must be completed at Loyola College.

Visiting: There are regularly scheduled orientations for prospective students, including a general information session, an interview, and a campus tour. There are guides for informal visits and visitors may sit in on classes. To schedule a visit, contact the Admissions Office.

Financial Aid: In 2009-2010, at least 57% of all full-time freshmen and 46% of continuing full-time students received some form of financial aid. At least 53% of all full-time freshmen and 43% of continuing full-time students received need-based aid. The average freshman award was $26,345. Need-based scholarships or need-based grants averaged $18,750; need-based self-help aid (loans and jobs) averaged $7,595; non-need-based athletic scholarships averaged $32,280. Institutional awards averaged $12,530. 15% of undergraduate students work part-time. Average annual earnings from campus work are $1380. The average financial indebtedness of the 2009 graduate was $26,855. Loyola College is a member of CSS. The CSS/Profile, FAFSA, and if applicable, a noncustodial parent's statement and business/farm supplement are required. The deadline for filing freshman financial aid applications for fall entry is February 15.

International Students: There are 17 international students enrolled. The school actively recruits these students. They must take the TOEFL. They must also take the SAT or ACT.

Computers: All students may access the system. There are no time limits and no fees.

Graduates: From July 1, 2008 to June 30, 2009, 808 bachelor's degrees were awarded. The most popular majors were business/marketing (37%), communications/journalism (11%), and public administration/social services (7%). In an average class, 77% graduate in 4 years or less, 86% graduate in 5 years or less, and 83% graduate in 6 years or less.

Admissions Contact: William Bossemeyer, Dean of Admissions. A campus DVD is available. Web: *www.loyola.edu*

MARYLAND INSTITUTE COLLEGE OF ART

Baltimore, MD 21217 — D-2 — (410) 225-2222; (410) 225-2337

Full-time: 560 men, 1100 women	Faculty: n/av
Part-time: 10 men, 10 women	Ph.D.s: 82%
Graduate: 80 men, 160 women	Student/Faculty: n/av
Year: semesters, summer session	Tuition: $31,000
Application Deadline: see profile	Room & Board: $8500
Freshman Class: n/av	
SAT: required	SPECIAL

Maryland Institute College of Art, founded in 1826, is a private accredited institution offering undergraduate and graduate degrees in the fine arts. Figures in the above capsule and this profile are approximate. There are 9 graduate schools. In addition to regional accreditation, MICA has baccalaureate program accreditation with NASAD. The library contains 83,564 volumes and 5600 audio/video tapes/CDs/DVDs, and subscribes to 402 periodicals including electronic. Computerized library services include interlibrary loans, database searching, Internet access, and laptop Internet portals. Special learning facilities include a learning resource center, an art gallery, 12 large art galleries, open to the public year-round and featuring work by MICA faculty, students, and nationally and internationally known artists, a slide library containing 220,000 slides, and 8 other galleries for undergraduate and graduate exhibitions. The 13-acre campus is in an urban area. Including any residence halls, there are 25 buildings.

Student Life: 80% of undergraduates are from out of state, mostly the Northeast. Students are from 47 states, 44 foreign countries, and Canada. 76% are from public schools. 67% are white. The average age of freshmen is 18; all undergraduates, 20. 15% do not continue beyond their first year; 76% remain to graduate.

Housing: 657 students can be accommodated in college housing, which includes coed dorms, on-campus apartments, and off-campus apartments. Residence halls include project rooms where students can do artwork 24 hours a day. On-campus housing is guaranteed for the freshman year only, is available on a first-come, first-served basis, and is available on a lottery system for upperclassmen. 88% of students live on campus; of those, 95% remain on campus on weekends. Alcohol is not permitted. All students may keep cars.

Activities: There are no fraternities or sororities. There are 50 groups on campus, including animation, art, ballet, belly dance, bowling, choir, chorale, comic, dance, drama, environmental, ethnic, film, faming, gay, humor magazine, international, knitting, literary magazine, orchestra, outdoor, photography, pirate, playwriting, political, professional, radio, religious, running, social, social service, student government, ultimate Frisbee, vampire, and Viking. Popular campus events include International Education Week, Fashion Show, and Caribbean Carnival

Sports: There are 4 intramural sports for men and 4 for women. Facilities include an outdoor volleyball court and fitness center for weight lifting and aerobics on campus. The fitness center also includes a fitness studio where students take classes like yoga, meditation, aerobics, belly dancing, ballet, ballroom dancing, and break dancing. There is also a recreation center 5 blocks from campus with a basketball court and other fitness equipment.

Disabled Students: 85% of the campus is accessible. Facilities include wheelchair ramps, elevators, special parking, specially equipped restrooms, special class scheduling, lowered drinking fountains, lowered telephones, and lowered fire extinguishers.

Services: Counseling and information services are available, as is tutoring in some subjects, including writing and study skills. There is remedial writing.

Campus Safety and Security: Measures include 24-hour foot and vehicle patrol, self-defense education, and security escort services. There are shuttle buses, emergency telephones, lighted pathways/sidewalks, building monitors in most buildings, and periodic discussions and seminars on safety.

Programs of Study: MICA confers B.F.A. degrees. Master's degrees are also awarded. Bachelor's degrees are awarded in COMMUNICATIONS AND THE ARTS (animation, art history and appreciation, ceramic art and design, drawing, fiber/textiles/weaving, fine arts, graphic design, illustration, media arts, painting, photography, printmaking, sculpture, and video), ENGINEERING AND ENVIRONMENTAL DESIGN (environmental design). Painting, illustration, and general fine arts are the largest.

Required: All students complete a foundation program in their first year, including courses in painting, drawing, two- and three-dimensional design, liberal arts, and electronic arts. Of a total 126 credits, students must take one-third of the courses in liberal arts and two-thirds in studio arts, with 60 credits in the major and a minimum 2.0 GPA. Seniors must complete a focused, professionally oriented body of work.

Special: Exchange programs are offered with Goucher College, Loyola and Notre Dame Colleges, Johns Hopkins University, the Peabody Conservatory of Music, the University of Baltimore, University of Maryland Baltimore County, Towson University, Morgan State University, and Baltimore Hebrew College. Cross-registration is possible with any member schools in the Alliance of Independent Colleges of Art and the East Coast Art Schools Consortium. A New York studio semester is available as well as a semester of study with any member schools in the Association of Independent Colleges of Art and Design. Study abroad is possible in the junior year in any of 45 schools in 24 countries.

Faculty/Classroom: 50% of faculty are male; 50% are female. 87% teach undergraduates. No introductory courses are taught by graduate students. The average class size in an introductory lecture is 24 and in a regular course is 17.

Admissions: There were 2 National Merit finalists in a recent year.

Requirements: The SAT is required. Admission is based on a comprehensive set of criteria with the most emphasis placed on artistic ability as demonstrated in the portfolio and on academic achievement as demonstrated in test scores, GPA, and level of course work. Essays, recommendations, interview, and extracurricular activities are also considered. AP credits are accepted. Important factors in the admissions decision are evidence of special talent, advanced placement or honors courses, and extracurricular activities record.

Procedure: Freshmen are admitted fall and spring. Entrance exams should be taken in the spring of the junior year. There are early decisions, early admissions and deferred admissions plans. Check with the school for current application deadlines. The fall 2009 application fee was $50. A waiting list is maintained.

Transfer: 60 transfer students enrolled in a recent year. Transfer applicants must submit high school and college transcripts, a personal essay, a portfolio of artwork, letters of recommendation, and course descriptions. 63 of 126 credits required for the bachelor's degree must be completed at MICA.

Visiting: There are regularly scheduled orientations for prospective students, including campus tours and presentations about curriculum, student life, admission, and financial aid. There are guides for informal visits and visitors may sit in on classes. To schedule a visit, contact the Office of Undergraduate Admission.

Financial Aid: In a recent year, 85% of all full-time students received some form of financial aid. 62% of all full-time freshmen and 65% of continuing full-time students received need-based aid. The average freshman award was $17,006. 60% of undergraduate students work part-time. Average annual earnings from campus work are $1100. The average financial indebtedness of a recent graduate was $18,919. MICA is a member of CSS. The FAFSA and the college's own financial statement are required. Check with the school for current application deadlines.

International Students: There were 71 international students enrolled in a recent year. The school actively recruits these students. They must take the TOEFL, with a minimum score of 550 on the paper-based TOEFL (PBT) or 80 on the Internet-based version (iBT), the Comprehensive English Language Test, the SAT, or the IELTS.

Computers: Wireless access is available. More than 350 PCs are available in more than 30 classrooms, labs, and public areas. 60% of the campus has wireless access. Students can use the student portal, Web galleries, student blogs, e-mail, and blackboard e-learning. All students may access the system 24 hours a day. There are no time limits and no fees. It is strongly recommended that all students have a personal computer.

Graduates: In a recent year, 312 bachelor's degrees were awarded. The most popular majors were general fine arts (17%), painting (16%), and graphic design (13%). 30 companies recruited on campus in a recent year. In an average class, 1% graduate in 3 years or less, 64% graduate in 4 years or less, 74% graduate in 5 years or less, and 76% graduate in 6 years or less. Of a recent graduating class, 23% were enrolled in graduate school within 6 months of graduation and 89% were employed.

Admissions Contact: Dean of Admission. E-Mail: *admissions@mica.edu* Web: *www.mica.edu*

MCDANIEL COLLEGE
Westminster, MD 21157-4390

D-1

(410) 857-2230
(800) 638-5005; (410) 857-2757

Full-time: 750 men, 940 women	**Faculty:** IIB, av$
Part-time: 30 men, 30 women	**Ph.D.s:** 95%
Graduate: 450 men, 1520 women	**Student/Faculty:** n/av
Year: 4-1-4	**Tuition:** $32,000
Application Deadline: see profile	**Room & Board:** $6600
Freshman Class: n/av	
SAT: required	**VERY COMPETITIVE**

McDaniel College, founded in 1867 as Western Maryland College, is a private college offering programs in the liberal arts. Figures in the above capsule and this profile are approximate. There is 1 graduate school. In addition to regional accreditation, The Hill has baccalaureate program accreditation with CSWE and NCATE. The library contains 206,483 volumes, 1.4 million microform items, and 12,942 audio/video tapes/CDs/DVDs, and subscribes to 21,062 periodicals including electronic. Computerized library services include interlibrary loans, database searching, Internet access, and laptop Internet portals. Special learning facilities include an art gallery, radio station, TV station, physics observatory, and student research science labs. The 160-acre campus is in a suburban area 30 miles northwest of Baltimore. Including any residence halls, there are 62 buildings.

Student Life: 70% of undergraduates are from Maryland. Others are from 35 states, 12 foreign countries, and Canada. 80% are from public schools. 80% are white. The average age of freshmen is 18; all undergraduates, 20. 16% do not continue beyond their first year; 72% remain to graduate.

Housing: 1306 students can be accommodated in college housing, which includes single-sex and coed dorms and on-campus apartments. In addition, there are honors houses, language houses, special-interest houses, fraternity and sorority floors, academic clusters, and substance-free floors. On-campus housing is guaranteed for all 4 years. 75% of students live on campus; of those, 85% remain on campus on weekends. Upperclassmen may keep cars.

Activities: 13% of men belong to 1 local and 3 national fraternities; 12% of women belong to 1 local and 2 national sororities. There are 132 groups on campus, including art, band, cheerleading, choir, chorale, chorus, computers, dance, drama, environmental, ethnic, film, forensics, gay, honors, international, jazz band, literary magazine, musical theater, newspaper, orchestra, outdoors, pep band, photography, political, professional, radio and TV, religious, social, social service, student government, ultimate Frisbee, and yearbook. Popular campus events include Spring Fling, Senior Week, and Reunion Weekend.

Sports: There are 11 intercollegiate sports for men and 11 for women, and 13 intramural sports for men and 12 for women. Facilities include a 9-hole golf course, tennis courts, a swimming pool, a football stadium with a track, a squash/racquetball court, a weight-training center, basketball and volleyball courts, and soccer, softball, and lacrosse fields.

Disabled Students: 85% of the campus is accessible. Facilities include wheelchair ramps, elevators, special parking, specially equipped restrooms, special class scheduling, lowered drinking fountains, lowered telephones, and special housing.

Services: Counseling and information services are available, as is tutoring in most subjects. There is a reader service for the blind and remedial math, reading, and writing.

Campus Safety and Security: Measures include 24-hour foot and vehicle patrol and security escort services. There are emergency telephones and lighted pathways/sidewalks.

Programs of Study: The Hill confers B.A. degrees. Master's degrees are also awarded. Bachelor's degrees are awarded in BIOLOGICAL SCIENCE (biology/biological science), BUSINESS (business administration and management), COMMUNICATIONS AND THE ARTS (art history and appreciation, communications, dramatic arts, English, fine arts, French, German, music, and Spanish), COMPUTER AND PHYSICAL SCIENCE (chemistry, computer science, mathematics, and physics), EDUCATION (physical education), ENGINEERING AND ENVIRONMENTAL DESIGN (environmental science), SOCIAL SCIENCE (economics, history, philosophy, political science/government, psychology, religion, social work, and sociology). Business administration, psychology, and biology are the largest.

Required: Distribution requirements for all students include cross-cultural studies, literature and fine arts, humanities, natural sciences, quantitative analysis, and social sciences. All students must take English composition, foreign language, and phys ed (4 courses) and pass a math proficiency exam. A total of 128 credit hours is required for graduation, including 38 to 50 in the major. The college uses a 4-course system, with most courses 4 credits. The minimum GPA for graduation is 2.0.

Special: Internships are available in all majors. Study abroad is available around the world including McDaniel's program in Budapest. There is a Washington semester in conjunction with American University and 3-2 engineering programs with Washington University and the University of Maryland. The college offers work-study programs, dual and student-designed majors, credit by exam (in foreign languages), and pass/fail options. McDaniel College has a 5-year deaf education program and offers certification in elementary and secondary education. The college also offers advanced standing for international baccalaureate recipients. There are 20 national honor societies, including Phi Beta Kappa, a freshman honors program, and 24 departmental honors programs.

Faculty/Classroom: 53% of faculty are male; 47% are female. All teach undergraduates. No introductory courses are taught by graduate students. The average class size in an introductory lecture is 18; in a laboratory, 17; and in a regular course, 17.

Admissions: 8 freshmen graduated first in their class in a recent year.

Requirements: The SAT is required. In addition, applicants must be graduates of an accredited secondary school or have a GED. A minimum of 16 academic credits are required, including 4 years of English, 3 each of foreign language, math, and social studies, and 2 of a lab science. SAT Subject tests and an interview are recommended. An essay and academic recommendations are required. The Hill requires applicants to be in the upper 50% of their class. A GPA of 2.5 is required. AP and CLEP credits are accepted. Important factors in the admissions decision are advanced placement or honors courses, leadership record, and evidence of special talent.

Procedure: Freshmen are admitted fall and spring. Entrance exams should be taken at the end of the junior year. There is a deferred admissions plan. Check with the school for current application deadlines. The fall 2009 application fee was $50. Applications are accepted on-line. 111 applicants were on a recent waiting list, 23 were accepted.

Transfer: 66 transfer students enrolled in a recent year. A minimum college GPA of 2.5 is required. 32 of 128 credits required for the bachelor's degree must be completed at The Hill.

Visiting: There are regularly scheduled orientations for prospective students, including an information session conducted by a counselor and/or the Director or Dean of Admissions and a student-led tour of campus. Individual visits and fall visit days include a class visit and lunch on campus. There are guides for informal visits and visitors may sit in on classes. To schedule a visit, contact the Admissions Office.

Financial Aid: In a recent year, 89% of all full-time freshmen and 83% of continuing full-time students received some form of financial aid. 71% of all full-time freshmen and 65% of continuing full-time students received need-based aid. The average freshman award was $23,294. 18% of undergraduate students work part-time. Average annual earnings from campus work are $866. The average financial indebtedness of a recent graduate was $22,753. The FAFSA and the college's own financial statement are required. Check with the school for current application deadlines.

International Students: There were 11 international students enrolled in a recent year. The school actively recruits these students. They must take the TOEFL.

Computers: Wireless access is available. All students may access the system. 1 lab is open 24 hours per day; other labs are open 8:30 A.M. to midnight daily. There are no time limits and no fees.

Graduates: In a recent year, 407 bachelor's degrees were awarded. The most popular majors were communication (10%), psychology (10%), and sociology (9%). 49 companies recruited on campus in a recent year. In an average class, 65% graduate in 4 years or less and 72% graduate in 6 years or less. Of a recent graduating class, 33% were enrolled in graduate school within 6 months of graduation and 88% were employed.

Admissions Contact: Dean of Admissions.
E-mail: *admissions@mcdaniel.edu* Web: *www.mcdaniel.edu*

MORGAN STATE UNIVERSITY   D-2
Baltimore, MD 21251   (443) 885-3000
                                        (800) 332-6674; (443) 319-3684

Full-time: 2075 men, 2945 women	**Faculty:** n/av
Part-time: 355 men, 445 women	**Ph.D.s:** 80%
Graduate: 205 men, 300 women	**Student/Faculty:** n/av
Year: semesters, summer session	**Tuition:** $6500 ($14,500)
Application Deadline: see profile	**Room & Board:** $8000
Freshman Class: n/av	
SAT or ACT: required	**COMPETITIVE**

Morgan State University, founded in 1867, is a comprehensive public institution offering undergraduate and graduate programs leading to liberal arts, preprofessional, and professional degrees. Figures in the above capsule and this profile are approximate. There are 6 undergraduate schools and 4 graduate schools. In addition to regional accreditation, Morgan State has baccalaureate program accreditation with AACSB, ABET, ADA, ASLA, CSWE, NAAB, NASAD, NASM, and NCATE. The library contains 389,516 volumes, 738,311 microform items, and 45,855 audio/video tapes/CDs/DVDs, and subscribes to 3011 periodicals including electronic. Computerized library services include interlibrary loans and database searching. Special learning facilities include a learning resource center, art gallery, radio station, and TV station. The 140-acre campus is in a suburban area in the northeast corner of Baltimore. Including any residence halls, there are 41 buildings.

Student Life: 60% of undergraduates are from Maryland. Others are from 40 states, 20 foreign countries, and Canada. 91% are from public schools. 92% are African American. The average age of freshmen is 18; all undergraduates, 21. 24% do not continue beyond their first year; 45% remain to graduate.

Housing: 1800 students can be accommodated in college housing, which includes single-sex dorms and on-campus apartments. In addition, there are honors houses. On-campus housing is guaranteed for the freshman year only and is available on a first-come, first-served basis. 70% of students commute. Alcohol is not permitted. All students may keep cars.

Activities: 4% of men belong to 2 local and 4 national fraternities; 3% of women belong to 3 local and 4 national sororities. There are 150 groups on campus, including art, band, cheerleading, chess, choir, chorale, chorus, computers, dance, debate, drama, drill team, drum and bugle corps, ethnic, film, forensics, gay, honors, international, jazz band, literary magazine, marching band, musical theater, newspaper, opera, orchestra, pep band, photography, political, professional, radio and TV, religious, social, social service, student government, symphony, and yearbook. Popular campus events include Kwanzaa and I Love Morgan Day.

Sports: There are 6 intercollegiate sports for men and 6 for women, and 17 intramural sports for men and 16 for women. Facilities include a field house, a gym, a weight room, a swimming pool, tennis and racquetball courts, and various playing fields.

Disabled Students: 90% of the campus is accessible. Facilities include wheelchair ramps, elevators, special parking, specially equipped restrooms, special class scheduling, and lowered drinking fountains.

Services: Counseling and information services are available, as is tutoring in every subject. There is a reader service for the blind and remedial math, reading, and writing. There are also note takers and sign language interpreters for disabled students.

Campus Safety and Security: Measures include 24-hour foot and vehicle patrol, self-defense education, and security escort services. There are shuttle buses, emergency telephones, and lighted pathways/sidewalks.

Programs of Study: Morgan State confers B.A., B.S., A.B., and B.S.Ed. degrees. Master's and doctoral degrees are also awarded. Bachelor's degrees are awarded in BIOLOGICAL SCIENCE (biology/biological science), BUSINESS (accounting, business administration and management, hospitality management services, and marketing/retailing/merchandising), COMMUNICATIONS AND THE ARTS (dramatic arts, English, fine arts, music, speech/debate/rhetoric, and telecommunications), COMPUTER AND PHYSICAL SCIENCE (chemistry, computer science, information sciences and systems, mathematics, and physics), EDUCATION (elementary education, health education, and physical education), ENGINEERING AND ENVIRONMENTAL DESIGN (civil engineering, electrical/electronics engineering, engineering physics, and industrial engineering technology), HEALTH PROFESSIONS (medical laboratory technology and mental health/human services), SOCIAL SCIENCE (African American studies, economics, history, home economics, philosophy, political science/government, psychology, religion, social work, and sociology). Engineering, chemistry, and social work are the strongest academically. Business administration, accounting, and electrical engineering are the largest.

Required: To graduate, students must complete at least 120 credit hours, including 74 in the major, with a 2.0 GPA. All students must pass speech and writing proficiency exams prior to their senior year. The 46-credit general education requirement includes courses in English, humanities, logic, history, behavioral science, science, math, African American history, and health and phys ed. Seniors must pass a proficiency exam in their major.

Special: Co-op programs in public and private institutions may be arranged for pharmacy honors, predentistry, premedicine, and special education students. The university also offers internships for juniors and seniors, study abroad in 3 countries, work-study programs, and preprofessional physical therapy and prelaw programs. Dual majors may be pursued but do not lead to a dual degree. There are 28 national honor societies and a freshman honors program.

Faculty/Classroom: 60% of faculty are male; 40% are female. All teach undergraduates, 76% do research, and 76% do both. No introductory courses are taught by graduate students. The average class size in an introductory lecture is 25; in a laboratory, 26; and in a regular course, 21.

Requirements: The SAT or ACT is required, with a satisfactory score. In addition, applicants should be high school graduates or have earned the GED and are encouraged to have 4 years of English, 3 of math, 2 each of science, social studies, and history, and 1 of a foreign language. A personal essay is recommended and, when appropriate, an audition. A GPA of 2.5 is required. AP and CLEP credits are accepted. Important factors in the admissions decision are recommendations by school officials, evidence of special talent, and parents or siblings attended your school.

Procedure: Freshmen are admitted fall and spring. Entrance exams should be taken during the fall semester of the junior or senior year. There is a rolling admissions plan. Check with the school for current application deadlines. The fall 2009 application fee was $25.

Transfer: Applicants with fewer than 24 credits must submit high school transcripts; those with fewer than 12 credits must also submit SAT scores. Applicants are expected to have at least a 2.0 GPA in all college work attempted and be in good standing at the last institution attended. 30 of 120 credits required for the bachelor's degree must be completed at Morgan State.

Visiting: There are regularly scheduled orientations for prospective students, including placement testing and academic advising. There are guides for informal visits; visitors may sit in on classes and stay overnight. To schedule a visit, contact Admissions.

Financial Aid: Morgan State is a member of CSS. The FAFSA and the college's own financial statement are required. Check with the school for current application deadlines.

International Students: They must take the TOEFL or the ALIGU. They must also take the SAT or ACT. Students who have not attended any school during the preceding 3 years are not required to submit standardized test scores.

Computers: All students may access the system. There are no time limits and no fees.

Graduates: In a recent year, 821 bachelor's degrees were awarded. The most popular majors were telecommunications (8%), electrical engineering (8%), and biology (7%). 79 companies recruited on campus in a recent year. In an average class, 12% graduate in 4 years or less, 34% graduate in 5 years or less, and 41% graduate in 6 years or less. Of a recent graduating class, 47% were enrolled in graduate school within 6 months of graduation and 89% were employed.

Admissions Contact: Director of Admission and Recruitment. A campus DVD is available. E-mail: *admissions@morgan.edu* Web: *www.morgan.edu*

MOUNT SAINT MARY'S UNIVERSITY   D-1
Emmitsburg, MD 21727

(301) 447-5214
(800) 448-4347; (301) 447-5860

Full-time: 648 men, 853 women	**Faculty:** 103; II A, --$
Part-time: 39 men, 80 women	**Ph.D.s:** 87%
Graduate: 279 men, 181 women	**Student/Faculty:** 14 to 1
Year: semesters, summer session	**Tuition:** $29,020
Application Deadline: see profile	**Room & Board:** $9878
Freshman Class: 2963 applied, 2497 accepted, 465 enrolled	
SAT CR/M: 520/520	**ACT:** 23 COMPETITIVE

Mount Saint Mary's University, founded in 1808, is a private liberal arts institution affiliated with the Roman Catholic Church. There are 4 undergraduate schools and 4 graduate schools. In addition to regional accreditation, The Mount has baccalaureate program accreditation with NASDTEC and NCATE. The library contains 216,740 volumes, 21,945 microform items, and 3,642 audio/video tapes/CDs/DVDs, and subscribes to 912 periodicals including electronic. Computerized library services include interlibrary loans, database searching, Internet access, and laptop Internet portals. Special learning facilities include a learning resource center, art gallery, radio station, TV station, and archives. The 1400-acre campus is in a rural area 60 miles northwest of Washington, D.C., and 50 miles west of Baltimore. Including any residence halls, there are 25 buildings.

Student Life: 57% of undergraduates are from Maryland. Others are from 35 states, 13 foreign countries, and Canada. 55% are from public

schools. 81% are white. 80% are Catholic; 16% Protestant. The average age of freshmen is 18; all undergraduates, 20. 22% do not continue beyond their first year; 72% remain to graduate.

Housing: 1272 students can be accommodated in college housing, which includes coed dorms and on-campus apartments. In addition, there are special-interest houses, wellness floors, and quiet floors. On-campus housing is guaranteed for all 4 years. 84% of students live on campus; of those, 80% remain on campus on weekends. All students may keep cars.

Activities: There are no fraternities or sororities. There are 70 groups on campus, including art, band, cheerleading, chess, choir, chorale, computers, dance, debate, drama, environmental, ethnic, honors, international, literary magazine, musical theater, newspaper, pep band, political, professional, radio and TV, religious, social, social service, student government, and yearbook. Popular campus events include Christmas Dance, Halloween Dance, and Crab Feast.

Sports: There are 9 intercollegiate sports for men and 10 for women, and 23 intramural sports for men and 18 for women. Facilities include multipurpose indoor courts, a track, a pool, aerobics facilities, a sauna, a weight room, a basketball arena, lighted tennis courts, and playing fields.

Disabled Students: 85% of the campus is accessible. Facilities include wheelchair ramps, elevators, special parking, specially equipped restrooms, special class scheduling, lowered drinking fountains, and lowered telephones.

Services: Counseling and information services are available, as is tutoring in every subject. There is a reader service for the blind, and remedial math. There is a study skills and language lab and a writing center. Closed-caption TV and software for sight-impaired students are also available.

Campus Safety and Security: Measures include 24-hour foot and vehicle patrol, emergency notification system, and security escort services. There are emergency telephones, lighted pathways/sidewalks, and controlled access to dorms/residences.

Programs of Study: The Mount confers B.A. and B.S. degrees. Master's degrees are also awarded. Bachelor's degrees are awarded in BIOLOGICAL SCIENCE (biochemistry and biology/biological science), BUSINESS (accounting, business administration and management, and sports management), COMMUNICATIONS AND THE ARTS (communications, English, fine arts, French, German, and Spanish), COMPUTER AND PHYSICAL SCIENCE (chemistry, computer science, information sciences and systems, and mathematics), EDUCATION (elementary education), ENGINEERING AND ENVIRONMENTAL DESIGN (environmental science), SOCIAL SCIENCE (criminal justice, economics, history, interdisciplinary studies, international studies, philosophy, political science/government, psychology, social studies, sociology, and theological studies). Business, biology, and elementary education are the largest.

Required: Students are required to take a 4-year, 52-credit core curriculum (with an additional foreign language proficiency requirement) in liberal arts, which includes a freshman seminar, a 4-course Western civilization sequence including art and literature, and courses in science and math, American culture, philosophy, theology, non-Western culture, and ethics. Graduation requirements include 120 credits, with most majors requiring 36 credits (30 to 36 in the major) and a minimum GPA of 2.0.

Special: Mount Saint Mary's offers cross-registration with an area community college, study abroad in the U.K., Europe, and South America, and secondary teacher certification in English, foreign languages, math, and social studies. Dual majors, interdisciplinary majors in biopsychology, American culture, and classical studies, a general studies degree, 3 dual degree programs, and nondegree and accelerated study are possible. A number of independently designed internships, work-study programs, and pass/fail options are available. There also is an integrated freshman year program. There are 19 national honor societies, a freshman honors program, and 14 departmental honors programs.

Faculty/Classroom: 53% of faculty are male; 47% are female. 90% teach undergraduates, 72% do research, and 72% do both. No introductory courses are taught by graduate students. The average class size in an introductory lecture is 23; in a laboratory is 16; and in a regular course is 20.

Admissions: 84% of the 2009-2010 applicants were accepted. The SAT scores for the 2009-2010 freshman class were: Critical Reading--33% below 500, 49% between 500 and 599, 16% between 600 and 700, and 2% above 700; Math--38% below 500, 40% between 500 and 599, 20% between 600 and 700, and 2% above 700; Writing--36% below 500, 47% between 500 and 599, 15% between 600 and 700, and 2% above 700. The ACT scores were 9% below 21, 43% between 21 and 23, 33% between 24 and 26, 9% between 27 and 28, and 5% above 28. 37% of the current freshmen were in the top fifth of their class; 67% were in the top two fifths. 2 freshmen graduated first in their class.

Requirements: The SAT is required. In addition, applicants should be graduates of an accredited secondary school or hold the GED. Secondary preparation should include 4 years of English, 3 each of math, history, natural science, and social sciences, and 2 of a foreign language. An interview is recommended. AP and CLEP credits are accepted. Important factors in the admissions decision are recommendations by school officials, advanced placement or honors courses, and extracurricular activities record.

Procedure: Freshmen are admitted fall and spring. Entrance exams should be taken by January of the senior year. There are early admissions, deferred admissions, and rolling admissions plans. Check with the school for current application deadlines. The fall 2009 application fee was $35. Applications are accepted on-line.

Transfer: 37 transfer students enrolled in 2008-2009. Transfer applicants should have at least a 2.0 GPA in previous college work, be in good academic and disciplinary standing, and account for all time elapsed since graduation from high school. 30 of 120 credits required for the bachelor's degree must be completed at The Mount.

Visiting: There are regularly scheduled orientations for prospective students, including campus tours and information sessions on academic programs, community life, admissions, and financial aid. There are guides for informal visits, visitors may sit in on classes, and stay overnight. To schedule a visit, conqact the Admissions Office at admissions@msmary.edu.

Financial Aid: In 2009-2010, 98% of all full-time freshmen and 98% of continuing full-time students received some form of financial aid. 72% of all full-time freshmen and 60% of continuing full-time students received need-based aid. The average freshman award was $17,925, with $2,909 ($8,000 maximum) from need-based scholarships or need-based grants; $5,150 ($6,700 maximum) from need-based self-help aid (loans and jobs); $11,550 ($38,898 maximum) from non-need-based athletic scholarships; and $13,600 ($28,420 maximum) from other non-need-based awards and non-need-based scholarships. 38% of undergraduate students work part-time. Average annual earnings from campus work are $1500. The average financial indebtedness of the 2009 graduate was $24,000. The FAFSA and the college's own financial statement are required. The deadline for filing freshman financial aid applications for fall entry is March 1.

International Students: There are 16 international students enrolled. They must take the TOEFL with a minimum score of 550 on the paper-based TOEFL (PBT) or 79 on the Internet-based version (iBT). They must also take the SAT or ACT.

Computers: There are 5 computer labs on campus with a total of 100 PCs available. Wireless service is available in all classrooms, dorm rooms, student union, dining areas, and library. All students may access the system 24 hours per day. There are no time limits and no fees. It is strongly recommended that all students have a personal computer.

Graduates: From July 1, 2008 to June 30, 2009, 403 bachelor's degrees were awarded. The most popular majors were business (19%), elementary education (11%), and communication studies (9%). 44 companies recruited on campus in 2008-2009. In an average class, 1% graduate in 3 years or less, 70% graduate in 4 years or less, 73% graduate in 5 years or less, and 73% graduate in 6 years or less. Of the 2008 graduating class, 30% were enrolled in graduate school within 6 months of graduation, and 90% were employed.

Admissions Contact: Michael Post, Dean of Admissions and Enrollment Management. A campus DVD is available. E-Mail: admissions@msmary.edu Web: www.msmary.edu

SAINT JOHN'S COLLEGE
Annapolis, MD 21404   E-3

(410) 626-2523
(800) 727-9238; (410) 269-7916

Full-time: 260 men, 230 women	**Faculty:** n/av
Part-time: none	**Ph.D.s:** 78%
Graduate: 50 men, 40 women	**Student/Faculty:** n/av
Year: semesters	**Tuition:** $37,000
Application Deadline: open	**Room & Board:** $9000
Freshman Class: n/av	
SAT or ACT: not required	**HIGHLY COMPETITIVE**

St. John's College, founded as King William's School in 1696 and chartered as St. John's in 1784, is a private institution that offers a single, all-required curriculum sometimes called the Great Books Program. Students and faculty work together in small discussion classes without lecture courses, written finals, or emphasis on grades. The program is a rigorous interdisciplinary curriculum based on the great works of literature, math, philosophy, theology, sciences, political theory, music, history, and economics. There is also a campus in Santa Fe, New Mexico. Figures in the above capsule and this profile are approximate. There is 1 graduate school. The 2 libraries contain 133,000 volumes, 2000 microform items, and 5000 audio/video tapes/CDs/DVDs, and subscribe to 240 periodicals including electronic. Computerized library services include interlibrary loans, database searching, Internet access, and laptop Internet portals. Special learning facilities include an art gallery and planetarium. The 36-acre campus is in a small town 35 miles east of Washington, D.C., and 32 miles south of Baltimore. Including any residence halls, there are 18 buildings.

Student Life: 83% of undergraduates are from out of state, mostly the South. Students are from 43 states, 12 foreign countries, and Canada.

60% are from public schools. 90% are white. 58% claim no religious affiliation; 22% Protestant. The average age of freshmen is 19; all undergraduates, 20. 20% do not continue beyond their first year; 76% remain to graduate.

Housing: 375 students can be accommodated in college housing, which includes single-sex and coed dorms. In addition, there are special-interest houses. On-campus housing is guaranteed for the freshman year only and is available on a lottery system for upperclassmen. 75% of students live on campus; of those, 95% remain on campus on weekends. Upperclassmen may keep cars.

Activities: There are no fraternities or sororities. There are 49 groups on campus, including art, chess, chorus, Christian fellowship, community, computers, dance, drama, environmental, fencing, film, garden, gay, international, Jewish fellowship, literary magazine, newspaper, orchestra, photography, poetry, political, religious, social, social service, student government, vegetarian, waltz and swing, and woodshop. Popular campus events include Reality Weekend, Senior Prank, and College Navy Croquet Match.

Sports: There are 4 intercollegiate sports for men and 4 for women, and 19 intramural sports for men and 19 for women. Facilities include a gym with a weight room, cardio room, and indoor running track, tennis courts, a boathouse for sailing and crew, a pier with floating docks, and playing fields.

Disabled Students: 70% of the campus is accessible. Facilities include wheelchair ramps, elevators, special parking, specially equipped restrooms, special class scheduling, lowered drinking fountains, lowered telephones, and special housing.

Services: Counseling and information services are available, as is tutoring in some subjects, including Greek, French, math, and writing. There is remedial math and writing.

Campus Safety and Security: Measures include 24-hour foot and vehicle patrol, emergency notification system, self-defense education, and security escort services. There are emergency telephones, lighted pathways/sidewalks, and controlled access to dorms/residences.

Programs of Study: St. John's confers B.A. degrees. Master's degrees are also awarded. Bachelor's degrees are awarded in SOCIAL SCIENCE (liberal arts/general studies, Western European studies, and Western civilization/culture).

Required: The common curriculum, equivalent to 132 credits, covers a range of classic to modern works. Students attend small seminars; 9-week preceptorials on specific works or topics; language, music, and math tutorials; and a 3-year natural sciences lab. Active learning occurs through discussion, translations, writing, experiment, mathematical demonstration, and musical analysis. Students take oral exams each semester and submit annual essays. Sophomores also take a math exam and seniors an oral exam that admits them to degree candidacy. Seniors also present a final essay to the faculty and take a 1-hour public oral exam.

Special: St. John's offers summer internships and an informal study-abroad program.

Faculty/Classroom: 73% of faculty are male; 27% are female. 93% teach undergraduates. No introductory courses are taught by graduate students. The average class size in a laboratory is 15 and in a regular course is 15.

Admissions: There were 4 National Merit finalists in a recent year.

Requirements: Applicants need not be high school graduates; some students are admitted before they complete high school. Test scores may be submitted but are not required. Secondary preparation should include 4 years of English, 3 years of math, and 2 years each of foreign language, science, and history. Applicants must submit written essays, which are critical to the admissions decision, and are strongly urged to visit. Important factors in the admissions decision are recommendations by school officials, advanced placement or honors courses, and personality/intangible qualities.

Procedure: Freshmen are admitted fall. There are early admissions, deferred admissions, and rolling admissions plans. Application deadlines are open. Notification is sent on a rolling basis. Applications are accepted on-line.

Transfer: 16 transfer students enrolled in a recent year. Transfer students may enter only as freshmen and must complete the entire program at St. John's. The admissions criteria are the same as for regular students. Students in good academic standing may transfer to the Santa Fe campus at the beginning of any academic year.

Visiting: There are regularly scheduled orientations for prospective students, consisting of an overnight stay on campus, class visits, and a tour. There are guides for informal visits, and visitors may sit in on classes and stay overnight. To schedule a visit, contact the Admission Office at (410) 626-2522.

Financial Aid: In a recent year, 61% of all full-time freshmen and 68% of continuing full-time students received some form of financial aid. 57% of all full-time freshmen and 65% of continuing full-time students received need-based aid. The average freshman award was $30,545. 75% of undergraduate students work part-time. Average annual earnings from campus work are $2700. The average financial indebtedness of a recent graduate was $23,760. St. John's is a member of CSS. The CSS/

Profile, the FAFSA, and parent and student federal tax returns are required. Check with the school for current application deadlines.

International Students: There were 12 international students enrolled in a recent year. The school actively recruits these students. They must take the TOEFL. They must also take the SAT.

Computers: Wireless access is available. PCs are located in student computer labs and the library. Wireless access in some dorms and public areas. All students may access the system 24 hours a day. There are no time limits and no fees.

Graduates: In a recent year, 104 bachelor's degrees were awarded. 7 companies recruited on campus in a recent year. In an average class, 63% graduate in 4 years or less, 71% graduate in 5 years or less, and 76% graduate in 6 years or less. Of a recent graduating class, 13% were enrolled in graduate school within 6 months of graduation and 60% were employed.

Admissions Contact: Director of Admissions. A campus DVD is available. E-Mail: *admissions@sjca.edu* Web: *www.sjca.edu*

SAINT MARY'S COLLEGE OF MARYLAND E-4

St. Marys City, MD 20686
(240) 895-5000
(800) 492-7181; (240) 895-5001

Full-time: 826 men, 1114 women	**Faculty:** 142; IIB
Part-time: 17 men, 21 women	**Ph.D.s:** 97%
Graduate: 8 men, 35 women	**Student/Faculty:** 12 to 1
Year: semesters, summer session	**Tuition:** $13,234 ($24,627)
Application Deadline: January 1	**Room & Board:** $9,950
Freshman Class: 2411 applied, 1381 accepted, 488 enrolled	
SAT CR/M/W: 640/610/620	**ACT:** 26 HIGHLY COMPETITIVE

St. Mary's College of Maryland, founded in 1840, is a small public liberal arts college designated by law as a Maryland honors college in 1992. There are no undergraduate schools and one graduate school. The library contains 1.7 million volumes, 40,602 microform items, 11,122 audio/video tapes/CDs/DVDs, and subscribes to 17,930 periodicals including electronic. Computerized library services include interlibrary loans, database searching, Internet access, and laptop Internet portals. Special learning facilities include a learning resource center, art gallery, radio station, TV station, historic archeological site, and estuarine research facilities. The 319-acre campus is in a rural area 70 miles southeast of Washington, D.C. Including any residence halls, there are 450 buildings.

Student Life: 84% of undergraduates are from Maryland. Students are from 33 states, 39 foreign countries, and Canada. 80% are white. The average age of freshmen is 18; all undergraduates, 20. 10% do not continue beyond their first year; 79% remain to graduate.

Housing: 1571 students can be accommodated in college housing, which includes single-sex and coed dorms and on-campus apartments. In addition, there are language houses and special-interest houses. On-campus housing is guaranteed for all 4 years. 80% of students live on campus; of those, 75% remain on campus on weekends. All students may keep cars.

Activities: There are no fraternities or sororities. There are 117 groups on campus, including academic, and sports, art, cheerleading, chess, choir, chorale, chorus, computers, dance, debate, drama, environmental, ethnic, film, gay, honors, international, jazz band, literary magazine, musical theater, newspaper, orchestra, outdoors, photography, political, professional, radio and TV, religious, social, social service, student government, symphony, and yearbook. Popular campus events include World Carnival, River Concert Series, and the Great Cardboard-Boat Race.

Sports: There are 8 intercollegiate sports for men and 9 for women, and 10 intramural sports for men and 10 for women. Facilities include an Olympic-size 50 meter pool, a 25-yard swimming pool, a 1,200-seat basketball and volleyball arena, an expanded health and fitness center, weight room, training room, exercise room, 2 gymnasiums, and locker and team rooms. Physical education, athletics, and recreation facilities also include 5 varsity practice fields, a track, 6 lighted tennis courts, an outdoor stadium, rowing center, and baseball facilities.

Disabled Students: 92% of the campus is accessible. Facilities include wheelchair ramps, elevators, special parking, specially equipped rest rooms, special class scheduling, lowered drinking fountains, lowered telephones, special housing, and living suites that meet ADA standards are also available.

Services: Counseling and information services are available, as is tutoring in some subjects, anthropology, biology, chemistry, computer science, economics, English, foreign languages, history, mathematics, physics, psychology, sociology, and writing. There is a reader service for the blind.

Campus Safety and Security: Measures include 24-hour foot and vehicle patrol, emergency notification system, self-defense education, and security escort services. There are emergency telephones, lighted pathways/sidewalks, access controls for dorms/residences, student security-assistant foot patrols, and nighthawk program from 8 P.M. until midnight.

Programs of Study: SMCM confers B.A. degrees. Master's degrees are also awarded. Bachelor's degrees are awarded in BIOLOGICAL SCI-

ENCE (biochemistry and biology/biological science), COMMUNICATIONS AND THE ARTS (art, art history and appreciation, dramatic arts, English, film arts, languages, music, and visual and performing arts), COMPUTER AND PHYSICAL SCIENCE (chemistry, computer science, mathematics, natural sciences, and physics), SOCIAL SCIENCE (anthropology, Asian/Oriental studies, economics, history, human development, philosophy, political science/government, psychology, public affairs, religion, and sociology). Biology, psychology, and economics are the largest.

Required: Students must complete complete core curriculum requirements, six breadth categories, and experiencing liberal arts in the world. There is also a St. Mary's Project or a senior experience. Students must meet additional requirements in their major fields and complete at least 128 semester hours with at least a 2.0 GPA.

Special: St. Mary's offers internships, study abroad, national and international exchange programs, and work-study. Dual and student-designed majors and a 3-2 engineering degree with the University of Maryland, College Park, also are offered. Non-degree study and pass/fail options are possible. There are 8 national honor societies, including Phi Beta Kappa, and a freshman honors program.

Faculty/Classroom: 56% of faculty are male; 44% are female. All teach and do research. No introductory courses are taught by graduate students.

Admissions: 57% of the 2009-2010 applicants were accepted. The SAT scores for the 2009-2010 freshman class were: Critical Reading--7% below 500, 24% between 500 and 599, 51% between 600 and 700, and 17% above 700; Math--12% below 500, 30% between 500 and 599, 52% between 600 and 700, and 6% above 700; Writing--9% below 500, 34% between 500 and 599, 48% between 600 and 700, and 9% above 700. The ACT scores were 7% below 21, 15% between 21 and 23, 30% between 24 and 26, 20% between 27 and 28, and 28% above 28. 71% of the current freshmen were in the top fifth of their class; 92% were in the top two fifths. 9 freshmen graduated first in their class.

Requirements: The SAT is required. In addition, applicants should have graduated from an accredited secondary school or earned the GED. Minimum high school preparation should include 4 units of English, 3 each of math, social studies, and science, and 7 electives. An essay, a resume of co-curricular activities, and 2 letters of recommendation are required. AP and CLEP credits are accepted. Important factors in the admissions decision are recommendations by school officials, extracurricular activities record, and advanced placement or honors courses.

Procedure: Freshmen are admitted fall. Entrance exams should be taken by the spring of their junior year. There is an early decision plan. Early decision applications should be filed by December 1; regular applications by January 1 for fall entry and November 1 for spring entry. The fall 2008 application fee was $50. Notification of early decision is sent January 1; regular decision, April 1. Applications are accepted on-line. 181 applicants were on a recent waiting list, 24 were accepted.

Transfer: 76 transfer students enrolled in 2008-2009. Transfer applicants must have a 2.0 GPA. Most successful applicants have at least a 3.0 GPA. 38 of 128 credits required for the bachelor's degree must be completed at SMCM.

Visiting: There are regularly scheduled orientations for prospective students, including personal interviews, group presentations, open house programs, meetings with faculty and students, and campus tours. There are guides for informal visits, visitors may sit in on classes, and stay overnight. To schedule a visit, contact the Office of Admissions at 800-492-7181.

Financial Aid: In 2009-2010, 80% of all full-time freshmen and 71% of continuing full-time students received some form of financial aid. 60% of all full-time freshmen and 51% of continuing full-time students received need-based aid. The average freshmen award was $7,000, with $2,000 ($7,000 maximum) from need-based scholarships or need-based grants; $2,000 ($3,250 maximum) from need-based self-help aid (loans and jobs); and $3,000 ($7,000 maximum) from other non-need-based awards and non-need-based scholarships. 25% of undergraduate students work part-time. Average annual earnings from campus work are $1000. The average financial indebtedness of the 2009 graduate was $17,125. SMCM is a member of CSS. The FAFSA is required. The priority date for freshman financial aid applications for fall entry is February 15. The deadline for filing freshman financial aid applications for fall entry is March 1.

International Students: There are 73 international students enrolled. The school actively recruits these students. They must take the TOEFL with a minimum score of 550 on the paper-based TOEFL (PBT) and the college's own test. They must also take the SAT or ACT.

Computers: Wireless access is available. Throughout the campus, there are approximately 400 PCs in computer labs across campus, featuring Microsoft Windows XP and the Apple MacOS operating systems. These computer labs are available to all students for word processing, spreadsheet, and database work. There are also several smart classrooms and discipline-specific labs on campus. All of the computer labs have access to the library system, e-mail, and the Internet. There is also wireless access in all academic building areas of the campus for those who own wireless-ready laptop computers. All students may access the system during all lab hours. There are no time limits and no fees.

Graduates: From July 1, 2008 to June 30, 2009, 488 bachelor's degrees were awarded. The most popular majors were English (13%), biology (11%), and psychology (10%). 32 companies recruited on campus in 2008-2009. In an average class, 70% graduate in 4 years or less, 75% graduate in 5 years or less, and 79% graduate in 6 years or less.

Admissions Contact: Dr. Wesley P. Jordan, Dean of Admissions and Financial Aid. A campus DVD is available. E-Mail: *admissions@smcm.edu* Web: *http://www.smcm.edu*

SALISBURY UNIVERSITY   F-4

Salisbury, MD 21801   **(410) 543-6161; (410) 546-6016**

Full-time: 2845 men, 3515 women	**Faculty:** IIA, -$
Part-time: 265 men, 320 women	**Ph.Ds:** 82%
Graduate: 175 men, 470 women	**Student/Faculty:** n/av
Year: 4-1-4, summer session	**Tuition:** $6500 ($14,500)
Application Deadline: see profile	**Room & Board:** $8000
Freshman Class: n/av	
SAT: required	**COMPETITIVE**

Salisbury University, founded in 1925, is a public comprehensive university providing undergraduate programs in the liberal arts, sciences, pre-professional and professional programs, and select applied graduate programs in business, education, nursing, psychology, English, and history. Figures in the above capsule and this profile are approximate. There are 4 undergraduate schools and 1 graduate school. In addition to regional accreditation, SU has baccalaureate program accreditation with AACSB, CSWE, NCATE, and NLN. The library contains 268,426 volumes, 752,217 microform items, and 1216 audio/video tapes/CDs/DVDs, and subscribes to 1241 periodicals including electronic. Computerized library services include interlibrary loans, database searching, and Internet access. Special learning facilities include a learning resource center, an art gallery, a radio station, a TV station, the Research Center for Delmarva History and Culture, the Enterprise Development Group, the Shorecan Small Business Resources Center, and the Scarborough Leadership Center. The 154-acre campus is in a rural area 110 miles southeast of Baltimore and 100 miles east of Washington, D.C. Including any residence halls, there are 55 buildings.

Student Life: 85% of undergraduates are from Maryland. Others are from 32 states, 56 foreign countries, and Canada. 82% are white; 11% African American. The average age of freshmen is 18; all undergraduates, 21. 19% do not continue beyond their first year; 70% remain to graduate.

Housing: 1700 students can be accommodated in college housing, which includes single-sex and coed dorms and off-campus apartments. On-campus housing is available on a first-come, first-served basis and is available on a lottery system for upperclassmen. 76% of students commute. Upperclassmen may keep cars.

Activities: 5% of men belong to 4 national fraternities; 6% of women belong to 4 national sororities. There are 104 groups on campus, including art, band, cheerleading, chess, choir, chorale, chorus, computers, dance, drama, ethnic, film, gay, honors, international, jazz band, literary magazine, musical theater, newspaper, orchestra, pep band, political, professional, radio and TV, religious, social, social service, student government, symphony, and yearbook. Popular campus events include October Fest, Spring Fling, and Festival of Culture.

Sports: There are 10 intercollegiate sports for men and 11 for women, and 16 intramural sports for men and 16 for women. Facilities include a 3000-seat stadium, a 2000-seat gym, a multipurpose gym, a 25-meter, 6-lane swimming pool, indoor climbing walls, a dance studio, racquetball and indoor and outdoor tennis courts, a baseball diamond, varsity and practice fields, an all-weather track, a fitness center, a strength room, lighted intramural fields, and outdoor sand volleyball courts.

Disabled Students: 90% of the campus is accessible. Facilities include wheelchair ramps, elevators, special parking, specially equipped restrooms, special class scheduling, lowered drinking fountains, and lowered telephones.

Services: Counseling and information services are available, as is tutoring in some subjects. There is a reader service for the blind, remedial math, reading, and writing, and extended test-taking time.

Campus Safety and Security: Measures include 24-hour foot and vehicle patrol, emergency notification system, self-defense education, and security escort services. There are shuttle buses, emergency telephones, and lighted pathways/sidewalks.

Programs of Study: SU confers B.A., B.S., B.A.S.W., and B.F.A. degrees. Master's degrees are also awarded. Bachelor's degrees are awarded in AGRICULTURE (environmental studies), BIOLOGICAL SCIENCE (biology/biological science), BUSINESS (accounting, banking and finance, business administration and management, management information systems, and marketing/retailing/merchandising), COMMUNICATIONS AND THE ARTS (art, communications, English, fine arts, French, music, Spanish, and theater management), COMPUTER AND PHYSICAL SCIENCE (chemistry, computer science, mathematics, and

physics), EDUCATION (athletic training, early childhood education, elementary education, health education, and physical education), HEALTH PROFESSIONS (environmental health science, exercise science, medical technology, nursing, and respiratory therapy), SOCIAL SCIENCE (economics, geography, history, interdisciplinary studies, international studies, peace studies, philosophy, political science/government, psychology, social work, and sociology). Chemistry, business, and education are the strongest academically. Business administration, elementary education, and biology are the largest.

Required: Students must complete 45 semester hours of general education requirements, including specific courses in English composition and literature, world civilization, humanities, social studies, math, and phys ed. The core curriculum also includes courses in art and physical or life science. The bachelor's degree requires completion of at least 120 semester hours, including 30 or more in the major field, with a minimum GPA of 2.0. Some majors may have higher requirements. 30 of the last 37 credit hours must be completed at SU, except for special co-op programs.

Special: Cross-registration with schools in the University System of Maryland and study abroad in numerous countries are offered. SU also offers an Annapolis semester, a Washington semester, internships, work-study programs, accelerated degree programs in dentistry, optometry, podiatric medicine, and pharmacy, dual majors in biology/environmental marine science, social work/sociology, and physical engineering, interdisciplinary and student-designed majors including physics/microelectronics, a 3-2 engineering degree with the University of Maryland at College Park, Old Dominion University, and Widener University, a co-op program in electrical engineering, and pass/fail options. There are 20 national honor societies, a freshman honors program, and 15 departmental honors programs.

Faculty/Classroom: 56% of faculty are male; 44% are female. All teach undergraduates, and 16% teach and do research. Graduate students teach 1% of introductory courses. The average class size in an introductory lecture is 32; in a laboratory, 21; and in a regular course, 26.

Requirements: The SAT is required. The ACT Optional Writing test is also required. In addition, applicants must be graduates of accredited secondary schools or have earned a GED. The university requires 14 academic credits or 20 Carnegie units, including 4 in English, 3 each in math and social studies, 3 in science (2 with labs), and 2 in foreign language. Auditions are required for admission into the music and B.F.A. programs once admission to the university is granted. Essays are recommended but not required. A campus visit is recommended for all students. The SAT is not required for any enrolling student with a 3.5 or greater GPA. A GPA of 2.0 is required. AP and CLEP credits are accepted. Important factors in the admissions decision are advanced placement or honors courses, leadership record, and extracurricular activities record.

Procedure: Freshmen are admitted to all sessions. Entrance exams should be taken by December of the senior year. Check with the school for current application deadlines. The fall 2009 application fee was $45. Applications are accepted on-line.

Transfer: 1136 transfer students enrolled in a recent year. Applicants must present a minimum GPA of 2.0 in at least 24 transferable credit hours earned. Students with fewer than 24 credit hours must be eligible for freshman admission in addition to maintaining at least a 2.0 GPA in college courses. 30 of 125 credits required for the bachelor's degree must be completed at SU.

Visiting: There are regularly scheduled orientations for prospective students, including presentations, tours, meetings with faculty and staff, and Saturday open house programs. There are guides for informal visits and visitors may sit in on classes. To schedule a visit, contact the Admissions Office.

Financial Aid: In a recent year, 73% of all full-time freshmen and 67% of continuing full-time students received some form of financial aid. 32% of all full-time freshmen and 27% of continuing full-time students received need-based aid. The average freshman award was $9832. Need-based scholarships or need-based grants averaged $5875 ($22,352 maximum); need-based self-help aid (loans and jobs) averaged $2250 ($24,258 maximum); and other non-need-based awards and non-need-based scholarships averaged $4145 ($20,600 maximum). 30% of undergraduate students work part-time. Average annual earnings from campus work are $2000. The average financial indebtedness of a recent graduate was $17,669. The FAFSA is required. Check with the school for current application deadlines.

International Students: There were 41 international students enrolled in a recent year. They must take the TOEFL and provide proof of VISA. They must also take the SAT or ACT.

Computers: Wireless access is available. The university's labs are all connected to the campus network, which provides Internet access. SU has 7 PC (30 units or more) computer labs as well as a 19 station Mac labs. Scanning and printing stations are available for student use in the main Fulton Hall labs. The campus network extends to all residence halls through the RESNET program. There are 2350 ports in residence halls. Each room has 1 connection for each student. All students may access the system 24 hours daily via modem or in residence halls. There are no time limits. The fee in 2009 was $150. It is strongly recommended that all students have a personal computer.

Graduates: In a recent year, 1439 bachelor's degrees were awarded. The most popular majors were business administration (19%), education (13%), and social sciences and history (10%). 250 companies recruited on campus in a recent year. In an average class, 52% graduate in 4 years or less, 67% graduate in 5 years or less, and 70% graduate in 6 years or less. Of a recent graduating class, 33% were enrolled in graduate school within 6 months of graduation and 95% were employed.

Admissions Contact: Aaron Basko, Director of Admissions. E-Mail: *admissions@salisbury.edu* Web: *www.salisbury.edu*

SOJOURNER-DOUGLASS COLLEGE

Baltimore, MD 21202

(410) 276-0306
(800) 732-2630; (410) 675-1810

Full-time: 40 men, 150 women	**Faculty:** n/av
Part-time: 20 men, 40 women	**Ph.D.s:** 18%
Graduate: none	**Student/Faculty:** n/av
Year: varies	**Tuition:** $9160
Application Deadline: open	
Freshman Class: n/av	
SAT or ACT: not required	**LESS COMPETITIVE**

Sojourner-Douglass College, established in 1980, is a private institution offering undergraduate programs in administration, human and social resources, and human growth and development to a predominantly black student body. Figures in the above capsule and this profile are approximate. The library contains 20,000 volumes. Special learning facilities include a learning resource center. The campus is in an urban area in Baltimore.

Student Life: All undergraduates are from Maryland.

Housing: There are no residence halls. All students commute.

Activities: There are no fraternities or sororities. There are 5 groups on campus, including student government and yearbook.

Sports: There is no sports program at Sojourner-Douglass.

Disabled Students: Facilities include wheelchair ramps, elevators, and special parking.

Services: Counseling and information services are available, as is tutoring in some subjects, including reading, writing, math, and study skills.

Programs of Study: Sojourner-Douglass confers B.A. degrees. Bachelor's degrees are awarded in BUSINESS (business administration and management and tourism), COMMUNICATIONS AND THE ARTS (broadcasting), EDUCATION (early childhood education), HEALTH PROFESSIONS (health care administration), SOCIAL SCIENCE (criminal justice, gerontology, psychology, public administration, and social work).

Required: To graduate, students must earn 63 to 66 general education credits, with 15 credits in English literature and composition; 15 credits in political science, history, economics, sociology, geography, psychology, and anthropology; 12 credits in the humanities; 9 credits in natural science and math; and 3 credits each in career planning and personal development, psychology of the black family in America, and psychology of racism. 12 credits must be earned in a project that demonstrates competence in the major. 6 credits must be earned in the sociology of work. There is also a 3-credit education seminar requirement. A total of 132 credits is needed to graduate, with 54 to 69 in the major.

Special: Credit may be granted for life, military, and work experience. Faculty-supervised independent study is possible for adult students.

Requirements: The SAT or ACT is not required. Applicants must be graduates of an accredited secondary school or have a GED certificate. They must have completed 4 years of English and 2 years each of math, history, and social studies. Autobiographical essays, resumes, and interviews are required.

Procedure: Freshmen are admitted to all sessions. There is a rolling admissions plan. Application deadlines are open.

Transfer: Transfer criteria are the same as for entering freshmen; however, transfers are not accepted to all classes.

Visiting: There are regularly scheduled orientations for prospective students. To schedule a visit, contact the Office of Admissions.

Financial Aid: The CCS/Profile, FAFSA, FFS, or SFS and federal income tax form is required. Check with the school for current application deadlines.

Computers: There are no time limits and no fees.

Admissions Contact: Coordinator, Admissions. Web: *www.sdc.edu*

STEVENSON UNIVERSITY
Villa Julia College

D-2

Stevenson, MD 21153

443-352-4444
(877) GO TO VJC; 443-352-4440

Full-time: 800 men, 1750 women	**Faculty:** IIB, -$
Part-time: 110 men, 425 women	**Ph.D.s:** 69%
Graduate: 75 men, 160 women	**Student/Faculty:** n/av
Year: semesters, summer session	**Tuition:** $22,090
Application Deadline: see profile	**Room & Board:** $9000
Freshman Class: n/av	
SAT or ACT: required	**COMPETITIVE**

Stevenson University, formerly Villa Julie College, was founded in 1947 and is an independent, comprehensive college offering a liberal arts education combined with career preparation. Figures in the above capsule and this profile are approximate. There is 1 graduate school. In addition to regional accreditation, Stevenson has baccalaureate program accreditation with NCATE and NLN. The library contains 84,047 volumes, 199,324 microform items, and 13,950 audio/video tapes/CDs/DVDs, and subscribes to 22,915 periodicals including electronic. Computerized library services include interlibrary loans, database searching, and Internet access. Special learning facilities include a learning resource center, art gallery, theater, and video studio. The 139-acre campus is in a suburban area 10 miles northwest of Baltimore. Including any residence halls, there are 30 buildings.

Student Life: 94% of undergraduates are from Maryland. Others are from 27 states and 7 foreign countries. 75% are from public schools. 71% are white; 15% African American. The average age of freshmen is 18; all undergraduates, 23. 17% do not continue beyond their first year.

Housing: 1157 students can be accommodated in college housing, which includes coed dorms and on-campus apartments. On-campus housing is available on a first-come, first-served basis. 61% of students commute. All students may keep cars.

Activities: There are no fraternities; 2% of women belong to 1 national sorority. There are 40 groups on campus, including art, band, cheerleading, chess, chorus, computers, dance, drama, environmental, ethnic, film, forensics, gay, honors, international, jazz band, literary magazine, newspaper, orchestra, pep band, photography, political, professional, religious, social, social service, and student government. Popular campus events include Welcome Picnic, Founder's Day, and SGA Haunted Trail and Bonfire.

Sports: There are 10 intercollegiate sports for men and 11 for women, and 6 intramural sports for men and 6 for women. Facilities include tennis courts, an athletic field, a 1000-seat gym, a fitness center, a NATA-certified training room, and an aerobics room.

Disabled Students: 99% of the campus is accessible. Facilities include wheelchair ramps, elevators, special parking, specially equipped restrooms, special class scheduling, lowered drinking fountains, lowered telephones, and special housing.

Services: Counseling and information services are available, as is tutoring in most subjects. There is remedial math, reading, and writing. Free individual tutoring as well as study groups led by a tutor, peer tutoring, paraprofessional tutoring, and faculty tutoring are available.

Campus Safety and Security: Measures include 24-hour foot and vehicle patrol, emergency notification system, self-defense education, and security escort services. There are shuttle buses, emergency telephones, and lighted pathways/sidewalks.

Programs of Study: Stevenson confers B.A. and B.S. degrees. Master's degrees are also awarded. Bachelor's degrees are awarded in BIOLOGICAL SCIENCE (biology/biological science and biotechnology), BUSINESS (accounting, banking and finance, business administration and management, business communications, business systems analysis, and marketing management), COMMUNICATIONS AND THE ARTS (art, dramatic arts, English literature, film arts, video, and visual design), COMPUTER AND PHYSICAL SCIENCE (applied mathematics, chemistry, computer security and information assurance, information sciences and systems, and mathematics), EDUCATION (early childhood education and elementary education), HEALTH PROFESSIONS (medical laboratory technology and nursing), SOCIAL SCIENCE (history, human services, interdisciplinary studies, paralegal studies, psychology, and public affairs). Education, nursing, and paralegal are the strongest academically. Paralegal, nursing, and business are the largest.

Required: The core curriculum includes courses in writing, communication, fine arts, social sciences, math, natural science, humanities, and phys ed. Courses in computer information systems are also required. Students must complete a minimum of 120 hours, including 45 hours in upper-level courses, with at least a 2.0 overall GPA. The number of hours required per major varies. Many majors require a capstone course or an internship.

Special: Co-op programs and internships are available. In addition, study abroad, service learning, field placements, independent study and research, and other experiential learning opportunities are offered as part of classes. Cross-registration, work study, accelerated degree programs, and student-designed majors are possible. There are 10 national honor societies and a freshman honors program.

Faculty/Classroom: 43% of faculty are male; 57% are female. 99% teach undergraduates. No introductory courses are taught by graduate students.

Admissions: 5 freshmen graduated first in their class in a recent year. **Requirements:** The SAT or ACT is required. In addition, applicants must be graduates of an accredited secondary school. Although a secondary transcript is required, particular secondary preparation is not stipulated for all programs. Some degree programs do require specific high school courses, however. An essay is required and an interview is recommended. AP and CLEP credits are accepted. Important factors in the admissions decision are advanced placement or honors courses, recommendations by school officials, and leadership record.

Procedure: Freshmen are admitted fall, spring, and summer. Entrance exams should be taken between September and November of the senior year. There are deferred admissions and rolling admissions plans. Application deadlines are open. The application fee is $25. Applications are accepted on-line.

Transfer: 235 transfer students enrolled in a recent year. Transfer applicants must provide both college and high school transcripts and have a minimum 2.5 GPA. Transfer students with a 2.0 cumulative GPA and other accomplishments or experience may be granted conditional admission to the college. 30 of 120 credits required for the bachelor's degree must be completed at Stevenson.

Visiting: There are regularly scheduled orientations for prospective students, including a general overview, information on how to apply and how to finance a college education, special academic presentations, tours, meetings with faculty and students, and lunch. There are guides for informal visits and visitors may sit in on classes. To schedule a visit, contact the Admissions Office.

Financial Aid: Steveson is a member of CSS. The FAFSA is required. Check with the school for current application deadlines.

International Students: There were 8 international students enrolled in a recent year. They must take the TOEFL with a minimum score of 550 on the paper-based TOEFL (PBT) or 80 on the Internet-based version (iBT).

Computers: Wireless access is available. All students may access the system at all times. There are no time limits and no fees.

Graduates: In a recent year, 553 bachelor's degrees were awarded. The most popular majors were business/marketing (22%), health professions and related sciences (22%), and visual and performing arts (11%). 55 companies recruited on campus in a recent year. In an average class, 49% graduate in 4 years or less, 61% graduate in 5 years or less, and 61% graduate in 6 years or less. Of a recent graduating class, 17% were enrolled in graduate school within 6 months of graduation and 97% were employed.

Admissions Contact: Mark J. Hergan, Vice President for Enrollment Management. A campus DVD is available. E-Mail: *admissions@vjc.edu* Web: *www.vjc.edu*

TOWSON UNIVERSITY   D-2
Towson, MD 21252-0001

	(410) 704-2113
	(888) 4-TOWSON; (410) 704-3030
Full-time: 5540 men, 8645 women	**Faculty:** IIA, -$
Part-time: 940 men, 1105 women	**Ph.D.s:** 52%
Graduate: 890 men, 2655 women	**Student/Faculty:** n/av
Year: semesters, summer session	**Tuition:** $8000 ($17,500)
Application Deadline: see profile	**Room & Board:** $8000
Freshman Class: n/av	
SAT or ACT: required	**VERY COMPETITIVE**

Towson University, founded in 1866, is part of the University System of Maryland and offers undergraduate and graduate programs in liberal arts and sciences, allied health sciences, education, fine arts, communication, and business and economics. Figures in the above capsule and this profile are approximate. There are 7 undergraduate schools and 1 graduate school. In addition to regional accreditation, Towson has baccalaureate program accreditation with AACSB, CAHEA, NASDTEC, NASM, NCATE, and NLN. The library contains 364,468 volumes, 830,286 microform items, and 14,174 audio/video tapes/CDs/DVDs, and subscribes to 2164 periodicals including electronic. Computerized library services include interlibrary loans, database searching, and Internet access. Special learning facilities include a learning resource center, art gallery, planetarium, radio station, TV station, curriculum center, herbarium, animal museum, observatory, and greenhouse. The 328-acre campus is in a suburban area 2 miles north of Baltimore. Including any residence halls, there are 44 buildings.

Student Life: 80% of undergraduates are from Maryland. 69% are white; 12% African American. The average age of freshmen is 19; all undergraduates, 22.

Housing: 3518 students can be accommodated in college housing, which includes coed dorms and on-campus apartments. In addition, there are honors houses, special-interest houses, separate floors that are alcohol-free, smoke-free, and substance-free, leadership and quiet floors, and an international house. On-campus housing is available on a first-come, first-served basis and is available on a lottery system for upperclassmen. Priority is given to out-of-town students. 78% of students commute. Upperclassmen may keep cars.

Activities: 8% of men belong to 13 national fraternities; 6% of women belong to 11 national sororities. Groups on campus include art, band, cheerleading, choir, chorale, chorus, computers, dance, drama, drill team, environmental, ethnic, forensics, gay, honors, international, jazz band, literary magazine, marching band, musical theater, orchestra, pep band, photography, political, professional, religious, social, social service, student government, and symphony. Popular campus events include fraternity and sorority dances, Ethics Forum, and Tiger Fest.

Sports: There are 7 intercollegiate sports for men and 12 for women. Facilities include an athletic center, a stadium, baseball and softball fields, tennis courts, a pool, a soccer field, and 3 practice fields. Recreation facilities include 3 gyms, a weight room, a pool, lighted playing fields, and an indoor climbing wall.

Disabled Students: 85% of the campus is accessible. Facilities include wheelchair ramps, elevators, special parking, specially equipped restrooms, special class scheduling, lowered drinking fountains, lowered telephones, special housing, automatic doors, assistive listening devices in theaters and concert halls, and interior and exterior signage.

Services: Counseling and information services are available, as is tutoring in most subjects. There is a reader service for the blind and remedial math, reading, and writing. There are also note takers, English language and tutorial services centers, a writing lab, and signers for the hearing impaired.

Campus Safety and Security: Measures include 24-hour foot and vehicle patrol, emergency notification system, self-defense education, and security escort services. There are shuttle buses, emergency telephones, lighted pathways/sidewalks, controlled access to dorms/residences, Operation ID, and a police dog on campus.

Programs of Study: Towson confers B.A., B.S., B.F.A., and B.M. degrees. Master's and doctoral degrees are also awarded. Bachelor's degrees are awarded in BIOLOGICAL SCIENCE (biology/biological science and molecular biology), BUSINESS (accounting, business administration and management, and sports management), COMMUNICATIONS AND THE ARTS (art, communications, dance, English, French, German, media arts, music, Spanish, and theater design), COMPUTER AND PHYSICAL SCIENCE (chemistry, computer science, earth science, geology, geoscience, information sciences and systems, mathematics, and physics), EDUCATION (art education, athletic training, dance education, early childhood education, education, education of the deaf and hearing impaired, elementary education, music education, physical education, and special education), ENGINEERING AND ENVIRONMENTAL DESIGN (environmental science), HEALTH PROFESSIONS (exercise science, health care administration, health science, medical laboratory technology, nursing, occupational therapy, speech pathology/audiology, and sports medicine), SOCIAL SCIENCE (anthropology, crosscultural studies, economics, family/consumer studies, geography, gerontology, history, interdisciplinary studies, international studies, law, philosophy, political science/government, psychology, religion, social science, sociology, and women's studies). Fine arts, business, and education are the strongest academically. Business disciplines, mass communications, and psychology are the largest.

Required: Students must complete course work in the arts, English, humanities, math, biological or physical science, social science, information technology, and global awareness.

Special: Towson University offers cooperative programs with other institutions in the University System of Maryland and at Loyola College, the College of Notre Dame, and Johns Hopkins University, cross-registration at more than 80 colleges through the National Student Exchange, and study abroad. Students may pursue a dual major in physics and engineering, an interdisciplinary studies degree, which allows them to design their own majors, a 3-2 engineering program with the University of Maryland at College Park and Penn State, or nondegree study. There are pass/fail options, extensive evening offerings, and opportunities to earn credits between semesters. Internships are available in most majors, and work-study programs are offered both on and off campus. There are 20 national honor societies, a freshman honors program, and 12 departmental honors programs.

Faculty/Classroom: 50% of faculty are male; 50% are female. No introductory courses are taught by graduate students. The average class size in an introductory lecture is 25; in a laboratory, 24; and in a regular course, 25.

Admissions: 9 freshmen graduated first in their class in a recent year. **Requirements:** The SAT or ACT is required. The ACT Optional Writing test is also required. In addition, applicants should have graduated from an accredited secondary school or earned the GED. Secondary preparation should include 4 years of English, 3 each of math, lab science, and social studies, and 2 of foreign language. Prospective music and dance majors must audition. A GPA of 3.1 is required. AP and CLEP credits are accepted. Important factors in the admissions decision are advanced placement or honors courses, recommendations by school officials, and leadership record.

Procedure: Freshmen are admitted fall and spring. Entrance exams should be taken in the junior or senior year. There are deferred admissions and rolling admissions plans. Check with the school for current application deadlines. The fall 2009 application fee was $45. Notification is sent on a rolling basis. Applications are accepted on-line. A waiting list is maintained.

Transfer: 2500 transfer students enrolled in a recent year. Transfer applicants should have earned at least 30 academic credits. For those with fewer than 30 attempted, freshmen requirements must be met. Minimum GPA requirements range from 2.0 to 2.5, depending on the number of credits completed. Transcripts are required. 30 of 120 credits required for the bachelor's degree must be completed at Towson.

Visiting: There are regularly scheduled orientations for prospective students, including campus tours, a session for parents, a session on the admissions process for transfers and freshmen, and a roundtable discussion. There are guides for informal visits. To schedule a visit, contact the Admissions Office.

Financial Aid: In a recent year, 70% of all full-time freshmen and 62% of continuing full-time students received some form of financial aid. 43% of all full-time freshmen and 39% of continuing full-time students received need-based aid. The average freshman award was $12,131. 72% of undergraduate students work part-time. Average annual earnings from campus work are $1185. The average financial indebtedness of a recent graduate was $14,085. The FAFSA is required. Check with the school for current application deadlines.

International Students: The school actively recruits these students. They must take the TOEFL and the college's own test. The TOEFL is required at preadmission; a college test is required at postadmission. They must also take the SAT or ACT; the school accepts the TOEFL as a substitute for the verbal SAT.

Computers: Wireless access is available. All students may access the system. Systems are accessible 24 hours daily except 5 P.M. to 9 P.M. Fridays. There are no time limits and no fees.

Graduates: In a recent year, 3120 bachelor's degrees were awarded. The most popular majors were business administration (16%), psychology (8%), and mass communication (7%). 115 companies recruited on campus in a recent year.

Admissions Contact: Director of Admissions. A campus DVD is available. E-mail: *admissions@towson.edu* Web: *www.towson.edu*

UNITED STATES NAVAL ACADEMY
E-3

Annapolis, MD 21402-5018
(410) 293-4361
(888) 249-7707; (410) 293-1815

Full-time: 3640 men, 928 women	Faculty: 525; IIB, ++$
Part-time: none	Ph.D.s: 64%
Graduate: none	Student/Faculty: 9 to 1
Year: semesters, summer session	Tuition: n/app
Application Deadline: January 31	
Freshman Class: 4644 applied, 1464 accepted, 1251 enrolled	
SAT or ACT: required	MOST COMPETITIVE

The United States Naval Academy, founded in 1845, is a national military service college offering undergraduate degree programs and professional training in aviation, surface ships, submarines, and various military, maritime, and technical fields. The U.S. Navy pays tuition, room and board, medical and dental care, and a monthly stipend to all Naval Academy students. Graduates earn a Bachelor of Science degree and a commission in the United States Navy or the United States Marine Corp and have a five year obligation of active military service. In addition to regional accreditation, Annapolis has baccalaureate program accreditation with ABET and CSAB. The library contains 701,505 volumes, 201,854 microform items, and 7,317 audio/video tapes/CDs/DVDs, and subscribes to 1,979 periodicals including electronic. Computerized library services include interlibrary loans, database searching, Internet access, and laptop Internet portals. Special learning facilities include a learning resource center, planetarium, radio station, a propulsion lab, a nuclear reactor, an oceanographic research vessel, towing tanks, a flight simulator, and a naval history museum. The 329-acre campus is in a small town 30 miles southeast of Baltimore and 35 miles east of Washington, D.C. Including any residence halls, there are 75 buildings.

Student Life: 96% of undergraduates are from out of state, mostly the Northeast. Others are from 49 states, and 28 foreign countries. 71% are white. 38% are Protestant; 36% Catholic. The average age of freshmen is 18; all undergraduates, 20. 6% do not continue beyond their first year; 86% remain to graduate.

Housing: 4700 students can be accommodated in college housing, which includes coed dorms. On-campus housing is guaranteed for all 4 years. Upperclassmen may keep cars.

Activities: There are no fraternities or sororities. There are 75 groups on campus, including bagpipe, cheerleading, chess, choir, chorus, computers, debate, drama, drill team, drum and bugle corps, ethnic, honors, international, jazz band, literary magazine, marching band, musical theater, orchestra, pep band, photography, professional, radio and TV, religious, social, social service, student government, and yearbook. Popular campus events include Commissioning Week, which includes the Plebe Recognition Ceremony, Ring Dance, and graduation.

Sports: There are 19 intercollegiate sports for men and 11 for women, and 23 intramural sports for men and 23 for women. Facilities include a 34,000-seat stadium, a 5700-seat basketball arena, an Olympic pool with a diving well for 10-meter diving boards, a wrestling arena, a 200-meter indoor track, a 400-meter outdoor track, an indoor ice rink, 6 nautilus and weight rooms, facilities for gymnastics, boxing, volleyball, swimming, water polo, racquetball, basketball and personal conditioning, squash courts, climbing wall, baseball stadium, crew house, 18 hole golf course, soccer facility, sailing center, indoor and outdoor tennis courts, and 2 athletic field houses.

Disabled Students: All of the campus is accessible. Facilities include wheelchair ramps, elevators, special parking, and specially equipped restrooms.

Services: Counseling and information services are available, as is tutoring in most subjects. There is remedial math, reading, and writing.

Campus Safety and Security: Measures include 24-hour foot and vehicle patrol, emergency notification system, and self-defense education. There are emergency telephones, lighted pathways/sidewalks, controlled access to dorms/residences, in-room safes, and gate guards.

Programs of Study: Annapolis confers B.S. degrees. Bachelor's degrees are awarded in COMMUNICATIONS AND THE ARTS (Arabic, Chinese, and English), COMPUTER AND PHYSICAL SCIENCE (applied mathematics, chemistry, computer science, information sciences and systems, mathematics, oceanography, physics, and science), ENGINEERING AND ENVIRONMENTAL DESIGN (aeronautical engineering, aerospace studies, aerospace studies, electrical/electronics engineering technology, engineering, marine engineering, mechanical engineering, naval architecture and marine engineering, ocean engineering, and systems engineering), SOCIAL SCIENCE (economics, history, and political science/government). Political science, mechanical engineering, and systems engineering are the largest.

Required: Students must complete approximately 140 semester hours, including core requirements in mathematics, engineering, natural sciences, humanities, and social sciences. Physical education is required during all 4 years. Physical readiness test must be passed semi-annually. During required summer training sessions, students train aboard U.S. Navy ships, submarines, and aircraft and with units of the U.S. Marine Corps. Graduates serve at least 5 years on active duty as commissioned officers of the Navy or Marine Corps.

Special: A voluntary graduate program is available for those midshipmen who complete academic graduation requirements by the end of their seventh semester and wish to begin master's work at nearby universities, such as Georgetown, Johns Hopkins, or Maryland. Trident Scholars spend their senior year in independent research at the Naval Academy. Study abroad is available in 6 countries. There are 10 national honor societies and 5 departmental honors programs.

Faculty/Classroom: 80% of faculty are male; 20% are female. All teach undergraduates. No introductory courses are taught by graduate students. The average class size in an introductory lecture, 23, in a laboratory, 10, and in a regular course is, 15.

Admissions: 32% of the 2009-2010 applicants were accepted. The SAT scores for the 2009-2010 freshman class were: Critical Reading--8% below 500, 35% between 500 and 599, 41% between 600 and 700, and 16% above 700; Math--5% below 500, 25% between 500 and 599, 49% between 600 and 700, and 21% above 700. 76% of the current freshmen were in the top fifth of their class; 91% were in the top two fifths.

Requirements: The SAT or ACT is required. In addition, candidates must be unmarried with no dependents, U.S. citizens of good moral character, and between 17 and 23 years of age. Candidates should have a sound secondary school background, including 4 years each of English and math, 2 years of a foreign language, and 1 year each of U.S. history, world or European history, chemistry, physics, and computer literacy. Candidates must obtain an official nomination from congressional or military sources. An interview is conducted, and medical and physical exams must be passed to qualify for admission. AP credits are accepted.

Procedure: Freshmen are admitted in the summer. Entrance exams should be taken after December of the junior year. There are early admissions and rolling admissions plans. Applications should be filed by January 31 for fall entry. Notifications are sent April 15. Applications are accepted on-line. A waiting list is maintained.

Transfer: All students enter as freshmen. 140 of 140 credits required for the bachelor's degree must be completed at Annapolis.

Visiting: There are regularly scheduled orientations for prospective students, including visitation weekends for highly competitive candidates for admission, and summer seminar weeks for rising high school seniors. There are guides for informal visits; visitors may sit in on classes and stay overnight..

Financial Aid: Check with the school for current application deadlines.

International Students: There are 53 international students enrolled. The school actively recruits these students. They must take the TOEFL. They must also take the SAT or ACT.

Computers: There are no time limits and no fees. All students are required to have a personal computer. A Each student is issued a standardized personal computer.

Graduates: From July 1, 2008 to June 30, 2009, 1055 bachelor's degrees were awarded. The most popular majors were political science (17%), economics (12%), and mechanical engineering (9%). 2 companies recruited on campus in 2008-2009. In an average class, 85% graduate in 4 years or less. Of the 2008 graduating class, 2% were enrolled in graduate school within 6 months of graduation, and 100% were employed.

Admissions Contact: Candidate Guidance Office
Web: www.usna.edu

UNIVERSITY OF MARYLAND/BALTIMORE COUNTY D-2

Baltimore, MD 21250   (410) 455-2291; (410) 455-1094

Full-time: 4360 men, 3605 women	Faculty: I, -$
Part-time: 760 men, 745 women	Ph.D.s: 85%
Graduate: 1160 men, 1420 women	Student/Faculty: n/av
Year: 4-1-4, summer session	Tuition: $9000 ($18,000)
Application Deadline: see profile	Room & Board: $9000
Freshman Class: n/av	
SAT or ACT: required	**VERY COMPETITIVE**

UMBC, founded in 1966, is a public research university offering programs in liberal arts and sciences and engineering. There are 4 undergraduate schools and 3 graduate schools. Figures in the above capsule and this profile are approximate. In addition to regional accreditation, UMBC has baccalaureate program accreditation with ABET, CSWE, and NCATE. The library contains 1.0 million volumes, 1.1 million microform items, and 1.9 million audio/video tapes/CDs/DVDs, and subscribes to 4138 periodicals including electronic. Computerized library services include interlibrary loans, database searching, and Internet access. Special learning facilities include a learning resource center, an art gallery, a radio station, the Imaging Research Center, the Howard Hughes Medical Institute, and a telescope. The 530-acre campus is in a suburban area 5 miles southwest of Baltimore and 35 miles north of Washington, D.C. Including any residence halls, there are 50 buildings.

Student Life: 89% of undergraduates are from Maryland. Others are from 43 states, 95 foreign countries, and Canada. 52% are white; 18% Asian American; 15% African American. The average age of freshmen is 18; all undergraduates, 22. 15% do not continue beyond their first year; 56% remain to graduate.

Housing: 3850 students can be accommodated in college housing, which includes single-sex and coed dorms and on-campus apartments. In addition, there are honors houses, language houses, special-interest houses, wellness and quiet-study floors, and same-sex floors. On-campus housing is guaranteed for the freshman year only and is available on a first-come, first-served basis. 66% of students commute. Alcohol is not permitted. All students may keep cars.

Activities: 4% of men belong to 11 national fraternities; 4% of women belong to 8 national sororities. There are 180 groups on campus, including art, band, cheerleading, chess, choir, chorus, computers, Council of Majors, dance, debate, drama, ethnic, film, gay, honors, Intellectual Sports Council, international, jazz band, literary magazine, Model United Nations, musical threater, newspaper, opera, orchestra, pep band, political, professional, radio and TV, religious, social, social service, student government, and symphony. Popular campus events include Quadmania, Welcome Week, and Family Weekend.

Sports: There are 8 intercollegiate sports for men and 9 for women, and 16 intramural sports for men and 16 for women. Facilities include a multipurpose arena, an aquatic center, a fitness center, tennis courts, a 4500-seat stadium, playing and practice fields, an indoor track, an outdoor cross-country course, a golf driving range, a track and field complex, and a soccer stadium.

Disabled Students: 95% of the campus is accessible. Facilities include wheelchair ramps, elevators, special parking, specially equipped rest rooms, special class scheduling, lowered drinking fountains, lowered telephones, a Braille writer, tape recorders, talking book machines, TTY, talking calculators, Optacon, and information on the talking computer.

Services: Counseling and information services are available, as is tutoring in most subjects. There is a reader service for the blind and remedial math, reading, and writing. Other services include notetakers, readers, mobility training, American Sign Language interpreters, and scribes for students who have a need based on a manual or learning disability.

Campus Safety and Security: Measures include self-defense education and security escort services. There are shuttle buses, emergency telephones, lighted pathways/sidewalks, a 24-hour police department, and a campus risk management department.

Programs of Study: UMBC confers B.A., B.S., B.F.A., and B.S.E. degrees. Master's and doctoral degrees are also awarded. Bachelor's degrees are awarded in AGRICULTURE (environmental studies), BIO-

LOGICAL SCIENCE (biochemistry, bioinformatics, and biology/biological science), COMMUNICATIONS AND THE ARTS (communications, dance, dramatic arts, English, fine arts, French, German, linguistics, modern language, music, Russian, Spanish, theater design, and visual and performing arts), COMPUTER AND PHYSICAL SCIENCE (chemistry, computer science, information sciences and systems, mathematics, physics, and statistics), ENGINEERING AND ENVIRONMENTAL DESIGN (chemical engineering, computer engineering, environmental science, and mechanical engineering), HEALTH PROFESSIONS (emergency medical technologies and health science), SOCIAL SCIENCE (African American studies, American studies, anthropology, classical/ancient civilization, economics, gender studies, geography, history, interdisciplinary studies, philosophy, political science/government, psychology, social work, sociology, and women's studies). Information systems, computer science, and biological sciences are the largest.

Required: To graduate, students are required to complete at least 120 credits, including 45 at the upper-division level, with a minimum GPA of 2.0. The core curriculum includes courses in arts and humanities, social sciences, math and natural sciences, phys ed, and modern or classical language and culture. Students must pass an English composition course with a C or better.

Special: Dual and student-designed majors, cooperative education programs in all majors, a Washington semester, the Sondheim Public Affairs Scholars Program, cross-registration with University of Maryland schools and Johns Hopkins University, internships, both paid and nonpaid, in public, private, and nonprofit organizations, study abroad in 19 countries, work-study programs, B.A.-B.S. degrees, pass/fail options, and nondegree study are available. UMBC also offers various opportunities in interdisciplinary studies and in such fields as artificial intelligence and optical communications. There are 15 national honor societies, including Phi Beta Kappa, a freshman honors program, and 17 departmental honors programs.

Faculty/Classroom: 61% of faculty are male; 39% are female. No introductory courses are taught by graduate students. The average class size in an introductory lecture is 41; in a laboratory, 28; and in a regular course, 30.

Requirements: The SAT or ACT is required. In addition, minimum high school preparation should include 4 years of English, 3 years each of social science/history and math, including algebra I and II and geometry, 3 years of lab sciences and 2 of a foreign language. An essay is required of all freshman applicants. A GPA of 3.0 is required. AP and CLEP credits are accepted. Important factors in the admissions decision are advanced placement or honors courses, recommendations by school officials, and leadership record.

Procedure: Freshmen are admitted to all sessions. Entrance exams should be taken by fall of the senior year. There is an early admissions plan. Check with the school for current application deadlines. The fall 2009 application fee was $50. Applications are accepted on-line. A waiting list is maintained.

Transfer: 1454 transfer students enrolled in a recent year. A 2.5 cumulative GPA for all previous college work is recommended. Applicants with fewer than 30 semester hours should submit SAT scores and the high school transcript; they must also meet freshman admission requirements. 30 of 120 credits required for the bachelor's degree must be completed at UMBC.

Visiting: There are regularly scheduled orientations for prospective students, including a group information session with an admissions counselor followed by a student-guided walking tour of campus. Saturday information sessions and 4 campus open houses are also scheduled each fall. Summer preview days are in July and August. There are 2 transfer open houses. There are guides for informal visits, and visitors may sit in on classes and stay overnight. To schedule a visit, contact Office of Undergraduate Admissions.

Financial Aid: In a recent year, 46% of all full-time freshmen and 45% of continuing full-time students received some form of financial aid. 39% of all full-time freshmen and 43% of continuing full-time students received need-based aid. All undergraduate students work part-time. Average annual earnings from campus work are $1335. The average financial indebtedness of a recent graduate was $20,298. The FAFSA is required. Check with the school for current application deadlines.

International Students: There were 316 international students enrolled in a recent year. They must take the TOEFL with a minimum score of 550 on the paper-based TOEFL (PBT) or 80 on the Internet-based version (iBT).

Computers: There is wireless access throughout most academic buildings. There are 800 open, wired network connections available to students in the library, 107 in classrooms, 800 in computer labs, and 6000 elsewhere in the university. All college-owned and affiliated housing units are wired for high-speed Internet access. All students may access the system. For modem dial-up access, there is a 200 hour per month limit). All other access is unlimited. There are no fees. It is strongly recommended that all students have a personal computer.

Graduates: In a recent year, 1914 bachelor's degrees were awarded. The most popular majors were psychology (12%), information systems

(11%), and biological sciences (11%). In an average class, 1% graduate in 3 years or less, 35% graduate in 4 years or less, 53% graduate in 5 years or less, and 59% graduate in 6 years or less.

Admissions Contact: Director of Admissions. E-Mail: *admissions@umbc.edu* Web: *www.umbc.edu*

UNIVERSITY OF MARYLAND/COLLEGE PARK   D-3

| College Park, MD 20742 | (301) 314-8385 |
| | (800) 422-5867; (301) 314-9693 |

Full-time: 12,893 men, 11,724 women	**Faculty:** 1644; I, +$
Part-time: 1066 men, 859 women	**Ph.D.s:** n/av
Graduate: 5552 men, 5101 women	**Student/Faculty:** 15 to 1
Year: semesters, summer session	**Tuition:** $8052 ($23,989)
Application Deadline: January 20	**Room & Board:** $9375
Freshman Class: 28,443 applied, 11,976 accepted, 4202 enrolled	
SAT or ACT: required	**HIGHLY COMPETITIVE**

The University of Maryland/College Park, founded in 1856, is a land-grant institution and the flagship campus of the state's university system, offering undergraduate and graduate degrees. There are 11 undergraduate schools and 13 graduate schools. In addition to regional accreditation, Maryland has baccalaureate program accreditation with AACSB, ABET, ACEJMC, ASLA, NASM, and NCATE. The 7 libraries contain 3.8 million volumes, 5.8 million microform items, and 405,567 audio/video tapes/CDs/DVDs, and subscribe to 51,989 periodicals including electronic. Computerized library services include interlibrary loans, database searching, Internet access, and laptop Internet portals. Special learning facilities include a learning resource center, art gallery, radio station, TV station, and observatory. The 1250-acre campus is in a suburban area 3 miles northeast of Washington, D.C., and 35 miles south of Baltimore. Including any residence halls, there are 273 buildings.

Student Life: 76% of undergraduates are from Maryland. Others are from 50 states, 139 foreign countries, and Canada. 58% are white; 15% Asian American; 12% African American. The average age of freshmen is 18; all undergraduates, 21. 7% do not continue beyond their first year; 82% remain to graduate.

Housing: 10,974 students can be accommodated in college housing, which includes single-sex and coed dorms and on-campus apartments. In addition, there are honors houses, language houses, special-interest houses, fraternity houses, and sorority houses. On-campus housing is available on a lottery system for upperclassmen. 59% of students commute. Alcohol is not permitted. Upperclassmen may keep cars.

Activities: 9% of men belong to 36 national fraternities; 11% of women belong to 27 national sororities. There are 574 groups on campus, including art, band, cheerleading, chess, choir, chorale, chorus, computers, dance, debate, drama, drill team, environmental, ethnic, film, forensics, gay, honors, international, jazz band, literary magazine, marching band, musical theater, newspaper, opera, orchestra, pep band, photography, political, professional, radio and TV, religious, social, social service, student government, symphony, and yearbook. Popular campus events include Art Attack, Union All-Niter, and Maryland Day.

Sports: There are 12 intercollegiate sports for men and 15 for women, and 17 intramural sports for men and 17 for women. Facilities include 2 indoor and 2 outdoor swimming pools, intramural fields, tennis, squash, racquetball, volleyball, and basketball courts, a fitness center including weight rooms, aerobic rooms, martial arts rooms, saunas, and an indoor track, a bowling alley, a golf course, and an outdoor artificial turf field. Athletic facilities include a 51,000-seat stadium, a 17,950-seat gym, and indoor and outdoor artificial turf practice fields.

Disabled Students: 95% of the campus is accessible. Facilities include wheelchair ramps, elevators, special parking, specially equipped restrooms, special class scheduling, lowered drinking fountains, lowered telephones, a special shuttle service, and electronic doors.

Services: Counseling and information services are available, as is tutoring in most subjects, including all 100- and 200-level courses. There is a reader service for the blind and remedial math.

Campus Safety and Security: Measures include 24-hour foot and vehicle patrol, emergency notification system, self-defense education, and security escort services. There are shuttle buses, emergency telephones, lighted pathways/sidewalks, and video surveillance.

Programs of Study: Maryland confers B.A., B.S., B.L.A., B.M., and B.M.E. degrees. Master's and doctoral degrees are also awarded. Bachelor's degrees are awarded in AGRICULTURE (agricultural business management, agricultural economics, agriculture, animal science, natural resource management, and plant science), BIOLOGICAL SCIENCE (biochemistry, biology/biological science, microbiology, and nutrition), BUSINESS (accounting, banking and finance, business administration and management, international business management, logistics, management information systems, marketing management, operations management, supply chain management, and transportation management), COMMUNICATIONS AND THE ARTS (art history and appreciation, Chinese, classics, communications, dance, dramatic arts, English, English literature, French, Germanic languages and literature, Japanese, journalism, linguistics, music, music performance, music theory and composition, romance languages and literature, Russian, Spanish, and studio art), COMPUTER AND PHYSICAL SCIENCE (astronomy, chemistry, computer science, geology, information sciences and systems, mathematics, natural sciences, physical sciences, and physics), EDUCATION (art education, drama education, early childhood education, education, elementary education, English education, foreign languages education, mathematics education, music education, physical education, science education, secondary education, social studies education, and special education), ENGINEERING AND ENVIRONMENTAL DESIGN (aeronautical engineering, architecture, bioresource engineering, chemical engineering, civil engineering, computer engineering, electrical/electronics engineering, engineering, environmental science, fire protection engineering, landscape architecture/design, materials engineering, and mechanical engineering), HEALTH PROFESSIONS (community health work, preveterinary science, speech pathology/audiology, and veterinary science), SOCIAL SCIENCE (African American studies, American studies, anthropology, criminal justice, criminology, dietetics, economics, family/consumer studies, food science, geography, history, Italian studies, Judaic studies, philosophy, political science/government, psychology, Russian and Slavic studies, sociology, and women's studies). Engineering, computer science, and business are the strongest academically. Economics, criminology and criminal justice, and government and politics are the largest.

Required: Most programs require a minimum of 120 credits for graduation; the number of hours required in the major varies. All students must take 43 to 46 credits in a multidisciplinary core curriculum, including 10 in math and science, 9 each in social sciences, and humanities and the arts, 6 in advanced studies, and 3 diversity credits. Freshman and junior composition are also required, and students must maintain a 2.0 GPA.

Special: Each of the 11 undergraduate schools offers special programs, and there is a campus-wide co-op education program offering engineering and other majors. In addition, the university offers cross-registration with other colleges in the Consortium of Universities of the Washington Metropolitan Area, several living-learning programs for undergraduates, the B.A.-B.S. degree in most majors, dual and student-designed majors, nondegree study, an accelerated veterinary medicine program, varied study-abroad opportunities, work-study programs with government and nonprofit organizations, and internship opportunities with federal and state legislators, the local media, and various federal agencies. There are 53 national honor societies, including Phi Beta Kappa, a freshman honors program, and 39 departmental honors programs.

Faculty/Classroom: 63% of faculty are male; 37% are female. 57% teach undergraduates, and 43% do research. Graduate students teach 13% of introductory courses. The average class size in an introductory lecture is 47; in a laboratory, 20; and in a regular course, 36.

Admissions: 42% of the 2009-2010 applicants were accepted. The SAT scores for the 2009-2010 freshman class were: Critical Reading--4% below 500, 29% between 500 and 599, 49% between 600 and 700, and 18% above 700; Math--3% below 500, 15% between 500 and 599, 50% between 600 and 700, and 32% above 700.

Requirements: he SAT or ACT is required. The university evaluates exam scores along with GPA, curriculum, and other criteria. Applicants should be graduates of accredited secondary schools or have the GED. Secondary preparation should include 4 years of English, 3 of history or social sciences, 2 of algebra and 1 of plane geometry, and 2 of lab sciences. An essay and counselor recommendation are required. Music majors must also audition. AP and CLEP credits are accepted. Important factors in the admissions decision are advanced placement or honors courses, recommendations by school officials, and evidence of special talent.

Procedure: Freshmen are admitted fall, spring, and summer. Entrance exams should be taken at the end of the junior year or the beginning of the senior year. There are deferred admissions and rolling admissions plans. Applications should be filed by January 20 for fall entry and December 1 for spring entry. The fall 2008 application fee was $55. Notifications are sent April 1. Applications are accepted on-line.

Transfer: 2344 transfer students enrolled in 2008-2009. Transfer applicants from regionally accredited institutions should have attempted at least 12 credits and have earned at least a 2.5 GPA, although this requirement varies depending on space available. Applicants from Maryland community colleges may be given special consideration. 30 of 120 credits required for the bachelor's degree must be completed at Maryland.

Visiting: There are regularly scheduled orientations for prospective students, consisting of 3 fall and 4 spring open house programs for admitted students, as well as regularly scheduled information sessions followed by a campus tour. There are guides for informal visits, visitors may sit in on classes, and stay overnight. To schedule a visit, contact the Office of Undergraduate Admissions.

Financial Aid: 19% of undergraduate students work part-time. Average annual earnings from campus work are $5789. The FAFSA is required. The priority date for freshman financial aid applications for fall entry is February 15.

International Students: There are 598 international students enrolled. They must take the TOEFL or the IELTS. They must also take the SAT or ACT.

Computers: Wireless access is available. There are 1800 computers provided for student use in computer labs throughout the campus; the wireless network is available in all college-owned housing, libraries, and classrooms as well as in many administration buildings across campus. All students may access the system 24 hours a day, 7 days a week. There are no time limits and no fees.

Graduates: From July 1, 2008 to June 30, 2009, 6704 bachelor's degrees were awarded. The most popular majors were criminology and criminal justice (7%), economics (7%), and psychology (5%). In an average class, 63% graduate in 4 years or less, 80% graduate in 5 years or less, and 82% graduate in 6 years or less.

Admissions Contact: Admissions Officer. A campus DVD is available. E-Mail: *um-admit@uga.umd.edu* Web: *www.umd.edu*

UNIVERSITY OF MARYLAND/EASTERN SHORE   F-4

Princess Anne, MD 21853   **(410) 651-6410; (410) 651-7922**

Full-time: 1225 men, 1810 women	**Faculty:** IIA, --$
Part-time: 125 men, 175 women	**Ph.D.s:** 80%
Graduate: 190 men, 255 women	**Student/Faculty:** n/av
Year: semesters, summer session	**Tuition:** $7000 ($14,000)
Application Deadline: see profile	**Room & Board:** $7000
Freshman Class: n/av	
SAT: required	**COMPETITIVE**

The University of Maryland/Eastern Shore, founded in 1886, is a public university and part of the University of Maryland System offering undergraduate and graduate programs in the arts and sciences, professional studies, and agricultural sciences. Figures in the above capsule and this capsule are approximate. There are 3 undergraduate schools and 1 graduate school. The library contains 150,000 volumes. Computerized library services include interlibrary loans and database searching. Special learning facilities include a learning resource center, art gallery, and radio station. The 700-acre campus is in a rural area 15 miles south of Salisbury. Including any residence halls, there are 40 buildings.

Student Life: 71% of undergraduates are from Maryland. Others are from 32 states, 48 foreign countries, and Canada. 85% are from public schools. 76% are African American; 18% white. 90% are Protestant. The average age of freshmen is 18; all undergraduates, 24. 25% do not continue beyond their first year; 36% remain to graduate.

Housing: 1530 students can be accommodated in college housing, which includes single-sex dorms, on-campus apartments, and off-campus apartments. In addition, there are honors houses and a residential complex. On-campus housing is available on a first-come, first-served basis and is available on a lottery system for upperclassmen. 50% of students commute. All students may keep cars.

Activities: 20% of men belong to 4 national fraternities; 20% of women belong to 4 national sororities. There are 25 groups on campus, including art, band, cheerleading, choir, chorale, chorus, computers, dance, drama, drill team, ethnic, honors, international, jazz band, literary magazine, musical theater, newspaper, pep band, photography, political, professional, radio and TV, religious, social, social service, student government, and yearbook. Popular campus events include Parents Day, Spring Festival, and Ethnic Festival.

Sports: There are 5 intercollegiate sports for men and 5 for women, and 4 intramural sports for men and 4 for women. Facilities include an indoor swimming pool and a 3000-seat stadium.

Disabled Students: 20% of the campus is accessible. Facilities include wheelchair ramps, elevators, special parking, specially equipped restrooms, special class scheduling, lowered drinking fountains, and lowered telephones.

Services: Counseling and information services are available, as is tutoring in every subject. There is remedial math, reading, and writing.

Campus Safety and Security: Measures include 24-hour foot and vehicle patrol and security escort services. There are shuttle buses, emergency telephones, lighted pathways/sidewalks, and a student security team.

Programs of Study: UMES confers B.A., B.S., B.G.S., and B.M. degrees. Master's and doctoral degrees are also awarded. Bachelor's degrees are awarded in AGRICULTURE (agriculture and poultry science), BIOLOGICAL SCIENCE (biology/biological science), BUSINESS (accounting, business administration and management, and hotel/motel and restaurant management), COMMUNICATIONS AND THE ARTS (English), COMPUTER AND PHYSICAL SCIENCE (chemistry, computer science, and mathematics), EDUCATION (agricultural education, art education, business education, elementary education, health education, home economics education, industrial arts education, mathematics education, music education, physical education, science education, secondary education, and social science education), ENGINEERING AND ENVIRONMENTAL DESIGN (aeronautical science, construction technology, engineering technology, and environmental science), HEALTH PROFESSIONS (physical therapy and rehabilitation therapy),

SOCIAL SCIENCE (criminal justice, history, home economics, liberal arts/general studies, and sociology). Physical therapy, engineering, and environmental science are the strongest academically. Business, hotel restaurant management, and biology are the largest.

Required: Students must complete 122 hours, including 36 hours in the major, 15 in communicative and quantitative skills, 9 in humanities, 7 in natural sciences, 6 in social sciences, and 4 in health and phys ed. A minimum 2.0 overall GPA is required.

Special: Students may cross-register at Salisbury State University. A cooperative education program, internships, a winter term, work-study programs, a general studies degree, and dual and student-designed majors are offered. Also available are an accelerated degree program and a 3-2 engineering degree with the University of Maryland/College Park. There are pass/fail options. There is 1 national honor society, a freshman honors program, and 10 departmental honors programs.

Faculty/Classroom: 45% of faculty are male; 55% are female. 85% teach undergraduates, and 15% do research. Graduate students teach 1% of introductory courses. The average class size in an introductory lecture is 75; in a laboratory, 18; and in a regular course, 30.

Requirements: The SAT is required. In addition, applicants should be graduates of accredited secondary schools or have the GED. High school preparation should include 4 years of English, 3 each of social science or history and math, including 2 of algebra and 1 of geometry, and 2 of lab science. An essay and interview are recommended. UMES recommends that prospective art education majors submit a portfolio. A GPA of 2.5 is required. AP and CLEP credits are accepted. Important factors in the admissions decision are advanced placement or honors courses, leadership record, and recommendations by school officials.

Procedure: Freshmen are admitted to all sessions. Entrance exams should be taken in April. There are early decision, early admissions, deferred admissions, and rolling admissions plans. Check with the school for current application deadlines. The fall 2009 application fee was $25.

Transfer: Transfer applicants must have attempted at least 9 credits at another institution and have at least a cumulative GPA of 2.0 or have earned an associate degree or completed 56 hours of community college work. 75 of 122 credits required for the bachelor's degree must be completed at UMES.

Visiting: There are regularly scheduled orientations for prospective students, including 2 formal orientation sessions and 9 visitation/open house days. There are guides for informal visits and visitors may sit in on classes. To schedule a visit, contact the Office of Recruitment at (410) 651-6178.

Financial Aid: UMES is a member of CSS. The college's own financial statement is required. Check with the school for current application deadlines.

International Students: They must take the TOEFL. They must also take the SAT, scoring 800.

Computers: There are no fees. It is strongly recommended that all students have a personal computer.

Admissions Contact: Cheryll Collier-Mills, Director of Admissions and Recruitment. E-Mail: *ccmills@umes.edu* Web: *www.umes.edu*

UNIVERSITY OF MARYLAND/UNIVERSITY COLLEGE   D-3

Adelphi, MD 20783   **(249) 684-2101**
(800) 888-8682; (240) 684-2153

Full-time: 1401 men, 2007 women	**Faculty:** 103
Part-time: 9311 men, 11565 women	**Ph.D.s:** 83%
Graduate: 5729 men, 7334 women	**Student/Faculty:** n/av
Year: semesters, summer session	
Application Deadline: open	
Freshman Class: n/av	**SPECIAL**

University of Maryland University College, founded in 1947, serves the needs of the adult continuing education student, offering daytime, evening, weekend, and online programs in convenient locations in the Maryland, D.C. Metro, and Virginia areas. It There is one undergraduate school and one graduate school. The library contains 1,248 volumes and subscribes to 76,287 periodicals including electronic. Computerized library services include interlibrary loans, database searching, and Internet access. Special learning facilities include a learning resource center, art gallery, and TV station. The campus is in an urban area.

Student Life: 60% of undergraduates are from Maryland. Others are from 50 states, 21 foreign countries, and Canada. 40% are white; 31% African American. The average age of all undergraduates is 32.

Housing: There are no residence halls. All students commute.

Activities: There are no fraternities or sororities.

Sports: There is no sports program at UMUC.

Disabled Students: Facilities include wheelchair ramps, elevators, special parking, specially equipped restrooms, special class scheduling, and lowered drinking fountains.

Services: Counseling and information services are available, as is tutoring in some subjects, including math, writing, accounting, economics, introductory finance, and computing. There is a reader service for the blind.

Campus Safety and Security: Measures include 24-hour foot and vehicle patrol, emergency notification system, and self-defense education. There are emergency telephones and lighted pathways/sidewalks.

Programs of Study: UMUC confers B.A. and B.S. degrees. Associate, master's, and doctoral degrees are also awarded. Bachelor's degrees are awarded in BIOLOGICAL SCIENCE (biotechnology), BUSINESS (accounting, business administration and management, human resources, management information systems, management science, and marketing management), COMMUNICATIONS AND THE ARTS (communications and English), COMPUTER AND PHYSICAL SCIENCE (computer science and information sciences and systems), ENGINEERING AND ENVIRONMENTAL DESIGN (computer technology, emergency/disaster science, and environmental science), SOCIAL SCIENCE (Asian/Oriental studies, criminal justice, fire science, gerontology, history, humanities, liberal arts/general studies, paralegal studies, political science/government, psychology, and social science).

Required: A general education requirement of 41 credit hours includes courses in communications, humanities, social sciences, biological and social science, math/science, and interdisciplinary studies.

Special: UMUC offers cooperative programs in several career programs. There are work-study programs with local employers. Credit by exam, credit for prior learning, 6 nondegree study, and pass/fail options are available. Through UMUC's open learning program, a number of independent learning courses are available. There are 64 national honor societies.

Faculty/Classroom: 41% of faculty are male; 59% are female. 80% teach undergraduates. No introductory courses are taught by graduate students. The average class size in a regular course is 23.

Requirements: Students should be graduates of an accredited secondary school or have a GED equivalent. AP and CLEP credits are accepted.

Procedure: Freshmen are admitted to all sessions. There is a rolling admissions plan. Application deadlines are open. Application fee is $50. Applications are accepted on-line.

Transfer: 11,763 transfer students enrolled in 2008-2009. 30 of 120 credits required for the bachelor's degree must be completed at UMUC.

Financial Aid: The FAFSA and SAR (for Pell grants) are required. Check with the school for current application deadlines.

International Students: There are 107 international students enrolled. They must take the TOEFL with a minimum score of 550 on the paper-based TOEFL (PBT) or 79 on the Internet-based version (iBT) and the college's own test.

Computers: Wireless access is available. All students may access the system. There are no time limits and no fees.

Graduates: From July 1, 2008 to June 30, 2009, 2698 bachelor's degrees were awarded. The most popular majors were business and management (38%), computer and information (21%), and general studies (8%).

Admissions Contact: Jessica Sadaka, Director of Admissions. E-Mail: *emteam@umuc.edu* Web: *www.umuc.edu*

UNIVERSITY SYSTEM OF MARYLAND

The University System of Maryland, established in 1856, is a public system in Maryland. It is governed by a board of regents, whose chief administrator is chancellor. The primary goal of the system is research, teaching, and public service. Profiles of the 4-year campuses are included in this section.

VILLA JULIE COLLEGE
(See Stevenson University)

WASHINGTON COLLEGE   E-2
Chestertown, MD 21620-1197

(410) 778-7700
(800) 422-1782; (410) 778-7287

Full-time: 527 men, 758 women	**Faculty:** 98; IIB, +$
Part-time: 10 men, 19 women	**Ph.D.s:** 95%
Graduate: 23 men, 35 women	**Student/Faculty:** 13 to 1
Year: semesters	**Tuition:** $35,350
Application Deadline: March 1	**Room & Board:** $7460
Freshman Class: 4498 applied, 3240 accepted, 378 enrolled	
SAT CR/M: 560/570	**ACT:** required
	VERY COMPETITIVE

Washington College, founded in 1782, is an independent college offering programs in the liberal arts and sciences, business management, and teacher preparation. There is 1 graduate school. The library contains 219,461 volumes, 100,635 microform items, and 8,701 audio/video tapes/CDs/DVDs, and subscribes to 28,222 periodicals including electronic. Computerized library services include interlibrary loans, database searching, Internet access, and laptop Internet portals. Special learning facilities include a learning resource center, art gallery, the Center for the

American Experience, the Center for Environment and Society, and the Rose O'Neill Literary House. The 112-acre campus is in a small town 75 miles from Baltimore. Including any residence halls, there are 71 buildings.

Student Life: 52% of undergraduates are from Maryland. Others are from 31 states, 36 foreign countries, and Canada. 59% are from public schools. 85% are white. The average age of freshmen is 18; all undergraduates, 19. 16% do not continue beyond their first year; 80% remain to graduate.

Housing: 1076 students can be accommodated in college housing, which includes single-sex and coed dorms and on-campus apartments. In addition, there are special-interest houses, an international house, a science house, and substance-free housing. On-campus housing is guaranteed for the freshman year only and is available on a lottery system for upperclassmen. 86% of students live on campus; of those, 65% remain on campus on weekends. All students may keep cars.

Activities: 8% of men belong to 3 national fraternities; 14% of women belong to 3 national sororities. There are 52 groups on campus, including chorale, chorus, computers, dance, debate, drama, education and leadership, environmental, ethnic, gay, honors, international, jazz band, literary magazine, minority and human rights, newspaper, opera, orchestra, photography, political, professional, radio and TV, religious, social, social service, student government, and yearbook. Popular campus events include fall and spring convocations, George Washington Birthday Ball, and May Day.

Sports: There are 8 intercollegiate sports for men and 10 for women, and 12 intramural sports for men and 11 for women. Facilities include a stadium, a swim center, a gym, a field house, squash and racquetball courts, a fitness center, playing and practice fields, and a boathouse. There are riding facilities nearby.

Disabled Students: 80% of the campus is accessible. Facilities include wheelchair ramps, elevators, special parking, specially equipped rest rooms, special class scheduling, lowered drinking fountains, and lowered telephones.

Services: Counseling and information services are available, as is tutoring in every subject. There is remedial math and writing, a writing center, a math lab, a study skills tutor, and peer tutors.

Campus Safety and Security: Measures include 24-hour foot and vehicle patrol, emergency notification system, and security escort services. There are emergency telephones, lighted pathways/sidewalks, and peer education through student groups.

Programs of Study: WC confers B.A. and B.S. degrees. Master's degrees are also awarded. Bachelor's degrees are awarded in BIOLOGICAL SCIENCE (biology/biological science), BUSINESS (business administration and management), COMMUNICATIONS AND THE ARTS (art, dramatic arts, English, fine arts, French, German, music, and Spanish), COMPUTER AND PHYSICAL SCIENCE (chemistry, computer science, mathematics, and physics), ENGINEERING AND ENVIRONMENTAL DESIGN (environmental science), SOCIAL SCIENCE (American studies, anthropology, economics, history, humanities, international studies, philosophy, political science/government, psychology, and sociology). English, psychology, and business management are the strongest academically.

Required: All students are required to take a freshman Global Perspectives seminar and courses distributed among the social sciences, natural sciences, humanities, quantitative studies, foreign languages, and a writing requirement. The Senior Capstone Experience consists of a comprehensive exam, thesis, or independent project. Students must complete 128 credit hours, including at least 32 in the major, to graduate. A minimum GPA of 2.0 is required.

Special: Internships are available in all majors. There is study abroad in 26 countries and a Washington semester. The college offers a 3-2 engineering degree with the University of Maryland at College Park as well as a 3-2 nursing program with Johns Hopkins University and student-designed majors. There are 7 national honor societies, including Phi Beta Kappa.

Faculty/Classroom: 57% of faculty are male; 43% are female. All teach undergraduates. No introductory courses are taught by graduate students. The average class size in an introductory lecture is 15; in a laboratory, 16; and in a regular course, 15.

Admissions: 72% of the 2009-2010 applicants were accepted. The SAT scores for the 2009-2010 freshman class were: Critical Reading-- 12% below 500, 53% between 500 and 599, 28% between 600 and 700, and 7% above 700; Math--14% below 500, 52% between 500 and 599, 30% between 600 and 700, and 4% above 700. The ACT scores were 9% below 21, 30% between 21 and 23, 32% between 24 and 26, 18% between 27 and 28, and 11% above 28. 65% of the current freshmen were in the top fifth of their class; 81% were in the top two fifths. There were 3 National Merit finalists.

Requirements: The SAT or ACT is required. In addition, applicants must be graduates of an accredited secondary school or have a GED. 16 Carnegie units are required. Applicants should take high school courses in English, foreign language, history, math, science, and social studies. An essay is required, and an interview is recommended. A GPA of 2.5

is required. AP credits are accepted. Important factors in the admissions decision are advanced placement or honors courses, recommendations by school officials, and leadership record.

Procedure: Freshmen are admitted fall and spring. Entrance exams should be taken in the spring of the junior year or fall of the senior year. There are early decision, deferred admissions and rolling admissions plans. Early decision applications should be filed by November 1; regular applications, by March 1 for fall entry and December 1 for spring entry, along with a $55 fee. Notification is sent on a rolling basis. 45 early decision candidates were accepted for the 2009-2010 class. 400 applicants were on the 2009 waiting list; 100 were admitted. Applications are accepted on-line.

Transfer: 18 transfer students enrolled in 2008-2009. A minimum GPA of 2.5 is required. An interview is recommended. 56 of 128 credits required for the bachelor's degree must be completed at WC.

Visiting: There are regularly scheduled orientations for prospective students, consisting of weekday visits. There are guides for informal visits and visitors may sit in on classes. To schedule a visit, contact the Admissions Office.

Financial Aid: In 2009-2010, 88% of all full-time freshmen and 82% of continuing full-time students received some form of financial aid. The average freshman award was $25,412. The average financial indebtedness of the 2009 graduate was $28,727. 40% of undergraduate students work part-time. Average annual earnings from campus work are $1000. WC is a member of CSS. The FAFSA, the college's own financial state-ment, and signed copies of the student's and parents' federal tax returns and W2s are required. The deadline for filing freshman financial aid applications for fall entry is February 15.

International Students: There are 43 international students enrolled. The school actively recruits these students. They must take the TOEFL with a minimum score of 550 on the paper-based TOEFL (PBT) or 79 on the Internet-based version (iBT). They must also take the SAT or ACT.

Computers: Wireless access is available. Students may use the college's network and/or wireless system for personal and academic use. There is a portal log-in for wireless use. All students may access the system. There are no time limits and no fees. It is strongly recommended that all students have a personal computer.

Graduates: From July 1, 2008 to June 30, 2009, 293 bachelor's degrees were awarded. The most popular majors were business management (14%), English (13%), and psychology (12%). In an average class, 2% graduate in 3 years or less, 75% graduate in 4 years or less, 77% graduate in 5 years or less, and 80% graduate in 6 years or less. 75 companies recruited on campus in 2008-2009. Of the 2008 graduating class, 30% were enrolled in graduate school within 6 months of graduation, and 60% were employed.

Admissions Contact: Kevin Coveney, Vice President of Admissions. A campus DVD is available. E-mail: *adm_off@washcoll.edu* Web: *www.washcoll.edu*

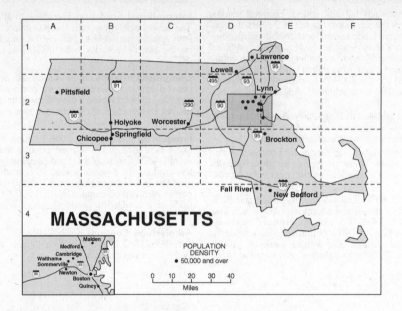

MASSACHUSETTS

AMERICAN INTERNATIONAL COLLEGE   B-3
Springfield, MA 01109

(413) 205-3201
(800) 242-3142; (413) 205-3051

Full-time: 677 men, 904 women	**Faculty:** 75
Part-time: 42 men, 106 women	**Ph.D.s:** 47%
Graduate: 364 men, 1308 women	**Student/Faculty:** 18 to 1
Year: semesters, summer session	**Tuition:** $25,500
Application Deadline: open	**Room & Board:** $10,600
Freshman Class: 1469 applied, 1162 accepted, 364 enrolled	
SAT CR/M/W: 467/471/461	**ACT:** 19 **LESS COMPETITIVE**

American International College, founded in 1885, is an independent institution offering programs in liberal arts, business, health science, and teacher preparation. There are 4 undergraduate schools and 3 graduate schools. In addition to regional accreditation, AIC has baccalaureate program accreditation with APTA, NASDTEC, and NLN. The library contains 70,741 volumes, 293 microform items, and 1,749 audio/video tapes/CDs/DVDs, and subscribes to 7,211 periodicals including electronic. Computerized library services include interlibrary loans, database searching, Internet access, and laptop Internet portals. Special learning facilities include a learning resource center, art gallery, radio station, and an anatomical lab for health sciences. The 58-acre campus is in an urban area 75 miles west of Boston. Including any residence halls, there are 22 buildings.

Student Life: 63% of undergraduates are from Massachusetts. Students are from 30 states, 15 foreign countries, and Canada. 85% are from public schools. 50% are white; 32% African American; 11% Hispanic. The average age of freshmen is 20; all undergraduates, 25. 32% do not continue beyond their first year; 60% remain to graduate.

Housing: 781 students can be accommodated in college housing, which includes single-sex and coed dorms and on-campus apartments. On-campus housing is guaranteed for all 4 years, is available on a first-come, first-served basis, and is available on a lottery system for upperclassmen. 50% of students commute. All students may keep cars.

Activities: 1% of men belong to 5 national fraternities; 1% of women belong to 2 national sororities. There are 40 groups on campus, including cheerleading, computers, dance, drama, ethnic, film, gay, honors, international, literary magazine, newspaper, pep band, photography, political, professional, radio and TV, religious, social, social service, student government, women's, and yearbook. Popular campus events include holiday semi-formals, international festival, and Caribbean and Asian-American Festival.

Sports: There are 12 intercollegiate sports for men and 10 for women, and 16 intramural sports for men and 12 for women. Facilities include a football stadium, tennis courts, playing fields, and a health and fitness center.

Disabled Students: 75% of the campus is accessible. Facilities include wheelchair ramps, elevators, special parking, specially equipped restrooms, special class scheduling, and lowered drinking fountains.

Services: Counseling and information services are available, as is tutoring in every subject. There is remedial math and writing.

Campus Safety and Security: Measures include 24-hour foot and vehicle patrol, emergency notification system, self-defense education, and security escort services. There are shuttle buses, emergency telephones, lighted pathways/sidewalks, and controlled access to dorms/residences.

Programs of Study: AIC confers B.A., B.S., B.B.A., B.S.B.A., B.S.N., and B.S.O.T. degrees. Associates, master's, and doctoral degrees are also awarded. Bachelor's degrees are awarded in BIOLOGICAL SCIENCE (biochemistry and biology/biological science), BUSINESS (accounting, business administration and management, business economics, entrepreneurial studies, human resources, international business management, and marketing/retailing/merchandising), COMMUNICATIONS AND THE ARTS (advertising, communications, English, and Spanish), COMPUTER AND PHYSICAL SCIENCE (chemistry, mathematics, and science), EDUCATION (early childhood education, elementary education, foreign languages education, middle school education, science education, secondary education, and special education), HEALTH PROFESSIONS (medical laboratory technology, nursing, occupational therapy, physical therapy, predentistry, and premedicine), SOCIAL SCIENCE (criminal justice, economics, history, international relations, liberal arts/general studies, philosophy, political science/government, prelaw, psychology, public administration, and sociology). Psychology, preprofessional, and health sciences are the strongest academically. Criminal justice, physical therapy, and nursing are the largest.

Required: Distribution requirements include 12 credits of social sciences, 9 of English, 8 of lab science, 6 of humanities, and 3 each of math and computer-oriented courses. A total of 120 credit hours is required for graduation, with 30 to 36 hours in the major. A minimum 2.0 GPA is required for graduation.

Special: Cross-registration with the Cooperative Colleges of Greater Springfield is permitted. Internships are available in all programs, for up to 6 credits in every major, and study abroad is offered, as is a Washington semester. There are 4 national honor societies, a freshman honors program, and 9 departmental honors programs.

Faculty/Classroom: 40% of faculty are male; 60% are female. All teach undergraduates, 15% do research, and 15% do both. No introductory courses are taught by graduate students. The average class size in an introductory lecture is 27; in a laboratory is 16; and in a regular course is 19.

Admissions: 79% of the 2009-2010 applicants were accepted. The SAT scores for the 2009-2010 freshman class were: Critical Reading--67% below 500, 28% between 500 and 599, 4% between 600 and 700, and 1% above 700; Math--64% below 500, 26% between 500 and 599, 10% between 600 and 700, and 1% above 700; Writing--66% below 500, 29% between 500 and 599, 5% between 600 and 700, and % above 700. The ACT scores were 60% below 21, 30% between 21 and 23, 4% between 24 and 26, 4% between 27 and 28, and 2% above 28. 50% of the current freshmen were in the top fifth of their class; 73% were in the top two fifths.

Requirements: The SAT or ACT is required. In addition, applicants must be graduates of an accredited secondary school or have a GED. They must have completed 16 academic credits of secondary school work with a minimum of 4 years of English, 2 each of history, math, and science, and 1 of social studies. An interview is recommended. A GPA of 2.0 is required. AP and CLEP credits are accepted.

Procedure: Freshmen are admitted to all sessions. Entrance exams should be taken by March of the senior year. There are deferred admissions and rolling admissions plans. Application deadlines are open. Application fee is $25. Notification is sent on a rolling basis. Applications are accepted on-line.

Transfer: 220 transfer students enrolled in 2008-2009. Transfer applicants must have at least a 2.0 GPA. 30 of 120 credits required for the bachelor's degree must be completed at AIC.

Visiting: There are regularly scheduled orientations for prospective students, open houses with faculty, a student life panel, departmental faculty presentations, a financial aid presentation, a tour, and brunch. There are guides for informal visits, visitors may sit in on classes, and stay overnight. To schedule a visit, contact the Admissions Office at (413) 205-3201.

Financial Aid: In 2009-2010, 85% of all full-time freshmen and 88% of continuing full-time students received some form of financial aid. 85% of all full-time freshmen and 88% of continuing full-time students received need-based aid. The average freshmen award was $23,912. 17% of undergraduate students work part-time. Average annual earnings from campus work are $1542. The average financial indebtedness of the 2009 graduate was $34,839. AIC is a member of CSS. The FAFSA is required. The deadline for filing freshman financial aid applications for fall entry is April 1.

International Students: There are 40 international students enrolled. The school actively recruits these students. They must take the TOEFL with a minimum score of 550 on the paper-based TOEFL (PBT) or 80 on the Internet-based version (iBT). They must also take the SAT or ACT.

Computers: Wireless access is available. Wireless access is available campus-wide. In addition, approximately 100 PC stations are available for student access across campus including the library, residence halls, dining hall, and computer laboratories. All students may access the system. 7 days per week. There are no time limits and no fees. It is strongly recommended that all students have a personal computer.

Graduates: From July 1, 2008 to June 30, 2009, 291 bachelor's degrees were awarded. The most popular majors were health professions (26%), business (18%), and criminal justice (12%). 50 companies recruited on campus in 2008-2009. In an average class, 25% graduate in 4 years or less, 50% graduate in 5 years or less, and 60% graduate in 6 years or less. Of the 2008 graduating class, 21% were enrolled in graduate school within 6 months of graduation, and 58% were employed.

Admissions Contact: Peter Miller, Vice President Admission Services. E-Mail: *inquiry@aic.edu* Web: *www.aic.edu*

AMHERST COLLEGE	B-2
Amherst, MA 01002-5000	**(413) 542-8417; (413) 542-2040**
Full-time: 850 men,800 women	**Faculty:** IIB, ++$
Part-time: none	**Ph.D.s:** 94%
Graduate: none	**Student/Faculty:** n/av
Year: semesters	**Tuition:** $35,000
Application Deadline: see profile	**Room & Board:** $10,000
Freshman Class: n/av	
SAT or ACT: required	**MOST COMPETITIVE**

Amherst College, founded in 1821, is a private liberal arts institution. Figures in the above capsule and in this profile are approximate. The 5 libraries contain 1 million volumes, 530,038 microform items, and 60,826 audio/video tapes/CDs/DVDs, and subscribe to 5,563 periodicals including electronic. Computerized library services include interlibrary loans, database searching, and Internet access. Special learning facilities include a learning resource center, art gallery, natural history museum, planetarium, radio station, an observatory, the Emily Dickinson Museum, and the Amherst Center for Russian Culture. The 1015-acre campus is in a small town 90 miles west of Boston. Including any residence halls, there are 75 buildings.

Student Life: 81% of undergraduates are from out of state, mostly the Middle Atlantic. Students are from 50 states, 31 foreign countries, and Canada. 58% are from public schools. 44% are white; 13% Asian American. The average age of freshmen is 18; all undergraduates, 19. 3% do not continue beyond their first year; 97% remain to graduate.

Housing: 1650 students can be accommodated in college housing, which includes single-sex and coed dorms. In addition, there are language houses, special-interest houses, and 1 cooperative house. On-campus housing is guaranteed for all 4 years. 98% of students live on campus; of those, 95% remain on campus on weekends. Upperclassmen may keep cars.

Activities: There are no fraternities or sororities. There are 110 groups on campus, including art, band, chess, choir, chorale, chorus, communications, computers, dance, debate, drama, ethnic, film, gay, honors, international, jazz band, literary magazine, mock trial, musical theater, newspaper, opera, orchestra, pep band, photography, political, professional, radio and TV, religious, social, social service, student govern-

ment, and symphony. Popular campus events include Newport Jazz, Harlem Renaissance, and Spring Weekend Concert.

Sports: There are 13 intercollegiate sports for men and 14 for women, and 6 intramural sports for men and 6 for women. Facilities include 2 gyms, a pool, a field house, a hockey rink, an outdoor track, a fitness center, 10 international squash courts, an indoor jogging track, 3 indoor and 30 outdoor tennis courts, baseball and softball diamonds, a 9-hole golf course, and playing fields.

Disabled Students: Facilities include wheelchair ramps, elevators, special parking, specially equipped restrooms, special class scheduling, lowered drinking fountains, and lowered telephones.

Services: Counseling and information services are available, as is tutoring in every subject. There is a reader service for the blind. A quantitative skills center and a writing center are also available.

Campus Safety and Security: Measures include 24-hour foot and vehicle patrol, self-defense education, and security escort services. There are shuttle buses, emergency telephones, lighted pathways/sidewalks, ACEMS (Amherst College Emergency Medical Service), access code pad security to dorms, and "blue light" emergency telephones placed in 19 locations around campus.

Programs of Study: Amherst confers B.A. degrees. Bachelor's degrees are awarded in BIOLOGICAL SCIENCE (biology/biological science and neurosciences), COMMUNICATIONS AND THE ARTS (classics, dance, dramatic arts, English, fine arts, French, German, Greek, Latin, music, Russian, and Spanish), COMPUTER AND PHYSICAL SCIENCE (astronomy, chemistry, computer science, geology, mathematics, and physics), SOCIAL SCIENCE (African American studies, American studies, anthropology, Asian/Oriental studies, economics, European studies, history, interdisciplinary studies, law, philosophy, political science/government, psychology, religion, sociology, and women's studies). English, psychology, and economics are the largest.

Required: To earn the B.A., all students must complete 32 courses, equivalent to 128 credits, 8 to 14 of which are in the major, with at least a C average. Other than a 1-semester freshman seminar in liberal studies, there are no specific course requirements. A thesis or comparable work is required for honors candidates.

Special: Students may cross-register through the Five College Consortium, the other members of which are all within 10 miles of Amherst, or through the Twelve College Exchange Program. A number of interterm and summer internships are available, as is study-abroad in 40 countries. Dual majors, student-designed interdisciplinary majors based on independent study as of junior or senior year, and work-study programs are possible. There are limited pass/fail options. There are 2 national honor societies, including Phi Beta Kappa, and 30 departmental honors programs.

Faculty/Classroom: 57% of faculty are male; 43% are female. All teach and do research. No introductory courses are taught by graduate students. The average class size in a laboratory, 18, and in a regular course, 15.

Requirements: The SAT or ACT is required. In addition, plus 2 SAT: Subject tests are required for admission. Amherst strongly recommends that applicants take 4 years of English, math through calculus, 3 or 4 years of a foreign language, 2 years of history and social science, and at least 2 years of natural science, including a lab science. 2 essays are required. Important factors in the admissions decision are advanced placement or honors courses, recommendations by school officials, and evidence of special talent.

Procedure: Freshmen are admitted fall. Entrance exams should be taken no later than December of the senior year. There are early decision and deferred admissions plans. Check with the school for current application deadlines and fees. Applications are accepted on-line.

Transfer: Applicants must have full sophomore standing prior to applying and a minimum 3.0 GPA in previous college work. Transfers are accepted for the sophomore and junior classes only, and Amherst recommends that they submit SAT or ACT scores, plus high school and college transcripts, and seek a personal interview. 64 of 128 credits required for the bachelor's degree must be completed at Amherst.

Visiting: There are regularly scheduled orientations for prospective students, consisting of information sessions led by a dean and student-led tours. There are guides for informal visits; visitors may sit in on classes and stay overnight. To schedule a visit, contact the Admission Office at admission@amherst.edu.

Financial Aid: The CSS/Profile and FAFSA are required. Check with the school for current application deadlines.

International Students: The school actively recruits these students. They must take the TOEFL or MELAB, or the SAT: ELAP if English is not the applicant's first language. They must also take the SAT or ACT.

Computers: Wireless access is available. All dorm rooms provide Internet access as well as libraries and academic buildings. All libraries and academic resource centers provide wireless Internet along with a handful of outdoor areas. There are approximately 270 PC terminals available for student use. All students may access the system 24 hours a day.

Admissions Contact: Peter Roomey, Director of Public Affairs. E-Mail: *admission@amherst.edu* Web: *www.amherst.edu*

ANNA MARIA COLLEGE
C-2

Paxton, MA 01612-1198

(508) 849-3360
(800) 344-4586; (508) 849-3362

Full-time: 310 men, 400 women	**Faculty:** n/av
Part-time: 100 men, 120 women	**Ph.D.s:** 50%
Graduate: 125 men, 210 women	**Student/Faculty:** n/av
Year: semesters, summer session	**Tuition:** $25,000
Application Deadline: open	**Room & Board:** $9600
Freshman Class: n/av	
SAT or ACT: required	**LESS COMPETITIVE**

Anna Maria College, founded in 1946, is a small, comprehensive Catholic college offering career-oriented programs in liberal and fine arts, business, and teacher preparation. Figures in the above capsule and this profile are approximate. There are 5 undergraduate schools and 1 graduate school. In addition to regional accreditation, AMC has baccalaureate program accreditation with CSWE and NLN. The library contains 75,789 volumes, 1702 microform items, and 6095 audio/video tapes/CDs/DVDs, and subscribes to 291 periodicals including electronic. Computerized library services include interlibrary loans, database searching, and Internet access. Special learning facilities include a learning resource center, art gallery, audiovisual center, and nature trail. The 180-acre campus is in a rural area 8 miles northwest of Worcester. Including any residence halls, there are 13 buildings.

Student Life: 84% of undergraduates are from Massachusetts. Others are from 14 states, 2 foreign countries, and Canada. 78% are white. The average age of freshmen is 19; all undergraduates, 20. 36% do not continue beyond their first year; 49% remain to graduate.

Housing: 459 students can be accommodated in college housing, which includes coed dorms. In addition, there is substance-free housing. On-campus housing is guaranteed for the freshman year only, is available on a first-come, first-served basis, and is available on a lottery system for upperclassmen. Priority is given to out-of-town students. 54% of students commute. All students may keep cars.

Activities: There are no fraternities or sororities. There are 25 groups on campus, including art, cheerleading, choir, chorus, computers, dance, drama, ethnic, gay, honors, international, jazz band, musical theater, newspaper, political, professional, religious, social, social service, student government, and yearbook. Popular campus events include Harvest Weekend, Mr. AMC, and Trick or Treating for Children.

Sports: There are 5 intercollegiate sports for men and 5 for women, and 3 intramural sports for men and 2 for women. Facilities include an activities center with a basketball court, locker rooms, and weight and fitness equipment, soccer, baseball, and softball fields, an outdoor basketball court, and a fitness trail.

Disabled Students: 80% of the campus is accessible. Facilities include wheelchair ramps, elevators, special parking, specially equipped restrooms, special class scheduling, lowered drinking fountains, and special housing.

Services: Counseling and information services are available, as is tutoring in every subject through a tutoring lab There is a reader service for the blind and remedial math, reading, and writing.

Campus Safety and Security: Measures include 24-hour foot and vehicle patrol and security escort services. There are shuttle buses, emergency telephones, and lighted pathways/sidewalks.

Programs of Study: AMC confers B.A., B.S., B.M., and B.S.N. degrees. Associate and master's degrees are also awarded. Bachelor's degrees are awarded in BUSINESS (business administration and management and sports management), COMMUNICATIONS AND THE ARTS (art, English, graphic design, media arts, modern language, music, music performance, studio art, and visual and performing arts), COMPUTER AND PHYSICAL SCIENCE (computer science), EDUCATION (early childhood education, elementary education, and music education), ENGINEERING AND ENVIRONMENTAL DESIGN (environmental science), HEALTH PROFESSIONS (art therapy, music therapy, and nursing), SOCIAL SCIENCE (criminal justice, fire science, history, human development, humanities, liberal arts/general studies, paralegal studies, political science/government, psychology, religion, social science, social work, and sociology). Criminal justice, fire science, and business are the largest.

Required: The 60-credit core curriculum consists of classes in English, literature, math, computers, natural science, foreign language, fine arts, history, philosophy, social/behavioral sciences, and religious studies. A total of 120 credits is required for graduation, with a minimum of 30 in the major and a 2.0 GPA.

Special: Cross-registration with the Colleges of the Worcester Consortium and internships in all majors are available. The college offers study abroad, a Washington semester, student-designed majors, accelerated degree programs, a general studies degree, credit by exam, work-study programs, and 5-year advanced degree programs in business, counseling psychology, criminal justice, education, visual art, and fire science. There are 6 national honor societies.

Faculty/Classroom: 53% of faculty are male; 47% are female. All teach undergraduates. No introductory courses are taught by graduate students. The average class size in an introductory lecture is 20; in a laboratory, 20; and in a regular course, 13.

Requirements: The SAT or ACT is required. A GED is accepted. 16 academic units are recommended, including 4 years of English, 2 years each of foreign language, history, math, and sciences, and 1 year of social studies. An interview is recommended. When applicable, an audition and portfolio are required. Students who have been out of high school for 3 or more years, or transfer students with 10 or more college-level courses, do not need to submit standardized test scores. An essay is required. A GPA of 2.0 is required. AP and CLEP credits are accepted. Important factors in the admissions decision are advanced placement or honors courses, extracurricular activities record, and leadership record.

Procedure: Freshmen are admitted fall and spring. Entrance exams should be taken in spring of the junior year or fall of the senior year. There are deferred admissions and rolling admissions plans. Application deadlines are open. The fall 2009 application fee was $40. Notification is sent on a rolling basis. Applications are accepted on-line.

Transfer: 34 transfer students enrolled in a recent year. Transfers with a minimum GPA of 2.0 are accepted for upper-division work. High school and college transcripts are required. An essay or personal statement and a statement of good standing from prior institutions are also required. 60 of 120 credits required for the bachelor's degree must be completed at AMC.

Visiting: There are regularly scheduled orientations for prospective students, including on-campus interviews, campus tours, day visitation program by appointment, and a fall open house. There are guides for informal visits, and visitors may sit in on classes and stay overnight. To schedule a visit, contact the Undergraduate Admission Office at (508) 849-3365.

Financial Aid: In a recent year, 93% of all full-time freshmen and 85% of continuing full-time students received some form of financial aid. 77% of all full-time freshmen and 70% of continuing full-time students received need-based aid. The average freshman award was $15,703. 19% of undergraduate students work part-time. Average annual earnings from campus work are $1200. The average financial indebtedness of a recent graduate was $30,000. The FAFSA and the state aid form are required. Check with the school for current application deadlines.

International Students: There were 2 international students enrolled in a recent year. The school actively recruits these students. They must take the TOEFL with a minimum score of 470 on the paper-based TOEFL (PBT). They must also take the SAT or ACT.

Computers: Wireless access is available. Students utilize the college network through the use of college-owned computers in classrooms, computer labs, and residence halls. There are 4 computer labs used strictly in a teaching environment, including 1 teaching lab, 1 graphic arts lab, 1 health sciences lab, and 1 MIDI lab for the music program. All college-owned computers have access to Microsoft Office as well as Internet access at a minimum. In addition to college-owned computers, students have the opportunity to access the college network from any location on campus through the use of the college wireless network and their personally owned computer. In addition, resident students may connect to the college network from residence halls through a wired connection. All students may access the system.

Graduates: In a recent year, 157 bachelor's degrees were awarded. The most popular majors were criminal justice (18%), social work and psychology (15%), and fire science (14%). 9 companies recruited on campus in a recent year. In an average class, 49% graduate in 4 years or less and 55% graduate in 6 years or less.

Admissions Contact: Director of Admission.
E-mail: *admission@annamaria.edu* Web: *www.annamaria.edu*

ART INSTITUTE OF BOSTON AT LESLEY UNIVERSITY
E-2

Boston, MA 02215-2598

(617) 585-6710
(800) 773-0494, ext. 6706; (617) 585-6720

Full-time: 301 men, 903 women	**Faculty:** n/a
Part-time: 18 men, 45 women	**Ph.D.s:** 43%
Graduate: none	**Student/Faculty:** n/av
Year: semesters, summer session	**Tuition:** $27,330
Application Deadline: February 15	**Room & Board:** $12,400
Freshman Class: 2523 applied, 1639 accepted, 328 enrolled	**SPECIAL**

The Art Institute of Boston at Lesley University, founded in 1912, is a private institution offering undergraduate visual art programs leading to baccalaureate degrees, 3-year diplomas, and advanced professional certificates, as well as continuing and professional education, intensive workshops, and precollege courses. There are 2 undergraduate schools and 1 graduate school. In addition to regional accreditation, AIB has baccalaureate program accreditation with NASAD. The 2 libraries contain 124,022 volumes, 878,938 microform items, and 42,680 audio/video tapes/CDs/DVDs, and subscribe to 3,935 periodicals including electronic. Computerized library services include interlibrary loans, database searching, Internet access, and laptop Internet portals. Special learning facilities include a learning resource center, art gallery, computer labs, state-of-the-art animation lab, print-making studio, clay studio, wood-working studio, photo lab, and digital-printing lab. The 2-acre campus is in an urban area in the Kenmore Square area of Boston. Including any residence halls, there are 53 buildings.

Student Life: 56% of undergraduates are from Massachusetts. Others are from 34 states, 10 foreign countries, and Canada. 83% are from public schools. 63% are white. The average age of freshmen is 18; all undergraduates, 20. 33% do not continue beyond their first year; 63% remain to graduate.

Housing: 650 students can be accommodated in college housing, which includes single-sex and coed dorms. On-campus housing is available on a first-come and first-served basis. 50% of students commute. All students may keep cars.

Activities: There are no fraternities or sororities. There are 25 groups on campus, including art, chorale, chorus, drama, ethnic, gay, international, literary magazine, musical theater, religious, social service, and student government. Popular campus events include student lunches, student and faculty coffee hours, and Edible Art.

Sports: There are 7 intercollegiate sports for men and 7 for women, and 3 intramural sports for men and 5 for women. Facilities include an outdoor tennis court, a fitness center with Nautilus circuit, free weights, and cardiovascular equipment on the main campus. In addition, students may use an Olympic-size swimming pool, playing field facilities, basketball and racquetball courts, a rowing tank, a softball court, an indoor track, and a lighted outdoor soccer field at a nearby school.

Disabled Students: 85% of the campus is accessible. Facilities include wheelchair ramps, elevators, specially equipped restrooms, special class scheduling, and lowered drinking fountains.

Services: Counseling and information services are available, as is tutoring in some subjects. There is a reader service for the blind, and remedial math and writing.

Campus Safety and Security: Measures include 24-hour foot and vehicle patrol, self-defense education, and security escort services. There are shuttle buses, emergency telephones, lighted pathways/sidewalks, alarms, and electronically operated entrances in some buildings.

Programs of Study: AIB confers B.F.A. degrees. Master's degrees are also awarded. Bachelor's degrees are awarded in COMMUNICATIONS AND THE ARTS (design, fine arts, illustration, and photography). Design and photography are the strongest academically. Illustration/animation is the largest.

Required: All students must complete 123 to 128 credits, including 31 credits in the foundation program and 82 or more in the major. Senior juries are required.

Special: There is cross-registration with Lesley University. Internships are required for design majors and encouraged for all other majors. Accelerated degree programs in all majors, study abroad in 6 countries and dual majors in fine art/illustration, design/illustration, illustration/animation, and art education are offered. There is a freshman honors program and 2 departmental honors programs.

Faculty/Classroom: 44% of faculty are male; 56% are female. All teach undergraduates. No introductory courses are taught by graduate students. The average class size in an introductory lecture, 20, in a laboratory, 14, and in a regular course, 14.

Admissions: 65% of the 2009-2010 applicants were accepted. The SAT scores for the 2009-2010 freshman class were: Critical Reading--27% below 500, 47% between 500 and 599, 24% between 600 and 700, and 2% above 700; Math--41% below 500, 46% between 500 and 599, 12% between 600 and 700, and 1% above 700; Writing--27% below 500, 50% between 500 and 599, 20% between 600 and 700, and 3% above 700. The ACT scores were 9% below 21, 50% between 21 and 23, 13% between 24 and 26, 24% between 27 and 28, and 4% above 28. 38% of the current freshmen were in the top fifth of their class; 70% were in the top two fifths.

Requirements: Applicants must submit an official high school transcript, an essay, and do a portfolio review. Letters of recommendation and a campus tour are encouraged. AP and CLEP credits are accepted. Important factors in the admissions decision are evidence of special talent, personality/intangible qualities, and advanced placement or honors courses.

Procedure: Freshmen are admitted fall and spring. Entrance exams should be taken by February 15. There is a deferred admissions plan. Applications should be filed by February 15 for fall entry and November 15 for spring entry. The fall 2009 application fee was $40. Applications are accepted on-line. A waiting list is maintained.

Transfer: High school and college transcripts, a portfolio review, an essay, and SAT or ACT scores (if graduated since 1995) are required. 45 of 123 credits required for the bachelor's degree must be completed at AIB.

Visiting: There are regularly scheduled orientations for prospective students, meeting with faculty and students. There are guides for informal visits and visitors may sit in on classes. To schedule a visit, contact the Office of Admissions at (800) 773-0494 or (617) 585-6700.

Financial Aid: In 2009-2010, 72% of all full-time freshmen received some form of financial aid. 72% of all full-time freshmen received need-based aid. The average freshmen award was $20,328. 18% of undergraduate students work part-time. Average annual earnings from campus work are $2000. The average financial indebtedness of the 2009 graduate was $14,000. The FAFSA and the college's own financial statement are required. The priority date for freshman financial aid applications for fall entry is February 15.

International Students: There are 44 international students enrolled. The school actively recruits these students. They must take the TOEFL with a minimum score of 500 on the paper-based TOEFL (PBT) or 61 on the Internet-based version (iBT).

Computers: The university offers students 12 computer labs, each with an average of 15 computers. In addition, Internet access is provided in all classroom dorms, and lounge areas, and wireless access is available in 50% of all classrooms. A campus-wide network gives all students access to course and extracurricular activity information free of charge. All students may access the system. There are no time limits and no fees.

Graduates: In a recent year, 390 bachelor's degrees were awarded. The most popular majors were illustration (33%), design (24%), and photography (21%). In an average class, 36% graduate in 4 years or less, 53% graduate in 5 years or less, and 63% graduate in 6 years or less. Of the 2008 graduating class, 11% were enrolled in graduate school within 6 months of graduation, and 75% were employed.

Admissions Contact: Bob Gielow, Director of Admissions. E-Mail: *admissions@aiboston.edu* Web: *www.aiboston.edu*

ASSUMPTION COLLEGE

C-2

Worcester, MA 01609-1296

(508) 767-7285
(866) 477-7776; (508) 799-4412

Full-time: 886 men, 1228 women	**Faculty:** 154; IIB, -$
Part-time: no men, 3 women	**Ph.D.s:** 93%
Graduate: 126 men, 358 women	**Student/Faculty:** 14 to 1
Year: semesters, summer session	**Tuition:** $30,171
Application Deadline: February 15	**Room & Board:** $10,070
Freshman Class: 3719 applied, 2947 accepted, 515 enrolled	
SAT CR/M: 520/530	**ACT:** 22 — COMPETITIVE

Assumption College, founded in 1904 by Augustinians of the Assumption, offers a Catholic, liberal arts and sciences education to undergraduates, along with programs for graduate and continuing education students. There is 1 graduate school. The library contains 230,180 volumes, 5,418 microform items, and 43,479 audio/video tapes/CDs/DVDs, and subscribes to 3,550 periodicals including electronic. Computerized library services include interlibrary loans, database searching, Internet access, and laptop Internet portals. Special learning facilities include a learning resource center and TV station. The 180-acre campus is in a suburban area 45 miles west of Boston. Including any residence halls, there are 48 buildings.

Student Life: 66% of undergraduates are from Massachusetts. Others are from 26 states, 9 foreign countries, and Canada. 62% are from public schools. 76% are white. The average age of freshmen is 19; all undergraduates, 20. 19% do not continue beyond their first year; 66% remain to graduate.

Housing: 2056 students can be accommodated in college housing, which includes single-sex dorms and on-campus apartments. In addition, there are special-interest houses, freshman dorms, substance-free dorms, and a living/learning center. On-campus housing is guaranteed for all 4 years. 90% of students live on campus; of those, 80% remain on campus on weekends. Upperclassmen may keep cars.

Activities: There are no fraternities or sororities. There are 50 groups on campus, including art, band, cheerleading, choir, chorale, chorus, computers, dance, drama, environmental, ethnic, film, honors, international, jazz band, literary magazine, musical theater, newspaper, orchestra, pep band, photography, political, professional, radio and TV, religious, social, social service, and student government. Popular campus events include Midnight madness basketball kickoff, Campus concert, and Duck Day.

Sports: There are 10 intercollegiate sports for men and 11 for women, and 9 intramural sports for men and 8 for women. Facilities include a 1200-seat multi-sports stadium, a 3000-seat gym, baseball and softball diamonds, a field hockey area, a soccer field, and tennis courts. A recreation center houses a 6-lane swimming pool, a jogging/walking track, 4 racquetball courts, an aerobics/dance studio, fully equipped Bodymaster and free-weight rooms, a fitness center, and a field house with 3 multipurpose courts for basketball, volleyball, and floor hockey.

Disabled Students: 71% of the campus is accessible. Facilities include wheelchair ramps, elevators, special parking, specially equipped restrooms, special class scheduling, lowered drinking fountains, lowered telephones, and special housing.

Services: Counseling and information services are available, as is tutoring in most subjects. There is a reader service for the blind, signing for the deaf, and technology services for the disabled.

Campus Safety and Security: Measures include 24-hour foot and vehicle patrol, emergency notification system, self-defense education, and security escort services. There are shuttle buses, emergency telephones, lighted pathways/sidewalks, and controlled access to dorms/residences.

Programs of Study: Assumption confers B.A. degrees. Master's degrees are also awarded. Bachelor's degrees are awarded in BIOLOGICAL SCIENCE (biology/biological science and biotechnology), BUSINESS (accounting, business administration and management, international business management, international economics, marketing management, and organizational behavior), COMMUNICATIONS AND THE ARTS (classics, English, French, languages, music, Spanish, and visual and performing arts), COMPUTER AND PHYSICAL SCIENCE (chemistry, computer science, and mathematics), ENGINEERING AND ENVIRONMENTAL DESIGN (environmental science), HEALTH PROFESSIONS (rehabilitation therapy), SOCIAL SCIENCE (economics, history, international studies, Italian studies, Latin American studies, philosophy, political science/government, psychology, sociology, and theological studies). Natural sciences, political science, and philosophy are the strongest academically. Business studies, English, and psychology are the largest.

Required: Students must complete a core curriculum of 3 courses from different disciplines in social science: 2 courses in 1 and 1 course in another of the 3 areas of math, natural science, and foreign languages; 2 courses each of English composition, philosophy, and theology; 1 each of literature, history, and either art, music, or theater arts, and 1 additional course in 2 of the 3 areas of philosophy and theology, literature, and history. A minimum of 120 semester credit hours, with a minimum of 38 semester courses, must be completed; 8 to 14 courses must be in the upper division of the major. A minimum 2.0 GPA is required.

Special: There are co-op programs in gerontology studies and marine studies. Cross-registration with the Colleges of Worcester Consortium is offered. The college offers internships, study abroad, a Washington semester, student-designed and dual majors, credit by exam, and credit for military experience. 6-in-5 programs, accounting (BA/MBA), special education(BA/MA), and school counseling (BA/MA). There are 11 national honor societies and a freshman honors program.

Faculty/Classroom: 56% of faculty are male; 44% are female. All teach undergraduates. No introductory courses are taught by graduate students. The average class size in an introductory lecture, 22, in a laboratory, 15, and in a regular course, 20.

Admissions: 79% of the 2009-2010 applicants were accepted. The SAT scores for the 2009-2010 freshman class were: Critical Reading--28% below 500, 53% between 500 and 599, 17% between 600 and 700, and 2% above 700; Math--27% below 500, 50% between 500 and 599, 22% between 600 and 700, and 1% above 700. The ACT scores were 28% below 21, 35% between 21 and 23, 26% between 24 and 26, 8% between 27 and 28, and 3% above 28. 34% of the current freshmen were in the top fifth of their class; 74% were in the top two fifths.

Requirements: Applicants must graduate from an accredited secondary school or have a GED. 18 academic units are required, including 4 years of English, 3 of math, and 2 each of history, science, and foreign language. An essay and an interview are recommended. AP and CLEP credits are accepted. Important factors in the admissions decision are advanced placement or honors courses, leadership record, and recommendations by school officials.

Procedure: Freshmen are admitted fall and spring. Entrance exams should be taken in May of the junior year or November of the senior year. There are early admissions, deferred admissions, and rolling admissions plans. Applications should be filed by February 15 for fall entry and December 21 for spring entry, along with a $50 fee. Notification is sent on a rolling basis. Applications are accepted on-line. 302 applicants were on a recent waiting list, 73 were accepted.

Transfer: 57 transfer students enrolled in 2008-2009. Transfer students must have maintained a minimum 2.5 GPA at their previous college. SAT scores and high school and college transcripts are required. 60 of 120 credits required for the bachelor's degree must be completed at Assumption.

Visiting: There are regularly scheduled orientations for prospective students, consisting of new student orientation, meetings with future classmates, choosing roommates, registration, testing, conferences with academic advisers, and discussions of aspects of college life. There are guides for informal visits and visitors may sit in on classes. To schedule a visit, contact the Office of Admissions at (866) 477-7776.

Financial Aid: In 2009-2010, 94% of all full-time freshmen and 95% of continuing full-time students received some form of financial aid. 78% of all full-time freshmen and 74% of continuing full-time students received need-based aid. The average freshman award was $26,021. Need-based scholarships or need-based grants averaged $16,670 ($35,000 maximum); need-based self-help aid (loans and jobs) averaged $3,500 ($5,500 maximum);non-need-based athletic scholarships averaged $36,926 ($40,712 maximum); other non-need-based awards and non-need-based scholarships averaged $10,007 ($29,806 maximum). 68% of undergraduate students work part-time. Average annual earnings from campus work are $630. The average financial indebtedness of the 2009 graduate was $24,382. The FAFSA is required. The deadline for filing freshman financial aid applications for fall entry is February 15.

International Students: There are 12 international students enrolled. The school actively recruits these students. They must take the TOEFL with a minimum score of 550 on the paper-based TOEFL (PBT) or 80 on the Internet-based version (iBT).

Computers: Wireless access is available. Every classroom has wired and wireless connections. In classrooms, the total wired ports equal 500. There are 315 computers across campus available for general student use. All are connected to the Internet and have a full suite of applications. There are approximately 520 wired connections across the campus in the library, campus center, IT center, and other public locations. The campus is fully wireless, including residence halls and other campus buildings. All students may access the system. There are no time limits. The fee is $200.

Graduates: From July 1, 2008 to June 30, 2009, 443 bachelor's degrees were awarded. The most popular majors were psychology (12%), accounting (9%), and English (7%). In an average class, 64% graduate in 4 years or less, 66% graduate in 5 years or less, and 66% graduate in 6 years or less. Of the 2008 graduating class, 26% were enrolled in graduate school within 6 months of graduation, and 77% were employed.

Admissions Contact: Evan E. Lipp, Vice President for Enrollment Management. A campus DVD is available. E-Mail: *admiss@assumption.edu*
Web: *www.assumption.edu/admissions/undergratuate/default/.aspx*

ATLANTIC UNION COLLEGE
South Lancaster, MA 01561

C-2

(978) 368-2239
(800) 282-2030; (978) 368-2517

Full-time: 150 men, 250 women	**Faculty:** n/av
Part-time: 20 men, 30 women	**Ph.Ds:** 42%
Graduate: 5 men, 10 women	**Student/Faculty:** n/av
Year: semesters, summer session	**Tuition:** $17,000
Application Deadline: see profile	**Room & Board:** $7600
Freshman Class: n/av	
SAT or ACT: required	**LESS COMPETITIVE**

Atlantic Union College, established in 1882, is a private liberal arts institution associated with the Seventh-Day Adventist church and offers professional and preprofessional programs. Figures in the above capsule and this profile are approximate. In addition to regional accreditation, AUC has baccalaureate program accreditation with CSWE, NASM, and NLN. The library contains 139,000 volumes, 17,336 microform items, and 4754 audio/video tapes/CDs/DVDs, and subscribes to 469 periodicals including electronic. Computerized library services include interlibrary loans, database searching, and Internet access. Special learning facilities include a learning resource center, art gallery, model elementary and secondary schools, and music conservatory. The 135-acre campus is in a small town 50 miles west of Boston. Including any residence halls, there are 54 buildings.

Student Life: 55% of undergraduates are from out of state, mostly the Northeast. Students are from 14 states, 21 foreign countries, and Canada. 53% are African American; 22% Hispanic; 20% white; 15% foreign nationals. The average age of freshmen is 21; all undergraduates, 23. 27% do not continue beyond their first year.

Housing: 469 students can be accommodated in college housing, which includes single-sex dorms, on-campus apartments, and married student housing. On-campus housing is guaranteed for all 4 years. 56% of students live on campus; of those, 85% remain on campus on weekends. Alcohol is not permitted. All students may keep cars.

Activities: There are no fraternities or sororities. There are 13 groups on campus, including art, band, choir, chorale, drama, ethnic, honors, newspaper, orchestra, religious, social, student government, and yearbook. Popular campus events include fall picnic, Cultural Heritage Weeks, and Fine Arts Week.

Sports: There are 7 intramural sports for men and 7 for women. Facilities include a gym and field house with a weight room and tennis/volleyball/badminton, racquetball/handball, and basketball courts, a swimming pool, and athletic fields for flag football, soccer, softball, and baseball.

Disabled Students: 73% of the campus is accessible. Facilities include wheelchair ramps, elevators, special parking, specially equipped restrooms, special class scheduling, and lowered drinking fountains.

Services: Counseling and information services are available, as is tutoring in most subjects. There is remedial math, reading, and writing. Additional services are provided upon request

Campus Safety and Security: Measures include self-defense education and security escort services. There are lighted pathways/sidewalks.

Programs of Study: AUC confers B.A., B.S., and B.M. degrees. Associate and master's degrees are also awarded. Bachelor's degrees are awarded in BIOLOGICAL SCIENCE (biology/biological science and life science), BUSINESS (accounting and business administration and management), COMMUNICATIONS AND THE ARTS (art, English, and music), COMPUTER AND PHYSICAL SCIENCE (computer science, information sciences and systems, and mathematics), EDUCATION (early childhood education, elementary education, and music education), HEALTH PROFESSIONS (nursing), SOCIAL SCIENCE (culinary arts, history, liberal arts/general studies, ministries, psychology, religion, social work, and theological studies). Nursing, business, and psychology are the strongest academically. Nursing, business, and education are the largest.

Required: Students must complete 9 hours each in humanities, science, and social science and 12 hours in religion/ethics. Foreign language proficiency, a phys ed requirement, 40 hours of community service, and a course in college writing must also be completed. AUC requires 128 to 143 credit hours for the bachelor's degree, with 30 to 60 in the major, and a 2.0 GPA.

Special: There is cross-registration with Mount Wachusett Community College and the Colleges of Worcester Consortium. Students may study abroad in 6 countries. AUC also offers newspaper and biology research internships, cooperative programs in several majors, pass/fail options, and nondegree study. The Summer Advantage in New England program offers precollege credit to high school honor students. There is also an adult degree program, in which most study is done at home and in which student-designed majors are permitted. Dual majors, an accelerated degree in management and professional studies, a 1-3 engineering degree with Walla Walla College, and preprofessional curricula in dentistry, dental hygiene, medicine, respiratory therapy, radiologic technology, and veterinary medicine in conjunction with Loma Linda University are offered. There are 3 national honor societies, a freshman honors program, and 4 departmental honors programs.

Faculty/Classroom: 45% of faculty are male; 55% are female. All teach undergraduates, and 10% both teach and do research. No introductory courses are taught by graduate students. The average class size in an introductory lecture is 18; in a laboratory, 30; and in a regular course, 16.

Requirements: The SAT or ACT is required. In addition, applicants should be graduates of an accredited secondary school. The GED is accepted with a minimum score of 250. Required academic credits include 4 years of high school English and 2 years each of a foreign language, math, history, and science. A GPA of 2.2 is required. AP and CLEP credits are accepted. Important factors in the admissions decision are recommendations by school officials, recommendations by alumni, and personality/intangible qualities.

Procedure: Freshmen are admitted fall and spring. Entrance exams should be taken during the senior year of high school. There is a rolling admissions plan. Check with the school for current application deadlines. The fall 2009 application fee was $25. Notification is sent on a rolling basis. Applications are accepted on-line.

Transfer: Applicants who have completed at least 24 semester hours are not required to submit SAT or ACT scores. Applicants from junior colleges may receive credit for up to 72 semester hours. Only a grade of C or better transfers for credit. 30 of 128 credits required for the bachelor's degree must be completed at AUC.

Visiting: There are regularly scheduled orientations for prospective students, including campus tours, class visits, and financial aid and admissions information sessions. There are guides for informal visits, and visitors may sit in on classes and stay overnight. To schedule a visit, contact Wayne Dunbar at (978) 368-2259.

Financial Aid: AUC is a member of CSS. The FAFSA is required. Check with the school for current application deadlines.

International Students: The school actively recruits these students. They must take the TOEFL. They must also take the ACT, scoring 17.

Computers: Wireless access is available. Students may apply for network and/or wireless access seperately. Both allow Internet access. Access is also accomplished by using laptops (wireless labs only) or through campus labs (network) located in the science complex (3 main computer labs), the library, and the dorms. Some academic departments also have small labs. All students may access the system. There are no time limits. There is a fee. It is strongly recommended that all students have a personal computer.

Admissions Contact: Director of Admissions. A campus DVD is available. E-mail: *enroll@atlanticuc.edu* Web: *www.atlanticuc.edu*

BABSON COLLEGE D-2
Babson Park, MA 02457

(781) 239-5522
(800) 488-3696; (781) 239-4135

Full-time: 1070 men, 730 women	Faculty: n/av
Part-time: none	Ph.D.s: 72%
Graduate: 1200 men, 440 women	Student/Faculty: n/av
Year: semesters, summer session	Tuition: $39,040
Application Deadline: see profile	Room & Board: $12,900
Freshman Class: n/av	
SAT or ACT: required	HIGHLY COMPETITIVE

Babson College, founded in 1919, is a private business school. All students start their own businesses during their freshman year with money loaned by the college. Figures in the above capsule and this capsule are approximate. There is 1 graduate school. In addition to regional accreditation, Babson has baccalaureate program accreditation with AACSB. The library contains 132,024 volumes, 346,941 microform items, and 4645 audio/video tapes/CDs/DVDs, and subscribes to 511 periodicals including electronic. Computerized library services include interlibrary loans, database searching, and Internet access. Special learning facilities include a learning resource center, art gallery, radio station, performing arts theater, and centers for entrepreneurial studies, management, language and culture, writing, math, visual arts, executive education, and women's leadership. The 370-acre campus is in a suburban area 14 miles west of Boston. Including any residence halls, there are 53 buildings.

Student Life: 70% of undergraduates are from out of state, mostly the Northeast. Students are from 47 states, 60 foreign countries, and Canada. 50% are from public schools. 44% are white; 18% foreign nationals; 11% Asian American. The average age of freshmen is 18; all undergraduates, 20. 5% do not continue beyond their first year; 85% remain to graduate.

Housing: 1441 students can be accommodated in college housing, which includes single-sex and coed dorms, on-campus apartments, and married student housing. In addition, there are special-interest houses, substance-free living, fraternity and sorority towers, and a cultural house. On-campus housing is guaranteed for all 4 years. 85% of students live on campus; of those, 80% remain on campus on weekends. All students may keep cars.

Activities: 10% of men belong to 7 national fraternities; 12% of women belong to 3 national sororities. There are 60 groups on campus, including art, band, cappella , cheerleading, choir, chorus, dance, drama, ethnic, gay, honors, international, jazz band, literary magazine, musical theater, newspaper, photography, political, professional, radio and TV, religious, social, social service, student government, and yearbook. Popular campus events include Multicultural Week.

Sports: There are 11 intercollegiate sports for men and 11 for women, and 11 intramural sports for men and 11 for women. Facilities include a sports complex with an indoor pool, a 200-meter, 6-lane indoor track, a 1500-square-foot field house, a 600-seat gym with 3 basketball courts, 5 squash and 2 racquetball courts, a fitness center, a dance aerobics studio, locker rooms with saunas, and a sports medicine facility.

Disabled Students: 75% of the campus is accessible. Facilities include wheelchair ramps, elevators, special parking, specially equipped restrooms, special class scheduling, lowered drinking fountains, and special housing.

Services: Counseling and information services are available, as is tutoring in most subjects. There are writing/speech skills and math/science skills centers.

Campus Safety and Security: Measures include 24-hour foot and vehicle patrol, self-defense education, and security escort services. There are shuttle buses, emergency telephones, lighted pathways/sidewalks, a motorist assist program, a transportation service for the cross-registration program, vans available to students for school activities, and crime prevention programs.

Programs of Study: Babson confers B.S.M. degrees. Master's degrees are also awarded. Bachelor's degrees are awarded in BUSINESS (business administration and management).

Required: Students must complete a curriculum of general management and liberal arts, with 50% in management and 50% in liberal arts. A total of 128 semester hours is required for graduation. A minimum GPA of 2.0 is required.

Special: There is cross-registration with Brandeis University, Wellesley College, and F.W. Olin College of Engineering. Internships and study abroad in 27 countries are available. There is a freshman honors program and 10 departmental honors programs.

Faculty/Classroom: 69% of faculty are male; 31% are female. No introductory courses are taught by graduate students. The average class size in an introductory lecture is 34; in a laboratory, 20; and in a regular course, 27.

Requirements: The SAT or ACT is required. In addition, applicants must be graduates of an accredited secondary school or have a GED. 16 academic courses are required, including 4 credits of English, 3 of math, 2 of social studies, and 1 of science. A fourth year of math is strongly recommended. Essays are required. SAT Subject tests in math are recommended. AP credits are accepted. Important factors in the admissions decision are advanced placement or honors courses, evidence of special talent, and leadership record.

Procedure: Freshmen are admitted fall. Entrance exams should be taken prior to application (SAT or ACT). There are early decision, early admissions and deferred admissions plans. Check with the school for current application deadlines. The fall 2009 application fee was $60. Applications are accepted on-line. A waiting list is maintained.

Transfer: Transfer applicants are expected to demonstrate solid academic performance at their prior institution and must submit 1 essay and 1 recommendation from a college teacher or administrator, in addition to a high school transcript and SAT scores. They must also submit course descriptions and syllabi for any courses they have taken. 64 of 128 credits required for the bachelor's degree must be completed at Babson.

Visiting: There are regularly scheduled orientations for prospective students, including an open house each year, personal interviews, campus tours, group information sessions and Fall Preview Days (select Saturdays). There are guides for informal visits. To schedule a visit, contact the Admission Office.

Financial Aid: In a recent year, 4% of all full-time freshmen and 41% of continuing full-time students received some form of financial aid. 45% of all full-time freshmen and 41% of continuing full-time students received need-based aid. The average freshman award was $26,171. 32% of undergraduate students work part-time. Average annual earnings from campus work are $1580. The average financial indebtedness of a recent graduate was $24,900. The CSS/Profile, the FAFSA, and tax returns are required. Check with the school for current application deadlines.

International Students: There were 318 international students enrolled in a recent year. The school actively recruits these students. They must take the TOEFL with a minimum score of 600, or take the English Language Proficiency Test. They must also take the SAT or ACT.

Computers: Wireless access is available. All students may access the system. There are no time limits and no fees. It is strongly recommended that all students have a personal computer. An IBM ThinkPad is recommended.

Graduates: In a recent year, 424 bachelor's degrees were awarded. 301 companies recruited on campus in a recent year. In an average class, 80% graduate in 4 years or less, 85% graduate in 5 years or less, and 85% graduate in 6 years or less. Of a recent graduating class, 3% were enrolled in graduate school within 6 months of graduation and 92% were employed.

Admissions Contact: Dean of Undergraduate Admission. A campus DVD is available. E-mail: *ugradadmission@babson.edu* Web: *www.babson.edu*

BAY PATH COLLEGE
Longmeadow, MA 01106

(413) 565-1331
(800) 782-7284; (413) 565-1105

Full-time: 1110 women	**Faculty:** n/av
Part-time: 235 women	**Ph.D.s:** 54%
Graduate: 25 men, 90 women	**Student/Faculty:** n/av
Year: semesters	**Tuition:** $21,000
Application Deadline: open	**Room & Board:** $9000
Freshman Class: n/av	
SAT or ACT: required	**COMPETITIVE**

Bay Path College, founded in 1897, is a comprehensive, private college offering innovative undergraduate programs for women onnly and graduate programs for men and women. Figures in the above capsule and this profile are approximate. There is 1 graduate school. The library contains 47,415 volumes, 4326 microform items, and 3632 audio/video tapes/CDs/DVDs, and subscribes to 156 periodicals including electronic. Computerized library services include interlibrary loans, database searching, and Internet access. Special learning facilities include a learning resource center, radio station, and TV station. The 48-acre campus is in a suburban area 3 miles south of Springfield. Including any residence halls, there are 17 buildings.

Student Life: 59% of undergraduates are from Massachusetts. Others are from 15 states and 6 foreign countries. 93% are from public schools. 79% are white; 11% African American. The average age of freshmen is 18; all undergraduates, 35.

Housing: 376 students can be accommodated in college housing, which includes single-sex dorms. On-campus housing is guaranteed for all 4 years. 66% of students live on campus; of those, 60% remain on campus on weekends. Alcohol is not permitted. All students may keep cars.

Activities: There are no fraternities or sororities. There are 39 groups on campus, including cheerleading, choir, chorale, computers, dance, drama, ethnic, forensics, gay, Habitat for Humanity, honors, international, literary magazine, musical threater, newspaper, political, political awareness, professional, radio and TV, religious, social, social service, student government, Winter Guard, and yearbook. Popular campus events include father/daughter and mother/daughter banquets, Karaoke Unplugged, and Dinner with the President.

Sports: There are 5 intercollegiate sports for women. Facilities include a fitness center that houses a weight-training room, a dance studio, and an aerobics room and a nearby 12-acre playing field with soccer and softball fields, a walking/jogging track, and a field house.

Disabled Students: 50% of the campus is accessible. Facilities include wheelchair ramps, elevators, special parking, and specially equipped rest rooms.

Services: Counseling and information services are available, as is tutoring in every subject.

Campus Safety and Security: Measures include 24-hour foot and vehicle patrol, self-defense education, and security escort services. There are emergency telephones, lighted pathways/sidewalks, and fire, vehicle, and driving safety education programs.

Programs of Study: Bay Path confers B.A. and B.S. degrees. Associate and master's degrees are also awarded. Bachelor's degrees are awarded in BIOLOGICAL SCIENCE (biology/biological science), BUSINESS (business administration and management, international business management, and marketing/retailing/merchandising), COMMUNICATIONS AND THE ARTS (communications), EDUCATION (early childhood education and elementary education), ENGINEERING AND ENVIRONMENTAL DESIGN (interior design), HEALTH PROFESSIONS (occupational therapy), SOCIAL SCIENCE (child psychology/development, criminal justice, forensic studies, law, liberal arts/general studies, and psychology).

Required: To graduate, students must complete at least 120 credits with a minimum GPA of 2.0. The 46-hour core curriculum includes course work in communication, science, social science, math, and fine and performing arts.

Special: Cross-registration is possible with other member schools of the Cooperating Colleges of Greater Springfield Consortium. Bay Path's capital of the world program allows students to visit a different world center during each spring break.

Faculty/Classroom: 40% of faculty are male; 60% are female. All teach undergraduates. No introductory courses are taught by graduate students.

Requirements: The SAT or ACT is required. In addition, applicants should have completed at least 4 academic courses each year, including 4 years of English, 3 of math, at least 2 each of social studies and lab sciences, and 2 of a foreign language. An essay is required, as are letters of recommendation from a guidance counselor and a teacher. An interview is strongly recommended. A GPA of 2.0 is required. AP and CLEP credits are accepted.

Procedure: Freshmen are admitted fall and spring. Entrance exams should be taken in the spring of the junior year or by December of the senior year. There are deferred admissions and rolling admissions plans. Application deadlines are open. The fall 2009 application fee was $25. Applications are accepted on-line.

Transfer: Applicants must be in good standing at their previous school and are encouraged to arrange for an interview at Bay Path. Students who have earned fewer than 12 credits must submit SAT or ACT scores. 30 of 120 credits required for the bachelor's degree must be completed at Bay Path.

Visiting: There are regularly scheduled orientations for prospective students. There are guides for informal visits, and visitors may sit in on classes and stay overnight. To schedule a visit, contact Admissions.

Financial Aid: Bay Path is a member of CSS. The FAFSA, the college's own financial statement, and parent and student income tax forms are required. Check with the school for current application deadlines.

International Students: The school actively recruits these students. They must take the TOEFL. They must also take the SAT or ACT, scoring 800 on the SAT.

Computers: Wireless access is available. All students may access the system. There are no time limits and no fees.

Admissions Contact: Director of Admissions.
E-mail: *admiss@baypath.edu* Web: *www.baypath.edu*

BECKER COLLEGE
Worcester, MA 01615-0071

C-2

(508) 791-9241, ext. 245
(877) 523-2537; (508) 890-1500

Full-time: 185 men, 625 women	**Faculty:** n/av
Part-time: 120 men, 550 women	**Ph.D.s:** 33%
Graduate: none	**Student/Faculty:** n/av
Year: semesters, summer session	**Tuition:** $25,000
Application Deadline: open	**Room & Board:** $8500
Freshman Class: n/av	
SAT or ACT: required	**LESS COMPETITIVE**

Becker College, founded in 1887, is an independent undergraduate liberal arts and sciences institution offering baccalaureate degrees in various programs. Figures in the above capsule and this profile are approximate. In addition to regional accreditation, Becker has baccalaureate program accreditation with NLN. The 2 libraries contain 75,000 volumes and subscribe to 253 periodicals including electronic. Computerized library services include interlibrary loans, database searching, and Internet access. Special learning facilities include a learning resource center, a day care center, a veterinary clinic, and a preschool facility. The 100-acre campus is in an urban area 40 miles west of Boston. Including any residence halls, there are 27 buildings.

Student Life: 68% of undergraduates are from Massachusetts. Others are from 18 states and 6 foreign countries. 52% are white. The average age of all undergraduates is 22. 36% do not continue beyond their first year; 30% remain to graduate.

Housing: 200 students can be accommodated in college housing, which includes single-sex and coed dorms. In addition, there is 21 and over housing. On-campus housing is guaranteed for all 4 years. 60% of students commute. All students may keep cars.

Activities: There are no fraternities or sororities. There are 22 groups on campus, including animal, art, chorus, dance, drama, ethnic, gay, honors, international, newspaper, outdoor, photography, professional, social, social service, student government, and yearbook. Popular campus events include Family Day, Class Day, and Spree Day.

Sports: There are 6 intercollegiate sports for men and 8 for women, and 5 intramural sports for men and 5 for women. Facilities include a gym, on-campus field hockey and soccer fields, and tennis courts.

Disabled Students: 80% of the campus is accessible. Facilities include wheelchair ramps, elevators, special parking, specially equipped restrooms, lowered drinking fountains, lowered telephones, and special housing. All classes are accessible.

Services: Counseling and information services are available, as is tutoring in most subjects. There is remedial math and writing. There is also an academic support center for students.

Campus Safety and Security: Measures include 24-hour foot and vehicle patrol, self-defense education, and security escort services. There are shuttle buses, emergency telephones, and lighted pathways/sidewalks.

Programs of Study: Becker confers B.A. and B.S. degrees. Associate degrees are also awarded. Bachelor's degrees are awarded in BUSINESS (accounting, banking and finance, business administration and management, hospitality management services, human resources, marketing and distribution, and sports management), COMMUNICATIONS AND THE ARTS (communications, design, and graphic design), EDUCATION (early childhood education and elementary education), ENGINEERING AND ENVIRONMENTAL DESIGN (interior design), HEALTH PROFESSIONS (exercise science, health, and veterinary science), SOCIAL SCIENCE (criminal justice, human development, law, and psychology). Nursing and veterinary science are the strongest academically. Business administration is the largest.

Required: To graduate, baccalaureate students must complete 122 semester hours and maintain a 2.0 minimum GPA. Distribution requirements vary with the program of study.

Special: Cross-registration is offered through the Worcester Consortium of Higher Education. There are co-op programs, internships, study abroad, student-designed majors, work-study programs, and B.A.-B.S. degrees. There is 1 national honor society and a freshman honors program.

Faculty/Classroom: 31% of faculty are male; 69% are female. All teach undergraduates. The average class size in an introductory lecture is 20; in a laboratory, 15; and in a regular course, 25.

Requirements: The SAT is required. The ACT is recommended. In addition, a high school transcript is required. A GPA of 2.0 is required. AP and CLEP credits are accepted.

Procedure: Freshmen are admitted to all sessions. Entrance exams should be taken before submitting the application. There is a rolling admissions plan. Application deadlines are open. The fall 2009 application fee was $30. Notification is sent on a rolling basis. Applications are accepted on-line.

Transfer: Requirements for transfer students depend on the program. 62 of 122 credits required for the bachelor's degree must be completed at Becker.

Visiting: There are regularly scheduled orientations for prospective students, consisting of 2 open houses each year and group tours. There are guides for informal visits and visitors may sit in on classes. To schedule a visit, contact the Admissions Receptionist.

Financial Aid: The FAFSA is required. Check with the school for current application deadlines.

International Students: The school actively recruits these students. They must take the TOEFL. The ELPT is also accepted. They must also take the SAT or ACT.

Computers: All students may access the system. There are no time limits and no fees.

Admissions Contact: Director of Recruitment and Admissions. E-mail: *admissions@beckercollege.edu* Web: *www.becker.edu*

BENJAMIN FRANKLIN INSTITUTE OF TECHNOLOGY   E-2
Boston, MA 02116   (617) 423-4630; (617) 482-3706

Full-time: 400 men and women	**Faculty:** n/av
Part-time: none	**Ph.D.s:** 3%
Graduate: none	**Student/Faculty:** n/av
Year: semesters, summer session	**Tuition:** $15,000
Application Deadline: see profile	**Room & Board:** $10,000
Freshman Class: n/av	
SAT or ACT: not requried	**SPECIAL**

Benjamin Franklin Institute of Technology, founded in 1908, is a private technical college offering degree programs in industrial and engineering technologies. A bachelor's degree is offered in automotive technology. Figures in the above capsule and this profile are approximate. In addition to regional accreditation, BFIT has baccalaureate program accreditation with ABET. The library contains 10,000 volumes and subscribes to 70 periodicals including electronic. Computerized library services include interlibrary loans, database searching, and Internet access. Special learning facilities include a learning resource center. The 3-acre campus is in an urban area. Including any residence halls, there are 3 buildings.

Student Life: 95% of undergraduates are from Massachusetts. Others are from 7 states and 7 foreign countries. 35% are white; 35% African American; 14% Hispanic; 12% Asian American. The average age of freshmen is 22; all undergraduates, 22.

Housing: 20 students can be accommodated in college housing, which includes single-sex dorms. On-campus housing is available on a first-come, first-served basis. Priority is given to out-of-town students. Alcohol is not permitted. No one may keep cars.

Activities: There are no fraternities or sororities. There are 2 groups on campus, including student government and women's. Popular campus events include Technology Olympics and International Culture Day.

Sports: There are 2 intercollegiate sports for men and 2 intramural sports for men.

Disabled Students: 50% of the campus is accessible. Facilities include elevators and specially equipped restrooms.

Services: Counseling and information services are available, as is tutoring in every subject. There is remedial math, reading, and writing.

Programs of Study: BFIT confers B.S. degrees. Associate degrees are also awarded. Bachelor's degrees are awarded in ENGINEERING AND ENVIRONMENTAL DESIGN (automotive technology).

Required: To graduate, students must earn a minimum cumulative GPA of 2.0. 2 college English courses are required.

Special: If qualified, 2-year BFIT graduates may transfer to Northeastern University. Automotive technology management students have access to Northeastern's facilities and resources.

Faculty/Classroom: 74% of faculty are male; 26% are female. All teach undergraduates. The average class size in an introductory lecture is 30; in a laboratory, 12; and in a regular course, 25.

Requirements: Applicants should be high school graduates or have the GED. A GPA of 2.0 is required.

Procedure: Freshmen are admitted fall and spring. There is a rolling admissions plan. Check with the school for current application deadlines. The fall 2009 application fee was $25.

Visiting: Visitors may sit in on classes. To schedule a visit, contact the Office of Admission at (617) 423-4630, ext. 121.

Financial Aid: BFIT is a member of CSS. The FAFSA and federal tax returns are required. Check with the school for current application deadlines.

International Students: They must take the TOEFL and the college's own test, or satisfactorily complete Franklin's or another recognized ESL program.

Computers: All students may access the system. There are no time limits and no fees. It is strongly recommended that all students have a personal computer.

Admissions Contact: Dean of Enrollment Services. E-Mail: *admissions@bfit.edu* Web: *www.bfit.edu*

BENTLEY UNIVERSITY   D-2
Bentley College

Waltham, MA 02452-4705   (781) 891-2244
(800) 523-2354; (781) 891-3414

Full-time: 2389 men, 1641 women	**Faculty:** 231; IIA, ++$
Part-time: 133 men, 72 women	**Ph.D.s:** 82%
Graduate: 772 men, 609 women	**Student/Faculty:** 17 to 1
Year: semesters, summer session	**Tuition:** $35,828
Application Deadline: January 15	**Room & Board:** $11,740
Freshman Class: 6675 applied, 2842 accepted, 949 enrolled	
SAT CR/M/W: 580/650/600	**ACT: 26 HIGHLY COMPETITIVE**

Bentley University, formerly Bentley College, is a private institution that offers advanced business education along with a strong foundation in the arts and sciences. There is 1 graduate school. In addition to regional accreditation, Bentley has baccalaureate program accreditation with AACSB. The library contains 170,300 volumes, 3,700 microform items, and 9,500 audio/video tapes/CDs/DVDs, and subscribes to 39,000 periodicals including electronic. Computerized library services include interlibrary loans, database searching, Internet access, and laptop Internet portals. Special learning facilities include a learning resource center, art gallery, radio station, TV station, Academic Technology Center, Accounting Center (ACELAB), Alliance for Ethics and Social Responsibility, Valente Center for Arts and Sciences, Center for Business Ethics (CBE), Center for International Students and Scholars (CISS), Center for Languages and International Collaboration (CLIC), Center for Marketing Technology (CMT), Cronin International Center, Cyberlaw Center, Design and Usability Center (DUC), Enterprise Risk Management Program, Hughey Center for Financial Services, Library, Service-Learning Center, Trading Room, and Women's Leadership Institute. The 163-acre campus is in a suburban area Waltham, Massachusetts. Including any residence halls, there are 38 buildings.

Student Life: 52% of undergraduates are from out of state, mostly the Northeast. Students are from 42 states, 79 foreign countries, and Canada. 66% are from public schools. 67% are white; 14% foreign nationals. The average age of freshmen is 18; all undergraduates, 20. 7% do not continue beyond their first year; 87% remain to graduate.

Housing: 3365 students can be accommodated in college housing, which includes coed dorms, on-campus apartments, and off-campus apartments. In addition, there are special-interest houses and 3 wellness houses with an overall health and wellness theme are available to upper class students. Global living floors with a focus on connecting international and US students are available to residents. On-campus housing is guaranteed for all 4 years. 79% of students live on campus; of those, 85% remain on campus on weekends. Upperclassmen may keep cars.

Activities: 12% of men belong to 1 local and 5 national fraternities; 11% of women belong to 5 national sororities. There are 100 groups on campus, including art, band, cheerleading, chess, choir, chorus, computers, dance, debate, drama, environmental, ethnic, film, gay, honors, international, jazz band, literary magazine, newspaper, pep band, photography, political, professional, radio and TV, religious, social, social service, and student government. Popular campus events include Halloween Party, Culture Fest, Festival of Colors, Spring Day, and fashion shows.

Sports: There are 12 intercollegiate sports for men and 11 for women, and 8 intramural sports for men and 6 for women. Facilities include the Dana Center, a 118,000-square foot multipurpose facility, which, features a field house, a two-story fitness center, a fitness center for varsity athletes, general locker rooms, competition size swimming pool, athletic training room and rehabilitation area, athletic team and locker rooms, and 24 athletic offices.

Disabled Students: 70% of the campus is accessible. Facilities include wheelchair ramps, elevators, special parking, specially equipped restrooms, special class scheduling, lowered drinking fountains, lowered telephones, and special housing.

Services: Counseling and information services are available, as is tutoring in most subjects. There is a reader service for the blind, and remedial math, reading, and writing. There is a Kurzweil 3000 (text to speech), Dragon Naturally Speaking (speech to text) available, and additional assistive programs upon request

Campus Safety and Security: Measures include 24-hour foot and vehicle patrol, emergency notification system, self-defense education, and security escort services. There are shuttle buses, emergency telephones, lighted pathways/sidewalks, and ID card access system for residence halls.

Programs of Study: Bentley confers B.A., B.S., B.S.MBA, B.A.MBA, B.S.MS, B.A.MS. degrees. Associate, master's, and doctoral degrees are also awarded. Bachelor's degrees are awarded in BUSINESS (accounting, banking and finance, management information systems, management science, and marketing and distribution), COMMUNICATIONS AND THE ARTS (design and media arts), COMPUTER AND PHYSICAL SCIENCE (information sciences and systems and mathematics), ENGINEERING AND ENVIRONMENTAL DESIGN (computer technology), SOCIAL SCIENCE (economics, history, international studies, liberal arts/general studies, and philosophy). Management, finance, and marketing are the strongest academically.

Required: All undergraduate students complete general education courses in areas such as information technology, expository writing, mathematical sciences, natural sciences, humanities, behavioral sciences, history, philosophy, and economics. Students in B.S. programs take a common core of 9 courses covering major business areas such as accounting, business law, and strategic management. All students take elective courses that fulfill a diversity, international, and communication intensive requirement. A total of 122 credit hours is required for graduation, with a minimum GPA of 2.0. All students must take a first-year seminar.

Special: There is cross-registration with Regis College and Brandeis University, and internships are available in business and public service. The college offers study abroad in 24 countries, work-study programs, accelerated degree programs, student-designed majors, credit by exam, and nondegree study. There is also liberal studies major through which business majors can broaden their exposure to the arts and sciences, and arts and science majors can minor in business or interdisciplinary topics. There are 2 national honor societies, a freshman honors program, and 11 departmental honors programs.

Faculty/Classroom: 59% of faculty are male; 41% are female. 86% teach undergraduates. No introductory courses are taught by graduate students. The average class size in an introductory lecture, 23, in a laboratory, 20, and in a regular course, 24.

Admissions: 43% of the 2009-2010 applicants were accepted. The SAT scores for the 2009-2010 freshman class were: Critical Reading--8% below 500, 47% between 500 and 599, 39% between 600 and 700, and 6% above 700; Math--3% below 500, 18% between 500 and 599, 63% between 600 and 700, and 16% above 700; Writing--9% below 500, 41% between 500 and 599, 43% between 600 and 700, and 7% above 700. The ACT scores were 1% below 21, 13% between 21 and 23, 36% between 24 and 26, 28% between 27 and 28, and 22% above 28. 67% of the current freshmen were in the top fifth of their class; 93% were in the top two fifths. 7 freshmen graduated first in their class.

Requirements: The SAT or ACT is required. In addition, applicants must be graduates of an accredited high school or have a GED. Recommended high school preparation is 4 units each in English and math, geometry, and a senior-year math course; 3 units science; 3 units in a foreign language; 3 units in history; and 2 additional units in English, math, social science or lab science, foreign language, or speech. AP and CLEP credits are accepted. Important factors in the admissions decision are recommendations by school officials, extracurricular activities record, and leadership record.

Procedure: Freshmen are admitted fall and spring. Scores must be received by January 15. There are early decision and deferred admissions plans. Early decision applications should be filed by November 1; regular applications, by January 15 for fall entry; and November 1 for spring entry, along with a $50 fee. Notification of early decision is sent December 18; regular decision, April 1. 148 early decision candidates were accepted for the 2009-2010 class. 410 applicants were on the 2009 waiting list; 118 were admitted. Applications are accepted on-line.

Transfer: 142 transfer students enrolled in 2008-2009. Transfer application, personal statement, mid-year progress report and two letters of recommendation required. SAT or ACT is required of all applicants who have completed fewer than 10 college courses. All official college transcripts must be submitted. 60 of 122 credits required for the bachelor's degree must be completed at Bentley.

Visiting: There are regularly scheduled orientations for prospective students, including fall, spring, and summer open house programs. Interviews are arranged by appointment; campus tours and group information sessions take place regularly throughout the year. Visits are available during the week and some selected Saturdays. There are guides for informal visits. To schedule a visit, contact the Office of Undergraduate Admission at ugavisits@bentley.edu.

Financial Aid: In 2009-2010, 79% of all full-time freshmen and 76% of continuing full-time students received some form of financial aid. 42% of all full-time freshmen and 43% of continuing full-time students received need-based aid. The average freshman award was $29,106. Need-based scholarships or need-based grants averaged $20,801; need-based self-help aid (loans and jobs) averaged $5,479; non-need-based athletic scholarships averaged $31,526; and other non-need-based awards and non-need-based scholarships averaged $17,052. 28% of undergraduate students work part-time. Average annual earnings from campus work are $1477. The average financial indebtedness of the 2009 graduate was $33,079. Bentley is a member of CSS. The CSS/Profile, FAFSA, and federal tax returns, including all schedules for parents and student are required. The deadline for filing freshman financial aid applications for fall entry is February 1.

International Students: There are 425 international students enrolled. The school actively recruits these students. They must take the TOEFL with a minimum score of 550 on the paper-based TOEFL (PBT) or 80 on the Internet-based version (iBT). They must also take the SAT or ACT.

Computers: Wireless access is available. The entire campus including resident halls, is fully covered with 802.11n wireless access utilizing WPA2 enterprise encryption. Additionally, approximately 500 desktop computers are available for student usage in specialty classroom laboratories and public areas such as the library. Wired network ports are also available throughout the campus All students may access the system 24/7. There are no time limits and no fees. All students are required to have a personal computer. All undergraduate students are provided an HP6930p Elitebook notebook computer.

Graduates: From July 1, 2008 to June 30, 2009, 1073 bachelor's degrees were awarded. The most popular majors were finance (19%), business administration (16%), and marketing (16%). 850 companies recruited on campus in 2008-2009. In an average class, 82% graduate in 4 years or less, 87% graduate in 5 years or less, and 88% graduate in 6 years or less. Of the 2008 graduating class, 18% were enrolled in graduate school within 6 months of graduation.

Admissions Contact: Erik Vardaro, Director of Undergraduate Admission. E-Mail: ugadmission@bentley.edu Web: www.bentley.edu

BERKLEE COLLEGE OF MUSIC   E-2

Boston, MA 02215-3693

(617) 266-1400, ext. 2222
(800) BERKLEE; (617) 747-2047

Full-time: 3740 men and somen	**Faculty:** n/av
Part-time: 355 men and women	**Ph.Ds:** 12%
Graduate: none	**Student/Faculty:** n/av
Year: semesters, summer session	**Tuition:** $31,300
Application Deadline: see profile	**Room & Board:** $15,800
Freshman Class: n/av	
SAT or ACT: required	**SPECIAL**

Berklee College of Music, founded in 1945, is a private institution offering programs in music production and engineering, film scoring, music business/management, composition, music synthesis, music education, music therapy, performance, contemporary writing and production, jazz composition, songwriting, and professional music. Figures in the above capsule and this profile are approximate. The library contains 47,993 volumes and 36,214 audio/video tapes/CDs/DVDs, and subscribes to 1232 periodicals including electronic. Computerized library services include interlibrary loans, database searching, Internet access, and laptop Internet portals. Special learning facilities include a learning resource center, a radio station, 12 recording studios, 5 performance venues, and film scoring, music synthesis, and songwriting labs. The campus is in an urban area in the Fenway Cultural District, Back Bay, Boston. Including any residence halls, there are 20 buildings.

Student Life: 79% of undergraduates are from out of state, mostly the Northeast. Students are from 50 states, 106 foreign countries, and Canada. 66% are white; 45% Asian American; 25% foreign nationals. The average age of freshmen is 20; all undergraduates, 22. 16% do not continue beyond their first year; 49% remain to graduate.

Housing: 840 students can be accommodated in college housing, which includes coed dorms. On-campus housing is available on a first-come, first-served basis and is available on a lottery system for upperclassmen. 88% of students commute. Alcohol is not permitted. No one may keep cars.

Activities: There are no fraternities or sororities. There are 62 groups on campus, including art, band, choir, chorale, chorus, computers, dance, ethnic, gay, international, jazz band, marching band, musical theater, newspaper, orchestra, pep band, political, professional, radio and TV, religious, social, social service, and student government. Popular campus events include International Night, daily recitals and concerts, and Singer Showcase.

Sports: There are 4 intramural sports for men and 4 for women. Discount memberships at the YMCA, a student rate at the Massachusetts College of Art fitness room, and membership at the Sheraton Fitness Center and the Tennis and Racquet Club of Boston are available.

Disabled Students: All of the campus is accessible. Facilities include wheelchair ramps, elevators, special class scheduling, lowered drinking fountains, and lowered telephones.

Services: Counseling and information services are available, as is tutoring in every subject. There is a reader service for the blind. Tape recorders, untimed testing, and learning center resources are available.

Campus Safety and Security: Measures include 24-hour foot and vehicle patrol and security escort services. There are emergency telephones and lighted pathways/sidewalks.

Programs of Study: Berklee confers B.M. degrees. Master's degrees are also awarded. Bachelor's degrees are awarded in COMMUNICATIONS AND THE ARTS (film arts, jazz, music, music business management, music performance, music technology, and music theory and composition), EDUCATION (music education), HEALTH PROFESSIONS (music therapy). Performance, professional music, and music production and engineering are the largest.

Required: Students working toward a degree must take general education courses in English composition/literature, history, physical science, and social sciences. Music course programs vary by specialization. A total of 120 credits must be completed with a minimum GPA of 2.0.

Special: Berklee offers cross-registration with the Pro-Arts Consortium, study abroad in the Netherlands, internships in music education, music therapy, and music production and engineering, 5-year dual majors, and a 4-year professional (nondegree) diploma program. Work-study programs, an accelerated degree program, student-designed majors, and credit by exam are available.

Faculty/Classroom: 74% of faculty are male; 26% are female. All teach undergraduates. The average class size in an introductory lecture is 14; in a laboratory, 7; and in a regular course, 6.

Requirements: The SAT or ACT is required. The ACT Optional Writing test is also required. In addition, applicants must be graduates of an accredited secondary school that has a college preparatory program or have their GED. An audition and interview are recommended. Applicants must also submit a detailed reference letter regarding their training and experience in music and a letter from a private instructor, school music director, or professional musician. A GPA of 2.0 is required. AP credits are accepted. Important factors in the admissions decision are evidence of special talent, extracurricular activities record, and recommendations by alumni.

Procedure: Freshmen are admitted to all sessions. Entrance exams should be taken in the fall of the senior year of high school. There are early decision, deferred admissions and rolling admissions plans. Check with the school for current application deadlines. The fall 2009 application fee was $150. Applications are accepted on-line. A waiting list is maintained.

Transfer: Applicants must go through the same application procedures as entering freshmen, as well as submit all previous college records. 60 of 120 credits required for the bachelor's degree must be completed at Berklee.

Visiting: There are regularly scheduled orientations for prospective students, consisting of 2 tours scheduled daily during semesters, with a morning tour followed by an information session given by an admissions counselor. There are guides for informal visits. To schedule a visit, contact the Admissions Office.

Financial Aid: In a recent year, 57% of all full-time freshmen and 38% of continuing full-time students received some form of financial aid. 26% of undergraduate students work part-time. Average annual earnings from campus work are $1880. Berklee is a member of CSS. The CSS/Profile, the FFS, and the college's own financial statement are required. Check with the school for current application deadlines.

International Students: There were 912 international students enrolled in a recent year. The school actively recruits these students. They must take the TOEFL and the college's own test. They must also take the SAT or ACT.

Computers: Wireless access is available. All students may access the system. There are no time limits and no fees. All students are required to have a personal computer. An Apple Mac Book Pro is recommended.

Graduates: In a recent year, 851 bachelor's degrees were awarded. The most popular majors were professional music (22%), music business/management (19%), and music production and engineering (11%).

Admissions Contact: Director of Admissions. A campus DVD is available. E-mail: *admissions@berklee.edu* Web: *www.berklee.edu*

BOSTON ARCHITECTURAL COLLEGE   E-2

Boston, MA 02115   (617) 262-5000; (617) 585-0121

Full-time: 425 men, 195 women	Faculty: n/av
Part-time: 9 men, 6 women	Ph.D.s: 80%
Graduate: 272 men, 239 women	Student/Faculty: n/av
Year: semesters, summer session	Tuition: $10,500
Application Deadline: open	
Freshman Class: 452 applied, 370 accepted, 190 enrolled	SPECIAL

Boston Architectural College, founded in 1889 as the Boston Architectural Club, is an independent commuter institution offering professional programs in architecture and interior design. Students work in architectural and interior design offices during the day and attend classes at night. The BAC also offers a bachelor of design studies degree. A first professional degree in landscape architecture is offered at the undergraduate level. The tuition figures in the above capsule are approximate. There is 1 graduate school. In addition to regional accreditation, the BAC has baccalaureate program accreditation with ASLA, FIDER, and NAAB. The library contains 40,300 volumes, and 350 audio/video tapes/CDs/DVDs, and subscribes to 140 periodicals including electronic. Computerized library services include interlibrary loans, database searching, and Internet access. Special learning facilities include a learning resource center and art gallery. The campus is in an urban area in Boston. Including any residence halls, there are 4 buildings.

Student Life: 50% of undergraduates are from out of state, mostly the Northeast. Students are from 23 states and 12 foreign countries. 72% are white. The average age of freshmen is 24; all undergraduates, 25. 41% do not continue beyond their first year; 25% remain to graduate.

Housing: There are no residence halls. All students commute.

Activities: There are no fraternities or sororities. There are 5 groups on campus, including professional and student government.

Sports: There is no sports program at the BAC.

Disabled Students: All of the campus is accessible. Facilities include wheelchair ramps, elevators, special parking, specially equipped restrooms, and special class scheduling.

Services: Counseling and information services are available, as is tutoring in every subject. The writing center provides one-on-one writing assistance and special services for ESL students.

Campus Safety and Security: Measures include 24-hour foot and vehicle patrol and security escort services. There are lighted pathways/sidewalks, and full-time building security during operating hours.

Programs of Study: The BAC confers B.Arch., B. Design Studies, B.Int.Design., and B.L.A. degrees. Master's degrees are also awarded. Bachelor's degrees are awarded in COMMUNICATIONS AND THE ARTS (design), ENGINEERING AND ENVIRONMENTAL DESIGN (architecture, interior design, and landscape architecture/design). Architecture is the largest.

Required: To graduate, all students must complete 123 academic credits, 93 of which must be in professional subjects and 30 in general education courses; 21 credits must be earned in liberal arts courses. Students must earn 54 additional credits by working in architectural or interior-design offices or related fields. Academic study is divided into 3 segments, the final segment being the thesis year, which consists of 2 semesters of student-designed study under the guidance of a faculty adviser. A minimum 2.5 GPA is required.

Special: BAC offers study abroad and cross-registration with schools in the Professional Arts Consortium in Boston and with the Art Institute of Boston for studio and professional courses. The participating schools are the BAC, Berklee College of Music, Boston Conservatory, Emerson College, Massachusetts College of Art, and School of the MFA.

Faculty/Classroom: 86% of faculty are male; 14% are female. All teach undergraduates. No introductory courses are taught by graduate students. The average class size in an introductory lecture, 33, and in a laboratory, 8.

Admissions: 82% of the 2009-2010 applicants were accepted. 16% of the current freshmen were in the top fifth of their class; 25% were in the top two fifths. 6 freshmen graduated first in their class.

Requirements: All applicants who have graduated from high school or have a college degree are admitted on a first-come, first-served basis. Official transcripts from previously attended secondary schools and colleges must be submitted to determine qualification for admission and advanced placement. AP and CLEP credits are accepted.

Procedure: Freshmen are admitted fall and spring. There are deferred admissions and rolling admissions plans. Application deadlines are open. Application fee is $50. Notification is sent on a rolling basis. Applications are accepted on-line.

Transfer: 105 transfer students enrolled in 2008-2009. Applicants for transfer must have a 2.0 GPA to receive transfer credit in most courses; 3.0 in math. 45 credits required for the bachelor's degree must be completed at the BAC.

Visiting: There are regularly scheduled orientations for prospective students, consisting of monthly presentations. There are guides for informal visits and visitors may sit in on classes. To schedule a visit, contact the Admissions Office at (617) 585-0123.

Financial Aid: In 2009-2010, 81% of all full-time freshmen and 77% of continuing full-time students received some form of financial aid. 73% of all full-time freshmen and 68% of continuing full-time students received need-based aid. The average freshman award was $4,354. Need-based scholarships or need-based grants averaged $4,094 ($7,600 maximum); need-based self-help aid (loans and jobs) averaged $3,463 ($7,500 maximum); and other non-need-based awards and non-need-based scholarships averaged $1,232 ($3,915 maximum). 7% of undergraduate students work part-time. Average annual earnings from campus work are $2062. The average financial indebtedness of the 2009 graduate was $38,854. the BAC is a member of CSS. The FAFSA and the college's own financial statement are required. The priority date for freshman financial aid applications for fall entry is April 15.

International Students: There are 50 international students enrolled. They must take the TOEFL.

Computers: Wireless access is available. There are personal laptops for wireless, and 4 classrooms and 1 computer homework lab provide access for 75 students. All students may access the system. There are no time limits and no fees.

Graduates: From July 1, 2008 to June 30, 2009, 39 bachelor's degrees were awarded. The most popular majors were architecture (54%), interior design (26%), and design studies (20%).

Admissions Contact: Richard Moyer, Director of Admissions. E-Mail: *admissions@the-bac.edu* Web: *www.the-bac.edu*

BOSTON COLLEGE   E-2
Chestnut Hill, MA 02467

| | (617) 552-3100 |
| | (800) 360-2522; (617) 552-0798 |

Full-time: 4369 men, 4691 women	**Faculty:** I, +$
Part-time: none	**Ph.D.s:** 98%
Graduate: 2118 men, 2725 women	**Student/Faculty:** n/av
Year: semesters, summer session	**Tuition:** $39,130
Application Deadline: January 1	**Room & Board:** $12,909
Freshman Class: 30,845 applied, 8093 accepted, 2167 enrolled	
SAT CR/M/W: 655/685/665	**ACT:** 30 **MOST COMPETITIVE**

Boston College, founded in 1863, is an independent institution affiliated with the Roman Catholic Church and the Jesuit Order. It offers undergraduate programs in the arts and sciences, business, nursing, and education as well as graduate and professional programs. There are 4 undergraduate schools and 7 graduate schools. In addition to regional accreditation, BC has baccalaureate program accreditation with AACSB, CSWE, NCATE, and NLN. The 8 libraries contain 2.5 million volumes, 4.2 million microform items, and 2099 audio/video tapes/CDs/DVDs, and subscribe to 31,644 periodicals including electronic. Computerized library services include interlibrary loans, database searching, and Internet access. Special learning facilities include a learning resource center, art gallery, radio station, and TV station. The 386-acre campus is in a suburban area 6 miles west of Boston. Including any residence halls, there are 137 buildings.

Student Life: 74% of undergraduates are from out of state, mostly the Northeast. Students are from 50 states, 58 foreign countries, and Canada. 53% are from public schools. 71% are white. 73% are Catholic; 22% Protestant; 13% claim no religious affiliation. The average age of freshmen is 18; all undergraduates, 21. 5% do not continue beyond their first year; 91% remain to graduate.

Housing: 7315 students can be accommodated in college housing, which includes single-sex and coed dorms and on-campus apartments. In addition, there are honors houses, special-interest houses, community and multicultural housing, quiet residences, single-sex freshman halls, perspectives academic program housing, and a substance-free residence. On-campus housing is guaranteed for the freshman year only and is available on a lottery system for upperclassmen. 82% of students live on

campus; of those, 90% remain on campus on weekends. A limited number of upperclassmen may keep cars.

Activities: There are no fraternities or sororities. There are 223 groups on campus, including art, band, cheerleading, chess, choir, chorale, chorus, computers, dance, debate, drama, ethnic, film, honors, international, jazz band, literary magazine, marching band, musical theater, newspaper, orchestra, pep band, photography, political, professional, radio and TV, religious, social, social service, student government, symphony, and yearbook. Popular campus events include Middlemarch Ball, Christmas Chorale, and Senior Week.

Sports: There are 12 intercollegiate sports for men and 15 for women, and 28 intramural sports for men and 25 for women. Facilities include a 44,500-seat stadium, a forum that seats 8500 for basketball and 7600 for ice hockey, soccer fields, a track, and a student recreation complex with cardio equipment, weights, indoor pool, and tennis courts.

Disabled Students: 95% of the campus is accessible. Facilities include wheelchair ramps, elevators, special parking, specially equipped restrooms, special class scheduling, lowered drinking fountains, lowered telephones, and special housing.

Services: Counseling and information services are available, as is tutoring in most subjects. There is a reader service for the blind and an academic development center that serves all students.

Campus Safety and Security: Measures include 24-hour foot and vehicle patrol, emergency notification system, self-defense education, and security escort services. There are shuttle buses, emergency telephones, and lighted pathways/sidewalks. Safety seminars and safety walking tours are offered for incoming students during orientation. A fire safety awareness week is held every year with a mock dorm room fire demonstration, distribution of fire safety education materials, and drills.

Programs of Study: BC confers B.A. and B.S. degrees. Master's and doctoral degrees are also awarded. Bachelor's degrees are awarded in BIOLOGICAL SCIENCE (biochemistry and biology/biological science), BUSINESS (accounting, banking and finance, business administration and management, business economics, human resources, management science, marketing/retailing/merchandising, and operations research), COMMUNICATIONS AND THE ARTS (art history and appreciation, classics, communications, dramatic arts, English, film arts, French, Italian, linguistics, music, romance languages and literature, and studio art), COMPUTER AND PHYSICAL SCIENCE (chemistry, computer science, geology, geophysics and seismology, information sciences and systems, mathematics, and physics), EDUCATION (early childhood education, elementary education, secondary education, and special education), ENGINEERING AND ENVIRONMENTAL DESIGN (environmental science), HEALTH PROFESSIONS (nursing), SOCIAL SCIENCE (classical/ancient civilization, economics, German area studies, Hispanic American studies, history, human development, philosophy, political science/government, psychology, Russian and Slavic studies, sociology, and theological studies). Finance, economics, and chemistry are the strongest academically. Finance, communications, and English are the largest.

Required: Core requirements include 2 courses each in natural science, social science, history, philosophy, and theology; 1 course each in literature, writing, math, and cultural diversity; and proficiency in a foreign language for College of Arts and Sciences students. To graduate, students must complete 114 credits (121 in nursing), including at least 30 in the major with a minimum 1.667 GPA (1.5 in management). Computer science is required for management majors, and a freshman writing seminar for all students except honors and AP students. Students in the honors program and most students seeking departmental honors must complete a thesis; honors program students may elect to take courses in lieu of a thesis. Scholars of the college must complete a scholar's project before graduation.

Special: There are internship programs in management and in arts and sciences. Students may cross-register with Boston University, Brandeis University, Hebrew College, Pine Manor College, Regis College, and Tufts University. BC also offers a Washington semester in cooperation with American University, work-study programs with nonprofit agencies, study abroad in 28 countries, and dual and student-designed majors. Students may pursue a 3-2 engineering program with Boston University and accelerated 5-year programs in social work and education. There are 12 national honor societies, including Phi Beta Kappa, a freshman honors program, and 4 departmental honors programs.

Faculty/Classroom: 62% of faculty are male; 38% are female. All teach and do research. Graduate students teach 14% of introductory courses. The average class size in a laboratory is 15 and in a regular course, 30.

Admissions: 26% of the 2009-2010 applicants were accepted. The SAT scores for the 2009-2010 freshman class were: Critical Reading--3% below 500, 15% between 500 and 599, 53% between 600 and 700, and 29% above 700; Math--2% below 500, 11% between 500 and 599, 45% between 600 and 700, and 42% above 700; Writing--2% below 500, 13% between 500 and 599, 48% between 600 and 700, and 37% above 700. 62% of ACT scores were above 28. 95% of the current freshmen were in the top fifth of their class; 99% were in the top two fifths.

Requirements: The SAT or ACT is required. Students may take either the SAT test with Writing and 2 Subject tests of their choice or the ACT test with Writing. Applicants must be graduates of an accredited high school, completing 4 units each of English, foreign language, science, and math. Those students applying to the school of nursing must complete at least 2 years of a lab science including 1 unit of chemistry. Applicants to the school of management are strongly encouraged to take 4 years of college preparatory math. An essay is required. AP credits are accepted.

Procedure: Freshmen are admitted fall and spring. Entrance exams should be taken no later than January of the senior year. There are early decision, early action and deferred admissions plans. Early decision applications should be filed by November 1; regular applications, by January 1 for fall entry and November 1 for spring entry, along with a $70 fee. Early action notifications are sent December 25; regular decision, April 15. 2300 applicants were on the 2009 waiting list; 317 were admitted. Applications are accepted on-line.

Transfer: 78 transfer students enrolled in 2008-2009. Applicants must have a current GPA of at least 3.0 and must have earned a minimum of 9 semester hours. High school transcripts, letters of recommendation, and SAT or ACT scores are required. 54 of 114 credits required for the bachelor's degree must be completed at BC.

Visiting: There are regularly scheduled orientations for prospective students, consisting of group information sessions and campus tours Monday through Friday. There are guides for informal visits; visitors may sit in on classes. To schedule a visit, contact the Office of Undergraduate Admission.

Financial Aid: In 2009-2010, 42% of all full-time freshmen and 42% of continuing full-time students received some form of financial aid. 39% of all full-time freshmen and 40% of continuing full-time students received need-based aid. The average freshman award was $29,349. Need-based scholarships or need-based grants averaged $26,241; need-based self-help aid (loans and jobs) averaged $5014; non-need-based athletic scholarships averaged $39,975; and other non-need-based awards and non-need-based scholarships averaged $14,828. 26% of undergraduate students work part time. Average annual earnings from campus work are $1700. The average financial indebtedness of the 2009 graduate was $19,358. BC is a member of CSS. The CSS/Profile, FAFSA, federal IRS income tax form, W-2s, and Divorced/Separated Statement (when applicable) are required. The deadline for filing freshman financial aid applications for fall entry is February 1.

International Students: There are 230 international students enrolled. The school actively recruits these students. They must take the TOEFL with a minimum score of 600 on the paper-based TOEFL (PBT)or 100 on the Internet-based version (iBT). They must also take the ACT or the SAT and 2 SAT Subject tests of student's choice.

Computers: Wireless access is available. All dorm rooms are wired for the college's network, and wireless coverage is available in most buildings on campus, including classrooms, cafeterias, and administration buildings. All students may access the system at all times. There are no time limits and no fees. It is strongly recommended that all students have a personal computer. BC offers special network-ready bundles through both Dell and Apple.

Graduates: From July 1, 2008 to June 30, 2009, 2236 bachelor's degrees were awarded. The most popular majors were finance (11%), communications (9%), and English (7%). 300 companies recruited on campus in 2008-2009. In an average class, 88% graduate in 4 years or less, and 91% graduate in 6 years or less. Of the 2008 graduating class, 26% were enrolled in graduate school within 6 months of graduation, and 70% were employed.

Admissions Contact: John L. Mahoney Jr., Director Undergraduate Admission. A campus DVD is available. Web: *www.bc.edu*

BOSTON CONSERVATORY   E-2

Boston, MA 02215   (617) 536-6340; (617) 536-3176

Full-time: 100 men, 240 women	**Faculty:** n/av
Part-time: 10 men, 15 women	**Ph.D.s:** 1%
Graduate: none	**Student/Faculty:** n/av
Year: semesters, summer session	**Tuition:** $31,900
Application Deadline: open	**Room & Board:** $15,880
Freshman Class: n/av	
SAT or ACT: recommended	**SPECIAL**

Boston Conservatory, founded in 1867, is a private college providing degree programs in music, musical theater, and dance. Figures in the above capsule and this profile are approximate. There are 3 graduate schools. In addition to regional accreditation, the Conservatory has baccalaureate program accreditation with NASM. The library contains 40,000 volumes and subscribes to 120 periodicals including electronic. Computerized library services include interlibrary loans and database searching. The campus is in an urban area in Boston's Back Bay. Including any residence halls, there are 7 buildings.

Student Life: Students are from 36 states, 29 foreign countries, and Canada. 90% are white. The average age of freshmen is 18. 23% do not continue beyond their first year; 44% remain to graduate.

Housing: 164 students can be accommodated in college housing, which includes single-sex and coed dorms. In addition, there are special-interest houses and international housing. On-campus housing is guaranteed for all 4 years. 67% of students commute. Alcohol is not permitted. All students may keep cars.

Activities: There is 1 national fraternity and 2 national sororities. There are 19 groups on campus, including band, choir, chorale, chorus, dance, drama, ethnic, gay, international, musical theater, newspaper, opera, orchestra, political, professional, religious, social service, student government, and yearbook. Popular campus events include Parents Weekend.

Sports: There is no sports program at the Conservatory.

Disabled Students: 20% of the campus is accessible. Facilities include elevators.

Services: Counseling and information services are available, as is tutoring in every subject. A fee is required.

Campus Safety and Security: Measures include 24-hour foot and vehicle patrol and self-defense education.

Programs of Study: The Conservatory confers B.F.A. and B.Mus. degrees. Bachelor's degrees are awarded in COMMUNICATIONS AND THE ARTS (dance, guitar, music, music performance, music theory and composition, musical theater, opera, and piano/organ), EDUCATION (music education).

Required: All students must successfully complete the curriculum with no more than 12 credit hours of D-grade work. In addition, music performance majors must present recitals, music education majors must present a recital from memory, and composition majors must pass an exam on their primary instrument, present a portfolio of original composition, and perform a recital.

Special: There are 3 national honor societies and 1 departmental honors program.

Faculty/Classroom: All faculty teach undergraduates. The average class size in an introductory lecture is 15; in a laboratory, 5; and in a regular course, 15.

Requirements: The SAT or ACT is recommended, and scores are reviewed. An audition is required. An academic high school diploma or GED also is required. A GPA of 2.0 is required. AP and CLEP credits are accepted. Important factors in the admissions decision are evidence of special talent, extracurricular activities record, and personality/intangible qualities.

Procedure: Freshmen are admitted fall. Entrance exams should be taken as early as possible. There are deferred admissions and rolling admissions plans. Application deadlines are open.

Transfer: A successful audition and a 2.0 GPA are required. Transfer credits are determined by exam or review by the division head and the dean. The high school transcript is required if fewer than 30 college credits have been earned.

Visiting: Visitors may sit in on classes. To schedule a visit, contact the Admissions Office.

Financial Aid: The Conservatory is a member of CSS. The CSS/Profile and the college's own financial statement are required. Check with the school for current application deadlines.

International Students: The school actively recruits these students. They must take the TOEFL or the MELAB and the college's own test. They must also take the SAT, scoring 950. An audition also is required.

Computers: There are no time limits and no fees.

Admissions Contact: Director of Enrollment Management. e-mail: *admissions@bostonconservatory.edu* Web: *www.bostonconservatory.edu*

BOSTON UNIVERSITY   E-2

Boston, MA 02215   (617) 353-2300; (617) 353-9695

Full-time: 7100 men, 10300 women	**Faculty:** I, av$
Part-time: 675 men, 640 women	**Ph.D.s:** 85%
Graduate: 5665 men, 6610 women	**Student/Faculty:** n/av
Year: semesters, summer session	**Tuition:** $39,850
Application Deadline: see profile	**Room & Board:** $12,000
Freshman Class: n/av	
SAT or ACT: required	**HIGHLY COMPETITIVE+**

Boston University, founded in 1839, is a private institution offering undergraduate and graduate programs in basic studies, liberal arts, communication, hotel and food administration, allied health education management, and fine arts. Figures in the above capsule and this capsule are approximate. There are 11 undergraduate schools and 15 graduate schools. In addition to regional accreditation, BU has baccalaureate program accreditation with ABET and NASM. The 23 libraries contain 2.4 million volumes, 4.5 million microform items, and 72,542 audio/video tapes/CDs/DVDs, and subscribe to 34,214 periodicals including electronic. Computerized library services include interlibrary loans and database searching. Special learning facilities include a learning resource center, art gallery, planetarium, radio station, TV station, astronomy observatory, 20th-century archives, theater and theater company in residence, scientific computing and visualization lab, the Geddes language lab, speech, language, and hearing clinic, hotel/food administration culinary center, performance center, multimedia center, center for photonics research, center for remote sensing, and the Metcalf Center for Science and Engineering. The 132-acre campus is in an urban area on the Charles River in Boston's Back Bay. Including any residence halls, there are 349 buildings.

Student Life: 77% of undergraduates are from out of state, mostly the Middle Atlantic. Students are from 50 states, 135 foreign countries, and Canada. 75% are from public schools. 57% are white; 13% Asian American. 34% are Catholic; 23% Protestant; 20% claim no religious affiliation; 13% Jewish. The average age of freshmen is 19; all undergraduates, 21. 9% do not continue beyond their first year; 77% remain to graduate.

Housing: 10,616 students can be accommodated in college housing, which includes single-sex and coed dorms, on-campus apartments, off-campus apartments, and married student housing. In addition, there are honors houses, language houses, special-interest houses, international floors and houses, and student residences. On-campus housing is guaranteed for all 4 years. 66% of students live on campus; of those, 80% remain on campus on weekends. All students may keep cars.

Activities: 3% of men belong to 1 local and 8 national fraternities; 5% of women belong to 9 national sororities. There are 400 groups on campus, including art, band, cheerleading, chess, choir, chorale, chorus, computers, dance, drama, ethnic, film, gay, honors, international, jazz band, literary magazine, marching band, multicultural, musical theater, newspaper, opera, orchestra, pep band, photography, political, professional, radio and TV, religious, social, social service, sports, student government, symphony, and yearbook. Popular campus events include the Fall Welcome (Splash), World Fair and Culture Fest, and Head of the Charles River Regatta.

Sports: There are 12 intercollegiate sports for men and 14 for women, and 23 intramural sports for men and 23 for women. Facilities include 2 gyms, an ice-skating rink, saunas, a pool, a dance studio, a crew tank, a weight room, indoor and outdoor tracks, tennis and volleyball courts, multipurpose playing fields, and a boathouse.

Disabled Students: 90% of the campus is accessible. Facilities include wheelchair ramps, elevators, special parking, specially equipped restrooms, special class scheduling, lowered drinking fountains, lowered telephones, special housing. on-campus transportation, relocation of classes/events for access, tactile and access maps, visual fire alarms for the deaf, adaptive computers, and readers, note takers, and ASL interpreters.

Services: Counseling and information services are available, as is tutoring in most subjects, including liberal arts, science, engineering, and management. There is a reader service for the blind. Comprehensive learning strategies for the learning disabled are available.

Campus Safety and Security: Measures include 24-hour foot and vehicle patrol, self-defense education, and security escort services. There are shuttle buses, emergency telephones, lighted pathways/sidewalks, and a mountain bicycle patrol system. There is a uniformed safety/security assistant on duty 24 hours a day in large residence halls and 60 academy-trained officers in the university police department.

Programs of Study: BU confers B.A., B.S., B.F.A., B.L.S., B.Mus., and B.S.B.A. degrees. Master's and doctoral degrees are also awarded. Bachelor's degrees are awarded in AGRICULTURE (environmental studies), BIOLOGICAL SCIENCE (biochemistry, biology/biological science, ecology, environmental biology, neurosciences, nutrition, and physiology), BUSINESS (accounting, banking and finance, business administration and management, entrepreneurial studies, hotel/motel and restaurant management, international business management, management information systems, management science, marketing/retailing/merchandising, operations research, and organizational behavior), COMMUNICATIONS AND THE ARTS (apparel design, classics, communications, dramatic arts, East Asian languages and literature, English, film arts, French, German, Germanic languages and literature, graphic design, Greek (classical), Greek (modern), Italian, journalism, Latin, linguistics, music, music history and appreciation, music performance, music theory and composition, painting, performing arts, public relations, sculpture, Spanish, theater design, and theater management), COMPUTER AND PHYSICAL SCIENCE (astronomy, astrophysics, chemistry, computer science, earth science, geophysics and seismology, mathematics, physics, and planetary and space science), EDUCATION (art education, athletic training, bilingual/bicultural education, drama education, early childhood education, education, education of the deaf and hearing impaired, elementary education, English education, foreign languages education, mathematics education, music education, physical education, science education, social studies education, and special education), ENGINEERING AND ENVIRONMENTAL DESIGN (aeronautical engineering, biomedical engineering, computer engineering, electrical/electronics engineering, engineering, environmental science, manufacturing engineering, and mechanical engineering), HEALTH PROFESSIONS (exercise science, health, health science, physical therapy, rehabilitation therapy, and speech pathology/audiology), SOCIAL SCIENCE (American studies, anthropology, archeology, Asian/Oriental studies, classical/ancient civilization, East Asian studies, Eastern European studies, economics, French studies, geography, Hispanic American studies, history, interdisciplinary studies, international relations, Italian studies, Japanese studies, Latin American studies, philosophy, physical fitness/movement, political science/government, psychology, religion, sociology, and urban studies). The University Professors Program, accelerated medical and dental programs, and the management honors program are the strongest academically. Communications, business, and marketing are the largest.

Required: Most students are required to complete 128 credit hours to qualify for graduation. Hours in the major, specific disciplines, curricula, distribution requirements, and minimum GPA vary, depending on the school or college of BU attended. In addition students in the College of Arts and Sciences must complete the College Writing Program, which includes 1 full year of formal instruction in writing, reading, research, and speaking.

Special: Cross-registration is permitted with Brandeis University, Tufts University, Boston College, and Hebrew College in Massachusetts. Opportunities are provided for internships, co-op programs in engineering, a Washington semester, on- and off-campus work-study, accelerated degree programs, B.A.-B.S. degrees, dual majors, student-designed majors, credit by exam, nondegree studies, pass/fail options, and study abroad in 18 countries. A 3-2 engineering degree is offered with 16 schools and 2-2 engineering agreements with 6 schools, plus 107 other 2-2 agreements. The University Professors Program offers a creative cross-disciplinary approach, and the College of Basic Studies offers team teaching. There are 16 national honor societies, a freshman honors program, and 6 departmental honors programs.

Faculty/Classroom: 69% of faculty are male; 31% are female. 56% teach undergraduates. No introductory courses are taught by graduate students. The average class size in an introductory lecture is 58; in a laboratory, 16; and in a regular course, 19.

Requirements: The SAT or ACT is required. The ACT Optional Writing test is also required. Applicants are evaluated on an individual basis. Evidence of strong academic performance in a college prep curriculum, including 4 years of English, at least 3 years of math (through precalculus), 3 years of lab sciences, and 3 years of social studies/history with at least 2 years of a foreign language, is the most important aspect of a student's application review. Subject tests in chemistry and math (level 2) are required for the accelerated medical and dental programs. Students planning to take the SAT are required to submit the SAT with the writing section along with 2 SAT Subject tests in different subject areas of their choice. Students selected as finalists in the accelerated programs in medicine and dentistry will be invited to interview in Boston. Candidates for the College of Fine Arts must present a portfolio or participate in an audition. AP and CLEP credits are accepted. Important factors in the admissions decision are advanced placement or honors courses.

Procedure: Freshmen are admitted fall and spring. Entrance exams should be taken in the junior year or early in the senior year. There are early decision, early admissions and deferred admissions plans. Check with the school for current application deadlines. The fall 2009 application fee was $70. Applications are accepted on-line. A waiting list is maintained.

Transfer: College transcripts, SAT (with writing test) or ACT scores, and a complete high school transcript (or GED) should be submitted. Recommendations and an essay are also recommended.

Visiting: There are regularly scheduled orientations for prospective students. The Admissions Reception Center is open Monday through Friday and some Saturdays during the academic year. Appointments can be made for class visits or lunch with current students. Campus tours and information sessions are also offered. There are guides for informal visits; visitors may sit in on classes and stay overnight. To schedule a visit, contact the Admissions Reception Center at (617) 353-2318.

Financial Aid: BU is a member of CSS. The CSS/Profile and FAFSA are required. Check with the school for current application deadlines.

International Students: The school actively recruits these students. They must take the TOEFL. They must also take the SAT or ACT.

Computers: Wireless access is available. A shared cluster of UNIX systems consisting of several IBM RS/600 machines support the approximately 40,000 users. The BU campus network provides direct access to the Internet, e-mail, the Web, and many other resources. Tens of thousands of ports support communications that are available throughout the campus, including residence halls. All students may access the system 24 hours a day. Students enrolled in the School of Management and the College of Engineerin must have a personal computer.

Admissions Contact: Director, Undergraduate Admissions.
E-mail: *admissions@bu.edu* Web: *www.bu.edu*

BRANDEIS UNIVERSITY   D-2
Waltham, MA 02454

(781) 736-3500
(800) 622-0622; (781) 736-3536

Full-time: 1425 men, 1795 women	**Faculty:** I, av$
Part-time: 5 men, 15 women	**Ph.D.s:** 96%
Graduate: 1055 men, 1050 women	**Student/Faculty:** n/av
Year: semesters, summer session	**Tuition:** $40,500
Application Deadline: see profile	**Room & Board:** $11,200
Freshman Class: n/av	
SAT or ACT: required	**MOST COMPETITIVE**

Brandeis University, founded in 1948, is a private liberal arts institution. Figures in the above capsule and this profile are approximate. There are 4 graduate schools. The 3 libraries contain 1.2 million volumes, 950,610 microform items, and 39,201 audio/video tapes/CDs/DVDs, and subscribe to 38,393 periodicals including electronic. Computerized library services include interlibrary loans, database searching, Internet access, and laptop Internet portals. Special learning facilities include a learning resource center, art gallery, radio station, TV station, astronomical observatory, cultural center, treasure hall, art museum, and audiovisual center. The 235-acre campus is in a suburban area 10 miles west of Boston. Including any residence halls, there are 88 buildings.

Student Life: 75% of undergraduates are from out of state, mostly the Northeast. Students are from 46 states, 54 foreign countries, and Canada. 75% are white. The average age of freshmen is 18; all undergraduates, 20. 6% do not continue beyond their first year; 88% remain to graduate.

Housing: 2558 students can be accommodated in college housing, which includes coed dorms, on-campus apartments, and off-campus apartments. In addition, there are special-interest houses. On-campus housing is available on a first-come, first-served basis and is available on a lottery system for upperclassmen. 77% of students live on campus; of those, 90% remain on campus on weekends. Upperclassmen may keep cars.

Activities: There are no fraternities or sororities. There are 246 groups on campus, including art, cheerleading, chess, choir, chorale, chorus, computers, dance, debate, drama, environmental, ethnic, film, gay, honors, international, jazz band, literary magazine, musical theater, newspaper, orchestra, pep band, photography, political, professional, radio and TV, religious, social, social service, student government, symphony, and yearbook. Popular campus events include Pachanga, Halloween for the Hungry, and Louispalooza.

Sports: There are 10 intercollegiate sports for men and 10 for women, and 12 intramural sports for men and 12 for women. Facilities include a 7000-seat field house, a basketball arena, an indoor swimming pool, 3 indoor tennis courts, 10 squash and racquetball courts, an indoor track, several multipurpose rooms for fencing, aerobics, dance, and wrestling, sauna and steam rooms, Nautilus and free weight rooms, soccer and practice fields, baseball and softball diamonds, a cross-country and fitness trail, and 10 outdoor tennis courts.

Disabled Students: 78% of the campus is accessible. Facilities include wheelchair ramps, elevators, special parking, specially equipped restrooms, special class scheduling, lowered drinking fountains, and lowered telephones. Libraries, student centers, several other buildings, sports facilities, and the majority of residence halls are fully accessible.

Services: Counseling and information services are available, as is tutoring in most subjects.

Campus Safety and Security: Measures include 24-hour foot and vehicle patrol, emergency notification system, self-defense education, and security escort services. There are shuttle buses, emergency telephones, and lighted pathways/sidewalks.

Programs of Study: Brandeis confers B.A. and B.S. degrees. Master's and doctoral degrees are also awarded. Bachelor's degrees are awarded in AGRICULTURE (environmental studies), BIOLOGICAL SCIENCE (biochemistry, biology/biological science, biophysics, and neurosciences), COMMUNICATIONS AND THE ARTS (American literature, art history and appreciation, classics, comparative literature, dramatic arts, English literature, French, German, Greek (classical), linguistics, music, Russian languages and literature, and Spanish), COMPUTER AND PHYSICAL SCIENCE (chemistry, computer science, mathematics, and physics), HEALTH PROFESSIONS (health science), SOCIAL SCIENCE (African American studies, American studies, anthropology, classical/ancient civilization, East Asian studies, economics, European studies, history, interdisciplinary studies, international studies, Islamic studies, Italian studies, Judaic studies, Latin American studies, Middle Eastern studies, Near Eastern studies, philosophy, political science/government, psychology, sociology, and women's studies). Biology, history, and politics are the strongest academically. Economics, psychology, and international studies are the largest.

Required: All candidates for a bachelor's degree must satisfactorily complete a major, a writing requirement, a foreign language requirement, a group of courses designed to provide a strong foundation in general education, and the phys ed requirement. Oral communication, quantitative reasoning, and non-Western and comparative studies requirements also must be met. No courses used to fulfill any general university requirement may be taken on the pass/fail grading option.

Special: Students may pursue interdepartmental programs in 18 different fields. Students may cross-register with Boston, Wellesley, Babson, and Bentley Colleges and Boston and Tufts Universities. Study abroad is possible in 69 countries. Internships are available in virtually every field, and work-study is also available. Dual and student-designed majors can be arranged. The university also offers credit by exam, nondegree study, and pass/fail options. Opportunities for early acceptance to area medical schools are offered. There are 4 national honor societies, including Phi Beta Kappa, a freshman honors program, and 51 departmental honors programs.

Faculty/Classroom: 58% of faculty are male; 42% are female. All teach and do research. Graduate students teach 10% of introductory courses. The average class size in a regular course is 28.

Admissions: There were 32 National Merit finalists in a recent year. 19 freshmen graduated first in their class.

Requirements: The SAT or ACT is required. In addition, Brandeis requires the SAT Reasoning test with Writing and 2 SAT Subject tests of different subjects. Students may submit the ACT with writing as a substitute for the SAT Reasoning test and SAT Subject tests. Applicants should prepare with 4 years of high school English, 3 each of foreign language and math, and at least 1 each of science and social studies. An essay is required, and an interview is recommended. AP credits are accepted. Important factors in the admissions decision are advanced placement or honors courses, recommendations by school officials, and extracurricular activities record.

Procedure: Freshmen are admitted fall and spring. Entrance exams should be taken by January of the senior year. There are early decision and deferred admissions plans. Check with the school for current application deadlines. The fall 2009 application fee was $55. Applications are accepted on-line. A waiting list is maintained.

Transfer: 34 transfer students enrolled in a recent year. Major consideration is given to the quality of college-level work completed, the secondary school record, testing, professors' and deans' evaluations, and the impression made by the candidate. Because there is a 2-year residence requirement, students should apply before entering their junior year. 64 credits required for the bachelor's degree must be completed at Brandeis.

Visiting: There are regularly scheduled orientations for prospective students, including year-round student-led campus tours and, in the summer, information sessions given by the admissions staff. There are guides for informal visits, and visitors may sit in on classes and stay overnight. To schedule a visit, contact the Office of Admissions.

Financial Aid: In a recent year, 53% of all full-time freshmen and 47% of continuing full-time students received some form of financial aid. 41% of all full-time freshmen and 45% of continuing full-time students received need-based aid. The average freshman award was $27,354. 40% of undergraduate students work part-time. Average annual earnings from campus work are $1588. The average financial indebtedness of a recent graduate was $22,381. Brandeis is a member of CSS. The CSS/Profile, the FAFSA, and copies of student and parent income tax returns for matriculating students are required. Check with the school for current application deadlines.

International Students: There were 240 international students enrolled in a recent year. The school actively recruits these students. They must take the TOEFL with a minimum score of 600 on the paper-based TOEFL (PBT) or 100 on the Internet-based version (iBT). Applicants whose native language is English must take the SAT and SAT: Subject tests.

Computers: Wireless access is available. Wireless connectivity is campus-wide. All students may access the system. There are no time limits and no fees.

Graduates: In a recent year, 812 bachelor's degrees were awarded. The most popular majors were economics (14%), biology (9%), and psychology (8%). 60 companies recruited on campus in a recent year. In an average class, 84% graduate in 4 years or less, 88% graduate in 5 years or less, and 88% graduate in 6 years or less. Of a recent graduating class, 28% were enrolled in graduate school within 6 months of graduation and 54% were employed.

Admissions Contact: Dean of Admissions.
E-mail: *admissions@brandeis.edu* Web: *www.brandeis.edu*

BRIDGEWATER STATE COLLEGE   E-3

Bridgewater, MA 02325   (508) 531-1237; (508) 531-1746

Full-time: 2780 men, 3995 women	Faculty: n/av
Part-time: 575 men, 820 women	Ph.D.s: 89%
Graduate: 490 men, 1300 women	Student/Faculty: n/av
Year: semesters, summer session	Tuition: $6500 ($12,500)
Application Deadline: see profile	Room & Board: $8000
Freshman Class: n/av	
SAT or ACT: required	COMPETITIVE

Bridgewater State College, founded in 1840, is a state-supported college offering undergraduate and graduate programs in liberal arts, education, business, aviation science, and preprofessional studies. Figures in the above capsule and this profile are approximate. There are 3 undergraduate schools and 1 graduate school. In addition to regional accreditation, Bridgewater has baccalaureate program accreditation with CSWE and NCATE. The library contains 285,380 volumes, 225 microform items, and 14,337 audio/video tapes/CDs/DVDs, and subscribes to 2923 periodicals including electronic. Computerized library services include interlibrary loans and database searching. Special learning facilities include a learning resource center, art gallery, radio station, astronomical observatory, human performance lab and flight simulators, electronic classrooms, teleconferencing facility with satellite dish, and children's developmental clinic. The 235-acre campus is in a small town 28 miles south of Boston. Including any residence halls, there are 41 buildings.

Student Life: 95% of undergraduates are from Massachusetts. Others are from 21 states, 12 foreign countries, and Canada. 77% are white. The average age of freshmen is 18; all undergraduates, 21. 25% do not continue beyond their first year; 49% remain to graduate.

Housing: 2465 students can be accommodated in college housing, which includes single-sex and coed dorms and on-campus apartments. On-campus housing is guaranteed for all 4 years. 67% of students commute. All students may keep cars.

Activities: There are 2 local and 3 national fraternities and 3 national sororities. There are 74 groups on campus, including band, cheerleading, choir, chorale, computers, dance, drama, ethnic, gay, honors, international, jazz band, literary magazine, marching band, music ensembles, musical theater, newspaper, pep band, photography, political, professional, religious, social, social service, student government, and yearbook. Popular campus events include Convocation, Multicultural Day, and Christmas and spring balls.

Sports: There are 10 intercollegiate sports for men and 11 for women, and 6 intramural sports for men and 4 for women. Facilities include 2 gyms, an Olympic-size swimming pool, tennis courts, a football stadium, a 9-lane track, soccer, lacrosse, and field hockey fields, and a baseball and softball complex.

Disabled Students: 96% of the campus is accessible. Facilities include wheelchair ramps, elevators, special parking, specially equipped restrooms, special class scheduling, lowered drinking fountains, lowered telephones, special housing, a handicapped van service, and a college-operated transit system.

Services: Counseling and information services are available, as is tutoring in most subjects. There is a reader service for the blind and remedial math, reading, and writing. There are taped texts, classroom interpreters, scribes and note takers, testing accommodations, and a speech/hearing/language center.

Campus Safety and Security: Measures include 24-hour foot and vehicle patrol, self-defense education, and security escort services. There are shuttle buses, emergency telephones, lighted pathways/sidewalks, a college-operated transit system that runs from 7 A.M. to midnight, Monday through Friday, and a safety-escort van that runs from 6 P.M. to 3 A.M.

Programs of Study: The college confers B.A., B.S., and B.S.Ed. degrees. Master's degrees are also awarded. Bachelor's degrees are awarded in BIOLOGICAL SCIENCE (biology/biological science), BUSINESS (accounting and management science), COMMUNICATIONS AND THE ARTS (art, communications, English, music, and Spanish), COMPUTER AND PHYSICAL SCIENCE (chemistry, computer science, earth science, geology, mathematics, and physics), EDUCATION (early childhood education, elementary education, health education, physical education, and special education), ENGINEERING AND ENVIRONMENTAL DESIGN (aviation administration/management), SOCIAL SCIENCE (anthropology, criminal justice, economics, geography, history, philosophy, political science/government, psychology, social work, and sociology). Management science, aviation science, and education are the strongest academically. Management science, psychology, and education are the largest.

Required: Students are required to complete a minimum of 120 semester hours, with 30 to 36 hours in the major and 52 to 55 hours in general education courses. Students must maintain a minimum GPA of 2.0 and complete an introduction to information resources course.

Special: Opportunities are provided for cross-registration with other Massachusetts schools, internships in most majors, dual majors in any 2 subjects, core requirement credit for military service and work experience, nondegree study, and study abroad in England and Canada. A

Washington semester offers possible internship experience in political science. There are 11 national honor societies, a freshman honors program, and 14 departmental honors programs.

Faculty/Classroom: 52% of faculty are male; 48% are female. All teach undergraduates. No introductory courses are taught by graduate students. The average class size in an introductory lecture is 32; in a laboratory, 18; and in a regular course, 24.

Requirements: The SAT or ACT is required. In addition, graduation from an accredited secondary school is required; a GED will be accepted. Applicants must have successfully completed 16 Carnegie units, including 4 years of English, 3 of math, 3 of science with 2 lab sciences, 2 of a foreign language, 1 each of history and social studies, and 2 in other college preparatory electives. An essay is recommended. A GPA of 2.0 is required. AP and CLEP credits are accepted. Important factors in the admissions decision are advanced placement or honors courses, leadership record, and extracurricular activities record.

Procedure: Freshmen are admitted fall and spring. Entrance exams should be taken no later than January. There is a deferred admissions plan. Check with the school for current application deadlines. The fall 2009 application fee was $25. Notification is sent on a rolling basis. Applications are accepted on-line.

Transfer: Transfer students must have maintained a minimum GPA of 2.5 from 12 to 24 credits or 2.0 from more than 24 credits at the previous college, although this alone does not guarantee admission. College transcripts and an essay are required of all transfer students; some students must submit high school transcripts and standardized test scores. 30 of 120 credits required for the bachelor's degree must be completed at Bridgewater.

Visiting: There are regularly scheduled orientations for prospective students, including tours Monday through Friday and information sessions on Fridays when college is in session. Visitations are available on a limited basis Saturdays during the fall. Campus tours are available year round. There are guides for informal visits and visitors may sit in on classes. To schedule a visit, contact the Office of Admissions.

Financial Aid: In a recent year, 46% of all full-time freshmen and 51% of continuing full-time students received some form of financial aid. 37% of all full-time freshmen and 45% of continuing full-time students received need-based aid. The average freshman award was $3040. 25% of undergraduate students work part-time. Average annual earnings from campus work are $4000. The average financial indebtedness of a recent graduate was $15,065. The college is a member of CSS. The FAFSA and the parents' tax returns are required. Check with the school for current application deadlines.

International Students: There were 157 international students enrolled in a recent year. They must take the TOEFL. They must also take the SAT or ACT.

Computers: All students may access the system 7 days a week. There are no time limits and no fees.

Admissions Contact: Director of Admissions. E-Mail: *admission@bridgew.edu* Web: *www.bridgew.edu*

CAMBRIDGE COLLEGE   D-2

Cambridge, MA 02138   (617) 868-1000
                                 800-877-4723; (617) 349-3561

Full-time: 214 men, 191 women	Faculty: n/av
Part-time: 587 men, 253 women	Ph.D.s: 63%
Graduate: 2135 men, 582 women	Student/Faculty: n/av
Year: semesters, summer session	Tuition: $13,280
Application Deadline: open	
Freshman Class: 375 applied, 256 accepted, 188 enrolled	
SAT or ACT: not required	SPECIAL

Founded in 1971, Cambridge College is a private, non-profit commuter institution dedicated to providing educational opportunities for working adults and underserved learners. Cambridge College is approved and accredited to offer programs through its main campus and 8 regional centers in Springfield and Lawrence, MA; Chesapeake and South Boston, VA; Augusta, GA; San Juan, PR; Ontario, CA; and Memphis, TN. There is 1 undergraduate school and 3 graduate schools. Computerized library services include interlibrary loans, database searching, Internet access, and laptop Internet portals. Special learning facilities include a learning resource center. The campus is in an urban area in Cambridge. Including any residence halls, there are 3 buildings.

Student Life: 90% of undergraduates are from Massachusetts. 28% are African American; 19% Hispanic; 16% white. The average age of freshmen is 30; all undergraduates, 32.

Housing: There are no residence halls. All students commute.

Activities: There are no fraternities or sororities.

Sports: There is no sports program.

Disabled Students: All of the campus is accessible. Facilities include elevators, special parking, specially equipped restrooms, special class scheduling, lowered drinking fountains, and lowered telephones.

Services: Counseling and information services are available, as is tutoring in most subjects. There is remedial math, reading, and writing.

Campus Safety and Security: Measures include emergency notification system, emergency telephones, and lighted pathways/sidewalks.

Programs of Study: Cambridge College confers B.A. and B.S. degrees. Master's and doctoral degrees are also awarded. Bachelor's degrees are awarded in BUSINESS (management science) and SOCIAL SCIENCE (human services, interdisciplinary studies, and psychology). Multidisciplinary studies, management, and psychology are the strongest academically and the largest.

Required: Students must complete 120 credit hours, including 60 in general education requirements and 30 to 39 in the major to graduate. Students also must complete a final capstone project near the end of their program.

Faculty/Classroom: 38% of faculty are male; 62% are female. No introductory courses are taught by graduate students.

Admissions: 68% of the 2009-2010 applicants were accepted.

Requirements: CLEP credits are accepted.

Procedure: Freshmen are admitted to all sessions. There are deferred admissions and rolling admissions plans. Application deadlines are open. The fall 2008 application fee was $30. Applications are accepted on-line.

Transfer: 108 transfer students enrolled in 2008-2009. High school and college transcripts are required; an interview and a statement of good standing from the previous institution is recommended. 30 of 120 credits required for the bachelor's degree must be completed at .

Visiting: There are guides for informal visits.

Financial Aid: In 2009-2010, 61% of all full-time freshmen and 72% of continuing full-time students received some form of financial aid. At least 61% of all full-time freshmen and 72% of continuing full-time students received need-based aid. The average freshman award was $3478. Need-based scholarships or need-based grants averaged $5092, and need-based self-help aid (loans and jobs) averaged $3574. The FAFSA and the college's own financial statement are required.

International Students: There are 33 international students enrolled. The school actively recruits these students. They must take the TOEFL with a minimum score of 550 on the paper-based TOEFL (PBT) or 79 on the Internet-based version (iBT).

Computers: Wireless access is available. All students may access the system.

Graduates: From July 1, 2008 to June 30, 2009, 202 bachelor's degrees were awarded. The most popular majors were multidisciplinary studies (46%), management studies (31%), and psychology (23%).

Admissions Contact: Stephen Lyons, Director of Admissions.
E-mail: *admit@cambridgecollege.edu* Web: *www.cambridgecollege.edu*

CLARK UNIVERSITY   C-2
Worcester, MA 01610-1477

(508) 793-7431
(800) 462-5275; (508) 793-8821

Full-time: 860 men, 1634 women	Faculty: 187; IIA, +$
Part-time: 49 men, 78 women	Ph.D.s: 96%
Graduate: 494 men, 589 women	Student/Faculty: 13 to 1
Year: semesters, summer session	Tuition: $35,220
Application Deadline: January 15	Room & Board: $6750
Freshman Class: 4271 applied, 2741 accepted, 550 enrolled	
SAT CR/M/W: 600/590/600	ACT: 26 HIGHLY COMPETITIVE

Clark University, founded in 1887, is an independent liberal arts and research institution. There are 2 undergraduate schools and 3 graduate schools. In addition to regional accreditation, Clark has baccalaureate program accreditation with AACSB and NASDTEC. The 6 libraries contain 617,838 volumes, 60,363 microform items, and 1372 audio/video tapes/CDs/DVDs, and subscribe to 1303 periodicals including electronic. Computerized library services include interlibrary loans, database searching, Internet access, and laptop Internet portals. Special learning facilities include a learning resource center, art gallery, radio station, TV studio, campus cable network, center for music with 2 studios for electronic music, 2 theaters, and magnetic resonance imaging facility. The 50-acre campus is in an urban area 50 miles west of Boston. Including any residence halls, there are 69 buildings.

Student Life: 61% of undergraduates are from out of state, mostly the Northeast. Students are from 42 states and 77 foreign countries. 75% are from public schools. 81% are white. 39% claim no religious affiliation; 21% Protestant; 17% Catholic; 15% Jewish. The average age of freshmen is 19; all undergraduates, 20. 12% do not continue beyond their first year; 78% remain to graduate.

Housing: 1809 students can be accommodated in college housing, which includes single-sex and coed dorms and on-campus apartments. In addition, there are special-interest houses, nonsmoking, quiet, substance awareness, and year-round houses. On-campus housing is guaranteed for the freshman year only and is available on a lottery system for upperclassmen. 70% of students live on campus. All students may keep cars.

Activities: There are no fraternities or sororities. There are 115 groups on campus, including art, band, chess, choir, chorale, chorus, computers, dance, debate, drama, environmental, ethnic, film, gay, honors, in-

ternational, jazz band, literary magazine, musical theater, newspaper, orchestra, pep band, photography, political, professional, radio and TV, religious, social, social service, student government, symphony, and yearbook. Popular campus events include Gryphon and Pleiades Honor Society Variety Show, International Gala, and Speaker's Forum.

Sports: There are 8 intercollegiate sports for men and 9 for women, and 14 intramural sports for men and 14 for women. Facilities include an athletic center with a 2000-seat gym, a pool, a fitness center, tennis courts, outdoor fields, and baseball and softball diamonds.

Disabled Students: 95% of the campus is accessible. Facilities include wheelchair ramps, elevators, special parking, specially equipped restrooms, special class scheduling, lowered drinking fountains, lowered telephones, and special housing.

Services: Counseling and information services are available, as is tutoring in math, biology, chemistry, economics, and psychology. For learning-disabled students, the university provides early orientation, alternative test-taking accommodations, and a learning specialist.

Campus Safety and Security: Measures include 24-hour foot and vehicle patrol, emergency notification system, self-defense education, and security escort services. There are shuttle buses, emergency telephones, lighted pathways/sidewalks, and controlled access to dorms/residences.

Programs of Study: Clark confers B.A. degrees. Master's and doctoral degrees are also awarded. Bachelor's degrees are awarded in BIOLOGICAL SCIENCE (biochemistry and biology/biological science), BUSINESS (business administration and management), COMMUNICATIONS AND THE ARTS (art history and appreciation, communications, comparative literature, dramatic arts, English, film arts, fine arts, French, languages, music, romance languages and literature, Spanish, studio art, and visual and performing arts), COMPUTER AND PHYSICAL SCIENCE (chemistry, computer science, mathematics, and physics), ENGINEERING AND ENVIRONMENTAL DESIGN (environmental science), HEALTH PROFESSIONS (predentistry and premedicine), SOCIAL SCIENCE (classical/ancient civilization, economics, geography, history, international relations, international studies, philosophy, political science/government, prelaw, psychology, sociology, and women's studies). Psychology, government/international, and biology are the largest.

Required: Each student is required to complete 2 critical thinking courses in 2 categories of verbal expression and formal analysis, and 6 perspectives courses, representing the categories of aesthetics, comparative, historical, language and culture, science, and values. A student must receive passing grades in a minimum of 32 full courses, with a C- or better in at least 24 of these courses, and maintain a minimum 2.0 GPA to graduate.

Special: For-credit internships are available in all disciplines with private corporations and small businesses, medical centers, and government agencies. There is cross-registration with members of the Worcester Consortium, including 9 other colleges and universities. Clark also offers study abroad in 16 countries, a Washington semester with American University, work-study programs, accelerated degree programs, dual and student-designed majors, pass/no record options, and a 3-2 engineering degree with Columbia University. A gerontology certificate is offered with the Worcester Consortium for Higher Education. There are 8 national honor societies, including Phi Beta Kappa, and 21 departmental honors programs.

Faculty/Classroom: 57% of faculty are male; 43% are female. All teach and do research. No introductory courses are taught by graduate students. The average class size in an introductory lecture is 28; in a laboratory, 15; and in a regular course, 16.

Admissions: 64% of the 2009-2010 applicants were accepted. The SAT scores for the 2009-2010 freshman class were: Critical Reading--11% below 500, 37% between 500 and 599, 40% between 600 and 700, and 12% above 700; Math--12% below 500, 42% between 500 and 599, 38% between 600 and 700, and 8% above 700; Writing--10% below 500, 37% between 500 and 599, 44% between 600 and 700, and 9% above 700. The ACT scores were 6% below 21, 15% between 21 and 23, 31% between 24 and 26, 17% between 27 and 28, and 31% above 28. 60% of the current freshmen were in the top fifth of their class; 91% were in the top two fifths. 2 freshmen graduated first in their class.

Requirements: The SAT or ACT is required. In addition, the SAT Writing test is also recommended. Applicants must graduate from an accredited secondary school or have a GED. 16 Carnegie units are required, including 4 years of English, 3 each of math and science, and 2 each of foreign language and social studies, including history. An interview is recommended. AP credits are accepted. Important factors in the admissions decision are advanced placement or honors courses, recommendations by alumni, and recommendations by school officials.

Procedure: Freshmen are admitted fall and spring. Entrance exams should be taken by November of the senior year. There ae early decision and deferred admissions plans. Early decision applications should be filed by November 15; regular applications, by January 15 for fall entry and November 15 for spring entry, along with a $55 fee. Notification of early decision is sent January 1; regular decision, April 1. 56 early decision candidates were accepted for the 2009-2010 class. 35 applicants were on the 2009 waiting list; 12 were admitted. Applications are accepted on-line.

Transfer: 48 transfer students enrolled in 2008-2009. Applicants should have a minimum GPA of about 2.8. At least one full semester of college course work is required. High school and college transcripts, recent SAT or ACT test scores, a statement of good standing from previous institutions attended, and a transfer statement are required. Grades of C or better in comparable course work transfer for credit. 16 of 32 course units required for the bachelor's degree must be completed at Clark.

Visiting: There are regularly scheduled orientations for prospective students, consisting of open houses during fall and spring semesters, which include tours, information sessions, and talks with faculty, administration, and coaches. There are guides for informal visits, and visitors may sit in on classes. To schedule a visit, contact the Admissions Office.

Financial Aid: In 2009-2010, 91% of all full-time freshmen and 82% of continuing full-time students received some form of financial aid. 56% of all full-time freshmen and 56% of continuing full-time students received need-based aid. The average freshman award was $20,962. Need-based scholarships or need-based grants averaged $20,705; need-based self-help aid (loans and jobs) averaged $4844; and non-need-based awards and non-need-based scholarships averaged $34,900. 75% of undergraduate students work part-time. Average annual earnings from campus work are $1901. The average financial indebtedness of the 2009 graduate was $21,925. Clark is a member of CSS. The CSS/Profile and FAFSA are required. The deadline for filing freshman financial aid applications for fall entry is January 15.

International Students: There are 183 international students enrolled. The school actively recruits these students. They must take the TOEFL with a minimum score of 550 on the paper-based TOEFL (PBT) or 80 on the Internet-based version (iBT), or take the IELTS, scoring 6.5. They must also take the ACT or SAT, scoring 400.

Computers: Wireless access is available. All students may access the system 7 days per week. There are no time limits and no fees. It is strongly recommended that all students have a personal computer.

Graduates: From July 1, 2008 to June 30, 2009, 521 bachelor's degrees were awarded. The most popular majors were psychology (16%), government (11%), and biology and biochemistry (9%). 60 companies recruited on campus in 2008-2009. In an average class, 1% graduate in 3 years or less, 73% graduate in 4 years or less, 78% graduate in 5 years or less, and 78% graduate in 6 years or less. Of the 2008 graduating class, 40% were enrolled in graduate school within 6 months of graduation.

Admissions Contact: Donald Honeman, Dean of Admissions.
E-mail: *admissions@clarku.edu* Web: *www.clarku.edu*

COLLEGE OF THE HOLY CROSS   C-2
Worcester, MA 01610

(508) 793-2443
(800) 442-2421; (508) 793-3888

Full-time: 1315 men, 1582 women	Faculty: 244; IIB, +$
Part-time: 21 men, 15 women	Ph.D.s: 98%
Graduate: none	Student/Faculty: 12 to 1
Year: semesters	Tuition: $38,722
Application Deadline: January 15	Room & Board: $10,620
Freshman Class: 6652 applied, 2426 accepted, 747 enrolled	
SAT CR/M: 634/647	ACT: 28 MOST COMPETITIVE

The College of the Holy Cross is the only liberal arts college that embraces a Catholic, Jesuit identity. And of the 28 Jesuit colleges and universities in the United States, Holy Cross stands alone in its exclusive commitment to undergraduate education. Students enjoy a full array of athletic facilities, a state-of the-art fitness center, and outstanding arts spaces. The 4 libraries contain 627,742 volumes, 16,518 microform items, and 30,320 audio/video tapes/CDs/DVDs, and subscribe to 1,334 periodicals including electronic. Computerized library services include interlibrary loans, database searching, Internet access, and laptop Internet portals. Special learning facilities include a learning resource center, art gallery, radio station, greenhouses, facilities for aquatic research, and a multimedia resource center. The 174-acre campus is in a suburban area 45 miles west of Boston. Including any residence halls, there are 34 buildings.

Student Life: 63% of undergraduates are from out of state, mostly the Northeast. Students are from 45 states, 18 foreign countries, and Canada. 47% are from public schools. 67% are white. 72% are Catholic; 15% Protestant. The average age of freshmen is 18; all undergraduates, 20. 4% do not continue beyond their first year; 89% remain to graduate.

Housing: 2342 students can be accommodated in college housing, which includes coed dorms and on-campus apartments. In addition, there are special-interest houses, substance-free housing, and first-year living and learning housing. On-campus housing is guaranteed for all 4 years. 88% of students live on campus; of those, 90% remain on campus on weekends. Upperclassmen may keep cars.

Activities: There are no fraternities or sororities. There are 105 groups on campus, including art, band, cheerleading, choir, chorale, chorus, computers, dance, debate, drama, drill team, environmental, ethnic, film, gay, honors, international, investing club, jazz band, literary magazine, marching band, musical theater, newspaper, orchestra, pep band,

photography, political, professional, religious, social, social service, student government, and yearbook. Popular campus events include Spring Weekend, Family Weekend, and Senior Week.

Sports: There are 13 intercollegiate sports for men and 14 for women, and 6 intramural sports for men and 6 for women. Facilities include an astroturf playing field, baseball, football fields, and soccer stadiums, indoor and outdoor running tracks, a swimming pool, an ice rink, indoor crew tanks, a basketball arena, weight and exercise rooms, a wellness center and tennis, squash, and racquetball courts.

Disabled Students: 85% of the campus is accessible. Facilities include wheelchair ramps, elevators, special parking, specially equipped restrooms, special class scheduling, lowered drinking fountains, lowered telephones, and special housing. There are special diets, tutors, readers, interpreters, note takers, academic accommodations, and library and laboratory assistance.

Services: Counseling and information services are available, as is tutoring in some subjects, including calculus, statistics, chemistry, physics, economics, classics, Spanish, and writing.

Campus Safety and Security: Measures include 24-hour foot and vehicle patrol, emergency notification system, self-defense education, and security escort services. There are shuttle buses, emergency telephones, lighted pathways/sidewalks, and a card access control system.

Programs of Study: Holy Cross confers A.B. degrees. Bachelor's degrees are awarded in AGRICULTURE (environmental studies), BIOLOGICAL SCIENCE (biology/biological science), BUSINESS (accounting), COMMUNICATIONS AND THE ARTS (art history and appreciation, classics, dramatic arts, English, French, German, Italian, literature, music, Russian, Spanish, and studio art), COMPUTER AND PHYSICAL SCIENCE (chemistry, computer science, mathematics, and physics), EDUCATION (agricultural education), ENGINEERING AND ENVIRONMENTAL DESIGN (architecture), SOCIAL SCIENCE (anthropology, Asian/Oriental studies, economics, German area studies, history, medieval studies, philosophy, political science/government, psychology, religion, Russian and Slavic studies, and sociology). Economics, English, and psychology are the largest.

Required: Distribution requirements include social science, natural and mathematical science, cross-cultural studies, religious and philosophical studies, historical studies and the arts, and literature. In addition, students must demonstrate competence in a classical or modern language or American sign language. A total of 32 courses worth at least 1 unit each is required for graduation, with 10 to 14 courses in the major. The minimum GPA for graduation is 2.0.

Special: Academic internships are available through the Center for Interdisciplinary and Special Studies. Student-designed majors, dual majors including economics-accounting major, a Washington semester, and study abroad in approximately 17 countries are possible. There is a 3-2 engineering program with Columbia University or Dartmouth College, internships, and an accelerated degree program. Students may cross-register with other universities in the Colleges of Worcester Consortium. There are 2 national honor societies, including Phi Beta Kappa, and 5 departmental honors programs.

Faculty/Classroom: 54% of faculty are male; 46% are female. All teach and do research. No introductory courses are taught by graduate students. The average class size in an introductory lecture, 23, in a laboratory, 16, and in a regular course, 19.

Admissions: 36% of the 2009-2010 applicants were accepted. The SAT scores for the 2009-2010 freshman class were: Critical Reading--3% below 500, 21% between 500 and 599, 57% between 600 and 700, and 19% above 700; Math--3% below 500, 16% between 500 and 599, 61% between 600 and 700, and 20% above 700. 89% of the current freshmen were in the top fifth of their class; 99% were in the top two fifths. There was 1 National Merit finalist. 13 freshmen graduated first in their class.

Requirements: Applicants should be graduates of an accredited secondary school or hold the GED. Recommended preparatory courses include English, foreign language, history, math, and science. An essay is required. Students have the option to submit standardized test scores if they believe the results represent a fuller picture of their achievements and potential; students who opt not to submit scores will not be at any disadvantage in admissions decisions. An interview is recommended. AP credits are accepted. Important factors in the admissions decision are extracurricular activities record, recommendations by school officials, and advanced placement or honors courses.

Procedure: Freshmen are admitted in the fall. Entrance exams should be taken no later than January 15th of the senior year. There is an early decision and a deferred admissions plan. Early decision applications should be filed by December 15; regular applications by January 15 for fall entry. The fall 2009 application fee was $60. Notification of early decision is sent January 1; regular decision, April 1. Applications are accepted on-line. 526 applicants were on a recent waiting list.

Transfer: 29 transfer students enrolled in 2008-2009. Standardized test scores are not required but applicants must provide transcripts and 2 teacher recommendations. Personal interviews are highly recommended. 64 of 128 credits required for the bachelor's degree must be completed at Holy Cross.

Visiting: There are regularly scheduled orientations for prospective students, including fall open houses in October and November consisting of informational panels on academics, admissions, financial aid, and student life, as well as tours of the facilities. There are guides for informal visits; visitors may sit in on classes and stay overnight. To schedule a visit, contact the Admissions Office at (800) 442-2421.

Financial Aid: In 2009-2010, 64% of all full-time freshmen and 58% of continuing full-time students received some form of financial aid. 62% of all full-time freshmen and 57% of continuing full-time students received need-based aid. The average freshman award was $32,441. Need-based scholarships or need-based grants averaged $25,182 ($48,800 maximum); need-based self-help aid (loans and jobs) averaged $7,091 ($7,500 maximum); non-need based athletic scholarships averaged $49,748 ($48,800 maximum); and other non-need based awards and non-need based scholarships averaged $29,105 ($38,180 maximum). 45% of undergraduate students work part-time. Average annual earnings from campus work are $1800. The average financial indebtedness of the 2009 graduate was $23,785. Holy Cross is a member of CSS. The CSS/Profile, FAFSA, and student and parent federal tax returns are required. The deadline for filing freshman financial aid applications for fall entry is February 1.

International Students: There are 52 international students enrolled. The school actively recruits these students. They must take the TOEFL with a minimum score of 550 on the paper-based TOEFL (PBT) or 79 on the Internet-based version (iBT).

Computers: Wireless access is available. Students have full access to the college's computer network system, including broadband Internet access in all residential rooms and common areas as well as 485 college-provided PCs and Macs located throughout the campus. All students may access the system 24 hours per day. There are no time limits and no fees.

Graduates: From July 1, 2008 to June 30, 2009, 678 bachelor's degrees were awarded. The most popular majors were economics (17%), English (11%), and psychology (11%). 29 companies recruited on campus in 2008-2009. In an average class, 87% graduate in 4 years or less, 89% graduate in 5 years or less, and 89% graduate in 6 years or less. Of the 2008 graduating class, 24% were enrolled in graduate school within 6 months of graduation, and 60% were employed.

Admissions Contact: Admissions Office A campus DVD is available. E-Mail: *admissions@holycross.edu* Web: *www.holycross.edu*

CURRY COLLEGE   E-2
Milton, MA 02186-9984

	(617) 333-2210
	(800) 669-0686; (617) 333-2114
Full-time: 932 men, 1056 women	**Faculty:** 119; IIB, av$
Part-time: 287 men, 530 women	**Ph.D.s:** 57%
Graduate: 152 men, 168 women	**Student/Faculty:** 18 to 1
Year: semesters, summer session	**Tuition:** $29,830
Application Deadline: April 1	**Room & Board:** $11,110
Freshman Class: 4355 applied, 3268 accepted, 716 enrolled	
SAT CR/M/W: 463/466/464	**ACT:** 20 **COMPETITIVE**

Curry College, founded in 1879, is a private liberal arts institution. There are no undergraduate schools and one graduate school. In addition to regional accreditation, Curry has baccalaureate program accreditation with NLN. The library contains 139,000 volumes, 0 microform items, and 2,700 audio/video tapes/CDs/DVDs, and subscribes to 29,800 periodicals including electronic. Computerized library services include interlibrary loans, database searching, Internet access, and laptop Internet portals. Special learning facilities include a learning resource center, radio station, and TV station. The 135-acre campus is in a suburban area 7 miles southwest of Boston. Including any residence halls, there are 43 buildings.

Student Life: 77% of undergraduates are from Massachusetts. Students are from 40 states, 18 foreign countries, and Canada. 63% are white. The average age of freshmen is 18; all undergraduates, 25. 32% do not continue beyond their first year; 48% remain to graduate.

Housing: 1410 students can be accommodated in college housing, which includes single-sex and coed dorms. In addition, there are honors houses and special-interest houses. On-campus housing is available on a first-come, first-served basis, and is available on a lottery system for upperclassmen. 68% of students live on campus; of those, 80% remain on campus on weekends. Upperclassmen may keep cars.

Activities: There are no fraternities or sororities. There are 33 groups on campus, including art, cheerleading, chorale, dance, drama, ethnic, film, gay, honors, international, literary magazine, musical theater, newspaper, photography, political, professional, radio and TV, religious, social, social service, and student government. Popular campus events include formal dances, a concert series, and Curry Connections Fair.

Sports: There are 7 intercollegiate sports for men and 6 for women, and 5 intramural sports for men and 5 for women. Facilities include a 500-seat gym, a dance studio, 13 outdoor tennis courts, an outdoor pool, 5 athletic fields, a 2,000-seat stadium, a 500-seat auditorium, and a 5,000-meter cross-country trail.

Disabled Students: 60% of the campus is accessible. Facilities include wheelchair ramps, elevators, special parking, specially equipped restrooms, and special class scheduling.

Services: Counseling and information services are available, as is tutoring in most subjects. There is a reader service for the blind, and remedial math, reading, and writing. General development courses in writing, reading, and math are designed to develop the student's basic skills.

Campus Safety and Security: Measures include 24-hour foot and vehicle patrol, emergency notification system, self-defense education, and security escort services. There are shuttle buses, emergency telephones, lighted pathways/sidewalks, and a campus safety office offers security services.

Programs of Study: Curry confers B.A., B.S., and B.S.N. degrees. Master's degrees are also awarded. Bachelor's degrees are awarded in BIOLOGICAL SCIENCE (biology/biological science), BUSINESS (business administration and management), COMMUNICATIONS AND THE ARTS (communications, English, graphic design, and visual and performing arts), COMPUTER AND PHYSICAL SCIENCE (chemistry, information sciences and systems, and physics), EDUCATION (early childhood education, elementary education, health education, and special education), ENGINEERING AND ENVIRONMENTAL DESIGN (environmental science), HEALTH PROFESSIONS (nursing), SOCIAL SCIENCE (criminal justice, history, philosophy, political science/government, psychology, and sociology). Nursing is the strongest academically. Business, communications, and education are the largest.

Required: Successful completion of the liberal arts core curriculum and a total of 120 semester hours (121 for nursing), completion of a major, and a minimum 2.0 GPA, are required for graduation. Nursing students must pass a comprehensive exam. Transfer students have modified liberal arts requirements.

Special: Curry offers internships in all majors, an accelerated degree with approval of the dean, study abroad, work-study programs, dual and student-designed majors, credit by exam and for life, work, and military experience, non-degree study, and pass/fail options. There are 2 national honor societies and a freshman honors program.

Faculty/Classroom: 40% of faculty are male; 60% are female. 97% teach undergraduates, and 5% do both. No introductory courses are taught by graduate students. The average class size in an introductory lecture is 20; in a laboratory is 12; and in a regular course is 20.

Admissions: 75% of the 2009-2010 applicants were accepted. The SAT scores for the 2009-2010 freshman class were: Critical Reading--73% below 500, 23% between 500 and 599, 3% between 600 and 700, and 1% above 700; Math--69% below 500, 27% between 500 and 599, 4% between 600 and 700, and % above 700; Writing--70% below 500, 27% between 500 and 599, 3% between 600 and 700, and % above 700. The ACT scores were 23% below 21, 66% between 21 and 23, 11% between 24 and 26, % between 27 and 28, and % above 28. 54% of the current freshmen were in the top fifth of their class; 26% were in the top two fifths.

Requirements: The SAT or ACT is required. In addition, applicants should have combined average scores of 950-1100 on the SAT. Applicants must be graduates of an accredited secondary school or have a GED. 16 credits are required, including 4 years of English, 2 each of foreign language, history, science and social studies and 3 of math. An essay is required and an interview recommended. Applications are available on the college web site. A GPA of 2.5 is required. AP and CLEP credits are accepted. Important factors in the admissions decision are recommendations by school officials, extracurricular activities record, and evidence of special talent.

Procedure: Freshmen are admitted fall and spring. Entrance exams should be taken during the junior year or in November of the senior year. There are early decision, deferred admissions and rolling admissions plans. Early decision applications should be filed by December 1; regular applications, April 1 for fall entry and November 1 for spring entry, along with a $50 fee. Notification is sent on a rolling basis. Applications are accepted on-line. 107 applicants were on a recent waiting list, 35 were accepted.

Transfer: 89 transfer students enrolled in 2008-2009. Transfer applicants must be in good academic standing at their previous colleges, with a minimum GPA of 2.0. An interview is recommended. 30 of 120 credits required for the bachelor's degree must be completed at Curry.

Visiting: There are regularly scheduled orientations for prospective students, visits consist of interviews with an admissions counselor and tours with a student. There are guides for informal visits, visitors may sit in on classes, and stay overnight. To schedule a visit, contact the Admissions Office at (617) 333-2210.

Financial Aid: In 2009-2010, 67% of all full-time freshmen and 66% of continuing full-time students received some form of financial aid. 64% of all full-time freshmen and 63% of continuing full-time students received need-based aid. The average freshmen award was $17,478, with $4,359 ($4,359 maximum) from need-based self-help aid (loans and jobs) and $4,560 ($12,000 maximum) from other non-need-based awards and non-need-based scholarships. 13% of undergraduate students work part-time. Average annual earnings from campus work are

$525. The average financial indebtedness of the 2009 graduate was $34,877. Curry is a member of CSS. The FAFSA is required. The priority date for freshman financial aid applications for fall entry is March 1.

International Students: The school actively recruits these students. They must take the TOEFL with a minimum score of 525 on the paper-based TOEFL (PBT) or 71 on the Internet-based version (iBT). They must also take the SAT or ACT.

Computers: Wireless access is available. Computer labs are available throughout the campus as well as wireless access in select locations. All students may access the system. There are no time limits and no fees. It is strongly recommended that all students have a personal computer.

Graduates: From July 1, 2008 to June 30, 2009, 335 bachelor's degrees were awarded. The most popular majors were criminal justice (22%), nursing (21%), and business management (20%). In an average class, 47% graduate in 4 years or less and 50% graduate in 5 years or less.

Admissions Contact: Jane Fidler, Dean of Admissions. E-Mail: *curryadm@curry.edu* Web: *www.curry.edu*

EASTERN NAZARENE COLLEGE   E-2
Quincy, MA 02170

	(617) 745-3711
	(800) 883-6288; (617) 745-3980
Full-time: 245 men, 355 women	**Faculty:** n/av
Part-time: 15 men, 25 women	**Ph.D.s:** 57%
Graduate: 30 men, 140 women	**Student/Faculty:** n/av
Year: 4-1-4, summer session	**Tuition:** $22,000
Application Deadline: see profile	**Room & Board:** $8000
Freshman Class: n/av	
SAT or ACT: required	**COMPETITIVE**

Eastern Nazarene College, founded in 1918, is a private college affiliated with the Church of the Nazarene and offers a program in the liberal arts. Figures in the above capsule and this profile are approximate. There is 1 graduate school. In addition to regional accreditation, ENC has baccalaureate program accreditation with CSWE. The library contains 115,000 volumes and subscribes to 600 periodicals including electronic. Computerized library services include interlibrary loans and database searching. Special learning facilities include a learning resource center and radio station. The 15-acre campus is in a suburban area 6 miles south of Boston. Including any residence halls, there are 16 buildings.

Student Life: 55% of undergraduates are from out of state, mostly the Northeast. Students are from 27 states, 24 foreign countries, and Canada. 88% are white. 88% are Protestant. The average age of freshmen is 18; all undergraduates, 20. 25% do not continue beyond their first year; 60% remain to graduate.

Housing: 638 students can be accommodated in college housing, which includes single-sex dorms and married student housing. On-campus housing is guaranteed for all 4 years. 75% of students live on campus; of those, 75% remain on campus on weekends. Alcohol is not permitted. All students may keep cars.

Activities: There are no fraternities or sororities. There are 34 groups on campus, including band, cheerleading, choir, chorale, chorus, drama, jazz band, literary magazine, musical theater, newspaper, pep band, photography, professional, radio and TV, religious, social service, student government, and yearbook. Popular campus events include Freshmen Breakout, All-School Outing, and Junior/Senior Banquet.

Sports: There are 5 intercollegiate sports for men and 5 for women, and 4 intramural sports for men and 5 for women. Facilities include a phys ed center equipped with a basketball area, batting cage, and playing courts.

Disabled Students: 65% of the campus is accessible. Facilities include wheelchair ramps, elevators, special parking, and specially equipped restrooms.

Services: Counseling and information services are available, as is tutoring in most subjects. There is remedial math, reading, and writing.

Campus Safety and Security: Measures include 24-hour foot and vehicle patrol, self-defense education, and security escort services. There are emergency telephones and lighted pathways/sidewalks.

Programs of Study: ENC confers B.A. and B.S. degrees. Associate and master's degrees are also awarded. Bachelor's degrees are awarded in BIOLOGICAL SCIENCE (biology/biological science and marine biology), BUSINESS (accounting and business administration and management), COMMUNICATIONS AND THE ARTS (advertising, broadcasting, communications, dramatic arts, English, French, journalism, literature, music, music performance, Spanish, and speech/debate/rhetoric), COMPUTER AND PHYSICAL SCIENCE (chemistry, computer science, mathematics, physics, and science), EDUCATION (athletic training, education, elementary education, music education, science education, and social science education), ENGINEERING AND ENVIRONMENTAL DESIGN (computer engineering, engineering physics, and environmental science), HEALTH PROFESSIONS (sports medicine), SOCIAL SCIENCE (child psychology/development, Christian studies, clinical psychology, history, ministries, physical fitness/movement, psychology, religion, religious music, social studies, social work, and sociol-

ogy). Chemistry, physics, and history are the strongest academically. Education, business, and psychology are the largest.

Required: All students must complete the core curriculum of writing and rhetoric, biblical history, social science, science or math, symbolic systems and intercultural awareness, philosophy and religion, and phys ed. A total of 130 credits is required for the B.A. or B.S., with 32 to 40 in the major. Minimum GPA for graduation is 2.0.

Special: Internships are available in the metropolitan Boston area. Study abroad in Costa Rica, a Washington semester, a 3-2 engineering degree with Boston University, and a cooperative program with the Massachusetts College of Pharmacy are offered. Work-study programs, dual majors, credit for life, military, and work experience, and pass/fail options are available. An off-campus degree-completion program for adults in business administration is offered. There is 1 national honor society.

Faculty/Classroom: 72% of faculty are male; 28% are female. 83% teach undergraduates. No introductory courses are taught by graduate students. The average class size in an introductory lecture is 75; in a laboratory, 20; and in a regular course, 22.

Requirements: The SAT or ACT is required. In addition, applicants must be graduates of an accredited secondary school or have a GED. They must have a minimum of 16 academic credits, including 4 of English, 2 to 4 each of math and foreign language, 1 to 4 of science, and 1 to 2 each of history and social studies. Music students must audition. An essay and interview are recommended. A GPA of 2.3 is required. AP and CLEP credits are accepted. Important factors in the admissions decision are advanced placement or honors courses, recommendations by school officials, and leadership record.

Procedure: Freshmen are admitted to all sessions. Entrance exams should be taken in the spring of the junior year. There are deferred admissions and rolling admissions plans. Check with the school for current application deadlines. The fall 2009 application fee was $25.

Transfer: A minimum 2.0 GPA is required. An interview is recommended. 60 of 130 credits required for the bachelor's degree must be completed at ENC.

Visiting: There are regularly scheduled orientations for prospective students. There are guides for informal visits, and visitors may sit in on classes and stay overnight. To schedule a visit, contact the Office of Admissions.

Financial Aid: ENC is a member of CSS. The FAFSA and the college's own financial statement are required. Check with the school for current application deadlines.

International Students: They must take the TOEFL.

Computers: All students may access the system. There are no time limits.

Admissions Contact: Director of Admissions. E-Mail: *admission@enc.edu* Web: *www.enc.edu*

ELMS COLLEGE   B-3
Chicopee, MA 01013

	(413) 592-3189
	(800) 255-ELMS; (413) 594-2781
Full-time: 65 men, 360 women	**Faculty:** n/av
Part-time: 25 men, 190 women	**Ph.D.s:** 76%
Graduate: 20 men, 80 women	**Student/Faculty:** n/av
Year: semesters	**Tuition:** $14,100
Application Deadline: open	**Room & Board:** $9800
Freshman Class: n/av	
SAT or ACT: required	**VERY COMPETITIVE**

Elms College, founded in 1928 as College of Our Lady of the Elms, is a Roman Catholic institution offering undergraduate degrees in liberal arts and sciences and graduate degrees in liberal arts, education, and theology. Figures in the above capsule and this profile are approximate. In addition to regional accreditation, Elms has baccalaureate program accreditation with CSWE and NLN. The library contains 103,136 volumes, 77,784 microform items, and 2208 audio/video tapes/CDs/DVDs, and subscribes to 695 periodicals including electronic. Computerized library services include interlibrary loans and database searching. Special learning facilities include a learning resource center, art gallery, radio station, TV station, and rare books collection. The 32-acre campus is in a suburban area 2 miles north of Springfield and 90 miles west of Boston. Including any residence halls, there are 11 buildings.

Student Life: 85% of undergraduates are from Massachusetts. Others are from 9 states and 10 foreign countries. 74% are from public schools. 80% are white. 60% are Catholic. The average age of freshmen is 20; all undergraduates, 22. 11% do not continue beyond their first year.

Housing: 315 students can be accommodated in college housing, which includes single-sex and coed dorms. On-campus housing is guaranteed for all 4 years. 60% of students commute. All students may keep cars.

Activities: There are no fraternities or sororities. There are 41 groups on campus, including art, choir, chorale, chorus, computers, dance, drama, ethnic, honors, international, literary magazine, musical theater, newspaper, photography, professional, radio and TV, religious, social,

social service, student government, and yearbook. Popular campus events include Soph Show, Cap and Gown, and Ring Ceremony.

Sports: There are 6 intercollegiate sports for men and 9 for women, and 6 intramural sports for men and 6 for women. Facilities include fitness and athletic center housing a suspended indoor track, a 25-meter, 6-lane pool, a weight and aerobics room, a multipurpose arena, a basketball court, and a volleyball court.

Disabled Students: 40% of the campus is accessible. Facilities include wheelchair ramps, elevators, special parking, specially equipped restrooms, special class scheduling, lowered drinking fountains, lowered telephones, and automated doors.

Services: Counseling and information services are available, as is tutoring in every subject. There is a reader service for the blind and remedial math, reading, and writing. There also is an academic advising and resource center, a counseling service office, career services, wellness services, a campus ministry office, and resident advisers.

Campus Safety and Security: Measures include 24-hour foot and vehicle patrol, self-defense education, and security escort services. There are emergency telephones and lighted pathways/sidewalks. A safety and security manual is published each year, and there is a safety and security committee of administrators, students, faculty, and staff.

Programs of Study: Elms confers B.A. and B.S. degrees. Associate and master's degrees are also awarded. Bachelor's degrees are awarded in BIOLOGICAL SCIENCE (biology/biological science), BUSINESS (accounting, business administration and management, international business management, and marketing/retailing/merchandising), COMMUNICATIONS AND THE ARTS (English, fine arts, and Spanish), COMPUTER AND PHYSICAL SCIENCE (chemistry, computer science, mathematics, and natural sciences), EDUCATION (bilingual/bicultural education, early childhood education, elementary education, foreign languages education, middle school education, science education, secondary education, special education, and teaching English as a second/foreign language (TESOL/TEFOL)), HEALTH PROFESSIONS (health science, medical laboratory technology, nursing, predentistry, premedicine, and speech pathology/audiology), SOCIAL SCIENCE (American studies, international studies, paralegal studies, prelaw, psychology, religion, social work, and sociology). Nursing, education, and biology are the strongest academically. Education, business, and nursing are the largest.

Required: To graduate, all students must complete 120 hours with a 2.0 GPA. 54 hours are required in courses in rhetoric, computer science, history, religion, phys ed, philosophy, sociology, fine arts, humanities, foreign language, math, senior seminar, and service learning experience.

Special: Students may cross-register at any of the Cooperating Colleges of Greater Springfield or Consortium of Sisters of St. Joseph Colleges. Internships are available with local hospitals, businesses, and schools. Study abroad, student-designed interdepartmental majors, accelerated degree programs, work-study, dual majors, nondegree study, and pass/fail options are offered. There are 5 national honor societies, including Phi Beta Kappa, and a freshman honors program.

Faculty/Classroom: 35% of faculty are male; 65% are female. 90% teach undergraduates, 93% do research, and 92% do both. No introductory courses are taught by graduate students. The average class size in an introductory lecture is 13; in a laboratory, 8; and in a regular course, 11.

Requirements: The SAT or ACT is required. In addition, applicants should be graduates of accredited high schools or have earned the GED. Secondary preparation should include 4 units of English, 3 each of math and science, and 2 each of foreign language, history, and social studies. A personal essay is required; an interview is recommended. A GPA of 2.5 is required. AP and CLEP credits are accepted. Important factors in the admissions decision are advanced placement or honors courses, recommendations by school officials, and extracurricular activities record.

Procedure: Freshmen are admitted fall and spring. Entrance exams should be taken no later than November of the senior year. There are early admissions, deferred admissions, and rolling admissions plans. Application deadlines are open. The fall 2009 application fee was $30. Applications are accepted on-line.

Transfer: Applicants must have a minimum 2.0 GPA. 45 of 120 credits required for the bachelor's degree must be completed at Elms.

Visiting: There are regularly scheduled orientations for prospective students, including tours and interviews scheduled weekdays between 9 A.M. and 4 P.M. as well as 2 open houses in the fall and 1 in the spring. There are guides for informal visits,and visitors may sit in on classes and stay overnight. To schedule a visit, contact the Admission Office.

Financial Aid: Elms is a member of CSS. The FAFSA and the college's own financial statement are required. Check with the school for current application deadlines.

International Students: The school actively recruits these students.

Computers: All students may access the system 8 A.M. to 10 P.M. Monday through Friday and 12 noon to 9 P.M. Saturday and Sunday. Residence hall labs are open 24 hours. There are no time limits and no fees.

Admissions Contact: Director of Admission.
E-mail: *admissions@elms.edu* Web: *www.elms.edu*

EMERSON COLLEGE
E-2

Boston, MA 02116-4624 | (617) 824-8600; (617) 824-8609

Full-time: 1402 men, 2020 women	Faculty: 141; IIA, av$
Part-time: 78 men, 196 women	Ph.D.s: 72%
Graduate: 213 men, 637 women	Student/Faculty: 24 to 1
Year: semesters, summer session	Tuition: $30,080
Application Deadline: January 5	Room & Board: $12,280
Freshman Class: 6943 applied, 2926 accepted, 766 enrolled	
SAT CR/M/W: 623/592/622	ACT: 26 HIGHLY COMPETITIVE

Founded in 1880, Emerson is one of the premier colleges in the United States for the study of communication and the arts. There are 2 undergraduate schools and 2 graduate schools. The library contains 179,380 volumes, 9899 microform items, and 11,596 audio/video tapes/CDs/DVDs, and subscribes to 23,446 periodicals including electronic. Computerized library services include interlibrary loans, database searching, Internet access, and laptop Internet portals. Special learning facilities include a learning resource center, art gallery, radio station, TV station, sound-treated television studios, film production facilities and digital production labs, speech-language-hearing clinics, a proscenium stage theater, 2 radio stations, marketing research suite, and digital newsroom. The 8-acre campus is in an urban area on Boston Common in the Theater District. Including any residence halls, there are 10 buildings.

Student Life: 80% of undergraduates are from out of state, mostly the Middle Atlantic. Students are from 43 states, 19 foreign countries, and Canada. 75% are from public schools. 77% are white. The average age of freshmen is 18; all undergraduates, 20. 12% do not continue beyond their first year; 78% remain to graduate.

Housing: 1934 students can be accommodated in college housing, which includes coed dorms and living and learning communities such as a writers' block and digital culture floors. On-campus housing is guaranteed for the freshman year only, is available on a first-come, first-served basis, and is available on a lottery system for upperclassmen. 55% of students live on campus; of those, 75% remain on campus on weekends. No one may keep cars.

Activities: 3% of men belong to 2 local and 1 national fraternity; 3% of women belong to 2 local and 1 national sorority. There are 65 groups on campus, including chorale, computers, dance, debate, digital media, drama, environmental, ethnic, film, forensics, gay, honors, international, literary magazine, marketing/PR, musical theater, newspaper, photography, political, professional, radio and TV, religious, social, social service, student government, theatre troupes, and yearbook. Popular campus events include Evvy's Award Show and Hand-Me-Down Night.

Sports: There are 7 intercollegiate sports for men and 8 for women. Facilities include a gymnasium, 10,000-square-foot fitness center, and lighted athletic field.

Disabled Students: 85% of the campus is accessible. Facilities include wheelchair ramps, elevators, specially equipped restrooms, special class scheduling, and special housing.

Services: Counseling and information services are available, as is tutoring in most subjects. There is remedial math, reading, and writing.

Campus Safety and Security: Measures include 24-hour foot and vehicle patrol, emergency notification system, self-defense education, and security escort services. There are shuttle buses, emergency telephones, lighted pathways/sidewalks, and access controls for dorms/residences.

Programs of Study: Emerson confers B.A., B.S., and B.F.A. degrees. Master's and doctoral degrees are also awarded. Bachelor's degrees are awarded in BUSINESS (marketing management), COMMUNICATIONS AND THE ARTS (advertising, broadcasting, communications, creative writing, dramatic arts, film arts, journalism, media arts, musical theater, performing arts, public relations, publishing, radio/television technology, speech/debate/rhetoric, theater design, and theater management), HEALTH PROFESSIONS (speech pathology/audiology), SOCIAL SCIENCE (interdisciplinary studies). Visual and media arts, writing, and literature are the strongest academically. Visual and media arts, performing arts, and communication are the largest.

Required: All students must complete 128 credit hours, with 40 to 64 in their major and a minimum GPA of 2.0. The general education curriculum consists of 4 foundations courses (oral and written communication and quantitative reasoning), 7 perspectives courses (liberal arts humanities), and 2 global/U.S. diversity courses.

Special: Student-designed, interdisciplinary, and dual majors are available. Cross-registration is offered with the 6-member Boston ProArts consortium and Suffolk University. Nearly 800 internships are possible, 600 in Boston and 200 in Los Angeles. Internships bear credit and are graded. Emerson has nondegree study as well as study abroad in the Netherlands, Taiwan, Czech Republic, and a summer film program in Prague. There is 1 national honor society and a freshman honors program.

Faculty/Classroom: 55% of faculty are male; 45% are female. All teach undergraduates. Graduate students teach 4% of introductory courses. The average class size in an introductory lecture is 35; in a laboratory, 18; and in a regular course, 24.

Admissions: 42% of the 2009-2010 applicants were accepted. The SAT scores for the 2009-2010 freshman class were: Critical Reading--4% below 500, 31% between 500 and 599, 48% between 600 and 700, and 17% above 700; Math--7% below 500, 44% between 500 and 599, 43% between 600 and 700, and 6% above 700; Writing--4% below 500, 30% between 500 and 599, 51% between 600 and 700, and 15% above 700. The ACT scores were 4% below 21, 17% between 21 and 23, 32% between 24 and 26, 21% between 27 and 28, and 26% above 28. 77% of the current freshmen were in the top fifth of their class; 98% were in the top two fifths. 5 freshmen graduated first in their class.

Requirements: The SAT or ACT is required. The ACT Optional Writing test is also required. Emerson is a member of the Common Application and requires an Application Supplement. Candidates must have graduated from high school (or have a GED) and present 4 years of English and 3 each in science, social studies, foreign language, and math. Candidates for performing arts programs are required to submit a theater-related resume and either audition or interview, or submit a portfolio or an essay. Candidates for film are required to submit either a 5- to 8-minute video sample and statement, or a 5- to 10-page script. AP and CLEP credits are accepted. Important factors in the admissions decision are advanced placement or honors courses, evidence of special talent, and recommendations by school officials.

Procedure: Freshmen are admitted fall and spring. Entrance exams should be taken before December of the senior year. There are early decision and deferred admissions plan. Early decision applications should be filed by November 1; regular applications, by January 5 for fall entry and November 1 for spring entry, along with a $65 fee. Notifications of early decision are sent December 15, regular decision, April 1. 798 applicants were on the 2009 waiting list; 104 were admitted. Applications are accepted on-line.

Transfer: 210 transfer students enrolled in 2008-2009. Requirements for transfer students are the same as for all students. 48 of 128 credits required for the bachelor's degree must be completed at Emerson.

Visiting: There are regularly scheduled orientations for prospective students, including an admission session with an admission representative and a tour led by a current student. There are guides for informal visits, and visitors may sit in on classes. Visits may be scheduled on-line at *http://www.emerson.edu/admission/undergraduate/experience/visit.cfm*.

Financial Aid: In 2009-2010, 63% of all full-time freshmen and 55% of continuing full-time students received some form of financial aid. 53% of all full-time freshmen and 43% of continuing full-time students received need-based aid. The average freshman award was $15,685. Need-based scholarships or need-based grants averaged $14,243; need-based self-help aid (loans and jobs) averaged $4394; and other non-need-based awards and non-need-based scholarships averaged $12,396. 60% of undergraduate students work part-time. Average annual earnings from campus work are $1600. The average financial indebtedness of the 2009 graduate was $15,262. The CSS/Profile and FAFSA are required. The priority date for freshman financial aid applications for fall entry is March 1.

International Students: There are 100 international students enrolled. The school actively recruits these students. They must take the TOEFL with a minimum score of 550 on the paper-based TOEFL (PBT) or 80 on the Internet-based version (iBT), or take the IELTS. They must also take the SAT or ACT.

Computers: Wireless access is available. There are very few restrictions on network or wireless access with more than 3000 ports on campus. All students may access the system 24 hours a day. There are no time limits and no fees. It is strongly recommended that all students have a personal computer.

Graduates: From July 1, 2008 to June 30, 2009, 840 bachelor's degrees were awarded. The most popular majors were communications/journalism (33%), performing arts (31%), writing, literature, and publishing (19%). In an average class, 78% graduate in 6 years or less. Of the 2008 graduating class, 9% were enrolled in graduate school within 6 months of graduation, and 76% were employed.

Admissions Contact: Director of Undergraduate Admission. E-mail: *admission@emerson.edu* Web: *www.emerson.edu*

EMMANUEL COLLEGE

	E-2
Boston, MA 02115	(617) 735-9715; (617) 735-9801
Full-time: 458 men, 1190 women	**Faculty:** 82; IIB, av$
Part-time: 58 men, 301 women	**Ph.D.s:** 84%
Graduate: 70 men, 209 women	**Student/Faculty:** 16 to 1
Year: semesters, summer session	**Tuition:** $29,365
Application Deadline: March 1	**Room & Board:** $11,950
Freshman Class: 5518 applied, 3100 accepted, 424 enrolled	
SAT CR/M/W: 540/520/540	**ACT:** 22 COMPETITIVE

Emmanuel College, founded in 1919 by the Sisters of Notre Dame de Namur, is a Catholic college offering a liberal arts and sciences curriculum. There is 1 graduate school. The library contains 135,000 volumes and 800 audio/video tapes/CDs/DVDs, and subscribes to 1063 periodicals including electronic. Computerized library services include interlibrary loans, database searching, Internet access, and laptop Internet portals. Special learning facilities include a learning resource center and art gallery. The 17-acre campus is in an urban area in Boston. Including any residence halls, there are 10 buildings.

Student Life: 62% of undergraduates are from Massachusetts. Others are from 29 states and 34 foreign countries. 75% are from public schools. 65% are white. The average age of freshmen is 18; all undergraduates, 23. 21% do not continue beyond their first year; 63% remain to graduate.

Housing: 1184 students can be accommodated in college housing, which includes coed dorms. In addition, there are special-interest houses. On-campus housing is guaranteed for all 4 years. 71% of students live on campus; of those, 75% remain on campus on weekends. Alcohol is not permitted. Upperclassmen may keep cars.

Activities: There are no fraternities or sororities. There are 90 groups on campus, including art, band, cheerleading, choir, chorus, dance, debate, drama, environmental, ethnic, film, forensics, gay, honors, international, jazz band, literary magazine, musical theater, newspaper, orchestra, pep band, photography, political, professional, radio and TV, religious, social, social service, student government, and yearbook. Popular campus events include Moonlight Breakfast, Student Leadership Reception, and Latin Explosion.

Sports: There are 8 intercollegiate sports for men and 9 for women. Facilities a 1430-seat gym with basketball/volleyball courts, a fitness center, a training room, locker rooms, and athletic staff offices and conference rooms. There are also softball, soccer, and lacrosse fields.

Disabled Students: 90% of the campus is accessible. Facilities include wheelchair ramps, elevators, special parking, specially equipped restrooms, special class scheduling, lowered drinking fountains, lowered telephones, and special housing.

Services: Counseling and information services are available, as is tutoring in every subject. There is a reader service for the blind and remedial math and writing.

Campus Safety and Security: Measures include 24-hour foot and vehicle patrol, emergency notification system, self-defense education, and security escort services. There are shuttle buses, lighted pathways/sidewalks, 24-hour staffed residence hall desks and security office, closed-circuit surveillance in public areas, off-campus escorts, a bike patrol, a first responders program, and a Rape Agression Defense program.

Programs of Study: Emmanuel confers B.A., B.S., and B.F.A. degrees. Master's degrees are also awarded. Bachelor's degrees are awarded in AGRICULTURE (environmental studies), BIOLOGICAL SCIENCE (biochemistry, biology/biological science, biomathematics, and neurosciences), BUSINESS (business administration and management), COMMUNICATIONS AND THE ARTS (communications, English, English literature, Spanish, and studio art), COMPUTER AND PHYSICAL SCIENCE (chemistry and mathematics), EDUCATION (elementary education and secondary education), ENGINEERING AND ENVIRONMENTAL DESIGN (graphic arts technology), HEALTH PROFESSIONS (art therapy and nursing), SOCIAL SCIENCE (American studies, counseling/psychology, developmental psychology, history, interdisciplinary studies, international studies, liberal arts/general studies, political science/government, psychology, religion, and sociology). English, management, and the sciences are the largest.

Required: Students must complete a total of 128 credit hours with 40 to 48 in the major and a 2.0 GPA to graduate. Distribution requirements include 15 general ed courses, 10 to 17 courses for the major, and 5 to 7 elective or minor courses. A capstone experience and first-year seminar are required.

Special: There is cross-registration with Wheelock College, Simmons College, Massachusetts College of Art, Massachusetts College of Pharmacy, and the Wentworth Institute of Technology. The college offers internships, study abroad, a Washington semester, work-study programs on campus and in Boston-area organizations, an accelerated degree program in business administration for nontraditional students, dual and student-designed majors, and prelaw/prehealth preparation. There are 11 national honor societies and a freshman honors program. All departments have honors programs.

Faculty/Classroom: 38% of faculty are male; 62% are female. All teach undergraduates. No introductory courses are taught by graduate students. The average class size in an introductory lecture is 18; in a laboratory, 15; and in a regular course, 17.

Admissions: 56% of the 2009-2010 applicants were accepted. The SAT scores for the 2009-2010 freshman class were: Critical Reading--18% below 500, 58% between 500 and 599, 20% between 600 and 700, and 4% above 700; Math--31% below 500, 52% between 500 and 599, 15% between 600 and 700, and 2% above 700; Writing--20% below 500, 55% between 500 and 599, 22% between 600 and 700, and 3% above 700.

Requirements: The SAT or ACT is required. In addition, applicants must be graduates of an accredited secondary school or have a GED. 16 academic credits are required, including 4 years of English, 3 years of math, and 2 years each of foreign language, lab science, and social studies. An essay and an interview are encouraged but not required. AP and CLEP credits are accepted.

Procedure: Freshmen are admitted fall and spring. Entrance exams should be taken by November of the senior year. There are early decision and deferred admissions plans. Early decision applications should be filed by November 1; regular applications, by March 1 for fall entry, along with a $40 fee. Notification of early decision is sent December 1; regular decision, on a rolling basis. A waiting list is an active part of the admissions procedure. Applications are accepted on-line. A waiting list is maintained.

Transfer: 62 transfer students enrolled in 2008-2009. Students must submit essays, college and high school transcripts, and 2 letters of recommendation. They must be financially and academically eligible to return to the previously attended institution. 64 of 128 credits required for the bachelor's degree must be completed at Emmanuel.

Visiting: There are regularly scheduled orientations for prospective students, consisting of 2 open houses and weekday and weekend information sessions. There are guides for informal visits, and visitors may sit in on classes, and stay overnight. To schedule a visit, contact the Admissions Office.

Financial Aid: In 2009-2010, 94% of all full-time freshmen and 88% of continuing full-time students received some form of financial aid. 74% of all full-time freshmen and 77% of continuing full-time students received need-based aid. The FAFSA, the college's own financial statement, and parents' and students' income tax forms are required. The priority date for freshman financial aid applications for fall entry is April 1.

International Students: There are 29 international students enrolled. The school actively recruits these students. They must take the TOEFL, with a minimum score of 550 on the paper-based TOEFL (PBT) or 80 on the Internet-based version (iBT), or take ELS level 109 or the equivalent. They must also take the SAT or ACT.

Computers: Wireless access is available. All students may access the system. There are no time limits and no fees.

Graduates: From July 1, 2008 to June 30, 2009, 459 bachelor's degrees were awarded. The most popular majors were management (16%), psychology (13%), and English (9%). 50 companies recruited on campus in 2008-2009. In an average class, 1% graduate in 3 years or less, 55% graduate in 4 years or less, 62% graduate in 5 years or less, and 63% graduate in 6 years or less.

Admissions Contact: Sandra Robbins, Dean of Enrollment. E-Mail: *enroll@emmanuel.edu* Web: *www.emmanuel.edu*

ENDICOTT COLLEGE E-2

Beverly, MA 01915

(978) 921-1000
(800) 325-1114; (978) 232-2520

Full-time: 830 men, 1194 women	**Faculty:** 77; IIB, av$
Part-time: 63 men, 82 women	**Ph.D.s:** 56%
Graduate: 152 men, 305 women	**Student/Faculty:** 26 to 1
Year: 4-1-4, summer session	**Tuition:** $25,376
Application Deadline: February 15	**Room & Board:** $11,836
Freshman Class: 3885 applied, 2072 accepted, 561 enrolled	
SAT CR/M/W: 530/550/530	**COMPETITIVE**

Endicott College, founded in 1939, is a private institution offering bachelor and master degree programs in the professional and liberal arts. Education is built upon a combination of theory and practice, which is tested through internships and work experience. There are 8 undergraduate schools and 1 graduate school. In addition to regional accreditation, Endicott has baccalaureate program accreditation with CAATE, CIDA, and NLN. The library contains 121,485 volumes, 2304 microform items, and 1595 audio/video tapes/CDs/DVDs, and subscribes to 47,274 periodicals including electronic. Computerized library services include interlibrary loans, database searching, Internet access, and laptop Internet portals. Special learning facilities include a learning resource center, art gallery, radio station, TV station, archives museum, student-run restaurant, nature trails, and private beaches and marshland. The 231-acre campus is in a suburban area 20 miles north of Boston. Including any residence halls, there are 47 buildings.

Student Life: 52% of undergraduates are from out of state, mostly the Northeast. Students are from 28 states and 26 foreign countries. 85% are white. The average age of freshmen is 18; all undergraduates, 19. 17% do not continue beyond their first year; 72% remain to graduate.

Housing: 1724 students can be accommodated in college housing, which includes single-sex and coed dorms, on-campus apartments, and off-campus apartments. In addition, there are honors houses, special-interest houses, international housing, and single-parent housing. On-campus housing is guaranteed for the freshman year only, is available on a first-come, first-served basis, and is available on a lottery system for upperclassmen. 85% of students live on campus; of those, 87% remain on campus on weekends. Upperclassmen may keep cars.

Activities: There are no fraternities or sororities. There are 47 groups on campus, including art, cheerleading, chorale, chorus, computers, crew, dance, debate, drama, environmental, ethnic, film, fitness, gay, honors, international, jazz band, literary magazine, musical theater,

newspaper, outdoor adventure, political, professional, radio and TV, religious, sailing, social, social service, student government, and yearbook. Popular campus events include performing arts events and ice skating.

Sports: There are 13 intercollegiate sports for men and 14 for women, and 9 intramural sports for men and 9 for women. Facilities include a 1400-seat gym with a racquetball, indoor tennis and basketball courts, weight, fitness, and aerobics rooms, indoor track, rock climbing wall, and a field house. Outdoor facilities include 6 outdoor tennis courts, field hockey, softball, lighted baseball, lacrosse, and soccer fields, and a 2200-seat stadium.

Disabled Students: 90% of the campus is accessible. Facilities include wheelchair ramps, elevators, special parking, specially equipped restrooms, special class scheduling, and lowered drinking fountains.

Services: Counseling and information services are available, as is tutoring in every subject. There is a reader service for the blind. An interpreter service for hearing-impaired students is available.

Campus Safety and Security: Measures include 24-hour foot and vehicle patrol, emergency notification system, self-defense education, and security escort services. There are shuttle buses, emergency telephones, lighted pathways/sidewalks, controlled access to dorms/residences, license plate recognition system, security cameras, property identification, crime prevention workshops, and alcohol safety programs.

Programs of Study: Endicott confers B.A., B.S., and B.F.A. degrees. Associate and master's degrees are also awarded. Bachelor's degrees are awarded in AGRICULTURE (environmental studies), BIOLOGICAL SCIENCE (biotechnology), BUSINESS (accounting, business administration and management, and sports management), COMMUNICATIONS AND THE ARTS (communications, English, and fine arts), COMPUTER AND PHYSICAL SCIENCE (computer science and information sciences and systems), EDUCATION (athletic training, education, and physical education), ENGINEERING AND ENVIRONMENTAL DESIGN (interior design), HEALTH PROFESSIONS (nursing), SOCIAL SCIENCE (criminal justice, history, human services, international studies, liberal arts/general studies, and psychology). Business is the largest.

Required: To graduate, students must complete 126 credit hours with a minimum GPA of 2.0 (2.5 in education and nursing). Core requirements include 9 credits in science, humanities, social sciences, math, and writing courses, 12 upper-division electives, 3 credits in seminar in academic inquiry, senior seminar, and capstone. A senior thesis is required.

Special: Cross-registration is available with NECCUM. Internships are required in every major. Students may study abroad, and there are accelerated degree programs in business administration and psychology. Student-designed majors are available in liberal studies. There are 7 national honor societies, a freshman honors program, and 8 departmental honors programs. Students from all programs may be part of the institutionwide honors program.

Faculty/Classroom: 44% of faculty are male; 66% are female. All teach undergraduates. No introductory courses are taught by graduate students. The average class size in an introductory lecture is 18; in a laboratory, 9; and in a regular course, 18.

Admissions: 53% of the 2009-2010 applicants were accepted. The SAT scores for the 2009-2010 freshman class were: Critical Reading--28% below 500, 56% between 500 and 599, 15% between 600 and 700, and 1% above 700; Math--21% below 500, 56% between 500 and 599, 22% between 600 and 700, and 1% above 700; Writing--30% below 500, 51% between 500 and 599, 18% between 600 and 700, and 1% above 700.

Requirements: The SAT or ACT is required. In addition, essays and 2 science and math recommendations are required for nursing (including chemistry) and athletic training majors. AP and CLEP credits are accepted. Important factors in the admissions decision are recommendations by school officials.

Procedure: Freshmen are admitted fall and spring. Entrance exams should be taken in fall of the senior year. There are deferred admissions and rolling admissions plans. Applications should be filed by February 15 for fall entry and December 15 for spring entry, along with a $40 fee. 191 applicants were on the 2009 waiting list; 5 were admitted. Applications are accepted on-line.

Transfer: 35 transfer students enrolled in 2008-2009. The SAT or ACT is required, as are official high school and college transcripts and a letter of recommendation. 24 of 126 credits required for the bachelor's degree must be completed at Endicott.

Visiting: There are regularly scheduled orientations for prospective students, including testing, preregistration, and an introduction to general student life. There are guides for informal visits; visitors may sit in on classes and stay overnight. To schedule a visit, contact the Admission Office.

Financial Aid: In 2009-2010, 86% of all full-time freshmen and 83% of continuing full-time students received some form of financial aid. 49% of all full-time freshmen and 47% of continuing full-time students received need-based aid. Need-based scholarships or need-based grants averaged $9439; need-based self-help aid (loans and jobs) averaged $4627; and non-need-based awards and non-need-based scholarships averaged $6306. 24% of undergraduate students work part-time. Average annual earnings from campus work are $1500. The average financial indebtedness of the 2009 graduate was $33,783. Endicott is a member of CSS. The FAFSA and the college's own financial statement are required. The priority date for freshman financial aid applications for fall entry is March 15.

International Students: There are 56 international students enrolled. The school actively recruits these students. They must take the TOEFL with a minimum score of 550 on the paper-based TOEFL (PBT) or 79 on the Internet-based version (iBT). They must also take the SAT or ACT.

Computers: Wireless access is available. Common areas such as computer labs, cybercafé, and library contain 232 computers for general student use. Cybercafé is available 24 hours a day, 7 days a week. All academic and leisure buildings and most residence halls have wireless access. Residence halls are wired for 1 port per pillow. All students may access the system 24 hours a day, 7 days a week. There are no time limits and no fees. It is strongly recommended that all students have a personal computer. Students enrolled in business and interior design must have a personal computer.

Graduates: From July 1, 2008 to June 30, 2009, 458 bachelor's degrees were awarded. The most popular majors were business administration (24%), sport management (12%), and communication (10%). 60 companies recruited on campus in 2008-2009. In an average class, 68% graduate in 4 years or less, 71% graduate in 5 years or less, and 72% graduate in 6 years or less. Of the 2008 graduating class, 26% were enrolled in graduate school within 6 months of graduation, and 78% were employed.

Admissions Contact: Thomas J. Redman, Vice President Admissions. A campus DVD is available. E-mail: *admissio@endicott.edu* Web: *www.endicott.edu*

FITCHBURG STATE COLLEGE   C-2

Fitchburg, MA 01420-2697

(978) 665-3144
(800) 705-9692; (978) 665-4540

Full-time: 1676 men, 1843 women	**Faculty:** 179
Part-time: 323 men, 388 women	**Ph.D.s:** 91%
Graduate: 713 men, 2107 women	**Student/Faculty:** 19 to 1
Year: semesters	**Tuition:** $6900 ($12,980)
Application Deadline: March 1	**Room & Board:** $7870
Freshman Class: n/av	
SAT or ACT: required	**COMPETITIVE**

Fitchburg State College, founded in 1894, is a public college offering programs in liberal arts, business, communications, health sciences, and education. In addition to regional accreditation, Fitchburg State has baccalaureate program accreditation with ABET and NCATE. The library contains 248,644 volumes, 347,845 microform items, and 1950 audio/video tapes/CDs/DVDs, and subscribes to 2104 periodicals including electronic. Computerized library services include interlibrary loans, database searching, Internet access, and laptop Internet portals. Special learning facilities include a learning resource center, art gallery, radio station, campus school, graphics center, and TV studio. The 43-acre campus is in a suburban area 45 miles west of Boston. Including any residence halls, there are 35 buildings.

Student Life: 91% of undergraduates are from Massachusetts. Others are from 20 states, 4 foreign countries, and Canada. 80% are from public schools. 90% are white. The average age of freshmen is 18; all undergraduates, 22. 23% do not continue beyond their first year; 52% remain to graduate.

Housing: 1688 students can be accommodated in college housing, which includes coed dorms and on-campus apartments. In addition, there are special-interest houses. Priority is given to out-of-town students. 60% of students commute. All students may keep cars.

Activities: 2% of men belong to 42 national fraternities; 3% of women belong to 3 national sororities. There are 60 groups on campus, including band, cheerleading, choir, chorus, computers, dance, debate, drama, environmental, ethnic, film, gay, honors, international, jazz band, literary magazine, newspaper, photography, political, professional, radio and TV, religious, social, social service, student government, and yearbook. Popular campus events include Falcon Fest and Center Stage Performing Arts Series.

Sports: There are 8 intercollegiate sports for men and 7 for women, and 8 intramural sports for men and 8 for women. Facilities include a 1000-seat gym, an indoor/outdoor track, a weight room, varsity and intramural fields, a student union, volleyball, basketball, racquetball, and tennis courts, a swimming pool, and a dance studio.

Disabled Students: 80% of the campus is accessible. Facilities include wheelchair ramps, elevators, special parking, specially equipped rest rooms, special class scheduling, lowered drinking fountains, lowered telephones, special housing, and an adaptive computer lab.

Services: Counseling and information services are available, as is tutoring in most subjects. There is a reader service for the blind and remedial math, reading, and writing.

Campus Safety and Security: Measures include 24-hour foot and vehicle patrol, emergency notification system, self-defense education, and security escort services. There are shuttle buses, emergency telephones, and lighted pathways/sidewalks.

Programs of Study: Fitchburg State confers B.A., B.S., and B.S.Ed. degrees. Master's degrees are also awarded. Bachelor's degrees are awarded in BIOLOGICAL SCIENCE (biology/biological science), BUSINESS (business administration and management), COMMUNICATIONS AND THE ARTS (communications and English), COMPUTER AND PHYSICAL SCIENCE (computer science, earth science, and mathematics), EDUCATION (early childhood education, elementary education, industrial arts education, middle school education, secondary education, and special education), ENGINEERING AND ENVIRONMENTAL DESIGN (industrial engineering technology), HEALTH PROFESSIONS (exercise science and nursing), SOCIAL SCIENCE (criminal justice, economics, geography, history, human services, liberal arts/general studies, political science/government, psychology, and sociology). Communications and English are the strongest academically. Business administration, communications, and nursing are the largest.

Required: All students must complete a minimum of 120 credit hours with a GPA of at least 2.0 overall and in the major (some majors require a higher GPA). Core coursework is required in the arts, science/math and technology, citizenship and the world, and global diversity. Also required are 2 introductory semesters of writing.

Special: Students may cross-register at any other Massachusetts state college. Internships in a variety of fields, study abroad in 11 countries, B.A.-B.S. degrees, dual majors, and a student-designed interdisciplinary studies major are offered. There are 9 national honor societies, a freshman honors program, and 8 departmental honors programs.

Faculty/Classroom: 51% of faculty are male; 49% are female. All teach undergraduates. No introductory courses are taught by graduate students. The average class size in an introductory lecture is 26, in a laboratory, 15, and in a regular course, 21.

Requirements: The SAT or ACT is required. In addition, applicants should be graduates of accredited high schools or have the GED. Secondary preparation should include 4 years of English, 3 years each of math and liberal arts or phys ed, and 2 years each of a foreign language, social studies, including U.S. history, and science. A GPA of 2.0 is required. AP and CLEP credits are accepted. Important factors in the admissions decision are advanced placement or honors courses, leadership record, and extracurricular activities record.

Procedure: Freshmen are admitted fall and spring. Entrance exams should be taken in the junior or senior year. There are deferred admissions and rolling admissions plans. Applications should be filed by March 1 for fall entry and December 1 for spring entry, along with a $25 fee. Notification is sent on a rolling basis. Applications are accepted on-line.

Transfer: 357 transfer students enrolled in 2008-2009. Applicants should present a minimum GPA of 2.0 in at least 12 credits of transferable college work. 45 of 120 credits required for the bachelor's degree must be completed at Fitchburg State.

Visiting: There are regularly scheduled orientations for prospective students, including tours of the campus and residence halls, admissions/financial aid information, and academic program advising. There are guides for informal visits and visitors may sit in on classes. To schedule a visit, contact the Admissions Office.

Financial Aid: The FAFSA is required. The deadline for filing freshman financial aid applications for fall entry is March 1.

International Students: There are 110 international students enrolled. The school actively recruits these students. They must take the TOEFL with a minimum score of 550 on the paper-based TOEFL (PBT) or 79 on the Internet-based version (iBT). They must also take the SAT or ACT.

Computers: Wireless access is available. Open PC and Mac labs are available to students; wireless Internet access is available in the library campus center and all classroom buildings. All students may access the system 24 hours per day. There are no time limits and no fees. It is strongly recommended that all students have a personal computer.

Graduates: From July 1, 2008 to June 30, 2009, 639 bachelor's degrees were awarded. The most popular majors were communications (17%), business administration (15%), and interdisciplinary studies (10%). In an average class, 24% graduate in 4 years or less, 47% graduate in 5 years or less, and 52% graduate in 6 years or less. Of the 2008 graduating class, 5% were enrolled in graduate school within 6 months of graduation and 90% were employed.

Admissions Contact: Pamela McCafferty, Dean of Enrollment. E-Mail: *admissions@fsc.edu* Web: *www.fsc.edu*

FRAMINGHAM STATE COLLEGE D-2

Framingham, MA 01701-9101 (508) 626-4500; (508) 626-4017

Full-time: 1083 men, 2024 women **Faculty:** 168
Part-time: 308 men, 567 women **Ph.D.s:** 83%
Graduate: 454 men, 1670 women **Student/Faculty:** 18 to 1
Year: semesters, summer session **Tuition:** $6540 ($12,620)
Application Deadline: February 15 **Room & Board:** $8018
Freshman Class: 3964 applied, 2417 accepted, 650 enrolled
SAT CR/M: 517/521 **COMPETITIVE**

Framingham State College, founded in 1839, is a comprehensive public institution offering degree programs based on a liberal arts foundation that includes unique career programs. There is 1 graduate school. In addition to regional accreditation, FSC has baccalaureate program accreditation with ADA and NLN. The library contains 216,436 volumes, 688,330 microform items, and 3,493 audio/video tapes/CDs/DVDs, and subscribes to 424 periodicals including electronic. Computerized library services include interlibrary loans, database searching, Internet access, and laptop Internet portals. Special learning facilities include a learning resource center, art gallery, planetarium, radio station, a greenhouse, TV studio, early childhood demonstration lab, curriculum library, and McAuliffe Challenger Learning Center. The 50-acre campus is in a suburban area 20 miles west of Boston. Including any residence halls, there are 22 buildings.

Student Life: 95% of undergraduates are from Massachusetts. Others are from 20 states and 12 foreign countries. 80% are from public schools. 87% are white. The average age of freshmen is 19; all undergraduates, 21. 27% do not continue beyond their first year; 43% remain to graduate.

Housing: 1578 students can be accommodated in college housing, which includes single-sex and coed dorms. On-campus housing is available on a first-come and first-served basis. 55% of students commute. Alcohol is not permitted. Upperclassmen may keep cars.

Activities: There are no fraternities or sororities. There are 52 groups on campus, including art, cheerleading, chorale, chorus, computers, dance, drama, ethnic, gay, honors, international, literary magazine, newspaper, political, professional, radio and TV, religious, social, social service, and student government. Popular campus events include the Sandbox Festival, Super Weekends, and Semi-Formal Dance.

Sports: There are 6 intercollegiate sports for men and 7 for women, and 10 intramural sports for men and 10 for women. Facilities include an athletic and recreation center, a gym, and a student center. There is an all-weather turf field for soccer, and football, field hockey, and intramural sports are available on lower campus fields.

Disabled Students: 95% of the campus is accessible. Facilities include wheelchair ramps, elevators, special parking, specially equipped restrooms, special class scheduling, lowered drinking fountains, and lowered telephones.

Services: Counseling and information services are available, as is tutoring in most subjects. There is a reader service for the blind, and remedial math, reading, and writing. The Center for Academic Support and Advising offers free tutoring in writing, math, and reading. Subject tutoring may be arranged for an hourly fee.

Campus Safety and Security: Measures include 24-hour foot and vehicle patrol, emergency notification system, self-defense education, and security escort services. There are shuttle buses, emergency telephones, lighted pathways/sidewalks, security cameras, residence hall security, and card access.

Programs of Study: FSC confers B.A., B.S., and B.S.Ed degrees. Master's degrees are also awarded. Bachelor's degrees are awarded in BIOLOGICAL SCIENCE (biology/biological science and nutrition), BUSINESS (business administration and management and fashion merchandising), COMMUNICATIONS AND THE ARTS (art history and appreciation, communications, English, modern language, and studio art), COMPUTER AND PHYSICAL SCIENCE (chemistry, computer science, and mathematics), EDUCATION (business education, early childhood education, and elementary education), ENGINEERING AND ENVIRONMENTAL DESIGN (environmental science), HEALTH PROFESSIONS (nursing), SOCIAL SCIENCE (economics, family/consumer studies, fashion design and technology, food science, geography, history, interdisciplinary studies, political science/government, psychology, sociology, and textiles and clothing). Business administration, communication arts, and psychology are the largest.

Required: The college's goal-based general education model includes writing; math; language; literature or philosophy; visual or performing arts; physical science; life science; historical studies; social and behavioral sciences; forces in the United States; study of Constitutions, gender, class, and race; and non-Western studies. Every student must take 12 general education courses and fulfill all required goals. A total of 128 credits (32 courses), including 40 to 68 credits in the major, and a 2.0 GPA are required to graduate.

Special: The college offers a 2-3 preengineering program in cooperation with the University of Massachusetts at Amherst, Lowell, and Dartmouth. Cross-registration is possible at any of the state colleges. Study abroad in 8 countries, a Washington semester, and various internships are available. Pass/fail options are limited to 2 courses. There are 11 national honor societies, a freshman honors program, and 8 departmental honors programs.

Faculty/Classroom: 45% of faculty are male; 55% are female. All teach undergraduates. No introductory courses are taught by graduate students. The average class size in an introductory lecture, 16, and in a laboratory, 30.

Admissions: 61% of the 2009-2010 applicants were accepted.

Requirements: The SAT is required. In addition, applicants must have a high school diploma or the GED. Secondary preparation must total 16 college-preparatory credits, including 4 years of English, 3 each of math and science (2 with lab), and 2 each of foreign language and social science. The required 2 years of electives may include additional academic subjects or art, music, or computer courses. Prospective studio art majors must submit a portfolio. A GPA of 3.0 is required. AP and CLEP credits are accepted. Important factors in the admissions decision are advanced placement or honors courses, leadership record, and recommendations by school officials.

Procedure: Freshmen are admitted fall and spring. Entrance exams should be taken in the spring of the junior year or fall of the senior year. There are early admissions, deferred admissions, and rolling admissions plans. Applications should be filed by February 15 for fall entry and December 1 for spring entry, along with a $45 fee. Notification is sent on a rolling basis. Applications are accepted on-line.

Transfer: 341 transfer students enrolled in 2008-2009. Applicants with more than 24 college credits must present a college GPA of at least 2.5; those with fewer than 24 credits must also meet freshman admission requirements. Official transcripts must be submitted from all colleges previously attended at the time of application. 32 of 128 credits required for the bachelor's degree must be completed at FSC.

Visiting: There are regularly scheduled orientations for prospective students, including campus tours and information sessions. There are guides for informal visits and visitors may sit in on classes. To schedule a visit, contact the Office of Undergraduate Admissions at (508) 626-4500.

Financial Aid: In 2009-2010, 84% of all full-time freshmen and 67% of continuing full-time students received some form of financial aid. 53% of all full-time freshmen and 47% of continuing full-time students received need-based aid. The average freshman award was $8,239. 60% of undergraduate students work part-time. Average annual earnings from campus work are $1050. The average financial indebtedness of the 2009 graduate was $18,200. The FAFSA is required. The priority date for freshman financial aid applications for fall entry is March 1.

International Students: There were 18 international students enrolled in a recent year. They must take the TOEFL with a minimum score of 80 on the Internet-based version (iBT). They must also take the SAT or ACT.

Computers: Wireless access is available. Students have 24-hour wireless access in all of the campus environs. In addition, there are 6 academic computer labs, 5 general labs and PC classrooms, each of the 6 residence halls has a computer lab, and there is a 24-hour lab in the commuter lounge of the College Center. All students may access the system at any time. There are no time limits and no fees. All students are required to have a personal computer. A Dell or the equivalent is recommended.

Graduates: From July 1, 2008 to June 30, 2009, 664 bachelor's degrees were awarded. The most popular majors were business and management (15%), psychology (9%), and sociology and communications (9%). 669 companies recruited on campus in 2008-2009. In an average class, 52% graduate in 6 years or less.

Admissions Contact: Nick Figueroa, Dean of Admissions. E-Mail: admissions@framingham.edu Web: www.framingham.edu

FRANKLIN W. OLIN COLLEGE OF ENGINEERING

Needham, MA 02492-1200 (781) 292-2222; (781) 292-2210

Full-time: 175 men, 130 women **Faculty:** n/av
Part-time: none **Ph.D.s:** 98%
Graduate: none **Student/Faculty:** n/av
Year: semesters **Tuition:** $42,000
Application Deadline: see profile **Room & Board:** $13,500
Freshman Class: n/av
SAT or ACT: required **SPECIAL**

Franklin W. Olin College of Engineering, founded in 1997, is a private technical college degree programs in engineering. Figures in the above capsule and this profile are approximate. In addition to regional accreditation, Olin has baccalaureate program accreditation with ABET. Computerized library services include interlibrary loans, database searching, Internet access, and laptop Internet portals. Special learning facilities include an art gallery. The 75-acre campus is in a suburban area 12 miles southwest of Boston. Including any residence halls, there are 10 buildings.

Student Life: 91% of undergraduates are from out of state. Students are from 43 states, 5 foreign countries, and Canada. 46% are white;

11% Asian American. The average age of freshmen is 18; all undergraduates, 19. 1% do not continue beyond their first year; 90% remain to graduate.

Housing: College-sponsored housing includes coed dorms. On-campus housing is guaranteed for all 4 years. 98% of students live on campus; of those, 99% remain on campus on weekends. All students may keep cars.

Activities: There are no fraternities or sororities. There are 50 groups on campus, including art, band, chess, chorus, computers, dance, drama, environmental, film, gay, jazz band, literary magazine, orchestra, photography, political, professional, religious, social, social service, student government, and yearbook. Popular campus events include convocation, Big Conversation, and Club Fair.

Sports: There is no sports program at Olin. Facilities include soccer and frisbee fields and extensive indoor facilities, including a pool, track, and exercise equipment.

Disabled Students: All of the campus is accessible. Facilities include wheelchair ramps, elevators, special parking, specially equipped rest rooms, special class scheduling, lowered drinking fountains, lowered telephones, and special housing.

Services: Counseling and information services are available, as is tutoring in every subject.

Campus Safety and Security: Measures include 24-hour foot and vehicle patrol, emergency notification system, self-defense education, and security escort services. There are shuttle buses, emergency telephones, lighted pathways/sidewalks, controlled access to dorms/residences, and an e-mail emergency notification system.

Programs of Study: Olin confers B.S. degrees. Bachelor's degrees are awarded in ENGINEERING AND ENVIRONMENTAL DESIGN (computer engineering, electrical/electronics engineering, engineering, and mechanical engineering).

Required: To graduate, students must complete 120 credit hours, of which at least 46 must be in engineering, 30 in math and science, and 28 in art, humanities, and social sciences.

Special: There is cross-registration with Babson College, Brandeis University, and Wellesley College. The college offers study abroad in more than 40 countries.

Faculty/Classroom: 61% of faculty are male; 39% are female. All teach undergraduates. The average class size in an introductory lecture is 20; in a laboratory, 15; and in a regular course, 20.

Admissions: There were 39 National Merit finalists in a recent year. 15 freshmen graduated first in their class.

Requirements: The SAT or ACT is required. In addition, SAT Subject tests in math and science or the ACT with Writing are required. Also required are a high school profile with a counselor's letter of recommendation, letters of recommendation from a core math or science teacher and 1 other teacher, and 2 essays (of 300 and 500 words in length). All finalists for admission must have an on-campus interview.

Procedure: Freshmen are admitted fall. Entrance exams should be taken by December of the senior year. There is a deferred admissions plan. Check with the school for current application deadlines. The application fee is $80. Applications are accepted on-line. 41 applicants were on a recent waiting list, 11 were accepted.

Transfer: Olin has no transfer policy; all students enter as first-year students.

Visiting: There are guides for informal visits, and visitors may sit in on classes and stay overnight. To schedule a visit, go to http://olin.edu/admission/visits_tours.asp.

Financial Aid: In a recent year, all full-time students received some form of financial aid. 7% of all full-time freshmen and 13% of continuing full-time students received need-based aid. The FAFSA is required. Check with the school for current application deadlines.

International Students: They must take the SAT or ACT.

Computers: Wireless access is available across campus (inside and outside). There are 4 category, 6 ports per pillow in residence halls and computer labs with high-end equipment including workstations, reprographic printers, color copier, scanner, and video and audio editing stations. Students utilize the network for blended courses, Internet access, social networking, group work in and out of class, shared resources with partner institutions (Babson, Brandeis, Wellesley), research projects with internal and external partners, funded senior projects, and student services such as registration, financial aid, and billing. A dual boot environment (Windows and Linux) provides Web development and production space and services and personal, group, and project storage. All students may access the system 24 hours a day, 7 days a week. There are no time limits and no fees. All students are required to have a personal computer. A Dell is recommended.

Graduates: In a recent year, 71 bachelor's degrees were awarded. The most popular majors were mechanical engineering (37%), general engineering (37%), and electrical and computer engineering (26%). 53 companies recruited on campus in a recent year. In an average class, 96% graduate in 4 years or less and 100% graduate in 5 years or less. Of a recent graduating class, 18% were enrolled in graduate school within 6 months of graduation and 58% were employed.

Admissions Contact: Charles Nolan, Dean of Admission.
E-mail: *info @olin.edu* Web: *www.olin.edu*

GORDON COLLEGE · E-2
Wenham, MA 01984
(978) 867-4218
(866) 464-6736; (978) 867-4682

Full-time: 582 men, 972 women	Faculty: 97; IIB, av$
Part-time: 11 men, 21 women	Ph.D.s: 75%
Graduate: 15 men, 80 women	Student/Faculty: 16 to 1
Year: semesters	Tuition: $28,352
Application Deadline: March 1	Room & Board: $7720
Freshman Class: 1664 applied, 1106 accepted, 382 enrolled	
SAT CR/M/W: 588/567/586	ACT: 26 VERY COMPETITIVE+

Gordon College, founded in 1889, is a private, nondenominational Christian college offering liberal arts and sciences. There are 2 graduate schools. In addition to regional accreditation, Gordon has baccalaureate program accreditation with CSWE, NASDTEC, and NASM. The library contains 191,404 volumes, 31,666 microform items, and 5225 audio/video tapes/CDs/DVDs, and subscribes to 510 periodicals including electronic. Computerized library services include interlibrary loans, database searching, Internet access, and laptop Internet portals. Special learning facilities include a learning resource center and art gallery. The 440-acre campus is in a small town 25 miles north of Boston. Including any residence halls, there are 30 buildings.

Student Life: 71% of undergraduates are from out of state, mostly the Northeast. Students are from 45 states, 23 foreign countries, and Canada. 85% are white. 96% are Protestant. The average age of freshmen is 18; all undergraduates, 20. 13% do not continue beyond their first year; 72% remain to graduate.

Housing: 1370 students can be accommodated in college housing, which includes single-sex dorms, on-campus apartments, and married student housing. In addition, there are special-interest houses. On-campus housing is guaranteed for all 4 years. 88% of students live on campus; of those, 70% remain on campus on weekends. Alcohol is not permitted. All students may keep cars.

Activities: There are no fraternities or sororities. There are 35 groups on campus, including art, bagpipe, band, cheerleading, choir, chorale, chorus, dance, debate, drama, ethnic, film, honors, international, jazz band, literary magazine, musical theater, newspaper, off-campus ministries, opera, orchestra, pep band, photography, political, professional, religious, social, social service, student government, student outreach, symphony, and yearbook. Popular campus events include Symposium Days, Day of Prayer, and International Week.

Sports: There are 8 intercollegiate sports for men and 9 for women, and 15 intramural sports for men and 15 for women. Facilities include a gym, weight rooms, tennis courts, athletic fields, a training room, a swimming pool, a climbing wall, racquetball courts, an aerobics room, ski/running trails, an outdoor ropes course, a sauna, and a walking track.

Disabled Students: 90% of the campus is accessible. Facilities include wheelchair ramps, elevators, special parking, specially equipped rest rooms, special class scheduling, lowered drinking fountains, lowered telephones, and special housing.

Services: Counseling and information services are available, as is tutoring in some subjects, including math, writing, and core science. There is a reader service for the blind and remedial math, reading, and writing. There are writing and academic support centers.

Campus Safety and Security: Measures include 24-hour foot and vehicle patrol, emergency notification system, self-defense education, and security escort services. There are emergency telephones and lighted pathways/sidewalks.

Programs of Study: Gordon confers B.A., B.S., and B.Mu. degrees. Master's degrees are also awarded. Bachelor's degrees are awarded in BIOLOGICAL SCIENCE (biology/biological science), BUSINESS (accounting, banking and finance, business administration and management, and recreation and leisure services), COMMUNICATIONS AND THE ARTS (art, communications, dramatic arts, English, French, German, languages, music, music performance, and Spanish), COMPUTER AND PHYSICAL SCIENCE (chemistry, computer science, mathematics, and physics), EDUCATION (early childhood education, elementary education, middle school education, music education, secondary education, and special education), SOCIAL SCIENCE (biblical studies, economics, history, international studies, philosophy, political science/government, psychology, social work, sociology, and youth ministry). English, biology, and psychology are the strongest academically. English, psychology, and communications are the largest.

Required: All students must demonstrate competency in writing, speech, and foreign language. The core curriculum consists of 8 credits in biblical studies, 8 in social and behavioral sciences, 8 in natural sciences, math, and computer science, 6 in humanities, and 4 each in fine arts and freshman seminar. A total of 124 credits is required for graduation, with 18 or more in the major and a minimum GPA of 2.0.

Special: Gordon offers cooperative education, internships, and cross-registration with other institutions in the Northeast Consortium of Colleges and Universities in Massachusetts. There is a 3-2 engineering program with the University of Massachusetts at Lowell and a 2-2 program in allied health with the Thomas Jefferson College of Allied Health Science in Philadelphia. B.A.-B.S. degrees, dual majors, student-designed majors, nondegree study, and pass/fail options are available. A 3-2 engineering degree is available with the University of Massachusetts at Lowell. Off-campus study opportunities include a Washington semester, the Christian College Consortium Visitor Program, the LaVida Wilderness Expedition, and study abroad in Europe, the Middle East, and China. There are 2 national honor societies and 12 departmental honors programs.

Faculty/Classroom: 59% of faculty are male; 38% are female. All teach undergraduates. No introductory courses are taught by graduate students. The average class size in an introductory lecture is 30; in a laboratory, 14; and in a regular course, 19.

Admissions: 66% of the 2009-2010 applicants were accepted. The SAT scores for the 2009-2010 freshman class were: Critical Reading--15% below 500, 38% between 500 and 599, 36% between 600 and 700, and 11% above 700; Math--21% below 500, 36% between 500 and 599, 35% between 600 and 700, and 6% above 700; Writing--14% below 500, 39% between 500 and 599, 36% between 600 and 700, and 11% above 700. 50% of the current freshmen were in the top fifth of their class; 75% were in the top two fifths. There were 3 National Merit finalists.

Requirements: The SAT or ACT is required. The ACT Optional Writing test is also required. In addition, applicants must graduate from an accredited secondary school or have a GED. A minimum of 17 Carnegie units is required, including 4 English courses and 2 courses each in math, science, and social studies. Foreign language is a recommended elective. An essay, a personal reference, and an interview are required. Music majors must audition. Art majors must submit a portfolio for acceptance to the program. AP credits are accepted. Important factors in the admissions decision are advanced placement or honors courses, leadership record, and personality/intangible qualities.

Procedure: Freshmen are admitted fall and spring. Entrance exams should be taken in the spring of the junior year or the fall of the senior year. There are early decision, deferred admissions and rolling admissions plans. Early decision applications should be filed by November 15; regular applications, by March 1 for fall entry and November 1 for spring entry, along with a $50 fee. Notification of early decision is sent December 15; regular decision, January 1. Applications are accepted on-line.

Transfer: 45 transfer students enrolled in 2008-2009. Applicants must have a minimum GPA of 2.5. College transcripts, high school transcripts, and SAT or ACT scores if the applicant has completed less than 1 year of full-time study, an essay, an interview, and personal and academic references are required. 32 of 124 credits required for the bachelor's degree must be completed at Gordon.

Visiting: There are regularly scheduled orientations for prospective students, consisting of numerous open house programs throughout the fall, winter, and spring. There are guides for informal visits, and visitors may sit in on classes and stay overnight. To schedule a visit, contact Kristy Walker, Director of Admissions Visits.

Financial Aid: In 2009-2010, 94% of all full-time freshmen and 91% of continuing full-time students received some form of financial aid. 63% of all full-time freshmen and 66% of continuing full-time students received need-based aid. The average freshman award was $17,040. 48% of undergraduate students work part-time. Average annual earnings from campus work are $1830. The average financial indebtedness of the 2009 graduate was $33,332. Gordon is a member of CSS. The CSS/Profile and FAFSA are required. The deadline for filing freshman financial aid applications for fall entry is March 1.

International Students: There are 65 international students enrolled. The school actively recruits these students. They must take the TOEFL, the SAT, or the ACT.

Computers: Wireless access is available. Most of the campus is wireless, including common areas. All residence hall rooms are wired. All students may access the system at any time. There are no time limits and no fees.

Graduates: From July 1, 2008 to June 30, 2009, 374 bachelor's degrees were awarded. The most popular majors were business (13%), education (9%), and psychology (8%). In an average class, 64% graduate in 4 years or less, 70% graduate in 5 years or less, and 72% graduate in 6 years or less.

Admissions Contact: Brook Berry, Vice President for Enrollment. E-mail: *admissions@gordon.edu* Web: *www.gordon.edu*

MASSACHUSETTS 127

HAMPSHIRE COLLEGE
Amherst, MA 01002 (413) 559-5471; (413) 559-5631

Full-time: 570 men, 780 women	Faculty: IIB, +$
Part-time: none	Ph.D.s: 90%
Graduate: none	Student/Faculty: n/av
Year: 4-1-4	Tuition: $39,000
Application Deadline: see profile	Room & Board: $10,500
Freshman Class: n/av	
SAT or ACT: not required	**HIGHLY COMPETITIVE**

Hampshire College, founded in 1965, is a private institution offering a liberal arts education with an emphasis on independent research, creative work, and multidisciplinary study. Figures in the above capsule and this profile are approximate. The library contains 124,710 volumes, 4534 microform items, and 8727 audio/video tapes/CDs/DVDs, and subscribes to 731 periodicals including electronic. Computerized library services include interlibrary loans and database searching. Special learning facilities include an art gallery, multimedia center, farm center, music and dance studios, optics lab, electronics shop, integrated greenhouse, aquaculture facility, fabrication shop, and performing arts center. The 800-acre campus is in a rural area 20 miles north of Springfield. Including any residence halls, there are 28 buildings.

Student Life: 86% of undergraduates are from out of state, mostly the Northeast. Students are from 46 states, 25 foreign countries, and Canada. 76% are white. The average age of freshmen is 18; all undergraduates, 20. 21% do not continue beyond their first year.

Housing: 1100 students can be accommodated in college housing, which includes single-sex and coed dorms and on-campus apartments. In addition, there are special-interest houses. On-campus housing is guaranteed for all 4 years. 92% of students live on campus. All students may keep cars.

Activities: There are no fraternities or sororities. There are 80 groups on campus, including art, chorus, computers, dance, drama, ethnic, film, gay, international, literary magazine, musical theater, orchestra, photography, political, radio and TV, religious, social, social service, and student government. Popular campus events include Southern Exposure, Spring Jam, and Casino Night.

Sports: There are 3 intercollegiate sports for men and 2 for women, and 18 intramural sports for men and 18 for women. Facilities include 2 multipurpose sports centers housing a glass-enclosed swimming pool, a 12,000-square-foot playing floor, a 30-foot climbing wall, a weightlifting area, 4 indoor tennis courts, and a jogging track. Other facilities include soccer fields, 10 outdoor tennis courts, 2 softball diamonds, and a 2-mile nature trail.

Disabled Students: 90% of the campus is accessible. Facilities include wheelchair ramps, elevators, special parking, specially equipped restrooms, special class scheduling, lowered drinking fountains, and lowered telephones. The college provides a variety of support services to meet individual special needs.

Services: Counseling and information services are available, as is tutoring in most subjects. There is a reader service for the blind, an advising center, a writing and reading program, and a lab quantitative skills program.

Campus Safety and Security: Measures include 24-hour foot and vehicle patrol and security escort services. There are lighted pathways/sidewalks, an EMT on-call program, and dorm doors accessible by students only.

Programs of Study: Hampshire confers B.A. degrees. Bachelor's degrees are awarded in AGRICULTURE (agriculture and animal science), BIOLOGICAL SCIENCE (biology/biological science, botany, ecology, marine biology, nutrition, and physiology), COMMUNICATIONS AND THE ARTS (art history and appreciation, communications, comparative literature, creative writing, dance, dramatic arts, film arts, fine arts, journalism, linguistics, literature, media arts, music, performing arts, photography, and video), COMPUTER AND PHYSICAL SCIENCE (chemistry, computer science, geology, mathematics, physics, and science), EDUCATION (education), ENGINEERING AND ENVIRONMENTAL DESIGN (architecture, environmental design, and environmental science), HEALTH PROFESSIONS (health science and premedicine), SOCIAL SCIENCE (African studies, African American studies, American studies, anthropology, Asian/Oriental studies, cognitive science, crosscultural studies, economics, family/consumer studies, geography, history, humanities, international relations, international studies, Judaic studies, Latin American studies, law, Middle Eastern studies, peace studies, philosophy, political science/government, psychology, religion, sociology, urban studies, and women's studies). Film/photography/video is the strongest academically. Social sciences is the largest.

Required: All students must complete 3 divisions of study. In Division I: Basic Studies, students complete courses in cognitive science, humanities, arts and cultural studies, natural science, interdisciplinary arts, and social science and must complete 2 courses or the Division I exam project. In Division II: Concentration, students explore their field or fields of emphasis through individually designed internships or field studies. In Division III: Advanced Studies, students complete a major independent study project centered on a specific topic, question, or idea. Students must also partcipate in service to the college or the surrounding community and consider some aspect of their work from a non-Western perspective.

Special: Cross-registration is possible with other members of the Five College Consortium (Amherst College, the University of Massachusetts, Smith College, and Mount Holyoke). Internships, multidisciplinary dual majors, and study abroad (in the ISEP program, Tibetan Center, or a Costa Rica semester) are offered. All majors are student-designed. Students may complete their programs in fewer than 4 years.

Faculty/Classroom: 50% of faculty are male; 50% are female. All teach undergraduates. The average class size in a regular course is 17.

Requirements: Applicants must submit all transcripts from ninth grade on or GED/state equivalency exam results. Students are required to submit a personal statement and an analytic essay or academic paper. An interview is recommended. AP credits are accepted. Important factors in the admissions decision are personality/intangible qualities, evidence of special talent, and extracurricular activities record.

Procedure: Freshmen are admitted fall and spring. There are early decision, early admissions and deferred admissions plans. Check with the school for current application deadlines. The fall 2009 application fee was $55. Applications are accepted on-line. A waiting list is maintained.

Transfer: A proposed program of study, high school and college transcripts, and 1 recommendation must be submitted.

Visiting: There are regularly scheduled orientations for prospective students, including interviews, information sessions, campus tours, Discover Hampshire Days, Campus Visitation Days, and an overnight program. There are guides for informal visits; visitors may sit in on classes and stay overnight. To schedule a visit, contact the Admissions Office.

Financial Aid: Hampshire is a member of CSS. The CSS/Profile, the FAFSA, the college's own financial statement, and noncustodial parent statement are required. Check with the school for current application deadlines.

International Students: The school actively recruits these students. They must take the TOEFL.

Computers: All students may access the system 24 hours per day via their own PCs or at designated hours in the labs, generally 8 A.M. to midnight, but up to 24 hours at semester's end.

Admissions Contact: Director of Admissions. E-Mail: *admissions@hampshire.edu* Web: *www.hampshire.edu*

HARVARD UNIVERSITY/HARVARD COLLEGE	D-2
Cambridge, MA 02138	(617) 495-1551; (617) 495-8821
Full-time: 3510 men, 3140 women	**Faculty:** I, ++$
Part-time: 10 men, 10 women	**Ph.D.s:** n/av
Graduate: 5565 men, 5350 women	**Student/Faculty:** n/av
Year: semesters, summer session	**Tuition:** $37,000
Application Deadline: see profile	**Room & Board:** $12,000
Freshman Class: n/av	
SAT or ACT: required	**MOST COMPETITIVE**

Harvard College is the undergraduate college of Harvard University. Harvard College was founded in 1636. Harvard University also has 10 graduate schools. Figures in the above capsule and this profile are approximate. In addition to regional accreditation, Harvard has baccalaureate program accreditation with ABET. The 97 libraries contain 15.0 million volumes and subscribe to 100,000 periodicals including electronic. Computerized library services include interlibrary loans and database searching. Special learning facilities include a learning resource center, art gallery, natural history museum, planetarium, and radio station. The 380-acre campus is in an urban area across the Charles River from Boston. Including any residence halls, there are 400 buildings.

Student Life: 81% of undergraduates are from out of state, mostly the Middle Atlantic. Students are from 50 states, 118 foreign countries, and Canada. 67% are from public schools. 43% are white; 17% Asian American. The average age of freshmen is 18; all undergraduates, 20. 96% remain to graduate.

Housing: 6325 students can be accommodated in college housing, which includes coed dorms and on-campus apartments. On-campus housing is guaranteed for all 4 years. 97% of students live on campus. All students may keep cars.

Activities: There are no fraternities or sororities. There are 250 groups on campus, including art, band, cheerleading, chess, choir, chorale, chorus, computers, dance, debate, drama, ethnic, film, gay, honors, international, jazz band, literary magazine, marching band, musical theater, newspaper, opera, orchestra, pep band, photography, political, professional, radio and TV, religious, social, social service, student government, symphony, and yearbook. Popular campus events include Harvard/Yale football, Head of the Charles crew regatta, and Cultural Rhythms Festival.

Sports: There are 21 intercollegiate sports for men and 20 for women, and 16 intramural sports for men and 16 for women. Facilities include several gyms and athletic centers, pools, a track, boat houses, a sailing center, a hockey rink, and various courts and playing fields.

Disabled Students: Facilities include wheelchair ramps, elevators, special parking, specially equipped restrooms, special class scheduling, lowered drinking fountains, and lowered telephones.

Services: Counseling and information services are available, as is tutoring in every subject. There is a reader service for the blind.

Campus Safety and Security: Measures include 24-hour foot and vehicle patrol, self-defense education, and security escort services. There are shuttle buses, emergency telephones, and lighted pathways/sidewalks.

Programs of Study: Harvard confers A.B. and S.B. degrees. Master's and doctoral degrees are also awarded. Bachelor's degrees are awarded in BIOLOGICAL SCIENCE (biochemistry, biology/biological science, and biophysics), COMMUNICATIONS AND THE ARTS (art history and appreciation, Chinese, classics, creative writing, English, fine arts, folklore and mythology, French, German, Greek, Hebrew, Italian, Japanese, Latin, linguistics, literature, music, Portuguese, Russian, and Spanish), COMPUTER AND PHYSICAL SCIENCE (applied mathematics, astronomy, chemistry, computer science, geology, geophysics and seismology, mathematics, physical sciences, physics, and statistics), ENGINEERING AND ENVIRONMENTAL DESIGN (engineering, environmental design, environmental science, and preengineering), SOCIAL SCIENCE (African American studies, American studies, anthropology, Asian/Oriental studies, economics, European studies, history, humanities, Middle Eastern studies, philosophy, political science/government, psychology, religion, Russian and Slavic studies, Sanskrit and Indian studies, social science, social studies, sociology, and women's studies). Economics, government, and biology are the largest.

Required: In 8 semesters, students must pass a minimum of 32 1-semester courses. The average course load is 4 courses per semester, but the course rate may be varied for special reasons. A typical balanced program devotes about one-fourth of its courses to core curriculum requirements, one-half to the concentration (or major field), and the remaining one-fourth to electives.

Special: Students may cross-register with MIT and with other schools within the university and may design their own concentrations or enroll for nondegree study. Internships and study abroad may be arranged. Accelerated degree programs, dual majors, a 3-2 engineering degree, and a combined A.B.-S.B. in engineering are offered. There are pass/fail options. There is a Phi Beta Kappa honors program.

Faculty/Classroom: 98% teach undergraduates, 97% do research, and 95% do both. No introductory courses are taught by graduate students. The average class size in a regular course is 25.

Requirements: The SAT or ACT is required, as well as 3 SAT Subject tests. Applicants need not be high school graduates but are expected to be well prepared academically. An essay and an interview are required, in addition to a transcript, a counselor report, and 2 teacher recommendations from academic disciplines. AP credits are accepted. Important factors in the admissions decision are evidence of special talent, personality/intangible qualities, and recommendations by school officials.

Procedure: Freshmen are admitted fall. Entrance exams should be taken by January of the senior year. There is a deferred admissions plan. Check with the school for current application deadlines. The fall 2009 application fee was $65. Applications are accepted on-line. A waiting list is maintained.

Transfer: Transfer applicants must have completed at least 1 full year of daytime study in a degree-granting program at 1 institution. Students are required to submit the SAT or ACT, 2 letters of recommendation, high school and college transcripts with a dean's report, and several essays. 16 of 32 credits required for the bachelor's degree must be completed at Harvard.

Visiting: There are regularly scheduled orientations for prospective students, consisting of group information sessions and tours. There are guides for informal visits, visitors may sit in on classes, and stay overnight. To schedule a visit, contact the Undergraduate Admissions Office.

Financial Aid: Harvard is a member of CSS. The CSS/Profile, FAFSA, the college's own financial statement, and federal tax forms are required. Check with the school for current application deadlines.

International Students: The school actively recruits these students. They must also take the SAT or ACT.

Computers: All students may access the system 24 hours per day. There are no time limits and no fees.

Admissions Contact: Director of Admissions. A campus DVD is available. E-Mail: *college@harvard.edu* Web: *www.college.harvard.edu*

HELLENIC COLLEGE/HOLY CROSS GREEK ORTHODOX SCHOOL OF THEOLOGY

D-2

Brookline, MA 02445   (617) 731-3500, ext.1260; (617) 850-1460

Full-time: 50 men, 35 women	**Faculty:** 13
Part-time: none	**Ph.Ds:** 90%
Graduate: 110 men, 17 women	**Student/Faculty:** 7 to 1
Year: semesters	**Tuition:** $18,850
Application Deadline: May 1	**Room & Board:** $11,780
Freshman Class: 61 applied, 44 accepted, 35 enrolled	
SAT or ACT: required	**VERY COMPETITIVE**

Hellenic College, founded in 1937, is a private college affiliated with the Greek Orthodox Church. It offers programs in the classics, elementary education, religious studies, human development, management and leadership, and literature and history. There is 1 graduate school. In addition to regional accreditation, HCHC has baccalaureate program accreditation with NASDTEC. The library contains 75,000 volumes, 863 microform items, and 2,849 audio/video tapes/CDs/DVDs, and subscribes to 721 periodicals including electronic. Computerized library services include interlibrary loans, database searching, and Internet access. The 59-acre campus is in an urban area 4 miles southwest of Boston. Including any residence halls, there are 7 buildings.

Student Life: 95% of undergraduates are from out of state, mostly the Midwest. Students are from 25 states, 10 foreign countries, and Canada. 95% are from public schools. 97% are white. 95% are Most are Greek or Eastern Orthodox.. The average age of freshmen is 20; all undergraduates, 22. 5% do not continue beyond their first year; 95% remain to graduate.

Housing: 220 students can be accommodated in college housing, which includes coed dorms, on-campus apartments, and married student housing. On-campus housing is guaranteed for all 4 years. 95% of students live on campus; of those, 95% remain on campus on weekends. Alcohol is not permitted. All students may keep cars.

Activities: There are no fraternities or sororities. Groups on campus include choir, ethnic, religious, social, social service, and student government. Popular campus events include Feast of the Holy Cross, Matriculation Day, and Campus Christmas Party.

Sports: There are 4 intramural sports for men and 3 for women. Facilities include a gym, tennis, basketball, and racquetball courts, and a soccer field.

Disabled Students: 10% of the campus is accessible. Facilities include wheelchair ramps, elevators, special parking, specially equipped restrooms, and lowered drinking fountains.

Services: Counseling and information services are available, as is tutoring in some subjects, including Greek, music writing, and composition. There is remedial math, reading, and writing.

Campus Safety and Security: There are shuttle buses, lighted pathways/sidewalks, and a 16-hour security patrol.

Programs of Study: HCHC confers B.A. degrees. Master's degrees are also awarded. Bachelor's degrees are awarded in BUSINESS (business administration and management), COMMUNICATIONS AND THE ARTS (classics and literature), EDUCATION (elementary education), SOCIAL SCIENCE (history, human development, and religion). Religious studies and elementary education are the strongest academically. Religious studies and human development are the largest.

Required: To graduate, students must complete 129 credits, with 39 in the major, and maintain a minimum overall GPA of 2.0. General education requirements include 72 credits, with courses in English language and literature, music, history, science, philosophy, and social science.

Special: The college offers cross-registration with Boston Theological Institute, Newbury College, and Boston College, credit by examination, and study abroad in Greece. There is a freshman honors program.

Faculty/Classroom: 60% of faculty are male; 40% are female. All teach undergraduates. The average class size in an introductory lecture is 20; in a laboratory, 20; and in a regular course, 15.

Admissions: 72% of the 2009-2010 applicants were accepted. The SAT scores for the 2009-2010 freshman class were: Critical Reading--50% below 500, 25% between 500 and 599, 15% between 600 and 700; and 10% above 700; Math--50% below 500, 40% between 500 and 599, and 10% between 600 and 700; Writing--50% below 500, 25% between 500 and 599, 15% between 600 and 700; and 10% above 700. The ACT scores were 10% below 21, 60% between 21 and 23, 20% between 24 and 26, and 10% between 27 and 28.

Requirements: The SAT or ACT is required. In addition, applicants should graduate from an accredited secondary school or have a GED. 15 academic credits are required, including 4 units of English, 2 each of math, foreign language, and social studies, and 1 of science. An essay is required. A GPA of 2.5 is required. AP and CLEP credits are accepted. Important factors in the admissions decision are recommendations by school officials, advanced placement or honors courses, and recommendations by alumni.

Procedure: Freshmen are admitted fall and spring. There are early decision, deferred, and rolling admissions plans. Early decision applications should be filed by December 1; regular applications, by May 1 for fall entry and December 1 for spring entry. The fall 2009 application fee was $50. Notification of early decision is sent February 1; regular decision, June 15.

Transfer: 11 transfer students enrolled in 2009-2010. An essay, college transcripts, recommendation letters, an interview, and a health certificate are required. SAT scores and high school transcripts are waived if the student has 24 or more college credit hours. 60 of 129 credits required for the bachelor's degree must be completed at HCHC.

Visiting: There are regularly scheduled orientations for prospective students, including observation of classroom and student life. There are guides for informal visits; visitors may sit in on classes and stay overnight. To schedule a visit, contact Agnes Desses, Office of Admissions at admissions@hchc.edu.

Financial Aid: In a recent year, 95% of all full-time students received some form of financial aid, including need-based aid. 33% of undergraduate students work part-time. Average annual earnings from campus work are $1600. The average financial indebtedness of the 2009 graduate was $31,000. The FAFSA and the college's own financial statement are required. The priority date for freshman financial aid applications for fall entry is April 1. The deadline for filing freshman financial aid applications for fall entry is July 1.

International Students: There are 8 international students enrolled. They must take the TOEFL, scoring 500 on the paper-based version or 61 on the Internet-based version.

Computers: Wireless access is available. All students may access the system. There are no time limits and no fees.

Graduates: From July 1, 2008 to June 30, 2009, 21 bachelor's degrees were awarded. The most popular majors were religious studies (50%), elementary education (25%), and human development (25%). In an average class, 97% graduate in 4 years or less and 100% graduate in 5 years or less. Of a recent graduating class, 60% were enrolled in graduate school within 6 months of graduation and 30% were employed.

Admissions Contact: Agnes Desses, Assistant Director, Admissions. A campus DVD is available. E-mail: *admissions@hchc.edu*
Web: *www.hchc.edu*

LASELL COLLEGE

D-2

Newton, MA 02466   (617) 243-2225
(888) LASELL-4; (617) 243-2380

Full-time: 496 men, 1008 women	**Faculty:** 67; IIB, -$
Part-time: 5 men, 11 women	**Ph.Ds:** 87%
Graduate: none	**Student/Faculty:** 22 to 1
Year: semesters	**Tuition:** $25,300
Application Deadline: n/av	**Room & Board:** $10,500
Freshman Class: 3760 applied, 2156 accepted, 522 enrolled	
SAT CR/M/W: 485/490/490	**ACT:** 20 **COMPETITIVE**

Lasell College, founded in 1851, is a comprehensive coeducational college offering professionally oriented programs in the sciences, business, education, and health fields. There is one undergraduate school and one graduate school. The library contains 52,466 volumes and 2,579 audio/video tapes/CDs/DVDs, and subscribes to 221 periodicals including electronic. Computerized library services include interlibrary loans, database searching, and Internet access. Special learning facilities include a learning resource center, art gallery, radio station, an early childhood curriculum library, Lasell Village (retirement community), a nursery school, and a daycare center. The 50-acre campus is in a suburban area 8 miles west of Boston. Including any residence halls, there are 48 buildings.

Student Life: 56% of undergraduates are from Massachusetts. Others are from 22 states and 13 foreign countries. 95% are from public schools. 81% are white. The average age of freshmen is 18; all undergraduates, 20. 27% do not continue beyond their first year.

Housing: 1202 students can be accommodated in college housing, which includes single-sex and coed dorms and on-campus apartments. In addition, there are special-interest houses. On-campus housing is guaranteed for all 4 years. 79% of students live on campus; of those, 50% remain on campus on weekends. No one may keep cars.

Activities: There are no fraternities or sororities. There are 43 groups on campus, including art, cheerleading, chorale, chorus, dance, drama, environmental, ethnic, gay, honors, international, jazz band, literary magazine, newspaper, political, professional, radio and TV, religious, social, social service, student government, and yearbook. Popular campus events include River Day, Torchlight Parade, and Awards Night.

Sports: There are 7 intercollegiate sports for men and 8 for women, and 9 intramural sports for men and 9 for women. Facilities include an athletic center with a basketball court, a volleyball court, an indoor track, a dance studio, and locker rooms, plus tennis courts, 2 exercise rooms, and 2 athletic fields.

Disabled Students: Facilities include wheelchair ramps, elevators, special parking, specially equipped restrooms, special class scheduling, lowered drinking fountains, and lowered telephones.

Services: Counseling and information services are available, as is tutoring in most subjects. There is remedial math and writing. The Academic

Achievement Center offers individual assistance in math, accounting, and many other subjects, as well as in techniques for writing, coaching on presentation skills, and improving reading comprehension, as well as providing special resources for students with documented learning disabilities.

Campus Safety and Security: Measures include 24-hour foot and vehicle patrol, emergency notification system, and self-defense education. There are shuttle buses, emergency telephones, and lighted pathways/sidewalks.

Programs of Study: Lasell confers B.A. and B.S. degrees. Master's degrees are also awarded. Bachelor's degrees are awarded in AGRICULTURE (environmental studies), BUSINESS (accounting, banking and finance, business administration and management, entrepreneurial studies, fashion merchandising, hospitality management services, international business management, marketing/retailing/merchandising, sports management, and tourism), COMMUNICATIONS AND THE ARTS (advertising, communications, English, graphic design, journalism, media arts, multimedia, public relations, sports media, and video), COMPUTER AND PHYSICAL SCIENCE (applied mathematics and web technology), EDUCATION (athletic training, early childhood education, elementary education, secondary education, and sports studies), SOCIAL SCIENCE (child care/child and family studies, criminal justice, fashion design and technology, history, human services, humanities, interdisciplinary studies, law, liberal arts/general studies, paralegal studies, physical fitness/movement, psychology, and sociology). Allied health is the strongest academically. Business, education, and criminal justice are the largest.

Required: To graduate, students must complete 124 credit hours with a minimum GPA of 2.0. Requirements include 2 courses in writing and math, one course in literature, art, music, or drama, one in history, philosophy, or language, one in social science, one in science, and a computer literacy course. An internship is also required.

Special: Internships are built into the curriculum, and work-study programs are available on campus. Student-designed majors and student-arranged study-abroad programs are possible. All programs feature connected learning, which is an ongoing practical application of classroom theory. There is a freshman honors program and an honors program with students from all majors.

Faculty/Classroom: 37% of faculty are male; 62% are female. All teach undergraduates. No introductory courses are taught by graduate students. The average class size in an introductory lecture is 18; in a laboratory 14; and in a regular course 15.

Admissions: 57% of the 2009-2010 applicants were accepted. The SAT scores for the 2009-2010 freshman class were: Critical Reading--54% below 500, 39% between 500 and 599, 7% between 600 and 700, and 0.2% above 700; Math--53% below 500, 39% between 500 and 599, 8% between 600 and 700, and 0.4% above 700; Writing--54% below 500, 38% between 500 and 599, 7% between 600 and 700, and 1% above 700. The ACT scores were 54% below 21, 29% between 21 and 23, 15% between 24 and 26, and 2% between 27 and 28.

Requirements: The SAT is required. In addition, applicants should have completed 16 Carnegie units of high school study. The GED is accepted. Two letters of recommendation and a personal essay are required, and an interview is recommended. AP and CLEP credits are accepted. Important factors in the admissions decision are advanced placement or honors courses, personality/intangible qualities, and leadership record.

Procedure: Freshmen are admitted fall and spring. There is a rolling admissions plan. Application deadlines are open. Application fee is $40. Notifications are sent December 15. Applications are accepted on-line.

Transfer: 61 transfer students enrolled in 2008-2009. Applicants must have a minimum 2.3 GPA. 60 of 120 credits required for the bachelor's degree must be completed at Lasell.

Visiting: There are regularly scheduled orientations for prospective students, consisting of the president's welcome, faculty presentations, tours, and student panels. There are guides for informal visits and visitors may sit in on classes and stay overnight. To schedule a visit, contact the Office of Undergraduate Admission at (617) 243-2225.

Financial Aid: In 2009-2010, 99% of all full-time freshmen and 94% of continuing full-time students received some form of financial aid. 82% of all full-time freshmen and 76% of continuing full-time students received need-based aid. The average freshmen award was $21,300, with $8,690 ($19,650 maximum) from need-based scholarships or need-based grants; $6,112 ($11,500 maximum) from need-based self-help aid (loans and jobs); and $8,896 ($18,750 maximum) from other non-need-based awards and non-need-based scholarships. 32% of undergraduate students work part-time. Lasell is a member of CSS. The FAFSA and the college's own financial statement are required. The priority date for freshman financial aid applications for fall entry is March 1.

International Students: There are 22 international students enrolled. The school actively recruits these students. They must take the TOEFL with a minimum score of 525 on the paper-based TOEFL (PBT) or 61 on the Internet-based version (iBT), and the IELTS and the SAT or ACT.

Computers: Wireless access is available. Windows PC and Mac computers are available in 7 public labs and 2 specialized departmental labs.

Most residence halls and academic buildings have wireless access to the Internet. All students may access the system. 24 hours/day, 7 days/week. There are no time limits and no fees. It is strongly recommended that all students have a personal computer. A Dell Windows PC or a Macintosh is recommended.

Graduates: From July 1, 2008 to June 30, 2009, 222 bachelor's degrees were awarded. The most popular majors were business (47%), fashion/graphic design (14%), and sports management/science (13%). Of the 2008 graduating class, 20% were enrolled in graduate school within 6 months of graduation, and 90% were employed.

Admissions Contact: James M. Tweed, Dean of Admission. E-Mail: *info@lasell.edu* Web: *www.lasell.edu*

LESLEY UNIVERSITY

D-2

Cambridge, MA 02138-2790

(617) 349-8800
(800) 999-1959; (617) 349-8810

Full-time: 301 men, 903 women	**Faculty:** n/av
Part-time: 18 men, 45 women	**Ph.D.s:** 43%
Graduate: none	**Student/Faculty:** n/av
Year: semesters, summer session	**Tuition:** $29,200
Application Deadline: November 16	**Room & Board:** $12,400
Freshman Class: n/av	
SAT or ACT: required	**COMPETITIVE**

Lesley University, founded in 1909, is a private undergraduate institution, offering degree programs in education, human services, and the arts. Expanded resources, course work, and opportunities are available to students through the larger coeducational Lesley University system, including cross-registration with the Art Institute of Boston. There are 2 undergraduate schools and 2 graduate schools. In addition to regional accreditation, Lesley has baccalaureate program accreditation with NASAD and TEAC. The 2 libraries contain 124,022 volumes, 878,938 microform items, and 42,680 audio/video tapes/CDs/DVDs, and subscribe to 861 periodicals including electronic. Computerized library services include interlibrary loans, database searching, Internet access, and laptop Internet portals. Special learning facilities include a learning resource center, art gallery, center for teaching resources, media production facility, and instructional computing and math achievement center. The 5-acre campus is in an urban area just outside of Harvard Square in Cambridge. Including any residence halls, there are 53 buildings.

Student Life: 56% of undergraduates are from Massachusetts. Others are from 34 states, 10 foreign countries, and Canada. 83% are from public schools. 63% are white. The average age of freshmen is 18; all undergraduates, 20. 33% do not continue beyond their first year; 63% remain to graduate.

Housing: 650 students can be accommodated in college housing, which includes single-sex and coed dorms. In addition, there are special-interest houses and social interest and themed housing. On-campus housing is available on a first-come and first-served basis. 50% of students commute. All students may keep cars.

Activities: There are no fraternities or sororities. There are 25 groups on campus, including choir, chorus, dance, drama, ethnic, gay, international, literary magazine, musical theater, photography, political, professional, religious, Second Start, social, social service, student athlete advisory committee, student government, and Third Wave (a womens's group). Popular campus events include Family and Friends Weekend, Quad Fest, and World Fest.

Sports: There are 7 intercollegiate sports for men and 7 for women, and 3 intramural sports for men and 5 for women. Facilities include outdoor tennis courts, and a fitness center with Nautilus circuit, free weights, and cardiovascular equipment. Students may also use an Olympic-size swimming pool at a nearby school as well as the indoor and outdoor facilities at a nearby school, including two full size basketball courts, two racquetball courts, a rowing tank, a softball court, an indoor track and a lighted outdoor soccer field.

Disabled Students: 85% of the campus is accessible. Facilities include wheelchair ramps, elevators, special parking, specially equipped restrooms, special class scheduling, and lowered drinking fountains. The Disability Services Office provides document review and arranges for reasonable accommodations for special needs students.

Services: Counseling and information services are available, as is tutoring in most subjects. There is a reader service for the blind, and remedial math. There are study skills and interpreter services.

Campus Safety and Security: Measures include 24-hour foot and vehicle patrol, self-defense education, and security escort services. There are shuttle buses, emergency telephones, lighted pathways/sidewalks, and watch tours.

Programs of Study: Lesley confers B.S., B.F.A. degrees. Associates, master's, and doctoral degrees are also awarded. Bachelor's degrees are awarded in BUSINESS (management science), COMMUNICATIONS AND THE ARTS (visual and performing arts), COMPUTER AND PHYSICAL SCIENCE (natural sciences), EDUCATION (early childhood education, elementary education, middle school education, and special education), SOCIAL SCIENCE (human services, humanities, psychology, and social science). Education, counseling, photography and art therapy are the largest.

Required: Students must complete 45 hours of general education requirements, including 15 of humanities, 12 of natural science, 9 of social science, 6 of multicultural perspectives, and 3 of first-year seminar; emphasis is given to cross-curriculum components in writing, critical and quantitative reasoning, global perspectives, and leadership and ethics. Art Institute of Boston Students must also complete a Foundation year. To graduate, students need 128 total credit hours, including 30 to 33 in the liberal arts majors or 41 to 43 in professional majors.

Special: Study abroad in Cuba, England, and Sweden, and 6 others by arrangement, a Washington Justice semester, and on-campus work-study programs are offered. All students participate in at least 3 field placement experiences, beginning in their freshman year. There are combined accelerated degree programs in management, counseling, and education majors. Dual majors and student-designed majors are also available. Accelerated and weekend course programs as well as cross-registration with AIB are offered for Adult Baccalaureate College and School of Education. There is a freshman honors program and 2 departmental honors programs.

Faculty/Classroom: 44% of faculty are male; 56% are female. All teach and do research. No introductory courses are taught by graduate students. The average class size in an introductory lecture, 20, in a laboratory, 14, and in a regular course, 14.

Admissions: The SAT scores for the 2009-2010 freshman class were: Critical Reading--27% below 500, 47% between 500 and 599, 24% between 600 and 700, and 2% above 700; Math--41% below 500, 46% between 500 and 599, 12% between 600 and 700, and 1% above 700; Writing--27% below 500, 50% between 500 and 599, 20% between 600 and 700, and 3% above 700. The ACT scores were 9% below 21, 50% between 21 and 23, 13% between 24 and 26, 24% between 27 and 28, and 4% above 28. 38% of the current freshmen were in the top fifth of their class; 70% were in the top two fifths.

Requirements: The SAT or ACT is required. In addition, it is recommended that students complete 20 academic units in high school, including 4 in English, 3 in science, 3 in math, and 2 in U.S. history. SAT or ACT scores, a writing sample, and 2 recommendations are also required as part of the application; a personal interview is recommended. Applicants must have a high school diploma from an accredited secondary school or a GED. AP and CLEP credits are accepted. Important factors in the admissions decision are evidence of special talent, personality/intangible qualities, and advanced placement or honors courses.

Procedure: Freshmen are admitted fall and spring. Entrance exams should be taken by February 15. There are deferred admissions and rolling admissions plans. Applications should be filed by November 15 for spring entry, along with a $50 fee. Notification is sent on a rolling basis. Applications are accepted on-line. A waiting list is maintained.

Transfer: Applicants must have a minimum 2.5 GPA. They must provide high school and college transcripts, complete an essay or personal statement, and have a statement of good standing from prior institution. An interview is recommended for all Lesley College students and required of all Art Institute of Boston Students. 45 of 124 credits required for the bachelor's degree must be completed at Lesley.

Visiting: There are regularly scheduled orientations for prospective students, includes personal interviews with professional staff, student campus tours, information sessions, class visits, and meetings with financial aid. There are guides for informal visits, visitors may sit in on classes, and stay overnight. To schedule a visit, contact Lesley College Admissions, AIB Admissions at lcadmissions@lesley.edu or admissions@aiboston.edu.

Financial Aid: In 2009-2010, 72% of all full-time freshmen received some form of financial aid. 72% of all full-time freshmen received need-based aid. The average freshmen award was $15,652. 27% of undergraduate students work part-time. Average annual earnings from campus work are $1800. The average financial indebtedness of the 2009 graduate was $14,000. The FAFSA, the college's own financial statement, and parent and student federal tax returns are required. The priority date for freshman financial aid applications for fall entry is March 1. The deadline for filing freshman financial aid applications for fall entry is February 15.

International Students: There are 44 international students enrolled. The school actively recruits these students. They must take the TOEFL with a minimum score of 500 on the paper-based TOEFL (PBT).

Computers: Wireless access is available. The university offers students 12 computer labs, each with an average of 15 computers. In addition Internet access is provided in all classrooms, dorms and lounge areas and wireless access is available in 50% of all classrooms. A campus wide network is in place which gives all students access to course and extracurricular activity information free of charge. All students may access the system 24/7, except for some computer labs. There are no time limits and no fees.

Graduates: From July 1, 2008 to June 30, 2009, 390 bachelor's degrees were awarded. The most popular majors were liberal studies (31%), visual and performing arts (27%), and psychology (13%). 28 companies recruited on campus in 2008-2009. In an average class, 36%

graduate in 4 years or less, 17% graduate in 5 years or less, and 10% graduate in 6 years or less. Of the 2008 graduating class, 11% were enrolled in graduate school within 6 months of graduation, and 75% were employed.

Admissions Contact: Deb Kocar, Director of Admissions. E-Mail: lcadmission@lesley.edu Web: www.hchc.edu

MASSACHUSETTS BOARD OF HIGHER EDUCATION

The Massachusetts Board of Higher Education, established in 1980, is a public system in Massachusetts. It is governed by a 16-member board of regents appointed by the governor., whose chief administrator is chancellor. The primary goal of the system is the central governing authority for the state's public higher education system. Profiles of the 4-year campuses are included in this section.

MASSACHUSETTS COLLEGE OF ART AND DESIGN   E-2

Boston, MA 02115   (617) 879-7221; (617) 879-7250

Full-time: 538 men, 1049 women	**Faculty:** 101
Part-time: 53 men, 132 women	**Ph.D.s:** 78%
Graduate: 60 men, 100 women	**Student/Faculty:** 16 to 1
Year: semesters, summer session	**Tuition:** $8400 ($24,400)
Application Deadline: February 1	**Room & Board:** $11,288
Freshman Class: 1631 applied, 837 accepted, 315 enrolled	
SAT CR/M/W: 560/540/540	SPECIAL

Massachusetts College of Art and Design, founded in 1873, is a public institution offering undergraduate and graduate programs in art, design, and education. There is 1 graduate school. In addition to regional accreditation, MassArt has baccalaureate program accreditation with NASAD. The library contains 231,586 volumes and 8700 microform items, and subscribes to 757 periodicals including electronic. Computerized library services include interlibrary loans, database searching, and Internet access. Special learning facilities include 7 art galleries, a foundry, glass furnaces, ceramic kilns, video and film studios, performance and studio spaces, and a Polaroid 20 x 24 camera. The 5-acre campus is in an urban area in Boston. Including any residence halls, there are 6 buildings.

Student Life: 70% of undergraduates are from Massachusetts. Others are from 40 states, 28 foreign countries, and Canada. 85% are from public schools. 79% are white. The average age of freshmen is 18; all undergraduates, 22. 12% do not continue beyond their first year; 64% remain to graduate.

Housing: 375 students can be accommodated in college housing, which includes coed dorms and on-campus apartments. In addition, there is a visual art college residence hall with ventilated workrooms, a visiting artist suite, and gallery space. On-campus housing is guaranteed for the freshman year only, is available on a first-come, first-served basis, and is available on a lottery system for upperclassmen. Priority is given to out-of-town students. 77% of students commute. Alcohol is not permitted. No one may keep cars.

Activities: There are no fraternities or sororities. There are 30 groups on campus, including art, computers, ethnic, film, gay, international, literary magazine, newspaper, photography, political, professional, radio and TV, social, social service, and student government. Popular campus events include Eventworks, Annual Iron Pour, and First Night Ice Sculpture.

Sports: There are 7 intercollegiate sports for men and 6 for women, and 8 intramural sports for men and 6 for women. Facilities include a gym, a fitness center, and courts for squash, volleyball, and basketball.

Disabled Students: 95% of the campus is accessible. Facilities include wheelchair ramps, elevators, special parking, specially equipped restrooms, special class scheduling, lowered drinking fountains, and lowered telephones.

Services: There is remedial reading and writing.

Campus Safety and Security: Measures include 24-hour foot and vehicle patrol, self-defense education, and security escort services. There are shuttle buses, emergency telephones, and lighted pathways/sidewalks.

Programs of Study: MassArt confers B.F.A. degrees. Master's degrees are also awarded. Bachelor's degrees are awarded in COMMUNICATIONS AND THE ARTS (animation, art history and appreciation, ceramic art and design, fiber/textiles/weaving, film arts, fine arts, glass, graphic design, illustration, industrial design, media arts, metal/jewelry, painting, photography, printmaking, sculpture, and studio art), EDUCATION (art education), ENGINEERING AND ENVIRONMENTAL DESIGN (architecture), SOCIAL SCIENCE (fashion design and technology). Painting, illustration, and graphic design are the largest.

Required: A total of 120 semester credits is required for graduation; the minimum GPA varies by major. Typically, students take 42 credits in liberal arts, 18 in studio foundations, 36 in the major, and 24 in electives. Beginning in the sophomore year, the student's work is reviewed by panels of faculty and visiting artists.

Special: MassArt offers cross-registration with several consortiums, internships for advanced students, on- and off-campus work-study programs, study abroad and foreign-exchange programs, an open major for exceptional students, and dual majors in most combinations of concentrations.

Faculty/Classroom: 55% of faculty are male; 45% are female. All teach undergraduates. No introductory courses are taught by graduate students. The average class size in an introductory lecture is 23; in a laboratory, 12; and in a regular course, 14.

Admissions: 51% of the 2009-2010 applicants were accepted. The SAT scores for the 2009-2010 freshman class were: Critical Reading--18% below 500, 47% between 500 and 599, 30% between 600 and 700; and 5% above 700; Math--26% below 500, 49% between 500 and 599, 22% between 600 and 700, and 3% above 700; Writing--23% below 500, 49% between 500 and 599, 24% between 600 and 700; and 3% above 700. 35% of the current freshmen were in the top fifth of their class; 72% were in the top two fifths.

Requirements: The SAT is required. In addition, applicants should be graduates of an accredited secondary school or have earned the GED. College preparatory studies should include as a minimum 4 years of English, 2 each of social studies, math, and science, 2 academic electives (1 math or science and 1 art elective), and a foreign language. A personal essay and portfolio are required, and an interview and letters of reference are recommended. A GPA of 3.0 is required. AP and CLEP credits are accepted. Important factors in the admissions decision are evidence of special talent, recommendations by school officials, and personality/intangible qualities.

Procedure: Freshmen are admitted fall and spring. Entrance exams should be taken in early fall of the senior year. There are deferred admissions and rolling admissions plans. Applications should be filed by February 1 for fall entry; November 1 for spring entry, along with an application fee of $30 (Massachusetts residents) or $65 (nonresidents). Notification is sent April 1. Applications are accepted on-line. 56 applicants were on a recent waiting list, 8 were accepted.

Transfer: 130 transfer students enrolled in 2008-2009. Applicants must submit secondary school and postsecondary school transcripts, a statement of purpose, and a portfolio of at least 15 pieces, preferably in slides. An interview is recommended. 60 of 120 credits required for the bachelor's degree must be completed at MassArt.

Visiting: There are regularly scheduled orientations for prospective students, including an information session and a campus tour. There are guides for informal visits and visitors may sit in on classes. To schedule a visit, contact the Admissions Office.

Financial Aid: In a recent year, 81% of all full-time freshmen and 76% of continuing full-time students received some form of financial aid. 60% of all full-time freshmen and 62% of continuing full-time students received need-based aid. The average freshman award was $8508. 84% of undergraduate students work part-time. Average annual earnings from campus work are $1000. The FAFSA is required. The priority deadline for filing freshman financial aid applications is March 1.

International Students: There are 36 international students enrolled. They must take the TOEFL with a minimum score of 550 on the paper-based TOEFL (PBT) or 85 on the Internet-based version (iBT). They may take the SAT or ACT in lieu of the TOEFL.

Computers: Wireless access is available. All students may access the system. There are no time limits. There is a fee.

Graduates: From July 1, 2008 to June 30, 2009, 290 bachelor's degrees were awarded. The most popular majors were painting (11%), graphic design/studio (10%), and photography (10%). 8 companies recruited on campus in 2008-2009. In an average class, 1% graduate in 3 years or less, 42% graduate in 4 years or less, 58% graduate in 5 years or less, and 64% graduate in 6 years or less. Of the 2008 graduating class, 5% were enrolled in graduate school within 6 months of graduation and 89% were employed.

Admissions Contact: Karen Townsend, Director of Admissions. A campus DVD is available. E-mail: *admissions@massart.edu* Web: *www.massart.edu*

MASSACHUSETTS COLLEGE OF LIBERAL ARTS   A-1

North Adams, MA 01247-4100   (413) 662-5410; (413) 662-5179

Full-time: 604 men, 863 women	Faculty: 87; IIB, av$
Part-time: 70 men, 138 women	Ph.D.s: 82%
Graduate: 105 men, 182 women	Student/Faculty: 17 to 1
Year: semesters, summer session	Tuition: $
Application Deadline: open	Room & Board: $7870
Freshman Class: n/av	
SAT CR/M: 533/510	ACT: required COMPETITIVE

Massachusetts College of Liberal Arts (MCLA) is a public, liberal arts institution providing an educational experience that integrates the fundamentals of liberal arts into all major programs. MCLA provides unmatched, hands-on growth opportunities, in an inspiring, creative community. Unique to MCLA are the low faculty to student ratio, the ability to collaborate with the regions cultural venues for the fine and performing arts, and the Berkshire Hills Internship Program. MCLA also offers diverse campus residence halls, more than 50 clubs and organiza-

tions, and a very active student government association. There are no undergraduate schools. In addition to regional accreditation, MCLA has baccalaureate program accreditation with NCATE. The library contains 167,549 volumes, 291,450 microform items, 6,204 audio/video tapes/CDs/DVDs, and subscribes to 69 periodicals including electronic. Computerized library services include interlibrary loans, database searching, and Internet access. Special learning facilities include a learning resource center, art gallery, radio station, and TV station. The 80-acre campus is in a rural area 45 miles east of Albany, NY. Including any residence halls, there are 19 buildings.

Student Life: 74% of undergraduates are from Massachusetts. Students are from 18 states, and 2 foreign countries. 81% are white. The average age of freshmen is 18; all undergraduates, 23. 25% do not continue beyond their first year; 50% remain to graduate.

Housing: 1100 students can be accommodated in college housing, which includes single-sex and coed dorms and on-campus apartments. On-campus housing is guaranteed for all 4 years. 68% of students live on campus; of those, 85% remain on campus on weekends. Upperclassmen may keep cars.

Activities: There are 50 groups on campus, including band, cheerleading, choir, chorus, computers, dance, drama, environmental, ethnic, gay, honors, international, jazz band, literary magazine, musical theater, newspaper, photography, political, professional, radio and TV, religious, social, social service, and student government.

Sports: There are 5 intercollegiate sports for men and 6 for women, and 10 intramural sports for men and 10 for women. Facilities include an campus center with a swimming pool, weight rooms, a fitness center, and handball, squash, and racquetball courts. The campus also features an outdoor complex with tennis courts and soccer, baseball, and softball fields, a 1,750-seat gym, and a 5-mile cross-country running trail.

Disabled Students: 95% of the campus is accessible. Facilities include wheelchair ramps, elevators, special parking, specially equipped restrooms, and special class scheduling.

Services: Counseling and information services are available, as is tutoring in some subjects, most general education requirements. There is remedial math, reading, and writing. The Tutoring Exchange Network has qualified peers tutoring small groups.

Campus Safety and Security: Measures include 24-hour foot and vehicle patrol, self-defense education, and security escort services. There are emergency telephones and lighted pathways/sidewalks.

Programs of Study: MCLA confers B.A. and B.S. degrees. Master's degrees are also awarded. Bachelor's degrees are awarded in BIOLOGICAL SCIENCE (biology/biological science), BUSINESS (business administration and management), COMMUNICATIONS AND THE ARTS (English and fine arts), COMPUTER AND PHYSICAL SCIENCE (computer science, mathematics, and physics), EDUCATION (education), SOCIAL SCIENCE (history, interdisciplinary studies, philosophy, psychology, and sociology). English, business, and education are the largest.

Required: All students must complete at least 120 credits, including 50 in the core curriculum, and maintain a GPA of at least 2.0. Phys ed and computer science courses are required.

Special: MCLA offers cross-registration with Williams College and Berkshire Community College, dual majors, internships in all majors, and study abroad in many countries within the International College Program. Student-designed majors, pass/fail options, nondegree study, and independent study also are available. There are 8 national honor societies, a freshman honors program, and 6 departmental honors programs.

Faculty/Classroom: 55% of faculty are male; 45% are female. 91% teach undergraduates. No introductory courses are taught by graduate students. The average class size in an introductory lecture is 13; in a laboratory is 13; and in a regular course is 14.

Admissions: n/av

Requirements: The SAT or ACT is required. In addition, MCLA uses an eligibility index to determine a minimum SAT score. Applicants should have completed 16 Carnegie units, including 4 courses in English, 3 each in science and math, and 2 each in foreign language, history/social science, and electives. The GED is also accepted. A GPA of 2.0 is required. AP and CLEP credits are accepted.

Procedure: Freshmen are admitted fall and spring. Entrance exams should be taken by January of the senior year. There are early decision, deferred admissions and rolling admissions plans. Early decision applications should be filed by December 1; regular application deadlines are open. Application fee is $35. Notification is sent on a rolling basis. Applications are accepted on-line.

Transfer: 160 transfer students enrolled in 2008-2009. Between 12-23 transfer credits and minimum GPA of 2.5 is accepted from transfer students. In addition, applicants with 24 or more transfer credits, with a minimum GPA of 2.0 is also accepted. 45 of 120 credits required for the bachelor's degree must be completed at MCLA.

Visiting: There are regularly scheduled orientations for prospective students. There are guides for informal visits and visitors may sit in on classes. To schedule a visit, contact Admissions Office at admissions@mcla.edu.

Financial Aid: In 2009-2010, 80% of all full-time freshmen and 71% of continuing full-time students received some form of financial aid. 74%

of all full-time freshmen and 67% of continuing full-time students received need-based aid. The average financial indebtedness of the 2009 graduate was $22,168. MCLA is a member of CSS. The FAFSA and the college's own financial statement are required. The priority date for freshman financial aid applications for fall entry is March 1.

International Students: The school actively recruits these students. They must take the TOEFL with a minimum score of 550 on the paper-based TOEFL (PBT). They must also take the SAT.

Computers: Wireless access is available. All students may access the system. Limits on student access to the system vary with the time of year. There are no fees. All students are required to have a personal computer.

Graduates: From July 1, 2008 to June 30, 2009, 293 bachelor's degrees were awarded. The most popular majors were English communications (21%), Business (19%), and Sociology (15%). In an average class, 38% graduate in 4 years or less, 47% graduate in 5 years or less, and 50% graduate in 6 years or less.

Admissions Contact: Steve King, Director of Admissions. E-Mail: *admissions@mcla.edu*

MASSACHUSETTS COLLEGE OF PHARMACY AND HEALTH SCIENCES

E-2

Boston, MA 02115

(617) 732-2850
(800) 225-5506; (617) 732-2118

Full-time: 888 men, 1882 women	Faculty: 202
Part-time: 28 men, 85 women	Ph.D.s: 86%
Graduate: 447 men, 922 women	Student/Faculty: 21 to 1
Year: semesters, summer session	Tuition: $24,550
Application Deadline: February 1	Room & Board: $11,900
Freshman Class: 3194 applied, 1383 accepted, 764 enrolled	
SAT CR/M/W: 525/570/540	ACT: 24	SPECIAL

The Massachusetts College of Pharmacy and Health Sciences, established in 1823, is a private institution offering undergraduate programs in chemistry, the pharmaceutical sciences, and the health sciences. There are 5 undergraduate schools and 1 graduate school. In addition to regional accreditation, MCPHS has baccalaureate program accreditation with ACPE and ADA. The library contains 54,800 volumes, microform items, and audio/video tapes/CDs/DVDs, and subscribes to 32,800 periodicals including electronic. Computerized library services include interlibrary loans, database searching, Internet access, and laptop Internet portals. Special learning facilities include a learning resource center, pharmacy labs, dental hygiene clinic, and nursing labs. The 2-acre campus is in an urban area 1 mile from the center of Boston. Including any residence halls, there are 3 buildings.

Student Life: 56% of undergraduates are from Massachusetts. Others are from 43 states, 32 foreign countries, and Canada. 54% are white; 26% Asian American. The average age of freshmen is 18; all undergraduates, 21. 17% do not continue beyond their first year; 69% remain to graduate.

Housing: 785 students can be accommodated in college housing, which includes single-sex and coed dorms and on-campus apartments. On-campus housing is guaranteed for the freshman year only, is available on a first-come, first-served basis, and is available on a lottery system for upperclassmen. 74% of students commute. Alcohol is not permitted. No one may keep cars.

Activities: There are 5 national fraternities. There are 66 groups on campus, including academic, art, band, choir, chorale, chorus, cultural, dance, drama, environmental, ethnic, gay, honors, international, musical theater, newspaper, orchestra, professional, religious, social service, and student government. Popular campus events include International Fair and Mission Hill Walk for Health.

Sports: There are 6 intramural sports for men and 6 for women. Facilities are shared with the Massachusetts College of Art and include a wellness center with weight training equipment and a gym with court space for basketball, volleyball, and badminton.

Disabled Students: All of the campus is accessible. Facilities include wheelchair ramps, elevators, special parking, specially equipped restrooms, lowered drinking fountains, lowered telephones, and special housing. All dorm rooms have elevator access and meet ADA requirements.

Services: Counseling and information services are available, as is tutoring in some subjects. Tutoring is free of charge and includes both group and individual peer tutoring.

Campus Safety and Security: Measures include emergency notification system, self-defense education, and security escort services. There are shuttle buses, lighted pathways/sidewalks, controlled access to dorms/residences, security guards at all entrances, and admission to all buildings by means of a security pass worn by all students, faculty, and staff.

Programs of Study: MCPHS confers B.S. and B.S.N. degrees. Master's and doctoral degrees are also awarded. Bachelor's degrees are awarded in COMPUTER AND PHYSICAL SCIENCE (chemistry and radiological technology), HEALTH PROFESSIONS (dental hygiene, health science, nuclear medical technology, nursing, pharmaceutical science, and pre-medicine). Pharmacy and nursing are the largest.

Required: Graduation requirements vary by program. Students must complete course work in expository writing, history and politics, psychology, sociology, interpersonal communications in the health professions, evolution of the health professions, biomedical ethics, and humanities. Students must maintain a minimum GPA of 2.0 overall and a professional GPA that varies by program.

Special: MCPHS offers cross-registration with the other colleges of the Fenway Consortium and cooperative programs with several schools. Accelerated degrees and dual majors are available in some programs. There are 2 national honor societies.

Faculty/Classroom: 35% of faculty are male; 65% are female. All teach and do research. No introductory courses are taught by graduate students.

Admissions: 43% of the 2009-2010 applicants were accepted. The SAT scores for the 2009-2010 freshman class were: Critical Reading--31% below 500, 55% between 500 and 599, 13% between 600 and 700, and 1% above 700; Math--16% below 500, 47% between 500 and 599, 34% between 600 and 700, and 4% above 700; Writing--26% below 500, 51% between 500 and 599, 22% between 600 and 700, and 1% above 700. The ACT scores were 20% below 21, 28% between 21 and 23, 34% between 24 and 26, 14% between 27 and 28, and 4% above 28.

Requirements: The SAT or ACT is required. In addition, applicants must graduate from an accredited secondary school with 16 units, including 4 of English, 3 of math, 2 of lab science, 1 of history, and 6 of other college-preparatory subjects. The college also advises advanced chemistry or physics with lab and an extra unit of math. Interviews are recommended. Letters of reference from a guidance counselor and a science or math teacher and 2 student essays are required. AP and CLEP credits are accepted. Important factors in the admissions decision are evidence of special talent, recommendations by school officials, and advanced placement or honors courses.

Procedure: Freshmen are admitted in fall. Entrance exams should be taken by December of the senior year. There are early admissions and deferred admissions plans. Applications should be filed by February 1 for fall entry. The fall 2009 application fee was $70. Notifications are sent April 1. Applications are accepted on-line.

Transfer: 224 transfer students enrolled in 2008-2009. Applicants must have a minimum GPA of 2.5. Those with 1 year or less of college credit must submit secondary school transcripts. 30 of 124 credits required for the bachelor's degree must be completed at MCPHS.

Visiting: There are regularly scheduled orientations for prospective students, including a campus tour and information sessions. There are guides for informal visits, and visitors may sit in on classes. To schedule a visit, contact the Admissions Office.

Financial Aid: The average freshman award in 2009-2010 was $14,986. 20% of undergraduate students work part-time. Average annual earnings from campus work are $1200. MCPHS is a member of CSS. The FAFSA is required. The deadline for filing freshman financial aid applications for fall entry is March 15.

International Students: There are 153 international students enrolled. The school actively recruits these students. They must take the TOEFL with a minimum score of 550 on the paper-based TOEFL (PBT) or 79 on the Internet-based version (iBT) and the college's own test. They must also take the SAT or ACT.

Computers: Wireless access is available. MPCHS provides Internet access in dorms, computer labs, hallway kiosks, and the library. There are more than 500 computers available to students. All students may access the system. There are no time limits and no fees. It is strongly recommended that all students have a personal computer.

Graduates: From July 1, 2008 to June 30, 2009, 279 bachelor's degrees were awarded. The most popular majors were pharmacy (64%), nursing (8%), and dental hygiene (6%). 150 companies recruited on campus in 2008-2009. In an average class, 19% graduate in 3 years or less, 60% graduate in 4 years or less, 66% graduate in 5 years or less, and 69% graduate in 6 years or less.

Admissions Contact: Kathleen Ryan, Executive Director of Admissions. A campus DVD is available. E-mail: *admissions@mcphs.edu* Web: *www.mcphs.edu*

MASSACHUSETTS INSTITUTE OF TECHNOLOGY   D-2

Cambridge, MA 02139   (617) 253-3400; (617) 258-8304

Full-time: 2300 men, 1901 women	**Faculty:** 1018; I, ++$
Part-time: 16 men, 15 women	**Ph.D.s:** 98%
Graduate: 4236 men, 1916 women	**Student/Faculty:** 4 to 1
Year: 4-1-4, summer session	**Tuition:** $37,782
Application Deadline: January 1	**Room & Board:** $11,360
Freshman Class: 15663 applied, 1676 accepted, 1072 enrolled	
SAT CR/M/W: 715/770/710	**ACT:** 33 **MOST COMPETITIVE**

Massachusetts Institute of Technology, founded in 1861, is a private, independent institution offering programs in architecture and planning, engineering, humanities, arts, and social sciences, management, science, and health sciences, and technology. There are 5 undergraduate schools and 6 graduate schools. In addition to regional accreditation, MIT has baccalaureate program accreditation with AACSB, ABET, and CSAB. The 7 libraries contain 3.1 million volumes, 2.4 million microform items, and 41,523 audio/video tapes/CDs/DVDs, and subscribe to 60,105 periodicals including electronic. Computerized library services include interlibrary loans, database searching, Internet access, and laptop Internet portals. Special learning facilities include an art gallery, radio station, TV station, and numerous labs and centers. The 168-acre campus is in an urban area 1 mile north of Boston. Including any residence halls, there are 142 buildings.

Student Life: 91% of undergraduates are from out of state, mostly the Middle Atlantic. Students are from 50 states, 92 foreign countries, and Canada. 36% are white; 26% Asian American; 13% Hispanic. The average age of freshmen is 18; all undergraduates, 20. 3% do not continue beyond their first year; 97% remain to graduate.

Housing: 3150 students can be accommodated in college housing, which includes single-sex and coed dorms, on-campus apartments, and married student housing. In addition, there are language houses, special-interest houses, fraternity houses, off-campus independent living groups, and non-Greek cooperative houses. On-campus housing is guaranteed for all 4 years. 74% of students live on campus. Upperclassmen may keep cars.

Activities: 50% of men belong to 2 local and 25 national fraternities; 34% of women belong to 6 national sororities. Groups on campus include art, band, cheerleading, chess, choir, chorale, chorus, computers, dance, debate, drama, environmental, ethnic, film, gay, honors, international, jazz band, literary magazine, marching band, musical theater, newspaper, orchestra, photography, political, professional, radio and TV, religious, social, social service, student government, symphony, and yearbook. Popular campus events include Independent Activities Period and Spring Weekend.

Sports: There are 18 intercollegiate sports for men and 17 for women, and 20 intramural sports for men and 20 for women. Facilities include an athletic complex with 10 buildings and 26 acres of playing fields.

Disabled Students: Facilities include wheelchair ramps, elevators, special parking, specially equipped restrooms, special class scheduling, lowered drinking fountains, lowered telephones. wheelchair lifts, and automatic doors. An assistive technology lab and assistance with library services are available, upon determination of need.

Services: Counseling and information services are available, as is tutoring in most subjects. There is a reader service for the blind. Accommodations for students with documented disabilities are determined on an individual basis.

Campus Safety and Security: Measures include 24-hour foot and vehicle patrol, emergency notification system, self-defense education, and security escort services. There are shuttle buses, emergency telephones, and lighted pathways/sidewalks. Automated external defibrillators (AEDs) are stationed across campus.

Programs of Study: MIT confers B.S. degrees. Master's and doctoral degrees are also awarded. Bachelor's degrees are awarded in BIOLOGICAL SCIENCE (biology/biological science and neurosciences), BUSINESS (management science), COMMUNICATIONS AND THE ARTS (creative writing, digital communications, linguistics, literature, media arts, and music), COMPUTER AND PHYSICAL SCIENCE (chemistry, computer science, earth science, mathematics, physics, and science technology), ENGINEERING AND ENVIRONMENTAL DESIGN (aeronautical engineering, aerospace studies, architecture, biomedical engineering, chemical engineering, civil engineering, electrical/electronics engineering, engineering, environmental engineering, materials engineering, materials science, mechanical engineering, nuclear engineering, and ocean engineering), SOCIAL SCIENCE (anthropology, archeology, cognitive science, economics, French studies, history, humanities, philosophy, political science/government, Spanish studies, and urban studies). Engineering is the largest.

Required: To graduate, students must fulfill the General Institute Requirements, as well as communication and phys ed requirements, and earn an additional 180 to 198 credit units, while fulfilling departmental program requirements. The General Institute Requirements consist of 6 courses in science, 1 in lab science, 2 in restricted science and technolo-

gy electives, and 8 in humanities, arts, and social sciences for a total of 17 courses.

Special: MIT offers cross-registration with Harvard, Wellesley, the Massachusetts College of Art and Design, and the School of the Museum of Fine Arts. Internships are offered in a number of programs. Study abroad is offered at the Cambridge University in England as part of the Cambridge-MIT Undergraduate Exchange. The Department of Aeronautics and Astronautics and Materials, Science, and Engineering have specific exchange programs. The Undergraduate Research Opportunities Program (UROP) offers students research work with faculty. There are 10 national honor societies, including Phi Beta Kappa.

Faculty/Classroom: 79% of faculty are male; 21% are female. All teach and do research. No introductory courses are taught by graduate students.

Admissions: 11% of the 2009-2010 applicants were accepted. The SAT scores for the 2009-2010 freshman class were: Critical Reading--1% below 500, 5% between 500 and 599, 34% between 600 and 700, and 60% above 700; Math--12% between 600 and 700 and 88% above 700; Writing--6% between 500 and 599, 34% between 600 and 700, and 60% above 700. The ACT scores were 1% between 24 and 26, 4% between 27 and 28, and 95% above 28. All of the current freshmen were in the top fifth of their class. 232 freshmen graduated first in their class.

Requirements: The SAT or ACT is required. The ACT Optional Writing test is also required. In addition, 2 SAT Subject tests, including 1 math and 1 science, are required. 14 academic units are recommended, including 4 each of English, math, and science, 2 of social studies, and a foreign language. The GED is accepted. Essays, 2 teacher evaluations, an official transcript, and a guidance counselor report are required. An interview is strongly recommended. AP credits are accepted.

Procedure: Freshmen are admitted in the fall. Entrance exams should be taken by the January test date. There are early admissions and deferred admissions plans. Applications should be filed by January 1 for fall entry. The fall 2008 application fee was $75. Notifications are sent March 20. Applications are accepted on-line. 455 applicants were on a recent waiting list, 78 were accepted.

Transfer: 18 transfer students enrolled in 2008-2009. Applicants must have a minimum of 2 semesters but not more than 5 semesters of college at the time of enrollment. Transfer credit is assessed on a course by course basis. Transfer students must complete at least 3 semesters at MIT for the bachelor's degree, and only U.S. citizens and permanent residents are allowed to apply for spring entry. Others may apply for entry in the fall.

Visiting: There are regularly scheduled orientations for prospective students, including daily tours (Monday through Friday) preceded by an information session with admissions staff. Visitors may sit in on classes and stay overnight. To schedule a visit, contact the Office of Admissions at (617) 253-3400.

Financial Aid: In 2009-2010, 87% of all full-time freshmen and 76% of continuing full-time students received some form of financial aid. 67% of all full-time freshmen and 63% of continuing full-time students received need-based aid. The average freshman award was $32,430. Need-based scholarships or need-based grants averaged $35,271 ($57,389 maximum); need-based self-help aid (loans and jobs) averaged $3260 ($4750 maximum). 64% of undergraduate students work part-time. Average annual earnings from campus work are $2930. The average financial indebtedness of the 2009 graduate was $15,043. MIT is a member of CSS. The CSS/Profile, FAFSA, parent W-2s and 1040s, and the business tax form are required. The deadline for filing freshman financial aid applications for fall entry is February 15.

International Students: There are 394 international students enrolled. The school actively recruits these students. They must take the SAT or ACT. Non-English speakers may substitute the TOEFL for the SAT or ACT.

Computers: Wireless access is available. Students may use the wireless network with their own computers; students in dorms can access wireless as well as wired networks. All students have their own computers and/or loaners. In addition, there are more than 1000 public-access computers on campus. All students may access the system at all times. There are no time limits and no fees.

Graduates: From July 1, 2008 to June 30, 2009, 1146 bachelor's degrees were awarded. The most popular majors were computer science and engineering (11%), mathematics (8%), and mechanical engineering (7%). 265 companies recruited on campus in 2008-2009. In an average class, 2% graduate in 3 years or less, 83% graduate in 4 years or less, 90% graduate in 5 years or less, and 91% graduate in 6 years or less. Of the 2008 graduating class, 37% were enrolled in graduate school within 6 months of graduation and 47% were employed.

Admissions Contact: Stuart Schmill, Dean of Admissions.
E-mail: *admissions@mit.edu* Web: *www.mit.edu*

MASSACHUSETTS MARITIME ACADEMY — E-4
Buzzards Bay, MA 02532-1803 (508) 830-5000
(800) 544-3411; (508) 830-5077

Full-time: 820 men, 105 women **Faculty:** n/av
Part-time: 40 men, 10 women **Ph.D.s:** n/av
Graduate: 40 men, 5 women **Student/Faculty:** n/av
Year: semesters **Tuition:** $6340 ($20,000)
Application Deadline: see profile **Room & Board:** $9000
Freshman Class: n/av
SAT or ACT: required **COMPETITIVE**

Massachusetts Maritime Academy, founded in 1891, is the oldest continuously operating maritime academy in the country. Cooperative educational learning and leadership training opportunities prepare graduates for professional positions within private industry or, if opted, military commissions. Figures in the above capsule and this profile are approximate. The library contains 40,171 volumes, 11,674 microform items, and 1113 audio/video tapes/CDs/DVDs, and subscribes to 505 periodicals including electronic. Computerized library services include interlibrary loans, database searching, Internet access, and laptop Internet portals. Special learning facilities include a learning resource center, planetarium, full bridge-training simulator, oil-spill management simulator, liquid cargo-handling simulator, and computer-aided design lab. The 55-acre campus is in a small town 60 miles south of Boston. Including any residence halls, there are 9 buildings.

Student Life: 70% of undergraduates are from Massachusetts. Others are from 26 states and 11 foreign countries. 73% are from public schools. 90% are white. The average age of freshmen is 18; all undergraduates, 21. 15% do not continue beyond their first year; 70% remain to graduate.

Housing: 800 students can be accommodated in college housing, which includes coed dorms. On-campus housing is guaranteed for all 4 years. 97% of students live on campus; of those, 35% remain on campus on weekends. Alcohol is not permitted. All students may keep cars.

Activities: There are no fraternities or sororities. There are 15 groups on campus, including band, choir, chorus, computers, drill team, jazz band, marching band, newspaper, photography, professional, religious, scuba, social service, student government, and yearbook. Popular campus events include Ring Dance, Emory Rice Day, and Recognition.

Sports: There are 8 intercollegiate sports for men and 6 for women, and 13 intramural sports for men and 5 for women. Facilities include football and baseball fields, a pistol range, outdoor tennis and basketball courts, a sailing center, an Olympic-size swimming pool, 2 weight rooms, 3 multipurpose handball courts, and wrestling courts and fitness rooms. An indoor gym/auditorium seats 2500.

Disabled Students: 90% of the campus is accessible. Facilities include wheelchair ramps, elevators, special parking, and specially equipped restrooms.

Services: Counseling and information services are available, as is tutoring in most subjects.

Campus Safety and Security: Measures include 24-hour foot and vehicle patrol. There are lighted pathways/sidewalks.

Programs of Study: MMA confers B.S. degrees. Master's degrees are also awarded. Bachelor's degrees are awarded in BUSINESS (international business management and transportation management), ENGINEERING AND ENVIRONMENTAL DESIGN (environmental engineering, industrial engineering, and marine engineering). Marine engineering is the strongest academically and the largest.

Required: All students must complete 164 credit hours with a minimum of 60 hours in the major and a GPA of 2.0. Requirements include 4 courses in phys ed, 2 each in chemistry and naval science, and 1 each in algebra/trigonometry, introduction to computers, English composition, American literature, Western civilization, economics, analysis, American government, first aid, admiralty law, introduction to marine transportation, introduction to marine engineering, and calculus. All students must complete at least 1 sea term.

Special: MMA offers a junior-year internship in a commercial shipping program. Educational experience includes a minimum of 120 days aboard a training ship, with visits to foreign ports. There are cooperative programs in facilities and environmental engineering and in marine safety and environmental protection. A dual major is available in marine engineering and marine transportaton. A concentration is available in emergency management.

Faculty/Classroom: 96% of faculty are male; 4% are female. All teach undergraduates, and 3% do research. No introductory courses are taught by graduate students. The average class size in an introductory lecture is 25; in a laboratory, 12; and in a regular course, 22.

Requirements: The SAT or ACT is required. In addition, applicants must have graduated from an accredited secondary school or hold a GED certificate. They should have completed 16 Carnegie units, including 4 in English, 3 in math, and 2 each in a foreign language, science, and social science. An essay is required, and an interview is strongly recommended. A GPA of 2.0 is required. AP and CLEP credits are accept-

ed. Important factors in the admissions decision are advanced placement or honors courses, leadership record, and extracurricular activities record.

Procedure: Freshmen are admitted fall. There are early decision, deferred admissions and rolling admissions plans. Application deadlines are open. The fall 2009 application fee was $50. Applications are accepted on-line.

Transfer: Students must have a minimum GPA of 2.0. 30 of 164 credits required for the bachelor's degree must be completed at MMA.

Visiting: There are regularly scheduled orientations for prospective students, including a campus tour and an admissions interview. An optional overnight visit can be arranged. There are also open house programs and guides for informal visits. To schedule a visit, contact Admissions.

Financial Aid: MMA is a member of CSS. The CSS/Profile, the FAFSA, and the college's own financial statement are required. Check with the school for current application deadlines.

International Students: They must take the TOEFL. They must also take the SAT or ACT.

Computers: All students may access the system 8 A.M. to 11 P.M. There are no time limits and no fees. All students are required to have a personal computer.

Admissions Contact: Dean of Enrollment Services. A campus DVD is available. E-mail: admissions@maritime.edu Web: www.maritime.edu

MERRIMACK COLLEGE — E-2
North Andover, MA 01845 (978) 837-5100; (978) 837-5133

Full-time: 900 men, 925 women **Faculty:** n/av
Part-time: 115 men, 125 women **Ph.D.s:** 77%
Graduate: 5 men, 45 women **Student/Faculty:** n/av
Year: semesters, summer session **Tuition:** $29,800
Application Deadline: see profile **Room & Board:** $11,000
Freshman Class: n/av
SAT or ACT: recommended **COMPETITIVE**

Merrimack College, founded in 1947 by the Augustinian clergy of the Roman Catholic Church, is a private institution that offers undergraduate programs in science, engineering, business administration, and liberal arts. Figures in the above capsule and this profile are approximate. In addition to regional accreditation, Merrimack has baccalaureate program accreditation with ABET. The library contains 118,420 volumes, 12,238 microform items, and 2134 audio/video tapes/CDs/DVDs, and subscribes to 896 periodicals including electronic. Computerized library services include interlibrary loans, database searching, and Internet access. Special learning facilities include a learning resource center, art gallery, planetarium, TV station, chemistry center, observatory, and center for the arts. The 220-acre campus is in a suburban area 25 miles north of Boston. Including any residence halls, there are 34 buildings.

Student Life: 72% of undergraduates are from Massachusetts. Others are from 29 states, 13 foreign countries, and Canada. 60% are from public schools. 78% are white. The average age of freshmen is 18; all undergraduates, 20. 18% do not continue beyond their first year; 74% remain to graduate.

Housing: 1590 students can be accommodated in college housing, which includes single-sex and coed dorms and on-campus apartments. In addition, there are special-interest houses and international, wellness, and theme housing, including Austin Scholars housing. On-campus housing is guaranteed for all 4 years. 76% of students live on campus; of those, 90% remain on campus on weekends. Upperclassmen may keep cars.

Activities: 3% of men belong to 3 national fraternities; 5% of women belong to 3 national sororities. There are 45 groups on campus, including art, cheerleading, choir, chorale, chorus, computers, dance, drama, ethnic, gay, honors, international, jazz band, literary magazine, musical theater, newspaper, pep band, photography, political, professional, radio and TV, religious, social, social service, and student government. Popular campus events include Springfest, Peace and Social Justice Awareness Week, and Global Village.

Sports: There are 8 intercollegiate sports for men and 8 for women, and 6 intramural sports for men and 6 for women. Facilities include an athletic complex, including an ice rink, a basketball court, an aerobics studio, and an exercise room and outdoor facilities including 2 sets of tennis courts, baseball, football, softball, soccer, lacrosse, and field hockey fields, and a turf field.

Disabled Students: All of the campus is accessible. Facilities include wheelchair ramps, elevators, special parking, specially equipped restrooms, special class scheduling, lowered drinking fountains, and lowered telephones.

Services: Counseling and information services are available, as is tutoring in every subject. Math, science, and writing resource centers are available to all students.

Campus Safety and Security: Measures include 24-hour foot and vehicle patrol, emergency notification system, self-defense education, and security escort services. There are shuttle buses, emergency telephones, and lighted pathways/sidewalks. An and Rape Aggressive Defense program is available through police services.

Programs of Study: Merrimack confers B.A. and B.S. degrees. Associate and master's degrees are also awarded. Bachelor's degrees are awarded in BIOLOGICAL SCIENCE (biochemistry and biology/ biological science), BUSINESS (accounting, business administration and management, business economics, international business management, and marketing/retailing/merchandising), COMMUNICATIONS AND THE ARTS (communications, English, and modern language), COMPUTER AND PHYSICAL SCIENCE (chemistry, computer science, mathematics, and physics), EDUCATION (elementary education and secondary education), ENGINEERING AND ENVIRONMENTAL DESIGN (civil engineering, electrical/electronics engineering, and environmental science), HEALTH PROFESSIONS (allied health, predentistry, premedicine, and sports medicine), SOCIAL SCIENCE (economics, history, philosophy, political science/government, prelaw, psychology, religion, and sociology). Science, engineering, and business are the strongest academically. Business, psychology, and sports medicine are the largest.

Required: All students are required to complete 50% of degree in the liberal arts with a variety of courses that must include 3 each in humanities, social science, and math and science, 2 each in theology and philosophy, and 1 each in English composition and freshman seminar. Students also must maintain a minimum GPA of 2.0 while taking a total of 120 credit hours, including 30 in the major.

Special: Merrimack offers cooperative programs in business, engineering, liberal arts, and computer science, cross-registration through the Northeast Consortium, internships in all arts and science programs, study abroad in 15 countries, and a Washington semester at American University. Work-study programs, a 5-year combined B.A.-B.S. degree in many major fields, and dual and self-designed majors are available. General studies, nondegree study, and pass/fail options are possible. There are 7 national honor societies and 3 departmental honors programs.

Faculty/Classroom: 58% of faculty are male; 42% are female. All teach undergraduates, 60% do research, and 60% do both. No introductory courses are taught by graduate students. The average class size in an introductory lecture is 25; in a laboratory, 15; and in a regular course, 15.

Admissions: 4 freshmen graduated first in their class in a recent year.

Requirements: The SAT or ACT is recommended. In addition, for business administration, humanities, and social science majors, Merrimack recommends that applicants complete 4 units of English, 3 each of math and science, 2 of social studies, and a foreign language. For other majors, an additional math course and 1 additional course in science are needed. An essay is required, and an interview is recommended. Applicants should have completed 16 Carnegie units. Merrimack requires applicants to be in the upper 50% of their class. A GPA of 2.7 is required. AP and CLEP credits are accepted. Important factors in the admissions decision are recommendations by school officials, advanced placement or honors courses, and leadership record.

Procedure: Freshmen are admitted fall and spring. Entrance exams should be taken during the spring of the junior year and the fall of the senior year. There is a deferred admissions plan. Check with the school for current application deadlines. The fall 2009 application fee was $60. Applications are accepted on-line. A waiting list is maintained.

Transfer: 103 transfer students enrolled in a recent year. Applicants must have maintained a minimum 2.5 GPA; some programs require a higher GPA. Transfer students must complete the transfer application and essay and must submit official college/university transcript (from each college/university attended), course descriptions of all courses completed from each college/university (needed for evaluation and determination of transfer credit), and a letter of recommendation. The SAT, an interview, and a letter of recommendation are recommended. A high school transcript and an official AP or CLEAP score report (if applicable) are required of the transfer applicant with fewer than 30 semester hours of college-level credit completed at the time of application. 45 of 128 credits required for the bachelor's degree must be completed at Merrimack.

Visiting: There are regularly scheduled orientations for prospective students, including campus open houses (total of 3) and several Saturday information sessions for prospective freshman candidates during the fall months. Transfer students have 1 fall semester open house/information session and 2 during the winter/spring months. Additionally, the admissions office hosts weekly information sessions and interviews throughout the calendar year. All open houses and information sessions for prospective freshman and transfer students include curriculum information, application process information, student life information, housing information and financial aid/scholarship information. Tours of the campus by current Merrimack students are provided at all campus events and interviews. Visitors may sit in on classes. To schedule a visit, contact the Office of Admissions.

Financial Aid: In a recent year, 88% of all full-time freshmen and 78% of continuing full-time students received some form of financial aid. 81% of all full-time freshmen and 70% of continuing full-time students received need-based aid. The average freshman award was $17,500. 78% of undergraduate students work part-time. Average annual earnings from campus work are $1800. The average financial indebtedness of a recent graduate was $25,000. Merrimack is a member of CSS. The FAFSA is required. Check with the school for current application deadlines.

International Students: There were 27 international students enrolled in a recent year. The school actively recruits these students. They must take the TOEFL with a minimum score of 550 on the paper-based TOEFL (PBT) or 75 on the Internet-based version (iBT).

Computers: Wireless access is available. The campus center has computers available for commuter students, and the library has several computer labs available to all students. Both buildings are wireless. All students may access the system. There are no time limits and no fees. It is strongly recommended that all students have a personal computer. The business school provides a laptop to each student as part of its tuition.

Graduates: In a recent year, 530 bachelor's degrees were awarded. The most popular majors were marketing (10%), psychology (10%), and management (9%). 169 companies recruited on campus in a recent year. In an average class, 53% graduate in 4 years or less, 70% graduate in 5 years or less, and 71% graduate in 6 years or less. Of a recent graduating class, 8% were enrolled in graduate school within 6 months of graduation, and 93% were employed.

Admissions Contact: Vice President for Enrollment Management. E-mail: *admissions@merrimack.edu* Web: *www.merrimack.edu*

MONTSERRAT COLLEGE OF ART | E-2

Beverly, MA 01915

(978) 921-4242
(800) 836-0487; (978) 921-4241

Full-time: 100 men, 180 women	**Faculty:** n/av
Part-time: 10 men, 15 women	**Ph.D.s:** 16%
Graduate: none	**Student/Faculty:** n/av
Year: semesters	**Tuition:** $24,000
Application Deadline: open	**Room & Board:** $7000
Freshman Class: n/av	
SAT or ACT: required	**SPECIAL**

Montserrat College of Art, founded in 1970, is a private residential, professional institution offering degrees in painting and drawing, fine arts, printmaking, graphic design, illustration, photography, and sculpture, with a complementary program in art education. Figures in the above capsule and this profile are approximate. In addition to regional accreditation, Montserrat has baccalaureate program accreditation with ACBSP and NASAD. The library contains 11,484 volumes and 677 audio/video tapes/CDs/DVDs, and subscribes to 79 periodicals including electronic. Computerized library services include interlibrary loans and database searching. Special learning facilities include a learning resource center and art gallery. The 10-acre campus is in a suburban area 26 miles north of Boston. Including any residence halls, there are 17 buildings.

Student Life: 50% of undergraduates are from out of state, mostly the Northeast. Students are from 19 states. 93% are white. The average age of freshmen is 19; all undergraduates, 23. 49% do not continue beyond their first year; 49% remain to graduate.

Housing: 162 students can be accommodated in college housing, which includes single-sex and coed on-campus apartments. In addition, there is quiet housing. All housing is smoke-free. On-campus housing is available on a first-come, first-served basis and is available on a lottery system for upperclassmen. 52% of students commute. Alcohol is not permitted. All students may keep cars.

Activities: There are no fraternities or sororities. There are 6 groups on campus, including art, international, literary magazine, newspaper, radio and TV, social, and student government. Popular campus events include Forum Days, Halloween and holiday parties, and gallery openings.

Sports: There are 2 intramural sports for men and 2 for women. Montserrat uses the facilities of the local YMCA.

Disabled Students: 50% of the campus is accessible. Facilities include wheelchair ramps, elevators, special parking, specially equipped restrooms, and special class scheduling.

Services: Counseling and information services are available, as is tutoring in some subjects, including art history. There is remedial writing and a reader service for students with dyslexia.

Campus Safety and Security: There are emergency telephones and lighted pathways/sidewalks. In addition, there is a security guard in the main building and resident assistants trained in first aid and CPR who patrol the buildings.

Programs of Study: Montserrat confers B.F.A. degrees. Bachelor's degrees are awarded in COMMUNICATIONS AND THE ARTS (fine arts, graphic design, illustration, painting, photography, printmaking, and sculpture), EDUCATION (art education).

Required: To graduate, all students are required to complete 120 credits, including 78 in studio courses and 42 in liberal arts courses, with a 2.0 GPA. Requirements include 12 credits in art history, 9 in humanitites, and 6 each in English composition and liberal arts. Distribution requirements include 33 credits freshman year, 30 sophomore and junior year, and 27 senior year. To enter the senior program, Montserrat students must have a portfolio. During semester-end evaluations, each student displays work from all courses and is evaluated by a faculty panel.

Special: Montserrat is a member of the Northeast Consortium of Colleges and Universities in Massachusetts, which allows students to take classes at any member college for the same cost. Credit study is available through the continuing education department. Montserrat also offers internships, summer study in New York City or Italy, dual and student-designed majors in fine arts and in art education, and a mobility program that allows students to spend a semester at another school within the Association of Independent Colleges of Art and Design.

Faculty/Classroom: 44% of faculty are male; 55% are female. All teach undergraduates. The average class size in a regular course is 15.

Requirements: The SAT or ACT is required. In addition, students must submit an artist's statement, a portfolio, 2 letters of recommendation, and a high school transcript, although no specific program of study is required. A portfolio interview is strongly recommended. A GPA of 2.3 is required. AP and CLEP credits are accepted. Important factors in the admissions decision are evidence of special talent, advanced placement or honors courses, and personality/intangible qualities.

Procedure: Freshmen are admitted fall and spring. There are deferred admissions and rolling admissions plans. Application deadlines are open. The application fee is $50.

Transfer: Applicants are required to submit a portfolio, transcripts from previous colleges, and an artist's statement. An interview is recommended. 60 of 120 credits required for the bachelor's degree must be completed at Montserrat.

Visiting: There are regularly scheduled orientations for prospective students, including tours of college studios, observation of classes, and portfolio consultations. There are guides for informal visits and visitors may sit in on classes. To schedule a visit, contact the Admissions Coordinator.

Financial Aid: The FAFSA and the college's own financial statement are required. Check with the school for current application deadlines.

International Students: The school actively recruits these students. They must take the TOEFL.

Computers: Wireless access is available. The college offers computer labs for work in design, illustration, photography, and video as well as for research, writing, and communication. Computers are available in classroom and studio spaces across campus; "smart classrooms" give instructors interactive control over visuals from electronic media. Printing is available at several campus locations. Wireless access is available in the senior design and sculpture studios. All students may access the system 8 A.M. to 11 P.M. daily. There are no time limits and no fees.

Admissions Contact: Dean of Admissions and Enrollment Management. E-Mail: *admiss@montserrat.edu* Web: *www.montserrat.edu*

MOUNT HOLYOKE COLLEGE

B-3

South Hadley, MA 01075 (413) 538-2023; (413) 538-2409

Full-time: no men, 2224 women	Faculty: 224; IIB, ++$
Part-time: 5 men, 59 women	Ph.D.s: 95%
Graduate: 1 man, 15 women	Student/Faculty: 9 to 1
Year: semesters	Tuition: $39,126
Application Deadline: January 15	Room & Board: $11,450
Freshman Class: 3061 applied, 1771 accepted, 574 enrolled	
SAT CR/M/W: 660/660/670	ACT: 29

HIGHLY COMPETITIVE+

Mount Holyoke, founded in 1837, is an independent, liberal arts college and the oldest institution of higher learning for women in the United States. The 3 libraries contain 116,118 volumes, 24,173 microform items, and 9470 audio/video tapes/CDs/DVDs, and subscribe to 4119 periodicals including electronic. Computerized library services include interlibrary loans, database searching, Internet access, and laptop Internet portals. Special learning facilities include a learning resource center, art gallery, radio station, observatory, child study center, botanical garden and greenhouse, equestrian center, conference center, and centers for global initiatives, leadership, and the environment. The 800-acre campus is in a small town 90 miles west of Boston and 160 miles north of New York City. Including all residence halls, there are 62 buildings.

Student Life: 73% of undergraduates are from out of state, mostly the Northeast. Students are from 45 states, 69 foreign countries, and Canada. 59% are from public schools. 46% are white; 20% foreign nationals. The average age of freshmen is 18; all undergraduates, 21. 8% do not continue beyond their first year; 82% remain to graduate.

Housing: 2125 students can be accommodated in college housing, which includes single-sex dorms and on-campus apartments. Special accommodations are available by need. On-campus housing is guaranteed for all 4 years. 93% of students live on campus; of those, 70% remain on campus on weekends. All students may keep cars.

Activities: There are no fraternities or sororities. There are 150 groups on campus, including art, band, cheerleading, choir, chorale, chorus, computers, dance, debate, drama, environmental, ethnic, film, gay, honors, international, jazz band, literary magazine, musical theater, newspaper, orchestra, photography, political, radio and TV, religious, social, social service, student government, and symphony. Popular campus events include Glascock Intercollegiate Poetry Contest, Founders Day Ceremony, and Las Vegas Night.

Sports: There are 13 intercollegiate sports for women, and 13 intramural sports for women. Facilities include a sports and dance complex that houses 2 rehearsal dance studios, a performance dance studio, and a classroom; a gym with basketball, volleyball, and badminton courts; an 8-lane, 25-meter pool and separate diving tank; a 3,100-square-foot weight room; and a field house with a 1/8-mile 4-lane track, indoor pole vault pit, indoor long jump pit, 6 tennis courts, cardiovascular area, 5 international squash courts, and 2 racquetball courts. Outdoor facilities include 12 tennis courts, a 1/4-mile 6-lane track, field hockey, soccer, lacrosse, rugby, and softball fields, a rowing tank, a cross-country course, an equestrian center, and a 18-hole golf course.

Disabled Students: 95% of the campus is accessible. Facilities include wheelchair ramps, elevators, special parking, specially equipped restrooms, special class scheduling, lowered drinking fountains, and special housing.

Services: Counseling and information services are available, as is tutoring in every subject. The writing center is available to all students at all levels. There is a reader service for the blind. Special testing accommodations, diagnostic testing services, note-taking services, as well as readers and tutors, are available. There is also an adaptive technology lab.

Campus Safety and Security: Measures include 24-hour foot and vehicle patrol, self-defense education, and security escort services. There are shuttle buses, emergency telephones, lighted pathways/sidewalks, and controlled access to dorms/residences.

Programs of Study: Mount Holyoke confers A.B. degrees. Master's degrees are also awarded. Bachelor's degrees are awarded in AGRICULTURE (environmental studies), BIOLOGICAL SCIENCE (biochemistry, biology/biological science, and neurosciences), BUSINESS (organizational leadership and management), COMMUNICATIONS AND THE ARTS (art, art history and appreciation, classics, dance, dramatic arts, English, film arts, French, Greek, Italian, Latin, music, romance languages and literature, Russian, Russian languages and literature, Spanish, and studio art), COMPUTER AND PHYSICAL SCIENCE (astronomy, chemistry, computer science, geology, mathematics, physics, and statistics), EDUCATION (psychology education), ENGINEERING AND ENVIRONMENTAL DESIGN (architecture and engineering), SOCIAL SCIENCE (African American studies, American studies, anthropology, Asian/Oriental studies, classical/ancient civilization, economics, European studies, gender studies, geography, German area studies, history, international relations, Latin American studies, medieval studies, philosophy, political science/government, psychology, religion, social science, sociology, and women's studies). Sciences, social sciences, and international relations are the strongest academically. Biology, international relations, and English are the largest.

Required: Students must maintain a minimum GPA of 2.0 while taking 128 total credits, with 32 to 56 in the major. At least 68 credits must be earned from course work outside the major department. Students must complete 3 courses in the humanities, 2 courses each in science/math and social studies, a foreign language, a multicultural perspective course, and 6 credits in phys ed. A minor field of study is necessary for those not pursuing a double major, or an interdisciplinary major.

Special: Mount Holyoke offers students cross-registration through the Five College Consortium. Other opportunities include the 12 College Exchange Program, science and international studies internships, study abroad in 14 countries (semester or full-year), a Washington semester, work-study, student-designed majors, dual majors, a January program, accelerated degrees, nondegree study, and pass/fail options. A teacher licensure program is available. There are 2 national honor societies, including Phi Beta Kappa, and all departments have honors programs.

Faculty/Classroom: 45% of faculty are male; 55% are female. All teach and do research. No introductory courses are taught by graduate students. The average class size in an introductory lecture is 15; in a laboratory, 12; and in a regular course, 10.

Admissions: 58% of the 2009-2010 applicants were accepted. The SAT scores for the 2009-2010 freshman class were: Critical Reading--1% below 500, 17% between 500 and 599, 46% between 600 and 700, and 36% above 700; Math--4% below 500, 18% between 500 and 599, 45% between 600 and 700, and 31% above 700; Writing--1% below 500, 13% between 500 and 599, 55% between 600 and 700, and 31% above 700. The ACT scores were 4% between 21 and 23, 13% between 24 and 26, 23% between 27 and 28, and 60% above 28. 82% of the current freshmen were in the top fifth of their class; 95% were in the top two fifths. 24 freshmen graduated first in their class.

Requirements: The school recommends that applicants have 4 years each of English and foreign language, 3 each of math and science, and 2 of social studies. An essay is required and an interview is strongly recommended. AP credits are accepted. Important factors in the admissions decision are recommendations by school officials, leadership record, and advanced placement or honors courses.

Procedure: Freshmen are admitted fall. Entrance exams should be taken before the application deadline. There are early decision and deferred admissions plans. Early decision applications should be filed by November 15; regular applications, by January 15 for fall entry, along with a $60 fee. Notification of early decision is sent December 31; regular decision, April 1. Applications are accepted on-line. 292 applicants were on a recent waiting list.

Transfer: 49 transfer students enrolled in 2008-2009. A statement of good standing, transcripts of secondary school or college-level work, and an essay are required. An interview is recommended. SAT scores will be considered if submitted but are not required. 64 of 128 credits required for the bachelor's degree must be completed at Mount Holyoke.

Visiting: There are regularly scheduled orientations for prospective students, including tours, on-campus interviews, overnight stays, and meetings with professors and coaches. There are guides for informal visits, and visitors may sit in on classes and stay overnight. To schedule a visit, contact the Admission Office.

Financial Aid: In 2009-2010, 84% of all full-time freshmen and 76% of continuing full-time students received some form of financial aid. 72% of all full-time freshmen and 68% of continuing full-time students received need-based aid. The average freshman award was $35,797. 95% of undergraduate students work part-time. Average annual earnings from campus work are $2100. The average financial indebtedness of the 2009 graduate was $23,008. Mount Holyoke is a member of CSS. The CSS/Profile, FAFSA, parent and student tax returns, and noncustodial parent form are required. The priority date for freshman financial aid applications for fall entry is February 15. The deadline for filing freshman financial aid applications for fall entry is March 1.

International Students: There are 464 international students enrolled. The school actively recruits these students. They must take the TOEFL, with a minimum score of 600 on the paper-based TOEFL (PBT), if English is not their first language.

Computers: Wireless access is available. There are 586 publicly accessible computer workstations available for students on campus; students can access both the regular network and wireless system in the library, student center, and other locations throughout campus. All dorms, dining halls, libraries, and the student center are on a wireless network. All students may access the system. There are no time limits and no fees.

Graduates: From July 1, 2008 to June 30, 2009, 565 bachelor's degrees were awarded. The most popular majors were English (9%), biology (9%), and international relations (8%). 50 companies recruited on campus in 2008-2009. In an average class, 78% graduate in 4 years or less, 83% graduate in 5 years or less, and 83% graduate in 6 years or less. Of the 2008 graduating class, 16% were enrolled in graduate school within 6 months of graduation and 87% were employed.

Admissions Contact: Diane C. Anci, Dean of Admission. E-Mail: admission@mtholyoke.edu Web: www.mtholyoke.edu

MOUNT IDA COLLEGE D-2

Newton, MA 02459

(617) 928-4553; (617) 928-4507

Full-time: 400 men, 700 women	**Faculty:** 56; IIB
Part-time: 10 men, 20 women	**Ph.D.s:** 61%
Graduate: none	**Student/Faculty:** 19 to 1
Year: semesters, summer session	**Tuition:** $21,115
Application Deadline: open	**Room & Board:** $9,000
Freshman Class: n/av	
SAT or ACT: required	**LESS COMPETITIVE**

Mount Ida College, founded in 1899, is a private institution that prepares students for professional careers through a career centered curriculum that is integrated with liberal studies. Mount Ida has undergraduate schools, and is accredited with ABFSE, ADA, FIDER, and NASAD. The library contains 62,500 volumes, 68 micro-form items, 2,000 audio/video tapes/CDs/DVDs, and subscribes to 530 periodicals including electronic. Computerized library services include inter-library loans, database searching, and Internet access. Special learning facilities include a learning resource center, art gallery, radio station, TV station, communication lab, darkroom, sewing rooms, blueprint-making facility, and dental labs. The 72-acre campus is in a suburban area, 8 miles west of downtown Boston. Including residence halls, there are 18 buildings.

Student Life: 54% of undergraduates are from Massachusetts. Students are from 23 states, 33 foreign countries, and Canada. 80% are from public schools. 63% are white; 16% African American. The average age of freshmen is 19; all undergraduates, 21.

Housing: 803 students can be accommodated in college housing, which includes single-sex and coed dorms. In addition, there are honors houses and housing for students over age 21. On-campus housing is guaranteed for all 4 years. 60% of students live on campus. Upperclassmen may keep cars.

Activities: There are no fraternities or sororities. There are 25 groups on campus, including AIGA, commuter, equestrian, travel, vet technology, art, cheerleading, chess, choir, dance, drama, ethnic, fashion, gay, honors, international, literary magazine, newspaper, photography, professional, radio and TV, religious, social, social service, student government, and yearbook. Popular campus events include Welcome Week, Spring Fling, and Senior Week.

Sports: There are 7 intercollegiate sports for men and 6 for women; and 8 intramural sports for men and 10 for women. Facilities include a gym, playing fields, a fitness center, tennis courts, an outdoor swimming pool, athletic fields, and an athletic center.

Disabled Students: 75% of the campus is accessible. Facilities include wheelchair ramps, elevators, special parking, specially equipped rest rooms, special class scheduling, lowered drinking fountains, lowered telephones, and special housing.

Services: Counseling and information services are available, as is tutoring in most subjects. There is remedial math, reading, and writing. There is a program for learning disabled students, for which a fee is charged. Studies skills courses are also available. The Learning Circle is another innovative campus wide initiative that provides a professional learning specialist to assist students and monitor their academic progress.

Campus Safety and Security: Measures include 24-hour foot and vehicle patrol, self-defense education, and security escort services. There are shuttle buses, emergency telephones, and lighted pathways/sidewalks.

Programs of Study: Mount Ida confers B.A., B.S., and B.L.S. degrees. Associates degrees are also awarded. Bachelor's degrees are awarded in AGRICULTURE (equine science), BUSINESS (business administration and management, fashion merchandising, funeral home services, hospitality management services, marketing/retailing/merchandising, retailing, and small business management), COMMUNICATIONS AND THE ARTS (communications, graphic design, journalism, media arts, and radio/television technology), EDUCATION (early childhood education), ENGINEERING AND ENVIRONMENTAL DESIGN (interior design), HEALTH PROFESSIONS (veterinary science), SOCIAL SCIENCE (child psychology/development, criminal justice, fashion design and technology, law, and liberal arts/general studies). Veterinary technology, dental hygiene, and funeral service are the strongest academically. Business and veterinary technology is the largest.

Required: Candidates for a bachelor's degree must earn 128 credits with a 2.0 GPA. The distribution requirement varies for each major. 1 phys ed course is required. The all-college curriculum includes these common experiences for all students: a college success course, a junior year interdisciplinary seminar, and a senior capstone project.

Special: Internships in the form of work experience are available in each department. Work-study is provided by the college, student-designed majors, study abroad in 14 countries, exchange program with Strasbourg, France, a general studies degree, an interdisciplinary major in legal studies, non-degree study, and an accelerated degree program in funeral service are also available. There are 4 national honor societies, a freshman honors program, and 4 departmental honors programs.

Faculty/Classroom: 46% of faculty are male; 54% are female. All teach undergraduates. No introductory courses are taught by graduate students. The average class size in an introductory lecture is 25; in a laboratory it is 16; and in a regular course it is 20.

Requirements: The SAT or ACT is required. In addition, applicants are required to have 4 units of English, 2 of social studies, and 3 each of math and science. A portfolio is recommended for certain programs, while an interview is recommended for all applicants. The GED is accepted. A GPA of 2.0 is required. AP and CLEP credits are accepted. Important factors in the admissions decision are advanced placement or honors courses, evidence of special talent, and recommendations by school officials.

Procedure: Freshmen are admitted fall and spring. Entrance exams should be taken as early as possible by the junior year. There are early admissions, deferred admissions, and rolling admissions plans. Application deadlines are open. The application fee is $35. Applications are accepted on-line.

Transfer: 144 transfer students enrolled in 2008-2009. Applicants need a minimum GPA of C and must submit college and high school transcripts. 32 of 120 credits required for the bachelor's degree must be completed at Mount Ida.

Visiting: There are regularly scheduled orientations for prospective students, consisting of fall and spring open houses, Saturday sessions, and weekday appointments. There are guides for informal visits, visitors may sit in on classes, and stay overnight. To schedule a visit, contact the Admissions Office at admissions@mountida.edu.

Financial Aid: 70% of undergraduate students work part-time. Average annual earnings from campus work are $1500. The average financial indebtedness of the 2009 graduate was $19,268. Mount Ida is a member of CSS. The FAFSA is required. The priority date for freshman financial aid applications for fall entry is May 1.

International Students: There are 93 international students enrolled. The school actively recruits these students. They must take the TOEFL. They must also take the SAT or ACT.

Computers: All students may access the system. There are no time limits and no fees. It is strongly recommended that all students have a personal computer. A Mac for graphic design majors is recommended.

Graduates: From July 1, 2008 to June 30, 2009, 128 bachelor's degrees were awarded. The most popular majors were criminal justice (16%), graphic design (13%), and management (11%).

Admissions Contact: Judith A. Kaufman E-Mail: admissions@mountida.edu Web: www.mountida.edu

NEW ENGLAND CONSERVATORY OF MUSIC E-2

Boston, MA 02115 (617) 585-1101; (617) 585-1115

Full-time: 198 men, 162 women	**Faculty:** IIA, --$
Part-time: 22 men, 7 women	**Ph.D.s:** n/av
Graduate: 173 men, 221 women	**Student/Faculty:** 4 to 1
Year: semesters	**Tuition:** $30,975
Application Deadline: December 1	**Room & Board:** $11,300
Freshman Class: 1004 applied, 304 accepted, 107 enrolled	**SPECIAL**

The New England Conservatory of Music, founded in 1867, is the oldest private school of its kind in the United States. It combines classroom study of music with an emphasis on performance for talented young musicians. There are no undergraduate schools and one graduate school. In addition to regional accreditation, NEC has baccalaureate program accreditation with NASM. The 3 libraries contain 86,400 volumes, 265 microform items, and 60,000 audio/video tapes/CDs/DVDs, and subscribe to 295 periodicals including electronic. Computerized library services include inter-library loans, database searching, and Internet access. The 8-acre campus is in an urban area 2 miles south of downtown Boston. Including any residence halls, there are 4 buildings.

Student Life: 88% of undergraduates are from out of state, mostly the Northeast. Students are from 46 states, 36 foreign countries, and Canada. 75% are from public schools. 57% are white; 29% foreign nationals. The average age of freshmen is 18; all undergraduates, 21.

Housing: 169 students can be accommodated in college housing, which includes coed dorms. On-campus housing is guaranteed for the freshman year only. 75% of students commute. Alcohol is not permitted. No one may keep cars.

Activities: There are no fraternities or sororities. There are 6 groups on campus, including band, choir, chorale, chorus, gay, international, jazz band, newspaper, opera, orchestra, religious, social service, student government, and symphony. Popular campus events include visits of guest performers and 600 NEC concerts per year.

Sports: There is no sports program at NEC.

Disabled Students: All of the campus is accessible. Facilities include elevators, special parking, specially equipped rest rooms, and lowered drinking fountains.

Services: Counseling and information services are available, as is tutoring in most subjects. There is remedial writing.

Campus Safety and Security: Measures include security escort services.

Programs of Study: NEC confers B.Mus. degrees. Master's and doctoral degrees are also awarded. Bachelor's degrees are awarded in COMMUNICATIONS AND THE ARTS (applied music, jazz, music, music history and appreciation, music performance, music theory and composition, and visual and performing arts).

Required: Requirements for graduation include successful completion of all core music courses and an annual music promotional, participation in required ensembles, a minimum 2.0 GPA, an average of 120 total credits, and a senior recital.

Special: NEC offers cross-registration with Northeastern, Tufts University, and Simmons College, as well as 5 year double degree programs with Tufts University and Harvard University.

Faculty/Classroom: 68% of faculty are male; 32% are female. All teach undergraduates. No introductory courses are taught by graduate students. The average class size in an introductory lecture is 30 and in a regular course is 15.

Admissions: 30% of the 2009-2010 applicants were accepted.

Requirements: Applicants must be graduates of an accredited secondary school or have a GED. An artistic resume, repertoire list and essay is required, as is an audition after submitting the formal application. In some cases, taped auditions are accepted; these must be submitted with the admissions application. Applicants are expected to have reached an advanced level of musical accomplishment. A GPA of 2.8 is required. AP and CLEP credits are accepted. Important factors in the admissions decision are evidence of special talent, recommendations by school officials, and parents or siblings attended your school.

Procedure: Freshmen are admitted fall and spring. Entrance exams should be taken by March 1. There is a deferred admissions plan. Applications should be filed by December 1 for fall entry and November 1 for spring entry, along with a $100 fee. Notifications are sent April 1. Applications are accepted on-line. 100 applicants were on a recent waiting list, 3 were accepted.

Transfer: 23 transfer students enrolled in 2008-2009. Transfer students must audition and submit all college-level transcripts and a transfer statement. 60 of 120 credits required for the bachelor's degree must be completed at NEC.

Visiting: There are regularly scheduled orientations for prospective students, consisting of tours offered regularly during the week. Visitors may sit in on classes. To schedule a visit, contact the Admissions Office.

Financial Aid: In 2009-2010, 80% of all full-time freshmen and 98% of continuing full-time students received some form of financial aid. 61% of all full-time freshmen and 82% of continuing full-time students received need-based aid. The average freshmen award was $26,055, with $11,029 ($23,510 maximum) from need-based scholarships or need-based grants; $7,069 ($11,500 maximum) from need-based self-help aid (loans and jobs); and $10,436 ($15,500 maximum) from other non-need-based awards and non-need-based scholarships. 28% of undergraduate students work part-time. Average annual earnings from campus work is $1242. The average financial indebtedness of the 2009 graduate was $29,113. NEC is a member of CSS. The FAFSA and the college's own financial statement are required. The deadline for filing freshman financial aid applications for fall entry is December 1.

International Students: There are 47 international students enrolled. The school actively recruits these students. They must take the TOEFL with a minimum score of 500 on the paper-based TOEFL (PBT) or 61 on the Internet-based version (iBT).

Computers: Wireless access is available. There are PCs with Internet access in the computer lab, music technology classroom (doubles as a computer lab when not in use for classes), and libraries. Wireless access is available in our main and audio libraries, our student lounge, and dining hall. All students may access the system. There are no time limits and no fees.

Graduates: From July 1, 2008 to June 30, 2009, 90 bachelor's degrees were awarded. The most popular majors were performance (95%) and composition (5%). 50 companies recruited on campus in 2008-2009. Of the 2008 graduating class, 85% were enrolled in graduate school within 6 months of graduation.

Admissions Contact: Christina Daly, Acting Director of Admissions. E-Mail: admissions@newenglandconservatory.edu
Web: www.newenglandconservatory.edu

NEWBURY COLLEGE D-2

Brookline, MA 02445-5796

(617) 730-7007
(800) NEWBURY; (617) 731-9618

Full-time: 450 men, 500 women	**Faculty:** 54
Part-time: none	**Ph.D.s:** 20%
Graduate: none	**Student/Faculty:** 18 to 1
Year: semesters, summer session	**Tuition:** $20,000
Application Deadline: March 1	**Room & Board:** $9,000
Freshman Class: 1800 applied, 1460 accepted, 360 enrolled	
ACT: 20	**SAT:** recommended
	COMPETITIVE

Newbury College, founded in 1962, is a private institution offering career-relevant degree programs in business, graphic design, legal studies, computer science, interior design, communication, culinary arts, hotel and restaurant management, and psychology. There are 3 undergraduate schools. In addition to regional accreditation, Newbury has baccalaureate program accreditation with FIDER. The library contains 32,459 volumes, 74,000 microform items, 1,900 audio/video tapes/CDs/DVDs, and subscribes to 127,000 periodicals including electronic. Computerized library services include inter-library loans and database searching. Special learning facilities include a learning resource center, art gallery, radio station, and TV station. The 10-acre campus is in a suburban area 3 miles west of Boston. Including any residence halls, there are 10 buildings.

Student Life: 64% of undergraduates are from Massachusetts. Students are from 20 states, 42 foreign countries, and Canada. 60% are from public schools. 52% are white; 24% foreign nationals; 14% African American. The average age of freshmen is 19; all undergraduates, 21. 10% do not continue beyond their first year; 85% remain to graduate.

Housing: 202 students can be accommodated in college housing, which includes single-sex and coed dorms. In addition, there are special-interest houses. On-campus housing is guaranteed for the freshman year only, is available on a first-come, first-served basis, and is available on a lottery system for upperclassmen. Priority is given to out-of-town students. 50% of students commute. Alcohol is not permitted. Upperclassmen may keep cars.

Activities: There are no fraternities or sororities. There are 20 groups on campus, including debate, drama, ethnic, gay, honors, international, jazz band, literary magazine, professional, radio and TV, religious, social, social service, and student government. Popular campus events include Multicultural Week, Spring Fling, and Fall Fest.

Sports: There are 6 intercollegiate sports for men and 6 for women; and 9 intramural sports for men and 9 for women. Facilities include an off-site gym and a cardiovascular/weight room.

Disabled Students: 80% of the campus is accessible. Facilities include wheelchair ramps, elevators, special parking, and specially equipped rest rooms.

Services: Counseling and information services are available, as is tutoring in every subject. There is a reader service for the blind, and remedial math, reading, and writing.

Campus Safety and Security: Measures include 24-hour foot and vehicle patrol and security escort services. There are shuttle buses and lighted pathways/sidewalks.

Programs of Study: Newbury confers B.S. degrees. Associates degrees are also awarded. Bachelor's degrees are awarded in BUSINESS (accounting, business administration and management, hotel/motel and restaurant management, and international business management), COMMUNICATIONS AND THE ARTS (communications and graphic design), COMPUTER AND PHYSICAL SCIENCE (computer science), ENGINEERING AND ENVIRONMENTAL DESIGN (interior design), HEALTH PROFESSIONS (health care administration), SOCIAL SCIENCE (criminal justice, food production/management/services, paralegal studies, pre-law, and psychology). Legal studies and hotel and restaurant management are the strongest academically. Business administration, culinary arts, and interior design are the largest.

Required: Candidates for a bachelor's degree must earn 120 credits or 60 credits beyond the associate degree, with a 2.0 GPA. Distribution requirements include courses in math, lab science, literature, and social science, as well as 3 additional credits in arts and sciences.

Special: Internships are part of the bachelor degree program. Dual majors are available. Credits earned for associate degrees in professional areas can be applied toward the college's bachelor degree programs. There is a 3-3 law program with Massachusetts School of Law and study abroad in many countries. A fashion merchandising concentration is possible within the business administration B.S. degree. There are a freshman honors program.

Faculty/Classroom: 51% of faculty are male; 49% are female. All teach undergraduates. No introductory courses are taught by graduate students. The average class size in an introductory lecture is 20; in a laboratory it is 10; and in a regular course it is 16.

Admissions: 81% of the 2009-2010 applicants were accepted.

Requirements: The SAT or ACT is recommended. In addition, applicants must submit an application, 2 letters of recommendation, high school transcripts, and an essay. A personal interview is strongly recommended. A GPA of 2.0 is required. AP and CLEP credits are accepted. Important factors in the admissions decision are leadership record, recommendations by alumni, and extracurricular activities record.

Procedure: Freshmen are admitted fall and spring. Entrance exams should be taken following acceptance. There are early admissions, deferred admissions, and rolling admissions plans. Applications should be filed by March 1 for fall entry and November 1 for spring entry, along with a $50 fee. Notification is sent on a rolling basis. Applications are accepted on-line.

Transfer: 35 transfer students enrolled in 2008-2009. Transfer students must submit an application, 2 recommendations, high school and college transcripts, and an essay. 30 of 120 credits required for the bachelor's degree must be completed at Newbury.

Visiting: There are regularly scheduled orientations for prospective students, including fall and spring open houses, daily interviews, and campus tours. There are guides for informal visits and visitors may sit in on classes. To schedule a visit, contact the Office of Admission at info@newbury.edu.

Financial Aid: In 2009-2010, 80% of all full-time freshmen and 78% of continuing full-time students received some form of financial aid. 75% of all full-time freshmen and 75% of continuing full-time students received need-based aid. 58% of undergraduate students work part-time. Average annual earnings from campus work is $1250. Newbury is a member of CSS. The FAFSA and the college's own financial statement are required. The priority date for freshman financial aid applications for fall entry is November 1. The deadline for filing freshman financial aid applications for fall entry is March 1.

International Students: There are 230 international students enrolled. The school actively recruits these students. They must take the TOEFL.

Computers: All students may access the system. There are no time limits and no fees.

Graduates: From July 1, 2008 to June 30, 2009, 115 bachelor's degrees were awarded. The most popular majors were business management (34%), hotel and restaurant management (24%), and computer science (10%). 60 companies recruited on campus in 2008-2009. Of the 2008 graduating class, 12% were enrolled in graduate school within 6 months of graduation, and 96% were employed.

Admissions Contact: Salvadore Liberto, Vice President. E-Mail: info@newbury.edu Web: www.newbury.edu

NICHOLS COLLEGE   C-3
Dudley, MA 01571

(508) 213-2274
(800) 470-3379; (508) 943-9885

Full-time: 734 men, 425 women	Faculty: 36
Part-time: 61 men, 117 women	Ph.D.s: 61%
Graduate: 105 men, 105 women	Student/Faculty: 30 to 1
Year: semesters, summer session	Tuition: $28,040 ($25,700)
Application Deadline: open	Room & Board: $9200
Freshman Class: 2135 applied, 1553 accepted, 392 enrolled	
SAT CR/M/W: 450/470/450	ACT: 20 LESS COMPETITIVE

Nichols College, founded in 1815, is a private institution emphasizing business and liberal arts. There are campuses in Dudley, Auburn, and Worcester. There is 1 undergraduate school and 1 graduate school. The library contains 80,000 volumes, 2936 microform items, and 905 audio/video tapes/CDs/DVDs, and subscribes to 152 periodicals including electronic. Computerized library services include interlibrary loans, database searching, Internet access, and laptop Internet portals. Special learning facilities include a learning resource center, radio station, and the Robert C. Fischer Policy and Cultural Institute. The 200-acre campus is in a suburban area 20 miles south of Worcester. Including any residence halls, there are 24 buildings.

Student Life: 61% of undergraduates are from Massachusetts. Others are from 25 states, 4 foreign countries, and Canada. 88% are white. The average age of freshmen is 18; all undergraduates, 22. 34% do not continue beyond their first year; 53% remain to graduate.

Housing: 975 students can be accommodated in college housing, which includes coed dorms and on-campus apartments, substance-free housing, quiet lifestyle housing, and academic living housing. On-campus housing is guaranteed for all 4 years and is available on a lottery system for upperclassmen. 84% of students live on campus. All students may keep cars.

Activities: There are no fraternities or sororities. There are 25 groups on campus, including cheerleading, chess, computers, departmental, drama, ethnic, gay, honors, international, literary magazine, newspaper, political, professional, radio and TV, religious, social, social service, and student government. Popular campus events include Spring Weekend and 100 Days Social.

Sports: There are 8 intercollegiate sports for men and 7 for women. Facilities include a field house with basketball courts, a sauna, aerobics and weight training rooms, and athletic training facilities. There is also an athletic complex with a gym, a suspended jogging track, 2 racquetball courts, a squash court, an indoor climbing wall, and 2 fitness rooms. Outdoor facilities include 6 tennis courts, a volleyball court, and a basketball court.

Disabled Students: 67% of the campus is accessible. Facilities include wheelchair ramps, elevators, special parking, specially equipped restrooms, special class scheduling, lowered drinking fountains, and special housing. The college makes every effort to accommodate students with special needs.

Services: Counseling and information services are available, as is tutoring in most subjects. There is remedial math and writing, and ESL assistance by appointment.

Campus Safety and Security: Measures include 24-hour foot and vehicle patrol, emergency notification system, self-defense education, and security escort services. There are emergency telephones, lighted pathways/sidewalks, and access controls for dorms/residences.

Programs of Study: Nichols confers B.A. and B.S.B.A. degrees. Associate and master's degrees are also awarded. Bachelor's degrees are awarded in BUSINESS (accounting, business administration and management, business communications, human resources, international business management, management information systems, marketing/retailing/merchandising, and sports management), COMMUNICATIONS AND THE ARTS (arts administration/management and English), COMPUTER AND PHYSICAL SCIENCE (mathematics), SOCIAL SCIENCE (criminal justice, economics, history, law, and psychology). Accounting is the strongest academically. Sports management and criminal justice are the largest.

Required: All students must complete a program of study within 10 semesters and maintain a GPA of 2.0 overall and in their major. Business students need 33 hours of business core classes out of the total 122 hours required of all students for graduation. Students must complete 2 writing-intensive upper-level courses, and they must attend 28 events within the Cultural Experience: The Arts, Sciences, and Public Policy Program.

Special: Nichols offers cross-registration with the Worcester Consortium of Colleges, internships designed with departmental approval, study abroad at Regents College in London and European University, a Washington semester, a general business degree, a teacher certification program, an accelerated degree program in business administration, and nondegree study. There are 5 national honor societies, a freshman honors program, and 8 departmental honors programs.

Faculty/Classroom: 63% of faculty are male; 37% are female. All teach undergraduates and do research. No introductory courses are taught by graduate students. The average class size in an introductory lecture is 22; in a laboratory, 16; and in a regular course, 23.

Admissions: 73% of the 2009-2010 applicants were accepted. The SAT scores for the 2009-2010 freshman class were: Critical Reading--73% below 500, 24% between 500 and 599, and 3% between 600 and 700; Math--64% below 500, 27% between 500 and 599, and 9% between 600 and 700; Writing--72% below 500, 26% between 500 and 599, and 2% between 600 and 700. The ACT scores were 70% below 21, 13% between 21 and 23, 8% between 24 and 26, 7% between 27 and 28, and 2% above 28.

Requirements: The SAT or ACT is required. In addition, applicants must have graduated from an accredited secondary school or have earned a GED. Recommended preparation includes 4 years of high school English, 3 of math, and 2 each of science and social studies. A GPA of 2.0 is required. AP and CLEP credits are accepted. Important factors in the admissions decision are advanced placement or honors courses, recommendations by school officials, and personality/intangible qualities.

Procedure: Freshmen are admitted fall and spring. Entrance exams should be taken by November of the senior year. There are deferred admissions and rolling admissions plans. Application deadlines are open. Application fee is $25. Notification is sent on a rolling basis. Applications are accepted on-line.

Transfer: 40 transfer students enrolled in 2008-2009. Applicants need an average GPA of 2.6 in courses to be transferred and must submit official transcripts of all previous college study. 30 of 122 credits required for the bachelor's degree must be completed at Nichols.

Visiting: There are regularly scheduled orientations for prospective students, including meetings with faculty members and preregistration; separate orientation programs are tailored for transfers only. There are guides for informal visits, visitors may sit in on classes, and stay overnight. To schedule a visit, contact the Admissions Office.

Financial Aid: In a recent year, 90% of all full-time freshmen and 89% of continuing full-time students received some form of financial aid. 80% of all full-time freshmen and 79% of continuing full-time students received need-based aid. The average freshman award was $26,408. Need-based scholarships or need-based grants averaged $7215 ($22,610 maximum); need-based self-help aid (loans and jobs) averaged $3953 ($13,000 maximum); and non-need-based awards and non-need-based scholarships averaged $15,258 ($24,000 maximum). 17% of undergraduate students work part-time. Average annual earnings from campus work are $1008. The average financial indebtedness of a recent graduate was $27,764. The FAFSA is required. The deadline for filing freshman financial aid applications for fall entry is March 1.

International Students: There are 5 international students enrolled. The school actively recruits these students. They must take the TOEFL with a minimum score of 550 on the paper-based TOEFL (PBT), or have acceptable scores on the SAT or ACT.

Computers: Wireless access is available. Nichols students have 65 PCs available in the library, 24 in a classroom, and 8 in the alumni snack bar. All students may access the system 24 hours a day. There are no time limits and no fees. It is strongly recommended that all students have a personal computer. Nichols College has a discount agreement with Lenovo.

Graduates: From July 1, 2008 to June 30, 2009, 175 bachelor's degrees were awarded. The most popular majors were general business (23%), sport management (19%), and accounting (12%). In an average class, 45% graduate in 4 years or less, 52% graduate in 5 years or less, and 53% graduate in 6 years or less. Of the 2008 graduating class, 3% were enrolled in graduate school within 6 months of graduation, and 95% were employed.

Admissions Contact: Bob Martin, Associate Director of Admissions. E-mail: *admissions@nichols.edu* Web: *www.nichols.edu*

NORTHEASTERN UNIVERSITY | E-2

Boston, MA 02115	(617) 373-2200; (617) 373-8780
Full-time: 7751 men, 7948 women	Faculty: 984; I, av$
Part-time: none	Ph.D.s: 88%
Graduate: 3231 men, 3161 women	Student/Faculty: 16 to 1
Year: semesters, summer session	Tuition: $35,362
Application Deadline: January 15	Room & Board: $12,350
Freshman Class: 34,005 applied, 13,948 accepted, 2833 enrolled	
SAT CR/M/W: 630/660/630	HIGHLY COMPETITIVE

Northeastern University, founded in 1898, is a private research university. It offers an experiential learning program anchored in cooperative education. Students doing co-op in the United States and abroad alternate semesters of full-time study with semesters of full-time work in fields relevant to their professional interests and major. There are 6 undergraduate schools and 8 graduate schools. In addition to regional accreditation, Northeastern has baccalaureate program accreditation with AACSB, ABET, ACPE, APTA, CAHEA, CSAB, and NLN. The 3 libraries contain 966,923 volumes, 2.4 million microform items, and 17,953 audio/video tapes/CDs/DVDs, and subscribe to 31,331 periodicals including electronic. Computerized library services include interlibrary loans, database searching, Internet access, and laptop Internet portals. Special learning facilities include a learning resource center, art gallery, and radio station. The 73-acre campus is in an urban area in the heart of the Back Bay section of Boston. Including any residence halls, there are 88 buildings.

Student Life: 61% of undergraduates are from out of state, mostly the Northeast. Students are from 50 states, 108 foreign countries, and Canada. 52% are white. The average age of freshmen is 18; all undergraduates, 21. 9% do not continue beyond their first year; 75% remain to graduate.

Housing: 7853 students can be accommodated in college housing, which includes single-sex and coed dorms and on-campus apartments. In addition, there are honors houses, special-interest houses, leadership halls, and quiet, living and learning, international, wellness, multicultural, gender neutral, and community service housing. On-campus housing is guaranteed for the first three years, is available on a first-come, first-served basis, and is available on a lottery system for upperclassmen. 50% of students commute. Upperclassmen may keep cars.

Activities: 4% of men belong to 2 local and 12 national fraternities; 4% of women belong to 12 national sororities. There are 272 groups on campus, including art, band, cheerleading, chess, chorale, chorus, communications, computers, dance, debate, drama, environmental, ethnic, gay, honors, international, jazz band, literary magazine, musical theater, newspaper, orchestra, pep band, photography, political, professional, radio and TV, religious, Resident Student Association, social, social service, student government, symphony, and yearbook. Popular campus events include Springfest, Senior Week, and Tree Lighting.

Sports: There are 9 intercollegiate sports for men and 10 for women, and 24 intramural sports for men and 24 for women. Facilities include outdoor and indoor tracks, a football stadium, an indoor hockey arena, a swimming pool, indoor and outdoor tennis courts, racquetball, squash, volleyball, and basketball courts, and exercise and weight machines.

Disabled Students: 95% of the campus is accessible. Facilities include wheelchair ramps, elevators, special parking, specially equipped rest rooms, special class scheduling, lowered drinking fountains, lowered telephones, special housing, specially equipped labs, and a tunnel system connecting the major administrative and academic buildings.

Services: Counseling and information services are available, as is tutoring in most subjects and a central on-line source linking students to a range of academic services, including advising, tutoring, support centers, and enhancement opportunities. There is a reader service for the blind, and remedial math, reading, and writing.

Campus Safety and Security: Measures include 24-hour foot and vehicle patrol, emergency notification system, self-defense education, and security escort services. There are shuttle buses, emergency telephones, lighted pathways/sidewalks, controlled access to dorms/residences, and in-room safes. A fire and security alarm center monitors residence halls, academic buildings, and athletic facilities. A Campus Center for Violence Against Women produces and coordinates sexual assault and domestic violence education, awareness, and training programs for students and employees.

Programs of Study: Northeastern confers B.A., B.S., and B.F.A. degrees. Master's and doctoral degrees are also awarded. Bachelor's degrees are awarded in BIOLOGICAL SCIENCE (biochemistry, biology/ biological science, neurosciences, and toxicology), BUSINESS (accounting, business administration and management, human resources, international business management, management information systems, and marketing/retailing/merchandising), COMMUNICATIONS AND THE ARTS (advertising, art, communications, dramatic arts, English, journalism, languages, linguistics, music, performing arts, and public relations), COMPUTER AND PHYSICAL SCIENCE (applied physics, chemistry, computer programming, computer science, geology, information sciences and systems, mathematics, and physics), EDUCATION (athletic training, early childhood education, and elementary education), ENGINEERING AND ENVIRONMENTAL DESIGN (architecture, chemical engineering, civil engineering, computer engineering, computer technology, electrical/electronics engineering, electrical/electronics engineering technology, engineering, engineering technology, industrial engineering, mechanical engineering, and mechanical engineering technology), HEALTH PROFESSIONS (health science, medical laboratory science, nursing, pharmacy, physical therapy, rehabilitation therapy, and speech pathology/audiology), SOCIAL SCIENCE (African American studies, anthropology, criminal justice, economics, history, human services, interdisciplinary studies, international relations, philosophy, physical fitness/movement, political science/government, psychology, and sociology). Arts and sciences and business administration are the strongest academically. Engineering and computer science are the largest.

Required: Although each college has its own requirements, students must generally complete at least 128 semester hours with a minimum GPA of 2.0. Students must also fulfill the universitywide general education requirement.

Special: Northeastern offers paid professional internships with area companies in Boston, around the country, and throughout the world to integrate classroom instruction with professional experience. Cross-registration with the New England Conservatory of Music and Hebrew College, among other universities and colleges, study abroad in dozens of countries, a Washington semester, work-study through the university and in neighboring public and private agencies, dual majors, and student-designed majors in the arts and sciences are also offered. Nondegree adult and continuing education are available, as are programs and scholarships for racial minorities and women, and accelerated degrees in engineering, nursing, and arts and sciences. There are 11 national honor societies and a freshman honors program.

Faculty/Classroom: 61% of faculty are male; 39% are female. All teach undergraduates and do research. No introductory courses are taught by graduate students.

Admissions: 41% of the 2009-2010 applicants were accepted. The SAT scores for the 2009-2010 freshman class were: Critical Reading--5%

below 500, 27% between 500 and 599, 53% between 600 and 700, and 15% above 700; Math--2% below 500, 14% between 500 and 599, 58% between 600 and 700, and 26% above 700; Writing--4% below 500, 27% between 500 and 599, 54% between 600 and 700, and 15% above 700. The ACT scores were 7% below 21, 55% between 24 and 26, and 38% above 28. 75% of the current freshmen were in the top fifth of their class; 94% were in the top two fifths. 38 freshmen graduated first in their class.

Requirements: The SAT or ACT with Writing component is required. In addition, Northeastern recommends that applicants have 17 academic units, including 4 in English, 3 each in math, science, and social studies, and 2 each in foreign language and history. Recommended are 4 units in math and science, and a foreign language. An essay is required. AP credits are accepted. Important factors in the admissions decision are advanced placement or honors courses, leadership record, evidence of special talent, and extracurricular activities record.

Procedure: Freshmen are admitted fall and spring. Entrance exams should be taken from May of the junior year through December of the senior year. There are early admissions and deferred admissions plans. Early decision applications should be filed by November 1; regular applications, by January 15 for fall entry and November 1 for winter entry. The fall 2009 application fee was $70. Notification of early decision is sent December 31; regular decision, April 1. 4790 applicants were on the 2009 waiting list; 167 were admitted. Applications are accepted on-line.

Transfer: 589 transfer students enrolled in 2008-2009. The most successful transfer students have earned a cumulative GPA of 3.0 and have also completed the introductory-level courses for their intended majors. Transfer students with less than 27 semester hours of college-level credit must submit their high school transcripts and SAT or ACT scores. 32 of 128 credits required for the bachelor's degree must be completed at Northeastern.

Visiting: There are regularly scheduled orientations for prospective students. There are guides for informal visits. To schedule a visit, contact the Office of Undergraduate Admissions at (617) 373-2211.

Financial Aid: The CSS/Profile and FAFSA are required. The deadline for filing freshman financial aid applications for fall entry is February 15.

International Students: There are 1181 international students enrolled. The school actively recruits these students. They must take the TOEFL with a minimum score of 550 on the paper-based TOEFL (PBT) or 79 on the Internet-based version (iBT). They must also take the SAT or ACT. Minimum scores vary by program.

Computers: Wireless access is available. 26,800 simultaneous users can be accommodated on the wireless network, and there are 663 open-wired network connections. All academic buildings, classrooms, offices, and one 1200-bed residence hall are 100% wireless. All other residential halls have wireless in the lobby, lounges, and laundry rooms. All students may access the system 24 hours daily. There are no time limits and no fees. Students in the School of Architecture should have a MacBook Pro.

Graduates: From July 1, 2008 to June 30, 2009, 2808 bachelor's degrees were awarded. The most popular majors were business (21%), engineering (13%), and health sciences (11%). In an average class, 75% graduate in 6 years or less. 600 companies recruited on campus in 2008-2009. Of the 2008 graduating class, 20% were enrolled in graduate school within 6 months of graduation, and 85% were employed.

Admissions Contact: Ronne Turner, Director of Admissions. A campus DVD is available. E-mail: *admissions@neu.edu* Web: *www.northeastern.edu*

PINE MANOR COLLEGE	E-2
Chestnut Hill, MA 02467	**(617) 731-7104**
	(800) 762-1357; (617) 731-7102
Full-time: no men, 450 women	**Faculty:** 30; IIB, --$
Part-time: no men, 8 women	**Ph.D.s:** 77%
Graduate: none	**Student/Faculty:** 15 to 1
Year: semesters, summer session	**Tuition:** $32,659
Application Deadline: open	**Room & Board:** $11,670
Freshman Class: 387 applied, 364 accepted, 138 enrolled	
SAT or ACT: required	**LESS COMPETITIVE**

Pine Manor College, established in 1911, is a private liberal arts college for women. There are no undergraduate schools. The library contains 65,632 volumes, 62,386 microform items, and 1,944 audio/video tapes/CDs/DVDs, and subscribes to 272 periodicals including electronic. Computerized library services include interlibrary loans, database searching, and Internet access. Special learning facilities include a learning resource center, art gallery, radio station, TV station, a language lab. The 60-acre campus is in a suburban area 5 miles west of Boston. Including any residence halls, there are 28 buildings.

Student Life: 75% of undergraduates are from Massachusetts. Students are from 21 states, 15 foreign countries, and Canada. 39% are African American; 14% Hispanic; 13% white. The average age of freshmen is 18; all undergraduates, 20. 32% do not continue beyond their first year; 53% remain to graduate.

Housing: 481 students can be accommodated in college housing, which includes single-sex dorms. In addition, there are special-interest

houses, nonsmoking dorms, and a wellness floor (no alcohol allowed). On-campus housing is guaranteed for all 4 years. 68% of students live on campus; of those, 80% remain on campus on weekends. All students may keep cars.

Activities: There are no fraternities or sororities. There are 25 groups on campus, including student health (SHAB), interior design (ASID), minority (ALANA), psychology, art, chorus, dance, diversity, drama, environmental, ethnic, gay, honors, international, literary magazine, musical theater, newspaper, political, professional, radio and TV, religious, social, social service, student government, and yearbook. Popular campus events include Late Night Breakfast during finals, Stressbusters, and Casino Night.

Sports: There are 7 intercollegiate sports for women. Facilities include a modern gym, softball and soccer fields, cross-country trails, tennis courts, a dance studio, and a weight room.

Disabled Students: 40% of the campus is accessible. Facilities include wheelchair ramps, elevators, special parking, specially equipped restrooms, special class scheduling, lowered drinking fountains, and special housing.

Services: Counseling and information services are available, as is tutoring in every subject. There is remedial math, reading, and writing. The learning resource center has professional and peer tutoring and workshops.

Campus Safety and Security: Measures include 24-hour foot and vehicle patrol, self-defense education, and security escort services. There are shuttle buses, emergency telephones, and lighted pathways/sidewalks.

Programs of Study: PMC confers B.A. degrees. Associates and master's degrees are also awarded. Bachelor's degrees are awarded in BIOLOGICAL SCIENCE (biology/biological science), BUSINESS (business administration and management), COMMUNICATIONS AND THE ARTS (art, communications, and English), SOCIAL SCIENCE (ethics, politics, and social policy, history, and psychology). Psychology, visual arts, and biology are the largest.

Required: An outcomes-based general education program, with portfolio assessment, is a college requirement. A 4-year leadership program complements the portfolio program. This assists students in exploring inclusive and socially responsible leadership. In addition, students must maintain a minimum GPA of 2.0 and take a total of 132 semester hours.

Special: Pine Manor offers cross-registration with area colleges, internships at more than 1000 sites, and study abroad throughout the world, and at sea. A Washington semester, work-study programs, dual majors, student-designed majors, a B.A.-B.S. degree, non-degree study within continuing education, and pass/fail options for 1 course each semester also are available as is the English Language Institute for students whose native language is not English. There is 1 national honor society and a freshman honors program.

Faculty/Classroom: 26% of faculty are male; 74% are female. All teach undergraduates. No introductory courses are taught by graduate students. The average class size in an introductory lecture is 16; in a laboratory is 16; and in a regular course is 13.

Admissions: 94% of the 2009-2010 applicants were accepted.

Requirements: The SAT or ACT is required. In addition, applicants are required to have taken 4 courses in English and 3 in math. Additional courses in foreign language, social science, natural science, and elective areas are recommended. An essay is also required. An interview is recommended. The GED is accepted. AP and CLEP credits are accepted. Important factors in the admissions decision are advanced placement or honors courses, leadership record, and recommendations by school officials.

Procedure: Freshmen are admitted fall and spring. There are deferred admissions and rolling admissions plans. Application deadlines are open. Application fee is $25. Notification is sent on a rolling basis. Applications are accepted on-line.

Transfer: 24 transfer students enrolled in 2008-2009. Pine Manor requires transfer students to submit 2 letters of recommendation (1 from a professor) and college transcripts and recommends high school transcripts. The SAT or ACT also is recommended. 32 of 132 credits required for the bachelor's degree must be completed at PMC.

Visiting: There are regularly scheduled orientations for prospective students, including a campus tour and interview. There are guides for informal visits, visitors may sit in on classes, and stay overnight. To schedule a visit, contact the Admissions Office at admissions@Pmc.edu.

Financial Aid: In 2009-2010, 95% of all full-time freshmen and % of continuing full-time students received some form of financial aid. Average annual earnings from campus work are $1500. The average financial indebtedness of the 2009 graduate was $27,000. The FAFSA is required. The priority date for freshman financial aid applications for fall entry is May 1.

International Students: There are 39 international students enrolled. The school actively recruits these students. They must take the TOEFL.

Computers: Wireless access is available. Pine Manor College enjoys high-speed computing network. Students have access to e-mail, the Internet, a campus PC network, and PCs located throughout the campus.

Laptop connections are also available in some areas. Software for word processing, spreadsheets, databases, statistics, Web page development, graphic design, desktop and electronic publishing, digital media, and specialized course software is available for student use on college PCs in classrooms and labs. Students are provided with an e-mail account, network storage space for files, and 25MB of Web space on our community Web site. All students may access the system. There are no time limits and no fees.

Graduates: From July 1, 2008 to June 30, 2009, 89 bachelor's degrees were awarded. The most popular majors were psychology (25%), business administration (19%), and biology (18%). In an average class, 33% graduate in 4 years or less, 38% graduate in 5 years or less, and 40% graduate in 6 years or less.

Admissions Contact: William L. Boffi, Dean of Student Recruitment and Retention. E-Mail: *admissions@pmc.edu* Web: *www.pmc.edu*

REGIS COLLEGE D-2

Weston, MA 02493-1571

(781) 768-7100
(866) 438-7344; (781) 768-7071

Full-time: 153 men, 696 women	**Faculty:** 54; IIB, --$
Part-time: 20 men, 203 women	**Ph.D.s:** 70%
Graduate: 47 men, 567 women	**Student/Faculty:** 13 to 1
Year: semesters, summer session	**Tuition:** $28,900
Application Deadline: see profile	**Room & Board:** $12,190
Freshman Class: 1735 applied, 1270 accepted, 241 enrolled	
SAT CR/M/W: 460/455/470	**ACT:** 19 **LESS COMPETITIVE**

Regis College, founded in 1927, is a private liberal arts institution that is affiliated with the Roman Catholic Church. There is 1 graduate school. In addition to regional accreditation, Regis has baccalaureate program accreditation with CSWE, NASDTEC, and NLN. The library contains 134,669 volumes, 10,826 microform items, 7856 audio/video tapes/CDs/DVDs, and subscribes to 24,774 periodicals including electronic. Computerized library services include interlibrary loans, database searching, Internet access, and laptop Internet portals. Special learning facilities include a learning resource center, art gallery, radio station, museum of stamps and postal history, and fine arts center. The 131-acre campus is in a suburban area 12 miles west of Boston. Including any residence halls, there are 15 buildings.

Student Life: 92% of undergraduates are from Massachusetts. Others are from 18 states and 10 foreign countries. 70% are from public schools. 38% are white; 22% African American. The average age of freshmen is 18; all undergraduates, 19. 32% do not continue beyond their first year; 63% remain to graduate.

Housing: 475 students can be accommodated in college housing, which includes single-sex and coed dorms. In addition, there are quiet housing floors. On-campus housing is guaranteed for all 4 years. 60% of students live on campus; of those, 60% remain on campus on weekends. All students may keep cars.

Activities: There are no fraternities or sororities. There are 34 groups on campus, including art, band, choir, chorale, chorus, commuter, computers, dance, drama, ethnic, honors, international, literary magazine, musical theater, newspaper, photography, political, professional, radio and TV, religious, residential, SAINTS, social, social service, student government, and Tower Society. Popular campus events include Father/Daughter Dance, Role Model Brunch, and Family Weekend.

Sports: There are 8 intercollegiate sports for men and 10 for women, and 4 intramural sports for men and 4 for women. Facilities include an athletic facility, a softball diamond, a soccer field, 4 tennis courts, an aerobics and dance studio, squash courts, a pool, a sauna, and a Jacuzzi. The on-campus fitness center provides a full range of cardiovascular machines as well as free weights and Nautilus equipment.

Disabled Students: 87% of the campus is accessible. Facilities include wheelchair ramps, elevators, special parking, specially equipped restrooms, special class scheduling, lowered drinking fountains, and special housing.

Services: Counseling and information services are available, as is tutoring in most subjects. There is a reader service for the blind and remedial math, reading, and writing. There are academic support services for learning-disabled students.

Campus Safety and Security: Measures include 24-hour foot and vehicle patrol, self-defense education, and security escort services. There are shuttle buses, emergency telephones, lighted pathways/sidewalks, and controlled access to dorms/residences.

Programs of Study: Regis confers B.A., B.S.N., and B.S.W. degrees. Associate and master's degrees are also awarded. Bachelor's degrees are awarded in BIOLOGICAL SCIENCE (biochemistry and biology/biological science), BUSINESS (management science), COMMUNICATIONS AND THE ARTS (communications, dramatic arts, English, graphic design, public relations, and Spanish), COMPUTER AND PHYSICAL SCIENCE (chemistry, computer science, and information sciences and systems), EDUCATION (mathematics education and museum studies), HEALTH PROFESSIONS (nursing), SOCIAL SCIENCE (history, international relations, law, liberal arts/general studies, political

science/government, psychology, social work, and sociology). Nursing, communication, and management are the largest.

Required: To graduate, students must complete a total of 144 credits, including 8 to 12 in the major, as well as the general education program requirements with a minimum GPA of 2.0.

Special: Regis offers cross-registration with Boston, Babson, and Bentley Colleges and through the Sisters of St. Joseph Consortium. Students may study abroad at Regis affiliates in London, Ireland, and Kyoto, Japan, or through programs of other American colleges. Regis also offers internships, an accelerated degree program, a Washington semester at American University, dual and self-designed majors, work-study, nondegree study, and pass/fail options. Students have the option of pursuing a minor in addition to their major field of study. There are 10 national honor societies and a freshman honors program.

Faculty/Classroom: 17% of faculty are male; 83% are female. 72% teach undergraduates. No introductory courses are taught by graduate students. The average class size in an introductory lecture is 18; in a laboratory, 10; and in a regular course, 11.

Admissions: 73% of the 2009-2010 applicants were accepted. The SAT scores for the 2009-2010 freshman class were: Critical Reading--67% below 500, 29% between 500 and 599, 3% between 600 and 700, and 1% above 700; Math--70% below 500, 24% between 500 and 599, and 6% between 600 and 700; Writing--64% below 500, 29% between 500 and 599, and 7% between 600 and 700. The ACT scores were 73% below 21, 25% between 21 and 23, 1% between 24 and 26, and 1% between 27 and 28. 25% of the current freshmen were in the top fifth of their class; 60% were in the top two fifths.

Requirements: The SAT or ACT is required. In addition, applicants should have 4 years of English, 3 or 4 electives, 3 years of math, and 2 years each of foreign language, social studies, and natural science, including a lab science. An essay and 2 letters of recommendation are required. An interview is strongly encouraged. The GED is accepted. Online applications must be accompanied by the transcript, letters of recommendation, and official SAT or ACT scores. Regis requires applicants to be in the upper 50% of their class. A GPA of 2.5 is required. AP and CLEP credits are accepted. Important factors in the admissions decision are recommendations by school officials, extracurricular activities record, and ability to finance college education.

Procedure: Freshmen are admitted fall and spring. Entrance exams should be taken during the fall before enrollment. There are deferred admissions and rolling admissions plans. Check with the school for current application deadlines. The application fee is $50. Applications are accepted on-line.

Transfer: 47 transfer students enrolled in 2008-2009. Transfer students must complete an admission application and fee. In addition, an official high school transcript is required if the applicant has completed fewer than 9 college courses. If fewer than 16 courses have been completed, an official college transcript, 1 letter of recommendation from a professor at the previous college attended, the academic catalog of the previous college, an essay, and SAT or ACT scores are requried, in addition to health records. 64 of 144 credits required for the bachelor's degree must be completed at Regis.

Visiting: There are regularly scheduled orientations for prospective students, including a welcome tour, lunch, speaker panels, and overnight programs offering class participation. There are also guides for informal visits. To schedule a visit, contact the Admissions Office.

Financial Aid: Regis is a member of CSS. The FAFSA and the college's own financial statement are required. The priority date for freshman financial aid applications for fall entry is February 15.

International Students: There are 10 international students enrolled. The school actively recruits these students. They must take the TOEFL with a minimum score of 550 on the paper-based TOEFL (PBT) or 79 on the Internet-based version (iBT). They must also take the SAT or ACT.

Computers: Wireless access is available. Students can access network resources including e-mail, Blackboard, the Internet, and Web access to registration and grades either from their dorm room, a computer lab, or off campus through the Internet. All students may access the system. There are no time limits and no fees.

Graduates: From July 1, 2008 to June 30, 2009, 227 bachelor's degrees were awarded. The most popular majors were nursing (55%), communication (8%), and biology (8%). 15 companies recruited on campus in 2008-2009. In an average class, 51% graduate in 4 years or less, 60% graduate in 5 years or less, and 63% graduate in 6 years or less.

Admissions Contact: Office of Admission.
E-mail: *admission@regiscollege.edu* Web: *www.regiscollege.edu*

SALEM STATE COLLEGE
E-2

Salem, MA 01970
(978) 542-6200; (978) 542-6893

Full-time: 2045 men, 3425 women	**Faculty:** 296
Part-time: 631 men, 1197 women	**Ph.D.s:** 77%
Graduate: 579 men, 1988 women	**Student/Faculty:** 18 to 1
Year: semesters, summer session	**Tuition:** $5,594 ($11,734)
Application Deadline: open	**Room & Board:** $7,567
Freshman Class: 4827 applied, 4324 accepted, 1226 enrolled	
SAT or ACT: required	**LESS COMPETITIVE**

Salem State College, founded in 1854, is a public institution offering programs in liberal arts, business, education, and nursing. There are 5 undergraduate schools and one graduate school. In addition to regional accreditation, Salem State has baccalaureate program accreditation with CSWE, NASAD, NCATE, and NLN. The library contains 301,876 volumes, 566,592 microform items, and subscribes to 1,145 periodicals including electronic. Computerized library services include inter-library loans, database searching, and Internet access. Special learning facilities include a learning resource center, art gallery, radio station, TV station, and an observatory. The 62-acre campus is in an urban area 18 miles northeast of Boston. Including any residence halls, there are 19 buildings.

Student Life: 90% of undergraduates are from Massachusetts. Students are from 20 states, 40 foreign countries, and Canada. 98% are from public schools. 83% are white. The average age of freshmen is 19; all undergraduates, 24. 25% do not continue beyond their first year; 36% remain to graduate.

Housing: 1470 students can be accommodated in college housing, which includes single-sex and coed dorms and on-campus apartments. On-campus housing is available on a first-come and first-served basis. Priority is given to out-of-town students. 78% of students commute. Alcohol is not permitted. Upperclassmen may keep cars.

Activities: There are no fraternities or sororities. There are 44 groups on campus, including art, band, cheerleading, choir, chorale, chorus, communications, computers, dance, drama, ethnic, gay, honors, international, jazz band, literary magazine, musical theater, newspaper, photography, political, radio and TV, religious, social, social service, and student government. Popular campus events include Welcome Week, Arts Festival, and Senior Week.

Sports: There are 10 intercollegiate sports for men and 10 for women, and 15 intramural sports for men and 15 for women. Facilities include an athletic center with 27 facilities, including a 1600-seat gym, a 2800-seat ice rink, an 8-lane swimming pool, 4 tennis courts, a weight room, a dance studio, and a wellness fitness center.

Disabled Students: 90% of the campus is accessible. Facilities include wheelchair ramps, elevators, special parking, specially equipped rest rooms, lowered drinking fountains, and lowered telephones.

Services: Counseling and information services are available, as is tutoring in every subject. There is a reader service for the blind, and remedial math, reading, and writing.

Campus Safety and Security: Measures include 24-hour foot and vehicle patrol, self-defense education, and security escort services. There are shuttle buses, emergency telephones, and lighted pathways/sidewalks.

Programs of Study: Salem State confers B.A., B.S., B.F.A., B.G.S., B.S.B.A., B.S.Ed., B.S.N., and B.S.W. degrees. Master's degrees are also awarded. Bachelor's degrees are awarded in BIOLOGICAL SCIENCE (biology/biological science), BUSINESS (accounting, banking and finance, business administration and management, and marketing/retailing/merchandising), COMMUNICATIONS AND THE ARTS (advertising, communications, design, dramatic arts, English, fine arts, and photography), COMPUTER AND PHYSICAL SCIENCE (chemistry, computer programming, earth science, geology, and mathematics), EDUCATION (art education, business education, education, science education, and secondary education), ENGINEERING AND ENVIRONMENTAL DESIGN (cartography), HEALTH PROFESSIONS (medical laboratory technology and nursing), SOCIAL SCIENCE (criminal justice, economics, geography, history, psychology, social work, and sociology). Sciences is the strongest academically. Business administration is the largest.

Required: All students must demonstrate basic competence in reading, math, and computer literacy, and are required to take a distribution of classes that includes 36 to 38 credits in humanities, sciences, and social sciences. Specific courses required are English composition, speech, physical education, and the first-year seminar. All core and distribution requirements may be waived if the student passes a departmentally prescribed exemption exam. A minimum GPA of 2.0 and a total of 127 credits, with 36 in the major, are needed to graduate.

Special: Study abroad is available in 3 countries. Cross-registration through a consortium, internships, work-study programs, a Washington semester, student-designed and dual majors, B.A.-B.S. degrees, and a general studies degree are offered. Life experience credit, non-degree study, and pass/fail options also are possible. There are 13 national honor societies, a freshman honors program, and 9 departmental honors programs.

Faculty/Classroom: All teach undergraduates. No introductory courses are taught by graduate students. The average class size in an introductory lecture is 22; in a laboratory is 12; and in a regular course is 17.

Admissions: 90% of the 2009-2010 applicants were accepted.

Requirements: The SAT or ACT is required. In addition, Salem State requires that applicants earn 16 credits, including 4 years of English, 3 years each of math and science, and 2 years each of foreign language and history. Courses in music, art, drama, computer science, and psychology are suggested. Art majors must provide a portfolio. A GED is acceptable. Students with a GED, those out of school more than 3 years, and the learning disabled do not need the SAT. A GPA of 2.0 is required. AP and CLEP credits are accepted. Important factors in the admissions decision are advanced placement or honors courses, evidence of special talent, and recommendations by school officials.

Procedure: Freshmen are admitted fall. Entrance exams should be taken November and December of the senior year. There are deferred admissions and rolling admissions plans. Application deadlines are open. The application fee is $25. Applications are accepted on-line.

Transfer: 809 transfer students enrolled in 2008-2009. Transfer students are required to have a minimum GPA of 2.0 with more than 24 credits; 2.5 with fewer than 24 credits. 30 of 127 credits required for the bachelor's degree must be completed at Salem State.

Visiting: There are regularly scheduled orientations for prospective students. There are guides for informal visits and visitors may sit in on classes. To schedule a visit, contact the Admissions Office at admissions@salemstate.edu.

Financial Aid: 86% of undergraduate students work part-time. Average annual earnings from campus work is $1600. The FAFSA is required. Check with the school for current application deadlines.

International Students: There are 258 international students enrolled. The school actively recruits these students. They must take the TOEFL. They must also take the SAT or ACT.

Computers: Wireless access is available. All students may access the system. 7 days a week. There are no time limits and no fees. All students are required to have a personal computer.

Graduates: From July 1, 2008 to June 30, 2009, 845 bachelor's degrees were awarded. The most popular majors were business marketing (20%), education (12%), and psychology (10%).

Admissions Contact: Nate Bryant, Director of Admissions. E-Mail: admissions@salem.mass.edu Web: www.salemstate.edu

SIMMONS COLLEGE
E-2

Boston, MA 02115
(617) 521-2051
(800) 345-8468; (617) 521-3190

Full-time: 1746 women	**Faculty:** 188; IIA, av$
Part-time: 223 women	**Ph.D.s:** 65%
Graduate: 400 men, 2634 women	**Student/Faculty:** 9 to 1
Year: semesters, summer session	**Tuition:** $31,450
Application Deadline: April 1	**Room & Board:** $12,050
Freshman Class: 3522 applied, 2013 accepted, 357 enrolled	
SAT CR/M/W: 551/541/563	**ACT:** 24 **VERY COMPETITIVE**

Simmons College, founded in 1899, is a private institution with an undergraduate college for women that offers a comprehensive education combining the arts, sciences, and humanities with preprofessional training. All graduate programs are co-ed, with the exception of the women-only MBA program. There are 3 undergraduate schools and 5 graduate schools. In addition to regional accreditation, Simmons has baccalaureate program accreditation with ADA, APTA, CSWE, and NLN. The library contains 241,750 volumes, 13,515 microform items, and 7,867 audio/video tapes/CDs/DVDs, and subscribes to 1,873 periodicals including electronic. Computerized library services include interlibrary loans, database searching, Internet access, and laptop Internet portals. Special learning facilities include a learning resource center, art gallery, radio station, TV studio, modern language lab, physical therapy motion lab, nursing lab, and library science technology center. The 12-acre campus is in an urban area in Boston. Including any residence halls, there are 21 buildings.

Student Life: 61% of undergraduates are from Massachusetts. Others are from 36 states, 53 foreign countries, and Canada. 74% are from public schools. 64% are white. The average age of freshmen is 18; all undergraduates, 22. 26% do not continue beyond their first year; 71% remain to graduate.

Housing: 1030 students can be accommodated in college housing, which includes single-sex and coed dorms and off-campus apartments. In addition, there are special-interest houses. On-campus housing is available on a first-come, first-served basis, and is available on a lottery system for upperclassmen. 52% of students commute. No one may keep cars.

Activities: There are no fraternities or sororities. There are 79 groups on campus, including art, cheerleading, choir, chorale, chorus, dance, debate, drama, ethnic, film, gay, honors, international, literary magazine, musical theater, newspaper, orchestra, political, professional, radio and TV, religious, social, social service, student government, and yearbook. Popular campus events include Honors Convocation, May Day Breakfast, and Culture Shock.

Sports: There are 8 intercollegiate sports for women, and 4 intramural sports for women. Facilities include an 8-lane pool, a spa and sauna, 1 racquetball and 2 squash courts, 2 rowing tanks, 3 fitness rooms, a dance studio, an indoor running area, 2 volleyball courts, and a basketball court.

Disabled Students: 95% of the campus is accessible. Facilities include wheelchair ramps, elevators, special parking, specially equipped restrooms, special class scheduling, and lowered drinking fountains.

Services: Counseling and information services are available, as is tutoring in most subjects, basic freshman courses, languages, biology, chemistry, psychology, and math. There is a reader service for the blind. One on one course content tutoring, study groups for a number of the major courses are provided, study skills tutoring is provided to assist students with time management, test anxiety, motivation, and goal setting, and a math adviser is available to help students prepare to take/or retake the college required Math Competency Test.

Campus Safety and Security: Measures include 24-hour foot and vehicle patrol, emergency notification system, self-defense education, and security escort services. There are shuttle buses, emergency telephones, lighted pathways/sidewalks, closed-circuit TV, ID card access, and security training in first response and crisis intervention.

Programs of Study: Simmons confers B.A. and B.S. degrees. Master's and doctoral degrees are also awarded. Bachelor's degrees are awarded in BIOLOGICAL SCIENCE (biochemistry, biology/biological science, and nutrition), BUSINESS (banking and finance, management information systems, and marketing/retailing/merchandising), COMMUNICATIONS AND THE ARTS (art, arts administration/management, communications, English, English as a second/foreign language, French, music, public relations, and Spanish), COMPUTER AND PHYSICAL SCIENCE (chemistry, computer science, and mathematics), EDUCATION (early childhood education, elementary education, secondary education, and special education), ENGINEERING AND ENVIRONMENTAL DESIGN (environmental science), HEALTH PROFESSIONS (nursing, physical therapy, and premedicine), SOCIAL SCIENCE (African American studies, dietetics, East Asian studies, economics, food science, history, human services, international relations, philosophy, political science/government, prelaw, psychobiology, psychology, sociology, and women's studies). Physical therapy, biology, and communication are the strongest academically. Nursing, communications, and psychology are the largest.

Required: To graduate, students must complete 128 semester hours, including 24 to 48 in the major, and maintain a minimum GPA of 2.0. Eight semester hours in a supervised independent learning experience or an internship are also required. Students must also fulfill foreign language, math competency, and technology competency requirements. In addition to completing the multidisciplinary core courses, students must complete 1 course from each of the following 6 modes of inquiry categories: creative and performing arts; language, literature, and culture; quantitative analysis and reasoning; scientific inquiry; social and historical perspectives; and psychological and ethical development. A thesis is optional.

Special: Cross-registration is available with the New England Conservatory of Music, Hebrew, Emmanuel, and Wheelock Colleges, Massachusetts College of Art, Massachusetts College of Pharmacy and Health Sciences, and Wentworth Institute of Technology. Simmons offers study abroad in Europe through the Institute of European studies. A Washington semester at American University, accelerated degree programs, profit and nonprofit internship programs, a B.A.-B.S. degree, dual majors, interdisciplinary majors, student-designed majors, work-study programs, and pass/fail options are also offered. There is a dual-degree program in chemistry, pharmacy, and physician's assistant with Massachusetts College of Pharmacy. There are 3 national honor societies, a freshman honors program, and 23 departmental honors programs.

Faculty/Classroom: 25% of faculty are male; 75% are female. All teach and do research. No introductory courses are taught by graduate students. The average class size in an introductory lecture, 24, in a laboratory, 13, and in a regular course, 18.

Admissions: 57% of the 2009-2010 applicants were accepted. The SAT scores for the 2009-2010 freshman class were: Critical Reading--25% below 500, 50% between 500 and 599, 21% between 600 and 700, and 3% above 700; Math--27% below 500, 47% between 500 and 599, 25% between 600 and 700, and 1% above 700; Writing--15% below 500, 53% between 500 and 599, 29% between 600 and 700, and 3% above 700. The ACT scores were 21% below 21, 30% between 21 and 23, 28% between 24 and 26, 16% between 27 and 28, and 6% above 28. 46% of the current freshmen were in the top fifth of their class; 78% were in the top two fifths.

Requirements: The SAT or ACT is required. In addition, Simmons recommends that applicants have 4 years of English, 3 each of math, science, and social studies, and 2 of foreign language. An essay is required,

and an interview is strongly recommended. A GPA of 3.0 is required. AP and CLEP credits are accepted. Important factors in the admissions decision are advanced placement or honors courses, recommendations by school officials, and extracurricular activities record.

Procedure: Freshmen are admitted fall and spring. Entrance exams should be taken by February 1 of the senior year. There is a early decision, deferred admissions plan. Early decision applications should be filed by December 1; regular applications, by April 1 for fall entry and December 1 for spring entry, along with a $55 fee. Notification of early decision is sent January 20; regular decision, April 15. Applications are accepted on-line. A waiting list is maintained.

Transfer: 109 transfer students enrolled in 2008-2009. Applicants should have a GPA of 2.8, at least 9 college-level credit hours, official transcripts from all colleges attended, and a faculty recommendation and dean's report from the previous college attended. 48 of 128 credits required for the bachelor's degree must be completed at Simmons.

Visiting: There are regularly scheduled orientations for prospective students, including a campus tour, class attendance, an interview, and meetings with faculty and students. There are guides for informal visits; visitors may sit in on classes and stay overnight. To schedule a visit, contact the Admissions Office at (800) 345-8468.

Financial Aid: In 2009-2010, 78% of all full-time freshmen and 67% of continuing full-time students received some form of financial aid. 74% of all full-time freshmen and 65% of continuing full-time students received need-based aid. The average freshman award was $21,501. Need-based scholarships or need-based grants averaged $6,569 ($21,250 maximum); and need-based self-help aid (loans and jobs) averaged $4,804 ($10,000 maximum). 34% of undergraduate students work part-time. Average annual earnings from campus work are $2500. The average financial indebtedness of the 2009 graduate was $42,174. Simmons is a member of CSS. The FAFSA and federal tax returns or W2 forms are required. The priority date for freshman financial aid applications for fall entry is February 1. The deadline for filing freshman financial aid applications for fall entry is March 1.

International Students: There are 125 international students enrolled. The school actively recruits these students. They must take the TOEFL with a minimum score of 560 on the paper-based TOEFL (PBT) or 83 on the Internet-based version (iBT). They must also take the SAT or ACT.

Computers: Wireless access is available. Students may use the college's network and/or wireless system for personal or academic reasons, including legal media file sharing, but not for commercial purposes. There are over 630 Macintosh and Windows computers on campus available for student use. All buildings on campus include Internet access, and many are covered by our wireless network as well. All students may access the system. There are no time limits and no fees. It is strongly recommended that all students have a personal computer.

Graduates: From July 1, 2008 to June 30, 2009, 477 bachelor's degrees were awarded. The most popular majors were nursing (27%), communications (18%), and psychology (9%). 83 companies recruited on campus in 2008-2009. In an average class, 62% graduate in 4 years or less, 72% graduate in 5 years or less, and 73% graduate in 6 years or less. Of the 2008 graduating class, 27% were enrolled in graduate school within 6 months of graduation, and 68% were employed.

Admissions Contact: Catherine Childs-Capolupo, Director of Undergraduate Admission. E-Mail: *ugadm@simmons.edu*
Web: *www.simmons.edu*

SIMON'S ROCK COLLEGE OF BARD A-2
Simon's Rock College of Bard

Great Barrington, MA 01230-9702	(413) 528-7355
	(800) 235-7186; (413) 528-7334

Full-time: 170 men, 233 women	Faculty: n/av
Part-time: 3 men, 2 women	Ph.D.s: n/av
Graduate: none	Student/Faculty: n/av
Year: semesters	Tuition: $37,130
Application Deadline: open	Room & Board: $9,730
Freshman Class: 333 applied, 296 accepted, 194 enrolled	
SAT CR/M: 662/587	ACT: 27 VERY COMPETITIVE+

Bard College at Simon's Rock, formerly Simon's Rock College of Bard, founded in 1964, is a private liberal arts school especially designed to permit students who have completed the 10th or 11th grades to enroll for collegiate studies, earning either an associate's or a bachelor's degree. There are no undergraduate schools. The library contains 70,791 volumes, 7,550 microform items, 4,382 audio/video tapes/CDs/DVDs, and subscribes to 437 periodicals including electronic. Computerized library services include inter-library loans, database searching, and Internet access. Special learning facilities include a learning resource center, art gallery, radio station, TV station, language lab, greenhouse, and community garden. The 275-acre campus is in a small town 50 miles west of Springfield. Including any residence halls, there are 47 buildings.

Student Life: 82% of undergraduates are from out of state, mostly the Northeast. Students are from 41 states, and 11 foreign countries. 67%

are from public schools. 54% are white. The average age of freshmen is 17; all undergraduates, 18. 22% do not continue beyond their first year.

Housing: 356 students can be accommodated in college housing, which includes single-sex and coed dorms and on-campus apartments. In addition, there are special-interest houses. On-campus housing is guaranteed for all 4 years. 81% of students live on campus; of those, 85% remain on campus on weekends. Alcohol is not permitted. Upperclassmen may keep cars.

Activities: There are no fraternities or sororities. There are 21 groups on campus, including Greenagers, labor coalition, math, multicultural, QueerSA, art, choir, chorus, computers, dance, debate, drama, environmental, ethnic, film, gay, international, jazz band, literary magazine, musical theater, newspaper, opera, orchestra, photography, political, radio and TV, religious, social, social service, student government, womens center, and yearbook. Popular campus events include Winter Solstice, May Fest, and Prom Night.

Sports: There are 7 intercollegiate sports for men and 7 for women, and 11 intramural sports for men and 11 for women. Facilities include an 8-lane swimming pool, a multi-court gym, 3 racquetball courts, an elevated running track, a fitness and weight-training center, a rock-climbing wall, a soccer field, 4 tennis courts, and hiking trails.

Disabled Students: 80% of the campus is accessible. Facilities include wheelchair ramps, elevators, special parking, specially equipped rest rooms, special class scheduling, lowered drinking fountains, lowered telephones, and special housing.

Services: Counseling and information services are available, as is tutoring in every subject. There is a reader service for the blind. Study skills instruction is available.

Campus Safety and Security: Measures include self-defense education and security escort services. There are emergency telephones, lighted pathways/sidewalks, and security officers from 4 P.M. to 8 P.M. weekdays and 24 hours a day on weekends.

Programs of Study: Simon's Rock confers B.A. degrees. Associates degrees are also awarded. Bachelor's degrees are awarded in BIOLOGICAL SCIENCE (biology/biological science and ecology), COMMUNICATIONS AND THE ARTS (art, art history and appreciation, creative writing, dance, dramatic arts, drawing, English literature, fine arts, French, German, Germanic languages and literature, literature, modern language, music history and appreciation, music performance, music theory and composition, painting, performing arts, photography, Spanish, studio art, and visual and performing arts), COMPUTER AND PHYSICAL SCIENCE (applied mathematics, chemistry, mathematics, natural sciences, physics, quantitative methods, and science), HEALTH PROFESSIONS (premedicine), SOCIAL SCIENCE (African American studies, American studies, Asian/Oriental studies, crosscultural studies, East Asian studies, Eastern European studies, ethics, politics, and social policy, European studies, French studies, German area studies, interdisciplinary studies, Latin American studies, philosophy, political science/government, psychology, and Russian and Slavic studies). Cross-cultural relations, psychology, and music are the strongest academically. Politics, law, and society are the largest.

Required: All students must complete a writing and thinking workshop, a 2-semester freshman seminar, a sophomore seminar, and a cultural perspectives seminar. The core curriculum also includes distribution requirements in the arts, math, natural sciences, and foreign languages, and physical education. A total of 120 credits, including at least 32 in the major, at least 12 credits at the 300-level or above, at least one tutorial, ECP, course at Bard College or a semester abroad/away, plus an interdisciplinary B.A. seminar, an 8-credit senior thesis, and a minimum 2.0 GPA are needed for the B.A. in liberal arts.

Special: A major consists of selecting 2 concentrations from the 36 is available; one concentration may be self-designed. Independent study internships in many fields, study abroad, a cooperative program with Bard College, and a 3-2 engineering degree with Columbia University, Dartmouth College, or Washington University in St. Louis are available. Simon's Rock has an articulation agreement with Lincoln College and Oxford University that allows Simon's Rock students to spend their junior year in residence at Lincoln College. The Clark Early College Fellows Program is available.

Faculty/Classroom: 63% of faculty are male; 37% are female. All teach and do research. No introductory courses are taught by graduate students. The average class size in an introductory lecture is 14; in a laboratory is 10; in a regular course is 12.

Admissions: 89% of the 2009-2010 applicants were accepted. The SAT scores for the 2009-2010 freshman class were: Critical Reading--7% below 500, 32% between 500 and 599, 41% between 600 and 700, and 20% above 700; Math--16% below 500, 41% between 500 and 599, 30% between 600 and 700, and 13% above 700. The ACT scores were 6% below 21, 6% between 21 and 23, 63% between 24 and 26, % between 27 and 28, and 25% above 28.

Requirements: The ACT Optional Writing test is required. In addition, the admissions committee looks more toward the required interview, essay, recommendations, and special talent. The school recommends that prospective students finish 2 years each of English, foreign languages,

history, math, science, and social studies. A GPA of 2.0 is required. AP credits are accepted. Important factors in the admissions decision are advanced placement or honors courses, recommendations by school officials, and evidence of special talent.

Procedure: Freshmen are admitted fall and spring. Entrance exams should be taken prior to June 10. There are deferred admissions and rolling admissions plans. Check with the school for current application deadlines. The application fee is $50. Notification is sent on a Rolling basis.

Transfer: 2 transfer students enrolled in 2008-2009. Transfer students must be evaluated by the dean of academic affairs and registrar. 60 of 120 credits required for the bachelor's degree must be completed at Simon's Rock.

Visiting: There are regularly scheduled orientations for prospective students, including attending a class, a campus tour, and an interview. There are guides for informal visits and visitors may sit in on classes. To schedule a visit, contact Receptionist, Office of Admission at (413) 528-7355 or (800) 235-7186.

Financial Aid: In 2009-2010, 80% of all full-time freshmen and 84% of continuing full-time students received some form of financial aid. 67% of all full-time freshmen and 59% of continuing full-time students received need-based aid. The average freshmen award was $26,300, with $7,600 ($38,500 maximum) from need-based scholarships or need-based grants; $6,500 ($33,000 maximum) from need-based self-help aid (loans and jobs); $12,200 ($37,075 maximum) from other non-need-based awards and non-need-based scholarships; and $1,373 from other forms of aid. 20% of undergraduate students work part-time. Average annual earnings from campus work are $1500. The average financial indebtedness of the 2009 graduate was $13,525. Simon's Rock is a member of CSS. The CSS/Profile and FAFSA are required. The priority date for freshman financial aid applications for fall entry is April 15. The deadline for filing freshman financial aid applications for fall entry is May 31.

International Students: There are 4 international students enrolled. They must take the TOEFL.

Computers: Wireless access is available. Secure wireless coverage is available throughout the academic buildings, classroom buildings, the Student Union and the campus library. Wireless coverage will be expanded to dormitories and other campus buildings. Ethernet outlets are located in all student rooms, classrooms and throughout the academic buildings on campus. Computers are available for student use in the library and in academic buildings; some computer labs are configured and reserved for particular academic departments. All students may access the system. There are no time limits and no fees. It is strongly recommended that all students have a personal computer.

Graduates: From July 1, 2008 to June 30, 2009, 39 bachelor's degrees were awarded. The most popular majors were psychology (26%), pre-Engineering (13%), and art history (10%). In an average class, 71% graduate in 4 years or less, 88% graduate in 5 years or less, and 90% graduate in 6 years or less.

Admissions Contact: Office of Admission E-Mail: admit@simons-rock.edu Web: www.simons-rock.edu

SMITH COLLEGE
B-2

Northampton, MA 01063
(413) 585-2500; (413) 585-2527

Full-time: 2593 women	**Faculty:** 285; IIB, ++$
Part-time: 21 women	**Ph.D.s:** 98%
Graduate: 72 men, 435 women	**Student/Faculty:** 9 to 1
Year: semesters	**Tuition:** $37,758
Application Deadline: January 15	**Room & Board:** $12,622
Freshman Class: 4011 applied, 1904 accepted, 665 enrolled	
SAT CR/M/W: 660/640/660	**ACT:** 29 **MOST COMPETITIVE**

Smith College, founded in 1871, is the largest independent women's college in the United States and offers a liberal arts education. There is one undergraduate school and one graduate school. In addition to regional accreditation, Smith has baccalaureate program accreditation with ABET. The 4 libraries contain 1.4 million volumes, 149,174 microform items, and 75,525 audio/video tapes/CDs/DVDs, and subscribe to 40,000 periodicals including electronic. Computerized library services include interlibrary loans, database searching, Internet access, and laptop Internet portals. Special learning facilities include a learning resource center, art gallery, radio station, TV station, astronomy observatories, center for foreign languages and culture, digital design studio, plant and horticultural labs, art studios with casting, printmaking, and darkroom facilities, and specialized libraries for science, music, and art, and the Quantitative Learning Center, and the Jacobson Center for Writing, Teaching and Learning. The 147-acre campus is in a small town 90 miles west of Boston. Including any residence halls, there are 115 buildings.

Student Life: 80% of undergraduates are from out of state, mostly the Northeast. Students are from 50 states, 70 foreign countries, and Canada. 59% are from public schools. 41% are white; 13% Asian American. 16% are Protestant; 12% Catholic; 11% claim no religious affiliation;

11% Orthodox, Hindu, Latter Day Saints, Muslim, Unitarian, other. The average age of freshmen is 18; all undergraduates, 21. 9% do not continue beyond their first year; 88% remain to graduate.

Housing: 2446 students can be accommodated in college housing, which includes single-sex dorms and on-campus apartments. In addition, there are language houses, special-interest houses, nonsmoking houses, 2 cooperative houses, housing for nontraditional-age students, an apartment complex for a limited number of juniors and seniors, a senior house, and a French-speaking house. On-campus housing is guaranteed for all 4 years. 93% of students live on campus; of those, 95% remain on campus on weekends. Upperclassmen may keep cars.

Activities: There are no fraternities or sororities. There are 113 groups on campus, including art, chess, choir, chorale, chorus, computers, dance, debate, drama, environmental, ethnic, film, gay, honors, international, jazz band, literary magazine, musical theater, newspaper, orchestra, photography, political, professional, radio and TV, religious, social, social service, student government, symphony, and yearbook. Popular campus events include International Student Day, Spring and Winter Weekends, and Rally Day.

Sports: There are 15 intercollegiate sports for women, and 3 intramural sports for women. Facilities include indoor and outdoor tracks and tennis courts, riding rings, 2 gyms, a climbing wall, an indoor swimming pool with 1- and 3-meter diving boards, 2 weight-training rooms, a dance studio, 2 athletic training rooms, a human performance lab, squash courts, and field hockey, soccer, lacrosse, and softball fields. There is a performing arts center and a concert hall.

Disabled Students: 85% of the campus is accessible. Facilities include wheelchair ramps, elevators, special parking, specially equipped restrooms, special class scheduling, lowered drinking fountains, and lowered telephones.

Services: Counseling and information services are available, as is tutoring in every subject. There is a reader service for the blind. Numerous services are provided for learning-disabled students, including note taking, oral tests, readers, tutors, books on tape, reading software, voice recognition, tape recorders, extended-timed tests, and writing counselors.

Campus Safety and Security: Measures include 24-hour foot and vehicle patrol, emergency notification system, self-defense education, and security escort services. There are shuttle buses, emergency telephones, lighted pathways/sidewalks. First-year students are required to attend panel discussions on campus safety. Specialized personal safety presentations, including self defense and sexual assault information, are provided to various houses and organizations. There are crime prevention programs, including bicycle registration.

Programs of Study: Smith confers A.B. and B.S.E.S degrees. Master's and doctoral degrees are also awarded. Bachelor's degrees are awarded in BIOLOGICAL SCIENCE (biochemistry, biology/biological science, and neurosciences), COMMUNICATIONS AND THE ARTS (art history and appreciation, classics, comparative literature, creative writing, dance, dramatic arts, East Asian languages and literature, English, film arts, French, Germanic languages and literature, Greek, Italian, Latin, music, Russian, Spanish, and studio art), COMPUTER AND PHYSICAL SCIENCE (astronomy, chemistry, computer science, geology, mathematics, and physics), EDUCATION (early childhood education, education, and elementary education), ENGINEERING AND ENVIRONMENTAL DESIGN (architecture and engineering), HEALTH PROFESSIONS (exercise science), SOCIAL SCIENCE (African studies, African American studies, American studies, anthropology, classical/ancient civilization, cognitive science, economics, ethics, politics, and social policy, European studies, French studies, history, international relations, Japanese studies, Judaic studies, Latin American studies, Luso-Brazilian studies, medieval studies, Middle Eastern studies, philosophy, political science/government, psychology, religion, Russian and Slavic studies, sociology, urban studies, and women's studies). Art, government, and psychology are the largest.

Required: All students plan individual programs in consultation with faculty advisers and take 64 credits outside their major and 36 to 64 credits in the major. Students must maintain a minimum 2.0 GPA in all academic work and during the senior year. A total of 128 credits is needed to graduate. A writing-intensive course is required for first-year students. A thesis is required for departmental honors programs. Distribution requirements are necessary for Latin honors eligibility.

Special: Smith offers study abroad in more than 50 countries including the Smith College programs in Italy, France, Germany, and Switzerland, affiliated programs in India, Japan, Russia, China, South Africa, Peru, Brazil, and Spain, and many others. Other opportunities include cross-registration with 5 area colleges, a Washington semester, Smithsonian internships, exchanges with historically Black colleges and other liberal arts colleges, and at BioSphere2. A 3-2 engineering degree is offered with Dartmouth College. Support for nontraditional-age students and for international students is provided, and funding for a summer internship is available for every undergraduate. Accelerated degree programs, student-designed majors, dual majors, and non-degree study are offered. There are 3 national honor societies, including Phi Beta Kappa.

Faculty/Classroom: 47% of faculty are male; 53% are female. All teach and do research. No introductory courses are taught by graduate students. The average class size in an introductory lecture is 25; in a laboratory is 13; and in a regular course is 20.

Admissions: 47% of the 2009-2010 applicants were accepted. The SAT scores for the 2009-2010 freshman class were: Critical Reading--2% below 500, 20% between 500 and 599, 46% between 600 and 700, and 33% above 700; Math--4% below 500, 24% between 500 and 599, 48% between 600 and 700, and 25% above 700; Writing--1% below 500, 19% between 500 and 599, 49% between 600 and 700, and 32% above 700. The ACT scores were 4% below 21, 6% between 21 and 23, 16% between 24 and 26, 26% between 27 and 28, and 48% above 28. 87% of the current freshmen were in the top fifth of their class; 98% were in the top two fifths. 28 freshmen graduated first in their class.

Requirements: Smith highly recommends that applicants have 4 years of English, 3 years each of math, science, and a foreign language, and 2 years of history. SAT and ACT are considered but not required. Interviews are recommended. The GED is accepted. AP credits are accepted.

Procedure: Freshmen are admitted in the fall. Entrance exams should be taken before January of the senior year. There are early decision, early admissions, and deferred admissions plans. Early decision applications should be filed by November 15, along with a $60 fee. Notification of early decision is sent December 15; regular decision, April 1. 166 early decision candidates were accepted for the 2009-2010 class. 578 applicants were on the 2009 waiting list; 96 were admitted. Applications are accepted on-line.

Transfer: 89 transfer students enrolled in 2008-2009. Criteria for transfer students are similar to those for entering freshmen, with more emphasis on the college record. 59 of 128 credits required for the bachelor's degree must be completed at Smith.

Visiting: There are regularly scheduled orientations for prospective students, including student-guided tours available 4 times a day, Monday through Friday, when school is in full session and on Saturday mornings from September to January. Interviews may also be scheduled during these times. Information sessions are offered twice daily most of the year. There are guides for informal visits, visitors may sit in on classes, and stay overnight. To schedule a visit, contact the Office of Admissions receptionist at admission@smith.edu.

Financial Aid: In 2009-2010, 61% of all full-time freshmen and 63% of continuing full-time students received some form of financial aid. 57% of all full-time freshmen and 60% of continuing full-time students received need-based aid. The average freshman award was $33,269. Need-based scholarships or need-based grants averaged $31,980 ; and need-based self-help aid (loans and jobs) averaged $4,745. The average financial indebtedness of the 2009 graduate was $21,573. Smith is a member of CSS. The CSS/Profile, FAFSA, and the college's own financial statement are required. The deadline for filing freshman financial aid applications for fall entry is February 1.

International Students: There are 205 international students enrolled. The school actively recruits these students. They must take the TOEFL. They must also take the SAT or ACT if the language of instruction is English.

Computers: Students can access the campus network and the Internet from over 500 college-owned personal computers located throughout the campus in the libraries, classrooms, labs, and the Campus Center or by using their own computer in their on-campus residence. Wireless access is available in the libraries, Campus Center, houses, and classrooms. All students may access the system. There are no time limits and no fees.

Graduates: From July 1, 2008 to June 30, 2009, 679 bachelor's degrees were awarded. The most popular majors were government (11%), psychology (11%), and art (9%). 150 companies recruited on campus in 2008-2009. In an average class, 78% graduate in 4 years or less, 83% graduate in 5 years or less, and 84% graduate in 6 years or less.

Admissions Contact: Debra Shaver, Director of Admission. A campus DVD is available. E-Mail: *admission@smith.edu* Web: *www.smith.edu*

SPRINGFIELD COLLEGE B-3
Springfield, MA 01109 (413) 748-3136
(800) 343-1257; (413) 748-3694

Full-time: 2100 men and women	**Faculty:** 210; IIA, --$
Part-time: 100 men and women	**Ph.D.s:** 62%
Graduate: 900 men and women	**Student/Faculty:** 10 to 1
Year: semesters, summer session	**Tuition:** $18,000
Application Deadline:	**Room & Board:** $7,000
Freshman Class: n/av	
SAT or ACT: required	**COMPETITIVE**

Springfield College, established in 1885, is a private liberal arts and sciences institution. There are 3 undergraduate schools and one graduate school. In addition to regional accreditation, S.C. has baccalaureate program accreditation with APTA, CAHEA, and NRPA. The library contains 168,332 volumes, 736,056 microform items, 3,200 audio/video tapes/CDs/DVDs, and subscribes to 831 periodicals including electronic. Computerized library services include inter-library loans and database searching. Special learning facilities include an art gallery, radio station, and an outdoor center. The 160-acre campus is in a suburban area 26 miles north of Hartford, Connecticut. Including any residence halls, there are 38 buildings.

Student Life: Students are from 30 states, 12 foreign countries, and Canada. 83% are from public schools. 93% are white. The average age of freshmen is 18; all undergraduates, 21. 12% do not continue beyond their first year.

Housing: 1980 students can be accommodated in college housing, which includes single-sex and coed dorms, on-campus apartments, off-campus apartments, and married student housing. In addition, there are special-interest houses and a wellness dorm. On-campus housing is guaranteed for all 4 years. 85% of students live on campus; of those, 70% remain on campus on weekends. Alcohol is not permitted. Upperclassmen may keep cars.

Activities: There are no fraternities or sororities. There are 58 groups on campus, including art, band, cheerleading, choir, chorus, club sports, communications, computers, dance, drama, ethnic, film, gay, honors, international, jazz band, literary magazine, musical theater, newspaper, pep band, professional, radio and TV, religious, social, social service, student government, and yearbook. Popular campus events include Parents Weekend and Stepping Up Day.

Sports: There are 13 intercollegiate sports for men and 11 for women, and 10 intramural sports for men and 10 for women. Facilities include a 2000-seat stadium, a 2000-seat gym, a super turf football/soccer/lacrosse/field hockey field, 8 tennis courts, baseball and softball fields, and free weight and Nautilus rooms.

Disabled Students: 75% of the campus is accessible. Facilities include wheelchair ramps, elevators, special parking, specially equipped rest rooms, special class scheduling, and lowered drinking fountains.

Services: Counseling and information services are available, as is tutoring in every subject. There is remedial math and writing.

Campus Safety and Security: Measures include 24-hour foot and vehicle patrol, self-defense education, and security escort services. There are shuttle buses, emergency telephones, and lighted pathways/sidewalks.

Programs of Study: S.C. confers B.A. and B.S. degrees. Master's and doctoral degrees are also awarded. Bachelor's degrees are awarded in BIOLOGICAL SCIENCE (biochemistry, biology/biological science, and biotechnology), BUSINESS (business administration and management and sports management), COMMUNICATIONS AND THE ARTS (English and fine arts), COMPUTER AND PHYSICAL SCIENCE (chemistry, information sciences and systems, and mathematics), EDUCATION (early childhood education, elementary education, health education, middle school education, physical education, science education, and secondary education), ENGINEERING AND ENVIRONMENTAL DESIGN (computer graphics), HEALTH PROFESSIONS (art therapy, emergency medical technologies, environmental health science, health care administration, predentistry, premedicine, recreation therapy, and rehabilitation therapy), SOCIAL SCIENCE (gerontology, history, human services, parks and recreation management, physical fitness/movement, political science/government, prelaw, psychology, and sociology). Physical therapy and athletic training are the strongest academically. Physical education is the largest.

Required: To graduate, students must complete a total of 130 credits with a 2.0 GPA. Core requirements include 50 semester hours in English, social and natural sciences, health, religion, philosophy, and art, and 4 credits in phys ed.

Special: There is a co-op program and cross-registration with cooperating colleges in the greater Springfield area. Internships are required in most majors, and there is limited study abroad. There are 2 national honor societies.

Faculty/Classroom: 52% of faculty are male; 48% are female. No introductory courses are taught by graduate students. The average class size in an introductory lecture is 125; in a laboratory is 20; and in a regular course is 30.

Requirements: The SAT or ACT is required. In addition, Applicants must be graduates of an accredited secondary school and have completed 4 years of English and 3 years each of history, math, and science. The school accepts the GED. An essay is required and an interview is recommended. Applications are accepted on-line. AP and CLEP credits are accepted. Important factors in the admissions decision are advanced placement or honors courses, leadership record, and extracurricular activities record.

Procedure: Freshmen are admitted fall and spring. Entrance exams should be taken by November of the senior year. There are early decision, early admissions, deferred admissions, and rolling admissions plans. Early decision applications should be filed by December 1; check with the school for other current application deadlines. The application fee is $40. Notification of early decision is sent February 1; regular decision, March 15. Applications are accepted on-line. A waiting list is maintained.

Transfer: Grades of 2.0 transfer for credit. Transfer students are admitted in the fall and spring.

Visiting: There are guides for informal visits, visitors may sit in on classes, and stay overnight. To schedule a visit, contact the Admissions Office.

Financial Aid: The CSS/Profile and FAFSA, and tax returns for parents and the student are required. The deadline for filing freshman financial aid applications for fall entry is March 15.

International Students: There are 20 international students enrolled. The school actively recruits these students. They must take the TOEFL. They must also take the SAT or ACT.

Computers: All students may access the system. There are no time limits and no fees.

Graduates: Of the 2008 graduating class, 19% were enrolled in graduate school within 6 months of graduation, and 78% were employed.

Admissions Contact: Mary N. DeAngelo, Director of Admissions. A campus DVD is available. E-Mail: admissions@spfldcol.edu Web:www.springfieldcollege.edu

STONEHILL COLLEGE   E-3

Easton, MA 02357-0100   (508) 565-1373; (508) 565-1545

Full-time: 966 men, 1454 women	**Faculty:** 151; IIB, av$
Part-time: 20 men, 28 women	**Ph.Ds:** 83%
Graduate: none	**Student/Faculty:** 16 to 1
Year: semesters, summer session	**Tuition:** $31,210
Application Deadline: January 15	**Room & Board:** $12,240
Freshman Class: 5871 applied, 3313 accepted, 683 enrolled	
SAT CR/M: 590/610	**ACT:** 26 **HIGHLY COMPETITIVE**

Stonehill College, founded in 1948 by the Holy Cross Fathers, is a private Roman Catholic college offering undergraduate degrees in liberal arts and sciences, business, and other preprofessional disciplines. The library contains 246,055 volumes, 150,558 microform items, and 9296 audio/video tapes/CDs/DVDs, and subscribes to 13,488 periodicals including electronic. Computerized library services include interlibrary loans, database searching, Internet access, and laptop Internet portals. Special learning facilities include a learning resource center, art gallery, radio station, observatory, institute for the study of law and society, and several archives and special collections. The 375-acre campus is in a suburban area 20 miles south of Boston. Including any residence halls, there are 64 buildings.

Student Life: 53% of undergraduates are from Massachusetts. Others are from 28 states and 9 foreign countries. 64% are from public schools. 92% are white. 70% are Catholic; 13% claim no religious affiliation. The average age of freshmen is 18; all undergraduates, 20. 11% do not continue beyond their first year; 82% remain to graduate.

Housing: 1945 students can be accommodated in college housing, which includes single-sex and coed dorms. In addition, there are special-interest houses, substance-free/wellness housing, and community service housing. On-campus housing is guaranteed for all 4 years. 88% of students live on campus; of those, 85% remain on campus on weekends. Upperclassmen may keep cars.

Activities: There are no fraternities or sororities. There are 74 groups on campus, including art, band, cheerleading, choir, chorale, chorus, computers, dance, drama, environmental, ethnic, film, gay, honors, international, literary magazine, musical theater, newspaper, pep band, photography, political, professional, radio and TV, religious, social, social service, student government, and yearbook. Popular campus events include Skyhawk Weekend, Spring Weekend, and Halloween Mixer.

Sports: There are 9 intercollegiate sports for men and 10 for women, and 22 intramural sports for men and 20 for women. Facilities include a 2000-seat stadium for football, field hockey, soccer, and lacrosse, a 2000-seat field for men's and women's soccer, a gym with basketball and volleyball courts, 4200 square feet of weight and cardiovascular fitness areas, a recreational and intramural sports complex, tennis courts, baseball, softball, and field hockey fields, and 3 recreational fields for intramural and club sports.

Disabled Students: 85% of the campus is accessible. Facilities include wheelchair ramps, elevators, special parking, specially equipped rest rooms, special class scheduling, lowered drinking fountains, lowered telephones, and special housing.

Services: Counseling and information services are available, as is tutoring in most subjects. A learning disabilities specialist and free diagnostic testing are also available as are auxiliary aids for hearing-impaired students, note takers, and other resources based on need. There is a reader service for the blind and remedial writing.

Campus Safety and Security: Measures include 24-hour foot and vehicle patrol, emergency notification system, self-defense education, and security escort services. There are emergency telephones, lighted pathways/sidewalks, bicycle patrols, and a weekend guest sign-in policy.

Programs of Study: Stonehill confers B.A., B.S., and B.S.B.A. degrees. Bachelor's degrees are awarded in AGRICULTURE (environmental studies), BIOLOGICAL SCIENCE (biochemistry, biology/biological science, and neurosciences), BUSINESS (accounting, banking and finance, business administration and management, international business management, and marketing/retailing/merchandising), COMMUNICATIONS AND THE ARTS (art history and appreciation, communications, English, fine arts, French, and Spanish), COMPUTER AND PHYSICAL SCIENCE (chemistry, computer science, mathematics, and physics), EDU-

CATION (education), HEALTH PROFESSIONS (health care administration), SOCIAL SCIENCE (American studies, criminology, economics, gender studies, history, interdisciplinary studies, international studies, philosophy, political science/government, psychology, public administration, religion, and sociology). Business, biology, and psychology are the strongest academically.

Required: All students must complete a cornerstone program, which consists of 4 common courses within history/literature and philosophy/religious studies; a learning community consisting of 2 linked courses and a 3rd integrated course; a moral inquiry course; and a senior capstone experience within the major. Distribution requirements include 2 semesters of a foreign language and 1 course each in natural scientific inquiry, social scientific inquiry, and statistical reasoning. Students must complete 120 hours (40 3- to 4-credit courses) while maintaining a minimum GPA of 2.0.

Special: On-campus work-study, international and domestic internships, a Washington semester through the Washington Center, and a semester in New York City are available. Cross-registration with 8 other Massachusetts schools in the SACHEM consortium is also available. A 3-2 computer engineering degree is offered with the University of Notre Dame. Opportunities for study abroad include 120 programs in 35 countries. Nondegree, directed, and field study are available as well as a pass/fail option for upperclassmen. Programs in early childhood, elementary, and secondary education lead to the state's provisional teacher certification. Stonehill is also a member of the Marine Studies Consortium. Preprofessional preparation is available in medicine, dentistry, law, and theology. There are 19 national honor societies, a freshman honors program, and 15 departmental honors programs.

Faculty/Classroom: 62% of faculty are male; 38% are female. All teach and do research. No introductory courses are taught by graduate students. The average class size in an introductory lecture is 20 and in a laboratory, 20.

Admissions: 56% of the 2009-2010 applicants were accepted. The SAT scores for the 2009-2010 freshman class were: Critical Reading--4% below 500, 45% between 500 and 599, 46% between 600 and 700, and 5% above 700; Math--4% below 500, 32% between 500 and 599, 59% between 600 and 700, and 5% above 700. The ACT scores were 2% below 21, 12% between 21 and 23, 32% between 24 and 26, 28% between 27 and 28, and 26% above 28. 81% of the current freshmen were in the top fifth of their class; 98% were in the top two fifths. 10 freshmen graduated first in their class.

Requirements: Applicants should be graduates of an accredited high school or have earned the GED. Secondary preparation should include 4 units each of English and math, 3 units each of foreign language and science, and 3 combined units of history, political science, and social sciences plus 3 elective subjects. An essay, school report, 2 teacher evaluations, and a completed common application sent with a Stonehill Supplemental Information Form are required. AP credits are accepted. Important factors in the admissions decision are advanced placement or honors courses, leadership record, and extracurricular activities record.

Procedure: Freshmen are admitted fall and spring. There are early decision, early admissions, and deferred admissions plans. Early decision applications should be filed by November 1; regular applications, by January 15 for fall entry and November 1 for spring entry, along with a $60 fee. Notification of early decision is sent December 25; regular decision, April 1. 50 early decision candidates were accepted for the 2009-2010 class. 997 applicants were on the 2009 waiting list; 412 were admitted. Applications are accepted on-line.

Transfer: 44 transfer students enrolled in 2008-2009. Applicants must have a minimum GPA of 2.0.Official high school transcripts and college transcripts along with catalogs with course descriptions from all colleges attended are required. An essay and 2 recommendations are required, and an interview is recommended. 60 of 120 credits required for the bachelor's degree must be completed at Stonehill.

Visiting: There are regularly scheduled orientations for prospective students, consisting of group information sessions and guided campus tours available by appointment throughout the year. Visitors may sit in on classes. To schedule a visit, contact the Admissions Office.

Financial Aid: In 2009-2010, 97% of all full-time freshmen and 88% of continuing full-time students received some form of financial aid. 60% of all full-time freshmen and 57% of continuing full-time students received need-based aid. The average freshman award was $22,165. Need-based scholarships or need-based grants averaged $18,140 ($43,450 maximum); need-based self-help aid (loans and jobs) averaged $7700 ($9000 maximum); non-need-based athletic scholarships averaged $9126 ($43,450 maximum); and other non-need-based awards and non-need-based scholarships averaged $9001 ($31,210 maximum). 26% of undergraduate students work part-time. Average annual earnings from campus work are $1111. The average financial indebtedness of the 2009 graduate was $29,163. Stonehill is a member of CSS. The CSS/Profile, FAFSA, and noncustodial profile and business/farm supplement are required. The deadline for filing freshman financial aid applications for fall entry is February 1.

International Students: There are 10 international students enrolled. The school actively recruits these students. They must take the TOEFL.

Computers: Wireless access is available. The college provides students with wired and wireless computing facilities including 10 multimedia labs with over 300 computers for classroom and student use. The software available includes extensive instructional packages, web page development tools, language programming, and database tools. Each lab is equipped with printers. All students may access the system 7 days a week, 24 hours a day. There are no time limits and no fees. It is strongly recommended that all students have a personal computer.

Graduates: From July 1, 2008 to June 30, 2009, 569 bachelor's degrees were awarded. The most popular majors were business (24%), psychology (11%), and criminology and English (6%). 272 companies recruited on campus in 2008-2009. In an average class, 80% graduate in 4 years or less, 82% graduate in 5 years or less, and 82% graduate in 6 years or less. Of the 2008 graduating class, 32% were enrolled in graduate school within 6 months of graduation, and 65% were employed.

Admissions Contact: Brian P. Murphy, Dean of Admissions and Enrollment. E-mail: *admissions@stonehill.edu* Web: *www.stonehill.edu*

SUFFOLK UNIVERSITY   E-2
Boston, MA 02108-2770   (617) 573-8460
(800) 6SUFFOL; (617) 742-4291

Full-time: 2288 men, 2924 women	**Faculty:** 342; IIA, ++$
Part-time: 130 men, 153 women	**Ph.D.s:** 89%
Graduate: 691 men, 1000 women	**Student/Faculty:** 15 to 1
Year: semesters, summer session	**Tuition:** $27,208
Application Deadline: March 1	**Room & Board:** $14,544
Freshman Class: 9036 applied, 7611 accepted, 1254 enrolled	
SAT CR/M/W: 506/505/505	**ACT:** 22 COMPETITIVE

Suffolk University, founded in 1906, is a private institution offering undergraduate and graduate degrees in the arts and sciences, business, and law. There are 2 undergraduate schools and 3 graduate schools. In addition to regional accreditation, Suffolk has baccalaureate program accreditation with AACSB, ABET, FIDER, and NASAD. The 3 libraries contain 129,647 volumes, 144,151 microform items, 1,168 audio/video tapes/CDs/DVDs, and subscribe to 22,344 periodicals including electronic. Computerized library services include interlibrary loans, database searching, Internet access, and laptop Internet portals. Special learning facilities include a learning resource center, art gallery, radio station, and TV station. The 2-acre campus is in an urban area Boston. Including any residence halls, there are 18 buildings.

Student Life: 62% of undergraduates are from Massachusetts. Students are from 45 states, 100 foreign countries, and Canada. 66% are from public schools. 53% are white; 11% foreign nationals. The average age of freshmen is 18; all undergraduates, 21. 28% do not continue beyond their first year; 54% remain to graduate.

Housing: 1050 students can be accommodated in college housing, which includes coed dorms. On-campus housing is available on a first-come, first-served basis, and is available on a lottery system for upperclassmen. Alcohol is not permitted. No one may keep cars.

Activities: 1% of men belong to 1 national fraternity; % of women belong to 1 local sorority. There are 75 groups on campus, including evening students, recycling, transfer students, art, choir, chorale, chorus, computers, dance, debate, drama, ethnic, film, forensics, gay, honors, international, jazz band, literary magazine, musical threater, newspaper, orientation, photography, political, professional, radio and TV, religious, social, social service, and student government. Popular campus events include Hispanic Fiesta, Fallfest Talent Show, and Temple Street Fair.

Sports: There are 7 intercollegiate sports for men and 6 for women, and 2 intramural sports for men and 1 for women. Facilities include a basketball, volleyball, and aerobics facility, intramurals, and indoor baseball/softball practice and a fully equipped fitness center.

Disabled Students: 95% of the campus is accessible. Facilities include wheelchair ramps, elevators, specially equipped rest rooms, special class scheduling, lowered drinking fountains, and lowered telephones.

Services: Counseling and information services are available, as is tutoring in every subject. There is a reader service for the blind, and remedial math, reading, and writing.

Campus Safety and Security: Measures include 24-hour foot and vehicle patrol, emergency notification system, self-defense education, and security escort services. There are emergency telephones and lighted pathways/sidewalks.

Programs of Study: Suffolk confers B.A., B.S., B.F.A., B.S.B.A., B.S.G.S., and B.S.J. degrees. Associates, master's, and doctoral degrees are also awarded. Bachelor's degrees are awarded in AGRICULTURE (environmental studies), BIOLOGICAL SCIENCE (biochemistry, biology/biological science, biotechnology, life science, and marine science), BUSINESS (accounting, banking and finance, entrepreneurial studies, international business management, international economics, management science, and marketing/retailing/merchandising), COMMUNICATIONS AND THE ARTS (advertising, art history and appreciation, broadcasting, communications, creative writing, dramatic arts, English, film arts, fine arts, French, graphic design, journalism, media arts, music history and appreciation, performing arts, public relations, Spanish, and speech/debate/rhetoric), COMPUTER AND PHYSICAL SCIENCE (chemistry, computer programming, computer science, information sciences and systems, mathematics, and physics), EDUCATION (business education, elementary education, English education, mathematics education, and science education), ENGINEERING AND ENVIRONMENTAL DESIGN (computer engineering, electrical/electronics engineering, environmental engineering, environmental science, and interior design), HEALTH PROFESSIONS (medical laboratory technology, medical science, and radiological science), SOCIAL SCIENCE (African American studies, American studies, criminal justice, economics, European studies, German area studies, history, human development, human services, humanities, international relations, paralegal studies, philosophy, political science/government, psychology, public administration, social science, sociology, and women's studies). Business, sociology, and communications. are the strongest academically.

Required: All students must complete their semester hours with at least a 2.0 GPA. Distribution requirements vary by degree program.

Special: Numerous cooperative education and work-study programs are available in the Boston area. Cross-registration is offered with Emerson College. Study abroad in 25 countries with over 56 programs and over 35 cities to choose from. A semester internship in Washington, D.C., as well as local and international internships, are possible. B.A. and B.S. degrees in business and public administration, majors in medical biophysics and radiation biology taught in collaboration with Massachusetts General Hospital, dual and student-designed majors, and a lawyer's assistant certificate program are also available. Also, Suffolk has campuses in Spain and Senegal. There are 15 national honor societies, a freshman honors program, and 11 departmental honors programs.

Faculty/Classroom: 57% of faculty are male; 43% are female. All teach undergraduates, and 84% do research. No introductory courses are taught by graduate students. The average class size in an introductory lecture is 24; in a laboratory is 16; and in a regular course is 18.

Admissions: 84% of the 2009-2010 applicants were accepted. The SAT scores for the 2009-2010 freshman class were: Critical Reading-- 48% below 500, 40% between 500 and 599, 11% between 600 and 700, and 1 above 700; Math--47% below 500, 39% between 500 and 599, 13% between 600 and 700, and 1 above 700; Writing--45% below 500, 42% between 500 and 599, 12% between 600 and 700, and 1 above 700. The ACT scores were 38% below 21, 32% between 21 and 23, 16% between 24 and 26, 10% between 27 and 28, and 3% above 28. 30% of the current freshmen were in the top fifth of their class; 57% were in the top two fifths.

Requirements: The SAT or ACT is required. The ACT Optional Writing test is also required. In addition, applicants should have a high school diploma or the GED. Recommended secondary preparation includes 4 years of English, 3 of math, 2 each of a foreign language and science, and 1 of American history. Exact requirements differ by degree program. A personal essay is required, and an interview is recommended. A GPA of 2.0 is required. AP and CLEP credits are accepted. Important factors in the admissions decision are advanced placement or honors courses, recommendations by school officials, and leadership record.

Procedure: Freshmen are admitted fall, spring, and summer. Entrance exams should be taken by December of the senior year. There are early decision, early admissions and deferred admissions plans. Early decision applications should be filed by November 1; regular applications, by March 1 for fall entry and December 15 for spring entry, along with a $50 fee. Notification of early decision is sent December 15; regular decision, January 15. Applications are accepted on-line. 163 applicants were on a recent waiting list, 79 were accepted.

Transfer: 395 transfer students enrolled in 2008-2009. Applicants should have a minimum 2.5 GPA from an accredited college. Those with fewer than 15 college credits must submit a high school transcript. 30 credits required for the bachelor's degree must be completed at Suffolk.

Visiting: There are regularly scheduled orientations for prospective students, Students visits include a general presentation and an overview panel presentation of student life, career and co-op opportunities, learning center services, and athletics and academic department meetings, and campus tours. There are guides for informal visits and visitors may sit in on classes. To schedule a visit, contact the Admissions Office.

Financial Aid: In 2009-2010, 82% of all full-time freshmen and 75% of continuing full-time students received some form of financial aid. 71% of all full-time freshmen and 59% of continuing full-time students received need-based aid. The average freshman award was $27,908, with $12,953 ($45,407 maximum) from need-based scholarships or need-based grants; $5,543 ($9,000 maximum) from need-based self-help aid (loans and jobs); and $13,090 ($6,202 maximum) from other non-need-based awards and non-need-based scholarships. 44% of undergraduate students work part-time. Average annual earnings from campus work are $2392. The FAFSA and the college's own financial statement, and verification of income are required. The deadline for filing freshman financial aid applications for fall entry is March 1.

International Students: There are 573 international students enrolled. The school actively recruits these students. They must take the TOEFL with a minimum score of 550 on the paper-based TOEFL (PBT) or 80 on the Internet-based version (iBT). They must also take the SAT or ACT, and the college's own entrance exam.

Computers: Wireless access is available. The library supports an 802.11 a/b/g network. Students with their own laptops may complete a form available at the circulation desk and register their laptop's wireless network interface card to acquire access to the library's wireless network. Laptops are also available at the library's check-out center for student/school use. All library laptops are registered to the library's wireless network. All students may access the system. There are no time limits and no fees.

Graduates: From July 1, 2008 to June 30, 2009, 1119 bachelor's degrees were awarded. The most popular majors were business/marketing (40%), sociology (18%), and communications (12%). 121 companies recruited on campus in 2008-2009. In an average class, 1% graduate in 3 years or less, 37% graduate in 4 years or less, 52% graduate in 5 years or less, and 54% graduate in 6 years or less. Of the 2008 graduating class, 19% were enrolled in graduate school within 6 months of graduation, and 92% were employed.

Admissions Contact: John Hamel, Director of Undergraduate Admissions. A campus DVD is available. E-Mail: *admission@suffolk.edu* Web: *www.suffolk.edu*

TUFTS UNIVERSITY   D-2
Medford, MA 02155   (617) 627-3170; (617) 627-3860

Full-time: 2456 men, 2456 women	Faculty: 421; I, av$
Part-time: 22 men, 46 women	Ph.D.s: 95%
Graduate: 1215 men, 1808 women	Student/Faculty: 12 to 1
Year: semesters, summer session	Tuition: $36,700
Application Deadline: January 1	Room & Board: $10,160
Freshman Class: 15387 applied, 4231 accepted, 1373 enrolled	

MOST COMPETITIVE

Tufts University, founded in 1852, is a private institution offering undergraduate programs in liberal arts and sciences, and engineering. There are 2 undergraduate schools and 8 graduate schools. In addition to regional accreditation, Tufts has baccalaureate program accreditation with ABET, ADA, and CAHEA. The 2 libraries contain 1.2 million volumes, 1.3 million microform items, 42,952 audio/video tapes/CDs/DVDs, and subscribe to 19,817 periodicals including electronic. Computerized library services include inter-library loans, database searching, Internet access, and laptop Internet portals. Special learning facilities include a learning resource center, art gallery, radio station, TV station, 300 seat recital hall and theater in the round. The 150-acre campus is in a suburban area 5 miles northwest of Boston. Including any residence halls, there are 170 buildings.

Student Life: 75% of undergraduates are from out of state, mostly the Middle Atlantic. Students are from 49 states, 66 foreign countries, and Canada. 60% are from public schools. 57% are white; 13% Asian American. The average age of freshmen is 18; all undergraduates, 20. 5% do not continue beyond their first year; 92% remain to graduate.

Housing: 3550 students can be accommodated in college housing, which includes single-sex and coed dorms and on-campus apartments. In addition, there are language houses, special-interest houses, fraternity houses, cooperative houses. On-campus housing is available on a lottery system for upperclassmen. 70% of students live on campus. Upperclassmen may keep cars.

Activities: 11% of men belong to 8 national fraternities; 3% of women belong to 3 national sororities. There are 160 groups on campus, including art, band, cheerleading, chess, choir, chorale, chorus, computers, dance, debate, drama, environmental, ethnic, film, forensics, gay, honors, international, jazz band, literary magazine, marching band, musical theater, newspaper, orchestra, outdoors, pep band, photography, political, professional, radio and TV, religious, social, social service, student government, and symphony. Popular campus events include a dramatic arts series, national and international forums, and an international affairs symposium.

Sports: There are 14 intercollegiate sports for men and 16 for women, and 13 intramural sports for men and 14 for women. Facilities include a football stadium, 2 gyms, an 8-lane all-weather track, 9 tennis courts, a field house, an indoor cage, an indoor track, 7 squash courts, a swimming pool, a dance room, a weight room, a sauna, a sailing center, an exercise center, and baseball, softball, and playing fields.

Disabled Students: 90% of the campus is accessible. Facilities include wheelchair ramps, elevators, special parking, specially equipped rest rooms, special class scheduling, lowered drinking fountains, lowered telephones.

Services: Counseling and information services are available, as is tutoring in every subject, as needed through the Academic Resources Center. There is a reader service for the blind. Services are also available through the women's center, and African American, Hispanic and Asian culture houses.

Campus Safety and Security: Measures include 24-hour foot and vehicle patrol, emergency notification system, self-defense education, and security escort services. There are shuttle buses, emergency telephones, and lighted pathways/sidewalks.

Programs of Study: Tufts confers B.A., B.S., B.S.C.E., B.S.Ch.E., B.S. Comp. Eng., B.S.E., B.S.E.E., B.S.E.S., B.S. Environmental Eng., B.S.M.E., B.S.B.M.E., and B.S.C.S degrees. Master's and doctoral degrees are also awarded. Bachelor's degrees are awarded in BIOLOGICAL SCIENCE (biochemistry, biology/biological science, and biotechnology), COMMUNICATIONS AND THE ARTS (art history and appreciation, Chinese, classics, dramatic arts, English, French, German, Greek, Italian, Japanese, Latin, music, Russian, and Spanish), COMPUTER AND PHYSICAL SCIENCE (applied physics, astrophysics, chemical physics, chemistry, computer science, geology, mathematics, and physics), ENGINEERING AND ENVIRONMENTAL DESIGN (architecture, biomedical engineering, chemical engineering, civil engineering, computer engineering, electrical/electronics engineering, engineering, engineering and applied science, engineering physics, environmental engineering, environmental science, and mechanical engineering), HEALTH PROFESSIONS (community health work), SOCIAL SCIENCE (American studies, anthropology, archeology, Asian/Oriental studies, biopsychology, child psychology/development, economics, German area studies, history, international relations, Judaic studies, Middle Eastern studies, peace studies, philosophy, political science/government, psychology, religion, Russian and Slavic studies, sociology, and women's studies). International relations, economics, and political science are the largest.

Required: Liberal arts students must complete 34 courses, 10 of them in the area of concentration. Requirements include foundation courses in writing and foreign language or culture and courses in humanities, arts, social sciences, math, and natural sciences. Requirements for engineering students include a total of 38 courses, 12 of them in the area of concentration, and distribution requirements in English, math and science, humanities, and social sciences.

Special: The university offers cross-registration at Swarthmore College, Boston University, Boston College, and Brandeis University, a Washington semester, and study abroad in England, Spain, France, Chile, Japan, Ghana, China, Hong Kong, and Germany. Many internships are available. Double majors in the liberal arts are common; student-designed majors are possible. There is a 5-year B.A./M.A. or B.S./M.S. program in engineering or liberal arts, a B.A./B.F.A. program with the Museum School of Fine Arts, and a B.A./B.M. program with the New England Conservatory of Music. There are 4 national honor societies, including Phi Beta Kappa.

Faculty/Classroom: 59% of faculty are male; 41% are female. All teach and do research. No introductory courses are taught by graduate students. The average class size in a regular course is 20.

Admissions: 27% of the 2009-2010 applicants were accepted. 96% of the current freshmen were in the top fifth of their class; 99% were in the top two fifths. There were 41 National Merit finalists.

Requirements: In addition, the university accepts either the SAT Reasoning Test and the results of SAT Subject tests or the ACT. Liberal arts applicants should take the SAT Subject test of their choice; engineering applicants should take a math level I or II, and either physics or chemistry. In addition, all applicants should be high school graduates or hold the GED. Academic preparation is expected to include 4 years of English, 3 years each of humanities and a foreign language, 2 years each of social and natural sciences, and 1 year of history. AP credits are accepted. Important factors in the admissions decision are advanced placement or honors courses, recommendations by school officials, and extracurricular activities record.

Procedure: Freshmen are admitted in the fall. Entrance exams should be taken by January of the senior year. There is a deferred admissions plan. Applications should be filed by January 1 for fall entry, along with a $70 fee. Notifications are sent April 1. Applications are accepted online. A waiting list is maintained.

Transfer: 26 transfer students enrolled in 2008-2009. Admission is competitive. Primary consideration is given to college and secondary school achievement, and record of personal involvement. 17 of 34 credits required for the bachelor's degree must be completed at Tufts.

Visiting: There are regularly scheduled orientations for prospective students, including orientation sessions twice a day, Monday through Friday, April 1 to early December, followed by campus tours. There are additional orientation sessions and tours on selected Saturday mornings during the fall. There are guides for informal visits, visitors may sit in on classes, and stay overnight. To schedule a visit, contact the Admissions Office at admissions.inquiry@ase.tufts.edu.

Financial Aid: In 2009-2010, 44% of all full-time freshmen and 50% of continuing full-time students received some form of financial aid. 45% of all full-time freshmen and 50% of continuing full-time students received need-based aid. The average freshmen award was $29,147. 40% of undergraduate students work part-time. The average financial indebtedness of the 2009 graduate was $14,190. Tufts is a member of CSS. The CSS/Profile and FAFSA, and parent and student federal income tax forms are required. The deadline for filing freshman financial aid applications for fall entry is February 15.

International Students: There are 335 international students enrolled. The school actively recruits these students. They must take the TOEFL if English is not their first language. They must also take the SAT or ACT.

The student must also take the ACT, or the SAT Reasoning Test and 2 SAT subject tests.

Computers: Wireless access is available. All students may access the system. 24 hours a day. There are no time limits and no fees.

Graduates: From July 1, 2008 to June 30, 2009, 1144 bachelor's degrees were awarded. The most popular majors were international relations (15%), economics (10%), and psychology (8%). 150 companies recruited on campus in 2008-2009. In an average class, 92% graduate in 6 years or less.

Admissions Contact: Lee A. Coffin, Dean of Admissions. E-Mail: admissions.inquiry@ase.tufts.edu Web: www.tufts.edu

UNIVERSITY OF MASSACHUSETTS AMHERST B-2

Amherst, MA 01003	(413) 545-0222; (413) 545-4312
Full-time: 9801 men, 9514 women	Faculty: 971; I, av$
Part-time: 669 men, 889 women	Ph.D.s: 93%
Graduate: 3053 men, 3090 women	Student/Faculty: 20 to 1
Year: semesters, summer session	Tuition: $11,732 ($23,229)
Application Deadline: January 15	Room & Board: $8276
Freshman Class: 29452 applied, 19703 accepted, 4124 enrolled	
SAT CR/M: 575/594	ACT: 25　VERY COMPETITIVE

Established in 1863, University of Massachusetts Amherst is a public research, land-grant institution offering nearly 100 academic majors. There are 8 undergraduate schools and 8 graduate schools. In addition to regional accreditation, UMass Amherst has baccalaureate program accreditation with AACSB, ABET, ASLA, FIDER, NASM, NCATE, NLN, and SAF. The 2 libraries contain 3.3 million volumes, 2.6 million microform items, and 25,230 audio/video tapes/CDs/DVDs, and subscribe to 57,233 periodicals including electronic. Computerized library services include interlibrary loans, database searching, Internet access, and laptop Internet portals. Special learning facilities include a learning resource center, art gallery, radio station, TV station, botanical gardens. The 1463-acre campus is in a small town 90 miles west of Boston and 60 miles north of Hartford, Connecticut. Including any residence halls, there are 344 buildings.

Student Life: 81% of undergraduates are from Massachusetts. Others are from 50 states, 50 foreign countries, and Canada. 79% are white; 46% African American; 45% Hispanic. The average age of freshmen is 18; all undergraduates, 21. 13% do not continue beyond their first year; 66% remain to graduate.

Housing: 11850 students can be accommodated in college housing, which includes single-sex and coed dorms, on-campus apartments, and married student housing. In addition, there are honors houses, language houses, special-interest houses, fraternity houses, sorority houses, international housing, and first-year experience housing. On-campus housing is guaranteed for the freshman year only and is available on a lottery system for upperclassmen. 63% of students live on campus. All students may keep cars.

Activities: 5% of men belong to 1 local and 20 national fraternities; 5% of women belong to 1 local and 14 national sororities. There are 367 groups on campus, including art, band, cheerleading, chess, choir, chorale, chorus, computers, dance, debate, drama, environmental, ethnic, film, gay, honors, international, jazz band, literary magazine, marching band, musical theater, newspaper, opera, orchestra, pep band, photography, political, professional, radio and TV, religious, social, social service, student government, student-owned businesses, symphony, and yearbook. Popular campus events include First Week and Something Every Friday Movies.

Sports: There are 10 intercollegiate sports for men and 11 for women, and 9 intramural sports for men and 10 for women. Facilities include 120 acres of multipurpose fields, softball and soccer fields, a 20,000-seat football stadium, a track, and 22 tennis courts. Indoor facilities include a 120,000-sq-ft recreation center with weight and fitness equipment, a 3-court gym, a wellness center, and an elevated jogging track. Other facilities include 3 pools, 3 handball/squash, racquetball courts, 2 gyms, a wrestling room, 2 dance studios, weight-training rooms, fitness centers, basketball/volleyball/badminton courts, and an indoor track. The indoor sports arena has 10,500 seats and 2 Olympic-sized ice sheets. Body shops are also available in residential areas.

Disabled Students: All of the campus is accessible. Facilities include wheelchair ramps, elevators, special parking, specially equipped restrooms, special class scheduling, lowered drinking fountains, lowered telephones, special housing. All programs are made accessible through accommodations.

Services: Counseling and information services are available, as is tutoring in most subjects. There is a reader service for the blind.

Campus Safety and Security: Measures include 24-hour foot and vehicle patrol, emergency notification system, self-defense education, and security escort services. There are shuttle buses, emergency telephones, lighted pathways/sidewalks, and controlled access to dorms/residences.

Programs of Study: UMass Amherst confers B.A., B.S., B.B.A., B.F.A., B.G.S., and B.Mus. degrees. Associate, master's, and doctoral degrees are also awarded. Bachelor's degrees are awarded in AGRICULTURE (agricultural economics, animal science, forestry and related sciences, natural resource management, plant science, soil science, wildlife management, and wood science), BIOLOGICAL SCIENCE (biochemistry, biology/biological science, microbiology, and nutrition), BUSINESS (accounting, banking and finance, business administration and management, hospitality management services, marketing management, and sports management), COMMUNICATIONS AND THE ARTS (art history and appreciation, Chinese, classics, communications, comparative literature, dance, design, dramatic arts, English, Germanic languages and literature, Japanese, journalism, linguistics, music, music performance, Portuguese, Spanish, and studio art), COMPUTER AND PHYSICAL SCIENCE (astronomy, chemistry, computer science, earth science, geology, mathematics, physics, and science), ENGINEERING AND ENVIRONMENTAL DESIGN (chemical engineering, civil engineering, computer engineering, electrical/electronics engineering, environmental design, environmental science, industrial engineering, landscape architecture/design, and mechanical engineering), HEALTH PROFESSIONS (exercise science, nursing, public health, and speech pathology/audiology), SOCIAL SCIENCE (African American studies, anthropology, economics, food science, French studies, gender studies, geography, history, interdisciplinary studies, Italian studies, Judaic studies, law, liberal arts/general studies, Middle Eastern studies, philosophy, political science/government, psychology, Russian and Slavic studies, sociology, and women's studies). Psychology, management, and biology are the largest.

Required: Students must complete 120 credit hours and maintain a minimum GPA of 2.0 overall and in the major. For the general education requirement, students must take 4 courses in Social World with at least 2 of those in social and cultural diversity, 2 courses in Biological and Physical World, 1 each in Basic Math Skills, Integrative Experience, Writing,and Analytic Reasoning. There is an Interdisciplinary option.

Special: Cross-registration is possible with Smith, Mount Holyoke, Hampshire, and Amherst Colleges. Co-op programs, internships in every major, study abroad in more than 40 countries, a Washington semester, work-study programs, dual majors, and B.A.-B.S. degrees are available. The Bachelor's Degree with Individual Concentration (BDIC) is also available. The Commonwealth Honors College welcomes honor students who meet entrance requirements. There are also teacher certification, distance learning, independent study, and ESL programs. There are 30 national honor societies, including Phi Beta Kappa, a freshman honors program, and 74 departmental honors programs.

Faculty/Classroom: 60% of faculty are male; 40% are female. All teach and do research. No introductory courses are taught by graduate students.

Admissions: 67% of the 2009-2010 applicants were accepted. The SAT scores for the 2009-2010 freshman class were: Math--10% below 500, 41% between 500 and 599, 41% between 600 and 700, and 9% above 700; Writing--14% below 500, 48% between 500 and 599, 31% between 600 and 700, and 7% above 700. The ACT scores were 9% below 21, 22% between 21 and 23, 32% between 24 and 26, 20% between 27 and 28, and 17% above 28. 54% of the current freshmen were in the top fifth of their class; 90% were in the top two fifths. 3 freshmen graduated first in their class.

Requirements: The SAT is required. In addition, applicants must be graduates of an accredited secondary school or have the GED. The university recommends that students complete 16 Carnegie units including 4 years of English, 3 years each of math, and science (including 2 years lab), and 2 years each of electives, foreign language, and social studies. 4 years of math are required for business, computer science, and engineering majors. Students must present a portfolio for admission to the art program and must audition for admission to music and dance. A GPA of 2.0 is required. AP and CLEP credits are accepted. Important factors in the admissions decision are advanced placement or honors courses, extracurricular activities record, and recommendations by school officials.

Procedure: Freshmen are admitted fall and spring. Entrance exams should be taken as soon as possible after admissions deadline. There are early admissions, deferred admissions, and rolling admissions plans. Early decision applications should be filed by November 1; regular applications, by January 15 for fall entry; and October 1 for spring entry, along with a $40 fee. Notifications are sent in March. 214 applicants were on the 2009 waiting list; 170 were admitted. Applications are accepted online.

Transfer: 1626 transfer students enrolled in 2008-2009. Transfer applicants must submit transcripts from all colleges or universities attended and an essay. Those with fewer than 27 credits must submit high school transcripts and SAT scores. Priority is given to students with an associate degree. Grades of C- or better in comparable coursework transfer for credit. 45 of 120 credits required for the bachelor's degree must be completed at UMass Amherst.

Visiting: There are regularly scheduled orientations for prospective students, including 3 guided tours daily weekdays, 2 tours daily on weekends and twice-daily information sessions. There are guides for informal visits and visitors may sit in on classes. To schedule a visit, contact the University Tour Service at (413) 545-0306.

Financial Aid: In 2009-2010, 84% of all full-time freshmen and 71% of continuing full-time students received some form of financial aid. 52% of all full-time freshmen and 53% of continuing full-time students received need-based aid. The average freshman award was $9,590. Need-based scholarships or need-based grants averaged $8,892 ; need-based self-help aid (loans and jobs) averaged $4,232; non-need-based athletic scholarships averaged $15,623; and other non-need-based awards and non-need-based scholarships averaged $2,308. 19% of undergraduate students work part-time. Average annual earnings from campus work are $1400. The average financial indebtedness of the 2009 graduate was $23,847. UMass Amherst is a member of CSS. The FAFSA is required. The priority date for freshman financial aid applications for fall entry is February 14.

International Students: There are 182 international students enrolled. The school actively recruits these students. They must take the TOEFL with a minimum score of 550 on the paper-based TOEFL (PBT) or 80 on the Internet-based version (iBT). They must also take the SAT or ACT.

Computers: Wireless access is available. The university offers centralized computing services through the Office of Information Technologies. All students are required to have an account. This account provides students with access to numerous computers available for teaching and public use, a campuswide network accessible from residence halls, public buildings, and off campus, an e-mail account, the campus on-line course management system, and the campus wireless network, which is available at many on-campus locations. Registration, grades, and student information are available on-line. There is also an open learning space with computer terminals, work areas, printers, and support staff in the W.E.B. DuBois Library. All students may access the system. There are no time limits and no fees. It is strongly recommended that all students have a personal computer.

Graduates: From July 1, 2008 to June 30, 2009, 4573 bachelor's degrees were awarded. The most popular majors were psychology (8%), communication (6%), and hospitality and tourism management (5%). In an average class, 49% graduate in 4 years or less, 63% graduate in 5 years or less, and 66% graduate in 6 years or less. Of the 2008 graduating class, 22% were enrolled in graduate school within 6 months of graduation, and 70% were employed.

Admissions Contact: Kevin Kelly, Director of Admissions. A campus DVD is available. E-Mail: *mail@admissions.umass.edu* Web: *www.umass.edu*

UNIVERSITY OF MASSACHUSETTS BOSTON · E-2

Boston, MA 02125-3393	(617) 287-6000; (617) 287-5999
Full-time: 3334 men, 4347 women	**Faculty:** 499; I, -$
Part-time: 1447 men, 1913 women	**Ph.Ds:** 93%
Graduate: 1187 men, 2684 women	**Student/Faculty:** 15 to 1
Year: semesters, summer session	**Tuition:** $10,611 ($22,797)
Application Deadline: June 1	
Freshman Class: 6060 applied, 3728 accepted, 987 enrolled	
SAT CR/M: 510/530	**ACT:** required **COMPETITIVE**

The University of Massachusetts Boston, established in 1964, is a public research institution offering undergraduate studies in arts and sciences and in preprofessional training. There are 5 undergraduate schools and 7 graduate schools. In addition to regional accreditation, UMass Boston has baccalaureate program accreditation with AACSB and ABET. The library contains 600,000 volumes, 827,171 microform items, and 1902 audio/video tapes/CDs/DVDs, and subscribes to 2779 periodicals including electronic. Computerized library services include interlibrary loans, database searching, Internet access, and laptop Internet portals. Special learning facilities include a learning resource center, art gallery, planetarium, radio station, tropical greenhouse, observatory, adaptive computer lab, languages lab, and applied language and math center. The 177-acre campus is in an urban area 5 miles south of downtown Boston. Including any residence halls, there are 10 buildings.

Student Life: 95% of undergraduates are from Massachusetts. Others are from 40 states, 138 foreign countries, and Canada. 56% are white; 17% African American; 15% Asian American. The average age of freshmen is 18; all undergraduates, 25. 23% do not continue beyond their first year; 39% remain to graduate.

Housing: There are no residence halls. All students commute.

Activities: There are no fraternities or sororities. There are 75 groups on campus, including art, band, cheerleading, chess, choir, chorale, chorus, computers, dance, drama, ethnic, film, gay, honors, international, jazz band, literary magazine, musical theater, newspaper, orchestra, photography, political, professional, radio and TV, religious, social, social service, and student government. Popular campus events include Convocation Day, seasonal festivals, and lecture series.

Sports: There are 7 intercollegiate sports for men and 7 for women, and 12 intramural sports for men and 12 for women. Facilities include an athletic center with a 3500-seat gym with 4 basketball and 2 volleyball courts, an ice rink that seats 1000, a Olympic-size swimming pool with high-dive area, a multipurpose weight room, a sports medicine area, an 8-lane, 400-meter track, 8 tennis courts, a softball diamond, 3 multipurpose fields primarily used for soccer and lacrosse, and other recreational fields, a boat house, dock, and fleet of sailboats and rowing dories, and a fitness center with strength-training equipment.

Disabled Students: All of the campus is accessible. Facilities include wheelchair ramps, elevators, special parking, specially equipped rest rooms, special class scheduling, lowered drinking fountains, lowered telephones, amplified phones, powered doors, indoor-connected building access, an accessible shuttle bus, an adaptive computer lab, and a center for students with disabilities.

Services: Counseling and information services are available, as is tutoring in every subject. There is a reader service for the blind and remedial math, reading, and writing. There are also reading study skills workshops and a math resource center available.

Campus Safety and Security: Measures include 24-hour foot and vehicle patrol, emergency notification system, self-defense education, and security escort services. There are shuttle buses, emergency telephones, lighted pathways/sidewalks, Operation ID, motorist assistance, and crime prevention programs.

Programs of Study: UMass Boston confers B.A. and B.S. degrees. Master's and doctoral degrees are also awarded. Bachelor's degrees are awarded in BIOLOGICAL SCIENCE (biochemistry and biology/biological science), BUSINESS (labor studies and management science), COMMUNICATIONS AND THE ARTS (art, classical languages, classics, dramatic arts, English, French, Italian, music, and Spanish), COMPUTER AND PHYSICAL SCIENCE (chemistry, computer science, earth science, information sciences and systems, mathematics, and physics), ENGINEERING AND ENVIRONMENTAL DESIGN (engineering and engineering physics), HEALTH PROFESSIONS (exercise science, medical technology, and nursing), SOCIAL SCIENCE (African American studies, American studies, anthropology, community services, criminal justice, economics, ethics, politics, and social policy, geography, gerontology, Hispanic American studies, history, human services, paralegal studies, philosophy, political science/government, psychology, sociology, and women's studies). Management, nursing, and psychology are the largest.

Required: For graduation, students must complete 120 credit hours (123 hours in the College of Nursing) and maintain a minimum GPA of 2.0. Distribution requirements vary by college. All students must demonstrate writing proficiency.

Special: Students may cross-register with Boston Public Colleges, Massachusetts College of Art, Bunker Hill Community College, Roxbury Community College, and Hebrew College. UMass Boston also offers cooperative programs, internships, study abroad, work-study programs, student-designed majors, B.A.-B.S. degrees, nondegree study, pass/fail options, and dual and interdisciplinary majors, including anthropology/history, biology/medical technology, philosophy/public policy, and psychology/sociology. Also available are 3-1 and 2-2 engineering programs with various area institutions. The College of Public and Community Service provides social-oriented education. There are 3 national honor societies and a freshman honors program.

Faculty/Classroom: 52% of faculty are male; 48% are female. 90% teach undergraduates. No introductory courses are taught by graduate students. The average class size in an introductory lecture is 25; in a laboratory is 18; and in a regular course is 25.

Admissions: 62% of the 2009-2010 applicants were accepted. The SAT scores for the 2009-2010 freshman class were: Critical Reading--42% below 500, 43% between 500 and 599, 14% between 600 and 700, and 1% above 700; Math--32% below 500, 47% between 500 and 599, 19% between 600 and 700, and 2% above 700.

Requirements: The SAT or ACT is required. In addition, applicants should be graduates of an accredited secondary school. The GED is accepted. The university requires the completion of 16 Carnegie units, including 4 years of English, 3 of college preparatory math and science, 2 each of a foreign language and social studies, and 2 electives in the above academic areas or in humanities, arts, or computer science. A GPA of 3.0 is required. AP and CLEP credits are accepted.

Procedure: Freshmen are admitted fall and spring. Entrance exams should be taken by the fall of the senior year. There are deferred admissions and rolling admissions plans. Applications should be filed by June 1 for fall entry, along with a $40 fee. Notification is sent on a rolling basis. Applications are accepted on-line.

Transfer: 1746 transfer students enrolled in 2008-2009. Applicants with fewer than 24 credits must meet freshman requirements. To transfer, students must have a minimum GPA of 3.0. Grades of C- or better transfer for credit. 30 of 120 credits required for the bachelor's degree must be completed at UMass Boston.

Visiting: There are regularly scheduled orientations for prospective students, including general information sessions about the university and the admissions process and a tour of the campus. There are guides for informal visits and visitors may sit in on classes. To schedule a visit, contact Enrollment Information Services at (617) 287-6000.

Financial Aid: The FAFSA is required. Check with the school for current application deadlines.

International Students: The school actively recruits these students. They must take the TOEFL with a minimum score of 550 on the paper-based TOEFL (PBT) or 79 on the Internet-based version (iBT). They must also take the SAT or ACT if the language of instruction is English.

Computers: Wireless access is available. All students may access the system 24 hours a day. There are no time limits and no fees.

Graduates: From July 1, 2008 to June 30, 2009, 1608 bachelor's degrees were awarded. The most popular majors were management (19%), social science (14%), and health professions and related science (14%). In an average class, 1% graduate in 3 years or less, 10% graduate in 4 years or less, 30% graduate in 5 years or less, and 39% graduate in 6 years or less.

Admissions Contact: Liliana Mickle, Director, Undergraduate Admissions. E-Mail: *enrollmentinfo@umb.edu* Web: *www.umb.edu*

UNIVERSITY OF MASSACHUSETTS DARTMOUTH   E-4
North Dartmouth, MA 02747-2300 (508) 999-9106
(508) 999-8755

Full-time: 3776 men, 3292 women	**Faculty:** 357; IIA, +$
Part-time: 371 men, 543 women	**Ph.D.s:** 86%
Graduate: 588 men, 732 women	**Student/Faculty:** 20 to 1
Year: semesters, summer session	**Tuition:** $10,358 ($20,061)
Application Deadline: open	**Room & Board:** $9370
Freshman Class: 7155 applied, 4881 accepted, 1516 enrolled	
SAT CR/M/W: 520/550/520	**ACT:** 23 COMPETITIVE

University of Massachusetts Dartmouth, founded in 1895, is a public institution that provides undergraduate and graduate programs in the liberal and creative arts and sciences and in professional training. There are 5 undergraduate schools and 2 graduate schools. In addition to regional accreditation, UMass Dartmouth has baccalaureate program accreditation with AACSB, ABET, CSAB, NASAD, NASDTEC, and NLN. The library contains 461,338 volumes, 854,386 microform items, and 8115 audio/video tapes/CDs/DVDs, and subscribes to 2783 periodicals including electronic. Computerized library services include interlibrary loans, database searching, and Internet access. Special learning facilities include a learning resource center, art gallery, radio station, observatory, marine research vessels, and a number of cultural and research centers. The 710-acre campus is in a suburban area approximately 60 miles south of Boston and 35 miles east of Providence, Rhode Island. Including any residence halls, there are 28 buildings.

Student Life: 96% of undergraduates are from Massachusetts. Others are from 24 states, 15 foreign countries, and Canada. 88% are from public schools. 84% are white. The average age of freshmen is 19; all undergraduates, 21. 25% do not continue beyond their first year; 46% remain to graduate.

Housing: 4450 students can be accommodated in college housing, which includes coed dorms and on-campus apartments. In addition, there are honors houses, a quiet house, and apartments for upperclassmen. On-campus housing is guaranteed for the freshman year only, is available on a first-come, first-served basis, and is available on a lottery system for upperclassmen. Priority is given to out-of-town students. 56% of students live on campus; of those, 35% remain on campus on weekends. All students may keep cars.

Activities: 1% of men belong to 6 national fraternities; 1% of women belong to 1 local and 3 national sororities. There are 100 groups on campus, including art, band, cheerleading, choir, chorale, chorus, computers, drama, ethnic, film, gay, honors, international, jazz band, literary magazine, musical theater, newspaper, orchestra, pep band, political, professional, radio and TV, religious, social, social service, student government, and symphony. Popular campus events include Welcome Back Week and Spring Fling Week.

Sports: There are 12 intercollegiate sports for men and 13 for women, and 11 intramural sports for men and 11 for women. Facilities include a 3000-seat gym, an 1850-seat football stadium, an aquatic sports center, 13 tennis courts, a 10,000-sq-ft fitness center, a running track, and soccer, softball, and intramural fields.

Disabled Students: 94% of the campus is accessible. Facilities include wheelchair ramps, elevators, special parking, specially equipped rest-rooms, special class scheduling, lowered drinking fountains, lowered telephones, special housing, mobility assistance, note takers/readers, alternative testing, and an office of disabled student services.

Services: Counseling and information services are available, as is tutoring in most subjects through the writing/reading, science/engineering, math/business, and academic resource centers. There is a reader service for the blind, and remedial math, reading, and writing.

Campus Safety and Security: Measures include 24-hour foot and vehicle patrol, emergency notification system, self-defense education, and security escort services. There are shuttle buses, emergency telephones, lighted pathways/sidewalks, and a bicycle patrol.

Programs of Study: UMass Dartmouth confers B.A., B.S., and B.F.A. degrees. Master's and doctoral degrees are also awarded. Bachelor's degrees are awarded in BIOLOGICAL SCIENCE (biochemistry, biology/biological science, and marine biology), BUSINESS (accounting, banking and finance, business administration and management, human resources, management information systems, marketing/retailing/merchandising, and operations management), COMMUNICATIONS AND THE ARTS (art history and appreciation, ceramic art and design, design, English, fiber/textiles/weaving, French, graphic design, illustration, metal/jewelry, music, painting, photography, Portuguese, sculpture, Spanish, and technical and business writing), COMPUTER AND PHYSICAL SCIENCE (chemistry, computer science, mathematics, and physics), EDUCATION (art education), ENGINEERING AND ENVIRONMENTAL DESIGN (civil engineering, computer engineering, electrical/electronics engineering, materials science, mechanical engineering, and textile technology), HEALTH PROFESSIONS (medical laboratory science and nursing), SOCIAL SCIENCE (anthropology, criminal justice, economics, history, humanities and social science, interdisciplinary studies, philosophy, political science/government, psychology, sociology, and women's studies). Engineering, physical/life sciences, and design/fine arts are the strongest academically. Business systems administration, nursing, and psychology are the largest.

Required: The core curriculum requires 9 credits each of communication skills, cultural and artistic literacy, and math/science/technology, 6 each of global awareness and information/computer literacy, and 3 of ethics. A freshman English composition course is required. Colleges set some additional distribution course requirements. The B.A. requires foreign language study. To graduate, students must complete 120 to 132 credit hours and maintain a 2.0 GPA.

Special: The university permits cross-registration through the SACHEM Consortium of 9 schools in Massachusetts. Study abroad in 9 countries, an engineering or business co-op program, a Washington semester, internships, numerous work-study programs, dual majors, and student-designed majors are available. Teacher certification in elementary and secondary education is available as is a 3+3 law degree with a local law school. Nondegree study, pass/fail options, B.S.-M.S. degrees in chemistry, nursing, computer science, electrical engineering, computer engineering, and mechanical engineering, a B.A.-M.A. in psychology, and credit for life experience are possible. There are 5 national honor societies and a freshman honors program.

Faculty/Classroom: 57% of faculty are male; 43% are female. All teach undergraduates, and 60% do research. Graduate students teach 1% of introductory courses. The average class size in an introductory lecture is 41; in a laboratory, 18; and in a regular course, 22.

Admissions: 68% of the 2009-2010 applicants were accepted. The SAT scores for the 2009-2010 freshman class were: Critical Reading--37% below 500, 48% between 500 and 599, 14% between 600 and 700, and 1% above 700; Math--28% below 500, 49% between 500 and 599, 21% between 600 and 700, and 2% above 700; Writing--37% below 500, 50% between 500 and 599, 12% between 600 and 700, and 1% above 700. The ACT scores were 25% below 21, 37% between 21 and 23, 21% between 24 and 26, 9% between 27 and 28, and 8% above 28. 3 freshmen graduated first in their class.

Requirements: The SAT is required. In addition, applicants should have 4 years of English, 3 each of science and math, 2 of the same foreign language, 1 each of social studies and U.S. history, and 2 of college-preparatory electives. The GED is accepted. An audition is necessary for music majors, and a portfolio is recommended for studio arts and design applicants. All applicants must submit an essay. A GPA of 3.0 is required. AP and CLEP credits are accepted. Important factors in the admissions decision are recommendations by school officials, advanced placement or honors courses, and evidence of special talent.

Procedure: Freshmen are admitted fall and spring. Entrance exams should be taken during the spring of the junior year or early fall of the senior year. There are early decision, deferred admissions, and rolling admissions plans. Early decision applications should be filed by November 15; other application deadlines are open. Application fee is $40. Notification of early decision is sent December 15; other notification is sent on a rolling basis. 44 early decision candidates were accepted for the 2009-2010 class. Applications are accepted on-line.

Transfer: 470 transfer students enrolled in 2008-2009. Applicants must submit all official college transcripts and must take the SAT unless they graduated from high school more than 3 years prior to applying. Those with fewer than 30 transferable credits must submit high school records. 45 of 120 to 132 credits required for the bachelor's degree must be completed at UMass Dartmouth.

Visiting: There are regularly scheduled orientations for prospective students, including scheduled campus tours Monday through Friday and most Saturdays. There are guides for informal visits, and visitors may sit in on classes. To schedule a visit, contact the Admissions Office.

Financial Aid: In 2008-2009, 61% of all full-time freshmen and 57% of continuing full-time students received some form of financial aid. 50% of all full-time freshmen and 43% of continuing full-time students received need-based aid. Need-based scholarships or need-based grants averaged $6149, and need-based self-help aid (loans and jobs) averaged $6436. 27% of undergraduate students work part-time. Average annual earnings from campus work are $2155. The average financial indebtedness of the 2009 graduate was $18,900. The FAFSA is required.

The priority date for freshman financial aid applications for fall entry is March 1.

International Students: There are 31 international students enrolled. They must take the TOEFL with a minimum score of 520 on the paper-based TOEFL (PBT) or 68 on the Internet-based version (iBT). They must also take the SAT.

Computers: Wireless access is available. PCs and Macs are located in the library and academic buildings. Wireless access is available, as is Internet hookups in dorms. All students may access the system during the day and evening as well as on weekends. There are no time limits and no fees. It is strongly recommended that all students have a personal computer.

Graduates: From July 1, 2008 to June 30, 2009, 1245 bachelor's degrees were awarded. The most popular majors were marketing (8%), nursing (8%), and psychology (6%). 105 companies recruited on campus in 2008-2009. In an average class, 27% graduate in 4 years or less, 42% graduate in 5 years or less, and 46% graduate in 6 years or less. Of the 2008 graduating class, 14% were enrolled in graduate school within 6 months of graduation, and 22% were employed.

Admissions Contact: Kathy Magnusson, Associate Director of Admissions. E-mail: *admissions@umassd.edu* Web: *www.umassd.edu*

UNIVERSITY OF MASSACHUSETTS LOWELL   D-1

Lowell, MA 01854   **(978) 934-3931**
                                          (800) 410-4607; (978) 934-3086

Full-time: 4551 men, 3008 women	**Faculty:** I, +$
Part-time: 1755 men, 1234 women	**Ph.D.s:** 48%
Graduate: 1627 men, 1427 women	**Student/Faculty:** n/av
Year: semesters, summer session	**Tuition:** $10,681 ($26,067)
Application Deadline: open	**Room & Board:** $8635
Freshman Class: 5913 applied, 4287 accepted, 1522 enrolled	
SAT M/W: 555/528	**COMPETITIVE**

The University of Massachussetts Lowell, founded in 1895, is a public institution offering undergraduate programs through the schools of arts and sciences, engineering, health professions, management science, and music and graduate programs in education. There are 5 undergraduate schools and 1 graduate school. In addition to regional accreditation, UMass Lowell has baccalaureate program accreditation with AACSB, ABET, APTA, CAHEA, CSAB, NASAD, NASM, NCATE, and NLN. The 3 libraries contain 382,599 volumes, 91,022 microform items, and 14,353 audio/video tapes/CDs/DVDs, and subscribe to 32,744 periodicals including electronic. Computerized library services include interlibrary loans, database searching, Internet access, and laptop Internet portals. Special learning facilities include a learning resource center, art gallery, natural history museum, radio station, many experimental and investigative labs, and the Research Foundation, which includes a materials testing division and centers for atmospheric research and tropical disease. The 100-acre campus is in an urban area 30 miles northwest of Boston. Including any residence halls, there are 37 buildings.

Student Life: 85% of undergraduates are from Massachusetts. Others are from 43 states, 28 foreign countries, and Canada. 72% are white. The average age of freshmen is 18; all undergraduates, 23. 21% do not continue beyond their first year; 79% remain to graduate.

Housing: 3081 students can be accommodated in college housing, which includes single-sex and coed dorms, off-campus apartments, and married student housing. In addition, there are special-interest houses. On-campus housing is guaranteed for the freshman year only and is available on a first-come, first-served basis. 64% of students commute. All students may keep cars.

Activities: There are no fraternities or sororities. There are 100 groups on campus, including art, band, cheerleading, computers, drama, ethnic, gay, honors, international, marching band, musical theater, newspaper, pep band, photography, political, professional, radio and TV, religious, social, social service, and student government.

Sports: There are 15 intercollegiate sports for men and 10 for women, and 34 intramural sports for men and 34 for women. Facilities include a 2000-seat gym, a pool, weight-training facilities, and areas for gymnastics, wrestling, and judo. There are also courts for handball, squash, and tennis and various playing fields.

Disabled Students: 70% of the campus is accessible. Facilities include wheelchair ramps, elevators, special parking, specially equipped restrooms, special class scheduling, lowered drinking fountains, and lowered telephones.

Services: Counseling and information services are available, as is tutoring in most subjects. There is a reader service for the blind and remedial writing.

Campus Safety and Security: Measures include 24-hour foot and vehicle patrol, self-defense education, and security escort services. There are shuttle buses, emergency telephones, and lighted pathways/sidewalks.

Programs of Study: UMass Lowell confers B.A., B.F.A., B.L.A., B.M., B.S., B.S.B.A., B.S.E., B.S.E.T., B.S.I.M., and B.S.I.T. degrees. Associate, master's, and doctoral degrees are also awarded. Bachelor's degrees are awarded in BIOLOGICAL SCIENCE (biology/biological science), BUSINESS (business administration and management), COMMUNICATIONS AND THE ARTS (English, fine arts, modern language, and music performance), COMPUTER AND PHYSICAL SCIENCE (applied mathematics, chemistry, computer science, information sciences and systems, mathematics, and physics), ENGINEERING AND ENVIRONMENTAL DESIGN (chemical engineering, civil engineering, electrical/electronics engineering, engineering technology, environmental science, industrial administration/management, industrial engineering technology, mechanical engineering, and plastics engineering), HEALTH PROFESSIONS (clinical science, community health work, exercise science, and nursing), SOCIAL SCIENCE (American studies, criminal justice, economics, history, liberal arts/general studies, philosophy, political science/government, psychology, and sociology). Engineering and management are the largest.

Required: All students must complete a minimum of 120 credits with a 2.0 GPA. Core requirements include 6 credits of English composition, 3 credits of human values, and an area distribution requirement of 27 to 29 credits outside the major in behavioral and social science, fine arts and the humanities, and math and the sciences.

Special: Cross-registration, co-op, and work-study programs are available, as are opportunities for study abroad. The university offers a combined B.A.-B.S. degree in engineering, dual majors, nondegree study, and pass/fail options. There are 2 national honor societies, a freshman honors program, and 100 departmental honors programs.

Faculty/Classroom: 61% of faculty are male; 39% are female. No introductory courses are taught by graduate students.

Admissions: 73% of the 2009-2010 applicants were accepted. The SAT scores for the 2009-2010 freshman class were: Critical Reading--34% below 500, 48% between 500 and 599, 16% between 600 and 700, and 2% above 700; Math--23% below 500, 47% between 500 and 599, 27% between 600 and 700, and 3% above 700. 15% of the current freshmen were in the top fifth of their class; 58% were in the top two fifths. 8 freshmen graduated first in their class.

Requirements: The SAT or ACT is required; the SAT is preferred. In addition, applicants should have a high school diploma or the GED. The university recommends that secondary preparation include 4 courses in English, 3 each in social science/history and math, 2 each in science and a foreign language, and 2 academic electives. Prospective music majors must audition, and an interview is recommended for all students. A GPA of 3.0 is required. AP and CLEP credits are accepted.

Procedure: Freshmen are admitted fall and spring. Entrance exams should be taken by January of the senior year. There are deferred admissions and rolling admissions plans. Application deadlines are open. The application fee is $40. 89 applicants were on the 2009 waiting list; 27 were admitted. Applications are accepted on-line.

Transfer: 935 transfer students enrolled in 2008-2009. Transfer applicants must present at least a 2.0 GPA in previous college work. Those with fewer than 30 credits must meet freshman admission requirements. 30 of 120 credits required for the bachelor's degree must be completed at UMass Lowell.

Visiting: There are regularly scheduled orientations for prospective students. To schedule a visit, contact the Office of Student Services at (978) 934-2105.

Financial Aid: In 2009-2010, 94% of all full-time freshmen received some form of financial aid, including need-based aid. The average freshman award was $12,705. Need-based scholarships or need-based grants averaged $6805; need-based self-help aid (loans and jobs) averaged $6593; non-need-based athletic scholarships averaged $4834; and other non-need-based awards and non-need-based scholarships averaged $2435. 16% of undergraduate students work part-time. Average annual earnings from campus work are $3090. The average financial indebtedness of the 2009 graduate was $21,542. The FAFSA is required. The priority date for freshman financial aid applications for fall entry is March 1.

International Students: There are 55 international students enrolled. They must take the TOEFL with a minimum score of 550 on the paper-based TOEFL (PBT) or 79 on the Internet-based version (iBT). They must also take the SAT or ACT.

Computers: Wireless access is available. All students may access the system. There are no time limits and no fees.

Graduates: From July 1, 2008 to June 30, 2009, 1337 bachelor's degrees were awarded. The most popular majors were business administration (16%), engineering (11%), and criminal justice (7%). In an average class, 22% graduate in 4 years or less, 44% graduate in 5 years or less, and 46% graduate in 6 years or less.

Admissions Contact: Kerrie Johnston, Director, Admissions.
E-mail: *admissions@uml.edu* Web: *www.uml.edu*

WELLESLEY COLLEGE · D-2

Wellesley, MA 02481 · (781) 283-2270; (781) 283-3678

Full-time: 2185 women	Faculty: 259; IIB, ++$
Part-time: 83 women	Ph.D.s: 293%
Graduate: none	Student/Faculty: 8 to 1
Year: semesters	Tuition: $38,062
Application Deadline: January 15	Room & Board: $11,786
Freshman Class: 4156 applied, 1463 accepted, 589 enrolled	
SAT CR/M/W: 689/683/693	ACT: 30 MOST COMPETITIVE

Wellesley College, established in 1870, is a small, private, diverse liberal arts and sciences college for women. The 5 libraries contain 94,346 volumes, 536,499 microform items, and 36,439 audio/video tapes/CDs/DVDs, and subscribe to 1,945 periodicals including electronic. Computerized library services include interlibrary loans, database searching, and Internet access. Special learning facilities include a learning resource center, art gallery, radio station, a science center, a botanic greenhouse, an observatory, a center for developmental studies and services, centers for research on women and child study, and a media and technology center. The 500-acre campus is in a suburban area 12 miles west of Boston. Including any residence halls, there are 64 buildings.

Student Life: 86% of undergraduates are from out of state, mostly the Middle Atlantic. Students are from 50 states, 60 foreign countries, and Canada. 63% are from public schools. 41% are white; 25% Asian American. The average age of freshmen is 18; all undergraduates, 20. 6% do not continue beyond their first year; 943% remain to graduate.

Housing: 2188 students can be accommodated in college housing, which includes single-sex dorms. In addition, there are language houses, special-interest houses, language corridors, and co-ops. On-campus housing is guaranteed for all 4 years. 97% of students live on campus. Upperclassmen may keep cars.

Activities: There are no fraternities or sororities. There are 160 groups on campus, including art, choir, chorus, computers, dance, debate, drama, environmental, ethnic, film, gay, honors, international, jazz band, literary magazine, musical theater, newspaper, orchestra, photography, political, professional, radio and TV, religious, social, social service, student government, symphony, and yearbook. Popular campus events include Lake Day, Spring Weekend, and International Week.

Sports: There are 13 intercollegiate sports for women and 21 intramural sports for women. Facilities include an indoor pool, dance studios, a weight room, an indoor track, a golf course, and courts for racquetball, squash, tennis, and volleyball.

Disabled Students: All of the campus is accessible. Facilities include wheelchair ramps, elevators, special parking, specially equipped restrooms, special class scheduling, lowered drinking fountains, lowered telephones, special housing, and signage in braille.

Services: Counseling and information services are available, as is tutoring in every subject. There is a reader service for the blind.

Campus Safety and Security: Measures include 24-hour foot and vehicle patrol, emergency notification system, self-defense education, and security escort services. There are shuttle buses, emergency telephones, and lighted pathways/sidewalks.

Programs of Study: Wellesley confers B.A. degrees. Bachelor's degrees are awarded in AGRICULTURE (environmental studies), BIOLOGICAL SCIENCE (biochemistry, biology/biological science, and neurosciences), COMMUNICATIONS AND THE ARTS (art history and appreciation, Chinese, comparative literature, dramatic arts, English, film arts, French, German, Greek, Japanese, Latin, music, Russian, Russian languages and literature, Spanish, and studio art), COMPUTER AND PHYSICAL SCIENCE (astronomy, astrophysics, chemistry, computer science, geology, mathematics, and physics), ENGINEERING AND ENVIRONMENTAL DESIGN (architecture), SOCIAL SCIENCE (African American studies, American studies, anthropology, archeology, Asian/Oriental studies, classical/ancient civilization, cognitive science, economics, French studies, German area studies, history, international relations, Italian studies, Japanese studies, Judaic studies, Latin American studies, medieval studies, Middle Eastern studies, peace studies, philosophy, political science/government, psychology, religion, sociology, and women's studies). Psychology, English, and economics are the largest.

Required: All students must complete 32 units, at least 8 of which are in the major field, with a minimum 2.0 GPA. Requirements include 3 courses each in humanities, social science, and natural science and math; 1 multicultural course; 1 semester of expository writing in any department; and 8 credits in phys ed. Students must also possess proficiency in a modern or ancient foreign language. A thesis is required for departmental honors. A quantitative reasoning requirement must be satisfied by all students.

Special: Students may cross-register at MIT, Brandeis University, or Babson College. Exchange programs are available with Spelman College in Georgia and Mills College in California, with members of the Twelve College Exchange Program, with Williams College's maritime studies program, and with Connecticut College's National Theater Institute. Study abroad is possible through Wellesley-administered programs in France and Austria, exchange programs in Argentina, Japan, Korea, and the United Kingdom, and other programs in Italy, Japan, Spain, South Africa, and China. There are more than 150 approved study abroad programs available. There are summer internship programs in Boston and Washington, D.C. Dual majors, student-designed majors, nondegree study, and pass/fail options are possible. A 3-2 program with MIT, Dartmouth, and Columbia awards a B.A.-B.S. degree. There are 2 national honor societies, including Phi Beta Kappa, and 51 departmental honors programs.

Faculty/Classroom: 37% of faculty are male; 63% are female. All teach undergraduates. No introductory courses are taught by graduate students. The average class size in an introductory lecture, 30, and in a regular course, 19.

Admissions: 35% of the 2009-2010 applicants were accepted. The SAT scores for the 2009-2010 freshman class were: Critical Reading-- 10% between 500 and 599, 38% between 600 and 700, and 52% above 700; Math-- 11% between 500 and 599, 45% between 600 and 700, and 43% above 700; Writing-- 8% between 500 and 599, 41% between 600 and 700, and 51% above 700. The ACT scores were 69% above 28. 96% of the current freshmen were in the top fifth of their class; All were in the top two fifths. 78 freshmen graduated first in their class.

Requirements: The SAT or ACT is required. The SAT Reasoning Test and 2 SAT subject tests, or the ACT with Writing are required. Wellesley College does not require a fixed plan of secondary school course preparation. Entering students normally have completed 4 years of college preparatory studies in secondary school that include training in clear and coherent writing and interpreting literature; history; principles of math (typically 4 years); competence in at least 1 foreign language, ancient or modern (usually 4 years of study); and experience in at least 2 lab sciences. An essay is required, and an interview is recommended. AP credits are accepted. Important factors in the admissions decision are advanced placement or honors courses, extracurricular activities record, and recommendations by school officials.

Procedure: Freshmen are admitted in the fall. Entrance exams should be taken during the spring of the junior year or fall of the senior year. December is the last month in which standaradized test should be taken. There are early decision and deferred admissions plans. Early decision applications should be filed by November 1; regular applications, by January 15 for fall entry. The fall 2008 application fee was $50. Notification of early decision is sent december 15; regular decision, April 1. Applications are accepted on-line and the application fee is waived. 543 applicants were on a recent waiting list, 30 were accepted.

Transfer: 27 transfer students enrolled in 2008-2009. Applicants must provide high school and college transcripts, SAT or ACT scores, a personal statement, and a statement of good standing from institutions previously attended. An interview is required. 16 of 32 credits required for the bachelor's degree must be completed at Wellesley.

Visiting: There are guides for informal visits; visitors may sit in on classes and stay overnight. To schedule a visit, contact the Admissions Office at (781) 283-2270.

Financial Aid: In 2009-2010, 56% of all full-time freshmen and 54% of continuing full-time students received some form of financial aid. 58% of all full-time freshmen and 58% of continuing full-time students received need-based aid. The average freshmen award was $36,064. Average annual earnings from campus work are $2000. The average financial indebtedness of the 2009 graduate was $13,324. Wellesley is a member of CSS. The CSS/Profile, FAFSA, and the college's own financial statement, and and the most recent income tax returns of parents and student. are required. The deadline for filing freshman financial aid applications for fall entry is January 15.

International Students: There are 211 international students enrolled. The school actively recruits these students. They must take the SAT or ACT. It is strongly recommended that they take an English proficiency exam. It is strongly recommended they take the TOEFL, especially for students who have not studied for at least 5 years in an English-based curriculum. If a student does not take the ACT, she must submit scores from SAT and SAT II subject tests.

Computers: Wireless access is available. Computer terminals are available in the libraries. Wireless access is available in the libraries, academic buildings, and residence halls. All students may access the system. There are no time limits and no fees.

Graduates: From July 1, 2008 to June 30, 2009, 594 bachelor's degrees were awarded. The most popular majors were economics (15%), political science (12%), and English (10%). In an average class, 86% graduate in 4 years or less, 89% graduate in 5 years or less, and 89% graduate in 6 years or less.

Admissions Contact: Board of Admission A campus DVD is available. E-Mail: *admission@wellesley.edu* Web: *www.wellesley.edu*

WENTWORTH INSTITUTE OF TECHNOLOGY   E-2

Boston, MA 02115

(617) 989-4000
(800) 556-0610; (617) 989-4010

Full-time: 2653 men, 680 women	**Faculty:** 135
Part-time: none 343 men, 52 women	**Ph.D.s:** 50%
Graduate: none	**Student/Faculty:** 25 to 1
Year: semesters, summer session	**Tuition:** $20,150
Application Deadline:	**Room & Board:** $9,650
Freshman Class: 2329 applied, 1867 accepted, 859 enrolled	
ACT: 23	**SAT:** required **COMPETITIVE**

Wentworth Institute of Technology, founded in 1904, is a private college specializing in architecture, design, engineering, technology, and management. There are no undergraduate schools. In addition to regional accreditation, Wentworth has baccalaureate program accreditation with ABET, ACCE, FIDER, and NAAB. The library contains 77,000 volumes, 90 microform items, 750 audio/video tapes/CDs/DVDs, and subscribes to 500 periodicals including electronic. Computerized library services include interlibrary loans, database searching, and Internet access. Special learning facilities include a learning resource center, radio station, printed-circuit lab, CAD/CAM/CAE labs, design studios, and numerically controlled manufacturing systems. The 35-acre campus is in an urban area in Boston. Including any residence halls, there are 27 buildings.

Student Life: 60% of undergraduates are from Massachusetts. Students are from 39 states, 51 foreign countries, and Canada. 72% are white. The average age of freshmen is 19; all undergraduates, 22. 31% do not continue beyond their first year; 52% remain to graduate.

Housing: 1665 students can be accommodated in college housing, which includes coed dorms and on-campus apartments. On-campus housing is guaranteed for all 4 years and is guaranteed for the freshman year only. 60% of students live on campus. Alcohol is not permitted. Upperclassmen may keep cars.

Activities: There are no fraternities or sororities. There are 50 groups on campus, including communications, computers, dance, drama, ethnic, gay, honors, international, literary magazine, musical threater, newspaper, orchestra, professional, radio and TV, religious, social, social service, student government, and yearbook. Popular campus events include Design Lecture Series, Beaux Arts Ball, and Women's History Month.

Sports: There are 9 intercollegiate sports for men and 6 for women, and 5 intramural sports for men and 5 for women. Facilities include gyms, tennis courts, a riflery range, a fitness center, an outdoor basketball court, and softball, soccer, and lacrosse playing fields.

Disabled Students: 30% of the campus is accessible. Facilities include wheelchair ramps, elevators, special parking, specially equipped rest rooms, special class scheduling, lowered drinking fountains, and lowered telephones.

Services: Counseling and information services are available, as is tutoring in every subject. There is remedial math and writing. Free tutoring is available to all students through the learning center.

Campus Safety and Security: Measures include 24-hour foot and vehicle patrol, self-defense education, and security escort services. There are shuttle buses, emergency telephones, lighted pathways/sidewalks, and campus police officers have emergency medical training.

Programs of Study: Wentworth confers B.S. and B.Arch. degrees. Associates degrees are also awarded. Bachelor's degrees are awarded in COMMUNICATIONS AND THE ARTS (industrial design), COMPUTER AND PHYSICAL SCIENCE (computer science and information sciences and systems), ENGINEERING AND ENVIRONMENTAL DESIGN (architecture, biomedical engineering, civil engineering technology, computer technology, construction management, construction technology, electrical/electronics engineering technology, electromechanical technology, environmental science, industrial administration/management, interior design, mechanical engineering technology, and technological management). Architecture, computer science, and electronic engineering technology are the largest.

Required: For a bachelor's degree, students must complete a total of 136 to 176 hours, depending on the major, with a minimum GPA of 2.0 overall and 2.5 in the major. An introductory computer course is required of all students. All full-time bachelor's degree candidates must complete 2 semesters of co-op, beginning after the first 2 years of study. A writing competency assessment is required at the end of the sophomore year.

Special: Wentworth offers extensive cooperative programs, cross-registration with other members of the Colleges of the Fenway Consortium, study abroad, including study in France for third-year architecture students, interdisciplinary majors, including engineering technology and facilities planning and management, a dual major in technical management, and nondegree study. Most students at the bachelor's level attend school in the summer, as most cooperative work occurs during the academic year. There is 1 national honor society.

Faculty/Classroom: 76% of faculty are male; 24% are female. All teach undergraduates. No introductory courses are taught by graduate students. The average class size in an introductory lecture is 25; in a laboratory is 25; and in a regular course is 21.

Admissions: 80% of the 2009-2010 applicants were accepted.

Requirements: The SAT or ACT is required. In addition, applicants must be graduates of an accredited secondary school or have the GED. High school course requirements vary by major. AP and CLEP credits are accepted. Important factors in the admissions decision are advanced placement or honors courses, leadership record, and extracurricular activities record.

Procedure: Freshmen are admitted fall and spring. Entrance exams should be taken in the spring of the junior year or the fall of the senior year. There are deferred admissions and rolling admissions plans. Check with the school for current application deadlines. Notification is sent on a rolling basis. Applications are accepted on-line. A waiting list is maintained.

Transfer: 197 transfer students enrolled in 2008-2009. Requirements for transfer students vary by program. All applicants must submit official college and high school transcripts. Portfolios and faculty reviews are recommended of applicants to industrial design, interior design, and architecture programs. Grades of C or better transfer for credit. Transfer students must take 50% of the course work in their degree program at Wentworth to graduate.

Visiting: There are regularly scheduled orientations for prospective students, including daily tours and information programs, Monday to Friday. There are guides for informal visits and visitors may sit in on classes. To schedule a visit, contact the Admissions Office.

Financial Aid: In 2009-2010, 80% of all full-time freshmen and 80% of continuing full-time students received some form of financial aid. 60% of all full-time freshmen and 65% of continuing full-time students received need-based aid. 29% of undergraduate students work part-time. The FAFSA is required. The priority date for freshman financial aid applications for fall entry is March 1. The deadline for filing freshman financial aid applications for fall entry is June 1.

International Students: There are 120 international students enrolled. The school actively recruits these students. They must also take the SAT or ACT. with the SAT recommended.

Computers: Wireless access is available. All students are issued a laptop with the software needed for their majors. This is included in tuition. All students may access the system. There are no time limits and no fees. It is strongly recommended that all students have a personal computer.

Graduates: n/av

Admissions Contact: Office of Admissions E-Mail: admissions@wit.edu Web: www.wit.edu

WESTERN NEW ENGLAND COLLEGE B-3

Springfield, MA 01119

(413) 782-1321
(800) 325-1122 ext. 1321; (413) 782-1777

Full-time: 1479 men, 984 women	Faculty: 155; IIA, +$
Part-time: 174 men, 102 women	Ph.D.s: 89%
Graduate: 442 men, 529 women	Student/Faculty: 16 to 1
Year: semesters, summer session	Tuition: $28,816
Application Deadline: open	Room & Board: $10,980
Freshman Class: 4769 applied, 3861 accepted, 689 enrolled	
SAT CR/M: 520/540	ACT: 23 COMPETITIVE

Western New England College, founded in 1919, is a private nonsecretarian institution offering undergraduate programs in business, engineering, and arts and sciences. There are 3 undergraduate schools and 2 graduate schools. In addition to regional accreditation, WNEC has baccalaureate program accreditation with AACSB, ABET, and CSWE. The library contains 130,900 volumes, 194,268 microform items, and 5,200 audio/video tapes/CDs/DVDs, and subscribes to 208 periodicals including electronic. Computerized library services include interlibrary loans, database searching, Internet access, and laptop Internet portals. Special learning facilities include an art gallery and radio station. The 215-acre campus is in a suburban area 90 miles west of Boston. Including any residence halls, there are 23 buildings.

Student Life: 51% of undergraduates are from out of state, mostly the Middle Atlantic. Students are from 39 states, 3 foreign countries, and Canada. 80% are white. 82% claim no religious affiliation; 13% Catholic. The average age of freshmen is 18; all undergraduates, 20. 25% do not continue beyond their first year; 57% remain to graduate.

Housing: 2070 students can be accommodated in college housing, which includes coed dorms and on-campus apartments. Freshmen are grouped by academic interest areas or theme housing. On-campus housing is guaranteed for all 4 years. 75% of students live on campus. All students may keep cars.

Activities: There are no fraternities or sororities. There are 58 groups on campus, including art, cheerleading, chorus, computers, dance, drama, environmental, ethnic, gay, honors, international, jazz band, literary magazine, newspaper, pep band, photography, political, professional, radio and TV, religious, social, social service, student government, and yearbook. Popular campus events include Spring Week, Family and Friends Weekend, and Winter Week.

Sports: There are 10 intercollegiate sports for men and 9 for women, and 9 intramural sports for men and 9 for women. Facilities include a healthful living center equipped for basketball (2,000 seats), wrestling, racquetball, squash, aerobics, fitness, and volleyball, as well as a weight room, an 8-lane pool, and a track.

Disabled Students: 90% of the campus is accessible. Facilities include wheelchair ramps, elevators, special parking, specially equipped restrooms, special class scheduling, lowered drinking fountains, and lowered telephones.

Services: Counseling and information services are available, as is tutoring in most subjects.

Campus Safety and Security: Measures include 24-hour foot and vehicle patrol, emergency notification system, self-defense education, and security escort services. There are emergency telephones, lighted pathways/sidewalks, controlled access to dorms/residences, security cameras, medical response, fire response, and a comprehensive public safety awareness program.

Programs of Study: WNEC confers B.A., B.S., B.B.A., B.A.L.S., B.S.B.A., B.S.B.E., B.S.C.J., B.S.E.E., B.S.H.S., B.S.I.E., and B.S.M.E. degrees. Associates, master's, and doctoral degrees are also awarded. Bachelor's degrees are awarded in BIOLOGICAL SCIENCE (biology/biological science, ecology, and molecular biology), BUSINESS (accounting, banking and finance, business administration and management, management science, marketing/retailing/merchandising, and sports management), COMMUNICATIONS AND THE ARTS (advertising, communications, creative writing, English, and public relations), COMPUTER AND PHYSICAL SCIENCE (chemistry, computer science, information sciences and systems, and mathematics), EDUCATION (elementary education and secondary education), ENGINEERING AND ENVIRONMENTAL DESIGN (bioengineering, biomedical engineering, computer engineering, electrical/electronics engineering, industrial engineering, and mechanical engineering), SOCIAL SCIENCE (criminal justice, economics, forensic studies, history, international studies, law, liberal arts/general studies, philosophy, political science/government, psychology, social work, and sociology). Criminal justice, management, psychology, and engineering are the largest.

Required: To graduate, students must complete 122 credit hours, with a minimum GPA of 2.0. Requirements include 2 courses each in English, math, lab science, and phys ed, and 1 course each in history, culture, and computers. A first-year seminar is also required for freshmen. Other requirements vary according to the major.

Special: Students may cross-register with cooperating colleges of Greater Springfield. The college offers internships, study abroad, a Washington semester, work-study programs, B.A.-B.S. degrees, an accelerated degree program, and dual and student-designed majors. The 3+3 law program offers qualified students the opportunity to earn a J.D. in 6 years. There is also a 6-year biomedical engineering/law program, a 5-year Bachelor/M.B.A., and a 5-year accounting/M.S.A. There are 9 national honor societies and a freshman honors program.

Faculty/Classroom: 63% of faculty are male; 37% are female. No introductory courses are taught by graduate students. The average class size in an introductory lecture is 20; in a laboratory 17; and in a regular course 19.

Admissions: 81% of the 2009-2010 applicants were accepted. The SAT scores for the 2009-2010 freshman class were: Critical Reading--37% below 500, 48% between 500 and 599, 14% between 600 and 700, and 1% above 700; Math--29% below 500, 43% between 500 and 599, 25% between 600 and 700, and 3% above 700. The ACT scores were 29% below 21, 30% between 21 and 23, 26% between 24 and 26, 9% between 27 and 28, and 6% above 28. 33% of the current freshmen were in the top fifth of their class; 61% were in the top two fifths. 2 freshmen graduated first in their class.

Requirements: The SAT is required. In addition, applicants must be graduates of an approved secondary school and must have completed 4 years of high school English, 2 or more years of math, 1 or more years of science, and 1 year of history and social science. An interview is recommended. ACT is accepted in lieu of SAT. AP and CLEP credits are accepted. Important factors in the admissions decision are advanced placement or honors courses, extracurricular activities record, and recommendations by school officials.

Procedure: Freshmen are admitted fall and spring. Entrance exams should be taken in the spring of the junior year or fall of the senior year. There are deferred admissions and rolling admissions plans. Application deadlines are open. The fall 2009 application fee was $50. Notification is sent on a rolling basis. Applications are accepted on-line.

Transfer: 90 transfer students enrolled in 2008-2009. Applicants must have a minimum GPA of 2.3. Grades of C or better transfer for credit. The college admits transfer students in the fall and spring. 30 of 122 credits required for the bachelor's degree must be completed at WNEC.

Visiting: There are regularly scheduled orientations for prospective students, including multiple open houses. There are guides for informal visits and visitors may sit in on classes and stay overnight. To schedule a visit, contact the Undergraduate Admissions Office at 800-325-1122.

Financial Aid: In 2009-2010, 92% of all full-time freshmen received some form of financial aid. 77% of all full-time freshmen received need-based aid. The average freshmen award was $18,700. WNEC is a member of CSS. The FAFSA, and federal tax returns and W-2s are required. The priority date for freshman financial aid applications for fall entry is April 1. The deadline for filing freshman financial aid applications for fall entry is rolling.

International Students: There are 3 international students enrolled. The school actively recruits these students. They must take the TOEFL, or SAT or ACT.

Computers: Wireless access is available. All students may access the system at varying hours from campus labs; 24 hours a day from residence halls. There are no time limits and no fees.

Graduates: From July 1, 2008 to June 30, 2009, 584 bachelor's degrees were awarded. The most popular majors were psychology (12%), management (11%), and engineering (combined) (9%). In an average class, 5% graduate in 3 years or less, 44% graduate in 4 years or less, 53% graduate in 5 years or less, and 55% graduate in 6 years or less.

Admissions Contact: Dr. Charles R. Pollock, Vice President for Enrollment Management. A campus DVD is available. E-Mail: ugradmis@wnec.edu Web: www.wnec.edu

WESTFIELD STATE COLLEGE	B-3
Westfield, MA 01086-1630	**(413) 572-5218; (413) 572-0520**
Full-time: n/av none	Faculty: 176
Part-time: n/av none	Ph.Ds: 88%
Graduate: n/av none	Student/Faculty: 24 to 1
Year: semesters, summer session	Tuition: $6,210 ($12,290)
Application Deadline: March 1	Room & Board: $6,470
Freshman Class: 5080 applied, 2845 accepted, 950 enrolled	
SAT CR/M: 500/520	ACT: 20	COMPETITIVE

Westfield State College, founded in 1838, is a public college with liberal arts and teacher preparation programs and professional training. There are no undergraduate schools and one graduate school. In addition to regional accreditation, Westfield State has baccalaureate program accreditation with CSWE, NASM, and NCATE. The library contains 147,668 volumes, 471,522 microform items, 4,110 audio/video tapes/CDs/DVDs, and subscribes to 18,885 periodicals including electronic. Computerized library services include interlibrary loans, database searching, and Internet access. Special learning facilities include a learning resource center, art gallery, natural history museum, radio station, TV station, a geology museum. The 257-acre campus is in a suburban area 15 miles west of Springfield. Including any residence halls, there are 14 buildings.

Student Life: 93% of undergraduates are from Massachusetts. Students are from 20 states, 1 foreign country, and Canada. 83% are white. The average age of freshmen is 18; all undergraduates, 20. 24% do not continue beyond their first year; 56% remain to graduate.

Housing: 2510 students can be accommodated in college housing, which includes coed dorms, on-campus apartments, a living/learning unit, and special housing for international students. On-campus housing is guaranteed for all 4 years. 61% of students live on campus; of those, 70% remain on campus on weekends. Upperclassmen may keep cars.

Activities: There are no fraternities or sororities. There are 50 groups on campus, including art, band, chess, choir, chorale, chorus, communications, drama, ethnic, gay, honors, jazz band, literary magazine, musical threater, newspaper, orchestra, pep band, photography, political, professional, radio and TV, religious, social service, and student government. Popular campus events include Halloween Dance, Spring Weekend, and Comedy Night.

Sports: There are 7 intercollegiate sports for men and 11 for women, and 19 intramural sports for men and 19 for women. Facilities include a track, baseball and softball fields, tennis courts, a 400-seat gym, and a 5,000-seat stadium.

Disabled Students: 65% of the campus is accessible. Facilities include wheelchair ramps, elevators, special parking, specially equipped rest rooms, special class scheduling, lowered telephones, and special housing.

Services: Counseling and information services are available, as is tutoring in every subject. There is a reader service for the blind, and remedial math, reading, and writing.

Campus Safety and Security: Measures include 24-hour foot and vehicle patrol and security escort services. There are shuttle buses, emergency telephones, and lighted pathways/sidewalks.

Programs of Study: Westfield State confers B.A., B.S., B.S.E., and B.S.W. degrees. Master's degrees are also awarded. Bachelor's degrees are awarded in BIOLOGICAL SCIENCE (biology/biological science), BUSINESS (business administration and management), COMMUNICATIONS AND THE ARTS (communications, dramatic arts, English, fine arts, and music), COMPUTER AND PHYSICAL SCIENCE (computer science, information sciences and systems, and mathematics), EDUCATION (art education, business education, early childhood education, elementary education, middle school education, music education, science education, secondary education, and special education), ENGINEERING AND ENVIRONMENTAL DESIGN (environmental science), SOCIAL SCIENCE (criminal justice, economics, history, interdisciplinary

studies, physical fitness/movement, political science/government, psychology, social work, sociology, and urban studies). Criminal justice, education, and business are the largest.

Required: Students must complete a total of 120 credit hours, with 43 or more credits in 9 specified areas and 30 to 40 hours in the major. The college requires a 2.0 GPA overall and 2.0 in major courses. U.S. history or government and diversity awareness courses are required.

Special: Students may cross-register through College Academic Program Sharing, National Student Exchange, and Cooperating Colleges of Greater Springfield. Internships are for credit only in conjunction with all major programs. The college offers study abroad in 36 countries, a Washington semester for political science, criminal justice, and psychology majors, dual majors, student-designed majors, and some credit for military experience. There are 8 national honor societies and a freshman honors program.

Faculty/Classroom: 48% of faculty are male; 52% are female. All teach undergraduates. No introductory courses are taught by graduate students. The average class size in an introductory lecture is 26; in a laboratory is 15; and in a regular course is 24.

Admissions: 56% of the 2009-2010 applicants were accepted. The SAT scores for the 2009-2010 freshman class were: Critical Reading--45% below 500, 44% between 500 and 599, 10% between 600 and 700, and 1 above 700; Math--40% below 500, 47% between 500 and 599, 13% between 600 and 700, and above 700. The ACT scores were 51% below 21, 29% between 21 and 23, 14% between 24 and 26, 3% between 27 and 28, and 3% above 28.

Requirements: The SAT is required. In addition, applicants must achieve between a 2.0 and 3.0 cumulative average in academic subjects, contingent upon the SAT scores. They must be graduates of an accredited secondary school and must have completed 4 years of college preparatory level English, 3 years of math (algebra I and II and geometry), 2 years of social sciences (including 1 year of U.S history), 3 sciences, including 2 with lab, 2 foreign language, and 2 years of electives. The GED is accepted. A portfolio is required for admission to the art program, and an audition is necessary for admission to the music program. A GPA of 2.0 is required. AP and CLEP credits are accepted. Important factors in the admissions decision are advanced placement or honors courses, leadership record, and evidence of special talent.

Procedure: Freshmen are admitted fall and spring. Entrance exams should be taken in the spring of the junior year and fall of the senior year. There are deferred admissions and rolling admissions plans. Applications should be filed by March 1 for fall entry and December 1 for spring entry. The fall 2008 application fee was $25. Applications are accepted on-line.

Transfer: 250 transfer students enrolled in 2008-2009. Transfer students must have 24 transferable credits with a minimum cumulative GPA of 2.0 (higher for some majors). A grade of C- or better with a 2.0 GPA will transfer for credit. Transfer students are admitted in the fall and spring. 30 of 120 credits required for the bachelor's degree must be completed at Westfield State.

Visiting: There are regularly scheduled orientations for prospective students, including a campus tour, classroom observation, academic department presentations, lunch with faculty, staff, and students, and a question-and-answer session moderated by a panel of administrators. There are guides for informal visits. To schedule a visit, contact the Admission Office.

Financial Aid: In 2009-2010, 66% of all full-time freshmen and 65% of continuing full-time students received some form of financial aid. 39% of all full-time freshmen and 43% of continuing full-time students received need-based aid. The average freshmen award was $8,239. 8% of undergraduate students work part-time. Average annual earnings from campus work are $879. The average financial indebtedness of the 2009 graduate was $11,211. Westfield State is a member of CSS. The FAFSA is required. The deadline for filing freshman financial aid applications for fall entry is March 1.

International Students: There are 12 international students enrolled. They must take the TOEFL with a minimum score of 550 on the paper-based TOEFL (PBT) or 80 on the Internet-based version (iBT). They must also take the SAT.

Computers: Wireless access is available. All students may access the system. There are no time limits and no fees.

Graduates: From July 1, 2008 to June 30, 2009, 929 bachelor's degrees were awarded. The most popular majors were criminal justice (19%), business management (15%), and elementary education (12%). 100 companies recruited on campus in 2008-2009. In an average class, 39% graduate in 4 years or less, 54% graduate in 5 years or less, and 56% graduate in 6 years or less.

Admissions Contact: Michelle Mattie, Associate Dean, Enrollment Management. A campus DVD is available. E-Mail: admission@wsc.ma.edu Web: www.wsc.ma.edu

WHEATON COLLEGE   D-3
Norton, MA 02766

(508) 286-8251
(800) 394-6003; (508) 286-8271

Full-time: 625 men, 1002 women	Faculty: 139; IIB, +$
Part-time: 1 man, 4 women	Ph.D.s: 88%
Graduate: none	Student/Faculty: 12 to 1
Year: semesters	Tuition: $39,850
Application Deadline: January 15	Room & Board: $9590
Freshman Class: 3304 applied, 1947 accepted, 424 enrolled	
SAT CR/M: 630/620	ACT: 29

HIGHLY COMPETITIVE+

Wheaton College, established in 1834, is an independent liberal arts institution. The library contains 376,616 volumes, 74,078 microform items, and 17,133 audio/video tapes/CDs/DVDs, and subscribes to 15,299 periodicals including electronic. Computerized library services include interlibrary loans, database searching, Internet access, and laptop Internet portals. Special learning facilities include a learning resource center, art gallery, planetarium, radio station, a greenhouse, and an observatory. The 400-acre campus is in a suburban area 35 miles south of Boston and 15 miles north of Providence. Including any residence halls, there are 92 buildings.

Student Life: 68% of undergraduates are from out of state, mostly the Northeast. Students are from 42 states, 38 foreign countries, and Canada. 62% are from public schools. 76% are white. The average age of freshmen is 18; all undergraduates, 20. 12% do not continue beyond their first year; 75% remain to graduate.

Housing: 1489 students can be accommodated in college housing, which includes single-sex and coed dorms. In addition, there are language houses and special-interest houses including, among others, House of Living Arts, Women of Color/Social Responsibility, Global Awareness, and Outdoors Education. On-campus housing is guaranteed for all 4 years. 93% of students live on campus; of those, 73% remain on campus on weekends. Upperclassmen may keep cars; freshman parking is available but limited, with priority for those with medical conditions or off-campus jobs.

Activities: There are no fraternities or sororities. There are 70 groups on campus, including art, BACCHUS, band, choir, chorale, chorus, dance, debate, drama, environmental, ethnic, film, gay, Habitat for Humanity, honors, international, jazz band, literary magazine, musical theater, newspaper, orchestra, photography, political, professional, radio and TV, religious, social, social service, student government, symphony, Voices United to Jam (gospel choir), yearbook, and Zen Meditation Group. Popular campus events include Otis Social Justice Symposium and Award, Spring Weekend, and Season of Service.

Sports: There are 9 intercollegiate sports for men and 12 for women, and 9 intramural sports for men and 9 for women. Facilities include an 8-lane stretch pool, a field house with 5 tennis courts, 1 outdoor and 5 indoor basketball courts, a 200-meter track, a golf/archery range and batting cage, an 850-seat gym, 7 lighted outdoor tennis courts, a running course, a baseball stadium, 2 athletic fields, a softball field, an aerobics/dance studio, and a fitness center.

Disabled Students: 50% of the campus is accessible. Facilities include wheelchair ramps, elevators, special parking, specially equipped rest rooms, special class scheduling, and lowered telephones.

Services: Counseling and information services are available, as is tutoring in most subjects. There is a reader service for the blind and remedial writing. Peer tutoring and note takers for hearing-impaired students are available.

Campus Safety and Security: Measures include 24-hour foot and vehicle patrol, emergency notification system, self-defense education, and security escort services. There are emergency telephones and lighted pathways/sidewalks.

Programs of Study: Wheaton confers A.B. degrees. Bachelor's degrees are awarded in BIOLOGICAL SCIENCE (biochemistry, bioinformatics, and biology/biological science), COMMUNICATIONS AND THE ARTS (art history and appreciation, classics, creative writing, dramatic arts, English, fine arts, German, Greek, Latin, literature, music, Russian, and studio art), COMPUTER AND PHYSICAL SCIENCE (astronomy, chemistry, computer mathematics, computer science, mathematics, and physics), ENGINEERING AND ENVIRONMENTAL DESIGN (environmental science), SOCIAL SCIENCE (African studies, African American studies, American studies, anthropology, Asian/Oriental studies, classical/ancient civilization, economics, French studies, German area studies, Hispanic American studies, history, international relations, Italian studies, philosophy, political science/government, psychobiology, psychology, religion, Russian and Slavic studies, sociology, and women's studies). Arts and sciences are the strongest academically. Psychology, English, and economics are the largest.

Required: Among the requirements for graduation are 32 course credits (4 semester hours each), with a minimum of 10 courses in the major. The requirements for each major are determined by the department. The core classes consist of English, quantitative skills, foreign language, and non-Western history. Students must maintain a minimum GPA of 2.0 (C-) in all courses to remain in good academic standing.

Special: Students may cross-register with Brown University as well as with colleges in the Southeastern Association for Cooperation in Higher Education in Massachusetts and with schools participating in the 12 College Exchange Program. Wheaton offers study abroad in 54 countries, internship programs, nondegree study, dual majors, student-designed majors, a Washington semester at American University, and interdisciplinary majors, including math and economics, math and computer science, physics and astronomy, and theater and English dramatic literature. Dual-degree programs exist with the following institutions: Thayer School of Engineering, Dartmouth College (B.S. Engineering); Emerson College (M.A. Integrated Marketing Communication); Graduate School of Management, University of Rochester (M.B.A.); George Washington University (B.S. Engineering); School of the Museum of Fine Arts (B.F.A.); Andover-Newton Theological School (M.A. Religion); and New England School of Optometry (Doctor of Optometry). There are 8 national honor societies, including Phi Beta Kappa, and a freshman honors program. All departments have honors programs.

Faculty/Classroom: 46% of faculty are male; 54% are female. All teach undergraduates and do research. The average class size in an introductory lecture is 60; in a laboratory, 22; and in a regular course, 30.

Admissions: 59% of the 2009-2010 applicants were accepted. The SAT scores for the 2009-2010 freshman class were: Critical Reading--6% below 500, 26% between 500 and 599, 46% between 600 and 700, and 22% above 700; Math--3% below 500, 36% between 500 and 599, 45% between 600 and 700, and 16% above 700. The ACT scores were 2% below 21, 16% between 24 and 26, 35% between 27 and 28, and 47% above 28. 75% of the current freshmen were in the top fifth of their class; 92% were in the top two fifths. 6 freshmen graduated first in their class.

Requirements: Submission of SAT or ACT scores in optional. Applicants must be graduates of an accredited secondary school. Recommended courses include English with emphasis on composition skills, 4 years; foreign language and math, 4 years each; social studies, 3 years; and lab science, 2 to 3 years. Wheaton requires an essay and a graded writing sample and strongly recommends an interview. AP credits are accepted. Important factors in the admissions decision are advanced placement or honors courses, extracurricular activities record, and personality/intangible qualities.

Procedure: Freshmen are admitted fall and spring. Entrance exams should be taken in October and/or November. There are early decision and deferred admissions plans. Early decision applications should be filed by November 15; regular applications, by January 15 for fall entry and November 1 for spring entry, along with a $55 fee. Notification of early decision is sent December 15; regular decision, April 1. 140 early decision candidates were accepted for the 2009-2010 class. 380 applicants were on the 2009 waiting list; 18 were admitted. Applications are accepted on-line.

Transfer: 9 transfer students enrolled in 2008-2009. Transfer students are encouraged to present a strong B average in their college work to date. Preference will be given to college over high school work. High school and college transcripts, an essay or personal statement, a statement of good standing, 2 instructor recommendations, and a midterm evaluation are required. 16 of 32 course credits required for the bachelor's degree must be completed at Wheaton.

Visiting: There are regularly scheduled orientations for prospective students, including class visits, tours, panels on financial aid, student life, and athletics, lunch with faculty, and department open houses. There are guides for informal visits, and visitors may sit in on classes and stay overnight. To schedule a visit, contact the Admissions Office.

Financial Aid: In 2009-2010, 76% of all full-time freshmen and 66% of continuing full-time students received some form of financial aid.61% of all full-time freshmen and 54% of continuing full-time students received need-based aid. The average freshman award was $27,200. Need-based scholarships or need-based grants averaged $25,818 ($46,800 maximum); need-based self-help aid (loans and jobs) averaged $5,787 ($7,000 maximum); and other non-need-based awards and non-need-based scholarships averaged $11,250 ($15,000 maximum). The average financial indebtedness of the 2009 graduate was $25,540. 55% of undergraduate students work part-time. Average annual earnings from campus work are $1175. Wheaton is a member of CSS. The CSS/Profile or FAFSA and parents' and student's federal tax returns and if applicable, noncustodial profile and business/farm supplement are required. The deadline for filing freshman financial aid applications for fall entry is February 1.

International Students: There are 76 international students enrolled. The school actively recruits these students. They must take the TOEFL with a minimum score of 580 on the paper-based TOEFL (PBT) or 90 on the Internet-based version (iBT).

Computers: The campus has both wireless and wired Internet access from every residence hall and college classroom. While nearly all students bring a computer with them to Wheaton, there are 375 computers available in public spaces, labs, and classrooms. Many faculty members use Moodle, a course management software system, to post documents

such as syllabi and assignments, have electronic discussions, give quizzes, make announcements, and more. Services including registration and access to academic records and campus news and events are all available through the Internet. All students may access the system 24 hours a day, 7 days a week. There are no time limits. The fee is $120 per year. It is strongly recommended that all students have a personal computer.
Graduates: From July 1, 2008 to June 30, 2009, 460 bachelor's degrees were awarded. The most popular majors were psychology (10%), English (6%), and economics (6%). In an average class, 73% graduate in 4 years or less, 75% graduate in 5 years or less, and 75% graduate in 6 years or less. Of the 2008 graduating class, 29% were enrolled in graduate school within 6 months of graduation, and 50% were employed. 22 companies recruited on campus in 2008-2009.
Admissions Contact: Gail Berson, Vice President for Enrollment and Dean of Admission and Student Aid.
E-mail: *admission@wheatoncollege.edu* Web: *wheatoncollege.edu*

WHEELOCK COLLEGE
Boston, MA 02215-4176

E-2

(617) 879-2206
(800) 734-5212; (617) 879-2449

Full-time: 40 men, 600 women	**Faculty:** 65; IIA, av$
Part-time: 3 men, 37 women	**Ph.D.s:** 89%
Graduate: 23 men, 330 women	**Student/Faculty:** 10 to 1
Year: semesters	**Tuition:** $23,625
Application Deadline: March 1	**Room & Board:** $9,450
Freshman Class: 703 applied, 535 accepted, 181 enrolled	
SAT: required	**COMPETITIVE**

Wheelock College, established in 1888, is a private institution with programs in education, child life and family studies, social work, juvenile justice and youth advocacy, and human services. There are no undergraduate schools and one graduate school. In addition to regional accreditation, Wheelock has baccalaureate program accreditation with CSWE and NCATE. The library contains 83,573 volumes, 483,257 microform items, 3,633 audio/video tapes/CDs/DVDs, and subscribes to 12,629 periodicals including electronic. Computerized library services include interlibrary loans, database searching, Internet access, and laptop Internet portals. Special learning facilities include a learning resource center, art gallery, and the Wheelock Family Theater. The 7-acre campus is in an urban area in Boston. Including any residence halls, there are 12 buildings.
Student Life: 63% of undergraduates are from Massachusetts. Students are from 22 states, and 2 foreign countries. 90% are from public schools. 85% are white. The average age of freshmen is 18; all undergraduates, 20. 29% do not continue beyond their first year; 73% remain to graduate.
Housing: 500 students can be accommodated in college housing, which includes single-sex and coed dorms. a cooperative living house, nonsmoking floors, and a wellness floor. On-campus housing is guaranteed for all 4 years. 73% of students live on campus; of those, 50% remain on campus on weekends. Upperclassmen may keep cars.
Activities: There are no fraternities or sororities. There are 25 groups on campus, including Sign Choir, women's center, Best Buddies, choir, chorale, chorus, dance, drama, ethnic, gay, honors, international, professional, religious, social, social service, and student government. Popular campus events include Kids Day, Family Weekend, and COF Concerts.
Sports: There are 5 intercollegiate sports for women, and 9 intramural sports for men and 9 for women. Facilities include a sports complex at a neighboring college with a pool and diving board, racquetball courts, a weight room, an indoor track, a basketball court, crew tanks, and cardiovascular equipment.
Disabled Students: 67% of the campus is accessible. Facilities include wheelchair ramps, elevators, special parking, specially equipped rest rooms, special class scheduling, lowered drinking fountains, lowered telephones, and assistive technology availabe in the learning center.
Services: Counseling and information services are available, as is tutoring in every subject. There is a reader service for the blind, and remedial math, reading, and writing. Academic support services provide individualized assistance upon request.
Campus Safety and Security: Measures include 24-hour foot and vehicle patrol and security escort services. There are emergency telephones and lighted pathways/sidewalks.
Programs of Study: Wheelock confers B.A., B.S., and B.S.W. degrees. Associates and master's degrees are also awarded. Bachelor's degrees are awarded in EDUCATION (early childhood education, elementary education, and special education), SOCIAL SCIENCE (child care/child and family studies, human development, and social work). Teaching, social work, and child life are the strongest academically and have the largest enrollments. are the strongest academically.
Required: To graduate, students must complete between 134 and 140 credit hours, with a minimum GPA of 2.0. Wheelock requires at least a 32-credit major combined with a 36-credit professional studies program. Students must earn 26 credits in English composition, math, human

growth and development, children and their environments, first-year seminar, visual and performing arts, and 1 course in first aid.
Special: Wheelock offers cross-registration with all colleges in the Colleges of the Fenway and internships that include student teaching and social work practice. Dual majors, study-abroad programs, and pass/fail options are available. Students may receive credit for life and work experience. Students begin practical fieldwork their freshman year and continue for all 4 years. There is 1 national honor society.
Faculty/Classroom: 13% of faculty are male; 87% are female. 70% teach undergraduates. No introductory courses are taught by graduate students. The average class size in an introductory lecture is 20; in a laboratory is 17; and in a regular course is 15.
Admissions: 76% of the 2009-2010 applicants were accepted. The ACT scores were 56% below 21, 11% between 21 and 23, 33% between 24 and 26, % between 27 and 28, and % above 28. 28% of the current freshmen were in the top fifth of their class; 54% were in the top two fifths.
Requirements: The SAT is required. In addition, applicants must be graduates of an accredited secondary school and must have completed 4 years of English, 3 years of math, and 2 years each of science and history. The GED is accepted. The college requires a graded writing sample and recommends an interview. A GPA of 2.0 is required. AP and CLEP credits are accepted. Important factors in the admissions decision are advanced placement or honors courses, evidence of special talent, and personality/intangible qualities.
Procedure: Freshmen are admitted fall and spring. Entrance exams should be taken in the spring of the junior year and/or fall of the senior year. There are early decision, deferred admissions and rolling admissions plans. Early decision applications should be filed by December 1; regular applications, by March 1 for fall entry and December 1 for spring entry, along with a $35 fee. Notification of early decision is sent December 15; other notification is sent on a rolling basis. Applications are accepted on-line.
Transfer: 75 transfer students enrolled in 2008-2009. Transfer students must have a minimum GPA of 2.0 and must present 1 letter of recommendation. Grades of C- or better transfer for credit. Applicants must submit all official high school and college transcripts. 67 of 134 credits required for the bachelor's degree must be completed at Wheelock.
Visiting: There are regularly scheduled orientations for prospective students, and information sessions are held on select Saturdays in the fall and spring. Students hear a presentation from a counselor, have a tour, and may speak to a counselor individually. There are guides for informal visits, visitors may sit in on classes, and stay overnight. To schedule a visit, contact the Undergraduate Admissions Office.
Financial Aid: In 2009-2010, 94% of all full-time freshmen and 82% of continuing full-time students received some form of financial aid. 63% of all full-time freshmen and 70% of continuing full-time students received need-based aid. The average freshmen award was $23,709, with $6,821 ($19,200 maximum) from need-based scholarships or need-based grants; $4,425 ($8,425 maximum) from need-based self-help aid (loans and jobs); and $18,026 ($23,600 maximum) from other non-need-based awards and non-need-based scholarships. 33% of undergraduate students work part-time. Average annual earnings from campus work are $1800. The average financial indebtedness of the 2009 graduate was $21,125. The FAFSA is required. The priority date for freshman financial aid applications for fall entry is February 15.
International Students: There are 5 international students enrolled. They must take the TOEFL. They must also take the SAT or ACT. Applicants should submit SAT or ACT scores or TOEFL scores if English is not their official language.
Computers: All students may access the system. 24 hours a day any time school is in session. There are no time limits and no fees.
Graduates: From July 1, 2008 to June 30, 2009, 81 bachelor's degrees were awarded. The most popular majors were teacher education (68%), child life (16%), and social work (16%). 35 companies recruited on campus in 2008-2009. In an average class, 48% graduate in 4 years or less, 52% graduate in 5 years or less, and 53% graduate in 6 years or less. Of the 2008 graduating class, 22% were enrolled in graduate school within 6 months of graduation, and 95% were employed.
Admissions Contact: Lynne Harding, Dean of Admissions. E-Mail: undergrad@wheelock.edu Web: www.wheelock.edu

WILLIAMS COLLEGE
Williamstown, MA 01267

A-1

(413) 597-2211

Full-time: 987 men, 977 women	**Faculty:** 257; IIB, ++$
Part-time: 9 men, 24 women	**Ph.D.s:** 99%
Graduate: 18 men, 31 women	**Student/Faculty:** 8 to 1
Year: 4-1-4	**Tuition:** $35,670
Application Deadline: January 1	**Room & Board:** $9,470
Freshman Class: 6448 applied, 1194 accepted, 540 enrolled	
SAT CR/M: 720/710	**ACT:** 31 **MOST COMPETITIVE**

Williams College, founded in 1793, is a private institution offering undergraduate degrees in liberal arts and graduate degrees in art history and development economics. There are no undergraduate schools and 2 graduate schools. The 11 libraries contain 948,365 volumes, 492,374 microform items, 39,133 audio/video tapes/CDs/DVDs, and subscribe to 13,493 periodicals including electronic. Computerized library services include interlibrary loans, database searching, and Internet access. Special learning facilities include a learning resource center, art gallery, planetarium, radio station, a 2500-acre experimental forest, an environmental studies center, a center for foreign languages, literatures, and cultures, a rare book library, a studio art center, and a 3 stage center for the performing arts. The 450-acre campus is in a small town 150 miles north of New York City. Including any residence halls, there are 97 buildings.

Student Life: 86% of undergraduates are from out of state, mostly the Northeast. 64% are white; 11% Asian American. The average age of freshmen is 18; all undergraduates, 20. 3% do not continue beyond their first year; 95% remain to graduate.

Housing: 1972 students can be accommodated in college housing, which includes single-sex and coed dorms, on-campus apartments, and cooperative housing, in which students prepare their own meals. On-campus housing is guaranteed for all 4 years. Upperclassmen may keep cars.

Activities: There are no fraternities or sororities. Groups on campus include acapella singing groups, handbell choir, art, band, chess, choir, chorale, chorus, comedy group, computers, dance, debate, drama, environmental, ethnic, film, gay, honors, international, jazz band, literary magazine, marching band, musical theater, newspaper, orchestra, pep band, photography, political, radio and TV, religious, social service, student government, symphony, and yearbook. Popular campus events include Winter Carnival, Mountain Day, and Multicultural Center-sponsored activities.

Sports: There are 16 intercollegiate sports for men and 15 for women, and 17 intramural sports for men and 17 for women. Facilities include 2 gyms, a 50-meter pool, a dance studio, a weight room, rowing tanks, a boathouse, a golf course, playing fields, artificial turf field, indoor and outdoor tracks, and courts for tennis, squash, and paddle tennis.

Disabled Students: Facilities include wheelchair ramps, elevators, special parking, specially equipped rest rooms, special class scheduling, lowered drinking fountains, and lowered telephones.

Services: Counseling and information services are available, as is tutoring in every subject. There is a reader service for the blind, and remedial math, reading, and writing. Other services include a peer health program, rape and sexual assault hotline, and 10-1 counseling service.

Campus Safety and Security: Measures include 24-hour foot and vehicle patrol, emergency notification system, self-defense education, and security escort services. There are emergency telephones, lighted pathways/sidewalks, and controlled access to dorms/residences.

Programs of Study: Williams confers B.A. degrees. Master's degrees are also awarded. Bachelor's degrees are awarded in BIOLOGICAL SCIENCE (biology/biological science), COMMUNICATIONS AND THE ARTS (art, art history and appreciation, classics, dramatic arts, English, fine arts, French, German, literature, music, Russian, and Spanish), COMPUTER AND PHYSICAL SCIENCE (astronomy, astrophysics, chemistry, computer science, geology, mathematics, and physics), SOCIAL SCIENCE (American studies, anthropology, Asian/Oriental studies, economics, history, philosophy, political science/government, psychology, religion, sociology, and women's studies).

Required: All students must complete 4 winter studies and 32 courses, 9 of which are in the major field, with a C- or higher. Requirements include 3 semester-long courses in each of 3 academic divisions: languages and arts, social sciences, and science and math. Also required are 1 course in cultural pluralism and 4 semesters of phys ed.

Special: Students may cross-register at Bennington or Massachusetts College of Liberal Arts and study abroad in Madrid, Oxford, Cairo, Beijing, and Kyoto, or any approved program with another college or university. Teaching and medical field experiences, dual and student-designed majors, internships, and a 3-2 engineering program with Columbia University and Washington University are offered. There are pass/fail options during the winter term. Each department offers at least 1 Oxford-model tutorial every year. There are 2 national honor societies, including Phi Beta Kappa.

Faculty/Classroom: 59% of faculty are male; 41% are female. All teach and do research. No introductory courses are taught by graduate students. The average class size in an introductory lecture is 30; in a laboratory is 13; and in a regular course is 16.

Admissions: 19% of the 2009-2010 applicants were accepted. The SAT scores for the 2009-2010 freshman class were: Critical Reading--% below 500, 6% between 500 and 599, 28% between 600 and 700, and 66 above 700; Math--% below 500, 6% between 500 and 599, 32% between 600 and 700, and 61 above 700.

Requirements: The SAT is required. In addition, SAT: Subject tests in 3 subjects are required. Secondary preparation should include 4 years each of English and math, 3 to 4 years of foreign language, and at least 2 years each of science and social studies. A personal essay must be submitted. Williams accepts the Common Application AP credits are accepted. Important factors in the admissions decision are advanced placement

or honors courses, recommendations by school officials, and evidence of special talent.

Procedure: Freshmen are admitted in the fall. There is a early decision and deferred admissions plans. Early decision applications should be filed by November 10; regular applications, by January 1 for fall entry. The fall 2008 application fee was $60. Applications are accepted on-line. 682 applicants were on a recent waiting list, 53 were accepted.

Transfer: 8 transfer students enrolled in 2008-2009. Transfer applicants should present a 3.5 GPA in previous college work and must submit either the SAT or ACT scores.

Visiting: There are regularly scheduled orientations for prospective students, consisting of panels, forums, class visits, and campus tours. There are guides for informal visits, visitors may sit in on classes, and stay overnight. To schedule a visit, contact the Purple Key Society office at (413) 597-3148.

Financial Aid: In 2009-2010, 51% of all full-time freshmen and 45% of continuing full-time students received some form of financial aid. 51% of all full-time freshmen and 45% of continuing full-time students received need-based aid. The average freshmen award was $35,625. Average annual earnings from campus work are $800. The average financial indebtedness of the 2009 graduate was $9,727. The CSS/Profile, FAFSA, and the college's own financial statement are required. The deadline for filing freshman financial aid applications for fall entry is February 1.

International Students: There are 132 international students enrolled. The school actively recruits these students. They must take the TOEFL, if English is not the applicant's first language. They must also take the SAT or ACT.

Computers: Wireless access is available. Every student dorm room is wired for high-speed Internet access. Many public spaces on campus have wireless Internet availability. Numerous public computer terminals are located in the Computer Center and library as well as in other student spaces around campus. All students may access the system. There are no time limits and no fees.

Graduates: From July 1, 2008 to June 30, 2009, 517 bachelor's degrees were awarded. The most popular majors were economics (18%), English (11%), and Art (8%). In an average class, 91% graduate in 4 years or less, 95% graduate in 5 years or less, and 95% graduate in 6 years or less.

Admissions Contact: Richard Nesbitt, Director of Admission. E-Mail: admission@williams.edu Web: www.williams.edu

WORCESTER POLYTECHNIC INSTITUTE   C-2

Worcester, MA 01609-2280   (508) 831-5286; (508) 831-5875

Full-time: 2346 men, 927 women	**Faculty:** 263; IIA, +$
Part-time: 97 men, 21 women	**Ph.D.s:** 94%
Graduate: 847 men, 306 women	**Student/Faculty:** 12 to 1
Year: trimesters, summer session	**Tuition:** $37,440
Application Deadline: February 1	**Room & Board:** $11,360
Freshman Class: 6284 applied, 3989 accepted, 928 enrolled	
SAT CR/M/W: 610/670/600	**ACT:** 28
	HIGHLY COMPETITIVE+

Worcester Polytechnic Institute, founded in 1865, is a private technological university offering degrees in the sciences, engineering, computer science, business management, and the liberal arts. The academic program emphasizes professional-level project work. There is 1 undergraduate school and 1 graduate school. In addition to regional accreditation, WPI has baccalaureate program accreditation with AACSB and ABET. The library contains 271,361 volumes, 111,000 microform items, and 1654 audio/video tapes/CDs/DVDs, and subscribes to 36,000 periodicals including electronic. Computerized library services include interlibrary loans, database searching, Internet access, and laptop Internet portals. Special learning facilities include a learning resource center, art gallery, radio station, TV station, robotics lab, wind tunnel, and greenhouse. The 80-acre campus is in a suburban area 40 miles west of Boston. Including any residence halls, there are 48 buildings.

Student Life: 54% of undergraduates are from out of state, mostly the Northeast. Students are from 43 states, 70 foreign countries, and Canada. 74% are from public schools. 74% are white. The average age of freshmen is 18; all undergraduates, 20. 5% do not continue beyond their first year; 80% remain to graduate.

Housing: 1591 students can be accommodated in college housing, which includes coed dorms, on-campus apartments, and off-campus apartments. In addition, there are special-interest houses, fraternity houses, and sorority houses. On-campus housing is guaranteed for the freshman year only and is available on a lottery system for upperclassmen. 60% of students live on campus; of those, 75% remain on campus on weekends. Upperclassmen may keep cars.

Activities: 30% of men belong to 13 national fraternities; 34% of women belong to 3 national sororities. There are 200 groups on campus, including art, band, cheerleading, chess, choir, chorale, chorus, computers, dance, debate, drama, environmental, ethnic, forensics, gay, honors, international, jazz band, literary magazine, marching band, musical theater, newspaper, orchestra, pep band, photography, political, professional, radio and TV, religious, social, social service, student government, symphony, and yearbook. Popular campus events include Traditions Day, New Voices Festival, and Winter Carnival.

Sports: There are 10 intercollegiate sports for men and 10 for women, and 10 intramural sports for men and 10 for women. Facilities include an aerobics area, baseball and softball fields, bowling alleys, an 8-lane synthetic surface track, a fitness center, a crew center, a playing field with artificial turf, a pool, basketball, tennis, racquetball and squash courts, and a 2800-seat gym. The sports and recreation center holds a 4-court gym, an indoor track, 11,000-sq-ft of fitness space, a rowing rank, and a 25-meter competition pool.

Disabled Students: 96% of the campus is accessible. Facilities include wheelchair ramps, elevators, special parking, specially equipped restrooms, special class scheduling, and lowered drinking fountains.

Services: Counseling and information services are available, as is tutoring in every subject.

Campus Safety and Security: Measures include 24-hour foot and vehicle patrol, emergency notification system, self-defense education, and security escort services. There are shuttle buses, emergency telephones, lighted pathways/sidewalks, and a student-run emergency medical service supervised by the campus police department.

Programs of Study: WPI confers B.A. and B.S. degrees. Master's and doctoral degrees are also awarded. Bachelor's degrees are awarded in AGRICULTURE (environmental studies), BIOLOGICAL SCIENCE (biochemistry and biotechnology), BUSINESS (business administration and management, management engineering, and management information systems), COMMUNICATIONS AND THE ARTS (technical and business writing), COMPUTER AND PHYSICAL SCIENCE (actuarial science, chemistry, computer science, digital arts/technology, mathematics, and physics), ENGINEERING AND ENVIRONMENTAL DESIGN (aeronautical engineering, biomedical engineering, chemical engineering, civil engineering, computer graphics, electrical/electronics engineering, engineering physics, environmental engineering, industrial engineering, materials engineering, mechanical engineering, and technology and public affairs), SOCIAL SCIENCE (economics, fire protection, humanities, interdisciplinary studies, social science, and systems science). Engineering, biology, and computer science are the largest.

Required: For a B.S. degree, WPI requires that students in science and engineering complete an individual project in the humanities. Students must also complete 2 major team projects. Distribution requirements vary according to the major, and all students must take courses in social sciences and phys ed.

Special: Students may cross-register with 9 other colleges in the Colleges of Worcester Consortium. Co-op programs in all majors, internships, work-study programs, dual majors in every subject, student-designed majors, 3-2 engineering degrees, a Washington semester, non-degree study, and pass/fail options are all available. There are accelerated degree programs in fire protection engineering and math. There are 26 special project centers in 17 countries. There are 10 national honor societies.

Faculty/Classroom: 76% of faculty are male; 24% are female. All teach undergraduates. No introductory courses are taught by graduate students. The average class size in a laboratory is 24 and in a regular course, 25.

Admissions: 63% of the 2009-2010 applicants were accepted. The SAT scores for the 2009-2010 freshman class were: Critical Reading--8% below 500, 35% between 500 and 599, 43% between 600 and 700, and 14% above 700; Math--% below 500, 12% between 500 and 599, 54% between 600 and 700, and 34% above 700; Writing--6% below 500, 28% between 500 and 599, 45% between 600 and 700, and 11% above 700. The ACT scores were 2% below 21, 9% between 21 and 23, 20% between 24 and 26, 25% between 27 and 28, and 44% above 28. 80% of the current freshmen were in the top fifth of their class; 96% were in the top two fifths. There were 6 National Merit finalists. 37 freshmen graduated first in their class.

Requirements: Applicants must have completed 4 years of math, including precalculus, 4 years of English, and 2 lab sciences. An essay is required as well as a letter of recommendation from either a math or science teacher and the guidance counselor. Those opting for Flex Path will submit academic work in place of the SAT or ACT. AP credits are accepted. Important factors in the admissions decision are advanced placement or honors courses, recommendations by school officials, and extracurricular activities record.

Procedure: Freshmen are admitted fall and spring. Entrance exams should be taken between April and January. There is a deferred admissions plan. Applications should be filed by February 1 for fall entry and November 15 for spring entry, along with a $60 fee. Notifications are sent April 1. 852 applicants were on the 2009 waiting list; 2 were admitted. Applications are accepted on-line.

Transfer: 41 transfer students enrolled in 2008-2009. Grades of C or better transfer for credit. A high school transcript or GED is required. Students who have been out of school for a year or more must present a resume or personal biography and 2 academic recommendations. Also

they must have completed a calculus course and 2 lab sciences courses. 75 of 135 credits required for the bachelor's degree must be completed at WPI.

Visiting: There are regularly scheduled orientations for prospective students, consisting of meetings and presentations from various academic and extracurricular groups. There are guides for informal visits; visitors may sit in on classes and stay overnight. To schedule a visit, contact the Admissions Office.

Financial Aid: In 2009-2010, 99% of all full-time freshmen and 97% of continuing full-time students received some form of financial aid. 76% of all full-time freshmen and 64% of continuing full-time students received need-based aid. The average freshman award was $25,229. Need-based scholarships and need-based grants averaged $18,073; and need-based self-help aid (loans and jobs) averaged $7156. 19% of undergraduate students work part-time. Average annual earnings from campus work are $1322. The average financial indebtedness of the 2009 graduate was $44,340. WPI is a member of CSS. The CSS/Profile, FAFSA, CSS Noncustodial Profile, and WPI Upper-Class Application are required, The deadline for filing freshman financial aid applications for fall entry is February 1.

International Students: There are 293 international students enrolled. The school actively recruits these students. They must take the TOEFL with a minimum score of 550 on the paper-based TOEFL (PBT) or 80 on the Internet-based version (iBT) or take the MELAB, the college's own test, or IELTS. They must also take the SAT or ACT or submit a Flex Path Supplement.

Computers: Wireless access is available. WPI has a state-of-the-art network infrastructure as well as wireless access in all academic and residential buildings. There are 28 computer labs/classrooms, including several with 24/7 card access. WPI students can also access network resources from off campus via our Virtual Private Network. All students may access the system 24 hours daily. There are no time limits and no fees.

Graduates: From July 1, 2008 to June 30, 2009, 615 bachelor's degrees were awarded. The most popular majors were mechanical engineering (25%), electrical and computer engineering (13%), and civil and environmental enginerring (9%). 200 companies recruited on campus in 2008-2009. In an average class, 70% graduate in 4 years or less, 78% graduate in 5 years or less, and 80% graduate in 6 years or less. Of the 2008 graduating class, 25% were enrolled in graduate school within 6 months of graduation, and 67% were employed.

Admissions Contact: Edward J. Connor, Director of Admissions. A campus DVD is available. E-mail: *admissions@wpi.edu* Web: *www.wpi.edu*

WORCESTER STATE COLLEGE   C-2
Worcester, MA 01602-2597

(508) 929-8040
(866) 972-2255; (508) 929-8183

Full-time: 1429 men, 1913 women	**Faculty:** 174
Part-time: 450 men, 810 women	**Ph.Ds:** 73%
Graduate: 201 men, 555 women	**Student/Faculty:** 15 to 1
Year: semesters, summer session	**Tuition:** $5,864 ($11,944)
Application Deadline: open	**Room & Board:** $7958
Freshman Class: 3810 applied, 2030 accepted, 699 enrolled	
SAT CR/M: 500/510	**ACT:** 21 **COMPETITIVE**

Worcester State College, established in 1874, is part of the Massachusetts public higher education system and offer undergraduate and graduate programs. A liberal arts core is emphasized, as are selected areas of science, the health professions, education, business and management. There are no undergraduate schools and one graduate school. In addition to regional accreditation, WSC has baccalaureate program accreditation with NLN. The library contains 198,408 volumes, 16,383 microform items, 4,093 audio/video tapes/CDs/DVDs, and subscribes to 734 periodicals including electronic. Computerized library services include interlibrary loans, database searching, and Internet access. Special learning facilities include a learning resource center, radio station, TV station, photographic labs, audiovisual center, multimedia classrooms with satellite connectivity, discipline-specific computer labs, and a speech, language, and hearing clinic. The 53-acre campus is in an urban area 45 miles west of Boston. Including any residence halls, there are 10 buildings.

Student Life: 96% of undergraduates are from Massachusetts. Students are from 16 states, 23 foreign countries, and Canada. 78% are white. The average age of freshmen is 18; all undergraduates, 24. 24% do not continue beyond their first year; 40% remain to graduate.

Housing: 1000 students can be accommodated in college housing, which includes single-sex and coed dorms, and on-campus apartments. On-campus housing is available on a first-come and first-served basis. Priority is given to out-of-town students. 75% of students commute. Alcohol is not permitted. Upperclassmen may keep cars.

Activities: There are no fraternities or sororities. There are 56 groups on campus, including cheerleading, chorale, computers, dance, drama, environmental, ethnic, gay, honors, jazz band, newspaper, political, professional, radio and TV, religious, social, social service, student government, and yearbook. Popular campus events include Winter Carnival, Senior Week, and a lecture series.

Sports: There are 10 intercollegiate sports for men and 10 for women, and 11 intramural sports for men and 11 for women. Facilities include an auditorium, a gym, a fitness center, tennis courts, a track, baseball and softball diamonds, and football, field hockey, and all-purpose fields.

Disabled Students: All of the campus is accessible. Facilities include wheelchair ramps, elevators, special parking, specially equipped rest rooms, lowered drinking fountains, lowered telephones, and special housing.

Services: Counseling and information services are available, as is tutoring in most subjects. There is a reader service for the blind, and remedial math, reading, and writing. In conjunction with Quinsigamond Community College courses and WSC instructors are also available.

Campus Safety and Security: Measures include 24-hour foot and vehicle patrol, emergency notification system, self-defense education, and security escort services. There are emergency telephones, lighted pathways/sidewalks, controlled access to dorms/residences, and crime prevention programs offered throughout the year to both students and faculty/staff.

Programs of Study: WSC confers B.A. and B.S. degrees. Master's degrees are also awarded. Bachelor's degrees are awarded in BIOLOGICAL SCIENCE (biology/biological science and biotechnology), BUSINESS (business administration and management), COMMUNICATIONS AND THE ARTS (communications, English, and Spanish), COMPUTER AND PHYSICAL SCIENCE (chemistry, computer science, mathematics, and natural sciences), EDUCATION (early childhood education and elementary education), HEALTH PROFESSIONS (health, health science, nursing, occupational therapy, and speech pathology/audiology), SOCIAL SCIENCE (criminal justice, economics, geography, history, psychology, sociology, and urban studies). Occupational therapy and nursing is the strongest academically. Business Administration, Psychology, and Criminal Justice are the largest.

Required: To graduate, students must complete a foundation requirement, including English composition, math, and the study of the U.S. and Massachusetts constitutions. Distribution requirements include 12 credits each in humanities, and behavioral & social sciences, and 13 in natural sciences and math; 9 in fine arts; and 3 in health studies. Students must complete 120 credits, 30 to 48 in the major, with a minimum 2.0 GPA overall and in the major.

Special: Cross-registration with the Worcester Consortium for Higher Education is available, as are internships, study abroad, a Washington semester, work-study, B.A.-B.S. degrees, dual majors, non-degree study, and a pass/fail option. There are 17 national honor societies and a freshman honors program.

Faculty/Classroom: 49% of faculty are male; 51% are female. 84% teach undergraduates. No introductory courses are taught by graduate students. The average class size in an introductory lecture is 22; in a laboratory is 16; and in a regular course is 19.

Admissions: 53% of the 2009-2010 applicants were accepted. The SAT scores for the 2009-2010 freshman class were: Critical Reading--48% below 500, 43% between 500 and 599, 8% between 600 and 700, and 1 above 700; Math--41% below 500, 49% between 500 and 599, 10% between 600 and 700, and above 700. The ACT scores were 39% below 21, 36% between 21 and 23, 19% between 24 and 26, 3% between 27 and 28, and 3% above 28.

Requirements: The SAT or ACT is required. In addition, for students with a GPA of 2.9 or above, a minimum SAT or ACT score may be required. For students whose GPA is below 2.9, a minimum SAT or ACT score is applied according to a scale established by WSC. Applicants must graduate from an accredited secondary school. They should have completed 4 years of English, 3 of math, 2 each of a foreign language, a lab science, and social studies, including 1 year of U.S. history and government, and 2 electives. The College Board Student Descriptive questionnaire must be submitted. A GPA of 2.0 is required. AP and CLEP credits are accepted. A GPA of 2.0 is required. AP and CLEP credits are accepted.

Procedure: Freshmen are admitted fall, spring, and summer. Entrance exams should be taken in spring of the junior year or fall of the senior year. There is a rolling admissions plan. Check with the school for current application deadlines. The application fee is $20. Notification is sent on a rolling basis. Applications are accepted on-line. 86 applicants were on a recent waiting list.

Transfer: 472 transfer students enrolled in 2008-2009. Transfer applicants must have earned a minimum of 12 college credits with a minimum 2.5 GPA or 13 to 23 credits with a minimum 2.0 GPA. Students with fewer than 24 transfer credits may be admitted under the same criteria as first-time freshmen. 30 of 120 credits required for the bachelor's degree must be completed at WSC.

Visiting: There are regularly scheduled orientations for prospective students, including a campus tour and review of campus life and organizations, success in college, special opportunities, and available services. Visitors may sit in on classes. To schedule a visit, contact Admissions at (508) 929-8040.

Financial Aid: Average annual earnings from campus work are $924. The average financial indebtedness of the 2009 graduate was $13,605. WSC is a member of CSS. The FAFSA and the college's own financial statement are required. The priority date for freshman financial aid applications for fall entry is March 1. The deadline for filing freshman financial aid applications for fall entry is May 1.

International Students: There are 50 international students enrolled. They must take the TOEFL with a minimum score of 550 on the paper-based TOEFL (PBT) or 79 on the Internet-based version (iBT). They must also take the SAT or ACT.

Computers: Wireless access is available. All students may access the system. There are no time limits and no fees. All students are required to have a personal computer. A Dell is recommended.

Graduates: From July 1, 2008 to June 30, 2009, 758 bachelor's degrees were awarded. The most popular majors were psychology (11%), business administration (8%), and communications (7%). In an average class, 21% graduate in 4 years or less, 38% graduate in 5 years or less, and 40% graduate in 6 years or less.

Admissions Contact: Beth Axelson, Director of Admissions. A campus DVD is available. E-Mail: admissions@worcester.edu Web: www.worcester.edu

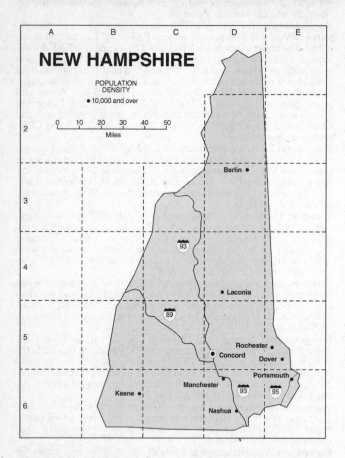

NEW HAMPSHIRE

POPULATION
DENSITY

● 10,000 and over

0   10   20   30   40   50
Miles

Berlin ●

Laconia ●

Rochester ●
Concord ●   Dover ●

Portsmouth ●
Manchester ●

Keene ●

Nashua ●

mental, film, gay, honors, international, Key Association, literary magazine, musical theater, newspaper, outing, photography, political, professional, radio and TV, religious, social, social service, student academic counselors, and student government. Popular campus events include Fall and Spring Weekends and Mountain Day.

Sports: There are 8 intercollegiate sports for men and 9 for women, and 15 intramural sports for men and 15 for women. Facilities include 6 outdoor and 3 indoor tennis courts, a fitness center, an NCAA-approved swimming pool, a suspended indoor track, squash and racquetball courts, 4 outdoor competitive fields, and nearby golf courses, ski and biking trails, and an indoor riding arena.

Disabled Students: 50% of the campus is accessible. Facilities include wheelchair ramps, elevators, special parking, specially equipped restrooms, special class scheduling, and special housing.

Services: Counseling and information services are available, as is tutoring in every subject. There is a reader service for the blind, and remedial math, reading, and writing.

Campus Safety and Security: Measures include 24-hour foot and vehicle patrol, emergency notification system, self-defense education, and security escort services. There are shuttle buses, emergency telephones, lighted pathways/sidewalks, controlled access to dorms/residences, and monthly meetings between students and campus safety personnel.

Programs of Study: Colby-Sawyer confers B.A., B.S., and B.F.A. degrees. Associates degrees are also awarded. Bachelor's degrees are awarded in AGRICULTURE (environmental studies), BIOLOGICAL SCIENCE (biology/biological science), BUSINESS (business administration and management and sports management), COMMUNICATIONS AND THE ARTS (art, communications, English, and graphic design), EDUCATION (art education, athletic training, early childhood education, English education, and social studies education), HEALTH PROFESSIONS (exercise science and nursing), SOCIAL SCIENCE (child psychology/development, history, and psychology). Exercise and sport sciences, business administration, and nursing are the largest.

Required: Required courses include writing, math, and computer literacy. Each pathway is a set of five courses that all relate to a theme. Each student is required to take a total of eight Exploration courses: 1 course each in fne and performing arts, history, humanities, literature, social sciences, and laboratory science course, and 1 course from 2 of the following areas: environmental literacy, media literacy, global perspectives, and wellness. Most majors must also complete an internship or a senior research project. A total of 120 credit hours, with a minimum GPA of 2.0, is required for graduation.

Special: There is cross-registration through the New Hampshire College and University Council. Students may choose internships (required in some majors) and may study abroad in Australia, Canada, and several European countries. A Washington semester with American University is available. Other options include education certification, credit by exam, and interdisciplinary majors such as history, society, and culture. There are 4 national honor societies and a freshman honors program.

Faculty/Classroom: 48% of faculty are male; 52% are female. All teach undergraduates. No introductory courses are taught by graduate students. The average class size in a regular course is 17.

Requirements: The SAT or ACT is required. The ACT Optional Writing test is also required. The GED is accepted. A minimum of 15 college preparatory credits is recommended for admission, including 4 years of English, 3 or more of social studies, 3 of math, 2 of the same foreign language, and 3 or more of lab science. An essay is required, as are 2 letters of recommendation. Interviews are strongly recommended. A GPA of 2.0 is required. AP and CLEP credits are accepted.

Procedure: Freshmen are admitted fall and spring. Entrance exams should be taken in the fall of the senior year. There are early decision, deferred admissions and rolling admissions plans. Early decision applications should be filed by December 1; heck with the school for other current application deadlines. The application fee is $45. Notification of early decision is sent December 15; regular decision, sent on a rolling basis. Applications are accepted on-line.

Transfer: 17 transfer students enrolled in in a recent year. College-level work will be emphasized. College transcripts, course descriptions, and a dean's form are required in addition to the standard requirements. 60 of 120 credits required for the bachelor's degree must be completed at Colby-Sawyer.

Visiting: There are regularly scheduled orientations for prospective students, including tours and interviews. Open house programs offer tours as well as academic, athletic, campus life, career development, and academic development presentations; several visiting-day programs offer tours, interviews, and class visits. There are guides for informal visits; visitors may sit in on classes and stay overnight. To schedule a visit, contact the Admissions Office at (603) 526-3700 or 1(800) 272-1015.

Financial Aid: In a recent year, 81% of all full-time freshmen and 78% of continuing full-time students received some form of financial aid. 81% of all full-time freshmen and 78% of continuing full-time students re-

COLBY-SAWYER COLLEGE   C-5
New London, NH 03257

(603) 526-3700
(800) 272-1015; (603) 526-3452

Full-time: 320 men, 610 women	**Faculty:** n/av
Part-time: 15 men, 10 women	**Ph.D.s:** n/av
Graduate: none	**Student/Faculty:** n/av
Year: semesters	**Tuition:** $29,000
Application Deadline: open	**Room & Board:** $10,000
Freshman Class: n/av	
SAT or ACT: required	**COMPETITIVE**

Colby-Sawyer College, established in 1837, is an independent institution offering programs of study that innovatively integrate liberal arts and sciences with professional preparation. Undergraduate majors include environmental studies, graphic design, child development, education, exercise and sport sciences, studio arts, nursing, business, biology, English, psychology, communications, and history, society, and culture, as well as education certification. Figures in the above capsule and in this profile are approximate. The library contains 93,861 volumes, 204,109 microform items, and 2,400 audio/video tapes/CDs/DVDs, and subscribes to 32,019 periodicals including electronic. Computerized library services include interlibrary loans, database searching, and Internet access. Special learning facilities include a learning resource center, art gallery, radio station, academic development center, laboratory school (K-3), weather station, and the Curtis L.Ivey Science Center. The 200-acre campus is in a small town 100 miles northwest of Boston, MA. Including any residence halls, there are 29 buildings.

Student Life: 68% of undergraduates are from out of state, mostly the Northeast. Students are from 25 states, 11 foreign countries, and Canada. 83% are from public schools. 89% are white. The average age of freshmen is 18; all undergraduates, 20. 19% do not continue beyond their first year; 64% remain to graduate.

Housing: 870 students can be accommodated in college housing, which includes single-sex and coed dorms. In addition, there is a substance-free residence hall. On-campus housing is guaranteed for all 4 years. 90% of students live on campus; of those, 70% remain on campus on weekends. All students may keep cars.

Activities: There are no fraternities or sororities. There are 40 groups on campus, including art, chorus, counselors, dance, drama, environ-

ceived need-based aid. The average financial indebtedness of the 2009 graduate was $13,578. Colby-Sawyer is a member of CSS. The FAFSA is required. Check with the school for current application deadlines.

International Students: There were 13 international students enrolled in a recent year. The school actively recruits these students. They must take the TOEFL.

Computers: Wireless access is available. All students may access the system. There are no time limits and no fees.

Graduates: In a recent year, 216 bachelor's degrees were awarded. The most popular majors were psychology (13%), business administration (12%), and nursing (11%). In an average class, 51% graduate in 4 years or less, 59% graduate in 5 years or less, and 60% graduate in 6 years or less. Of the 2008 graduating class, 11% were enrolled in graduate school within 6 months of graduation, and 90% were employed.

Admissions Contact: Admissions Office E-Mail: *admissions@colby-sawyer.edu* Web: *www.colby-sawyer.edu*

DANIEL WEBSTER COLLEGE   D-6

Nashua, NH 03063-1300   (603) 577-6600
                                      (800) 325-6876; (603) 577-6001

Full-time: 555 men, 135 women	**Faculty:** n/av
Part-time: 25 men, 10 women	**Ph.D.s:** n/av
Graduate: 75 men, 70 women	**Student/Faculty:** n/av
Year: semesters, summer session	**Tuition:** $27,282
Application Deadline: open	**Room & Board:** $9369
Freshman Class: n/av	
SAT: required	**COMPETITIVE**

Daniel Webster College, founded in 1965, is a private college offering study in the fields of aviation, business, computer sciences, engineering, sports management, and social sciences. The 1 graduate school. The library contains 32,000 volumes, 55,294 microform items, and 1,457 audio/video tapes/CDs/DVDs, and subscribes to 390 periodicals including electronic. Computerized library services include interlibrary loans, database searching, and Internet access. Special learning facilities include a learning resource center, a flight center, a flight tower, air traffic control labs, flight simulators, a hangar, and a fleet of airplanes. The 54-acre campus is in a suburban area 35 miles northwest of Boston. Including any residence halls, there are 14 buildings.

Student Life: 66% of undergraduates are from out of state, mostly the Northeast. Students are from 22 states, 15 foreign countries, and Canada. 91% are white. The average age of freshmen is 18; all undergraduates, 21. 24% do not continue beyond their first year.

Housing: 500 students can be accommodated in college housing, which includes single-sex and coed dorms and on-campus apartments. In addition, there are suites, quiet floors in residence halls, smoke-free areas, and a substance-free, 10-month housing option. On-campus housing is guaranteed for all 4 years. 68% of students live on campus; of those, 80% remain on campus on weekends. All students may keep cars.

Activities: There are no fraternities or sororities. There are 26 groups on campus, including computers, culinary, drama, film, golf, honors, jazz band, newspaper, off reading, professional, religious, ski, social, social service, student government, and yearbook. Popular campus events include Ski Day, Family Weekend, and a whitewater rafting trip.

Sports: There are 7 intercollegiate sports for men and 7 for women, and 6 intramural sports for men and 5 for women. Facilities include an indoor basketball/volleyball court, a weight room, soccer, lacrosse, and softball fields, and cross-country trails.

Disabled Students: 75% of the campus is accessible. Facilities include wheelchair ramps, elevators, special parking, specially equipped restrooms, special class scheduling, and lowered drinking fountains.

Services: Counseling and information services are available, as is tutoring in every subject. There is remedial math and writing, study skills and test skills workshops, study groups, a math/science center, a writing center, and accommodations for students with learning disabilities.

Campus Safety and Security: Measures include 24-hour foot and vehicle patrol, emergency notification system, self-defense education, and security escort services. There are emergency telephones, lighted pathways/sidewalks, and controlled access to dorms/residences.

Programs of Study: DWC confers B.S. degrees. Associates and master's degrees are also awarded. Bachelor's degrees are awarded in BUSINESS (business administration and management, management information systems, marketing management, and sports management), COMPUTER AND PHYSICAL SCIENCE (computer science and information sciences and systems), ENGINEERING AND ENVIRONMENTAL DESIGN (aeronautical engineering, air traffic control, airline piloting and navigation, aviation administration/management, computer technology, and mechanical engineering), SOCIAL SCIENCE (psychology and social science). Aviation, computer science, and information systems are the strongest academically. Aviation is the largest.

Required: Students must complete general education courses in communication, computer literacy, math, natural science, the humanities, and the social sciences. At least 120 credits, with 45 to 58 in the major,

are required for graduation. Students must maintain a minimum overall GPA of 2.0. and grades of C or better in their major.

Special: There is cross-registration with the New Hampshire College and University Council. All programs offer credit by exam. Interdisciplinary majors, including aviation flight operations and aviation management/air traffic management are available. Study abroad, internships in aviation, business management, computer sciences, and sport management, a general studies degree, and a 2-2 engineering program with the universities of New Hampshire and Massachusetts at Lowell, Kettering University, and Clarkson University are additional options. There is 1 national honor society and 1 departmental honors program.

Faculty/Classroom: 76% of faculty are male; 24% are female. All teach and do research. No introductory courses are taught by graduate students. The average class size in an introductory lecture is 17; in a laboratory is 12; and in a regular course is 20.

Requirements: The SAT is required. In addition, applicants must be graduates of an accredited secondary school or submit the GED. Students should have taken 4 years of English, 3 of math, 2 each of social studies and science, and 1 of history. An essay and an interview are recommended. A GPA of 2.0 is required. AP and CLEP credits are accepted. Important factors in the admissions decision are advanced placement or honors courses, recommendations by school officials, and leadership record.

Procedure: Freshmen are admitted to all sessions. There are early decision, deferred admissions and rolling admissions plans. Application deadlines are open. Application fee is $35. Applications are accepted on-line.

Transfer: Transfer students must have a minimum college GPA of 2.0. The SAT is required. Grades of C or better transfer for credit. 30 of 120 credits required for the bachelor's degree must be completed at DWC.

Visiting: There are regularly scheduled orientations for prospective students, including a tour and an admissions interview; also available are meetings with faculty and coaches and an aerial tour of the campus as well as sitting in on class. There are guides for informal visits; visitors may sit in on classes and stay overnight. To schedule a visit, contact the Office of Admissions at (603) 577-6600.

Financial Aid: The FAFSA and the college's own financial statement are required. Check with the school for current application deadlines.

International Students: They must take the TOEFL. They must also take the SAT or ACT.

Computers: Wireless access is available. There are computer labs on campus with some doubling as classrooms. There are 4 labs that are open 8 am to midnight. Students have the ability to use all of these computers. The majority of their use is during the day between the hours of 10:00 am and 3:00 pm. All students may access the system when the computer center is open. There are no time limits. The fee is $120. It is strongly recommended that all students have a personal computer. A IBM-compatible, recommended Dell is recommended.

Admissions Contact: Daniel P. Monahan, Dean of Admissions. E-Mail: *admissions@dwc.edu* Web: *www.dwc.edu*

DARTMOUTH COLLEGE   B-4

Hanover, NH 03755   (603) 646-2875; (603) 646-1216

Full-time: 2064 men, 2037 women	**Faculty:** 482
Part-time: 25 men, 21 women	**Ph.D.s:** n/av
Graduate: 988 men, 713 women	**Student/Faculty:** 8 to 1
Year: quarters, summer session	**Tuition:** $36,690
Application Deadline: January 1	**Room & Board:** $10,779
Freshman Class: 16538 applied, 2228 accepted, 1095 enrolled	
SAT or ACT: required	**MOST COMPETITIVE**

Dartmouth College, chartered in 1769, is a private liberal arts institution offering a wide range of graduate and undergraduate programs. There is a year-round academic calendar of 4 10-week terms. There are 4 graduate schools. The 10 libraries contain 2.5 million volumes, 2.6 million microform items, and 772,660 audio/video tapes/CDs/DVDs, and subscribe to 42,116 periodicals including electronic. Computerized library services include interlibrary loans, database searching, Internet access, and laptop Internet portals. Special learning facilities include a learning resource center, art gallery, radio station, creative and performing arts center, life sciences lab, physical and social sciences centers, and observatory. The 265-acre campus is in a rural area 140 miles northwest of Boston. Including any residence halls, there are 100 buildings.

Student Life: 96% of undergraduates are from out of state, mostly the Middle Atlantic. Students are from 50 states, 80 foreign countries, and Canada. 62% are from public schools. 55% are white; 14% Asian American. 30% are Protestant; 28% claim no religious affiliation; 23% Catholic; 11% Jewish. The average age of freshmen is 18; all undergraduates, 20. 2% do not continue beyond their first year; 95% remain to graduate.

Housing: 3500 students can be accommodated in college housing, which includes coed dorms, on-campus apartments, off-campus apartments, and married student housing. In addition, there are language houses, special-interest houses, fraternity houses, sorority houses, substance- and smoke-free residence halls, and faculty-in-residence and academic affinity programs. On-campus housing is guaranteed for the freshman year only and is available on a lottery system for upperclassmen. 85% of students live on campus. Upperclassmen may keep cars.

Activities: 39% of men belong to 9 local and 5 national fraternities; 34% of women belong to 3 local and 6 national sororities. There are 300 groups on campus, including art, band, cheerleading, chess, choir, chorale, chorus, computers, dance, debate, drama, environmental, ethnic, film, forensics, gay, honors, international, jazz band, literary magazine, marching band, musical theater, newspaper, opera, orchestra, outing, pep band, photography, political, professional, radio and TV, religious, social, social service, student government, symphony, and yearbook. Popular campus events include Dartmouth Night/Homecoming Weekend, Winter Carnival, and Green Key Service Weekend.

Sports: There are 17 intercollegiate sports for men and 17 for women, and 25 intramural sports for men and 25 for women. Facilities include a 2100-seat arena, a 16,000-square-foot fitness center, squash and racquetball courts, a dance studio, a 5000-seat ice-hockey arena, a gym, a 20,000-seat football stadium, a boat house, a tennis center with indoor and outdoor courts, a golf course, a ski slope with 3 chairlifts, and a riding farm.

Disabled Students: All of the campus is accessible. Facilities include wheelchair ramps, elevators, special parking, specially equipped restrooms, special class scheduling, lowered drinking fountains, lowered telephones, and special housing.

Services: Counseling and information services are available, as is tutoring in every subject. There is a reader service for the blind. There is an academic skills center for all students. Readers, note takers, tape recorders, and support for learning-disabled students are available.

Campus Safety and Security: Measures include 24-hour foot and vehicle patrol, emergency notification system, self-defense education, and security escort services. There are shuttle buses, emergency telephones, and lighted pathways/sidewalks.

Programs of Study: Dartmouth confers B.A. and B.Eng. degrees. Master's and doctoral degrees are also awarded. Bachelor's degrees are awarded in AGRICULTURE (environmental studies), BIOLOGICAL SCIENCE (biochemistry, biology/biological science, genetics, and neurosciences), COMMUNICATIONS AND THE ARTS (Arabic, art history and appreciation, Chinese, classical languages, classics, comparative literature, dramatic arts, English, film arts, French, German, Italian, linguistics, music, Portuguese, romance languages and literature, Russian, Spanish, and studio art), COMPUTER AND PHYSICAL SCIENCE (astrophysics, chemistry, computer science, earth science, mathematics, and physics), ENGINEERING AND ENVIRONMENTAL DESIGN (engineering and applied science, engineering physics, and environmental science), SOCIAL SCIENCE (African American studies, anthropology, Asian/Oriental studies, classical/ancient civilization, cognitive science, economics, French studies, geography, German area studies, history, Latin American studies, Middle Eastern studies, Native American studies, philosophy, psychology, religion, Russian and Slavic studies, sociology, Spanish studies, and women's studies). Economics, government, and psychological and brain sciences are the largest.

Required: All students must pass 35 courses, 10 of which must be distributed in the following fields: arts; social analysis; literature; quantitative or deductive science; philosophical, religious, or historical analysis; natural science; technology or applied science; and international or comparative study. 3 world culture courses are required from the U.S., Europe, and at least 1 non-Western society. A multidisciplinary or interdisciplinary course, a freshman seminar, a senior project, and foreign language proficiency are also required.

Special: Students may design programs using the college's unique Dartmouth Plan, which divides the academic calendar into 4 10-week terms, based on the seasons. The plan permits greater flexibility for vacations and for the 45 study-abroad programs in 23 countries in Latin America, Europe, Asia, and Africa. Cross-registration is offered through the Twelve College Exchange Network. Exchange programs also exist with the University of California at San Diego, Stanford, Oxford, and McGill Universities, selected German universities, Keio University in Tokyo, and Beijing Normal University in China. Students may design their own interdisciplinary majors involving multiple departments, take dual majors in all fields, or create a modified major involving 2 departments, with emphasis in 1. Hands-on computer science education, internships, and work-study programs also are available. A 3-2 engineering degree is offered with Dartmouth's Thayer School of Engineering. There are 3 national honor societies, including Phi Beta Kappa.

Faculty/Classroom: 62% of faculty are male; 38% are female. All teach and do research. No introductory courses are taught by graduate students. The average class size in an introductory lecture, 34, in a laboratory, 16 and in a regular course, 23.

Admissions: 13% of the 2009-2010 applicants were accepted. 95% of the current freshmen were in the top fifth of their class; all were in the top two fifths. 323 freshmen graduated first in their class.

Requirements: The SAT or ACT is required. The ACT Optional Writing test is also required. In addition, as are 2 SAT subject tests. Evidence of intellectual capacity, motivation, and personal integrity are important factors in the highly competitive admissions process, which also consid-

ers talent, accomplishment, and involvement in nonacademic areas. Course requirements are flexible, but students are urged to take English, foreign language, math, lab science, and history. The GED is accepted. AP credits are accepted.

Procedure: Freshmen are in the admitted fall. Entrance exams should be taken no later than November or January of the senior year. There is a early decision and deferred admissions plans. Early decision applications should be filed by November 1; regular applications, by January 1 for fall entry. The fall 2009 application fee was $70. Notification of early decision is sent December 15; regular decision, April 1. 958 applicants were on the 2009 waiting list; 95 were admitted. Applications are accepted on-line.

Transfer: 23 transfer students enrolled in 2008-2009. Applicants must demonstrate high achievement and intellectual motivation through college transcripts as well as standardized test scores and high school transcripts. 18 of 35 credits required for the bachelor's degree must be completed at Dartmouth.

Visiting: There are regularly scheduled orientations for prospective students, including a campus tour, a group information session, and a student forum. There are guides for informal visits; visitors may sit in on classes and stay overnight. To schedule a visit, contact the Office of Admissions at (603) 646-2875.

Financial Aid: In 2009-2010, 49% of all full-time freshmen and 53% of continuing full-time students received some form of financial aid. 49% of all full-time freshmen and 53% of continuing full-time students received need-based aid. The average financial award was $37,055. The average financial indebtedness of the 2009 graduate was $18,095. Dartmouth is a member of CSS. The CSS/Profile, FAFSA, and parents' and student's federal income tax returns are required. The deadline for filing freshman financial aid applications for fall entry is February 1.

International Students: There are 286 international students enrolled. The school actively recruits these students. They must take the TOEFL. They must also take the SAT or ACT.

Computers: Wireless access is available. All students may access the system 24 hours daily. There are no time limits and no fees. All students are required to have a personal computer.

Graduates: From July 1, 2008 to June 30, 2009, 1084 bachelor's degrees were awarded. In an average class, 95% graduate in 6 years or less.

Admissions Contact: Maria Laskaris, Dean of Admissions. E-Mail: *admissions.office@dartmouth.edu* Web: *www.dartmouth.edu*

FRANKLIN PIERCE UNIVERSITY C-8
Rindge, NH 03461-

(603) 899-4050
(800) 437-0048; (603) 899-4394

Full-time: 890 men, 850 women	**Faculty:** n/av
Part-time: 10 men, 15 women	**Ph.D.s:** n/av
Graduate: none	**Student/Faculty:** n/av
Year: semesters, summer session	**Tuition:** $27,000
Application Deadline: see profile	**Room & Board:** $9000
Freshman Class: n/av	
SAT or ACT: required	**COMPETITIVE**

Franklin Pierce University, founded in 1962, is a private liberal arts institution that also has an extensive continuing education program, which offers undergraduate and graduate degrees at locations in Concord, Keene, Lebanon, Manchester, and Portsmouth in New Hampshire. The figures in the above capsule and in this profile are approximate. The library contains 123,004 volumes, 5,409 microform items, and 13,368 audio/video tapes/CDs/DVDs, and subscribes to 10,275 periodicals including electronic. Computerized library services include interlibrary loans, database searching, Internet access, and laptop Internet portals. Special learning facilities include a learning resource center, art gallery, radio station, TV station, computer labs, theaters, and studios. The 1200-acre campus is in a rural area 65 miles northwest of Boston. Including any residence halls, there are 30 buildings.

Student Life: 82% of undergraduates are from out of state, mostly the Northeast. Students are from 34 states, 29 foreign countries, and Canada. 78% are white. The average age of freshmen is 18; all undergraduates, 20. 32% do not continue beyond their first year; 48% remain to graduate.

Housing: 1460 students can be accommodated in college housing, which includes single-sex and coed dorms, on-campus apartments, and off-campus apartments. On-campus housing is guaranteed for all 4 years. 85% of students live on campus; of those, 70% remain on campus on weekends. All students may keep cars.

Activities: There are no fraternities or sororities. There are 35 groups on campus, including art, cheerleading, chess, choir, chorale, chorus, computers, dance, drama, ethnic, forensics, gay, honors, international, jazz band, literary magazine, musical theater, newspaper, outing, photography, political, professional, radio and TV, religious, social, social service, student government, and yearbook. Popular campus events include Winter Carnival, Spring and Fall Weekends, and Up All Night Mardi Gras.

Sports: There are 9 intercollegiate sports for men and 11 for women, and 32 intramural sports for men and 32 for women. Facilities include a 72,000-square-foot airframe activity center, (with tennis courts, indoor turf soccer field, basketball courts, track, fitness center, and volleyball courts) a field house, a fitness center, an 800-seat gym, an athletic training facility, playing fields including an artificial turf baseball field, and artificial turf soccer/lacrosse and field hockey field, a softball field, and another all-purpose field, a lake with a beach, a fleet of sailboats and kayaks, cross-country and hiking trails, and courts for tennis, basketball, and volleyball.

Disabled Students: 70% of the campus is accessible. Facilities include wheelchair ramps, elevators, special parking, specially equipped restrooms, special class scheduling, and special housing.

Services: Counseling and information services are available, as is tutoring in every subject. There is a reader service for the blind, and remedial math, reading, and writing, note takers, a professional reading specialist, alternative testing, reduced course loads, study skills workshops, and content-area study skills courses

Campus Safety and Security: Measures include 24-hour foot and vehicle patrol, emergency notification system, self-defense education, and security escort services. There are shuttle buses, emergency telephones, and lighted pathways/sidewalks.

Programs of Study: FP confers B.A. and B.S. degrees. Associates, master's, and doctoral degrees are also awarded. Bachelor's degrees are awarded in BIOLOGICAL SCIENCE (biology/biological science), BUSINESS (accounting, banking and finance, business administration and management, management science, marketing/retailing/merchandising, and sports management), COMMUNICATIONS AND THE ARTS (arts administration/management, communications, dramatic arts, English, fine arts, graphic design, and music), COMPUTER AND PHYSICAL SCIENCE (information sciences and systems and mathematics), EDUCATION (education, elementary education, and secondary education), ENGINEERING AND ENVIRONMENTAL DESIGN (environmental science), SOCIAL SCIENCE (American studies, anthropology, criminal justice, history, political science/government, psychology, and social work). Anthropology, biology, and history are the strongest academically. Criminal justice, mass communication, and management are the largest.

Required: Students must complete 120 semester hours with a cumulative GPA of at least 2.0 and pass exams for writing and math competency. Individual and Community core requirements total 11 courses, including Individual and Community, College Writing, Integrated Science, American Experience, Challenge of Business in Society, Twentieth Century, Mathematics, Experiencing the Arts or Music in our World, Ancient and Medieval Worlds or Reason and Romanticism, Science of Society, and a senior liberal arts seminar.

Special: Cross-registration is offered in nearly every subject through the New Hampshire College and University Council, a 13-member consortium of area institutions. Study abroad in 8 countries, the Walk Across Europe, internships in most majors on or off campus, a Washington semester, and work-study through the college are possible. In addition, accelerated degree programs in all majors, dual majors in most fields, student-designed majors, credit for life experience, and nondegree study are available. There are 7 national honor societies and a freshman honors program.

Faculty/Classroom: 60% of faculty are male; 40% are female. All teach undergraduates, and 50% do both. No introductory courses are taught by graduate students. The average class size in an introductory lecture is 60; in a laboratory is 16; and in a regular course is 19.

Requirements: The SAT or ACT is required. The ACT Optional Writing test is also required. In addition, applicants must have earned 10 academic units or 16 Carnegie units in high school, including 4 years of English, 3 each in math and social studies, and 3 in science. An interview is recommended. The GED is accepted. AP and CLEP credits are accepted. Important factors in the admissions decision are recommendations by school officials, advanced placement or honors courses, and extracurricular activities record.

Procedure: Freshmen are admitted to all sessions. Entrance exams should be taken in the spring of junior year or the fall of the senior year. There are deferred admissions and rolling admissions plans. Application deadlines are open. Application fee is $40. Notification is sent on a rolling basis. Applications are accepted on-line.

Transfer: 41 transfer students enrolled in a recent year. A minimum 2.0 GPA in college work is required. Students with fewer than 30 credits must submit SAT results (no minimum score) and official high school transcripts. A personal recommendation is necessary, and an interview is recommended. 30 of 120 credits required for the bachelor's degree must be completed at FP.

Visiting: There are regularly scheduled orientations for prospective students, including open houses held each spring and fall and interviews and tours available weekdays and most Saturdays. There are guides for informal visits; visitors may sit in on classes and stay overnight. To schedule a visit, contact the Admissions Office.

Financial Aid: In a recent year, 93% of all full-time freshmen and 97% of continuing full-time students received some form of financial aid. 83% of all full-time freshmen and 88% of continuing full-time students received need-based aid. The average freshmen award was $18,331. 43% of undergraduate students worked part-time. Average annual earnings from campus work are $618. The average financial indebtedness of the 2009 graduate was $24,156. The FAFSA is required. Check with the school for current application deadlines.

International Students: There were 60 international students enrolled in a recent year. The school actively recruits these students. They must take the TOEFL, and also take ELS Level 109. The SAT or ACT may be substituted for the TOEFL.

Computers: Wireless access is available. There is 1 PC lab always available for general use by any student, and there are 2 PC labs available during the day if not in use by classes and always available in evenings. There is 1 Mac lab available in the evenings. Students can save important documents to their personal folder on the network and can access the Internet and the colleges intranet; software used in the classes is available in the labs. All students may access the system 24 hours a day, 7 days a week. There are no time limits and no fees. It is strongly recommended that all students have a personal computer.

Graduates: In a recent year, 278 bachelor's degrees were awarded. The most popular majors were mass communication (11%), management (9%), and biology (8%). 30 companies recruited on campus in 2008-2009. In an average class, 2% graduate in 3 years or less, 43% graduate in 4 years or less, 46% graduate in 5 years or less, and 47% graduate in 6 years or less. Of the 2008 graduating class, 19% were enrolled in graduate school within 6 months of graduation, and 79% were employed.

Admissions Contact: Linda Quimby, Associate Director. A campus DVD is available. E-Mail: *admissions@franklinpierce.edu* Web: *www.franklinpierce.edu*

GRANITE STATE COLLEGE   D-4

Concord, NH 03301-7317   (603) 513-1320
                                   (888) 228-3000; (603) 513-1387

Full-time: 215 men, 472 women	**Faculty:** n/av
Part-time: 195 men, 636 women	**Ph.D.s:** 25%
Graduate: 35 men, 181 women	**Student/Faculty:** n/av
Year: trimesters, summer session	**Tuition:** $6195 ($6555)
Application Deadline: open	
Freshman Class: 746 applied, 746 accepted, 492 enrolled	**SPECIAL**

Since 1972, Granite State College, has been the University System of New Hampshire's leader in providing access to public higher education for adults. The college features online degrees, community-based academic centers, and innovative programs such as self-designed bachelor degrees. There is one undergraduate school. Computerized library services include interlibrary loans, database searching, and Internet access. Special learning facilities include a learning resource center and a virtual library that serves all 9 Centers and online students. The campus is in a small town.

Student Life: 91% of undergraduates are from New Hampshire. Others are from 22 states, 1 foreign country, and Canada. 86% are white. The average age of all undergraduates is 36.

Housing: There are no residence halls. All students commute.

Activities: There are no fraternities or sororities.

Sports: There is no sports program at GSC.

Disabled Students: All of the campus is accessible. Facilities include wheelchair ramps, special parking, and specially equipped restrooms.

Services: Counseling and information services are available, as is tutoring in every subject. There is remedial math, reading, and writing. other accommodations may be requested.

Campus Safety and Security: Measures include an emergency notification system. There are lighted pathways/sidewalks and controlled access to dorms/residences.

Programs of Study: GSC confers B.A. and B.S. degrees. Associate degrees are also awarded. Bachelor's degrees are awarded in BUSINESS (management science), COMPUTER AND PHYSICAL SCIENCE (applied science), EDUCATION (early childhood education), SOCIAL SCIENCE (behavioral science, criminal justice, and liberal arts/general studies). Individualized studies majors and business management are the largest.

Required: Students must complete 124 credits, at least 32 to 39 in the major, and must maintain a minimum GPA of 2.0. All students are required to complete general education courses in critical thinking, written communication, quantitative reasoning, oral communication, information technology literacy, arts and culture, literature and ideas, history and politics, social science, science, and global perspectives.

Special: Opportunities are provided for internships, cross-registration with all USNH schools, student-designed majors, credit by exam, nondegree study, and pass/fail options (for degree students only). GSC offers programs throughout the state through a network of 9 local Academic Centers. There is 1 national honor society.

Faculty/Classroom: 42% of faculty are male; 58% are female. All teach undergraduates. No introductory courses are taught by graduate students. The average class size in a regular course is 10.

Admissions: 100% of the 2009-2010 applicants were accepted.

Requirements: Applicants must self-certify that they have received a high school diploma or GED. An essay is required, and an advising interview is recommended. The college no longer requires the taking of the Accuplacer for admissions; instead, the tests are used for skills assessment and placement purposes. AP and CLEP credits are accepted.

Procedure: Freshmen are admitted to all sessions. There is a rolling admissions plan. Application deadlines are open. The fall 2009 application fee was $45. Notification is sent on a rolling basis. Applications are accepted on-line.

Transfer: 246 transfer students enrolled in 2008-2009. Transfer credits will be accepted via transcript if they are from a regionally accredited institution and will be evaluated to determine whether they contribute toward meeting GSC degree requirements. Minimum grade for transferred course credits is a C. There is no time limit on past college credits. 30 of 124 credits required for the bachelor's degree must be completed at GSC.

Visiting: There are regularly scheduled orientations for prospective students, consisting of an overview of college programs, financial aid, services, and transfer policies. Visitors may sit in on classes. To schedule a visit, contact local Academic Center at (888) 228-3000.

Financial Aid: The average financial indebtedness of the 2009 graduate was $21,500. The FAFSA is required. Check with the school for current application deadlines.

International Students: They must take the TOEFL with a minimum score of 550 on the paper-based TOEFL (PBT).

Computers: Wireless access is available. Computer labs (average of 16 PCs each), along with designated computers in resource rooms, are available for student use at all local Centers. Wireless routers are also available at each Center providing access to the Internet. All students may access the system during regular operating hours. There are no time limits and no fees. It is strongly recommended that all students have a personal computer.

Graduates: From July 1, 2008 to June 30, 2009, 221 bachelor's degrees were awarded. The most popular majors were individualized studies (31%), business management (27%), and behavioral science (18%). In an average class, 47% graduate in 4 years or less, 51% graduate in 5 years or less, and 53% graduate in 6 years or less.

Admissions Contact: Ruth Nawn, Associate Director of Admissions. A campus DVD is available. E-Mail: *ruth.nawn@granite.edu* Web: *www.granite.edu*

HESSER COLLEGE

Manchester, NH 03101

(603) 668-6660
(800) 526-9231; (603) 666-4722

Full-time: 135 men, 285 women	**Faculty:** n/av
Part-time: 90 men, 225 women	**Ph.D.s:** n/av
Graduate: none	**Student/Faculty:** n/av
Year: semesters, summer session	**Tuition:** $14,500
Application Deadline: see profile	**Room & Board:** $7000
Freshman Class: n/av	**NONCOMPETITIVE**

Hesser College, founded in 1900, is a small, private institution affiliated with the Kaplan Education Corporation and offering more than 13 associate and bachelor degree programs. Students must have an associate degree from Hesser in order to pursue a bachelor's degree in Psychology. The figures in the above capsule and in this profile are approximate. The library contains 24,000 volumes, and 1,800 audio/video tapes/CDs/DVDs, and subscribes to 30,107 periodicals including electronic. Computerized library services include interlibrary loans, database searching, and Internet access. Special learning facilities include a learning resource center, radio station, medical labs, G4 graphic design lab, and massage therapy lab. The 2-acre campus is in a suburban area. Hesser College has 5 Instructional Sites. The main campus is located in Manchester, NH.

Student Life: 75% of undergraduates are from New Hampshire. Others are from 13 states. 63% are white. The average age of freshmen is 27; all undergraduates, 29. 52% do not continue beyond their first year; 34% remain to graduate.

Housing: 3440 students can be accommodated in college housing, which includes single-sex dorms. On-campus housing is guaranteed for all 4 years, is available on a first-come, and first-served basis. 9% of students commute. Alcohol is not permitted. All students may keep cars.

Activities: There are no fraternities or sororities. Groups on campus include chess, choir, chorale, chorus, debate, drama, environmental, honors, international, musical theater, newspaper, radio and TV, social, social service, student government, and yearbook.

Sports: There are 43 intercollegiate sports for men and 4 for women, and 10 intramural sports for men and 10 for women. Basketball, volleyball, soccer, and softball programs are available.

Disabled Students: Facilities include elevators and special parking.

Services: Counseling and information services are available, as is tutoring in every subject. There is remedial math, reading, and writing. There is an academic skills center.

Campus Safety and Security: Measures include 24-hour foot and vehicle patrol and security escort services.

Programs of Study: confers B.S. degrees. Associates degrees are also awarded. Bachelor's degrees are awarded in BUSINESS (accounting and business administration and management), SOCIAL SCIENCE (criminal justice and psychology). Physical therapist assistant is the strongest academically. Criminal justice is the largest.

Required: Contact the school for specific program information.

Special: Internships and work-study programs are available. The college offers a J.D. degree through an articulation agreement with the Massachusetts School of Law, Andover. There are 2 national honor societies, including Phi Beta Kappa, and a freshman honors program.

Faculty/Classroom: 67% of faculty are male; 33% are female. All teach undergraduates. No introductory courses are taught by graduate students. The average class size in an introductory lecture is 18; in a laboratory is 15; and in a regular course is 25.

Requirements: Applicants must be high school graduates. The GED is accepted. An interview is required. CLEP credits are accepted. Important factors in the admissions decision are ability to finance college education, personality/intangible qualities, and recommendations by school officials.

Procedure: Freshmen are admitted to all sessions. Entrance exams should be taken at orientation. There is a rolling admissions plan. Application deadlines are open. Application fee is $20. Applications are accepted on-line.

Transfer: 386 transfer students enrolled in a recent year. 60 of 120 credits required for the bachelor's degree must be completed at Hesser.

Visiting: There are regularly scheduled orientations for prospective students, including campus tours Monday through Friday during the school year and Monday through Thursday during the summer. Open House and Saturday tour days are also available. There are guides for informal visits and visitors may sit in on classes. To schedule a visit, contact Michael Fischer, Dean of Students at (603) 668-6660, ext. 6377.

Financial Aid: In a recent year, 84% of all full-time freshmen and 79% of continuing full-time students received some form of financial aid. 63% of all full-time freshmen and 65% of continuing full-time students received need-based aid. 13% of undergraduate students worked part-time. Average annual earnings from campus work were $1486. The FAFSA and the college's own financial statement are required. Check with the school for current application deadlines.

Computers: All students may access the system. There are no time limits and no fees.

Graduates: In a recent year, 164 bachelor's degrees were awarded. The most popular majors were business (49%), criminal justice (35%), and accounting (15%). 50 companies recruited on campus in 2008-2009.

Admissions Contact: Lee Ann Gray & Jamie LaCourse, Director of Admissions. A campus DVD is available. E-Mail: *lgray@hesser.edu jlacourse@hesser.edu* Web: *www.hesser.edu*

KEENE STATE COLLEGE
B-6

Keene, NH 03435

(603) 358-2276
(800) KSC-1909; (603) 358-2767

Full-time: 1910 men, 2580 women	**Faculty:** IIA, av$
Part-time: 70 men, 115 women	**Ph.D.s:** n/av
Graduate: 25 men, 90 women	**Student/Faculty:** n/av
Year: semesters, summer session	**Tuition:** $9000 ($16,500)
Application Deadline: April 1	**Room & Board:** $8000
Freshman Class: n/av	
SAT: required	**COMPETITIVE**

Keene State College, founded in 1909, is part of the public University System of New Hampshire and offers a liberal arts program that includes teacher preparation, art, and business emphases. The figures in the above capsule and in this profile are approximate. There are 3 undergraduate schools and 1 graduate school. In addition to regional accreditation, KSC has baccalaureate program accreditation with NASM and NCATE. The library contains 324,176 volumes, 766,806 microform items, and 8,160 audio/video tapes/CDs/DVDs, and subscribes to 1,486 periodicals including electronic. Computerized library services include interlibrary loans, database searching, Internet access, and laptop Internet portals. Special learning facilities include a learning resource center, art gallery, radio station, TV station, the Cohen Center for Holocaust Studies/Holocaust Resource Center. The 150-acre campus is in a small town 90 miles northwest of Boston and 100 miles north of Hartford, CT. Including any residence halls, there are 70 buildings.

Student Life: 52% of undergraduates are from New Hampshire. Others are from 28 states, and 4 foreign countries. 95% are white. The average age of freshmen is 18; all undergraduates, 20. 20% do not continue beyond their first year; 58% remain to graduate.

Housing: 2800 students can be accommodated in college housing, which includes single-sex and coed dorms, on-campus apartments, and married student housing. In addition, there are honors houses, language houses, special-interest houses, fraternity houses, sorority houses, diversity, alcohol/drug-free, quiet study, leadership, language/cultural learning, honors, and wellness. On-campus housing is guaranteed for the freshman year only and is available on a lottery system for upperclassmen. 60% of students live on campus; of those, 65% remain on campus on weekends. Upperclassmen may keep cars.

Activities: 3% of men belong to 3 local fraternities; 3% of women belong to 5 local sororities. There are 88 groups on campus, including art, band, books, cheerleading, choir, chorale, chorus, computers, dance, drama, environmental, ethnic, feminisms, film, gay, history, honors, international, jazz band, languages, literary magazine, musical theater, newspaper, orchestra, photography, political, professional, radio and TV, religious, science/math, social, social service, sports/physical activities, student government, and yearbook. Popular campus events include Spring Weekend, Pumpkin Festival, and Alternative Spring Break.

Sports: There are 8 intercollegiate sports for men and 10 for women, and 18 intramural sports for men and 18 for women. Facilities include a 46,000-square foot recreational center, a 2100-seat gym, a 1300-seat stadium for soccer, field hockey, baseball and softball diamonds, and lacrosse, an indoor pool, a fitness center, racquetball, tennis, squash, basketball, volleyball, and indoor soccer courts, a jogging track, and a training room.

Disabled Students: 95% of the campus is accessible. Facilities include wheelchair ramps, elevators, special parking, specially equipped restrooms, lowered drinking fountains, and lowered telephones.

Services: Counseling and information services are available, as is tutoring in most subjects, There is a writing process center, a reading center, and a math center. There is a reader service for the blind, and remedial math, reading, and writing.

Campus Safety and Security: Measures include 24-hour foot and vehicle patrol, self-defense education, and security escort services. There are shuttle buses, emergency telephones, lighted pathways/sidewalks, and controlled access to dorms/residences.

Programs of Study: KSC confers B.A., B.S., B.F.A., and B.M. degrees. Associates and master's degrees are also awarded. Bachelor's degrees are awarded in BIOLOGICAL SCIENCE (biology/biological science and nutrition), BUSINESS (management science), COMMUNICATIONS AND THE ARTS (art, choral music, communications, dance, dramatic arts, English, film arts, French, graphic design, journalism, music, music history and appreciation, music performance, music technology, music theory and composition, Spanish, studio art, and theater design), COMPUTER AND PHYSICAL SCIENCE (applied mathematics, chemistry, computer mathematics, computer science, geology, mathematics, physical sciences, and science), EDUCATION (early childhood education, education, elementary education, foreign languages education, mathematics education, music education, physical education, science education, secondary education, social science education, and special education), ENGINEERING AND ENVIRONMENTAL DESIGN (architecture and environmental science), HEALTH PROFESSIONS (health science and preventive/wellness health care), SOCIAL SCIENCE (addiction studies, American studies, economics, geography, history, philosophy, psychology, safety management, social science, and sociology). French, Spanish, chemistry, and music education are the strongest academically. Education, safety studies, and management are the largest.

Required: All students must take 120 to 139 credits, with 34 to 95 hours in their major, while maintaining a 2.0 GPA. Distribution requirements include 8 credits in writing/reading comprehension, 16 credits in arts and humanities, 16 credits in sciences, and 4 credits in interdisciplinary studies. Students must have a minimum of 30 credits in residence at KSC to graduate.

Special: Internships and co-op programs in most areas of study, study abroad anywhere in the world, and work-study at the college are available. Student teaching is required for education majors. Students also may pursue dual majors, a general studies degree, individualized majors, accelerated degrees in the psychology honors program, and a 3-2 engineering degree with Clarkson University or the University of New Hampshire. In addition, there are pass/fail options and credit for life experience. There are 20 national honor societies, a freshman honors program, and 2 departmental honors programs.

Faculty/Classroom: 50% of faculty are male; 50% are female. 91% teach undergraduates. No introductory courses are taught by graduate students. The average class size in an introductory lecture is 22; in a laboratory is 14; and in a regular course is 20.

Requirements: The SAT is required. In addition, applicants must submit completed application with fee, official high school transcript including first marking period grades for senior year, SAT test scores (or ACT test scores), essay, and a letter of recommendation. Applicants need at least 14 academic credits, including 4 years of English, and 3 years each of math and science, 2 years each of social studies, and academic electives. A portfolio or an audition is required for certain programs. AP and CLEP credits are accepted.

Procedure: Freshmen are admitted fall and spring. Entrance exams should be taken during the spring of the junior year or fall of the senior year. There are deferred admissions and rolling admissions plans. Applications should be filed by April 1 for fall entry and December 1 for spring

entry. The fall 2009 application fee was $35. Notifications are sent December 1. Applications are accepted on-line.

Transfer: 185 transfer students enrolled in a recent year. Applicants must submit completed application with fee, official school transcripts from all previous colleges, SAT test scores (or ACT test scores), essay, and a letter of reference from a college administrator. A portfolio or an audition is required for certain programs. 30 of 120 credits required for the bachelor's degree must be completed at KSC.

Visiting: There are regularly scheduled orientations for prospective students, consisting of a personal interview with the professional staff and a tour. There are guides for informal visits and visitors may sit in on classes. To schedule a visit, contact the Admissions Office at (603) 358-2276.

Financial Aid: The FAFSA and IRS tax returns are required. Check with the school for current application deadlines.

International Students: There were 19 international students enrolled in a recent year. They must take the TOEFL.

Computers: Wireless access is available. The wireless network is available in the library and some classrooms. Laptop computers with wireless access cards are available at the library. All residence halls are wired for high speed Internet access, and there are 750 open, wired network connections on campus including all classrooms. The wireless network can accommodate 200 simultaneous users. All students may access the system 24 hours per day. There are no time limits and no fees.

Graduates: In a recent year, 1046 bachelor's degrees were awarded. The most popular majors were education (19%), psychology (11%), and management (10%). 80 companies recruited on campus in 2008-2009. In an average class, 1% graduate in 3 years or less, 36% graduate in 4 years or less, 54% graduate in 5 years or less, and 58% graduate in 6 years or less. Of the 2008 graduating class, 10% were enrolled in graduate school within 6 months of graduation, and 43% were employed.

Admissions Contact: Peggy Richmond, Director of Admissions. E-Mail: *admissions@keene.edu* Web: *www.keene.edu*

NEW ENGLAND COLLEGE   C-5
Henniker, NH 03242

(603) 428-2223
(800) 521-7642; (608) 428-3155

Full-time: 472 men, 467 women	**Faculty:** 65
Part-time: 30 men, 28 women	**Ph.D.s:** 80%
Graduate: 303 men, 599 women	**Student/Faculty:** 14 to 1
Year: semesters, summer session	**Tuition:** $25,100
Application Deadline: open	**Room & Board:** $8794
Freshman Class: 1767 applied, 1428 accepted, 258 enrolled	
SAT or ACT: not required	**LESS COMPETITIVE**

New England College, founded in 1946, is an independent liberal arts institution emphasizing small classes and a cocurricular leadership program. There are no undergraduate schools and one graduate school. The library contains 110,000 volumes, 36,000 microform items, and 2,000 audio/video tapes/CDs/DVDs, and subscribes to 700 periodicals including electronic. Computerized library services include interlibrary loans, database searching, Internet access, and laptop Internet portals. Special learning facilities include a learning resource center, art gallery, radio station, and the Center for Educational Innovation, with a high-tech classroom building. The 225-acre campus is in a small town 17 miles west of Concord and 80 miles north of Boston, Massachusetts. Including any residence halls, there are 31 buildings.

Student Life: 64% of undergraduates are from out of state, mostly the Northeast. Students are from 38 states, 20 foreign countries, and Canada. 73% are from public schools. 86% are white. The average age of freshmen is 19; all undergraduates, 21. 42% do not continue beyond their first year; 44% remain to graduate.

Housing: 685 students can be accommodated in college housing, which includes coed dorms and on-campus apartments. In addition, there are special-interest houses, and cooperative substance-free housing. On-campus housing is guaranteed for all 4 years and is available on a lottery system for upperclassmen. 58% of students live on campus; of those, 80% remain on campus on weekends. All students may keep cars.

Activities: 8% of men belong to 2 local and 1 national fraternities; 8% of women belong to 3 local and 1 national sororities. There are 34 groups on campus, including cheerleading, chorus, dance, drama, environmental, ethnic, film, gay, honors, international, literary magazine, newspaper, photography, political, professional, radio and TV, religious, social, social service, sports, student government, and yearbook. Popular campus events include International Week, Snow Day, and Spring Weekend.

Sports: There are 6 intercollegiate sports for men and 7 for women, and 7 intramural sports for men and 7 for women. Facilities include a gym, a field house, 26 acres of playing fields, indoor and outdoor basketball and tennis courts, cross-country ski trails, Alpine skiing at a local ski area, and a fitness center.

Disabled Students: 80% of the campus is accessible. Facilities include wheelchair ramps, elevators, special parking, specially equipped restrooms, and special class scheduling.

Services: Counseling and information services are available, as is tutoring in most subjects. There is remedial math and writing. The mentor program provides both academic and social advising.

Campus Safety and Security: Measures include 24-hour foot and vehicle patrol, emergency notification system, and security escort services. There are shuttle buses, emergency telephones, and lighted pathways/sidewalks.

Programs of Study: NEC confers B.A. and B.S. degrees. Associate and master's degrees are also awarded. Bachelor's degrees are awarded in BIOLOGICAL SCIENCE (biology/biological science), BUSINESS (business administration and management, recreation and leisure services, and sports management), COMMUNICATIONS AND THE ARTS (art history and appreciation, communications, comparative literature, creative writing, dramatic arts, English literature, and fine arts), COMPUTER AND PHYSICAL SCIENCE (mathematics), EDUCATION (elementary education, physical education, secondary education, and special education), ENGINEERING AND ENVIRONMENTAL DESIGN (environmental science), HEALTH PROFESSIONS (health science), SOCIAL SCIENCE (criminal justice, philosophy, physical fitness/movement, political science/government, psychology, sociology, and women's studies). Business, education, and psychology are the strongest academically. Business, education, and biology/health science are the largest.

Required: All students must earn a minimum GPA of 2.0 and take 120 credit hours, including an average of 40 in their major. Distribution requirements cover 5 general education areas, including science, humanities, social science, and math. Specific requirements include College Writing I and II, a math course (or a passing grade on a placement test), and science courses.

Special: Cross-registration is available with the New Hampshire College and University Council. Also available are internships for juniors and seniors with a GPA of 2.5, study abroad in most countries, work-study programs, dual majors, student-designed majors, interdisciplinary majors, nondegree study, pass/fail options, and a 3-2 engineering degree with Clarkson University. A 4+1 MBA at Union University; and 3+3 Law program at New York Law School are also offered. There are 1 national honor societies.

Faculty/Classroom: 52% of faculty are male; 48% are female. All teach undergraduates, and 20% do both. No introductory courses are taught by graduate students. The average class size in an introductory lecture is 18; in a laboratory is 12; and in a regular course is 17.

Admissions: 81% of the 2009-2010 applicants were accepted. 3% of the current freshmen were in the top fifth of their class; 23% were in the top two fifths.

Requirements: In addition, 4 years of English, 3 years each of math and social studies, and 2 years each of science and electives are recommended. An essay is required and an interview is recommended. A GPA of 2.0 is required. AP and CLEP credits are accepted. Important factors in the admissions decision are personality/intangible qualities, extracurricular activities record, and leadership record.

Procedure: Freshmen are admitted fall, spring, and summer. There are deferred admissions and rolling admissions plans. Application deadlines are open. Application fee is $30. Notification is sent on a rolling basis. Applications are accepted on-line.

Transfer: 62 transfer students enrolled in 2008-2009. Transfer students should have a 2.0 minimum GPA from the previous college. A recommendation from the dean of students is required. An interview is recommended. 30 of 120 credits required for the bachelor's degree must be completed at NEC.

Visiting: There are regularly scheduled orientations for prospective students, including class registration and meeting faculty and other students. There are guides for informal visits, visitors may sit in on classes, and stay overnight. To schedule a visit, contact Muriel Schlosser in the Admissions Office at (603) 428-2223.

Financial Aid: In 2009-2010, 98% of all full-time freshmen and 95% of continuing full-time students received some form of financial aid. 81% of all full-time freshmen and 71% of continuing full-time students received need-based aid. The average freshman award was $25,105. Need-based scholarships or need-based grants averaged $16,469 ; need-based self-help aid (loans and jobs) averaged $9,436; and other non-need-based awards and non-need-based scholarships averaged $10,387. 58% of undergraduate students work part-time. Average annual earnings from campus work are $1750. The average financial indebtedness of the 2009 graduate was $33,466. The FAFSA and the college's own financial statement are required. The priority date for freshman financial aid applications for fall entry is March 15. The deadline for filing freshman financial aid applications for fall entry is September 2.

International Students: There are 69 international students enrolled. The school actively recruits these students. They must take the TOEFL with a minimum score of 550 on the paper-based TOEFL (PBT) or 79 on the Internet-based version (iBT) or take the MELAB, the Comprehensive English Language Test, and the college's own test.

Computers: Wireless access is available. Wireless service is available at all locations across campus. PCs are located in several computer labs, the library, and the writing lab. All students may access the system. 24

hours a day, 7 days a week. There are no time limits and no fees. It is strongly recommended that all students have a personal computer. A See website for details. is recommended.

Graduates: From July 1, 2008 to June 30, 2009, 162 bachelor's degrees were awarded. The most popular majors were business (20%), sport and recreation management (15%), and education (11%). 30 companies recruited on campus in 2008-2009. In an average class, 40% graduate in 4 years or less, 42% graduate in 5 years or less, and 43% graduate in 6 years or less. Of the 2008 graduating class, 22% were enrolled in graduate school within 6 months of graduation, and 89% were employed.

Admissions Contact: Office of Admission A campus DVD is available. E-Mail: *admission@necl.nec.edu* Web: *www.nec.edu*

PLYMOUTH STATE UNIVERSITY   D-4
Plymouth, NH 03264-1595

	(603) 535-2237
	(800) 842-6900; (603) 535-2714
Full-time: 2169 men, 1856 women	**Faculty:** IIA, av$
Part-time: 133 men, 103 women	**Ph.Ds:** 81%
Graduate: 494 men, 1490 women	**Student/Faculty:** 17 to 1
Year: semesters, summer session	**Tuition:** $8944 ($17,114)
Application Deadline: April 1	**Room & Board:** $8594
Freshman Class: 4239 applied, 2957 accepted, 966 enrolled	
SAT or ACT: required	**COMPETITIVE**

Plymouth State University, founded in 1871, is a comprehensive regional university located in central New Hampshire at the gateway to the White Mountains and Lakes Region and offering programs in business, education, and liberal arts and sciences. In addition to regional accreditation, PSU has baccalaureate program accreditation with ABET, ACB-SP, CSWE, and NCATE. The library contains 349,390 volumes, 661,820 microform items, and 13,447 audio/video tapes/CDs/DVDs, and subscribes to 1,043 periodicals including electronic. Computerized library services include interlibrary loans, database searching, Internet access, and laptop Internet portals. Special learning facilities include a learning resource center, art gallery, planetarium, radio station, a major performing arts center, an NAEYC-accredited lab school for children ages 2 to 6, geographic information systems lab, meteorology lab, graphic design, computer lab, MIDI lab, and weather technology evaluation center. The 177-acre campus is in a small town 2 hours north of Boston. Including any residence halls, there are 64 buildings.

Student Life: 59% of undergraduates are from New Hampshire. Others are from 27 states, 9 foreign countries, and Canada. 90% are white. The average age of freshmen is 18; all undergraduates, 21. 19% do not continue beyond their first year; 54% remain to graduate.

Housing: 2497 students can be accommodated in college housing, which includes coed dorms, on-campus apartments, and married student housing. In addition, there are special-interest houses. There is a wellness residence hall and special interest areas in the residence halls for skiing, snowboarding, biking, hiking, music/theater, fine arts, community service, fitness, and quiet study/academic. On-campus housing is guaranteed for all 4 years and is available on a lottery system for upperclassmen. All students may keep cars.

Activities: There are no fraternities; 3% of women belong to 1 local sorority and 2 national sororities. There are more than 100 groups on campus, including art, band, cheerleading, choir, chorale, computers, dance, debate, drama, ethnic, film, gay, honors, international, jazz band, literary magazine, musical theater, newspaper, political, professional, radio and TV, religious, social, social service, and student government. Popular campus events include Spring Fling, Earth Week, and Winter Carnival.

Sports: There are 8 intercollegiate sports for men and 11 for women, and 10 intramural sports for men and 10 for women. Facilities include a 2500-seat stadium, a 2000-seat gym, playing fields, and facilities for basketball, racquetball, indoor soccer, swimming, tennis, volleyball, softball, and lacrosse. There is also a 75,000 sq.ft. recreation student center separate from athletics, as well as a ropes course. An indoor hockey arena is nearing completion.

Disabled Students: 75% of the campus is accessible. Facilities include wheelchair ramps, elevators, special parking, specially equipped restrooms, lowered drinking fountains, lowered telephones, and special housing. The shuttle service is wheelchair-accessible, and there are handicap-accessible student apartment units, ADA compliant alarm systems, and TDD/TTY.

Services: Counseling and information services are available, as is tutoring in 100- and 200-level courses and some upper-level courses. There is remedial writing. Peer tutoring is available.

Campus Safety and Security: Measures include 24-hour foot and vehicle patrol, emergency notification system, self-defense education, and security escort services. There are shuttle buses, emergency telephones, and lighted pathways/sidewalks, and programs in defensive driving, alcohol awareness, drug identification, and personal safety.

Programs of Study: PSU confers B.A., B.S., and B.F.A. degrees. Master's degrees are also awarded. Bachelor's degrees are awarded in BIOLOGICAL SCIENCE (biology/biological science, biotechnology, and environmental biology), BUSINESS (accounting, business administration and management, marketing management, and recreation and leisure services), COMMUNICATIONS AND THE ARTS (art, communications, English, French, graphic design, music, performing arts, and Spanish), COMPUTER AND PHYSICAL SCIENCE (atmospheric sciences and meteorology, chemistry, computer science, information sciences and systems, and mathematics), EDUCATION (art education, athletic training, health education, music education, physical education, recreation education, and science education), ENGINEERING AND ENVIRONMENTAL DESIGN (city/community/regional planning), SOCIAL SCIENCE (anthropology, child care/child and family studies, criminal justice, early childhood studies, economics, geography, history, humanities, interdisciplinary studies, medieval studies, philosophy, political science/government, psychology, public administration, social science, and social work). Art/graphic design, business administration, and criminal justice are the strongest academically. Childhood studies, management, and phys ed are the largest.

Required: All students must maintain a minimum GPA of 2.0 while enrolled in 120 semester hours, including 1 course each in composition and math foundations, a 3-credit first year seminar, and the general education program, which requires 6 credits each in creative thought, scientific inquiry, and self and society directions, and 3 credits each in diversity, global awareness, integration, and wellness connections. Also required are quantitative reasoning in the disciplines as well as technology and writing connections in the major.

Special: Cross-registration with the New Hampshire College and University Council is available. Internships, study abroad in 3 countries, and college work-study programs are available. Dual majors, an accelerated degree program, offering an undergraduate business and M.B.A. degree in 5 years, and student-designed majors are possible. There are 13 national honor societies, a freshman honors program, and 2 departmental honors programs.

Faculty/Classroom: 52% of faculty are male; 48% are female. No introductory courses are taught by graduate students. The average class size in an introductory lecture is 25; in a laboratory is 17; and in a regular course is 20.

Admissions: 70% of the 2009-2010 applicants were accepted. The SAT scores for the 2009-2010 freshman class were: Critical Reading-- 45% below 500, 34% between 500 and 599, 7% between 600 and 700, and 1% above 700; Math--44% below 500, 36% between 500 and 599, 7% between 600 and 700, and 1% above 700. The ACT scores were 64% below 21, 12% between 24 and 26, 12% between 27 and 28, and 1% above 28.

Requirements: The SAT or ACT is required. In addition, PSU requires that applicants have completed 4 units of English, 3 of math, 2 of social studies and science, and 1 of history, and recommends 2 in foreign language. An audition for certain programs is required, and an essay is required. The GED is accepted. AP and CLEP credits are accepted. Important factors in the admissions decision are advanced placement or honors courses, recommendations by school officials, and leadership record.

Procedure: Freshmen are admitted fall and spring. Entrance exams should be taken in November of the senior year. There are deferred admissions and rolling admissions plans. Applications should be filed by April 1 for fall entry; December 1 for spring entry, along with a $45 fee. Notification is sent on a rolling basis. Applications are accepted on-line.

Transfer: 193 transfer students enrolled in 2008-2009. Transfer students must have a minimum GPA of 2.0 on prior work to be considered. 30 of 120 credits required for the bachelor's degree must be completed at PSU.

Visiting: There are regularly scheduled orientations for prospective students, including an admission presentation, a tour of the campus, and a meal in the dining hall. There are guides for informal visits and visitors may sit in on classes. To schedule a visit, contact the Admission Office at plymouthadmit@plymouth.edu.

Financial Aid: In 2008-2009, 88% of all full-time freshmen and 81% of continuing full-time students received some form of financial aid. 62% of all full-time freshmen and 59% of continuing full-time students received need-based aid. The average freshman award was $7,162. Need-based scholarships or need-based grants averaged $4,854; need-based self-help aid (loans and jobs) averaged $4,304; and other non-need-based awards and non-need-based scholarships averaged $2,985. 14% of undergraduate students work part-time. Average annual earnings from campus work are $850. The average financial indebtedness of the 2009 graduate was $26,636. The FAFSA is required. The priority date for freshman financial aid applications for fall entry is March 1.

International Students: There are 17 international students enrolled. The school actively recruits these students. They must take the TOEFL and proof of English proficiency during secondary education.

Computers: Wireless access is available. All students may access the system. There are no time limits. The fee is $330. It is strongly recommended that all students have a personal computer.

Graduates: From July 1, 2008 to June 30, 2009, 806 bachelor's degrees were awarded. The most popular majors were business (27%), ed-

ucation (14%), and art/graphic design (8%). 20 companies recruited on campus in 2008-2009. In an average class, 35% graduate in 4 years or less and 54% graduate in 6 years or less.

Admissions Contact: Eugene D. Fahey, Senior Associate Director of Admission. E-Mail: *plymouthadmit@plymouth.edu* Web: *www.plymouth.edu*

RIVIER COLLEGE   D-6
Nashua, NH 03060-5086   (603) 897-8507
                                              (800) 44-RIVIER; (603) 891-1799

Full-time: 310 men, 610 women	**Faculty:** n/av
Part-time: 205 men, 505 women	**Ph.D.s:** n/av
Graduate: 255 men, 625 women	**Student/Faculty:** n/av
Year: semesters, summer session	**Tuition:** $26,000
Application Deadline: open	**Room & Board:** $9000
Freshman Class: n/av	
SAT: required	**COMPETITIVE**

Rivier College, founded in 1933 by the Sisters of the Presentation of Mary, is a private Roman Catholic college offering a liberal arts and professional curriculum. The figures in the above capsule and in this profile are approximate. There is 1 graduate school. In addition to regional accreditation, Rivier has baccalaureate program accreditation with NLN. The library contains 107,200 volumes, 89,572 microform items, and 29,094 audio/video tapes/CDs/DVDs, and subscribes to 480 periodicals including electronic. Computerized library services include interlibrary loans and database searching. Special learning facilities include a learning resource center, art gallery, radio station, TV station, education curriculum resources center, legal reference center, early childhood center/ laboratory school, and language lab. The 68-acre campus is in a suburban area 45 miles north of Boston. Including any residence halls, there are 44 buildings.

Student Life: 68% of undergraduates are from New Hampshire. Others are from 13 states, 13 foreign countries, and Canada. 80% are from public schools. 93% are white. 80% are Catholic. The average age of freshmen is 18; all undergraduates, 28. 29% do not continue beyond their first year.

Housing: 425 students can be accommodated in college housing, which includes coed dorms. In addition, there is a substance-free/ wellness residence hall. On-campus housing is guaranteed for all 4 years, is available on a first-come, and first-served basis. 56% of students commute. All students may keep cars.

Activities: There are no fraternities or sororities. There are 32 groups on campus, including paralegal, art, chorus, computers, debate, drama, ethnic, history, honors, international, literary magazine, newspaper, nursing, paralegal, political, professional, religious, social, social sciences, social service, student government, and yearbook. Popular campus events include Spirit Week, Black History Month, and Women's History Month.

Sports: There are 5 intercollegiate sports for men and 5 for women, and 7 intramural sports for men and 7 for women. Facilities include a 300-seat gym, a weight room, and soccer and softball fields.

Disabled Students: 75% of the campus is accessible. Facilities include wheelchair ramps, elevators, special parking, specially equipped restrooms, and lowered drinking fountains.

Services: Counseling and information services are available, as is tutoring in some subjects, including math, English, business, and languages. Tutoring is available in other subjects. There is remedial math and writing. There is a full-service writing center.

Campus Safety and Security: Measures include 24-hour foot and vehicle patrol and security escort services. There are emergency telephones, lighted pathways/sidewalks, 24-hour access by telephone or walkie-talkie, and electronically operated dorm entrances using security cards.

Programs of Study: Rivier confers B.A., B.S., and B.F.A. degrees. Associates and master's degrees are also awarded. Bachelor's degrees are awarded in BIOLOGICAL SCIENCE (biology/biological science), BUSINESS (business administration and management, management information systems, and management science), COMMUNICATIONS AND THE ARTS (communications, English, graphic design, illustration, and studio art), COMPUTER AND PHYSICAL SCIENCE (computer science and mathematics), EDUCATION (art education, early childhood education, elementary education, English education, mathematics education, secondary education, and social studies education), HEALTH PROFESSIONS (nursing, predentistry, premedicine, and preveterinary science), SOCIAL SCIENCE (history, human development, liberal arts/general studies, political science/government, prelaw, psychology, and sociology). Art, education, and nursing are the strongest academically. Education, psychology, and business are the largest.

Required: A writing sample is required at entry, and a demonstration of writing proficiency must be shown prior to graduation. Students must complete at least 120 credit hours, ordinarily consisting of 40 3-credit courses with 35 to 60 credits in the student's major, and they must maintain a minimum GPA of 2.0. Distribution requirements include 17 core courses in basic skills of writing and math, the humanities, and the sciences. These courses include religious studies, philosophy, physical and life sciences, fine arts, modern languages, literature, behavioral and social sciences, and Western civilization.

Special: Rivier offers cross-registration through the New Hampshire College and University Council, internships in most majors, an accelerated master's program in English, dual majors, a liberal studies degree, credit by challenge examination, nondegree study, and pass/fail options. There is 1 national honor society and a freshman honors program.

Faculty/Classroom: 38% of faculty are male; 62% are female. 88% teach undergraduates. No introductory courses are taught by graduate students. The average class size in an introductory lecture is 25; in a laboratory is 20; and in a regular course is 17.

Requirements: The SAT is required. In addition, applicants must be high school graduates or hold the GED. The recommended college preparatory curriculum includes 4 years of English, 3 of math, 2 or more each of foreign language and social studies, 1 of lab science, and 4 academic electives. An essay and 1 or 2 letters of recommendation are required, and an interview is highly recommended. Prospective art majors must submit a portfolio. A GPA of 2.5 is required. AP and CLEP credits are accepted. Important factors in the admissions decision are advanced placement or honors courses, recommendations by school officials, and extracurricular activities record.

Procedure: Freshmen are admitted fall and spring. Entrance exams should be taken in the junior or senior year. There are deferred admissions and rolling admissions plans. Application deadlines are open. The fall 2009 application fee was $25. Notification is sent on a rolling basis. Applications are accepted on-line.

Transfer: Transfer applicants should have a minimum GPA of 2.5 and submit SAT or ACT scores if they have earned fewer than 12 credits at the previous institution. Official college transcripts are required and an interview is recommended. 60 of 120 credits required for the bachelor's degree must be completed at Rivier.

Visiting: There are regularly scheduled orientations for prospective students, including an opportunity to interview, a tour, class visits, and opportunities to meet with faculty, coaches, and current students. There are guides for informal visits; visitors may sit in on classes and stay overnight. To schedule a visit, contact the Office of Undergraduate Admissions.

Financial Aid: Rivier is a member of CSS. The FAFSA is required. Check with the school for current application deadlines.

International Students: The school actively recruits these students. They must take the TOEFL and the college's own test.

Computers: All students may access the system 24 hours a day. There are no time limits. The fee varies. A Windows-based Pentium-class PC is recommended.

Admissions Contact: David A. Boisvert, Director of Undergraduate Admissions. E-Mail: rivadmit@rivier.edu Web: www.rivier.edu

---

SAINT ANSELM COLLEGE   D-6
Manchester, NH 03102

	(603) 641-7500
	(888)-4-ANSELM; (603) 641-7550
Full-time: 850 men, 1100 women	**Faculty:** IIB, av$
Part-time: 30 men, 25 women	**Ph.D.s:** n/av
Graduate: none	**Student/Faculty:** n/av
Year: semesters, summer session	**Tuition:** $27,800
Application Deadline: March 1	**Room & Board:** $11,000
Freshman Class: n/av	
SAT: required	**COMPETITIVE**

Saint Anselm College, founded in 1889, is a private Roman Catholic institution offering a liberal arts education. The figures in the above capsule and in this profile are approximate. In addition to regional accreditation, Saint Anselm has baccalaureate program accreditation with NLN. The library contains 219,000 volumes, 65,000 microform items, and 8,000 audio/video tapes/CDs/DVDs, and subscribes to 3,900 periodicals including electronic. Computerized library services include interlibrary loans, database searching, and Internet access. Special learning facilities include a learning resource center, art gallery, planetarium, radio station, and TV station. The 404-acre campus is in a suburban area 50 miles north of Boston. Including any residence halls, there are 63 buildings.

Student Life: 78% of undergraduates are from out of state, mostly the Northeast. Students are from 28 states, 21 foreign countries, and Canada. 67% are from public schools. 93% are white. 78% are Catholic. The average age of freshmen is 18; all undergraduates, 20. 12% do not continue beyond their first year; 74% remain to graduate.

Housing: 1644 students can be accommodated in college housing, which includes single-sex and coed dorms and on-campus apartments. In addition, there are special-interest houses and substance-free housing. On-campus housing is guaranteed for all 4 years. 87% of students live on campus; of those, 85% remain on campus on weekends. All students may keep cars.

Activities: There are no fraternities or sororities. There are 65 groups on campus, including art, band, cheerleading, chess, choir, chorale, cho-

rus, computers, dance, debate, drama, environmental, ethnic, honors, international, jazz band, literary magazine, musical theater, newspaper, orchestra, pep band, photography, political, professional, radio and TV, religious, social, social service, student government, and yearbook. Popular campus events include Winter Weekend, Family Weekend, and Road for Hope.

Sports: There are 10 intercollegiate sports for men and 10 for women, and 13 intramural sports for men and 13 for women. Facilities include a 1500-seat gym, an ice hockey arena, an activity center that houses basketball, volleyball, tennis, and racquetball courts, and weight and training rooms; a 2500-seat football stadium; a 500-seat baseball stadium; and athletic fields.

Disabled Students: 60% of the campus is accessible. Facilities include wheelchair ramps, elevators, special parking, specially equipped restrooms, special class scheduling, and lowered drinking fountains.

Services: Counseling and information services are available, as is tutoring in most subjects. There is a reader service for the blind.

Campus Safety and Security: Measures include 24-hour foot and vehicle patrol. There are emergency telephones, lighted pathways/sidewalks, and security escort upon request.

Programs of Study: Saint Anselm confers B.A. and B.S.N. degrees. Bachelor's degrees are awarded in BIOLOGICAL SCIENCE (biochemistry and biology/biological science), BUSINESS (accounting, banking and finance, and business administration and management), COMMUNICATIONS AND THE ARTS (classics, English, fine arts, French, and Spanish), COMPUTER AND PHYSICAL SCIENCE (chemistry, computer science, mathematics, and natural sciences), EDUCATION (secondary education), ENGINEERING AND ENVIRONMENTAL DESIGN (engineering and environmental science), HEALTH PROFESSIONS (nursing, predentistry, and premedicine), SOCIAL SCIENCE (criminal justice, economics, history, liberal arts/general studies, philosophy, political science/government, prelaw, psychology, sociology, and theological studies). Business, English, and psychology are the largest.

Required: All students must maintain a GPA of 2.0 in the major while completing at least 40 semester courses, including 4 semesters in the humanities, 3 each in philosophy and theology, 2 each in English and lab science, and 2 to 4 in foreign language; 10 to 13 courses are required in the major area of study.

Special: Saint Anselm offers a 5-year liberal arts and a 3-2 engineering program in cooperation with Manhattan College, University of Notre Dame, University of Massachusetts Lowell, and Catholic University of America. Cross-registration is possible. In addition, internships, work-study, a Washington semester, a New York City semester, study abroad, and nondegree study are available. There are 11 national honor societies, a freshman honors program, and 20 departmental honors programs.

Faculty/Classroom: 60% of faculty are male; 40% are female. All teach undergraduates. No introductory courses are taught by graduate students. The average class size in an introductory lecture is 20; in a laboratory is 14; and in a regular course is 24.

Requirements: The SAT is required. In addition, applicants must have 16 academic credits and 16 Carnegie units, including 4 years of English, 3 each of math and science, 2 of foreign language, and 1 each of history and social studies. An essay is required, and an interview is recommended. The GED is accepted. A GPA of 2.5 is required. AP and CLEP credits are accepted. Important factors in the admissions decision are advanced placement or honors courses, leadership record, and recommendations by school officials.

Procedure: Freshmen are admitted fall and spring. Entrance exams should be taken during the spring of the junior year or fall of the senior year. There are early decision, deferred admissions and rolling admissions plans. Early decision applications should be filed by November 15; regular applications, by March 1 for fall entry and December 1 for spring entry, along with a $55 fee. Notification of early decision is sent December 1. Applications are accepted on-line. A waiting list is maintained.

Transfer: 22 transfer students enrolled in a recent year. Transfer students must have a minimum GPA of 2.5 after earning at least 30 college credits. The SAT is required and an interview is recommended. In addition, 2 letters of recommendation are necessary. 20 of 40 credits required for the bachelor's degree must be completed at Saint Anselm.

Visiting: There are regularly scheduled orientations for prospective students, consisting of daily individual interviews and/or group information sessions followed by a campus tour. There are guides for informal visits; visitors may sit in on classes and stay overnight. To schedule a visit, contact the Office of Admission.

Financial Aid: In a recent year, 68% of all full-time freshmen and 68% of continuing full-time students received some form of financial aid. 68% of all full-time freshmen and 67% of continuing full-time students received need-based aid. The average freshmen award was $19,693. Saint Anselm is a member of CSS. The CSS/Profile and FAFSA are required. Check with the school for current application deadlines.

International Students: There were 10 international students enrolled in a recent year. The school actively recruits these students. They must take the TOEFL. They must also take the SAT or ACT.

Computers: Wireless access is available. Mac lab, PC lab, and desktop PC's are available in the library. All students may access the system 8:30 A.M. to 12 A.M., Monday through Friday; 10 A.M. to 6 P.M. Saturday; 1 P.M. to 12 A.M. Sunday. There are no time limits and no fees.

Graduates: In a recent year, 459 bachelor's degrees were awarded. The most popular majors were social sciences and history (28%), business/marketing (22%), and protective services (14%). In an average class, 66% graduate in 4 years or less, 70% graduate in 5 years or less, and 70% graduate in 6 years or less.

Admissions Contact: Nancy Griffin, Dean of Admission. E-Mail: admission@anselm.edu Web: www.anselm.edu

---

SOUTHERN NEW HAMPSHIRE UNIVERSITY D-6
Manchester, NH 03106-1045
(603) 645-9611
(800) 642-4968; (603) 645-9693

Full-time: 870 men, 1070 women	**Faculty:** IIA, av$
Part-time: 25 men, 30 women	**Ph.D.s:** n/av
Graduate: 965 men, 1415 women	**Student/Faculty:** n/av
Year: semesters, summer session	**Tuition:** $24,400
Application Deadline: see profile	**Room & Board:** $9000
Freshman Class: n/av	
SAT or ACT: required	**COMPETITIVE**

Southern New Hampshire University, founded in 1932, is a private university offering academic programs in business, education, liberal arts, culinary arts, and community economic development. SNHU also has continuing education and online education programs. The figures in the above capsule and in this profile are approximate. There are 5 undergraduate schools and 4 graduate schools. In addition to regional accreditation, SNHU has baccalaureate program accreditation with ACBSP. The library contains 94,042 volumes, 378,319 microform items, and 3,170 audio/video tapes/CDs/DVDs, and subscribes to 755 periodicals including electronic. Computerized library services include interlibrary loans, database searching, Internet access, and laptop Internet portals. Special learning facilities include a learning resource center, art gallery, radio station, a center for financial studies, an advertising agency (on campus), an audiovisual studio, a psychology observation lab, a career development center, and an iMAC graphics lab. The 280-acre campus is in a suburban area 55 miles north of Boston. Including any residence halls, there are 28 buildings.

Student Life: 54% of undergraduates are from out of state, mostly the Northeast. Students are from 28 states, 54 foreign countries, and Canada. 88% are from public schools. 77% are white. 36% are Catholic; 29% claim no religious affiliation; 20% Protestant. The average age of freshmen is 19; all undergraduates, 20. 25% do not continue beyond their first year; 50% remain to graduate.

Housing: 1668 students can be accommodated in college housing, which includes single-sex and coed dorms and on-campus apartments. In addition, there are special-interest houses and a wellness housing area. On-campus housing is guaranteed for all 4 years. 76% of students live on campus; of those, 65% remain on campus on weekends. All students may keep cars.

Activities: 4% of men belong to 2 national fraternities; 5% of women belong to 3 local and 1 national sorority. There are 52 groups on campus, including cheerleading, chess, chorus, crew club, dance, debate, drama, ethnic, field hockey, gay, honors, international, musical theater, newspaper, political, professional, radio and TV, religious, social, social service, sports club, student government, and yearbook. Popular campus events include Fall, Winter, and Spring Weekends, International Night, and trips abroad (Italy, Greece, and England).

Sports: There is no sports program at SNHU. Facilities include 2 gyms, an Olympic-sized swimming pool, 4 lighted tennis courts, a lighted artificial surface game field, a fitness room, natural grass baseball , softball, and practice fields, a racquetball court, and an aerobic/exercise room.

Disabled Students: 80% of the campus is accessible. Facilities include wheelchair ramps, elevators, special parking, specially equipped restrooms, special class scheduling, lowered drinking fountains, lowered telephones, special housing, and automatic door openers.

Services: Counseling and information services are available, as is tutoring in every subject. There is a reader service for the blind and remedial math and writing. Peer mentoring and structured learning assistance services are also available. There is also a Jump Start program available for the summer of pre-college.

Campus Safety and Security: Measures include 24-hour foot and vehicle patrol, emergency notification system, and security escort services. There are emergency telephones, lighted pathways/sidewalks, controlled access to dorms/residences, winter driving seminars for international students, and public safety officers.

Programs of Study: SNHU confers B.A., B.S., and B.A.S.H.A. degrees. Associates, master's, and doctoral degrees are also awarded. Bachelor's degrees are awarded in AGRICULTURE (environmental studies), BUSINESS (accounting, business administration and management, fashion merchandising, hospitality management services, international business management, marketing management, marketing/ retailing/merchandising, retailing, sports management, and tourism), COMMUNICATIONS AND THE ARTS (advertising, communications, creative writing, English, English literature, and graphic design), COMPUTER AND PHYSICAL SCIENCE (computer science, digital arts/technology, and information sciences and systems), EDUCATION (business education, early childhood education, education, elementary education, English education, secondary education, social studies education, and special education), SOCIAL SCIENCE (child psychology/development, culinary arts, history, liberal arts/general studies, political science/government, psychology, public affairs, and social science). Business administration is the strongest academically. Business administration, sports management, and psychology are the largest.

Required: To graduate, students must complete a minimum of 120 credit hours, including 39 in their majors, with a GPA of 2.0. Distribution requirements total 45 credits from the college core, including 2 to 3 courses in writing, and 2 math, information technology, public speaking, statistics, behavioral, social and natural sciences, courses and electives in fine arts and literature.

Special: There are co-ops available, a choice of over 35 study abroad opportunities through the University Studies Abroad Consortium, work-study positions throughout the campus, dual majors, and a 3-year bachelor's degree that is an accelerated degree program in business administration. There are 6 national honor societies, a freshman honors program, and 1 departmental honors program.

Faculty/Classroom: 60% of faculty are male; 40% are female. 90% teach undergraduates, 78% do research, and 73% do both. No introductory courses are taught by graduate students. The average class size in an introductory lecture is 20; in a laboratory is 15; and in a regular course is 21.

Requirements: The SAT or ACT is required. The ACT Optional Writing test is also required. In addition, students must have completed 4 years of English and 3 of math. An essay, high school transcript, and a letter of recommendation from a guidance counselor or 2 teachers are required. An interview is strongly recommended. The GED is accepted. A GPA of 2.0 is required. AP and CLEP credits are accepted.

Procedure: Freshmen are admitted fall and spring. There are deferred admissions and rolling admissions plans. Application deadlines are open. Application fee is $40. Notification is sent on a rolling basis. Applications are accepted on-line.

Transfer: 164 transfer students enrolled in a recent year. Transfer applicants must submit a completed application, essay, official high school transcript, official college transcripts, supplemental transfer form, and a letter of recommendation. An interview is also highly recommended. Most successful applicants for transfer admission have a cumulative GPA of 2.5 or higher 30 of 120 credits required for the bachelor's degree must be completed at SNHU.

Visiting: There are regularly scheduled orientations for prospective students, including a greeting from college administrators, campus tours with students, and informal presentation/discussions with faculty and staff. There are guides for informal visits and visitors may sit in on classes. To schedule a visit, contact Admission Office at admission@snhu.edu.

Financial Aid: In a recent year, 95% of all full-time freshmen and 92% of continuing full-time students received some form of financial aid. 76% of all full-time freshmen and 68% of continuing full-time students received need-based aid. SNHU is a member of CSS. The FAFSA is required. Check with the school for current application deadlines.

International Students: There were 89 international students enrolled in a recent year. The school actively recruits these students. They must take the TOEFL.

Computers: Wireless access is available. The university provides over 500 publicly accessible PCs around the main campus and at the continuing education centers, located in general computer labs, specialty computer labs, and in classrooms. All students may use these PCs for Internet and e-mail access. Wireless Internet access is available in all classrooms at the main campus and at the continuing education centers. All students may access the system 8 A.M. to 12 P.M. daily; extended hours during final exams. There are no time limits and no fees. All students are required to have a personal computer. Students enrolled in Students in the School of Business, School of Liberal Arts, and School of Education. must have a personal computer. A Dell Latitude D610 or D810 are recommended is recommended.

Graduates: In a recent year, 1141 bachelor's degrees were awarded. The most popular majors were business administration (42%), psychology (6%), and accounting (6%). 75 companies recruited on campus in 2008-2009. In an average class, 40% graduate in 4 years or less, 48% graduate in 5 years or less, and 50% graduate in 6 years or less. Of the 2008 graduating class, 11% were enrolled in graduate school within 6 months of graduation, and 85% were employed.

Admissions Contact: Steven Soba, Director of Admission. A campus DVD is available. E-Mail: admission@snhu.edu Web: www.snhu.edu

THOMAS MORE COLLEGE OF LIBERAL ARTS

D-6

Merrimack, NH 03054

(603) 880-8308
(800) 880-8308; (603) 880-9280

Full-time: 40 men, 30 women	**Faculty:** 5
Part-time: none	**Ph.D.s:** 100%
Graduate: none	**Student/Faculty:** 14 to 1
Year: semesters	**Tuition:** $14,500
Application Deadline: open	**Room & Board:** $9100
Freshman Class: n/av	
SAT or ACT: required	**COMPETITIVE**

Thomas More College of Liberal Arts, founded in 1978 by Roman Catholic educators, is an undergraduate institution that combines intensive reading of the Great Books with lectures and seminar discussions placing those works in their historical, cultural, and theological context. Thomas More welcomes students of all faiths. In addition to regional accreditation, TMC has baccalaureate program accreditation with AALE. The library contains 50,000 volumes. The 12-acre campus is in a suburban area between Nashua and Manchester, 40 miles north of Boston. Including any residence halls, there are 5 buildings.

Student Life: 81% of undergraduates are from out of state, mostly the Northeast. Students are from 20 states, 2 foreign countries, and Canada. 84% are white. The average age of freshmen is 18; all undergraduates, 20. 9% do not continue beyond their first year.

Housing: College-sponsored housing includes single-sex dorms. On-campus housing is guaranteed for all 4 years. 95% of students live on campus. Alcohol is not permitted. All students may keep cars.

Activities: There are no fraternities or sororities. Groups on campus include art, choir, newspaper, photography, and radio and TV.

Disabled Students: 70% of the campus is accessible. Facilities include wheelchair ramps, special parking, and specially equipped restrooms.

Services: Informal tutoring is available by request.

Campus Safety and Security: Measures include security escort services. There are lighted pathways/sidewalks.

Programs of Study: TMC confers B.A. degrees. Bachelor's degrees are awarded in SOCIAL SCIENCE (liberal arts/general studies).

Required: To graduate, students in the classes of 2013 and beyond must complete 121 credit hours, including 32 in humanities, 12 each in classical languages, tutorials, philosophy, and Sacred Scripture, 9 in writing/rhetoric/poetics, 7 in fine arts, and 6 each in math, natural science, and theology. In addition, students must complete a junior project of independent study and a senior thesis and seminar.

Special: A semester in Rome for sophomores is required unless waived. Internships are available at Vatican Radio, Zenit News, and the United Nations.

Faculty/Classroom: 80% of faculty are male; 20% are female. All teach undergraduates, and 80% also do research.

Requirements: The SAT or ACT is required. In addition, applicants should be high school graduates with 4 college preparatory units of English, 3 of math, and 2 each of foreign language, social science, and lab science. The GED is accepted. An essay and 2 letters of recommendation are required. An interview is strongly recommended. Important factors in the admissions decision are personality/intangible qualities, evidence of special talent, and leadership record.

Procedure: Freshmen are admitted fall and spring. There is a rolling admissions plan. Application deadlines are open. Applications are accepted on-line.

Transfer: Applicants must submit a transcript from all higher institutions attended.

Visiting: There are guides for informal visits, and visitors may sit in on classes and stay overnight. To schedule a visit, contact Mark Schwerdt, Director of Admissions.

Financial Aid: In a recent year, 80% of all full-time freshmen and 90% of continuing full-time students received some form of financial aid. 65% of all full-time freshmen and 77% of continuing full-time students received need-based aid. The average freshman award was $8768. 59% of undergraduate students work part-time. Average annual earnings from campus work are $1960. TMC is a member of CSS. The FAFSA is required. Check with the school for current application deadlines.

International Students: The school actively recruits these students.

Computers: Wireless access is available. All students may access the system during library hours. There are no time limits and no fees.

Admissions Contact: Mark Schwerdt, Director of Admissions.
E-mail: *admissions@thomasmorecollege.edu*
Web: *www.thomasmorecollege.edu*

UNIVERSITY OF NEW HAMPSHIRE

E-5

Durham, NH 03824

(603) 862-1360; (603) 862-0077

Full-time: 5045 men, 6513 women	**Faculty:** 610; I, av$
Part-time: 117 men, 137 women	**Ph.D.s:** 84%
Graduate: 1084 men, 1636 women	**Student/Faculty:** 19 to 1
Year: 4-1-4, summer session	**Tuition:** $12,743 ($26,713)
Application Deadline: February 1	**Room & Board:** $8874
Freshman Class: 15656 applied, 11145 accepted, 2837 enrolled	
SAT CR/M: 553/570	**ACT:** required
	VERY COMPETITIVE

The University of New Hampshire, founded in 1866, is part of the public university system of New Hampshire and offers degree programs in liberal arts, engineering, physical sciences, business, economics, life sciences, agriculture, and health and human services. There are 6 undergraduate schools and 1 graduate school. In addition to regional accreditation, UNH has baccalaureate program accreditation with AACSB, ABET, ADA, AHEA, CAHEA, CSAB, CSWE, NASM, NLN, NRPA, and SAF. The 5 libraries contain 2.4 million volumes, 3.0 million microform items, and 302,135 audio/video tapes/CDs/DVDs, and subscribe to 50,043 periodicals including electronic. Computerized library services include interlibrary loans, database searching, Internet access, and laptop Internet portals. Special learning facilities include a learning resource center, art gallery, radio station, TV station, optical observatory, marine research lab, experiential learning center, electron microscope, child development center, journalism lab, various agricultural and equine facilities, sawmill, language labs, performing arts center, and survey center. The 2600-acre campus is in a rural area 50 miles north of Boston. Including any residence halls, there are 183 buildings.

Student Life: 58% of undergraduates are from New Hampshire. Others are from 41 states, 29 foreign countries, and Canada. 82% are from public schools. 76% are white. The average age of freshmen is 18; all undergraduates, 20. 14% do not continue beyond their first year; 73% remain to graduate.

Housing: 7500 students can be accommodated in college housing, which includes single-sex and coed dorms, on-campus apartments, and married student housing. In addition, there are honors houses, language houses, special-interest houses, and international and substance-free residence halls. On-campus housing is available on a first-come, first-served basis. 59% of students live on campus; of those, 65% remain on campus on weekends. Upperclassmen may keep cars.

Activities: 9% of men belong to 11 national fraternities; 9% of women belong to 7 national sororities. There are 187 groups on campus, including art, band, cheerleading, chess, choir, chorale, chorus, computers, dance, debate, drama, environmental, ethnic, film, gay, honors, international, jazz band, literary magazine, marching band, musical theater, newspaper, orchestra, pep band, photography, political, professional, radio and TV, religious, social, social service, student government, symphony, and yearbook. Popular campus events include Jukebox, Student Activities Fair (in conjunction with University Day), and Winter Carnival.

Sports: There are 7 intercollegiate sports for men and 12 for women, and 17 intramural sports for men and 18 for women. Facilities include indoor and outdoor swimming pools, tracks, tennis courts, gyms, wrestling and gymnastics rooms, a dance studio, playing fields, an indoor ice rink, and cross-country ski trails. A 3-story recreation and sports complex, which seats 6500 for hockey and 7500 for basketball and special events, includes a fitness center, jogging track, weight room, racquetball courts, international squash court, aerobics and martial arts studios, multipurpose courts, and basketball courts.

Disabled Students: 85% of the campus is accessible. Facilities include wheelchair ramps, elevators, special parking, specially equipped restrooms, special class scheduling, lowered drinking fountains, lowered telephones, and special housing. Accommodations made on a case-by-case basis include sign language interpreters, reduced course loads, extended exam time, accessible transportation, academic modifications, note takers, text on tape, and note takers.

Services: Instruction in learning strategies, study skills, time management, and organizational skills is available. The university writing center offers free assistance by trained consultants.

Campus Safety and Security: Measures include 24-hour foot and vehicle patrol, emergency notification system, self-defense education, and security escort services. There are shuttle buses, emergency telephones, lighted pathways/sidewalks, limited access to dorms, and prevention awareness programs.

Programs of Study: UNH confers B.A., B.F.A., B.M., B.S., and B.S.F. degrees. Associates, master's, and doctoral degrees are also awarded. Bachelor's degrees are awarded in AGRICULTURE (animal science, dairy science, environmental studies, forestry and related sciences, horticulture, plant science, soil science, and wildlife management), BIOLOGICAL SCIENCE (biochemistry, biology/biological science, genetics, microbiology, molecular biology, neurosciences, nutrition, and zoology), BUSINESS (business administration and management, hospitality management services, hotel/motel and restaurant management, recreation and leisure services, and tourism), COMMUNICATIONS AND THE

ARTS (classics, communications, English, English literature, fine arts, French, German, Greek, Latin, linguistics, music, music performance, music theory and composition, Russian, Spanish, studio art, and voice), COMPUTER AND PHYSICAL SCIENCE (chemistry, computer science, earth science, geology, information sciences and systems, mathematics, and physics), EDUCATION (athletic training, English education, environmental education, mathematics education, music education, physical education, recreation education, and science education), ENGINEERING AND ENVIRONMENTAL DESIGN (chemical engineering, city/community/regional planning, civil engineering, computer engineering, electrical/electronics engineering, environmental engineering, environmental science, and mechanical engineering), HEALTH PROFESSIONS (biomedical science, health care administration, health science, medical laboratory science, nursing, occupational therapy, preveterinary science, and speech pathology/audiology), SOCIAL SCIENCE (anthropology, economics, European studies, family/consumer studies, French studies, history, humanities, philosophy, physical fitness/movement, political science/government, psychology, social work, sociology, water resources, and women's studies). Business, engineering, and English are the strongest academically. Business, psychology, and English are the largest.

Required: To graduate, all students must maintain a GPA of 2.0 and complete at least 128 credits, with a minimum of 36 credits and 10 classes in the major. General education requirements include 4 writing-intensive courses, including freshman composition, 3 courses in biological/physical science, and 1 course each in quantitative reasoning, historical perspectives, social science, fine arts, foreign culture, and philosophy/literature. Honors students and most seniors write a thesis or complete a project.

Special: Joint programs with Cornell University in marine science are available. Extensive cross-registration is possible through the New Hampshire College and University Council Consortium. There also is nationwide study through the National Student Exchange and worldwide study through the Center for International Education. Internships, study abroad throughout the world, a Washington semester, work-study, and B.A.-B.S. degrees, dual majors, a general studies degree, student-designed majors, extensive 3-2 B.S.-M.B.A. programs and other bachelor's-graduate degree plans, nondegree study, and pass/fail options are also available. A 3-2 engineering degree is offered with the New Hampshire Technical Institute, Vermont Technical College, Keene State College, and other institutions. There are 18 national honor societies, including Phi Beta Kappa, a freshman honors program, and 42 departmental honors programs.

Faculty/Classroom: 54% of faculty are male; 44% are female. 98% teach undergraduates, all do research, and 98% do both. Graduate students teach 2% of introductory courses. The average class size in an introductory lecture is 57; in a laboratory, 22; and in a regular course, 26.

Admissions: 71% of the 2009-2010 applicants were accepted. The SAT scores for the 2009-2010 freshman class were: Critical Reading--21% below 500, 51% between 500 and 599, 24% between 600 and 700, and 4% above 700; Math--16% below 500, 46% between 500 and 599, 34% between 600 and 700, and 4% above 700. 51% of the current freshmen were in the top fifth of their class; 90% were in the top two fifths. 62 freshmen graduated first in their class.

Requirements: The SAT or ACT is required. The ACT Optional Writing test is also required. In addition, applicants should have 18 academic credits, including 4 each in English and math, 3 each in science and foreign language, and 2 in social studies. An essay is required for all students. An audition is required for music students. AP and CLEP credits are accepted. Important factors in the admissions decision are advanced placement or honors courses, recommendations by school officials, and evidence of special talent.

Procedure: Freshmen are admitted fall and spring. Entrance exams should be taken before February 1 of the senior year. There are early decision, early admissions and deferred admissions plans. Early decision applications should be filed by November 15; regular applications by February 1 for fall entry and October 15 for spring entry. The application fee is $50 for New Hampshire residents and $60 for nonresidents. Notification of early decision is sent January 15; regular decision, April 15. Applications are accepted on-line.

Transfer: 572 transfer students enrolled in 2008-2009. Applicants must submit an overall minimum GPA of 2.8 in a general education curriculum. The SAT or the ACT is required unless waived. An essay is required. A letter of recommendation is optional. 32 of 128 credits required for the bachelor's degree must be completed at UNH.

Visiting: There are regularly scheduled orientations for prospective students, including campus tours, group information session, and open house programs. Visitors may sit in on classes. To schedule a visit, contact the Admissions Office.

Financial Aid: In 2009-2010, 84% of all full-time freshmen and 79% of continuing full-time students received some form of financial aid. 60% of all full-time freshmen and 59% of continuing full-time students received need-based aid. The average freshmen award was $18,637, with $7416 ($28,331 maximum) from need-based scholarships or need-based grants; $5275 ($10,000 maximum) from need-based self-help aid (loans and jobs); $24,504 ($33,832 maximum) from non-need-based athletic scholarships; and $10,123 ($35,000 maximum) from other non-need-based awards and non-need-based scholarships. 33% of undergraduate students work part-time. Average annual earnings from campus work are $3719. The average financial indebtedness of the 2009 graduate was $30,760. The FAFSA is required. The deadline for filing freshman financial aid applications for fall entry is March 1.

International Students: There are 76 international students enrolled. The school actively recruits these students. They must take the TOEFL with a minimum score of 550 on the paper-based TOEFL (PBT) or 80 on the Internet-based version (iBT). They must also take the SAT or ACT.

Computers: Wireless access is available. Students can access the system from residence halls, PC clusters, classrooms, and the library, as well as the student union and the front lawn of the main administrative building. All students may access the system. There are no time limits and no fees. It is strongly recommended that all students have a personal computer.

Graduates: From July 1, 2008 to June 30, 2009, 2592 bachelor's degrees were awarded. The most popular majors were business administration (14%), psychology (7%), and communication (6%). 250 companies recruited on campus in 2008-2009. In an average class, 53% graduate in 4 years or less, 70% graduate in 5 years or less, and 73% graduate in 6 years or less. Of the 2008 graduating class, 30% were enrolled in graduate school within 6 months of graduation and 50% were employed.

Admissions Contact: Robert McGann, Director, Admissions. E-Mail: *admissions@unh.edu* Web: *www.unh.edu*

UNIVERSITY SYSTEM OF NEW HAMPSHIRE

The University System of New Hampshire, established in 1963, is a public system in New Hampshire. It is governed by a board of trustees, whose chief administrator is the chancellor. The primary goal of the system is to serve the higher educational needs of the people of New Hampshire. The main priorities are to provide a well-coordinated system of higher education, student access and diversity, and quality programs through a commitment to excellence. Profiles of the 4-year campuses are included in this section.

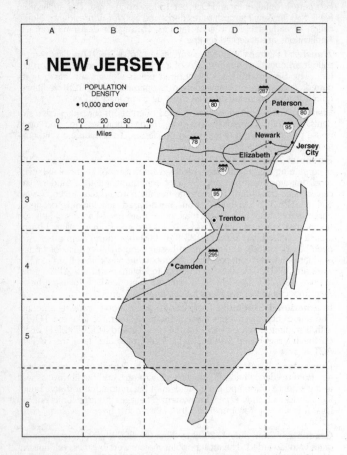

NEW JERSEY

POPULATION DENSITY

• 10,000 and over

0 10 20 30 40
Miles

Paterson
Newark
Jersey City
Elizabeth
Trenton
Camden

---

missions plans. Application deadlines are open. The application fee is $50. Notification is sent on a rolling basis. Applications are accepted on-line.

Transfer: A transcript from each college or university attended must be submitted to receive credit. 60 of 180 credits required for the bachelor's degree must be completed at Berkeley.

Visiting: There are guides for informal visits.

Financial Aid: The FAFSA, the college's own financial statement, and state income tax form are required. Check with the school for current application deadlines.

International Students: The school actively recruits these students. They must take the TOEFL.

Computers: All students may access the system. There are no time limits and no fees.

Graduates: In a recent year, 242 bachelor's degrees were awarded.

Admissions Contact: Admissions Officer
E-mail: *info@berkeleycollege.edu* Web: *www.berkeleycollege.edu*

BLOOMFIELD COLLEGE   E-2
Bloomfield, NJ 07003

(973) 748-9000, ext. 219
(800) 848-4555; (973) 748-0916

Full-time: 629 men, 1102 women	**Faculty:** 68; IIB, +$
Part-time: 128 men, 296 women	**Ph.D.s:** 74%
Graduate: none	**Student/Faculty:** 25 to 1
Year: semesters, summer session	**Tuition:** $20,000
Application Deadline: March 14	**Room & Board:** $11,300
Freshman Class: n/av	
SAT or ACT: required	**COMPETITIVE**

Bloomfield College, founded in 1868 and affiliated with the Presbyterian Church (U.S.A.), is an independent institution offering programs in liberal arts and sciences, creative arts and technology, professional studies, and the clinical and health sciences. There is one undergraduate school. In addition to regional accreditation, Bloomfield has baccalaureate program accreditation with NLN. The library contains 65,000 volumes, 59 microform items, and 5,000 audio/video tapes/CDs/DVDs, and subscribes to 560 periodicals including electronic. Computerized library services include interlibrary loans, database searching, Internet access, and laptop Internet portals. Special learning facilities include a learning resource center, art gallery, and electronic classrooms. The 12-acre campus is in a suburban area 15 miles from New York City. Including any residence halls, there are 46 buildings.

Student Life: 94% of undergraduates are from New Jersey. Others are from 20 states, and 4 foreign countries. 69% are from public schools. 50% are African American; 29% Hispanic; 15% white. The average age of freshmen is 19; all undergraduates, 24. 29% do not continue beyond their first year; 26% remain to graduate.

Housing: 547 students can be accommodated in college housing, which includes coed dorms and on-campus apartments. In addition, there are honors houses, special-interest houses, sorority houses, an off-campus hotel, and residential houses. On-campus housing is available on a first-come, first-served basis. Priority is given to out-of-town students. 81% of students commute. Alcohol is not permitted. All students may keep cars.

Activities: 3% of men belong to 1 local fraternity and 3 national fraternities; 1% of women belong to 6 national sororities. There are 43 groups on campus, including DEEP Retreat, chorus, ethnic, film, gay, honors, international, newspaper, professional, radio and TV, religious, social, social service, STEP Retreat, and student government. Popular campus events include formal dinners, multicultural festivals, and cultural events (including musical events, lectures, speakers).

Sports: There are 6 intercollegiate sports for men and 5 for women, and 2 intramural sports for men and 2 for women. Facilities include a 500-seat gym, weight-lifting facilities, and a basketball and volleyball court.

Disabled Students: 55% of the campus is accessible. Facilities include wheelchair ramps, elevators, special parking, specially equipped restrooms, lowered drinking fountains, and special housing.

Services: Counseling and information services are available, as is tutoring in most subjects. There is a reader service for the blind, and remedial math, reading, and writing.

Campus Safety and Security: Measures include 24-hour foot and vehicle patrol, emergency notification system, security escort services, emergency telephones, and lighted pathways/sidewalks. Security cameras are installed in all high-traffic areas.

Programs of Study: Bloomfield confers B.A. and B.S. degrees. Bachelor's degrees are awarded in BIOLOGICAL SCIENCE (biology/biological science), BUSINESS (accounting and business administration and management), COMMUNICATIONS AND THE ARTS (English and fine arts), COMPUTER AND PHYSICAL SCIENCE (applied mathematics,

---

BERKELEY COLLEGE/NEW JERSEY
West Paterson, NJ 07424

(973) 278-5400
(800)446-5400; (273-278-9141)

Full-time: 790 men, 1845 women	**Faculty:** n/av
Part-time: 70 men, 355 women	**Ph.D.s:** n/av
Graduate: none	**Student/Faculty:** n/av
Year: trimesters	**Tuition:** $20,000
Application Deadline: open	**Room & Board:** $10,000
Freshman Class: n/av	
SAT or ACT: required	**LESS COMPETITIVE**

Berkeley College of New Jersey, founded in 1931, is a private institution offering undergraduate programs in business. Figures in the above capsule and this profile are approximate. The library contains 11,000 volumes and subscribes to 130 periodicals including electronic. Computerized library services include interlibrary loans and database searching. Special learning facilities include a learning resource center. The campus is in a suburban area in West Paterson, approximately 20 miles from New York City. Including any residence halls, there are 2 buildings.

Student Life: 93% of undergraduates are from New Jersey. Others are from 4 states and 4 foreign countries. 34% are African American; 23% white; 23% Hispanic.

Housing: College-sponsored housing includes dorms. 96% of students commute.

Activities: There are no fraternities or sororities.

Sports: There is no sports program at Berkeley.

Services: Counseling and information services are available, as is tutoring in most subjects. There is remedial math, reading, and writing.

Programs of Study: Berkeley confers B.B.A. degrees. Associate degrees are also awarded. Bachelor's degrees are awarded in BUSINESS (accounting, business administration and management, international business management, and marketing/retailing/merchandising), HEALTH PROFESSIONS (health care administration).

Requirements: The SAT or ACT is required. In addition, graduation from an accredited high school or the GED, and an entrance exam or SAT or ACT scores are basic requirements for admission. A personal interview is strongly recommended. AP and CLEP credits are accepted.

Procedure: Freshmen are admitted to all sessions. Entrance exams should be taken any time. There are deferred admissions and rolling ad-

chemistry, information sciences and systems, and mathematics), EDUCATION (education), ENGINEERING AND ENVIRONMENTAL DESIGN (graphic arts technology), HEALTH PROFESSIONS (allied health, clinical science, and nursing), SOCIAL SCIENCE (history, philosophy, political science/government, psychology, religion, and sociology). Nursing and education is the strongest academically. Business, education, and creative arts and technology are the largest.

Required: All students must complete a Common Core, meet general education requirements, and maintain a 2.0 GPA. At least 33 course units are required for graduation.

Special: Internships, study abroad, and work-study programs are available. Double majors and contract majors are also possible. There are 4 national honor societies and a freshman honors program.

Faculty/Classroom: 49% of faculty are male; 51% are female. All teach undergraduates. The average class size in an introductory lecture is 17; in a laboratory is 13; and in a regular course is 15.

Admissions: 19% of the current freshmen were in the top fifth of their class; 45% were in the top two fifths.

Requirements: The SAT or ACT is required. In addition, the college requires at least 14 academic units, which should include English, math, history, and lab science. An essay and 2 personal recommendations are required. A GPA of 2.8 is required. AP and CLEP credits are accepted. Important factors in the admissions decision are advanced placement or honors courses, recommendations by school officials, and extracurricular activities record.

Procedure: Freshmen are admitted in fall, spring, and summer. Entrance exams should be taken during the senior year. There are early admissions, deferred admissions, and rolling admissions plans. Applications should be filed by March 14 for fall entry; December 1 for spring entry, along with a $40 fee. Notification is sent on a rolling basis. Applications are accepted on-line.

Transfer: 360 transfer students enrolled in 2008-2009. Applicants must present a minimum GPA of 2.0 from an accredited institution and submit official transcripts from all previously attended colleges. 8 of 33 credits required for the bachelor's degree must be completed at Bloomfield.

Visiting: There are regularly scheduled orientations for prospective students, consisting of a campus tour, an admissions interview, and other activities by request. There are guides for informal visits, and visitors may sit in on classes and stay overnight. To schedule a visit, contact the Office of Admissions at (973) 748-9000, ext. 230.

Financial Aid: In 2009-2010, 98% of all full-time freshmen and 96% of continuing full-time students received some form of financial aid. 94% of all full-time freshmen and 90% of continuing full-time students received need-based aid. The average freshman award was $24,032. Need-based scholarships or need-based grants averaged $15,855 ($22,500 maximum); need-based self-help aid (loans and jobs) averaged $4,105 ($5,900 maximum); non-need-based athletic scholarships averaged $12,721 ($29,044 maximum); and other non-need-based awards and non-need-based scholarships averaged $6,424 ($32,000 maximum). 20% of undergraduate students work part-time. Average annual earnings from campus work are $2335. The average financial indebtedness of the 2009 graduate was $25,015. The FAFSA is required. The priority date for freshman financial aid applications for fall entry is March 15. The deadline for filing freshman financial aid applications for fall entry is June 1.

International Students: There are 29 international students enrolled. The school actively recruits these students. They must take the TOEFL with a minimum score of 550 on the paper-based TOEFL (PBT) or 79 on the Internet-based version (iBT). They must also take the SAT or ACT.

Computers: Wireless access is available through labs, dorms, library, student center, and walk-up stations at various locations. All students may access the system. There are no time limits and no fees.

Graduates: From July 1, 2008 to June 30, 2009, 281 bachelor's degrees were awarded. The most popular majors were business administration (17%), sociology (16%), and psychology (15%). 485 companies recruited on campus in 2008-2009. In an average class, 11% graduate in 4 years or less, 23% graduate in 5 years or less, and 26% graduate in 6 years or less. Of the 2008 graduating class, 7% were enrolled in graduate school within 6 months of graduation, and 75% were employed.

Admissions Contact: Adam Castro, Director of Admissions. E-Mail: admission@bloomfield.edu Web: www.bloomfield.edu

CALDWELL COLLEGE E-2
Caldwell, NJ 07006

(973) 618-3000
(888) 864-9516; (973) 618-3600

Full-time: 380 men, 700 women	**Faculty:** IIB, av$
Part-time: 165 men, 460 women	**Ph.D.s:** n/av
Graduate: 120 men, 460 women	**Student/Faculty:** n/av
Year: semesters, summer session	**Tuition:** $22,200
Application Deadline: see profile	**Room & Board:** $8000
Freshman Class: n/av	
SAT: required	**LESS COMPETITIVE**

Caldwell College, founded in 1939, is a private school offering programs in liberal arts, science, business, fine arts, and education. It is affiliated with the Roman Catholic Church. The figures in the above capsule and in this profile are approximate. There is 1 graduate school. In addition to regional accreditation, Caldwell has baccalaureate program accreditation with TEAC. The library contains 144,909 volumes, 6,228 microform items, and 2,112 audio/video tapes/CDs/DVDs, and subscribes to 370 periodicals including electronic. Computerized library services include interlibrary loans, database searching, and Internet access. Special learning facilities include a learning resource center and art gallery. The 80-acre campus is in a suburban area 20 miles west of New York City. Including any residence halls, there are 9 buildings.

Student Life: 87% of undergraduates are from New Jersey. Others are from 14 states, 31 foreign countries, and Canada. 75% are from public schools. 68% are white; 13% African American. The average age of freshmen is 18; all undergraduates, 34. 27% do not continue beyond their first year; 56% remain to graduate.

Housing: 380 students can be accommodated in college housing, which includes coed dorms. On-campus housing is guaranteed for all 4 years. 61% of students commute. All students may keep cars.

Activities: There are no fraternities or sororities. There are 21 groups on campus, including art, band, cheerleading, choir, ethnic, honors, international, literary magazine, newspaper, orchestra, professional, religious, social, social service, student government, and yearbook. Popular campus events include Founders Day, Freshman Investiture, and Fall Festival.

Sports: There are 5 intercollegiate sports for men and 5 for women, and 4 intramural sports for men and 4 for women. Facilities include a multipurpose gym, a training room, tennis courts, weight rooms, playing fields, and a pool.

Disabled Students: 85% of the campus is accessible. Facilities include wheelchair ramps, elevators, special parking, specially equipped restrooms, special class scheduling, lowered drinking fountains, and lowered telephones.

Services: Counseling and information services are available, as is tutoring in most subjects. There is a reader service for the blind, and remedial math, reading, and writing, and a writing lab.

Campus Safety and Security: Measures include 24-hour foot and vehicle patrol, self-defense education, and security escort services. There are emergency telephones and lighted pathways/sidewalks.

Programs of Study: Caldwell confers B.A., B.S., and B.F.A. degrees. Master's degrees are also awarded. Bachelor's degrees are awarded in BIOLOGICAL SCIENCE (biology/biological science), BUSINESS (accounting, business administration and management, international business management, management science, and marketing and distribution), COMMUNICATIONS AND THE ARTS (art, communications, English, fine arts, French, music, Spanish, and studio art), COMPUTER AND PHYSICAL SCIENCE (chemistry, computer management, computer science, information sciences and systems, and mathematics), EDUCATION (elementary education), HEALTH PROFESSIONS (medical laboratory technology), SOCIAL SCIENCE (criminal justice, history, political science/government, psychology, social studies, sociology, and theological studies). Liberal arts, education, and sciences are the strongest academically. Business, education, and psychology are the largest.

Required: Students must maintain a minimum GPA of 2.0 while taking 120 credit hours, including a minimum of 30 in the major. The 55-credit core includes 15 credits in religion/philosophy, 6 each in history, English, language, social science, math and computer science, and fine arts, and 2 in communication arts. Students must participate in an outcome assessment that is unique for each department. It is a comprehensive exam for some.

Special: Caldwell offers co-op and internship programs in all majors; study abroad in 6 countries; a Washington semester; 1-semester internships; and work-study with Dominican Adult Day Care, Hill Top Day Care, and Family and Child Services of North Essex. B.A.-B.S. degrees in 29 fields, dual majors in all majors, credit for life experience in adult education, nondegree study, student-designed majors, and pass/fail options are possible. The Continuing Education Program offers adults (23 years or older) a chance to complete degree requirements in the evening and Saturdays, and the External Degree Program gives adults an opportunity to earn a degree off without attending on-campus classes. There are 15 national honor societies and a freshman honors program.

Faculty/Classroom: 49% of faculty are male; 51% are female. 89% teach undergraduates. No introductory courses are taught by graduate students. The average class size in an introductory lecture is 15; in a laboratory is 13; and in a regular course is 12.

Requirements: The SAT is required. In addition, applicants need 16 academic credits or 16 Carnegie units, including 4 years in English, 2 each in foreign language, math, and science, and 1 in history. A written recommendation from a high school counselor is required. A portfolio, audition, and interview are recommended, depending on the field of study. The GED is accepted. A GPA of 2.0 is required. AP and CLEP credits are accepted. Important factors in the admissions decision are advanced placement or honors courses, leadership record, and recommendations by school officials.

Procedure: Freshmen are admitted to all sessions. Entrance exams should be taken in fall of the senior year. There are early admissions and rolling admissions plans. Application deadlines are open. Application fee is $40. Applications are accepted on-line.

Transfer: Transfer students must have a minimum GPA of 2.0 (2.5 in teacher education) and 12 transferable credits. 45 of 120 credits required for the bachelor's degree must be completed at Caldwell.

Visiting: There are regularly scheduled orientations for prospective students, including a brief presentation by faculty and students, followed by a tour. There are guides for informal visits; visitors may sit in on classes and stay overnight. To schedule a visit, contact the Admissions Office.

Financial Aid: The FAFSA and the college's own financial statement are required. Check with the school for current application deadlines.

International Students: The school actively recruits these students. They must take the TOEFL.

Computers: All students may access the system Monday to Thursday 9 A.M. to 9:30 P.M., Friday 10:30 A.M. to 4 P.M., and weekends, 12 P.M. to 5 P.M. There are no time limits and no fees.

Admissions Contact: Kathryn Reilly, Director of Admissions. A campus DVD is available. E-Mail: *admissions@caldwell.edu* Web: *www.caldwell.edu*

CENTENARY COLLEGE   C-2
Hackettstown, NJ 07840

(908) 852-1400
(800) 236-8679; (908) 852-3454

Full-time: 732 men, 1231 women	**Faculty:** 68; IIB, --$
Part-time: 69 men, 108 women	**Ph.D.s:** 56%
Graduate: 245 men, 554 women	**Student/Faculty:** 34 to 1
Year: semesters, summer session	**Tuition:** $23,950
Application Deadline: open	**Room & Board:** $8900
Freshman Class: 753 applied, 672 accepted, 272 enrolled	
SAT CR/M/W: 462/461/458	**ACT:** 18 **LESS COMPETITIVE**

Centenary College, founded in 1867, is a private institution affiliated with the United Methodist Church. The college offers undergraduate and graduate programs in liberal arts, business, international studies, education, equine studies, fashion, and fine arts. There is 1 graduate school. In addition to regional accreditation, Centenary has baccalaureate program accreditation with NASDTEC. The library contains 68,000 volumes, 20,000 microform items, and 5000 audio/video tapes/CDs/DVDs, and subscribes to 375 periodicals including electronic. Computerized library services include interlibrary loans, database searching, Internet access, and laptop Internet portals. Special learning facilities include a learning resource center, art gallery, radio station, TV station, equestrian center, and CAD lab. The 42-acre campus is in a suburban area 55 miles west of New York City. Including any residence halls, there are 22 buildings.

Student Life: 88% of undergraduates are from New Jersey. Others are from 21 states, 14 foreign countries, and Canada. 80% are from public schools. 67% are white. The average age of freshmen is 18; all undergraduates, 24. 24% do not continue beyond their first year; 48% remain to graduate.

Housing: 756 students can be accommodated in college housing, which includes single-sex and coed dorms and on-campus apartments. On-campus housing is available on a first-come, first-served basis and is available on a lottery system for upperclassmen. 53% of students live on campus; of those, 70% remain on campus on weekends. All students may keep cars.

Activities: 10% of men belong to 1 local fraternity; 15% of women belong to 3 local sororities. There are 31 groups on campus, including art, cheerleading, chorus, dance, drama, environmental, ethnic, honors, international, literary magazine, newspaper, photography, political, professional, radio and TV, religious, social, social service, student government, and yearbook. Popular campus events include Presidents Ball and Community Plunge.

Sports: There are 7 intercollegiate sports for men and 7 for women. Facilities include a gym, a fitness center, an indoor pool, tennis courts, playing fields, and an equine center and stables.

Disabled Students: 60% of the campus is accessible. Facilities include wheelchair ramps, special parking, specially equipped restrooms, special class scheduling, and lowered telephones.

Services: Counseling and information services are available, as is tutoring in some subjects. There is remedial math, reading, and writing. Learning associates provide personalized subject-matter support.

Campus Safety and Security: Measures include 24-hour foot and vehicle patrol, emergency notification system, and security escort services. There are lighted pathways/sidewalks.

Programs of Study: Centenary confers B.A., B.F.A., and B.S. degrees. Associates and master's degrees are also awarded. Bachelor's degrees are awarded in AGRICULTURE (equine science), BIOLOGICAL SCIENCE (biology/biological science), BUSINESS (accounting and business administration and management), COMMUNICATIONS AND THE ARTS (applied art, communications, dramatic arts, and English), COMPUTER AND PHYSICAL SCIENCE (mathematics), EDUCATION (elementary education and secondary education), SOCIAL SCIENCE (criminal justice, fashion design and technology, history, interdisciplinary studies, international studies, political science/government, psychology, and sociology). Equine studies, business, and education certification. are the strongest academically.

Required: Students must complete a distribution of 40 to 46 semester hours in core courses, including college seminars, and 9 credits in liberal arts studies, as well as the required number of credits, usually 48, for their majors. At least 128 semester hours and a minimum GPA of 2.0 are needed to earn the bachelor's degree.

Special: Centenary offers internships in every major. The college offers study abroad in England and other countries, dual majors, as long as they are covered under the same degree, an accelerated degree program in liberal arts and business administration, student-designed majors, work-study on-campus, and a pass/fail option. Students ages 25 or older may earn life experience credits. There is 1 national honor society and a freshman honors program.

Faculty/Classroom: 50% of faculty are male; 50% are female. All teach and do research. No introductory courses are taught by graduate students. The average class size in an introductory lecture is 25; in a laboratory, 20; and in a regular course, 15.

Admissions: 89% of the 2009-2010 applicants were accepted. The SAT scores for the 2009-2010 freshman class were: Critical Reading--71% below 500, 25% between 500 and 599, 3% between 600 and 700, and 1% above 700; Math--72% below 500, 24% between 500 and 599, 3% between 600 and 700, and 1% above 700; Writing--68% below 500, 27% between 500 and 599, 4% between 600 and 700, and 1% above 700. The ACT scores were 68% below 21, 11% between 21 and 23, and 21% between 24 and 26. 1 freshman graduated first in the class.

Requirements: The SAT or ACT is required. In addition, minimum scores include a satisfactory SAT score or an ACT composite of 18. Applicants must be graduates of accredited secondary schools or have earned a GED. Centenary requires 16 academic credits or Carnegie units, based on 4 years of English, math, and science and 2 years each of foreign language and history. An essay is required for freshmen, and an interview is recommended. Applicants to specific fine arts programs must also submit a portfolio. A GPA of 2.0 is required. AP and CLEP credits are accepted. Important factors in the admissions decision are advanced placement or honors courses, leadership record, and ability to finance college education.

Procedure: Freshmen are admitted fall and spring. Entrance exams should be taken as early as possible in the senior year. There are deferred admissions and rolling admissions plans. Application deadlines are open. The application fee is $30. Notification is sent on a rolling basis. Applications are accepted on-line.

Transfer: 220 transfer students enrolled in 2008-2009. Applicants must have a minimum college GPA of 2.0 and submit proof of high school graduation or the equivalent. 32 of 128 credits required for the bachelor's degree must be completed at Centenary.

Visiting: There are regularly scheduled orientations for prospective students, including basic skills testing, advising, registration, and social events. Visitors may sit in on classes and stay overnight. To schedule a visit, contact the Admissions Office.

Financial Aid: In 2008-2009, 85% of all full-time freshmen and 88% of continuing full-time students received some form of financial aid. 84% of all full-time freshmen and 85% of continuing full-time students received need-based aid. The average freshmen award was $19,100. 75% of undergraduate students work part-time. Average annual earnings from campus work are $1200. The average financial indebtedness of a recent graduate was $28,104. The FAFSA and other forms as requested are required. The priority date for freshman financial aid applications for fall entry is March 15. The deadline for filing freshman financial aid applications for fall entry is September 1.

International Students: There were 111 international students enrolled in a recent year. The school actively recruits these students. They must take the TOEFL, with a minimum score of 500 on the paper-based TOEFL (PBT) or 60 on the Internet-based version (iBT), or the IELTS with a score of 5.0. They must also take the SAT or ACT.

Computers: Wireless access is available. All full-time undergraduates are provided laptops. Computer facilities are also available throughout the campus. All students may access the system. Computer and CAD lab use depends on lab hours. The fee is $700.

Graduates: From July 1, 2008 to June 30, 2009, 481 bachelor's degrees were awarded. The most popular majors were business administration (58%), social sciences (21%), and equine (7%). 35 companies recruited on campus in 2008-2009. In an average class, 46% graduate in 4 years or less, 44% graduate in 5 years or less, and 48% graduate in 6 years or less. Of a recent graduating class, 15% were enrolled in graduate school within 6 months of graduation and 75% were employed.

Admissions Contact: Glenna Warren, Dean of Admissions. E-Mail: *admissions@centenarycollege.edu* Web: *www.centenarycollege.edu*

COLLEGE OF NEW JERSEY   D-3
Ewing, NJ 08628-0718   (609) 771-2131
(800) 624-0967; (609) 637-5174

Full-time: 2519 men, 3561 women	**Faculty:** 347; IIA, +$
Part-time: 62 men, 95 women	**Ph.D.s:** 88%
Graduate: 150 men, 593 women	**Student/Faculty:** 18 to 1
Year: semesters, summer session	**Tuition:** $12,722 ($21,408)
Application Deadline: January 15	**Room & Board:** $9996
Freshman Class: 9238 applied, 1284 accepted, 4267 enrolled	
SAT CR/M/W: 630/660/630	**MOST COMPETITIVE**

The College of New Jersey, founded in 1855, is a public institution offering programs in the liberal arts, sciences, business, engineering, nursing, and education. There are 7 undergraduate schools and 1 graduate school. In addition to regional accreditation, TCNJ has baccalaureate program accreditation with AACSB, ABET, NASM, NCATE, and NLN. The library contains 561,250 volumes, 18,204 microform items, and 33,464 audio/video tapes/CDs/DVDs, and subscribes to 6194 periodicals including electronic. Computerized library services include interlibrary loans, database searching, Internet access, and laptop Internet portals. Special learning facilities include a learning resource center, art gallery, planetarium, radio station, TV station, electron microscopy lab, nuclear magnetic resonance lab, optical spectroscopy lab, observatory, planetarium, and greenhouse. The 289-acre campus is in a suburban area between Princeton and Trenton. Including any residence halls, there are 61 buildings.

Student Life: 94% of undergraduates are from New Jersey. Others are from 23 states and 16 foreign countries. 70% are from public schools. 65% are white. 48% are Catholic; 17% Protestant; 15% claim no religious affiliation; 15% Eastern Orthodox, Buddhist, Muslim, Islamic, Quaker. The average age of freshmen is 18; all undergraduates, 20. 5% do not continue beyond their first year; 84% remain to graduate.

Housing: 3626 students can be accommodated in college housing, which includes single-sex and coed dorms, on-campus apartments, and off-campus apartments. In addition, there are honors houses and special-interest houses. All freshman participate in the First Seminar Program and are housed in learning communities that connect the academic and social aspects of the college environment. On-campus housing is guaranteed for the freshman year only and is available on a lottery system for upperclassmen. 58% of students live on campus; of those, 70% remain on campus on weekends. Upperclassmen may keep cars.

Activities: 16% of men belong to 2 local and 9 national fraternities; 13% of women belong to 15 national sororities. There are 205 groups on campus, including foreign language, art, band, cheerleading, chess, choir, chorale, chorus, computers, dance, drama, environmental, ethnic, film, gay, honors, international, jazz band, literary magazine, musical theater, newspaper, opera, orchestra, pep band, photography, political, professional, radio and TV, recreational, religious, social, social service, student government, symphony, and yearbook. Popular campus events include Lallanobozza, Mystique of the EAST, and TCNJ Later Nighter.

Sports: There are 9 intercollegiate sports for men and 9 for women, and 14 intramural sports for men and 14 for women. Facilities include a 5000-seat stadium with an Astroturf field, an aquatic center, baseball and softball diamonds, a Sportexe-surface soccer/multipurpose field, an all-weather track, a sand volleyball court, 5 grass playing fields, a 1200-seat gym, a physical enhancement center, a student recreation center, tennis, racquetball, and basketball/volleyball courts, and a free weight room.

Disabled Students: 90% of the campus is accessible. Facilities include wheelchair ramps, elevators, special parking, specially equipped restrooms, special class scheduling, lowered drinking fountains, lowered telephones, and special housing.

Services: Counseling and information services are available, as is tutoring in most subjects. There is a reader service for the blind, and remedial math, reading, and writing.

Campus Safety and Security: Measures include 24-hour foot and vehicle patrol, emergency notification system, self-defense education, and security escort services. There are emergency telephones, lighted pathways/sidewalks, and controlled access to dorms/residences.

Programs of Study: TCNJ confers B.A., B.S., B.A.B.M.E., B.F.A., B.M., B.S.C.E., B.S.Co.E., B.S.E.E., B.S.M.E., and B.S.N. degrees. Master's degrees are also awarded. Bachelor's degrees are awarded in BIOLOGICAL SCIENCE (biology/biological science), BUSINESS (accounting and business administration and management), COMMUNICATIONS AND THE ARTS (art, art history and appreciation, communications, English, fine arts, graphic design, multimedia, music, and Spanish), COMPUTER AND PHYSICAL SCIENCE (chemistry, computer science, digital arts/technology, mathematics, and physics), EDUCATION (art education, early childhood education, education of the deaf and hearing impaired, elementary education, English education, health education, mathematics education, music education, physical education, science education, social science education, social studies education, special education, and technical education), ENGINEERING AND ENVIRONMENTAL DESIGN (biomedical engineering, civil engineering, computer engineering, electrical/electronics engineering, engineering and applied science, and mechanical engineering), HEALTH PROFESSIONS (exercise science and nursing), SOCIAL SCIENCE (criminal justice, economics, history, international studies, philosophy, political science/government, psychology, sociology, and women's studies). Biology, education, and engineering are the strongest academically. Psychology, biology, and elementary education are the largest.

Required: To graduate, students must complete a liberal learning curriculum of 128 to 136 credit hours that includes at least 1 major, as well as a suite of courses that address 3 interdependent structural elements: intellectual and scholarly growth; civic responsibilities; and the broad sectors of human inquiry within the arts and humanities, social sciences, natural sciences, and quantitative reasoning.

Special: TCNJ offers cross-registration with the New Jersey Marine Science Consortium, a limited number of overseas internship possibilities, numerous internships in the public and private sectors, a Washington semester, and study abroad in more than a dozen countries. Pass/fail options and some dual majors are possible. Specially designed research courses allow students to participate in collaborative scholarly projects with members of the faculty, and the Bonner Center offers opportunities for community-engaged initiatives. Combined advanced and accelerated degree programs are offered in education of the deaf and hard of hearing, special education, medicine, and optometry. There are 16 national honor societies, including Phi Beta Kappa, a freshman honors program, and 40 departmental honors programs.

Faculty/Classroom: 49% of faculty are male; 51% are female. All teach undergraduates, and 85% also do research. No introductory courses are taught by graduate students. The average class size in an introductory lecture is 25; in a laboratory, 17; and in a regular course, 21.

Admissions: 14% of the 2009-2010 applicants were accepted. The SAT scores for the 2009-2010 freshman class were: Critical Reading--2% below 500, 31% between 500 and 599, 53% between 600 and 700, and 15% above 700; Math--1% below 500, 16% between 500 and 599, 62% between 600 and 700, and 22% above 700; Writing--1% below 500, 26% between 500 and 599, 59% between 600 and 700, and 14% above 700. 87% of the current freshmen were in the top fifth of their class; 98% were in the top two fifths. 13 freshmen graduated first in their class.

Requirements: The SAT is required. In addition, applicants must have earned 16 academic credits in high school, consisting of 4 in English, 3 each in math and science, 2 each in foreign language and social studies, and 6 others distributed among math, science, social studies, and a foreign language. An essay is required. Art majors must submit a portfolio, and music majors must audition. The GED is accepted. A GPA of 2.0 is required. AP and CLEP credits are accepted. Important factors in the admissions decision are advanced placement or honors courses, leadership record, and evidence of special talent.

Procedure: Freshmen are admitted fall and spring. Entrance exams should be taken by the end of the junior year or early in the senior year. There are early decision and rolling admissions plans. Early decision applications should be filed by November 15; regular applications, by January 15 for fall entry and November 1 for spring entry, along with a $70 fee. Notification of early decision is sent December 15; other notifications are sent on a rolling basis beginning January 15. 288 early decision candidates were accepted for the 2009-2010 class. 550 applicants were on the 2009 waiting list; 288 were admitted. Applications are accepted on-line.

Transfer: 324 transfer students enrolled in 2008-2009. Transfer students must have a minimum GPA of 2.5, and those with fewer than 33 credits must submit SAT scores. An associate degree is recommended. All transfer students must submit high school transcripts. 12 of 32 to 34 course units required for the bachelor's degree must be completed at TCNJ.

Visiting: There are regularly scheduled orientations for prospective students, consisting of an admissions presentation and a tour of campus. Reservations are required. There are guides for informal visits; visitors may sit in on classes and stay overnight. To schedule a visit, contact the Admissions Office.

Financial Aid: In 2009-2010, 86% of all full-time freshmen and 72% of continuing full-time students received some form of financial aid. 42% of all full-time freshmen and 40% of continuing full-time students received need-based aid. The average freshmen award was $11,258, with $3912 ($8000 maximum) from need-based self-help aid (loans and jobs) and $7255 ($35,172 maximum) from other non-need-based awards and non-need-based scholarships. 21% of undergraduate students work part-time. Average annual earnings from campus work are $1863. The average financial indebtedness of the 2009 graduate was $22,088. TCNJ is a member of CSS. The FAFSA and copies of students' and parents' tax returns as applicable are required. The priority date for freshman financial aid applications for fall entry is March 1. The deadline for filing freshman financial aid applications for fall entry is October 1.

International Students: There are 23 international students enrolled. They must take the TOEFL with a minimum score of 550 on the paper-based TOEFL (PBT) or 90 on the Internet-based version (iBT). They must also take the SAT or ACT. The SAT is required for merit scholarship consideration.

Computers: There are 631 computers in 30 computer labs on campus, classrooms, and the library. All classrooms are connected to the college network. The majority of TCNJ's campus is wireless. All residence hall rooms have access to the college network. All students may access the system. There are no time limits. The fee is $189. It is strongly recommended that all students have a personal computer.

Graduates: From July 1, 2008 to June 30, 2009, 1487 bachelor's degrees were awarded. The most popular majors were psychology (8%), business/finance (7%), and biology (6%). More than 400 companies recruited on campus in 2008-2009. In an average class, 1% graduate in 3 years or less, 67% graduate in 4 years or less, 82% graduate in 5 years or less, and 85% graduate in 6 years or less. Of the 2008 graduating class, 27% were enrolled in graduate school within 6 months of graduation, and 96% were employed.

Admissions Contact: Lisa Angeloni, Dean of Admissions.
E-mail: *tcnjinfo@tcnj.edu* Web: *www.tcnj.edu*

COLLEGE OF SAINT ELIZABETH   E-2

Morristown, NJ 07960-6989   **(973) 290-4700**
                                                    (800) 210-7900; (973) 290-4710

Full-time: 15 men, 663 women	**Faculty:** 51; IIB, av$
Part-time: 118 men, 485 women	**Ph.D.s:** 86%
Graduate: 143 men, 733 women	**Student/Faculty:** 13 to 1
Year: semesters, summer session	**Tuition:** $25,058
Application Deadline: March 1	**Room & Board:** $10,904
Freshman Class: 424 accepted, 178 enrolled	
SAT CR/M/W: 442/430/452	**LESS COMPETITIVE**

The College of St. Elizabeth, founded in 1899, is a private Roman Catholic college primarily for women. Undergraduate programs are offered in the arts and sciences, business administration, education, foods and nutrition, and upper-level nursing. There are graduate programs in education, management, health care management, nutrition, psychology, and theology. Adult undergraduate degree programs and graduate programs are coed. There is 1 graduate school. In addition to regional accreditation, CSE has baccalaureate program accreditation with ADA, NLN, and TEAC. The library contains 119,438 volumes, 142,451 microform items, and 1,744 audio/video tapes/CDs/DVDs, and subscribes to 977 periodicals including electronic. Computerized library services include interlibrary loans, database searching, Internet access, and laptop Internet portals. Special learning facilities include a learning resource center, art gallery, and a television studio. The 188-acre campus is in a suburban area 30 miles west of New York City. Including any residence halls, there are 12 buildings.

Student Life: 92% of undergraduates are from New Jersey. Others are from 13 states and 49 foreign countries. 74% are from public schools. 41% are white; 17% African American; 15% Hispanic. 48% are Catholic. The average age of freshmen is 18; all undergraduates, 30. 28% do not continue beyond their first year; 62% remain to graduate.

Housing: 411 students can be accommodated in college housing, which includes single-sex dorms. On-campus housing is guaranteed for all 4 years. 63% of students live on campus; of those, 10% remain on campus on weekends. All students may keep cars.

Activities: There are no fraternities or sororities. There are 15 groups on campus, including chorale, dance, drama, ethnic, honors, international, literary magazine, newspaper, professional, religious, social, social service, and student government. Popular campus events include Rathskellers, Oktoberfest, and International Night.

Sports: There are 8 intercollegiate sports for women. Facilities include a student center that houses a swimming pool, a weight room, an archery range, and a gym. Tennis courts are also available, as is a bike and fitness trail.

Disabled Students: 75% of the campus is accessible. Facilities include wheelchair ramps, elevators, special parking, specially equipped restrooms, special class scheduling, and handrails.

Services: Counseling and information services are available, as is tutoring in most subjects. There is remedial math, reading, and writing. Other services include books on tape, large monitor computers, and note takers.

Campus Safety and Security: Measures include 24-hour foot and vehicle patrol, emergency notification system, and security escort services. There are emergency telephones and lighted pathways/sidewalks.

Programs of Study: CSE confers B.A., B.S., and B.S.N. degrees. Master's and doctoral degrees are also awarded. Bachelor's degrees are awarded in BIOLOGICAL SCIENCE (biochemistry, biology/biological science, and nutrition), BUSINESS (business administration and management), COMMUNICATIONS AND THE ARTS (art, communications, English, fine arts, music, and Spanish), COMPUTER AND PHYSICAL SCIENCE (chemistry, computer science, and mathematics), EDUCATION (education and elementary education), HEALTH PROFESSIONS (nursing), SOCIAL SCIENCE (American studies, economics, history, international studies, philosophy, psychology, sociology, and theological studies). Math, chemistry, and education are the strongest academically. Nursing, education, and business administration are the largest.

Required: To graduate, students must complete 128 semester hours, with a minimum of 32 in the major, while maintaining a GPA of 2.0, or 2.75 for education majors. Core requirements include 27 credits in specific humanities courses focusing on theology, philosophy, literature, history, foreign language, and fine arts, 6 to 8 in math and science, and 6 in social science. In addition, 2 credits in fitness/wellness and an interdisciplinary course are required. Students must also demonstrate proficiency in writing and complete a comprehensive or capstone experience.

Special: There is cross-registration with Drew and Fairleigh Dickinson Universities. CSE also offers internships in business, law, technology, health, government, sports, and television. On-campus work-study, accelerated degree programs, dual majors, student-designed majors, study abroad, credit for life experience, pass/fail options, and nondegree study are also available. Continuing studies programs are geared to the working student. There are 10 national honor societies, a freshman honors program, and 1 departmental honors program.

Faculty/Classroom: 31% of faculty are male; 69% are female. 76% teach undergraduates, and 5% both teach and do research. No introductory courses are taught by graduate students. The average class size in an introductory lecture is 15; in a laboratory, 12; and in a regular course, 13.

Admissions: The SAT scores for the 2009-2010 freshman class were: Critical Reading--74% below 500, 21% between 500 and 599, 4% between 600 and 700, and 2% above 700; Math--76% below 500, 18% between 500 and 599, 5% between 600 and 700, and 1% above 700; Writing--68% below 500, 23% between 500 and 599, 6% between 600 and 700, and 2% above 700. 29% of the current freshmen were in the top fifth of their class; 57% were in the top two fifths.

Requirements: The SAT is required. In addition, applicants must be graduates of an accredited secondary school or have earned a GED. The college requires 16 academic units, including 3 each in English and math/science, 2 in foreign language, and 1 in history. An essay and 2 letters of recommendation are required, and an interview is recommended. A GPA of 2.0 is required. AP and CLEP credits are accepted. Important factors in the admissions decision are advanced placement or honors courses, recommendations by school officials, and leadership record.

Procedure: Freshmen are admitted fall and spring. Entrance exams should be taken early in the senior year. There are deferred admissions and rolling admissions plans. Applications should be filed by March 1 for fall entry; November 1 for spring entry, along with a $35 fee. Applications are accepted on-line.

Transfer: 64 transfer students enrolled in 2008-2009. Applicants must present a minimum GPA of 2.0 in course work from an accredited college. SAT or ACT scores, an associate degree, and an interview are also recommended. 32 of 128 credits required for the bachelor's degree must be completed at CSE.

Visiting: There are regularly scheduled orientations for prospective students, including interviews, tours, and class visitation. There are guides for informal visits, and visitors may sit in on classes and stay overnight. To schedule a visit, contact Donna Tatarka at (973) 290-4705.

Financial Aid: 31% of undergraduate students work part-time. Average annual earnings from campus work are $4350. CSE is a member of CSS. The FAFSA is required. The priority date for freshman financial aid applications for fall entry is March 1. The deadline for filing freshman financial aid applications for fall entry is September 1.

International Students: There are 45 international students enrolled. The school actively recruits these students. They must take the TOEFL or other approved assessment tests. Applicants from English-speaking countries may submit scores from either the TOEFL or the SAT.

Computers: Wireless access is available. Students may access the campus network and Internet through computer labs on campus or through the college Wi-Fi network using their own computer. 127 lab computers are available for student use. Dorm rooms have wired Ethernet connections, and all dorms have full Wi-Fi network coverage. Wi-Fi is available in 5 of the 7 buildings on campus. All students may access the system. There are no time limits and no fees.

Graduates: From July 1, 2008 to June 30, 2009, 253 bachelor's degrees were awarded. The most popular majors were nursing (22%), business (16%), and communication (11%). In an average class, 56% graduate in 4 years or less, 61% graduate in 5 years or less, and 62% graduate in 6 years or less.

Admissions Contact: Donna Tatarka, Dean of Admission. A campus DVD is available. E-mail: *apply@www.cse.edu* Web: *www.cse.edu*

DEVRY COLLEGE OF TECHNOLOGY/NORTH BRUNSWICK D-3

North Brunswick, NJ 08902   (732) 435-4850
    (800) 33-DEVRY; (732) 435-4856

Full-time: 618 men, 218 women	**Faculty:** n/av
Part-time: 408 men, 188 women	**Ph.D.s:** n/av
Graduate: none	**Student/Faculty:** n/av
Year: semesters, summer session	
Application Deadline: open	
Freshman Class: n/av	**LESS COMPETITIVE**

DeVry College of Technology/North Brunswick, founded in 1969, is a private institution offering hands-on programs in electronics, business administration, computer information systems, and information technology. The school is 1 of 67 DeVry University locations throughout the United States and Canada. There are no undergraduate schools. In addition to regional accreditation, DeVry has baccalaureate program accreditation with ABET. The library contains 32,201 volumes, 1,870 audio/video tapes/CDs/DVDs, and subscribes to 210 periodicals including electronic. Computerized library services include interlibrary loans and database searching. Special learning facilities include a learning resource center. The 15-acre campus is in a small town North Brunswick, NJ. Including any residence halls, there are 1 buildings.

Student Life: 15% of undergraduates are from out of state, mostly the Middle Atlantic. 43% are white; 25% African American; 19% Hispanic. The average age of all undergraduates is 24.

Housing: There are no residence halls. All students commute.

Activities: There are no fraternities or sororities. There are 11 groups on campus, including ethnic, honors, and professional. Popular campus events include Student Appreciation Day.

Sports: There is no sports program at DeVry.

Disabled Students: All of the campus is accessible. Facilities include wheelchair ramps, elevators, special parking, specially equipped restrooms, special class scheduling, lowered drinking fountains, and lowered telephones.

Services: Counseling and information services are available, as is tutoring in every subject.

Campus Safety and Security: n/av

Programs of Study: DeVry confers B.S. degrees. Associates and master's degrees are also awarded. Bachelor's degrees are awarded in BUSINESS (business administration and management), COMMUNICATIONS AND THE ARTS (telecommunications), COMPUTER AND PHYSICAL SCIENCE (information sciences and systems), EDUCATION (computer education), ENGINEERING AND ENVIRONMENTAL DESIGN (biomedical engineering and electrical/electronics engineering technology). Telecommunications is the largest.

Required: To graduate, students must achieve a GPA of at least 2.0, complete 48 to 154 credit hours, and satisfactorily complete all curriculum requirements. Course requirements vary according to program. All first-semester students take courses in business organization, computer applications, algebra, psychology, and student success strategies.

Special: Evening and weekend classes, distance learning, co-op programs, and an accelerated degree program are offered. There are 2 national honor societies and including Phi Beta Kappa.

Faculty/Classroom: All teach undergraduates. No introductory courses are taught by graduate students.

Requirements: In addition, admissions requirements include graduation from a secondary school; the GED is also accepted. Applicants must pass the DeVry entrance exam or present satisfactory ACT or SAT I scores. An interview is required. CLEP credits are accepted.

Procedure: Freshmen are admitted fall, spring, and summer. There are early admissions, deferred admissions, and rolling admissions plans. Application deadlines are open. Application fee is $50. Notification is sent on a rolling basis. Applications are accepted on-line.

Transfer: 196 transfer students enrolled in 2008-2009. Applicants must present passing grades in all completed college course work, demonstrate language skills proficiency with at least 24 completed semester hours, and present evidence of math proficiency by appropriate college-level credits. A minimum GPA of 2.0 is required. 30 of 48 credits required for the bachelor's degree must be completed at DeVry.

Visiting: There are regularly scheduled orientations for prospective students. There are guides for informal visits and visitors may sit in on classes. To schedule a visit, contact Danielle DiNapoli, Dean of Admissions.

Financial Aid: In 2009-2010, 49% of all full-time freshmen and 63% of continuing full-time students received some form of financial aid. 48% of all full-time freshmen and 61% of continuing full-time students received need-based aid. The average freshmen award was $6,840. The FAFSA is required. Check with the school for current application deadlines.

International Students: There are 52 international students enrolled. They must take the TOEFL.

Computers: Computer information students may access the system during published lab hours. There are no fees. Students enrolled in the Information Technology program have DeVry-issued laptop computers. Students must have a personal computer.

Graduates: From July 1, 2008 to June 30, 2009, 259 bachelor's degrees were awarded. The most popular majors were computer and information sciences (46%), business/marketing (37%), and engineering technologies (16%). 173 companies recruited on campus in 2008-2009.

Admissions Contact: Danielle DiNapoli, Dean of Admissions. E-Mail: *admissions@devry.edu* Web: *www.nj.devry.edu*

DREW UNIVERSITY/COLLEGE OF LIBERAL ARTS D-2

Madison, NJ 07940   (973) 408-DREW; (973) 408-3068

Full-time: 640 men, 975 women	**Faculty:** IIA, +$
Part-time: 25 men, 45 women	**Ph.D.s:** n/av
Graduate: 350 men, 420 women	**Student/Faculty:** n/av
Year: semesters, summer session	**Tuition:** $35,600
Application Deadline: February 15	**Room & Board:** $10,000
Freshman Class: n/av	**VERY COMPETITIVE**

The College of Liberal Arts was added to Drew University in 1928 and is part of an educational complex that includes a theological school and a graduate school. Drew is a private, nonprofit, independent institution. The figures in the above capsule and in this profile are approximate. There are 2 graduate schools. The library contains 571,850 volumes, 485,288 microform items, and 2,611 audio/video tapes/CDs/DVDs, and subscribes to 21,997 periodicals including electronic. Computerized library services include interlibrary loans, database searching, Internet access, and laptop Internet portals. Special learning facilities include a learning resource center, art gallery, radio station, TV station, observatory, photography gallery, and TV satellite dish. The 186-acre campus is in a small town 30 miles west of New York City. Including any residence halls, there are 57 buildings.

Student Life: 57% of undergraduates are from New Jersey. Others are from 45 states, and 11 foreign countries. 65% are from public schools. 63% are white. The average age of freshmen is 18; all undergraduates, 20. 83% remain to graduate.

Housing: 1354 students can be accommodated in college housing, which includes single-sex and coed dorms, on-campus apartments, and married student housing. In addition, there are language houses and special-interest houses. On-campus housing is guaranteed for all 4 years. 85% of students live on campus; of those, 70% remain on campus on weekends. Upperclassmen may keep cars.

Activities: There are no fraternities or sororities. There are 80 groups on campus, including art, cheerleading, choir, chorale, computers, dance, drama, ecology, ethnic, film, gay, honors, international, jazz band, literary magazine, newspaper, orchestra, pep band, photography, political, professional, radio and TV, religious, social, social service, student government, and women's. Popular campus events include Holiday Semiformal, Annual Picnic, and Multicultural Awareness Day.

Sports: There are 11 intercollegiate sports for men and 12 for women, and 12 intramural sports for men and 12 for women. Facilities include an artificial turf athletic field with a 1000-seat gym, a 1000-seat auditorium, a swimming pool, a lighted tennis complex, a weight training room, a game room, an indoor track, a forest preserve, and an arboretum.

Disabled Students: Facilities include wheelchair ramps, elevators, special parking, specially equipped restrooms, special class scheduling, lowered drinking fountains, lowered telephones. The main dining facility, the student center and commons, and the ground floor of every dorm and classroom building are accessible to students with physical disabilities.

Services: Counseling and information services are available, as is tutoring in most subjects. There is a reader service for the blind.

Campus Safety and Security: Measures include 24-hour foot and vehicle patrol, emergency notification system, self-defense education, and security escort services. There are emergency telephones and lighted pathways/sidewalks.

Programs of Study: Drew confers B.A. degrees. Master's and doctoral degrees are also awarded. Bachelor's degrees are awarded in BIOLOGICAL SCIENCE (biochemistry, biology/biological science, and neurosciences), COMMUNICATIONS AND THE ARTS (art, art history and appreciation, Chinese, classics, dramatic arts, English, French, German, music, and Spanish), COMPUTER AND PHYSICAL SCIENCE (chemistry, computer science, mathematics, and physics), SOCIAL SCIENCE (African studies, anthropology, behavioral science, economics, history, philosophy, political science/government, psychology, religion, sociology, and women's studies). Psychology, political science, and English are the largest.

Required: To graduate, students must earn at least 128 credits, of which at least 64 must be beyond the lower level and at least 32 must be at the upper level. All students must fulfill the requirements of a major and those of the general education program. For graduation, the cumulative GPA, both overall and in the major, must be at least 2.0. General education requirements include a first-year seminar, demonstration of writing competency, at least 8 credits in foreign language and fulfillment of a language-in-context requirement, and completion of at least 4 credits in each of 2 different departments in the following 4 divisions: natural and mathematical sciences, social sciences, humanities, and arts and literature. Each student must also complete a minor.

Special: Drew offers co-op programs with Duke University, as well as cross-registration with the College of Saint Elizabeth and Fairleigh Dickinson University. There are also dual majors, study abroad, a Wall Street semester, a Washington semester, student-designed majors, internships, 3-2 engineering programs with Washington University in St. Louis, the Stevens Institute of Technology, and Columbia University in New York City, and a 7-year B.A.-M.D. program in medicine with UMDNJ. There are 11 national honor societies, including Phi Beta Kappa, and 12 departmental honors programs.

Faculty/Classroom: 54% of faculty are male; 46% are female. All teach and do research. Graduate students teach 1% of introductory courses. The average class size in an introductory lecture is 25; in a laboratory is 20; and in a regular course is 18.

Requirements: The university strongly recommends 18 academic credits or Carnegie units, including 4 in English, 3 in math, and 2 each in foreign language, science, social studies, and history, with the remaining 3 in additional academic courses. An essay is also required, and an interview is recommended. AP and CLEP credits are accepted. Important factors in the admissions decision are ability to finance college education, advanced placement or honors courses, and extracurricular activities record.

Procedure: Freshmen are admitted fall and spring. Entrance exams should be taken by January of the senior year. There are early decision, early admissions and deferred admissions plans. Early decision applications should be filed by December 1; regular applications, by February 15 for fall entry and December 1 for spring entry, along with a $50 fee. Notification of early decision is sent December 24; regular decision, March 15. Applications are accepted on-line. A waiting list is maintained.

Transfer: 40 transfer students enrolled in a recent year. Applicants must submit satisfactory high school and college academic records, a personal essay, and a statement of good standing from previous schools attended. An interview also may be required. Students with fewer then 12 credits must apply as entering freshman. 64 of 128 credits required for the bachelor's degree must be completed at Drew.

Visiting: There are regularly scheduled orientations for prospective students. There are guides for informal visits; visitors may sit in on classes and stay overnight. To schedule a visit, contact the Admissions Office at (973) 408-3739.

Financial Aid: In a recent year, 51% of all full-time freshmen and 49% of continuing full-time students received some form of financial aid. 51% of all full-time freshmen and 48% of continuing full-time students received need-based aid. The average freshmen award was $23,523. 29% of undergraduate students worked part-time. Average annual earnings from campus work were $1200. The average financial indebtedness of the 2009 graduate was $18,275. Drew is a member of CSS. The CSS/Profile and FAFSA are required. Check with the school for current application deadlines.

International Students: There are 24 international students enrolled. The school actively recruits these students. They must take the TOEFL.

Computers: Wireless access is available. All students may access the system. There are no time limits and no fees. A IBM thinkpad is recommended.

Graduates: In a recent year, 355 bachelor's degrees were awarded. The most popular majors were social sciences (32%), English (11%), and psychology (11%). 78 companies recruited on campus in 2008-2009. In an average class, 69% graduate in 4 years or less, 75% graduate in 5 years or less, and 76% graduate in 6 years or less. Of the 2008 graduating class, 22% were enrolled in graduate school within 6 months of graduation, and 49% were employed.

Admissions Contact: Mary Beth Carey, Dean of Admissions and Financial Assistance. E-Mail: *cadm@drew.edu*
Web: *http://www.drew.edu*

FAIRLEIGH DICKINSON UNIVERSITY SYSTEM

The Fairleigh Dickinson University System, established in 1942, is a private system in New Jersey. It is governed by Board of Trustees, whose chief administrator is President. The primary goal of the system is Teaching/Research. The main priorities are To provide an academically challenging learning experience to prepare students for employment or enrollment in graduate and professional schools; To promote independent thinking and collaborative learning in students as part of the educational process; and To cultivate a holistic, integrated living-learning experience as part of the educational process, and to foster the ideals of good citizenship and community service. Profiles of the 4-year campuses are included in this section.

FAIRLEIGH DICKINSON UNIVERSITY/COLLEGE AT FLORHAM   D-3

Madison, NJ 07940
(973) 443-8900
(800) 338-8803; (973) 443-8088

Full-time: 1076 men, 1205 women	**Faculty:** n/av
Part-time: 98 men, 101 women	**Ph.D.s:** n/av
Graduate: 512 men, 517 women	**Student/Faculty:** n/av
Year: semesters, summer session	**Tuition:** $31,084
Application Deadline: open	**Room & Board:** $11,058
Freshman Class: 3907 applied, 2601 accepted, 646 enrolled	
SAT CR/M/W: 520/530/520	**ACT:** required **COMPETITIVE**

Fairleigh Dickinson University/College at Florham, founded in 1942, is an independent university offering undergraduate, graduate, and professional level programs. Studies are rooted in the liberal arts but also offer hands-on opportunities in business and professional internships, cooperative education, and global studies abroad. There are 3 undergraduate schools and 2 graduate schools. In addition to regional accreditation, College at Florham has baccalaureate program accreditation with AACSB and NASDTEC. The library contains 149,850 volumes, 19,236 microform items, and 689 audio/video tapes/CDs/DVDs, and subscribes to 1182 periodicals including electronic. Computerized library services include interlibrary loans, database searching, Internet access, and laptop Internet portals. Special learning facilities include a learning resource center, art gallery, radio station, web-lab, ITV multimedia classrooms, and theaters. The 166-acre campus is in a suburban area 27 miles west of New York City. Including any residence halls, there are 36 buildings.

Student Life: 85% of undergraduates are from New Jersey. Others are from 27 states, 12 foreign countries, and Canada. 69% are white. The average age of freshmen is 18; all undergraduates, 20. 25% do not continue beyond their first year; 52% remain to graduate.

Housing: 1500 students can be accommodated in college housing, which includes coed dorms. In addition, there are honors houses and special-interest houses. On-campus housing is available on a first-come, first-served basis. Priority is given to out-of-town students. 60% of students live on campus; of those, 75% remain on campus on weekends. Upperclassmen may keep cars.

Activities: There are 6 national fraternities and 4 national sororities. There are 44 groups on campus, including cheerleading, chorale, computers, dance, environmental, ethnic, gay, honors, international, literary magazine, newspaper, political, professional, radio and TV, religious, social, social service, and student government. Popular campus events include Florham Fest and Haunted Mansion.

Sports: There are 9 intercollegiate sports for men and 9 for women, and 7 intramural sports for men and 5 for women. Facilities include a state-of-the-art synthetic turf field for football, field hockey, soccer, and lacrosse.

Disabled Students: 34% of the campus is accessible. Facilities include wheelchair ramps, elevators, special parking, specially equipped restrooms, special class scheduling, lowered drinking fountains, lowered telephones, and special housing.

Services: Counseling and information services are available, as is tutoring in most subjects. There is a reader service for the blind, remedial math, reading, and writing, and oral interpretation for the hearing impaired. Workshops also offer assistance with study skills and time management, and support services for basic skills students and freshmen are available. There is a Regional Center for College Students with Learning Disabilities that offers comprehensive support to students admitted to the program.

Campus Safety and Security: Measures include 24-hour foot and vehicle patrol, emergency notification system, self-defense education, and security escort services. There are shuttle buses, emergency telephones, and lighted pathways/sidewalks.

Programs of Study: College at Florham confers B.A., B.S., B.S.A.H.T, B.S.C.L.S., and B.S.N. degrees. Master's degrees are also awarded. Bachelor's degrees are awarded in BIOLOGICAL SCIENCE (biochemistry and biology/biological science), BUSINESS (accounting, banking and finance, business administration and management, entrepreneurial studies, hotel/motel and restaurant management, and marketing/retailing/merchandising), COMMUNICATIONS AND THE ARTS (animation, communications, creative writing, dramatic arts, film arts, fine arts, literature, and video), COMPUTER AND PHYSICAL SCIENCE (chemistry, computer science, mathematics, and radiological technology), HEALTH PROFESSIONS (allied health, clinical science, medical laboratory technology, and nursing), SOCIAL SCIENCE (economics, French studies, history, humanities, liberal arts/general studies, philosophy, political science/government, psychology, sociology, and Spanish studies). Psychology, business management, and communications are the largest.

Required: To graduate, students must complete a 120 to 128 credits, including 30 to 44 in the major, with an overall minimum 2.0 GPA (2.5 in the major). Distribution requirements include courses in English, communications, math, phys ed, foreign language, humanities, social and behavioral sciences, lab and computer science, an integrated, interdisciplinary university core sequence, and freshman seminar.

Special: The college offers co-op programs in most majors, internships, and study abroad. A Washington semester, work-study, accelerated degrees, and student-designed majors in the humanities and general studies are possible. Prepharmacy and joint baccalaureate dental programs are available. There are 10 national honor societies, a freshman honors program, and 11 departmental honors programs.

Faculty/Classroom: No introductory courses are taught by graduate students.

Admissions: 67% of the 2009-2010 applicants were accepted. The SAT scores for the 2009-2010 freshman class were: Critical Reading--36% below 500, 51% between 500 and 599, 13% between 600 and 700, and 1% above 700; Math--31% below 500, 49% between 500 and 599, 18% between 600 and 700, and 1% above 700; Writing--36% below 500, 50% between 500 and 599, 13% between 600 and 700, and 1% above 700. 32% of the current freshmen were in the top fifth of their class; 62% were in the top two fifths. 5 freshmen graduated first in their class.

Requirements: The SAT or ACT is required. In addition, applicants should be graduates of an accredited high school or have a GED certificate. They should have completed a minimum of 16 academic units, including 4 in English, 3 in math, 2 each in history, foreign language, and lab science (3 are recommended), and 3 in electives. Those students applying to science and health sciences programs must meet additional requirements. An interview may be requested. AP and CLEP credits are accepted. Important factors in the admissions decision are leadership record, recommendations by school officials, and extracurricular activities record.

Procedure: Freshmen are admitted to all sessions. Entrance exams should be taken May of their junior year. There are early admissions, deferred admissions, and rolling admissions plans. Application deadlines are open; March 1 is recommended for fall entry. The application fee is $40. Notification is sent on a rolling basis. Applications are accepted online.

Transfer: 131 transfer students enrolled in 2008-2009. All transfer applicants must submit official transcripts for all college work taken. Those students with fewer than 24 credits must also submit a high school transcript or a copy of their state department of education's equivalency score and SAT scores. 32 of 120 to 128 credits required for the bachelor's degree must be completed at College at Florham.

Visiting: There are regularly scheduled orientations for prospective students, including standardized placement testing, faculty advisement, class registration, and educational and social activities to prepare students for entrance. There are guides for informal visits; visitors may sit in on classes and stay overnight. To schedule a visit, contact the Admissions Office.

Financial Aid: The FAFSA is required. The priority date for freshman financial aid applications for fall entry is February 15.

International Students: There are 14 international students enrolled. The school actively recruits these students. They must take the TOEFL with a minimum score of 550 on the paper-based TOEFL (PBT) or 79 on the Internet-based version (iBT) or the IELTS. SAT or ACT is highly recommended.

Computers: Wireless access is available. All students may access the system. There are no time limits. The fee is $692. It is strongly recommended that all students have a personal computer. An IBM ThinkPad or NetVista is recommended.

Graduates: From July 1, 2008 to June 30, 2009, 522 bachelor's degrees were awarded. The most popular majors were psychology (14%), business/marketing (12%), and communications (8%). 200 companies recruited on campus in 2008-2009. In an average class, 35% graduate in 4 years or less, 48% graduate in 5 years or less, and 52% graduate in 6 years or less.

Admissions Contact: Jonathan Wexler, Associate Vice President of Enrollment Management. E-mail: *globaleducation@fdu.edu* Web: *www.fdu.edu*

FAIRLEIGH DICKINSON UNIVERSITY/METROPOLITAN CAMPUS E-2

Teaneck, NJ 07666

(201) 692-2553
(800) 338-8803; (201) 692-7319

Full-time: 983 men, 1488 women	**Faculty:** n/av
Part-time: 1567 men, 2006 women	**Ph.D.s:** n/av
Graduate: 1126 men, 1634 women	**Student/Faculty:** n/av
Year: semesters, summer session	**Tuition:** $28,886
Application Deadline: March 15	**Room & Board:** $11,368
Freshman Class: 5108 applied, 2916 accepted, 711 enrolled	
SAT CR/M/W: 510/530/500	**ACT:** required **COMPETITIVE**

Farleigh Dickinson University/Metropolitan Campus, founded in 1942, is an independent university offering undergraduate and graduate degrees in business, arts and sciences, professional studies, public administration, and hotel, restaurant, and tourism management. There are 3 undergrad-

uate schools and 3 graduate schools. In addition to regional accreditation, FDU has baccalaureate program accreditation with AACSB, ABET, and TEAC. The 3 libraries contain 196,703 volumes, 103,808 microform items, and 1311 audio/video tapes/CDs/DVDs, and subscribe to 1601 periodicals including electronic. Computerized library services include interlibrary loans, database searching, and Internet access. Special learning facilities include a learning resource center, art gallery, radio station, computer labs, ITV multimedia classrooms, photonics lab, theater, art galleries, Web lab, Center for Psychological Sevices, cyber crime lab, and the Regional Center for College Students with Learning Disabilities. The 88-acre campus is in a suburban area 13 miles from midtown Manhattan, New York City. Including any residence halls, there are 55 buildings.

Student Life: 87% of undergraduates are from New Jersey. Others are from 25 states, 64 foreign countries, and Canada. 33% are white; 20% Hispanic; 18% African American. The average age of freshmen is 18; all undergraduates, 22. 27% do not continue beyond their first year; 40% remain to graduate.

Housing: 982 students can be accommodated in college housing, which includes single-sex and coed dorms. In addition, there are honors houses, special-interest houses, a L.I.F.E. house, and Global Scholar houses. On-campus housing is available on a first-come, first-served basis and is available on a lottery system for upperclassmen. 79% of students commute. Alcohol is not permitted. All students may keep cars.

Activities: 1% of men belong to 5 national fraternities; 1% of women belong to 7 national sororities. There are 72 groups on campus, including cheerleading, chorus, computers, dance, drama, environmental, ethnic, film, gay, honors, international, literary magazine, newspaper, pep band, photography, political, professional, radio and TV, religious, social, social service, student government, and student programming board. Popular campus events include Welcome Back Week, Spring Fest, and dances.

Sports: There are 7 intercollegiate sports for men and 10 for women, and 7 intramural sports for men and 7 for women. Facilities include a 5000-seat facility with a 6-lane, 200-meter track, 4 full basketball courts, 2 volleyball courts, 4 racquetball courts, and a fully equipped weight room; 6 outdoor tennis courts; a baseball field and soccer field with bleachers; 2 training room facilities; a softball field; and a state-of-the-art fitness center with aerobics room, selectorized weight room, and cardio room.

Disabled Students: 41% of the campus is accessible. Facilities include wheelchair ramps, elevators, special parking, specially equipped restrooms, special class scheduling, lowered drinking fountains, lowered telephones, special housing, and oral interpretation for the hearing impaired.

Services: Counseling and information services are available, as is tutoring in every subject. There is a reader service for the blind and remedial math, reading, and writing. Workshops offer assistance with academic study skills, time management, and advanced reading and writing. Support services for basic skills students and freshmen are available. There is also a Regional Center for College Students with Learning Disabilities that offers comprehensive support to students admitted to the program.

Campus Safety and Security: Measures include 24-hour foot and vehicle patrol, emergency notification system, self-defense education, and security escort services. There are emergency telephones and lighted pathways/sidewalks.

Programs of Study: FDU confers B.A., B.S., B.S.Civ.E.T., B.S.C.L.S., B.S.Con.E.T., B.S.E.E., B.S.E.E.T., B.S.M.E.T., and B.S.N. degrees. Associate, master's, and doctoral degrees are also awarded. Bachelor's degrees are awarded in BIOLOGICAL SCIENCE (biochemistry, biology/biological science, and marine biology), BUSINESS (accounting, business administration and management, business economics, entrepreneurial studies, hotel/motel and restaurant management, and marketing/retailing/merchandising), COMMUNICATIONS AND THE ARTS (communications, English literature, and fine arts), COMPUTER AND PHYSICAL SCIENCE (chemistry, computer science, information sciences and systems, mathematics, radiological technology, and science), ENGINEERING AND ENVIRONMENTAL DESIGN (civil engineering technology, construction engineering, electrical/electronics engineering, electrical/electronics engineering technology, and mechanical engineering technology), HEALTH PROFESSIONS (allied health, clinical science, medical laboratory technology, nursing, and physical therapy), SOCIAL SCIENCE (criminal justice, economics, history, humanities, interdisciplinary studies, international studies, liberal arts/general studies, philosophy, political science/government, psychology, and Spanish studies). Nursing, psychology, and business management are the largest.

Required: To graduate, students must complete 120 to 128 credits, including 30 to 44 in the major, with an overall minimum 2.0. GPA. Students must complete a 4-semester interdisciplinary sequence and 1 course in freshman seminar. The core curriculum includes 6 credits in English, 12 in university core, and 3 each in math and computer science.

Special: FDU offers co-op programs in most majors, cross-registration, internships, and study abroad in England and Vancouver. A Washington semester, work-study, accelerated degrees, and student-designed majors in the humanities and general studies are possible. A 7-year medical program is available with Karol Marcinkowski School of Medicine in Poland, as is an accelerated chiropractic program with New York Chiropractic College and Logan Chiropractic College (B.S., B.A./M.A.T.). There are 12 national honor societies, a freshman honors program, and 16 departmental honors programs.

Faculty/Classroom: No introductory courses are taught by graduate students.

Admissions: 57% of the 2009-2010 applicants were accepted. The SAT scores for the 2009-2010 freshman class were: Critical Reading--42% below 500, 46% between 500 and 599, and 11% between 600 and 700; Math--30% below 500, 52% between 500 and 599, 16% between 600 and 700, and 2% above 700; Writing--43% below 500, 49% between 500 and 599, and 8% between 600 and 700. 30% of the current freshmen were in the top fifth of their class; 62% were in the top two fifths. 1 freshman graduated first in the class.

Requirements: The SAT or ACT is required. In addition, applicants should be graduates of an accredited high school or have a GED certificate. They should have completed a minimum of 16 academic units, including 4 in English, 3 in math, 2 each in history, foreign language, and lab science (3 are recommended), and 3 in electives. Those students applying to science, engineering, and health sciences programs must meet additional requirements. An interview may be required. AP and CLEP credits are accepted. Important factors in the admissions decision are leadership record, recommendations by school officials, and extracurricular activities record.

Procedure: Freshmen are admitted to all sessions. Entrance exams should be taken by May of the junior year. There are deferred admissions and rolling admissions plans. Applications should be filed by March 15 for fall entry, along with a $40 fee. Notification is sent on a rolling basis. Applications are accepted on-line.

Transfer: 499 transfer students enrolled in 2008-2009. All applicants must submit official transcripts for all college work taken. Those students with fewer than 24 credits must also submit a high school transcript or a copy of their state department of education's equivalency score and SAT scores. 32 of 128 credits required for the bachelor's degree must be completed at FDU.

Visiting: There are regularly scheduled orientations for prospective students, including standardized placement testing, faculty advisement, class registration, and educational and social activities to prepare students for entrance. There are guides for informal visits, and visitors may sit in on classes and stay overnight. To schedule a visit, contact the Admissions Office.

Financial Aid: Check with the school for current application deadlines.

International Students: There are 243 international students enrolled. The school actively recruits these students. They must take the TOEFLm with a minimum score of 550 on the paper-based TOEFL (PBT) or 79 on the Internet-based version (iBT), or take the IELTS. The ACT or SAT is highly recommended.

Computers: Wireless access is available. All students may access the system. There are no time limits. The fee is $692. It is strongly recommended that all students have a personal computer. A IBM ThinkPad or NetVista is recommended.

Graduates: From July 1, 2008 to June 30, 2009, 784 bachelor's degrees were awarded. The most popular majors were psychology (7%), nursing (6%), and criminal justice (6%). 201 companies recruited on campus in 2008-2009. In an average class, 21% graduate in 4 years or less, 37% graduate in 5 years or less, and 40% graduate in 6 years or less.

Admissions Contact: Jonathan Wexler, Associate Vice President of Enrollment Management. E-mail: *globaleducation@fdu.edu* Web: *www.fdu.edu*

FELICIAN COLLEGE   E-2

Lodi, NJ 07644   (201) 559-6131; (201) 559-6188

Full-time: 316 men, 1033 women	Faculty: 96
Part-time: 83 men, 300 women	Ph.D.s: 55%
Graduate: 78 men, 275 women	Student/Faculty: 14 to 1
Year: semesters, summer session	Tuition: $25,050
Application Deadline: open	Room & Board: $9700
Freshman Class: 1618 applied, 1358 accepted, 254 enrolled	
SAT: required	COMPETITIVE

Felician College, founded in 1942, is a private, Roman Catholic, liberal arts school with concentrations in health science, teacher education, and arts and sciences. There are 4 undergraduate schools and 4 graduate schools. In addition to regional accreditation, Felician has baccalaureate program accreditation with CAHEA and NLN. The library contains 107,000 volumes, 89,191 microform items, and 3611 audio/video tapes/CDs/DVDs, and subscribes to 351 periodicals including electronic. Computerized library services include interlibrary loans, database searching, Internet access, and laptop Internet portals. Special learning facilities include a learning resource center, radio station, and a nursing clinical lab. The 32-acre campus is in a suburban area 10 miles west of New York City. Including any residence halls, there are 15 buildings.

Student Life: 94% of undergraduates are from New Jersey. Others are from 8 states, 6 foreign countries, and Canada. 65% are from public schools. 45% are white; 24% Hispanic; 17% African American; 11% Asian American. The average age of freshmen is 18; all undergraduates, 27. 32% do not continue beyond their first year; 37% remain to graduate.

Housing: 580 students can be accommodated in college housing, which includes single-sex and coed dorms. On-campus housing is guaranteed for all 4 years. 76% of students commute. Alcohol is not permitted. Upperclassmen may keep cars.

Activities: There are no fraternities or sororities. There are 18 groups on campus, including art, cheerleading, chess, choir, computers, drama, education, ethnic, free enterprise, honors, international, karate, literary magazine, professional, religious, science, social service, and student government. Popular campus events include College festival, springfest, and sibling weekend.

Sports: There are 5 intercollegiate sports for men and 5 for women. Facilities include 2 fitness centers and a gym.

Disabled Students: 90% of the campus is accessible. Facilities include wheelchair ramps, elevators, special parking, specially equipped restrooms, lowered drinking fountains, lowered telephones, special housing, and wheelchair lifts.

Services: Counseling and information services are available, as is tutoring in most subjects. There is remedial math, reading, and writing.

Campus Safety and Security: Measures include 24-hour foot and vehicle patrol, emergency notification system, and self-defense education. There are shuttle buses, emergency telephones, and lighted pathways/sidewalks.

Programs of Study: Felician confers B.A., B.S., and B.S.N. degrees. Associate and master's degrees are also awarded. Bachelor's degrees are awarded in BIOLOGICAL SCIENCE (biology/biological science), BUSINESS (accounting, business administration and management, international business management, and marketing management), COMMUNICATIONS AND THE ARTS (art, communications, English, fine arts, graphic design, journalism, and music), COMPUTER AND PHYSICAL SCIENCE (computer security and information assurance, information sciences and systems, mathematics, and natural sciences), EDUCATION (early childhood education, education, elementary education, secondary education, and special education), HEALTH PROFESSIONS (allied health and nursing), SOCIAL SCIENCE (criminal justice, history, humanities, liberal arts/general studies, philosophy, psychology, religion, and social science). Education and nursing are the strongest academically.

Required: All students must earn a minimum GPA of 2.0 (2.5 in medical lab technology, 2.75 in nursing, and 3.0 in education), while taking 120 credit hours (128 to 130 in education), with 39 to 57 hours in their majors. Distribution requirements include 45 to 47 hours from a core curriculum, including courses in English, philosophy, religious studies, humanities, historical tradition, science, and social-cultural studies.

Special: Co-op programs are available in clinical lab sciences with the University of Medicine and Dentistry of New Jersey and with SUNY College of Optometry, New York Chiropractic College, New York College of Podiatric Medicine, and Bloomsburg University of Pennsylvania (Audiology Program). In addition, internships for credit, work-study at the college, dual majors in education, an interdisciplinary studies degree, an accelerated degree in nursing, student-designed majors within humanities and social and behavioral sciences, and pass/fail options are possible. There is a freshman honors program.

Faculty/Classroom: 42% of faculty are male; 58% are female. No introductory courses are taught by graduate students. The average class size in an introductory lecture is 25; in a laboratory, 20; and in a regular course, 15.

Admissions: 84% of the 2009-2010 applicants were accepted. 20% of the current freshmen were in the top fifth of their class; 44% were in the top two fifths.

Requirements: The SAT is required, with a minimum composite score of 850 recommended (Critical Reading and Math). The college also recommends that applicants have 16 academic credits, including 4 in English, 2 to 3 each in math, science, and social studies, and 3 to 6 in academic electives, including foreign language. An interview is recommended. The GED is accepted. A GPA of 2.0 is required. AP and CLEP credits are accepted. Important factors in the admissions decision are recommendations by school officials, advanced placement or honors courses, and extracurricular activities record.

Procedure: Freshmen are admitted fall and spring. There is a rolling admissions plan. Application deadlines are open. Application fee is $30. Notification is sent on a rolling basis. Applications are accepted on-line.

Transfer: Applicants must have maintained a minimum GPA of 2.5 (2.75 in nursing and 3.0 in education). An interview is recommended. Nursing majors require previous college-level lab science. 30 of 120 credits required for the bachelor's degree must be completed at Felician.

Visiting: There are regularly scheduled orientations for prospective students. There are guides for informal visits, and visitors may sit in on classes. To schedule a visit, contact the Office of Undergraduate Admission.

Financial Aid: In 2009-2010, 87% of all full-time freshmen and 80% of continuing full-time students received some form of financial aid. 73% of all full-time freshmen and 63% of continuing full-time students received need-based aid. The average freshman award was $11,130. Need-based scholarships or need-based grants averaged $7256; need-based self-help aid (loans and jobs) averaged $5445; non-need-based athletic scholarships averaged $12,456; and other non-need-based awards and non-need-based scholarships averaged $7012. 97% of undergraduate students work part-time. Average annual earnings from campus work are $3000. The average financial indebtedness of the 2009 graduate was $40,000. The FAFSA and the college's own financial statement are required. Check with the school for current application deadlines.

International Students: There are 48 international students enrolled. The school actively recruits these students. They must take the TOEFL with a minimum score of 500 on the paper-based TOEFL (PBT) or 61 on the Internet-based version (iBT), or take the IELTS.

Computers: Wireless access is available. All students may access the system. There are no time limits and no fees.

Graduates: From July 1, 2008 to June 30, 2009, 317 bachelor's degrees were awarded. The most popular majors were business/marketing (31%), nursing (27%), and education (17%). In an average class, 21% graduate in 4 years or less, 36% graduate in 5 years or less, and 37% graduate in 6 years or less. 17 companies recruited on campus in 2008-2009.

Admissions Contact: Alex Scott, Director of Undergraduate Admissions. A campus DVD is available. E-mail: *admissions@felician.edu* Web: *www.felician.edu*

GEORGIAN COURT UNIVERSITY E-4
Lakewood, NJ 08701-2697 (800) 458-8422

Full-time: 75 men, 1441 women	Faculty: IIA, -$
Part-time: 111 men, 343 women	Ph.D.s: 87%
Graduate: 187 men, 866 women	Student/Faculty: 15 to 1
Year: semesters, summer session	Tuition: $24,490
Application Deadline:	Room & Board: $9386
Freshman Class: n/av	
SAT or ACT: recommended	LESS COMPETITIVE

Georgian Court University, founded in 1908, is an independent Roman Catholic university. The day division matriculates women; the University College division is coeducational. Undergraduate programs are offered in the arts and sciences, business, and education. There are 4 undergraduate schools. In addition to regional accreditation, The Court has baccalaureate program accreditation with ACBSP, CSWE, and TEAC. The library contains 148,026 volumes, 749,524 microform items, and 6519 audio/video tapes/CDs/DVDs, and subscribes to 1808 periodicals including electronic. Computerized library services include interlibrary loans, database searching, Internet access, and laptop Internet portals. Special learning facilities include a learning resource center, art gallery, and arboretum. The 156-acre campus is in a suburban area 60 miles south of New York City and 60 miles east of Philadelphia. Including any residence halls, there are 24 buildings.

Student Life: 97% of undergraduates are from New Jersey. Others are from 13 states, 5 foreign countries, and Canada. 75% are white; 13% African American. 70% are Catholic; 42% claim no religious affiliation. The average age of freshmen is 18; all undergraduates, 24. 22% do not continue beyond their first year; 58% remain to graduate.

Housing: 447 students can be accommodated in college housing, which includes single-sex dorms. On-campus housing is guaranteed for the freshman year only, is available on a first-come, first-served basis, and is available on a lottery system for upperclassmen. 75% of students commute. All students may keep cars.

Activities: There are no fraternities or sororities. There are 48 groups on campus, including art, band, choir, chorale, chorus, dance, ethnic, gay, honors, international, jazz band, literary magazine, newspaper, orchestra, professional, religious, social, social service, and student government. Popular campus events include Latin Night, Diversifest, and Comedy Night.

Sports: There are 8 intercollegiate sports for women. Facilities include a wellness center and athletic complex with fitness and aerobic facilities as well as a dance studio.

Disabled Students: 77% of the campus is accessible. Facilities include wheelchair ramps, elevators, special parking, specially equipped restrooms, special class scheduling, lowered drinking fountains, lowered telephones, and special equipment for the visually and hearing impaired.

Services: Counseling and information services are available, as is tutoring in most subjects. There is remedial math, reading, and writing.

Campus Safety and Security: Measures include 24-hour foot and vehicle patrol, emergency notification system, and security escort services. There are shuttle vans, emergency telephones, lighted pathways/sidewalks, and access controls to dorms/residences.

Programs of Study: The Court confers B.A., B.S., B.F.A., and B.S.W. degrees. Master's degrees are also awarded. Bachelor's degrees are awarded in BIOLOGICAL SCIENCE (biochemistry and biology/biological science), BUSINESS (accounting, business administration and management, and tourism), COMMUNICATIONS AND THE ARTS (applied art, art, communications, dance, English, music, and Spanish), COMPUTER AND PHYSICAL SCIENCE (chemistry, mathematics, and natural sciences), EDUCATION (education), HEALTH PROFESSIONS (allied health, clinical science, exercise science, health, medical records administration/services, and nursing), SOCIAL SCIENCE (criminal justice, history, humanities, psychology, religion, social work, and sociology). Psychology is the largest.

Required: All students must complete 128 total credit hours, including 30 in the major, and must maintain a 2.0 GPA overall, 2.5 in the major.

Special: Georgian Court offers co-op programs in business administration, internships, an accelerated degree in education (teacher certification) and dual majors with education. There are 18 national honor societies and a freshman honors program.

Faculty/Classroom: 39% of faculty are male; 61% are female. No introductory courses are taught by graduate students. The average class size in an introductory lecture is 17; in a laboratory is 10; and in a regular course, 14.

Requirements: The SAT or ACT and ACT Writing Test are recommended. In addition, applicants must be graduates of accredited secondary schools or have earned a GED. The university requires 16 academic credits or Carnegie units based on 6 years of academic electives, 4 of English, 2 each of foreign language and math, and 1 each of history and a lab science. An interview is recommended for all students, and an audition is required for applied music majors. AP and CLEP credits are accepted.

Procedure: Freshmen are admitted fall and spring. Entrance exams should be taken by January of the senior year. There is a rolling admissions plan. Applications should be filed by January 1 for spring entry. The fall 2009 application fee was $40. Notification is sent on a rolling basis. Applications are accepted on-line.

Transfer: 277 transfer students enrolled in 2008-2009. Applicants with fewer than 24 credits must fulfill freshman requirements. 30 of 128 credits required for the bachelor's degree must be completed at The Court.

Visiting: There are regularly scheduled orientations for prospective students, including visits with faculty and students and a tour of facilities. There are guides for informal visits; visitors may sit in on classes and stay overnight. To schedule a visit, contact the Director of Admissions at (732) 987-2765.

Financial Aid: In 2008-2009, 99% of all full-time freshmen and 94% of continuing full-time students received some form of financial aid. The average freshman award was $25,000. The Court is a member of CSS. The FAFSA, the college's own financial statement, and parent and student 1040 tax forms are required. Check with the school for current application deadlines.

International Students: There are 7 international students enrolled. The school actively recruits these students. They must take the TOEFL.

Computers: Wireless access is available. All students may access the system. There are no time limits. The annual fee is $420.

Graduates: From July 1, 2008 to June 30, 2009, 438 bachelor's degrees were awarded. The most popular majors were psychology (31%), business (20%), and English (13%). In an average class, 35% graduate in 4 years or less, 53% graduate in 5 years or less, and 56% graduate in 6 years or less.

Admissions Contact: Kathie Gallant, Director of Admissions. E-mail: *admissions@georgian.edu* Web: *www.georgian.edu*

KEAN UNIVERSITY E-2
Union, NJ 07083-0411 (908) 737-7100; (908) 737-7105

Full-time: 3729 men, 5626 women	Faculty: 352; IIA, +$
Part-time: 890 men, 1827 women	Ph.D.s: 91%
Graduate: 681 men, 2298 women	Student/Faculty: 16 to 1
Year: semesters, summer session	Tuition: $9446 ($14,081)
Application Deadline: May 31	Room & Board: $12,264
Freshman Class: 5955 applied, 3693 accepted, 1548 enrolled	
SAT: required	COMPETITIVE

Kean University, founded in 1855, is a public institution offering undergraduate and graduate programs in the arts and sciences, business, education, government, nursing, and technology. Kean is primarily a metropolitan commuter university. There are 5 undergraduate schools and 1 graduate school. In addition to regional accreditation, Kean has baccalaureate program accreditation with CSWE, NASM, NCATE, and NLN. The library contains 254,700 volumes, 538,170 microform items, and 6000 audio/video tapes/CDs/DVDs, and subscribes to 27,826 periodicals including electronic. Computerized library services include interlibrary loans, database searching, Internet access, and laptop Internet portals. Special learning facilities include a learning resource center, art gallery, planetarium, radio station, TV station, the New Jersey Center for Science, Technology, and Mathematics Education, the Holocaust Resource Center, the Wynona Moore Lipman Ethnic Studies Center, the Institute for Foreign Service and Diplomacy, the Liberty Hall Museum, and the

Human Rights Institute. The 186-acre campus is in a suburban area 12 miles west of New York City. Including any residence halls, there are 35 buildings.

Student Life: 98% of undergraduates are from New Jersey. Others are from 16 states, 63 foreign countries, and Canada. 47% are white; 21% Hispanic; 19% African American. The average age of freshmen is 18; all undergraduates, 24. 19% do not continue beyond their first year; 45% remain to graduate.

Housing: 2045 students can be accommodated in college housing, which includes single-sex and coed dorms and on-campus apartments. In addition there is freshman housing and a women-only floor. On-campus housing is guaranteed for the freshman year if the housing application is received by May 1 and is available on a lottery system for upperclassmen. 85% of students commute. Alcohol is not permitted. Upperclassmen may keep cars.

Activities: 4% of men belong to 5 local and 11 national fraternities; 4% of women belong to 6 local and 9 national sororities. There are 143 groups on campus, including art, band, choir, chorale, chorus, computers, dance, drama, environmental, ethnic, film, gay, honors, international, jazz band, literary magazine, musical theater, newspaper, orchestra, pep band, photography, political, professional, radio and TV, religious, social, social service, and student government. Popular campus events include University Weekend, Unity Week, and Campus Awareness Festival.

Sports: There are 6 intercollegiate sports for men and 8 for women, 3 intramural sports for men and 3 for women, and 7 coed intramural sports. Facilities include a 5300-seat stadium, an 8-lane track, a 800-seat soccer stadium, a 350-seat baseball stadium, a 250-seat softball stadium, 3 practice fields, a 3000-seat arena, 5 indoor basketball courts, 2 outdoor basketball courts, 10 outdoor tennis courts, 2 indoor swimming pools, 3 fitness rooms, pool tables, pinball machines, and video games.

Disabled Students: All of the campus is accessible. Facilities include wheelchair ramps, elevators, special parking, specially equipped restrooms, lowered drinking fountains, lowered telephones, and special housing.

Services: Counseling and information services are available, as is tutoring in most subjects. There is a reader service for the blind, remedial math, reading, and writing, and a full program for learning-disabled students.

Campus Safety and Security: Measures include 24-hour foot and vehicle patrol, emergency notification system, self-defense education, and security escort services. There are shuttle buses, emergency telephones, and lighted pathways/sidewalks.

Programs of Study: Kean confers B.A., B.S., B.F.A., B.I.D., and B.S.N. degrees. Master's and doctoral degrees are also awarded. Bachelor's degrees are awarded in BIOLOGICAL SCIENCE (biology/biological science), BUSINESS (accounting, banking and finance, management science, marketing/retailing/merchandising, and recreational facilities management), COMMUNICATIONS AND THE ARTS (art history and appreciation, broadcasting, communications, dramatic arts, English, film arts, fine arts, graphic design, industrial design, media arts, music, performing arts, Spanish, studio art, telecommunications, theater design, and visual and performing arts), COMPUTER AND PHYSICAL SCIENCE (chemistry, computer science, earth science, mathematics, and science technology), EDUCATION (athletic training, early childhood education, elementary education, middle school education, music education, physical education, secondary education, and special education), ENGINEERING AND ENVIRONMENTAL DESIGN (environmental science and interior design), HEALTH PROFESSIONS (medical technology, nursing, and speech pathology/audiology), SOCIAL SCIENCE (criminal justice, economics, history, philosophy and religion, political science/government, psychology, public administration, and sociology). Science/technology and education are the strongest academically. Business and education are the largest.

Required: Students must complete a writing emphasis course within their major, a capstone course, and at least 30 credits in a major field. The B.A. requires completion of 124 to 147 semester hours with a minimum GPA of 2.0. Freshmen students must complete a Transition to Kean course.

Special: Students may study abroad in 38 countries. Kean offers cooperative programs, a B.A. or B.S. degree in biology, chemistry, or earth science, internships in many majors, a Washington semester, credit for life experience, and pass/fail options. There are 23 national honor societies, a freshman honors program, and 10 departmental honors programs.

Faculty/Classroom: 54% of faculty are male; 46% are female. All teach undergraduates. No introductory courses are taught by graduate students. The average class size in a regular course is 21.

Admissions: 62% of the 2009-2010 applicants were accepted. 20% of the current freshmen were in the top fifth of their class; 51% were in the top two fifths.

Requirements: The SAT is required. In addition, applicants must be graduates of accredited secondary schools or have earned a GED. College preparatory study includes 4 courses in English, 3 in math, 2 each in lab science and social studies, and 5 in academic electives. An essay and 2 letters of recommendation are also required. A GPA of 3.0 is required. AP and CLEP credits are accepted.

Procedure: Freshmen are admitted fall and spring. Entrance exams should be taken by October of the senior year at the latest. There is a rolling admissions plan. Applications should be filed by May 31 for fall entry; November 1 for spring entry, along with a $50 fee. Applications are accepted on-line.

Transfer: 1733 transfer students enrolled in 2008-2009. Transcripts from any foreign institution attended undergo NACES evaluation. 32 of 124 credits required for the bachelor's degree must be completed at Kean.

Visiting: There are regularly scheduled orientations for prospective students. There are guides for informal visits. To schedule a visit, contact the Undergraduate Admissions Office.

Financial Aid: In 2009-2010, 79% of all full-time freshmen and 74% of continuing full-time students received some form of financial aid. 68% of all full-time freshmen and 65% of continuing full-time students received need-based aid. 6% of undergraduate students work part-time. Average annual earnings from campus work are $1935. The average financial indebtedness of the 2009 graduate was $19,698. The FAFSA is required. The priority date for freshman financial aid applications for fall entry is March 15.

International Students: There are 182 international students enrolled. The school actively recruits these students. They must take the SAT or ACT.

Computers: Wireless access is available. Students may access the Internet wirelessly from within every building on campus, as well as right outside the entrances. There are also more than 50 campus labs with an average of 24 PCs loaded with Microsoft Office Suite, IE, Adobe Acrobat Reader, and many other productivity programs. All students may access the system. There are no time limits and no fees.

Graduates: From July 1, 2008 to June 30, 2009, 2082 bachelor's degrees were awarded. The most popular majors were management science (10%), psychology (10%), and criminal justice (6%). In an average class, 19% graduate in 4 years or less, 38% graduate in 5 years or less, and 45% graduate in 6 years or less.

Admissions Contact: Valerie Winslow, Director of Admissions. A campus DVD is available. E-mail: *admitme@kean.edu* Web: *www.kean.edu*

MONMOUTH UNIVERSITY
West Long Branch, NJ 07764-1898

E-3

(732) 571-3456
(800) 543-9671; (732) 263-5166

Full-time: 1867 men, 2439 women	**Faculty:** 212; IIA, av$
Part-time: 111 men, 264 women	**Ph.Ds:** 82%
Graduate: 500 men, 1318 women	**Student/Faculty:** 19 to 1
Year: semesters, , summer session	**Tuition:** $25,013
Application Deadline: March 1	**Room & Board:** $9,554
Freshman Class: 6738 applied, 4160 accepted, 998 enrolled	
SAT CR/M/W: 530/550/530	**ACT:** 23 **VERY COMPETITIVE**

Monmouth University, founded in 1933, is a private comprehensive institution offering both undergraduate and graduate programs in the arts and sciences, business, education, upper-level nursing, technology, and professional training. There are 7 undergraduate schools and one graduate school. In addition to regional accreditation, Monmouth has baccalaureate program accreditation with AACSB, ABET, CSWE, and NLN. The library contains 248,000 volumes, and subscribes to 22,500 periodicals including electronic. Computerized library services include interlibrary loans, database searching, Internet access, and laptop Internet portals. Special learning facilities include a learning resource center, art gallery, radio station, TV station, theater, and a greenhouse. The 156-acre campus is in a suburban area 60 miles south of New York City. Including any residence halls, there are 56 buildings.

Student Life: 88% of undergraduates are from New Jersey. Students are from 26 states, 18 foreign countries, and Canada. 77% are white. The average age of freshmen is 18; all undergraduates, 21. 22% do not continue beyond their first year; 61% remain to graduate.

Housing: 1883 students can be accommodated in college housing, which includes coed dorms, on-campus apartments, and off-campus apartments. In addition, there are honors houses and special-interest houses. On-campus housing is guaranteed for the freshman year only, is available on a first-come, first-served basis, and is available on a lottery system for upperclassmen. Priority is given to out-of-town students. 56% of students commute. All students may keep cars.

Activities: 14% of men belong to 7 national fraternities; 14% of women belong to 7 national sororities. There are 65 groups on campus, including band, cheerleading, choir, chorus, computers, dance, debate, drama, ethnic, gay, honors, international, jazz band, literary magazine, musical threater, newspaper, pep band, political, professional, radio and TV, religious, social service, student government, and yearbook. Popular campus events include Springfest, Ebony Night, and Winter Ball.

Sports: There are 8 intercollegiate sports for men and 9 for women, and 8 intramural sports for men and 9 for women. Facilities include a 4100 seat competition arena, 200 meter 6-lane indoor track, a 2500-seat gym, a 4600-seat football field, outdoor tennis courts, 3 basketball courts, an 8-lane all-weather track, an indoor Olympic-size pool, exercise, and weight rooms, and baseball, softball, soccer, and field hockey fields.

Disabled Students: 90% of the campus is accessible. Facilities include wheelchair ramps, elevators, special parking, specially equipped rest rooms, special class scheduling, lowered drinking fountains, special housing, and academic assistance provided within the classroom.

Services: Counseling and information services are available, as is tutoring in every subject. There is a reader service for the blind, and remedial math, reading, and writing.

Campus Safety and Security: Measures include 24-hour foot and vehicle patrol, self-defense education, and security escort services. There are emergency telephones, lighted pathways/sidewalks, university police force, and a student watch organization.

Programs of Study: Monmouth confers B.A., B.S., B.F.A., B.S.N., and B.S.W. degrees. Associates and master's degrees are also awarded. Bachelor's degrees are awarded in BIOLOGICAL SCIENCE (biology/biological science and marine biology), BUSINESS (accounting, banking and finance, business administration and management, business economics, international business management, marketing management, and real estate), COMMUNICATIONS AND THE ARTS (art, art history and appreciation, communications, English, graphic design, modern language, music, music business management, and Spanish), COMPUTER AND PHYSICAL SCIENCE (chemistry, computer science, mathematics, and software engineering), EDUCATION (art education, English education, foreign languages education, health education, mathematics education, music education, physical education, science education, secondary education, and special education), ENGINEERING AND ENVIRONMENTAL DESIGN (computer graphics), HEALTH PROFESSIONS (clinical science, medical laboratory technology, nursing, and premedicine), SOCIAL SCIENCE (anthropology, criminal justice, history, political science/government, prelaw, psychology, social work, and sociology). Business, education, and communication are the largest.

Required: To graduate, students must earn at least 128 credits, including 30 to 81 in a major, with a minimum GPA of 2.0 overall and 2.1 in the major. Education majors are required to have a cumulative GPA of 2.75.

Special: Students may study abroad. There are cooperative and internship programs and a Washington semester. Monmouth also offers work-study programs, dual majors, flexible studies programs, and credit for life experience. Nondegree study is possible. There are 22 national honor societies and a freshman honors program.

Faculty/Classroom: 48% of faculty are male; 52% are female. 80% teach undergraduates. No introductory courses are taught by graduate students. The average class size in an introductory lecture is 26; in a laboratory is 10; and in a regular course is 22.

Admissions: 62% of the 2009-2010 applicants were accepted. The SAT scores for the 2009-2010 freshman class were: Critical Reading--28% below 500, 57% between 500 and 599, 14% between 600 and 700, and 1 above 700; Math--19% below 500, 55% between 500 and 599, 24% between 600 and 700, and 2 above 700; Writing--25% below 500, 58% between 500 and 599, 16% between 600 and 700, and 2 above 700. The ACT scores were 6% below 21, 47% between 21 and 23, 31% between 24 and 26, 11% between 27 and 28, and 5% above 28. 37% of the current freshmen were in the top fifth of their class; 71% were in the top two fifths.

Requirements: The SAT or ACT is required. The ACT Optional Writing test is also required. In addition, applicants must be graduates of accredited secondary schools or have earned a GED. The college requires 16 Carnegie units, based on 4 years of English, 3 of math, and 2 each of history and science, with the remaining 5 units in academic electives. An essay and an interview are also recommended. The personal statement is option. A GPA of 2.3 is required. AP and CLEP credits are accepted. Important factors in the admissions decision are advanced placement or honors courses, leadership record, and extracurricular activities record.

Procedure: Freshmen are admitted fall, spring, and summer. Entrance exams should be taken by December of the senior year. There is a deferred admissions plan. Applications should be filed by March 1 for fall entry and January 1 for spring entry, along with a $50 fee. Notifications are sent April 1. Applications are accepted on-line.

Transfer: 507 transfer students enrolled in 2008-2009. Transfer applicants with fewer than 24 transferable college credits must provide a high school transcript and SAT I scores. All transfer applicants must submit college transcripts and a statement of good standing. A minimum college GPA of 2.25 is required. For education majors, a minimum cumulative GPA of 2.75 is required. 32 of 128 credits required for the bachelor's degree must be completed at Monmouth.

Visiting: There are regularly scheduled orientations for prospective students, including campus tours and interviews. There are guides for infor-mal visits and visitors may sit in on classes. To schedule a visit, contact the Admissions Office at (800) 543-9671.

Financial Aid: In 2009-2010, 99% of all full-time freshmen and 97% of continuing full-time students received some form of financial aid. 30% of all full-time freshmen and 40% of continuing full-time students received need-based aid. Average annual earnings from campus work are $1500. The average financial indebtedness of the 2009 graduate was $25,000. The FAFSA is required. Check with the school for current application deadlines.

International Students: There are 26 international students enrolled. The school actively recruits these students. They must take the TOEFL with a minimum score of 550 on the paper-based TOEFL (PBT) or 79 on the Internet-based version (iBT) or take the MELAB, the IELTS, or the Cambridge ESOL (CAE). They must also take the SAT or ACT, scoring 1620. Students from English speaking countries must take the SAT or ACT.

Computers: Wireless access is available. There are more than 670 computers available for students use in computer labs on campus in academic buildings, the library, the student center, and residence halls, and 2 of these labs are open 24 hours. There is wireless network service in the library, academic buildings, the student center, the resident dining hall, the administration building, and outside locations. Students are provided with campus-wide network connectivity, controlled Internet access, access to personal e-mail accounts, on campus, and access to netwrok servers. All students may access the system. 24 hours a day, 7 days a week. There are no time limits and no fees. A Pentium III, 80 GB hard drive, 256 MB RAM PC with CD is recommended.

Graduates: From July 1, 2008 to June 30, 2009, 1061 bachelor's degrees were awarded. The most popular majors were business (32%), education (15%), and communication (13%). 175 companies recruited on campus in 2008-2009. In an average class, 36% graduate in 4 years or less, 59% graduate in 5 years or less, and 61% graduate in 6 years or less.

Admissions Contact: Victoria Bobik, Director of Undergraduate Admission. E-Mail: admission@monmouth.edu
Web: www.monmouth.edu

MONTCLAIR STATE UNIVERSITY   E-2
Upper Montclair, NJ 07043-1624   (973) 655-4444
(800) 331-9205; (973) 655-7700

Full-time: 4225 men, 6670 women	**Faculty:** IIA, +$
Part-time: 765 men, 1375 women	**Ph.Ds:** n/av
Graduate: 1020 men, 2710 women	**Student/Faculty:** n/av
Year: semesters, summer session	**Tuition:** $9500 ($17,000)
Application Deadline: March 1	**Room & Board:** $10,000
Freshman Class: n/av	
SAT: required	**COMPETITIVE**

Montclair State University, established in 1908, is a public institution offering programs in liberal arts and sciences, business administration, fine and performing arts, and professional studies. The figures in the above capsule and in this profile are approximate. There are 5 undergraduate schools and 1 graduate school. In addition to regional accreditation, Montclair has baccalaureate program accreditation with AACSB, ABET, ADA, CSAB, NASAD, NASDTEC, NASM, NCATE, and NRPA. The library contains 459,034 volumes, 1.2 million microform items, and 21,145 audio/video tapes/CDs/DVDs, and subscribes to 21,145 periodicals including electronic. Computerized library services include interlibrary loans, database searching, and Internet access. Special learning facilities include a learning resource center, art gallery, radio station, TV station, a psycho-educational center, and Academic Success Center. The 275-acre campus is in a suburban area 14 miles west of New York City. Including any residence halls, there are 57 buildings.

Student Life: 97% of undergraduates are from New Jersey. Others are from 31 states, 129 foreign countries, and Canada. 80% are from public schools. 58% are white; 20% Hispanic. 47% are Catholic; 33% Muslim 3%, Hindu 1%, Buddhist 1%, No Preference 14%, Unknown 14%; 17% Protestant. The average age of freshmen is 19; all undergraduates, 23. 18% do not continue beyond their first year; 61% remain to graduate.

Housing: 3423 students can be accommodated in college housing, which includes single-sex and coed dorms and on-campus apartments. In addition, there are honors houses and special-interest houses. On-campus housing is available on a first-come and first-served basis. Priority is given to out-of-town students. 74% of students commute. Alcohol is not permitted. All students may keep cars.

Activities: 4% of men belong to 1 local and 17 national fraternities; 4% of women belong to 4 local and 18 national sororities. There are 120 groups on campus including band, cheerleading, choir, chorus, dance, drama, ethnic, gay, honors, international, jazz band, literary magazine, marching band, musical theater, newspaper, orchestra, pep band, political, professional, radio and TV, religious, social, social service, student government, and yearbook. Popular campus events include Welcome Week, Montclairfest, and Spring Week.

Sports: There are 8 intercollegiate sports for men and 8 for women, and 12 intramural sports for men and 12 for women. Facilities include a gym complex with competitive pool, 2 basketball courts, an auxiliary gym, wrestling room, a 6000-seat Astroturf stadium, a baseball stadium, a softball stadium, soccer park, all weather track, tennis courts, and a fitness center.

Disabled Students: 90% of the campus is accessible. Facilities include wheelchair ramps, elevators, special parking, specially equipped restrooms, special class scheduling, lowered drinking fountains, lowered telephones, special housing. curb cuts, speaker phones, special building signs, TDDs, and priority registration. There is a disability resource center on campus.

Services: Counseling and information services are available, as is tutoring in most subjects. There is a reader service for the blind, and remedial math, reading, and writing. Audio textbooks are available.

Campus Safety and Security: Measures include 24-hour foot and vehicle patrol, emergency notification system, self-defense education, and security escort services. There are shuttle buses, emergency telephones, lighted pathways/sidewalks, controlled access to dorms/residences, a full-time campus police force, a crime prevention officer, and crime prevention programs.

Programs of Study: Montclair confers B.A., B.S., B.F.A., and B.Mus. degrees. Master's and doctoral degrees are also awarded. Bachelor's degrees are awarded in BIOLOGICAL SCIENCE (biochemistry, biology/biological science, environmental biology, marine science, molecular biology, and nutrition), BUSINESS (accounting, banking and finance, business administration and management, business economics, hospitality management services, international business management, management information systems, marketing management, recreation and leisure services, retailing, and tourism), COMMUNICATIONS AND THE ARTS (art, art history and appreciation, broadcasting, classics, communications, communications technology, creative writing, dance, dramatic arts, English, film arts, fine arts, French, graphic design, Italian, Latin, linguistics, music, music performance, music theory and composition, musical theater, public relations, Spanish, speech/debate/rhetoric, studio art, and theater design), COMPUTER AND PHYSICAL SCIENCE (applied mathematics, astronomy, chemistry, computer science, geoscience, information sciences and systems, mathematics, and physics), EDUCATION (art education, athletic training, business education, early childhood education, health education, home economics education, middle school education, music education, and physical education), HEALTH PROFESSIONS (allied health, community health work, music therapy, predentistry, premedicine, prepharmacy, and public health), SOCIAL SCIENCE (anthropology, criminal justice, dietetics, economics, family and community services, food production/management/services, geography, gerontology, history, home economics, human ecology, humanities, law, paralegal studies, parks and recreation management, philosophy, political science/government, psychology, religion, sociology, and women's studies). Business administration, family and child studies, and psychology are the largest.

Required: Students must successfully complete a minimum of 120 semester hours, with 33 to 82 in the major, while maintaining a minimum GPA of 2.0. General education requirements include courses in communications, contemporary issues, art appreciation, a foreign language, humanities, math, natural/physical science, social sciences, and multicultural awareness, as well as 1 semester hour in phys ed and 3 semester hours in computer science.

Special: Internships, co-op programs in all majors, credit by exam, pass/fail options, work-study, credit for life experience, independent study, and study abroad in 51 countries are offered. Joint-degree programs are offered in practical anthropology and applied economics, and a 5-year B.A.-B.Mus. program in music is available, as is an articulated medical, dental, physical therapy, and physician assistant program with the University of Medicine and Dentistry of New Jersey and an articulated program leading to a Pharm.D. with Rutgers University. There are 28 national honor societies, a freshman honors program, and 3 departmental honors programs.

Faculty/Classroom: 47% of faculty are male; 53% are female. All teach undergraduates. No introductory courses are taught by graduate students. The average class size in an introductory lecture is 26; in a laboratory is 18; and in a regular course is 25.

Requirements: The SAT is required. In addition, applicants must submit 16 Carnegie units, including 4 in English, 3 to 4 in math (including algebra I and II and geometry), 2 each in lab science, social studies, and a foreign language, and the remainder in additional courses in these fields. The GED is accepted. A portfolio, audition, or interview is required for students planning to major in fine arts, music, speech, or theater. Admission to computer science requires 4 years of math, including trigonometry. AP and CLEP credits are accepted. Important factors in the admissions decision are advanced placement or honors courses, recommendations by school officials, and leadership record.

Procedure: Freshmen are admitted fall and spring. Entrance exams should be taken in October, November, or December of the senior year. There is a rolling admissions plan. Applications should be filed by March 1 for fall entry and November 1 for spring entry. The fall 2009 application fee was $55. Notification is sent on a rolling basis. Applications are accepted on-line.

Transfer: 1617 transfer students enrolled in in a recent year. Applicants must have completed a minimum of 15 credits from an accredited college. A cumulative GPA of 2.5 is required for most majors, with higher required in select programs. Applicants must have completed English composition. High school and college transcripts are required. 32 of 120 credits required for the bachelor's degree must be completed at Montclair.

Visiting: There are regularly scheduled orientations for prospective students. There are guides for informal visits. To schedule a visit, contact the Admissions Office at (973) 655-5322.

Financial Aid: In a recent year, 63% of all full-time freshmen and 63% of continuing full-time students received some form of financial aid. 45% of all full-time freshmen and 50% of continuing full-time students received need-based aid. The average freshmen award was $10,638, with $6,752 ($12,986 maximum) from need-based scholarships or need-based grants; $4,181 ($8,500 maximum) from need-based self-help aid (loans and jobs); and $4,370 ($19,788 maximum) from other non-need-based awards and non-need-based scholarships. All of undergraduate students worked part-time. Average annual earnings from campus work were $2071. The average financial indebtedness of the 2009 graduate was $17,456. The FAFSA is required. Check with the school for current application deadlines.

International Students: There were 566 international students enrolled in a recent year. The school actively recruits these students. They must take the TOEFL.

Computers: Wireless access is available. PC and Mac labs are located throughout the campus, with about 250 computers and PC printers. A network of Sun workstations is also available. A wide variety of general and discipline-specific software is offered. Residence hall rooms are wired for network connections and Internet access is available. All students may access the system. There are no time limits and no fees. Students enrolled in Business Administration must have a personal computer.

Graduates: In a recent year 2482 bachelor's degrees were awarded. The most popular majors were business administration (19%), family and child studies (14%), and psychology (10%). 150 companies recruited on campus in 2008-2009. In an average class, 1% graduate in 3 years or less, 27% graduate in 4 years or less, 54% graduate in 5 years or less, and 61% graduate in 6 years or less. Of the 2008 graduating class, 21% were enrolled in graduate school within 6 months of graduation, and 90% were employed.

Admissions Contact: Jason Langdon, Director of Admissions. E-Mail: *msuadm@mail.montclair.edu* Web: *www.montclair.edu*

NEW JERSEY CITY UNIVERSITY   E-2

Jersey City, NJ 07305
(201) 200-3073
(888) 441-NJCU; (201) 200-3288

Full-time: 1874 men, 2821 women	**Faculty:** 243
Part-time: 604 men, 1068 women	**Ph.Ds:** 89%
Graduate: 530 men, 1502 women	**Student/Faculty:** 19 to 1
Year: semesters, summer session	**Tuition:** $8897 ($16,265)
Application Deadline: April 1	**Room & Board:** $10,136
Freshman Class: 4360 applied, 1726 accepted, 614 enrolled	
SAT CR/M/W: 460/470/450	**COMPETITIVE+**

New Jersey City University, founded in 1927, is a public institution offering undergraduate and graduate programs in the arts and sciences, business administration, education, health science, upper-level nursing, and other professional fields. There are 3 undergraduate schools and 1 graduate school. In addition to regional accreditation, NJCU has baccalaureate program accreditation with AACSB, NASAD, NASM, NCATE, and NLN. The library contains 319,360 volumes, 1.8 million microform items, and 3618 audio/video tapes/CDs/DVDs, and subscribes to 24,214 periodicals including electronic. Computerized library services include interlibrary loans, database searching, and Internet access. Special learning facilities include a learning resource center, art gallery, radio station, media arts center, and lab school for special education instruction. The 51-acre campus is in an urban area 5 miles west of New York City. Including any residence halls, there are 19 buildings.

Student Life: 99% of undergraduates are from New Jersey. Others are from 18 states, and 47 foreign countries. 35% are Hispanic; 27% white; 20% African American. The average age of freshmen is 18; all undergraduates, 27. 23% do not continue beyond their first year; 35% remain to graduate.

Housing: 250 students can be accommodated in college housing, which includes coed dorms. On-campus housing is guaranteed for all 4 years. 95% of students commute. Alcohol is not permitted. All students may keep cars.

Activities: 1% of men belong to 6 national fraternities; 1% of women belong to 2 local and 5 national sororities. There are 24 groups on campus, including art, band, choir, chorale, chorus, computers, dance, drama, ethnic, film, gay, honors, international, jazz band, literary magazine, musical theater, newspaper, opera, orchestra, photography, political, professional, radio and TV, religious, social, social service, student government, and symphony. Popular campus events include President's Picnic, Town and Gown Concert, and lecture series.

Sports: There are 8 intercollegiate sports for men and 8 for women, and 22 intramural sports for men and 22 for women. Facilities include an athletic and fitness center with a 2000-seat arena, jogging track, fitness facilities, 6-lane pool, sauna, racquetball courts, and soccer, tennis, baseball, and softball facilities.

Disabled Students: All of the campus is accessible. Facilities include wheelchair ramps, elevators, special parking, specially equipped restrooms, special class scheduling, lowered drinking fountains, and lowered telephones.

Services: Counseling and information services are available, as is tutoring in most subjects. There is remedial math, reading, and writing.

Campus Safety and Security: Measures include 24-hour foot and vehicle patrol, emergency notification system, and security escort services. There are shuttle buses, emergency telephones, lighted pathways/sidewalks, and controlled access to dorms/residences.

Programs of Study: NJCU confers B.A., B.F.A., B.S., and B.S.N. and accelerated B.S.N. degrees. Master's degrees are also awarded. Bachelor's degrees are awarded in BIOLOGICAL SCIENCE (biology/biological science), BUSINESS (business administration and management and retailing), COMMUNICATIONS AND THE ARTS (design, English, fine arts, media arts, music, photography, and Spanish), COMPUTER AND PHYSICAL SCIENCE (chemistry, computer science, geology, mathematics, and physics), EDUCATION (art education, early childhood education, elementary education, health education, music education, secondary education, and special education), HEALTH PROFESSIONS (medical laboratory technology, nuclear medical technology, nursing, and public health), SOCIAL SCIENCE (criminal justice, economics, geography, history, philosophy, political science/government, psychology, and sociology). Business, computer science, criminal justice are the largest.

Required: Students must complete 66 semester hours in general education courses, satisfy college requirements in English, communication, and math, and complete the introductory career exploration and computer usage courses. The bachelor's degree requires completion of at least 128 semester hours, including 36 to 54 in a major field, with a minimum GPA of 2.0. Distribution requirements include 9 credits each in natural science, social science, humanities, and fine and performing arts and 6 credits in communications and contemporary world.

Special: Co-op programs in all majors and internships in some are available. NJCU also offers study abroad, work-study programs, numerous health science programs, and some programs affiliated with New Jersey College of Medicine and Dentistry in Newark. Nondegree study and dual majors are possible. There is an accelerated degree program in nursing. There are 4 national honor societies, a freshman honors program, and 1 departmental honors program.

Faculty/Classroom: 50% of faculty are male; 50% are female. All teach undergraduates. No introductory courses are taught by graduate students. The average class size in a regular course is 21.

Admissions: 40% of the 2009-2010 applicants were accepted. The SAT scores for the 2009-2010 freshman class were: Critical Reading--73% below 500, 23% between 500 and 599, and 4% between 600 and 700; Math--66% below 500, 30% between 500 and 599, and 4% between 600 and 700; Writing--72% below 500, 26% between 500 and 599, and 1% between 600 and 700. 25% of the current freshmen were in the top fifth of their class; 60% were in the top two fifths.

Requirements: The SAT is required. In addition, applicants must be graduates of accredited secondary schools or have earned a GED. The college requires 16 Carnegie units, including 4 in English, 3 in math, and 2 each in social studies and a lab science, with the remaining 5 units in a foreign language and additional academic courses. An essay is also required, and an interview is recommended. NJCU requires applicants to be in the upper 50% of their class. A GPA of 2.5 is required. AP and CLEP credits are accepted. Important factors in the admissions decision are advanced placement or honors courses, evidence of special talent, and recommendations by school officials.

Procedure: Freshmen are admitted fall and spring. Entrance exams should be taken in the spring of the junior year or fall of the senior year. There are deferred admissions and rolling admissions plans. Applications should be filed by april 1 for fall entry, along with a $35 fee. Notification is sent January 1. Applications are accepted on-line. A waiting list is maintained.

Transfer: 869 transfer students enrolled in 2008-2009. Applicants must present a minimum GPA of 2.0 in at least 12 credit hours completed at the college level. Students transferring fewer than 12 credits must also submit SAT scores of at least 480 verbal and 440 math. An interview is recommended for all transfers. A basic skills test is required for transfers who have fewer than 30 credits or have not taken English or math at their previous school. College transcripts are required. 36 of 128 credits required for the bachelor's degree must be completed at NJCU.

Visiting: There are regularly scheduled orientations for prospective students, including a financial aid workshop, guided tours, and open house.

There is a summer orientation. There are guides for informal visits and visitors may sit in on classes. To schedule a visit, contact the Admissions Office.

Financial Aid: In a recent year, 75% of all full-time freshmen and 73% of continuing full-time students received some form of financial aid. 37% of all full-time freshmen and 49% of continuing full-time students received need-based aid. The average freshman award was $8171. The FAFSA is required. Check with the school for current application deadlines.

International Students: There are 88 international students enrolled. They must take the TOEFL. They must also take the SAT.

Computers: All students may access the system 24 hours a day. There are no time limits and no fees.

Graduates: From July 1, 2008 to June 30, 2009, 1002 bachelor's degrees were awarded. The most popular majors were business administration (23%), psychology (10%), and criminal justice (9%). 350 companies recruited on campus in a recent year. In an average class, 6% graduate in 4 years or less, 23% graduate in 5 years or less, and 32% graduate in 6 years or less.

Admissions Contact: Jose BaldaDirector of Admissions. E-mail: *admissions@njcu.edu* Web: *www.njcu.edu*

NEW JERSEY INSTITUTE OF TECHNOLOGY   E-2

Newark, NJ 07102-1982   (973) 596-3300; (973) 596-6085

Full-time: 3450 men, 910 women	Faculty: I, av$
Part-time: 1210 men, 310 women	Ph.D.s: n/av
Graduate: 2105 men, 1005 women	Student/Faculty: n/av
Year: semesters, summer session	Tuition: $9500 ($14,500)
Application Deadline: see profile	Room & Board: $9000
Freshman Class: n/av	
SAT: required	**VERY COMPETITIVE**

New Jersey Institute of Technology is a public research university providing instruction, research, and public service in engineering, computer science, management, architecture, engineering technology, applied sciences, and related fields. The figures in the above capsule and in this profile are approximate. There are 6 undergraduate schools and 1 graduate school. In addition to regional accreditation, NJIT has baccalaureate program accreditation with AACSB, ABET, and NAAB. The 2 libraries contain 220,000 volumes, 7,325 microform items, and 73,807 audio/video tapes/CDs/DVDs, and subscribe to 2,500 periodicals including electronic. Computerized library services include interlibrary loans and database searching. Special learning facilities include a learning resource center, art gallery, radio station, 3 TV studios. NJIT is home to many government- and industry-sponsored labs and research centers, including the EPA Northeast Hazardous Substance Research Center, the National Center for Transportation and Industrial Productivity, the Center for Manufacturing Systems, the Emission Reduction Research Center, the Microelectronics Research Center, the Center for Microwave and Lightwave Engineering, and the Multi-Lifecycle Engineering Center. The 45-acre campus is in an urban area 10 miles west of New York City. Including any residence halls, there are 25 buildings.

Student Life: 94% of undergraduates are from New Jersey. Others are from 36 states, 109 foreign countries, and Canada. 80% are from public schools. 31% are white; 22% Asian American; 14% foreign nationals. The average age of freshmen is 18; all undergraduates, 23. 15% do not continue beyond their first year; 49% remain to graduate.

Housing: 1434 students can be accommodated in college housing, which includes coed dorms. On-campus housing is available on a first-come, first-served basis, and is available on a lottery system for upperclassmen. Priority is given to out-of-town students. 75% of students commute. All students may keep cars.

Activities: 7% of men belong to 4 local and 10 national fraternities; 5% of women belong to 4 local and 5 national sororities. There are 92 groups on campus, including art, chess, computers, drama, drum and bugle corps, ethnic, gay, honors, international, musical theater, newspaper, photography, professional, radio and TV, religious, social, social service, student government, and yearbook. Popular campus events include Miniversity, International Students Food Festival, and Leadership Training Weekend.

Sports: There are 9 intercollegiate sports for men and 6 for women, and 13 intramural sports for men and 7 for women. Facilities include a 1000-seat stadium, a fitness center with an indoor track, a 6-lane swimming pool, 4 tennis courts, 4 racket sport courts, playing fields, bowling lanes, a table tennis and billiards area, and 3 gyms, the largest of which seats 1200.

Disabled Students: 95% of the campus is accessible. Facilities include wheelchair ramps, elevators, special parking, specially equipped restrooms, special class scheduling, lowered drinking fountains, and lowered telephones.

Services: Counseling and information services are available, as is tutoring in most subjects. There is a reader service for the blind, and remedial math, reading, and writing.

Campus Safety and Security: Measures include 24-hour foot and vehicle patrol, self-defense education, and security escort services. There are shuttle buses, emergency telephones, and lighted pathways/sidewalks.

Programs of Study: NJIT confers B.A., B.S., and B.Arch. degrees. Master's and doctoral degrees are also awarded. Bachelor's degrees are awarded in BIOLOGICAL SCIENCE (biology/biological science), BUSINESS (management science), COMMUNICATIONS AND THE ARTS (communications and technical and business writing), COMPUTER AND PHYSICAL SCIENCE (applied mathematics, applied physics, chemistry, computer management, computer science, information sciences and systems, and mathematics), ENGINEERING AND ENVIRONMENTAL DESIGN (architecture, biomedical engineering, chemical engineering, civil engineering, computer engineering, computer technology, electrical/electronics engineering, engineering and applied science, engineering technology, environmental engineering, environmental science, geophysical engineering, industrial engineering, manufacturing engineering, mechanical engineering, technological management, and technology and public affairs), SOCIAL SCIENCE (history). Engineering, computer science, and architecture are the strongest academically. Engineering is the largest.

Required: General university requirements include 9 credits of humanities and social science electives, 7 of natural sciences, 6 each of math, cultural history, basic social sciences, and engineering technology, 3 each of English and management, and 2 of computer science. Students must also complete 2 courses in phys ed. To graduate, students must earn between 124 and 164 credits, depending on the program, including 50 in the major, with a minimum GPA of 2.0 in upper-level major courses.

Special: Cross-registration is offered in conjunction with Essex County College, Rutgers University's Newark campus, and the University of Medicine and Dentistry of New Jersey. Cooperative programs, available in all majors, include two 6-month internships. There are 3-2 engineering degree programs with Stockton State College and Lincoln and Seton Hall Universities. NJIT also offers work-study programs, study abroad in 18 countries, dual and interdisciplinary majors, accelerated degree programs, distance learning, and nondegree study. There is 1 national honor society and a freshman honors program.

Faculty/Classroom: 84% of faculty are male; 16% are female. 74% teach undergraduates, all do research, and 74% do both. Graduate students teach 10% of introductory courses. The average class size in an introductory lecture is 30; in a laboratory is 27; and in a regular course is 25.

Requirements: The SAT is required. In addition, the SAT: Subject test in math I or II is also required. Applicants should have completed 16 secondary school units, including 4 each in English and math, 2 in a lab science, and 6 in a distribution of social studies, foreign language, math, and science courses. AP and CLEP credits are accepted. Important factors in the admissions decision are advanced placement or honors courses, recommendations by school officials, and geographical diversity.

Procedure: Freshmen are admitted fall and spring. Entrance exams should be taken in May of the junior year or November of the senior year. There is a rolling admissions plan. Applications should be filed by November 15 for spring entry, along with a $35 fee. Notifications are sent January 2. Applications are accepted on-line. A waiting list is maintained.

Transfer: 494 transfer students enrolled in a recent year. A minimum college GPA of 2.0 is required, but 2.5 or higher is recommended. Students must submit transcripts of all attempted postsecondary academic work. Applicants with fewer than 30 credits may be asked to provide scores on the SAT and the SAT: Subject test in math, as well as high school transcripts. Engineering technology students must present an associate degree. Admission to the School of Architecture is very competitive for transfer students. 33 of 124 credits required for the bachelor's degree must be completed at NJIT.

Visiting: There are regularly scheduled orientations for prospective students, including tours and meetings with admissions personnel, students, and faculty. There are guides for informal visits; visitors may sit in on classes and stay overnight. To schedule a visit, contact Kathy Kelly, Director of Admissions.

Financial Aid: The FAFSA and the college's own financial statement are required. Check with the school for current application deadlines.

International Students: The school actively recruits these students. They must take the TOEFL. They must also take the SAT.

Computers: All students may access the system. There are no time limits and no fees. All students are required to have a personal computer. All full-time freshmen are given a PC and a variety of software is recommended.

Admissions Contact: Kathy Kelly, Director of Admissions. E-Mail: *admissions@admin.njit.edu* Web: *www.njit.edu*

PRINCETON UNIVERSITY   D-3

Princeton, NJ 08544-0430   (609) 258-3000; (609) 258-6743

Full-time: 2600 men, 2275 women	Faculty: I, ++$
Part-time: none	Ph.D s: n/av
Graduate: 1410 men, 950 women	Student/Faculty: n/av
Year: semesters	Tuition: $35,000
Application Deadline: January 1	Room & Board: $12,000
Freshman Class: n/av	
SAT or ACT: required	**MOST COMPETITIVE**

Princeton University, established in 1746, is a private institution offering degrees in the liberal arts and sciences, engineering, applied science, architecture, public and international affairs, interdisciplinary and regional studies, and the creative arts. The figures in the above capsule and in this profile are approximate. There are 4 graduate schools. In addition to regional accreditation, Princeton has baccalaureate program accreditation with ABET and NAAB. The 16 libraries contain 6.2 million volumes, 6.3 million microform items, and 60,000 audio/video tapes/CDs/DVDs, and subscribe to 15,000 periodicals including electronic. Computerized library services include interlibrary loans and database searching. Special learning facilities include an art gallery, natural history museum, radio station, a music center, a visual and performing arts center, several theaters, an observatory, a plasma physics lab, and a center for environmental and energy studies. The 500-acre campus is in a small town 50 miles south of New York City. Including any residence halls, there are 160 buildings.

Student Life: 84% of undergraduates are from out of state, mostly the Middle Atlantic. Students are from 50 states, 70 foreign countries, and Canada. 52% are white; 14% Asian American. The average age of freshmen is 18; all undergraduates, 20. 3% do not continue beyond their first year; 97% remain to graduate.

Housing: 6729 students can be accommodated in college housing, which includes coed dorms, on-campus apartments, off-campus apartments, and married student housing. Freshmen and sophomores are assigned to 5 residential colleges; most juniors and seniors live in upperclass dorms and select from among such dining options as co-ops and private clubs. On-campus housing is guaranteed for all 4 years. 98% of students live on campus; of those, 100% remain on campus on weekends. Upperclassmen may keep cars.

Activities: There are no fraternities or sororities. There are 200 groups on campus, including art, band, cheerleading, chess, choir, chorale, chorus, computers, dance, drama, ethnic, forensics, gay, honors, international, jazz band, literary magazine, marching band, Model UN, musical theater, opera, orchestra, pep band, photography, political, professional, religious, social, social service, student government, symphony, and yearbook.

Sports: There are 20 intercollegiate sports for men and 18 for women, and 35 intramural sports for men and 35 for women. Facilities include a 250,000-square-foot gymnasium for intercollegiate sports; a gymnasium for recreational sports; a fitness center; an Olympic-size pool with complete diving facilities; separate stadiums for football (28,000 seats), track and field, and lacrosse and field hockey; a hockey rink; and outdoor facilities such as tennis courts, an 18-hole golf course, and more than 50 acres of fields for baseball, lacrosse, rugby, soccer, and softball.

Disabled Students: Facilities include wheelchair ramps, elevators, special parking, specially equipped restrooms, lowered drinking fountains, lowered telephones, and special housing. Each student's needs are assessed individually. Accommodations may include additional testing time, sign language translators, and dietary accommodations for food allergies. Princeton has an Office of Disability Services.

Services: Counseling and information services are available, as is tutoring in every subject. There is a reader service for the blind. Princetonüs McGraw Center for Teaching and Learning offers workshops and individual consultations in which students can learn to manage large reading loads, problem-solve, take effective notes and create study tools, prepare for long-term projects and oral presentations; prepare for exams, manage time, and overcome test anxiety. Princetonüs Writing Program works to ensure freshmen and others can master college-level writing.

Campus Safety and Security: Measures include 24-hour foot and vehicle patrol, emergency notification system, self-defense education, and security escort services. There are shuttle buses, emergency telephones, lighted pathways/sidewalks, and controlled access to dorms/residences.

Programs of Study: Princeton confers A.B. and B.S.E. degrees. Master's and doctoral degrees are also awarded. Bachelor's degrees are awarded in BIOLOGICAL SCIENCE (ecology, evolutionary biology, and molecular biology), BUSINESS (operations research), COMMUNICATIONS AND THE ARTS (classics, comparative literature, English, French, German, Italian, music, Portuguese, Slavic languages, and Spanish), COMPUTER AND PHYSICAL SCIENCE (astrophysics, chemistry, computer science, geoscience, mathematics, and physics), ENGINEERING AND ENVIRONMENTAL DESIGN (aeronautical engineering, architectural engineering, architecture, chemical engineering, civil engineering, electrical/electronics engineering, and mechanical engineering), SOCIAL SCIENCE (anthropology, archeology, East Asian studies, economics, history, international relations, Near Eastern studies, philosophy, political science/government, psychology, religion, and sociology). Economics, politics, and history are the largest.

Required: To graduate, students must complete 8 semesters, or academic units. Candidates for the A.B. degree must demonstrate proficiency in English composition and a foreign language and they must complete distribution requirements in 7 academic areas. Candidates for the B.S.E. must satisfy the English composition requirement and complete a minimum of 7 courses in the humanities and social sciences spread over 4 distribution areas. A junior project and senior thesis are required of virtually all students.

Special: Princeton offers independent study, accelerated degree programs, student-proposed courses and majors, field study, community-based learning course that enrich course work with related service projects, study abroad, freshman seminars, and independent work in the junior and senior year. They also offer a Program in Teacher Preparation. There are 2 national honor societies, including Phi Beta Kappa, and all departments have honors programs.

Faculty/Classroom: 69% of faculty are male; 31% are female. All teach and do research. No introductory courses are taught by graduate students.

Requirements: The SAT or ACT is required. The ACT is accepted in lieu of SAT Reasoning test when every other school to which the student applies requires only the ACT. Three SAT Subject tests are also required for all applicants. Recommended college preparatory courses include 4 years each of English, math, science, and a foreign language; 2 years each of lab science and history; and some study of art and music. Essays are required as part of the application and an interview is recommended. Students with special talent in visual or performing arts may supplement tapes, CDs or DVDs. AP credits are accepted. Important factors in the admissions decision are personality/intangible qualities, recommendations by school officials, and advanced placement or honors courses.

Procedure: Freshmen are admitted in the fall. Entrance exams should be taken by January of the senior year at the latest. There are early admissions and deferred admissions plans. Applications should be filed by January 1 for fall entry, along with a $65 fee. Notifications are sent April 1. Applications are accepted on-line. A waiting list is maintained.

Transfer: Princeton does not have a transfer admissions option.

Visiting: There are regularly scheduled orientations for prospective students, Including information sessions on Monday to Friday within the Admission Office, and some Saturdays in the fall. Also, Princeton has an open campus, with many free and public events, and students are welcome to attend such events. Visitors may sit in on classes. To schedule a visit, contact Undergraduate Admission Office at (609) 258-3060.

Financial Aid: In a recent year, 55% of all full-time freshmen and 51% of continuing full-time students received some form of financial aid. 55% of all full-time freshmen and 51% of continuing full-time students received need-based aid. The average freshmen award was $31,114. 67% of undergraduate students worked part-time. Average annual earnings from campus work were $1500. The average financial indebtedness of the 2009 graduate was $5,592. Princeton is a member of CSS. The FAFSA and the college's own financial statement are required. Check with the school for current application deadlines.

International Students: There were 377 international students enrolled in a recent year. The school actively recruits these students. They must take the TOEFL, The SAT: Writing Test may be substituted for the TOEFL. Students must take the SAT or ACT, plus three SAT Subject Tests.

Computers: Wireless access is available. Students have access to a varied and powerful computing network at Princeton. High-speed data connections and wireless service are available in every undergraduate dorm room, and wireless service also is provided in many areas across campus. Additionally, students have access to more than 250 Windows-based and Macintosh computers in the two dozen computer clusters around campus. Most of the clusters are available 24 hours a day and also provide access to scanners and free printing. These resources allow students to take advantage of networked resources such as e-mail, central printing, online library systems, streaming video, and specialty course software. All students may access the system. There are no time limits and no fees. It is strongly recommended that all students have a personal computer.

Graduates: in a recent year, 1144 bachelor's degrees were awarded. The most popular majors were social sciences (25%), engineering (15%), and history (9%). 310 companies recruited on campus in 2008-2009. In an average class, 88% graduate in 4 years or less, 94% graduate in 5 years or less, and 95% graduate in 6 years or less.

Admissions Contact: Jonathan R. LeBouef, Associate Registrar. E-Mail: *uaoffice@princeton.edu* Web: *www.princeton.edu*

RAMAPO COLLEGE OF NEW JERSEY — D-2

Mahwah, NJ 07430

(201) 684-7300
(800) 9-RAMAPO; (201) 684-7964

Full-time: 2196 men, 3028 women
Part-time: 224 men, 328 women
Graduate: 60 men, 190 women
Year: semesters, , summer session
Application Deadline: March 1
Freshman Class: 5556 applied, 2550 accepted, 880 enrolled
SAT CR/M/W: 550/590/570

Faculty: 213; IIB, +$
Ph.D.s: 94%
Student/Faculty: 18 to 1
Tuition: n/av
Room & Board: $11,290

HIGHLY COMPETITIVE

Ramapo College, founded in 1969, is a public institution offering undergraduate programs in the arts and sciences, American and international studies, business administration, and human services. Personal interaction is incorporated throughout the curriculum as is an international and multicultural component including telecommunications and computer technology. There are 5 undergraduate schools and 3 graduate schools. In addition to regional accreditation, Ramapo has baccalaureate program accreditation with CSWE and TEAC. The library contains 176,128 volumes, 2,500 microform items, 9,663 audio/video tapes/CDs/DVDs, and subscribes to 950 periodicals including electronic. Computerized library services include inter-library loans, database searching, Internet access, and laptop Internet portals. Special learning facilities include a learning resource center, radio station, TV station, astronomical observatory, international telecommunications satellite center, the Marge Roukema Center for International Education and Entrepreneurship, a solar greenhouse center, a spirituality center, and a sustainability education center is under construction. The 314-acre campus is in a suburban area 25 miles northwest of New York City. Including any residence halls, there are 71 buildings.

Student Life: 95% of undergraduates are from New Jersey. Students are from 20 states, 40 foreign countries, and Canada. 76% are white. The average age of freshmen is 18; all undergraduates, 22.

Housing: 3066 students can be accommodated in college housing, which includes coed dorms and on-campus apartments. In addition, there are honors houses, special-interest houses, and blocks of rooms that are reserved for scholars and honors students. On-campus housing is guaranteed for all 4 years, is available on a first-come, and first-served basis. 53% of students live on campus. All students may keep cars.

Activities: 10% of men belong to 9 national fraternities; 9% of women belong to 10 national sororities. There are 100 groups on campus, including cheerleading, choir, chorale, chorus, computers, dance, debate, drama, environmental, ethnic, film, gay, honors, international, jazz band, literary magazine, musical theater, newspaper, pep band, photography, political, professional, radio and TV, religious, social, social service, and student government. Popular campus events include Stroll Competition, Relay for Life, and the Senior Send-Off.

Sports: There are 13 intramural sports for men and 12 for women. Facilities include a 1200-seat stadium that includes an 8-lane, 400-meter track and a Field Turf field, 12 lighted tennis courts, and baseball, softball, field hockey, and soccer fields. A 1457-seat competition arena houses basketball and volleyball courts, and there is an auxiliary gym for intramurals and recreation. A 5000-square-foot fitness center includes cardio machines, machine weight stations, and free weights. Also available is a new athletic training room, a 6-lane swimming pool, and multiple locker rooms.

Disabled Students: All of the campus is accessible. Facilities include wheelchair ramps, elevators, special parking, specially equipped rest rooms, special class scheduling, lowered drinking fountains, lowered telephones, and special housing.

Services: Counseling and information services are available, as is tutoring in every subject. There is a reader service for the blind, and remedial math, reading, and writing.

Campus Safety and Security: Measures include 24-hour foot and vehicle patrol, emergency notification system, and security escort services. There are shuttle buses, emergency telephones, lighted pathways/sidewalks, surveillance cameras.

Programs of Study: Ramapo confers B.A., B.S., B.S.N., and B.S.W. degrees. Master's degrees are also awarded. Bachelor's degrees are awarded in AGRICULTURE (environmental studies), BIOLOGICAL SCIENCE (biochemistry, bioinformatics, and biology/biological science), BUSINESS (accounting, business administration and management, and international business management), COMMUNICATIONS AND THE ARTS (art, communications, dramatic arts, literature, music, and visual and performing arts), COMPUTER AND PHYSICAL SCIENCE (chemistry, computer science, information sciences and systems, and mathematics), ENGINEERING AND ENVIRONMENTAL DESIGN (engineering physics and environmental science), HEALTH PROFESSIONS (allied health, clinical science, and nursing), SOCIAL SCIENCE (American studies, economics, history, international studies, law, liberal arts/general studies, political science/government, psychology, science and society, social science, social work, sociology, and Spanish studies). Physics, bioinformatics, and biology are the strongest academically. Psychology, business administration, and communication arts are the largest.

Required: Students must complete general education requirements of approximately 50 credits in science, social science, humanities, and English composition, as well as core requirements in their school of study and their particular major. A senior seminar is also required. To graduate, students must earn at least 128 credits with a minimum GPA of 2.0.

Special: Ramapo's curriculum emphasizes the interdependence of global society and includes an international dimension in all academic programs. Students may study abroad in many countries. Cooperative programs are available with various corporations and in foreign countries. Cross-registration is possible with local state colleges. Ramapo offers accelerated degree programs, dual and student-designed majors, credit for life experience, pass/fail options, internships, work-study programs, and certificate programs in gerontology and substance abuse. A teachers education program is offered. There are 20 national honor societies and a freshman honors program.

Faculty/Classroom: 55% of faculty are male; 45% are female. All teach undergraduates. No introductory courses are taught by graduate students. The average class size in an introductory lecture is 26; in a laboratory is 19; and in a regular course is 23.

Admissions: 46% of the 2009-2010 applicants were accepted. The SAT scores for the 2009-2010 freshman class were: Critical Reading--10% below 500, 63% between 500 and 599, 23% between 600 and 700, and 4 above 700; Math--5% below 500, 51% between 500 and 599, 40% between 600 and 700, and 5 above 700; Writing--10% below 500, 56% between 500 and 599, 29% between 600 and 700, and 5 above 700. 51% of the current freshmen were in the top fifth of their class; 97% were in the top two fifths. 3 freshmen graduated first in their class.

Requirements: The SAT is required. In addition, applicants must be graduates of an accredited secondary schools or have earned a GED. The college requires 18 academic credits, including 4 in English, 3 each in math, science, and social studies, 2 in foreign language, and the remaining 3 in academic electives. Students must also submit an essay. An interview is recommended. A GPA of 3.0 is required. AP and CLEP credits are accepted. Important factors in the admissions decision are advanced placement or honors courses, recommendations by school officials, and evidence of special talent.

Procedure: Freshmen are admitted fall and spring. Entrance exams should be taken during the senior year. There are early admissions, deferred admissions, and rolling admissions plans. Applications should be filed by March 1 for fall entry and December 1 for spring entry. The fall 2008 application fee was $60. Notification is sent on a rolling basis. Applications are accepted on-line. 505 applicants were on a recent waiting list, 104 were accepted.

Transfer: 608 transfer students enrolled in 2008-2009. Applicants must supply a completed admission application, official transcripts from all previously attended colleges, and an official high school transcript (if fewer than 60 credits from another college attempted). 48 of 128 credits required for the bachelor's degree must be completed at Ramapo.

Visiting: There are regularly scheduled orientations for prospective students, Student visits include orientation, advisement, registration, and immediate decision days (that follow the early action plan). There are guides for informal visits and visitors may sit in on classes. To schedule a visit, contact the Admissions Office.

Financial Aid: In 2009-2010, 73% of all full-time freshmen and 71% of continuing full-time students received some form of financial aid. 47% of all full-time freshmen and 49% of continuing full-time students received need-based aid. The average freshmen award was $11,414, with $11,114 ($32,851 maximum) from need-based scholarships or need-based grants; $3,495 ($6,749 maximum) from need-based self-help aid (loans and jobs); and $13,539 ($25,480 maximum) from other non-need-based awards and non-need-based scholarships. 17% of undergraduate students work part-time. Average annual earnings from campus work are $2332. The average financial indebtedness of the 2009 graduate was $19,789. The FAFSA is required. The priority date for freshman financial aid applications for fall entry is March 1. The deadline for filing freshman financial aid applications for fall entry is March 15.

International Students: There are 125 international students enrolled. The school actively recruits these students. They must take the TOEFL with a minimum score of 550 on the paper-based TOEFL (PBT) and the Comprehensive English Language Test. They must also take the SAT.

Computers: Wireless access is available. All residential halls are wired for Internet access. All students have access to computers on campus. There are approximately 908 PCs and 150 Mac computers networked in labs, academic cores, and the student center. All students may access the system according to posted schedules for lab times. There are no time limits and no fees.

Graduates: From July 1, 2008 to June 30, 2009, 1142 bachelor's degrees were awarded. The most popular majors were business administration (15%), psychology (15%), and communication arts (11%). 14 companies recruited on campus in 2008-2009. In an average class, 64% graduate in 4 years or less, 73% graduate in 5 years or less, and 70% graduate in 6 years or less.

Admissions Contact: Peter Rice, Director of Admissions. A campus DVD is available. E-Mail: *admissions@ramapo.edu* Web: *www.ramapo.edu*

RICHARD STOCKTON COLLEGE OF NEW JERSEY D-5

Pomona, NJ 08240-0195 (609) 652-4261; (609) 748-5541

Full-time: 2460 men, 3420 women	**Faculty:** IIB, +$
Part-time: 350 men, 560 women	**Ph.D.s:** n/av
Graduate: 160 men, 440 women	**Student/Faculty:** n/av
Year: semesters, summer session	**Tuition:** $10,000 ($14,500)
Application Deadline: see profile	**Room & Board:** $10,000
Freshman Class: n/av	
SAT or ACT: required	**VERY COMPETITIVE**

Richard Stockton College of New Jersey, founded in 1969, is a public liberal arts college with 28 undergraduate programs and 6 graduate specialty areas. The figures in the above capsule and in this profile are approximate. There is 1 graduate school. In addition to regional accreditation, Stockton has baccalaureate program accreditation with APTA, CSWE, NASDTEC, and NLN. The library contains 627,318 volumes, 1.1 million microform items, and 15,342 audio/video tapes/CDs/DVDs, and subscribes to 26,375 periodicals including electronic. Computerized library services include interlibrary loans, database searching, and Internet access. Special learning facilities include a learning resource center, art gallery, radio station, TV station, astronomical observatory, marine science field lab, marina with a fleet of small boats, Holocaust resource center, educational technology, training center, and performing arts center. The 1600-acre campus is in a suburban area 12 miles northwest of Atlantic City. Including any residence halls, there are 55 buildings.

Student Life: 98% of undergraduates are from New Jersey. Others are from 21 states, 10 foreign countries, and Canada. 74% are from public schools. 78% are white. The average age of freshmen is 18; all undergraduates, 22. 17% do not continue beyond their first year; 67% remain to graduate.

Housing: 2081 students can be accommodated in college housing, which includes coed dorms and on-campus apartments. In addition, there are special-interest houses, and wellness, substance-free, academic, and smoke-free housing. On-campus housing is guaranteed for the freshman year only, is available on a first-come, first-served basis, and is available on a lottery system for upperclassmen. 68% of students commute. All students may keep cars.

Activities: 4% of men belong to 11 national fraternities; 5% of women belong to 10 national sororities. There are 94 groups on campus, including art, band, cheerleading, chess, choir, chorale, chorus, computers, dance, drama, ethnic, gay, honors, international, jazz band, literary magazine, newspaper, orchestra, pep band, photography, political, professional, radio and TV, religious, social, social service, and student government. Popular campus events include Spring Concert, Spring Fling, and Black History Month.

Sports: There are 7 intercollegiate sports for men and 10 for women, and 10 intramural sports for men and 10 for women. Facilities include an indoor 6-lane swimming pool, an outdoor track, a weight-lifting gym, 2 multipurpose gyms, a sauna, steam baths, and dance studios, as well as playing fields, a 60-acre lake for fishing and canoeing, cross-country courses, bike trails, an all-weather track, and tennis, racquetball, and basketball courts. There are 9 club sports in addition to intramurals.

Disabled Students: 99% of the campus is accessible. Facilities include wheelchair ramps, elevators, special parking, specially equipped restrooms, special class scheduling, lowered drinking fountains, and lowered telephones.

Services: Counseling and information services are available, as is tutoring in most subjects. There is a reader service for the blind, and remedial math, reading, and writing. In addition, there is a skills center and a learning access program for learning-disabled students.

Campus Safety and Security: Measures include 24-hour foot and vehicle patrol, emergency notification system, self-defense education, and security escort services. There are emergency telephones, lighted pathways/sidewalks, and a fully commissioned police department.

Programs of Study: Stockton confers B.A., B.S., and B.S.N. degrees. Master's and doctoral degrees are also awarded. Bachelor's degrees are awarded in BIOLOGICAL SCIENCE (biochemistry, biology/biological science, and marine science), BUSINESS (accounting, banking and finance, business administration and management, and management science), COMMUNICATIONS AND THE ARTS (communications, dance, dramatic arts, fine arts, languages, literature, and music), COMPUTER AND PHYSICAL SCIENCE (chemistry, computer science, geology, information sciences and systems, mathematics, and physics), EDUCATION (education), ENGINEERING AND ENVIRONMENTAL DESIGN (computational sciences, environmental science, and preengineering), HEALTH PROFESSIONS (nursing, physical therapy, public health, and speech pathology/audiology), SOCIAL SCIENCE (anthropology, criminal justice, economics, history, liberal arts/general studies, philosophy, political science/government, psychology, and social work). Sciences is the strongest academically. Business, psychology, and criminal justice. are the largest.

Required: To graduate, students must earn 128 credit hours, with 32 in the general studies curriculum and maintain a minimum GPA of 2.0. 3 quantitative reasoning and 4 writing courses as well as freshman seminar are required.

Special: Stockton offers internships in all fields with a wide variety of companies, work-study with various government agencies and corporations, a Washington semester, independent study, and study abroad in 53 countries. Dual majors in all programs, student-designed majors, an accelerated degree in medicine and criminal justice, 3-2 engineering degrees with the New Jersey Institute of Technology and Rutgers University, and general studies degrees are also offered. Nondegree study, pass/fail options, and credit for life, military, and work experience are possible. There are 5 national honor societies and a freshman honors program.

Faculty/Classroom: 54% of faculty are male; 46% are female. No introductory courses are taught by graduate students. The average class size in an introductory lecture is 33; in a laboratory is 18; and in a regular course is 19.

Requirements: The SAT or ACT is required. In addition, applicants must be high school graduates; the GED is accepted. 16 academic credits are required, including 4 years in English, 3 each in math and social studies, 2 in science, and 4 additional years of any of the above or a foreign language, or both. An essay and an interview are recommended, and a portfolio or audition is necessary where appropriate. AP and CLEP credits are accepted. Important factors in the admissions decision are advanced placement or honors courses, leadership record, and evidence of special talent.

Procedure: Freshmen are admitted fall and spring. Entrance exams should be taken once in the junior year and again before January in the senior year. There is a rolling admissions plan. Applications should be filed by December 1 for spring entry. The fall 2009 application fee was $50. Notification is sent on a rolling basis. Applications are accepted online. A waiting list is maintained.

Transfer: 1088 transfer students enrolled in a recent year. Transfer students must have earned at least 16 credits at other colleges and must submit college and high school transcripts as well as SAT scores. 32 of 128 credits required for the bachelor's degree must be completed at Stockton.

Visiting: There are regularly scheduled orientations for prospective students, including academic advising and orientation. There are guides for informal visits and visitors may sit in on classes. To schedule a visit, contact Enrollment Management at (609) 652-4251.

Financial Aid: In a recent year, 77% of all full-time freshmen and 90% of continuing full-time students received some form of financial aid. 40% of all full-time freshmen and 41% of continuing full-time students received need-based aid. The average freshmen award was $11,772, with $8,170 ($15,396 maximum) from need-based scholarships or need-based grants; $3,702 ($9,900 maximum) from need-based self-help aid (loans and jobs); and $3,602 ($23,555 maximum) from other non-need-based awards and non-need-based scholarships. 16% of undergraduate students worked part-time. Average annual earnings from campus work were $1394. The average financial indebtedness of the 2009 graduate was $15,624. The FAFSA is required. Check with the school for current application deadlines.

International Students: There were 25 international students enrolled in a recent year. They must take the TOEFL. They must also take the SAT or ACT.

Computers: Wireless access is available. All students have access to the wireless network from their personally owned computers. All residential students have access to the campus network through a hard-wired Ethernet connection. All students have access to the network from 850 computers in 40 different computer labs. Three of these labs (64 computers) are open 24/7. The remaining labs are open 94 hours per week. All students may access the system 24 hours a day. There are no time limits and no fees.

Graduates: In a recent year, 1632 bachelor's degrees were awarded. The most popular majors were social science (30%), business and management (19%), and natural sciences (15%). 250 companies recruited on campus in 2008-2009. In an average class, 2% graduate in 3 years or less, 43% graduate in 4 years or less, 65% graduate in 5 years or less, and 67% graduate in 6 years or less. Of the 2008 graduating class, 34% were enrolled in graduate school within 6 months of graduation, and 83% were employed.

Admissions Contact: John Lacovelli, Interim Dean, Enrollment Management. E-Mail: *admissions@stockton.edu* Web: *www.stockton.edu*

RIDER UNIVERSITY
Rider College
D-3

Lawrenceville, NJ 08648-3099
(609) 896-5042
(800) 257-9026; (609) 895-6645

Full-time: 1605 men, 2469 women	**Faculty:** 228; IIA, +$
Part-time: 328 men, 489 women	**Ph.D.s:** 97%
Graduate: 364 men, 818 women	**Student/Faculty:** 17 to 1
Year: semesters, summer session	**Tuition:** $29,060
Application Deadline: open	**Room & Board:** $10,720
Freshman Class: 7372 applied, 5534 accepted, 1026 enrolled	
SAT CR/M/W: 510/510/520	**ACT:** 21 **COMPETITIVE**

Rider University, founded in 1865, is a private institution offering undergraduate programs in the areas of business administration, liberal arts, education, sciences, and continuing studies. Westminster Choir College, located in nearby Princeton, is Rider's fourth college. There are 4 undergraduate schools and 2 graduate schools. In addition to regional accreditation, Rider has baccalaureate program accreditation with AACSB and NCATE. The library contains 458,102 volumes, 1.1 million microform items, and 3,873 audio/video tapes/CDs/DVDs, and subscribes to 37,685 periodicals including electronic. Computerized library services include interlibrary loans, database searching, Internet access, and laptop Internet portals. Special learning facilities include a learning resource center, art gallery, radio station, TV station, journalism and sociology labs, and a holocaust/genocide center. The 280-acre campus is in a suburban area 3 miles north of Trenton and 7 miles south of Princeton. Including any residence halls, there are 39 buildings.

Student Life: 78% of undergraduates are from New Jersey. Others are from 35 states, 50 foreign countries, and Canada. 67% are white. 38% claim no religious affiliation; 31% Catholic; 20% Baptist, Congregational, Christian Scientist, Church of Christ. The average age of freshmen is 18; all undergraduates, 22. 20% do not continue beyond their first year; 60% remain to graduate.

Housing: 2515 students can be accommodated in college housing, which includes single-sex and coed dorms and on-campus apartments. In addition, there are special-interest houses, fraternity houses, learning community, wellness, quiet, science area, and first-year experience housing. On-campus housing is available on a lottery system for upperclassmen. 56% of students live on campus; of those, 50% remain on campus on weekends. All students may keep cars.

Activities: 4% of men belong to 4 local and 4 national fraternities; 9% of women belong to 8 national sororities. There are 130 groups on campus, including art, band, cheerleading, choir, chorale, chorus, computers, dance, drama, environmental, ethnic, gay, honors, international, jazz band, literary magazine, musical threater, opera, orchestra, pep band, photography, political, professional, religious, social, social service, student government, symphony, and yearbook. Popular campus events include Cranberry Fest, Family Day, and Unity Day.

Sports: There are 10 intercollegiate sports for men and 10 for women, and 10 intramural sports for men and 6 for women. Facilities include a recreation center with basketball, volleyball, and tennis courts, and an elevated jogging/walking track, and a fitness center with cardio equipment, weight room machines, and free weights.

Disabled Students: 75% of the campus is accessible. Facilities include wheelchair ramps, elevators, special parking, specially equipped rest rooms, special class scheduling, lowered drinking fountains, and lowered telephones.

Services: Counseling and information services are available, as is tutoring in most subjects. There is remedial math, reading, and writing.

Campus Safety and Security: Measures include 24-hour foot and vehicle patrol, emergency notification system, self-defense education, and security escort services. There are shuttle buses, emergency telephones, lighted pathways/sidewalks, a shuttle car, a staffed kiosk at the entrance, a security system in residence halls, video camera surveillance, bike patrol, and a property ID program.

Programs of Study: Rider confers B.A., B.S., and B.S.B.A. degrees. Associates and master's degrees are also awarded. Bachelor's degrees are awarded in BIOLOGICAL SCIENCE (biochemistry, biology/biological science, and marine science), BUSINESS (accounting, banking and finance, business administration and management, business economics, human resources, international business management, management science, marketing/retailing/merchandising, and office supervision and management), COMMUNICATIONS AND THE ARTS (advertising, communications, dance, dramatic arts, English, English literature, fine arts, French, German, journalism, multimedia, music, piano/organ, public relations, Russian, Spanish, and voice), COMPUTER AND PHYSICAL SCIENCE (actuarial science, chemistry, geoscience, information sciences and systems, mathematics, and physics), EDUCATION (business education, early childhood education, elementary education, English education, foreign languages education, marketing and distribution education, mathematics education, music education, science education, secondary education, and social studies education), ENGINEERING AND ENVIRONMENTAL DESIGN (environmental science), HEALTH

PROFESSIONS (premedicine), SOCIAL SCIENCE (American studies, biopsychology, economics, history, liberal arts/general studies, philosophy, political science/government, prelaw, psychology, and sociology). Elementary education, accounting, and business administration are the largest.

Required: To graduate, all students must maintain a minimum GPA of 2.0 while taking 120 semester hours. Students also must fulfill core curriculum requirements, including 9 hours in humanities, 7 to 8 in science, 6 each in English writing and foreign language (may be waived if proficiency is demonstrated), social sciences/communications, and history, and 3 in math. 30 to 76 credits are required in the major. A thesis is required in the honors program and some science majors.

Special: Internships in many programs, a co-op program in retail marketing, work-study, study abroad in 14 countries, a B.A.-B.S. degree in all liberal arts and sciences, dual majors in education, a liberal studies degree, and nondegree study are possible. There are 24 national honor societies, a freshman honors program, and 17 departmental honors programs.

Faculty/Classroom: 53% of faculty are male; 47% are female. All teach undergraduates. No introductory courses are taught by graduate students. The average class size in an introductory lecture is 26; in a laboratory is 14; and in a regular course is 20.

Admissions: 75% of the 2009-2010 applicants were accepted. The SAT scores for the 2009-2010 freshman class were: Critical Reading-- 40% below 500, 45% between 500 and 599, 14% between 600 and 700, and 1% above 700; Math--36% below 500, 45% between 500 and 599, 18% between 600 and 700, and 1% above 700; Writing--39% below 500, 45% between 500 and 599, 15% between 600 and 700, and 1% above 700. The ACT scores were 36% below 21, 34% between 21 and 23, 24% between 24 and 26, 4% between 27 and 28, and 2% above 28. 49% of the current freshmen were in the top fifth of their class; 65% were in the top two fifths.

Requirements: The SAT or ACT is required. In addition, applicants need 16 Carnegie units, including 4 years of English and 2 of math. 3 units of math are required for prospective math, science, and business majors. An essay is recommended. An audition is required for theater scholarships. The GED is accepted. AP and CLEP credits are accepted. Important factors in the admissions decision are advanced placement or honors courses, extracurricular activities record, and leadership record.

Procedure: Freshmen are admitted fall and spring. Entrance exams should be taken by January of the senior year. There are early decision, deferred admissions and rolling admissions plans. Early decision applications should be filed by November 15; regular application deadlines are open. Application fee is $50. Notification of early decision is sent December 15; regular decision, sent on a rolling basis. Applications are accepted on-line. A waiting list is maintained.

Transfer: 241 transfer students enrolled in 2008-2009. A GPA of 2.5 or better is required for applicants. If students have fewer than 30 credits, they also must submit high school transcripts and SAT scores. An essay or personal statement is required, and an interview is recommended. 30 of 120 credits required for the bachelor's degree must be completed at Rider.

Visiting: There are regularly scheduled orientations for prospective students, including 3 open houses, Saturday information sessions and other programs that consist of a welcome, a campus tour, and a variety of formal and informal activities to meet faculty, staff, current students, and alumni. There are guides for informal visits and visitors may sit in on classes. To schedule a visit, contact the Office of Admissions at (609) 896-5042.

Financial Aid: In 2009-2010, 77% of all full-time freshmen and 70% of continuing full-time students received some form of financial aid. 76% of all full-time freshmen and 68% of continuing full-time students received need-based aid. The average freshmen award was $22,721, with $3,590 from other forms of aid. The FAFSA is required. The priority date for freshman financial aid applications for fall entry is March 1. The deadline for filing freshman financial aid applications for fall entry is June 30.

International Students: There are 74 international students enrolled. The school actively recruits these students. They must take the TOEFL with a minimum score of 550 on the paper-based TOEFL (PBT) or 80 on the Internet-based version (iBT). They must also take the SAT or ACT.

Computers: Wireless is available campus wide. All students may access the system during regular lab hours and at any time in residence halls. There are no time limits. The annual fee is $330 for full-time students and $35 per course for part-time students. All business students must have a personal computer.

Graduates: From July 1, 2008 to June 30, 2009, 865 bachelor's degrees were awarded. The most popular majors were business (30%), education (16%), and English (14%). 150 companies recruited on campus in 2008-2009. In an average class, 47% graduate in 4 years or less, 58% graduate in 5 years or less, and 60% graduate in 6 years or less.

Admissions Contact: Susan C. Christian, Director of Admissions. A campus DVD is available. E-Mail: *admissions@rider.edu* Web: *www.rider.edu*

ROWAN UNIVERSITY C-4
Glassboro, NJ 08028

(855) 256-4200
(800) 447-1165; (856) 256-4430

Full-time: 4114 men, 4221 women	**Faculty:** 380
Part-time: 469 men, 861 women	**Ph.D.s:** 82%
Graduate: 419 men, 922 women	**Student/Faculty:** 15 to 1
Year: semesters, summer session	**Tuition:** $11,234 ($18,308)
Application Deadline: n/av	**Room & Board:** $10,000
Freshman Class: n/av	
SAT: required	**VERY COMPETITIVE**

Rowan University was founded in 1923 as a public institution offering undergraduate programs in the arts and sciences, business administration, communication, education, fine and performing arts, and engineering. There are 6 undergraduate schools and one graduate school. In addition to regional accreditation, Rowan has baccalaureate program accreditation with AACSB, ABET, CSAB, NASAD, NASDTEC, NASM, and NCATE. The library contains 345,926 volumes, 497,842 microform items, 47,525 audio/video tapes/CDs/DVDs, and subscribes to 5,789 periodicals including electronic. Computerized library services include interlibrary loans, database searching, and Internet access. Special learning facilities include a learning resource center, art gallery, planetarium, radio station, TV station, an observatory. The 200-acre campus is in a suburban area 20 miles southeast of Philadelphia. Including any residence halls, there are 41 buildings.

Student Life: 95% of undergraduates are from New Jersey. Students are from 11 states, 25 foreign countries, and Canada. 65% are from public schools. 79% are white. The average age of freshmen is 19; all undergraduates, 21. 14% do not continue beyond their first year; 62% remain to graduate.

Housing: 2300 students can be accommodated in college housing, which includes coed dorms, on-campus apartments, off-campus apartments, and married student housing. In addition, there are honors houses, language houses, special-interest houses, and healthy living facilities. On-campus housing is guaranteed for the freshman year only and is available on a lottery system for upperclassmen. Priority is given to out-of-town students. 60% of students live on campus; of those, 85% remain on campus on weekends. Alcohol is not permitted. Upperclassmen may keep cars.

Activities: 5% of men belong to 1 local and 12 national fraternities; 6% of women belong to 5 local and 8 national sororities. There are 150 groups on campus, including and concert band, art, band, cheerleading, chess, choir, chorale, chorus, computers, dance, drama, ethnic, film, gay, honors, international, jazz band, literary magazine, music ensembles, musical theater, newspaper, opera, orchestra, pep band, photography, political, professional, radio and TV, religious, social, social service, student government, and symphony. Popular campus events include Spring Fling, Unity Day, and The Big Event.

Sports: There are 8 intercollegiate sports for men and 10 for women, and 7 intramural sports for men and 6 for women. Facilities include a 3000-seat stadium, a 1800-seat gym, a 1000-seat auditorium, a swimming pool, tennis courts, and playing fields.

Disabled Students: 95% of the campus is accessible. Facilities include wheelchair ramps, elevators, special parking, specially equipped restrooms, special class scheduling, lowered drinking fountains, lowered telephones, and special housing.

Services: Counseling and information services are available, as is tutoring in every subject. There is remedial math, reading, and writing.

Campus Safety and Security: Measures include 24-hour foot and vehicle patrol, self-defense education, and security escort services. There are shuttle buses, emergency telephones, and lighted pathways/ sidewalks.

Programs of Study: Rowan confers B.A., B.S., B.F.A., and B.M. degrees. Master's and doctoral degrees are also awarded. Bachelor's degrees are awarded in BIOLOGICAL SCIENCE (biology/biological science), BUSINESS (accounting, business administration and management, marketing/retailing/merchandising, personnel management, and small business management), COMMUNICATIONS AND THE ARTS (art, broadcasting, communications, dramatic arts, English, fine arts, journalism, music, Spanish, and speech/debate/rhetoric), COMPUTER AND PHYSICAL SCIENCE (chemistry, computer science, mathematics, and physics), EDUCATION (early childhood education, elementary education, foreign languages education, music education, and science education), ENGINEERING AND ENVIRONMENTAL DESIGN (civil engineering and engineering), HEALTH PROFESSIONS (health), SOCIAL SCIENCE (criminal justice, economics, geography, history, liberal arts/general studies, political science/government, psychology, and sociology). Engineering, communications, and business administration are the strongest academically. Elementary education, communications, and business administration are the largest.

Required: General education requirements include 12 to 18 semester hours of social and behavioral sciences, 12 to 16 of science and math, 6 to 9 of communications, 6 of fine and performing arts, and 3 to 6 of history/humanities/languages/arts. Students must also complete 6 semester hours of writing, 3 of phys ed, lab science, computer literacy, and math. Students also must attend the Roman Seminar. The bachelor's degree requires completion of 120 to 132 semester hours, including 30 to 39 in a major field, with a minimum GPA of 2.0.

Special: Students may study abroad in 50 countries. Internships are available in all majors both with and without pay. Rowan also offers accelerated degree programs and 3-2 degrees in optometry, podiatry, and pharmacy. There are dual majors, pass/fail options, and credit for military experience. There are 12 national honor societies, a freshman honors program, and 100 departmental honors programs.

Faculty/Classroom: 58% of faculty are male; 42% are female. All teach undergraduates. No introductory courses are taught by graduate students. The average class size in an introductory lecture is 22; in a laboratory is 16; and in a regular course is 22.

Admissions: n/av

Requirements: The SAT is required. In addition, students are required to score an 1080, or no less than 500 on either part. Students submitting ACT scores should have a minimum composite score of 23. Applicants must be graduates of accredited secondary schools or have earned a GED. Rowan requires 16 academic credits or Carnegie units, including 4 in English, 3 each in math and college preparatory electives, and 2 each in foreign language, history, and lab science. A portfolio or audition is required for specific majors. A GPA of 3.0 is required. AP and CLEP credits are accepted. Important factors in the admissions decision are advanced placement or honors courses, evidence of special talent, and leadership record.

Procedure: Freshmen are admitted fall and spring. Entrance exams should be taken by May or June of the junior year, or by December of the sen. There is a deferred admissions plan. Applications should be filed by November 1 for spring entry, along with a $50 fee. Notifications are sent April 15. Applications are accepted on-line. 100 applicants were on a waiting list, 40 were accepted.

Transfer: 962 transfer students enrolled in 2008-2009. Applicants must have a minimum GPA of 2.0, but should present a GPA of 2.5 to be competitive. An associate degree is recommended. Students who have earned fewer than 24 semester hours must also submit a high school transcript and SAT I results. 30 of 120 credits required for the bachelor's degree must be completed at Rowan.

Visiting: There are regularly scheduled orientations for prospective students, a 2-day summer program providing schedule confirmation/adjustment, student activities updates, and workshops for students and parents. There are guides for informal visits and visitors may sit in on classes. To schedule a visit, contact the Admissions Office at admissions@rowan.edu.

Financial Aid: In 2009-2010, 70% of all full-time freshmen and 70% of continuing full-time students received some form of financial aid. 81% of all full-time freshmen and 81% of continuing full-time students received need-based aid. The average freshmen award was $8,793. 10% of undergraduate students work part-time. Average annual earnings from campus work are $1200. The FAFSA is required. The priority date for freshman financial aid applications for fall entry is January 1. The deadline for filing freshman financial aid applications for fall entry is March 15.

International Students: The school actively recruits these students. They must take the TOEFL. They must also take the SAT or ACT. Applicants from English-speaking countries must also submit an SAT I score.

Computers: Wireless access is available. All students may access the system. 24 hours a day. There are no time limits and no fees. Students enrolled in engineering must have a personal computer.

Graduates: From July 1, 2008 to June 30, 2009, 2096 bachelor's degrees were awarded. The most popular majors were business administration (18%), communications (13%), and elementary education (11%). 106 companies recruited on campus in 2008-2009. In an average class, 20% graduate in 4 years or less, 48% graduate in 5 years or less, and 55% graduate in 6 years or less. Of the 2008 graduating class, 95% were enrolled in graduate school within 6 months of graduation, and 95% were employed.

Admissions Contact: Albert Betts, Director of Admissions. E-Mail: *admissions@rowan.edu* Web: *www.rowan.edu*

RUTGERS, THE STATE UNIVERSITY OF NEW JERSEY

The Rutgers, the State University of New Jersey, established in 1766, is a public system in New Jersey. It is governed by a board of governors, whose chief administrator is the president. The primary goal of the system is instruction, research, and service. The main priorities are to continue development as a distinguished comprehensive public university, to enhance undergraduate education, to strengthen graduate education and research, and to develop and improve programs to serve society New Jersey's needs. Profiles of the 4-year campuses are included in this section.

RUTGERS, THE STATE UNIVERSITY OF NEW JERSEY/CAMDEN CAMPUS

C-4

Camden, NJ 08102-1461	(856) 225-6104
Full-time: 1568 men, 1769 women	Faculty: 252; IIA, ++$
Part-time: 271 men, 459 women	Ph.Ds: 99%
Graduate: 917 men, 743 women	Student/Faculty: 13 to 1
Year: semesters, summer session	Tuition: $11,698 ($22,330)
Application Deadline: open	Room & Board: $9788
Freshman Class: n/av	
SAT CR/M/W: 510/560/520	ACT: required

VERY COMPETITIVE

Rutgers, The State University of New Jersey/Camden Campus, founded in 1927, comprises 3 undergraduate, degree-granting schools: College of the Arts and Sciences, University College-Camden, and the School of Business-Camden. Each school has individual requirements, policies, and fees. There are also 3 graduate schools. In addition to regional accreditation, Camden has baccalaureate program accreditation with AACSB and CSWE. The 2 libraries contain 729,987 volumes, 974,491 microform items, and 591 audio/video tapes/CDs/DVDs, and subscribe to 12,325 periodicals including electronic. Computerized library services include interlibrary loans, database searching, and Internet access. Special learning facilities include a learning resource center, art gallery, and radio station. The 31-acre campus is in an urban area 1 mile east of Philadelphia. Including any residence halls, there are 34 buildings.

Student Life: 98% of undergraduates are from New Jersey. Others are from 17 states and 11 foreign countries. 62% are white; 16% African American. The average age of freshmen is 18; all undergraduates, 22. 19% do not continue beyond their first year; 59% remain to graduate.

Housing: 478 students can be accommodated in college housing, which includes coed dorms and on-campus apartments. 89% of students commute. Alcohol is not permitted.

Activities: There are no fraternities or sororities. There are 70 groups on campus, including computers, drama, ethnic, gay, honors, international, literary magazine, political, professional, radio and TV, religious, social, social service, and student government. Popular campus events include Raptor Day, Springfest, and Bill Maher Lecture.

Sports: There are 6 intercollegiate sports for men and 6 for women.

Disabled Students: 95% of the campus is accessible. Facilities include wheelchair ramps, elevators, special parking, specially equipped restrooms, special class scheduling, lowered drinking fountains, lowered telephones, and special housing. Facilities vary from building to building, but all classes are scheduled in accessible locations for disabled students.

Services: Counseling and information services are available, as is tutoring in introductory classes. There is a reader service for the blind, and remedial math, reading, and writing.

Campus Safety and Security: Measures include 24-hour foot and vehicle patrol, emergency notification system, self-defense education, and security escort services. There are shuttle buses, emergency telephones, and lighted pathways/sidewalks. The police department is supplemented by security guards.

Programs of Study: Camden confers B.A., B.S., and B.H.M. degrees. Master's degrees are also awarded. Bachelor's degrees are awarded in BIOLOGICAL SCIENCE (biochemistry and biology/biological science), BUSINESS (accounting, banking and finance, hospitality management services, management science, and marketing/retailing/merchandising), COMMUNICATIONS AND THE ARTS (art, art history and appreciation, dramatic arts, English, French, German, music, and Spanish), COMPUTER AND PHYSICAL SCIENCE (chemistry, computer science, mathematics, physics, and science), HEALTH PROFESSIONS (medical laboratory technology and nursing), SOCIAL SCIENCE (African American studies, criminal justice, economics, history, liberal arts/general studies, philosophy, political science/government, psychology, religion, social work, sociology, and urban studies). Psychology, criminal justice, and biology are the largest.

Required: To graduate, students must complete 120 credits, with 30 to 48 in the major, and maintain a minimum GPA of 2.0. A core curriculum of 60 credits is required, including 3 credits each in literary masterpieces, art, music or theater arts, and a foreign language, with an additional 3 credits in English or a foreign language, and 3 credits in math, with an additional 3 credits in math, computer science, or statistics. 1 interdisciplinary course is required, as are 9 credits from social science disciplines, 6 credits in English composition, 6 credits in history, 6 credits in the natural science disciplines, and an additional 9 credits in courses offered outside the major department.

Special: The university offers co-op programs, cross-registration, internships, accelerated degrees, student-designed majors, dual majors, non-degree study, and pass/fail options. Students may study abroad in 28 countries. There is an 8-year B.A./M.D. program with the University of Medicine and Dentistry of New Jersey and many combined bachelor's and master's programs. There are programs in distance learning, English as a Second Language, honors, and independent study. There is a freshman honors program.

Faculty/Classroom: 61% of faculty are male; 39% are female. No introductory courses are taught by graduate students. The average class size in an introductory lecture is 30; in a laboratory, 20; and in a regular course, 30.

Admissions: The SAT scores for the 2009-2010 freshman class were: Critical Reading--26% below 500, 49% between 500 and 599, 20% between 600 and 700, and 4% above 700; Math--20% below 500, 49% between 500 and 599, 26% between 600 and 700, and 5% above 700. 31% of the current freshmen were in the top fifth of their class; 63% were in the top two fifths.

Requirements: The SAT or ACT is required, except for students who have been out of high school for 2 years or more. SAT Subject tests are required of students without a high school diploma from an accredited high school and from some GED holders. A high school diploma is required; the GED is accepted. Students must have completed a general college-preparatory program, including 16 academic credits or Carnegie units, with 4 years of English, 3 years of math (4 recommended), and 2 years each of a foreign language and science, plus 5 in electives. AP and CLEP credits are accepted. Important factors in the admissions decision are advanced placement or honors courses, evidence of special talent, and leadership record.

Procedure: Freshmen are admitted in the fall. Entrance exams should be taken by December of senior year, but this is not required. There are early admissions and rolling admissions plans. Application deadlines are open. Application fee is $60. Notifications are sent March 1. Applications are accepted on-line. A waiting list is maintained.

Transfer: 398 transfer students enrolled in 2008-2009. Applicants must have a minimum of 12 credit hours. Grades of C or better in courses that correspond in content and credit to those offered by the college transfer for credit. Transfer students are admitted in the fall and spring semesters. All high school and previous college transcripts are required. 30 of 120 credits required for the bachelor's degree must be completed at Camden.

Visiting: There are regularly scheduled orientations for prospective students, including an information session with an admissions officer and a campus tour. Visitors may sit in on classes. To schedule a visit, contact the Admissions Office (Camden).

Financial Aid: In 2009-2010, 93% of all full-time freshmen and 93% of continuing full-time students received some form of financial aid. 69% of all full-time freshmen and 73% of continuing full-time students received need-based aid. The average freshman award was $13,051. Need-based scholarships and need-based grants averaged $11,001; need-based self-help aid (loans and jobs) averaged $7453; and non-need-based awards and non-need-based scholarships averaged $8539. Average annual earnings from campus work are $1424. The average financial indebtedness of the 2009 graduate was $25,119. The FAFSA is required. The priority date for freshman financial aid applications for fall entry is March 15. The deadline for filing freshman financial aid applications for fall entry is open.

International Students: International students must take the TOEFL with a score of 550 on the paper-based TOEFL (PBT) or 79 on the Internet-based version (iBT), or the IELTS, scoring 7, and also take the SAT or ACT.

Computers: All students may access the system. Public labs are open whenever the building housing the lab is open. There are no time limits. The fee is $200.

Graduates: In a recent year, 873 bachelor's degrees were awarded. The most popular majors were business/marketing (24%), psychology (15%), and social sciences (12%). In an average class, 43% graduate in 5 years or less and 52% graduate in 6 years or less.

Admissions Contact: Dr. Deborah Bowles, Associate Provost for Enrollment Management. Web: *www.rutgers.edu*

RUTGERS, THE STATE UNIVERSITY OF NEW JERSEY/NEW BRUNSWICK/PISCATAWAY CAMPUS

D-3

Piscataway, NJ 08854   (732) 932-4636; (732) 445-0237

Full-time: 14,239 men, 13,349 women	**Faculty:** 1678; I, +$
Part-time: 757 men, 750 women	**Ph.D.s:** 99%
Graduate: 3155 men, 5114 women	**Student/Faculty:** 14 to 1
Year: semesters, summer session	**Tuition:** $11,886 ($22,518)
Application Deadline: open	**Room & Board:** $10,676
Freshman Class: 28,624 applied, 17,598 accepted, 5835 enrolled	
SAT CR/M/W: 580/620/590	**ACT:** required
	HIGHLY COMPETITIVE

Rutgers, The State University of New Jersey, New Brunswick Campus, founded in 1766, comprises 9 undergraduate units. Students in New Brunswick enroll in the School of Arts and Sciences, the liberal arts college, and/or in 1 of 8 professional schools: School of Environmental and Biological Sciences (formerly Cook College); Mason Gross School of the Arts; Rutgers Business School: Undergraduate-New Brunswick; School of Communication, Information, and Library Studies; School of Engineering; Edward J. Bloustein School of Planning and Public Policy; the School of Management and Labor Relations; or Ernest Mario School of

Pharmacy. Each school within the New Brunswick campus has individual requirements, policies, and fees. There are also 10 graduate schools. In addition to regional accreditation, RU-New Brunswick has baccalaureate program accreditation with AACSB, ABET, ASLA, CSWE, and NASM. The 13 libraries contain 5.1 million volumes, 357,753 microform items, and 110,808 audio/video tapes/CDs/DVDs, and subscribe to 195,296 periodicals including electronic. Computerized library services include interlibrary loans, database searching, and Internet access. Special learning facilities include a learning resource center, art gallery, radio station, TV station, geology museum, and various research centers. The 2683-acre campus is in a small town 33 miles south of New York City. Including any residence halls, there are 647 buildings.

Student Life: 93% of undergraduates are from New Jersey. Others are from 45 states, 54 foreign countries, and Canada. 51% are white; 25% Asian American. The average age of freshmen is 18; all undergraduates, 21. 8% do not continue beyond their first year; 75% remain to graduate.

Housing: 14,071 students can be accommodated in college housing, which includes single-sex and coed dorms and married student housing. In addition, there are language and cultural houses, special-interest houses, fraternity houses, sorority houses, substance-free house, Math/Science/Engineering House for women, first-year residence, transfer center, and residence for single mothers and children. 50% of students commute. Alcohol is not permitted. Upperclassmen may keep cars.

Activities: 9% of men belong to 27 national fraternities; there are 15 national sororities. There are more than 400 groups on campus, including art, band, cheerleading, chess, choir, chorale, chorus, computers, dance, drama, drill team, ethnic, film, gay, honors, international, jazz band, literary magazine, marching band, newspaper, opera, orchestra, pep band, photography, political, professional, radio and TV, religious, social, social service, student government, symphony, and yearbook. Popular campus events include Ag Field Day, UC Festival, and theater trips.

Sports: There are 9 intercollegiate sports for men and 13 for women.

Disabled Students: Facilities include wheelchair ramps, elevators, special parking, specially equipped restrooms, special class scheduling, lowered drinking fountains, lowered telephones, and special housing. Facilities vary from building to building, but all classes are scheduled in accessible locations for disabled students.

Services: Counseling and information services are available, as is tutoring in most subjects, with specific assistance in difficult first- and second-level courses, as well as reading assistance. There is remedial math, reading, and writing. There is computer software with aids, library technology, and assistance.

Campus Safety and Security: Measures include 24-hour foot and vehicle patrol, self-defense education, security escort services, shuttle buses, emergency telephones, and lighted pathways/sidewalks. The police department is supplemented by security guards and student safety officers.

Programs of Study: RU-New Brunswick confers B.A., B.S., B.F.A., and B.Mus. degrees. Master's and doctoral degrees are also awarded. Bachelor's degrees are awarded in AGRICULTURE (agriculture, animal science, natural resource management, and plant science), BIOLOGICAL SCIENCE (biochemistry, biology/biological science, biomathematics, biotechnology, botany, cell biology, ecology, evolutionary biology, genetics, marine science, microbiology, molecular biology, nutrition, and physiology), BUSINESS (accounting, banking and finance, business administration and management, labor studies, management information systems, management science, and marketing/retailing/merchandising), COMMUNICATIONS AND THE ARTS (art, art history and appreciation, Chinese, classics, communications, comparative literature, dance, dramatic arts, East Asian languages and literature, English, French, German, Italian, journalism, Latin, linguistics, music, Portuguese, Russian, Spanish, and visual and performing arts), COMPUTER AND PHYSICAL SCIENCE (astrophysics, chemistry, computer science, geology, information sciences and systems, mathematics, physics, and statistics), ENGINEERING AND ENVIRONMENTAL DESIGN (bioresource engineering, ceramic engineering, chemical engineering, civil engineering, electrical/electronics engineering, engineering and applied science, environmental science, industrial engineering, and mechanical engineering), HEALTH PROFESSIONS (biomedical science, exercise science, medical technology, pharmacy, and public health), SOCIAL SCIENCE (African American studies, American studies, anthropology, Asian/Oriental studies, criminal justice, economics, food science, geography, Hispanic American studies, history, humanities, Judaic studies, Latin American studies, medieval studies, Middle Eastern studies, philosophy, political science/government, psychology, religion, Russian and Slavic studies, social work, sociology, urban studies, and women's studies). Business, engineering, and biological sciences are the largest.

Required: To graduate, students must complete 120 credits, with a minimum GPA of 2.0. A liberal arts core requirement includes writing (6 credits), quantitative reasoning (6 credits), natural sciences (6 credits), social sciences and humanities (12 credits), diversity (3 credits), and global awareness (3 credits). Check with the individual college for specific program requirements.

Special: The college offers co-op programs, cross registration, and study abroad in 28 countries. A Washington semester, work-study, accelerated degree programs, B.A.-B.S. degrees, student-designed majors, nondegree study, and pass/fail options are available. There is an 8-year B.A. or B.S./M.D. program with the University of Medicine and Dentistry New Jersey and several dual-degree (5-year and 6-year) programs. There are 2 national honor societies, including Phi Beta Kappa, and a freshman honors program.

Faculty/Classroom: 58% of faculty are male; 42% are female. No introductory courses are taught by graduate students. The average class size in an introductory lecture is 30; in a laboratory, 20; and in a regular course, 30.

Admissions: 61% of the 2009-2010 applicants were accepted. The SAT scores for the 2009-2010 freshman class were: Critical Reading--11% below 500, 49% between 500 and 599, 31% between 600 and 700, and 9% above 700; Math--6% below 500, 33% between 500 and 599, 42% between 600 and 700, and 19% above 700; Writing--17% below 500, 55% between 500 and 599, 22% between 600 and 700, and 6% above 700. 72% of the current freshmen were in the top fifth of their class; 95% were in the top two fifths.

Requirements: The SAT or ACT is required. In addition, a high school diploma is required. The GED is accepted. Students must have completed a general college-preparatory program, including 16 academic credits or Carnegie units, with 4 years of English, 3 years of math (4 recommended), including algebra I and II and geometry, 2 years each of a foreign language and science, and 5 in electives. Engineering students need 4 years of math and must take chemistry and physics; nursing and pharmacy students must take biology and chemistry. SAT Subject tests are required for students without a high school diploma from an accredited high school and from some GED holders. AP and CLEP credits are accepted. Important factors in the admissions decision are evidence of special talent, extracurricular activities record, and ability to finance college education.

Procedure: Freshmen are admitted in the fall. Entrance exams should be taken December of senior year but this is not required. There are early admissions and rolling admissions plans. Application deadlines are open. Application fee is $65. Notifications are sent March 1. Applications are accepted on-line. A waiting list is maintained.

Transfer: 1477 transfer students enrolled in 2008-2009. Applicants must have a minimum of 12 credit hours earned. High school and college transcripts are required. Transfers are admitted in the fall or spring. 30 of 120 credits required for the bachelor's degree must be completed at RU-New Brunswick.

Visiting: There are regularly scheduled orientations for prospective students, including a preadmission orientation. To schedule a visit, contact University Undergraduate Admissions.

Financial Aid: In 2009-2010, 88% of all full-time freshmen and 86% of continuing full-time students received some form of financial aid. 59% of all full-time freshmen and 60% of continuing full-time students received need-based aid. The average freshman award was $15,306. Need-based scholarships and need-based grants averaged $9882; need-based self-help aid (loans and jobs) averaged $6479; non-need-based athletic scholarships averaged $11,798; and other non-need-based awards and non-need-based scholarships averaged $6300. Average annual earnings from campus work are $1324. The average financial indebtedness of the 2009 graduate was $24,687. The FAFSA is required. The priority date for freshman financial aid applications for fall entry is March 15.

International Students: They must take the TOEFL with a score of 550 on the paper-based TOEFL (PBT) or 79 on the Internet-based version (iBT), or the IELTS, scoring 7.

Computers: Wireless access is available. All students may access the system 24 hours per day. There are no time limits. The fee is $283.

Graduates: From July 1, 2008 to June 30, 2009, 5752 bachelor's degrees were awarded. The most popular majors were social sciences (17%), psychology (11%), and biological/life sciences (10%). 1000 companies recruited on campus in 2008-2009. In an average class, 69% graduate in 5 years or less and 75% graduate in 6 years or less.

Admissions Contact: Office of University Undergraduate Admissions
Web: *www.rutgers.edu*

RUTGERS, THE STATE UNIVERSITY OF NEW JERSEY/NEWARK CAMPUS   E-2

Newark, NJ 07102-1897 (973) 353-5205; (973) 353-1440

Full-time: 2705 men, 3049 women	**Faculty:** 447; I, +$
Part-time: 697 men, 856 women	**Ph.D.s:** 99%
Graduate: 2308 men, 1885 women	**Student/Faculty:** 13 to 1
Year: semesters, summer session	**Tuition:** $11,414 ($22,046)
Application Deadline: open	**Room & Board:** $11,155
Freshman Class: 12,462 applied, 7430 accepted, 872 enrolled	
SAT CR/M/W: 510/560/520	**ACT:** required
	VERY COMPETITIVE

Rutgers, The State University of New Jersey/Newark Campus, founded in 1930, comprises 4 undergraduate, degree-granting schools: Newark College of Arts and Sciences, University College-Newark, Rutgers Business School: Undergraduate-Newark, and College of Nursing. Each school has individual requirements, policies, and fees. There are also 4 graduate schools. In addition to regional accreditation, RU-Newark has baccalaureate program accreditation with AACSB, CSWE, and NASM. The 4 libraries contain 1 million volumes, 1.5 million microform items, and 42,504 audio/video tapes/CDs/DVDs, and subscribe to 23,731 periodicals including electronic. Computerized library services include interlibrary loans, database searching, and Internet access. Special learning facilities include a learning resource center, art gallery, radio station, molecular and behavioral neuroscience center, and institutes of jazz and animal behavior. The 348-acre campus is in an urban area 7 miles west of New York City. Including any residence halls, there are 33 buildings.

Student Life: 97% of undergraduates are from New Jersey. Others are from 27 states, 35 foreign countries, and Canada. 27% are white; 24% Asian American; 20% Hispanic; 18% African American. The average age of freshmen is 18; all undergraduates, 23. 14% do not continue beyond their first year; 59% remain to graduate.

Housing: 1255 students can be accommodated in college housing, which includes coed dorms and on-campus apartments. In addition, there are fraternity houses. 83% of students commute. Alcohol is not permitted.

Activities: There are no fraternities or sororities. There are 85 groups on campus, including chess, chorale, chorus, drama, newspaper, outreach, radio and TV, and student government. Popular campus events include Black History month, Honors convocation, and Alpha Sigma Lambda.

Sports: There are 5 intercollegiate sports for men and 5 for women.

Disabled Students: 80% of the campus is accessible. Facilities include wheelchair ramps, elevators, special parking, specially equipped restrooms, special class scheduling, lowered drinking fountains, lowered telephones, and special housing. Facilities vary from building to building, but all classes are scheduled in accessible locations for disabled students.

Services: Counseling and information services are available, as is tutoring in most subjects. There is a reader service for the blind, and remedial math, reading, and writing.

Campus Safety and Security: Measures include 24-hour foot and vehicle patrol, self-defense education, and security escort services. There are shuttle buses, emergency telephones, and lighted pathways/sidewalks. Security guards assist Rutgers police in providing public safety services. There is also a student marshal program.

Programs of Study: RU-Newark confers B.A., B.S., and B.F.A. degrees. Master's and doctoral degrees are also awarded. Bachelor's degrees are awarded in BIOLOGICAL SCIENCE (biology/biological science, botany, and zoology), BUSINESS (accounting, banking and finance, business administration and management, management science, and marketing/retailing/merchandising), COMMUNICATIONS AND THE ARTS (art, dramatic arts, English, French, German, journalism, music, Portuguese, Spanish, and visual and performing arts), COMPUTER AND PHYSICAL SCIENCE (applied mathematics, applied physics, chemistry, computer science, geology, geoscience, information sciences and systems, mathematics, and physics), ENGINEERING AND ENVIRONMENTAL DESIGN (environmental science), HEALTH PROFESSIONS (allied health, clinical science, and nursing), SOCIAL SCIENCE (African American studies, American studies, anthropology, criminal justice, Eastern European studies, economics, history, medieval studies, philosophy, political science/government, psychology, Puerto Rican studies, science and society, social work, sociology, and women's studies). Accounting, biology, and nursing are the largest.

Required: To graduate, students must complete 124 credits with a minimum GPA of 2.0. Distribution requirements include 8 credits in natural science and math or 3 courses in nonlab science, math, or computer science; 6 credits each in history, literature, social sciences, humanities, and fine arts; 1 course in critical thinking; and 15 credits of electives. All students must take English composition and demonstrate math proficiency either by exam or by successfully completing a college algebra course or any other advanced course in math, a college calculus course (with a grade of C or better), or a precalculus course (with a grade of B or better).

Special: Students may cross-register with the New Jersey Institute of Technology and the University of Medicine and Dentistry of New Jersey. Internships are available. The school offers study abroad in 28 countries, accelerated degree programs in business administration and criminal justice, co-op programs, independent study, distance learning, English as a second language, dual majors, student-designed majors, nondegree study, and pass/fail options. Contact the school for information on the Honors College. There are 12 national honor societies, including Phi Beta Kappa, and a freshman honors program.

Faculty/Classroom: 57% of faculty are male; 43% are female. All teach and do research. No introductory courses are taught by graduate students. The average class size in an introductory lecture is 30; in a laboratory, 20; and in a regular course, 30.

Admissions: 60% of the 2009-2010 applicants were accepted. The SAT scores for the 2009-2010 freshman class were: Critical Reading--38% below 500, 45% between 500 and 599, 15% between 600 and 700, and 2% above 700; Math--20% below 500, 45% between 500 and 599, 31% between 600 and 700, and 4% above 700; Writing--36% below 500, 45% between 500 and 599, 16% between 600 and 700, and 3% above 700. 49% of the current freshmen were in the top fifth of their class; 78% were in the top two fifths.

Requirements: The SAT or ACT is required. In addition, a high school diploma is required; the GED is accepted. SAT Subject tests are required of students without a high school diploma from an accredited high school and from some GED holders. Students should have completed a general college-preparatory program, including 16 high school academic credits or Carnegie units, with 4 years of English, 3 years of math (4 recommended), 2 years each of science and foreign language, and 5 electives. Biology and chemistry are required for nursing students. AP and CLEP credits are accepted. Important factors in the admissions decision are advanced placement or honors courses, evidence of special talent, and leadership record.

Procedure: Freshmen are admitted in the fall. Entrance exams should be taken by December of senior year, but this is not required. There are early admissions and rolling admissions plans. Application deadlines are open. Application fee is $65. Notifications are sent March 1. Applications are accepted on-line. A waiting list is maintained.

Transfer: 664 transfer students enrolled in 2008-2009. Students who have completed at least 12 credit hours at another college with a cumulative GPA of 2.0 are considered for admission as transfer students. Transfers are admitted in the fall and spring. High school and college transcripts are required. 30 of 124 credits required for the bachelor's degree must be completed at RU-Newark.

Visiting: There are regularly scheduled orientations for prospective students, including an information session with an admissions counselor and a tour of the campus. There are guides for informal visits, and visitors may sit in on classes. To schedule a visit, contact the Admissions Office (Newark).

Financial Aid: In 2009-2010, 85% of all full-time freshmen and 89% of continuing full-time students received some form of financial aid. 71% of all full-time freshmen and 83% of continuing full-time students received need-based aid. The average freshman award was $13,561. Need-based scholarships and need-based grants averaged $12,504; need-based self-help aid (loans and jobs) averaged $8457; non-need-based athletic scholarships averaged $7500; and other non-need-based awards and non-need-based scholarships averaged $3507. Average annual earnings from campus work are $1272. The average financial indebtedness of the 2009 graduate was $23,710. The FAFSA is required. The priority date for freshman financial aid applications for fall entry is March 15. The deadline for filing freshman financial aid applications for fall entry is open.

International Students: International students must take the TOEFL with a score of 550 on the paper-based TOEFL (PBT) or 79 on the Internet-based version (iBT), or the IELTS, scoring 6, and the college's own test.

Computers: All students may access the system. There are no time limits. The fee is $283. All students are required to have a personal computer.

Graduates: From July 1, 2008 to June 30, 2009, 1357 bachelor's degrees were awarded. The most popular majors were business management (32%), nursing (16%), and biological sciences (11%). In an average class, 48% graduate in 5 years or less and 59% graduate in 6 years or less.

Admissions Contact: Bruce Neimeyer, Director of Admissions-Newark. Web: *www.rutgers.edu*

SAINT PETER'S COLLEGE   E-2
Jersey City, NJ 07306-5997   (201) 915-9213
                                               (888) SPC-9933; (201) 432-5860

Full-time: 2215 men and women	**Faculty:** IIA, -$
Part-time: 630 men and women	**Ph.D.s:** n/av
Graduate: none	**Student/Faculty:** n/av
Year: semesters, summer session	**Tuition:** $23,800
Application Deadline: open	**Room & Board:** $10,000
Freshman Class: n/av	
SAT or ACT: required	**LESS COMPETITIVE**

Saint Peter's College, founded in 1872, is a private liberal arts and business college affiliated with the Roman Catholic Church and known as New Jersey's Jesuit College. Figures in the above capsule and in this profile are approximate. There are 2 undergraduate schools and 3 graduate schools. In addition to regional accreditation, SPC has baccalaureate program accreditation with NLN. The 2 libraries contain 285,000 volumes, 70,000 microform items, and 3,800 audio/video tapes/CDs/DVDs, and subscribe to 1,800 periodicals including electronic. Computerized library services include interlibrary loans and database searching. Special learning facilities include a learning resource center, art gallery, radio station, and TV station. The 15-acre campus is in an urban area 2 miles west of New York City. Including any residence halls, there are 29 buildings.

Student Life: 87% of undergraduates are from New Jersey. Others are from 26 states and 10 foreign countries. 56% are from public schools. 44% are white; 27% Hispanic; 21% African American. 68% are Catholic. The average age of freshmen is 18; all undergraduates, 24. 23% do not continue beyond their first year; 51% remain to graduate.

Housing: 863 students can be accommodated in college housing, which includes single-sex and coed dorms and on-campus apartments. In addition, there are community service houses. On-campus housing is guaranteed for all 4 years. 50% of students commute. Upperclassmen may keep cars.

Activities: There are no fraternities or sororities. There are 50 groups on campus, including cheerleading, chess, chorus, computers, debate, drama, ethnic, forensics, honors, international, literary magazine, newspaper, pep band, political, professional, radio and TV, religious, social, social service, and student government. Popular campus events include International Day, career fairs, and SpringFest.

Sports: There are 10 intercollegiate sports for men and 8 for women, and 20 intramural sports for men and 18 for women. Facilities include a recreational center, a 2000-seat gym, and an athletic field.

Disabled Students: 80% of the campus is accessible. Facilities include wheelchair ramps, elevators, special parking, specially equipped restrooms, special class scheduling, lowered drinking fountains, and lowered telephones.

Services: Counseling and information services are available, as is tutoring in every subject. There is a reader service for the blind, and remedial math, reading, and writing.

Campus Safety and Security: Measures include 24-hour foot and vehicle patrol, self-defense education, and security escort services. There are shuttle buses, emergency telephones, security desk monitoring of access to residence halls.

Programs of Study: SPC confers B.A., B.S., and B.S.N. degrees. Associates and master's degrees are also awarded. Bachelor's degrees are awarded in BIOLOGICAL SCIENCE (biochemistry and biology/biological science), BUSINESS (accounting, business administration and management, international business management, and marketing/retailing/merchandising), COMMUNICATIONS AND THE ARTS (art history and appreciation, classical languages, communications, English, fine arts, graphic design, modern language, Spanish, and visual and performing arts), COMPUTER AND PHYSICAL SCIENCE (chemistry, computer science, mathematics, natural sciences, and physics), EDUCATION (elementary education and secondary education), HEALTH PROFESSIONS (biomedical science, health care administration, medical laboratory technology, nursing, predentistry, and premedicine), SOCIAL SCIENCE (African American studies, American studies, classical/ancient civilization, criminal justice, economics, history, humanities, interdisciplinary studies, international studies, Latin American studies, philosophy, political science/government, prelaw, psychology, social science, sociology, theological studies, and urban studies). Natural sciences and accounting are the strongest academically. Business management, accounting, and computer sciences are the largest.

Required: To graduate, students must complete 129 credit hours, including 57 in the core curriculum, 12 in core electives, between 30 and 45 in the major, and the rest in subjects related to the major. The core curriculum requires 9 credits of natural sciences, 6 to 8 of math, and 3 each of social science, philosophy, history, literature, a modern language, fine arts, and composition. Students must earn a GPA of 2.0.

Special: There are co-op programs with local companies, as well as departmental programs, and many internships available in Jersey City and nearby New York City. A Washington semester and study abroad in any of 60 countries are offered. There are preprofessional programs in dentistry, pharmacy, physician assistant, and physical therapy.The college also offers dual majors and student-designed majors, credit for life, military, and work experience, nondegree study, and pass/fail options. There are 9 national honor societies, a freshman honors program, and 1 departmental honors program.

Faculty/Classroom: 64% of faculty are male; 36% are female. All teach undergraduates. No introductory courses are taught by graduate students. The average class size in an introductory lecture is 23; in a laboratory is 14; and in a regular course is 16.

Requirements: The SAT or ACT is required. In addition, applicants must be high school graduates or submit the GED certificate. Students should have completed 16 Carnegie units of high school study, including 4 years of English, 3 of math, 2 each of science, history, and a foreign language, and another 3 of additional work in any of these subjects. An essay and 2 letters of recommendation are required, and an interview is recommended. AP and CLEP credits are accepted. Important factors in the admissions decision are advanced placement or honors courses, extracurricular activities record, and recommendations by school officials.

Procedure: Freshmen are admitted fall and spring. Entrance exams should be taken by the fall of the senior year. There are early admissions, deferred admissions, and rolling admissions plans. Application deadlines are open. Notification is sent on a rolling basis. Applications are accepted on-line.

Transfer: The school requires a 2.0 college GPA of transfer students, as well as a high school transcript and a satisfactory composite SAT score for students less than 2 years out of high school. An interview is recommended. 30 of 129 credits required for the bachelor's degree must be completed at SPC.

Visiting: There are regularly scheduled orientations for prospective students, including open houses, weekend and weekday visit days with a tour and class and information sessions, as well as tours and interviews by appointment. There are guides for informal visits; visitors may sit in on classes and stay overnight. To schedule a visit, contact the Admissions Office.

Financial Aid: SPC is a member of CSS. The FAFSA is required. Check with the school for current application deadlines.

International Students: The school actively recruits these students. They must take the TOEFL.

Computers: All students may access the system. The system may be used for remote access 24 hours a day; for local access, about 94 hours a week. There are no time limits and no fees.

Admissions Contact: Joseph Giglio, Director of Admissions. E-Mail: *admissions@spc.edu* Web: *www.spc.edu*

SETON HALL UNIVERSITY
South Orange, NJ 07079-2691

E-2

(973) 313-6146
(800) THE-HALL; (973) 275-2040

Full-time: 1979 men, 2692 women	**Faculty:** I, -$
Part-time: 199 men, 343 women	**Ph.D.s:** n/av
Graduate: 1962 men, 2421 women	**Student/Faculty:** n/av
Year: semesters, summer session	**Tuition:** $
Application Deadline: March 1	**Room & Board:** $10,514
Freshman Class: 10851 applied, 8602 accepted, 1139 enrolled	
SAT CR/M/W: 530/535/540	**ACT:** 23 COMPETITIVE

Seton Hall University, founded in 1856, is a major Catholic University. Seton Hall's 58 acre campus is located in South Orange, New Jersey, only 14 miles from New York City. The University is home to 10,000 students and eight schools that offer degrees at the baccalaureate, master, and doctoral and professional levels. There are 5 undergraduate schools and 8 graduate schools. In addition to regional accreditation, Seton Hall has baccalaureate program accreditation with AACSB, CSWE, NCATE, and NLN. The 2 libraries contain 573,728 volumes, 552,000 microform items, and 4,085 audio/video tapes/CDs/DVDs, and subscribe to 21,000 periodicals including electronic. Computerized library services include interlibrary loans, database searching, Internet access, and laptop Internet portals. Special learning facilities include a learning resource center, art gallery, natural history museum, radio station, TV station, various institutes, and centers for learning and research. The 58-acre campus is in a suburban area 14 miles west of New York City. Including any residence halls, there are 44 buildings.

Student Life: 73% of undergraduates are from New Jersey. Students are from 44 states, 34 foreign countries, and Canada. 68% are from public schools. 53% are white; 14% African American; 12% Hispanic. 65% are Catholic; 15% Protestant. The average age of freshmen is 18; all undergraduates, 21. 17% do not continue beyond their first year; 61% remain to graduate.

Housing: 2300 students can be accommodated in college housing, which includes single-sex and coed dorms and off-campus apartments. In addition, there are special-interest houses, sophomore discovery program, and alcohol free buildings. On-campus housing is available on a lottery system for upperclassmen. Priority is given to out-of-town students. 54% of students commute. Upperclassmen may keep cars.

Activities: 8% of men belong to 12 national fraternities; 7% of women belong to 14 national sororities. There are 124 groups on campus, including volunteer, recreation, student ambassador society, art, cheerleading, chess, choir, commuter council, computers, dance, drama, drill team, ethnic, forensics, honors, international, literary magazine, musical theater, newspaper, pep band, photography, political, professional, radio and TV, religious, social, social service, and student government. Popular campus events include University Day, Theatre-in-the-Round, and Career Day.

Sports: There are 8 intercollegiate sports for men and 9 for women, and 12 intramural sports for men and 12 for women. Facilities include a 2000-seat on-campus arena, recreational field house, indoor track, indoor pool, fitness and aerobics rooms, a soccer and baseball field, a softball field, and tennis and racquetball courts. Men's basketball also uses the Continental Arena, which seats 19,759.

Disabled Students: 75% of the campus is accessible. Facilities include wheelchair ramps, elevators, special parking, specially equipped restrooms, special class scheduling, and lowered drinking fountains.

Services: Counseling and information services are available, as is tutoring in most subjects. There is a reader service for the blind, and remedial math, reading, and writing. The Academic Resource Center also offers support for students interested in national scholarship opportunities and aids students who are pursuing interdisciplinary and pre-professional majors.

Campus Safety and Security: Measures include 24-hour foot and vehicle patrol, emergency notification system, self-defense education, and security escort services. There are shuttle buses, emergency telephones, lighted pathways/sidewalks, controlled access to dorms/residences, and security attendants are posted at residence hall entrances.

Programs of Study: Seton Hall confers B.A., B.S., B.A.B.A., B.S.B., B.S.E., B.S.I.R., and B.S.N. degrees. Master's and doctoral degrees are also awarded. Bachelor's degrees are awarded in AGRICULTURE (environmental studies), BIOLOGICAL SCIENCE (biochemistry and biology/biological science), BUSINESS (accounting, banking and finance, business administration and management, business economics, management information systems, marketing management, and sports management), COMMUNICATIONS AND THE ARTS (applied music, art history and appreciation, broadcasting, communications, English, fine arts, French, graphic design, Italian, journalism, modern language, and Spanish), COMPUTER AND PHYSICAL SCIENCE (chemistry, computer science, mathematics, and physics), EDUCATION (elementary education, secondary education, and special education), HEALTH PROFESSIONS (nursing), SOCIAL SCIENCE (African American studies, anthropology, Asian/Oriental studies, Christian studies, classical/ancient civilization, criminal justice, economics, history, international relations, liberal arts/general studies, philosophy, political science/government, psychology, religion, social science, social work, and sociology). Business, biology, and diplomacy are the strongest academically. Nursing, diplimacy, and finance are the largest.

Required: To graduate, students must complete the University Core Curriculum and complete at least 120 credit hours earning a minimum GPA of 2.0.

Special: Co-op and work-study are possible through the College of Arts and Sciences and the School of Business; internships are available through the college of arts and sciences and school of diplomacy. Education majors go into the field during their sophomore year. Cross-registration is available in engineering, including 3-2 engineering degrees, with the New Jersey Institute of Technology. Study abroad is available in 15 countries. An accelerated B.S.N. degree is offered. There are a total of 16 bachelor/graduate dual degree programs. Non-degree study is permitted. There are 27 national honor societies, a freshman honors program, and 5 departmental honors programs.

Faculty/Classroom: No introductory courses are taught by graduate students. The average class size in an introductory lecture is 28; in a laboratory is 13; and in a regular course is 21.

Admissions: 79% of the 2009-2010 applicants were accepted. The SAT scores for the 2009-2010 freshman class were: Critical Reading-- 32% below 500, 51% between 500 and 599, 15% between 600 and 700, and 2% above 700; Math--33% below 500, 44% between 500 and 599, 21% between 600 and 700, and 2% above 700; Writing--27% below 500, 49% between 500 and 599, 21% between 600 and 700, and 2% above 700. The ACT scores were 24% below 21, 32% between 21 and 23, 28% between 24 and 26, 8% between 27 and 28, and 9% above 28. 43% of the current freshmen were in the top fifth of their class; 73% were in the top two fifths. 3 freshmen graduated first in their class.

Requirements: The SAT or ACT is required. In addition, Seton Hall recommends a satisfactory score on the SAT or a minimum composite score on the ACT. Applicants must supply high school transcripts or a GED certificate. Students should have completed 16 Carnegie units of high school study, including 4 years of English, 3 of math, 2 each of a foreign language and either history or social studies, 1 of science, and 4 academic electives. An essay is optional and an interview is recommended. AP and CLEP credits are accepted. Important factors in the admissions decision are advanced placement or honors courses, leadership record, and parents or siblings attended your school.

Procedure: Freshmen are admitted fall and spring. Entrance exams should be taken by January of the senior year. There are early admissions, deferred admissions, and rolling admissions plans. Applications should be filed by March 1 for fall entry and December 1 for spring entry, along with a $55 fee. Notification is sent on a rolling basis. Applications are accepted on-line.

Transfer: 309 transfer students enrolled in 2008-2009. Applicants should have earned 30 hours of college credit, with a minimum GPA of 2.5, or 2.8 for the business and science schools. The SAT is required for students with fewer than 30 credits of college-level work at the time of application, and an interview is recommended. 30 of 120 credits required for the bachelor's degree must be completed at Seton Hall.

Visiting: There are regularly scheduled orientations for prospective students, including campus tours weekdays and Saturdays during the academic year and on weekdays during the summer. Open houses for prospective applicants are available each fall. Visitors may sit in on classes. To schedule a visit, contact the Enrollment Services Office at (973) 761-9332.

Financial Aid: 18% of undergraduate students work part-time. Average annual earnings from campus work are $2000. The FAFSA is required. The priority date for freshman financial aid applications for fall entry is March 1. The deadline for filing freshman financial aid applications for fall entry is open.

International Students: There are 141 international students enrolled. The school actively recruits these students. They must take the TOEFL with a minimum score of 550 on the paper-based TOEFL (PBT) or 79 on the Internet-based version (iBT). They must also take the SAT.

Computers: Wireless access is available. All undergraduate and select graduate students are issued laptop computers as part of their tuition and fees. Students have access to a network of tools used by more than 80% of the faculty to enhance the teaching and learning experience. Over 5000 laptop computers are handed out to students and approximately 400 computers are in computer labs and the library for public computing use. All students may access the system. Public labs are available until 11 P.M.; there is 24-hour remote network access. There are no time limits and no fees. All students are required to have a personal computer. Students enrolled in All full-time graduates are required to participate in the Mobile Computing Program. Students must have a personal computer. A Lenovo T500 and X200 is recommended.

Graduates: From July 1, 2008 to June 30, 2009, 1017 bachelor's degrees were awarded. The most popular majors were nursing (9%), finance (7%), and criminal justice (6%). 300 companies recruited on campus in 2008-2009. In an average class, 45% graduate in 4 years or less, 58% graduate in 5 years or less, and 61% graduate in 6 years or less. Of the 2008 graduating class, 26% were enrolled in graduate school within 6 months of graduation, and 64% were employed.

Admissions Contact: Peter Nacy, Assistant Vice President. A campus DVD is available. E-Mail: *thehall@shu.edu* Web: *www.shu.edu*

STEVENS INSTITUTE OF TECHNOLOGY E-2
Hoboken, NJ 07030

(201) 216-5194
(800) 458-5323; (201) 216-8348

Full-time: 1654 men, 579 women	**Faculty:** 226; IIA, +$
Part-time: 1 man	**Ph.D.s:** 90%
Graduate: 2761 men, 867 women	**Student/Faculty:** 10 to 1
Year: semesters, summer session	**Tuition:** $37,980
Application Deadline: February 1	**Room & Board:** $12,150
Freshman Class: 3232 applied, 1609 accepted, 614 enrolled	
SAT CR/M/W: 600/670/600	**ACT:** 27 **HIGHLY COMPETITIVE**

Stevens Institute of Technology, founded in 1870, is a private institution offering programs of study in science, computer science, engineering, business, and humanities. There are 4 undergraduate schools and 3 graduate schools. In addition to regional accreditation, Stevens has baccalaureate program accreditation with ABET and CSAB. The library contains 123,063 volumes and subscribes to 39,500 periodicals including electronic. Computerized library services include interlibrary loans, database searching, Internet access, and laptop Internet portals. Special learning facilities include a radio station, TV station, a lab for ocean and coastal engineering, an environmental lab, a design and manufacturing institute, a technology center, a telecommunications institute, a computer vision lab, an ultrafast laser spectroscopy and high-speed communications lab, and a wireless network security center. The 55-acre campus is in an urban area on the banks of the Hudson River, overlooking the Manhattan skyline. Including any residence halls, there are 25 buildings.

Student Life: 60% of undergraduates are from New Jersey. Others are from 42 states, 30 foreign countries, and Canada. 80% are from public schools. 54% are white; 11% Asian American. The average age of freshmen is 18; all undergraduates, 20. 10% do not continue beyond their first year; 76% remain to graduate.

Housing: 1358 students can be accommodated in college housing, which includes coed dorms, on-campus apartments, off-campus apartments, and married student housing. In addition, there are special-interest houses, fraternity houses, sorority houses, and special-interest

floors. On-campus housing is guaranteed for all 4 years. 85% of students live on campus; of those, 70% remain on campus on weekends. Alcohol is not permitted. Upperclassmen may keep cars.

Activities: 19% of men belong to 11 national fraternities; 20% of women belong to 1 local and 3 national sororities. There are 105 groups on campus, including anime, art, band, chess, choir, chorus, computers, dance, debate, drama, Engineers without Borders, environmental, ethnic, film, gamers, honors, international, jazz band, literary magazine, musical theater, newspaper, paintball, pep band, photography, political, professional, radio and TV, religious, SAE, social, social service, and student government. Popular campus events include Fall Tech Fest, Spring Boken Festival, and Midnight Breakfast.

Sports: There are 13 intercollegiate sports for men and 13 for women, and 12 intramural sports for men and 12 for women. Facilities include a 60,000-square-foot complex with an NCAA regulation swimming pool, a 1400-seat basketball arena, fitness rooms, racquetball/squash courts, a playing field, a student union, and several outdoor courts.

Disabled Students: All of the campus is accessible. Facilities include wheelchair ramps, elevators, special parking, specially equipped restrooms, lowered drinking fountains, and special housing.

Services: Counseling and information services are available, as is tutoring in every subject.

Campus Safety and Security: Measures include 24-hour foot and vehicle patrol, emergency notification system, self-defense education, and security escort services. There are emergency telephones, lighted pathways/sidewalks, and controlled access to dorms/residences.

Programs of Study: Stevens confers B.A., B.S., and B.E. degrees. Master's and doctoral degrees are also awarded. Bachelor's degrees are awarded in BIOLOGICAL SCIENCE (biochemistry and bioinformatics), BUSINESS (business administration and management), COMMUNICATIONS AND THE ARTS (literature and music technology), COMPUTER AND PHYSICAL SCIENCE (chemistry, computer science, computer security and information assurance, digital arts/technology, information sciences and systems, mathematics, physics, and science technology), ENGINEERING AND ENVIRONMENTAL DESIGN (biomedical engineering, chemical engineering, civil engineering, computational sciences, computer engineering, electrical/electronics engineering, engineering management, engineering physics, environmental engineering, mechanical engineering, naval architecture and marine engineering, and systems engineering), SOCIAL SCIENCE (history and philosophy). Engineering is the strongest academically. Mechanical engineering, civil engineering, and business are the largest.

Required: To graduate, the student must have earned 122 to 150 credit hours (dependent on program) with a minimum 2.0 GPA; the total hours in the major vary by program. The core curriculum includes courses in engineering, science, computer science, math, liberal arts, and phys ed.

Special: Stevens offers cross-registration and a 3-2 engineering degree with New York University, a work-study program within the school, co-op programs, corporate and research internships through the Undergraduate Projects in Technology and Medicine, study abroad in 7 countries, and pass/fail options for extra courses. Students may undertake dual majors as well as accelerated degree programs in medicine, dentistry, and law and can receive a B.A.-B.E. degree or a B.A.-B.S. degree in all majors. Undergraduates may take graduate courses. There are 9 national honor societies and a freshman honors program.

Faculty/Classroom: 80% of faculty are male; 20% are female. 75% do both. No introductory courses are taught by graduate students. The average class size in an introductory lecture, 75, in a laboratory, 20, and in a regular course, 25.

Admissions: 50% of the 2009-2010 applicants were accepted. The SAT scores for the 2009-2010 freshman class were: Critical Reading--9% below 500, 41% between 500 and 599, 41% between 600 and 700, and 9% above 700; Math--% below 500, 14% between 500 and 599, 58% between 600 and 700, and 28% above 700; Writing--11% below 500, 39% between 500 and 599, 41% between 600 and 700, and 9% above 700. The ACT scores were % below 21, 18% between 21 and 23, % between 24 and 26, 58% between 27 and 28, and 24% above 28. 78% of the current freshmen were in the top fifth of their class; 95% were in the top two fifths. 9 freshmen graduated first in their class.

Requirements: The SAT or ACT is required. In addition, applicants must provide official high school transcripts. Students should have taken 4 years of English, math, and science. An interview, essay, and 2 letters of recommendation are required. AP credits are accepted. Important factors in the admissions decision are advanced placement or honors courses, extracurricular activities record, and personality/intangible qualities.

Procedure: Freshmen are admitted in the fall. Entrance exams should be taken by February of the senior year. There are early decision and deferred admissions plans. Early decision applications should be filed by November 15; regular applications, by February 1 for fall entry and December 1 for spring entry, along with a $55 fee. Notification of early decision is sent December 15; regular decision, March 21. Applications are accepted on-line. 481 applicants were on a recent waiting list, 30 were accepted.

Transfer: 45 transfer students enrolled in 2008-2009. Applicants should have a minimum GPA of 3.0. They must submit all college transcripts, including course descriptions; SAT or ACT scores are required of those students with fewer than 30 hours of college credit. 50 of 122 to 150 (depending on the major)of credits required for the bachelor's degree must be completed at Stevens.

Visiting: There are regularly scheduled orientations for prospective students, including interviews and campus tours. There are guides for informal visits; visitors may sit in on classes and stay overnight. To schedule a visit, contact the Admissions Office at (201) 216-5194.

Financial Aid: In 2009-2010, 93% of all full-time freshmen and 90% of continuing full-time students received some form of financial aid. 84% of all full-time freshmen and 80% of continuing full-time students received need-based aid. The average freshman award was $24,380. Need-based scholarships or need-based grants averaged $15,021; need-based self-help aid (loans and jobs) averaged $4,613; and other non-need based awards and non-need based scholarships averaged $7,878. 24% of undergraduate students work part-time. Average annual earnings from campus work are $1202. The average financial indebtedness of the 2009 graduate was $1,587. Stevens is a member of CSS. The CSS/Profile and FAFSA are required. The priority date for freshman financial aid applications for fall entry is February 15.

International Students: There are 92 international students enrolled. The school actively recruits these students. They must take the TOEFL with a minimum score of 550 on the paper-based TOEFL (PBT) or 83 on the Internet-based version (iBT). They must also take the SAT or ACT.

Computers: Wireless access is available. All undergraduates receive a laptop as part of their admission to the institution. These laptops are all wireless enabled, and wireless access is available all over the campus. All students may access the system at all times. There are no time limits and no fees. All students are required to have a personal computer. Each student is provided with an HP 8530W with an Intel Core 2.

Graduates: From July 1, 2008 to June 30, 2009, 419 bachelor's degrees were awarded. The most popular majors were mechanical engineering (18%), electrical engineering (12%), and business (11%). 380 companies recruited on campus in 2008-2009. In an average class, 25% graduate in 4 years or less, 72% graduate in 5 years or less, and 76% graduate in 6 years or less. Of the 2008 graduating class, 20% were enrolled in graduate school within 6 months of graduation, and 75% were employed.

Admissions Contact: Daniel Gallagher, Dean of University Admissions. E-Mail: *admissions@stevens.edu* Web: *www.stevens.edu*

THOMAS EDISON STATE COLLEGE — D-3
Trenton, NJ 08608-1176 — (888) 442-8372; (609) 984-8447

Full-time: none	Faculty: n/av
Part-time: 10662 men, 6658 women	Ph.Ds: n/av
Graduate: 348 men, 538 women	Student/Faculty: n/av
Year: see profile	Tuition: $4695(6720)
Application Deadline: open	
Freshman Class: n/av	SPECIAL

Thomas Edison State College, founded in 1972, is a public institution of higher education. The college provides many ways to complete a degree in more than 100 areas of study, including credit by examination, assessment of experiential learning, guided independent study, and credit for corporate and military training. The college offers two tuition plans, a comprehensive tuition plan and a per-service tuition plan. There are 4 undergraduate schools. In addition to regional accreditation, Thomas Edison State College has baccalaureate program accreditation with NLN. The 2-acre campus is in an urban area 40 miles north of Philadelphia. Including any residence halls, there are 4 buildings.

Student Life: 67% of undergraduates are from out of state, mostly the South. Students are from 50 states, 74 foreign countries, and Canada. 66% are white; 18% African American. The average age of all undergraduates is 35.

Housing: There are no residence halls. All students commute.

Activities: There are no fraternities or sororities.

Sports: There is no sports program at Thomas Edison State College.

Disabled Students: 97% of the campus is accessible. Facilities include wheelchair ramps, elevators, special parking, specially equipped restrooms, lowered drinking fountains. textbooks on tape, interpreter services for the hearing-impaired, and examinations formatted to accommodate the student's need.

Services: n/av

Campus Safety and Security: There are emergency telephones, lighted pathways/sidewalks, a guard on the premises 7 A.M. to 11 P.M., and the perimeter is patrolled by the New Jersey State Police.

Programs of Study: Thomas Edison State College confers B.A., B.S., B.S.A.S.T., B.S.B.A., B.S.H.S., B.S.He.S., and B.S.N. degrees. Associates and master's degrees are also awarded. Bachelor's degrees are awarded in AGRICULTURE (environmental studies, forestry and related sciences, and horticulture), BIOLOGICAL SCIENCE (biology/biological

science), BUSINESS (accounting, entrepreneurial studies, hospitality management services, human resources, international business management, labor studies, marketing and distribution, operations management, real estate, and recreation and leisure services), COMMUNICATIONS AND THE ARTS (art, communications, dramatic arts, English, journalism, music, and photography), COMPUTER AND PHYSICAL SCIENCE (computer science, information sciences and systems, mathematics, and natural sciences), EDUCATION (health education), ENGINEERING AND ENVIRONMENTAL DESIGN (air traffic control, architecture, aviation computer technology, aviation maintenance management, civil engineering technology, computer technology, construction technology, electrical/electronics engineering technology, emergency/disaster science, energy management technology, engineering, environmental science, manufacturing technology, marine engineering, mechanical engineering technology, and nuclear engineering technology), HEALTH PROFESSIONS (cytotechnology, dental hygiene, health care administration, hospital administration, mental health/human services, nuclear medical technology, nursing, radiation therapy, and respiratory therapy), SOCIAL SCIENCE (anthropology, community services, criminal justice, dietetics, economics, fire protection, gerontology, history, humanities, law, liberal arts/general studies, philosophy, political science/government, psychology, public administration, religion, social science, social work, and sociology). Liberal studies, nuclear engineering technology, and general management are the largest.

Required: The baccalaureate student must complete a General Education requirement that includes courses in English composition, humanities, social sciences, natural sciences, and math for a total of approximately 60 general education credits. To graduate, 120 semester hours are required, with a minimum GPA of 2.0.

Special: Students may take dual majors in all degree programs except nursing. Graduates of associate degree and diploma programs of nursing may enroll for a B.S.N. degree only or both a B.S.N. and a M.S.N. degree with preparation as a nurse educator at the master's level. The B.S. in health sciences is available as a joint degree with the University of Medicine and Dentistry of New Jersey. Credit for college-level knowledge gained through life, military, and work experience is an option. Students work on their own, proceeding at their own pace, depending on the option selected for earning credit. Thomas Edison State College has a 12 semester calendar. There is 1 national honor society.

Faculty/Classroom: No introductory courses are taught by graduate students.

Admissions: n/av

Requirements: In addition, applicants must have a high school diploma or the equivalent and be at least 21 years old. Certain health-related and other areas of study are limited to persons holding appropriate certification. Admission to the bachelor's degree nursing program is limited to registered nurses (RNs) who are currently licensed in the United States. Admission to Master of Arts in Educational Leadership degree is limited to persons with valid Teacher's Certificate. Applicants under the age of 21 may be accepted on a case-by-case basis, or if they are a member of a special population, such as a corporate partner or a memberof the U.S. Military. AP and CLEP credits are accepted.

Procedure: Freshmen are admitted to all sessions. There is a rolling admissions plan. Application deadlines are open. The fall 2009 application fee was $75. Applications are accepted on-line.

Transfer: Transfers, like other students, must be at least 21 and be high school graduates or the equivalent. Certain health related and other areas of study are limited to persons holding appropriate certification. Admission to bachelor's degree nursing program limited to registered nurses (RNs) who are currently licensed in the United States. The granting of credit for course work successfully completed elsewhere is an intrinsic part of the school's system.

Visiting: There are regularly scheduled orientations for prospective students, 3 on-campus information sessions and an online admissions Video Guide. To schedule a visit, contact Director of Admissions at admissions@tesc.edu.

Financial Aid: Thomas Edison State College is a member of CSS. The FAFSA and the college's own financial statement are required. Check with the school for current application deadlines.

International Students: They must take the TOEFL with a minimum score of 500 on the paper-based TOEFL (PBT) or 173 on the Internet-based version (iBT).

Computers: Wireless access is available. There is an online course management system that utilizes the blackboard platform. The system provides students an opportunity to communicate with fellow students and mentors directly through the portal. All students may access the system. There are no time limits. The fee is $97.

Graduates: From July 1, 2008 to June 30, 2009, 1970 bachelor's degrees were awarded. The most popular majors were liberal studies (16%), nuclear engineering technology (11%), and psychology (5%).

Admissions Contact: Mr. David Hoftiezer, Director of Admissions. E-Mail: *admissions@tesc.edu* Web: *www.tesc.edu*

WESTMINSTER CHOIR COLLEGE   D-3

Princeton, NJ 08540   (609) 921-7100; (800) 962-4647

Full-time: 125 men, 215 women	**Faculty:** n/av
Part-time: 10 men, 5 women	**Ph.D.s:** n/av
Graduate: 40 men, 85 women	**Student/Faculty:** n/av
Year: semesters, summer session	**Tuition:** $26,000
Application Deadline: open	**Room & Board:** $10,000
Freshman Class: n/av	
SAT or ACT: required	**SPECIAL**

Westminster Choir College is a residential college of music located on a 23 acre campus in Princeton, N.J. offering a Bachelors in Music, a Bachelor of Arts in Music and a Master''s of Music. WCC also offers two summer study degree programs: Masters of Music Education and Voice Pedagogy. The figures in the above capsule and in this profile are approximate. There is 1 graduate school. In addition to regional accreditation, Westminster has baccalaureate program accreditation with NASDTEC, NASM, and NCATE. The library contains 455,809 volumes, 874,019 microform items, and 20,890 audio/video tapes/CDs/DVDs, and subscribes to 21,931 periodicals including electronic. Special learning facilities include a TV station. The 23-acre campus is in a suburban area 50 miles south of New York City. Including any residence halls, there are 13 buildings.

Student Life: 56% of undergraduates are from out of state, mostly the Middle Atlantic. Students are from 26 states and 10 foreign countries. 80% are white. The average age of freshmen is 19. 21% do not continue beyond their first year.

Housing: College-sponsored housing includes single-sex and coed dorms. In addition, there are special-interest houses. On-campus housing is available on a first-come, first-served basis, and is available on a lottery system for upperclassmen. 57% of students live on campus. Upperclassmen may keep cars.

Activities: There are no fraternities or sororities. Groups on campus include choir, chorale, chorus, ethnic, gay, honors, international, musical theater, newspaper, opera, professional, religious, social, social service, and student government. Popular campus events include Family Day and Spring Fling.

Sports: There is no sports program at Westminster.

Disabled Students: 43% of the campus is accessible. Facilities include elevators, special parking, and specially equipped restrooms.

Services: Counseling and information services are available, as is tutoring in most subjects. There is remedial math, reading, and writing, music theory and music history

Campus Safety and Security: Measures include 24-hour foot and vehicle patrol, self-defense education, and security escort services. There are emergency telephones and lighted pathways/sidewalks.

Programs of Study: confers B.A.M. and B.M. degrees. Master's degrees are also awarded. Bachelor's degrees are awarded in COMMUNICATIONS AND THE ARTS (music, music theory and composition, musical theater, piano/organ, and voice), EDUCATION (music education).

Required: To graduate,all students must maintain a minimum GPA of 2.0 while taking 120 semester hours.

Special: Internships in many programs, work study, summer study in Europe, and dual majors are available. There is a freshman honors program.

Faculty/Classroom: No introductory courses are taught by graduate students.

Requirements: The SAT or ACT is required. In addition, All undergraduate students must submit official high school transcripts and official SAT or ACT scores. All undergraduate applicants must complete an academic course of study in high school. The GED is accepted. Two letters of recommendation, at least one of which must be from a music reference, are required, as is a personal essay. Graduate students must submit official college transcripts showing proof of graduation. All applicants must audition.

Procedure: Application deadlines are open. The fall 2009 application fee was $45.

Visiting: There are guides for informal visits. To schedule a visit, contact the Office of Admissions at 1-800-962-4647.

Financial Aid: Check with the school for current application deadlines.

Admissions Contact: Katherine Shields, Director of Admissions. E-Mail: wccadmission@rider.edu Web: www.rider.edu

WILLIAM PATERSON UNIVERSITY OF NEW JERSEY   E-2

Wayne, NJ 07470   (973) 720-2125
                              Î877ù WOU EXCEL; (973) 720-2910

Full-time: 3275 men, 4240 women	**Faculty:** IIA, ++$
Part-time: 615 men, 1030 women	**Ph.D.s:** n/av
Graduate: 425 men, 1445 women	**Student/Faculty:** n/av
Year: semesters, summer session	**Tuition:** $10,000 ($16,000)
Application Deadline: May 1	**Room & Board:** $10,000
Freshman Class: n/av	
SAT or ACT: required	**COMPETITIVE**

William Paterson University of New Jersey, founded in 1855 as a college, is a public institution comprised of the colleges of Arts and Communication; Education; Humanities; and Social Sciences; Science and Health; and Business. Figures in the above capsule and in this profile are approximate. There are 5 undergraduate schools and 5 graduate schools. In addition to regional accreditation, WPUNJ has baccalaureate program accreditation with ASLA, NASM, NCATE, and NLN. The library contains 300,000 volumes, 1 million microform items, and 20,000 audio/video tapes/CDs/DVDs, and subscribes to 5,000 periodicals including electronic. Computerized library services include interlibrary loans and database searching. Special learning facilities include an art gallery, radio station, TV station, a speech and hearing clinic, an academic support center, a computerized writing center, and a teleconference center. The 320-acre campus is in a suburban area 25 miles west of New York City. Including any residence halls, there are 35 buildings.

Student Life: 98% of undergraduates are from New Jersey. Others are from 22 states, 58 foreign countries, and Canada. 75% are from public schools. 63% are white; 15% Hispanic; 12% African American. The average age of freshmen is 18; all undergraduates, 24.

Housing: College-sponsored housing includes coed dorms and on-campus apartments. In addition, there are honors houses. On-campus housing is guaranteed for all 4 years. 76% of students commute. Upperclassmen may keep cars.

Activities: 2% of men belong to 3 local and 8 national fraternities; 3% of women belong to 3 local and 11 national sororities. There are 50 groups on campus, including art, cheerleading, chorus, computers, dance, drama, ethnic, film, gay, honors, international, jazz band, literary magazine, musical theater, newspaper, opera, orchestra, photography, political, professional, radio and TV, religious, student government, and yearbook. Popular campus events include Midday Artist Series, Puerto Rican Heritage Month, and Latin American Week.

Sports: There are 7 intercollegiate sports for men and 7 for women, and 24 intramural sports for men and 24 for women. Facilities include a recreation center with courts for basketball, tennis, racquetball, volleyball, and badminton, weight and exercise rooms, saunas and whirlpools, and a 4000-seat auditorium. The university also offers an Olympic-size pool, 8 additional tennis courts, and an athletic complex with fields for baseball, field hockey, football, soccer, softball, and track.

Disabled Students: Facilities include wheelchair ramps, elevators, special parking, specially equipped restrooms, special class scheduling, lowered drinking fountains, lowered telephones, and special housing.

Services: Counseling and information services are available, as is tutoring in most subjects. There is remedial math, reading, and writing. There is a science enrichment center, a writing center, and a business tutorial lab.

Campus Safety and Security: Measures include 24-hour foot and vehicle patrol and security escort services. There are shuttle buses, emergency telephones, and lighted pathways/sidewalks.

Programs of Study: WPUNJ confers B.A., B.S., B.F.A., and B.M. degrees. Master's degrees are also awarded. Bachelor's degrees are awarded in BIOLOGICAL SCIENCE (biology/biological science and biotechnology), BUSINESS (accounting, banking and finance, and business administration and management), COMMUNICATIONS AND THE ARTS (art history and appreciation, communications, dramatic arts, English, fine arts, music, Spanish, and studio art), COMPUTER AND PHYSICAL SCIENCE (chemistry, computer science, and mathematics), EDUCATION (health education, music education, physical education, and special education), ENGINEERING AND ENVIRONMENTAL DESIGN (environmental science), HEALTH PROFESSIONS (community health work, health science, and nursing), SOCIAL SCIENCE (African American studies, anthropology, economics, geography, history, philosophy, political science/government, psychology, and sociology). Biology/biotechnology, computer science, and English are the strongest academically. Management, communications, and education are the largest.

Required: All students must maintain a cumulative GPA of at least 2.0 and take 128 credit hours, typically including 30 to 40 in their major. General education requirements include 21 credits in the humanities, 11 or 12 in science, 9 in the social sciences, and 6 in art and communication. Also required are 1 course in health or movement science, 1 course dealing with racism or sexism, and 1 course in non-Western culture. Students also complete 6 credits of general education electives and a minimum of 9 credits of upper-level elective courses.

Special: Study abroad in 33 countries, cross-registration, internships, work-study programs on campus, accelerated degree programs, dual majors, individual curriculum design, and credit for military experience are available. Nondegree study and some pass/fail options are also possible. In the Learning Clusters Project, students experience how 3 general education courses, taken together, reinforce and better integrate each other. There is a professional program in teacher education leading to certification in early childhood, elementary, middle, and secondary education. There are 6 national honor societies and 4 departmental honors programs.

Faculty/Classroom: 52% of faculty are male; 48% are female. All teach undergraduates, and 40% do research. No introductory courses are taught by graduate students. The average class size in an introductory lecture is 32; in a laboratory is 24; and in a regular course is 19.

Requirements: The SAT or ACT is required. In addition, applicants must have 16 academic credits or Carnegie units, including 4 in English, 3 in math, 2 each in science lab and social studies, and 5 electives such as foreign language and history. An essay and interview are recommended for some applicants, as are a portfolio and audition. The GED is accepted. AP and CLEP credits are accepted. Important factors in the admissions decision are advanced placement or honors courses, recommendations by school officials, and evidence of special talent.

Procedure: Freshmen are admitted fall and spring. Entrance exams should be taken by January 31. There are early admissions, deferred admissions, and rolling admissions plans. Applications should be filed by May 1 for fall entry. The fall 2009 application fee was $50. Notification is sent on a rolling basis. Applications are accepted on-line. A waiting list is maintained.

Transfer: Transfer students need a minimum GPA of 2.0 (business, nursing, computer science, and education students need a 2.5 GPA) and at least 12 credit hours earned. 38 of 128 credits required for the bachelor's degree must be completed at WPUNJ.

Visiting: There are regularly scheduled orientations for prospective students, including a campus tour, guest speakers, and dissemination of printed information. There are guides for informal visits and visitors may sit in on classes. To schedule a visit, contact the Admissions Office.

Financial Aid: WPUNJ is a member of CSS. The FAFSA and parent and student federal income tax forms are required. Check with the school for current application deadlines.

International Students: They must take the TOEFL.

Computers: All students may access the system at all times. There are no time limits. The fee is $30.

Admissions Contact: Director of Admissions E-Mail: *admissions@wpunj.edu* Web: *www.wpunj.edu*

NEW YORK

POPULATION
DENSITY

• 50,000 and over

0 20 40 60 80 100

Miles

ADELPHI UNIVERSITY

Garden City, NY 11530

D-5

(516) 877-3050
(800) ADELPHI; (516) 877-3039

Full-time: 1307 men, 2993 women	**Faculty:** 308; I, -$
Part-time: 151 men, 503 women	**Ph.Ds:** 86%
Graduate: 635 men, 2362 women	**Student/Faculty:** 14 to 1
Year: semesters, summer session	**Tuition:** $25,300
Application Deadline: open	**Room & Board:** $10,500
Freshman Class: 7349 applied, 5125 accepted, 1005 enrolled	
SAT CR/M/W: 530/540/520	**ACT:** 22 COMPETITIVE

Adelphi University, founded in 1896, is a private institution. The figure for tuition and fees in the above capsule is for first-year students; continuing students pay $22,200. There are 8 undergraduate schools and 7 graduate schools. In addition to regional accreditation, Adelphi has baccalaureate program accreditation with AACSB, CSWE, NCATE, and NLN. The library contains 588,987 volumes, 806,092 microform items, and 24,850 audio/video tapes/CDs/DVDs, and subscribes to 1507 periodicals including electronic. Computerized library services include interlibrary loans, database searching, Internet access, and laptop Internet portals. Special learning facilities include a learning resource center, an art gallery, a radio station, an observatory, a theater, sculpture and ceramics studios, a bronze-casting foundry, and language labs. The 75-acre campus is in a suburban area 20 miles east of New York City. Including any residence halls, there are 25 buildings.

Student Life: 92% of undergraduates are from New York. Others are from 38 states, 64 foreign countries, and Canada. 73% are from public schools. 68% are white; 14% African American. 58% are Catholic; 18% claim no religious affiliation; 11% Jewish. The average age of freshmen is 18; all undergraduates, 23. 20% do not continue beyond their first year; 62% remain to graduate.

Housing: 1219 students can be accommodated in college housing, which includes coed dorms. In addition, there are special-interest houses and honors dorms. On-campus housing is available on a first-come, first-served basis, and is available on a lottery system for upperclassmen. Priority is given to out-of-town students. 77% of students commute. Alcohol is not permitted. All students may keep cars.

Activities: 8% of men belong to 2 national fraternities; 11% of women belong to 5 national sororities. There are 80 groups on campus, including art, band, cheerleading, chorale, chorus, computers, dance, debate, drama, environmental, ethnic, film, gay, honors, international, jazz band, literary magazine, musical theater, newspaper, opera, orchestra, political, professional, radio and TV, religious, social, social service, student government, and yearbook. Popular campus events include Senior Week, Halloween Party, and Fall Fest.

Sports: There are 9 intercollegiate sports for men and 11 for women, and 14 intramural sports for men and 14 for women. Facilities include a 3000-seat stadium, a 600-seat gym, a 4-lane swimming pool, a finess center, racquetball, squash, and tennis courts, a dance studio, an indoor track, a baseball field, and a softball field.

Disabled Students: 95% of the campus is accessible. Facilities include wheelchair ramps, elevators, special parking, specially equipped rest rooms, special class scheduling, lowered drinking fountains, lowered telephones, and special housing.

Services: Counseling and information services are available, as is tutoring in most subjects, A learning center offers tutoring in writing and quantitative skills and help with class assignments. There is a reader service for the blind. A writing center is also available.

Campus Safety and Security: Measures include 24-hour foot and vehicle patrol, emergency notification system, self-defense education, and security escort services. There are shuttle buses, emergency telephones, and lighted pathways/sidewalks. Dorm main entrances are videotaped, and dorm doors are locked 24 hours a day.

Programs of Study: Adelphi confers B.A., B.S., B.B.A., B.F.A., B.S.Ed., and B.S.S.W. degrees. Associates, master's, and doctoral degrees are also awarded. Bachelor's degrees are awarded in AGRICULTURE (environmental studies), BIOLOGICAL SCIENCE (biochemistry and biology/biological science), BUSINESS (accounting, banking and finance, business administration and management, human resources, and management information systems), COMMUNICATIONS AND THE ARTS (art history and appreciation, communications, dance, design, dramatic arts, English, fine arts, French, languages, music, performing arts, Spanish, and theater design), COMPUTER AND PHYSICAL SCIENCE (chemistry, computer science, mathematics, and physics), EDUCATION (art education and physical education), HEALTH PROFESSIONS (nursing and speech pathology/audiology), SOCIAL SCIENCE (anthropology, criminal justice, economics, history, Latin American studies, philosophy, political science/government, psychology, social science, social work, and sociology). Nursing, biology, and psychology are the largest.

Required: To graduate, students need at least a 2.0 cumulative GPA (higher in some programs) and 120 credit hours with a minimum of 27 in the major. 6 credits each are required in the arts, humanities, and languages, natural sciences and math, and social sciences. Other course requirements include English composition, freshman seminar (3 credits each), and a 1-credit freshman orientation experience, and a capstone experience for seniors.

Special: Cross-registration is possible with New York University College of Dentistry, Tufts University School of Dental Medicine, Columbia University, New York Law School, SUNY State College of Optometry, and New York Medical College. Internships are available in accounting, banking and money management, and communications, among others. Study abroad is available in 65 countries, including Spain, France, Denmark, and England. A 5-year bachelor's/master's degree in a number of fields, including biology, social work, and education is offered. In addition, work-study programs, double majors, B.A.-B.S. degrees, an accelerated degree program, student-designed majors, and a Washington semester are available. A 3-2 engineering degree is offered with Rensselaer Polytechnic, Columbia, Polytechnic, and Stevens Institute of Technology, and joint degree programs are offered in computer science, dentistry, engineering, environmental studies, law, optometry, and physical therapy with other universities and technical institutions. Credit for life experience for adult students, nondegree study in special cases, and pass/fail options are possible. There are 19 national honor societies and a freshman honors program.

Faculty/Classroom: 38% of faculty are male; 62% are female. All teach undergraduates. No introductory courses are taught by graduate students. The average class size in a laboratory is 17 and in a regular course is 22.

Admissions: 70% of the 2009-2010 applicants were accepted. The SAT scores for the 2009-2010 freshman class were: Critical Reading--34% below 500, 47% between 500 and 599, 15% between 600 and 700, and 4% above 700; Math--27% below 500, 51% between 500 and 599, 20% between 600 and 700, and 3% above 700; Writing--35% below 500, 45% between 500 and 599, 16% between 600 and 700, and 4% above 700. The ACT scores were 27% below 21, 42% between 21 and 23, 17% between 24 and 26, 4% between 27 and 28, and 10% above 28. 38% of the current freshmen were in the top fifth of their class; 75% were in the top two fifths.

Requirements: The SAT or ACT is required. In addition, applicants should have 16 academic credits, including a recommended 4 units of

English, history, and social studies, 3 each of math and science, and 2 or 3 of foreign language. An essay is required and an interview recommended for all applicants. A portfolio for art and technical theater candidates, an audition for music, dance, and theater candidates, and an interview for nursing, social work, and honors candidates are required. The SAT is recommended for the general studies and learning disabilities programs. A GPA of 2.5 is required. AP credits are accepted. Important factors in the admissions decision are advanced placement or honors courses, leadership record, and personality/intangible qualities.

Procedure: Freshmen are admitted fall and spring. Entrance exams should be taken in October of the senior year or May of the junior year. There are early admissions, deferred admissions, and rolling admissions plans. Application deadlines are open. The fall 2008 application fee was $35. Applications are accepted on-line.

Transfer: 574 transfer students enrolled in a recent year. A GPA of 2.5 is recommended in addition to an essay, an official high school transcript, and official records of all work completed or in progress from previous colleges and universities. An interview is required for students in social work and nursing, and an audition is needed for music, dance, and theater students and a portfolio for art and technical theater students. 30 of 120 credits required for the bachelor's degree must be completed at Adelphi.

Visiting: There are regularly scheduled orientations for prospective students, including a campus tour, an interview, and information sessions. There are guides for informal visits and visitors may sit in on classes. To schedule a visit, contact Undergraduate Admissions.

Financial Aid: In 2009-2010, 91% of all full-time freshmen and 88% of continuing full-time students received some form of financial aid. 73% of all full-time freshmen and 69% of continuing full-time students received need-based aid. The average freshmen award was $17,850, with $6340 ($6500 maximum) from need-based scholarships or need-based grants; $5576 ($8000 maximum) from need-based self-help aid (loans and jobs); and $12,754 ($36,800 maximum) from non-need-based athletic scholarships. 19% of undergraduate students work part-time. Average annual earnings from campus work are $2156. The average financial indebtedness of the 2009 graduate was $28,307. Adelphi is a member of CSS. The FAFSA is required. The priority date for freshman financial aid applications for fall entry is March 1. The deadline for filing freshman financial aid applications for fall entry is February 15.

International Students: There are 166 international students enrolled. The school actively recruits these students. They must take the TOEFL with a minimum score of 550 on the paper-based TOEFL (PBT) or 80 on the Internet-based version (iBT). They must also take the SAT or ACT.

Computers: Wireless access is available. Each residence hall room and lounge provides wired connectivity. Access is available via more than 650 computers in approximately 35 public areas or labs. Wireless is available in academic buildings and some residence halls. All students may access the system. There are no time limits. The fee is $200.

Graduates: From July 1, 2008 to June 30, 2009, 1134 bachelor's degrees were awarded. The most popular majors were health professions (31%), business (13%), and social science (11%). 300 companies recruited on campus in 2008-2009. In an average class, 53% graduate in 4 years or less, 60% graduate in 5 years or less, and 62% graduate in 6 years or less. Of a recent graduating class, 38% were enrolled in graduate school within 6 months of graduation and 96% were employed.

Admissions Contact: Christine Murphy, Director, Office of University Admissions. E-mail: *admissions@adelphi.edu* Web: *www.adelphi.edu*

ALBANY COLLEGE OF PHARMACY AND HEALTH SCIENCES
D-3

Albany College of Pharmacy

Albany, NY 12208

	(518) 694-7328; (518) 694-7202
Full-time: 425 men, 589 women	Faculty: 70
Part-time: 1 men, 2 women	Ph.D.s: n/av
Graduate: 178 men, 229 women	Student/Faculty: 14 to 1
Year: semesters, summer session	Tuition: $21,150
Application Deadline: February 1	Room & Board: $7300
Freshman Class: 1136 applied, 702 accepted, 193 enrolled	
SAT CR/M/W: 580/620/560	ACT: 26 SPECIAL

Albany College of Pharmacy, founded in 1881, is a private, 6-year institution and a division of Union University. There are no undergraduate schools. In addition to regional accreditation, the college has baccalaureate program accreditation with ACPE. The library contains 14,500 volumes, 28,388 microform items, and 275 audio/video tapes/CDs/DVDs, and subscribes to 9,000 periodicals including electronic. Computerized library services include interlibrary loans, database searching, and Internet access. Special learning facilities include a learning resource center and a pharmacy museum. The 21-acre campus is in an urban area Albany, NY. Including any residence halls, there are 9 buildings.

Student Life: 80% of undergraduates are from New York. Students are from 20 states, 8 foreign countries, and Canada. 75% are from public

schools. 73% are white; 12% Asian American. The average age of freshmen is 18; all undergraduates, 21. 20% do not continue beyond their first year; 65% remain to graduate.

Housing: 615 students can be accommodated in college housing, which includes coed dorms, on-campus apartments, and off-campus apartments. On-campus housing is available on a lottery system for upperclassmen. 65% of students live on campus; of those, 65% remain on campus on weekends. Alcohol is not permitted. All students may keep cars.

Activities: 15% of men belong to 6 national fraternities.there are no sororities. There are 30 groups on campus, including cross-country, multicultural, outdoors, ski, bowling, choir, chorus, dance, ethnic, honors, international, literary magazine, newspaper, photography, professional, social service, and student government. Popular campus events include Interview Day, White Coat Ceremony, and Spring Fest.

Sports: There are 2 intercollegiate sports for men and 2 for women, and 3 intramural sports for men and 3 for women. Facilities include a gym, a fitness center, an outdoor track, and a soccer field.

Disabled Students: 98% of the campus is accessible. Facilities include wheelchair ramps, elevators, special parking, and specially equipped restrooms.

Services: Counseling and information services are available, as is tutoring in most subjects.

Campus Safety and Security: Measures include 24-hour foot and vehicle patrol, emergency notification system, and self-defense education. There are emergency telephones and lighted pathways/sidewalks.

Programs of Study: confers B.S. Biomedical Technology, B.S. Pharmaceutical Sciences, and B.S. Health and Human Sciences degrees. Master's and doctoral degrees are also awarded. Bachelor's degrees are awarded in HEALTH PROFESSIONS (medical laboratory science and pharmaceutical science). The Doctor of Pharmacy program is the strongest academically.

Required: To graduate, students must complete between 129 and 162 credits, depending on the degree program, including core curriculum courses, with a minimum GPA of 2.0.

Special: The college offers cross-registration with other area colleges, dual majors leading to master's and doctoral degrees, an accelerated degree, and applied professional pharmacy experience in the sixth year. There is an Early Assurance Program with Albany Medical College and articulation agreements with Albany Medical College (Physician Assistant Program) and Albany Law School (J.D.). There are 1 national honor societies.

Faculty/Classroom: 47% of faculty are male; 53% are female. No introductory courses are taught by graduate students. The average class size in an introductory lecture is 130; in a laboratory is 23; and in a regular course is 50.

Admissions: 62% of the 2009-2010 applicants were accepted. The SAT scores for the 2009-2010 freshman class were: Critical Reading-- 15% below 500, 52% between 500 and 599, 30% between 600 and 700, and 3% above 700; Math--3% below 500, 30% between 500 and 599, 57% between 600 and 700, and 10% above 700; Writing--21% below 500, 45% between 500 and 599, 33% between 600 and 700, and 1% above 700. The ACT scores were 4% below 21, 8% between 21 and 23, 38% between 24 and 26, 32% between 27 and 28, and 18% above 28. 88% of the current freshmen were in the top fifth of their class; 12% were in the top two fifths. 8 freshmen graduated first in their class.

Requirements: The SAT or ACT is required. In addition, applicants must be graduates of an accredited high school with at least 17 credits, including 4 each of English and math through pre-calculus and 3 of science, including chemistry. The GED is accepted. AP and CLEP credits are accepted. Important factors in the admissions decision are advanced placement or honors courses, extracurricular activities record, and recommendations by alumni.

Procedure: Freshmen are admitted fall. Entrance exams should be taken by the junior year. There are early decision admission plans. Early decision applications should be filed by November 1; regular applications, by February 1 for fall entry and December 1 for spring entry, along with a $75 fee. Notification of early decision is sent December 15; regular decision, March 15. Applications are accepted on-line. 104 applicants were on a recent waiting list.

Transfer: 118 transfer students enrolled in 2008-2009. Applicants must have a GPA of 3.2.

Visiting: There are regularly scheduled orientations for prospective students, including a tour of the school and residence halls and a discussion of admissions requirements, financial aid, and student activities. There are guides for informal visits, visitors may sit in on classes, and stay overnight. To schedule a visit, contact the Office of Admissions at (518) 694-7221.

Financial Aid: In 2009-2010, 88% of all full-time freshmen and 88% of continuing full-time students received some form of financial aid. 63% of all full-time freshmen and 68% of continuing full-time students received need-based aid. The average freshmen award was $10,382. 95% of undergraduate students work part-time. Average annual earnings from campus work are $1000. The FAFSA is required. The priority date for freshman financial aid applications for fall entry is February 1.

International Students: There are 113 international students enrolled. They must take the TOEFL with a minimum score of 600 on the paper-based TOEFL (PBT) or 100 on the Internet-based version (iBT), or the TSE. They must also take the SAT or ACT.

Computers: Wireless access is available. All students may access the system. 24 hours a day. There are no time limits. The fee is $200 per semester. All students are required to have a personal computer. A Gateway Tablet PC is recommended.

Graduates: From July 1, 2008 to June 30, 2009, 3 bachelor's degrees were awarded. The most popular majors were Doctor of Pharmacy (First Professional) (98%), B.S. Pharmaceutical Sciences (2%), and (%). 50 companies recruited on campus in 2008-2009. Of the 2008 graduating class, 13% were enrolled in graduate school within 6 months of graduation, and 87% were employed.

Admissions Contact: Matthew Stever, Director of Admissions. E-Mail: matthew.stever@acphs.edu Web: www.acphs.edu

ALBERT A. LIST COLLEGE OF JEWISH STUDIES   D-5

New York, NY 10027-4649	(212) 678-8832; (212) 678-8947
Full-time: 90 men, 90 women	Faculty: n/av
Part-time: 15 men, 15 women	Ph.D.s: n/av
Graduate: none	Student/Faculty: n/av
Year: semesters, summer session	Tuition: $11,600
Application Deadline: see profile	Room & Board: $10,000
Freshman Class: n/av	
SAT or ACT: required	

Albert A. List College of Jewish Studies, the undergraduate division of the Jewish Theological Seminary, founded in 1886, is a private institution affiliated with the Conservative branch of the Jewish faith. List College offers programs in all aspects of Judaism, including Bible, rabbinics, literature, history, philosophy, education, and communal service. There is also a combined liberal arts program with Columbia University and Barnard College. The figures in the above capsule and in this profile are approximate. The library contains 320,000 volumes, 3,500 microform items, and subscribes to 750 periodicals including electronic. Computerized library services include interlibrary loans and database searching. Special learning facilities include a learning resource center, art gallery, a music center, a Jewish education, research center, and the Jewish Museum Archives Center. The 1-acre campus is in an urban area on the upper west side of Manhattan. Including any residence halls, there are 6 buildings.

Student Life: 75% of undergraduates are from out of state, mostly the Middle Atlantic. Students are from 12 states, 3 foreign countries, and Canada. 70% are from public schools. All are white. All are Jewish. The average age of freshmen is 18; all undergraduates, 20. 96% remain to graduate.

Housing: 212 students can be accommodated in college housing, which includes coed dorms, on-campus apartments, off-campus apartments, and married student housing. In addition, there is kosher housing. On-campus housing is guaranteed for all 4 years. 93% of students live on campus; of those, 95% remain on campus on weekends. Alcohol is not permitted. All students may keep cars.

Activities: There are no fraternities or sororities. Groups on campus include art, band, choir, chorus, computers, dance, drama, ethnic, film, gay, honors, international, List College students have access to all clubs and organizations at Columbia and Barnard, literary magazine, musical theater, newspaper, orchestra, photography, political, professional, radio and TV, religious, social, social service, student government, and yearbook. Popular campus events include Purim, Simchat Torah, and Orientation.

Sports: There are 3 intramural sports for men and 3 for women. List College students may use the facilities at Columbia University.

Disabled Students: All of the campus is accessible. Facilities include wheelchair ramps, elevators, special parking, specially equipped restrooms, lowered drinking fountains, lowered telephones, and elevators with braille panels.

Services: Counseling and information services are available, as is tutoring in most subjects.

Campus Safety and Security: Measures include 24-hour foot and vehicle patrol and security escort services. There are emergency telephones and lighted pathways/sidewalks.

Programs of Study: List College confers B.A. degrees. Bachelor's degrees are awarded in SOCIAL SCIENCE (biblical studies and Judaic studies).

Required: Students must take a Hebrew language requirement, 24 credits in Jewish history, 9 in literature, and 6 each in Bible, Jewish philosophy, and Talmud. In addition, there are 60 required credits in liberal arts, including 6 credits each in English, history/philosophy/social science, and math or lab science to be completed at another college or university. A total of 156 credits (96 taken at List College) is required for graduation, with 21 in a major field.

Special: There is a joint program with Columbia University and a double-degree program with Barnard College, which enable students to earn 2 B.A. degrees in 4 to 4 1/2 years. Study abroad is available in Israel, England, France, and Spain. Student-designed majors, credit by exam, and nondegree study are also offered. There is a Phi Beta Kappa and a freshman honors program.

Faculty/Classroom: 68% of faculty are male; 32% are female. All teach and do research. No introductory courses are taught by graduate students. The average class size in an introductory lecture is 30 and in a regular course is 10.

Requirements: The SAT or ACT is required, as are SAT II: Subject tests. Applicants must be graduates of an accredited secondary school or have the GED. An essay and 2 recommendations are required; an interview is strongly recommended. AP credits are accepted. Important factors in the admissions decision are advanced placement or honors courses, extracurricular activities record, and personality/intangible qualities.

Procedure: Freshmen are admitted fall and spring. Entrance exams should be taken in the spring of the junior year. There are early decision, early admissions and deferred admissions plans. Early decision applications should be filed by November 15; regular applications, by November 1 for spring entry. The fall 2009 application fee was $60. Notification of early decision is sent December 15; regular decision, April 15.

Transfer: Applicants must submit SAT or ACT scores, an essay, high school and college transcripts, and 2 academic recommendations. A minimum college GPA of 2.5 is required. An interview is recommended. 48 of 156 credits required for the bachelor's degree must be completed at List College.

Visiting: There are regularly scheduled orientations for prospective students, including a tour of the campus and of Columbia University, an interview with the dean, and an overnight dormitory stay. There are guides for informal visits; visitors may sit in on classes and stay overnight. To schedule a visit, contact Reena Kamins, Admissions Director at (212) 678-8832.

Financial Aid: List College is a member of CSS. The CSS/Profile, the college's own financial statement, and 1040 tax forms are required. Check with the school for current application deadlines.

International Students: They must take the TOEFL and the college's own test, or the American Language English Placement Test. They must also take the SAT or ACT.

Computers: All students may access the system.

Admissions Contact: Reena Kamins, Director of Admissions. E-Mail: lcadmissions@jtsa.edu Web: www.jtsa.edu

ALFRED UNIVERSITY   B-4

Alfred, NY 14802-1205	(607) 871-2115
	(800) 541-9229; (607) 871-2198
Full-time: 896 men, 931 women	Faculty: 165
Part-time: 34 men, 48 women	Ph.D.s: 91%
Graduate: 122 men, 288 women	Student/Faculty: 11 to 1
Year: semesters, summer session	Tuition: $25,246
Application Deadline: February 1	Room & Board: $11,174
Freshman Class: 2579 applied, 1816 accepted, 465 enrolled	
SAT CR/M/W: 540/560/530	ACT: 24 VERY COMPETITIVE

Alfred University, founded in 1836, is composed of the privately endowed College of Business, College of Liberal Arts and Sciences, and New York State College of Ceramics (Inamori School of Engineering and School of Art and Design). Bachelor's, master's, and doctoral degrees and certificates of advanced study are awarded. There are 4 undergraduate schools and 1 graduate school. In addition to regional accreditation, AU has baccalaureate program accreditation with AACSB, ABET, ACS, CAAHEP, and NASAD. The 2 libraries contain 297,996 volumes, 86,536 microform items, and 176,336 audio/video tapes/CDs/DVDs, and subscribe to 48,886 periodicals including electronic. Computerized library services include interlibrary loans, database searching, and Internet access. Special learning facilities include a learning resource center, art gallery, radio station, TV station, and an observatory. The 232-acre campus is in a rural area 70 miles south of Rochester. Including any residence halls, there are 57 buildings.

Student Life: 69% of undergraduates are from New York. Others are from 38 states, 10 foreign countries, and Canada. 90% are from public schools. 68% are white. The average age of freshmen is 18; all undergraduates, 20. 29% do not continue beyond their first year; 69% remain to graduate.

Housing: 1456 students can be accommodated in college housing, which includes single-sex and coed dorms and on-campus apartments. In addition, there are honors houses, language houses, and special-interest houses. On-campus housing is guaranteed for the freshman year only, is available on a first-come, first-served basis, and is available on a lottery system for upperclassmen. 77% of students live on campus; of those, 90% remain on campus on weekends. All students may keep cars.

Activities: There are no fraternities or sororities. There are more than 75 groups on campus, including art, band, cheerleading, chess, chorale, chorus, computers, dance, drama, ethnic, film, gay, honors, international, jazz band, literary magazine, musical theater, newspaper, orchestra, pep band, photography, political, professional, radio and TV, religious, social, social service, Student Activities Board, student government, and yearbook. Popular campus events include Alumni Weekend, Hot Dog Day, and Glam Slam.

Sports: There are 10 intercollegiate sports for men and 11 for women, and 14 intramural sports for men and 13 for women. Facilities include an omniturf field for football, soccer and lacrosse, an Olympic-size pool, tennis courts, racquetball and squash courts, a weight room, and a dance and exercise studio. Merrill Field seats approximately 5000; the indoor gym seats approximately 3500. There is also a fitness center, an equestrian center, many hiking trails, and easy access to cross-country skiing.

Disabled Students: 50% of the campus is accessible. Facilities include wheelchair ramps, elevators, special parking, specially equipped restrooms, special class scheduling, and lowered drinking fountains.

Services: Counseling and information services are available, as is tutoring in most subjects. Time management, study skills workshops, and a writing center are available. There are also services for students with learning and physical disabilities.

Campus Safety and Security: Measures include security escort services. There are emergency telephones, lighted pathways/sidewalks, and vehicle and foot patrol.

Programs of Study: AU confers B.A., B.S., and B.F.A. degrees. Master's and doctoral degrees are also awarded. Bachelor's degrees are awarded in BIOLOGICAL SCIENCE (biology/biological science), BUSINESS (accounting, business administration and management, management science, and marketing/retailing/merchandising), COMMUNICATIONS AND THE ARTS (art history and appreciation, ceramic art and design, communications, dramatic arts, English, fine arts, French, German, glass, performing arts, and Spanish), COMPUTER AND PHYSICAL SCIENCE (chemistry, geology, mathematics, physics, and science), EDUCATION (art education, athletic training, business education, early childhood education, mathematics education, science education, secondary education, and social studies education), ENGINEERING AND ENVIRONMENTAL DESIGN (ceramic engineering, electrical/electronics engineering, environmental science, materials engineering, and mechanical engineering), SOCIAL SCIENCE (criminal justice, crosscultural studies, economics, gerontology, history, interdisciplinary studies, philosophy, political science/government, psychology, public administration, and sociology). Ceramic engineering, electrical engineering, and mechanical engineering are the strongest academically. Art and design, business administration, and ceramic engineering are the largest.

Required: To graduate, students must complete 120 to 137 credits, depending on the major, with 36 to 48 credits in the major. Students must demonstrate basic competencies in writing, oral communication, math, and computers. Freshmen must meet a physical education requirement. Distribution requirements include 8 credits each of social studies and natural science and 4 credits each of philosophy or religion, literature, art, and history. A minimum GPA of 2.0 and at least 30 semester hours have to be earned at AU.

Special: There are cooperative programs in engineering and business with Duke, Clarkson, and Columbia Universities and SUNY/Brockport. There is cross-registration with the SUNY College of Technology and a 5-year program in environmental management/forestry with Duke. Alfred offers internships in all programs, extensive study abroad, Washington and Albany semesters, work-study, a general studies degree, student-designed majors, dual majors, credit by exam, and pass/fail options. There are 16 national honor societies, including Phi Beta Kappa, and a freshman honors program.

Faculty/Classroom: 58% of faculty are male; 42% are female. 90% both teach undergraduates and do research. No introductory courses are taught by graduate students. The average class size in an introductory lecture is 25; in a laboratory, 15; and in a regular course, 18.

Admissions: 70% of the 2009-2010 applicants were accepted. The SAT scores for the 2009-2010 freshman class were: Critical Reading--26% below 500, 46% between 500 and 599, 23% between 600 and 700, and 5% above 700; Math--20% below 500, 49% between 500 and 599, 25% between 600 and 700, and 6% above 700; Writing--34% below 500, 44% between 500 and 599, 21% between 600 and 700, and 1% above 700. The ACT scores were 12% below 21, 31% between 21 and 23, 27% between 24 and 26, 13% between 27 and 28, and 17% above 28. 40% of the current freshmen were in the top fifth of their class; 76% were in the top two fifths. There were 3 National Merit finalists. 10 freshmen graduated first in their class.

Requirements: The SAT or ACT is required. A GED is accepted. In addition, a minimum of 16 Carnegie units is required, including 4 years of English and 2 to 3 years each of math, history/social studies, and science. The remaining units may be either in a foreign language or any of the previously mentioned fields. An essay is required, and applicants to B.F.A. programs must submit a portfolio. Interviews are encouraged. AP credits are accepted. Important factors in the admissions decision are advanced placement or honors courses, personality/intangible qualities, and extracurricular activities record.

Procedure: Freshmen are admitted fall and spring. Entrance exams should be taken in the junior year. There are early decision, deferred ad-

missions and rolling admissions plans. Early decision applications should be filed by December 1; regular applications, by February 1 for fall entry and December 1 for spring entry, along with a $50 fee. Notification of early decision is sent December 15; regular decision, on a rolling basis. 33 early decision candidates were accepted for the 2009-2010 class. Applications are accepted on-line.

Transfer: 64 transfer students enrolled in 2008-2009. Transfer applicants must have a GPA of at least 2.5. They must submit at least 1 letter of recommendation and official high school and college transcripts. Art students must submit a portfolio. 30 of 120 to 137 credits required for the bachelor's degree must be completed at AU.

Visiting: There are regularly scheduled orientations for prospective students, including a campus tour, a social activities panel, a financial aid presentation, faculty discussions, and on-campus interviews. There are guides for informal visits, and visitors may sit in on classes and stay overnight. To schedule a visit, contact the Admissions Office.

Financial Aid: In 2009-2010, 84% of all full-time students received some form of financial aid. 78% of all full-time freshmen and 76% of continuing full-time students received need-based aid. Need-based scholarships or need-based grants averaged $17,882; need-based self-help aid (loans and jobs) averaged $6471; and other non-need-based awards and non-need-based scholarships averaged $8755. 50% of undergraduate students work part-time. Average annual earnings from campus work are $1500. The average financial indebtedness of the 2009 graduate was $24,665. AU is a member of CSS. The FAFSA, the college's own financial statement, the business/farm supplement, and the noncustodial parent statement are required. The deadline for filing freshman financial aid applications for fall entry is May 1.

International Students: There are 39 international students enrolled. The school actively recruits these students. They must take the TOEFL with a minimum score of 550 on the paper-based TOEFL (PBT) or 80 on the Internet-based version (iBT), or take the IELTS. If students do not submit an SAT or ACT, they must submit the TOEFL or IELTS.

Computers: Wireless access is available. Each dorm room is wired; wireless is available in libraries, the campus center, and some classrooms. There are approximately 400 PCs available across campus for student use. All students may access the system 24 hours a day, 7 days a week. There are no time limits and no fees.

Graduates: From July 1, 2008 to June 30, 2009, 399 bachelor's degrees were awarded. The most popular majors were art and design (25%), psychology (9%), and business administration/education (6%). In an average class, 1% graduate in 3 years or less, 50% graduate in 4 years or less, 68% graduate in 5 years or less, and 69% graduate in 6 years or less. 79 companies recruited on campus in 2008-2009. Of the 2008 graduating class, 26% were enrolled in graduate school within 6 months of graduation, and 71% were employed.

Admissions Contact: Jeremy Spencer, Director of Admissions. E-mail: *spencer@alfred.edu or admissions@alfred.edu* Web: *www.alfred.edu*

BARD COLLEGE   D-4

Annandale-on-Hudson, NY 12504-5000   (845) 758-7472
                                                 (845) 758-5208

Full-time: 799 men, 1067 women	**Faculty:** 145; IIB, +$
Part-time: 36 men, 37 women	**Ph.Ds:** 96%
Graduate: 114 men, 181 women	**Student/Faculty:** 13 to 1
Year: 4-1-4	**Tuition:** $39,880
Application Deadline: January 15	**Room & Board:** $11,300
Freshman Class: 5510 applied, 1826 accepted, 505 enrolled	

VERY COMPETITIVE+

Bard College, founded in 1860, is an independent liberal arts and sciences institution affiliated historically with the Association of Episcopal Colleges. Discussion-oriented seminars and independent study are encouraged, tutorials are on a one-to-one basis, and most classes are kept small. There are 2 undergraduate schools and 8 graduate schools. The library contains 351,163 volumes, 7,995 microform items, and 3,916 audio/video tapes/CDs/DVDs, and subscribes to 32,413 periodicals including electronic. Computerized library services include interlibrary loans, database searching, Internet access, and laptop Internet portals. Special learning facilities include a learning resource center, art gallery, radio station, an ecology field station, the Levy Economics Institute, the Institute for Writing and Thinking, the Institute for Advanced Theology, the Center for Curatorial Studies and Art in Contemporary Culture, and an archeological station. The 600-acre campus is in a rural area 100 miles north of New York City. Including any residence halls, there are 70 buildings.

Student Life: 67% of undergraduates are from out of state, mostly the Middle Atlantic. Students are from 47 states, 59 foreign countries, and Canada. 64% are from public schools. 54% are white; 12% foreign nationals. The average age of freshmen is 18; all undergraduates, 20. 13% do not continue beyond their first year; 79% remain to graduate.

Housing: 1421 students can be accommodated in college housing, which includes single-sex and coed dorms. In addition, there are special-interest houses, a single-sex dorm, and quiet dorms. On-campus housing is guaranteed for the freshman year only and is available on a lottery system for upperclassmen. 64% of students live on campus; of those, 75% remain on campus on weekends. All students may keep cars.

Activities: There are no fraternities or sororities. There are more than 100 groups on campus, including art, band, chamber groups, chess, choir, chorus, computers, dance, debate, drama, environmental, ethnic, film, forensics, gay, international, jazz band, literary magazine, model UN, musical theater, newspaper, opera, orchestra, photography, political, radio and TV, religious, social, social service, student government, and symphony. Popular campus events include Winter Carnival, Spring Festival, and International Students Cultural Show.

Sports: There are 8 intercollegiate sports for men and 7 for women, and 9 intramural sports for men and 9 for women. Facilities include a gym and pool, fitness and weight facilities, rugby, soccer and lacrosse fields, squash and tennis courts, cross-country trails, bike paths, and multipurpose fields for activities such as ultimate frisbee and open recreation.

Disabled Students: 70% of the campus is accessible. Facilities include wheelchair ramps, elevators, special parking, specially equipped restrooms, lowered drinking fountains, and lowered telephones.

Services: Counseling and information services are available, as is tutoring in every subject. There is a reader service for the blind.

Campus Safety and Security: Measures include 24-hour foot and vehicle patrol, emergency notification system, self-defense education, and security escort services. There are shuttle buses, emergency telephones, lighted pathways/sidewalks, volunteer emergency medical technicians on call 24 hours a day, and Bard Response to Rape and Associated Violence Education (BRAVE).

Programs of Study: Bard confers B.A. and B.S. degrees. Associate, master's, and doctoral degrees are also awarded. Bachelor's degrees are awarded in BIOLOGICAL SCIENCE (biochemistry, biology/biological science, cell biology, ecology, microbiology, and molecular biology), COMMUNICATIONS AND THE ARTS (American literature, art history and appreciation, Chinese, classical languages, classics, creative writing, dance, dramatic arts, drawing, English, English literature, film arts, French, German, Germanic languages and literature, Italian, music history and appreciation, music performance, music theory and composition, painting, photography, Russian, sculpture, and Spanish), COMPUTER AND PHYSICAL SCIENCE (chemistry, mathematics, natural sciences, and physics), ENGINEERING AND ENVIRONMENTAL DESIGN (environmental science), HEALTH PROFESSIONS (predentistry and premedicine), SOCIAL SCIENCE (African studies, American studies, anthropology, archeology, area studies, Asian/Oriental studies, British studies, Celtic studies, clinical psychology, developmental psychology, Eastern European studies, economics, European studies, French studies, history, history of philosophy, history of science, human development, interdisciplinary studies, Italian studies, Judaic studies, Latin American studies, medieval studies, philosophy, political science/government, prelaw, religion, Russian and Slavic studies, social psychology, social science, sociology, and Spanish studies). Social studies, visual and/performing arts, and languages and literature are the largest.

Required: All students must complete a 3-week workshop in language and thinking, a first-year seminar, and a senior project. A conference in the junior year is required, and through a moderation process in the sophomore year, the student chooses a concentration in an academic department. A distribution of at least 1 course in each of the 9 academic areas is required, with a maximum of 84 hours in the student's major and a total of 124 credit hours needed to graduate. "Rethinking Differences", a course fulfilling the diversity requirement, is also required.

Special: Bard offers opportunities for study abroad, internships (no academic credit), Washington and New York semesters, dual majors, student-designed majors, accelerated degree programs, and pass/fail options. A 3-2 engineering degree is available with the Columbia University, Washington University (St. Louis), and Dartmouth College Schools of Engineering. Other 3-2 degrees are available in forestry and environmental studies, social work, architecture, city and regional planning, public health, and business administration. There are also opportunities for independent study, multicultural and ethnic studies, area studies, human rights, and globalization and international affairs.

Faculty/Classroom: 56% of faculty are male; 44% are female. All teach and do research. No introductory courses are taught by graduate students.

Admissions: 33% of the 2009-2010 applicants were accepted.

Requirements: Bard places strong emphasis on the academic background and intellectual curiosity of applicants, as well as indications of the student's commitment to social and environmental concerns, independent research, volunteer work, and other important extracurricular activities. Students applying for admission are expected to have graduated from an accredited secondary school (the GED is accepted) and must submit written essays with the application. The high school record should include a full complement of college-preparatory courses. Honors and advanced placement courses are also considered. A GPA of 3.0 is required. AP credits are accepted. Important factors in the admissions

decision are advanced placement or honors courses, recommendations by school officials, and extracurricular activities record.

Procedure: Freshmen are admitted fall. There are early admissions and deferred admissions plans. Applications should be filed by January 15 for fall entry and November 1 for spring entry, along with a $50 fee. Notifications are sent April 1. Applications are accepted on-line. 235 applicants were on a recent waiting list, 10 were accepted.

Transfer: 79 transfer students enrolled in 2008-2009. Admission requirements are the same as for regular applicants. A minimum GPA of 3.0 and an interview are recommended. High School transcript (when less than 2 years of college-level study completed), transfer questionnaire, and dean's report are required. 64 of 124 credits required for the bachelor's degree must be completed at Bard.

Visiting: There are regularly scheduled orientations for prospective students, consisting of regularly scheduled daily tours and information sessions. Visitors may sit in on classes. To schedule a visit, contact the Admissions Office at (845) 758-7472.

Financial Aid: In 2009-2010, 72% of all full-time freshmen and 66% of continuing full-time students received some form of financial aid. 66% of all full-time freshmen and 60% of continuing full-time students received need-based aid. The average freshman award was $31,959-$31,540. Need-based scholarships or need-based grants averaged $31,540 ($39,540) and need-based self-help aid (loans and jobs) averaged $4949 ($6,650 maximum). 38% of undergraduate students work part-time. Average annual earnings from campus work are $1200. The average financial indebtedness of the 2009 graduate was $26,131. Bard is a member of CSS. The CSS/Profile, FAFSA, the state aid form, and Non-custodial Profile and/or Business/Farm supplement if applicable are required. The priority date for freshman financial aid applications for fall entry is February 1. The deadline for filing freshman financial aid applications for fall entry is February 15.

International Students: There are 240 international students enrolled. The school actively recruits these students. They must take the TOEFL with a minimum score of 600 on the paper-based TOEFL (PBT).

Computers: Wireless access is available. All students may access the system. There are no time limits and no fees.

Graduates: From July 1, 2008 to June 30, 2009, 404 bachelor's degrees were awarded. The most popular majors were social studies (39%), visual and performing (30%), and language and literature (22%). 40 companies recruited on campus in 2008-2009. In an average class, 71% graduate in 4 years or less, 78% graduate in 5 years or less, and 80% graduate in 6 years or less.

Admissions Contact: Mary Backlund, Director of Admissions. A campus DVD is available. E-Mail: *admissions@bard.edu* Web: *www.bard.edu*

BERKELEY COLLEGE/NEW YORK CITY   D-5
New York, NY 10017

(212) 986-4343
(800) 446-5400; (212) 697-3371

Full-time: 750 men, 1620 women	Faculty: n/av
Part-time: 75 men, 200 women	Ph.Ds: n/av
Graduate: none	Student/Faculty: n/av
Year: trimesters	Tuition: $19,500
Application Deadline: open	
Freshman Class: n/av	
SAT or ACT: required	LESS COMPETITIVE

Berkeley College of New York City, founded in 1931, is a private institution offering undergraduate programs in business. The library contains 11,000 volumes, and subscribes to 130 periodicals including electronic. Computerized library services include interlibrary loans and database searching. Special learning facilities include a learning resource center. The campus is in an urban area in midtown Manhattan, a short walk from Grand Central Station. Including any residence halls, there are 2 buildings.

Student Life: 76% of undergraduates are from New York. 24% are Hispanic; 23% African American; 18% foreign nationals; 15% white. The average age of freshmen is 20; all undergraduates, 24.

Housing: There are no residence halls. All students commute.

Activities: There are no fraternities or sororities.

Sports: There is no sports program at Berkeley.

Services: Counseling and information services are available, as is tutoring in most subjects. There is remedial math, reading, and writing.

Programs of Study: Berkeley confers B.B.A. degrees. Associate degrees are also awarded. Bachelor's degrees are awarded in BUSINESS (accounting, business administration and management, international business management, and marketing/retailing/merchandising).

Faculty/Classroom: All teach undergraduates. No introductory courses are taught by graduate students.

Requirements: The SAT or ACT is required. In addition, graduation from an accredited high school or the GED, and an entrance exam or SAT or ACT scores are basic requirements for admission. A personal interview is strongly recommended. AP and CLEP credits are accepted.

Procedure: Freshmen are admitted to all sessions. Entrance exams should be taken any time. There are deferred admissions and rolling admissions plans. Application deadlines are open. Fall 2008 application fee was $50. Notification is sent on a rolling basis. Applications are accepted on-line.

Transfer: A transcript from each college or university attended must be submitted to receive credit. 60 of 180 credits required for the bachelor's degree must be completed at.

Visiting: There are guides for informal visits.

Financial Aid: In in a recent year, 90% of all full-time freshmen received some form of financial aid. The FAFSA, the college's own financial statement, and state income tax form are required. Check with the school for current application deadlines.

International Students: There were 130 international students enrolled in a recent year. The school actively recruits these students. They must take the TOEFL.

Computers: All students may access the system. There are no time limits and no fees.

Graduates: In a recent year, 2009, 311 bachelor's degrees were awarded.

Admissions   Contact: Admissions   Officer   E-Mail: *info@berkeleycollege.edu* Web: *www.berkeleycollege.edu*

BERKELEY COLLEGE/WESTCHESTER CAMPUS   D-5
White Plains, NY 10601   **(914) 694-1122**
(800) 446-5400; (914) 328-9469

Full-time: 170 men, 410 women	Faculty: n/av
Part-time: 15 men, 45 women	Ph.D.s: n/av
Graduate: none	Student/Faculty: n/av
Year: semesters	Tuition: $18,500
Application Deadline: open	Room & Board: $10,000
Freshman Class: n/av	**LESS COMPETITIVE**

Berkeley College, established in 1945, is a private institution with 5 campuses in New York and New Jersey. Its programs are designed to prepare students for careers in business by providing an education that balances academic studies, professional training, and hands-on experience. The information in this profile refers to the Westchester campus. The figures in the above capsule and in this profile are approximate. The library contains 9,500 volumes, and 800 audio/video tapes/CDs/DVDs, and subscribes to 80 periodicals including electronic. Computerized library services include interlibrary loans and database searching. Special learning facilities include a learning resource center. The 10-acre campus is in a suburban area. Including any residence halls, there are 3 buildings.

Student Life: 80% of undergraduates are from New York. Others are from 8 states, and 14 foreign countries. 66% are white; 16% African American; 11% Hispanic. The average age of freshmen is 19; all undergraduates, 20.

Housing: 96 students can be accommodated in college housing, which includes coed dorms. Priority is given to out-of-town students. 86% of students commute. Alcohol is not permitted. All students may keep cars.

Activities: There are no fraternities or sororities. There are 6 groups on campus, including international, newspaper, professional, social, social service, and student government. Popular campus events include Multicultural Month and Commuter Appreciation Day.

Sports: There is no sports program at Berkeley. Students have access to the sports and exercise facilities at nearby Manhattanville College.

Disabled Students: Facilities include wheelchair ramps, elevators, and special parking.

Services: Counseling and information services are available, as is tutoring in every subject. There is remedial math, reading, and writing.

Campus Safety and Security: There are lighted pathways/sidewalks and night patrols by trained security personnel.

Programs of Study: Berkeley confers B.B.A. degrees. Associates degrees are also awarded. Bachelor's degrees are awarded in BUSINESS (accounting, business administration and management, international business management, and marketing/retailing/merchandising).

Faculty/Classroom: No introductory courses are taught by graduate students.

Requirements: Graduation from an accredited high school or the equivalent (GED) and an entrance exam or the SAT or ACT scores are basic requirements for admission. A personal interview is strongly recommended. AP and CLEP credits are accepted.

Procedure: Freshmen are admitted to all sessions. Entrance exams should be taken as soon as the application is submitted, if possible. There are deferred admissions and rolling admissions plans. Application deadlines are open. The fall 2009 application fee was $35. Notification is sent on a rolling basis. Applications are accepted on-line.

Transfer: Applicants must submit a transcript from each college attended and a high school transcript or equivalent (GED). 60 of 180 credits required for the bachelor's degree must be completed at Berkeley.

Visiting: There are guides for informal visits.

Financial Aid: The FAFSA, the college's own financial statement, and state income tax return are required. Check with the school for current application deadlines.

International Students: The school actively recruits these students. They must take the TOEFL.

Computers: All students may access the system. There are no time limits and no fees.

Admissions   Contact: Admissions   Officer   E-Mail: *info@berkeleycollege.edu* Web: *www.berkeleycollege.edu*

BORICUA COLLEGE   D-5
New York, NY 10032   **(212) 694-1000 or (718) 782-2200**
(212) 694-1015 or (718) 782-2050

Full-time: 260 men, 910 women	Faculty: n/av
Part-time: none	Ph.D.s: n/av
Graduate: none	Student/Faculty: n/av
Year: semesters	Tuition: $8600
Application Deadline: see profiles	
Freshman Class: n/av	**COMPETITIVE**

Boricua College, founded in 1974, is a private college for bilingual students, designed to meet the needs of a Spanish-speaking population. Figures in the above capsule and in this profile are approximate. There are 2 graduate schools. The library contains 128,727 volumes, and 3,000 audio/video tapes/CDs/DVDs, and subscribes to 227 periodicals including electronic. Computerized library services include database searching. Special learning facilities include a learning resource center and art gallery. The campus is in an urban area in Manhattan and Brooklyn. Including any residence halls, there are 4 buildings.

Student Life: All of undergraduates are from New York. 70% are from public schools. 85% are Hispanic. The average age of freshmen is 29; all undergraduates, 32. 12% do not continue beyond their first year; 80% remain to graduate.

Housing: There are no residence halls. All students commute.

Activities: There are no fraternities or sororities. There are 5 groups on campus, including art, chorus, drama, newspaper, and student government. Popular campus events include cultural programs, Puerto Rican Discovery Day and Christmas and Spring concerts with chorus and orchestra.

Sports: Facilities include a gym.

Disabled Students: Facilities include elevators and specially equipped restrooms.

Services: Counseling and information services are available, as is tutoring in most subjects.

Campus Safety and Security: There are shuttle buses, emergency telephones, and lighted pathways/sidewalks.

Programs of Study: Boricua confers B.A. degrees. Bachelor's degrees are awarded in BUSINESS (business administration and management), EDUCATION (elementary education), SOCIAL SCIENCE (human services and liberal arts/general studies).

Faculty/Classroom: No introductory courses are taught by graduate students.

Requirements: Boricua administers its own tests to prospective students, although either the SAT or ACT is accepted. Applicants must be graduates of an accredited secondary school or have a GED. 2 letters of recommendation and an admissions interview are required. Applicants must demonstrate a working knowledge of English and Spanish to a faculty panel. CLEP credits are accepted. Important factors in the admissions decision are leadership record, personality/intangible qualities, and recommendations by school officials.

Procedure: Freshmen are admitted fall, spring, and summer. Entrance exams should be taken when called by the admissions staff. There are early decision and rolling admissions plan. Application deadlines are open. Application fee is $30.

Transfer: Applicants with associate degrees may transfer up to 60 credits. All college credits passed with grade C and above are accepted. 80 of 124 credits required for the bachelor's degree must be completed at Boricua.

Visiting: There are regularly scheduled orientations for prospective students. Letters are sent to prospective students advising them of scheduled orientations. To schedule a visit, contact Abraham Cruzat or Miriam Prefferat at (212) 694-1000 or (718) 782-2200.

Financial Aid: Boricua is a member of CSS. The FAFSA and income tax forms are required. Check with the school for current application deadlines.

Computers: All students may access the system. There are no time limits and no fees.

Admissions Contact: Abraham Cruz (Manhattan) or Miriam Pfeffer, Director of Student Services. E-Mail: *mpfeffer@boricuacolleg* Web: *www.boricuacollege.edu*

CANISIUS COLLEGE
A-3

Buffalo, NY 14208

(716) 888-2200
(800) 843-1517; (716) 888-3230

Full-time: 1444 men, 1606 women	**Faculty:** 223; IIA, av$
Part-time: 81 men, 65 women	**Ph.D.s:** 92%
Graduate: 634 men, 944 women	**Student/Faculty:** 11 to 1
Year: semesters, summer session	**Tuition:** $29,512
Application Deadline: March 1	**Room & Board:** $10,556
Freshman Class: 3996 applied, 3084 accepted, 708 enrolled	
SAT CR/M: 549/569	**ACT:** 24 **VERY COMPETITIVE**

Canisius College, founded in 1870, is a private Roman Catholic college in the Jesuit tradition. It offers undergraduate programs in the liberal arts and sciences, business, education, and human services. There are 3 undergraduate schools and 3 graduate schools. In addition to regional accreditation, Canisius has baccalaureate program accreditation with AACSB, CAHEA, and NCATE. The library contains 353,617 volumes, 599,947 microform items, and 11,361 audio/video tapes/CDs/DVDs, and subscribes to 37,240 periodicals including electronic. Computerized library services include interlibrary loans, database searching, Internet access, and laptop Internet portals. Special learning facilities include a learning resource center, art gallery, radio station, a television studio, foreign language lab, 87 media-assisted classrooms, digital media lab, and musical instrument digital interface classroom. The 36-acre campus is in an urban area in Buffalo. Including any residence halls, there are 51 buildings.

Student Life: 89% of undergraduates are from New York. Others are from 32 states, 14 foreign countries, and Canada. 70% are from public schools. 85% are white. The average age of freshmen is 18; all undergraduates, 20. 18% do not continue beyond their first year; 68% remain to graduate.

Housing: 1599 students can be accommodated in college housing, which includes single-sex and coed dorms, on-campus apartments, and off-campus apartments. In addition, there are honors houses, special-interest houses, an intercultural hall, and townhouses. On-campus housing is guaranteed for all 4 years, is available on a first-come, first-served basis, and is available on a lottery system for upperclassmen. 54% of students commute. All students may keep cars.

Activities: 1% of men belong to 1 national fraternity; 1% of women belong to 1 national sorority. There are 100 groups on campus, including art, band, cheerleading, chess, choir, chorale, computers, dance, drama, drill team, ethnic, gay, honors, international, jazz band, literary magazine, musical theater, newspaper, orchestra, pep band, political, professional, radio and TV, religious, social, social service, and student government. Popular campus events include Fall Semiformal, International Fest, and Canisius Concert Series.

Sports: There are 8 intercollegiate sports for men and 8 for women, and 12 intramural sports for men and 12 for women. Facilities include an 1800-seat athletic center with a 25-yard pool, training rooms, a 1000-seat sports complex with Astroturf playing fields, a rifle range, and a mirrored dance studio.

Disabled Students: 90% of the campus is accessible. Facilities include wheelchair ramps, elevators, special parking, specially equipped rest rooms, special class scheduling, lowered drinking fountains, lowered telephones, automatic doors, TDD, a shuttle service for students with disabilities, distraction-free testing spaces, and adjustable classroom desks.

Services: Counseling and information services are available, as is tutoring in every subject. There is a reader service for the blind, and remedial math, reading, and writing.

Campus Safety and Security: Measures include 24-hour foot and vehicle patrol, emergency notification system, self-defense education, and security escort services. There are shuttle buses, emergency telephones, lighted pathways/sidewalks, a crime prevention officer, bicycle patrols, and crime prevention programs.

Programs of Study: Canisius confers B.A. and B.S., B.A.Ed., and B.S.Ed. degrees. Master's degrees are also awarded. Bachelor's degrees are awarded in BIOLOGICAL SCIENCE (biochemistry, bioinformatics, biology/biological science, environmental biology, and zoology), BUSINESS (accounting, banking and finance, business administration and management, business communications, business economics, entrepreneurial studies, fashion merchandising, international business management, investments and securities, management information systems, management science, marketing management, and marketing/retailing/merchandising), COMMUNICATIONS AND THE ARTS (art history and appreciation, communications, digital communications, English, French, German, media arts, modern language, music, Spanish, and speech/debate/rhetoric), COMPUTER AND PHYSICAL SCIENCE (chemistry, computer science, information sciences and systems, mathematics, and physics), EDUCATION (athletic training, early childhood education, elementary education, English education, foreign languages education, mathematics education, middle school education, physical education, science education, social studies education, and special education), ENGINEERING AND ENVIRONMENTAL DESIGN (environmental science and preengineering), HEALTH PROFESSIONS (medical laboratory technology, predentistry, premedicine, prepharmacy, preveterinary science, and sports medicine), SOCIAL SCIENCE (anthropology, criminal justice, European studies, history, humanities and social science, international relations, liberal arts/general studies, philosophy, prelaw, psychology, sociology, and urban studies). Accounting, biology, and chemistry are the strongest academically. Psychology, biology, and communications studies are the largest.

Required: Students take 12 required courses and complete 6 knowledge and skills requirement areas to satisfy their requirements. In addition, students must take 10 3-credit courses in the major. A minimum of 120 credit hours and a GPA of 2.0 are required for graduation.

Special: Canisius offers internships, credit by exam, pass/fail options, dual majors, a Washington semester, work-study programs, and study abroad in 13 countries. Cooperative programs are available with the Fashion Institute of Technology in New York City. Cross-registration is permitted with 14 schools in the Western New York Consortium of Higher Education. Canisius also offers early assurance and joint degree programs, with SUNY health professions schools in Buffalo and Syracuse, and a 3-2 MBA. There are 9 national honor societies, a freshman honors program, and 5 departmental honors programs.

Faculty/Classroom: 63% of faculty are male; 37% are female. All teach and do research. No introductory courses are taught by graduate students. The average class size in an introductory lecture, 23, in a laboratory, 18, and in a regular course, 20.

Admissions: 77% of the 2009-2010 applicants were accepted. The SAT scores for the 2009-2010 freshman class were: Critical Reading-- 24% below 500, 48% between 500 and 599, 25% between 600 and 700, and 3% above 700; Math--19% below 500, 43% between 500 and 599, 33% between 600 and 700, and 5% above 700. The ACT scores were 8% below 21, 17% between 21 and 23, 22% between 24 and 26, 23% between 27 and 28, and 30% above 28. 51% of the current freshmen were in the top fifth of their class; 78% were in the top two fifths. 4 freshmen graduated first in their class.

Requirements: The SAT or ACT is required. In addition, all students must submit official high school transcript (or GED) and SAT or ACT results. College preparatory course work should include 4 units each of English and social science, 3 units each of math, science, and foreign language. Students with a B+ average and a satisfactory SAT score are most competitive. An essay and an interview are recommended. A GPA of 2.0 is required. AP and CLEP credits are accepted. Important factors in the admissions decision are leadership record, recommendations by school officials, and advanced placement or honors courses.

Procedure: Freshmen are admitted fall, spring, and summer. Entrance exams should be taken during the junior or senior year. There are deferred admissions and rolling admissions plans. Applications should be filed by March 1 for fall entry, along with a $40 fee. Notification is sent on a rolling basis. Applications are accepted on-line.

Transfer: 124 transfer students enrolled in 2008-2009. Applicants must present a minimum GPA of 2.0 and a Transfer Recommendation Form. 30 of 120 credits required for the bachelor's degree must be completed at Canisius.

Visiting: There are regularly scheduled orientations for prospective students, including an admissions interview or group session, campus tour, and financial aid appointment by request. Also available are summer visitations for families, selected Saturday visits, multiple fall open houses, an open house in the spring, a financial aid workshop workshop in January, and overnights for admitted students. There are guides for informal visits and visitors may sit in on classes. To schedule a visit, contact the Admissions Office at admissions@canisius.edu.

Financial Aid: In 2009-2010, 98% of all full-time freshmen and 94% of continuing full-time students received some form of financial aid. 82% of all full-time freshmen and 75% of continuing full-time students received need-based aid. The average freshman award was $26,843. Need-based scholarships or need-based grants averaged $9,552 ($36,848 maximum); need-based self-help aid (loans and jobs) averaged $4,471 ($7,300 maximum); non-need-based athletic scholarships averaged $19,919 ($42,636 maximum); and other non-need-based awards and non-need-based scholarships averaged $13,582 ($40,418 maximum). 24% of undergraduate students work part-time. Average annual earnings from campus work are $1676. The average financial indebtedness of the 2009 graduate was $33,645. Canisius is a member of CSS. The FAFSA is required. The priority date for freshman financial aid applications for fall entry is February 15.

International Students: There are 139 international students enrolled. The school actively recruits these students. They must take the TOEFL with a minimum score of 500 on the paper-based TOEFL (PBT) or 64 on the Internet-based version (iBT). They must also take the SAT or ACT.

Computers: Wireless access is available. Students may access more than 527 PCs throughout campus including kiosk stations in academic buildings. All computers are connected to the Internet and have access to extensive on-line research database provided by the library. Laptops with wireless access are available for use in the library. All students may access the system. The web can be accessed at any time. There are no time limits and no fees. It is strongly recommended that all students have a personal computer.

Graduates: From July 1, 2008 to June 30, 2009, 824 bachelor's degrees were awarded. The most popular majors were psychology (9%), communication studies (9%), and marketing (8%). 29 companies recruited on campus in 2008-2009. In an average class, 55% graduate in 4 years or less, 66% graduate in 5 years or less, and 68% graduate in 6 years or less. Of the 2008 graduating class, 26% were enrolled in graduate school within 6 months of graduation, and 63% were employed.

Admissions Contact: Ann Marie Moscovic, Director of Admissions. E-mail: *admissions@canisius.edu* Web: *www.canisius.edu*

CAZENOVIA COLLEGE C-3

Cazenovia, NY 13035   (315) 655-7208
(800) 654-3210; (315) 655-2190

Full-time: 250 men, 700 women	Faculty: IIB,--$
Part-time: 35 men, 120 women	Ph.D.s: n/av
Graduate: none	Student/Faculty: n/av
Year: semesters, summer session	Tuition: $21,800
Application Deadline: open	Room & Board: $9000
Freshman Class: n/av	
SAT or ACT: recommended	**COMPETITIVE**

Cazenovia College, founded in 1824, is a private institution offering degree programs in liberal arts and preprofessional studies. The figures in the above capsule and in this profile are approximate. The library contains 83,340 volumes, 14,727 microform items, and 4,160 audio/video tapes/CDs/DVDs, and subscribes to 61,000 periodicals including electronic. Computerized library services include interlibrary loans, database searching, Internet access, and laptop Internet portals. Special learning facilities include a learning resource center, art gallery, radio station, and a nearby campus farm with equine center. The 40-acre campus is in a small town 18 miles southeast of Syracuse. Including any residence halls, there are 26 buildings.

Student Life: 80% of undergraduates are from New York. Others are from 24 states, 4 foreign countries, and Canada. 90% are from public schools. 86% are white; 54% African American. The average age of freshmen is 18.

Housing: 817 students can be accommodated in college housing, which includes single-sex and coed dorms, on-campus apartments, and off-campus apartments. In addition, there are all-female residence hall, and upperclass-only housing. 90% of students live on campus. Upperclassmen may keep cars.

Activities: There are no fraternities or sororities. There are 52 groups on campus, including art, band, cheerleading, choir, chorale, computers, debate, drama, environmental, ethnic, gay, honors, literary magazine, musical theater, newspaper, political, professional, religious, social, social service, student government, and yearbook.

Sports: There are 10 intercollegiate sports for men and 10 for women, and 9 intramural sports for men and 9 for women. Facilities include an athletic center with a pool, 2 gyms, a fitness center, outdoor tennis courts, and athletic fields.

Disabled Students: 86% of the campus is accessible. Facilities include wheelchair ramps, elevators, special parking, specially equipped restrooms, special class scheduling, lowered telephones, and special housing.

Services: Counseling and information services are available, as is tutoring in most subjects. There is a reader service for the blind, and remedial math, reading, and writing.

Campus Safety and Security: Measures include 24-hour foot and vehicle patrol, emergency notification system, and security escort services. There are emergency telephones, lighted pathways/sidewalks, and controlled access to dorms/residences.

Programs of Study: Cazenovia confers B.A., B.S., B.F.A., and B.P.S. degrees. Associates degrees are also awarded. Bachelor's degrees are awarded in AGRICULTURE (environmental studies), BUSINESS (business administration and management and management science), COMMUNICATIONS AND THE ARTS (communications, English, studio art, and visual design), EDUCATION (early childhood education and elementary education), ENGINEERING AND ENVIRONMENTAL DESIGN (commercial art and interior design), SOCIAL SCIENCE (criminology, fashion design and technology, human services, liberal arts/general studies, psychology, and social science). Interior design and equine management are the strongest academically. Management is the largest.

Required: A total of 120 semester credits and a GPA of 2.0 are required for the bachelor's degree. Students must take courses in speech, academic writing, diversity and social consciousness, science or math, visual literacy, communications, ethics, cultural literacy, and research methods. They must also demonstrate math proficiency and complete a senior capstone course.

Special: Cazenovia offers internships, a Washington semester, work-study, B.A.-B.S. degrees in liberal studies and liberal and professional studies. There is a study-abroad program at Canterbury Christ Church

University in the United Kingdom. There are 3 national honor societies, a freshman honors program, and 2 departmental honors programs.

Faculty/Classroom: 40% of faculty are male; 60% are female. All teach undergraduates, and 1% do research. No introductory courses are taught by graduate students. The average class size in an introductory lecture is 20; in a laboratory is 15; and in a regular course is 16.

Requirements: The SAT or ACT is recommended. In addition, applicants should be graduates of an accredited secondary school or the equivalent. A recommendation from a guidance counselor or teacher is required. AP and CLEP credits are accepted. Important factors in the admissions decision are advanced placement or honors courses and leadership record.

Procedure: Freshmen are admitted fall and spring. Entrance exams should be taken by the fall of the senior year. There are deferred admissions and rolling admissions plans. Application deadlines are open. Application fee is $30. Applications are accepted on-line. A waiting list is maintained.

Transfer: 66 transfer students enrolled in a recent year. Applicants must present at least 12 college credits, with a minimum GPA of 2.0, and official transcripts from previous colleges attended. Students with fewer than 24 credits must also submit a high school transcript. 30 of 120 credits required for the bachelor's degree must be completed at Cazenovia.

Visiting: There are regularly scheduled orientations for prospective students, consisting of a welcome by the president and deans, financial aid sessions, placement testing, academic advising, and registration. There are guides for informal visits; visitors may sit in on classes and stay overnight. To schedule a visit, contact the Admissions and Financial Aid Office.

Financial Aid: Cazenovia is a member of CSS. The FAFSA and Express TAP are required. Check with the school for current application deadlines.

International Students: There were 4 international students enrolled in a recent year. The school actively recruits these students. They must take the TOEFL.

Computers: Wireless access is available. All students may access the system.

Graduates: In a recent year, 163 bachelor's degrees were awarded. The most popular majors were management (39%), human services (25%), and visual communications (19%).

Admissions Contact: Robert A. Croot, Dean for Admissions and Financial Aid. E-Mail: *admission@cazcollege.edu* Web: *www.cazenovia.edu*

CITY UNIVERSITY OF NEW YORK

The City University of New York, established in 1847, is a public system in New York. It is governed by a Board of Trustees, whose chief administrator is Chancellor. The primary goal of the system is To maintain and expand its commitment to academic excellence, and to the provision of equal access and opportunity. The main priorities are Providing access for all students who seek to enroll, Insuring student success. Enhancing instructional and research excellence. Profiles of the 4-year campuses are included in this section.

CITY UNIVERSITY OF NEW YORK/BARUCH COLLEGE D-5

New York, NY 10010-5585   (646) 312-1400; (646) 312-1361

Full-time: 4750 men, 4880 women	Faculty: IIA, ++$
Part-time: 1420 men, 1860 women	Ph.D.s: n/av
Graduate: 1550 men, 1700 women	Student/Faculty: n/av
Year: semesters, summer session	Tuition: $5400 ($9900)
Application Deadline: February 1	
Freshman Class: n/av	
SAT or ACT: required	**VERY COMPETITIVE**

Baruch College was founded in 1919 and became a separate unit of the City University of New York in 1968. It offers undergraduate programs in business and public administration and liberal arts and sciences. The figures in the above capsule and in this profile are approximate. There are 3 undergraduate schools and 3 graduate schools. In addition to regional accreditation, Baruch has baccalaureate program accreditation with AACSB. The library contains 456,132 volumes, 2.1 million microform items, and 1,246 audio/video tapes/CDs/DVDs, and subscribes to 15,860 periodicals including electronic. Computerized library services include interlibrary loans, database searching, and Internet access. Special learning facilities include an art gallery and radio station. The 39-acre campus is in an urban area Manhattan. Including any residence halls, there are 6 buildings.

Student Life: 84% of undergraduates are from New York. Others are from 151 foreign countries and Canada. 62% are from public schools. 30% are white; 30% Asian American; 17% Hispanic; 13% foreign nationals; 11% African American. The average age of freshmen is 18; all undergraduates, 24. 12% do not continue beyond their first year; 60% remain to graduate.

Housing: There are no residence halls. All students commute.

Activities: 1% of men belong to 1 local and 3 national fraternities; 1% of women belong to 1 local and 3 national sororities. There are 172 groups on campus, including cheerleading, chess, chorus, computers, dance, debate, drama, ethnic, gay, honors, international, literary magazine, newspaper, photography, political, professional, radio and TV, religious, social, social service, student government, and yearbook. Popular campus events include club fairs, street fairs, Relay for Life and Caribbean Week.

Sports: There are 7 intercollegiate sports for men and 7 for women, and 5 intramural sports for men and 5 for women. Facilities include two gyms, a swimming pool, a weight room, an exercise room, and racquetball courts.

Disabled Students: All of the campus is accessible. Facilities include wheelchair ramps, elevators, specially equipped restrooms, special class scheduling, lowered drinking fountains, and lowered telephones.

Services: Counseling and information services are available, as is tutoring in most subjects. There is a reader service for the blind, and remedial math and writing. Note takers and large-print computer screens are available. There are also interpreters for the deaf.

Campus Safety and Security: Measures include 24-hour foot and vehicle patrol, self-defense education, and security escort services. There are lighted pathways/sidewalks, controlled access to dorms/residences, fire safety directors and an ID system that uses card swipe in turnstiles for entry.

Programs of Study: Baruch confers B.A., B.S., and B.B.A. degrees. Master's and doctoral degrees are also awarded. Bachelor's degrees are awarded in BUSINESS (accounting, investments and securities, management science, marketing management, marketing/retailing/merchandising, operations research, personnel management, and real estate), COMMUNICATIONS AND THE ARTS (advertising, communications, English, journalism, music, and Spanish), COMPUTER AND PHYSICAL SCIENCE (actuarial science, information sciences and systems, mathematics, and statistics), SOCIAL SCIENCE (economics, history, industrial and organizational psychology, philosophy, political science/government, psychology, public affairs, and sociology). Economics, English, and math are the strongest academically. Accounting, finance, and computer information systems are the largest.

Required: Students must complete a minimum of 120 credits for the B.A. or B.S. and 124 for the B.B.A., with at least 24 hours in the major, and maintain a GPA of 2.0 overall in the major. Students' core curriculum should include courses in English, literature, communications, history, philosophy, psychology, microeconomics, and fine and performing arts.

Special: Students may take courses at all CUNY schools. The college offers internships and study abroad in Great Britain, France, Germany, Mexico, and Israel. Students may design their own liberal arts major. A federal work-study program is available, and pass/fail options are permitted for liberal arts majors. Students may combine any undergraduate major with a master's in accountancy. There are 7 national honor societies, a freshman honors program, and 3 departmental honors programs.

Faculty/Classroom: 62% of faculty are male; 38% are female. 93% teach undergraduates, and 89% do research. Graduate students teach 8% of introductory courses. The average class size in an introductory lecture is 275; in a laboratory is 20; and in a regular course is 35.

Requirements: The SAT or ACT is required. In addition, applicants must present an official high school transcript (a GED will be accepted) indicating a minimum average grade of 81% in academic subjects (minimum of 14 credits). A GPA of 80.0 is required. AP and CLEP credits are accepted.

Procedure: Freshmen are admitted fall and spring. There are early decision admission plans. Entrance exams should be taken March 1. Applications should be filed by February 1 for fall entry and October 1 for spring entry. The fall 2009 application fee was $65.

Transfer: 1337 transfer students enrolled in a recent year. Applicants must have a minimum GPA of 2.5 for 12 to 34.9 credits submitted, a minimum GPA of 2.25 for 35 to 59.9 credits, and a minimum GPA of 2.0 for 60 or more credits. Business applicants must have a 2.75 GPA. Students applying for transfer with fewer than 12 credits earned must have a minimum GPA of 2.5 and a minimum high school average of 80%. 32 of 128 credits required for the bachelor's degree must be completed at Baruch.

Visiting: There are regularly scheduled orientations for prospective students, including a meeting with an admissions counselor. There are guides for informal visits. To schedule a visit, contact the Admissions Office.

Financial Aid: The FAFSA is required. Check with the school for current application deadlines.

International Students: There were 1234 international students enrolled in a recent year. They must take the TOEFL.

Computers: Wireless access is available. All students receive a network account upon acceptance. They may use it for both wired and wireless network access. There are 1300 PCs in the 25 computer labs plus kiosks in high-traffic areas. All students may access the system. There are no time limits and no fees.

Graduates: In a recent year, 2550 bachelor's degrees were awarded. The most popular majors were finance and investments (25%), accounting (23%), and marketing (13%). 350 companies recruited on campus in 2008-2009. In an average class, 5% graduate in 4 years or less, 23% graduate in 5 years or less, and 35% graduate in 6 years or less. Of the 2008 graduating class, 7% were enrolled in graduate school within 6 months of graduation, and 66% were employed.

Admissions Contact: Marybeth Murphy, Director of Undergraduate Admissions. A campus DVD is available. E-Mail: *marybeth_murphy@baruch.cuny.edu* Web: *www.cuny.edu*

CITY UNIVERSITY OF NEW YORK/BROOKLYN COLLEGE

D-5

Brooklyn, NY 11210-2889   **(718) 951-5001; (718) 951-4506**

Full-time: 3813 men, 5455 women	Faculty: 533; IIA, +$
Part-time: 1452 men, 2349 women	Ph.D.s: 93%
Graduate: 1217 men, 2808 women	Student/Faculty: 17 to 1
Year: semesters, summer session	Tuition: $5051 ($12,901)
Application Deadline: October 1	
Freshman Class: 17497 applied, 4873 accepted, 977 enrolled	
SAT or ACT: required	COMPETITIVE+

Brooklyn College, established in 1930, is a publicly supported college of liberal arts, sciences, preprofessional, and professional studies. It is part of the City University of New York and serves the commuter student. There are 2 undergraduate schools and 1 graduate school. In addition to regional accreditation, Brooklyn College has baccalaureate program accreditation with ADA and NCATE. The library contains 1.4 million volumes, 1.7 million microform items, and 22,627 audio/video tapes/CDs/DVDs, and subscribes to 44,470 periodicals including electronic. Computerized library services include interlibrary loans, database searching, and Internet access. Special learning facilities include a learning resource center, art gallery, radio station, TV station, 3 color studios, and a speech and hearing clinic. The 26-acre campus is in an urban area in Brooklyn, New York. Including any residence halls, there are 10 buildings.

Student Life: 99% of undergraduates are from New York. Others are from 31 states, 102 foreign countries, and Canada. 77% are from public schools. 39% are white; 26% African American; 16% Asian American; 13% Hispanic. The average age of freshmen is 18; all undergraduates, 24. 22% do not continue beyond their first year; 78% remain to graduate.

Housing: There are no residence halls. All students commute.

Activities: 3% of men belong to 8 national fraternities; 3% of women belong to 4 local and 4 national sororities. There are 150 groups on campus, including academic, art, chess, computers, dance, drama, ethnic, film, forensics, gay, honors, international, literary magazine, musical theater, newspaper, political, professional, radio and TV, religious, social, social service, student government, symphony, and yearbook. Popular campus events include Welcome Back Bash, Fall Festival, and Make a Difference Day.

Sports: There are 6 intercollegiate sports for men and 6 for women, and 14 intramural sports for men and 14 for women. Facilities include a swimming pool, a soccer field, softball field, volleyball, racquetball, squash, tennis, and basketball courts, a fitness center, and a jogging track.

Disabled Students: All of the campus is accessible. Facilities include wheelchair ramps, elevators, special parking, specially equipped restrooms, special class scheduling, lowered drinking fountains, and lowered telephones.

Services: Counseling and information services are available, as is tutoring in every subject. There is a reader service for the blind.

Campus Safety and Security: Measures include 24-hour foot and vehicle patrol and security escort services. There are shuttle buses, emergency telephones, lighted pathways/sidewalks, controlled access to dorms/residences, CCTV cameras, and informational assistants.

Programs of Study: Brooklyn College confers B.A., B.S., B.F.A., and B.Mus. degrees. Master's degrees are also awarded. Bachelor's degrees are awarded in AGRICULTURE (environmental studies), BIOLOGICAL SCIENCE (biology/biological science), BUSINESS (accounting, banking and finance, business administration and management, and business systems analysis), COMMUNICATIONS AND THE ARTS (art, art history and appreciation, broadcasting, classics, communications, comparative literature, creative writing, English, film arts, French, Italian, journalism, linguistics, multimedia, music, music performance, music theory and composition, radio/television technology, Russian, Spanish, speech/debate/rhetoric, theater management, and visual and performing arts), COMPUTER AND PHYSICAL SCIENCE (chemistry, computer science, earth science, geology, information sciences and systems, mathematics, and physics), EDUCATION (art education, bilingual/bicultural education, early childhood education, elementary education, English education, foreign languages education, mathematics education, music education, physical education, science education, secondary education, and social studies education), HEALTH PROFESSIONS (health science and speech pathology/audiology), SOCIAL SCIENCE (African studies, American studies, anthropology, Caribbean studies, child care/child and family studies, economics, Hispanic American studies, history, Judaic studies, Latin American studies, philosophy, political science/government, psychology, religion, sociology, and women's studies). Business, accounting, and education are the largest.

Required: 11 required, interrelated courses cover the following core curriculum areas: classics, art, music, political science, sociology, history, literature, math, computer science, chemistry, physics, biology, geology, philosophy, and comparative cultures. There are basic skills requirements in reading, composition, speech, and math, as well as a foreign language requirement. A 2.0 GPA and a minimum of 120 credit hours, with 31 to 36 in the major (67 to 70 for chemistry), are required to graduate.

Special: There are numerous cross-registration programs with colleges and universities in the area. Many internships and work-study programs are available. Study abroad is possible in more than 29 countries. A B.A.-M.D., B.S.-M.P.S., and accelerated B.A.-M.A. programs are available. A number of B.A.-B.S. degrees, dual majors, a 3-2 engineering degree, and student-designed majors are possible. Credit by exam, credit for life experience, nondegree study, and pass/fail options are offered. There is a Latin and Greek Institute offered during the summer through the Graduate Center. There are 9 national honor societies, including Phi Beta Kappa, a freshman honors program, and 6 departmental honors programs.

Faculty/Classroom: 54% of faculty are male; 46% are female. No introductory courses are taught by graduate students. The average class size in a laboratory, 16, and in a regular course, 32.

Admissions: 28% of the 2009-2010 applicants were accepted. 38% of the current freshmen were in the top fifth of their class; 67% were in the top two fifths.

Requirements: SAT or ACT is required. Requirements for freshman applicants applying directly from high school: 81% GPA with 5 units of math and English with no less than 2 years of either combined (critical reading and math) SAT score or ACT equivalent of 1000 for regular freshmen admissions. Students will be admitted with GED score of 3000 and have the equivalent of 2 years of high school math.

Procedure: Freshmen are admitted fall and spring. There are early admissions and rolling admissions plans. Applications should be filed by October 1 for fall entry and February 1 for spring entry, along with a $65 fee. Notification is sent on a rolling basis. Applications are accepted online.

Transfer: 2605 transfer students enrolled in 2008-2009. Transfer students must have 24 credits; 2.5 GPA and freshman requirements: 25 and over credits, a 2.3 GPA. 30 of 120 credits required for the bachelor's degree must be completed at Brooklyn College.

Visiting: There are regularly scheduled orientations for prospective students, including campus tours, presentations, and meetings with faculty. There are guides for informal visits. To schedule a visit, contact Christopher Milton, Asst. Director for Recruitment at (718) 951-5001.

Financial Aid: In 2009-2010, 71% of all full-time freshmen and 69% of continuing full-time students received some form of financial aid. 71% of all full-time freshmen and 69% of continuing full-time students received need-based aid. The average freshmen award was $8,100, with $4,500 ($10,500 maximum) from need-based scholarships or need-based grants; $3,500 ($3,500 maximum) from need-based self-help aid (loans and jobs); and $4,000 ($10,500 maximum) from other non-need-based awards and non-need-based scholarships. 71% of undergraduate students work part-time. Average annual earnings from campus work are $1200. The average financial indebtedness of the 2009 graduate was $12,300. The FAFSA is required. The priority date for freshman financial aid applications for fall entry is April 1.

International Students: There are 649 international students enrolled. The school actively recruits these students. They must take the TOEFL with a minimum score of 500 on the paper-based TOEFL (PBT) or 61 on the Internet-based version (iBT) and the college's own test.

Computers: Wireless access is available. All students may access the system 1 hour, when other students are waiting. There are no fees.

Graduates: From July 1, 2008 to June 30, 2009, 2200 bachelor's degrees were awarded. The most popular majors were business (21%), education (13%), and psychology (12%). 330 companies recruited on campus in 2008-2009. In an average class, 37% graduate in 5 years or less and 43% graduate in 6 years or less.

Admissions Contact: Admissions Office A campus DVD is available. E-Mail: *adminqry@brooklyn.cuny.edu* Web: *www.brooklyn.cuny.edu*

CITY UNIVERSITY OF NEW YORK/CITY COLLEGE   D-5

New York, NY 10031-9101

Full-time: 4655 men, 4986 women	Faculty: 510; IIA, ++$
Part-time: 1650 men, 1669 women	Ph.D.s: 87%
Graduate: 1337 men, 2011 women	Student/Faculty: 19 to 1
Year: semesters, summer session	Tuition: $4929 ($415/cr)
Application Deadline: December 1	

(212) 650-6977; (212) 650-6417

Freshman Class: 8901 accepted, 1775 enrolled
SAT CR/M: 500/542   **COMPETITIVE**

City College, founded in 1847, is a public liberal arts college that is part of the City University of New York system. There are 6 undergraduate schools and 6 graduate schools. In addition to regional accreditation, CCNY has baccalaureate program accreditation with ABET, ABFSE, NAAB, and NCATE. The 47 libraries contain 1.5 million volumes, 901,300 microform items, and 27,377 audio/video tapes/CDs/DVDs, and subscribe to 56,476 periodicals including electronic. Computerized library services include interlibrary loans, database searching, Internet access, and laptop Internet portals. Special learning facilities include a learning resource center, art gallery, planetarium, radio station, TV station, weather station, laser labs, microwave labs, and Structural Biology Lab. The 35-acre campus is in an urban area in New York City. Including any residence halls, there are 14 buildings.

Student Life: 96% of undergraduates are from New York. Others are from 40 states, 158 foreign countries, and Canada. 84% are from public schools. 25% are Hispanic; 23% African American; 21% Asian American. The average age of freshmen is 18; all undergraduates, 22. 22% do not continue beyond their first year; 37% remain to graduate.

Housing: 580 students can be accommodated in college housing, which includes single-sex and coed on-campus apartments. On-campus housing is available on a first-come, first-served basis. Priority is given to out-of-town students. 97% of students commute. Alcohol is not permitted. All students may keep cars.

Activities: There are 3 national fraternities and 2 national sororities. There are 170 groups on campus, including , art, band, cheerleading, chess, chorus, computers, debate, drama, ethnic, film, gay, honors, international, jazz band, literary magazine, newspaper, orchestra, photography, political, professional, radio and TV, religious, social, social service, and student government. Popular campus events include Langston Hughes Poetry Contest, Dance Theater of Harlem performances at Davis Center, and Architecture Lecture Series.

Sports: There are 9 intercollegiate sports for men and 9 for women, and 9 intramural sports for men and 9 for women. Facilities include swimming pools, 2 gyms, and weight room.

Disabled Students: 94% of the campus is accessible. Facilities include wheelchair ramps, elevators, special parking, specially equipped restrooms, special class scheduling, lowered drinking fountains, and lowered telephones.

Services: Counseling and information services are available, as is tutoring in most subjects. There is a reader service for the blind.

Campus Safety and Security: Measures include 24-hour foot and vehicle patrol, emergency notification system, and security escort services. There are shuttle buses, emergency telephones, lighted pathways/sidewalks, access controls for dorms/residences, bicycle patrols, IDs, criminal investigations, and security systems.

Programs of Study: CCNY confers B.A., B.S., B.Arch., B.E., B.F.A., B.M.E., and B.S.Ed. degrees. Master's degrees are also awarded. Bachelor's degrees are awarded in BIOLOGICAL SCIENCE (biology/biological science), BUSINESS (business administration and management), COMMUNICATIONS AND THE ARTS (art, communications, comparative literature, dramatic arts, English, film arts, fine arts, French, multimedia, music, performing arts, romance languages and literature, Spanish, and video), COMPUTER AND PHYSICAL SCIENCE (atmospheric sciences and meteorology, chemistry, computer science, earth science, geology, mathematics, physics, and quantitative methods), EDUCATION (art education, bilingual/bicultural education, early childhood education, education of the emotionally handicapped, education of the mentally handicapped, elementary education, English education, foreign languages education, mathematics education, secondary education, social studies education, and special education), ENGINEERING AND ENVIRONMENTAL DESIGN (architecture, biomedical engineering, chemical engineering, civil engineering, computer engineering, electrical/electronics engineering, environmental engineering, environmental science, landscape architecture/design, and mechanical engineering), HEALTH PROFESSIONS (biomedical science, physician's assistant, predentistry, and premedicine), SOCIAL SCIENCE (American studies, anthropology, area studies, Asian/Oriental studies, economics, ethnic studies, history, international studies, Latin American studies, philosophy, political science/government, prelaw, psychology, sociology, and urban studies). Engineering, architecture, and sciences are the strongest academically. Engineering, architecture, and psychology are the largest.

Required: Students must successfully complete 120 credits, with 32 to 48 in the major, and maintain a minimum GPA of 2.0. A core curriculum must be met, including courses in anthropology, art, English, psychology, and sociology. Students must complete a college proficiency exam.

Special: Cross-registration is permitted with other City University colleges. A 7-year biomedical education degree is available. Opportunities are provided for a co-op program in engineering, internships, a Washington semester, work-study programs, a wide variety of accelerated degree programs, dual majors, credit by exam, credit for life experience, study abroad in 12 countries, and a B.A.-B.S. degree in biomedical engineering, math, physics, and psychology. There are 2 national honor societies, including Phi Beta Kappa, a freshman honors program, and 100 departmental honors programs.

Faculty/Classroom: 56% of faculty are male; 44% are female. 77% teach undergraduates, 65% do research, and 53% do both. No introductory courses are taught by graduate students. The average class size in an introductory lecture is 29; in a laboratory, 15; and in a regular course, 19.

Admissions: The SAT scores for the 2009-2010 freshman class were: Critical Reading--43% below 500, 34% between 500 and 599, 11% between 600 and 700, and 3% above 700; Math--32% below 500, 38% between 500 and 599, 20% between 600 and 700, and 7% above 700. 60% of the current freshmen were in the top fifth of their class; 87% were in the top two fifths.

Requirements: The SAT is required, with a satisfactory minimum score or an ACT score of 22. Graduation from an accredited secondary school is generally required, but a GED will be accepted. 14 academic credits should be presented with a minimum grade average of 80%. AP credits are accepted.

Procedure: Freshmen are admitted fall and spring. Entrance exams should be taken prior to registration. There is a rolling admissions plan. Applications should be filed by December 1 for fall entry and October 15 for spring entry, along with a $65 fee. Notifications are sent January 15. Applications are accepted on-line.

Transfer: 1536 transfer students enrolled in 2008-2009. Transfer applicants must have earned a minimum of 24 credit hours and maintained a GPA of 2.0. Selected programs have more competitive requirements. 32 of 120 credits required for the bachelor's degree must be completed at CCNY.

Visiting: There are regularly scheduled orientations for prospective students. There are guides for informal visits, and visitors may sit in on classes. To schedule a visit, contact the Admissions Office at (212) 650-6476.

Financial Aid: In 2009-2010, 71% of all full-time freshmen and 75% of continuing full-time students received some form of financial aid. 70% of all full-time freshmen and 73% of continuing full-time students received need-based aid. Need-based scholarships or need-based grants averaged $8310 (maximum $9950); need-based self-help aid (loans and jobs) averaged $7500 ($8500 maximum); and other non-need-based awards and non-need-based scholarships averaged $2800 ($10,000 maximum). The average financial indebtedness of the 2009 graduate was $15,300. The FAFSA and the state aid form are required. The priority date for freshman financial aid applications for fall entry is April 1. The deadline for filing freshman financial aid applications for fall entry is rolling.

International Students: There are 1758 international students enrolled. They must take the TOEFL with a minimum score of 500 on the paper-based TOEFL (PBT) or 61 on the Internet-based version (iBT). They must also take the ACT and the CUNY Placement Exam.

Computers: Wireless access is available. All students may access the system. There are no time limits and no fees.

Graduates: In a recent year, 1278 bachelor's degrees were awarded. The most popular majors were engineering (16%), psychology (13%), and visual and performing arts (12%). 850 companies recruited on campus in 2008-2009. In an average class, 6% graduate in 4 years or less, 25% graduate in 5 years or less, and 37% graduate in 6 years or less. Of the 2008 graduating class, 18% were enrolled in graduate school within 6 months of graduation.

Admissions Contact: Joe Fantozzi, Director of Admissions. A campus DVD is available. E-mail: *admissions@admin.ccny.cuny.edu* Web: *www.ccny.cuny.edu*

CITY UNIVERSITY OF NEW YORK/COLLEGE OF STATEN ISLAND
D-5

Staten Island, NY 10314   (718) 982-2090; (718) 982-2500

Full-time: 4119 men, 5092 women	Faculty: 348; IIA, +$
Part-time: 1189 men, 2178 women	Ph.D.s: 30%
Graduate: 258 men, 714 women	Student/Faculty: 26 to 1
Year: semesters, summer session	Tuition: $4978 ($5358)
Application Deadline: open	
Freshman Class: 9730 applied, 9730 accepted, 2404 enrolled	
SAT CR/M/W: 480/500/480	**NONCOMPETITIVE**

The College of Staten Island, a public institution founded in 1955, is a senior college of the City University of New York (CUNY), offering master, baccalaureate, associate degrees and post-master certificates in the liberal arts, sciences, and professional studies. There is 1 graduate school. In addition to regional accreditation, CSI has baccalaureate program accreditation with ABET, CSAB, NCATE, and NLN. The library contains 235,000 volumes, 605,465 microform items, and 7,762 audio/video tapes/CDs/DVDs, and subscribes to 43,446 periodicals including electronic. Computerized library services include interlibrary loans, database searching, Internet access, and laptop Internet portals. Special learning facilities include a learning resource center, art gallery, radio station, and an astrophysical observatory. The 204-acre campus is in an urban area in New York City's borough of Staten Island. Including any residence halls, there are 22 buildings.

Student Life: 80% of undergraduates are from New York. Others are from 15 states, 105 foreign countries, and Canada. 59% are white; 17% Hispanic; 12% African American; 12% Asian American. The average age of freshmen is 22; all undergraduates, 24. 21% do not continue beyond their first year; 46% remain to graduate.

Housing: There are no residence halls. All students commute.

Activities: There are no fraternities or sororities. There are 50 groups on campus, including art, cheerleading, chess, chorus, computers, dance, debate, drama, ethnic, film, gay, honors, international, jazz band, literary magazine, newspaper, photography, political, professional, radio and TV, religious, social, social service, student government, and yearbook. Popular campus events include Rocktoberfest, Fall and Spring Carnivals, and cultural dances.

Sports: There are 6 intercollegiate sports for men and 7 for women, and 8 intramural sports for men and 8 for women. Facilities include a 1200-seat main arena, an indoor pool, baseball, softball, and soccer fields, tennis courts, outdoor recreational basketball courts, outdoor track and field facilities, 3 indoor volleyball courts, and an auxiliary gym.

Disabled Students: 95% of the campus is accessible. Facilities include wheelchair ramps, elevators, special parking, specially equipped restrooms, special class scheduling, lowered drinking fountains, and lowered telephones.

Services: Counseling and information services are available, as is tutoring in most subjects. There is a reader service for the blind, and remedial math, reading, and writing. There are study groups, academic skills workshops, and various test preparation initiatives.

Campus Safety and Security: Measures include 24-hour foot and vehicle patrol, emergency notification system, and security escort services. There are shuttle buses, emergency telephones, lighted pathways/sidewalks, a radar-controlled traffic monitoring, and bicycle patrol.

Programs of Study: CSI confers B.A., B.S. degrees. Associate, master's, and doctoral degrees are also awarded. Bachelor's degrees are awarded in BIOLOGICAL SCIENCE (biochemistry and biology/biological science), BUSINESS (accounting and business administration and management), COMMUNICATIONS AND THE ARTS (art, communications, dramatic arts, English, film arts, music, and Spanish), COMPUTER AND PHYSICAL SCIENCE (chemistry, computer science, information sciences and systems, mathematics, and physics), ENGINEERING AND ENVIRONMENTAL DESIGN (engineering and applied science), HEALTH PROFESSIONS (medical technology and nursing), SOCIAL SCIENCE (African American studies, American studies, anthropology, economics, history, international studies, philosophy, political science/government, psychology, science and society, social work, sociology, and women's studies). Accounting, business, and education are the largest.

Required: The curriculum varies for each degree, but phys ed and English are required for all majors as well as courses from each of three areas: science/technology/math, social sciences/history/philosophy, and humanities. A minimum 2.0 GPA and 120 credit hours are required to graduate, except in select disciplines which may require a higher GPA or a greater number of credits.

Special: Cross-registration is available with any other CUNY college. Internships are available in most fields. Study abroad is possible in more than 38 countries, including Italy, Ecuador, England, China, Greece, Denmark, and Spain. There are student-designed majors and interdisciplinary majors, including computer science-math, sociology-anthropology, political science and philosophy, and science, letters, and society. Credit by exam, credit for life experience, dual majors, and non-degree study are available. There are 7 national honor societies, a freshman honors program, and 19 departmental honors programs.

Faculty/Classroom: 53% of faculty are male; 47% are female. 90% teach undergraduates. No introductory courses are taught by graduate students. The average class size in an introductory lecture, 25, in a laboratory, 25, and in a regular course, 29.

Admissions: All of the 2009-2010 applicants were accepted. The SAT scores for the 2009-2010 freshman class were: Critical Reading--54% below 500, 30% between 500 and 599, 9% between 600 and 700, and 1% above 700; Math--44% below 500, 41% between 500 and 599, 11% between 600 and 700, and 1% above 700; Writing--47% below 500, 35% between 500 and 599, 8% between 600 and 700, and 1% above 700.

Requirements: Admissions to a bachelor's degree is determined by an applicant's score on the college's admission index. The index is based on the applicant's high school courses and academic average and the combined verbal and mathematics SAT scores. An applicant whose score reaches or exceeds the college's minimum index number and meets the proficiency requirements in reading, writing and mathematics will be admitted to a bachelor's degree program. Applicants who are not admitted to a bachelor's degree program may enter an associate's degree program. AP and CLEP credits are accepted.

Procedure: Freshmen are admitted fall and spring. Entrance exams should be taken as soon as possible after admission. There are deferred admissions for 1 semester and rolling admissions plans. Application deadlines are open. Application fee is $65. Applications are accepted on-line.

Transfer: 678 transfer students enrolled in 2008-2009. Applicants must have a minimum 2.0 GPA and official transcripts. 30 of 120 credits required for the bachelor's degree must be completed at CSI.

Visiting: There are regularly scheduled orientations for prospective students, including pre-admission, campus tours and presentations. There are guides for informal visits and visitors may sit in on classes. To schedule a visit, contact the Office of Recruitment/Admissions at (718) 982-2259.

Financial Aid: 2% of undergraduate students work part-time. Average annual earnings from campus work are $800. CSI is a member of CSS. The FAFSA, the state aid form, and TAP/APTS are required. Check with the school for current application deadlines.

International Students: There were 260 international students enrolled in a recent year. The school actively recruits these students. They must take the TOEFL with a minimum score of 450 on the paper-based TOEFL (PBT) or 45 on the Internet-based version (iBT).

Computers: Wireless access is available. There are over 1254 computers available throughout campus and a multitude of access points. All students may access the system. Depending on the labs, hours vary. There are no time limits. The fee is $75/a semester. It is strongly recommended that all students have a personal computer.

Graduates: From July 1, 2008 to June 30, 2009, 1266 bachelor's degrees were awarded. The most popular majors were science, letters and society (16%), business (12%), and psychology (9%). 83 companies recruited on campus in 2008-2009. In an average class, 23% graduate in 4 years or less, 39% graduate in 5 years or less, and 46% graduate in 6 years or less. Of the 2008 graduating class, 35% were enrolled in graduate school within 6 months of graduation.

Admissions Contact: Emmanuel Esperance, Interim Director of Recruitment and Admissions. A campus DVD is available. E-Mail: *Emmanuel.Esperance@csi.cuny.edu* Web: *www.csi.cuny.edu*

CITY UNIVERSITY OF NEW YORK/HERBERT H. LEHMAN COLLEGE
D-5

Bronx, NY 10468

(718) 960-8700
(877) LEHMAN-1; (718) 960-8712

Full-time: 4215 men and women	Faculty: IIA,+$
Part-time: 3015 men and women	Ph.D.s: n/av
Graduate: 1875 men and women	Student/Faculty: n/av
Year: semesters, summer session	Tuition: $5000 ($8000)
Application Deadline: see profile	
Freshman Class: n/av	
SAT or ACT: recommended	LESS COMPETITIVE

Lehman College, established in 1968 as an independent unit of the City University of New York, is a commuter institution offering programs in the arts and humanities, natural and social sciences, nursing, and professional studies. The figures in the above capsule and in this profile are approximate. There are 5 undergraduate schools and 4 graduate schools. In addition to regional accreditation, Lehman has baccalaureate program accreditation with ADA, CSWE, NCATE, and NLN. The library contains 556,275 volumes, 620,660 microform items, and 1,832 audio/video tapes/CDs/DVDs, and subscribes to 1,513 periodicals including electronic. Computerized library services include database searching. Special learning facilities include a learning resource center, art gallery, radio station, TV station, and center for performing arts. The 37-acre campus is in an urban area in the Bronx, New York City. Including any residence halls, there are 15 buildings.

Student Life: 98% of undergraduates are from New York. Others are from 90 foreign countries. 74% are from public schools. 44% are Hispanic; 33% African American; 16% white. 54% are Catholic; 14% claim no religious affiliation. The average age of freshmen is 20; all undergraduates, 29.

Housing: There are no residence halls. All students commute.

Activities: There are 54 groups on campus, including art, band, chess, choir, chorus, computers, dance, drama, ethnic, film, honors, international, literary magazine, musical theater, newspaper, professional, radio and TV, religious, social, social service, student government, and yearbook.

Sports: There are 9 intercollegiate sports for men and 7 for women, and 9 intramural sports for men and 9 for women. Facilities include 3

gyms, an exercise room, a swimming pool, outdoor tennis courts, soccer and baseball fields, and a dance studio.

Disabled Students: 90% of the campus is accessible. Facilities include wheelchair ramps, elevators, special parking, specially equipped restrooms, and special class scheduling.

Services: Counseling and information services are available, as is tutoring in every subject. There is a reader service for the blind, and remedial math, reading, and writing. A writing center offers individual and small group tutorials and workshops.

Campus Safety and Security: Measures include 24-hour foot and vehicle patrol. There are emergency telephones and lighted pathways/sidewalks.

Programs of Study: Lehman confers B.A., B.S., and B.F.A. degrees. Master's degrees are also awarded. Bachelor's degrees are awarded in BIOLOGICAL SCIENCE (biology/biological science), BUSINESS (accounting, business administration and management, and management science), COMMUNICATIONS AND THE ARTS (communications, comparative literature, dance, English, fine arts, French, German, Greek, Hebrew, Italian, languages, Latin, linguistics, music, Russian, Spanish, and speech/debate/rhetoric), COMPUTER AND PHYSICAL SCIENCE (chemistry, computer science, geology, mathematics, and physics), EDUCATION (art education, business education, early childhood education, elementary education, foreign languages education, health education, science education, and secondary education), HEALTH PROFESSIONS (health care administration, nursing, predentistry, premedicine, and speech pathology/audiology), SOCIAL SCIENCE (African American studies, American studies, anthropology, dietetics, economics, geography, history, international relations, philosophy, political science/government, prelaw, psychology, social work, and sociology). Economics and accounting, education, and nursing are the largest.

Required: To graduate, students must successfully complete 120 credits, including 64 in the major, with a minimum GPA of 2.0. Requirements include 17 credits of core courses, 8 of English composition, 3 to 10 of a foreign language, and 3 of oral communication, as well as 22 credits distributed among courses in comparative culture, historical studies, social science, natural science, literature, art, and knowledge, self, and values. Students must demonstrate proficiency in basic reading, writing, and math skills before entering the upper division.

Special: Lehman offers internships, study abroad, work-study programs, dual and student-designed majors, nondegree study, pass/fail options, and credit for life experience. A 3-2 social work degree is offered in conjunction with the senior college of CUNY, Bard, and Sarah Lawrence. Transfer programs in preengineering, prepharmacy, and preenvironmental science and forestry allow students to complete their degrees at specialized colleges of other New York universities. There are 21 national honor societies, including Phi Beta Kappa, a freshman honors program, and 60 departmental honors programs.

Faculty/Classroom: 53% of faculty are male; 47% are female. No introductory courses are taught by graduate students. The average class size in an introductory lecture is 25 and in a laboratory is 12.

Requirements: The SAT or ACT is recommended. This requirement may also be satisfied by a satisfactory SAT score. Graduation from an accredited secondary school is required; a GED will be accepted. A GPA of 80.0 is required. AP and CLEP credits are accepted.

Procedure: Freshmen are admitted fall and spring. Entrance exams should be taken before registration. There are early decision, early admissions, deferred admissions, and rolling admissions plans. Check with the school for current application deadlines. The application fee is $40.

Transfer: Applicants must submit all educational records and show a minimum GPA of 2.0 in previous college work. Applicants with fewer than 13 college credits must also have a high school average of 80 in academic subjects. 38 of 120 credits required for the bachelor's degree must be completed at Lehman.

Visiting: There are regularly scheduled orientations for prospective students. There are guides for informal visits and visitors may sit in on classes. To schedule a visit, contact the Office of Student Recruitment at (718) 960-8713.

Financial Aid: The college's own financial statement is required. Check with the school for current application deadlines.

International Students: They must take the TOEFL and the college's own test.

Computers: All students may access the system. There are no time limits and no fees.

Admissions Contact: Clarence A. Wilkes, Director of Admissions. A campus DVD is available. E-Mail: *enroll@alpha.lehman.cuny.edu* Web: *www.lehman.cuny.edu*

CITY UNIVERSITY OF NEW YORK/HUNTER COLLEGE   D-5

New York, NY 10065	**(212) 772-4490; (800) 772-4000**
Full-time: 3820 men, 7352 women	Faculty: 686; IIA, +$
Part-time: 1462 men, 3226 women	Ph.D.s: 88%
Graduate: 1421 men, 4867 women	Student/Faculty: 15 to 1
Year: semesters, summer session	Tuition: $4999 ($10,359)
Application Deadline: open	Room & Board: $3500
Freshman Class: n/av	
SAT CR/M: 557/575	**VERY COMPETITIVE**

Hunter College, a comprehensive, nonprofit institution established in 1870, is part of the City University of New York and is both city- and state-supported. Primarily a commuter college, it emphasizes liberal arts in its undergraduate and graduate programs. There are 3 undergraduate schools and 4 graduate schools. In addition to regional accreditation, Hunter has baccalaureate program accreditation with ADA, APTA, ASLA, CSWE, NCATE, and NLN. The library contains 815,668 volumes, 1.2 million microform items, and 14,982 audio/video tapes/CDs/DVDs, and subscribes to 5,749 periodicals including electronic. Computerized library services include database searching. Special learning facilities include a learning resource center, art gallery, radio station, a geography/geology lab, on-campus elementary and secondary schools, and a theater. The 3-acre campus is in an urban area in New York City. Including any residence halls, there are 6 buildings.
Student Life: 98% of undergraduates are from New York. Others are from 40 states, 150 foreign countries, and Canada. 84% are from public schools. 36% are white; 32% Asian American; 24% Hispanic; 12% African American. The average age of freshmen is 18; all undergraduates, 24. 17% do not continue beyond their first year.
Housing: 629 students can be accommodated in college housing, which includes coed dorms. On-campus housing is available on a first-come, first-served basis, and is available on a lottery system for upperclassmen. 99% of students commute. No one may keep cars.
Activities: 2% of men belong to 1 local and 1 national fraternities.1% of women belong to There are 150 groups on campus, including art, band, cheerleading, choir, chorale, chorus, drama, ethnic, film, gay, honors, international, jazz band, literary magazine, musical theater, newspaper, orchestra, political, professional, radio and TV, religious, social, social service, student government, and symphony. Popular campus events include Major Day Fair.
Sports: There are 9 intercollegiate sports for men and 11 for women. Facilities include fencing, dance, and weight rooms, racquetball courts, a pool, outdoor tennis courts, and a gym.
Disabled Students: All of the campus is accessible. Facilities include wheelchair ramps, elevators, special parking, specially equipped restrooms, special class scheduling, lowered drinking fountains, lowered telephones.
Services: Counseling and information services are available, as is tutoring in every subject, There is a reader service for the blind, and remedial math, reading, and writing. Review of graduate-level papers through the writing center and a math tutoring center are available.
Campus Safety and Security: Measures include self-defense education. There are shuttle buses, emergency telephones, 24-hour foot patrol.
Programs of Study: Hunter confers B.A., B.S., B.F.A., B.Mus., and B.S.Ed degrees. Master's degrees are also awarded. Bachelor's degrees are awarded in BIOLOGICAL SCIENCE (biology/biological science and nutrition), BUSINESS (accounting), COMMUNICATIONS AND THE ARTS (Chinese, classics, comparative literature, creative writing, dance, dramatic arts, English, English literature, film arts, fine arts, French, German, Greek, Hebrew, Italian, languages, Latin, media arts, music, Russian, and Spanish), COMPUTER AND PHYSICAL SCIENCE (chemistry, computer science, mathematics, physics, and statistics), EDUCATION (art education, early childhood education, elementary education, foreign languages education, health education, middle school education, music education, science education, and secondary education), ENGINEERING AND ENVIRONMENTAL DESIGN (energy management technology, environmental science, and preengineering), HEALTH PROFESSIONS (medical laboratory technology, nursing, physical therapy, predentistry, premedicine, and public health), SOCIAL SCIENCE (African American studies, anthropology, archeology, economics, geography, Hispanic American studies, history, international relations, Judaic studies, Latin American studies, philosophy, political science/government, prelaw, psychology, religion, social science, sociology, urban studies, and women's studies). Nursing is the strongest academically. Psychology is the largest.
Required: To graduate, students must complete 120 credits. The total number of hours in a major varies from 24 credits for a liberal arts major to 63 credits for a professional concentration; a minimum GPA of 2.0 is needed overall and in the major. Distribution requirements include 12 credits of social sciences, up to 12 credits of a foreign language, 10 or more of math and science, 9 of humanities and the arts, 6 of literature, and 3 of English composition.
Special: Special academic programs include internships, student-designed majors, work-study, study abroad in 24 countries, and dual

majors. There is cross-registration with the Brooklyn School of Law, Marymount Manhattan College, and the YIVO Institute. Through the National Student Exchange Program, Hunter students can study for 1 or 2 semesters at any of 150 U.S. campuses. Accelerated degree programs are offered in anthropology, biopharmacology, economics, English, history, math, physics, sociology, and social research. Exchange programs in Paris or Puerto Rico are possible. There are 2 national honor societies, including Phi Beta Kappa, a freshman honors program, and 19 departmental honors programs.
Faculty/Classroom: No introductory courses are taught by graduate students. The average class size in a laboratory is 19 and in a regular course is 30.
Admissions: The SAT scores for the 2009-2010 freshman class were: Critical Reading--21% below 500, 55% between 500 and 599, 24% between 600 and 700, and % above 700; Math--12% below 500, 51% between 500 and 599, 30% between 600 and 700, and 7% above 700.
Requirements: The SAT is required. In addition, admission is based on a combination of high school grade average, high school academic credits, including English and math, and SAT scores. AP and CLEP credits are accepted.
Procedure: Freshmen are admitted fall and spring. Entrance exams should be taken by October of the junior year. There are early admissions, deferred admissions, and rolling admissions plans. Application deadlines are open. Application fee is $65. Notification of early decision is sent December 15; regular decision, January 1. 4 early decision candidates were accepted for the 2009-2010 class. Applications are accepted on-line.
Transfer: 2411 transfer students enrolled in 2008-2009. Applicants must have at least a 2.0 GPA. All students must complete 30 of the 120 to 131 credits required for a bachelor's degree at the college, including half of those needed for both the major and the minor.
Visiting: There are regularly scheduled orientations for prospective students, presentations and tours every Friday. . There are guides for informal visits and visitors may sit in on classes. To schedule a visit, contact the Office of Admissions at admissions@hunter.cuny.edu.
Financial Aid: The FAFSA and the college's own financial statement are required. The deadline for filing freshman financial aid applications for fall entry is May 1.
International Students: There are 1352 international students enrolled. They must take the TOEFL with a minimum score of 500 on the paper-based TOEFL (PBT) or 175 on the Internet-based version (iBT) and the college's own test.
Computers: All students may access the system. 24 hours a day. There are no time limits and no fees.
Graduates: From July 1, 2008 to June 30, 2009, 2052 bachelor's degrees were awarded. The most popular majors were Psychology (15%), English (11%), and Sociology (10%). In an average class, 42% graduate in 6 years or less.
Admissions Contact: Bill Zlata, Director of Admissions. E-Mail: admissions@hunter.cuny.edu Web: www.hunter.cuny.edu

CITY UNIVERSITY OF NEW YORK/JOHN JAY   D-5
COLLEGE OF CRIMINAL JUSTICE

New York, NY 10019	**(212) 237-8878; (212) 237-8777**
Full-time: 3215 men, 5205 women	Faculty: IIA, +$
Part-time: 1305 men, 1705 women	Ph.D.s: n/av
Graduate: 505 men, 1005 women	Student/Faculty: n/av
Year: semesters, summer session	Tuition: $15,904 ($20,544)
Application Deadline: open	
Freshman Class: n/av	
SAT: recommended	**COMPETITIVE**

John Jay College of Criminal Justice, established in 1964, is a liberal arts college and part of the City University of New York, with special emphasis in the fields of criminology, forensic science, correction administration, and other areas of the criminal justice system. Figures in the above capsule and in the this profile are approximate. There are 5 graduate schools. The library contains 215,609 volumes, 198,832 microform items, and 3,000 audio/video tapes/CDs/DVDs, and subscribes to 10,335 periodicals including electronic. Computerized library services include interlibrary loans and database searching. Special learning facilities include a learning resource center, art gallery, radio station, TV station, a fire science lab, a security technology lab, and an explosion-proof forensic science/toxicology lab. The 1-acre campus is in an urban area in midtown Manhattan. Including any residence halls, there are 3 buildings.
Student Life: 95% of undergraduates are from New York. 80% are from public schools. 35% are Hispanic; 25% African American; 23% white. The average age of freshmen is 19; all undergraduates, 23. 26% do not continue beyond their first year; 40% remain to graduate.
Housing: There are no residence halls. All students commute.
Activities: There are no fraternities or sororities. There are 26 groups on campus, including art, cheerleading, chess, choir, chorale, chorus, computers, dance, drama, ethnic, film, gay, honors, international, liter-

ary magazine, musical theater, newspaper, photography, political, professional, radio and TV, religious, social, social service, student government, and yearbook.

Sports: There are 5 intercollegiate sports for men and 5 for women, and 15 intramural sports for men and 15 for women. Facilities include 2 gyms, 2 racquetball courts, a fitness center, a swimming pool, a strength training center, and a rooftop outdoor tennis court and jogging track.

Disabled Students: 99% of the campus is accessible. Facilities include wheelchair ramps, elevators, special parking, specially equipped restrooms, special class scheduling, lowered drinking fountains, and lowered telephones.

Services: Counseling and information services are available, as is tutoring in most subjects, English, math and reading There is a reader service for the blind, and remedial math, reading, and writing.

Campus Safety and Security: Measures include 24-hour foot and vehicle patrol and self-defense education. There are emergency telephones and lighted pathways/sidewalks.

Programs of Study: John Jay confers B.A. and B.S. degrees. Associates and master's degrees are also awarded. Bachelor's degrees are awarded in BIOLOGICAL SCIENCE (toxicology), COMPUTER AND PHYSICAL SCIENCE (information sciences and systems), SOCIAL SCIENCE (corrections, criminal justice, criminology, fire science, forensic studies, law enforcement and corrections, political science/government, public administration, and safety management). Forensic science is the strongest academically. Criminal justice, forensic psychology, and police science are the largest.

Required: Students are required to complete 128 credit hours, with 36 to 42 of these hours in the student's major, and must maintain a minimum GPA of 2.0. 1 credit in phys ed is required of all students.

Special: The school offers co-op programs, and cross-registration with other schools in the City University of New York. Internships are available with the Manhattan District Attorney, the Queens Supreme Court, the New York City Police Department, the United States Marshal's Service, and the New York City Corrections Department. Opportunities are provided for work-study programs, a Washington semester in public administration, interdisciplinary and student-designed majors, including forensic psychology, pass/fail options, nondegree study, credit for life experience, B.A.-M.A. programs in forensic psychology, criminal justice, and public administration, and study abroad in 5 countries, including England, Barbados, and Israel. There is 1 national honor society and a freshman honors program.

Faculty/Classroom: 54% of faculty are male; 46% are female. 94% teach undergraduates, and 80% do both. Graduate students teach 5% of introductory courses. The average class size in an introductory lecture is 25; in a laboratory is 15; and in a regular course is 20.

Requirements: The SAT is recommended. In addition, applicants must have graduated from an accredited secondary school or a GED certificate will be accepted. Admission to associate degree programs requires a satisfactory SAT score, a high school average of 72, or a GED score of 300. Admission to baccalaureate degree program requires a minimum SAT I score of 1020 or a high school average of 80, and 12 academic units, with 4 units in English and math and 1 unit in each discipline. A GPA of 80.0 is required. AP and CLEP credits are accepted.

Procedure: Freshmen are admitted fall and spring. There are early admissions and rolling admissions plans. Application deadlines are open. The fall 2009 application fee was $40. Notification is sent on a rolling basis.

Transfer: Applicants must have completed 24 credits with a cumulative GPA of 2.0. If fewer than 24 credits are presented, a high school transcript should be presented. Half of the credits required for the major must be completed at John Jay.

Visiting: There are regularly scheduled orientations for prospective students, consisting of a freshman/transfer workshop. There are guides for informal visits and visitors may sit in on classes.

Financial Aid: The FAFSA is required. The deadline for filing freshman financial aid applications for fall entry is open.

International Students: They must take the TOEFL.

Computers: All students may access the system. There are no time limits and no fees.

Admissions Contact: Richard Saulnier, Dean of Admissions and Registration. E-Mail: *rsaulnier@jjay.cuny.edu* Web: *www.johnjay.cuny.edu*

CITY UNIVERSITY OF NEW YORK/MEDGAR EVERS COLLEGE D-5

Brooklyn, NY 11225-2201	(718) 270-6021; (718) 270-6198
Full-time: 1253 men, 3399 women	**Faculty:** 179; IIB, +$
Part-time: 509 men, 1920 women	**Ph.D.s:** 55%
Graduate: none	**Student/Faculty:** 26 to 1
Year: semesters, summer session	**Tuition:** $4920 ($11,120)
Application Deadline: open	
Freshman Class: 7178 applied, 1450 accepted, 1378 enrolled	
SAT CR/M/W: 380/380/380	**NONCOMPETITIVE**

Medgar Evers College, established in 1969 as part of the City University of New York, is an undergraduate commuter institution offering programs in business, education, natural sciences and math, nursing, and social sciences. In addition to regional accreditation, MEC has baccalaureate program accreditation with NCATE and NLN. The library contains 120,000 volumes, 42,225 microform items, and 6,000 audio/video tapes/CDs/DVDs, and subscribes to 36,282 periodicals including electronic. Computerized library services include interlibrary loans, database searching, and Internet access. Special learning facilities include a learning resource center, radio station, TV station, and a TV lab. The 8-acre campus is in an urban area located in Central Brooklyn of New York City. Including any residence halls, there are 3 buildings.

Student Life: 97% of undergraduates are from New York. Others are from 4 states, 75 foreign countries, and Canada. 99% are from public schools. 90% are African American. 50% are Islamic 2%, Buddhist 1%, others 47%; 22% Catholic; 14% Protestant; 12% claim no religious affiliation. The average age of freshmen is 21; all undergraduates, 27.7. 58% do not continue beyond their first year; 10% remain to graduate.

Housing: There are no residence halls. All students commute.

Activities: There are no fraternities or sororities. There are 25 groups on campus, including cheerleading, choir, dance, drama, ethnic, gay, jazz band, newspaper, political, professional, radio and TV, religious, social, social service, and student government. Popular campus events include Kwaanza and Black Solidarity Day.

Sports: There are 4 intercollegiate sports for men and 3 for women, and 5 intramural sports for men and 3 for women. Facilities include a swimming pool, a gym, and an exercise room.

Disabled Students: All of the campus is accessible. Facilities include wheelchair ramps, elevators, special parking, specially equipped rest rooms, lowered drinking fountains, and lowered telephones.

Services: Counseling and information services are available, as is tutoring in every subject. There is a reader service for the blind, and remedial math, reading, and writing.

Campus Safety and Security: Measures include 24-hour foot and vehicle patrol.

Programs of Study: MEC confers B.A. and B.S. degrees. Associates degrees are also awarded. Bachelor's degrees are awarded in BIOLOGICAL SCIENCE (biology/biological science), BUSINESS (accounting, business administration and management, and management information systems), COMMUNICATIONS AND THE ARTS (English), COMPUTER AND PHYSICAL SCIENCE (computer science and mathematics), EDUCATION (elementary education and special education), ENGINEERING AND ENVIRONMENTAL DESIGN (environmental science), HEALTH PROFESSIONS (nursing), SOCIAL SCIENCE (liberal arts/general studies, psychology, and public administration). Nursing is the strongest academically. Education is the largest.

Required: To graduate, students must complete 120 credits (depending on program) with a minimum GPA of 2.0. The core curriculum requires a total of 42 credits in English, philosophy, speech, math, liberal arts, career planning, and phys ed. Students must demonstrate proficiency in basic reading, writing, and math skills prior to entering their junior year.

Special: MEC offers exchange programs with other CUNY institutions, evening and weekend classes, credit for military and prior learning experience, pass/fail options, and nondegree study. Study abroad in 3 countries is also possible. There is 1 national honor society, a freshman honors program, and 11 departmental honors programs.

Faculty/Classroom: 54% of faculty are male; 46% are female. All teach undergraduates, 8% do research, and 8% do both. No introductory courses are taught by graduate students. The average class size in an introductory lecture, 26, in a laboratory, 20, and in a regular course, 25.

Admissions: 20% of the 2009-2010 applicants were accepted. The SAT scores for the 2009-2010 freshman class were: Critical Reading-- 91% below 500, 8% between 500 and 599, and 1% between 600 and 700; Math--92% below 500, and 8% between 500 and 599; Writing-- 93% below 500, 6% between 500 and 599, and 1% between 600 and 700.

Requirements: The SAT is recommended. In addition, MEC accepts all applicants who either are graduates of an accredited secondary school or have earned a GED with a score of 225 or higher. Students must meet the university's health standards. CLEP credits are accepted.

Procedure: Freshmen are admitted fall and spring. Entrance exams should be taken during the last year of high school. There is a rolling admissions plan. Application deadlines are open. The fall 2008 application fee was $65.

Transfer: 779 transfer students enrolled in 2008-2009. Applicants must have a minimum GPA of 2.0. Those students with fewer than 24 college credits must also submit a high school transcript. 32 of 120 credits required for the bachelor's degree must be completed at MEC.

Visiting: .

Financial Aid: In 2009-2010, 85% of all full-time freshmen and 81% of continuing full-time students received some form of financial aid. 85% of all full-time freshmen and 81% of continuing full-time students received need-based aid. The average freshmen award was $3,406, with $3,707 ($5,225 maximum) from need-based scholarships or need-based grants and $710 ($1,742 maximum) from need-based self-help aid (loans and jobs). 40% of undergraduate students work part-time. Average annual earnings from campus work are $1500. The FAFSA and CUNY Student Aid Form (CSAF) are required. The priority date for freshman financial aid applications for fall entry is January 1. The deadline for filing freshman financial aid applications for fall entry is July 31.

International Students: There are 112 international students enrolled. The school actively recruits these students. They must take the TOEFL with a minimum score of 475 on the paper-based TOEFL (PBT). They must also take the ACT and the college's own entrance exam.

Computers: Wireless access is available. Students can access PCs in any of the college's 3 computer labs and in the library. All students may access the system. There are no time limits. The fee is $75 per semester.

Graduates: From July 1, 2008 to June 30, 2009, 329 bachelor's degrees were awarded. The most popular majors were public administration (17%), psychology (15%), and business (15%). 15 companies recruited on campus in 2008-2009. In an average class, 5% graduate in 4 years or less, 11% graduate in 5 years or less, and 19% graduate in 6 years or less.

Admissions Contact: Julie Augustin, Acting Director of Admissions. Web: *www.mec.cuny.edu*

CITY UNIVERSITY OF NEW YORK/NEW YORK CITY COLLEGE OF TECHNOLOGY D-5

Brooklyn, NY 11201-2983	(718) 260-5500; (718) 260-5504
Full-time: 5110 men, 4020 women	Faculty: 411; IIB, +$
Part-time: 2950 men, 3324 women	Ph.D.s: n/av
Graduate: none	Student/Faculty: 22 to 1
Year: semesters, summer session	Tuition: $4939 ($12,789)
Application Deadline: March 15	
Freshman Class: n/av	
	NONCOMPETITIVE

New York City College of Technology, founded in 1946 and made part of the City University of New York system in 1964, is an undergraduate commuter college offering day and evening programs in technology. It is the largest public college of technology in the state and offers 61 degree and specialized certificate programs in the technologies of art and design, business, computer systems, engineering, entertainment, health care, hospitality, human services, law-related professions, career and technology teacher education, and the liberal arts and sciences. There are 3 undergraduate schools. In addition to regional accreditation, City Tech has baccalaureate program accreditation with ABET, ADA, NCATE, and NLN. The library contains 179,062 volumes, 14,079 microform items, and 3,136 audio/video tapes/CDs/DVDs, and subscribes to 39,942 periodicals including electronic. Computerized library services include interlibrary loans, database searching, Internet access, and laptop Internet portals. Special learning facilities include a learning resource center and art gallery. The campus is in an urban area. Including any residence halls, there are 9 buildings.

Student Life: 99% of undergraduates are from New York. Others are from 14 states, and 57 foreign countries. 35% are African American; 31% Hispanic; 18% Asian American; 11% white. The average age of freshmen is 19; all undergraduates, 24. 20% do not continue beyond their first year; 80% remain to graduate.

Housing: There are no residence halls. All students commute.

Activities: There are no fraternities or sororities. There are 60 groups on campus, including computers, dance, drama, ethnic, gay, honors, international, musical theater, newspaper, professional, religious, social, social service, and student government. Popular campus events include Latino Heritage, Women's History Month, and Multicultural Week.

Sports: There are 6 intercollegiate sports for men and 6 for women, and 6 intramural sports for men and 6 for women. Facilities include a gym, basketball courts, and a weight room.

Disabled Students: Facilities include wheelchair ramps, elevators, specially equipped restrooms, and lowered drinking fountains.

Services: Counseling and information services are available, as is tutoring in most subjects. There is a reader service for the blind, and remedial math, reading, and writing. Tutoring Services are available at the College Learning Center.

Campus Safety and Security: Measures include 24-hour foot and vehicle patrol and security escort services. There are emergency telephones and lighted pathways/sidewalks.

Programs of Study: City Tech confers B.S., B.S.Ed., and B.T. degrees. Associates degrees are also awarded. Bachelor's degrees are awarded in BUSINESS (hospitality management services and institutional management), COMMUNICATIONS AND THE ARTS (communications and telecommunications), COMPUTER AND PHYSICAL SCIENCE (applied mathematics and information sciences and systems), EDUCATION (technical education and vocational education), ENGINEERING AND ENVIRONMENTAL DESIGN (architectural technology, computer engineering, electromechanical technology, and graphic and printing production), HEALTH PROFESSIONS (health care administration), SOCIAL SCIENCE (human services, interdisciplinary studies, and paralegal studies). Computer system technology and nursing are the largest.

Required: Students must receive CUNY certification in reading, writing, and math and complete associate degree requirements. General education requirements include selections from African-American, Puerto Rican, and Latin American studies, sciences, humanities, and social sciences. A total of 120 credits is required for the B.S., B.S.Ed., or B.T. degree.

Special: B.A. and B.S. degrees are offered through CUNY's university-wide bachelor's exchange credits program. An alternative format program for adults offers credit for life/work experience. Nondegree study is possible. Internships are required in most majors.

Faculty/Classroom: 55% of faculty are male; 45% are female. All teach undergraduates. No introductory courses are taught by graduate students. The average class size in an introductory lecture is 30; in a laboratory is 17; and in a regular course is 24.

Requirements: Applicants should be graduates of an accredited secondary school or have the GED equivalent and meet the university's immunization requirements. A GPA of 2.0 is required. AP and CLEP credits are accepted.

Procedure: Freshmen are admitted fall, spring, and summer. Entrance exams should be taken during the spring or summer prior to fall entrance. There are deferred admissions and rolling admissions plans. Applications should be filed by March 15 for fall entry and October 1 for spring entry. The fall 2009 application fee was $65. Notification is sent on a rolling basis. Applications are accepted on-line.

Transfer: 1045 transfer students enrolled in 2008-2009. Candidates must have a 2.0 GPA. They must meet CUNY requirements in reading, writing, and math. 34 of 120 credits required for the bachelor's degree must be completed at City Tech.

Visiting: To schedule a visit, contact Alexis Chaconis at (718) 260-5500.

Financial Aid: In 2009-2010, 74% of all full-time freshmen and 75% of continuing full-time students received some form of financial aid. 60% of undergraduate students work part-time. The FAFSA, and CUNY Student Aid Form (CSAF) is required. Check with the school for current application deadlines.

International Students: There are 174 international students enrolled. The school actively recruits these students. They must take the TOEFL with a minimum score of 500 on the paper-based TOEFL (PBT) or 61 on the Internet-based version (iBT).

Computers: Wireless access is available. All students may access the system. There are no time limits and no fees.

Graduates: From July 1, 2008 to June 30, 2009, 647 bachelor's degrees were awarded. The most popular majors were computer information (20%), hospitality management (17%), and human services (12%). In an average class, 17% graduate in 6 years or less.

Admissions Contact: Alexis Chaconis, Director of Admissions. A campus DVD is available. E-Mail: *Achaconis@citytech.cuny.edu* Web: *www.citytech.cuny.edu*

CITY UNIVERSITY OF NEW YORK/QUEENS COLLEGE D-5

Flushing, NY 11367-1597	(718) 997-5608; (718) 997-5617
Full-time: 4893 men, 6869 women	Faculty: IIA, +$
Part-time: 1657 men, 2640 women	Ph.D.s: 85%
Graduate: 1346 men, 3306 women	Student/Faculty: n/av
Year: semesters, summer session	Tuition: $5047 ($10,407)
Application Deadline: January 1	Room & Board: $11,125
Freshman Class: 18028 applied, 6122 accepted, 1712 enrolled	
SAT: required	COMPETITIVE

Queens College, founded in 1937, is a public mostly commuter institution within the City University of New York system. There is 1 undergraduate school and 4 graduate schools. In addition to regional accreditation, Queens has baccalaureate program accreditation with ADA and NCATE. The 2 libraries contain 1.1 million volumes, 967,131 microform items, and 43,806 audio/video tapes/CDs/DVDs, and subscribe to 2689 periodicals including electronic. Computerized library services include interlibrary loans, database searching, Internet access, and laptop Internet portals. Special learning facilities include a learning resource center, art gallery, radio station, several small museums, and a theater. The 76-acre campus is in an urban area 10 miles from Manhattan. Including any residence halls, there are 20 buildings.

Student Life: 99% of undergraduates are from New York. Others are from 15 states, 79 foreign countries, and Canada. 70% are from public schools. 45% are white; 27% Asian American; 19% Hispanic. The average age of freshmen is 19; all undergraduates, 26. 15% do not continue beyond their first year; 48% remain to graduate.

Housing: 494 students can be accommodated in college housing, which includes coed dorms. On-campus housing is available on a first-come , first-served basis. 97% of students commute. Alcohol is not permitted. All students may keep cars.

Activities: 1% of men belong to 3 national fraternities; there are 3 national sororities. There are 140 groups on campus, including band, choir, chorus, debate, drama, ethnic, gay, honors, international, jazz band, literary magazine, musical theater, newspaper, orchestra, political, radio and TV, religious, social, social service, student government, symphony, and yearbook. Popular campus events include fall and spring campus fests and a spring job fair.

Sports: There are 9 intercollegiate sports for men and 12 for women, and 9 intramural sports for men and 9 for women. Facilities include a gym complex, swimming pool, dance studios, weight rooms, outdoor quarter-mile track, soccer, lacrosse, and baseball fields, and 18 tennis courts.

Disabled Students: 90% of the campus is accessible. Facilities include wheelchair ramps, elevators, special parking, specially equipped restrooms, special class scheduling, lowered drinking fountains, lowered telephones, and special housing.

Services: Counseling and information services are available, as is tutoring in most subjects. There is a reader service for the blind.

Campus Safety and Security: Measures include 24-hour foot and vehicle patrol and emergency notification system. There are emergency telephones and lighted pathways/sidewalks.

Programs of Study: Queens confers B.A., B.S., B.B.A., B.F.A., and B.Mus. degrees. Master's degrees are also awarded. Bachelor's degrees are awarded in AGRICULTURE (environmental studies), BIOLOGICAL SCIENCE (biology/biological science, environmental biology, neurosciences, and nutrition), BUSINESS (accounting, banking and finance, international business management, and labor studies), COMMUNICATIONS AND THE ARTS (art, art history and appreciation, Chinese, comparative literature, dance, dramatic arts, English, film arts, French, German, graphic design, Greek (modern), Hebrew, Italian, linguistics, media arts, music, music performance, Russian, Spanish, and studio art), COMPUTER AND PHYSICAL SCIENCE (actuarial science, chemistry, computer science, environmental geology, geology, mathematics, and physics), EDUCATION (art education, early childhood education, home economics education, music education, physical education, and science education), ENGINEERING AND ENVIRONMENTAL DESIGN (environmental science), HEALTH PROFESSIONS (exercise science and speech pathology/audiology), SOCIAL SCIENCE (African studies, American studies, anthropology, classical/ancient civilization, East Asian studies, economics, family/consumer studies, history, home economics, interdisciplinary studies, Judaic studies, Latin American studies, philosophy, political science/government, psychology, religion, sociology, urban studies, and women's studies). Accounting, computer science, and psychology are the largest.

Required: To graduate, students must complete 120 credits with a minimum GPA of 2.0. They must fulfill requirements in the major and 35 to 40 credits of a liberal arts core curriculum.

Special: Queens offers co-op programs, cross-registration with other CUNY campuses, internships in business, liberal arts, journalism, and social sciences, study abroad, work-study, accelerated degrees, dual majors, pass/fail options, and nondegree study. There are preprofessional programs in engineering, law, and prehealth. The SEEK program provides financial and educational resources for underprepared freshmen. There are 15 national honor societies, including Phi Beta Kappa, and a freshman honors program.

Faculty/Classroom: 53% of faculty are male; 47% are female. 85% teach and do research. Graduate students teach 1% of introductory courses.

Admissions: 34% of the 2009-2010 applicants were accepted. The SAT scores for the 2009-2010 freshman class were: Critical Reading-- 32% below 500, 48% between 500 and 599, 16% between 600 and 700, and 4% above 700; Math--15% below 500, 56% between 500 and 599, 25% between 600 and 700, and 4% above 700.

Requirements: The SAT is required. In addition, high school preparation should include 4 years each of English and social studies, 3 each of math and foreign language, and 2 of lab science. A GPA of 3.0 is required. AP and CLEP credits are accepted.

Procedure: Freshmen are admitted fall and spring. Entrance exams should be taken in the spring of the junior year or the fall of the senior year. There are early admissions and rolling admissions plans. Application deadlines are open. Application fee is $65. Notifications are sent February 1.

Transfer: 2305 transfer students enrolled in 2008-2009. Admissions requirements vary depending on the number of credits to be transferred; students should consult with the Admissions Office. 45 of 120 credits required for the bachelor's degree must be completed at Queens.

Visiting: There are regularly scheduled orientations for prospective students, including information sessions and a campus tour. Visitors may sit

in on classes. To schedule a visit, contact the Admissions Office at (718) 997-5614.

Financial Aid: In 2009-2010, 61% of all full-time freshmen and 55% of continuing full-time students received some form of financial aid. 52% of all full-time freshmen and 61% of continuing full-time students received need-based aid. The average freshman award was $4500. Need-based scholarships or need-based grants averaged $4000 ($7500 maximum). 2% of undergraduate students work part-time. Average annual earnings from campus work are $1000. The average financial indebtedness of the 2009 graduate was $12,000. The FAFSA and the state aid form are required. The priority date for freshman financial aid applications for fall entry is March 15. The deadline for filing freshman financial aid applications for fall entry is May 1.

International Students: There are 474 international students enrolled. They must take the TOEFL with a minimum score of 500 on the paper-based TOEFL (PBT) or 61 on the Internet-based version (iBT). They must also take the SAT or the CUNY Skills Assessment Test. Honors students should take SAT Subject tests.

Computers: Wireless access is available. Access to computers and the Internet is available in the library and computer labs across the campus. All students may access the system during day and evening hours, 7 days a week. There are no time limits. The fee is $75 per semester.

Graduates: From July 1, 2008 to June 30, 2009, 2646 bachelor's degrees were awarded. The most popular majors were accounting (17%), psychology (13%), and sociology (11%). 100 companies recruited on campus in 2008-2009. In an average class, 3% graduate in 3 years or less, 25% graduate in 4 years or less, 45% graduate in 5 years or less, and 53% graduate in 6 years or less. Of the 2008 graduating class, 21% were enrolled in graduate school within 6 months of graduation, and 70% were employed.

Admissions Contact: Dr. Vincent J. Angrisani, Executive Director of Admissions, Marketing, and Scholarship. A campus DVD is available. Web: *www.qc.edu*

CITY UNIVERSITY OF NEW YORK/YORK COLLEGE   D-5

Jamaica, NY 11451   (718) 262-2165; (718) 262-2601

Full-time: 1425 men, 2720 women	**Faculty:** IIB, +$
Part-time: 815 men, 1740 women	**Ph.D.s:** n/av
Graduate: 5 men, 20 women	**Student/Faculty:** n/av
Year: semesters, summer session	**Tuition:** $4700 ($9200)
Application Deadline: open	
Freshman Class: n/av	**NONCOMPETITIVE**

York College, established in 1966, is a public liberal arts commuter college and part of the City University of New York. The figures in the above capsule and in this profile are approximate. In addition to regional accreditation, York has baccalaureate program accreditation with CAHEA, CSWE, and NLN. The library contains 184,799 volumes, 140,461 microform items, and 4,613 audio/video tapes/CDs/DVDs, and subscribes to 7,613 periodicals including electronic. Computerized library services include interlibrary loans and database searching. Special learning facilities include a learning resource center, art gallery, TV station, a Cardio-pneumo simulator, and a theater. The 50-acre campus is in an urban area in New York City. Including any residence halls, there are 5 buildings.

Student Life: 88% of undergraduates are from New York. Others are from 6 states, 77 foreign countries, and Canada. 41% are African American; 15% Hispanic. The average age of freshmen is 19; all undergraduates, 24. 30% do not continue beyond their first year; 70% remain to graduate.

Housing: There are no residence halls. All students commute.

Activities: There are no fraternities or sororities. There are 50 groups on campus, including art, cheerleading, choir, chorus, computers, drama, ethnic, honors, international, jazz band, literary magazine, musical theater, newspaper, political, professional, radio and TV, religious, social, social service, and student government. Popular campus events include club fairs, talent shows, and ethnic fairs.

Sports: There are 9 intercollegiate sports for men and 8 for women, and 9 intramural sports for men and 8 for women. Facilities include a 1200-seat gym, a 25-meter, 6-lane swimming pool with diving boards, a health risk appraisal center, an exercise therapy room, outdoor track; tennis courts; soccer field; indoor walking/jogging track; weight room; aerobics room; handball courts; and multipurpose room.

Disabled Students: All of the campus is accessible. Facilities include wheelchair ramps, elevators, special parking, specially equipped restrooms, special class scheduling, lowered drinking fountains, and lowered telephones.

Services: Counseling and information services are available, as is tutoring in every subject. There is a reader service for the blind, and remedial math, reading, and writing.

Campus Safety and Security: Measures include 24-hour foot and vehicle patrol and security escort services. There are emergency telephones and lighted pathways/sidewalks.

Programs of Study: York confers B.A. and B.S. degrees. Master's degrees are also awarded. Bachelor's degrees are awarded in BIOLOGI-

CAL SCIENCE (biology/biological science and biotechnology), BUSINESS (accounting, business administration and management, and marketing/retailing/merchandising), COMMUNICATIONS AND THE ARTS (art history and appreciation, dramatic arts, English, French, music, Spanish, speech/debate/rhetoric, and studio art), COMPUTER AND PHYSICAL SCIENCE (chemistry, geology, information sciences and systems, mathematics, and physics), EDUCATION (physical education), HEALTH PROFESSIONS (community health work, environmental health science, exercise science, medical laboratory technology, nursing, and occupational therapy), SOCIAL SCIENCE (African American studies, anthropology, economics, gerontology, history, liberal arts/general studies, philosophy, political science/government, psychology, social work, and sociology). Liberal studies, business administration, and accounting are the largest.

Required: All students are required to complete 120 credits and maintain a minimum GPA of 2.0. The core curriculum of 61 credits includes courses in humanities, behavioral science, cultural diversity, math, natural science, and junior level writing. Students must also take a 2-credit phys ed course and complete 2 semesters of English.

Special: Cross-registration with all schools in the City University of New York is permitted. Also provided are work-study programs, credit by exam, dual majors in physics and math, nondegree study, pass/fail options, credit for life experience, internships, cooperative programs with other schools, and student-designed majors. There are 6 national honor societies and 4 departmental honors programs.

Faculty/Classroom: 55% of faculty are male; 45% are female. All teach undergraduates, and 7% do both. No introductory courses are taught by graduate students.

Requirements: Students should achieve a satisfactory score on the SAT. Applicants must have graduated from an accredited secondary school or present a GED certificate. An audition is recommended for music majors. AP and CLEP credits are accepted.

Procedure: Freshmen are admitted fall and spring. There are early admissions, deferred admissions, and rolling admissions plans. Application deadlines are open. The fall 2009 application fee was $65. Notifications are sent in monthly. Applications are accepted on-line.

Transfer: 700 transfer students enrolled in a recent year. Students must present a minimum GPA of 2.0. 40 of 120 credits required for the bachelor's degree must be completed at York.

Visiting: There are regularly scheduled orientations for prospective students, including workshops and group meetings with faculty and staff on matriculation; registration; financial aid, degree requirements; and advisement for classes. Visitors may sit in on classes. To schedule a visit, contact the Director of Admissions or Admissions counselor at (718) 262-2165.

Financial Aid: In a recent year, 77% of all full-time freshmen and 71% of continuing full-time students received some form of financial aid. 63% of all full-time freshmen and 54% of continuing full-time students received need-based aid. The FAFSA and the college's own financial statement are required. Check with the school for current application deadlines.

International Students: There were 723 international students enrolled in a recent year. They must take the TOEFL. They must also take the SAT or ACT and the Math placement test if the student comes from non-English-speaking country.

Computers: Wireless access is available. All students may access the system during hours of operation of college facilities. There are no time limits and no fees.

Graduates: In a recent year, 799 bachelor's degrees were awarded. The most popular majors were business administration (17%), psychology (15%), and accounting (11%). 100 companies recruited on campus in 2008-2009. In an average class, 6% graduate in 4 years or less, 20% graduate in 5 years or less, and 25% graduate in 6 years or less.

Admissions Contact: Diane Warmsley, Director of Admissions and Enrollment. A campus DVD is available. E-Mail: *admissions@york.cuny.edu* Web: *www.york.cuny.edu*

CLARKSON UNIVERSITY   D-2

Potsdam, NY 13699   (315) 268-6480; (315) 268-7647

Full-time: 1979 men, 756 women	**Faculty:** 178; I, -$
Part-time: 7 men, 4 women	**Ph.D.s:** 87%
Graduate: 302 men, 139 women	**Student/Faculty:** 15 to 1
Year: semesters, summer session	**Tuition:** $32,910
Application Deadline: January 15	**Room & Board:** $11,118
Freshman Class: 4054 applied, 2945 accepted, 777 enrolled	
SAT CR/M: 550/610	**ACT:** 25 **VERY COMPETITIVE**

Clarkson University, founded in 1896, is a private nationally ranked research institute offering undergraduate programs in engineering, business, science, and the humanities, and graduate programs in engineering, business, science, and health sciences. There are 3 undergraduate schools and 3 graduate schools. In addition to regional accreditation, Clarkson has baccalaureate program accreditation with AACSB, ABET, and APTA. The 2 libraries contain 338,321 volumes, 262,705 micro-

form items, and 2,079 audio/video tapes/CDs/DVDs, and subscribe to 3,127 periodicals including electronic. Computerized library services include interlibrary loans, database searching, Internet access, and laptop Internet portals. Special learning facilities include a learning resource center, radio station, and TV station. The 640-acre campus is in a rural area 70 miles north of Watertown and 75 miles south of Ottawa, Canada. Including any residence halls, there are 43 buildings.

Student Life: 70% of undergraduates are from New York. Others are from 41 states, 44 foreign countries, and Canada. 86% are from public schools. 81% are white. The average age of freshmen is 18; all undergraduates, 20. 15% do not continue beyond their first year; 70% remain to graduate.

Housing: 2204 students can be accommodated in college housing, which includes single-sex and coed dorms, on-campus apartments, and married student housing. In addition, there are special-interest houses, fraternity houses, and sorority houses. On-campus housing is guaranteed for all 4 years. 85% of students live on campus; of those, 90% remain on campus on weekends. All students may keep cars.

Activities: 9% of men belong to 2 local and 9 national fraternities; 9% of women belong to 3 national sororities. There are 117 groups on campus, including cheerleading, chess, chorus, computers, drama, environmental, ethnic, gay, honors, international, jazz band, literary magazine, musical theater, newspaper, orchestra, pep band, photography, professional, radio and TV, religious, social, social service, and student government. Popular campus events include Spring Fest, Holiday Hoops, and University Recognition Day.

Sports: There are 10 intercollegiate sports for men and 9 for women. Facilities include a 3000-seat multipurpose ice arena, a fitness center, a gym, a swimming pool, a weight room, a field house, tennis courts, and all purpose indoor and outdoor turf fields.

Disabled Students: 85% of the campus is accessible. Facilities include wheelchair ramps, elevators, special parking, specially equipped restrooms, special class scheduling, lowered drinking fountains, lowered telephones, and special housing.

Services: Counseling and information services are available, as is tutoring in most subjects, including all freshman-and sophomore-level courses and some junior-level courses.

Campus Safety and Security: Measures include 24-hour foot and vehicle patrol, emergency notification system, and security escort services. There are shuttle buses, emergency telephones, and lighted pathways/sidewalks.

Programs of Study: Clarkson confers B.S. and B.P.S. degrees. Master's and doctoral degrees are also awarded. Bachelor's degrees are awarded in BIOLOGICAL SCIENCE (biology/biological science and molecular biology), BUSINESS (business administration and management, business systems analysis, electronic business, entrepreneurial studies, management information systems, and supply chain management), COMMUNICATIONS AND THE ARTS (communications and technical and business writing), COMPUTER AND PHYSICAL SCIENCE (applied mathematics, chemistry, computer science, digital arts/technology, information sciences and systems, mathematics, physics, science, and software engineering), ENGINEERING AND ENVIRONMENTAL DESIGN (aeronautical engineering, chemical engineering, civil engineering, computer engineering, electrical/electronics engineering, engineering management, environmental engineering, environmental science, and mechanical engineering), SOCIAL SCIENCE (American studies, history, humanities, interdisciplinary studies, political science/government, psychology, social science, and sociology). Engineering, business, and interdisciplinary engineering and management are the strongest academically.

Required: Students must complete at least 120 credit hours, with 30 in the major and a minimum GPA of 2.0 to graduate. Students must meet a foundation curriculum requirement. All students entering as first-year students must take the First-Year Seminar or an equivalent course that may be offered by the University. Students in the Class of 2010 and beyond must meet the requirements of the Clarkson Common experience.

Special: Clarkson offers cross-registration with the SUNY Potsdam, SUNY Canton, and St. Lawrence University. Co-op programs in all academic areas, dual majors in business and liberal arts, interdisciplinary majors, internships, accelerated degree programs, student-designed majors in the B.P.S. degree program, and study abroad in England, Italy, New Zealand, Sweden, Germany, Australia, France, Austria, China, Korea, Mexico, Slovenia, Croatia, Spain, and Ireland are possible. There are 3-2 engineering programs with many institutions in the United States. Students who participate take the first 3 years of the prescribed program at a 4-year liberal arts institution and then transfer with junior standing into one of Clarkson's 4-year engineering curricula. There are 9 national honor societies, a freshman honors program, and 12 departmental honors programs.

Faculty/Classroom: 73% of faculty are male; 27% are female. 77% teach undergraduates, 13% do research, and 68% do both. No introductory courses are taught by graduate students. The average class size in an introductory lecture, 31, in a laboratory, 20, and in a regular course, 26.

Admissions: 73% of the 2009-2010 applicants were accepted. The SAT scores for the 2009-2010 freshman class were: Critical Reading-- 22% below 500, 47% between 500 and 599, 27% between 600 and 700, and 4% above 700; Math--7% below 500, 34% between 500 and 599, 50% between 600 and 700, and 9% above 700; Writing--28% below 500, 51% between 500 and 599, 18% between 600 and 700, and 3% above 700. The ACT scores were 9% below 21, 23% between 21 and 23, 35% between 24 and 26, 18% between 27 and 28, and 15% above 28. 59% of the current freshmen were in the top fifth of their class; 90% were in the top two fifths. 13 freshmen graduated first in their class.

Requirements: The SAT or ACT is required. In addition, SAT Subject tests are also recommended. Applicants must have graduated from an accredited secondary school or have the GED. A campus visit and interview are also recommended. SAT or ACT scores are required. AP and CLEP credits are accepted. Important factors in the admissions decision are advanced placement or honors courses, recommendations by school officials, and extracurricular activities record.

Procedure: Freshmen are admitted fall and spring. Entrance exams should be taken by November. There is an early decision and a deferred admissions plan. Early decision applications should be filed by December 1; regular applications, by January 15 for fall entry and December 1 for spring entry, along with a $50 fee. Notification of early decision is sent December 15; regular decision, February 1. Applications are accepted on-line. 143 applicants were on a recent waiting list, 20 were accepted.

Transfer: 92 transfer students enrolled in 2008-2009. Transfer students should submit transcripts from all colleges attended and 2 letters of recommendation, including 1 from an academic professor or instructor. An associate degree will be considered, and an interview is recommended. 30 of 120 credits required for the bachelor's degree must be completed at Clarkson.

Visiting: There are regularly scheduled orientations for prospective students, including meetings with administration and faculty. There are guides for informal visits; visitors may sit in on classes and stay overnight. To schedule a visit, contact the Admissions Office.

Financial Aid: In 2009-2010, 99% of all full-time freshmen and 95% of continuing full-time students received some form of financial aid. 82% of all full-time freshmen and 76% of continuing full-time students received need-based aid. The average freshmen award was $30,422, with $24,416 ($35,300 maximum) from need-based scholarships or need-based grants; $6,458 ($16,907 maximum) from need-based self-help aid (loans and jobs); $30,212 ($44,828 maximum) from non-need-based athletic scholarships; $14,715 ($32,910 maximum) from other non-need-based awards and non-need-based scholarships; and $2,243 from other forms of aid. 25% of undergraduate students work part-time. Average annual earnings from campus work are $914. The average financial indebtedness of the 2009 graduate was $32,125. The FAFSA is required. The deadline for filing freshman financial aid applications for fall entry is February 15.

International Students: There are 98 international students enrolled. The school actively recruits these students. They must take the TOEFL with a minimum score of 550 on the paper-based TOEFL (PBT) or 80 on the Internet-based version (iBT). They must also take the SAT or ACT.

Computers: Wireless access is available. The campus has 350 lab PCs, distributed between 8 public-access computer labs and 4 department labs. All campus computers (both wired and wireless) have unrestricted access to the Internet for both academic and recreational use. All students may access the system. There are no time limits and no fees. It is strongly recommended that all students have a personal computer.

Graduates: From July 1, 2008 to June 30, 2009, 587 bachelor's degrees were awarded. The most popular majors were engineering (45%), business (17%), and engineering and management (10%). 91 companies recruited on campus in 2008-2009. In an average class, 62% graduate in 4 years or less, 70% graduate in 5 years or less, and 72% graduate in 6 years or less. Of the 2008 graduating class, 23% were enrolled in graduate school within 6 months of graduation, and 77% were employed.

Admissions Contact: Brian T. Grant, Dean of Admission. E-Mail: bgrant@clarkson.edu Web: www.clarkson.edu

COLGATE UNIVERSITY C-3

Hamilton, NY 13346 (315) 228-7401; (315) 228-7544

Full-time: 1313 men, 1487 women	Faculty: 266; IIB, ++$
Part-time: 10 men, 15 women	Ph.D.s: 96%
Graduate: 4 men, 8 women	Student/Faculty: 11 to 1
Year: semesters	Tuition: $41,020
Application Deadline: January 15	Room & Board: $9910
Freshman Class: 7816 applied, 2464 accepted, 750 enrolled	
SAT CR/M: 661/680	ACT: 30 MOST COMPETITIVE

Colgate University, founded in 1819, is a private liberal arts institution. There is 1 graduate school. The 2 libraries contain 734,812 volumes, 593,646 microform items, and subscribe to 36,752 periodicals including

electronic. Computerized library services include interlibrary loans, database searching, Internet access, and laptop Internet portals. Special learning facilities include a learning resource center, art gallery, radio station, TV station, anthropology museum, and observatory. The 515-acre campus is in a rural area 45 miles southeast of Syracuse and 35 miles southwest of Utica. Including any residence halls, there are 87 buildings.

Student Life: 72% of undergraduates are from out of state, mostly the Northeast. Students are from 49 states, 35 foreign countries, and Canada. 62% are from public schools. 74% are white. The average age of freshmen is 18; all undergraduates, 20. 5% do not continue beyond their first year; 91% remain to graduate.

Housing: 2400 students can be accommodated in college housing, which includes coed dorms and on-campus apartments. In addition, there are language houses, special-interest houses, and fraternity houses. On-campus housing is guaranteed for all 4 years. 93% of students live on campus; of those, 96% remain on campus on weekends. All students may keep cars.

Activities: 40% of men belong to 6 national fraternities; 38% of women belong to 3 national sororities. Only sophomores, juniors, and seniors can join fraternities and sororities. There are 180 groups on campus, including art, band, cheerleading, chess, choir, chorale, chorus, computers, dance, debate, drama, environmental, ethnic, film, forensics, gay, honors, international, jazz band, literary magazine, musical threater, newspaper, orchestra, pep band, photography, political, professional, radio and TV, religious, social, social service, student government, symphony, and yearbook. Popular campus events include Winter Olympics, DanceFest, and Spring Party Weekend.

Sports: There are 11 intercollegiate sports for men and 12 for women, and 19 intramural sports for men and 19 for women. Facilities include numerous athletic fields, a softball diamond, an outdoor artificial surface field, a football stadium, an athletic center, a 3000-seat gym, a golf course, a field house, a 50-meter pool, a bowling center, a hockey rink, a 9000-square-foot fitness center, running trails, a trap range, and courts for basketball, tennis, squash, handball, and racquetball.

Disabled Students: 20% of the campus is accessible. Facilities include wheelchair ramps, elevators, special parking, specially equipped rest rooms, special class scheduling, and lowered drinking fountains.

Services: Counseling and information services are available, as is tutoring in every subject. There is a reader service for the blind and remedial writing. There is a note-taking service for students with learning and sensory disabilities and a writing center.

Campus Safety and Security: Measures include 24-hour foot and vehicle patrol, emergency notification system, self-defense education, and security escort services. There are shuttle buses, emergency telephones, and lighted pathways/sidewalks.

Programs of Study: Colgate confers B.A. degrees. Master's degrees are also awarded. Bachelor's degrees are awarded in BIOLOGICAL SCIENCE (biochemistry, biology/biological science, molecular biology, and neurosciences), COMMUNICATIONS AND THE ARTS (art history and appreciation, Chinese, classics, dramatic arts, English, French, German, Greek, Japanese, Latin, music, Russian, Spanish, and studio art), COMPUTER AND PHYSICAL SCIENCE (astronomy, astrophysics, chemistry, computer science, geology, geophysics and seismology, mathematics, natural sciences, physical sciences, and physics), EDUCATION (education), ENGINEERING AND ENVIRONMENTAL DESIGN (environmental science), SOCIAL SCIENCE (African studies, Asian/Oriental studies, economics, geography, history, humanities, international relations, Latin American studies, Native American studies, peace studies, philosophy, political science/government, psychology, religion, Russian and Slavic studies, social science, sociology, and women's studies). English, economics, and history are the largest.

Required: To graduate, students must complete a first-year seminar course and the core curriculum, including 4 general education courses and 2 courses each in the natural sciences, social sciences, and humanities. A total of 32 courses is required, with 8 to 12 courses in the major. Study in a foreign language, phys ed, and a swimming test are also required. Students need a minimum 2.0 GPA.

Special: Colgate offers various internships, semester and summer research opportunities with faculty, work-study, study abroad in 22 countries, accelerated degree programs, dual majors, and student-designed majors. A 3-2 engineering degree with Columbia and Washington Universities and Rensselaer Polytechnic Institute, an early assurance medical program with George Washington University, credit by exam, and pass/fail options are available. There are 12 national honor societies, including Phi Beta Kappa, and 10 departmental honors programs.

Faculty/Classroom: 57% of faculty are male; 43% are female. All teach and do research. No introductory courses are taught by graduate students. The average class size in an introductory lecture is 21; in a laboratory is 17; and in a regular course is 19.

Admissions: 32% of the 2009-2010 applicants were accepted. The SAT scores for the 2009-2010 freshman class were: Critical Reading--4% below 500, 12% between 500 and 599, 47% between 600 and 700, and 37% above 700; Math--2% below 500, 11% between 500 and 599, 45% between 600 and 700, and 42% above 700. The ACT scores were 1%

below 21, 3% between 21 and 23, 9% between 24 and 26, 13% between 27 and 28, and 76% above 28. 86% of the current freshmen were in the top fifth of their class; 98% were in the top two-fifths. 23 freshmen graduated first in their class.

Requirements: The SAT or ACT is required. In addition, 2 teacher recommendations and a counselor's report are required. An interview, though not evaluated, is recommended. Students should present 16 or more Carnegie credits, based on 4 years each of English and math and at least 3 of lab science, social science, and a foreign language, with electives in the arts. AP credits are accepted. Important factors in the admissions decision are advanced placement or honors courses, recommendations by school officials, and leadership record.

Procedure: Freshmen are admitted in the fall. Entrance exams should be taken in time for score reports to reach the university by January 15. There are early decision and deferred admissions plans. Early decision applications should be filed by November 15; regular applications, by January 15 for fall entry, along with a $55 fee. Notification of early decision is sent December 15; regular decision, April 1. Applications are accepted on-line. 709 applicants were on a recent waiting list, 22 were accepted.

Transfer: 22 transfer students enrolled in a recent year. Either the SAT or the ACT is required, as well as college and high school transcripts, a dean's report, and faculty recommendations. 16 of 32 credits required for the bachelor's degree must be completed at Colgate.

Visiting: There are regularly scheduled orientations for prospective students, including nonevaluative interviews, group information sessions, and student-led tours. There are guides for informal visits, visitors may sit in on classes and stay overnight. To schedule a visit, contact the Office of Admissions.

Financial Aid: In 2009-2010, 34% of all full-time freshmen and 35% of continuing full-time students received some form of financial aid, including need-based aid. The average freshmen award was $39,758. The average financial indebtedness of the 2009 graduate was $14,170. Colgate is a member of CSS. The CSS/Profile and FAFSA are required. International students need the International Student's Financial Aid Application. The deadline for filing freshman financial aid applications for fall entry is January 15.

International Students: There were 133 international students enrolled in a recent year. The school actively recruits these students. They must take the TOEFL and the SAT or ACT.

Computers: Wireless access is available. A general appropriate use policy exists for students using the university's network. Colgate provides 53 computer labs for students with an average of 16 computers in each lab. All classrooms allow for both wired and wireless connectivity to the Internet. All students may access the system. There are no time limits and no fees. It is strongly recommended that all students have a personal computer.

Graduates: From July 1, 2008 to June 30, 2009, 704 bachelor's degrees were awarded. 200 companies recruited on campus in 2008-2009. In an average class, 1% graduate in 3 years or less, 88% graduate in 4 years or less, 90% graduate in 5 years or less, and 91% graduate in 6 years or less. Of the 2008 graduating class, 20% were enrolled in graduate school within 6 months of graduation, and 80% were employed.

Admissions Contact: Gary L. Ross, Dean of Admission. E-Mail: admission@mail.colgate.edu Web: www.colgate.edu

COLLEGE OF MOUNT SAINT VINCENT   D-5

Riverdale, NY 10471   **(718) 405-3304**
                                      (800) 665-CMSV; (718) 549-7945

Full-time: 305 men, 1105 women	**Faculty:** n/av
Part-time: 30 men, 155 women	**Ph.Ds:** n/av
Graduate: 105 men, 310 women	**Student/Faculty:** n/av
Year: semesters, summer session	**Tuition:** $23,620
Application Deadline: March 1	**Room & Board:** $9370
Freshman Class: n/av	
SAT or ACT: required	**COMPETITIVE**

The College of Mount Saint Vincent, founded as an academy in 1847 and chartered as a college in 1911, is a private liberal arts institution in the Catholic tradition. The figures in the above capsule and in this profile are approximate. There are 3 graduate schools. In addition to regional accreditation, the Mount has baccalaureate program accreditation with ACBSP and NLN. The library contains 129,000 volumes, 7,000 microform items, and 6,500 audio/video tapes/CDs/DVDs, and subscribes to 234 periodicals including electronic. Computerized library services include interlibrary loans, database searching, and Internet access. Special learning facilities include a learning resource center, radio station, and TV station. The 70-acre campus is in an urban area 11 miles north of midtown Manhattan. Including any residence halls, there are 11 buildings.

Student Life: 89% of undergraduates are from New York. Others are from 19 states, and 4 foreign countries. 46% are from public schools. 38% are white; 32% Hispanic; 14% African American. 81% are Catho-

lic. The average age of freshmen is 18; all undergraduates, 22. 25% do not continue beyond their first year; 62% remain to graduate.

Housing: 540 students can be accommodated in college housing, which includes coed dorms. On-campus housing is guaranteed for all 4 years. 53% of students commute. All students may keep cars.

Activities: There are no fraternities or sororities. There are 30 groups on campus, including art, cheerleading, chess, choir, chorus, computers, dance, debate, drama, ethnic, film, gay, honors, international, literary magazine, musical theater, newspaper, photography, professional, radio and TV, religious, social, social service, student government, and yearbook. Popular campus events include Annual Block Party, Bachelor Auction, and Battle of the Dorms.

Sports: There are 7 intercollegiate sports for men and 8 for women, and 6 intramural sports for men and 6 for women. Facilities include a gym, a swimming pool, a weight room, a dance studio, a recreation room, a fitness center with aerobic and Nautilus facilities, and basketball, squash, and tennis courts.

Disabled Students: 90% of the campus is accessible. Facilities include wheelchair ramps, elevators, special parking, specially equipped restrooms, lowered drinking fountains, and lowered telephones.

Services: Counseling and information services are available, as is tutoring in most subjects, computer science, math, chemistry, biology, languages, psychology, sociology, writing, and economics. There is a reader service for the blind and remedial math, reading, and writing.

Campus Safety and Security: Measures include 24-hour foot and vehicle patrol and security escort services. There are shuttle buses, emergency telephones, lighted pathways/sidewalks, a college committee on safety and security on campus.

Programs of Study: The Mount confers B.A. and B.S. degrees. Associates and master's degrees are also awarded. Bachelor's degrees are awarded in BIOLOGICAL SCIENCE (biochemistry and biology/biological science), BUSINESS (business administration and management), COMMUNICATIONS AND THE ARTS (communications, English, French, modern language, and Spanish), COMPUTER AND PHYSICAL SCIENCE (chemistry, computer science, mathematics, and physics), EDUCATION (health education, physical education, and special education), HEALTH PROFESSIONS (allied health and nursing), SOCIAL SCIENCE (economics, history, liberal arts/general studies, philosophy, psychology, religion, sociology, and urban studies). Nursing and biology are the strongest academically. Nursing, psychology, and business are the largest.

Required: All students must complete a 56-credit core curriculum with courses in humanities, social sciences, math and computers, and natural sciences. A total of 120 credits for a B.A. or 126 credits for a B.S., with a minimum of 30 credits in the major, and a minimum GPA of 2.0 are required.

Special: Cross-registration with Manhattan College offers cooperative B.A. programs in international studies, philosophy, phys ed, physics, religious studies, and urban affairs. Internships, work-study, study abroad in 6 countries, a 3-2 engineering degree with Manhattan College, dual majors, and student-designed majors in liberal arts are available. B.A.-B.S. degrees in computer science, health education, math, and psychology, and teacher dual certification programs with special education and elementary, middle school, and secondary education are possible. There are 15 national honor societies, a freshman honors program, and 5 departmental honors programs.

Faculty/Classroom: 39% of faculty are male; 61% are female. All teach undergraduates, and 80% do both. No introductory courses are taught by graduate students. The average class size in an introductory lecture is 25; in a laboratory is 15; and in a regular course is 15.

Requirements: The SAT or ACT is required. In addition, applicants should have completed 4 high school academic units of English, 3 of science, and 2 each of math, foreign language, and social sciences, as well as electives. An essay is required, and an interview is recommended. 1 letter of recommendation is required, and additional letters are encouraged. A GPA of 80.0 is required. AP and CLEP credits are accepted. Important factors in the admissions decision are advanced placement or honors courses, recommendations by school officials, and extracurricular activities record.

Procedure: Freshmen are admitted fall and spring. Entrance exams should be taken during the junior year and/or fall of the senior year. There are early admissions and rolling admissions plans. Applications should be filed by March 1 for fall entry. The fall 2009 application fee was $35. Notification is sent on a rolling basis. Applications are accepted on-line.

Transfer: Transfer applicants should have a minimum GPA of 2.0. Those majoring in nursing, the sciences, math, or computer science need at least a 2.5 GPA. An interview is recommended. 45 of 120 credits required for the bachelor's degree must be completed at The Mount.

Visiting: There are regularly scheduled orientations for prospective students. Upon request, students may have an interview with an admissions counselor, sit in on classes, and tour the campus. All students are invited to an open house. Accepted students may have a one-on-one meeting with a student on campus. There are guides for informal visits; visitors may sit in on classes, and stay overnight. To schedule a visit, contact the Admissions Office.

Financial Aid: The Mount is a member of CSS. The FAFSA and the TAP application for New York state residents is required. Check with the school for current application deadlines.

International Students: The school actively recruits these students. They must take the TOEFL, or complete ELS Level 109, available on campus. They must also take the SAT or ACT.

Computers: All students may access the system 9 A.M. to 10 P.M. Monday through Thursday and 9 A.M. to 4 P.M. Friday, Saturday, and Sunday. There are no time limits. The fee is $150.

Admissions Contact: Timothy P. Nash, Dean of Admission and Financial Aid. A campus DVD is available. E-Mail: *admissions@mountsaintvincent.edu* Web: *www.cmsv.edu*

COLLEGE OF NEW ROCHELLE   D-5

New Rochelle, NY 10805-2339   **(914) 654-5452**
(800) 933-5923; (914) 654-5464

Full-time: 25 men, 605 women	**Faculty:** IIA, av$
Part-time: 60 men, 335 women	**Ph.D.s:** n/av
Graduate: 105 men, 930 women	**Student/Faculty:** n/av
Year: semesters, summer session	**Tuition:** $24,600
Application Deadline: August 15	**Room & Board:** $9000
Freshman Class: n/av	
SAT: required	**VERY COMPETITIVE**

The College of New Rochelle was founded in 1904 by the Ursuline order as the first Catholic college for women in New York State. Now independent, there are 3 undergraduate schools. The School of Arts and Sciences offers liberal arts baccalaureate education for women only; the School of Nursing is coeducational. The School of New Resources is described in a separate profile. The figures in the above profile and in this capsule are approximate. There are 3 undergraduate schools and 1 graduate school. In addition to regional accreditation, CNR has baccalaureate program accreditation with CSWE and NLN. The library contains 224,000 volumes, 277 microform items, and 5,700 audio/video tapes/CDs/DVDs, and subscribes to 1,432 periodicals including electronic. Computerized library services include interlibrary loans, database searching, and Internet access. Special learning facilities include a learning resource center, art gallery, and the Learning Center for Nursing. The 20-acre campus is in a suburban area 12 miles north of New York City. Including any residence halls, there are 20 buildings.

Student Life: 87% of undergrads are from New York. Others are from 17 states, and 10 foreign countries. 73% are from public schools. 52% are African American; 22% Hispanic; 18% white. 77% are Catholic; 18% Protestant. The average age of freshmen is 20; all undergraduates, 27. 29% do not continue beyond their first year; 71% remain to graduate.

Housing: 410 students can be accommodated in college housing, which includes single-sex dorms. On-campus housing is guaranteed for all 4 years. 56% of students live on campus; of those, 50% remain on campus on weekends. All students may keep cars.

Activities: There are no fraternities or sororities. There are 18 groups on campus, including art, cheerleading, choir, chorus, drama, environmental, ethnic, film, honors, international, literary magazine, musical theater, newspaper, photography, political, professional, religious, social, social service, and student government. Popular campus events include Junior Celebration, Family Weekend, and Strawberry Festival.

Sports: There are 6 intercollegiate sports for women. Facilities include a fitness center and tennis courts.

Disabled Students: 50% of the campus is accessible. Facilities include wheelchair ramps, elevators, special parking, specially equipped restrooms, and special class scheduling.

Services: Counseling and information services are available, as is tutoring in some subjects, science, languages. There is remedial math, reading, and writing. Individual counseling and educational workshops about self-development and personal concerns are available, as are self-help materials.

Campus Safety and Security: Measures include 24-hour foot and vehicle patrol, self-defense education, and security escort services. There are shuttle buses, emergency telephones, lighted pathways/sidewalks, card access to dorms, and surveillance cameras.

Programs of Study: CNR confers B.A., B.S., B.F.A., and B.S.N. degrees. Master's degrees are also awarded. Bachelor's degrees are awarded in AGRICULTURE (environmental studies), BIOLOGICAL SCIENCE (biology/biological science), BUSINESS (business administration and management), COMMUNICATIONS AND THE ARTS (art history and appreciation, classics, communications, English, French, and Spanish), COMPUTER AND PHYSICAL SCIENCE (chemistry and mathematics), EDUCATION (art education), HEALTH PROFESSIONS (art therapy and nursing), SOCIAL SCIENCE (economics, history, international studies, philosophy, political science/government, psychology, religion, social work, sociology, and women's studies). Nursing, art, and psychology are the largest.

Required: Students must complete 120 credit hours, 60 to 90 in liberal arts courses, depending on the major, meet specific course distribution requirements, and maintain a minimum GPA of 2.0 to graduate. 4 phys ed courses are also required.

Special: CNR provides cooperative programs in all disciplines, work-study programs, dual majors in all majors, interdisciplinary studies, an accelerated degree program in nursing, a Washington semester, internships, study abroad in 9 countries, nondegree study, pass/fail options, student-designed majors, and a general studies degree. There is 1 national honor society and a freshman honors program.

Faculty/Classroom: 25% of faculty are male; 75% are female. All teach and do research. No introductory courses are taught by graduate students. The average class size in an introductory lecture, 25, in a laboratory, 10, and in a regular course, 15.

Requirements: The SAT is required. In addition, graduation from an accredited secondary school is required; the GED is accepted. Applicants must have completed 15 academic credits, with 4 in English, 3 each in math, science, and social studies, and 2 in a foreign language. A portfolio is required for art majors. An essay and interview are recommended. AP and CLEP credits are accepted. Important factors in the admissions decision are advanced placement or honors courses, recommendations by school officials, and leadership record.

Procedure: Freshmen are admitted to all sessions. Entrance exams should be taken in the junior year or fall of the senior year. There are early admissions, deferred admissions, and rolling admissions plans. Applications should be filed by August 15 for fall entry and January 10 for spring entry. The fall 2009 application fee was $20. Notification is sent on a rolling basis.

Transfer: 68 transfer students enrolled in a recent year. Transfer students must submit a transcript from their previous college showing courses completed and a minimum GPA of 2.0. High school records and SAT scores are required. An interview is recommended. 30 of 120 credits required for the bachelor's degree must be completed at CNR.

Visiting: There are regularly scheduled orientations for prospective students, including several open houses providing information on admission. There are guides for informal visits; visitors may sit in on classes and stay overnight. To schedule a visit, contact the Office of Admissions at admission@cnr.edu.

Financial Aid: The FAFSA, CCS/Profile, FFS or SFS, the college's own financial statement, and income documentation are required. Check with the school for current application deadlines.

International Students: They must take the TOEFL or the ESL Language Test. They must also take the SAT or ACT. The SAT is preferred.

Computers: Wireless access is available. All students may access the system 24 hours per day. There are no time limits and no fees. It is strongly recommended that all students have a personal computer.

Graduates: In a recent year, 241 bachelor's degrees were awarded. The most popular majors were nursing (67%), psychology (9%), and commercial arts (4%). 27 companies recruited on campus in 2008-2009. In an average class, 50% graduate in 4 years or less, 51% graduate in 5 years or less, and 52% graduate in 6 years or less. Of the 2008 graduating class, 20% were enrolled in graduate school within 6 months of graduation, and 60% were employed.

Admissions Contact: Stephanie Decker, Director of Admission. A campus DVD is available. E-Mail: *sdecker@cnr.edu* Web: *www.cnr.edu*

COLLEGE OF NEW ROCHELLE - SCHOOL OF NEW RESOURCES   D-5

New Rochelle, NY 10805-2339   **(914) 654-5526**
(800) 288-4767; (914) 654-5664

Full-time: 405 men, 3505 women	**Faculty:** IIA,av$
Part-time: 50 men, 400 women	**Ph.D.s:** n/av
Graduate: none	**Student/Faculty:** n/av
Year: semesters, summer session	
Application Deadline: August 15	
Freshman Class: n/av	**SPECIAL**

The College of New Rochelle's School of New Resources is a liberal arts institution serving adult baccalaureate students. The figures in the above capsule and in this profile are approximate. There are no undergraduate schools. The library contains 224,000 volumes, 277 microform items, and 5,700 audio/video tapes/CDs/DVDs, and subscribes to 1,432 periodicals including electronic. Computerized library services include interlibrary loans, database searching, and Internet access. Special learning facilities include a learning resource center, art gallery, TV station, Access Centers to assist students in improving writing, reading, and math skills. The -acre campus is in an urban area 12 miles north of New York City. Five additional campuses are located within the city. Including any residence halls, there are 20 buildings.

Student Life: 98% of undergraduates are from New York. Others are from 3 states, and 3 foreign countries. 82% are African American; 14% Hispanic. The average age of freshmen is 33; all undergraduates, 36. 35% do not continue beyond their first year; 65% remain to graduate.

Housing: There are no residence halls. All students commute.

Activities: There are no fraternities or sororities. Groups on campus include drama, musical theater, religious, and student government. Popular campus events include Founders Day, College Bowl, and numerous women's and ethnic activities.

Sports: There is no sports program at SNR. Facilities include There is no sports program at SNR.

Disabled Students: None of the campus is accessible.

Services: Counseling and information services are available, as is tutoring in some subjects, communication skills, problem solving, and math skills. There is remedial math, reading, and writing.

Campus Safety and Security: Measures include 24-hour foot and vehicle patrol, self-defense education, and security escort services. There are shuttle buses, emergency telephones, lighted pathways/sidewalks, surveillance cameras.

Programs of Study: SNR confers B.A. degrees. Bachelor's degrees are awarded in SOCIAL SCIENCE (liberal arts/general studies).

Required: Students must complete 120 credit hours, meet specific course distribution requirements, and maintain a minimum GPA of 2.0 to graduate. Entrance, core, and exit seminars are required, as are degree-planning courses.

Special: SNR provides a voluntary work-study program. Student-designed internships, courses, and degree plans are available. Credit for prior learning may be obtained.

Faculty/Classroom: 54% of faculty are male; 46% are female. All teach undergraduates. No introductory courses are taught by graduate students. The average class size in an introductory lecture is 15; in a laboratory is 10; and in a regular course is 15.

Requirements: In addition, Enrolling students must be age 21 or older, have a high school diploma or its equivalent, and have successfully completed an English assessment. Test scores are not required. New students are expected to attend an orientation workshop. AP and CLEP credits are accepted.

Procedure: Freshmen are admitted to all sessions. Entrance exams should be taken in the junior year or fall of the senior year. There is a rolling admissions plan. Applications should be filed by August 15 for fall entry and January 10 for spring entry. Notification is sent on a rolling basis.

Transfer: Transfer students must obtain a transcript from their previous college. With some restrictions, course grades of C- or better will be accepted. 30 of 120 credits required for the bachelor's degree must be completed at SNR.

Visiting: .

Financial Aid: The FAFSA and the college's own financial statement, and income documentation are required. The deadline for filing freshman financial aid applications for fall entry is open.

Computers: All students may access the system. from 8:30 A.M. to 11 P.M. daily. Students are limited to 2 hours during peak usage. There are no fees.

Graduates: The most popular majors were (%), (%), and (%).

Admissions Contact: Director of Admissions A campus DVD is available. E-Mail: *admission@cnr.edu*
Web: *nyts.edu/college-of-new-rochelle*

COLLEGE OF SAINT ROSE
D-3

Albany, NY 12203

(518) 454-5111
(800) 637-8556; (518) 454-2013

Full-time: 830 men, 2105 women	**Faculty:** IIA, --$
Part-time: 80 men, 160 women	**Ph.D.s:** n/av
Graduate: 440 men, 1345 women	**Student/Faculty:** n/av
Year: semesters, summer session	**Tuition:** $18,600
Application Deadline: May 1	**Room & Board:** $8000
Freshman Class: n/av	
SAT or ACT: required	**COMPETITIVE**

The College of Saint Rose, established in 1920, is an independent liberal arts institution sponsored by the Sisters of St. Joseph of Carondelet. Tuition figures in the above capsule and in this profile are approximate. There are 4 undergraduate schools and 1 graduate school. In addition to regional accreditation, CSR has baccalaureate program accreditation with ACBSP, ASLA, and NASAD. The library contains 206,692 volumes, 307,904 microform items, and 1,510 audio/video tapes/CDs/DVDs, and subscribes to 902 periodicals including electronic. Computerized library services include interlibrary loans, database searching, and Internet access. Special learning facilities include a learning resource center, art gallery, and TV station. The 28-acre campus is in a suburban area in a residential section, 1 1/2 miles from downtown Albany. Including any residence halls, there are 77 buildings.

Student Life: 89% of undergraduates are from New York. Others are from 20 states, 9 foreign countries, and Canada. 79% are white. The average age of freshmen is 18; all undergraduates, 20. 18% do not continue beyond their first year; 65% remain to graduate.

Housing: 1102 students can be accommodated in college housing, which includes single-sex and coed dorms, on-campus apartments, and married student housing. In addition, there are apartments for single students. On-campus housing is available on a first-come, first-served basis, and is available on a lottery system for upperclassmen. 81% of students live on campus; of those, 50% remain on campus on weekends. All students may keep cars.

Activities: There are no fraternities or sororities. There are 37 groups on campus, including cheerleading, chorale, Circle K, commuter, computers, dance, departmental, disabled, drama, ethnic, international, jazz band, literary magazine, newspaper, political, professional, religious, social, social service, student government, women's, and yearbook. Popular campus events include Harvest Fest, Rose Rock, and Land and Water Olympics.

Sports: There are 6 intercollegiate sports for men and 6 for women, and 5 intramural sports for men and 5 for women. Facilities include a gym with basketball and volleyball courts, a weight room, an indoor swimming pool and access to city soccer fields, baseball fields, and softball fields.

Disabled Students: 98% of the campus is accessible. Facilities include wheelchair ramps, elevators, special parking, specially equipped restrooms, lowered drinking fountains, and lowered telephones.

Services: Counseling and information services are available, as is tutoring in most subjects, writing, math, accounting, computer science, and others as needed There is a reader service for the blind, and remedial math, reading, and writing. There is also a full-time assistant director of disabled student services.

Campus Safety and Security: Measures include 24-hour foot and vehicle patrol and security escort services. There are shuttle buses, emergency telephones, lighted pathways/sidewalks, a student volunteer escort service, and fire drills.

Programs of Study: CSR confers B.A., B.S., and B.F.A. degrees. Master's degrees are also awarded. Bachelor's degrees are awarded in BIOLOGICAL SCIENCE (biochemistry and biology/biological science), BUSINESS (accounting and business administration and management), COMMUNICATIONS AND THE ARTS (communications, English, graphic design, music, Spanish, and studio art), COMPUTER AND PHYSICAL SCIENCE (chemistry, information sciences and systems, and mathematics), EDUCATION (art education, early childhood education, elementary education, English education, foreign languages education, mathematics education, music education, science education, social studies education, special education, and technical education), ENGINEERING AND ENVIRONMENTAL DESIGN (environmental science), HEALTH PROFESSIONS (cytotechnology, medical technology, and speech pathology/audiology), SOCIAL SCIENCE (American studies, criminal justice, history, interdisciplinary studies, political science/government, psychology, religion, social work, and sociology). Education, art, and music are the strongest academically. Business, special education, and elementary education are the largest.

Required: To graduate, students must complete 122 credits with a minimum GPA of 2.0 overall and in the major; these requirements are higher for certain majors. Liberal education requirements consist of 6 credits in college writing and speech and 30 credits in the humanities, science and math, social science and business, English, computer literacy, foreign languages, history, philosophy, and the arts. Students must also complete 2 credits in phys ed.

Special: CSR offers cross-registration with the Hudson-Mohawk Association and the CSI Consortium, internships, work-study programs, study abroad in several countries, dual and student-designed majors, nondegree study, and pass/fail options. There are 3-2 engineering degree programs with Alfred and Clarkson Universities, Union College, and Rensselaer Polytechnic University, as well as a 6-year law program with Albany Law School. There are 6 national honor societies and 5 departmental honors programs.

Faculty/Classroom: 40% of faculty are male; 60% are female. No introductory courses are taught by graduate students. The average class size in a laboratory is 14 and in a regular course is 25.

Requirements: The SAT or ACT is required. In addition, applicants must be graduates of an accredited secondary school or have a GED certificate. They should have completed college preparatory programs including 4 years of English, social studies, history, math, science, and 3 years of math, science, and foreign language. All students must submit a letter of recommendation. Art students must submit portfolios, and music students must audition. AP and CLEP credits are accepted. Important factors in the admissions decision are advanced placement or honors courses, leadership record, and recommendations by school officials.

Procedure: Freshmen are admitted fall and spring. Entrance exams should be taken during spring of junior year or fall of senior year. There are early admissions, deferred admissions, and rolling admissions plans. Applications should be filed by May 1 for fall entry and November 1 for spring entry, along with a $35 fee. Notification is sent on a rolling basis. Applications are accepted on-line.

Transfer: 296 transfer students enrolled in a recent year. Applicants must submit official transcripts, a letter of recommendation, and a personal statement of the reasons for seeking transfer. An interview is recommended. Art majors must submit a portfolio, and music majors must audition. A minimum high school GPA is 3.0; minimum college GPA is 2.5 to 2.8. 60 of 122 credits required for the bachelor's degree must be completed at CSR.

Visiting: There are regularly scheduled orientations for prospective students, including visits with admissions and financial aid representatives, an overnight program hosted by students, Saturday information sessions in the fall, open house, and Accepted Student Day in April. There are guides for informal visits; visitors may sit in on classes and stay overnight. To schedule a visit, contact the Admissions Office at 800-637-8556.

Financial Aid: In a recent year, 83% of all full-time freshmen and 81% of continuing full-time students received some form of financial aid. 73% of all full-time freshmen and 77% of continuing full-time students received need-based aid. 1% of undergraduate students work part-time. The average financial indebtedness of the 2009 graduate was $24,920. CSR is a member of CSS. The FAFSA is required. Check with the school for current application deadlines.

International Students: There were 7 international students enrolled in a recent year. They must take the TOEFL.

Computers: All students may access the system. 24 hours a day Monday through Saturday, and additional hours on Sunday. There are no time limits. The fee is $100 per semester.

Graduates: In a recent year, 669 bachelor's degrees were awarded. The most popular majors were education (45%), business/marketing (9%), and visual and performing arts (8%). 45 companies recruited on campus in 2008-2009. In an average class, 49% graduate in 4 years or less, 67% graduate in 5 years or less, and 68% graduate in 6 years or less. Of the 2008 graduating class, 43% were enrolled in graduate school within 6 months of graduation, and 89% were employed.

Admissions Contact: Mary Grondahl, Associate Vice President for Undergraduate Admissions. A campus DVD is available. E-Mail: admit@rosnet.strose.edu Web: www.strose.edu

---

COLUMBIA UNIVERSITY SYSTEM

The Columbia University System, established in 1754, is a public system in New York. It is governed by a board of trustees, whose chief administrator is president. The primary goal of the system is teaching and research. The main priorities are providing outstanding undergraduate instruction; conducting research to develop new knowledge and methods; and training of professionals in law, business, social work, and medicine. Profiles of the 4-year campuses are included in this section.

COLUMBIA UNIVERSITY   D-5

New York, NY 10027	(212) 854-2522; (212) 854-1209
Full-time: 3005 men, 2700 women	Faculty: I, ++$
Part-time: none	Ph.D.s: n/av
Graduate: none	Student/Faculty: n/av
Year: semesters, summer session	Tuition: $38,000
Application Deadline: January 2	Room & Board: $10,000
Freshman Class: n/av	
SAT or ACT: required	MOST COMPETITIVE

Columbia University in the City of New York was founded in 1754. 4,100 undergraduates study liberal arts and science programs in Columbia College and 1,400 major in The Fu Foundation School of Engineering and Applied Science. Students also have access to our more than a dozen graduate and professional schools, a traditional college campus in the neighborhood of Morningside Heights, and all that New York City has to offer professionally, socially, and culturally. The figures in the above capsule and in this profile are approximate. The 25 libraries contain 9.5 million volumes. Computerized library services include interlibrary loans, database searching, Internet access, and laptop Internet portals. Special learning facilities include an art gallery, planetarium, radio station, TV station, and an observatory. The 36-acre campus is in an urban area New York City. Including any residence halls, there are 50 buildings.

Student Life: 75% of undergraduates are from out of state, mostly the Middle Atlantic. Students are from 49 states, 66 foreign countries, and Canada. 55% are from public schools. 41% are white; 18% Asian American. The average age of freshmen is 18; all undergraduates, 20. 3% do not continue beyond their first year; 93% remain to graduate.

Housing: 100 students can be accommodated in college housing, which includes single-sex and coed dorms and on-campus apartments. In addition, there are language houses, special-interest houses, and fraternity houses. On-campus housing is guaranteed for all 4 years. 94% of students live on campus. All students may keep cars.

Activities: 10% of men belong to 22 national fraternities; 6% of women belong to 11 national sororities. There are 300 groups on campus, including art, band, cheerleading, chess, choir, chorale, chorus, computers, dance, debate, drama, environmental, ethnic, film, forensics, gay, honors, international, jazz band, literary magazine, marching band, musical theater, newspaper, opera, orchestra, outdoor, pep band, photogra-

phy, political, professional, radio and TV, religious, social, social service, student government, symphony, and yearbook. Popular campus events include Columbia Fest, United Minorities Board Ethnic Festival, and Holiday Lighting Ceremony/Yule Log.

Sports: There are 14 intercollegiate sports for men and 15 for women, and 13 intramural sports for men and 13 for women. Facilities include a football stadium, indoor and outdoor track and field facilities, a baseball field, a soccer stadium, a recreational gym with a swimming pool, basketball/volleyball courts, aerobic, fencing, wrestling, martial arts, and weight rooms, a boat house, and tennis, squash, handball, and racquetball courts.

Disabled Students: All of the campus is accessible. Facilities include wheelchair ramps, elevators, special parking, specially equipped restrooms, special class scheduling, lowered drinking fountains, lowered telephones, and special housing.

Services: Counseling and information services are available, as is tutoring in every subject. There is a reader service for the blind.

Campus Safety and Security: Measures include 24-hour foot and vehicle patrol, self-defense education, and security escort services. There are shuttle buses, emergency telephones, and lighted pathways/sidewalks.

Programs of Study: Columbia confers A.B. degrees. Bachelor's degrees are awarded in BIOLOGICAL SCIENCE (biochemistry, biology/biological science, biophysics, environmental biology, and neurosciences), BUSINESS (operations research), COMMUNICATIONS AND THE ARTS (art history and appreciation, classics, comparative literature, dance, dramatic arts, English, film arts, French, German, Germanic languages and literature, Greek, Latin, linguistics, music, Russian, Spanish, and visual and performing arts), COMPUTER AND PHYSICAL SCIENCE (applied mathematics, applied physics, astronomy, astrophysics, chemistry, computer science, earth science, geochemistry, geology, geophysics and seismology, mathematics, physics, and statistics), EDUCATION (education), ENGINEERING AND ENVIRONMENTAL DESIGN (architecture, biomedical engineering, chemical engineering, civil engineering, computer engineering, electrical/electronics engineering, engineering management, engineering mechanics, environmental science, industrial engineering technology, materials science, mechanical engineering, metallurgical engineering, and mining and mineral engineering), SOCIAL SCIENCE (African American studies, American studies, anthropology, archeology, area studies, Asian/American studies, classical/ancient civilization, East Asian studies, economics, Hispanic American studies, history, Italian studies, Latin American studies, medieval studies, Middle Eastern studies, philosophy, political science/government, psychology, religion, Russian and Slavic studies, sociology, urban studies, and women's studies). Political science, economics, biomedical engineering, history, operations research, and mechanical engineering are the largest.

Required: All students complete a core curriculum consisting of classes in Western and non-Western cultures, literature and philosophy, history, social science, art, sculpture and architecture, and music of the Western tradition and science; 2 courses in non-Western areas are also required. Distribution requirements include 2 years of foreign language (unless competency can be demonstrated), 2 semesters of science, 1 year of phys ed, and 1 semester of writing. A thesis may be required for departmental honors in certain departments. A total of 124 credit hours is required; usually 30 to 40 of these are in the major. The engineering students are required to take Calculus, Physics, Chemistry and Economics and specific introductory engineering design courses in addition to half of the Columbia College core. The minimum required GPA is 2.0.

Special: There is a study abroad program at more than 100 locations, including France, Oxford and Cambridge Universities in England, and the Kyoto Center for Japanese Studies in Japan. Cross-registration is possible with the Juilliard School and Barnard College. Combined B.A.-B.S. degrees are offered via 3-2 or 4-1 engineering programs. A 3-2 engineering degree is offered with Columbia's Fu Foundation School of Engineering and Applied Science. There is also a 5-year B.A./M.I.A. with Columbia's School of International and Public Affairs. The college offers work-study, internships, credit by exam, pass/fail options, and dual, student-designed, and interdisciplinary majors, including regional studies and ancient studies. There are 31 departmental honors programs.

Faculty/Classroom: 68% of faculty are male; 32% are female. All teach and do research. No introductory courses are taught by graduate students. The average class size in an introductory lecture is 70; in a laboratory is 15; and in a regular course is 25.

Requirements: The SAT or ACT is required. The ACT Optional Writing test is also required. AP credits are accepted.

Procedure: Freshmen are admitted fall. Entrance exams should be taken by October or November of the senior year. There are early decision and deferred admissions plans. Early decision applications should be filed by November 1; regular applications, by January 2 for fall entry. The fall 2009 application fee was $70. Notification of early decision is sent December 15; regular decision, April 1. Applications are accepted on-line. A waiting list is maintained.

Transfer: 81 transfer students enrolled in a recent year. Applicants must have completed 1 full year of college (24 credits). They must submit high school and college transcripts. 60 of 128 credits required for the bachelor's degree must be completed at Columbia.

Visiting: There are regularly scheduled orientations for prospective students, consisting of group information sessions and student-led tours. There are guides for informal visits; visitors may sit in on classes and stay overnight. To schedule a visit, contact Visitors Center at (212) 854-4900.

Financial Aid: In a recent year, 63% of all full-time freshmen and 53% of continuing full-time students received some form of financial aid. 51% of all full-time freshmen and 48% of continuing full-time students received need-based aid. The average freshmen award was $34,577. The average financial indebtedness of the 2009 graduate was $17,144. Columbia is a member of CSS. The CSS/Profile, FAFSA, the college's own financial statement, federal tax returns, the business/farm supplement, and/or the divorced/separated parents statement, if applicable, are required. Check with the school for current application deadlines.

International Students: There were 482 international students enrolled in a recent year. The school actively recruits these students. They must take the TOEFL. They must also take the SAT or ACT.

Computers: Wireless access is available. There are computer labs and stand-alone terminals throughout the campus and computer clusters in residence halls. Every dorm room has an Ethernet connection. All students may access the system. 24 hours a day, 7 days a week. There are no time limits. There is a fee.

Graduates: In a recent year, 1390 bachelor's degrees were awarded. The most popular majors were political science (12%), English (11%), and economics (9%). 370 companies recruited on campus in 2008-2009. In an average class, 85% graduate in 4 years or less, 92% graduate in 5 years or less, and 93% graduate in 6 years or less.

Admissions Contact: Admissions Officer, Office of Undergraduate Admissions. A campus DVD is available. E-Mail: *ugradask@columbia.edu* Web: *www.columbia.edu*

COLUMBIA UNIVERSITY/BARNARD COLLEGE   D-5

New York, NY 10027-6598   (212) 854-5262; (212) 854-6220

Full-time: 2300 women	**Faculty:** n/av
Part-time: 55 women	**Ph.D.s:** n/av
Graduate: none	**Student/Faculty:** n/av
Year: semesters	**Tuition:** $29,000
Application Deadline: January 1	**Room & Board:** $12,000
Freshman Class: n/av	
SAT or ACT: required	**MOST COMPETITIVE**

Barnard College, founded in 1889, is an independent affiliate of Columbia University. It is an undergraduate womens' liberal arts college. Figures in the above capsule and in this profile are approximate. The library contains 204,906 volumes, 17,705 microform items, and 17,448 audio/video tapes/CDs/DVDs, and subscribes to 543 periodicals including electronic. Computerized library services include interlibrary loans, database searching, and Internet access. Special learning facilities include a learning resource center, art gallery, radio station, TV station, a greenhouse, history of physics lab, child development research and study center, dance studio, modern theater, womens' research archives within a womens' center, and multimedia labs and classrooms. The 4-acre campus is in an urban area occupying 4 city blocks of Manhattan's Upper West Side. Including any residence halls, there are 15 buildings.

Student Life: 68% of undergraduates are from out of state, mostly the Middle Atlantic. Students are from 48 states, 35 foreign countries, and Canada. 53% are from public schools. 66% are white; 16% Asian American. The average age of freshmen is 18; all undergraduates, 20. 5% do not continue beyond their first year; 84% remain to graduate.

Housing: 2057 students can be accommodated in college housing, which includes single-sex and coed dorms, on-campus apartments, and off-campus apartments. In addition, there are special-interest houses. On-campus housing is guaranteed for all 4 years. 90% of students live on campus; of those, 75% remain on campus on weekends. Alcohol is not permitted. All students may keep cars.

Activities: There are no fraternities or sororities. There are 100 groups on campus, including art, band, cheerleading, choir, chorale, chorus, dance, debate, drama, ethnic, film, gay, international, jazz band, literary magazine, marching band, Model UN, musical theater, newspaper, opera, orchestra, pep band, photography, political, professional, radio and TV, religious, social, social service, student government, symphony, and yearbook. Popular campus events include Spring and Winter Festivals, Founders Day, and Take Back the Night.

Sports: There are 15 intercollegiate sports for women, and 16 intramural sports for women. Facilities include pools, weight rooms, gyms, tennis courts, an indoor track, and a boat slip.

Disabled Students: 90% of the campus is accessible. Facilities include wheelchair ramps, elevators, special parking, specially equipped restrooms, special class scheduling, lowered drinking fountains, lowered telephones, and special housing. The Office of Disability Services provides a variety of support services to students with permanent and temporary disabilities.

Services: Counseling and information services are available, as is tutoring in every subject. There is a reader service for the blind. A student-staffed writing room is available for students of all levels of writing ability, and a math help room is also available to students in all math courses.

Campus Safety and Security: Measures include 24-hour foot and vehicle patrol and security escort services. There are shuttle buses, emergency telephones, lighted pathways/sidewalks, and safety and security education programs.

Programs of Study: Barnard College confers B.A. degrees. Bachelor's degrees are awarded in BIOLOGICAL SCIENCE (biochemistry and biology/biological science), COMMUNICATIONS AND THE ARTS (art history and appreciation, classics, comparative literature, dance, dramatic arts, English, film arts, French, German, Greek, Italian, Latin, linguistics, music, Russian, and Spanish), COMPUTER AND PHYSICAL SCIENCE (astronomy, chemistry, computer science, mathematics, physics, and statistics), ENGINEERING AND ENVIRONMENTAL DESIGN (architecture and environmental science), SOCIAL SCIENCE (American studies, anthropology, biopsychology, classical/ancient civilization, East Asian studies, economics, European studies, history, international studies, medieval studies, Middle Eastern studies, philosophy, political science/government, psychology, religion, sociology, urban studies, and women's studies). English, psychology, and economics and have the largest enrollments.

Required: A total of 120 credits is required, with a minimum GPA of 2.0. All students must take 4 semesters each of a foreign language, humanities, or social sciences outside the major, and geographic and cultural diversity courses that may satisfy the major or other requirements, 2 semesters each of lab science and phys ed, and 1 semester each in first-year seminar, first-year English, and quantitative reasoning.

Special: Barnard offers cross-registration with Columbia University, more than 2500 internships with New York City firms and institutions, and study abroad worldwide. A 3-2 engineering program with the Columbia School of Engineering and double-degree programs with the Columbia University Schools of International and Public Affairs, Law, and Dentistry, the Juilliard School, and the Jewish Theological Seminary are possible. The college offers dual and student-designed majors and multidisciplinary majors, including economic history. There is 1 national honor society and Phi Beta Kappa.

Faculty/Classroom: 35% of faculty are male; 65% are female. All teach and do research. No introductory courses are taught by graduate students. The average class size in an introductory lecture is 30; in a laboratory is 11; and in a regular course is 13.

Requirements: The SAT or ACT is required. If taking the SAT, an applicant must also take 3 SAT Subject tests, one of which must be in writing or literature. A GED is accepted. Applicants should prepare with 4 years of English, 3 of math and science, 3 or 4 of a foreign language, 2 of a lab science, and 1 of history. An interview is recommended. AP credits are accepted. Important factors in the admissions decision are advanced placement or honors courses, evidence of special talent, and extracurricular activities record.

Procedure: Freshmen are admitted fall. Entrance exams should be taken by January of the senior year. There are early decision, early admissions and deferred admissions plans. Early decision applications should be filed by November 15; regular applications, by January 1 for fall entry, along with a $55 fee. Notification of early decision is sent December 15; regular decision, April 1. Applications are accepted on-line. A waiting list is maintained.

Transfer: 80 transfer students enrolled in a recent year. Applicants must complete at least 1 college course. The SAT or ACT is required. Deadline for transfer applicants is April 1 (fall term) and November 1 (spring term). They must submit high school and college transcripts. They must be in good standing from prior institutions attended and submit an essay or personal statement. 60 of 120 credits required for the bachelor's degree must be completed at Barnard College.

Visiting: There are regularly scheduled orientations for prospective students, consisting of open house programs for prospective students regularly scheduled throughout the fall. There are guides for informal visits; visitors may sit in on classes and stay overnight. To schedule a visit, contact the Office of Admissions at (212) 854-2014.

Financial Aid: In a recent year, 44% of all full-time freshmen and 44% of continuing full-time students received some form of financial aid. 41% of all full-time freshmen and 42% of continuing full-time students received need-based aid. The average freshmen award was $30,644. 46% of undergraduate students worked part-time. The average financial indebtedness of the 2009 graduate was $17,630. Barnard College is a member of CSS. The CSS/Profile, FAFSA, the state aid form, the college's own financial statement, the parents' and student's federal tax returns, and the business and/or farm supplement are required. Check with the school for current application deadlines.

International Students: The school actively recruits these students. They must take the TOEFL. They must also take the SAT or ACT. Applicants who take the SAT must also take SAT Subject tests in writing or literature and 2 others.

Computers: All students may access the system. There are no time limits and no fees. It is strongly recommended that all students have a personal computer.

Graduates: In a recent year, 597 bachelor's degrees were awarded. The most popular majors were social sciences (25%), psychology (14%), and English (11%). In an average class, 2% graduate in 3 years or less, 82% graduate in 4 years or less, 88% graduate in 5 years or less, and 89% graduate in 6 years or less.

Admissions Contact: Jennifer Fondiller, Dean of Admissions. E-Mail: *admissions@barnard.edu* Web: *www.barnard.edu*

COLUMBIA UNIVERSITY/SCHOOL OF GENERAL STUDIES   D-5

New York, NY 10027	(212) 854-2772
	(800) 895-1169; (212) 854-6316

Full-time: 445 men, 367 women	**Faculty:** I, ++$
Part-time: 229 men, 310 women	**Ph.D.s:** 99%
Graduate: none	**Student/Faculty:** n/av
Year: semesters, summer session	**Tuition:** $36,058
Application Deadline: June 1	**Room & Board:** $14,066
Freshman Class: n/av	
SAT or ACT: recommended	**MOST COMPETITIVE**

The School of General Studies of Columbia University, founded in 1947, offers liberal arts degree programs and postgraduate studies for adult men and women whose post-high school education has been interrupted or postponed by at least 1 year. The 22 libraries contain 9.5 million volumes, 5.9 million microform items, and 107,850 audio/video tapes/CDs/DVDs, and subscribe to 117,264 periodicals including electronic. Computerized library services include interlibrary loans, database searching, Internet access, and laptop Internet portals. Special learning facilities include a learning resource center, art gallery, radio station, and TV station. The 36-acre campus is in an urban area on the upper west side of Manhattan in New York City.

Student Life: 42% of undergraduates are from out of state, mostly the Northeast. 50% are white; 17% foreign nationals; 13% Asian American. The average age of all undergraduates is 29.

Housing: 378 students can be accommodated in college housing, which includes single-sex and coed off-campus apartments and married student housing. In addition, there are fraternity houses and an international house. On-campus housing is available on a first-come, first-served basis. Priority is given to out-of-town students. 72% of students commute. Alcohol is not permitted. No one may keep cars.

Activities: 1% of men belong to 17 national fraternities; 1% of women belong to 11 national sororities. There are 250 groups on campus, including art, band, cheerleading, chess, choir, chorale, chorus, computers, dance, debate, drama, environmental, ethnic, film, gay, honors, international, jazz band, literary magazine, marching band, musical theater, newspaper, opera, orchestra, photography, political, professional, radio and TV, religious, social, social service, student government, symphony, women's, writers, and yearbook.

Sports: There are 14 intercollegiate sports for men and 15 for women, and 11 intramural sports for men and 11 for women. Facilities include 2 gyms, a swimming pool, tennis, squash, and racquetball courts, a training center, 2 dance/martial arts studios, a fencing room, a wrestling room, and an indoor track.

Disabled Students: All of the campus is accessible. Facilities include wheelchair ramps, elevators, specially equipped restrooms, lowered drinking fountains, and lowered telephones.

Services: Counseling and information services are available, as is tutoring in some subjects, including English composition, math, languages, and sciences.

Campus Safety and Security: Measures include 24-hour foot and vehicle patrol, emergency notification system, self-defense education, and security escort services. There are shuttle buses, emergency telephones, and lighted pathways/sidewalks.

Programs of Study: GS confers B.A. and B.S. degrees. Bachelor's degrees are awarded in BIOLOGICAL SCIENCE (biology/biological science), COMMUNICATIONS AND THE ARTS (art history and appreciation, classics, comparative literature, dance, dramatic arts, English literature, film arts, French, German, Italian, literature, music, Slavic languages, Spanish, and visual and performing arts), COMPUTER AND PHYSICAL SCIENCE (applied mathematics, astronomy, chemistry, computer science, geoscience, mathematics, physics, and statistics), ENGINEERING AND ENVIRONMENTAL DESIGN (architecture and environmental science), SOCIAL SCIENCE (African American studies, anthropology, archeology, classical/ancient civilization, East Asian studies, economics, French studies, German area studies, Hispanic American studies, history, Italian studies, Latin American studies, Middle Eastern studies, philosophy, political science/government, psychology, religion, sociology, urban studies, and women's studies). Political science, economics, and English are the largest.

Required: All students must complete 124 credit hours, including 56 distribution requirement credits in literature, humanities, foreign language or literature, social science, science, and cultural diversity. Proficiency in English composition and math is required. A GPA of 2.0 is necessary to graduate.

Special: Preprofessional studies in allied health and medical fields and interdisciplinary majors, minors, and concentrations are offered. Internships in New York City, work-study programs on campus, study abroad, a 3-2 engineering degree at Columbia University School of Engineering and Applied Science, B.A.-B.S. degrees, and dual majors are available. There is a Phi Beta Kappa honors program.

Faculty/Classroom: 63% of faculty are male; 37% are female.

Requirements: The SAT or ACT is recommended. SAT, ACT, or Columbia's General Studies Admissions Exam scores should be submitted along with high school and all college transcripts. An autobiographical statement is required. An interview is encouraged. AP credits are accepted. Important factors in the admissions decision are personality/intangible qualities, extracurricular activities record, and evidence of special talent.

Procedure: Freshmen are admitted to all sessions. Entrance exams should be taken as early as possible. There is a deferred admissions plan. Early decision applications should be filed by March 1 for fall entry and October 1 for spring entry. Regular decision applications should be filed by June 1 for fall entry, November 1 for pring entry, and April 1 for summer entry. The application fee is $65. Applications are accepted on-line. A waiting list is maintained.

Transfer: 184 transfer students enrolled in 2008-2009. Most students come to GS with some college credit. 64 of 124 credits required for the bachelor's degree must be completed at GS.

Visiting: There are regularly scheduled orientations for prospective students, consisting of an admissions information session every other Wednesday, preceded by a campus tour. There are guides for informal visits and visitors may sit in on classes. To schedule a visit, contact Office of Admissions and Financial Aid at (212) 854-5109.

Financial Aid: In 2009-2010, the average freshmen award was $8000. 75% of undergraduate students work part-time. Average annual earnings from campus work are $2500. The average financial indebtedness of the 2009 graduate was $65,000. GS is a member of CSS. The FAFSA and the college's own financial statement are required. Check with the school for current application deadlines.

International Students: There were 104 international students enrolled in a recent year. The school actively recruits these students. They must take the TOEFL, with a minimum score of 600 on the paper-based TOEFL (PBT) or 100 on the Internet-based version (iBT), or an English placement test administered by Columbia's American Language Program. Submission of recent SAT scores is encouraged. Students who have not taken the SAT must take the Columbia's General Studies Admissions Exam.

Computers: Wireless access is available. There are computer facilities in more than 65 buildings. All students may access the system. Students are limited to 1 hour. There are no fees. It is strongly recommended that all students have a personal computer.

Graduates: From July 1, 2008 to June 30, 2009, 271 bachelor's degrees were awarded. The most popular majors were economics (15%), English (13%), and history (11%). 300 companies recruited on campus in a recent year.

Admissions Contact: Curtis Rodgers, Dean of Admissions. E-Mail: *gsadmit@columbia.edu* Web: *www.gs.columbia.edu*

CONCORDIA COLLEGE-NEW YORK   D-5

Bronxville, NY 10708	(914) 337-9300
	(800) 937-2655; (914) 395-4636

Full-time: 275 men, 355 women	**Faculty:** n/a
Part-time: 35 men, 70 women	**Ph.D.s:** n/av
Graduate: none	**Student/Faculty:** n/av
Year: semesters	**Tuition:** $22,500
Application Deadline: March 15	**Room & Board:** $9000
Freshman Class: n/av	
SAT or ACT: required	**COMPETITIVE**

Concordia College, founded in 1881, is a Christian liberal arts college offering undergraduate majors, including business, education, music, social work, and professional training in ministry. The figures in the above capsule and in this profile are approximate. In addition to regional accreditation, Concordia has baccalaureate program accreditation with CSWE and NCATE. The library contains 85,000 volumes, 25,000 microform items, and 8,750 audio/video tapes/CDs/DVDs, and subscribes to 350 periodicals including electronic. Computerized library services include interlibrary loans, database searching, Internet access, and laptop Internet portals. Special learning facilities include a learning resource center, art gallery, education center, family center, and Lutheran education service. The 33-acre campus is in a suburban area 15 miles north of New York City. Including any residence halls, there are 21 buildings.

Student Life: 66% of undergraduates are from New York. Others are from 27 states, and 34 foreign countries. 54% are white; 11% African American. 40% are Protestant; 32% Catholic; 19% Unknown. The average age of freshmen is 18; all undergraduates, 24. 24% do not continue beyond their first year; 45% remain to graduate.

Housing: 424 students can be accommodated in college housing, which includes single-sex dorms. In addition, there are special-interest houses. On-campus housing is guaranteed for all 4 years. 66% of students live on campus; of those, 75% remain on campus on weekends. All students may keep cars.

Activities: 10% of men belong to 2 national fraternities; 10% of women belong to 2 national sororities. There are 25 groups on campus, including art, chamber and jazz ensembles, cheerleading, choir, chorus, drama, ethnic, honors, international, jazz band, literary magazine, musical theater, newspaper, orchestra, organist guild, photography, professional, religious, social, social service, student government, symphony, and yearbook. Popular campus events include guest lectures, dramatic presentations, and spring and fall festivals.

Sports: There are 5 intercollegiate sports for men and 6 for women, and 10 intramural sports for men and 10 for women. Facilities include an athletic center, a field house, indoor and outdoor tennis courts, squash and racquetball courts, a weight room, a fitness center, and 3 athletic fields.

Disabled Students: 50% of the campus is accessible. Facilities include wheelchair ramps, elevators, special parking, specially equipped restrooms, lowered drinking fountains, and lowered telephones.

Services: Counseling and information services are available, as is tutoring in most subjects. There is remedial math, reading, and writing.

Campus Safety and Security: Measures include 24-hour foot and vehicle patrol and security escort services. There are emergency telephones and lighted pathways/sidewalks.

Programs of Study: Concordia confers B.A., B.S. degrees. Associates degrees are also awarded. Bachelor's degrees are awarded in BIOLOGICAL SCIENCE (biology/biological science), BUSINESS (business administration and management), COMMUNICATIONS AND THE ARTS (applied music, arts administration/management, English, and music), COMPUTER AND PHYSICAL SCIENCE (mathematics), EDUCATION (early childhood education, education, elementary education, mathematics education, music education, and social studies education), ENGINEERING AND ENVIRONMENTAL DESIGN (environmental science), SOCIAL SCIENCE (behavioral science, history, interdisciplinary studies, international studies, religion, religious music, and social work). Education, behavioral sciences, and social work are the strongest academically. Education, business administration, and behavioral sciences are the largest.

Required: To graduate, students must complete 122 semester hours with a minimum GPA of 2.0. General education requirements include 21 hours of integrated learning courses and 18 credits of discipline support courses. Students are required to take 3 credits each of phys ed. A thesis is required in some majors.

Special: A registered professional nurse program is offered in cooperation with Mount Vernon Hospital School of Nursing. Concordia also offers co-op programs in social work and education, cross-registration with a consortium of nearby colleges, internships, study abroad in England, B.A.- B.S. degrees, an interdisciplinary studies degree and credit for life experience. Accelerated degree programs are available in business administration and behavioral sciences. There is1 national honor societies, a freshman honors program, and 10 departmental honors programs.

Faculty/Classroom: 55% of faculty are male; 45% are female. All teach undergraduates. No introductory courses are taught by graduate students. The average class size in an introductory lecture is 19; in a laboratory is 12; and in a regular course is 12.

Requirements: The SAT or ACT is required. In addition, applicants should be graduates of an accredited secondary school or have a GED certificate. Concordia prefers completion of 4 years of English, 3 of math,and 2 each of laboratory social studies, science and a foreign language. An interview is recommended, and those students applying to the music program must audition. A GPA of 2.5 is required. AP and CLEP credits are accepted. Important factors in the admissions decision are advanced placement or honors courses, evidence of special talent, and extracurricular activities record.

Procedure: Freshmen are admitted fall and spring. Entrance exams should be taken in the fall of the senior year. There are early decision, early admissions and rolling admissions plans. Early decision applications should be filed by November 15; regular applications, by March 15 for fall entry and December 30 for spring entry, along with a $40 fee. Notification of early decision is sent December 1; regular decision, January 15. Applications are accepted on-line.

Transfer: A 2.0 GPA is recommended. Applicants must submit official transcripts from previous colleges attended. Students must complete the last 30 credits at Concordia College. 30 of 122 credits required for the bachelor's degree must be completed at Concordia.

Visiting: There are regularly scheduled orientations for prospective students, Which include opportunities to interact with faculty, tour campus, learn about admission and financial aid, and discover academic and student life opportunities. There are guides for informal visits; visitors may sit in on classes and stay overnight. To schedule a visit, contact the Admissions Office.

Financial Aid: The FAFSA is required. Check with the school for current application deadlines.

International Students: The school actively recruits these students. They must take the TOEFL or take the SAT.

Computers: Wireless access is available. Concordia provides high-speed Internet access, e-mail services, individual disk storage file services, and access to library services and the college intranet. A total of 40 PCs are available for student use in the library, the Writing Center, and two computer labs. Resident students can also use their PCs for access to the local network from their dorm rooms. All students may access the system any time. There are no time limits and no fees.

Admissions Contact: Donna Hoyt E-Mail: *admissions@concordia-ny.edu* Web: *www.concordia-ny.edu*

COOPER UNION FOR THE ADVANCEMENT OF SCIENCE AND ART   D-5

New York, NY 10003-7120	(212) 353-4120; (212) 353-4342
Full-time: 561 men, 336 women	Faculty: 53; II B, ++$
Part-time: 1 men, no women	Ph.D.s: 89%
Graduate: 77 men, 11 women	Student/Faculty: 17 to 1
Year: semesters, summer session	Tuition: $1600
Application Deadline: January 1	Room & Board: $13,500
Freshman Class: 3387 applied, 249 accepted, 193 enrolled	
SAT CR/M: 660/720	ACT: 33 MOST COMPETITIVE

The Cooper Union for the Advancement of Science and Art, is an all honors college that provides full-tuition scholarships (estimated value $ 35000) to all undergradutes accepted. It offers degrees in architecture, art, and engineering. There are 3 undergraduate schools and one graduate school. In addition to regional accreditation, Cooper Union has baccalaureate program accreditation with ABET, NAAB, and NASAD. The library contains 104,000 volumes, 25,000 microform items, and 1,472 audio/video tapes/CDs/DVDs, and subscribes to 2,471 periodicals including electronic. Computerized library services include interlibrary loans, database searching, and Internet access. Special learning facilities include a learning resource center, art gallery, a center for speaking and writing, an electronic resources center, and a visual resources center. The campus is in an urban area located in the heart of lower Manhattan. Including any residence halls, there are 5 buildings.

Student Life: 60% of undergraduates are from New York. Others are from 43 states, 40 foreign countries, and Canada. 75% are from public schools. 42% are white; 19% Asian American; 15% foreign nationals. The average age of freshmen is 18; all undergraduates, 20. 5% do not continue beyond their first year; 90% remain to graduate.

Housing: 178 students can be accommodated in college housing, which includes coed dorms. 81% of students commute. No one may keep cars.

Activities: 15% of men belong to 1 national fraternity. There are no sororities. There are 85 groups on campus, including chess, chorale, computers, drama, environmental, ethnic, ethnic and musical, film, gay, honors, international, jazz band, literary magazine, newspaper, orchestra, political, professional, religious, social, social service, student government, and yearbook. Popular campus events include an end-of-the-year student art, architecture and engineering exhibit and ongoing events in the Great Hall, and the South Asia Society Culture Show.

Sports: There are 5 intercollegiate sports for men and 3 for women, and 12 intramural sports for men and 12 for women. Facilities include access to local gyms on weekends, a nearby swimming pool, and basketball courts.

Disabled Students: 80% of the campus is accessible. Facilities include wheelchair ramps, elevators, specially equipped restrooms, special class scheduling, and special housing.

Services: Counseling and information services are available, as is tutoring in some subjects, math, physics, speech, and writing.

Campus Safety and Security: There are emergency telephones and lighted pathways/sidewalks. There are security guards in all building lobbies and hand-scan technology in the residence hall.

Programs of Study: Cooper Union confers B.S., B.Arch., B.E., and B.F.A. degrees. Master's degrees are also awarded. Bachelor's degrees are awarded in COMMUNICATIONS AND THE ARTS (fine arts and graphic design), ENGINEERING AND ENVIRONMENTAL DESIGN (architecture, chemical engineering, civil engineering, electrical/electronics engineering, engineering, and mechanical engineering). Engineering is the strongest academically and the largest.

Required: The 5-year architecture program requires 160 credits, including 30 in liberal arts and electives, for graduation. Art students must complete 128 credits, including 38 in liberal arts and electives, with a minimum overall GPA of 2.0 to graduate. A 2.5 GPA is expected in studio work. Engineering students are required to complete a minimum of 135 credits, including a computer literacy course and 24 credits in humanities and social sciences, with a minimum GPA of 2.0.

Special: Cross-registration with New School University, internships, study abroad for art students in 15 countries, and for engineering students in 12 countries, and some pass/fail options are available. Nondegree study is possible. An accelerated degree in engineering is also available (combined bachelors and masters degree program). There are 4 national honor societies and 1 departmental honors program.

Faculty/Classroom: 77% of faculty are male; 23% are female. All teach and do research. No introductory courses are taught by graduate students. The average class size in an introductory lecture, 28, in a laboratory, 20, and in a regular course, 20.

Admissions: 7% of the 2009-2010 applicants were accepted. The SAT scores for the 2009-2010 freshman class were: Critical Reading--4% below 500, 22% between 500 and 599, 40% between 600 and 700, and 34% above 700; Math--7% below 500, 17% between 500 and 599, 21% between 600 and 700, and 5% above 700. The ACT scores were 25% between 27 and 28 and 75% above 28. 90% of the current freshmen were in the top fifth of their class; 98% were in the top two fifths. There were 8 National Merit finalists. 5 freshmen graduated first in their class.

Requirements: The SAT is required. In addition, engineering applicants must take SAT Subject Tests in mathematics I or II and physics or chemistry. Graduation from an approved secondary school is required. Applicants should have completed 16 to 18 high school academic credits, depending on their major. An essay is part of the application process. Art students must submit a portfolio. Art and architecture applicants must complete a project called the home test. AP credits are accepted. Important factors in the admissions decision are evidence of special talent, advanced placement or honors courses, and personality/intangible qualities.

Procedure: Freshmen are admitted in the fall. Entrance exams should be taken before February 1. There are early decision and deferred admissions plans. Early decision applications should be filed by December 1; regular applications, by January 1 for fall entry. The fall 2008 application fee was $65. Notification of early decision is sent February 1; regular decision, April 1. Applications are accepted on-line. 50 applicants were on a recent waiting list, 3 were accepted.

Transfer: 45 transfer students enrolled in 2008-2009. Art and architecture transfer applicants must present a portfolio and a minimum of 24 credits in studio classes. Engineering transfer applicants must submit a transcript with grades of B or better in at least 24 credits of appropriate courses.

Visiting: There are regularly scheduled orientations for prospective students, consisting of open house and portfolio review days for art and open house for engineering; architecture tours are by appointment. There are guides for informal visits and visitors may sit in on classes. To schedule a visit, contact the Office of Admissions and Records at (212) 353-4120.

Financial Aid: In 2009-2010, all full-time freshmen and all of continuing full-time students received some form of financial aid. 36% of all full-time freshmen and 35% of continuing full-time students received need-based aid. The average freshmen award was $35,000, with $3,249 ($5,000 maximum) from need-based scholarships or need-based grants; $2,084 ($3,000 maximum) from need-based self-help aid (loans and jobs); and $35,000 ($35,000 maximum) from other non-need-based awards and non-need-based scholarships. 47% of undergraduate students work part-time. Average annual earnings from campus work are $1001. The average financial indebtedness of the 2009 graduate was $9,900. Cooper Union is a member of CSS. The CSS/Profile and FAFSA are required. The priority date for freshman financial aid applications for fall entry is April 15. The deadline for filing freshman financial aid applications for fall entry is May 1.

International Students: There are 135 international students enrolled. They must take the TOEFL with a minimum score of 600 on the paper-based TOEFL (PBT) or 100 on the Internet-based version (iBT). They must also take the SAT or ACT, and the college's own entrance exam. All freshman applicants must take the SAT; art and architecture students must also take the home test.

Computers: Wireless access is available. All students may access the system whenever the Engineering Building is open. There are no time limits and no fees.

Graduates: From July 1, 2008 to June 30, 2009, 202 bachelor's degrees were awarded. The most popular majors were fine arts (27%), electrical engineering (14%), and mechanical engineering (13%). 110 companies recruited on campus in 2008-2009. In an average class, 1% graduate in 3 years or less, 75% graduate in 4 years or less, 90% graduate in 5 years or less, and 91% graduate in 6 years or less. Of the 2008 graduating class, 42% were enrolled in graduate school within 6 months of graduation, and 42% were employed.

Admissions Contact: Mitchell Lipton, Dean of Admissions and Records. A campus DVD is available. E-Mail: admissions@cooper.edu Web: www.cooper.edu

CORNELL UNIVERSITY   C-3

Ithaca, NY 14850   (607) 255-5241

Full-time: 7050 men, 6881 women	Faculty: 1432; I, +$
Part-time: none	Ph.D.s: 93%
Graduate: 3837 men, 2865 women	Student/Faculty: 10 to 1
Year: semesters, summer session	Tuition: $50,114
Application Deadline: January 1	Room & Board: $12,160
Freshman Class: 34371 applied, 6565 accepted, 3181 enrolled	
SAT or ACT: required	MOST COMPETITIVE

Cornell University was founded in 1865 as a land-grant institution. This private institution has undergraduate divisions that include the College of Architecture, Art, and Planning, the College of Arts and Sciences, the College of Engineering, and the School of Hotel Administration. State-assisted undergraduate divisions include the College of Agriculture and Life Sciences, the College of Human Ecology, and the School of Industrial and Labor Relations. There are 7 undergraduate schools and 4 graduate schools. In addition to regional accreditation, Cornell has baccalaureate program accreditation with AACSB, ABET, ASLA, and NAAB. The 19 libraries contain 7.5 million volumes, 8.5 million microform items, and 140,997 audio/video tapes/CDs/DVDs, and subscribe to 93,000 periodicals including electronic. Computerized library services include interlibrary loans, database searching, Internet access, and laptop Internet portals. Special learning facilities include a learning resource center, art gallery, planetarium, radio station, biotechnology institute, woods sanctuary, 4 designated national resource centers, 2 local optical observatories, Africana Studies and research center, arboretum, particle accelerator, supercomputers, national research centers, performing arts center, lab of ornithology, vertebrates museum, living and learning communities, campus orchard, dairy pilot plant, mineralogical museum, animal teaching hospital, 2 agricultural experiment stations, and a marine laboratory. The 745-acre campus is in a rural area 60 miles south of Syracuse, NY. Including any residence halls, there are 770 buildings.

Student Life: 58% of undergraduates are from out of state, mostly the Middle Atlantic. Students are from 49 states, 77 foreign countries, and Canada. 46% are white; 17% Asian American. The average age of freshmen is 18; all undergraduates, 20. 4% do not continue beyond their first year; 92% remain to graduate.

Housing: 8359 students can be accommodated in college housing, which includes single-sex and coed dorms, on-campus apartments, and married student housing. In addition, there are language houses, special-interest houses, fraternity houses, and sorority houses. On-campus housing is guaranteed for the freshman year only and is available on a lottery system for upperclassmen. 56% of students live on campus; of those, 90% remain on campus on weekends. All students may keep cars.

Activities: 32% of men belong to 2 local and 48 national fraternities; 23% of women belong to 19 national sororities. There are 820 groups on campus, including art, band, cheerleading, chess, choir, chorale, chorus, computers, dance, debate, drama, drill team; environmental, ethnic, film, forensics, gay, honors, international, jazz band, literary magazine, marching band, musical theater, newspaper, orchestra, pep band, photography, political, professional, radio and TV, religious, social, social service, student government, symphony, and yearbook. Popular campus events include Dragon Day, New Student Reading Project, and Third World Festival of the Arts.

Sports: There are 18 intercollegiate sports for men and 18 for women, and 27 intramural sports for men and 27 for women. Facilities include indoor and outdoor tracks, a 5000-seat indoor gym, 3 swimming pools, a 25000-seat stadium, 16 intercollegiate fields, a bowling alley, intramural fields, a boat house, indoor and outdoor tennis courts, and the Lindseth climbing wall.

Disabled Students: The campus is accessible. Facilities include wheelchair ramps, elevators, special parking, specially equipped restrooms, special class scheduling, lowered drinking fountains, lowered telephones, special housing, alternative test arrangements, and bus passes or van transportation.

Services: Counseling and information services are available, as is tutoring in some subjects. Many introductory courses in math, the sciences, and economics are available. There is a reader service for the blind. Biology and math student support centers, and writing workshops are also available. In addition, supplemental instruction in introductory math, chemistry, biology, economics, and physics courses are provided.

Campus Safety and Security: Measures include 24-hour foot and vehicle patrol, emergency notification system, self-defense education, and security escort services. There are shuttle buses, emergency telephones, and lighted pathways/sidewalks.

Programs of Study: Cornell confers B.A., B.S., B.Arch., and B.F.A. degrees. Master's and doctoral degrees are also awarded. Bachelor's degrees are awarded in AGRICULTURE (agricultural business management, agricultural economics, agriculture, animal science, horticulture, international agriculture, natural resource management, plant protection (pest management), plant science, and soil science), BIOLOGICAL SCIENCE (biochemistry, biology/biological science, ecology, entomology, microbiology, neurosciences, nutrition, plant genetics, and plant pathology), BUSINESS (hotel/motel and restaurant management and operations research), COMMUNICATIONS AND THE ARTS (art history and appreciation, Chinese, classics, communications, comparative literature, dance, dramatic arts, English, film arts, fine arts, French, German, Italian, linguistics, music, Russian, and Spanish), COMPUTER AND PHYSICAL SCIENCE (astronomy, atmospheric sciences and meteorology, chemistry, computer science, earth science, geology, information sciences and systems, mathematics, physics, science technology, and statistics), EDUCATION (education, home economics education, and science education), ENGINEERING AND ENVIRONMENTAL DESIGN (agricultural engineering, architectural history, architecture, bioengineering, chemical engineering, city/community/regional planning, civil engineering, computer engineering, electrical/electronics engineering, engineering physics, environmental engineering technology, environmental science, industrial administration/management, landscape architecture/design, materials science, and mechanical engineering), SOCIAL SCIENCE (African studies, American studies, anthropology, archeology, Asian/Oriental studies, classical/ancient civilization, consumer services, economics, family/consumer studies, food production/management/services, food science, gender studies, German area studies, history, human development, human services, Near Eastern studies, philosophy, political science/government, psychology, public affairs, religion, rural sociology, Russian and Slavic studies, sociology, textiles and clothing, urban studies, and women's studies). Engineering, business, and agriculture are the largest.

Required: Entering freshmen must meet basic swimming and water safety competency requirements. All undergraduates must take 2 semesters each of freshman writing seminar and phys ed. Graduation requirements vary by program, including a minimum of 120 credits.

Special: Cornell's colleges and schools offer nearly unlimited opportunities for international study internships and exchanges. There are opportunities for dual-majors, dual-degrees, and minors throughout the university. Refer to information provided by the individual schools, colleges, and programs for details. There are 47 national honor societies and including Phi Beta Kappa.

Faculty/Classroom: 69% of faculty are male; 31% are female. No introductory courses are taught by graduate students.

Admissions: 19% of the 2009-2010 applicants were accepted. The SAT scores for the 2009-2010 freshman class were: Critical Reading--1% below 500, 13% between 500 and 599, 44% between 600 and 700, and 42% above 700; Math--1% below 500, 6% between 500 and 599, 33% between 600 and 700, and 60% above 700. The ACT scores were % below 21, 2% between 21 and 23, 9% between 24 and 26, 11% between 27 and 28, and 78% above 28. 97% of the current freshmen were in the top fifth of their class; 100% were in the top two fifths.

Requirements: The SAT or ACT is required. The ACT Optional Writing test is also required. In addition, an essay is required as part of the application process. Other requirements vary by division or program, including specific SAT Subject tests and selection of courses within the minimum 16 secondary-school academic units needed. An interview and/or portfolio is required for specific majors. AP credits are accepted. Important factors in the admissions decision are advanced placement or honors courses, evidence of special talent, and leadership record.

Procedure: Freshmen are admitted fall and spring. Entrance exams should be taken by December of the senior year. There are early decision, early admissions and deferred admissions plans. Early decision applications should be filed by November 1; regular applications, by January 1 for fall entry and October 1 for spring entry. The fall 2009 application fee was $70. Notification of early decision is sent in December. Notifications are sent in April. Applications are accepted on-line. 1949 applicants were on a recent waiting list.

Transfer: 567 transfer students enrolled in 2008-2009. All applicants must submit high school and college transcripts, as well as scores from the SAT or ACT if taken previously. Other admission requirements vary by program, including the number of credits that must be completed at Cornell. 60 of 120 credits required for the bachelor's degree must be completed at Cornell.

Visiting: There are regularly scheduled orientations for prospective students, visits consist of campus tours and information sessions. There are guides for informal visits, visitors may sit in on classes, and stay overnight. To schedule a visit, contact the Red Carpet Society at (607) 255-3447.

Financial Aid: In 2009-2010, 60% of all full-time freshmen and 64% of continuing full-time students received some form of financial aid. 52% of all full-time freshmen and 46% of continuing full-time students received need-based aid. The average freshmen award was $36,062. The average financial indebtedness of the 2009 graduate was $21,549. The CSS/Profile, FAFSA, and the college's own financial statement, and The IRS form is required after enrollment are required. The deadline for filing freshman financial aid applications for fall entry is January 2.

International Students: There are 1216 international students enrolled. The school actively recruits these students. They must take the TOEFL with a minimum score of 600 on the paper-based TOEFL (PBT) or 100 on the Internet-based version (iBT). They must also take the SAT or ACT.

Computers: Wireless access is available. Students have access to campus wide PC centers and more than 30 departmental facilities with more than 2000 PCs, as well as networks in residence halls. Wireless connections are available in most campus locations. All networks are connected to the Internet. All students may access the system. There are no time limits and no fees. It is strongly recommended that all students have a personal computer. Students enrolled in engineering must have a personal computer.

Graduates: From July 1, 2008 to June 30, 2009, 3456 bachelor's degrees were awarded. The most popular majors were engineering (18%), business (14%), and agriculture (13%). 359 companies recruited on campus in 2008-2009. In an average class, 4% graduate in 3 years or less, 85% graduate in 4 years or less, 91% graduate in 5 years or less, and 92% graduate in 6 years or less. Of the 2008 graduating class, 32% were enrolled in graduate school within 6 months of graduation, and 55% were employed.

Admissions Contact: Jason Locke, Director of Undergraduate Admissions. A campus DVD is available. E-Mail: *admissions@cornell.edu* Web: *www.cornell.edu*

DAEMEN COLLEGE   A-3

Amherst, NY 14226-3592

(716) 839-8225
(800) 462-7652; (716) 839-8370

Full-time: 390 men, 975 women	**Faculty:** IIB, -$
Part-time: 60 men, 260 women	**Ph.D.s:** n/av
Graduate: 125 men, 725 women	**Student/Faculty:** n/av
Year: semesters, summer session	**Tuition:** $21,220
Application Deadline: open	**Room & Board:** $10,290
Freshman Class: n/av	
SAT or ACT: required	**COMPETITIVE**

Daemen College, founded in 1947, is a private institution offering undergraduate and graduate programs in the liberal and fine arts, business, education, allied health professions, and natural sciences. The figures in the above capsule and in this profile are approximate. There is 1 graduate school. In addition to regional accreditation, Daemen has baccalaureate program accreditation with APTA, CSWE, and NLN. The library contains 151,528 volumes, 27,768 microform items, and 5,394 audio/video tapes/CDs/DVDs, and subscribes to 17,924 periodicals including electronic. Computerized library services include interlibrary loans, database searching, Internet access, and laptop Internet portals. Special learning facilities include a learning resource center, art gallery, a video conference center. The 35-acre campus is in a suburban area 9 miles northeast of downtown Buffalo. Including any residence halls, there are 18 buildings.

Student Life: 96% of undergraduates are from New York. Others are from 16 states, 4 foreign countries, and Canada. 85% are white. 42% are Catholic; 15% Protestant; 12% Student designated . The average age of freshmen is 18; all undergraduates, 23. 26% do not continue beyond their first year; 54% remain to graduate.

Housing: 524 students can be accommodated in college housing, which includes coed dorms and on-campus apartments. In addition, there is a quiet dorm. On-campus housing is guaranteed for all 4 years. 65% of students commute. All students may keep cars.

Activities: 6% of men belong to 1 local fraternity; 4% of women belong to 4 local sororities. There are 47 groups on campus, including academic clubs, Amnesty International, art, athletic clubs, cheerleading, choir, dance, drama, environmental, ethnic, gay, honors, literary magazine, newspaper, prelaw, professional, social, social service, student government, student without borders, wellness, and yearbook. Popular campus events include Homecoming, Battle of the Bands, and Spring Fest.

Sports: There are 4 intercollegiate sports for men and 4 for women, and 4 intramural sports for men and 2 for women. Facilities include a gym, weight and exercise rooms, saunas, and a volleyball sand court.

Disabled Students: 83% of the campus is accessible. Facilities include wheelchair ramps, elevators, special parking, specially equipped restrooms, lowered drinking fountains, and lowered telephones.

Services: Counseling and information services are available, as is tutoring in every subject. There is remedial math, reading, and writing.

Campus Safety and Security: Measures include 24-hour foot and vehicle patrol and security escort services. There are emergency telephones, lighted pathways/sidewalks, and video monitors.

Programs of Study: Daemen confers B.A., B.S., B.S./M.S. (dual degree) and B.F.A. degrees. Master's and doctoral degrees are also awarded. Bachelor's degrees are awarded in BIOLOGICAL SCIENCE (biochemistry and biology/biological science), BUSINESS (accounting and business administration and management), COMMUNICATIONS AND THE ARTS (applied art, art, English, fine arts, French, graphic design, and Spanish), COMPUTER AND PHYSICAL SCIENCE (mathematics and natural sciences), EDUCATION (art education, early childhood education, elementary education, English education, foreign languages education, mathematics education, science education, and social studies education), HEALTH PROFESSIONS (health science, nursing, physician's assistant, and preventive/wellness health care), SOCIAL SCIENCE (history, political science/government, psychology, religion, and social work). Physical therapy, physician assistant, and natural science. are the strongest academically. Nursing, childhood education, physical therapy, and natural science are the largest.

Required: To graduate, students must complete 120 to 199 hours (depending on the degree program) with a minimum GPA of 2.0. Students are required to complete a minimum of 30 credit hours of course work in residence. The final semester's course work must be taken in residence.

Special: Daemen offers cooperative programs in all majors, internships, cross-registration within the Western New York Consortium of Colleges and Universities, student-designed majors, work-study programs, an accelerated degree program in nursing, dual majors, a Washington semester, and study abroad in 6 countries. There is an International Studies Program that leads to a minor in international studies. There are 8 national honor societies, a freshman honors program, and 20 departmental honors programs.

Faculty/Classroom: 40% of faculty are male; 60% are female. 64% teach undergraduates, and 1% do both. No introductory courses are taught by graduate students. The average class size in an introductory lecture is 17; in a laboratory is 10; and in a regular course is 14.

Requirements: The SAT or ACT is required. In addition, applicants must be graduates of an accredited secondary school or have the GED equivalent. Some departments have further admissions requirements, including a portfolio review for art majors, 3-year sequences of math and science for all natural science programs, and 2 essays, 3 letters of recommendation, and a supplemental application for the physician assistant program. A GPA of 2.0 is required. AP and CLEP credits are accepted. Important factors in the admissions decision are advanced placement or honors courses, leadership record, and evidence of special talent.

Procedure: Freshmen are admitted fall, spring, and summer. Entrance exams should be taken by the summer following the senior year. There are early admissions, deferred admissions, and rolling admissions plans. Application deadlines are open. The fall 2009 application fee was $25. Notification is sent on a rolling basis. Applications are accepted on-line. A waiting list is maintained.

Transfer: 243 transfer students enrolled in in a recent year. Applicants must present college transcripts and an indication of good standing from the last institution attended and a minimum GPA of 2.0. to 2.8. Physician assistant applicants should submit essays, 3 letters of recommendation, and supplemental applications. 30 of 120 credits required for the bachelor's degree must be completed at Daemen.

Visiting: There are regularly scheduled orientations for prospective students, Two 5-day orientations that includes a campus tour, an interview, and placement testing in math and English during July and August. Fall Open House in October, College Night in September, and Day @ Daemen in September and November are other regularly scheduled Admissions events. There are guides for informal visits; visitors may sit in on classes and stay overnight. To schedule a visit, contact the Admissions Office at (800) 462-7652 or (716) 839-8225.

Financial Aid: In a recent year, 88% of all full-time freshmen and 90% of continuing full-time students received some form of financial aid. 83% of all full-time freshmen and 82% of continuing full-time students received need-based aid. The average freshmen award was $12,769. 20% of undergraduate students worked part-time. Average annual earnings from campus work were $1077. The average financial indebtedness of the 2009 graduate was $20,465. The FAFSA, the state aid form, and foreign student certification of finances are required. Check with the school for current application deadlines.

International Students: There were 10 international students enrolled in a recent year. They must take the TOEFL.

Computers: Wireless access is available. PC's are available in the computer center, labs, library, and student center cyber café. Mac's are also available in science and graphic design labs. All dorm rooms are connected to the college's network. Wireless is available in the apartment-style residences and in the lounges of the freshman dorm. All students may access the system. There are no time limits and no fees.

Graduates: In a recent year, 279 bachelor's degrees were awarded. The most popular majors were nursing (18%), natural science (16%), and early childhood & childhood education (15%). 80 companies recruited on campus in 2008-2009. In an average class, 35% graduate in 4 years or less, 50% graduate in 5 years or less, and 54% graduate in 6 years or less. Of the 2008 graduating class, 25% were enrolled in graduate school within 6 months of graduation, and 90% were employed.

Admissions Contact: Donna Shaffner, Dean of Admissions. A campus DVD is available. E-Mail: *admissions@daemen.edu* Web: *www.daemen.edu*

DEVRY INSTITUTE OF TECHNOLOGY/NEW YORK   D-5

Long Island City, NY 11101-3051   (718) 472-2728
(888) 713-3879; (718) 361-0004

Full-time: 655 men, 256 women   **Faculty:** n/av
Part-time: 184 men, 71 women   **Ph.D.s:** n/av
Graduate: 124 men, 105 women   **Student/Faculty:** n/av
Year: semesters, summer session
Application Deadline: open

LESS COMPETITIVE

DeVry Institute of Technology/New York, founded in 1998, is a private institution offering hands-on programs in electronics, business administration, computer information systems, telecommunications, and computer technology. The school is 1 of 67 Devry University locations throughout the United States and Canada. There are no undergraduate schools. The library contains 9,752 volumes, and 708 audio/video tapes/CDs/DVDs, and subscribes to 120 periodicals including electronic. Computerized library services include interlibrary loans and database searching. Special learning facilities include a learning resource center, electronics and other labs. The 2-acre campus is in an urban area New York. Including any residence halls, there is 1 building.

Student Life: 10% of undergraduates are from out of state, mostly the Northeast.

Housing: There are no residence halls. All students commute.

Activities: There are no fraternities or sororities. There are 7 groups on campus, including chess, international, professional, social, and yearbook. Popular campus events include DSA Time Out, End of Semester Bashment, and Post Ramadan Celebration.

Sports: There is no sports program at DeVry.

Disabled Students: All of the campus is accessible. Facilities include elevators, special parking, specially equipped restrooms, special class scheduling, lowered drinking fountains, and lowered telephones.

Services: Counseling and information services are available, as is tutoring in every subject.

Campus Safety and Security: Measures include 24-hour foot and vehicle patrol and security escort services. There are emergency telephones and lighted pathways/sidewalks.

Programs of Study: DeVry confers B.S. degrees. Associates and master's degrees are also awarded. Bachelor's degrees are awarded in BUSINESS (accounting and business administration and management), COMMUNICATIONS AND THE ARTS (telecommunications), COMPUTER AND PHYSICAL SCIENCE (information sciences and systems), ENGINEERING AND ENVIRONMENTAL DESIGN (biomedical engineering, computer technology, and electrical/electronics engineering technology). Electronics, computer information systems, and business administration are the largest.

Required: To graduate, students must complete 48 to 154 credit hours with a 2.0 minimum GPA. Course requirements vary according to program. All first-semester students take courses in algebra, psychology, and student success strategies.

Special: Evening and weekend classes, co-op programs, distance learning, and an acclerated degree program are offered.

Faculty/Classroom: All teach undergraduates. No introductory courses are taught by graduate students.

Requirements: In addition, admissions requirements include graduation from a secondary school. The GED is also accepted. Applicants must pass the DeVry entrance exam or present satisfactory ACT or SAT I scores. An interview is required. CLEP credits are accepted.

Procedure: Freshmen are admitted fall, spring, and summer. There are early admissions, deferred admissions, and rolling admissions plans. Application deadlines are open. Application fee is $50. Notification is sent on a rolling basis. Applications are accepted on-line.

Transfer: 199 transfer students enrolled in 2008-2009. Applicants must present passing grades in all completed college course work, demonstrate language skills proficiency with at least 24 completed semester hours, and present evidence of math proficiency by appropriate college-level credits. A minimum GPA of 2.0 is required. 30 of 48 credits required for the bachelor's degree must be completed at DeVry.

Visiting: There are regularly scheduled orientations for prospective students. There are guides for informal visits and visitors may sit in on classes. To schedule a visit, contact the Director of Admissions.

Financial Aid: In 2009-2010, 66% of all full-time freshmen and 76% of continuing full-time students received some form of financial aid. 64% of all full-time freshmen and 74% of continuing full-time students received need-based aid. The average freshmen award was $8,821. The FAFSA is required. Check with the school for current application deadlines.

International Students: There are 101 international students enrolled. They must take the TOEFL.

Computers: Computer information systems students may access the system. during lab hours. There are no fees.

Graduates: From July 1, 2008 to June 30, 2009, 204 bachelor's degrees were awarded. The most popular majors were business/marketing

(53%), computer and information sciences (29%), and engineering technologies (18%). 21 companies recruited on campus in 2008-2009.

Admissions Contact: Director of Admissions E-Mail: *nyemailleads@ny.devry.edu* Web: *www.ny.devry.edu*

DOMINICAN COLLEGE   D-5
Orangeburg, NY 10962
(845) 848-7900
(866) 432-4636; (845) 365-3150

Full-time: 466 men, 897 women	**Faculty:** 64; IIA, --$
Part-time: 66 men, 248 women	**Ph.D.s:** 56%
Graduate: 64 men, 242 women	**Student/Faculty:** 21 to 1
Year: semesters, summer session	**Tuition:** $21,120
Application Deadline: open	**Room & Board:** $10,150
Freshman Class: 1474 applied, 1072 accepted, 375 enrolled	
SAT CR/M/W: 451/451/448	**ACT:** 18 COMPETITIVE

Dominican College, founded in 1952, is a private Catholic institution offering undergraduate and graduate programs in business, biology, education, liberal arts, nursing, premedicine, occupational therapy, and social sciences. There are 6 undergraduate schools and 5 graduate schools. In addition to regional accreditation, Dominican has baccalaureate program accreditation with CSWE and TEAC. The library contains 95,021 volumes, 17,000 microform items, and 1000 audio/video tapes/CDs/DVDs, and subscribes to 10,500 periodicals including electronic. Computerized library services include interlibrary loans, database searching, Internet access, and laptop Internet portals. Special learning facilities include a learning resource center. The 70-acre campus is in a suburban area 17 miles north of New York City. Including any residence halls, there are 16 buildings.

Student Life: 74% of undergraduates are from New York. Others are from 25 states, 18 foreign countries, and Canada. 70% are from public schools. 53% are white; 24% Hispanic; 20% African American; 12% Asian American. The average age of freshmen is 18; all undergraduates, 24. 34% do not continue beyond their first year; 47% remain to graduate.

Housing: 750 students can be accommodated in college housing, which includes coed dorms. On-campus housing is guaranteed for all 4 years. 52% of students live on campus; of those, 40% remain on campus on weekends. Alcohol is not permitted. All students may keep cars.

Activities: There are no fraternities or sororities. There are 27 groups on campus, including cheerleading, chorus, computers, debate, drama, ethnic, honors, literary magazine, musical theater, newspaper, professional, religious, social, social service, and student government. Popular campus events include Fire in the Sky, Family Day, and Fall Festival.

Sports: There are 5 intercollegiate sports for men and 7 for women, and 4 intramural sports for men and 4 for women. Facilities include a soccer and lacrosse field, a softball field, a practice field, a gym, an indoor track, a weight room, and a fitness center.

Disabled Students: All of the campus is accessible. Facilities include wheelchair ramps, special parking, specially equipped restrooms, lowered drinking fountains, and lowered telephones.

Services: Counseling and information services are available, as is tutoring in some subjects, including English and math. There is remedial math, reading, and writing. Content-based tutoring is also available.

Campus Safety and Security: Measures include 24-hour foot and vehicle patrol, emergency notification system, and security escort services. There are shuttle buses and lighted pathways/sidewalks.

Programs of Study: Dominican confers B.A., B.S., B.S.Ed., B.S.N., and B.S.W. degrees. Associates, master's, and doctoral degrees are also awarded. Bachelor's degrees are awarded in BIOLOGICAL SCIENCE (biology/biological science), BUSINESS (accounting, banking and finance, business administration and management, business economics, human resources, international business management, and marketing/retailing/merchandising), COMMUNICATIONS AND THE ARTS (English and Spanish), COMPUTER AND PHYSICAL SCIENCE (computer science, information sciences and systems, and mathematics), EDUCATION (athletic training, elementary education, mathematics education, science education, secondary education, and special education), HEALTH PROFESSIONS (health care administration, nursing, and occupational therapy), SOCIAL SCIENCE (criminal justice, history, humanities, psychology, social science, and social work). Occupational therapy, nursing, and physical therapy are the strongest academically. Nursing, occupational therapy, and biology are the largest.

Required: All students must complete courses in English and communications. Computer courses are required for business majors. To graduate, all students must complete 120 semester hours, including a general education curriculum of 36 to 39 credits. Distribution requirements include 12 to 15 credits in Communications and Analysis; 12 credits in Roots of Contemporary Life and Culture; and 12 credits in Issues in Contemporary Life and Culture. A minimum GPA of 2.7 must be maintained by nursing majors; 3.0 for occupational therapy majors. All other majors require a minimum of 2.0.

Special: There are internship opportunities available in various fields. A 3-2 engineering degree with Manhattan College is also offered. Dual

teacher certification in elementary or secondary education and special education is available. Credit for life experience is granted through submission of a portfolio. An accelerated B.S.N. and B.S. degree are available as well as a combined B.S./M.S. in occupational therapy. Weekend College, offered on a trimester basis, is designed to meet the needs of working adults. There are 7 national honor societies and a freshman honors program.

Faculty/Classroom: 28% of faculty are male; 72% are female. 88% teach undergraduates. No introductory courses are taught by graduate students. The average class size in an introductory lecture is 24; in a laboratory, 16; and in a regular course, 18.

Admissions: 73% of the 2009-2010 applicants were accepted. The SAT scores for the 2009-2010 freshman class were: Critical Reading--77% below 500, 20% between 500 and 599, 2% between 600 and 700, and 1% above 700; Math--75% below 500, 21% between 500 and 599, and 4% between 600 and 700; Writing--75% below 500, 21% between 500 and 599, 3% between 600 and 700, and 1% above 700. The ACT scores were 32% below 21, 58% between 21 and 23, 5% between 24 and 26, and 5% between 27 and 28.

Requirements: The SAT is required. The ACT Optional Writing test is also required. In addition, applicants should be graduates of an accredited secondary school or possess a GED equivalent. An interview and an essay are required for some professional programs. Recommended preparation includes 16 academic units of study distributed among English, math, natural sciences, and foreign language. AP and CLEP credits are accepted. Important factors in the admissions decision are advanced placement or honors courses, leadership record, and extracurricular activities record.

Procedure: Freshmen are admitted to all sessions. Entrance exams should be taken by November of the senior year. There are deferred admissions and rolling admissions plans. Application deadlines are open. The application fee is $35. Notification is sent on a rolling basis. Applications are accepted on-line. 29 applicants were on a recent waiting list.

Transfer: 250 transfer students enrolled in 2008-2009. Applicants must submit a transcript from their previous school. A minimum GPA of 2.0 is required. An interview may be required. 30 of 120 credits required for the bachelor's degree must be completed at Dominican.

Visiting: There are regularly scheduled orientations for prospective students. There are guides for informal visits and visitors may sit in on classes. To schedule a visit, contact Joyce Elbe, Director of Admissions.

Financial Aid: In 2009-2010, 97% of all full-time freshmen and 84% of continuing full-time students received some form of financial aid. 91% of all full-time freshmen and 84% of continuing full-time students received need-based aid. The average freshmen award was $14,526, with $11,745 ($15,000 maximum) from need-based scholarships or need-based grants; $3834 ($4625 maximum) from need-based self-help aid (loans and jobs); and $9101 ($10,000 maximum) from non-need-based athletic scholarships. 85% of undergraduate students work part-time. Average annual earnings from campus work are $1500. The average financial indebtedness of the 2009 graduate was $26,515. Dominican is a member of CSS. The FAFSA and the state aid form are required. The priority date for freshman financial aid applications for fall entry is February 15. The deadline for filing freshman financial aid applications for fall entry is June 15.

International Students: They must take the TOEFL. They must also take the SAT or ACT.

Computers: Wireless access is available. There are 3 computer labs in 3 separate buildings. The library provides an Internet-based circulation/card system that can be accessed using PCs. The library and 1 dorm have wireless service. All other residence halls have a network connection in every room. All students may access the system. There are no time limits and no fees. It is strongly recommended that all students have a personal computer.

Graduates: From July 1, 2008 to June 30, 2009, 298 bachelor's degrees were awarded. The most popular majors were health (33%), business (24%), and social sciences (15%). 25 companies recruited on campus in 2008-2009. In an average class, 27% graduate in 4 years or less, 42% graduate in 5 years or less, and 48% graduate in 6 years or less.

Admissions Contact: Joyce Elbe, Director of Admissions. E-Mail: *admissions@dc.edu* Web: *www.dc.edu*

DOWLING COLLEGE   E-5
Oakdale, NY 11769-1999
(631) 244-3436
(800) DOWLING; (631) 563-3271

Full-time: 980 men, 1210 women	**Faculty:** IIB, -$
Part-time: 480 men, 765 women	**Ph.D.s:** n/av
Graduate: 850 men, 1550 women	**Student/Faculty:** n/av
Year: 4-1-4, summer session	**Tuition:** $16,000
Application Deadline: see profile	**Room & Board:** $9000
Freshman Class: n/av	**LESS COMPETITIVE**

Dowling College, founded in 1955, is an independent comprehensive institution offering programs in the arts and sciences, aviation and transportation, business, and education. The figures in the above capsule and in this profile are approximate. There are 4 undergraduate schools and 3 graduate schools. In addition to regional accreditation, Dowling has baccalaureate program accreditation with NCATE. The 2 libraries contain 222,920 volumes, 394,000 microform items, and 2,843 audio/video tapes/CDs/DVDs, and subscribe to 961 periodicals including electronic. Computerized library services include interlibrary loans, database searching, Internet access, and laptop Internet portals. Special learning facilities include a learning resource center, art gallery, radio station, government documents, and the Federal Aviation Administration (FAA) Aviation Education Resource Center. The 156-acre campus is in a suburban area 50 miles east of New York City. Including any residence halls, there are 10 buildings.

Student Life: 88% of undergraduates are from New York. Others are from 31 states, 61 foreign countries, and Canada. 89% are from public schools. 61% are white. The average age of freshmen is 19; all undergraduates, 22. 33% do not continue beyond their first year; 48% remain to graduate.

Housing: 496 students can be accommodated in college housing, which includes coed on-campus apartments. On-campus housing is available on a first-come and first-served basis. Priority is given to out-of-town students. 82% of students commute. Alcohol is not permitted. All students may keep cars.

Activities: There are no fraternities or sororities. There are 39 groups on campus, including aeronautics, arts, cheerleading, choir, chorus, computers, drama, ethnic, gay, gospel choir, honors, international, literary magazine, martial arts, newspaper, orchestra, photography, professional, psychology, radio and TV, religious, social, and student government. Popular campus events include Freshman Mixer, Holiday Party, and Spring Cotillion.

Sports: There are 8 intercollegiate sports for men and 9 for women, and 1 intramural sports for men and 1 for women. Facilities include a basketball court, a weight room, tennis courts, and a fitness center.

Disabled Students: All of the campus is accessible. Facilities include wheelchair ramps, elevators, special parking, specially equipped restrooms, special class scheduling, lowered drinking fountains, and lowered telephones.

Services: Counseling and information services are available, as is tutoring in most subjects. There is remedial math, reading, and writing.

Campus Safety and Security: Measures include 24-hour foot and vehicle patrol and security escort services. There are shuttle buses, emergency telephones, and lighted pathways/sidewalks.

Programs of Study: Dowling confers B.A., B.S., and B.B.A. degrees. Master's and doctoral degrees are also awarded. Bachelor's degrees are awarded in BIOLOGICAL SCIENCE (biology/biological science and marine biology), BUSINESS (accounting, banking and finance, business administration and management, international business management, marketing/retailing/merchandising, sports management, tourism, and transportation management), COMMUNICATIONS AND THE ARTS (communications, English, fine arts, languages, music, romance languages and literature, speech/debate/rhetoric, and visual and performing arts), COMPUTER AND PHYSICAL SCIENCE (applied mathematics, computer science, information sciences and systems, mathematics, and natural sciences), EDUCATION (art education, elementary education, music education, secondary education, and special education), ENGINEERING AND ENVIRONMENTAL DESIGN (aeronautical science, aeronautical technology, and aviation administration/management), SOCIAL SCIENCE (economics, history, humanities, liberal arts/general studies, philosophy, political science/government, psychology, social science, and sociology). Business, education, and computer sciences are the largest.

Required: To graduate, students must complete 122 credits with a minimum GPA of 2.0. The required 36-credit general education core includes a senior seminar.

Special: Dowling offers a B.S. in professional and liberal studies, internships, independent study, work-study, and nondegree study. There are cooperative programs in several majors, including aeronautics and airway science majors, with the FAA. There are 10 national honor societies, a freshman honors program, and 3 departmental honors programs.

Faculty/Classroom: 58% of faculty are male; 42% are female. 63% teach undergraduates. No introductory courses are taught by graduate students. The average class size in an introductory lecture is 20; in a laboratory is 15; and in a regular course is 17.

Requirements: Applicants should be graduates of an accredited secondary school and have completed at least 16 Carnegie units, including 4 in English. An interview is strongly recommended. AP and CLEP credits are accepted. Important factors in the admissions decision are advanced placement or honors courses, evidence of special talent, and recommendations by school officials.

Procedure: Freshmen are admitted to all sessions. Entrance exams should be taken by January of the senior year. There are deferred admissions and rolling admissions plans. Application deadlines are open. Application fee is $25. Applications are accepted on-line.

Transfer: 617 transfer students enrolled in a recent year. Applicants must submit official transcripts from all colleges attended. Courses com-

pleted with a grade of C or better may transfer. 30 of 122 credits required for the bachelor's degree must be completed at Dowling.

Visiting: There are regularly scheduled orientations for prospective students, including a campus tour and meetings with enrollment services members, staff, and faculty. There are guides for informal visits; visitors may sit in on classes and stay overnight. To schedule a visit, contact the Enrollment Services Office at (631) 244-3303.

Financial Aid: In a recent year, 89% of all full-time freshmen and 73% of continuing full-time students received some form of financial aid. 79% of all full-time freshmen and 70% of continuing full-time students received need-based aid. The average freshmen award was $10,411. All of undergraduate students worked part-time. Average annual earnings from campus work were $2874. The average financial indebtedness of the 2009 graduate was $5,091. Dowling is a member of CSS. The FAFSA and the college's own financial statement are required. Check with the school for current application deadlines.

International Students: There were 158 international students enrolled in a recent year. The school actively recruits these students. They must take the TOEFL.

Computers: Wireless access is available. There are more than 200 PC's in computer labs, libraries, and students' lounges that can be used in wired network, and students laptops can be used wireless in certain stations, such as student lounges or libraries. All students may access the system 7 A.M. to 10:45 P.M. Monday through Thursday and 7 A.M. to 5 P.M. Friday through Sunday. There are no time limits and no fees.

Graduates: In a recent year, 2008 to June 30, 2009, 505 bachelor's degrees were awarded. The most popular majors were education (18%), liberal arts/general studies (10%), and social science (8%). 100 companies recruited on campus in 2008-2009. In an average class, 3% graduate in 3 years or less, 20% graduate in 4 years or less, 31% graduate in 5 years or less, and 34% graduate in 6 years or less.

Admissions Contact: Diane Kazanecki Kempter, Associate VP for of Enrollment and Systems Management. A campus DVD is available. E-Mail: KazanecD@dowling.edu Web: www.dowling.edu

D'YOUVILLE COLLEGE — A-3

Buffalo, NY 14201

(716) 829-7600
(800) 777-3921; (716) 829-7900

Full-time: 404 men, 1063 women	Faculty: 146
Part-time: 77 men, 322 women	Ph.D.s: n/av
Graduate: 329 men, 776 women	Student/Faculty: 12 to 1
Year: semesters, summer session	Tuition: $20,050
Application Deadline: open	Room & Board: $9800
Freshman Class: 822 applied, 791 accepted, 155 enrolled	
SAT CR/M/W: 520/530/510	ACT: 23 COMPETITIVE

D'Youville College, founded in 1908, is a private, nonsectarian liberal arts institution granting degrees at the Bachelors, Masters, First Professional and Doctoral levels. There is 1 graduate school. In addition to regional accreditation, D'Youville has baccalaureate program accreditation with ADA and APTA. The library contains 96,876 volumes, 205,411 microform items, and 4,246 audio/video tapes/CDs/DVDs, and subscribes to 683 periodicals including electronic. Computerized library services include interlibrary loans, database searching, Internet access, and laptop Internet portals. Special learning facilities include a learning resource center, and a professional theater. The 10-acre campus is in an urban area 1 mile north of downtown Buffalo and 1 mile from the Peace Bridge border crossing to Canada. Including any residence halls, there are 10 buildings.

Student Life: 95% of undergraduates are from New York. Others are from 20 states, 48 foreign countries, and Canada. 80% are from public schools. 65% are white; 12% African American. The average age of freshmen is 18; all undergraduates, 24. 27% do not continue beyond their first year; 63% remain to graduate.

Housing: 478 students can be accommodated in college housing, which includes single-sex and coed dorms and on-campus apartments. In addition, there are quiet floors and 21 and older floors. On-campus housing is guaranteed for all 4 years. 87% of students commute. All students may keep cars.

Activities: There are no fraternities or sororities. There are 35 groups on campus, including cheerleading, chorus, computers, dance, drama, drill team, ethnic, gay, honors, international, literary magazine, newspaper, professional, religious, social, social service, and student government. Popular campus events include Moving Up Days, International Fiesta, and Honors Convocation.

Sports: There are 7 intercollegiate sports for men and 7 for women. Facilities include a 500-seat gym that houses basketball and volleyball courts and an indoor batting cage, and a fitness facility with aerobic and free weights, swimming pool, and dance studio.

Disabled Students: 95% of the campus is accessible. Facilities include wheelchair ramps, elevators, special parking, specially equipped restrooms, lowered drinking fountains, and special housing.

Services: Counseling and information services are available, as is tutoring in some subjects, based on tutor accessibility. There is a reader service for the blind, and remedial math, reading, and writing.

Campus Safety and Security: Measures include 24-hour foot and vehicle patrol, emergency notification system, self-defense education, and security escort services. There are emergency telephones, lighted pathways/sidewalks, a special focus program, and a security committee.

Programs of Study: D'Youville confers B.A., B.S., BS/MS, and B.S.N. degrees. Master's and doctoral degrees are also awarded. Bachelor's degrees are awarded in BIOLOGICAL SCIENCE (biology/biological science), BUSINESS (accounting and business administration and management), COMMUNICATIONS AND THE ARTS (English), COMPUTER AND PHYSICAL SCIENCE (information sciences and systems and mathematics), HEALTH PROFESSIONS (exercise science, health care administration, nursing, and physician's assistant), SOCIAL SCIENCE (dietetics, history, interdisciplinary studies, international studies, philosophy, psychology, and sociology). Education and health professions are the strongest academically. Health professions, business, and nursing are the largest.

Required: All students must complete general program and core curriculum requirements, including 5 courses in humanities, 2 each in English and natural sciences, and 1 each in ethics, philosophy or religion, history, sociology, psychology, economics or political science, math, and computer science. A minimum of 120 to 144 credit hours, varying by major, with a minimum GPA of 2.0, (higher for some programs), is required to graduate.

Special: D'Youville has cross-registration with member colleges of the Western New York Consortium. Internships, work-study programs, dual majors, study abroad in 5 countries, and pass/fail options are available. Accelerated 5-year B.S.-M.S. programs in occupational therapy, international business, elementary education, Physician's Assistant and nursing, and dietetics are offered. For freshmen with undecided majors, the Career Discovery Program offers special courses, internships, and faculty advisers. There are 3 national honor societies and 2 departmental honors programs.

Faculty/Classroom: 43% of faculty are male; 67% are female. All teach and do research. No introductory courses are taught by graduate students.

Admissions: 96% of the 2009-2010 applicants were accepted. The SAT scores for the 2009-2010 freshman class were: Critical Reading--44% below 500, 48% between 500 and 599, 8% between 600 and 700, and % above 700; Math--33% below 500, 53% between 500 and 599, 14% between 600 and 700, and 1% above 700; Writing--49% below 500, 46% between 500 and 599, 6% between 600 and 700, and % above 700. The ACT scores were 20% below 21, 37% between 21 and 23, 27% between 24 and 26, 10% between 27 and 28, and 7% above 28. 40% of the current freshmen were in the top fifth of their class; 80% were in the top two fifths.

Requirements: The SAT or ACT is required. In addition, applicants should have completed 16 Carnegie units, including 4 years of high school English, 3 of social studies, and 1 each of math and science; some majors require additional years of math and science. The GED is accepted. A GPA of 2.0 is required. AP and CLEP credits are accepted.

Procedure: Freshmen are admitted fall and spring. Entrance exams should be taken by the end of the junior year. There are deferred admissions and rolling admissions plans. Application deadlines are open. Application fee is $25. Applications are accepted on-line.

Transfer: 235 transfer students enrolled in 2008-2009. Applicants need a minimum GPA of 2.0, or 2.5 for some programs. 30 of 120 credits required for the bachelor's degree must be completed at D'Youville.

Visiting: There are regularly scheduled orientations for prospective students. There are guides for informal visits; visitors may sit in on classes and stay overnight. To schedule a visit, contact the Admissions Office at (716) 829-7600.

Financial Aid: In 2009-2010, 86% of all full-time freshmen and 87% of continuing full-time students received some form of financial aid. 84% of all full-time freshmen and 84% of continuing full-time students received need-based aid. The average freshman award was $20,127. Need-based scholarships or need-based grants averaged $14,155 ($20,127 maximum); need-based self-help aid (loans and jobs) averaged $8,108 ($9,900 maximum); other non-need-based awards and non-need-based scholarships averaged $11,709 ($9,900 maximum). The average financial indebtedness of the 2009 graduate was $31,401. The FAFSA and the state aid form are required. The priority date for freshman financial aid applications for fall entry is March 1. The deadline for filing freshman financial aid applications for fall entry is April 15.

International Students: There are 156 international students enrolled. The school actively recruits these students. They must take the TOEFL with a minimum score of 500 on the paper-based TOEFL (PBT) or 61 on the Internet-based version (iBT). They must also take the SAT or ACT, scoring 900.

Computers: Wireless access is available. There are 2 general use PC labs, 2 classroom labs, a PC lab in each dorm, a lab in the library, and 10 wireless access areas on campus. All students may access the system.

There are no time limits and no fees. It is strongly recommended that all students have a personal computer.

Graduates: From July 1, 2008 to June 30, 2009, 318 bachelor's degrees were awarded. The most popular majors were health professions and related sciences (49%), business/marketing (20%), and interdisciplinary studies (10%). 92 companies recruited on campus in 2008-2009. In an average class, 40% graduate in 4 years or less, 63% graduate in 5 years or less, and 63% graduate in 6 years or less.

Admissions Contact: Steven Smith, Director of Undergraduate Admissions. E-Mail: *admiss@dyc.edu* Web: *www.dyc.edu*

EASTMAN SCHOOL OF MUSIC   B-3
Rochester, NY 14604   (585) 274-1060
(800) 388-9695; (585) 232-8601

Full-time: 255 men, 255 women	**Faculty:** n/av
Part-time: 10 men, no women	**Ph.D.s:** n/av
Graduate: 205 men, 205 women	**Student/Faculty:** n/av
Year: semesters	**Tuition:** $38,110
Application Deadline: see profile	**Room & Board:** $12,000
Freshman Class: n/av	
SAT or ACT: recommended	**SPECIAL**

Eastman School of Music, founded in 1921, is a private professional school of music within the University of Rochester .The figures in the above capsule and in this profile are approximate. There is 1 graduate school. In addition to regional accreditation, Eastman has baccalaureate program accreditation with NASM. The library contains 333,014 volumes, 14,116 microform items, and 78,154 audio/video tapes/CDs/DVDs, and subscribes to 620 periodicals including electronic. Computerized library services include interlibrary loans, database searching, and Internet access. Special learning facilities include a learning resource center, art gallery, recording studios, a music library, a theater, and 3 recital halls. The 3-acre campus is in an urban area in downtown Rochester. Including any residence halls, there are 5 buildings.

Student Life: 82% of undergraduates are from out of state, mostly the Middle Atlantic. Students are from 48 states, 32 foreign countries, and Canada. 90% are from public schools. 62% are white; 21% foreign nationals. The average age of freshmen is 18; all undergraduates, 20. 11% do not continue beyond their first year; 78% remain to graduate.

Housing: 360 students can be accommodated in college housing, which includes single-sex and coed dorms. In addition, there are special-interest houses, fraternity houses, and sorority houses. On-campus housing is guaranteed for all 4 years. 72% of students live on campus; of those, 100% remain on campus on weekends. All students may keep cars.

Activities: 5% of men belong to 2 national fraternities; 4% of women belong to 1 national sorority. There are 20 groups on campus, including Association for Injury Prevention, band, choir, chorale, chorus, computers, dance, gay, international, jazz band, literary magazine, newspaper, opera, orchestra, professional, religious, social, social service, student government, symphony, and yearbook. Popular campus events include Holiday Sing and Boo Blast.

Sports: There is no sports program at Eastman. All athletic facilities of the University of Rochester, as well as a nearby YMCA, are available to students.

Disabled Students: 95% of the campus is accessible. Facilities include wheelchair ramps, elevators, special parking, specially equipped restrooms, lowered drinking fountains, and lowered telephones.

Services: Counseling and information services are available, as is tutoring in every subject. There is a reader service for the blind, and remedial writing. English tutoring for nonnative English speakers is available.

Campus Safety and Security: Measures include 24-hour foot and vehicle patrol, self-defense education, and security escort services. There are shuttle buses, emergency telephones, lighted pathways/sidewalks, and security cameras.

Programs of Study: Eastman confers B.M. degrees. Master's and doctoral degrees are also awarded. Bachelor's degrees are awarded in COMMUNICATIONS AND THE ARTS (jazz, music, music performance, and music theory and composition), EDUCATION (music education). Performance is the largest.

Required: All students must complete core requirements in a major instrument or voice, music theory, music history, and Western cultural tradition, as well as English and humanities electives. A total of 120 to 148 credit hours, varying by program, with a minimum GPA of 2.0, is required to graduate.

Special: The school and the University of Rochester cooperatively offer the B.A. degree with a music concentration. All the facilities of the university are open to Eastman students. Cross-registration is also available with colleges in the Rochester Consortium. Dual majors are available in all areas of study. Internships, work-study, and study abroad (in 7 countries) are also possible. There are 1 national honor societies.

Faculty/Classroom: 60% of faculty are male; 40% are female. All teach and do research. Graduate students teach 10% of introductory courses. The average class size in an introductory lecture is 30 and in a regular course is 15.

Requirements: The SAT or ACT is recommended. The SAT or ACT is required only of home-schooled applicants. Applicants should be graduates of an accredited secondary school with 16 academic credits, including 4 years of English. The GED is accepted. An audition and an interview are required, as are 3 letters of recommendation. Some majors have other specific requirements. AP credits are accepted. Important factors in the admissions decision are evidence of special talent, recommendations by alumni, and personality/intangible qualities.

Procedure: Freshmen are admitted fall and spring. There are deferred admissions and rolling admissions plans. Applications should be filed by November 1 for spring entry, along with a $80 fee. Notifications are sent April 15. Applications are accepted on-line. A waiting list is maintained.

Transfer: Requirements include satisfactory academic standing at the previous institution, a successful audition, and an interview.

Visiting: There are regularly scheduled orientations for prospective students, including group information sessions and a tour of the facilities. To schedule a visit, contact the Admissions Office at admissions@esm.edu.

Financial Aid: Eastman is a member of CSS. The CSS/Profile, FAFSA, the state aid form, and the college's own financial statement are required. Check with the school for current application deadlines.

International Students: The school actively recruits these students. They must take the TOEFL.

Computers: All students may access the system. There are no time limits. The fee is $125. It is strongly recommended that all students have a personal computer.

Admissions Contact: Adrian Daly, Director of Admissions. E-Mail: *admissions.esm.rochester.edu* Web: *http://www.rochester.edu/Eastman*

ELMIRA COLLEGE · C-4

Elmira, NY 14901

(607) 735-1724
(800) 935-6472; (607) 735-1718

Full-time: 328 men, 797 women	Faculty: 82
Part-time: 52 men, 182 women	Ph.Ds: 100%
Graduate: 77 men, 221 women	Student/Faculty: 14 to 1
Year: see profile, summer session	Tuition: $34,800
Application Deadline: open	Room & Board: $10,800
Freshman Class: 2083 applied, 1648 accepted, 396 enrolled	
SAT CR/M: 540/530	ACT: 24	COMPETITIVE+

Elmira College, founded in 1855, is a private liberal arts institution offering general and preprofessional programs. In addition to regional accreditation, Elmira has baccalaureate program accreditation with NLN. The library contains 203,343 volumes, 591,429 microform items, and 5897 audio/video tapes/CDs/DVDs, and subscribes to 337 periodicals including electronic. Computerized library services include interlibrary loans, database searching, Internet access, and laptop Internet portals. Special learning facilities include a learning resource center, art gallery, radio station, speech and hearing clinic, and Mark Twain's study and exhibit. The 42-acre campus is in a suburban area 90 miles southwest of Syracuse and 50 miles west of Binghamton. Including any residence halls, there are 26 buildings.

Student Life: 52% of undergraduates are from out of state, mostly the Northeast. Students are from 35 states, 31 foreign countries, and Canada. 59% are from public schools. 71% are white. The average age of freshmen is 18; all undergraduates, 20. 27% do not continue beyond their first year; 66% remain to graduate.

Housing: 1097 students can be accommodated in college housing, which includes single-sex and coed dorms and on-campus apartments. In addition, there are quiet floors and alcohol- and tobacco-free floors. On-campus housing is guaranteed for all 4 years. 93% of students live on campus; of those, 90% remain on campus on weekends. All students may keep cars.

Activities: There are no fraternities or sororities. There are 107 groups on campus, including art, band, cheerleading, chorale, chorus, dance, drama, environmental, ethnic, honors, international, literary magazine, musical theater, newspaper, orchestra, pep band, political, professional, radio, religious, social, social service, and student government. Popular campus events include Mountain Day, Midnight Breakfast, and Spring Weekend.

Sports: There are 8 intercollegiate sports for men and 11 for women, and 17 intramural sports for men and 17 for women. Facilities include 2500-seat and 950-seat gyms, indoor tennis facilities, a 3500-seat hockey arena, racquetball courts, a fitness center, a dance studio, and a swimming pool.

Disabled Students: 25% of the campus is accessible. Facilities include wheelchair ramps, elevators, special parking, specially equipped restrooms, special class scheduling, lowered drinking fountains, and special housing.

Services: Counseling and information services are available, as is tutoring in most subjects. There is a reader service for the blind. Tutoring in math and freshman English is available in each freshman dorm.

Campus Safety and Security: Measures include 24-hour foot and vehicle patrol, emergency notification system, and security escort services. There are emergency telephones and lighted pathways/sidewalks.

Programs of Study: Elmira confers B.A. and B.S. degrees. Associate and master's degrees are also awarded. Bachelor's degrees are awarded in BIOLOGICAL SCIENCE (biochemistry and biology/biological science), BUSINESS (accounting, business administration and management, business economics, international business management, and marketing/retailing/merchandising), COMMUNICATIONS AND THE ARTS (art, classics, dramatic arts, English literature, fine arts, French, languages, music, and Spanish), COMPUTER AND PHYSICAL SCIENCE (chemistry and mathematics), EDUCATION (art education, elementary education, foreign languages education, science education, and secondary education), ENGINEERING AND ENVIRONMENTAL DESIGN (environmental science), HEALTH PROFESSIONS (medical laboratory technology, nursing, predentistry, premedicine, and speech pathology/audiology), SOCIAL SCIENCE (American studies, anthropology, criminal justice, history, human services, international studies, philosophy, political science/government, prelaw, psychology, and sociology). History, theater, and premedicine are the strongest academically. Psychology, business administration, and education are the largest.

Required: All students must complete general degree requirements, including communication skills, writing courses, math competency, and a core curriculum; distribution requirements in culture and civilization, contemporary social institutions, the scientific method, the creative process, and phys ed; and a field experience program. A total of 120 credit hours with a minimum GPA of 2.0 overall and in the major is required to graduate.

Special: The required field experience program provides a career-related internship as well as community service. A junior year abroad program, an accelerated degree program, a general studies degree, student-designed majors, and pass/fail options are available. A 3-2 chemical engineering degree is offered with Clarkson University. B.A.-B.S. degrees are offered in biochemistry, biology, chemistry, economics, education, environmental studies, history, math, political science, and psychology. There are 20 national honor societies, including Phi Beta Kappa.

Faculty/Classroom: 63% of faculty are male; 37% are female. All teach and do research. No introductory courses are taught by graduate students. The average class size in an introductory lecture is 24; in a laboratory, 10; and in a regular course, 16.

Admissions: 79% of the 2009-2010 applicants were accepted. The SAT scores for the 2009-2010 freshman class were: Critical Reading-- 37% below 500, 42% between 500 and 599, 16% between 600 and 700; and 5% above 700; Math--35% below 500, 46% between 500 and 599, 16% between 600 and 700, and 3% above 700. The ACT scores were 2% below 21, 55% between 21 and 23, 16% between 24 and 26, 20% between 27 and 28, and 7% above 29. 56% of the current freshmen were in the top fifth of their class; 91% were in the top two fifths.

Requirements: The SAT or ACT is required. In addition, applicants should have completed 4 years of high school English, 3 of math, and 2 of science. An essay is part of the application process. An interview is strongly recommended. A GPA of 2.0 is required. AP and CLEP credits are accepted. Important factors in the admissions decision are advanced placement or honors courses, extracurricular activities record, and recommendations by school officials.

Procedure: Freshmen are admitted fall and winter. Entrance exams should be taken by January of the entry year. There are early decision, deferred admissions and rolling admissions plans. Early decision applications should be filed by November 15; the regular application deadline is open fall entry. The application fee is $50. Notification of early decision is sent December 15; regular decision, on a rolling basis. Applications are accepted on-line. 26 applicants were on a recent waiting list, 2 were accepted.

Transfer: 49 transfer students enrolled in 2008-2009. Applicants should have a minimum GPA of 2.0. An interview is strongly recommended. 30 of 120 credits required for the bachelor's degree must be completed at Elmira.

Visiting: There are regularly scheduled orientations for prospective students, consisting of an open house and overview, tour, lunch, student panel, faculty panel, general admissions and scholarship information, and optional interview. Individual visits for interviews and tours are available year-round, including Saturday mornings. There are guides for informal visits, and visitors may sit in on classes and stay overnight. To schedule a visit, contact the Office of Admissions.

Financial Aid: In 2009-2010, 85% of all full-time freshmen and 81% of continuing full-time students received some form of financial aid. 83% of all full-time freshmen and 78% of continuing full-time students received need-based aid. The average freshman award was $21,877. Need-based scholarships or need-based grants averaged $23,653; need-based self-help aid (loans and jobs) averaged $3956. 50% of undergraduate students work part-time. Average annual earnings from campus work are $1500. The average financial indebtedness of the 2009 graduate was $21,805. The FAFSA and the state aid form are required. The priority date for freshman financial aid applications for fall entry is February 15. The deadline for filing freshman financial aid applications for fall entry is March 15.

International Students: There are 69 international students enrolled. The school actively recruits these students. They must take the TOEFL, with a minimum score of 500 on the paper-based TOEFL (PBT) or 61 on the Internet-based version (iBT), or take the Comprehensive English Language Test.

Computers: Wireless access is available. There are 145 computers for student use, with dedicated research computers in the library. There are wireless hot spots throughout campus and high-speed wired connections in every dorm room. All students may access the system. There are no time limits and no fees. It is strongly recommended that all students have a personal computer.

Graduates: From July 1, 2008 to June 30, 2009, 311 bachelor degrees were awarded. The most popular majors were business administration (24%), psychology (13%), and education (10%). 60 companies recruited on campus in 2008-2009. Of the 2008 graduating class, 45% were enrolled in graduate school within 6 months of graduation and 52% were employed.

Admissions Contact: Brett Moore, Director of Admissions. E-mail: *admissions@elmira.edu* Web: *www.elmira.edu*

EUGENE LANG COLLEGE NEW SCHOOL FOR LIBERAL ARTS

D-3

New York, NY 10011-8963 — (212) 229-5665; (212) 229-5166

Full-time: 380 men, 855 women	**Faculty:** n/av
Part-time: 30 men, 45 women	**Ph.D.s:** n/av
Graduate: none	**Student/Faculty:** n/av
Year: semesters	**Tuition:** $35,421
Application Deadline: February 1	**Room & Board:** $12,000
Freshman Class: n/av	**HIGHLY COMPETITIVE**

Eugene Lang College, established in 1978, is the liberal arts undergraduate division of the New School. The figures in the above capsule and in this profile are approximate. The 3 libraries contain 2.4 million volumes, 13,000 microform items, and 14,275 audio/video tapes/CDs/DVDs, and subscribe to 33,320 periodicals including electronic. Computerized library services include interlibrary loans, database searching, Internet access, a -acrnd laptop Internet portals. Special learning facilities include an art gallery and a writing center. The campus is in an urban area Greenwich Village, Manhattan. Including any residence halls, there are 14 buildings.

Student Life: 74% of undergraduates are from out of state, mostly the Middle Atlantic. Students are from 49 states, 32 foreign countries, and Canada. 61% are from public schools. 60% are white. The average age of freshmen is 19; all undergraduates, 20. 27% do not continue beyond their first year.

Housing: College-sponsored housing includes coed dorms, on-campus apartments, and off-campus apartments. On-campus housing is guaranteed for all 4 years, is available on a first-come, first-served basis, and is available on a lottery system for upperclassmen. 73% of students commute. Alcohol is not permitted. All students may keep cars.

Activities: There are no fraternities or sororities. There are 30 groups on campus, including choir, chorus, dance, debate, environmental, ethnic, film, gay, honors, international, jazz band, literary magazine, newspaper, opera, orchestra, photography, political, professional, religious, social, social service, student government, and symphony. Popular campus events include orchestra/chorus concerts, Christmas parties, and recitals.

Sports: There are 3 intramural sports for men and 3 for women. Facilities include a recreation room. A YMCA is also available for student use.

Disabled Students: 90% of the campus is accessible. Facilities include wheelchair ramps, elevators, specially equipped restrooms, lowered drinking fountains, and lowered telephones.

Services: Counseling and information services are available, as is tutoring in some subjects. center There is remedial writing.

Campus Safety and Security: Measures include self-defense education.

Programs of Study: Eugene Lang College confers B.A. degrees. Bachelor's degrees are awarded in AGRICULTURE (environmental studies), COMMUNICATIONS AND THE ARTS (creative writing, dramatic arts, English, and literature), EDUCATION (education), SOCIAL SCIENCE (crosscultural studies, economics, history, philosophy, political science/government, psychology, religion, social science, sociology, urban studies, and women's studies). Creative writing, history, urban studies, and education are the strongest academically. Writing and cultural studies are the largest.

Required: To graduate, students must complete 120 credit hours, with a GPA of 2.0 and a minimum of 36 hours in 1 of 11 paths of study: writing, literature, the arts (includes dance and theater, urban studies, social and historical inquiry, cultural studies, media, philosophy, religious studies, psychology, education studies, and science, technology, and society. Also required are 88 credit hours in Lang College courses and 4

credits of senior work. Required courses include a first-year writing seminar and a freshman workshop program.

Special: Lang College offers a concentration rather than a traditional major; there is no core curriculum and students are instructed in small seminars. Students may cross-register with other New School divisions. A large variety of internships for credit, study abroad, B.A./M.A. and B.A./M.S.T. options, a B.A./B.F.A. degree with Parsons The New School for Design and The New School for Jazz and Contemporary Music Program, student-designed majors, and nondegree study are available.

Faculty/Classroom: 51% of faculty are male; 49% are female. All teach undergraduates, 39% do research, and 39% do both. No introductory courses are taught by graduate students. The average class size in a laboratory is 14 and in a regular course is 14.

Requirements: The SAT or ACT is required. In addition, applicants must be enrolled in a strong college preparatory program. The GED is accepted. An essay and an interview are required. Art students must present a portfolio and complete a home exam. Jazz students are required to audition. AP credits are accepted. Important factors in the admissions decision are personality/intangible qualities, recommendations by school officials, and advanced placement or honors courses.

Procedure: Freshmen are admitted fall and spring. Entrance exams should be taken in May of the junior year or October of the senior year. There are early decision,–deferred admissions plan. Early decision applications should be filed by November 15; regular applications, by February 1 for fall entry and November 15 for spring entry, along with a $50 fee. Notification of early decision is sent December 15; regular decision, April 1. Applications are accepted on-line. A waiting list is maintained.

Transfer: 137 transfer students enrolled in a recent year. Applicants must have a minimum college GPA of 2.5 and must submit high school transcripts, ACT or SAT scores (if taken in the last 5 years), and 2 recommendations. An interview is recommended. Grades of C or better transfer for credit. 60 of 120 credits required for the bachelor's degree must be completed at Eugene Lang College.

Visiting: There are regularly scheduled orientations for prospective students, including a campus tour, visits to classes, and panel discussions. There are guides for informal visits and visitors may sit in on classes. To schedule a visit, contact the Office of Admissions at _lang@newschool.edu.

Financial Aid: In a recent year, 63% of all full-time freshmen and 64% of continuing full-time students received some form of financial aid. 61% of all full-time freshmen and 65% of continuing full-time students received need-based aid. The average freshmen award was $23,622, with $12,438 ($30,660 maximum) from need-based scholarships or need-based grants and $3,280 ($5,500 maximum) from need-based self-help aid (loans and jobs). Average annual earnings from campus work were $2000. The average financial indebtedness of the 2009 graduate was $14,770. Eugene Lang College is a member of CSS. The FAFSA, the state aid form, and the college's own financial statement are required. Check with the school for current application deadlines.

International Students: The school actively recruits these students. They must take the TOEFL. They must also take the SAT or ACT.

Computers: Wireless access is available. All students may access the system. There are no time limits and no fees.

Graduates: In a recent year, 2009, 221 bachelor's degrees were awarded. The most popular majors were liberal arts/general studies (100%). In an average class, 27% graduate in 4 years or less, 46% graduate in 5 years or less, and 53% graduate in 6 years or less.

Admissions Contact: Nicole Curvin, Director of Admissions. E-Mail: *lang@newschool.edu* Web: *www.lang.edu*

EXCELSIOR COLLEGE

D-3

Albany, NY 12203-5159 — (518) 464-8500; (888) 674-2388; (518) 464-8777

Full-time: none	**Faculty:** n/av
Part-time: 13,500 men, 20,000 women	**Ph.D.s:** n/av
Graduate: 320 men, 575 women	**Student/Faculty:** n/av
Year: see profile, summer session	**Tuition:** $1000
Application Deadline: see profile	
Freshman Class: n/av	**SPECIAL**

Excelsior College, founded in 1971, offers 34 degree programs designed to meet the needs of working adults, among whom are approximately 6,200 members of the U.S. armed forces. The college is home to a competency-based nursing program and the largest school of nursing in the United States. The college offers nondegree certificate programs as well as a series of ACE evaluated college-level proficiency exams that students can use to earn credit toward a degree at hundreds of colleges around the country. Figures in the above capsule and in this profile are approximate. There are 5 undergraduate schools and 3 graduate schools. In addition to regional accreditation, Excelsior has baccalaureate program accreditation with ABET and NLN. Computerized library services include interlibrary loans, database searching, and Internet access. The campus is in a suburban area in Albany. Including any residence halls, there are 3 buildings.

Student Life: 91% of undergraduates are from out of state. Students are from 50 states, 52 foreign countries, and Canada. 67% are white; 19% African American. The average age of all undergraduates is 40.

Housing: There are no residence halls. All students commute.

Activities: There are no fraternities or sororities. Popular campus events include commencement.

Sports: There is no sports program at Excelsior.

Disabled Students: All of the campus is accessible. Facilities include wheelchair ramps, elevators, special parking, specially equipped restrooms, and lowered drinking fountains.

Services: Counseling and information services are available, as is tutoring in some subjects, including statistics and writing.

Programs of Study: Excelsior confers B.A., B.S., B.S.Comp.Tech, B.S.Elect.Tech, B.S.N., B.S.Nuc.T, and B.S.T. degrees. Associate and master's degrees are also awarded. Bachelor's degrees are awarded in BIOLOGICAL SCIENCE (biology/biological science), BUSINESS (accounting, banking and finance, business administration and management, human resources, insurance and risk management, international business management, management information systems, and marketing/retailing/merchandising), COMMUNICATIONS AND THE ARTS (communications, English literature, languages, and music), COMPUTER AND PHYSICAL SCIENCE (chemistry, geology, information sciences and systems, mathematics, nuclear technology, and physics), ENGINEERING AND ENVIRONMENTAL DESIGN (computer technology, electrical/electronics engineering technology, and technological management), HEALTH PROFESSIONS (health science and nursing), SOCIAL SCIENCE (criminal justice, economics, geography, history, liberal arts/general studies, philosophy, political science/government, psychology, and sociology). Nursing and liberal studies are the largest.

Required: To graduate, students must complete 120 credits with 30 in the major and a minimum 2.0 GPA. At least 50% of course work must be in the arts and sciences. The required core courses include 6 to 12 credits each in humanities, math/science, and social science/history and 1 credit in information literacy. The nursing program requires a different set of core courses as well as the nursing performance exams. All students must fulfill a written English requirement.

Special: B.A. or B.S. candidates may major in liberal studies or in most traditional academic disciplines. Faculty consultants design curricula, approve sources of credit, create exams, and assess student learning. Students receive academic advising by telephone, letter, computer, or in person. The flexibility of this alternate program enables adults to pursue an undergraduate degree independently. Exams are available. Pass/fail options are possible. There is1 national honor society.

Faculty/Classroom: 40% of faculty are male; 60% are female. No introductory courses are taught by graduate students.

Requirements: There are no admissions requirements except for nursing students. Applicants need not be residents of New York State. Students without a high school diploma or equivalent are admitted as special students. Nursing enrollment is available only to students with certain health care backgrounds. AP and CLEP credits are accepted.

Procedure: Freshmen are admitted to all sessions. There is a rolling admissions plan. Check with school for current application deadlines and fees. Applications are accepted on-line.

Transfer: 12638 transfer students enrolled in a recent year.

Financial Aid: The FAFSA and the college's own financial statement are required. Check with the school for current application deadlines.

International Students: There were 355 international students enrolled in a recent year. The school actively recruits these students.

Computers: All students may access the system 24 hours a day, 7 days a week, via the Internet. There are no time limits and no fees.

Graduates: In a recent year, 2340 bachelor's degrees were awarded. The most popular majors were liberal arts (68%), business (9%), and nursing (8%).

Admissions Contact: Prospective Student Adviser E-Mail: info@excelsior.edu Web: www.excelsior.edu

FARMINGDALE STATE COLLEGE   E-5

Farmingdale, NY 11735   (631) 420-2200; (631) 420-2633

Full-time: 2720 men, 1740 women	**Faculty:** IIB, +$
Part-time: 1000 men, 1100 women	**Ph.D.s:** n/av
Graduate: none	**Student/Faculty:** n/av
Year: semesters, summer session	**Tuition:** $6000 ($12,000)
Application Deadline: open	**Room & Board:** $11,500
Freshman Class: n/av	
SAT: required	**COMPETITIVE**

Farmingdale State University of New York, formerly State University of New York/College of Technology at Farmingdale founded in 1912, is a public institution offering associate and bachelor's degrees in the applied sciences and technology. The figures in the above capsule and in this profile are approximate. There are 4 undergraduate schools. In addition to regional accreditation, SUNY Farmingdale has baccalaureate program accreditation with ABET and CAHEA. The library contains 150,000 volumes, 63,000 microform items, and 3,100 audio/video tapes/CDs/DVDs, and subscribes to 900 periodicals including electronic. Computerized library services include interlibrary loans, database searching, and Internet access. Special learning facilities include a learning resource center, art gallery, radio station, dental hygiene clinic, CAD/CAM and CIM labs, fleet of multi- and single-engine airplanes, and a greenhouse complex. The 380-acre campus is in a suburban area on Long Island, about 35 miles east of New York City. Including any residence halls, there are 40 buildings.

Student Life: 99% of undergraduates are from New York. Others are from 13 states, and 29 foreign countries. 92% are from public schools. 55% are white. The average age of freshmen is 22; all undergraduates, 26. 35% do not continue beyond their first year; 28% remain to graduate.

Housing: 500 students can be accommodated in college housing, which includes coed dorms. In addition there are honors wings and residences for students age 23 and older. On-campus housing is available on a first-come and first-served basis. 91% of students commute. Alcohol is not permitted. All students may keep cars.

Activities: There are no fraternities or sororities. There are 32 groups on campus, including art, cheerleading, computers, drama, ethnic, gay, honors, literary magazine, musical theater, newspaper, professional, radio and TV, religious, social, student government, and yearbook. Popular campus events include Comedy Nights, Spring Fling, and black, Hispanic, and women's history months.

Sports: There are 8 intercollegiate sports for men and 6 for women, and 11 intramural sports for men and 11 for women. Facilities include basketball, badminton, volleyball, racquetball, handball, squash, and tennis courts, a swimming pool, a wrestling room, bowling alleys, weight training rooms, indoor and outdoor tracks, a golf driving range and 3-hole golf layout, and baseball, softball, soccer/lacrosse, and multipurpose fields.

Disabled Students: 90% of the campus is accessible. Facilities include wheelchair ramps, elevators, special parking, specially equipped restrooms, special class scheduling, lowered drinking fountains, and lowered telephones.

Services: Counseling and information services are available, as is tutoring in most subjects. There is a reader service for the blind, and remedial math, reading, and writing. There is a learning disabilities specialist counselor available.

Campus Safety and Security: Measures include 24-hour foot and vehicle patrol and security escort services. There are emergency telephones and lighted pathways/sidewalks.

Programs of Study: SUNY Farmingdale confers B.S. and B.Tech. degrees. Associates degrees are also awarded. Bachelor's degrees are awarded in AGRICULTURE (horticulture), BIOLOGICAL SCIENCE (biology/biological science), ENGINEERING AND ENVIRONMENTAL DESIGN (aeronautical science, automotive technology, aviation administration/management, computer technology, construction management, electrical/electronics engineering technology, graphic arts technology, industrial administration/management, industrial engineering technology, and manufacturing technology), SOCIAL SCIENCE (applied psychology, economics, and safety and security technology). Electrical engineering technology, bioscience, and nursing are the strongest academically. Management of technology and computer programming is the largest.

Required: To graduate, students must complete 124 to 141 credits, including 60 to 70 in the major, with a minimum GPA of 2.0. The core curriculum includes 4 courses each in social science, math/science, and English/humanities, including English composition.

Special: Study abroad in 4 countries is available. There are 3 national honor societies and 1 departmental honors program.

Faculty/Classroom: 55% of faculty are male; 45% are female. All teach undergraduates. No introductory courses are taught by graduate students. The average class size in an introductory lecture is 25; in a laboratory is 15; and in a regular course is 21.

Requirements: The SAT is required. In addition, applicants must be graduates of an accredited secondary school or have earned a GED. Specific entrance requirements vary by program, but recommended preparation includes 4 units of English and 3 each of math, science, and social science. Art programs require a portfolio and an interview. A GPA of 2.0 is required. AP and CLEP credits are accepted.

Procedure: Freshmen are admitted fall and spring. There are deferred admissions and rolling admissions plans. Application deadlines are open. Application fee is $40. Notification is sent on a rolling basis.

Transfer: 559 transfer students enrolled in a recent year. Applicants must have a minimum GPA of 2.0 and be eligible to return to their previous college. 90 of 124 credits required for the bachelor's degree must be completed at SUNY Farmingdale.

Visiting: There are regularly scheduled orientations for prospective students, including a tour of the campus and general information about the college, admissions, financial aid, and residence life. There are guides for informal visits. To schedule a visit, contact the Admissions Office at admissions@farmingdale.edu.

Financial Aid: The FAFSA, the state aid form, and the college's own financial statement are required. Check with the school for current application deadlines.

International Students: There were 53 international students enrolled in a recent year. They must take the TOEFL.

Computers: Wireless access is available. Boot up and log on wireless is available across campus. All students may access the system during lab hours or through dial-in access. There are no time limits and no fees. It is strongly recommended that all students have a personal computer. Students enrolled in computer programming must have a personal computer.

Graduates: In a recent year, 535 bachelor's degrees were awarded. The most popular majors were management of technology (35%), engineering technology (17%), and computer/info sciences (13%). 50 companies recruited on campus in 2008-2009. In an average class, 17% graduate in 4 years or less, 17% graduate in 5 years or less, and 28% graduate in 6 years or less. Of the 2008 graduating class, 30% were employed within 6 months of graduation.

Admissions Contact: Jim Hall, Admissions Director. E-Mail: *jim.hall@farmingdale.edu* Web: *farmingdale.edu*

FASHION INSTITUTE OF TECHNOLOGY/STATE UNIVERSITY OF NEW YORK

D-5

New York, NY 10001-5992

(212) 217-7675
(800) Go-To-FIT; (212) 217-7481

Full-time: 1005 men, 5605 women	**Faculty:** n/av
Part-time: 805 men, 3305 women	**Ph.D.s:** n/av
Graduate: 15 men, 105 women	**Student/Faculty:** n/av
Year: 4-1-4, summer session	**Tuition:** $5468 ($12,904)
Application Deadline: see profile	**Room & Board:** $7000
Freshman Class: n/av	**COMPETITIVE**

The Fashion Institute of Technology, founded in 1944 as part of the State University of New York, is an art and design, business, and technology college that prepares students for careers in fashion and related design. The figures in the above capsule and in this profile are approximate. There is 1 graduate school. In addition to regional accreditation, FIT has baccalaureate program accreditation with FIDER and NASAD. The library contains 168,879 volumes, 4,712 microform items, and 244,335 audio/video tapes/CDs/DVDs, and subscribes to 502 periodicals including electronic. Computerized library services include interlibrary loans and database searching. Special learning facilities include an art gallery, radio station, design lab, lighting lab, quick response center, computer-aided design and communications facility, and the Annette Green Fragrance Foundation Studio Collections of the Museum at FIT. The 5-acre campus is in an urban area in Manhattan. Including any residence halls, there are 8 buildings.

Student Life: 63% of undergraduates are from New York. Others are from 49 states, 80 foreign countries, and Canada. 43% are white; 12% foreign nationals. The average age of freshmen is 22; all undergraduates, 29. 81% do not continue beyond their first year; 51% remain to graduate.

Housing: 1250 students can be accommodated in college housing, which includes single-sex and coed dorms and on-campus apartments. On-campus housing is available on a lottery system for upperclassmen. Priority is given to out-of-town students. 83% of students commute. Alcohol is not permitted. No one may keep cars.

Activities: There are no fraternities or sororities. There are 70 groups on campus, including art, cheerleading, choir, dance, drama, ethnic, gay, honors, literary magazine, musical theater, newspaper, photography, political, professional, radio and TV, religious, social, social service, student government, and yearbook. Popular campus events include fashion shows, a lecture series, and craft center events.

Sports: There are 4 intercollegiate sports for men and 4 for women, and 4 intramural sports for men and 4 for women. Facilities include 2 gyms, a dance studio, and a weight room.

Disabled Students: 95% of the campus is accessible. Facilities include wheelchair ramps, elevators, special parking, specially equipped restrooms, lowered drinking fountains, lowered telephones, services/facilities for the hearing impaired, and library tapes.

Services: Counseling and information services are available, as is tutoring in every subject. There is remedial math, reading, and writing. The school has a special program for the learning disabled.

Campus Safety and Security: Measures include 24-hour foot and vehicle patrol and self-defense education. There are emergency telephones, lighted pathways/sidewalks, and lectures by the New York City Police Department.

Programs of Study: FIT confers B.S. and B.F.A. degrees. Associates and master's degrees are also awarded. Bachelor's degrees are awarded in BUSINESS (apparel and accessories marketing, fashion merchandising, and marketing/retailing/merchandising), COMMUNICATIONS AND THE ARTS (advertising, design, fiber/textiles/weaving, graphic design, illustration, and toy design), ENGINEERING AND ENVIRONMENTAL DESIGN (computer graphics, interior design, and textile technology), SOCIAL SCIENCE (fashion design and technology, home furnishings and equipment management/production/services, and textiles and clothing). Fashion merchandising management, fashion design, and communication design are the largest.

Required: To graduate, students must complete the credit and course requirements for their majors with a 2.0 GPA. Students may qualify for a degree in two ways: by earning 60 credits, with half in the major while in residence at the upper-division level, or by earning 30 credits at the upper-division level in addition to an FIT associate degree. There is a 2-credit phys ed requirement.

Special: Internships are offered, and students may study abroad in 8 countries. Nondegree study is available. There iss1 departmental honors program.

Faculty/Classroom: 48% of faculty are male; 52% are female. All teach undergraduates. No introductory courses are taught by graduate students. The average class size in an introductory lecture is 25; in a laboratory is 18; and in a regular course is 25.

Requirements: Applicants must be high school graduates or have a GED certificate. An essay and, when appropriate, a portfolio are required. A GPA of 2.0 is required. AP and CLEP credits are accepted. Important factors in the admissions decision are personality/intangible qualities, leadership record, and evidence of special talent.

Procedure: Freshmen are admitted fall and spring. There are early decision and rolling admissions plans. Applications should be filed by October 1 for spring entry, along with a $40 fee. Applications are accepted on-line. A waiting list is maintained.

Transfer: Applicants must have a GPA of 2.0 and at least 30 college credits. An interview is required for art and design applicants, as well as a portfolio when appropriate. 30 of 60 credits required for the bachelor's degree must be completed at FIT.

Visiting: There are regularly scheduled orientations for prospective students, including a presentation and group information session with a counselor. To schedule a visit, contact the Admissions Office at fitinfo@fitnyc.edu.

Financial Aid: FIT is a member of CSS. The FAFSA and the state aid form are required. Check with the school for current application deadlines.

International Students: They must take the TOEFL.

Computers: All students may access the system. There are no time limits and no fees.

Admissions Contact: Dolores Lombardi, Director of Admissions. A campus DVD is available. E-Mail: *fitinfo@fitnyc.edu* Web: *www.fitnyc.edu*

FIVE TOWNS COLLEGE

E-5

Dix Hills, NY 11746 (631) 424-7000, ext. 2110; (631) 656-2172

Full-time: 793 men, 437 women	**Faculty:** n/av
Part-time: 20 men, 12 women	**Ph.D.s:** 51%
Graduate: 99 men, 86 women	**Student/Faculty:** n/av
Year: semesters, summer session	**Tuition:** $18,185
Application Deadline: rolling	**Room & Board:** $12,650
Freshman Class: 1179 applied, 639 accepted, 447 enrolled	
SAT CR/M/W: 400/390/400	**ACT:** 18 **SPECIAL**

Five Towns College, founded in 1972, is a private institution offering undergraduate programs in music, music business, business, liberal arts, theater, elementary education, and mass communication (broadcasting, journalism). There is 1 graduate school. In addition to regional accreditation, FTC has baccalaureate program accreditation with NCATE. The library contains 35,000 volumes, 50 microform items, and 12,000 audio/video tapes/CDs/DVDs, and subscribes to 500 periodicals including electronic. Computerized library services include interlibrary loans, database searching, Internet access, and laptop Internet portals. Special learning facilities include a learning resource center, radio station, TV station, 72-, 48-, and 24-track recording studios, a MIDI studio, and a film video/TV studio. The 40-acre campus is in a suburban area 48 miles east of New York City. Including any residence halls, there are 5 buildings.

Student Life: 95% of undergraduates are from New York. Others are from 20 states and 9 foreign countries. 91% are from public schools. 62% are white; 15% African American; 14% Hispanic. The average age of freshmen is 19; all undergraduates, 21. 30% do not continue beyond their first year; 58% remain to graduate.

Housing: 200 students can be accommodated in college housing, which includes coed dorms and off-campus apartments. Priority is given to out-of-town students. 90% of students commute. Alcohol is not permitted. All students may keep cars.

Activities: There are no fraternities or sororities. Groups on campus include art, band, barbershop quartets, broadcasting, choir, chorale, chorus, dance, drama, film, hip-hop, honors, international, jazz band, live audio, music business, musical theater, newspaper, orchestra, photography, professional, radio and TV, readers theater, social, student government, symphony, theatrical concert, and yearbook. Popular campus events include the Cultural Hour, the Annual Picnic, and spring and fall festivals.

Sports: There is no sports program at FTC. Facilities include a gym with basketball and volleyball courts, an outdoor baseball/soccer field, and a fitness center.

Disabled Students: All of the campus is accessible. Facilities include wheelchair ramps, special parking, specially equipped rest rooms, special class scheduling, lowered drinking fountains, lowered telephones, and special housing.

Services: Counseling and information services are available, as is tutoring in most subjects. There is remedial math, reading, and writing.

Campus Safety and Security: Measures include 24-hour foot and vehicle patrol and emergency notification system. There are shuttle buses and lighted pathways/sidewalks.

Programs of Study: FTC confers B.S., B.F.A., B.P.S., and Mus.B. degrees. Associate, master's, and doctoral degrees are also awarded. Bachelor's degrees are awarded in COMMUNICATIONS AND THE ARTS (audio technology, communications, dramatic arts, jazz, music business management, music performance, music theory and composition, and video), EDUCATION (elementary education and music education). Music and childhood education are the strongest academically. Business management with a concentration in audio recording technology is the largest.

Required: To graduate, all students must complete a total of 130 credits for a Mus.B. or B.F.A. degree, 128 for a B.S. degree, or 122 for a B.P.S. degree. Students must maintain at least a C average in their major concentration and have a minimum GPA of 2.0 to graduate. Distribution requirements include 45 credits in core courses in liberal arts. The core curriculum consists of English Composition 101 and 102, Speech 101, 3 credits of either psychology or sociology, and various upper-division liberal arts and social science courses. All music students must pass a jury exam. Music majors and elementary education majors must take a comprehensive exam.

Special: Cross-registration is available with schools in the Long Island Regional Advisory Council on Higher Education. Co-op programs are available, and work-study programs are offered on campus. Internships are available in business management (concentrations in audio recording technology and music business), film/video, mass communication (concentrations in broadcasting and journalism), theater, and education. A B.A.-B.S. degree in mass communication and childhood education is possible. There is 1 national honor society and 6 departmental honors programs.

Faculty/Classroom: 66% of faculty are male; 34% are female. All teach undergraduates and do research. No introductory courses are taught by graduate students. The average class size in an introductory lecture is 30; in a laboratory, 24.

Admissions: 54% of the 2009-2010 applicants were accepted. The SAT scores for the 2009-2010 freshman class were: Critical Reading-- 84% below 500, 12% between 500 and 599, 3% between 600 and 700, and 1% above 700; Math--81% below 500, 14% between 500 and 599, 4% between 600 and 700, and 1% above 700; Writing--83% below 500, 12% between 500 and 599, 4% between 600 and 700, and 1% above 700. The ACT scores were 95% below 21, 4% between 21 and 23, and 1% between 24 and 26. 8% of the current freshmen were in the top fifth of their class; 28% were in the top two fifths.

Requirements: The SAT or ACT is required. The ACT Optional Writing test is also required. In addition, a minimum high school average of 80 is required. A GED with a minimum score of 2500 is accepted. An audition is required for students in music and theater. AP and CLEP credits are accepted. Important factors in the admissions decision are advanced placement or honors courses, evidence of special talent, and parents or siblings attending the school.

Procedure: Freshmen are admitted fall, spring, and summer. Entrance exams should be taken prior to admission (placement exams are only for students who fall below FTC requirements). There are early decision, deferred admissions and rolling admissions plans. Early decision applications should be filed by December 1 for fall entry; for regular applications, deadlines are rolling. Application fee is $35. Notification is sent on a rolling basis 2 weeks after all admissions requirements are fulfilled. 5 early decision candidates were accepted for the 2009-2010 class.

Transfer: 150 transfer students enrolled in 2008-2009. Students must be in good academic standing at their former school and have a minimum GPA of 2.0. FTC accepts a maximum of 60 transfer credits. The residency requirement is 60 credits for the baccalaureate degree.

Visiting: There are regularly scheduled orientations for prospective students, including a campus tour, academic counseling, financial aid counseling, and educational workshops. Students also learn about student support services and how to become involved in student activities. There are guides for informal visits, and visitors may sit in on classes. To schedule a visit, contact the Admissions Office at (631) 656-2110.

Financial Aid: In 2009-2010, 90% of all full-time freshmen and 85% of continuing full-time students received some form of financial aid. 75% of all full-time freshmen and 73% of continuing full-time students received need-based aid. The average freshman award was $5,000. Need-

based scholarships or need-based grants averaged $6500 and need-based self-help aid (loans and jobs) averaged $3500. 74% of undergraduate students work part-time. Average annual earnings from campus work are $2000. The average financial indebtedness of the 2009 graduate was $18,000. The FAFSA and the college's own financial statement are required. Check with the school for current application deadlines.

International Students: There are 9 international students enrolled. The school actively recruits these students. They must take the TOEFL with a minimum score of 520 on the paper-based TOEFL (PBT) or 79 on the Internet-based version (iBT) and the college's own test. They must also take the SAT or ACT and the college's own entrance exam.

Computers: All students may access the system during school hours.

Admissions Contact: Jerry Cohen, Director of Admissions. A campus DVD is available. E-mail: *admissions@ftc.edu* Web: *www.ftc.edu*

FORDHAM UNIVERSITY SYSTEM

The Fordham University System, established in 1841, is a private system in New York affiliated with the Catholic Church in the Jesuit tradition. It is governed by a board of trustees, whose chief administrator is the president. The primary goal of the system is to foster the intellectual, moral, and religious development of its students and prepare them for leadership in a global society. The main priorities are excellence in undergraduate, graduate/professional programs, and commitment to teaching, research, and service. The total enrollment in a recent year of all 3 campuses was 14,448; there were 1403 faculty members. Altogether there are 69 baccalaureate, 71 master's, and 25 doctoral programs offered in the Fordham University System. Profiles of the 4-year campuses are included in this section.

FORDHAM UNIVERSITY
Bronx, NY 10458

D-5

(718) 817-4000
(800) FORDHAM; (718) 367-9404

Full-time: 4000 men, 4035 women	**Faculty:** I, av$
Part-time: 200 men, 330 women	**Ph.D.s:** n/av
Graduate: 2645 men, 4170 women	**Student/Faculty:** n/av
Year: semesters, summer session	**Tuition:** $33,500
Application Deadline: see profile	**Room & Board:** $13,000
Freshman Class: n/av	
SAT or ACT: required	**HIGHLY COMPETITIVE**

Fordham University, founded in 1841, is a private institution offering an education based on the Jesuit tradition, with 2 campuses in New York: 1 in the Bronx and 1 in Manhattan near Lincoln Center. The figures in the above capsule and in this profile are approximate. There are 3 undergraduate schools and 6 graduate schools. In addition to regional accreditation, has baccalaureate program accreditation with AACSB and NCATE. The 4 libraries contain 2 million volumes, 3.1 million microform items, and 19,295 audio/video tapes/CDs/DVDs, and subscribe to 15,940 periodicals including electronic. Computerized library services include interlibrary loans, database searching, and Internet access. Special learning facilities include a learning resource center, radio station, a seismic station, an archeological site, and a biological field station. The 85-acre campus is in an urban area adjacent to the Bronx Zoo and New York Botanical Garden. Including any residence halls, there are 32 buildings.

Student Life: 59% of undergraduates are from New York. Others are from 49 states, 50 foreign countries, and Canada. 40% are from public schools. 56% are white; 12% Hispanic. 66% are Catholic; 13% Buddhist, Greek Orthodox, Hindu, Muslim/Islam. The average age of freshmen is 18; all undergraduates, 20. 10% do not continue beyond their first year; 80% remain to graduate.

Housing: 3947 students can be accommodated in college housing, which includes coed dorms, on-campus apartments, and off-campus apartments. In addition, there are integrated learning communities. On-campus housing is guaranteed for all 4 years. 56% of students live on campus; of those, 90% remain on campus on weekends. All students may keep cars.

Activities: There are no fraternities or sororities. There are 133 groups on campus, including art, band, cheerleading, choir, chorale, chorus, computers, dance, drama, ethnic, film, gay, honors, international, jazz band, literary magazine, marching band, musical theater, newspaper, orchestra, pep band, photography, political, professional, radio and TV, religious, social, social service, student admission ambassadors, student government, and symphony. Popular campus events include Spring Weekend, Spring Semiformal, and Senior Week.

Sports: There are 19 intercollegiate sports for men and 17 for women, and 22 intramural sports for men and 22 for women. Facilities include a 6000-seat football stadium, an Olympic-size pool with a separate diving area, an indoor track, a 3200-seat gym, and tennis, squash, and racquetball courts.

Disabled Students: 80% of the campus is accessible. Facilities include wheelchair ramps, elevators, special parking, specially equipped rest-rooms, special class scheduling, and lowered drinking fountains.

Services: Counseling and information services are available, as is tutoring in most subjects.

Campus Safety and Security: Measures include 24-hour foot and vehicle patrol, emergency notification system, and security escort services. There are shuttle buses, emergency telephones, and lighted pathways/sidewalks.

Programs of Study: confers B.A., B.S., and B.F.A. degrees. Master's and doctoral degrees are also awarded. Bachelor's degrees are awarded in BIOLOGICAL SCIENCE (biology/biological science), BUSINESS (accounting, business administration and management, business economics, international business management, and marketing management), COMMUNICATIONS AND THE ARTS (art history and appreciation, broadcasting, classical languages, communications, comparative literature, dance, dramatic arts, English, film arts, fine arts, French, German, Italian, journalism, music, performing arts, Spanish, and visual and performing arts), COMPUTER AND PHYSICAL SCIENCE (chemistry, computer science, information sciences and systems, mathematics, physics, and science), ENGINEERING AND ENVIRONMENTAL DESIGN (engineering physics), SOCIAL SCIENCE (African studies, African American studies, American studies, anthropology, classical/ancient civilization, economics, French studies, German area studies, history, international studies, Italian studies, Latin American studies, medieval studies, Middle Eastern studies, philosophy, political science/government, psychology, religion, social science, social work, sociology, Spanish studies, theological studies, urban studies, and women's studies). Communications, social sciences, and English are the strongest academically. Business, psychology, and biology are the largest.

Required: All students must complete a core curriculum, including 2 courses each in English literature, history, philosophy, theology, natural sciences, social sciences, and foreign language competency and 1 each in math, English composition, and fine arts. A total of 124 credits with 30 in the major and a 2.0 minimum GPA are required. A thesis is required for the honors program.

Special: Fordham University offers career-oriented internships in communications and other majors during the junior or senior year with New York City companies and institutions. A combined 3-2 engineering program is available with Columbia and Case Western Reserve Universities. Study abroad, a Washington semester, accelerated degrees, dual and student-designed majors, and pass/fail options are available. There are 6 national honor societies, including Phi Beta Kappa, and a freshman honors program.

Faculty/Classroom: 64% of faculty are male; 36% are female. 74% do both. No introductory courses are taught by graduate students. The average class size in an introductory lecture is 21; in a laboratory is 11; and in a regular course is 17.

Requirements: The SAT or ACT is required. In addition, applicants should have completed 4 years of high school English and 3 each of math, science, social studies, history, and foreign language. Applicants should submit the Common Application, which includes an essay. A guidance counselor recommendation is also required. Auditions are required for theater and dance majors. AP credits are accepted. Important factors in the admissions decision are advanced placement or honors courses, extracurricular activities record, and recommendations by school officials.

Procedure: Freshmen are admitted fall and spring. Entrance exams should be taken by December of the senior year. There is a deferred admissions plan. Applications should be filed by November 1 for spring entry, along with a $50 fee. Notifications are sent April 1. Applications are accepted on-line. A waiting list is maintained.

Transfer: 280 transfer students enrolled in a recent year. A 3.0 minimum GPA is recommended. Applicants with less than 1 full year of full-time course work at a post-secondary institution should submit SAT or ACT scores. An interview is recommended. 64 of 124 credits required for the bachelor's degree must be completed at Fordham.

Visiting: There are regularly scheduled orientations for prospective students. There are guides for informal visits and visitors may sit in on classes. To schedule a visit, contact the Office of Undergraduate Admission at (800) FORDHAM.

Financial Aid: In a recent year, 63% of all full-time freshmen and 63% of continuing full-time students received some form of financial aid. 62% of all full-time freshmen and 61% of continuing full-time students received need-based aid. The average freshman award was $20,521. The average financial indebtedness of the 2009 graduate was $17,004. is a member of CSS. The CSS/Profile and FAFSA are required. Check with the school for current application deadlines.

International Students: There were 141 international students enrolled in a recent year. The school actively recruits these students. They must take the TOEFL and the college's own test. They must also take the SAT or ACT.

Computers: All students may access the system. There are no time limits and no fees.

Graduates: In a recent year, 1670 bachelor's degrees were awarded. The most popular majors were business (24%), social sciences/history (22%), and communications (14%). 500 companies recruited on campus in 2008-2009. In an average class, 1% graduate in 3 years or less, 68% graduate in 4 years or less, 72% graduate in 5 years or less, and 73% graduate in 6 years or less. Of the 2008 graduating class, 25% were enrolled in graduate school within 6 months of graduation, and 90% were employed.

Admissions Contact: Peter Farrell, Director of Admission. E-Mail: *enroll@fordham.edu* Web: *www.fordham.edu*

HAMILTON COLLEGE — C-3

Clinton, NY 13323

(315) 859-4421
(800) 843-2655; (315) 859-4457

Full-time: 870 men, 981 women	Faculty: 177; IIB, ++$
Part-time: 12 men, 19 women	Ph.D.s: 97%
Graduate: none	Student/Faculty: 10 to 1
Year: semesters	Tuition: $39,760
Application Deadline: January 1	Room & Board: $10,100
Freshman Class: 4661 applied, 1390 accepted, 466 enrolled	
SAT CR/M: 710/690	ACT: 30 MOST COMPETITIVE

Hamilton College, chartered in 1812, is a private, nonsectarian, liberal arts school offering undergraduate programs in the arts and sciences. The 3 libraries contain 617,080 volumes, 433,824 microform items, and 62,655 audio/video tapes/CDs/DVDs, and subscribe to 3800 periodicals including electronic. Computerized library services include interlibrary loans, database searching, and Internet access. Special learning facilities include an art gallery, radio station, and observatory. The 1300-acre campus is in a rural area 9 miles southwest of Utica. Including any residence halls, there are 104 buildings.

Student Life: 65% of undergraduates are from out of state, mostly the Northeast. Students are from 46 states, 40 foreign countries, and Canada. 60% are from public schools. 68% are white. 37% claim no religious affiliation; 25% Protestant; 22% Catholic; 13% Jewish. The average age of freshmen is 18; all undergraduates, 20. 4% do not continue beyond their first year; 86% remain to graduate.

Housing: 1813 students can be accommodated in college housing, which includes coed dorms, on-campus apartments, and married student housing. In addition, there are special-interest houses, quiet floors, and substance-free areas. On-campus housing is guaranteed for all 4 years. 97% of students live on campus; of those, 90% remain on campus on weekends. Upperclassmen may keep cars.

Activities: 34% of men belong to 11 national fraternities; 16% of women belong to 6 local and 1 national sororities. There are 153 groups on campus, including art, chess, choir, chorale, chorus, computers, dance, debate, drama, environmental, ethnic, film, gay, honors, international, jazz band, literary magazine, musical theater, newspaper, orchestra, photography, political, professional, radio, religious, social, social service, student government, and yearbook. Popular campus events include Class and Charter Day, Feb Fest (Winter Carnival), and Springfest.

Sports: There are 14 intercollegiate sports for men and 14 for women, and 17 intramural sports for men and 17 for women. Facilities include a gym, a field house, a fitness and dance center, squash and racquetball courts, indoor and outdoor tennis courts, an artificial grass football stadium, a 9-hole golf course, a swimming pool, indoor and outdoor tracks, baseball and softball fields, numerous grass fields, paddle tennis courts, and an ice rink.

Disabled Students: Facilities include wheelchair ramps, elevators, special parking, specially equipped rest rooms, special class scheduling, and special housing.

Services: Counseling and information services are available, as is tutoring in some subjects through the New York State Higher Education Opportunity Program (HEOP).

Campus Safety and Security: Measures include 24-hour foot and vehicle patrol, emergency notification system, self-defense education, and security escort services. There are shuttle buses, emergency telephones, lighted pathways/sidewalks, and access controls for dorms/residences.

Programs of Study: Hamilton confers B.A. degrees. Bachelor's degrees are awarded in AGRICULTURE (environmental studies), BIOLOGICAL SCIENCE (biochemistry, biology/biological science, and neurosciences), COMMUNICATIONS AND THE ARTS (art, art history and appreciation, Chinese, classics, communications, comparative literature, creative writing, dance, dramatic arts, English, English literature, French, languages, music, Spanish, and studio art), COMPUTER AND PHYSICAL SCIENCE (chemical physics, chemistry, computer science, geoscience, mathematics, and physics), SOCIAL SCIENCE (African studies, American studies, anthropology, archeology, Asian/Oriental studies, economics, German area studies, history, interdisciplinary studies, international relations, philosophy, political science/government, psychobiology, psychology, public affairs, religion, Russian and Slavic studies, sociology, and women's studies). Government, economics, and psychology are the largest.

Required: Students must successfully complete 128 credits, with 32 to 40 of these in the major, and must maintain at least a 72% average in half the courses taken.

Special: Cross-registration is permitted with Colgate University and Utica College. Opportunities are provided for a Washington semester. Student-designed majors and study abroad in many countries are available, and 3-2 engineering degrees are offered with Washington University, Rensselaer Polytechnic Institute, and Columbia University. There are 7 national honor societies, including Phi Beta Kappa.

Faculty/Classroom: 57% of faculty are male; 43% are female. All teach undergraduates.

Admissions: 30% of the 2009-2010 applicants were accepted. The SAT scores for the 2009-2010 freshman class were: Critical Reading--3% below 500, 8% between 500 and 599, 31% between 600 and 700, and 59% above 700; Math--2% below 500, 8% between 500 and 599, 45% between 600 and 700, and 45% above 700; Writing--2% below 500, 6% between 500 and 599, 37% between 600 and 700, and 54% above 700. The ACT scores were 5% between 21 and 23, 4% between 24 and 26, 12% between 27 and 28, and 78% above 28. 94% of the current freshmen were in the top fifth of their class; 99% were in the top two fifths. 24 freshmen graduated first in their class.

Requirements: The SAT or ACT is required. Although graduation from an accredited secondary school or a GED is desirable, and a full complement of college-preparatory courses is recommended, Hamilton will consider all highly recommended candidates who demonstrate an ability and desire to perform at intellectually demanding levels. Students can fulfill test requirements with the SAT, ACT, 3 SAT Subject tests, 3 AP exams, or any combination of these. An essay is required, and an interview is recommended. AP credits are accepted. Important factors in the admissions decision are advanced placement or honors courses, recommendations by school officials, and parents or siblings attended your school.

Procedure: Freshmen are admitted fall. Entrance exams should be taken prior to February of the senior year. There are early decision, early admissions and deferred admissions plans. Early decision applications should be filed by november 15; regular applications, by January 1 for fall entry. The fall 2008 application fee was $75. Notification of early decision is sent December 15; regular decision, April 1. Applications are accepted on-line. 1096 applicants were on a recent waiting list, 17 were accepted.

Transfer: 21 transfer students enrolled in 2008-2009. Transfer applicants must submit high school and college transcripts, an essay or personal statement, and standardized test scores and must present a minimum GPA of 3.0 in all college-level work. 64 of 128 credits required for the bachelor's degree must be completed at Hamilton.

Visiting: There are regularly scheduled orientations for prospective students, consisting of an interview, tour, class visit, and open house program. There are guides for informal visits, and visitors may sit in on classes and stay overnight. To schedule a visit, contact the Admissions Office.

Financial Aid: In 2009-2010, 45% of all full-time freshmen and 42% of continuing full-time students received some form of financial aid. 44% of all full-time freshmen and 40% of continuing full-time students received need-based aid. The average freshman award was $36,931. 56% of undergraduate students work part-time. Average annual earnings from campus work are $1300. The average financial indebtedness of the 2009 graduate was $19,466. The CSS/Profile, the FAFSA, the state aid form, and the college's own financial statement are required. The deadline for filing freshman financial aid applications for fall entry is February 8.

International Students: There are 92 international students enrolled. The school actively recruits these students. They must take the TOEFL. They must also take the SAT or ACT.

Computers: Wireless access is available. All students may access the system. There are no time limits and no fees.

Graduates: From July 1, 2008 to June 30, 2009, 472 bachelor's degrees were awarded. The most popular majors were economics (12%), government (9%), and psychology (8%). In an average class, 1% graduate in 3 years or less, 82% graduate in 4 years or less, 85% graduate in 5 years or less, and 86% graduate in 6 years or less. Of the 2008 graduating class, 18% were enrolled in graduate school within 6 months of graduation and 72% were employed.

Admissions Contact: Monica Inzer, Vice President and Dean of Admission and Financial Aid. E-mail: *admission@hamilton.edu* Web: *www.hamilton.edu*

HARTWICK COLLEGE D-3
Oneonta, NY 13820-4020

(607) 431-4150
(888) HARTWICK; (607) 431-4102

Full-time: 584 men, 839 women	Faculty: 100; IIB, -$
Part-time: 14 men, 18 women	Ph.D.s: 98%
Graduate: none	Student/Faculty: 15 to 1
Year: 4-1-4	Tuition: $33,330
Application Deadline: open	Room & Board: $9075
Freshman Class: n/av	
SAT or ACT: not required	COMPETITIVE+

Hartwick College, founded in 1797, is a private undergraduate liberal arts and sciences college. In addition to regional accreditation, Hartwick has baccalaureate program accreditation with ACS, CCNE, NASAD, NASM, NLN, and TEAC. The library contains 317,781 volumes, 123,518 microform items, and 4,700 audio/video tapes/CDs/DVDs, and subscribes to 400 periodicals including electronic. Computerized library services include interlibrary loans, database searching, Internet access, and laptop Internet portals. Special learning facilities include an art gallery, radio station, a museum, a 100-acre environmental study center, and an observatory. The 425-acre campus is in a small town 75 miles southwest of Albany. Including any residence halls, there are 28 buildings.

Student Life: 65% of undergraduates are from New York. Others are from 31 states, 20 foreign countries, and Canada. 86% are from public schools. 61% are white. The average age of freshmen is 18; all undergraduates, 20. 22% do not continue beyond their first year; 51% remain to graduate.

Housing: 1259 students can be accommodated in college housing, which includes single-sex and coed dorms and on-campus apartments. In addition, there are honors houses, special-interest houses, fraternity houses, sorority houses, substance-free housing, and an environmental campus. On-campus housing is guaranteed for all 4 years. 79% of students live on campus; of those, 90% remain on campus on weekends. All students may keep cars.

Activities: 5% of men belong to 1 local fraternity and 2 national fraternities; 4% of women belong to 1 local sorority and 2 national sororities. There are 70 groups on campus, including academic, art, band, cheerleading, choir, chorale, chorus, computers, dance, drama, environmental, ethnic, film, gay, honors, international, jazz band, literary magazine, musical theater, newspaper, orchestra, outing, photography, political, professional, radio and TV, religious, social, social service, student government, and yearbook. Popular campus events include Holiday Ball, Earth Day, and Multicultural Month.

Sports: There are 7 intercollegiate sports for men and 10 for women, and 5 intramural sports for men and 5 for women. Facilities include 2 gyms, an indoor pool, a dance room, athletic and training facilities, a track, a Nautilus exercise gym, a fitness center, a lighted all-weather playing field, a lighted soccer field, an equestrian complex, and courts for handball, racquetball, squash, and tennis.

Disabled Students: 50% of the campus is accessible. Facilities include wheelchair ramps, elevators, special parking, specially equipped rest rooms, special class scheduling, lowered drinking fountains, and lowered telephones.

Services: Counseling and information services are available, as is tutoring in every subject. There is a reader service for the blind. There are writing and math centers and an academic support center.

Campus Safety and Security: Measures include 24-hour foot and vehicle patrol, emergency notification system, self-defense education, and security escort services. There are emergency telephones, lighted pathways/sidewalks, and controlled access to dorms/residences.

Programs of Study: Hartwick confers B.A. and B.S. degrees. Bachelor's degrees are awarded in BIOLOGICAL SCIENCE (biochemistry and biology/biological science), BUSINESS (accounting and business administration and management), COMMUNICATIONS AND THE ARTS (art, art history and appreciation, dramatic arts, English, French, German, languages, music, and Spanish), COMPUTER AND PHYSICAL SCIENCE (chemistry, computer science, geology, information sciences and systems, mathematics, and physics), EDUCATION (music education), ENGINEERING AND ENVIRONMENTAL DESIGN (environmental science), HEALTH PROFESSIONS (medical technology and nursing), SOCIAL SCIENCE (anthropology, economics, history, philosophy, political science/government, psychology, religion, and sociology). Anthropology, biology, and English are the strongest academically. Psychology, management, and nursing are the largest.

Required: Students must complete 120 credit hours with at least a 2.0 GPA. The core curriculum consists of Hartwick's Liberal Arts in Practice. Distribution requirements include a first-year seminar; 9 credits spread through humanities, physical and life sciences, and social and behavioral sciences; 3 credits in quantitative and formal reasoning; foreign language (intermediate-level proficiency); attainment of writing level 4; and a senior capstone.

Special: Students may design their own majors and choose independent study. Cross-registration with SUNY College at Oneonta is possible, and local and international internships are available. There is a January thematic term, a Washington semester, and study abroad in 30 countries. First-year students may participate in specially designated off-campus programs. Experiential programs include Outward Bound and the National Outdoor Leadership School. All departments offer dual majors and accelerated degree options. There is a 3-2 engineering program with Clarkson University or Columbia University, and a 3-3 program with Albany Law School. There are 10 national honor societies and a freshman honors program.

Faculty/Classroom: 61% of faculty are male; 39% are female. All teach undergraduates. The average class size in an introductory lecture is 20; in a laboratory, 20; and in a regular course, 30.

Admissions: 22% of the current freshmen were in the top fifth of their class; 45% were in the top two fifths. 3 freshmen graduated first in their class.

Requirements: Reporting of SAT and ACT scores is optional. The recommended secondary course of study includes 4 years of English and 3 years each of math, a foreign language, history, and lab science. Hartwick strongly recommends that applicants plan a campus visit and interview. Prospective art majors should submit a portfolio, and music majors must audition. Computer disks are offered to all prospective students, providing information about the college as well as an application. A GPA of 2.5 is required (or grade average of 80%). AP and CLEP credits are accepted. Important factors in the admissions decision are advanced placement or honors courses, recommendations by school officials, and ability to finance college education.

Procedure: Freshmen are admitted to all sessions. Entrance exams should be taken in the spring of the junior year and/or the fall of the senior year. There are early decision, deferred admissions and rolling admissions plans. Early decision applications should be filed by November 1; deadlines for regular applications are open. Application fee is $35. Notification is sent on a rolling basis. 101 early decision candidates were accepted for a recent class. 97 applicants were on the 2009 waiting list; 51 were admitted. Applications are accepted on-line.

Transfer: 37 transfer students enrolled in a recent year. Applicants should present a minimum GPA of 2.0. 60 of 120 credits required for the bachelor's degree must be completed at Hartwick.

Visiting: There are regularly scheduled orientations for prospective students, consisting of an interview and tour, lunch, departmental open houses, presentations on student life, off-campus programs, and a career planning process. There are guides for informal visits, and visitors may sit in on classes and stay overnight. To schedule a visit, contact the Admissions Office.

Financial Aid: In 2009-2010, an estimated 76% of all full-time freshmen and 73% of continuing full-time students received some form of financial aid, including need-based aid. The estimated average freshman award was $25,720. Need-based scholarships or need-based grants averaged an estimated $21,421; need-based self-help aid (loans and jobs) averaged an estimated $5,565; institutional non-need-based scholarships averaged an estimated $17,166; and other institutional non-need-based awards and non-need-based scholarships averaged an estimated $10,081. 66% of undergraduate students work part-time. Average annual earnings from campus work are $1640. The average financial indebtedness of a recent year's graduate was $19,364. Hartwick is a member of CSS. The FAFSA and the college's own financial statement are required. Check with the school for current application deadlines.

International Students: There are 45 international students enrolled. The school actively recruits these students. They must take the TOEFL with a minimum score of 550 on the paper-based TOEFL (PBT) or 79 on the Internet-based version (iBT). They must also take the SAT, scoring 420 on the Critical Reading section.

Computers: Wireless access is available. All students may access the system 24 hours per day, 7 days per week. There are no time limits and no fees. It is strongly recommended that all students have a personal computer.

Graduates: From July 1, 2008 to June 30, 2009, 283 bachelor's degrees were awarded. The most popular majors were management (18%), psychology (11%), and history (8%). In an average class, 51% graduate in 4 years or less, 56% graduate in 5 years or less, and 60% graduate in 6 years or less. 20 companies recruited on campus in 2008-2009. Of the 2008 graduating class, 10% were enrolled in graduate school within 6 months of graduation, and 25% were employed.

Admissions Contact: David Conway, Vice President for Enrollment Management. E-mail: admissions@hartwick.edu
Web: www.hartwick.edu

HILBERT COLLEGE   A-3

Hamburg, NY 14075-1597

	(716) 649-7900, ext. 244
	(800) 649-8003; (716) 649-0702
Full-time: 350 men, 500 women	**Faculty:** IIB, --$
Part-time: 100 men, 150 women	**Ph.D.s:** 51%
Graduate: none	**Student/Faculty:** n/av
Year: semesters, summer session	**Tuition:** $17,600
Application Deadline: see pofile	**Room & Board:** $7400
Freshman Class: n/av	
SAT or ACT: recommended	**COMPETITIVE**

Hilbert College, founded in 1957, is a private institution offering degree programs in accounting, business, criminal justice, digital media and communications, economic crime investigation, English, forensic science, human services, liberal studies, paralegal, political science, psychology, and rehabilitation services. Some of the figures in the above capsule and in this profile are approximate. The library contains 36,076 volumes, 3,616 microform items, and 1,165 audio/video tapes/CDs/DVDs, and subscribes to 23,190 periodicals including electronic. Computerized library services include interlibrary loans, database searching,

Internet access, and laptop Internet portals. Special learning facilities include a learning resource center, creative and digital media lab, psychology research lab, forensic science/crime scene investigation lab, and economic crime computer lab. The 44-acre campus is in a suburban area about 10 miles south of Buffalo. Including any residence halls, there are 11 buildings.

Student Life: 95% of undergraduates are from New York. Others are from 8 states, 2 foreign countries, and Canada. 80% are from public schools. 87% are white. The average age of freshmen is 20; all undergraduates, 26. 26% do not continue beyond their first year; 74% remain to graduate.

Housing: 180 students can be accommodated in college housing, which includes coed dorms, on-campus apartments, and off-campus apartments. On-campus housing is guaranteed for all 4 years, is available on a first-come, first-served basis, and is available on a lottery system for upperclassmen. 79% of students commute. All students may keep cars.

Activities: There are no fraternities or sororities. There are 20 groups on campus, including academic, cheerleading, chorus, ethnic, film, honors, literary magazine, newspaper, professional, religious, social, social service, and student government. Popular campus events include Quad Party, Fall Fest, and Fall Family Weekend.

Sports: There are 5 intercollegiate sports for men and 6 for women, and 4 intramural sports for men and 4 for women. Facilities include a soccer/lacrosse field, baseball and softball diamonds, a practice field, a fitness center, and a 900-seat NCAA regulation indoor athletic facility.

Disabled Students: 95% of the campus is accessible. Facilities include wheelchair ramps, elevators, special parking, specially equipped restrooms, special class scheduling, lowered drinking fountains, and lowered telephones.

Services: Counseling and information services are available, as is tutoring in some subjects, writing, accounting, and math There is remedial math and writing.

Campus Safety and Security: Measures include 24-hour foot and vehicle patrol, emergency notification system, self-defense education, and security escort services. There are emergency telephones and lighted pathways/sidewalks.

Programs of Study: Hilbert confers B.A. and B.S. degrees. Associates degrees are also awarded. Bachelor's degrees are awarded in BUSINESS (accounting and business administration and management), COMMUNICATIONS AND THE ARTS (English), HEALTH PROFESSIONS (rehabilitation therapy), SOCIAL SCIENCE (criminal justice, criminology, forensic studies, human services, liberal arts/general studies, paralegal studies, political science/government, and psychology). Economic crime investigation, paralegal studies, psychology, and accounting are the strongest academically. Criminal justice, forensic science, and business administration are the largest.

Required: To graduate, students must complete 120 credit hours, including at least 36 in the major and 60 in liberal arts, with a minimum 2.0 GPA. Students must fulfill requirements in English, math, philosophy, and social sciences.

Special: Hilbert offers study abroad, cross-registration with the 17-member Western New York College Consortium, internships in most majors, and work-study programs. The college maintains articulation agreements with 22 New York State community colleges. There are 4 national honor societies, a freshman honors program, and 3 departmental honors programs.

Faculty/Classroom: 60% of faculty are male; 40% are female. All teach undergraduates, and 10% do research. No introductory courses are taught by graduate students. The average class size in an introductory lecture, 20, in a laboratory, 4, and in a regular course, 15.

Requirements: The SAT or ACT is recommended. AP and CLEP credits are accepted. Important factors in the admissions decision are leadership record, advanced placement or honors courses, and recommendations by school officials.

Procedure: Freshmen are admitted to all sessions. There are deferred admissions and rolling admissions plans. Application deadlines are open. The fall 2008 application fee was $20. Applications are accepted on-line.

Transfer: 163 transfer students enrolled in a recent year. Applicants must submit official transcripts from all colleges attended and, in some cases, the high school transcript. 30 of 120 credits required for the bachelor's degree must be completed at Hilbert.

Visiting: There are regularly scheduled orientations for prospective students. There are guides for informal visits and visitors may sit in on classes. To schedule a visit, contact the Office of Admissions.

Financial Aid: In a recent year, 88% of all full-time freshmen and 87% of continuing full-time students received some form of financial aid. 100% of all full-time freshmen and 98% of continuing full-time students received need-based aid. The average freshmen award was $10,552, with $2,570 ($5,000 maximum) from need-based scholarships or need-based grants; $3,642 ($5,500 maximum) from need-based self-help aid (loans and jobs); and $2,855 ($5,000 maximum) from other non-need-based awards and non-need-based scholarships. 7% of undergraduate students worked part-time. Average annual earnings from campus work were $1735. Hilbert is a member of CSS. The FAFSA is required. Check with the school for current application deadlines.

International Students: They must take the TOEFL.

Computers: Wireless access is available. All students may access the system. There are no time limits. The fee is $25 per semester.

Graduates: In a recent year, 240 bachelor's degrees were awarded. The most popular majors were criminal justice (40%), and business administration (18%). 50 companies recruited on campus in 2008-2009. In an average class, 34% graduated in 3 years or less, 40% graduated in 4 years or less, and 4% graduated in 5 years or less. Of the 2008 graduating class, 15% were enrolled in graduate school within 6 months of graduation, and 75% were employed.

Admissions Contact: Timothy Lee, Director of Admissions. E-Mail: *admissions@hilbert.edu* Web: *www.hilbert.edu*

HOBART AND WILLIAM SMITH COLLEGES   C-3

Geneva, NY 14456-3397   H: (315) 781-3622; (315) 781-3471

Full-time: 875 men, 1010 women	**Faculty:** IIB, +$
Part-time: 3 men and women	**Ph.D.s:** n/av
Graduate: none	**Student/Faculty:** n/av
Year: semesters	**Tuition:** $34,000
Application Deadline: February 1	**Room & Board:** $9000
Freshman Class: n/av	
SAT or ACT: required	**VERY COMPETITIVE**

Hobart College, a men's college founded in 1822, shares campus, classes, and faculty with William Smith College, a women's college founded in 1908. Together, these coordinate colleges offer degree programs in the liberal arts. Figures in the above capsule and in this profile are approximate. The library contains 375,762 volumes, 77,396 microform items, and 9,600 audio/video tapes/CDs/DVDs, and subscribes to 1,926 periodicals including electronic. Computerized library services include interlibrary loans, database searching, and Internet access. Special learning facilities include a learning resource center, art gallery, radio station, a 100-acre natural preserve, and a 70-foot research vessel. The 170-acre campus is in a small town 50 miles west of Syracuse and 50 miles east of Rochester, on the north shore of Seneca Lake. Including any residence halls, there are 95 buildings.

Student Life: 51% of undergraduates are from out of state, mostly the Northeast. Students are from 40 states, 19 foreign countries, and Canada. 65% are from public schools. 86% are white. 30% are Catholic; 30% Protestant; 20% claim no religious affiliation; 15% Jewish. The average age of freshmen is 18; all undergraduates, 20. 15% do not continue beyond their first year; 75% remain to graduate.

Housing: 1500 students can be accommodated in college housing, which includes single-sex and coed dorms and on-campus apartments. In addition, there are honors houses, language houses, special-interest houses, fraternity houses, cooperative houses in which students plan and prepare their own meals, and townhouses for upperclassmen. On-campus housing is guaranteed for all 4 years. 90% of students live on campus; of those, 93% remain on campus on weekends. All students may keep cars.

Activities: 15% of men belong to 5 national fraternities.there are no sororities. There are 70 groups on campus, including art, chess, choir, chorale, chorus, computers, dance, debate, drama, ethnic, film, forensics, gay, honors, international, jazz band, literary magazine, musical theater, newspaper, orchestra, photography, political, professional, radio and TV, religious, social, social service, student government, symphony, and yearbook. Popular campus events include Folk Festival, Charter Day, and Moving Up Day.

Sports: There are 11 intercollegiate sports for men and 11 for women, and 23 intramural sports for men and 23 for women. Facilities include a sport and recreation center, 2 gyms, numerous athletic fields, a swimming pool, 5 indoor tennis courts, 3 weight rooms, basketball and racquetball courts, an indoor track, international squash courts, a boathouse, and a crew facility.

Disabled Students: Facilities include wheelchair ramps, elevators, special parking, specially equipped restrooms, special class scheduling, and lowered drinking fountains.

Services: Counseling and information services are available, as is tutoring in every subject. There is a reader service for the blind, and remedial math, reading, and writing. There is a counseling center staffed by 5 therapists/counselors as well as various support groups and educational workshops.

Campus Safety and Security: Measures include 24-hour foot and vehicle patrol, self-defense education, and security escort services. There are shuttle buses, emergency telephones, and lighted pathways/sidewalks.

Programs of Study: HWS confers B.A. and B.S. degrees. Master's degrees are also awarded. Bachelor's degrees are awarded in BIOLOGICAL SCIENCE (biology/biological science), COMMUNICATIONS AND THE ARTS (art history and appreciation, classics, comparative literature, dance, English, fine arts, French, modern language, music, and studio art), COMPUTER AND PHYSICAL SCIENCE (chemistry, computer sci-

ence, geoscience, mathematics, and physics), ENGINEERING AND ENVIRONMENTAL DESIGN (architecture and environmental science), SOCIAL SCIENCE (African studies, American studies, anthropology, Asian/Oriental studies, economics, European studies, history, international relations, Latin American studies, philosophy, political science/government, psychology, religion, Russian and Slavic studies, sociology, Spanish studies, urban studies, and women's studies). Natural sciences, environmental studies, and creative writing are the strongest academically. English, economics, and political science are the largest.

Required: All first-year students must take a seminar. Students should complete a major of 14 to 18 courses and a minor of 6 to 8 courses, or a second major. Of the major or the minor (or second major), one must be disciplinary and the other interdisciplinary. Minimum grade and GPA standards apply. In addition, all students must meet the 8 goals established by the faculty to ensure breadth across the disciplines as well as depth in the major.

Special: Students are encouraged to spend at least 1 term in a study-abroad program, offered in more than 29 countries and locales within the United States. Options include a United Nations term, a Washington semester, an urban semester, and prearchitecture semesters in New York, Paris, Florence, or Copenhagen. HWS offers dual and student-designed majors, internships, credit for life/military/work experience, nondegree study, and pass/fail options. There are also advanced business degree programs with Clarkson University and Rochester Institute of Technology and 3-2 engineering degrees with Columbia University, Rensselaer Polytechnic Institute, and Dartmouth College. There are 9 national honor societies, including Phi Beta Kappa, and 100 departmental honors programs.

Faculty/Classroom: 60% of faculty are male; 40% are female. All teach and do research. No introductory courses are taught by graduate students. The average class size in an introductory lecture is 40; in a laboratory is 18; and in a regular course is 18.

Requirements: The SAT or ACT is required. SAT: Subject tests are not required but will be considered if taken. A GED may be is accepted. A total of 19 academic credits is required, including 4 years of English, 3 of math, and at least 3 each of lab science, foreign language, and history. An essay is required; an interview is recommended. AP credits are accepted. Important factors in the admissions decision are advanced placement or honors courses, evidence of special talent, and leadership record.

Procedure: Freshmen are admitted fall. Entrance exams should be taken no later than December of the senior year. There are early decision, early admissions and deferred admissions plans. Early decision applications should be filed by November 15; regular applications, by February 1 for fall entry, along with a $45 fee. Notification of early decision is sent December 15; regular decision, sent in March. Applications are accepted on-line. A waiting list is maintained.

Transfer: Applicants must have a 2.5 GPA and have completed 1 year of college study. They are required to take the SAT or ACT. An interview is recommended. 16 of 32 credits required for the bachelor's degree must be completed at HWS.

Visiting: There are regularly scheduled orientations for prospective students, including 7 open houses in the spring, summer, and fall and daily tours and personal interviews year round. Information sessions are offered February through April and on Saturdays in the summer. There are guides for informal visits; visitors may sit in on classes and stay overnight. To schedule a visit, contact the Office of Admissions at admissions@hws.edu.

Financial Aid: HWS is a member of CSS. The CSS/Profile and FAFSA are required. Check with the school for current application deadlines.

International Students: The school actively recruits these students. They must take the TOEFL. They must also take the SAT or ACT.

Computers: All students may access the system from 8 A.M. to 1 A.M., 7 days a week. There are no time limits and no fees. It is strongly recommended that all students have a personal computer. A Gateway Solo Laptop is recommended.

Admissions Contact: John W. Young, Director of Admissions. E-Mail: *jyoung@hws.edu* Web: *www.hws.edu*

HOFSTRA UNIVERSITY   D-5

Hempstead, NY 11549   (516) 463-6700
(800) HOFSTRA; (516) 463-7660

Full-time: 3505 men, 3822 women	**Faculty:** 420; I, av$
Part-time: 318 men, 274 women	**Ph.D.s:** 91%
Graduate: 1586 men, 2563 women	**Student/Faculty:** 17 to 1
Year: 4-1-4, summer session	**Tuition:** $30,130
Application Deadline: open	**Room & Board:** $11,330
Freshman Class: 20,829 applied, 11,801 accepted, 1568 enrolled	
SAT CR/M: 580/600	**ACT:** 26 **VERY COMPETITIVE+**

Hofstra University, founded in 1935, is an independent institution offering programs in liberal arts and sciences, business, communications, education, health and human services, honors studies, and law. There are 7 undergraduate schools and 6 graduate schools. In addition to regional accreditation, Hofstra has baccalaureate program accreditation with AACSB, ABA, ABET, ACEJMC, ACS, APA, ARC-PA, CAATE, and TEAC. The 3 libraries contain 1.1 million volumes, 3.5 million microform items, and 16,215 audio/video tapes/CDs/DVDs, and subscribe to 11,353 periodicals including electronic. Computerized library services include interlibrary loans, database searching, Internet access, and laptop Internet portals. Special learning facilities include a learning resource center, art gallery, radio station, TV station, financial trading room, comprehensive media production facility, converged newsroom learning center, career center, writing center, linux beowolf cluster, digital language lab, technology, science, and engineering labs, a rooftop observatory, 7 theaters, assessment centers for child observation and counseling, child care institute, a cultural center, a museum, an arboretum, and a bird sanctuary. The 240-acre campus is in a suburban area 25 miles east of New York City. Including any residence halls, there are 115 buildings.

Student Life: 63% of undergraduates are from New York. Others are from 45 states, 58 foreign countries, and Canada. 65% are white. The average age of freshmen is 18; all undergraduates, 21. 24% do not continue beyond their first year; 55% remain to graduate.

Housing: 4170 students can be accommodated in college housing, which includes single-sex and coed dorms. In addition, there are honors houses, special-interest houses, a living-learning center, quiet floors, women's floors, and freshman housing. On-campus housing is guaranteed for all 4 years. 51% of students commute. All students may keep cars.

Activities: 6% of men belong to 10 national fraternities; 8% of women belong to 3 local and 10 national sororities. There are 175 groups on campus, including art, band, cheerleading, chess, choir, chorale, chorus, Community Student Organization, computers, dance, debate, drama, drum and bugle corps, environmental, ethnic, film, forensics, gay, honors, international, jazz band, literary magazine, musical theater, newspaper, opera, orchestra, pep band, photography, political, professional, radio and TV, religious, Resident Student Association, social, social service, student government, and symphony. Popular campus events include New Student Convocation, Welcome Week, and Great Writers/Great Readings.

Sports: There are 8 intercollegiate sports for men and 9 for women, and 9 intramural sports for men and 8 for women. Facilities include a 15,000-seat stadium, a 5000-seat arena, a 1600-seat soccer stadium, a physical fitness center, a swim center with an Olympic-size swimming pool and high-dive area, a softball stadium, an intramurals field, and a recreation center with a multipurpose gym, an indoor track, and a weight room.

Disabled Students: All of the campus is accessible. Facilities include wheelchair ramps, elevators, special parking, specially equipped restrooms, special class scheduling, lowered drinking fountains, lowered telephones, and special housing.

Services: Counseling and information services are available, as is tutoring in most subjects. There is a reader service for the blind and tutoring offered in subjects such as English, math, reading, and writing.

Campus Safety and Security: Measures include 24-hour foot and vehicle patrol, emergency notification system, self-defense education, and security escort services. There are shuttle buses, emergency telephones, lighted pathways/sidewalks, controlled access to dorms/residences, security cameras in residence halls, a bike patrol, and a motorist assistance program.

Programs of Study: Hofstra confers B.A., B.S., B.B.A., B.E., B.F.A., and B.S.Ed. degrees. Master's and doctoral degrees are also awarded. Bachelor's degrees are awarded in AGRICULTURE (environmental studies), BIOLOGICAL SCIENCE (biochemistry, biology/biological science, and ecology), BUSINESS (accounting, banking and finance, business administration and management, business law, entrepreneurial studies, international business management, labor studies, management information systems, and marketing management), COMMUNICATIONS AND THE ARTS (American literature, art history and appreciation, audio technology, ceramic art and design, Chinese, classics, comparative literature, creative writing, dance, design, dramatic arts, English literature, film arts, fine arts, French, German, Hebrew, Italian, jazz, journalism, linguistics, media arts, metal/jewelry, music, music business management, music history and appreciation, music performance, music theory and composition, painting, photography, public relations, publishing, radio/television technology, Russian, Spanish, speech/debate/rhetoric, theater design, theater management, video, and visual and performing arts), COMPUTER AND PHYSICAL SCIENCE (applied mathematics, applied physics, chemistry, computer science, geology, mathematics, natural sciences, and physics), EDUCATION (art education, athletic training, business education, dance education, early childhood education, elementary education, English education, foreign languages education, health education, mathematics education, music education, physical education, science education, secondary education, and social studies education), ENGINEERING AND ENVIRONMENTAL DESIGN (biomedical engineering, civil engineering, computer engineering, electrical/electronics engineering, environmental engineering, industrial engineering, manufacturing engineering, and mechanical engineering),

HEALTH PROFESSIONS (allied health, community health work, exercise science, health science, physician's assistant, predentistry, premedicine, preoptometry, preosteopathy, prepodiatry, preveterinary science, and speech pathology/audiology), SOCIAL SCIENCE (African studies, American studies, anthropology, Asian/Oriental studies, Caribbean studies, economics, forensic studies, geography, Hispanic American studies, history, humanities, interdisciplinary studies, Judaic studies, Latin American studies, liberal arts/general studies, philosophy, political science/government, psychology, social science, sociology, and women's studies). Accounting, biology, and English are the strongest academically. Accounting, biology, and education are the largest.

Required: A total of 124 to 152 credit hours is required for graduation, with approximately 30 to 60 in the major depending on degree program. A minimum GPA of 2.0 is also required. Students must pass Writing Studies & Composition (WSC) 1 and 2 and pass a writing proficiency exam. A minimum of 6 semester hours each is required in humanities, natural sciences, math, and computer science, and in social science. Foreign language study is required for the B.A., the B.B.A., some B.S. programs, and in international business.

Special: Internships in numerous career fields, a Washington semester, an Albany State Assembly internship, study abroad in 16 countries, and dual and student-designed majors are offered. Credit for prior learning and credit by exam are given with proper credentials. Hofstra offers nondegree study and pass/fail options. There are 32 national honor societies, including Phi Beta Kappa, a freshman honors program, and 35 departmental honors programs.

Faculty/Classroom: 56% of faculty are male; 44% are female. 85% teach undergraduates, and all do research. No introductory courses are taught by graduate students. The average class size in an introductory lecture is 29; in a laboratory, 14; and in a regular course, 22.

Admissions: 57% of the 2009-2010 applicants were accepted. The SAT scores for the 2009-2010 freshman class were: Critical Reading--7% below 500, 50% between 500 and 599, 39% between 600 and 700, and 5% above 700; Math--4% below 500, 44% between 500 and 599, 47% between 600 and 700, and 4% above 700. The ACT scores were 3% below 21, 20% between 21 and 23, 38% between 24 and 26, 20% between 27 and 28, and 19% above 28. 49% of the current freshmen were in the top fifth of their class; 78% were in the top two fifths. 8 freshmen graduated first in their class.

Requirements: The SAT or ACT is required for some programs. In addition, applicants should graduate from an accredited secondary school or have a GED. Preparatory work should include 4 years of English, 3 each of history and social studies, math, and science, and 2 of foreign language. Engineering students are required to have 4 years of math and 1 each of chemistry and physics. An essay is required. Interviews are recommended. 1 counselor or teacher recommendation is recommended. AP and CLEP credits are accepted. Important factors in the admissions decision are advanced placement or honors courses, recommendations by school officials, and geographical diversity.

Procedure: Freshmen are admitted fall and spring. Entrance exams should be taken in the junior or senior year. There are early admissions, deferred admissions, and rolling admissions plans. Early decision applications should be filed by December 15; deadlines for regular applications are rolling. Application fee is $70. Notification of early decision is sent January 15; regular decision, February 1. 296 applicants were on the 2009 waiting list; 90 were admitted. Applications are accepted online.

Transfer: 526 transfer students enrolled in 2008-2009. Admission is based primarily on prior college work. A maximum of 64 credits from a 2-year school or 94 credits from a 4-year school is accepted. There is a 30-credit maximum on AP/CLEP credits. 30 of 124 to 152 credits required for the bachelor's degree must be completed at Hofstra.

Visiting: There are regularly scheduled orientations for prospective students, including a group information session, a campus tour, and an optional interview with an admission counselor. There are guides for informal visits, and visitors may sit in on classes and stay overnight. To schedule a visit, contact Andrea Nadler at (516) 463-6798.

Financial Aid: In 2009-2010, 89% of all full-time freshmen and 82% of continuing full-time students received some form of financial aid. 63% of all full-time freshmen and 57% of continuing full-time students received need-based aid. The average freshman award was $15,283. Need-based scholarships or need-based grants averaged $13,189 ($52,122 maximum); need-based self-help aid (loans and jobs) averaged $7,002 ($15,300 maximum); non-need-based athletic scholarships averaged $27,119 ($48,394 maximum); and other non-need-based awards and non-need-based scholarships averaged $10,589 ($33,100 maximum). 41% of undergraduate students work part-time. Average annual earnings from campus work are $3100. The FAFSA and the state aid form are required. The priority date for freshman financial aid applications for fall entry is February 15.

International Students: There are 128 international students enrolled. The school actively recruits these students. They must take the TOEFL with a minimum score of 550 on the paper-based TOEFL (PBT) or 80 on the Internet-based version (iBT).

Computers: Wireless access is available. Students have access to 1628 PCs in labs and classrooms. These computers are all connected to the campus network and have access to the Internet and Internet2. Students can use the extensive network of wireless hot spots or plug into public ports to gain access to the campus network and the Internet using their laptops. Residence hall rooms have wireless and a high-speed port per student for access to the network. All students may access the system. There are no time limits. The fee is $105. It is strongly recommended that all students have a personal computer. A Lenovo or Mac laptop (for certain majors) is recommended.

Graduates: From July 1, 2008 to June 30, 2009, 1750 bachelor's degrees were awarded. The most popular majors were marketing and international business (11%), journalism, media studies, and production (9%), and psychology (9%). In an average class, 41% graduate in 4 years or less, 53% graduate in 5 years or less, and 55% graduate in 6 years or less. 401 companies recruited on campus in 2008-2009. Of the 2008 graduating class, 30% were enrolled in graduate school within 6 months of graduation, and 93% were employed.

Admissions Contact: Jessica Eads, Vice President of Enrollment Management. A campus DVD is available. E-mail: *admission@hofstra.edu* Web: *www.hofstra.edu*

HOUGHTON COLLEGE   B-3

Houghton, NY 14744

(585) 567-9353
(800) 777-2556; (585) 567-9522

Full-time: 428 men, 824 women	**Faculty:** 88
Part-time: 28 men, 31 women	**Ph.D.s:** 88%
Graduate: 13 men, 12 women	**Student/Faculty:** 14 to 1
Year: semesters	**Tuition:** $24,440
Application Deadline: open	**Room & Board:** $7000
Freshman Class: 1000 applied, 889 accepted, 287 enrolled	
SAT CR/M/W: 600/578/582	**ACT:** 26 **VERY COMPETITIVE+**

Houghton College, founded in 1883, provides a residential educational experience integrating academic instruction with Christian faith. In addition to regional accreditation, Houghton has baccalaureate program accreditation with NASM. The library contains 230,070 volumes, 46,858 microform items, and 14,227 audio/video tapes/CDs/DVDs, and subscribes to 27,151 periodicals including electronic. Computerized library services include interlibrary loans, database searching, Internet access, and laptop Internet portals. Special learning facilities include a learning resource center, art gallery, radio station, an equestrian center, a ropes course, and a digital media lab. The 1300-acre campus is in a rural area 65 miles southeast of Buffalo and 70 miles southwest of Rochester. Including any residence halls, there are 20 buildings.

Student Life: 60% of undergraduates are from New York. Others are from 37 states, 23 foreign countries, and Canada. 63% are from public schools. 89% are white. 95% are Protestant. The average age of freshmen is 18; all undergraduates, 21. 14% do not continue beyond their first year; 70% remain to graduate.

Housing: 1066 students can be accommodated in college housing, which includes single-sex dorms, on-campus apartments, and married student housing. Equestrian students have the opportunity to live in housing on-site. On-campus housing is guaranteed for the freshman year only and is available on a lottery system for upperclassmen. Priority is given to out-of-town students. 89% of students live on campus; of those, 65% remain on campus on weekends. Alcohol is not permitted. All students may keep cars.

Activities: There are no fraternities or sororities. There are 40 groups on campus, including art, bagpipe, band, cheerleading, choir, chorale, chorus, drama, ethnic, honors, international, jazz band, literary magazine, ministry, mission organizations, musical theater, newspaper, opera, orchestra, political, professional, radio and TV, religious, social, social service, student government, and volunteer service. Popular campus events include Christian Life Emphasis Week, Winter Weekend, and Martin Luther King Jr. Service Day.

Sports: There are 4 intercollegiate sports for men and 6 for women, and 8 intramural sports for men and 6 for women. Facilities include 3 basketball and 4 racquetball courts, a swimming pool, an indoor track, a downhill ski slope, cross-country ski trails, 6 tennis courts, a climbing wall, an 8-lane all-weather track, a ropes course, and a 386-acre equestrian center with an indoor riding ring. The gym seats 1800; the auditorium, 1300.

Disabled Students: 85% of the campus is accessible. Facilities include wheelchair ramps, elevators, special parking, specially equipped rest rooms, special class scheduling, lowered drinking fountains, lowered telephones, and special housing.

Services: Counseling and information services are available, as is tutoring in some subjects, including general education courses. There is a reader service for the blind and support for learning-disabled students.

Campus Safety and Security: Measures include 24-hour foot and vehicle patrol and security escort services. There are shuttle buses, emergency telephones, and lighted pathways/sidewalks. There is a partnership with the state police to present personal safety information for new students.

Programs of Study: Houghton confers B.A., B.S., and B.Mus. degrees. Associate and master's degrees are also awarded. Bachelor's degrees are awarded in BIOLOGICAL SCIENCE (biochemistry and biology/biological science), BUSINESS (accounting, business administration and management, and recreation and leisure services), COMMUNICATIONS AND THE ARTS (art, communications, English, music performance, music theory and composition, and Spanish), COMPUTER AND PHYSICAL SCIENCE (chemistry, computer science, information sciences and systems, mathematics, physics, and science), EDUCATION (elementary education, music education, physical education, science education, secondary education, and teaching English as a second/foreign language (TESOL/TEFOL)), ENGINEERING AND ENVIRONMENTAL DESIGN (environmental science), HEALTH PROFESSIONS (medical technology), SOCIAL SCIENCE (biblical studies, crosscultural studies, history, humanities, international relations, ministries, philosophy, political science/government, psychology, religion, and sociology). Biology, religion, and music are the strongest academically. Education, biology, and business are the largest.

Required: Integrative studies courses are required in the following disciplines: writing, literature, Bible, foreign language, history, math, science, physical education, theology, philosophy, fine arts, social science, and humanities. A minimum GPA of 2.0 is required to graduate.

Special: Students may cross-register with members of the Western New York Consortium, the Christian College Consortium, and the Five College Committee. Internships are available in psychology, social work, business, educational ministries, physical fitness, political science, graphic design, communication, athletic training, recreation, English, and Christian education. Study abroad in 25 countries, a Washington semester, dual majors, and a 3-2 engineering degree with Clarkson and Washington Universities are available. Credit for military experience and nondegree study are possible. There are 2 national honor societies and a freshman honors program.

Faculty/Classroom: 62% of faculty are male; 38% are female. All teach undergraduates, and 20% also do research. No introductory courses are taught by graduate students. The average class size in an introductory lecture is 32; in a laboratory, 20; and in a regular course, 19.

Admissions: 89% of the 2009-2010 applicants were accepted. The SAT scores for the 2009-2010 freshman class were: Critical Reading--15% below 500, 38% between 500 and 599, 31% between 600 and 700, and 16% above 700; Math--17% below 500, 42% between 500 and 599, 33% between 600 and 700, and 8% above 700; Writing--17% below 500, 39% between 500 and 599, 33% between 600 and 700, and 11% above 700. The ACT scores were 12% below 21, 24% between 21 and 23, 22% between 24 and 26, 14% between 27 and 28, and 28% above 28. 57% of the current freshmen were in the top fifth of their class; 83% were in the top two fifths. There was 1 National Merit finalist. 16 freshmen graduated first in their class.

Requirements: The SAT or ACT is required. In addition, applicants must graduate from an accredited secondary school, be homeschooled, or have a GED. A total of 16 academic credits is recommended, including 4 of English, 3 of social studies, and 2 each of foreign language, math, and science. An essay is required. Music students must audition. An interview is recommended. Houghton requires applicants to be in the upper 50% of their class. A GPA of 2.5 is required. AP and CLEP credits are accepted. Important factors in the admissions decision are personality/intangible qualities, recommendations by school officials, and advanced placement or honors courses.

Procedure: Freshmen are admitted fall and spring. Entrance exams should be taken in the spring of the junior year or fall of the senior year. There are deferred admissions and rolling admissions plans. Application deadlines are open. Application fee is $40. Notification is sent January 1. Applications are accepted on-line.

Transfer: 54 transfer students enrolled in 2008-2009. Applicants should have a 2.75 or better GPA. A Christian character recommendation and high school transcripts must be submitted. The SAT or ACT and an interview are optional. 30 of 124 credits required for the bachelor's degree must be completed at Houghton.

Visiting: There are regularly scheduled orientations for prospective students, including a campus tour, an admissions interview, a financial aid session, a class visit, and an academic information session. There are guides for informal visits, and visitors may sit in on classes and stay overnight.

Financial Aid: In 2009-2010, 99% of all full-time freshmen and 98% of continuing full-time students received some form of financial aid. 97% of all full-time freshmen and 89% of continuing full-time students received need-based aid. The average freshman award was $22,000. Need-based scholarships or need-based grants averaged $8599 ($25,440 maximum); need-based self-help aid (loans and jobs) averaged $5819 ($9750 maximum); non-need-based athletic scholarships averaged $5764 ($15,220 maximum); and other non-need-based awards and non-need-based scholarships averaged $5786 ($21,250 maximum). 43% of undergraduate students work part-time. Average annual earnings from campus work are $888. The average financial indebtedness of the 2009 graduate was $32,580. Houghton is a member of

CSS. The FAFSA is required. The priority date for freshman financial aid applications for fall entry is March 1.

International Students: There are 54 international students enrolled. The school actively recruits these students. They must take the TOEFL with a minimum score of 550 on the paper-based TOEFL (PBT) or 80 on the Internet-based version (iBT). They must also take the SAT or ACT.

Computers: The campus is fully wired and has wireless capabilities. All students are provided with network access. All students may access the system. There are no time limits and no fees. It is strongly recommended that all students have a personal computer. The required model and make change from year to year.

Graduates: From July 1, 2008 to June 30, 2009, 335 bachelor's degrees were awarded. The most popular majors were business administration (25%), religion/religious studies (16%), and psychology (8%). In an average class, 3% graduate in 3 years or less, 61% graduate in 4 years or less, 70% graduate in 5 years or less, and 70% graduate in 6 years or less. 54 companies recruited on campus in 2008-2009. Of the 2008 graduating class, 44% were enrolled in graduate school within 6 months of graduation, and 87% were employed.

Admissions Contact: Wayne MacBeth, Vice President for Enrollment Management. E-mail: *admission@houghton.edu* Web: *www.houghton.edu*

IONA COLLEGE   D-5

New Rochelle, NY 10801-1890   (914) 633-2503
                                        (800) 231-IONA; (914) 633-2642

Full-time: 1406 men, 1839 women	**Faculty:** 183; IIA, +$
Part-time: 50 men, 49 women	**Ph.D.s:** 92%
Graduate: 342 men, 562 women	**Student/Faculty:** 18 to 1
Year: semesters, summer session	**Tuition:** $27,500
Application Deadline: February 15	**Room & Board:** $11,300
Freshman Class: 7313 applied, 4242 accepted, 789 enrolled	
SAT required	**ACT:** recommended

VERY COMPETITIVE

Iona College, founded in 1940, is a private college offering programs through schools of general studies, arts and science, and business. It has a graduate campus in Rockland County in addition to the main campus in New Rochelle. There are 2 undergraduate schools and 2 graduate schools. In addition to regional accreditation, Iona has baccalaureate program accreditation with AACSB, ABET, ACEJMC, CSWE, and NCATE.The 3 libraries contain 272,014 volumes, 510,100 microform items, and 3,922 audio/video tapes/CDs/DVDs, and subscribe to 475 periodicals including electronic. Computerized library services include interlibrary loans, database searching, Internet access, and laptop Internet portals. Special learning facilities include a learning resource center, art gallery, radio station, TV station, an electron microscope, and a speech and hearing clinic. The 35-acre campus is in a suburban area 20 miles northeast of New York City. Including any residence halls, there are 37 buildings.

Student Life: 77% of undergraduates are from New York. Others are from 41 states, 35 foreign countries, and Canada. 77% are white; 13% Hispanic. The average age of freshmen is 18; all undergraduates, 20. 15% do not continue beyond their first year; 62% remain to graduate.

Housing: 1076 students can be accommodated in college housing, which includes single-sex and coed dorms and off-campus apartments. In addition, there are honors houses and special-interest houses. On-campus housing is available on a first-come, first-served basis, and is available on a lottery system for upperclassmen. Priority is given to out-of-town students.69% of students commute. Upperclassmen may keep cars.

Activities: 4% of men belong to 2 local and 2 national fraternities; 6% of women belong to 5 local and 1 national sororities. There are 65 groups on campus, including bagpipe, cheerleading, choir, chorale, computers, dance, debate, drama, environmental, ethnic, film, gay, honors, international, literary magazine, musical theater, newspaper, pep band, photography, political, professional, radio and TV, religious, social, social service, student government, and yearbook. Popular campus events include Spring Concert, Involvement Fair, and Maroon Madness.

Sports: There are 10 intercollegiate sports for men and 11 for women, and 10 intramural sports for men and 10 for women. Facilities include an all-weather football-soccer/lacrosse field. Athletic center with a Nautilus, weight, and an aerobics rooms, and a swimming pool. The campus stadium seats 1200 and the indoor gym, 3000.

Disabled Students: 90% of the campus is accessible. Facilities include wheelchair ramps, elevators, special parking, specially equipped rest rooms, special class scheduling, lowered drinking fountains, lowered telephones, and special housing. All classes are on the first floor.

Services: Counseling and information services are available, as is tutoring in every subject. There is a reader service for the blind.

Campus Safety and Security: Measures include 24-hour foot and vehicle patrol, emergency notification system, self-defense education, and security escort services. There are shuttle buses, emergency telephones, and lighted pathways/sidewalks.

Programs of Study: Iona confers B.A., B.S., B.B.A., and B.P.S. degrees. Master's degrees are also awarded. Bachelor's degrees are awarded in BIOLOGICAL SCIENCE (biochemistry and biology/biological science), BUSINESS (accounting, business administration and management, international business management, management science, and marketing management), COMMUNICATIONS AND THE ARTS (advertising, communications, English, French, Italian, Spanish, and speech/debate/rhetoric), COMPUTER AND PHYSICAL SCIENCE (chemistry, computer science, mathematics, and physics), EDUCATION (early childhood education, elementary education, foreign languages education, middle school education, science education, and secondary education), HEALTH PROFESSIONS (medical technology and speech pathology/audiology), SOCIAL SCIENCE (behavioral science, criminal justice, economics, history, international studies, liberal arts/general studies, philosophy, political science/government, psychology, religion, social work, and sociology). Accounting, computer science, and mass communications are the strongest academically. Mass communications, psychology, and criminal justice are the largest.

Required: The core curriculum includes 24 credits of humanities, 12 credits of natural and symbolic languages, and 6 credits each of communications, social science, and science and technology. There is an arts core, a science core, and a business core. Computer literacy is required. The total number of credits required to graduate is at least 120, depending on the major, with at least 30 in the major. The minimum GPA is 2.0.

Special: There are internships for upperclassmen. Study abroad is available in 9 countries. There is work-study in Iona offices and academic departments. Students may earn a combined B.A.-B.S. degree in economics, psychology, childhood education, early adolescence education, and math education. There is a joint B.S./M.S. program with New York Medical College in physical therapy. 5-year programs are offered in computer science, psychology, history, and English. There are 23 national honor societies, a freshman honors program, and all departments have honors programs.

Faculty/Classroom: 66% of faculty are male; 34% are female. 93% teach undergraduates, and 76% do research. No introductory courses are taught by graduate students. The average class size in an introductory lecture, 24, in a laboratory, 18, and in a regular course, 20.

Admissions: 58% of the 2009-2010 applicants were accepted. The SAT scores for the 2009-2010 freshman class were: Critical Reading--43% below 500, 46% between 500 and 599, 9% between 600 and 700, and 2% above 700; Math--44% below 500, 44% between 500 and 599, 10% between 600 and 700, and 2% above 700; Writing--43% below 500, 46% between 500 and 599, 9% between 600 and 700, and 2% above 700. The ACT scores were 10% below 21, 36% between 21 and 23, 33% between 24 and 26, and 21% between 27 and 28. 49% of the current freshmen were in the top fifth of their class; 81% were in the top two fifths.

Requirements: The SAT is required. In addition, applicants must complete 16 academic credits, including 4 units of English, 3 of math, 2 of foreign language, and 1 each of history, science, and social studies. A GED is accepted. An essay is required, and an interview is recommended. A GPA of 2.5 is required. AP and CLEP credits are accepted. Important factors in the admissions decision are recommendations by school officials, leadership record, and advanced placement or honors courses.

Procedure: Freshmen are admitted fall and spring. Entrance exams should be taken in the spring of the junior year. There are early admissions and deferred admissions plans. Applications should be filed by February 15 for fall entry and January 1 for spring entry. The fall 2008 application fee was $50. Notifications are sent March 20. Applications are accepted on-line. 600 applicants were on a recent waiting list, 79 were accepted.

Transfer: 103 transfer students enrolled in 2008-2009. Transfer applicants must have a GPA of at least 2.5 and must submit high school transcripts if they have earned fewer than 30 college credits. An interview is recommended. 30 of 120 credits required for the bachelor's degree must be completed at Iona.

Visiting: There are regularly scheduled orientations for prospective students, including a meeting with an admissions counselor, a campus tour, and a variety of on-campus programs during the summer and fall. There are guides for informal visits and visitors may sit in on classes. To schedule a visit, contact Elizabeth English at (914) 633-2622.

Financial Aid: In 2009-2010, 98% of all full-time freshmen and 95% of continuing full-time students received some form of financial aid. 67% of all full-time freshmen and 56% of continuing full-time students received need-based aid. The average freshman award was $27,510. Need-based scholarships or need-based grants averaged $6,068 ($13,100 maximum); need-based self-help aid (loans and jobs) averaged $3,777 ($7,600 maximum); non-need based athletic scholarships averaged $14,146 ($43,482 maximum); and other non-need based awards and non-need based scholarships averaged $16,878 ($42,202 maximum). 20% of undergraduate students work part-time. Average annual earnings from campus work are $1125. The average financial indebtedness of the 2009 graduate was $24,212. Iona is a member of CSS. The FAFS, the college's own financial statement, and the TAP (Tuition Assistance Program) form are required. The priority date for freshman financial aid applications for fall entry is February 15. The deadline for filing freshman financial aid applications for fall entry is April 15.

International Students: There are 44 international students enrolled. The school actively recruits these students. They must take the TOEFL with a minimum score of 550 on the paper-based TOEFL (PBT). They must also take the SAT or ACT.

Computers: Wireless access is available. The campus WAN consists of 85 servers (57 NT, 15 LINUX, and 2 UNIX, 9VM, and 2 Apple OSx). There are 1500 college and student owned, high-end, wired and wireless Pentium systems available in computing labs, classrooms, residence halls, libraries, and the student center for student use. The entire college campus is wireless, all students may bring laptops and access the network. There is unlimited access. There are no time limits and no fees. It is strongly recommended that all students have a personal computer. The college negotiates discount pricing on laptops for our students with Dell, Lenovo, and Apple.

Graduates: From July 1, 2008 to June 30, 2009, 643 bachelor's degrees were awarded. The most popular majors were business (33%), mass communications (13%), and psychology (10%). 66 companies recruited on campus in 2008-2009. In an average class, 50% graduate in 4 years or less, 60% graduate in 5 years or less, and 62% graduate in 6 years or less. Of the 2008 graduating class, 32% were enrolled in graduate school within 6 months of graduation, and 66% were employed.

Admissions Contact: Kevin Cavanagh, Assistant VP for College Admissions. E-Mail: *icad@iona.edu* Web: *www.iona.edu*

ITHACA COLLEGE C-3

Ithaca, NY 14850-7000
(607) 274-3124
(800) 429-4274; (607) 274-1900

Full-time: 2749 men, 3621 women	**Faculty:** 463; IIA, av$
Part-time: 32 men, 38 women	**Ph.D.s:** 92%
Graduate: 139 men, 315 women	**Student/Faculty:** 12 to 1
Year: semesters, summer session	**Tuition:** $32,060
Application Deadline: February 1	**Room & Board:** $11,780
Freshman Class: 11917 applied, 9471 accepted, 2027 enrolled	
SAT CR/M/W: 580/580/580	**ACT:** required
	VERY COMPETITIVE

Ithaca College, founded in 1892, is a private college offering undergraduate and graduate programs in business, communications, health science and human performance, humanities, sciences, music, and interdisciplinary and international studies. There are 6 undergraduate schools and 1 graduate school. In addition to regional accreditation, Ithaca has baccalaureate program accreditation with AACSB, APTA, NASM, and NRPA. The library contains 304,015 volumes, 34,440 microform items, and 34,160 audio/video tapes/CDs/DVDs, and subscribes to 44,425 periodicals including electronic. Computerized library services include interlibrary loans, database searching, Internet access, and laptop Internet portals. Special learning facilities include an art gallery, a radio station, a TV station, digital audio and video labs, speech, hearing, wellness, and physical therapy clinics, a greenhouse, a financial "trading room," an observatory, and electroacoustic music studios. The 650-acre campus is in a small town 250 miles northwest of New York City. Including any residence halls, there are 86 buildings.

Student Life: 56% of undergraduates are from out of state, mostly the Middle Atlantic. Students are from 47 states, 75 foreign countries, and Canada. 84% are from public schools. 84% are white; 16% African American. The average age of freshmen is 18; all undergraduates, 20. 14% do not continue beyond their first year; 77% remain to graduate.

Housing: 4300 students can be accommodated in college housing, which includes single-sex and coed dorms and on-campus apartments. In addition, there are honors houses, language houses, first-year students only housing, a quiet study residence hall, service and music honor fraternities, smoke-free buildings and floors, coed housing by buildings, honors floors, a substance-free building, multicultural housing, and several freshman seminar groups housed together. On-campus housing is guaranteed for all 4 years. 70% of students live on campus; of those, 95% remain on campus on weekends. All students may keep cars.

Activities: 1% of men belong to 4 national fraternities; 1% of women belong to 1 local sorority. There are 185 groups on campus, including academic, art, band, cheerleading, chess, choir, chorale, chorus, computers, cultural, dance, drama, drum and bugle corps, ethnic, film, gay, honors, international, jazz band, literary magazine, musical theater, newspaper, opera, orchestra, pep band, photography, political, professional, radio and TV, religious, social, social service, sports clubs, student government, and symphony. Popular campus events include pep rallies, Student Involvement Fair, and various multicultural awareness events.

Sports: There are 11 intercollegiate sports for men and 13 for women, and 24 intramural sports for men and 24 for women. Facilities include 5 gyms, 2 dance studios, a student union, indoor and outdoor pools, a fitness center and wellness clinic, tennis courts, and baseball, football, lacrosse, field hockey, and soccer fields.

Disabled Students: Facilities include wheelchair ramps, elevators, special parking, specially equipped restrooms, special class scheduling, lowered drinking fountains, and lowered telephones.

Services: Nonremedial tutoring is available.

Campus Safety and Security: Measures include 24-hour foot and vehicle patrol and security escort services. There are emergency telephones, lighted pathways/sidewalks, and crime prevention programs.

Programs of Study: Ithaca confers B.A., B.S., B.F.A., and Mus.B. degrees. Master's and doctoral degrees are also awarded. Bachelor's degrees are awarded in BIOLOGICAL SCIENCE (biochemistry and biology/biological science), BUSINESS (accounting, banking and finance, business administration and management, business economics, human resources, international business management, management science, marketing management, marketing/retailing/merchandising, organizational behavior, personnel management, recreation and leisure services, and sports management), COMMUNICATIONS AND THE ARTS (art, art history and appreciation, audio technology, broadcasting, communications, creative writing, dramatic arts, English, film arts, fine arts, French, German, jazz, journalism, languages, media arts, modern language, music, music performance, music theory and composition, musical theater, performing arts, photography, public relations, Spanish, speech/debate/rhetoric, sports media, studio art, telecommunications, theater design, theater management, video, and visual and performing arts), COMPUTER AND PHYSICAL SCIENCE (chemistry, computer mathematics, computer science, information sciences and systems, mathematics, and physics), EDUCATION (art education, athletic training, education, education of the deaf and hearing impaired, educational media, English education, foreign languages education, health education, mathematics education, middle school education, music education, physical education, secondary education, social studies education, speech correction, and sports studies), ENGINEERING AND ENVIRONMENTAL DESIGN (environmental science), HEALTH PROFESSIONS (allied health, clinical science, community health work, exercise science, health, health science, hospital administration, occupational therapy, physical therapy, predentistry, premedicine, public health, recreation therapy, rehabilitation therapy, speech pathology/audiology, speech therapy, and sports medicine), SOCIAL SCIENCE (anthropology, economics, German area studies, gerontology, history, industrial and organizational psychology, interdisciplinary studies, Italian studies, liberal arts/general studies, philosophy, physical fitness/movement, political science/government, prelaw, psychology, social studies, and sociology). Physical therapy, theater, and music are the strongest academically. Music, business administration, and television/radio are the largest.

Required: Students must successfully complete a minimum of 120 credit hours. In addition, each student must meet the requirements of a core curriculum, which varies with each school within the college and includes courses in the liberal arts and professional courses outside the student's major.

Special: Cross-registration is available with Cornell University and Wells College. Opportunities are also provided for internships, study abroad in more than 9 countries, a Washington semester, work-study programs, accelerated degree programs, dual majors, nondegree study, pass/fail options, and student-designed majors. A 3-2 engineering degree with Cornell University, Clarkson University, Rensselaer Polytechnic Institute, and SUNY Binghamton is available. There is also a 4-1 B.S./M.B.A. program, a 3-1 optometry program, a pre-law advisory program, and a 1-semester program in marine biology with Duke University and the Sea Education Association. There are 25 national honor societies, a freshman honors program, and 16 departmental honors programs.

Faculty/Classroom: 51% of faculty are male; 49% are female. All teach undergraduates. Graduate students teach 7% of introductory courses. The average class size in an introductory lecture is 21 and in a regular course is 17.

Admissions: 79% of the 2009-2010 applicants were accepted. The SAT scores for the 2009-2010 freshman class were: Critical Reading--13% below 500, 46% between 500 and 599, 34% between 600 and 700, and 7% above 700; Math--14% below 500, 42% between 500 and 599, 40% between 600 and 700, and 4% above 700; Writing--14% below 500, 45% between 500 and 599, 35% between 600 and 700, and 6% above 700. 58% of the current freshmen were in the top fifth of their class; 88% were in the top two fifths. There were 4 National Merit finalists. 12 freshmen graduated first in their class.

Requirements: The SAT or ACT is required. The ACT Optional Writing test is also required. In addition, In addition, applicants should be graduates of an accredited secondary school with a minimum of 16 Carnegie units, including 4 years of English, 3 each of math, science, and social studies, 2 of foreign language, and other college-preparatory electives. The GED is accepted. An essay is required, as is an audition for music and theater students. In some majors, a portfolio and an interview are recommended. AP and CLEP credits are accepted.

Procedure: Freshmen are admitted fall and spring. Entrance exams should be taken in spring of the junior year or fall of the senior year. There are early decision, early admissions, deferred admissions, and rolling admissions plans. Early decision applications should be filed by November 1; regular applications, by February 1 for fall entry; and December 1 for spring entry, along with a $60 fee. Notification of early decision is sent December 15; regular decision, April 15. Applications are accepted on-line.

Transfer: 162 transfer students enrolled in 2008-2009. Transfer applicants must submit SAT or ACT scores, a high school transcript, transcripts from previously attended colleges, and a personal recommendation from their adviser or Dean of Students. A minimum college GPA of 2.75 is recommended. 30 of 120 credits required for the bachelor's degree must be completed at Ithaca.

Visiting: There are regularly scheduled orientations for prospective students, including a campus tour and an interview with an admissions counselor. Fall open house programs offering personal meetings with faculty are available by appointment. There are guides for informal visits, visitors may sit in on classes, and stay overnight. To schedule a visit, contact the Director of Admission at admissions@ithaca.edu.

Financial Aid: In 2009-2010, 96% of all full-time freshmen and 89% of continuing full-time students received some form of financial aid. 74% of all full-time freshmen and 67% of continuing full-time students received need-based aid. The average freshman award was $30,905. Need-based scholarships or need-based grants averaged $19,799 ($45,185 maximum); need-based self-help aid (loans and jobs) averaged $7,585 ($15,900 maximum); and other non-need-based awards and non-need-based scholarships averaged $6,204 ($46,562 maximum). 45% of undergraduate students work part-time. Average annual earnings from campus work are $2400. Ithaca is a member of CSS. The CSS/Profile and FAFSA are required. The deadline for filing freshman financial aid applications for fall entry is February 1.

International Students: There are 111 international students enrolled. The school actively recruits these students. They must take the TOEFL with a minimum score of 550 on the paper-based TOEFL (PBT) or 80 on the Internet-based version (iBT). They must also take the SAT or ACT.

Computers: Wireless access is available. Students may access Ithaca College's network from any of the approximately 640 computers available for general student use in labs, classrooms, and the library as well as via wireless networks in campus residence halls and many other areas on campus. All students may access the system 24 hours a day. There are no time limits and no fees. Students enrolled in the School of Business should have a Windows laptop; School of Communications students should have a Mac laptop.

Graduates: From July 1, 2008 to June 30, 2009, 1403 bachelor's degrees were awarded. The most popular majors were business administration (13%), television/radio (7%), and music (5%). 130 companies recruited on campus in 2008-2009. In an average class, 2% graduate in 3 years or less, 71% graduate in 4 years or less, 77% graduate in 5 years or less, and 77% graduate in 6 years or less. Of the 2008 graduating class, 33% were enrolled in graduate school within 6 months of graduation and 83% were employed.

Admissions Contact: Gerard Turbide, Director of Admission. A campus DVD is available. E-mail: *admission@ithaca.edu*
Web: *www.ithaca.edu*

JULLIARD SCHOOL   D-5
New York, NY 10023-6588

	(212) 799-5000, ext. 223
	(212) 724-6420
Full-time: 270 men, 225 women	**Faculty:** n/av
Part-time: none	**Ph.D.s:** n/av
Graduate: 185 men, 165 women	**Student/Faculty:** n/av
Year: semesters	**Tuition:** $32,180
Application Deadline: December 1	**Room & Board:** $12,280
Freshman Class: n/av	**SPECIAL**

The Juilliard School, founded in 1905, is a private conservatory for dance, drama, and music. Figures in the above capsule and in this profile are approximate. The library contains 96,013 volumes, 1,399 microform items, and 25,960 audio/video tapes/CDs/DVDs, and subscribes to 230 periodicals including electronic. Computerized library services include interlibrary loans, database searching, Internet access, and laptop Internet portals. The campus is in an urban area at the Lincoln Center in New York City. Including any residence halls, there are 2 buildings.

Student Life: 87% of undergraduates are from out of state, mostly the Northeast. Students are from 47 states, 47 foreign countries, and Canada. 50% are white; 25% foreign nationals; 15% Asian American. The average age of freshmen is 18; all undergraduates, 20. 3% do not continue beyond their first year; 80% remain to graduate.

Housing: 350 students can be accommodated in college housing, which includes single-sex dorms. In addition, there are special-interest houses, All floors are smoke-free. There are quiet, alcohol-free, and single sex (all female) floors. On-campus housing is guaranteed for the freshman year only, is available on a first-come, first-served basis, and is available on a lottery system for upperclassmen. 60% of students live on campus; of those, 95% remain on campus on weekends. No one may keep cars.

Activities: There are no fraternities or sororities. There are 15 groups on campus, including band, book discussion, choir, chorale, chorus, community service, dance, drama, environmental, ethnic, gay, international, jazz band, marching band, opera, orchestra, professional, recreation, religious, social, social service, student government, and symphony. Popular campus events include performances by the Juilliard orchestras at Lincoln Center, dance concerts, and drama and opera.

Sports: There is no sports program at Juilliard. Facilities include a fitness center in the residence hall.

Disabled Students: All of the campus is accessible. Facilities include wheelchair ramps, elevators, specially equipped restrooms, lowered drinking fountains, and lowered telephones.

Services: Counseling and information services are available, as is tutoring in some subjects, including ear training, literature and materials of music, and English.

Campus Safety and Security: Measures include 24-hour foot and vehicle patrol and self-defense education. There are emergency telephones, lighted pathways/sidewalks, and video cameras, and turnstiles with ID card access.

Programs of Study: Juilliard confers B.Mus. and B.F.A. degrees. Master's and doctoral degrees are also awarded. Bachelor's degrees are awarded in COMMUNICATIONS AND THE ARTS (dance, dramatic arts, and music). Piano, voice, and violin are the largest.

Required: Each division has its own requirements for graduation.

Special: A joint program with Columbia College and Barnard College (at Columbia University) allows students to obtain a 5-year B.A.-B.-MM. degree. Internships are available with cultural organizations in New York City. There is study abroad in music academy in England. Work-study programs, accelerated degrees and dual majors in music.

Faculty/Classroom: 67% of faculty are male; 33% are female. No introductory courses are taught by graduate students.

Requirements: A high school diploma or GED is required. Students are accepted primarily on the basis of personal auditions rather than tests. Important factors in the admissions decision are evidence of special talent.

Procedure: Freshmen are admitted in the fall. Personal auditions should be completed in December for opera, January & February for drama; February & March for dance; March for music; February & March for jazz. Applications should be filed by December 1 for fall entry, along with a $100 fee. Notifications are sent April 1. Applications are accepted on-line. A waiting list is maintained.

Transfer: 20 transfer students enrolled in a recent year. Transfer applicants must audition in person. 2 of 142 credits required for the bachelor's degree must be completed at Juilliard.

Visiting: There are regularly scheduled orientations for prospective students, including guided tours and question-and-answer sessions, Monday to Friday at noon. Visitors may sit in on classes. To schedule a visit, contact Admissions Office at admissions@juilliard.edu.

Financial Aid: In a recent year, 92% of all full-time freshmen and 85% of continuing full-time students received some form of financial aid. 90% of all full-time freshmen and 77% of continuing full-time students received need-based aid. The average freshmen award was $26,745, with $20,877 ($35,460 maximum) from need-based scholarships or need-based grants; $6,577 ($11,000 maximum) from need-based self-help aid (loans and jobs); and $2,234 ($5,000 maximum) from other non-need-based awards and non-need-based scholarships. 61% of undergraduate students worked part-time. Average annual earnings from campus work were $1094. The average financial indebtedness of the 2009 graduate was $25,332. The FAFSA and the college's own financial statement are required. Check with the school for current application deadlines.

International Students: There were 82 international students enrolled in a recent year. They must take the TOEFL and the college's own test, TWE. All students must audition in person.

Computers: Wireless access is available. All students may access the system. Students are limited to during lab hours. There are no fees.

Graduates: In a recent year, 102 bachelor's degrees were awarded. The most popular majors were music (70%), dance (20%), and drama (10%). In an average class, 2% graduate in 3 years or less, 69% graduate in 4 years or less, 71% graduate in 5 years or less, and 73% graduate in 6 years or less.

Admissions Contact: Office of Admissions E-Mail: *admissions@juilliard.edu* Web: *www.juilliard.edu*

KEUKA COLLEGE   B-3
Keuka Park, NY 14478   (315) 536-5254, ext. 254
(800) 33-KEUKA; (315) 536-5386

Full-time: 1185 men and women	Faculty: IIB, -$
Part-time: 445 men and women	Ph.D.s: n/av
Graduate: none	Student/Faculty: n/av
Year: 4-1-4, summer session	Tuition: $21,300
Application Deadline: open	Room & Board: $9000
Freshman Class: n/av	
SAT or ACT: required	COMPETITIVE

Keuka College, founded in 1890, is an independent college affiliated with American Baptist Churches and offers instruction in the liberal arts. The figures in the above capsule and in this profile are approximate. In addition to regional accreditation, Keuka has baccalaureate program accreditation with AHEA, CSWE, and NLN. The library contains 87,263 volumes, 4,190 microform items, and 4,190 audio/video tapes/CDs/DVDs, and subscribes to 18,151 periodicals including electronic. Computerized library services include interlibrary loans and database searching. Special learning facilities include a learning resource center, art gallery, and radio station. The 203-acre campus is in a rural area 60 miles south of Rochester. Including any residence halls, there are 19 buildings.

Student Life: 94% of undergraduates are from New York. Others are from 26 states, 2 foreign countries, and Canada. 80% are from public schools. 90% are white. The average age of freshmen is 18; all undergraduates, 23. 27% do not continue beyond their first year; 52% remain to graduate.

Housing: 719 students can be accommodated in college housing, which includes single-sex and coed dorms. In addition, there are honors houses, special-interest houses, cooperative living, and leadership and wellness housing. On-campus housing is guaranteed for all 4 years. 55% of students live on campus; of those, 60% remain on campus on weekends. Alcohol is not permitted. Upperclassmen may keep cars.

Activities: There are no fraternities or sororities. There are 45 groups on campus, including art, cheerleading, choir, chorale, community service, dance, drama, ethnic, honors, international, leadership, literary magazine, newspaper, political, professional, religious, social, social service, student government, and yearbook. Popular campus events include Spring Weekend, May Day, and Family Weekend.

Sports: There are 7 intercollegiate sports for men and 8 for women, and 8 intramural sports for men and 8 for women. Facilities include an Olympic-size pool, a gym, a fitness center, a weight room, and an outdoor athletic facility.

Disabled Students: 65% of the campus is accessible. Facilities include wheelchair ramps, elevators, special parking, specially equipped restrooms, special class scheduling, lowered drinking fountains, and special housing.

Services: Counseling and information services are available, as is tutoring in every subject. There is a reader service for the blind, and remedial math, reading, and writing. Individual and group tutoring is available free through the college's academic support services.

Campus Safety and Security: Measures include 24-hour foot and vehicle patrol and self-defense education. There are shuttle buses, emergency telephones, and lighted pathways/sidewalks.

Programs of Study: Keuka confers B.A. and B.S. degrees. Master's degrees are also awarded. Bachelor's degrees are awarded in BIOLOGICAL SCIENCE (biochemistry and biology/biological science), BUSINESS (accounting, business administration and management, hotel/motel and restaurant management, and marketing/retailing/merchandising), COMMUNICATIONS AND THE ARTS (American Sign Language, communications, and English), EDUCATION (elementary education and secondary education), ENGINEERING AND ENVIRONMENTAL DESIGN (environmental science), HEALTH PROFESSIONS (medical laboratory technology, nursing, occupational therapy, predentistry, premedicine, and preveterinary science), SOCIAL SCIENCE (criminal justice, political science/government, prelaw, psychology, social work, and sociology). Occupational therapy, biology, and education are the strongest academically. Occupational therapy, education, and management are the largest.

Required: Students must complete 1 field period combining academic study and professional experience for each year of enrollment. The core curriculum consists of 43 to 46 credits, including but not limited to required courses in phys ed, computer science, and integrative studies. A total of 120 credit hours is required for graduation with a minimum of 30 credits in the major and a major and cumulative GPA of 2.0.

Special: There are co-op programs with other members of the Rochester Area Colleges Consortium. The college offers internships, study abroad, a Washington semester, dual majors, and student-designed majors. Credit is also given by exam and for work experience. There are 16 national honor societies.

Faculty/Classroom: 42% of faculty are male; 58% are female. All teach undergraduates. No introductory courses are taught by graduate students. The average class size in an introductory lecture is 20; in a laboratory is 15; and in a regular course is 20.

Requirements: The SAT or ACT is required. In addition, students should graduate from an accredited secondary school with a minimum GPA of 2.8. The GED is accepted. A minimum of 15 Carnegie units is required, including 4 years of English, 3 of history, 2 to 3 of math and science, 2 of foreign language, and 1 of social studies. An essay is required, and an interview is recommended. AP and CLEP credits are accepted. Important factors in the admissions decision are recommendations by school officials, extracurricular activities record, and leadership record.

Procedure: Freshmen are admitted fall and spring. Entrance exams should be taken in the spring of the junior year or the fall of the senior year. There are early decision, deferred admissions and rolling admissions plans. Check with the school for current application deadlines. The fall 2009 application fee was $30. Notification is sent on a rolling basis. Applications are accepted on-line.

Transfer: Applicants must take the SAT or ACT and submit transcripts. An interview is recommended. A minimum GPA of 2.5 is required in college work. 30 of 120 credits required for the bachelor's degree must be completed at Keuka.

Visiting: There are regularly scheduled orientations for prospective students, including open houses held in October and April, when students can speak with faculty, student affairs and financial aid representatives, and current students. There are guides for informal visits; visitors may sit in on classes and stay overnight. To schedule a visit, contact the Admissions Office at (315) 279-4411.

Financial Aid: The FAFSA and the college's own financial statement are required. Check with the school for current application deadlines.

International Students: They must take the TOEFL.

Computers: All students may access the system. There are no time limits and no fees. It is strongly recommended that all students have a personal computer.

Admissions Contact: Claudine Ninestine, Director of Admissions. A campus DVD is available. E-Mail: *admissions@mail.keuka.edu* Web: *www.keuka.edu*

LABORATORA INSTITUTE OF MERCHANDISING
(See LIM College)

LE MOYNE COLLEGE   C-3
Syracuse, NY 13214-1301   (315) 445-4300
(800) 333-4733; (315) 445-4711

Full-time: 915 men, 1417 women	Faculty: 156; IIA, av$
Part-time: 112 men, 340 women	Ph.D.s: 94%
Graduate: 252 men, 488 women	Student/Faculty: 15 to 1
Year: semesters, summer session	Tuition: $25,780
Application Deadline: February 1	Room & Board: $9990
Freshman Class: 4526 applied, 3023 accepted, 608 enrolled	
SAT CR/M: 540/560	ACT: 23 VERY COMPETITIVE

Le Moyne College, founded in 1946, is a private liberal arts and sciences institution affiliated with the Roman Catholic Society of Jesus (Jesuit) and offers undergraduate and graduate degrees in a variety of disciplines. In addition to regional accreditation, Le Moyne has baccalaureate program accreditation with AACSB and TEAC. The library contains 268,041 volumes, 614,968 microform items, and 10,502 audio/video tapes/CDs/DVDs, and subscribes to 57,437 periodicals including electronic. Computerized library services include interlibrary loans, database searching, Internet access, and laptop Internet portals. Special learning facilities include a learning resource center, art gallery, radio station, TV station, and W. Carroll Coyne Performing Arts Center. The 161-acre campus is in a suburban area on the eastern edge of Syracuse. Including any residence halls, there are 37 buildings.

Student Life: 94% of undergraduates are from New York. Others are from 25 states, 33 foreign countries, and Canada. 84% are from public schools. 84% are white; 16% African American. 44% are Buddhist, Muslim, and other; 31% Catholic. The average age of freshmen is 18; all undergraduates, 20. 16% do not continue beyond their first year; 72% remain to graduate.

Housing: 1562 students can be accommodated in college housing, which includes single-sex and coed dorms, on-campus apartments, and off-campus apartments. In addition, there are special-interest houses and living learning communities. On-campus housing is guaranteed for all 4 years. 63% of students live on campus; of those, 85% remain on campus on weekends. All students may keep cars.

Activities: There are no fraternities or sororities. There are 70 groups on campus, including art, band, chess, choir, chorale, chorus, computers, dance, drama, environmental, ethnic, film, honors, international, jazz band, literary magazine, musical threater, newspaper, pep band, photography, political, professional, radio and TV, religious, social, social service, student government, and yearbook. Popular campus events include Spring Olympics, Halloween Dance, and Snowball Holiday Party.

Sports: There are 8 intercollegiate sports for men and 8 for women, and 9 intramural sports for men and 8 for women. Facilities include a

2500-seat gym, indoor batting cages, team rooms, a 25-yard lap pool with diving board, a whirlpool, a fitness center, an athletic training room, a jogging track, racquetball courts, a recreational gym, and locker rooms. Outdoor facilities include fields for intercollegiate baseball, softball, soccer, and lacrosse, tennis courts, a cross-country trail, and several intramural and club sports fields.

Disabled Students: 96% of the campus is accessible. Facilities include wheelchair ramps, elevators, special parking, specially equipped rest rooms, lowered drinking fountains, lowered telephones, special housing, automatic door openers, strobe fire alarm system, and wheelchair tables in classrooms.

Services: Counseling and information services are available, as is tutoring in some subjects, including math, biology, chemistry, physics, economics, philosophy, Spanish, French, German, and Latin. There is a reader service for the blind and remedial math and writing. Study groups are available for selected courses. Writing tutor support is available for all subjects.

Campus Safety and Security: Measures include 24-hour foot and vehicle patrol, emergency notification system, self-defense education, and security escort services. There are shuttle buses, emergency telephones, lighted pathways/sidewalks, access controls for dorms/residences, 8 blue-light security phones, 80 stationary closed-circuit security cameras, AT&T campuswide card access, and 7 pan/tilt/zoom closed-circuit security cameras.

Programs of Study: Le Moyne confers B.A. and B.S. degrees. Master's degrees are also awarded. Bachelor's degrees are awarded in BIOLOGICAL SCIENCE (biochemistry, biology/biological science, and ecology), BUSINESS (accounting, banking and finance, business administration and management, human resources, labor studies, management information systems, marketing management, operations management, and organizational leadership and management), COMMUNICATIONS AND THE ARTS (advertising, communications, creative writing, dramatic arts, English, film arts, French, journalism, literature, media arts, public relations, radio/television technology, and Spanish), COMPUTER AND PHYSICAL SCIENCE (actuarial science, applied mathematics, chemistry, computer science, information sciences and systems, mathematics, physical sciences, physics, science, and statistics), EDUCATION (elementary education, English education, foreign languages education, mathematics education, middle school education, science education, secondary education, social studies education, special education, and teaching English as a second/foreign language (TESOL/TEFOL)), ENGINEERING AND ENVIRONMENTAL DESIGN (environmental science), HEALTH PROFESSIONS (nursing, predentistry, premedicine, preoptometry, prepharmacy, prepodiatry, and preveterinary science), SOCIAL SCIENCE (anthropology, criminology, economics, forensic studies, history, human services, international studies, law enforcement and corrections, peace studies, philosophy, political science/government, prelaw, psychology, religion, and sociology). Biology, psychology, and accounting are the largest.

Required: A core curriculum of 14 courses in the humanities, natural sciences, and social sciences is required. Students must earn a GPA of 2.0, 30 hours in the major, and 120 total credit hours to graduate.

Special: Internships are available to students in all majors. A campus work-study program, study abroad in 10 countries, dual majors, and a Washington semester are offered. A 3-2 engineering degree is available with Manhattan College, Clarkson University, University of Detroit, and Syracuse University, and there are early assurance medical and dental programs. 3-3 and 3-4 dental, podiatry, and optometry programs are offered. Some pass/fail options are offered. There are 14 national honor societies, a freshman honors program, and 11 departmental honors programs.

Faculty/Classroom: 57% of faculty are male; 43% are female. All teach and do research. No introductory courses are taught by graduate students. The average class size in an introductory lecture is 21; in a laboratory is 17; and in a regular course is 20.

Admissions: 67% of the 2009-2010 applicants were accepted. The SAT scores for the 2009-2010 freshman class were: Critical Reading-- 25% below 500, 51% between 500 and 599, 22% between 600 and 700, and 2% above 700; Math--18% below 500, 50% between 500 and 599, 30% between 600 and 700, and 2% above 700. The ACT scores were 23% below 21, 34% between 21 and 23, 25% between 24 and 26, 8% between 27 and 28, and 10% above 28. 45% of the current freshmen were in the top fifth of their class; 81% were in the top two-fifths. 1 freshman graduated first in the class.

Requirements: The SAT or ACT is required. In addition, students should graduate from an accredited high school having completed 17 academic units that include 4 in English and social studies, 3 to 4 each in math and science, and 3 in foreign language. A personal statement and letters of recommendation from a teacher and a counselor are required. AP and CLEP credits are accepted. Important factors in the admissions decision are recommendations by school officials, advanced placement or honors courses, and extracurricular activities record.

Procedure: Freshmen are admitted fall and spring. Entrance exams should be taken in the spring of the junior year or fall of the senior year. There are early decision, early admissions, deferred admissions, and roll-

ing admissions plans. Early decision applications should be filed by December 1; regular applications, by February 1 for fall entry and December 1 for spring entry, along with a $35 fee. Notification of early decision is sent December 15; regular decision is sent on a rolling basis. Applications are accepted on-line. 95 applicants were on a recent waiting list, 7 were accepted.

Transfer: 240 transfer students enrolled in 2008-2009. A 2.6 GPA is required for admission to most programs. A completed application for transfer admission, official college transcripts, and a personal statement must be submitted. Official high school transcripts and SAT or ACT scores are needed for students with fewer than 24 completed college credits at the time of application. 30 of 120 credits required for the bachelor's degree must be completed at Le Moyne.

Visiting: There are regularly scheduled orientations for prospective students, including a campus tour and an interview with admissions counselors. Accepted students are invited to attend class and stay overnight in a residence hall. There are guides for informal visits and visitors may sit in on classes. To schedule a visit, contact the Admission Office at (315) 445-4300 or (800) 333-4733.

Financial Aid: In 2009-2010, 94% of all full-time freshmen and 91% of continuing full-time students received some form of financial aid. 81% of all full-time freshmen and 76% of continuing full-time students received need-based aid. The average freshmen award was $20,230, with $11,013 ($33,400 maximum) from need-based scholarships or need-based grants; $4,152 ($5,029 maximum) from need-based self-help aid (loans and jobs); $6,652 ($35,239 maximum) from non-need-based athletic scholarships; and $10,399 ($19,500 maximum) from other non-need-based awards and non-need-based scholarships. 41% of undergraduate students work part-time. Average annual earnings from campus work are $833. The average financial indebtedness of the 2009 graduate was $27,668. Le Moyne is a member of CSS. The FAFSA and the college's own financial statement are required. The deadline for filing freshman financial aid applications for fall entry is February 1.

International Students: There are 20 international students enrolled. The school actively recruits these students. They must take the TOEFL with a minimum score of 550 on the paper-based TOEFL (PBT) or 79 on the Internet-based version (iBT). They must also take the SAT or ACT.

Computers: Wireless access is available. About 325 PCs and Macs are connected to the campus network in public and departmental labs across campus, providing access to the library system, the Internet, and Novell servers with a multitude of applications. There is access to personal space on these servers. Access from residence hall rooms includes the library system, personal space, and the Internet. Wireless is available throughout most of the campus, including all academic areas. Most residential halls also have wireless capability. All students may access the system 24 hours a day. There are no time limits and no fees.

Graduates: From July 1, 2008 to June 30, 2009, 593 bachelor's degrees were awarded. The most popular majors were psychology (16%), biology (10%), and English (8%). 93 companies recruited on campus in 2008-2009. In an average class, 66% graduate in 4 years or less, 76% graduate in 5 years or less, and 78% graduate in 6 years or less. Of the 2008 graduating class, 38% were enrolled in graduate school within a year of graduation, and 88% were employed.

Admissions Contact: Dennis J. Nicholson, Director of Admission. A campus DVD is available. E-Mail: *admission@lemoyne.edu* Web: *www.lemoyne.edu*

LIM COLLEGE   D-5
Laboratory Institute of Merchandising

New York, NY 10022-5268

(212) 752-1530
(800) 677-1323; (212) 750-3432

Full-time: 76 men, 1226 women	**Faculty:** 24
Part-time: 6 men, 49 women	**Ph.Ds:** 29%
Graduate: none	**Student/Faculty:** 54 to 1
Year: semesters, summer session	**Tuition:** $20,425
Application Deadline: open	**Room & Board:** $19,400
Freshman Class: 898 applied, 717 accepted, 259 enrolled	
SAT CR/M: 480/468	**ACT:** 20 **LESS COMPETITIVE**

LIM College, formerly the Laboratory Institute of Merchandising, founded in 1939, is a private college offering programs in fashion merchandising, marketing, management, and visual merchandising. There is 1 undergraduate school. The library contains 17,500 volumes and 829 audio/video tapes/CDs/DVDs, and subscribes to 7000 periodicals including electronic. Computerized library services include database searching, Internet access, and laptop Internet portals. Special learning facilities include a learning resource center, color and materials lab, and CAD lab. The campus is in an urban area in mid-town Manhattan. Including any residence halls, there are 7 buildings.

Student Life: 58% of undergraduates are from out of state, mostly the Middle Atlantic. Students are from 34 states, 7 foreign countries, and Canada. 80% are from public schools. 67% are white; 15% Hispanic; 12% African American. The average age of freshmen is 18; all undergraduates, 20. 31% do not continue beyond their first year; 64% remain to graduate.

Housing: 355 students can be accommodated in college housing, which includes coed dorms. On-campus housing is available on a first-come, first-served basis. 75% of students commute. Alcohol is not permitted. No one may keep cars.

Activities: There are no fraternities or sororities. There are 12 groups on campus, including art, creative writing, dance, entrepreneurial, ethnic, fashion, film, newspaper, photography, professional, religious, SIFE, social service, student government, visual merchandising, and yearbook. Popular campus events include an annual fashion show, a ski trip, and a Halloween costume party.

Sports: There is no sports program at LIM.

Disabled Students: All of the campus is accessible. Facilities include elevators and specially equipped restrooms.

Services: Counseling and information services are available, as is tutoring in most subjects. There is remedial math, reading, and writing.

Campus Safety and Security: There is controlled access to dorms/residences.

Programs of Study: LIM confers B.B.A. and B.P.S. degrees. Associate and master's degrees are also awarded. Bachelor's degrees are awarded in BUSINESS (business administration and management, fashion merchandising, and marketing management). Fashion merchandising is the largest.

Required: Students must complete 32 credits in the liberal arts and a minimum of 82 in fashion/business courses. Freshmen and sophomores must successfully complete a 3-credit work project each year. Seniors must complete a 13-credit, semester-long co-op program. A total of 126 credits and a GPA of 2.0 are required to graduate.

Special: Internships are required in the first, second, and fourth years. Study abroad is available in China, Italy, Spain, France, and England. There are co-op programs as well as work-study programs with major department stores and specialty shops, manufacturers, showrooms, magazine publishers, and cosmetics companies. There is 1 national honor society and a freshman honors program.

Faculty/Classroom: 52% of faculty are male; 48% are female. All teach undergraduates. No introductory courses are taught by graduate students. The average class size in a regular course is 18.

Admissions: 80% of the 2009-2010 applicants were accepted. The SAT scores for the 2009-2010 freshman class were: Critical Reading--61% below 500, 34% between 500 and 599, and 5% between 600 and 700; Math--67% below 500, 28% between 500 and 599, and 5% between 600 and 700. The ACT scores were 58% below 21, 29% between 21 and 23, and 13% between 24 and 26.

Requirements: The SAT or ACT is required. In addition, applicants should be high school graduates or hold the GED. An essay and letters of recommendation are required. An interview and an activity sheet are recommended. AP and CLEP credits are accepted. Important factors in the admissions decision are leadership record, recommendations by school officials, and personality/intangible qualities.

Procedure: Freshmen are admitted fall and spring. Entrance exams should be taken the summer before the entering semester. There are early admissions, deferred admissions, and rolling admissions plans. Application deadlines are open. Application fee is $40. Applications are accepted on-line. A waiting list is maintained.

Transfer: 185 transfer students enrolled in 2008-2009. Applicants must also submit their official high school and college transcripts. Students with fewer than 30 college credits must submit SAT or ACT scores (waived for applicants over the age of 25). Interviews, essay, and letters of recommendation are required of all applicants. 46 of 126 credits required for the bachelor's degree must be completed at LIM.

Visiting: There are regularly scheduled orientations for prospective students, including tours and presentations on admissions, curriculum, career opportunities, and financial aid. There are guides for informal visits; visitors may sit in on classes and stay overnight. To schedule a visit, contact the Admissions Office.

Financial Aid: In a recent year, 79% of all full-time freshmen and 70% of continuing full-time students received some form of financial aid. 64% of all full-time freshmen and 53% of continuing full-time students received need-based aid. Need-based scholarships or need-based grants averaged $5037 ($12,310 maximum); need-based self-help aid (loans and jobs) averaged $3470 ($6300 maximum); and non-need-based awards and non-need-based scholarships averaged $3277 ($9050 maximum). Average annual earnings from campus work are $1491. The average financial indebtedness of a recent graduate was $22,027. The FAFSA and the college's own financial statement are required. The priority date for freshman financial aid applications for fall entry is April 1.

International Students: There are 134 international students enrolled. They must take the TOEFL with a minimum score of 550 on the paper-based TOEFL (PBT) or 80 on the Internet-based version (iBT). They must also take the SAT or ACT.

Computers: There are 335 computers connected to the college network throughout campus, all with Internet access. All campus locations have wireless access. Housing facilities all have high-speed Internet access. All students may access the system. There are no time limits and no fees.

Graduates: From July 1, 2008 to June 30, 2009, 222 bachelor's degrees were awarded. The most popular majors were fashion merchandising (55%), marketing (33%), and visual merchandising (7%). 70 companies recruited on campus in 2008-2009. In an average class, 1% graduate in 3 years or less, 54% graduate in 4 years or less, 57% graduate in 5 years or less, and 64% graduate in 6 years or less. Of the 2008 graduating class, 94% were employed within 6 months of graduation.

Admissions Contact: Kristina Ortiz, Assistant Dean of Admissions. E-mail: *admissions@limcollege.edu* Web: *www.limcollege.edu*

LONG ISLAND UNIVERSITY SYSTEM

The Long Island University System, established in 1886, is a private system in New York. It is governed by a board of trustees, whose chief administrator is the president. The primary goal of the system is to provide Long Island's communities with high-quality, humane higher education. The main priorities are teaching in the liberal arts and professions, extending higher education to underrepresented populations, and providing every student with opportunities for cooperative education placements in a field related to his or her major. Profiles of the 4-year campuses are included in this section.

LONG ISLAND UNIVERSITY/BROOKLYN CAMPUS D-5
Brooklyn, NY 11201

(718) 488-1292
(800) LIU-PLAN; (718) 797-2399

Full-time: 1305 men, 3005 women	**Faculty:** IIA, +$
Part-time: 255 men, 805 women	**Ph.D.s:** n/av
Graduate: 910 men, 1210 women	**Student/Faculty:** n/av
Year: semesters, summer session	**Tuition:** $19,000
Application Deadline: open	**Room & Board:** $7500
Freshman Class: n/av	
SAT or ACT: recommended	**COMPETITIVE**

Long Island University/Brooklyn Campus, founded in 1926, is part of the Long Island University system. It is a private institution offering programs in liberal arts and sciences, pharmacy, health professions, education, business, nursing, and special programs. It is largely a commuter school. The figures in the above capsule and in this profile are approximate. There are 6 undergraduate schools and 5 graduate schools. In addition to regional accreditation, LIU has baccalaureate program accreditation with ACPE and NLN. The library contains 2.1 million volumes, 813,544 microform items, and 7,902 audio/video tapes/CDs/DVDs, and subscribes to 8,042 periodicals including electronic. Computerized library services include interlibrary loans. Special learning facilities include a learning resource center, art gallery, radio station, and TV station. The 10-acre campus is in an urban area. Including any residence halls, there are 11 buildings.

Student Life: 86% of undergraduates are from New York. Others are from 35 states, 21 foreign countries, and Canada. 75% are from public schools. 43% are African American; 27% white; 19% Hispanic; 11% Asian American. The average age of freshmen is 21; all undergraduates, 25. 36% do not continue beyond their first year; 61% remain to graduate.

Housing: 525 students can be accommodated in college housing, which includes single-sex and coed dorms and married student housing. On-campus housing is available on a first-come and first-served basis. 89% of students commute. Alcohol is not permitted. No one may keep cars.

Activities: There are 75 groups on campus, including band, cheerleading, chess, chorale, computers, dance, ethnic, honors, international, jazz band, literary magazine, newspaper, pep band, photography, political, radio and TV, religious, student government, and yearbook.

Sports: There are 7 intercollegiate sports for men and 6 for women, and 6 intramural sports for men and 6 for women. Facilities include a baseball/soccer field and a basketball gym.

Disabled Students: All of the campus is accessible. Facilities include wheelchair ramps, elevators, specially equipped restrooms, special class scheduling, lowered drinking fountains, and lowered telephones.

Services: Counseling and information services are available, as is tutoring in most subjects. There is remedial math, reading, and writing.

Campus Safety and Security: Measures include 24-hour foot and vehicle patrol. There are emergency telephones and lighted pathways/sidewalks.

Programs of Study: LIU confers B.A., B.S., and B.F.A. degrees. Associates, master's, and doctoral degrees are also awarded. Bachelor's degrees are awarded in BIOLOGICAL SCIENCE (biology/biological science), BUSINESS (accounting, banking and finance, business administration and management, and marketing/retailing/merchandising), COMMUNICATIONS AND THE ARTS (broadcasting, communications, English, fine arts, journalism, languages, music, and speech/debate/rhetoric), COMPUTER AND PHYSICAL SCIENCE (chemistry, computer science, information sciences and systems, and mathematics), EDUCATION (art education, business education, early childhood education, elementary education, music education, science education, secondary education, special education, and teaching English as a second/foreign language (TESOL/TEFOL)), HEALTH PROFESSIONS (nursing, occupational therapy, pharmacy, physical therapy, physician's assistant, predentistry, and premedicine), SOCIAL SCIENCE (anthropology, economics, history, philosophy, political science/government, prelaw, psychology, social science, social work, and sociology). Health professions, pharmacy, and liberal arts are the strongest academically. Health professions, liberal arts, and business are the largest.

Required: Proficiency courses include basic English and math, English composition, and speech. Distribution requirements are 6 credits each in foreign language, math, and science. Students must complete a core curriculum of 18 credits in the humanities, 12 in social sciences, 8 in natural sciences, and 6 in math. A total of 128 credits (197 for pharmacy) is required for graduation, with 36 credits in the major, and a GPA of 2.0.

Special: Accelerated degree programs are available in all majors. Students may cross-register with other LIU campuses. Internships in career-related jobs provide cooperative education credits. Study abroad, dual-majors, credit for life, military, and work experience, and pass/fail options are also offered. There is a freshman honors program.

Faculty/Classroom: All teach undergraduates. No introductory courses are taught by graduate students. The average class size in a regular course is 22.

Requirements: The SAT or ACT is recommended. LIU requires applicants to be in the upper 75% of their class. A GPA of 2.0 is required. AP and CLEP credits are accepted. Important factors in the admissions decision are recommendations by school officials, advanced placement or honors courses, and evidence of special talent.

Procedure: Freshmen are admitted to all sessions. Entrance exams should be taken by January of the senior year. There are deferred admissions and rolling admissions plans. Application deadlines are open. Application fee is $30. Notification is sent on a rolling basis. Applications are accepted on-line.

Transfer: A GPA of 2.5 is required. 32 of 128 credits required for the bachelor's degree must be completed at LIU.

Visiting: There are regularly scheduled orientations for prospective students. Visitors may sit in on classes. To schedule a visit, contact the Admissions Office at (718) 488-1011.

Financial Aid: The CSS/Profile and the college's own financial statement are required. Check with the school for current application deadlines.

International Students: The school actively recruits these students. They must take the TOEFL. They must also take the SAT or ACT.

Computers: All students may access the system during library hours. There are no time limits and no fees.

Admissions Contact: Richard Sunday, Acting Dean of Admissions. E-Mail: *attend@liu.edu* Web: *www.liu.edu/campus/brooklyn*

LONG ISLAND UNIVERSITY/C.W. POST CAMPUS D-5

Brookville, NY 11548-1300

(516) 299-2900
(800) LIU-PLAN; (516) 299-2137

Full-time: 1600 men, 2400 women	**Faculty:** IIA, +$
Part-time: 1100 men, 1500 women	**Ph.D.s:** n/av
Graduate: 1000 men, 2600 women	**Student/Faculty:** n/av
Year: semesters, summer session	**Tuition:** $28,348
Application Deadline: open	**Room & Board:** $10,540
Freshman Class: 950 accepted, 803 enrolled	
SAT CR/M/W: 520/500/510	**ACT:** 21 **COMPETITIVE**

Long Island University/C.W. Post Campus, founded in 1954 as part of the private Long Island University system, offers 100 undergraduate and 63 graduate majors in education, liberal arts and sciences, accountancy, business, public service, health professions and nursing, and information and computer science. Enrollment figures in the above capsule are approximate. There are 6 undergraduate schools and 6 graduate schools. In addition to regional accreditation, C.W. Post has baccalaureate program accreditation with AACSB, ADA, ASLA, CAHEA, CSWE, and NLN. The library contains 1.1 million volumes, 834,413 microform items, and 9606 audio/video tapes/CDs/DVDs, and subscribes to 10,999 periodicals including electronic. Computerized library services include interlibrary loans and database searching. Special learning facilities include a learning resource center, art gallery, radio station, TV station, art museum, tax institute, speech and hearing center, center for business research, federal depository, and multimedia computer center. The 307-acre campus is in a suburban area 25 miles east of New York City, on the former estate of Marjorie Merriweather Post. Including any residence halls, there are 53 buildings.

Student Life: 91% of undergraduates are from New York. Others are from 32 states, 46 foreign countries, and Canada. 71% are from public schools. 13% are white. The average age of freshmen is 18; all undergraduates, 21. 31% do not continue beyond their first year; 37% remain to graduate.

Housing: 1710 students can be accommodated in college housing, which includes single-sex and coed dorms. In addition, there is a quiet hall. On-campus housing is guaranteed for all 4 years. 60% of students commute. All students may keep cars.

Activities: 1% of men belong to 4 national fraternities; 3% of women belong to 9 national sororities. There are 80 groups on campus, including art, band, chamber singing, cheerleading, choir, chorale, chorus, dance, drama, equestrian, ethnic, film, gay, honors, international, jazz band, literary magazine, Madrigal, musical theater, newspaper, orchestra, pep band, photography, political, professional, radio and TV, religious, Renaissance music, social, social service, student government, and vocal jazz. Popular campus events include Theater Festival, Spring Fling, and Cereal Bowl: The Inter-Residential Hall Competition.

Sports: There are 7 intercollegiate sports for men and 10 for women, and 5 intramural sports for men and 5 for women. Facilities include a 5000-seat football stadium, an equestrian center, tennis courts, 70 acres of baseball, soccer, lacrosse, softball, and practice fields, a recreational center with an 8-lane swimming pool, 3 basketball courts with spectator seating for 3000, racquetball courts, an indoor track, and weight and aerobic rooms.

Disabled Students: 75% of the campus is accessible. Facilities include wheelchair ramps, elevators, special parking, specially equipped rest rooms, special class scheduling, lowered drinking fountains, lowered telephones, special housing, and electric doors.

Services: Counseling and information services are available, as is tutoring in most subjects. There is a reader service for the blind, remedial math, reading, and writing, and an academic resource center for learning-disabled students.

Campus Safety and Security: Measures include 24-hour foot and vehicle patrol, self-defense education, and security escort services. There are shuttle buses, emergency telephones, lighted pathways/sidewalks, restricted night access to campus, card-access residence entrances, and an electronic keyless locking system for dorm rooms.

Programs of Study: C.W. Post confers B.A., B.F.A., B.S., and B.S.Ed. degrees. Associates, master's, and doctoral degrees are also awarded. Bachelor's degrees are awarded in AGRICULTURE (conservation and regulation), BIOLOGICAL SCIENCE (biology/biological science, molecular biology, and nutrition), BUSINESS (accounting, banking and finance, business administration and management, and marketing/retailing/merchandising), COMMUNICATIONS AND THE ARTS (arts administration/management, broadcasting, communications, dance, dramatic arts, English, film arts, fine arts, French, German, Italian, journalism, music, photography, public relations, and Spanish), COMPUTER AND PHYSICAL SCIENCE (chemistry, computer science, geology, information sciences and systems, mathematics, physics, and radiological technology), EDUCATION (art education, early childhood education, elementary education, English education, foreign languages education, health education, music education, science education, and secondary education), ENGINEERING AND ENVIRONMENTAL DESIGN (preengineering), HEALTH PROFESSIONS (art therapy, biomedical science, health care administration, medical laboratory technology, medical records administration/services, nursing, predentistry, premedicine, prepharmacy, and speech pathology/audiology), SOCIAL SCIENCE (criminal justice, economics, forensic studies, geography, history, international studies, philosophy, political science/government, prelaw, psychology, public administration, and social work). Accounting, radiologic technology, and biology are the strongest academically. Business, education, and media arts are the largest.

Required: Core requirements include 9 credits each of history and philosophy, 8 of lab science, 6 each of language and literature, arts, political science and economics, sociology, psychology, and geography or anthropology, and 3 of math. A minimum of 128 credits is required to graduate. GPA requirements range from 2.0 to 2.5 in most departments, 3.0 in interdisciplinary studies. Students must demonstrate competency in writing, quantitative skills, computer skills, oral communications, and library use.

Special: There is cross-registration with several other Long Island colleges. C.W. Post offers co-op programs in all majors, internships, study abroad in 11 countries, work-study in most departments, accelerated degree programs, and a Washington semester for outstanding criminal justice students. Dual and student-designed majors are available. There is a 3-2 engineering degree with Polytechnic University, Pratt Institute, and Arizona State University, and credit is available for life, military, and work experience. Nondegree study is available, as are pass/fail options. There are 14 national honor societies, a freshman honors program, and 16 departmental honors programs.

Faculty/Classroom: No introductory courses are taught by graduate students. The average class size in an introductory lecture is 26, in a laboratory, 20, and in a regular course, 19.

Admissions: The SAT scores for the 2009-2010 freshman class were: Critical Reading--62% below 500, 30% between 500 and 599, 7% between 600 and 700, and 1% above 700; Math--55% below 500, 33% between 500 and 599, 11% between 600 and 700, and 1% above 700; Writing--63% below 500, 30% between 500 and 599, and 7% between 600 and 700. The ACT scores were 44% below 21, 27% between 21 and 23, 10% between 24 and 26, and 4% between 27 and 28.

Requirements: The SAT or ACT is required, with a minimum composite SAT score of 900 or a minimum ACT score of 20. Applicants should be graduates of an accredited secondary school with a B average or have a GED. Preparatory work should include 4 years each of English and social science and 2 each of foreign language, college preparatory math, and lab science. A GPA of 75.0 is required. AP and CLEP credits are accepted. Important factors in the admissions decision are advanced placement or honors courses, recommendations by school officials, and evidence of special talent.

Procedure: Freshmen are admitted to all sessions. Entrance exams should be taken from May of the junior year through December of the senior year. There are early admissions, deferred admissions, and rolling admissions plans. application deadlines are open. The application fee is $30. Applications are accepted on-line.

Transfer: Applicants should have appropriate high school credentials and a minimum college GPA of 2.25. 32 of 128 credits required for the bachelor's degree must be completed at C.W. Post.

Visiting: There are regularly scheduled orientations for prospective students, consisting of Post Preview Days, which include meeting the faculty, an admissions and financial aid overview, and a campus tour. There are guides for informal visits and visitors may sit in on classes. To schedule a visit, contact the Office of Admissions.

Financial Aid: C.W. Post is a member of CSS. The CSS/Profile and FAFSA are required. Check with the school for current application deadlines.

International Students: The school actively recruits these students. They must take the TOEFL. SAT or ACT scores are recommended to help evaluate students' admissions eligibility and enable students to be considered for scholarships.

Computers: All students may access the system. Monday to Thursday 8 A.M. to 11 P.M. and Friday to Sunday 9 A.M. to 10 P.M. Dial-up capacity is available 24 hours a day. There are no time limits and no fees.

Admissions Contact: Joanne Grtzaiano, Executive Director of Admissions. E-Mail: *enroll@cwpost.liu.edu* Web: *www.liu.edu*

MANHATTAN COLLEGE   D-5
Riverdale, NY 10471

(718) 862-7200
(800) 622-9235; (718) 862-8019

Full-time: 1310 men, 1410 women	**Faculty:** IIA,+$
Part-time: 105 men, 105 women	**Ph.D.s:** 94%
Graduate: 205 men, 205 women	**Student/Faculty:** n/avn
Year: semesters, summer session	**Tuition:** $24,000
Application Deadline: March 1	**Room & Board:** $9500
Freshman Class: n/av	
SAT: required	**VERY COMPETITIVE**

Manhattan College, founded in 1853, is a private institution affiliated with the Christian Brothers of the Catholic Church. It offers degree programs in the arts and sciences, education and human services, business, and engineering. The figures in the above capsule and in this profile are approximate. There are 5 undergraduate schools and 3 graduate schools. In addition to regional accreditation, Manhattan has baccalaureate program accreditation with ABET, AHEA, and CAHEA. The 4 libraries contain 193,100 volumes, 383,480 microform items, and 3,244 audio/video tapes/CDs/DVDs, and subscribe to 1,527 periodicals including electronic. Computerized library services include interlibrary loans and database searching. Special learning facilities include a learning resource center, radio station, nuclear reactor lab, and media center. The 26-acre campus is in an urban area 10 miles north of midtown Manhattan. Including any residence halls, there are 28 buildings.

Student Life: 75% of undergraduates are from New York. Others are from 33 states, and 10 foreign countries. 60% are from public schools. 67% are white; 14% Hispanic. The average age of freshmen is 18; all undergraduates, 20. 15% do not continue beyond their first year; 68% remain to graduate.

Housing: 1440 students can be accommodated in college housing, which includes coed dorms and off-campus apartments. On-campus housing is guaranteed for all 4 years. 54% of students live on campus; of those, 80% remain on campus on weekends. All students may keep cars.

Activities: 2% of men belong to 3 local and 1 national fraternity; 1% of women belong to 4 local sororities. There are 70 groups on campus, including bagpipe, cheerleading, choir, chorus, computers, dance, debate, drama, ethnic, honors, international, jazz band, literary magazine, musical threater, newspaper, orchestra, pep band, political, professional, radio and TV, religious, social, social service, student government, and yearbook. Popular campus events include Annual Springfest, Special Olympics, and Jasper Jingle.

Sports: There are 8 intercollegiate sports for men and 8 for women, and 7 intramural sports for men and 7 for women. Facilities include 5 full basketball courts, which can also be used for volleyball and tennis, an indoor track, a weight room, a swimming pool, and a Nautilus center.

Disabled Students: All of the campus is accessible. Facilities include wheelchair ramps, elevators, special parking, and specially equipped rest rooms.

Services: Counseling and information services are available, as is tutoring in every subject.

Campus Safety and Security: Measures include 24-hour foot and vehicle patrol and security escort services. There are emergency telephones and lighted pathways/sidewalks.

Programs of Study: Manhattan confers B.A., B.S., and B.S.E. degrees. Master's degrees are also awarded. Bachelor's degrees are awarded in BIOLOGICAL SCIENCE (biochemistry and biology/biological science), BUSINESS (accounting, banking and finance, business economics, international business management, and marketing/retailing/merchandising), COMMUNICATIONS AND THE ARTS (communications, English, French, and Spanish), COMPUTER AND PHYSICAL SCIENCE (chemistry, computer science, information sciences and systems, mathematics, and physics), EDUCATION (early childhood education, elementary education, foreign languages education, health education, middle school education, physical education, science education, secondary education, and special education), ENGINEERING AND ENVIRONMENTAL DESIGN (chemical engineering, civil engineering, electrical/electronics engineering, environmental engineering, and mechanical engineering), HEALTH PROFESSIONS (predentistry, premedicine, and radiological science), SOCIAL SCIENCE (economics, history, peace studies, philosophy, political science/government, prelaw, psychology, religion, sociology, and urban studies). Engineering and business are the strongest academically. Arts, business, and education are the largest.

Required: All students must take courses in English composition and literature, religious studies, philosophy, humanities, social science, science, math, and a modern foreign language. About 130 credit hours are required for graduation, with about 36 in the major. The minimum GPA is 2.0.

Special: Manhattan offers co-op programs in 11 majors, cross-registration with the College of Mount St. Vincent, and off-campus internships in business, industry, government, and social or cultural organizations. Students may study abroad in 10 countries and enter work-study programs with major U.S. corporations, health services, or in the arts. A general studies degree, a 3-2 engineering degree, a dual major in international business, credit by exam, and nondegree study are also available. There are 22 national honor societies, including Phi Beta Kappa, a freshman honors program, and 28 departmental honors programs.

Faculty/Classroom: 70% of faculty are male; 30% are female. All teach undergraduates, and 80% do both. No introductory courses are taught by graduate students. The average class size in an introductory lecture is 15 and in a regular course is 22.

Requirements: The SAT is required. In addition, applicants must graduate from an accredited secondary school or have earned a GED. 16 academic units are required, including 4 of English, 3 each of math and social studies, and 2 of foreign language, lab sciences, and electives. An essay is required and an interview is recommended. AP and CLEP credits are accepted. Important factors in the admissions decision are advanced placement or honors courses, leadership record, and recommendations by school officials.

Procedure: Freshmen are admitted fall and spring. Entrance exams should be taken in the spring of the junior year or the fall of the senior year. There are early decision, deferred admissions and rolling admissions plans. Early decision applications should be filed by November 15; regular applications, by March 1 for fall entry and December 1 for spring entry. The fall 2008 application fee was $40. Notification of early decision is sent December 1; regular decision, December 15. Applications are accepted on-line. A waiting list is maintained.

Transfer: 125 transfer students enrolled in in a recent year. Applicants must have a GPA of 2.5 and meet subject course requirements according to their course of study. They must submit transcripts from colleges and high schools attended. An interview is recommended. 66 of 130 credits required for the bachelor's degree must be completed at Manhattan.

Visiting: There are regularly scheduled orientations for prospective students, during 2 days in the summer, which include scheduling, parent workshops, loan seminars, and English and math testing. There are guides for informal visits; visitors may sit in on classes and stay overnight. To schedule a visit, contact the Admission Center at admit@manhattan.edu.

Financial Aid: In a recent year, 82% of all full-time freshmen and 71% of continuing full-time students received some form of financial aid. 73% of all full-time freshmen and 63% of continuing full-time students received need-based aid. The average freshmen award was $12,688. 15% of undergraduate students worked part-time. Average annual earnings from campus work were $600. The average financial indebtedness of the 2009 graduate was $12,100. The FAFSA and the college's own financial statement are required. Check with the school for current application deadlines.

International Students: There were 39 international students enrolled in a recent year. The school actively recruits these students. They must take the TOEFL. They must also take the SAT or ACT.

Computers: All students may access the system 13 hours a day in the labs and 24 hours a day in residence halls or by modem. There are no time limits and no fees.

Graduates: In a recent year, 552 bachelor's degrees were awarded. The most popular majors were arts and science (33%), business (22%), and engineering (18%). 200 companies recruited on campus in 2008-2009. In an average class, 53% graduate in 4 years or less, 64% graduate in 5 years or less, and 68% graduate in 6 years or less. Of the 2008 graduating class, 16% were enrolled in graduate school within 6 months of graduation, and 61% were employed.

Admissions Contact: William J. Bisset, Jr., Assistant Vice President for Enrollment Management. A campus DVD is available. E-Mail: admit@manhattan.edu Web: www.manhattan.edu

MANHATTAN SCHOOL OF MUSIC　　　　D-5

New York, NY 10027-4678　　　　(212) 749-2802, ext. 4501
　　　　　　　　　　　　　　　　　　　　(212) 749-5471

Full-time: 210 men, 210 women	**Faculty:** n/av
Part-time: 5 men, 5 women	**Ph.D.s:** n/av
Graduate: 200 men, 245 women	**Student/Faculty:** n/av
Year: semesters	**Tuition:** $30,500
Application Deadline: see profile	**Room & Board:** $12,000
Freshman Class: n/av	
SAT or ACT: recommended	**SPECIAL**

The Manhattan School of Music, founded in 1917, is a private college offering undergraduate and graduate degrees in music performance and composition. The figures in the above capsule and in this profile are approximate. There is 1 graduate school. The library contains 73,405 volumes, and 31,500 audio/video tapes/CDs/DVDs, and subscribes to 128 periodicals including electronic. Computerized library services include interlibrary loans, database searching, and Internet access. The campus is in an urban area in New York City. Including any residence halls, there are 2 buildings.

Student Life: 83% of undergraduates are from out of state, mostly the Northeast. Students are from 31 states, 48 foreign countries, and Canada. 81% are from public schools. 36% are white; 36% foreign nationals. The average age of freshmen is 18; all undergraduates, 21. 9% do not continue beyond their first year; 54% remain to graduate.

Housing: 380 students can be accommodated in college housing, which includes single-sex and coed dorms. On-campus housing is guaranteed for the freshman year only and is available on a lottery system for upperclassmen. Priority is given to out-of-town students. 50% of students commute. All students may keep cars.

Activities: 10% of men belong to 2 local fraternities; 20% of women belong to 2 local sororities. There are 13 groups on campus, including choir, chorale, chorus, ethnic, gay, international, jazz band, musical theater, opera, orchestra, student government, and symphony. Popular campus events include a Halloween party, a Christmas/Chanukah party, and a post-opera party.

Sports: There is no sports program at MSM.

Disabled Students: 70% of the campus is accessible. Facilities include wheelchair ramps, elevators, specially equipped restrooms, special class scheduling, and lowered telephones.

Services: Counseling and information services are available, as is tutoring in most subjects. There is a reader service for the blind.

Campus Safety and Security: Measures include 24-hour foot and vehicle patrol. There are lighted pathways/sidewalks.

Programs of Study: MSM confers B.Mus. degrees. Master's and doctoral degrees are also awarded. Bachelor's degrees are awarded in COMMUNICATIONS AND THE ARTS (jazz music, music performance, music theory and composition, piano/organ, strings, and voice). Classical piano, classical voice, and jazz are the largest.

Required: All students must take 4 music theory courses, a 4-course core curriculum in the humanities, and 4 elective humanities courses and perform a final, senior-year recital. Composition majors must complete an original symphonic work. To graduate, students must earn 120 to 130 credit hours, including 90 to 100 in the major, with a minimum GPA of 2.0.

Special: There is cross-registration with Barnard College. Credit by exam in theory and music history is available.

Faculty/Classroom: 69% of faculty are male; 31% are female. All teach undergraduates. Graduate students teach 1% of introductory courses. The average class size in an introductory lecture is 20 and in a regular course is 15.

Requirements: The SAT or ACT is recommended. In addition, applicants should graduate from an accredited high school. The GED is accepted. Admission is based on a performance audition, evaluation of scholastic achievements, and available openings in the major field. AP and CLEP credits are accepted. Important factors in the admissions decision are evidence of special talent, personality/intangible qualities, and extracurricular activities record.

Procedure: Freshmen are admitted in the fall. Check with the school for current application deadlines. The application fee is $100. Notifications are sent April 1. A waiting list is maintained.

Transfer: Applicants must audition and submit college transcripts. 60 of 120 credits required for the bachelor's degree must be completed at MSM.

Visiting: There are regularly scheduled orientations for prospective students, consisting of a tour of the facility and a discussion with a counselor. There are guides for informal visits and visitors may sit in on classes. To schedule a visit, contact the Office of Admission and Financial Aid at (212) 749-2802, ext. 2.

Financial Aid: In a recent year, 52% of all full-time freshmen and 51% of continuing full-time students received some form of financial aid. 57% of all full-time freshmen and 44% of continuing full-time students received need-based aid. The average freshmen award was $18,263, with $14,494 ($36,000 maximum) from need-based scholarships or need-based grants and $14,083 ($28,750 maximum) from other non-need-based awards and non-need-based scholarships. 19% of undergraduate students worked part-time. Average annual earnings from campus work were $1443. The average financial indebtedness of the 2009 graduate was $17,658. The CSS/Profile, FAFSA, and the college's own financial statement are required. Check with the school for current application deadlines.

International Students: The school actively recruits these students. They must take the TOEFL. Applicants auditioning live whose first language is not English are required to take the English Placement Test (EPT). Applicants taking the EPT do not need to submit a TOEFL score. Applicants eligible for a recorded audition must submit a TOEFL score.

Computers: All students may access the system. There are no time limits and no fees.

Graduates: In a recent year, 2009, 85 bachelor's degrees were awarded. The most popular majors were voice (22%), piano (21%), and strings (16%). In an average class, 4% graduate in 3 years or less, 47% graduate in 4 years or less, 52% graduate in 5 years or less, and 54% graduate in 6 years or less.

Admissions Contact: Amy A. Anderson, Associate Dean for Enrollment Management. E-Mail: admission@msmnyc.edu Web: www.msmnyc.edu

MANHATTANVILLE COLLEGE　　　　D-5

Purchase, NY 10577　　　　　　　　　(914) 323-5464
　　　　　　　　　　(800) 32 VILLE; (914) 694-1732

Full-time: 588 men, 1129 women	**Faculty:** 102
Part-time: 48 men, 77 women	**Ph.D.s:** 99%
Graduate: 394 men, 745 women	**Student/Faculty:** 17 to 1
Year: semesters, summer session	**Tuition:** $32,760
Application Deadline: open	**Room & Board:** $13,500
Freshman Class: 4242 applied, 2240 accepted, 507 enrolled	
SAT CR/M: 530/540	**ACT:** 24　　**VERY COMPETITIVE**

Manhattanville College, founded in 1841, is an independent liberal arts institution offering more than 45 undergraduate areas of study. There are 2 graduate schools. The library contains 250,209 volumes, 259,230 microform items, and 5,312 audio/video tapes/CDs/DVDs, and subscribes to 36,923 periodicals including electronic. Computerized library services include interlibrary loans, database searching, and Internet access. Special learning facilities include a learning resource center, art gallery, radio station, TV station, and an environmental sciences building. The 100-acre campus is in a suburban area 25 miles north of New York City. Including any residence halls, there are 18 buildings.

Student Life: 53% of undergraduates are from New York. Others are from 39 states, 56 foreign countries, and Canada. 51% are white; 15% Hispanic; 11% foreign nationals. The average age of freshmen is 18; all undergraduates, 20. 19% do not continue beyond their first year; 60% remain to graduate.

Housing: 1330 students can be accommodated in college housing, which includes single-sex and coed dorms. On-campus housing is guaranteed for all 4 years. 77% of students live on campus; of those, 75% remain on campus on weekends. All students may keep cars.

Activities: There are no fraternities or sororities. There are 60 groups on campus, including art, band, cheerleading, chess, choir, chorale, chorus, computers, dance, debate, drama, environmental, ethnic, film, gay, honors, international, jazz band, literary magazine, musical theater, newspaper, orchestra, pep band, photography, political, professional, radio and TV, religious, social, social service, student government, and yearbook. Popular campus events include Quad Jam, Fall Jam, and The Global Pot.

Sports: There are 11 intercollegiate sports for men and 10 for women, and 5 intramural sports for men and 5 for women. Facilities include a 1000-seat gym, a 25-yard indoor pool, 6 deco-turf tennis courts, a healthworks-wellness center, baseball, turf lacrosse, field hockey, and softball fields, and batting cages.

Disabled Students: All of the campus is accessible. Facilities include wheelchair ramps, elevators, special parking, specially equipped rest rooms, special class scheduling, lowered drinking fountains, lowered telephones, and special housing.

Services: Counseling and information services are available, as is tutoring in every subject. There is a program for students with documented learning disabilities.

Campus Safety and Security: Measures include 24-hour foot and vehicle patrol, emergency notification system, and security escort services. There are shuttle buses, emergency telephones, lighted pathways/sidewalks, and controlled access to dorms/residences.

Programs of Study: M'ville confers B.A., B.S., B.F.A., and B.Mus. degrees. Master's degrees are also awarded. Bachelor's degrees are awarded in BIOLOGICAL SCIENCE (biochemistry and biology/biological science), BUSINESS (banking and finance and management science), COMMUNICATIONS AND THE ARTS (art, art history and appreciation, communications, dance, dramatic arts, English, French, music, and Spanish), COMPUTER AND PHYSICAL SCIENCE (chemistry, computer science, mathematics, and physics), EDUCATION (education), SOCIAL SCIENCE (American studies, Asian/Oriental studies, economics, history, international studies, philosophy, political science/government, psychology, religion, and sociology). English, art, and psychology are the strongest academically. Psychology, management, and history are the largest.

Required: All Manhattanville undergraduates must complete the indicated credit requirement in all 4 of the following curricular distribution areas: humanities (6 credits), social science (6 credits), mathematical and scientific (3 credits each), and fine arts (6 credits). A total of 120 credit hours and a minimum GPA of 2.0 are needed to graduate.

Special: Manhattanville offers cross-registration with SUNY Purchase, internships in all majors for credit, a Washington semester, and study abroad in 15 countries. Accelerated degree programs in behavioral studies, organizational management, and communications management are offered. Dual, student-designed, and interdisciplinary majors and pass/fail options are also available. Under the portfolio degree plan, students develop an individualized program combining both academic and nonacademic training. There is a freshman honors program and 16 departmental honors programs.

Faculty/Classroom: 50% of faculty are male; 50% are female. All teach undergraduates. No introductory courses are taught by graduate students. The average class size in an introductory lecture is 15; in a laboratory, 12; and in a regular course, 10.

Admissions: 53% of the 2009-2010 applicants were accepted. The SAT scores for the 2009-2010 freshman class were: Critical Reading--5% below 500, 74% between 500 and 599, 20% between 600 and 700, and 1% above 700; Math--5% below 500, 67% between 500 and 599, 26% between 600 and 700, and 2% above 700. The ACT scores were 25% below 21, 33% between 21 and 23, 26% between 24 and 26, 8% between 27 and 28, and 8% above 28. 100 freshmen graduated first in their class.

Requirements: The SAT or ACT is required. In addition, applicants should graduate in the upper 50% of their class with 4 years of English, 3 each of history, math, and science, including 2 of lab science, and 1 half-year each of art and music. The GED is accepted. Interviews are strongly encouraged. Art applicants must submit a portfolio; music applicants must audition. A GPA of 2.0 is required. AP and CLEP credits are accepted. Important factors in the admissions decision are leadership record, recommendations by alumni, and recommendations by school officials.

Procedure: Freshmen are admitted fall and spring. Entrance exams should be taken in the spring of the junior year or fall of the senior year. There are early decision, early admissions, deferred admissions, and rolling admissions plans. Early decision applications should be filed by December 1; for regular applications, deadlines are open. Application fee is $70. Notification of early decision is sent December 31; regular decision, on a rolling basis. 146 early decision candidates were accepted for the 2009-2010 class. 100 applicants were on the 2009 waiting list; 20 were admitted. Applications are accepted on-line.

Transfer: 104 transfer students enrolled in 2008-2009. Applicants must submit college transcripts. A minimum GPA of 2.5 and a statement of good standing are required. Applicants with fewer than 40 credits must submit all high school records and SAT scores. 60 of 120 credits required for the bachelor's degree must be completed at M'ville.

Visiting: There are regularly scheduled orientations for prospective students, including a campus tour and a meeting in Admissions. There are guides for informal visits, and visitors may sit in on classes and stay overnight. To schedule a visit, contact the Office of Admissions.

Financial Aid: In 2009-2010, 78% of all full-time freshmen and 76% of continuing full-time students received some form of financial aid. 63% of all full-time freshmen and 58% of continuing full-time students received need-based aid. The average freshmen award was $24,828. 33% of undergraduate students work part-time. Average annual earnings from campus work are $1750. The average financial indebtedness of the 2009 graduate was $23,294. The FAFSA, the state aid form, and the college's own financial statement are required. The deadline for filing freshman financial aid applications for fall entry is March 1.

International Students: There are 222 international students enrolled. The school actively recruits these students. They must take the TOEFL with a minimum score of 550 on the paper-based TOEFL (PBT) or 79-80 on the Internet-based version (iBT). They must also take the SAT or ACT.

Computers: Wireless access is available. All students may access the system. Internet and intranet are usable 24 hours per day, 7 days a week. Computer labs are open about 64 to 70 hours throughout the week. There are no time limits and no fees.

Graduates: From July 1, 2008 to June 30, 2009, 345 bachelor's degrees were awarded. The most popular majors were management (17%), psychology (11%), and communications (11%). In an average class, 56% graduate in 4 years or less, 60% graduate in 5 years or less, and 60% graduate in 6 years or less. 102 companies recruited on campus in 2008-2009. Of the 2008 graduating class, 32% were enrolled in graduate school within 6 months of graduation, and 28% were employed.

Admissions Contact: Jose Flores, Vice President, Enrollment Management. A campus DVD is available. E-mail: *admissions@mville.edu* Web: *www.manhattanville.edu*

MANNES COLLEGE NEW SCHOOL FOR MUSIC   D-5

New York, NY 10024
(212) 580-0210, ext. 4805
(800) 292-3040; (212) 580-1738

Full-time: 70 men, 100 women	**Faculty:** n/av
Part-time: 20 men, 20 women	**Ph.D.s:** n/av
Graduate: 75 men, 115 women	**Student/Faculty:** n/av
Year: semesters	**Tuition:** $32,500
Application Deadline: December 1	**Room & Board:** $12,000
Freshman Class: n/av	**SPECIAL**

Mannes College New School for music was founded in 1916 and is a private Classical music conservatory. The figures in the above capsule and in this profile are approximate. There is 1 graduate school. The 3 libraries contain 2.4 million volumes, 13,000 microform items, and 14,275 audio/video tapes/CDs/DVDs, and subscribe to 33,320 periodicals including electronic. Computerized library services include interlibrary loans, database searching, Internet access, and laptop Internet portals. The campus is in an urban area in Manhattan.

Student Life: 78% of undergraduates are from out of state, mostly the Middle Atlantic. Students are from 25 states, 13 foreign countries, and Canada. 59% are from public schools. 46% are white; 28% foreign nationals; 11% Asian American. The average age of freshmen is 19; all undergraduates, 21. 9% do not continue beyond their first year.

Housing: College-sponsored housing includes coed dorms, on-campus apartments, and off-campus apartments. On-campus housing is guaranteed for all 4 years, is available on a first-come, first-served basis, and is available on a lottery system for upperclassmen. 86% of students commute. Alcohol is not permitted.

Activities: There are no fraternities or sororities. There are 30 groups on campus, including art, choir, chorus, dance, debate, environmental, ethnic, film, gay, honors, international, jazz band, literary magazine, newspaper, opera, orchestra, photography, political, professional, religious, social, social service, student government, and symphony. Popular campus events include orchestra/chorus concerts, Christmas parties, and recitals.

Sports: There is no sports program at Mannes. Facilities include a recreation room. YMCA is also available for student use.

Disabled Students: 90% of the campus is accessible. Facilities include wheelchair ramps, elevators, specially equipped restrooms, lowered drinking fountains, and lowered telephones.

Services: Counseling and information services are available, as is tutoring in some subjects, including techniques of music.

Programs of Study: Mannes confers B.S. and B.Mus. degrees. Master's degrees are also awarded. Bachelor's degrees are awarded in COMMUNICATIONS AND THE ARTS (applied music, choral music, guitar, music, music performance, music theory and composition, piano/organ, strings, voice, and winds). Piano, voice, and violin are the largest.

Required: The required core curriculum includes courses in Techniques of Music. Students majoring in instruments and voice must participate in various ensemble classes. Courses are also required in English, western civilization, art history, literature, and history of music. To graduate, performance majors must perform before a faculty jury, and composition majors must submit 5 original pieces for juried consideration.

Special: Mannes offers cross-registration with New School. Internships and work-study are available.

Faculty/Classroom: 60% of faculty are male; 40% are female. All teach undergraduates, 3% do research, and 3% do both. No introductory courses are taught by graduate students. The average class size in an introductory lecture is 11 and in a regular course is 8.

Requirements: Applicants must be graduates of an accredited secondary school or have a GED certificate. An audition, an interview, a letter of recommendation, and a written test in music theory and musicianship are required. A GPA of 2.0 is required. AP credits are accepted. Important factors in the admissions decision are evidence of special talent, personality/intangible qualities, and recommendations by school officials.

Procedure: Freshmen are admitted in the fall. Entrance exams should be taken at the time of the audition. There is a deferred admissions plan. Applications should be filed by December 1 for fall entry and November 1 for spring entry, along with a $100 fee. Notifications are sent April 15. Applications are accepted on-line. 17 applicants were on a recent waiting list, 9 were accepted.

Transfer: 11 transfer students enrolled in a recent year. Transfer applicants must complete the same procedures as entering freshmen and submit transcripts from all secondary schools and colleges attended. 67 credits required for the bachelor's degree must be completed at Mannes.

Visiting: There are regularly scheduled orientations for prospective students. There are guides for informal visits and visitors may sit in on classes. To schedule a visit, contact the Admissions Office at (212) 580-0210, ext 4862.

Financial Aid: In a recent year, 61% of all full-time freshmen and 63% of continuing full-time students received some form of financial aid. 61% of all full-time freshmen and 63% of continuing full-time students received need-based aid. The average freshmen award was $15,508, with $14,502 ($29,800 maximum) from other non-need-based awards and non-need-based scholarships. Average annual earnings from campus work were $2000. The average financial indebtedness of the 2009 graduate was $17,938. Mannes is a member of CSS. The FAFSA, the state aid form, and the college's own financial statement are required. Check with the school for current application deadlines.

International Students: There were 64 international students enrolled in a recent year. They must take the TOEFL and the college's own test.

Computers: Wireless access is available. All students may access the system. There are no time limits and no fees.

Graduates: In a recent year, 25 bachelor's degrees were awarded. In an average class, 47% graduate in 4 years or less, 66% graduate in 5 years or less, and 66% graduate in 6 years or less.

Admissions Contact: Georgia Schmitt, Director of Admissions. E-Mail: *mannesadmissions@mannes.edu*
Web: *www.mannes.newschool.edu*

MARIST COLLEGE D-4
Poughkeepsie, NY 12601

	(845) 575-3226
	(800) 436-5483; (845) 575-3215
Full-time: 1900 men, 2600 women	**Faculty:** IIA, -$
Part-time: 185 men, 190 women	**Ph.D.s:** n/av
Graduate: 405 men, 485 women	**Student/Faculty:** n/av
Year: semesters, summer session	**Tuition:** $24,500
Application Deadline: February 15	**Room & Board:** $11,000
Freshman Class: n/av	
SAT or ACT: required	**COMPETITIVE**

Marist College, founded in 1929, is private liberal arts college with a Catholic tradition. The figures in the above capsule and in this profile are approximate. There are 7 undergraduate schools and 4 graduate schools. In addition to regional accreditation, Marist has baccalaureate program accreditation with AACSB and CSWE. The library contains 207,750 volumes, 12,206 microform items, and 5,657 audio/video tapes/CDs/DVDs, and subscribes to 30,127 periodicals including electronic. Computerized library services include interlibrary loans, database searching, Internet access, and laptop Internet portals. Special learning facilities include a learning resource center, art gallery, radio station, TV station, a gallery of Lowell Thomas memorabilia, estuarine and environmental studies lab, public opinion institute, and economic research center. The 180-acre campus is in a suburban area 75 miles north of New York City on the Hudson River. Including any residence halls, there are 49 buildings.

Student Life: 59% of undergraduates are from New York. Others are from 39 states, 9 foreign countries, and Canada. 70% are from public schools. 77% are white. The average age of freshmen is 18; all undergraduates, 22. 9% do not continue beyond their first year; 78% remain to graduate.

Housing: 2858 students can be accommodated in college housing, which includes coed dorms, on-campus apartments, and off-campus apartments. In addition, there are special-interest houses, freshman dorms with mentors, and housing for upperclassmen. 72% of students live on campus; of those, 90% remain on campus on weekends. Alcohol is not permitted. Upperclassmen may keep cars.

Activities: 1% of men belong to 3 national fraternities; 3% of women belong to 1 local and 3 national sororities. There are 81 groups on campus, including art, band, cheerleading, chess, choir, chorale, chorus, computers, dance, debate, drama, ethnic, film, gay, honors, international, jazz band, literary magazine, marching band, musical theater, newspaper, orchestra, pep band, photography, political, professional, radio and TV, religious, social, social service, student government, and symphony. Popular campus events include Activities Fair, Foxfest, and Giving Tree Program.

Sports: There are 11 intercollegiate sports for men and 12 for women, and 4 intramural sports for men and 4 for women. Facilities include a boathouse, a 3600-seat basketball arena, a 5000-seat stadium, 30 acres of playing fields, a field house, a swimming pool, a diving well, racquetball courts, a tennis pavilion, a dance and aerobics studio, a weight room, intramural basketball courts, an all-purpose playing space, and a fitness center.

Disabled Students: All of the campus is accessible. Facilities include wheelchair ramps, elevators, special parking, specially equipped restrooms, special class scheduling, lowered drinking fountains, and lowered telephones.

Services: Counseling and information services are available, as is tutoring in every subject. There is a reader service for the blind, and remedial math, reading, and writing.

Campus Safety and Security: Measures include 24-hour foot and vehicle patrol and security escort services. There are emergency telephones and lighted pathways/sidewalks.

Programs of Study: Marist confers B.A., B.S., and B.P.S. degrees. Master's degrees are also awarded. Bachelor's degrees are awarded in BIOLOGICAL SCIENCE (biology/biological science), BUSINESS (accounting, business administration and management, and fashion merchandising), COMMUNICATIONS AND THE ARTS (communications, English, fine arts, French, and Spanish), COMPUTER AND PHYSICAL SCIENCE (chemistry, computer mathematics, computer science, digital arts/technology, information sciences and systems, and mathematics), EDUCATION (athletic training and special education), ENGINEERING AND ENVIRONMENTAL DESIGN (environmental science), HEALTH PROFESSIONS (medical technology), SOCIAL SCIENCE (American studies, criminal justice, economics, fashion design and technology, history, interdisciplinary studies, philosophy, political science/government, psychology, and social work). Business administration, communications, and childhood/special education are the largest.

Required: To graduate, students must maintain a GPA of 2.0 in the major while taking 120 credits. A 30-credit core curriculum and 30 to 36 credits in a major are required. Distribution requirements include 6 credits each in natural sciences, social sciences, history, literature, and math and 3 credits each in fine arts and philosophy/religious studies. Specific course requirements include English writing skills and foundation courses in those areas defined by major programs.

Special: Marist offers cross-registration with schools in the Mid-Hudson Career Consortium and study abroad in 38 countries. The school also offers a 3-year degree in social work, co-op programs in computer science and computer information systems, information technology, accounting, and business, work-study programs, and dual and student-designed majors. There are internships available with more than 1100 organizations in the United States and abroad, including New York State Legislature and White House programs. There are 14 national honor societies and a freshman honors program.

Faculty/Classroom: 56% of faculty are male; 44% are female. 95% teach undergraduates, 68% do research, and 66% do both. No introductory courses are taught by graduate students. The average class size in an introductory lecture is 20; in a laboratory is 20; and in a regular course is 18.

Requirements: The SAT or ACT is required. The ACT Optional Writing test is also required. In addition, applicants should have 17 high school units, including at least 4 years in English, 3 each in math and science, 2 each in social studies, foreign language, and an elective, and 1 in American history. An essay and 2 letters of recommendation are also required. Marist requires applicants to be in the upper 50% of their class. AP and CLEP credits are accepted. Important factors in the admissions decision are advanced placement or honors courses, leadership record, and recommendations by school officials.

Procedure: Freshmen are admitted fall and spring. Entrance exams should be taken during the fall of the senior year. There are early decision and deferred admissions plans. Early decision applications should be filed by November 15; regular applications, by February 15 for fall entry and November 1 for spring entry, along with a $50 fee. Notification of early decision is sent December 15; regular decision, sent March 15. Applications are accepted on-line.

Transfer: 158 transfer students enrolled in a recent year. Applicants must have at least a 2.8 GPA (depending on the college and major program) in at least 30 college credits. Students with fewer than 25 credits will be treated as freshmen. Grades of C or better transfer. 30 of 120 credits required for the bachelor's degree must be completed at Marist.

Visiting: There are regularly scheduled orientations for prospective students, including 1-day June visits for freshmen and a 1-week welcome program. There are guides for informal visits; visitors may sit in on classes and stay overnight. To schedule a visit, contact the Admissions Office receptionist at www.marist.edu/admissions.

Financial Aid: In a recent year, 91% of all full-time freshmen and 80% of continuing full-time students received some form of financial aid. 59% of all full-time freshmen and 56% of continuing full-time students received need-based aid. The average freshmen award was $15,909, with $11,723 ($35,515 maximum) from need-based scholarships or need-based grants; $5,390 ($8,200 maximum) from need-based self-help aid (loans and jobs); and $9,804 ($36,885 maximum) from non-need-based athletic scholarships. 33% of undergraduate students worked part-time. Average annual earnings from campus work were $2088. The average financial indebtedness of the 2009 graduate was $28,374. The FAFSA is required. Check with the school for current application deadlines.

International Students: There were 12 international students enrolled in a recent year. The school actively recruits these students. They must take the TOEFL and the college's own test. The IELTS is accepted.

Computers: Wireless access is available. All residence halls and classrooms are connected to the campus network and the Internet. Students can also access Marist's wireless network from their residence halls and classrooms, as well as the library, dining room, lounges, athletic center, stadium, and laundry rooms. There are 36 computer labs and clusters with a total of 646 for student access. Internet 2 is available to all students to share resources with other Internet 2 institutions. All students may access the system. There are no time limits and no fees. It is strongly recommended that all students have a personal computer.

Graduates: In a recent year, 1152 bachelor's degrees were awarded. The most popular majors were business (24%), communications (20%), and childhood/special education (9%). 200 companies recruited on campus in 2008-2009. In an average class, 69% graduate in 4 years or less, 78% graduate in 5 years or less, and 78% graduate in 6 years or less. Of the 2008 graduating class, 22% were enrolled in graduate school within 6 months of graduation, and 85% were employed.

Admissions Contact: Kent Rinehart, Dean of Admission. E-Mail: *admissions@marist.edu* Web: *www.marist.edu*

MARYMOUNT MANHATTAN COLLEGE — D-5

New York, NY 10021
(212) 517-0555
(800) 627-9668; (212) 517-0448

Full-time: 445 men, 1284 women	**Faculty:** IIB, av$
Part-time: 22 men, 228 women	**Ph.D.s:** 91%
Graduate: none	**Student/Faculty:** n/av
Year: semesters, summer session	**Tuition:** $22,656
Application Deadline: open	**Room & Board:** $12,874
Freshman Class: 3447 applied, 2419 accepted, 487 enrolled	
SAT or ACT: required	**VERY COMPETITIVE**

Marymount Manhattan College is an urban, independent liberal arts college, offering programs in the arts and sciences for all ages, as well as substantial preprofessional preparation. There is 1 undergraduate school. The library contains 75,000 volumes, 70 microform items, and 4,000 audio/video tapes/CDs/DVDs, and subscribes to 2,740 periodicals including electronic. Computerized library services include interlibrary loans, database searching, Internet access, and laptop Internet portals. Special learning facilities include a learning resource center, art gallery, radio station, TV station, and a communications arts multimedia suite featuring digital editing technology. The 1-acre campus is in an urban area in Manhattan. Including any residence halls, there are 3 buildings.

Student Life: 55% of undergraduates are from out of state, mostly the Middle Atlantic. Students are from 44 states, 26 foreign countries, and Canada. 57% are from public schools. 68% are white; 14% Hispanic; 12% African American. The average age of freshmen is 18; all undergraduates, 20. 38% do not continue beyond their first year; 49% remain to graduate.

Housing: 780 students can be accommodated in college housing, which includes single-sex and coed dorms and off-campus apartments. On-campus housing is available on a first-come, first-served basis, and is available on a lottery system for upperclassmen. Priority is given to out-of-town students. 64% of students commute. Alcohol is not permitted. All students may keep cars.

Activities: There are no fraternities; 1% of women belong to 2 national sororities. There are 29 groups on campus, including art, choir, computers, dance, drama, ethnic, film, gay, honors, international, literary magazine, musical theater, newspaper, photography, political, professional, radio and TV, religious, social, social service, and student government. Popular campus events include Strawberry Festival, Honors Day, and Holiday Soiree.

Sports: There are 3 intramural sports for men and 3 for women. Facilities include a 300-seat auditorium.

Disabled Students: All of the campus is accessible. Facilities include wheelchair ramps, elevators, specially equipped restrooms, special class scheduling, and lowered drinking fountains.

Services: Counseling and information services are available, as is tutoring in every subject. There is remedial math, reading, and writing.

Campus Safety and Security: Measures include 24-hour foot and vehicle patrol and self-defense education. There are shuttle buses, lighted pathways/sidewalks, security cameras, and photo ID check-in.

Programs of Study: MMC confers B.A., B.S., and B.F.A. degrees. Associate degrees are also awarded. Bachelor's degrees are awarded in BIOLOGICAL SCIENCE (biology/biological science), BUSINESS (accounting and business administration and management), COMMUNICATIONS AND THE ARTS (communications, dance, dramatic arts, English, and fine arts), COMPUTER AND PHYSICAL SCIENCE (information sciences and systems), EDUCATION (elementary education), HEALTH PROFESSIONS (premedicine and speech pathology/audiology), SOCIAL SCIENCE (history, international studies, liberal arts/general studies, philosophy and religion, political science/government, psychology, and sociology). Theater, communications, and business are the strongest academically.

Required: To graduate, students must complete 120 credit hours, including 31 to 71 in the major, with a minimum GPA of 2.0. The core plus shared curriculum totals 48 credits in the areas of critical thinking, psychology and philosophy, quantitative reasoning and science, the modern world, communications/language, and the arts.

Special: MMC offers study abroad, interdisciplinary courses, pass/fail options, nondegree study, credit for life experience, and some 250 internships in all majors. Cooperative programs in business and finance, dance, music, languages, nursing, and urban education are offered in conjunction with local colleges and institutes. There is a January mini-session, cross-registration with Hunter College, and the China Institute, and a 5-year masters in publishing with Pace University. There are 7 national honor societies and 5 departmental honors programs.

Faculty/Classroom: 51% of faculty are male; 49% are female. 65% teach undergraduates, and 35% do both. No introductory courses are taught by graduate students. The average class size in an introductory lecture, 25, in a laboratory, 15, and in a regular course, 20.

Admissions: 70% of the 2009-2010 applicants were accepted.

Requirements: The SAT or ACT is required. In addition, applicants should be graduates of an accredited secondary school or have a GED certificate. MMC recommends completion of 16 academic units, including 4 each in English and electives, and 3 each in language, math, social science, and science. Recommendations are required, and an interview is strongly advised. Applicants to the dance and acting programs must audition. A GPA of 2.5 is required. AP and CLEP credits are accepted. Important factors in the admissions decision are personality/intangible qualities, evidence of special talent, and leadership record.

Procedure: Freshmen are admitted to all sessions. Entrance exams should be taken as early as possible. There are deferred admissions and rolling admissions plans. Application deadlines are open. The fall 2009 application fee was $60. Notification is sent on a rolling basis. Applications are accepted on-line. A waiting list is maintained.

Transfer: 151 transfer students enrolled in 2008-2009. Applicants who have graduated from high school less then 5 years ago must meet standard freshman requirements and must submit official transcripts from all colleges attended. 30 of 120 credits required for the bachelor's degree must be completed at MMC.

Visiting: There are regularly scheduled orientations for prospective students, including an interview with an admissions counselor, a tour of the school and dorms, and a meeting with a financial aid adviser. There are guides for informal visits and visitors may sit in on classes. To schedule a visit, contact the Admissions Office.

Financial Aid: In 2009-2010, at least 72% of all full-time freshmen and 75% of continuing full-time students received some form of financial aid. At least 70% of all full-time freshmen and 59% of continuing full-time students received need-based aid. The average freshman award was $14,025. Need-based scholarships or need-based grants averaged $11,158; need-based self-help aid (loans and jobs) averaged $3,686. Institutional awards averaged $5,263. 75% of undergraduate students work part-time. Average annual earnings from campus work are $2500. The average financial indebtedness of the 2009 graduate was $15,988. The FAFSA, and TAP for (New York state residents) is required. Check with the school for current application deadlines.

International Students: There are 58 international students enrolled. The school actively recruits these students. They must take the TOEFL. They must also take the SAT or ACT.

Computers: Wireless access is available. There are 2 PC labs with 22 stations each in the main building, and 1 PC lab for general use in the library. These are specialized computer labs for communications students and arts students. Wireless access is available in the library and in the Nugent building. There are 100 laptops in the library that can be used to access the Internet. All students may access the system. There are no time limits and no fees.

Graduates: From July 1, 2008 to June 30, 2009, 338 bachelor's degrees were awarded. The most popular majors were visual/performing arts (37%), journalism (27%), and social sciences (12%). 37 companies recruited on campus in 2008-2009. In an average class, 39% graduate in 4 years or less, 48% graduate in 5 years or less, and 49% graduate in 6 years or less. Of the 2008 graduating class, 23% were enrolled in graduate school within 6 months of graduation, and 63% were employed.

Admissions Contact: James Rogers, Dean of Admissions. E-Mail: *admissions@mmm.edu* Web: *www.mmm.edu*

MEDAILLE COLLEGE
C-1

Buffalo, NY 14214

(716) 880-2200; (716) 880-2007

Full-time: 630 men, 1081 women	**Faculty:** IIB, -$
Part-time: 13 men, 87 women	**Ph.D.s:** 66%
Graduate: 248 men, 864 women	**Student/Faculty:** n/av
Year: semesters, summer session	**Tuition:** $16,590
Application Deadline: see profile	**Room & Board:** $8424
Freshman Class: 1340 applied, 965 accepted, 392 enrolled	
SAT CR/M: 450/470	**ACT:** 20 **LESS COMPETITIVE**

Medaille College, founded in 1875, is a private, nonsectarian institution offering undergraduate programs in liberal arts, education, business, and sciences, and graduate programs in business and education, to a primarily commuter student body. Tuition figures in the above capsule are approximate. There is graduate school. The library contains 100,313 volumes, 1,887 audio/video tapes/CDs/DVDs, and subscribes to 25 periodicals including electronic. Computerized library services include interlibrary loans, database searching, Internet access, and laptop Internet portals. Special learning facilities include a learning resource center, radio station, TV station, and new media institute. The 13-acre campus is in an urban area 3 miles from downtown Buffalo. Including any residence halls, there are 17 buildings.

Student Life: 97% of undergraduates are from New York. Others are from 14 states, 2 foreign countries, and Canada. 67% are white; 15% foreign nationals; 13% African American. The average age of freshmen is 18; all undergraduates, 24. 32% do not continue beyond their first year; 39% remain to graduate.

Housing: 420 students can be accommodated in college housing, which includes single-sex and coed dorms, on-campus apartments, and off-campus apartments. On-campus housing is available on a first-come and first-served basis. 76% of students commute. All students may keep cars.

Activities: There are no fraternities or sororities. There are 20 groups on campus, including academic, cheerleading, ethnic, honors, literary magazine, newspaper, photography, professional, radio and TV, social, and student government. Popular campus events include Founders Day, Silent Auction, and Honors Convocation.

Sports: There are 7 intercollegiate sports for men and 7 for women, and 3 intramural sports for men and 3 for women. Facilities include an NCAA regulation gym located in the student center and a softball and soccer field.

Disabled Students: All of the campus is accessible. Facilities include wheelchair ramps, elevators, special parking, specially equipped restrooms, lowered drinking fountains, and lowered telephones.

Services: Counseling and information services are available, as is tutoring in most subjects. There is a reader service for the blind, and remedial math, reading, and writing.

Campus Safety and Security: Measures include 24-hour foot and vehicle patrol, self-defense education, and security escort services. There are shuttle buses, emergency telephones, and lighted pathways/sidewalks.

Programs of Study: Medaille confers B.A., B.S.,B.B.A., and B.S.Ed. degrees. Associates and master's degrees are also awarded. Bachelor's degrees are awarded in BIOLOGICAL SCIENCE (biology/biological science), BUSINESS (business administration and management and sports management), COMMUNICATIONS AND THE ARTS (communications and English), EDUCATION (early childhood education, elementary education, and middle school education), HEALTH PROFESSIONS (veterinary science), SOCIAL SCIENCE (criminal justice, liberal arts/general studies, psychology, and social science). Psychology and English are the strongest academically. Education, business administration, and veterinary technology are the largest.

Required: The bachelor's degree requires successful completion of 120 credit hours or 128 for elementary education and biology majors. In addition to specific course requirements for each major, students must maintain a minimum GPA of 2.0. Students must also complete a general education core curriculum of 30 required credits in Self and Others (3 credits); U.S. Colonial History (3 credits); Creative Expression (3 credits); Scientific Discovery, (3 credits); Mathematics (3 credits); Communication (9 credits) and 6 credits in baccalaureate capstone courses.

Special: Cross-registration is available with colleges in the Western New York Consortium. Most degree programs require internships. Opportunities are provided for student-designed majors, credit by examination, pass/fail options, accelerated degrees, dual majors, and credit for work experience. There are 2 national honor societies and a freshman honors program.

Faculty/Classroom: 74% of faculty are male; 26% are female. 95% teach undergraduates, 31% do research, and 31% do both. No introductory courses are taught by graduate students. The average class size in an introductory lecture, 20, in a laboratory, 10, and in a regular course, 14.

Admissions: 72% of the 2009-2010 applicants were accepted. The SAT scores for the 2009-2010 freshman class were: Critical Reading--73% below 500, 23% between 500 and 599, and 4% between 600 and

700; Math--64% below 500, 31% between 500 and 599, and 5% between 600 and 700.

Requirements: The SAT is required. In addition, applicants must be graduates of an accredited secondary school or hold the GED. An essay and an interview are required. A GPA of 70.0 is required. AP and CLEP credits are accepted. Important factors in the admissions decision are advanced placement or honors courses, personality/intangible qualities, and leadership record.

Procedure: Freshmen are admitted to all sessions. Entrance exams should be taken in May. There are deferred admissions and rolling admissions plans. Applications should be filed by January 15 for spring entry and May 15 for summer entry, along with a $25 fee. Notification is sent on a rolling basis. Applications are accepted on-line.

Transfer: 128 transfer students enrolled in 2008-2009. Transfer applicants must have a minimum GPA of 2.0 in their previous college work. An interview and recommendations are required. 30 of 120 credits required for the bachelor's degree must be completed at Medaille.

Visiting: There are regularly scheduled orientations for prospective students, including campus tours, academic program meetings, ice-breakers, and a review of policies and procedures. There are guides for informal visits; visitors may sit in on classes and stay overnight. To schedule a visit, contact Greg Florczak at (716) 880-2200.

Financial Aid: In 2009-2010, 92% of all full-time freshmen and 72% of continuing full-time students received some form of financial aid. 92% of all full-time freshmen and 72% of continuing full-time students received need-based aid. The average freshmen award was $15,800. 15% of undergraduate students work part-time. Average annual earnings from campus work are $1500. The average financial indebtedness of the 2009 graduate was $22,000. Medaille is a member of CSS. The FAFSA, the state aid form, and the college's own financial statement are required. The deadline for filing freshman financial aid applications for fall entry is March 1.

International Students: They must take the TOEFL. They must also take the SAT.

Computers: Wireless access is available. There are 120 workstations available for student use in the Library, dorms, Computer Center and Student Center. The College's wireless network extends to most buildings on each campus. Dorms are wired for high speed internet access and access to the campus-wide network. All students may access the system. There are no time limits and no fees.

Graduates: From July 1, 2008 to June 30, 2009, 276 bachelor's degrees were awarded. The most popular majors were business administration (40%), elementary teacher education (12%), and sport management (8%). 75 companies recruited on campus in 2008-2009. In an average class, 8% graduate in 3 years or less, 26% graduate in 4 years or less, 38% graduate in 5 years or less, and 39% graduate in 6 years or less. Of the 2008 graduating class, 20% were enrolled in graduate school within 6 months of graduation, and 95% were employed.

Admissions Contact: Greg Florczak, Director Enrollment Management. E-Mail: *gflorczak@medaille.edu* Web: *www.medaille.edu*

MERCY COLLEGE
D-5

Dobbs Ferry, NY 10522-1189

(914) 674-7704; (800) MERCY NY

Full-time: 1130 men, 2510 women	**Faculty:** IIA, -$
Part-time: 435 men, 1250 women	**Ph.D.s:** n/av
Graduate: 890 men, 2929 women	**Student/Faculty:** n/avn
Year: semesters, summer session	**Tuition:** $14,250
Application Deadline: open	**Room & Board:** $10,000
Freshman Class: n/av	
SAT or ACT: recommended	**NONCOMPETITIVE**

Mercy College, founded in 1950, is a private institution dedicated to offering a curriculum of liberal arts and sciences as well as preprofessional and professional programs. Graduate programs provide advanced preparation in selected disciplines. The figures in the above capsule and in this profile are approximate. There are 8 graduate schools. In addition to regional accreditation, Mercy has baccalaureate program accreditation with CSWE and NASAD. The 5 libraries contain 308,275 volumes, 1.1 million microform items, and 0 audio/video tapes/CDs/DVDs, and subscribe to 13,391 periodicals including electronic. Computerized library services include interlibrary loans, database searching, Internet access, and laptop Internet portals. Special learning facilities include a learning resource center, TV station, computer lab, reference library, and a digital arts center. The 60-acre campus is in a suburban area 12 miles north of New York City. Including any residence halls, there are 10 buildings.

Student Life: 93% of undergraduates are from New York. Others are from 35 states, 82 foreign countries, and Canada. 35% are white; 25% Hispanic; 24% African American. The average age of freshmen is 23; all undergraduates, 28. 25% do not continue beyond their first year; 60% remain to graduate.

Housing: 165 students can be accommodated in college housing, which includes coed dorms. On-campus housing is guaranteed for all 4 years, is available on a first-come, and first-served basis. Priority is given to out-of-town students. 97% of students commute. Alcohol is not permitted. All students may keep cars.

Activities: There are no fraternities or sororities. There are 18 groups on campus, including and mentoring program, cheerleading, chess, computers, dance, drama, environmental, ethnic, film, honors, international, literary magazine, newspaper, political, professional, religious, social, social service, student government, and veterinary club. Popular campus events include Open Houses, Poetry Readings, Club Fairs.

Sports: There are 6 intercollegiate sports for men and 6 for women. Facilities include gym, a soccer/baseball/softball field, 3 swimming pools, 2 tennis courts, a track, basketball/volleyball court and a fitness center.

Disabled Students: 75% of the campus is accessible. Facilities include wheelchair ramps, elevators, special parking, specially equipped restrooms, special class scheduling, and lowered drinking fountains.

Services: Counseling and information services are available, as is tutoring in every subject. There is a reader service for the blind, and remedial math, reading, and writing.

Campus Safety and Security: Measures include 24-hour foot and vehicle patrol and emergency notification system. There are emergency telephones and lighted pathways/sidewalks.

Programs of Study: Mercy confers B.A. and B.S. degrees. Associates, master's, and doctoral degrees are also awarded. Bachelor's degrees are awarded in BIOLOGICAL SCIENCE (biology/biological science), BUSINESS (accounting and business administration and management), COMMUNICATIONS AND THE ARTS (communications, English, journalism, media arts, music, and Spanish), COMPUTER AND PHYSICAL SCIENCE (computer science, information sciences and systems, and mathematics), EDUCATION (education of the deaf and hearing impaired, elementary education, special education, and teaching English as a second/foreign language (TESOL/TEFOL)), HEALTH PROFESSIONS (health science, medical laboratory technology, nursing, recreation therapy, and veterinary science); SOCIAL SCIENCE (behavioral science, criminal justice, history, interdisciplinary studies, law, paralegal studies, political science/government, psychology, social work, and sociology). Health professions programs are the strongest academically. Business and education are the largest.

Required: To graduate, students must complete 120 semester hours with a minimum GPA of 2.0 overall. In total 30 semester hours must be completed at Mercy. The Mercy College General Education Curriculum includes: 6 English credits, 3 speech credits, 6 history credits, 9 social science credits, 3 philosophy/religion credits, 3 art/music credits, 3 foreign language credits, 3 math credits, 3 computer science credits, and 3 natural science credits.

Special: Mercy offers internships and cooperative education in each major, an on-campus employment program with a community service component, study abroad, dual majors and degrees, credit for life experience, non-degree study, and pass/fail options. There are 14 national honor societies, including Phi Beta Kappa, a freshman honors program, and 14 departmental honors programs.

Faculty/Classroom: 47% of faculty are male; 54% are female. No introductory courses are taught by graduate students. The average class size in an introductory lecture is 17.

Requirements: The SAT or ACT is recommended. In addition, applicants must be graduates of an accredited secondary school or have a GED certificate. They should have completed at least 16 academic units. An interview is required and a letter of recommendation from the high school counselor or principal is required. AP and CLEP credits are accepted.

Procedure: Freshmen are admitted to all sessions. Entrance exams should be taken Between January and August of their senior year. There are early decision, deferred admissions and rolling admissions plans. Application deadlines are open. Application fee is $37. Notification is sent on a rolling basis. Applications are accepted on-line.

Transfer: 2312 transfer students enrolled in a recent year. Applicants must submit official transcripts from all colleges attended. Students with fewer than 15 college credits must also submit their high school transcript. An interview is required. 30 of 120 credits required for the bachelor's degree must be completed at Mercy.

Visiting: There are regularly scheduled orientations for prospective students, including spring and fall open houses and information sessions. There are guides for informal visits and visitors may sit in on classes. To schedule a visit, contact the Admissions Office at admissions@mercy.edu.

Financial Aid: Mercy is a member of CSS. The FAFSA is required. Check with the school for current application deadlines.

International Students: There were 163 international students enrolled in a recent year. The school actively recruits these students. They must take the TOEFL and the college's own test.

Computers: Wireless access is available. Students can log into computers at the libraries and at the computer labs using their AD credentials. There are several computer labs throughout all sites. When students logs in, they all get a mapped home directory where they store their files. At the labs and libraries, there are wireless access points where students who bring their own laptops can access the Internet. Initially, they must create an account with the authentication server prior to accessing the Internet. There is also a separate computer lab for students who reside in the dorms. All students may access the system.

Graduates: In a recent year, 1091 bachelor's degrees were awarded. The most popular majors were Behavioral Science (11%), Psychology (5%), and Health Science (5%). 242 companies recruited on campus in 2008-2009. In an average class, 16% graduate in 4 years or less, 24% graduate in 5 years or less, and 29% graduate in 6 years or less.

Admissions Contact: Jeff Cutting, Executive Director of Admissions and Marketing. Web: *www.mercy.edu*

METROPOLITAN COLLEGE OF NEW YORK   D-5

New York, NY 10013   (212) 343-1234, ext. 5001; (212) 343-8470

Full-time: 631 men and women	**Faculty:** n/av
Part-time: 45 men and women	**Ph.D.s:** 84%
Graduate: 409 men and women	**Student/Faculty:** n/av
Year: semesters, summer session	**Tuition:** $16,720
Application Deadline: open	
Freshman Class: 650 applied, 330 accepted, 126 enrolled	

VERY COMPETITIVE

Metropolitan College of New York, founded in 1964, is a private commuter institution offering programs in human services and business management. All bachelor degree programs involve a combination of class work and field work and may be completed in 2 years and 8 months. Most master's degree programs can be completed in 1 year. There are 2 undergraduate schools and 2 graduate schools. The library contains 32,000 volumes and 1800 microform items, and subscribes to 3300 periodicals including electronic. Computerized library services include interlibrary loans, database searching, and Internet access. Special learning facilities include a learning resource center. The campus is in an urban area in New York City. There is 1 building.

Student Life: 99% of undergraduates are from New York. Others are from 4 states, 9 foreign countries, and Canada. 68% are from public schools. 63% are African American; 19% Hispanic. The average age of freshmen is 32; all undergraduates, 32. 40% do not continue beyond their first year; 43% remain to graduate.

Housing: There are no residence halls. All students commute.

Activities: There are no fraternities or sororities. There are 10 groups on campus, including computers, ethnic, gay, honors, newspaper, professional, social, social service, and student government. Popular campus events include career fairs, admissions open house, and dean's list ceremonies.

Sports: There is no sports program at the college.

Disabled Students: All of the campus is accessible. Facilities include wheelchair ramps, elevators, specially equipped restrooms, special class scheduling, lowered drinking fountains, and lowered telephones.

Services: Counseling and information services are available, as is tutoring in every subject. There is remedial math, reading, and writing.

Campus Safety and Security: Measures include 24-hour foot and vehicle patrol emergency notification system, lighted pathways/sidewalks, fire drills, and a fire escape stairwell.

Programs of Study: The college confers B.B.A. and B.P.S. degrees. Associate and master's degrees are also awarded. Bachelor's degrees are awarded in BUSINESS (business administration and management), EDUCATION (early childhood education), HEALTH PROFESSIONS (mental health/human services), SOCIAL SCIENCE (child care/child and family studies, community services, gerontology, human services, prelaw, psychology, and social work). Business management is the strongest academically. Human services is the largest.

Required: To graduate, students must complete 128 credit hours with a minimum GPA of 2.0. The curriculum is prescribed; no electives are featured. A constructive action document based on performance in the field and mastery of course work is required each semester.

Special: Internships include required weekly 14-hour field sites. Study abroad in 3 countries, work-study programs, B.A.-B.S. degrees, and accelerated degree programs in human services, business management, and American urban studies are offered, as well as credit by exam and credit for life experience.

Faculty/Classroom: 51% of faculty are male; 49% are female. 95% teach undergraduates, 10% do research, and 99% do both. No introductory courses are taught by graduate students. The average class size in a laboratory is 15 and in a regular course, 15.

Admissions: 51% of the 2009-2010 applicants were accepted.

Requirements: Students must take the ETS's Accuplacer Test in reading and math; recent high school graduates who have a satisfactory SAT score may present the SAT instead. Applicants must have graduated from an accredited secondary school. The GED is accepted. An essay and an interview are required. CLEP credits are accepted. Important factors in the admissions decision are evidence of special talent, leadership record, and personality/intangible qualities.

Procedure: Freshmen are admitted to all sessions. Entrance exams should be taken in the senior year. There are deferred admissions and rolling admissions plans. Applications should be filed by December 1 for spring entry and April 1 for summer entry, along with a $30 fee. Applications are accepted on-line.

Transfer: 45 transfer students enrolled in a recent year. Admission is based on current skills and abilities as measured on the entrance exam and essay. 64 of 128 credits required for the bachelor's degree must be completed at the college.

Visiting: There are regularly scheduled orientations for prospective students. There are guides for informal visits and visitors may sit in on classes. To schedule a visit, contact the Admissions Office.

Financial Aid: In 2009-2010, 96% of all full-time freshmen and 90% of continuing full-time students received some form of financial aid. The average freshman award was $13,611. Need-based scholarships or need-based grants averaged $10,154; need-based self-help aid (loans and jobs) averaged $3517. The CSS/Profile, FAFSA, and the New York State Higher Education Financial Statement are required. The priority date for freshman financial aid applications for fall entry is March. The deadline for filing freshman financial aid applications for fall entry is August 15.

International Students: The school actively recruits international students. They must take the TOEFL and the Accuplacer test.

Computers: All students may access the system whenever the college is open. There are no time limits. The fee is $100. It is strongly recommended that all students have a personal computer.

Graduates: From July 1, 2008 to June 30, 2009, 166 bachelor's degrees were awarded. 70 companies recruited on campus in 2008-2009. In an average class, 42% graduate in 4 years or less. Of the 2008 graduating class, 50% were enrolled in graduate school within 6 months of graduation, and 80% were employed.

Admissions Contact: Steven Lenhart, Dean of Admissions.
E-mail: *slenhart@metropolitan.edu* Web: *www.metropolitan.edu*

MOLLOY COLLEGE   D-5

Rockville Centre, NY 11570   (516) 678-5000; (516) 256-2247

Full-time: 547 men, 1761 women	Faculty: IIB, av$
Part-time: 117 men, 612 women	Ph.D.s: 67%
Graduate: 180 men, 808 women	Student/Faculty: 14 to 1
Year: 4-1-4, summer session	Tuition: $20,960
Application Deadline: open	
Freshman Class: 1803 applied, 1064 accepted, 420 enrolled	
SAT CR/M/W: 500/520/500	ACT: 25 COMPETITIVE

Molloy College, an independent Catholic college founded in 1955, offers programs in nursing, business, education, social work, music therapy, and more. There are 6 undergraduate schools and 5 graduate schools. In addition to regional accreditation, Molloy has baccalaureate program accreditation with CSWE, NCATE, and NLN. The library contains 110,000 volumes and 3,170 audio/video tapes/CDs/DVDs, and subscribes to 720 periodicals including electronic. Computerized library services include interlibrary loans, database searching, and Internet access. Special learning facilities include a learning resource center, art gallery, and TV station. The 30-acre campus is in a suburban area 20 miles east of New York City. Including any residence halls, there are 5 buildings.

Student Life: 100% of undergraduates are from New York. Others are from 7 states and 9 foreign countries. 63% are white; 15% African American; 11% Hispanic. 64% are Catholic. The average age of freshmen is 18; all undergraduates, 22. 13% do not continue beyond their first year; 59% remain to graduate.

Housing: There are no residence halls. All students commute.

Activities: There are no fraternities or sororities. There are 23 groups on campus, including band, cheerleading, chess, choir, chorus, dance, drama, ethnic, honors, international, jazz band, literary magazine, musical theater, newspaper, professional, radio and TV, religious, social, social service, and student government. Popular campus events include Senior 55 Nights Party, Halloween Party, and Battle of the Bands.

Sports: There are 7 intercollegiate sports for men and 9 for women, and 1 intramural sport for men and 1 for women. Facilities include a gym, a dance studio, a weight room, sports fields, and basketball and tennis courts.

Disabled Students: All of the campus is accessible. Facilities include wheelchair ramps, elevators, special parking, specially equipped restrooms, special class scheduling, lowered drinking fountains, and lowered telephones.

Services: Counseling and information services are available, as is tutoring in every subject. There is a reader service for the blind, and remedial math, reading, and writing.

Campus Safety and Security: Measures include 24-hour foot and vehicle patrol, emergency notification system, and security escort services. There are shuttle buses, emergency telephones, lighted pathways/sidewalks, and a Campus Concerns Committee.

Programs of Study: Molloy confers B.A., B.S., B.F.A., and B.S.W degrees. Associates and master's degrees are also awarded. Bachelor's degrees are awarded in BIOLOGICAL SCIENCE (biology/biological science), BUSINESS (accounting and business administration and management), COMMUNICATIONS AND THE ARTS (art, communications, English, music, and Spanish), COMPUTER AND PHYSICAL SCIENCE (computer science, information sciences and systems, and mathe-

matics), EDUCATION (elementary education, secondary education, and special education), ENGINEERING AND ENVIRONMENTAL DESIGN (environmental science), HEALTH PROFESSIONS (music therapy, nursing, and speech pathology/audiology), SOCIAL SCIENCE (criminal justice, gerontology, history, interdisciplinary studies, peace studies, philosophy, political science/government, psychology, social work, sociology, and theological studies). Nursing, education, and social work are the strongest academically. Nursing, business, and education are the largest.

Required: General Education requirements consist of 45 to 54 credits. A total of 128 to 137 credit hours is required for graduation.

Special: Students may cross-register with 16 area colleges. The college offers internships, a Washington semester, study abroad, and dual and student-designed majors. Credit by examination and for life, military, and work experience, nondegree study, and pass/fail options are available. There are 19 national honor societies and a freshman honors program.

Faculty/Classroom: 27% of faculty are male; 73% are female. 78% teach undergraduates, 42% do research, and 31% do both. No introductory courses are taught by graduate students. The average class size in an introductory lecture is 18; in a laboratory 13; and in a regular course 17.

Admissions: 59% of the 2009-2010 applicants were accepted. The SAT scores for the 2009-2010 freshman class were: Critical Reading--43% below 500, 43% between 500 and 599, 13% between 600 and 700, and 1% above 700; Math--35% below 500, 45% between 500 and 599, 19% between 600 and 700, and 1% above 700; Writing--41% below 500, 46% between 500 and 599, 12% between 600 and 700, and 1% above 700. The ACT scores were 8% below 21, 26% between 21 and 23, 34% between 24 and 26, 15% between 27 and 28, and 17% above 28. 43% of the current freshmen were in the top fifth of their class; 81% were in the top two fifths.

Requirements: The SAT or ACT is required. The ACT Optional Writing test is also required. In addition, Applicants should be graduates of a secondary school or have a GED. Preparation should include 4 years of English, 3 each of math and history, and 2 each of foreign language and science. An essay is required and an interview is recommended. Music students must audition and take a theory exam. A GPA of 80.0 is required. AP and CLEP credits are accepted. Important factors in the admissions decision are advanced placement or honors courses, recommendations by school officials, and extracurricular activities record.

Procedure: Freshmen are admitted fall, spring, and summer. Entrance exams should be taken in the fall of the senior year. There are early admissions, deferred admissions, and rolling admissions plans. Application deadlines are open. Application fee is $30. Applications are accepted on-line.

Transfer: 458 transfer students enrolled in 2008-2009. A minimum college GPA of 2.0 is required, with some majors requiring a higher GPA. An interview is recommended. 30 of 128 credits required for the bachelor's degree must be completed at Molloy.

Visiting: There are regularly scheduled orientations for prospective students, including an address by the president of the college, department presentations, campus tours, and admissions, financial aid, and scholarship information. There are guides for informal visits and visitors may sit in on classes. To schedule a visit, contact the Admissions Office.

Financial Aid: In 2009-2010, 94% of all full-time freshmen and 75% of continuing full-time students received some form of financial aid. 78% of all full-time freshmen and 61% of continuing full-time students received need-based aid. All undergraduate students work part-time. Average annual earnings from campus work are $1584. The average financial indebtedness of the 2009 graduate was $29,823. Molloy is a member of CSS. The FAFSA is required. The priority date for freshman financial aid applications for fall entry is April 15. The deadline for filing freshman financial aid applications for fall entry is May 1.

International Students: There are 22 international students enrolled. They must take the college's own test.

Computers: Wireless access is available. Students may use 328 computers located in 19 labs and open space areas. The college has 100% wireless coverage. All students may access the system. There are no time limits and no fees.

Graduates: From July 1, 2008 to June 30, 2009, 576 bachelor's degrees were awarded. The most popular majors were nursing (48%), education (14%), and business (9%). 300 companies recruited on campus in 2008-2009. In an average class, 36% graduate in 4 years or less, 54% graduate in 5 years or less, and 59% graduate in 6 years or less.

Admissions Contact: Marguerite Lane, Director of Admissions. E-Mail: *mlane@molloy.edu* Web: *www.molloy.edu*

MONROE COLLEGE   D-5
Bronx, NY 10468

Full-time: 1410 men, 3510 women
Part-time: 155 men, 405 women
Graduate: none
Year: varies, summer session
Application Deadline: August 15
Freshman Class: n/av
SAT: recommended

(718) 933-6700
(800) 55 MONROE; (718) 364-3552
Faculty: n/a
Ph.D.s: n/av
Student/Faculty: n/av
Tuition: $11,200
Room & Board: $6500

COMPETITIVE

Monroe College, founded in 1933, offers bachelor's degrees in accounting, business management, computer information systems, criminal justice, hospitality management, and health services administration. The figures in the above capsule and in this profile are approximate. Computerized library services include interlibrary loans, database searching, Internet access, and laptop Internet portals. Special learning facilities include a learning resource center. The Bronx campus is located in the Fordham Road section of the Bronx. Including any residence halls, there are 5 buildings.

Student Life: 96% of undergraduates are from New York. 46% are African American; 42% Hispanic. The average age of freshmen is 23; all undergraduates, 26.

Housing: 620 students can be accommodated in college housing, which includes single-sex and coed dorms and off-campus apartments. In addition, there are honors houses. On-campus housing is guaranteed for all 4 years. 90% of students commute. All students may keep cars.

Activities: There are no fraternities or sororities. Groups on campus include cheerleading, computers, dance, drama, honors, literary magazine, newspaper, professional, and social service. Popular campus events include talent shows, President's and Deans' List Galas, and cultural trips to New York City.

Sports: There is no sports program at Monroe.

Disabled Students: All of the campus is accessible. Facilities include wheelchair ramps, elevators, special parking, specially equipped restrooms, special class scheduling, lowered drinking fountains, lowered telephones, and special housing.

Services: Counseling and information services are available, as is tutoring in every subject. There is a reader service for the blind, and remedial math, reading, and writing.

Campus Safety and Security: Measures include 24-hour foot and vehicle patrol, self-defense education, and security escort services. There are shuttle buses, emergency telephones, and lighted pathways/sidewalks.

Programs of Study: confers B.S. and B.B.A. degrees. Associates and master's degrees are also awarded. Bachelor's degrees are awarded in BUSINESS (accounting, business administration and management, and hospitality management services), COMPUTER AND PHYSICAL SCIENCE (information sciences and systems), HEALTH PROFESSIONS (health care administration), SOCIAL SCIENCE (criminal justice). Business management, criminal justice, and health services administration are the largest.

Required: To graduate, students must have 120 credit hours and at least a 2.0 GPA. The core curriculum includes courses in writing/literature, math, liberal arts, and business or technology.

Special: Co-op programs are available in all degree programs. Study abroad is available for culinary students interested in studying in Italy. There is 1 national honor society, a freshman honors program, and 1 departmental honors program.

Faculty/Classroom: All teach undergraduates. No introductory courses are taught by graduate students. The average class size in an introductory lecture is 30.

Requirements: The SAT is recommended. In addition, an application, an essay, and an interview are required. requires applicants to be in the upper 50% of their class. A GPA of 70.0 is required. AP and CLEP credits are accepted.

Procedure: Freshmen are admitted fall, winter, and spring. There are early decision and rolling admissions plans. Early decision applications should be filed by February 1; regular applications, by August 15 for fall entry, January 5 for winter entry, and April 15 for spring entry. The fall 2009 application fee was $35.

Transfer: Transfer students must provide an official transcript from any prior institution they have attended in addition to the application and an essay. 30 of 120 credits required for the bachelor's degree must be completed at Monroe.

Visiting: There are regularly scheduled orientations for prospective students, including a variety of open houses during the semester in which applicants can tour the campus and talk with faculty and/pr chairs of individual departments. There are guides for informal visits; visitors may sit in on classes and stay overnight. To schedule a visit, contact Evan Jerome (Bronx) Emerson Phillips (New Rochelle) at ejerome@monroecollege.edu or.

Financial Aid: The FAFSA, the state aid form, and the college's own financial statement are required. Check with the school for current application deadlines.

International Students: The school actively recruits these students.

Computers: Wireless access is available. There are a number of learning centers, libraries, and classrooms at both the Bronx and New Rochelle campuses where students have free use of more than 300 computers. Most of these computers have Internet access as well as access to the college's network. All students may access the system. There are no time limits and no fees.

Admissions Contact: Evan Jerome, Director of Admissions. A campus DVD is available. E-Mail: *admissions@monroecollege.edu* Web: *www.monroecollege.edu*

MOUNT SAINT MARY COLLEGE   D-4
Newburgh, NY 12550

Full-time: 473 men, 1394 women
Part-time: 86 men, 292 women
Graduate: 106 men, 366 women
Year: semesters, summer session
Application Deadline: open
Freshman Class: 2612 applied, 1877 accepted, 478 enrolled
SAT CR/M/W: 500/510/500

(845) 569-3248
(888) YES-MSMC; (845) 562-6762
Faculty: 78; IIB, av$
Ph.D.s: 84%
Student/Faculty: 23 to 1
Tuition: $21,930
Room & Board: $11,580

ACT: 21   COMPETITIVE

MSMC founded in 1959, is a private liberal arts college offering undergraduate programs leading to Bachelor of Arts and Bachelor of Science degrees, and graduate programs leading to the masters in education, nursing, and business administration. An accelerated evening program is offered for nontraditional and adult students. There are no undergraduate schools and 3 graduate schools. In addition to regional accreditation, the Mount has baccalaureate program accreditation with NCATE. The 2 libraries contain 105,999 volumes, 715,929 microform items, 7,927 audio/video tapes/CDs/DVDs, and subscribe to 29,775 periodicals including electronic. Computerized library services include interlibrary loans, database searching, Internet access, and laptop Internet portals. Special learning facilities include a learning resource center, radio station, elementary school, herbarium field station, and an arboretum. The 70-acre campus is in a suburban area 58 miles north of New York City. Including any residence halls, there are 40 buildings.

Student Life: 86% of undergraduates are from New York. Students are from 11 states. 50% are from public schools. 78% are white. 63% are Catholic; 27% Baptist, Christian, Episcopalian, Lutheran, and Methodist. The average age of freshmen is 18; all undergraduates, 23. 28% do not continue beyond their first year; 54% remain to graduate.

Housing: 875 students can be accommodated in college housing, which includes single-sex and coed dorms. on-campus townhouses. On-campus housing is guaranteed for all 4 years. 61% of students commute. Upperclassmen may keep cars.

Activities: There are no fraternities or sororities. There are 25 groups on campus, including art, choir, computers, dance, drama, ethnic, honors, literary magazine, musical theater, newspaper, photography, political, professional, radio and TV, religious, social, student government, and yearbook. Popular campus events include Octoberfest, Siblings Weekend, and Holiday Formal.

Sports: There are 7 intercollegiate sports for men and 8 for women, and 10 intramural sports for men and 10 for women. Facilities include a gym, a weight room, a tennis court, an indoor running track, a swimming pool, a cardiovascular room, a game room, and an aerobics/dance studio.

Disabled Students: All of the campus is accessible. Facilities include wheelchair ramps, elevators, special parking, specially equipped rest rooms, lowered telephones, special equipment in the library, and computer centers to accommodate students with low vision.

Services: Counseling and information services are available, as is tutoring in every subject. There is remedial math, reading, and writing.

Campus Safety and Security: Measures include 24-hour foot and vehicle patrol, self-defense education, and security escort services. There are shuttle buses, emergency telephones, and lighted pathways/sidewalks.

Programs of Study: Mount Saint Mary confers B.A., B.S., and B.S.Ed. degrees. Master's degrees are also awarded. Bachelor's degrees are awarded in BIOLOGICAL SCIENCE (biology/biological science), BUSINESS (accounting and business administration and management), COMMUNICATIONS AND THE ARTS (English, media arts, and public relations), COMPUTER AND PHYSICAL SCIENCE (chemistry, information sciences and systems, and mathematics), EDUCATION (education), HEALTH PROFESSIONS (medical laboratory technology, nursing, and physical therapy), SOCIAL SCIENCE (Hispanic American studies, history, human services, interdisciplinary studies, political science/government, psychology, social science, social work, and sociology). Education, nursing, and business are the strongest academically. Education, nursing, and psychology are the largest.

Required: A total of 120 credit hours is required for the B.A. or B.S., with 24 to 40 in the major and a minimum GPA of 2.0. Overall requirements are higher for nursing, medical technology, and education students. All students must achieve computer literacy before graduation.

Special: Co-op programs and internships are available in all majors. There is cross-registration with other mid-Hudson area colleges, as well as accelerated degree programs in business, accounting, and nursing, among others. There are several collaborative programs. The college also offers study abroad in more than 22 countries, a Washington semester, work-study, and dual and student-designed majors. Credit by exam and for life, military, and work experience is available for a maximum of 30 credits. There are 7 national honor societies and a freshman honors program.

Faculty/Classroom: 45% of faculty are male; 55% are female. 91% teach undergraduates. No introductory courses are taught by graduate students. The average class size in an introductory lecture is 25; in a laboratory is 14; and in a regular course is 21.

Admissions: 72% of the 2009-2010 applicants were accepted. The SAT scores for the 2009-2010 freshman class were: Critical Reading--48% below 500, 43% between 500 and 599, 8% between 600 and 700, and 1 above 700; Math--39% below 500, 45% between 500 and 599, 16% between 600 and 700, and 1 above 700; Writing--46% below 500, 45% between 500 and 599, 8% between 600 and 700, and 1 above 700. The ACT scores were 35% below 21, 41% between 21 and 23, 16% between 24 and 26, 5% between 27 and 28, and 3% above 28. 20% of the current freshmen were in the top fifth of their class; 40% were in the top two fifths.

Requirements: The SAT or ACT is required. The ACT Optional Writing test is also required. In addition, students should be graduates of an accredited secondary school. The GED is accepted. Applicants should prepare with 4 years each of English and history, and at least 3 each of math and science and 2 of foreign language. An essay and an interview are recommended. AP and CLEP credits are accepted. Important factors in the admissions decision are advanced placement or honors courses, evidence of special talent, and personality/intangible qualities.

Procedure: Freshmen are admitted to all sessions. Entrance exams should be taken by the junior year. There are deferred admissions and rolling admissions plans. Application deadlines are open. The fall 2008 application fee was $45. Notification is sent on a rolling basis. Applications are accepted on-line.

Transfer: 204 transfer students enrolled in 2008-2009. Applicants must have a GPA of at least 2.0 in all college work. The SAT or ACT, and an interview are recommended. 30 of 120 credits required for the bachelor's degree must be completed at the Mount.

Visiting: There are regularly scheduled orientations for prospective students, including 4 open houses per year, a new summer orientation program, and Spend a Day with a Current Student program in the spring. There are guides for informal visits, visitors may sit in on classes, and stay overnight. To schedule a visit, contact Admissions at 1-888-YES-MSMC.

Financial Aid: In 2009-2010, 94% of all full-time freshmen and 75% of continuing full-time students received some form of financial aid. 94% of all full-time freshmen and 74% of continuing full-time students received need-based aid. The average freshmen award was $15,800, with $7,900 ($36,400 maximum) from need-based scholarships or need-based grants; $7,300 ($32,600 maximum) from need-based self-help aid (loans and jobs); and $600 ($26,000 maximum) from other non-need-based awards and non-need-based scholarships. 13% of undergraduate students work part-time. Average annual earnings from campus work are $1158. The average financial indebtedness of the 2009 graduate was $20,000. The FAFSA is required. The priority date for freshman financial aid applications for fall entry is February 15. The deadline for filing freshman financial aid applications for fall entry is March 15.

International Students: They must take the TOEFL with a minimum score of 550 on the paper-based TOEFL (PBT) or 80 on the Internet-based version (iBT). They must also take the SAT or ACT, and the college's own entrance exam. freshman are required to take standard placement test.

Computers: Wireless access is available. The college provides students with access to over 300 computer workstations across campus for instruction and open laboratory access. There are 10 computer classrooms/laboratories, as well as computer facilities and clusters in the library, curriculum library, cyber-café, and the two major residence halls. Campus-wide high-speed wireless network provides students with access to college resources and the Internet from virtually anywhere on campus. All students may access the system. Networks are available 24/7. There are no time limits and no fees. It is strongly recommended that all students have a personal computer.

Graduates: From July 1, 2008 to June 30, 2009, 466 bachelor's degrees were awarded. The most popular majors were business (19%), nursing (13%), and history (12%). 90 companies recruited on campus in 2008-2009. In an average class, 1% graduate in 3 years or less, 39% graduate in 4 years or less, 50% graduate in 5 years or less, and 51% graduate in 6 years or less. Of the 2008 graduating class, 28% were en-

rolled in graduate school within 6 months of graduation, and 88% were employed.

Admissions Contact: Rodney Morrison, Director of Admissions. A campus DVD is available. E-Mail: *admissions@msmc.edu* Web: *www.msmc.edu*

NAZARETH COLLEGE OF ROCHESTER   B-3

Rochester, NY 14618-3790   **(585) 389-2860**
                                   (800) 462-3944; (585) 389-2826

Full-time: 500 men, 1500 women	**Faculty:** IIA, -$
Part-time: 50 men, 130 women	**Ph.Ds:** n/av
Graduate: 210 men, 830 women	**Student/Faculty:** n/av
Year: semesters, summer session	**Tuition:** $23,000
Application Deadline: February 15	**Room & Board:** $10,000
Freshman Class: n/av	**VERY COMPETITIVE**

Nazareth College of Rochester, founded in 1924, is an independent institution offering programs in the liberal arts and sciences and preprofessional areas. The figures in the above capsule and in this profile are approximate. There are 4 undergraduate schools and 4 graduate schools. In addition to regional accreditation, Nazareth has baccalaureate program accreditation with CSWE and NASM. The library contains 218,010 volumes, 460,199 microform items, and 12,417 audio/video tapes/CDs/DVDs, and subscribes to 1,432 periodicals including electronic. Computerized library services include interlibrary loans, database searching, and Internet access. Special learning facilities include a learning resource center, art gallery, and radio station. The 150-acre campus is in a suburban area 7 miles east of Rochester. Including any residence halls, there are 21 buildings.

Student Life: 95% of undergraduates are from New York. Others are from 25 states, 19 foreign countries, and Canada. 90% are from public schools. 84% are white. The average age of freshmen is 18; all undergraduates, 21. 17% do not continue beyond their first year; 76% remain to graduate.

Housing: 1205 students can be accommodated in college housing, which includes single-sex and coed dorms and on-campus apartments. In addition, there are language houses, special-interest houses, substance-free floors, freshman experience floors, and honors floors. On-campus housing is guaranteed for all 4 years. 55% of students live on campus; of those, 88% remain on campus on weekends. All students may keep cars.

Activities: There are no fraternities or sororities. There are 51 groups on campus, including art, band, choir, chorale, chorus, computers, dance, drama, ethnic, gay, honors, jazz band, literary magazine, musical theater, newspaper, opera, orchestra, political, professional, radio, religious, social, and student government. Popular campus events include Springfest and Siblings Weekend.

Sports: There are 11 intercollegiate sports for men and 13 for women, and 20 intramural sports for men and 20 for women. Facilities include a gym, a 25-meter swimming pool, soccer and lacrosse fields, including an outdoor turf field, tennis and racquetball courts, a fitness center, a sauna, a 2200-seat stadium, and a 400-meter all-weather track.

Disabled Students: 80% of the campus is accessible. Facilities include wheelchair ramps, elevators, special parking, specially equipped restrooms, special class scheduling, lowered drinking fountains, and special housing.

Services: Counseling and information services are available, as is tutoring in every subject.

Campus Safety and Security: Measures include 24-hour foot and vehicle patrol and security escort services. There are emergency telephones, lighted pathways/sidewalks, an alarm system, and security beepers free to all students.

Programs of Study: Nazareth confers B.A., B.S., and B.Mus. degrees. Master's and doctoral degrees are also awarded. Bachelor's degrees are awarded in BIOLOGICAL SCIENCE (biochemistry and biology/biological science), BUSINESS (accounting and business administration and management), COMMUNICATIONS AND THE ARTS (art, art history and appreciation, communications, dramatic arts, English, fine arts, French, German, Italian, music, music history and appreciation, music performance, Spanish, and speech/debate/rhetoric), COMPUTER AND PHYSICAL SCIENCE (chemistry, information sciences and systems, and mathematics), EDUCATION (art education, business education, elementary education, English education, foreign languages education, mathematics education, middle school education, music education, science education, social studies education, and special education), ENGINEERING AND ENVIRONMENTAL DESIGN (environmental science), HEALTH PROFESSIONS (music therapy, nursing, physical therapy, and speech pathology/audiology), SOCIAL SCIENCE (American studies, anthropology, economics, history, international studies, peace studies, philosophy, political science/government, psychology, religion, social science, social work, and sociology). Physical therapy, math, and English are the strongest academically. Business, psychology, and art are the largest.

Required: All students must take 1 course each in literature, math, lab science, philosophy, social science, history, fine arts, and religious studies. 2 semesters of phys ed, a course in computer literacy, and a writing competency exam in the junior year are required. Other requirements vary according to the major, with a total of 30 to 75 upper-division credits needed. A total of 120 credit hours is required to graduate. The minimum GPA is 2.0.

Special: There is cross-registration with members of the Rochester Area Colleges Consortium. Internships and a Washington semester are offered. There is study abroad in France, Spain, Italy, and Germany, and there are exchange programs in Australia, Japan, Italy, France, Peru, United Kingdom, Hungary, Wales. There are 20 national honor societies and 13 departmental honors programs.

Faculty/Classroom: 43% of faculty are male; 57% are female. All teach undergraduates. No introductory courses are taught by graduate students. The average class size in an introductory lecture is 21; in a laboratory is 13; and in a regular course is 19.

Requirements: Applicants should graduate from an accredited secondary school or have a GED. A minimum of 16 academic credits is required, including 4 years of English and 3 each of social studies, foreign language, math, and science. An essay is required, as is an audition for music and theater students and a portfolio for art students. An interview is recommended. Nazareth requires applicants to be in the upper 50% of their class. A GPA of 2.8 is required. AP and CLEP credits are accepted. Important factors in the admissions decision are geographical diversity, advanced placement or honors courses, and evidence of special talent.

Procedure: Freshmen are admitted fall and spring. Entrance exams should be taken by December of the senior year. There are early decision, early admissions and deferred admissions plans. Early decision applications should be filed by November 15; regular applications, by February 15 for fall entry and November 15 for spring entry, along with a $40 fee. Notification of early decision is sent December 15; regular decision, March 1. Applications are accepted on-line. A waiting list is maintained.

Transfer: 155 transfer students enrolled in a recent year. Applicants must have a college GPA of 2.5 (2.75 for education and physical therapy students). Those with fewer than 30 credits must submit high school transcripts. 30 of 120 credits required for the bachelor's degree must be completed at Nazareth.

Visiting: There are regularly scheduled orientations for prospective students, including individual appointments, group sessions, campus tours, open houses, and summer academic orientation. There are guides for informal visits; visitors may sit in on classes and stay overnight. To schedule a visit, contact the Admissions Office at admissions@naz.edu.

Financial Aid: In a recent year, 98% of all full-time freshmen and 96% of continuing full-time students received some form of financial aid. 77% of all full-time freshmen and 73% of continuing full-time students received need-based aid. The average freshman award was $16,446. 44% of undergraduate students worked part-time. Average annual earnings from campus work were $1421. The average financial indebtedness of the 2009 graduate was $26,795. Nazareth is a member of CSS. The FAFSA, and the CSS Profile are required for early decision applicants only. Check with the school for current application deadlines.

International Students: The school actively recruits these students. They must take the TOEFL.

Computers: Wireless access is available. All students may access the system. There are no time limits and no fees.

Graduates: In a recent year, 468 bachelor's degrees were awarded. The most popular majors were business (15%), English (11%), and psychology (10%). 36 companies recruited on campus in 2008-2009. In an average class, 71% graduate in 5 years or less and 76% graduate in 6 years or less. Of the 2008 graduating class, 49% were enrolled in graduate school within 6 months of graduation, and 72% were employed.

Admissions Contact: Thomas DaRin, Vice President of Enrollment Management. E-Mail: *admissions@naz.edu* Web: *ww.naz.edu*

NEW YORK INSTITUTE OF TECHNOLOGY D-5

Old Westbury, NY 11568-8000 (516) 686-7925
(800) 345-NYIT; (516) 686-7613

Full-time: 3235 men, 1910 women	**Faculty:** IIA,+$
Part-time: 1120 men, 635 women	**Ph.D.s:** n/av
Graduate: 2340 men, 1930 women	**Student/Faculty:** n/av
Year: semesters, summer session	**Tuition:** $21,600
Application Deadline: February 1	**Room & Board:** $10,500
Freshman Class: n/av	**VERY COMPETITIVE**

The New York Institute of Technology, founded in 1955, is a nonsectarian, institution of higher learning that provides undergraduate, graduate, and professional programs in allied health, architecture, art, business, culinary arts, communication, arts, education, engineering, hospitality management, and medicine and technology. Traditional and accelerated formats in day, evening, and weekend sessions are available, in addition to noncredit and personal enrichment programs and off-campus independent study. NYIT maintains additional campuses on Long Island and in Manhattan. NYIT'S on-line campus is an innovative virtual campus.

Students can take courses or acquire a 4-year degree entirely through Web-based computer conferencing with no campus classes required. The figures in the above capsule and in this profile are approximate. There are 7 undergraduate schools and 8 graduate schools. In addition to regional accreditation, NYIT has baccalaureate program accreditation with ABET, ADA, FIDER, and NAAB. The 5 libraries contain 169,905 volumes, 805,375 microform items, and 43,860 audio/video tapes/CDs/DVDs, and subscribe to 1,245 periodicals including electronic. Computerized library services include interlibrary loans, database searching, Internet access, and laptop Internet portals. Special learning facilities include a learning resource center, art gallery, radio station, TV station, and TV studios. The 525-acre campus is in a suburban area 25 miles east of New York City, 10 miles from Queens. Including any residence halls, there are 57 buildings.

Student Life: 91% of undergraduates are from New York. Others are from 49 states, 81 foreign countries, and Canada. 25% are white; 17% foreign nationals. The average age of freshmen is 18; all undergraduates, 23. 28% do not continue beyond their first year; 71% remain to graduate.

Housing: 1000 students can be accommodated in college housing, which includes single-sex and coed dorms, on-campus apartments, and off-campus apartments. In addition, there are special-interest houses, facilities for international, graduate, architecture, first year students, student leaders, student government executive board members, and Greek life organizations. On-campus housing is guaranteed for all 4 years. 93% of students commute. Alcohol is not permitted. All students may keep cars.

Activities: 1% of men belong to 1 local and 4 national fraternities; 1% of women belong to 2 local and 1 national sorority. There are 100 groups on campus, including academic, art, cheerleading, chorale, computers, dance, drama, ethnic, film, honors, international, literary magazine, musical theater, newspaper, political, professional, radio and TV, religious, social, social service, special interest, student government, student media, and yearbook. Popular campus events include May Fest, Club Fair Day, and Earth Day.

Sports: There are 7 intercollegiate sports for men and 7 for women, and 9 intramural sports for men and 9 for women. Facilities include a gym, soccer, softball and baseball fields, a track, courts for tennis, handball, and basketball, a fitness center, aquatic facilities, and a weight room.

Disabled Students: All of the campus is accessible. Facilities include wheelchair ramps, elevators, special parking, specially equipped restrooms, lowered drinking fountains, and special housing.

Services: Counseling and information services are available, as is tutoring in every subject. There is remedial math, reading, and writing.

Campus Safety and Security: Measures include 24-hour foot and vehicle patrol and security escort services. There are shuttle buses, emergency telephones, and lighted pathways/sidewalks.

Programs of Study: NYIT confers B.A., B.S., B.Arch., B.F.A., B.P.S., and B.Tech. degrees. Associates, master's, and doctoral degrees are also awarded. Bachelor's degrees are awarded in BIOLOGICAL SCIENCE (biology/biological science, life science, and nutrition), BUSINESS (accounting, banking and finance, business administration and management, hospitality management services, marketing and distribution, and marketing/retailing/merchandising), COMMUNICATIONS AND THE ARTS (advertising, communications, English, fine arts, graphic design, technical and business writing, and telecommunications), COMPUTER AND PHYSICAL SCIENCE (chemistry, computer science, mathematics, and physics), EDUCATION (art education, business education, education, elementary education, health education, middle school education, science education, secondary education, technical education, and trade and industrial education), ENGINEERING AND ENVIRONMENTAL DESIGN (aeronautical engineering, architecture, biomedical engineering, computer engineering, computer graphics, electrical/electronics engineering, electrical/electronics engineering technology, engineering technology, environmental design, environmental engineering technology, industrial engineering, interior design, manufacturing engineering, mechanical engineering, and technological management), HEALTH PROFESSIONS (clinical science, nursing, occupational therapy, physical therapy, physician's assistant, and preosteopathy), SOCIAL SCIENCE (behavioral science, interdisciplinary studies, political science/government, prelaw, social studies, and sociology). Architecture, allied health programs, and engineering are the strongest academically. Computer science, business administration, and architectural technology are the largest.

Required: All students take a core curriculum, sequenced over 8 semesters, that includes 42 credits in English, speech, behavioral and natural science, social science, philosophy, economics, and a capstone course in the major field. A total of 120 to 169 credits and a minimum GPA of 2.0, both overall and in the major, are required for graduation.

Special: NYIT offers cooperative programs, summer study abroad, internships, student-designed majors, a B.A.-B.S. degree in interdisciplinary studies, accelerated degree programs in osteopathic medicine, mechanical engineering, physical therapy, occupational therapy, and criminal justice, and nondegree study. There are 7 national honor societies, a freshman honors program, and 2 departmental honors programs.

Faculty/Classroom: 60% of faculty are male; 40% are female. 88% teach undergraduates, 28% do research, and 28% do both. No introductory courses are taught by graduate students. The average class size in an introductory lecture is 20; in a laboratory is 15; and in a regular course is 17.

Requirements: All students must present evidence of completion of high school degree or an equivalence. Architecture, engineering, combined baccalaureate/doctor of osteopathic medicine, nursing, occupational therapy, physical therapy, and physician assistant programs requirements include interviews, essays, letters of recommendation, volunteer hours, and Regents units. Recommendations are required for education program applicants. Portfolios are required for fine arts applicants. AP and CLEP credits are accepted. Important factors in the admissions decision are advanced placement or honors courses, recommendations by school officials, and leadership record.

Procedure: Freshmen are admitted fall, spring, and summer. Entrance exams should be taken in spring for fall enrollment. There are deferred admissions and rolling admissions plans. Applications should be filed by February 1 for fall entry. The fall 2009 application fee was $50. Notification is sent on a rolling basis. Applications are accepted on-line.

Transfer: 485 transfer students enrolled in a recent year. Applicants must submit official transcripts from all colleges attended. Students with less than 30 credits of previous college work must submit a high school transcript and standardized test scores. Some majors have specific requirements for their programs. 30 of 120 credits required for the bachelor's degree must be completed at NYIT.

Visiting: There are regularly scheduled orientations for prospective students, including open houses in fall and spring, with campus tours, a president's address, financial aid seminars, honors receptions, sessions with faculty advisers, and major-specific receptions. There are guides for informal visits and visitors may sit in on classes. To schedule a visit, contact the Admissions Office at (516) 686-7520.

Financial Aid: The FAFSA and NYS TAP form are required. Check with the school for current application deadlines.

International Students: There were 474 international students enrolled in a recent year. The school actively recruits these students. They must take the TOEFL and the college's own test. They must also take the SAT or ACT.

Computers: Wireless access is available. All students may access the system. There are no time limits and no fees. All students are required to have a personal computer. Students enrolled in architecture, engineering, and technology majors must have a personal computer.

Graduates: In a recent year, 1389 bachelor's degrees were awarded. The most popular majors were business (26%), interdisciplinary studies (16%), and architecture (9%). 120 companies recruited on campus in 2008-2009. In an average class, 1% graduate in 3 years or less, 15% graduate in 4 years or less, 24% graduate in 5 years or less, and 31% graduate in 6 years or less. Of the 2008 graduating class, 38% were enrolled in graduate school within 6 months of graduation, and 88% were employed.

Admissions Contact: Jacquelyn Nealon, Dean of Admissions and Financial Aid. A campus DVD is available. E-Mail: *admissions@nyit.edu* Web: *www.nyit.edu*

NEW YORK UNIVERSITY — D-5

New York, NY 10011 — (212) 998-4500; (212) 995-4902

Full-time: 7929 men, 12352 women	Faculty: ; I, +$
Part-time: 565 men, 792 women	Ph.D.s: 92%
Graduate: 9365 men, 12401 women	Student/Faculty: n/av
Year: semesters, summer session	Tuition: $38,765
Application Deadline: January 1	Room & Board: $13,228
Freshman Class: 37462 applied, 14159 accepted, 5000 enrolled	
SAT CR/M/W: 658/672/664	ACT: 29 MOST COMPETITIVE

New York University, founded in 1831, is the largest private university in the United States. NYU, which is composed of 14 schools, colleges, and divisions, occupies 5 major centers in Manhattan and operates branch campus and research programs in other parts of the United States and abroad. There are 8 undergraduate schools and 11 graduate schools. In addition to regional accreditation, NYU has baccalaureate program accreditation with AACSB, ACEJMC, ADA, CSWE, and NLN. The 12 libraries contain 5.7 million volumes, 5.6 million microform items,and 1.6 million audio/video tapes/CDs/DVDs, and subscribe to 67,960 periodicals including electronic. Computerized library services include interlibrary loans, database searching, Internet access, and laptop Internet portals. Special learning facilities include a learning resource center, art gallery, radio station, TV station, speech/language/hearing clinic, center for students with disabilities, and Speaking Freely (free non-credit foreign language classes). The campus is in an urban area in New York City's Greenwich Village. Including any residence halls, there are 150 buildings.

Student Life: 65% of undergraduates are from out of state, mostly the Northeast. Students are from 49 states, 91 foreign countries, and Canada. 65% are from public schools. 45% are white; 20% Asian American. The average age of freshmen is 18; all undergraduates, 20. 9% do not continue beyond their first year; 85% remain to graduate.

Housing: 10921 students can be accommodated in college housing, which includes coed dorms and on-campus apartments. In addition, there are special-interest houses, fraternity houses, SAFE (Substance and Alcohol-Free Environment), First Year Residential Experience, Sophomore Residential Experience, and Explorations Learning Communities. On-campus housing is guaranteed for all 4 years. 51% of students live on campus. All students may keep cars.

Activities: 1% of men belong to 14 national fraternities; 2% of women belong to 3 local and 3 national sororities. There are more than 400 groups on campus, including art, bagpipe, band, cheerleading, chess, choir, chorale, chorus, computers, dance, debate, drama, environmental, ethnic, film, forensics, gay, honors, international, jazz band, literary magazine, marching band, musical threater, newspaper, opera, orchestra, pep band, photography, political, professional, radio and TV, religious, social, social service, student government, and symphony. Popular campus events include Spring Strawberry Festival, Grad Alley, and Career Services Fair.

Sports: There are 11 intercollegiate sports for men and 10 for women, and 9 intramural sports for men and 9 for women. Facilities include 2 state-of-the-art sports and recreation facilities. The sports center houses multipurpose courts for basketball, volleyball, tennis, and badminton, squash courts, handball and racquetball courts, rooftop tennis courts and running track, a 25-meter swimming pool, a diving tank, saunas, weight-training facilities, an aerobic fitness room, rooms for wrestling, judo, fencing, physical fitness, exercise prescription, and dance, and a rock-climbing wall. The athletic center is equipped with a 25-yard swimming pool, basketball/activities courts, a foot aerobic fitness room with cardio equipment, and a 30-foot indoor climbing center.

Disabled Students: 95% of the campus is accessible. Facilities include wheelchair ramps, elevators, specially equipped rest rooms, special class scheduling, lowered drinking fountains, lowered telephones, special housing, buses with hydraulic lifts, adaptive computer equipment, CART or C-print services, a CTV enlargement system, a JAWS speech synthesizer, Dragon Dictate Voice Recognition, and Kurzweil Personal Readers.

Services: Counseling and information services are available, as is tutoring in every subject. There is a reader service for the blind. Other services include sign language interpreters, scribes, research aides, and note takers for special needs.

Campus Safety and Security: Measures include 24-hour foot and vehicle patrol, emergency notification system, self-defense education, and security escort services. There are shuttle buses, emergency telephones, lighted pathways/sidewalks, 24-hour security in residence halls, and a neighborhood-merchant emergency help service.

Programs of Study: NYU confers B.A., B.S., B.F.A., B.S./B.E., and Mus.B. degrees. Associates, master's, and doctoral degrees are also awarded. Bachelor's degrees are awarded in BIOLOGICAL SCIENCE (biochemistry, biology/biological science, neurosciences, and nutrition), BUSINESS (accounting, banking and finance, business administration and management, business economics, hotel/motel and restaurant management, international business management, management science, marketing/retailing/merchandising, operations research, organizational behavior, real estate, recreation and leisure services, and sports management), COMMUNICATIONS AND THE ARTS (American literature, art history and appreciation, classics, communications, communications technology, comparative literature, creative writing, dance, design, dramatic arts, English, English literature, film arts, fine arts, French, German, Germanic languages and literature, Greek, Greek (classical), Greek (modern), Hebrew, Italian, journalism, Latin, linguistics, media arts, music, music business management, music performance, music technology, music theory and composition, performing arts, photography, Portuguese, radio/television technology, romance languages and literature, Russian, Spanish, speech/debate/rhetoric, studio art, technical and business writing, theater management, and voice), COMPUTER AND PHYSICAL SCIENCE (actuarial science, chemistry, computer mathematics, computer science, digital arts/technology, earth science, information sciences and systems, mathematics, physics, and statistics), EDUCATION (art education, early childhood education, education, elementary education, English education, foreign languages education, mathematics education, music education, science education, secondary education, social studies education, special education, and speech correction), ENGINEERING AND ENVIRONMENTAL DESIGN (computer engineering, graphic arts technology, and urban design), HEALTH PROFESSIONS (dental hygiene, health care administration, nursing, predentistry, premedicine, and speech pathology/audiology), SOCIAL SCIENCE (African studies, African American studies, American studies, anthropology, applied psychology, area studies, Asian/American studies, classical/ancient civilization, early childhood studies, East Asian studies, economics, ethnic studies, European studies, gender studies, history, humanities, Iberian studies, international relations, Judaic studies, Latin American studies, Luso-Brazilian studies, medieval studies, Middle Eastern studies, philosophy, political science/government, psychology, public administration, religion, social science, social work, sociology, and urban studies). Theater, individualized studies, and finance are the largest.

Required: All students must complete a minimum of 128 credit hours and maintain a minimum GPA of 2.0. A course in expository writing is required. Students must complete a core liberal arts curriculum in addition to major and elective credit.

Special: A vast array of internships is available, as well as study worldwide at NYU's 10 sites: Berlin, Buenos Aires, Florence, Ghana, London, Madrid, Paris, Prague, Shanghai, and Tel Aviv. B.A.-B.S. degree options, accelerated degrees in more than 230 majors, dual and student-designed majors, credit by exam, and pass/fail options are also available. A Washington semester is available to political science majors. There are exchange programs with several historically black colleges. There is a Phi Beta Kappa and a freshman honors program.

Faculty/Classroom: 55% of faculty are male; 45% are female. No introductory courses are taught by graduate students.

Admissions: 38% of the 2009-2010 applicants were accepted. The SAT scores for the 2009-2010 freshman class were: Critical Reading--1% below 500, 17% between 500 and 599, 51% between 600 and 700, and 31% above 700; Math--1% below 500, 14% between 500 and 599, 49% between 600 and 700, and 37 above 700; Writing--1% below 500, 15% between 500 and 599, 51% between 600 and 700, and 33% above 700. The ACT scores were 16% between 24 and 26, 21% between 27 and 28, and 63% above 28. 92% of the current freshmen were in the top fifth of their class; 99% were in the top two-fifths. 235 freshmen graduated first in their class in a recent year.

Requirements: The SAT or ACT is required. The ACT Optional Writing test is also required. In addition, applicants must graduate from an accredited secondary school.The GED is accepted. Students must present at least 16 Carnegie units, including 4 in English. Some majors require an audition or submission of a creative portfolio. All applicants must submit an essay and 2 letters of recommendation. Applicants can submit the SAT and 2 SAT: Subject tests; the ACT with Writing; the SAT and 2 Advanced Placement (AP) exam scores; 3 SAT: Subject tests (1 in literature or the humanities, 1 in math/science, and 1 in any nonlanguage area); or 3 AP exam scores (1 in literature/humanities, 1 in math/science, and 1 in any nonlanguge area). AP credits are accepted. Important factors in the admissions decision are advanced placement or honors courses, extracurricular activities record, and leadership record.

Procedure: Freshmen are admitted fall and spring. Entrance exams should be taken by November of the senior year. There is an early decision admissions plan. Early decision applications should be filed by November 1; regular applications should be filed by January 1 for fall entry, along with a $65 fee. Notification of early decision is sent December 15; regular decision, April 1. Applications are accepted on-line. 2626 applicants were on a recent waiting list, 298 were accepted.

Transfer: 1115 transfer students enrolled in 2008-2009. Students must submit official college transcripts from all postsecondary institutions attended, a final high school transcript, and SAT scores. 64 of 128 credits required for the bachelor's degree must be completed at NYU.

Visiting: There are regularly scheduled orientations for prospective students, including campus tours and weekday information sessions by appointment. There are also 2 fall open houses. To schedule a visit, contact the Admissions Office at (212) 998-4524 or http://events.embark.com/.

Financial Aid: In 2009-2010, 52% of all full-time freshmen and 50% of continuing full-time students received some form of financial aid. 51% of all full-time freshmen and 47% of continuing full-time students received need-based aid. The average freshmen award was $26,287. 20% of undergraduate students work part-time. The average financial indebtedness of the 2009 graduate was $33,487. The FAFSA and the state aid form are required. The deadline for filing freshman financial aid applications for fall entry is February 15.

International Students: There are 1619 international students enrolled. The school actively recruits these students. They must take the TOEFL, the college's own test, or the IELTS, or have ESL testing. They must also take the SAT or ACT.

Computers: Wireless access is available. Facilities include Macs and PCs at 4 computer labs; more than 100 public terminals for walk-up access to e-mail and the Internet; laptop plug-in ports and circulating laptops at the library; modem connectors from home or while traveling; NYU Roam for wireless network access; and ResNet. All students may access the system 24 hours a day, 7 days a week. There are no time limits and no fees.

Graduates: From July 1, 2008 to June 30, 2009, 6059 bachelor's degrees were awarded. The most popular majors were visual and performing arts (20%), business/marketing (18%), and social sciences (16%). 695 companies recruited on campus in a recent year. In an average class, 79% graduate in 4 years or less, 84% graduate in 5 years or less, and 85% graduate in 6 years or less.

Admissions Contact: Office of Undergraduate Admissions. A campus DVD is available. Web: www.nyu.edu

NIAGARA UNIVERSITY   A-3

Niagara University, NY 14109

(716) 286-8700
(800) 462-2111; (716) 286-8710

Full-time: 1220 men, 1910 women	**Faculty:** IIA, -$
Part-time: 35 men, 105 women	**Ph.D.s:** n/av
Graduate: 290 men, 585 women	**Student/Faculty:** n/av
Year: semesters, summer session	**Tuition:** $24,700
Application Deadline: see profile	**Room & Board:** $10,250
Freshman Class: n/av	
SAT or ACT: required	COMPETITIVE

Niagara University, founded in 1856 by the Vincentian fathers and brothers, is a private institution rooted in a Roman Catholic tradition. Programs offered include those in liberal arts, business, education, nursing, and travel, hotel, and restaurant administration. The figures in the above capsule are approximate. There are 4 undergraduate schools and 3 graduate schools. In addition to regional accreditation, Niagara has baccalaureate program accreditation with AACSB, ACCE, CSWE, NCATE, and NLN. The library contains 273,753 volumes, 24,140 microform items, and 772 audio/video tapes/CDs/DVDs, and subscribes to 21,000 periodicals including electronic. Computerized library services include interlibrary loans, database searching, and Internet access. Special learning facilities include a learning resource center, art gallery, radio station, TV station, 2 theaters, and a greenhouse. The 160-acre campus is in a suburban area 4 miles north of Niagara Falls, overlooking the Niagara River gorge, 20 miles north of Buffalo. Including any residence halls, there are 25 buildings.

Student Life: 81% of undergraduates are from New York. Others are from 31 states, 10 foreign countries, and Canada. 75% are from public schools. 71% are white; 12% foreign nationals. 65% are Catholic; 20% Protestant. The average age of freshmen is 18; all undergraduates, 21. 18% do not continue beyond their first year; 63% remain to graduate.

Housing: 1531 students can be accommodated in college housing, which includes single-sex and coed dorms and on-campus apartments. In addition, there are honors houses, special-interest houses, and international housing. On-campus housing is guaranteed for all 4 years. 53% of students live on campus; of those, 75% remain on campus on weekends. All students may keep cars.

Activities: 2% of men belong to 2 national fraternities. There are no sororities. There are 78 groups on campus, including art, aviation, cheerleading, choir, chorale, computers, drama, drill team, ethnic, film, honors, international, musical theater, newspaper, pep band, political, professional, radio and TV, religious, social, social service, and student government. Popular campus events include Orientation, CARE, and Family Weekend.

Sports: There are 8 intercollegiate sports for men and 9 for women, and 25 intramural sports for men and 25 for women. Facilities include a 3400-seat gym, a 6-lane swimming and diving pool, exercise and weight rooms, saunas and dance areas, outdoor tennis courts, baseball and soccer fields, basketball and racquetball courts, a hockey arena, and multipurpose courts with an indoor track. Hiking and biking trails are nearby.

Disabled Students: 75% of the campus is accessible. Facilities include wheelchair ramps, elevators, special parking, specially equipped restrooms, special class scheduling, and lowered drinking fountains. There are campus accommodations for the vision impaired.

Services: Counseling and information services are available, as is tutoring in most subjects. There is a reader service for the blind, and remedial math, reading, and writing. Study skills development, note taking, and escort-assistance services are available, as are educational assistant services for the vision-impaired, educational/classroom assistance and machines for the hearing-impaired, and services for the learning disabled.

Campus Safety and Security: Measures include 24-hour foot and vehicle patrol, emergency notification system, self-defense education, and security escort services. There are emergency telephones, lighted pathways/sidewalks, and a campus security advisory board.

Programs of Study: Niagara confers B.A., B.S., B.B.A., and B.F.A. degrees. Associates and master's degrees are also awarded. Bachelor's degrees are awarded in BIOLOGICAL SCIENCE (biochemistry, biology/biological science, and life science), BUSINESS (accounting, business administration and management, business economics, hotel/motel and restaurant management, human resources, marketing/retailing/merchandising, tourism, and transportation management), COMMUNICATIONS AND THE ARTS (communications, dramatic arts, English, French, and Spanish), COMPUTER AND PHYSICAL SCIENCE (chemistry, computer science, information sciences and systems, and mathematics), EDUCATION (business education, early childhood education, elementary education, English education, foreign languages education, mathematics education, middle school education, science education, secondary education, social studies education, and special education), ENGINEERING AND ENVIRONMENTAL DESIGN (preengineering), HEALTH PROFESSIONS (nursing, predentistry, and premedicine), SOCIAL SCIENCE (criminal justice, history, international studies, liberal arts/general studies, philosophy, political science/government, prelaw, psychology, religion, social science, social work, and sociology). Business, social sciences, and biology are the strongest academically. Business administration, travel and tourism, and education are the largest.

Required: To graduate, students must earn 120 to 126 credit hours and a GPA of at least 2.0; 60 to 66 such hours are required in the major, 20 in specific disciplines, and 20 in liberal arts classes. A comprehensive exam is required in some majors; a thesis is required of honor students and some majors.

Special: Niagara offers a Washington semester, a semester at the state capitol in Albany, on-campus work-study, internships in most majors with such companies as the Big 6 accounting firms and Walt Disney World, and co-op programs in all areas except nursing, education, and social work. Students may study abroad in 8 countries and cross-register through the Western New York Consortium. An accelerated degree program in business, B.A.-B.S. degrees, dual majors, a 2-3 engineering program with the University of Detroit, nondegree study, credit for life, military, and work experience, pass/fail options, and research are also available. There is also an academic exploration program for undeclared majors. There are 14 national honor societies and a freshman honors program.

Faculty/Classroom: 64% of faculty are male; 36% are female. 80% teach undergraduates. No introductory courses are taught by graduate students. The average class size in an introductory lecture is 25 and in a regular course is 22.

Requirements: The SAT or ACT is required. In addition, applicants should be graduates of an accredited high school. The GED is accepted. The high school program should include 16 academic credits, with 4 in English and 2 each in foreign language, history, math, science, and social studies, as well as academic electives. Science, math, and computer majors should have 3 credits each in math and science. A GPA of 80.0 is required. AP and CLEP credits are accepted. Important factors in the admissions decision are advanced placement or honors courses, parents or siblings attended your school, and recommendations by school officials.

Procedure: Freshmen are admitted to all sessions. Entrance exams should be taken in the junior year or fall of the senior year. There are early decision, deferred admissions and rolling admissions plans. Check with the school for current application deadlines. The fall 2009 application fee was $30. Notification is sent on a rolling basis. Applications are accepted on-line.

Transfer: Applicants must have a minimum GPA of 2.0 in travel, hotel, and restaurant administration, arts and sciences, and academic exploration (except for 2.25 in business and 2.5 for nursing and education majors) and submit all high school and college transcripts. The SAT or ACT is recommended. 30 of 120 credits required for the bachelor's degree must be completed at Niagara.

Visiting: There are regularly scheduled orientations for prospective students, including individual interviews and campus tours. Other arrangements can be made individually, such as to attend a class, eat in the student cafeteria, and/or speak with a faculty member. There are guides for informal visits; visitors may sit in on classes and stay overnight. To schedule a visit, contact the Admissions Office appointment desk.

Financial Aid: Niagara is a member of CSS. The FAFSA is required. Check with the school for current application deadlines.

International Students: There were 159 international students enrolled in a recent year. The school actively recruits these students. They must take the TOEFL.

Computers: All students may access the system 9 A.M. to 11 P.M. Monday to Thursday, 9 A.M. to 5 P.M. Friday, noon to 5 P.M. Saturday, and 3 P.M. to 10 P.M. Sunday. There are no time limits and no fees. A PCs should be Windows-based for residence hall use.

Graduates: In a recent year, 551 bachelor's degrees were awarded. The most popular majors were education (22%), commerce and accounting (21%), and hospitality/tourism (11%). 139 companies recruited on campus in 2008-2009. In an average class, 55% graduate in 4 years or less, 60% graduate in 5 years or less, and 63% graduate in 6 years or less. Of the 2008 graduating class, 44% were enrolled in graduate school within 6 months of graduation, and 86% were employed.

Admissions Contact: Harry Gong, Director of Admissions. E-Mail: *admissions@niagara.edu* Web: *www.niagara.edu*

NYACK COLLEGE
D-5

Nyack, NY 10960

(845) 358-1710
(800) 336-9225; (845) 358-3047

Full-time: 710 men, 1015 women	**Faculty:** n/av
Part-time: 75 men, 115 women	**Ph.D.s:** n/av
Graduate: 315 men, 305 women	**Student/Faculty:** n/av
Year: semesters, summer session	**Tuition:** $20,000
Application Deadline: see profile	**Room & Board:** $8200
Freshman Class: n/av	
SAT or ACT: required	**COMPETITIVE**

Nyack College, founded in 1882, is a private liberal arts institution affiliated with the Christian and Missionary Alliance. The figures in the above capsule and in this profile are approximate. There is 1 graduate school. In addition to regional accreditation, Nyack has baccalaureate program accreditation with NASM. The 3 libraries contain 99,000 volumes, 208,000 microform items, and subscribe to 871 periodicals including electronic. Computerized library services include interlibrary loans and database searching. Special learning facilities include a learning resource center and radio station. The 102-acre campus is in a suburban area 20 miles north of New York City. Including any residence halls, there are 22 buildings.

Student Life: 67% of undergraduates are from New York. Others are from 42 states, 58 foreign countries, and Canada. 36% are white; 27% African American; 23% Hispanic. 94% are Protestant. The average age of freshmen is 21; all undergraduates, 27. 35% do not continue beyond their first year; 46% remain to graduate.

Housing: 715 students can be accommodated in college housing, which includes single-sex dorms and on-campus apartments. In addition, there are honors houses. On-campus housing is guaranteed for all 4 years. 81% of students live on campus. Alcohol is not permitted. All students may keep cars.

Activities: There are no fraternities or sororities. There are 17 groups on campus, including band, cheerleading, choir, chorale, drama, ethnic, hand bell choir, honors, ladies glee club, literary magazine, musical theater, newspaper, orchestra, professional, radio and TV, religious, social service, student government, and yearbook. Popular campus events include music festivals and the Cultural Events Series.

Sports: There are 5 intercollegiate sports for men and 5 for women. Facilities include a gym, soccer field, fitness center, training room, softball field, tennis courts, outdoor basketball courts, and a baseball field.

Disabled Students: 70% of the campus is accessible. Facilities include elevators, special parking, specially equipped restrooms, and lowered drinking fountains.

Services: Counseling and information services are available, as is tutoring in every subject. There is a reader service for the blind.

Campus Safety and Security: Measures include 24-hour foot and vehicle patrol and security escort services. There are lighted pathways/sidewalks.

Programs of Study: Nyack confers B.A., B.S., B.Mus., and S.M.B. degrees. Associates and master's degrees are also awarded. Bachelor's degrees are awarded in BUSINESS (accounting and business administration and management), COMMUNICATIONS AND THE ARTS (communications, English, music, music performance, music theory and composition, piano/organ, and voice), COMPUTER AND PHYSICAL SCIENCE (computer science and mathematics), EDUCATION (elementary education, music education, secondary education, and teaching English as a second/foreign language (TESOL/TEFOL)), SOCIAL SCIENCE (biblical studies, crosscultural studies, history, interdisciplinary studies, missions, pastoral studies, philosophy, psychology, religion, religious education, religious music, social science, social work, and youth ministry). Psychology, education, ministry-related programs, and business are the largest.

Required: To graduate, students must complete 126 to 130 credits with a minimum GPA of 2.0 or 2.5 for education majors. General education and major requirements vary by degree program. Students must adhere to the college's standards of Christian living and behavior and complete Bible courses.

Special: Nyack offers internships, cooperative programs with other schools, study abroad in 6 countries, a semester in Hollywood for communications majors, dual and student-designed majors, independent study, nondegree study, a Washington semester, and pass/fail options. The business program provides advanced standing for the M.B.A. program at St. Thomas Aquinas College in Sparkill, NY. There is a freshman honors program.

Faculty/Classroom: 60% of faculty are male; 40% are female. 70% teach undergraduates. No introductory courses are taught by graduate students. The average class size in a laboratory is 15 and in a regular course is 20.

Requirements: The SAT or ACT is required. In addition, high school graduation or its equivalent is essential. Completion of 16 academic credits is required; the college recommends 4 units of English, 3 of history or social science, 3 of any combination of math and science, 2 of a foreign language, and 4 of electives. Students must demonstrate sound Christian character through personal testimony and recommendations. An interview may be required. AP and CLEP credits are accepted.

Procedure: Freshmen are admitted fall and spring. There is a rolling admissions plan. Application deadlines are open. The fall 2009 application fee was $15. Notification is sent on a rolling basis.

Transfer: Applicants must provide all transcripts from previous schools attended. 30 of 126 credits required for the bachelor's degree must be completed at Nyack.

Visiting: There are regularly scheduled orientations for prospective students. There are guides for informal visits; visitors may sit in on classes and stay overnight. To schedule a visit, contact the Office of Admissions.

Financial Aid: The FAFSA and parent and student tax returns, if selected for verification are required. Check with the school for current application deadlines.

International Students: The school actively recruits these students. They must take the TOEFL. They must also take the SAT or ACT.
Computers: All students may access the system. There are no time limits and no fees.
Admissions Contact: Miguel Sanchez, Director of Admissions. A campus DVD is available. E-Mail: *enroll@nyack.edu*
Web: *www.nyackcollege.edu*

PACE UNIVERSITY   D-5

New York, NY 10038-1508   (212) 346-1225 or (914) 773-3321
                                     (800) 874-PACE: (212) 346-1040 or (914) 773-3851

Full-time: 2477 men, 4021 women   **Faculty:** 362; I, av$
Part-time: 714 men, 759 women   **Ph.D.s:** 89%
Graduate: 1902 men, 2833 women   **Student/Faculty:** 18 to 1
Year: semesters, summer session   **Tuition:** $32,626
Application Deadline: open   **Room & Board:** $11,560
Freshman Class: 8948 applied, 6613 accepted, 1672 enrolled
SAT CR/M: 539/547   **ACT:** required

                                           VERY COMPETITIVE

Pace University, founded in 1906, is a private institution offering programs in arts and sciences, business, nursing, education, and computer and information science on 3 campuses, with undergraduate studies in New York City and Pleasantville and graduate studies in White Plains. There are 5 undergraduate schools and 6 graduate schools. In addition to regional accreditation, Pace has baccalaureate program accreditation with AACSB and ABET. The 3 libraries contain 619,687 volumes, 60,453 microform items, and 2794 audio/video tapes/CDs/DVDs, and subscribe to 73,493 periodicals including electronic. Computerized library services include interlibrary loans and database searching. Special learning facilities include a learning resource center, radio station, TV station, 2 art galleries, a performing arts center, biological research labs, environmental center, language lab, and computer labs. The main campus is in an urban area in downtown New York City, and a 200-acre suburban campus is in Pleasantville/Briarcliff Manor. Including any residence halls, there are 65 buildings.
Student Life: 67% of undergraduates are from New York. Others are from 41 states, 30 foreign countries, and Canada. 70% are from public schools. 53% are white; 16% Hispanic; 13% African American. The average age of freshmen is 18; all undergraduates, 22. 26% do not continue beyond their first year; 57% remain to graduate.
Housing: 2921 students can be accommodated in college housing, which includes coed dorms, on-campus apartments, and off-campus apartments. In addition, there are honors houses, special-interest houses, and a wellness floor. 55% of students commute. All students may keep cars.
Activities: 5% of men belong to 3 local and 8 national fraternities; 5% of women belong to 3 local and 7 national sororities. There are 87 groups on campus, including art, cheerleading, chorus, computers, dance, debate, drama, environmental, ethnic, film, gay, honors, international, literary magazine, musical theater, newspaper, photography, political, professional, radio and TV, religious, social, social service, and student government. Popular campus events include Spring Fling, Springcoming, and Diade Comida.
Sports: There are 9 intercollegiate sports for men and 10 for women, and 8 intramural sports for men and 8 for women. Facilities include the Civic Center gym in New York City and gyms, tennis courts, playing fields, and a health, fitness, and recreation center at the Pleasantville/Briarcliff Manor campus.
Disabled Students: 70% of the campus is accessible. Facilities include wheelchair ramps, elevators, special parking, special class scheduling, lowered drinking fountains, lowered telephones, and other facilities that vary by campus.
Services: Counseling and information services are available, as is tutoring in every subject. There is remedial math, reading, and writing. All services are provided in the university's Center for Academic Excellence.
Campus Safety and Security: Measures include 24-hour foot and vehicle patrol and security escort services. There are shuttle buses, emergency telephones, lighted pathways/sidewalks, controlled access to dorms/residences, and closed circuit TV.
Programs of Study: Pace confers B.A., B.S., B.B.A., B.F.A., and B.S.N. degrees. Associate, master's, and doctoral degrees are also awarded. Bachelor's degrees are awarded in AGRICULTURE (environmental studies), BIOLOGICAL SCIENCE (biology/biological science), BUSINESS (accounting, banking and finance, business administration and management, business economics, entrepreneurial studies, hospitality management services, international business management, and marketing/retailing/merchandising), COMMUNICATIONS AND THE ARTS (art, art history and appreciation, communications, English, film arts, fine arts, modern language, Spanish, and theater design), COMPUTER AND PHYSICAL SCIENCE (chemistry, computer science, information sciences and systems, and mathematics), EDUCATION (elementary education), HEALTH PROFESSIONS (clinical science, nursing, and speech pathology/audiology), SOCIAL SCIENCE (American studies, biopsy-

chology, criminal justice, economics, forensic studies, history, philosophy and religion, political science/government, psychology, social science, sociology, and women's studies). Accounting is the strongest academically. Business and finance are the largest.

Required: To graduate, students must complete 128 to 133 credit hours, including 32 to 50 in the major, with a minimum GPA of 2.0. A core curriculum of 60 credits and an introductory computer science course are required as well as a community-based learning experience and 2 enhanced writing courses.

Special: Internships, study abroad, and a cooperative education program in all majors are available. Pace also offers accelerated degree programs, B.A.-B.S. degrees, dual majors, general studies degrees, and 3-2 engineering degrees with Manhattan College and Rensselaer Polytechnic Institute. Credit for life, military, and work experience, nondegree study, and pass/fail options are available. There are 24 national honor societies, a freshman honors program, and 19 departmental honors programs.

Faculty/Classroom: 58% of faculty are male; 42% are female. 84% teach undergraduates, and 24% do research. No introductory courses are taught by graduate students. The average class size in an introductory lecture is 35; in a laboratory, 11; and in a regular course, 23.

Admissions: 74% of the 2009-2010 applicants were accepted. The SAT scores for the 2009-2010 freshman class were: Critical Reading--28% below 500, 49% between 500 and 599, 21% between 600 and 700, and 2% above 700; Math--24% below 500, 51% between 500 and 599, 24% between 600 and 700, and 1% above 700. The ACT scores were 19% below 21, 30% between 21 and 23, 32% between 24 and 26, 12% between 27 and 28, and 7% above 28.

Requirements: The SAT or ACT is required. In addition, applicants should be graduates of an accredited secondary school with at least 16 academic credits, including 4 in English, 3 to 4 each in math, science, and history, and 2 to 3 in foreign language. The GED is accepted. An essay and an interview are recommended. A GPA of 3.0 is required. AP and CLEP credits are accepted. Important factors in the admissions decision are advanced placement or honors courses, recommendations by school officials, and leadership record.

Procedure: Freshmen are admitted fall and spring. Entrance exams should be taken by December of the senior year. There are early admissions, deferred admissions, and rolling admissions plans. Application deadlines are open. The fall 2009 application fee was $45. Notifications are sent December 15. Applications are accepted on-line.

Transfer: 682 transfer students enrolled in 2008-2009. Applicants are admitted in the fall or spring. A college GPA of 2.5 is required. Grades of C or better transfer for credit. A maximum of 68 credits will be accepted from a 2-year school. 32 of 128 to 133 credits required for the bachelor's degree must be completed at Pace.

Visiting: There are regularly scheduled orientations for prospective students, including student-for-a-day programs and overnight visits by appointment. There are guides for informal visits, and visitors may sit in on classes. To schedule a visit, contact the Office of Undergraduate Admission.

Financial Aid: In 2009-2010, 76% of all full-time freshmen and 71% of continuing full-time students received some form of financial aid. 76% of all full-time freshmen and 70% of continuing full-time students received need-based aid. The average freshman award was $27,024. Average annual earnings from campus work are $3633. The average financial indebtedness of the 2009 graduate was $29,622. The FAFSA is required. The deadline for filing freshman financial aid applications for fall entry is February 15.

International Students: There are 308 international students enrolled. The school actively recruits these students. They must take the TOEFL with a minimum score of 570 on the paper-based TOEFL (PBT) or 89 on the Internet-based version (iBT) and the college's own test.

Computers: All students may access the system 24 hours a day. There are no time limits and no fees.

Graduates: From July 1, 2008 to June 30, 2009, 1638 bachelor's degrees were awarded. The most popular majors were finance (13%), accounting (10%), and nursing (10%). 370 companies recruited on campus in 2008-2009. In an average class, 1% graduate in 3 years or less, 42% graduate in 4 years or less, 55% graduate in 5 years or less, and 57% graduate in 6 years or less. Of the 2008 graduating class, 20% were enrolled in graduate school within 6 months of graduation, and 84% were employed.

Admissions Contact: Donna J. Hoyt, Dean of Admissions.
E-mail: *infoctr@pace.edu* Web: *www.pace.edu*

PARSONS NEW SCHOOL FOR DESIGN
Parsons School of Design

D-5

New York, NY 10011	**(877) 528-3321**
	(877) 528-3324; (212) 229-5166
Full-time: 703 men, 2582 women	**Faculty:** 132
Part-time: 40 men, 212 women	**Ph.D.s:** n/av
Graduate: 137 men, 274 women	**Student/Faculty:** 25 to 1
Year: semesters, summer session	**Tuition:** $30,930
Application Deadline: open	**Room & Board:** $11,750
Freshman Class: n/av	
SAT or ACT required	**SPECIAL**

Parsons School of Design, founded in 1896, is a private professional art school and is part of the New School, a university. In addition to regional accreditation, Parsons has baccalaureate program accreditation with NAAB and NASAD. The 3 libraries contain 2.4 million volumes, 13,000 microform items, and 14,275 audio/video tapes/CDs/DVDs, and subscribe to 33,320 periodicals including electronic. Computerized library services include interlibrary loans, database searching, Internet access, and laptop Internet portals. Special learning facilities include an art gallery. The campus is in an urban area in Manhattan's Greenwich Village and in the Fashion District in Manhattan, on Seventh Avenue. Including any residence halls, there are 8 buildings.

Student Life: 83% of undergraduates are from out of state, mostly the Middle Atlantic. Students are from 50 states, 62 foreign countries, and Canada. 66% are from public schools. 30% are white; 29% foreign nationals; 20% Asian American. The average age of freshmen is 20; all undergraduates, 21. 14% do not continue beyond their first year.

Housing: College-sponsored housing includes coed dorms, on-campus apartments, and off-campus apartments. On-campus housing is guaranteed for all 4 years. 80% of students commute. Alcohol is not permitted. All students may keep cars.

Activities: There are no fraternities or sororities. There are 30 groups on campus, including art, choir, chorus, communications, dance, debate, environmental, ethnic, gay, honors, international, jazz band, literary magazine, newspaper, opera, orchestra, political, professional, religious, social, social service, student government, and symphony. Popular campus events include orchestra/chorus concerts, Christmas parties, and recitals.

Sports: There are 3 intramural sports for men and 3 for women. The University does not have an athletic facility but does have a recreation room. The intramural sports take place at an off site location. The off site location is the YMCA which has a regulation size basketball court, locker room/changing area, weight room and a 25 meter swimming pool. The recreation classes take place on campus in a multipurpose room that can accommodate 20 to 35 participants depending on recreation class being taught.

Disabled Students: 90% of the campus is accessible. Facilities include wheelchair ramps, elevators, specially equipped restrooms, lowered drinking fountains, and lowered telephones.

Services: Counseling and information services are available, as is tutoring in some subjects, English and art history. There is remedial reading and writing.

Programs of Study: Parsons confers B.A.-B.F.A., B.B.A., and B.F.A. degrees. Associates and master's degrees are also awarded. Bachelor's degrees are awarded in BUSINESS (marketing/retailing/merchandising), COMMUNICATIONS AND THE ARTS (advertising, design, fine arts, graphic design, illustration, industrial design, photography, and studio art), COMPUTER AND PHYSICAL SCIENCE (digital arts/technology), ENGINEERING AND ENVIRONMENTAL DESIGN (architectural engineering and interior design), SOCIAL SCIENCE (fashion design and technology). Fashion design, communication design, and management are the largest.

Required: To graduate, students must complete 134 credit hours, including 97 in the major, with a minimum GPA of 2.0. Parsons requires a minimum of 30 credits in liberal arts and 12 in art history.

Special: Students have increasing opportunities to enroll in courses offered by other divisions of the New School. Students may study abroad at the Parsons campus in Paris as well as several other programs. The 5-year combined B.A.-B.F.A. degree requires 180 credits for graduation.

Faculty/Classroom: 51% of faculty are male; 49% are female. All teach undergraduates, 13% do research, and 13% do both. No introductory courses are taught by graduate students. The average class size in an introductory lecture is 16 and in a regular course is 15.

Requirements: The SAT or ACT is required. In addition, applicants must be graduates of an accredited secondary school. The GED is accepted. Applicants should have completed 4 years each of art, English, history, and social studies. A portfolio and home exam are required, and an interview is recommended. A GPA of 3.0 is required. AP credits are accepted. Important factors in the admissions decision are personality/intangible qualities, advanced placement or honors courses, and evidence of special talent.

Procedure: Freshmen are admitted fall and spring. Entrance exams should be taken by spring of the junior year. There are deferred admissions and rolling admissions plans. Application deadlines are open. Application fee is $50. Notification is sent on a rolling basis. Applications are accepted on-line.

Transfer: 655 transfer students enrolled in a recent year. Applicants will receive credit for grade C work or better in college courses that are similar in content, purpose, and standards to the courses offered at Parsons. A high school transcript is required for undergraduates, and the SAT or ACT is recommended. All students must present a portfolio and Parsons Challenge. Transfers are admitted in the fall, and selected programs in the spring. 67 of 134 credits required for the bachelor's degree must be completed at Parsons.

Visiting: There are regularly scheduled orientations for prospective students. There are guides for informal visits. To schedule a visit, contact the Office of Admissions.

Financial Aid: In a recent year, 70% of all full-time freshmen and 71% of continuing full-time students received some form of financial aid. 70% of all full-time freshmen and 71% of continuing full-time students received need-based aid. The average freshmen award was $15,974, with $8,548 ($30,270 maximum) from need-based scholarships or need-based grants and $3,358 ($5,500 maximum) from need-based self-help aid (loans and jobs). Average annual earnings from campus work were $2000. The average financial indebtedness of the 2009 graduate was $17,339. Parsons is a member of CSS. The FAFSA, the state aid form, and the college's own financial statement are required. Check with the school for current application deadlines.

International Students: The school actively recruits these students. They must take the TOEFL with a minimum score of 580 on the paper-based TOEFL (PBT) or 92 on the Internet-based version (iBT). They must also take the SAT or ACT.

Computers: Wireless access is available. All students may access the system. There are no time limits and no fees. It is strongly recommended that all students have a personal computer.

Graduates: In a recent year, 455 bachelor's degrees were awarded. The most popular majors were visual and performing arts (97%), and architecture (3%). 212 companies recruited on campus in 2008-2009. In an average class, 53% graduate in 4 years or less, 66% graduate in 5 years or less, and 69% graduate in 6 years or less. Of the 2008 graduating class, 75% were employed within 6 months of graduation.

Admissions Contact: Anthony Padilla, Director of Admissions. E-Mail: *parsadm@newschool.edu* Web: *www.parsons.newschool..edu*

POLYTECHNIC INSTITUTE OF NEW YORK UNIVERSITY
Polytechnic University/Brooklyn

D-5

Brooklyn, NY 11201-3840	**(718) 260-3100**
	(800) 765-8324; (718) 260-3446
Full-time: 1155 men, 280 women	**Faculty:** I, -$
Part-time: 55 men, 15 women	**Ph.D.s:** n/av
Graduate: 1400 men, 435 women	**Student/Faculty:** n/av
Year: semesters, summer session	**Tuition:** $31,500
Application Deadline: see profile	**Room & Board:** $9000
Freshman Class: n/av	
SAT: required	**VERY COMPETITIVE**

Polytechnic University, founded in 1854, is a private, multi-campus university offering undergraduate and graduate programs through the divisions of arts and sciences, engineering, and management. The figures in the above capsule and in this profile are approximate. There are 2 graduate schools. In addition to regional accreditation, Brooklyn Poly has baccalaureate program accreditation with ABET and CSAB. The library contains 212,264 volumes, 60,106 microform items, and 337 audio/video tapes/CDs/DVDs, and subscribes to 1,621 periodicals including electronic. Computerized library services include interlibrary loans and database searching. Special learning facilities include a learning resource center and radio station. The 3-acre campus is in an urban area 5 minutes from downtown Manhattan. Including any residence halls, there are 6 buildings.

Student Life: 88% of undergraduates are from New York. Others are from 22 states, 30 foreign countries, and Canada. 85% are from public schools. 30% are Asian American; 27% white; 13% foreign nationals; 12% African American; 12% Hispanic. The average age of freshmen is 18; all undergraduates, 21. 16% do not continue beyond their first year; 47% remain to graduate.

Housing: 400 students can be accommodated in college housing, which includes coed dorms. In addition, there are fraternity houses. On-campus housing is available on a first-come and first-served basis. Priority is given to out-of-town students. 80% of students commute. Alcohol is not permitted. No one may keep cars.

Activities: 12% of men belong to 2 local and 3 national fraternities; 3% of women belong to 1 national sorority. There are 46 groups on campus, including chess, computers, ethnic, film, honors, international, literary magazine, newspaper, photography, professional, radio and TV, religious, social, social service, and student government. Popular campus events include Chinese New Year, film festivals, and International Food Fair.

Sports: There are 8 intercollegiate sports for men and 8 for women, and 9 intramural sports for men and 9 for women. Facilities include soccer, lacrosse, and baseball fields, basketball courts, ping-pong tables, and 2 student centers.

Disabled Students: All of the campus is accessible. Facilities include wheelchair ramps, elevators, special parking, specially equipped restrooms, lowered drinking fountains, and lowered telephones.

Services: Counseling and information services are available, as is tutoring in every subject. There is remedial math and writing.

Campus Safety and Security: Measures include 24-hour foot and vehicle patrol. There are emergency telephones and lighted pathways/sidewalks.

Programs of Study: Brooklyn Poly confers B.S. degrees. Master's and doctoral degrees are also awarded. Bachelor's degrees are awarded in BIOLOGICAL SCIENCE (molecular biology), BUSINESS (business administration and management), COMMUNICATIONS AND THE ARTS (technical and business writing), COMPUTER AND PHYSICAL SCIENCE (chemistry, computer science, information sciences and systems, mathematics, and physics), ENGINEERING AND ENVIRONMENTAL DESIGN (chemical engineering, civil engineering, computer engineering, construction management, electrical/electronics engineering, and mechanical engineering), SOCIAL SCIENCE (humanities, liberal arts/general studies, and social science). Engineering, management, and physical sciences are the strongest academically. Electrical engineering, computer engineering, and computer science are the largest.

Required: Students must complete all university and departmental course requirements, including 24 credits in humanities/social science, 16 in math, 12 in chemistry/physics, 4 in computers with Pascal, 4 in engineering design, and 3 in programming methodology. A total of 124 to 128 credits must be earned, with 32 in the major, and a minimum GPA of 2.0 is required to graduate. A senior design project is also required.

Special: Cooperative programs are available in all majors. Opportunities are provided for internships, work-study programs, study abroad, accelerated degree programs in engineering and computer science, dual majors, student-designed majors, and nondegree study. There are 9 national honor societies, a freshman honors program, and 3 departmental honors programs.

Faculty/Classroom: 81% of faculty are male; 19% are female. 68% teach undergraduates. No introductory courses are taught by graduate students. The average class size in an introductory lecture is 29; in a laboratory is 16; and in a regular course is 22.

Requirements: The SAT is required. In addition, graduation from an accredited secondary school is required; a GED will be accepted. Applicants must submit a minimum of 16 credit hours, including 4 each in English, math, and science and 1 each in foreign language, art, music, and social studies. An essay and an interview are recommended. AP credits are accepted. Important factors in the admissions decision are advanced placement or honors courses, leadership record, and evidence of special talent.

Procedure: Freshmen are admitted fall, spring, and summer. Entrance exams should be taken by November of the senior year. There are early admissions, deferred admissions, and rolling admissions plans. Application deadlines are open. The fall 2009 application fee was $50. Notification is sent on a rolling basis. Applications are accepted on-line.

Transfer: Transfer applicants must have a 2.75 cumulative GPA. Students with fewer than 30 credits must submit SAT scores and secondary school transcripts in addition to official college-level transcripts. 36 of 124 credits required for the bachelor's degree must be completed at Brooklyn Poly.

Visiting: There are regularly scheduled orientations for prospective students, including a keynote speaker, major presentations, financial aid and scholarship sessions, and student life and career services sessions. There are guides for informal visits and visitors may stay overnight. To schedule a visit, contact the Dean of Admissions at 718-637-5917.

Financial Aid: In a recent year, 98% of all full-time freshmen and 89% of continuing full-time students received some form of financial aid. 84% of all full-time freshmen and 82% of continuing full-time students received need-based aid. The average freshmen award was $21,685. 29% of undergraduate students worked part-time. Average annual earnings from campus work were $5720. The average financial indebtedness of the 2009 graduate was $22,332. Brooklyn Poly is a member of CSS. The FAFSA and the college's own financial statement are required. Check with the school for current application deadlines.

International Students: There were 193 international students enrolled in a recent year. The school actively recruits these students. They must take the TOEFL. They must also take the SAT.

Computers: All students may access the system. 24-hour dial-up service is available. Computer labs are open 13 hours a day. There are no time limits and no fees. All students are required to have a personal computer.

Graduates: In a recent year, 266 bachelor's degrees were awarded. The most popular majors were electrical engineering (19%), computer science (15%), and computer engineering (14%). 150 companies recruited on campus in 2008-2009. In an average class, 28% graduate in 4 years or less, 43% graduate in 5 years or less, and 47% graduate in 6 years or less. Of the 2008 graduating class, 13% were enrolled in graduate school within 6 months of graduation, and 70% were employed.

Admissions Contact: Joy Wexler, Dean of Undergraduate Admissions. E-Mail: *uadmit@poly.edu* Web: *www.poly.edu*

PRATT INSTITUTE   D-5
Brooklyn, NY 11205   (718) 636-3514
                                              (800) 331-0834; (718) 636-3670

Full-time: 1057 men, 1762 women	**Faculty:** IIA, -$
Part-time: 74 men, 80 women	**Ph.D.s:** n/av
Graduate: 471 men, 1218 women	**Student/Faculty:** n/av
Year: semesters, summer session	**Tuition:** $31,080
Application Deadline: January 15	**Room & Board:** $8918
Freshman Class: 5471 applied, 2268 accepted, 625 enrolled	
SAT or ACT: required	**SPECIAL**

Pratt Institute, founded in 1887, is a private institution offering undergraduate and graduate programs in architecture, art and design education, art history, industrial, interior, and communication design, fine arts, design management, arts and cultural management, writing for publication, performance and media, and professional studies. The tuition figures in the above capsule are approximate. There are 2 undergraduate schools and 3 graduate schools. In addition to regional accreditation, Pratt has baccalaureate program accreditation with FIDER, NAAB, and NASAD. The library contains 208,000 volumes, 50,000 microform items, and 3,500 audio/video tapes/CDs/DVDs, and subscribes to 700 periodicals including electronic. Computerized library services include database searching and Internet access. Special learning facilities include a learning resource center, art gallery, radio station, bronze foundry, and metal forge. The 25-acre campus is in an urban area 3 miles east of downtown Manhattan. Including any residence halls, there are 23 buildings.

Student Life: 63% of undergraduates are from out of state, mostly the Northeast. Students are from 46 states, 38 foreign countries, and Canada. 81% are from public schools. 54% are white; 15% Asian American. The average age of freshmen is 19; all undergraduates, 22. 17% do not continue beyond their first year; 65% remain to graduate.

Housing: 1500 students can be accommodated in college housing, which includes single-sex and coed dorms, on-campus apartments, and married student housing. In addition, there are honors houses. On-campus housing is guaranteed for the freshman year only, is available on a first-come, first-served basis, and is available on a lottery system for upperclassmen. Priority is given to out-of-town students. 51% of students commute. All students may keep cars.

Activities: There is 1 local and 1 national fraternity, and 1 local sorority. There are 50 groups on campus, including art, cheerleading, chess, ethnic, film, gay, honors, international, literary magazine, martial arts, newspaper, professional, radio and TV, religious, social, and student government. Popular campus events include Springfest, International Food Fair, and Holiday Ball.

Sports: There are 6 intercollegiate sports for men and 4 for women, and 3 intramural sports for men and 1 for women. Facilities include an activities resource center containing 5 indoor tennis courts, a 200-meter indoor track, volleyball and basketball courts, a weight room, and 2 dance studios.

Disabled Students: 75% of the campus is accessible. Facilities include wheelchair ramps, elevators, special parking, specially equipped restrooms, lowered drinking fountains, and special housing.

Services: Counseling and information services are available, as is tutoring in some subjects, including math, English, science, social science, and art history. There is a reader service for the blind and individual tutoring and testing services are also available.

Campus Safety and Security: Measures include 24-hour foot and vehicle patrol and security escort services. There are shuttle buses, emergency telephones, lighted pathways/sidewalks, and trained security officers.

Programs of Study: Pratt confers B.Arch., B.F.A., B.I.D., and B.P.S. degrees. Associate and master's degrees are also awarded. Bachelor's degrees are awarded in COMMUNICATIONS AND THE ARTS (art history and appreciation, communications, creative writing, film arts, fine arts, industrial design, and photography), EDUCATION (art education), ENGINEERING AND ENVIRONMENTAL DESIGN (architecture, computer graphics, construction management, and interior design), SOCIAL SCIENCE (fashion design and technology). Fine arts, industrial design, and communications design are the strongest academically. Architecture and communications design are the largest.

Required: The number of credits needed for graduation varies with the major, but a minimum of 132 is required, one quarter of which must be in liberal arts. Undergraduates must maintain a GPA of 2.0. All students must take 13 credits (15 for architecture majors) of liberal arts electives,

6 credits each of social sciences or philosophy, English, and cultural history, and 3 credits of science.

Special: Pratt offers co-op programs with the East Coast Consortium (art and design schools) and cross-registration with St. John's College and Queen's College. Internships, study abroad in 4 countries, accelerated degree programs, work-study programs, dual majors, credit for work experience, nondegree study, and pass/fail options are available. There are 4 national honor societies.

Faculty/Classroom: 58% of faculty are male; 42% are female. 92% teach undergraduates, and 1% do research. No introductory courses are taught by graduate students. The average class size in an introductory lecture, 22, in a laboratory, 20, and in a regular course, 15.

Admissions: 41% of the 2009-2010 applicants were accepted.

Requirements: The SAT or ACT is required. In addition, SAT: Subject tests in writing and mathematics level I or II are recommended for architecture applicants. Applicants must be graduates of an accredited secondary school. The GED is accepted. Students should have completed 4 years of English, 4 of math, and 2 each of science and history, and 1 of social studies. A portfolio is required, as is an interview for all applicants who live within 100 miles of Pratt. A GPA of 2.8 is required. AP and CLEP credits are accepted. Important factors in the admissions decision are evidence of special talent, advanced placement or honors courses, and recommendations by school officials.

Procedure: Freshmen are admitted in the fall. Entrance exams should be taken by November of the senior year. There is a deferred admissions plan. Applications should be filed by January 15 for fall entry, along with a $50 fee. Notifications are sent April 1. 820 applicants were on the 2009 waiting list; 213 were admitted. Applications are accepted on-line.

Transfer: 150 transfer students enrolled in 2008-2009. Applicants should present college transcripts and recommendations. Students with fewer than 30 college credits must submit SAT or ACT scores. All transfer applicants without an associate degree must submit high school transcripts as well. A portfolio is required for architecture and art and design students. An interview is recommended. Applicants must have a statement of good standing from prior institution(s). 48 of 132 credits required for the bachelor's degree must be completed at Pratt.

Visiting: There are regularly scheduled orientations for prospective students, including a campus tour, school wide presentations, departmental presentations, and financial aid workshops. There are guides for informal visits; visitors may sit in on classes and stay overnight. To schedule a visit, contact Olga Burger, the Office of Admissions at (800) 331-0834.

Financial Aid: Pratt is a member of CSS. The CSS/Profile, FAFSA, the college's own financial statement, and the parents' and student's tax returns are required. Check with the school for current application deadlines.

International Students: There are 395 international students enrolled. The school actively recruits these students. They must take the TOEFL and the college's own test.

Computers: All students may access the system 24 hours a day, 7 days a week. There are no time limits and no fees. It is strongly recommended that all students have a personal computer.

Graduates: From July 1, 2008 to June 30, 2009, 630 bachelor's degrees were awarded. The most popular majors were visual and performing arts (69%), architecture (16%), and liberal arts (4%).

Admissions Contact: Judith Aaron, Vice President for Enrollment. A campus DVD is available. E-Mail: *jaaron@pratt.edu* Web: *www.pratt.edu*

RENSSELAER POLYTECHNIC INSTITUTE	D-3
Troy, NY 12180-3590	(518) 276-6216
	(800) 448-6562; (518) 276-4072

Full-time: 4019 men, 1582 women	Faculty: 401; I, +$
Part-time: 41 men, 17 women	Ph.D.s: 92%
Graduate: 1482 men, 515 women	Student/Faculty: 14 to 1
Year: semesters, summer session	Tuition: $39,165
Application Deadline: January 15	Room & Board: $11,145
Freshman Class: 12350 applied, 5291 accepted, 1337 enrolled	
SAT CR/M/W: 650/700/630	ACT: 27 MOST COMPETITIVE

Rensselaer Polytechnic Institute, founded in 1824, is a private institution that offers bachelor's, master's and doctoral degrees in engineering, the sciences, information technology, architecture, management, and the humanities and social sciences. Institute programs serve undergraduates, graduate students, and working professionals around the world. There are 5 undergraduate schools and 5 graduate schools. In addition to regional accreditation, Rensselaer has baccalaureate program accreditation with AACSB, ABET, and NAAB. The 2 libraries contain 445,590 volumes, 173,901 microform items, and 6,439 audio/video tapes/CDs/DVDs, and subscribe to 44,214 periodicals including electronic. Computerized library services include interlibrary loans, database searching, Internet access, and laptop Internet portals. Special learning facilities include a learning resource center, art gallery, radio station, TV station, and an observatory. The 276-acre campus is in a suburban area 10 miles north of Albany. Including any residence halls, there are 200 buildings.

Student Life: 58% of undergraduates are from out of state, mostly the Northeast. Students are from 46 states, 65 foreign countries, and Canada. 78% are from public schools. 74% are white; 11% Asian American. The average age of freshmen is 18; all undergraduates, 20. 9% do not continue beyond their first year; 82% remain to graduate.

Housing: 3384 students can be accommodated in college housing, which includes single-sex and coed dorms, on-campus apartments, and married student housing. In addition, there are special-interest houses, fraternity houses, and a black cultural center. On-campus housing is available on a first-come, first-served basis, and is available on a lottery system for upperclassmen. 59% of students live on campus. Upperclassmen may keep cars.

Activities: 25% of men belong to 1 local and 31 national fraternities; 18% of women belong to 1 local and 4 national sororities. There are more than 160 groups on campus, including art, astrophysical, band, biomedical engineering, entrepreneurship, cheerleading, chess, choir, chorale, chorus, computers, dance, drama, drill team, environmental, ethnic, film, finance, gay, honors, international, jazz band, literary magazine, musical theater, orchestra, pep band, photography, political, professional, radio and TV, religious, Rensselaer biotechnology students, social, social service, student government, and symphony. Popular campus events include Big Red Freakout, Grand Marshal Week, and Performing Arts Series.

Sports: There are 12 intercollegiate sports for men and 11 for women, and 22 intramural sports for men and 21 for women. Facilities include a 4800-seat field house, a pool, a stadium,5 gyms, a sports and recreation center, several playing fields, 2 weight rooms, a fitness center, 6 tennis courts, 7 handball/squash courts, 3 artificial turf fields, an indoor track, an ice hockey rink, a 5200-seat stadium and a 1200-seat arena.

Disabled Students: 55% of the campus is accessible. Facilities include wheelchair ramps, elevators, special parking, specially equipped rest rooms, special class scheduling, lowered drinking fountains, and lowered telephones.

Services: Counseling and information services are available, as is tutoring in every subject. There is a reader service for the blind, and remedial math, reading, and writing. There is a writing center and an advising and learning assistance center.

Campus Safety and Security: Measures include 24-hour foot and vehicle patrol, self-defense education, and security escort services. There are shuttle buses, emergency telephones, lighted pathways/sidewalks, card-access residence halls, on-campus bicycle patrol, and a student volunteer program.

Programs of Study: Rensselaer confers B.S. and B.Arch. degrees. Master's and doctoral degrees are also awarded. Bachelor's degrees are awarded in BIOLOGICAL SCIENCE (biochemistry, biology/biological science, and biophysics), BUSINESS (management information systems, management science, and recreation and leisure services), COMMUNICATIONS AND THE ARTS (communications and media arts), COMPUTER AND PHYSICAL SCIENCE (applied physics, chemistry, computer science, geology, hydrogeology, mathematics, physics, and science technology), ENGINEERING AND ENVIRONMENTAL DESIGN (aeronautical engineering, architecture, biomedical engineering, chemical engineering, civil engineering, computer engineering, construction engineering, electrical/electronics engineering, engineering, engineering physics, environmental engineering, industrial engineering, materials engineering, mechanical engineering, and nuclear engineering), HEALTH PROFESSIONS (premedicine), SOCIAL SCIENCE (economics, interdisciplinary studies, philosophy, prelaw, and psychology). Engineering, sciences, and architecture are the strongest academically. General engineering, computer science, and management are the largest.

Required: For graduation, students must earn at least 124 credits in all majors except engineering (128 needed) and the B.Arch. Program (168 needed). The core curriculum includes 48 credits in math, science, humanities, and social sciences. Students must maintain a minimum GPA of 1.8 and must fulfill a writing requirement.

Special: Rensselaer offers co-op programs, internships, study abroad/exchange program, and pass/fail options are available. Students may pursue dual and student-designed majors, a 3-2 engineering degree with more than 40 universities, 2-2 agreements, an accelerated degree program in physician-scientist, law and MBA. There are 14 national honor societies and 8 departmental honors programs.

Faculty/Classroom: 79% of faculty are male; 21% are female. No introductory courses are taught by graduate students. The average class size in an introductory lecture, 35 in a laboratory, 18 and in a regular course, 28.

Admissions: 43% of the 2009-2010 applicants were accepted. The SAT scores for the 2009-2010 freshman class were: Critical Reading-19% between 500 and 599, 54% between 600 and 700, and 27% above 700; Math- 5% between 500 and 599, 43% between 600 and 700, and 52% above 700; Writing--2% below 500, 27% between 500 and 599, 53% between 600 and 700, and 18% above 700. The ACT scores were 3% below 21, 11% between 21 and 23, 25% between 24 and 26, 25% between 27 and 28, and 36% above 28. 80% of the current freshmen were in the top fifth of their class; 96% were in the top two fifths. 46 freshmen graduated first in their class.

Requirements: The SAT or ACT is required. In addition, SAT subject tests in critical reading, math and science are required for accelerated-program applicants or ACT, which must include the optional writing component in lieu of SAT and SAT. AP credits are accepted. Important factors in the admissions decision are advanced placement or honors courses, recommendations by school officials, and leadership record.

Procedure: Freshmen are admitted fall and spring. Entrance exams should be taken in the junior or senior year. There arean early decision and deferred admissions plans. Early decision I applications should be filed by November 2; early decision II by December 15; accelerated programs by November 2; and regular applications should be filed by January 15 for fall entry; along with a $70 fee. Notifications are sent December 5 for early decision I; early April for accelerated programs; January 16 for early decision II; and March 13 for regular decision. 3799 applicants were on the 2009 waiting list; 276 were admitted. Applications are accepted on-line.

Transfer: 103 transfer students enrolled in 2008-2009. Applicants should have completed 12 or more transferable college credits, and must be in good academic standing at the institutions they are attending or attended. 48 of 124 credits required for the bachelor's degree must be completed at Rensselaer.

Visiting: There are regularly scheduled orientations for prospective students. There are guides for informal visits and visitors may sit in on classes. To schedule a visit, contact the Admissions Office at admissions@rpi.edu.

Financial Aid: In 2009-2010, all full-time freshmen and 97% of continuing full-time students received some form of financial aid. 66% of all full-time freshmen and 65% of continuing full-time students received need-based aid. The average freshman award was $27,793. Need-based scholarships or need-based grants averaged $22,418; need-based self-help aid (loans and jobs) averaged $7,750; non-need based athletic scholarships averaged $43,106; and other non-need based awards and non-need based scholarships averaged $13,043. 24% of undergraduate students work part-time. Average annual earnings from campus work are $2000. The average financial indebtedness of the 2009 graduate was $30,838. Rensselaer is a member of CSS. The CSS/Profile and FAFSA are required. The deadline for filing freshman financial aid applications for fall entry is February 15.

International Students: There are 148 international students enrolled. The school actively recruits these students. They must take the TOEFL with a minimum score of 570 on the paper-based TOEFL (PBT) or 88 on the Internet-based version (iBT). They must also take the SAT or ACT.

Computers: Wireless access is available. Services include support for interactive learning (including WebCT courses), electronic information-retrieval services by the libraries, and on-line student and administrative services. All students may access the system. There are no time limits and no fees. A laptop computer is required of all undergraduates. An Lenovo ThinkPad T61 is recommended.

Graduates: From July 1, 2008 to June 30, 2009, 1076 bachelor's degrees were awarded. The most popular majors were engineering (53%), management (10%), and computer science (9%). 370 companies recruited on campus in 2008-2009. In an average class, 64% graduate in 4 years or less, 81% graduate in 5 years or less, and 82% graduate in 6 years or less. Of the 2008 graduating class, 27% were enrolled in graduate school within 6 months of graduation, and 68% were employed.

Admissions Contact: Karen Long, Director, Undergraduate Admissions. E-Mail: *admissions@rpi.edu* Web: *www.rpi.edu*

ROBERTS WESLEYAN COLLEGE B-3
Rochester, NY 14624-1997

(585) 594-6400
(800) 777-4792; (585) 594-6371

Full-time: 390 men, 875 women	Faculty: 87
Part-time: 40 men, 83 women	Ph.D.s: 66%
Graduate: 116 men, 424 women	Student/Faculty: 15 to 1
Year: semesters, summer session	Tuition: $23,780
Application Deadline: February 1	Room & Board: $8520
Freshman Class: 976 applied, 886 accepted, 259 enrolled	
SAT CR/M: 534/540	ACT: 24	COMPETITIVE+

Roberts Wesleyan College, founded in 1866, is a private institution affiliated with the Free Methodist Church. The curriculum offers a Christian liberal arts education. In addition to regional accreditation, Roberts has baccalaureate program accreditation with ACBSP, CSWE, NASAD, NASM, and NLN. The library contains 134,798 volumes, 170,345 microform items, and 4,229 audio/video tapes/CDs/DVDs, and subscribes to 1,845 periodicals including electronic. Computerized library services include interlibrary loans, database searching, Internet access, and laptop Internet portals. Special learning facilities include a learning resource center, art gallery, and radio station. The 75-acre campus is in a suburban area 8 miles southwest of Rochester. Including any residence halls, there are 32 buildings.

Student Life: 89% of undergraduates are from New York. Others are from 27 states, 18 foreign countries, and Canada. 81% are white. 87% are Protestant; 11% Catholic. The average age of freshmen is 19; all undergraduates, 22. 15% do not continue beyond their first year; 60% remain to graduate.

Housing: 792 students can be accommodated in college housing, which includes single-sex dorms, on-campus apartments, and off-campus apartments. On-campus housing is guaranteed for all 4 years. 65% of students live on campus; of those, 60% remain on campus on weekends. Alcohol is not permitted. All students may keep cars.

Activities: There are no fraternities or sororities. Groups on campus include band, choir, chorale, chorus, drama, ethnic, honors, international, jazz band, musical theater, newspaper, orchestra, pep band, radio and TV, religious, social, social service, student government, symphony, and yearbook. Popular campus events include Winter Weekend, Spring Formal, and talent and variety shows.

Sports: There are 6 intercollegiate sports for men and 6 for women, and 6 intramural sports for men and 6 for women. Facilities include an athletic center with facilities for basketball, volleyball, tennis, badminton, track, soccer, weight lifting, walleyball, racquetball, flag football, ultimate Frisbee, and swimming.

Disabled Students: 71% of the campus is accessible. Facilities include wheelchair ramps, elevators, special parking, specially equipped restrooms, special class scheduling, lowered drinking fountains, and lowered telephones.

Services: Counseling and information services are available, as is tutoring in every subject. Note takers for the hearing impaired are available. There is a reader service for the blind, and remedial math, reading, and writing.

Campus Safety and Security: Measures include 24-hour foot and vehicle patrol, emergency notification system, self-defense education, and security escort services. There are emergency telephones, lighted pathways/sidewalks, and personal-safety education programs.

Programs of Study: Roberts confers B.A. and B.S. degrees. Associate and master's degrees are also awarded. Bachelor's degrees are awarded in BIOLOGICAL SCIENCE (biochemistry and biology/biological science), BUSINESS (accounting, business administration and management, international business management, and marketing/retailing/merchandising), COMMUNICATIONS AND THE ARTS (applied art, applied music, art, communications, English, fine arts, graphic design, music, music performance, Spanish, and studio art), COMPUTER AND PHYSICAL SCIENCE (chemistry, computer science, mathematics, and physics), EDUCATION (art education, early childhood education, elementary education, English education, mathematics education, music education, physical education, secondary education, and special education), ENGINEERING AND ENVIRONMENTAL DESIGN (preengineering), HEALTH PROFESSIONS (nursing, pharmacy, premedicine, prepharmacy, and preveterinary science), SOCIAL SCIENCE (biblical studies, Christian studies, criminal justice, history, humanities, interdisciplinary studies, liberal arts/general studies, philosophy, prelaw, psychology, religion, and social work). Music, education, and social work are the strongest academically. Elementary education and nursing are the largest.

Required: To graduate, students must complete a minimum of 124 credit hours, with a minimum of 30 hours in the major. Required courses include first-year experience, phys ed, modern technology, world issues, speech, writing, history, Bible, and philosophy.

Special: Students may cross-register with members of the Rochester Area Colleges consortium. Internships, study abroad in 8 countries, a Washington semester, co-op programs, B.A.-B.S. degrees, dual majors, and 3-2 engineering degrees with Clarkson University, Rensselaer Polytechnic Institute, and Rochester Institute of Technology are available. Nondegree study and credit for life, military, and work experience are also offered. The organizational management program, geared to adults, consists of 4-hour weekly sessions, with reliance on out-of-class work. There is a freshman honors program, and all departments have honors programs.

Faculty/Classroom: 53% of faculty are male; 47% are female. 85% teach undergraduates. No introductory courses are taught by graduate students. The average class size in an introductory lecture is 38; in a laboratory, 15; and in a regular course, 23.

Admissions: 91% of the 2009-2010 applicants were accepted. The SAT scores for the 2009-2010 freshman class were: Critical Reading--33% below 500, 42% between 500 and 599, 18% between 600 and 700, and 4% above 700; Math--34% below 500, 35% between 500 and 599, 29% between 600 and 700, and 2% above 700; Writing--45% below 500, 39% between 500 and 599, 15% between 600 and 700, and 1% above 700. The ACT scores were 23% below 21, 18% between 21 and 23, 18% between 24 and 26, 23% between 27 and 28, and 18% above 28. 47% of the current freshmen were in the top fifth of their class; 71% were in the top two fifths. 8 freshmen graduated first in their class.

Requirements: The SAT or ACT is required. In addition, applicants must be graduates of an accredited secondary school. The GED is accepted. At least 12 academic credits are required, including 4 years of

English and 2 years each of math and science. A foreign language and 3 years of social studies are recommended. The chosen major may modify requirements. An essay is required, and an interview is recommended. Roberts requires applicants to be in the upper 50% of their class. A GPA of 2.3 is required. AP and CLEP credits are accepted. Important factors in the admissions decision are advanced placement or honors courses, personality/intangible qualities, and extracurricular activities record.

Procedure: Freshmen are admitted to all sessions. There are deferred admissions and rolling admissions plans. Applications should be filed by February 1 for fall entry and December 1 for spring entry. The fall 2009 application fee was $35. Notification is sent on a rolling basis. Applications are accepted on-line.

Transfer: 109 transfer students enrolled in 2008-2009. Applicants must submit transcripts from all previous institutions attended. Credit is usually accepted for courses with grade C or better. 30 of 124 credits required for the bachelor's degree must be completed at Roberts.

Visiting: There are regularly scheduled orientations for prospective students, including a campus tour, class visits, a student panel, an admissions overview, meetings with faculty, and a financial aid presentation. There are guides for informal visits, visitors may sit in on classes, and stay overnight. To schedule a visit, contact the Admissions Office at (800) 777-4792.

Financial Aid: In 2009-2010, 97% of all full-time freshmen and 92% of continuing full-time students received some form of financial aid. 90% of all full-time freshmen and 90% of continuing full-time students received need-based aid. The average freshman award was $26,588. 35% of undergraduate students work part-time. Average annual earnings from campus work are $1020. Roberts is a member of CSS. The FAFSA and TAP (New York residents only) are required. The priority date for freshman financial aid applications for fall entry is March 15. The deadline for filing freshman financial aid applications for fall entry is open.

International Students: There are 55 international students enrolled. They must take the TOEFL with a minimum score of 550 on the paper-based TOEFL (PBT) or 79 on the Internet-based version (iBT).

Computers: All students may access the system 24 hours a day, 7 days a week. There are no time limits and no fees.

Graduates: From July 1, 2008 to June 30, 2009, 361 bachelor's degrees were awarded. The most popular majors were organizational management (28%), nursing (22%), and elementary education (15%). In an average class, 48% graduate in 4 years or less, 57% graduate in 5 years or less, and 67% graduate in 6 years or less. Of the 2008 graduating class, 29% were enrolled in graduate school within 6 months of graduation, and 92% were employed.

Admissions Contact: Linda Kurtz Hoffman, Admissions and Marketing Specialist. A campus DVD is available.
E-mail: *admissions@roberts.edu* Web: *www.roberts.edu*

ROCHESTER INSTITUTE OF TECHNOLOGY   B-3

Rochester, NY 14623   (585) 475-6631; (585) 475-7424

Full-time: 8125 men, 3800 women	**Faculty:** IIA, +$
Part-time: 1080 men, 500 women	**Ph.D.s:** n/avn
Graduate: 1630 men, 915 women	**Student/Faculty:** n/av
Year: trimesters, summer session	**Tuition:** $30,501
Application Deadline: March 1	**Room & Board:** $10,044
Freshman Class: n/av	
SAT or ACT: required	**VERY COMPETITIVE**

Rochester Institute of Technology, a private institution founded in 1829, offers programs in art and design, science, computer science, medical sciences, engineering, fine arts, business, hotel management, graphic arts, information technology, and photography, as well as liberal arts, and includes the National Technical Institute for the Deaf. Most programs include a cooperative education component, which provides full-time work experience to complement classroom studies. The figures in the above capsule and in this profile are approximate. There are 8 undergraduate schools and 8 graduate schools. In addition to regional accreditation, RIT has baccalaureate program accreditation with AACSB, ABET, ADA, CAHEA, CSAB, CSWE, FIDER, and NASAD. The library contains 422,281 volumes, 498,703 microform items, and 54,935 audio/video tapes/CDs/DVDs, and subscribes to 21,208 periodicals including electronic. Computerized library services include interlibrary loans, database searching, Internet access, and laptop Internet portals. Special learning facilities include a learning resource center, art gallery, radio station, TV station, a computer chip manufacturing facility, a student-operated restaurant, an electronic prepress lab, an imaging science facility, and an observatory. The 1300-acre campus is in a suburban area 5 miles south of Rochester. Including any residence halls, there are 195 buildings.

Student Life: 55% of undergraduates are from New York. Others are from 49 states, 95 foreign countries, and Canada. 85% are from public schools. 70% are white. The average age of freshmen is 18; all undergraduates, 21. 11% do not continue beyond their first year; 64% remain to graduate.

Housing: 6854 students can be accommodated in college housing, which includes single-sex and coed dorms, on-campus apartments, and married student housing. In addition, there are honors houses, special-interest houses, fraternity houses, and sorority houses. On-campus housing is guaranteed for the freshman year only, is available on a first-come, first-served basis, and is available on a lottery system for upperclassmen. 65% of students live on campus; of those, 90% remain on campus on weekends. All students may keep cars.

Activities: 5% of men belong to 17 national fraternities; 5% of women belong to 12 national sororities. There are 175 groups on campus, including art, band, cheerleading, chess, choir, chorale, chorus, computers, dance, drama, environmental, ethnic, film, gay, gospel choir, honors, international, jazz band, literary magazine, newspaper, orchestra, pep band, photography, political, professional, radio and TV, religious, social, social service, and student government. Popular campus events include Fall, Spring, and Winter Weekends and Martin Luther King Celebration.

Sports: There are 11 intercollegiate sports for men and 12 for women, and 13 intramural sports for men and 13 for women. Facilities include 3 gyms, an ice rink, 2 swimming pools, 9 tennis courts, a field house, athletic fields, and a student life center with 8 racquetball courts, dance facilities, weight training facilities, and an indoor track.

Disabled Students: 95% of the campus is accessible. Facilities include wheelchair ramps, elevators, special parking, specially equipped restrooms, special class scheduling, lowered drinking fountains, lowered telephones, and special housing.

Services: Counseling and information services are available, as is tutoring in most subjects. There is a reader service for the blind. There are comprehensive support services for students with physical or learning disabilities and for first-generation college students.

Campus Safety and Security: Measures include 24-hour foot and vehicle patrol, emergency notification system, self-defense education, and security escort services. There are shuttle buses, emergency telephones, lighted pathways/sidewalks, and controlled access to dorms/residences.

Programs of Study: RIT confers B.S. and B.F.A. degrees. Associates, master's, and doctoral degrees are also awarded. Bachelor's degrees are awarded in BIOLOGICAL SCIENCE (biochemistry, bioinformatics, biology/biological science, biotechnology, and nutrition), BUSINESS (accounting, banking and finance, business administration and management, business systems analysis, hotel/motel and restaurant management, international business management, management information systems, management science, marketing management, and tourism), COMMUNICATIONS AND THE ARTS (animation, applied art, ceramic art and design, communications, communications technology, crafts, design, film arts, fine arts, glass, graphic design, illustration, industrial design, metal/jewelry, painting, photography, publishing, sculpture, studio art, telecommunications, and video), COMPUTER AND PHYSICAL SCIENCE (applied mathematics, chemistry, computer mathematics, computer science, information sciences and systems, mathematics, physics, polymer science, software engineering, statistics, and systems analysis), EDUCATION (education of the deaf and hearing impaired), ENGINEERING AND ENVIRONMENTAL DESIGN (aerospace studies, biomedical engineering, civil engineering technology, computer engineering, computer graphics, computer technology, electrical/electronics engineering, electrical/electronics engineering technology, engineering, engineering technology, environmental engineering technology, environmental science, furniture design, graphic arts technology, graphic and printing production, industrial engineering, interior design, manufacturing engineering, manufacturing technology, materials science, mechanical engineering, mechanical engineering technology, military science, printing technology, and woodworking), HEALTH PROFESSIONS (allied health, physician's assistant, predentistry, premedicine, preveterinary science, and ultrasound technology), SOCIAL SCIENCE (criminal justice, dietetics, economics, experimental psychology, food production/management/services, interpreter for the deaf, prelaw, psychology, and public affairs). Mechanical engineering, computer science, and film and animation are the strongest academically. Engineering, information technology, and photography are the largest.

Required: Students must have a GPA of 2.0 and have completed 180 quarter credit hours to graduate. Distribution requirements include 36 credits in the liberal arts (writing, humanities, and social sciences). B.S. programs also require a minimum of 20 quarter credit hours in science and math. There are no general science or math requirements for the B.F.A. programs in art, design, photography, or film/video.

Special: RIT offers internships in social science and allied health majors, and cooperative education programs with 1900 co-op employers. Cooperative education is required or recommended in most programs and provides full-time paid work experience. Cross-registration with Rochester-area colleges is available. There are accelerated dual degree (BS/MS, BS/ME, BS/MBA) programs in science, engineering, public policy, math, computer science, materials science, imaging science, and business. Students may study abroad in 15 countries, and student-designed majors are permitted in applied arts and sciences. There is an Honors Program in general education and home colleges. There are 6 national honor societies, a freshman honors program, and 7 departmental honors programs.

Faculty/Classroom: 68% of faculty are male; 32% are female. 97% teach undergraduates, 3% do research, and 90% do both. No introductory courses are taught by graduate students. The average class size in an introductory lecture is 30; in a laboratory is 16; and in a regular course is 20.

Requirements: The SAT or ACT is required. In addition, applicants must be high school graduates or have a GED certificate. Applicants are required to submit an essay, and an interview is recommended. The School of Art and the School of Design emphasize a required portfolio of artwork. Required high school math and science credits vary by program, with 3 years in each area generally acceptable. RIT requires applicants to be in the upper 50% of their class. AP and CLEP credits are accepted. Important factors in the admissions decision are advanced placement or honors courses, recommendations by school officials, and extracurricular activities record.

Procedure: Freshmen are admitted to all sessions. Entrance exams should be taken during the junior or senior year. There are early decision and deferred admissions plans. Early decision applications should be filed by December 1; regular applications, by March 1 for fall entry, along with a $50 fee. Notification of early decision is sent January 15; regular decision, March 15. Applications are accepted on-line. A waiting list is maintained.

Transfer: 1079 transfer students enrolled in a recent year. Transfer students must have a GPA of 2.5 for admission to most programs; those with fewer than 30 college credits must supply a high school transcript. Other requirements vary by program. 45 of 180 credits required for the bachelor's degree must be completed at RIT.

Visiting: There are regularly scheduled orientations for prospective students, including academic advising and information on housing and student services. There are guides for informal visits; visitors may sit in on classes and stay overnight. To schedule a visit, contact Admissions Receptionist at (585) 475-6736.

Financial Aid: In a recent year, 85% of all full-time freshmen and 75% of continuing full-time students received some form of financial aid. 73% of all full-time freshmen and 67% of continuing full-time students received need-based aid. The average freshmen award was $18,900. 70% of undergraduate students worked part-time. Average annual earnings from campus work were $2200. The average financial indebtedness of the 2009 graduate was $22,000. The FAFSA is required. Check with the school for current application deadlines.

International Students: There were 580 international students enrolled in a recent year. The school actively recruits these students. They must take the TOEFL. They must also take the SAT or ACT.

Computers: Wireless access is available. More than 2,500 PCs are available for student use in university computer labs. All students may access the system 7 days per week, 24-hour access. There are no time limits and no fees.

Graduates: I a recent year, 2432 bachelor's degrees were awarded. The most popular majors were engineering (14%), science (9%), and information technology (7%). 900 companies recruited on campus in 2008-2009. In an average class, 64% graduate in 6 years or less. Of the 2008 graduating class, 10% were enrolled in graduate school within 6 months of graduation, and 90% were employed.

Admissions Contact: Daniel Shelley, Director of Admissions. E-Mail: *admissions@rit.edu* Web: *www.rit.edu*

RUSSELL SAGE COLLEGE　　　D-3
Troy, NY 12180　　　　　　　　　**(518) 244-2217**
　　　　　　　　　(888) Very-Sage; (518) 244-6880

Full-time: no men, 805 women	**Faculty:** n/av
Part-time: no men, 55 women	**Ph.Ds:** n/av
Graduate: none	**Student/Faculty:** n/av
Year: semesters, summer session	**Tuition:** $20,800
Application Deadline: see profile	**Room & Board:** $8000
Freshman Class: n/av	
SAT or ACT: required	**COMPETITIVE**

Russell Sage, a private, comprehensive college, was founded in 1916 to prepare women for successful professional careers. Baccalaureate degrees in the traditional arts and sciences are offered, along with professional programs in nutrition, athletic training, nursing, physical and occupational therapy, theater, musical theater, creative arts in therapy, business, forensic science, communications, and education.. The figures in the above capsule and in this profile are approximate. There is 1 graduate school. In addition to regional accreditation, Russell Sage has baccalaureate program accreditation with ADA, APTA, NASAD, NCATE, and NLN. The library contains 342,021 volumes, 3,341 microform items, and 31,968 audio/video tapes/CDs/DVDs, and subscribes to 803 periodicals including electronic. Computerized library services include interlibrary loans and database searching. Special learning facilities include a learning resource center, the New York State Theater Institute, Robinson Athletic Center, and Helen Upton Center for Womens' Studies. The

14-acre campus is in an urban area 10 miles from Albany and Schenectady. Including any residence halls, there are 38 buildings.

Student Life: 92% of undergraduates are from New York. Others are from 13 states, and 2 foreign countries. 77% are white. The average age of freshmen is 18; all undergraduates, 22. 10% do not continue beyond their first year; 68% remain to graduate.

Housing: 738 students can be accommodated in college housing, which includes single-sex dorms and on-campus apartments. In addition, there are language houses, special-interest houses, 24-hour quiet housing and substance-free/wellness housing. On-campus housing is guaranteed for all 4 years and is available on a lottery system for upperclassmen. 55% of students commute. Upperclassmen may keep cars.

Activities: There are no fraternities or sororities. There are 26 groups on campus, including academic clubs in each major, choir, chorus, dance, drama, equestrian., ethnic, gay, honors, leadership, literary magazine, musical theater, newspaper, orchestra, political, religious, social, social service, student government, and yearbook. Popular campus events include Rally Day, Sage Fest, and Family Weekend.

Sports: There are 5 intercollegiate sports for women, and 8 intramural sports for women. Facilities include a weight and fitness center, a sports medicine facility, swimming pool, 4 tennis courts, a practice field, 2 gyms, and a large multipurpose room for indoor recreation.

Disabled Students: 70% of the campus is accessible. Facilities include wheelchair ramps, elevators, special parking, specially equipped restrooms, special class scheduling, computer center access, electronic access via blackboard for a variety of information and courses. There are specially equipped science labs and equipment and visits to administrative offices by arrangement.

Services: Counseling and information services are available, as is tutoring in most subjects. There is remedial math, reading, and writing.

Campus Safety and Security: Measures include 24-hour foot and vehicle patrol, self-defense education, and security escort services. There are emergency telephones, lighted pathways/sidewalks, an evening escort service, and monitored video cameras.

Programs of Study: Russell Sage confers B.A. and B.S. degrees. Master's degrees are also awarded. Bachelor's degrees are awarded in BIOLOGICAL SCIENCE (biochemistry, biology/biological science, and nutrition), BUSINESS (business administration and management), COMMUNICATIONS AND THE ARTS (communications, English, musical theater, and Spanish), COMPUTER AND PHYSICAL SCIENCE (chemistry, computer science, and mathematics), EDUCATION (athletic training and elementary education), ENGINEERING AND ENVIRONMENTAL DESIGN (environmental science), HEALTH PROFESSIONS (art therapy, nursing, occupational therapy, physical therapy, and public health), SOCIAL SCIENCE (applied psychology, biopsychology, criminal justice, forensic studies, history, interdisciplinary studies, international studies, political science/government, psychology, and sociology). Psychology, English, and nursing are the strongest academically. Health and rehabilitative sciences, education, and psychology are the largest.

Required: To graduate, students must complete 120 credits with a 2.0 GPA overall and at least 30 credits and a 2.2 GPA in the major. B.A. candidates must earn a minimum of 90 credits in the liberal arts and sciences and B.S. candidates must earn a minimum of 60. A general education requirement of 36 credits focuses on the experiences of women in a multicultural society, understanding technology, writing skills, and a broad exposure to the various arts and sciences. There is a course requiring community service and a writing-intensive course in the major. Students must also complete 6 credits in a single language or show proficiency and take technology-intensive and cross-cultured courses.

Special: Students may cross-register with the 14 area schools of the Hudson-Mohawk Association of Colleges. A theater major is offered in conjunction with NYSTI. Study abroad, internships, and work-study programs are available. There are several accelerated 5-year programs in the health sciences, a 5-year B.S./M.B.A., a 3-3 program with Albany Law School, and a 3-2 engineering degree with nearby Rensselaer Polytechnic Institute. 9 centers for interdisciplinary inquiry draw students from across majors. The college confers credit for life, military, or work experience. Nondegree study, student-designed majors, dual majors, and pass/fail options are also available. There are 14 national honor societies and a freshman honors program.

Faculty/Classroom: 38% of faculty are male; 62% are female. All teach and do research. No introductory courses are taught by graduate students. The average class size in an introductory lecture is 19; in a laboratory is 9; and in a regular course is 16.

Requirements: The SAT or ACT is required. In addition, applicants must be graduates of an accredited secondary school or have a GED. A minimum of 16 academic units are required, including courses in English, social sciences, natural sciences, math, and foreign language. An essay, for applicants still in high school, is required, and an interview is recommended. A GPA of 2.0 is required. AP and CLEP credits are accepted. Important factors in the admissions decision are advanced placement or honors courses, leadership record, and evidence of special talent.

Procedure: Freshmen are admitted fall and spring. Entrance exams should be taken during spring of the junior year or fall of the senior year.

There are early decision, early admissions, deferred admissions, and rolling admissions plans. Early decision applications should be filed by December 1; regular applications, check with the school for current application deadlines. The fall 2009 application fee was $30. Notification of early decision is sent December 15; others sent on a rolling basis. Applications are accepted on-line.

Transfer: Applicants must have a minimum GPA of 2.5. Interviews are strongly encouraged and may be required in some instances. 45 of 120 credits required for the bachelor's degree must be completed at Russell Sage.

Visiting: There are regularly scheduled orientations for prospective students, including meetings with faculty, a campus tour, a financial aid session, and an admissions interview. There are guides for informal visits; visitors may sit in on classes and stay overnight. To schedule a visit, contact the Office of Admission at (518) 244-2218.

Financial Aid: The FAFSA is required. Check with the school for current application deadlines.

International Students: The school actively recruits these students. They must take the TOEFL. International applicants with English as their native language must take the SAT or ACT.

Computers: All students may access the system. The public computer labs are open 14 hours per day, 7 days a week; dial-in access is available 24 hours a day. There are no time limits and no fees. It is strongly recommended that all students have a personal computer.

Admissions Contact: Elizabeth Robertson, Senior Associate Director of Admissions. E-Mail: rscadm@sage.edu Web: www.sage.edu

SAINT BONAVENTURE UNIVERSITY   A-3
St. Bonaventure, NY 14778-2284

(716) 375-2400
(800) 462-5050; (716) 375-4005

Full-time: 895 men, 970 women	**Faculty:** 141; IIA, --$
Part-time: 44 men, 58 women	**Ph.D.s:** 79%
Graduate: 194 men, 311 women	**Student/Faculty:** 13 to 1
Year: semesters, summer session	**Tuition:** $25,885
Application Deadline: April 1	**Room & Board:** $9199
Freshman Class: 1927 applied, 1617 accepted, 466 enrolled	
SAT CR/M/W: 500/520/500	**ACT:** 22 **COMPETITIVE**

Saint Bonaventure University, founded in 1858, is a private Roman Catholic institution in the Franciscan tradition, offering programs in the arts and sciences, education, business, and journalism and mass communication. There are 4 undergraduate schools and 1 graduate school. In addition to regional accreditation, SBU has baccalaureate program accreditation with AACSB and NCATE. The library contains 241,000 volumes, 97,000 microform items, and 7,000 audio/video tapes/CDs/DVDs, and subscribes to 1,500 periodicals including electronic. Computerized library services include interlibrary loans, database searching, Internet access, and laptop Internet portals. Special learning facilities include a learning resource center, art gallery, radio station, TV station, observatory. The 500-acre campus is in a small town 70 miles southeast of Buffalo. Including any residence halls, there are 30 buildings.

Student Life: 79% of undergraduates are from New York. Others are from 38 states, 9 foreign countries, and Canada. 78% are from public schools. 69% are white. The average age of freshmen is 18; all undergraduates, 20. 18% do not continue beyond their first year; 68% remain to graduate.

Housing: 1651 students can be accommodated in college housing, which includes single-sex and coed dorms and on-campus apartments. On-campus housing is guaranteed for all 4 years. 80% of students live on campus; of those, 90% remain on campus on weekends. All students may keep cars.

Activities: There are no fraternities or sororities. There are 74 groups on campus, including academic, art, band, cheerleading, chess, choir, chorale, chorus, computers, dance, drama, ethnic, honors, international, jazz band, literary magazine, newspaper, orchestra, photography, political, professional, radio and TV, religious, social, social service, student government, and yearbook. Popular campus events include Family Weekend, Spring and Winter Weekends, and varsity basketball games.

Sports: There are 7 intercollegiate sports for men and 7 for women, and 14 intramural sports for men and 13 for women. Facilities include a 6000-seat gym with basketball and volleyball courts, an indoor swimming pool, a 9-hole golf course, weight facilities and free weights, and a fitness center with state of the art strength, aerobics and conditioning areas, an indoor track, 3 multi-use courts, and a rock climbing wall. There is also a 77-acre area on campus with soccer, baseball, softball, rugby, and intramural fields.

Disabled Students: 90% of the campus is accessible. Facilities include wheelchair ramps, elevators, special parking, specially equipped restrooms, a counseling center staffed by 2 professionals, and a teaching and learning center with a coordinator for disabled services.

Services: Counseling and information services are available, as is tutoring in most subjects.

Campus Safety and Security: Measures include 24-hour foot and vehicle patrol and security escort services. There are shuttle buses, emergency telephones, and lighted pathways/sidewalks.

Programs of Study: SBU confers B.A., B.S., B.B.A., and B.S.Ed. degrees. Master's degrees are also awarded. Bachelor's degrees are awarded in BIOLOGICAL SCIENCE (biochemistry, bioinformatics, biology/biological science, and biophysics), BUSINESS (accounting, banking and finance, management science, and marketing/retailing/merchandising), COMMUNICATIONS AND THE ARTS (art history and appreciation, classical languages, dramatic arts, English, French, journalism, music, Spanish, and visual and performing arts), COMPUTER AND PHYSICAL SCIENCE (chemistry, computer science, information sciences and systems, mathematics, and physics), EDUCATION (elementary education, physical education, special education, and sports studies), ENGINEERING AND ENVIRONMENTAL DESIGN (engineering physics and environmental science), SOCIAL SCIENCE (child care/child and family studies, gerontology, history, international studies, philosophy, political science/government, psychology, social science, sociology, theological studies, and women's studies). Accounting, biology, and journalism /mass communications are the strongest academically and the largest.

Required: To graduate, students must complete 120 credit hours, 30 of them in the major, with a minimum GPA of 2.0. Students must also demonstrate writing competency through testing or course work.

Special: Cross-registration can be arranged almost anywhere in the United States through the Visiting Student Program. Internships are available in business, mass communication, political science, psychology, and social science. Study abroad in 18 countries, B.A.-B.S. degrees, accelerated degree programs, dual and student-designed majors, a Washington semester with American University, and pass/fail options are offered. Dual admissions with George Washington University School of Medicine, Lake Erie College of Osteopathic medicine, University at Buffalo School of Dental Medicine, Lake Erie College of Osteopathic Medicine School of Pharmacy, and University of Duquesne Law School is also possible. There are 10 national honor societies and a freshman honors program.

Faculty/Classroom: 63% of faculty are male; 37% are female. 92% teach undergraduates. No introductory courses are taught by graduate students. The average class size in an introductory lecture, 25, in a laboratory, 11, and in a regular course, 18.

Admissions: 84% of the 2009-2010 applicants were accepted. The SAT scores for the 2009-2010 freshman class were: Critical Reading--46% below 500, 39% between 500 and 599, 12% between 600 and 700, and 3% above 700; Math--38% below 500, 45% between 500 and 599, 15% between 600 and 700, and 2% above 700; Writing--49% below 500, 35% between 500 and 599, 13% between 600 and 700, and 3% above 700. The ACT scores were 33% below 21, 30% between 21 and 23, 20% between 24 and 26, 9% between 27 and 28, and 8% above 28. 31% of the current freshmen were in the top fifth of their class; 62% were in the top two fifths. 6 freshmen graduated first in their class.

Requirements: The SAT is required, the ACT is recommended, with a satisfactory score on the SAT or 24 on the ACT. Applicants must be graduates of an accredited secondary school or have a GED. 16 academic credits are required, including 4 years each of English and social studies, 3 each of math and science, and 2 of a foreign language. An essay and an interview are recommended. A GPA of 70.0 is required. AP and CLEP credits are accepted. Important factors in the admissions decision are recommendations by school officials, advanced placement and honors courses, and extracurricular activities record.

Procedure: Freshmen are admitted to all sessions. Entrance exams should be taken during the spring of the junior year or the fall of the senior year. There are early admissions, deferred admissions, and rolling admissions plans. Applications should be filed by April 1 for fall entry and December 1 for spring entry, along with a $30 fee. Notification is sent on a rolling basis. Applications are accepted on-line.

Transfer: 62 transfer students enrolled in 2008-2009. Applicants must have a minimum 2.0 GPA. High school and college transcripts, essay, and a letter of recommendation are required. 60 of 120 credits required for the bachelor's degree must be completed at SBU.

Visiting: There are regularly scheduled orientations for prospective students, including interviews, tours, class visits, and meetings with professors. There are guides for informal visits; visitors may sit in on classes and stay overnight. To schedule a visit, contact the Admissions Office at admissions@sbu.edu.

Financial Aid: In 2009-2010, 98% of all full-time freshmen and 95% of continuing full-time students received some form of financial aid. 95% of all full-time freshmen and 90% of continuing full-time students received need-based aid. The average freshman award was $21,777. Need-based scholarships or need-based grants averaged $12,100; need-based self-help aid (loans and jobs) averaged $5,100; non-need based athletic scholarships averaged $12,500; and other non-need based awards and non-need based scholarships averaged $9,300. 38% of undergraduate students work part-time. Average annual earnings from campus work are $800. The FAFSA is required. The priority date for freshman financial aid applications for fall entry is February 15.

International Students: The school actively recruits these students. They must take the TOEFL with a minimum score of 550 on the paper-based TOEFL (PBT) or 80 on the Internet-based version (iBT).

Computers: Wireless access is available. The university supports academic and administrative functions through a variety of systems. A combination of wired computer labs (more than 250 networked PCs) and wireless modems throughout campus provide access. All residence halls have Internet access. All students may access the system 24 hours per day via residence hall rooms or at designated lab hours. There are no time limits and no fees. Students enrolled in computer science and business information systems must have a personal computer.

Graduates: From July 1, 2008 to June 30, 2009, 397 bachelor's degrees were awarded. The most popular majors were business (38%), communications/journalism (17%), and education (12%). In an average class, 1% graduate in 3 years or less, 50% graduate in 4 years or less, 65% graduate in 5 years or less, and 67% graduate in 6 years or less. Of the 2008 graduating class, 46% were enrolled in graduate school within 6 months of graduation, and 51% were employed.

Admissions Contact: James Di Risio, Director of Admissions. A campus DVD is available. E-Mail: *admissions@sbu.edu* Web: *www.sbu.edu*

SAINT FRANCIS COLLEGE   D-5

Brooklyn, NY 11201   (718) 489-5200; (718) 802-0453

Full-time: 1011 men, 1166 women	**Faculty:** 80; IIB, av$
Part-time: 94 men, 180 women	**Ph.D.s:** 89%
Graduate: 19 men, 11 women	**Student/Faculty:** 18 to 1
Year: semesters, summer session	**Tuition:** $16,480
Application Deadline: April 1	**Room & Board:** $14,350
Freshman Class: 1944 applied, 1513 accepted, 581 enrolled	
SAT CR/M: 467/465	**LESS COMPETITIVE**

Saint Francis College, chartered in 1884 by the Franciscan Brothers, is a private, Catholic institution conferring degrees in the arts, sciences, business, education, and health sciences. There are no undergraduate schools. The library contains 140,000 volumes, 10,440 microform items, 2,050 audio/video tapes/CDs/DVDs, and subscribes to 14,300 periodicals including electronic. Computerized library services include interlibrary loans, database searching, Internet access, and laptop Internet portals. Special learning facilities include a learning resource center, a greenhouse, and a television studio. The 1-acre campus is in an urban area Brooklyn, NY. Including any residence halls, there are 6 buildings.
Student Life: 98% of undergraduates are from New York. Students are from 8 states, 50 foreign countries, and Canada. 49% are from public schools. 41% are white; 15% African American; 15% Hispanic. 56% are Catholic; 29% Protestant. The average age of freshmen is 19; all undergraduates, 21. 20% do not continue beyond their first year; 53% remain to graduate.

Housing: 100 students can be accommodated in college housing, which includes dorms. Students may apply for housing in the dorm at Polytechnic University, a short walk from St. Francis College. On-campus housing is available on a first-come and first-served basis. Alcohol is not permitted. All students commute. No one may keep cars.

Activities: There are no fraternities or sororities. There are 38 groups on campus, including art, cheerleading, choir, chorus, computers, dance, drama, ethnic, honors, international, literary magazine, newspaper, political, professional, radio and TV, religious, social, social service, and student government. Popular campus events include Terrier Tuesday, Sports events, and Student Government activities.

Sports: There are 9 intercollegiate sports for men and 10 for women, and 5 intramural sports for men and 5 for women. Facilities include an 1100-seat gym, an Olympic-size swimming pool, a weight-training room, a roof recreation area, and the Genovesi Center, which is a 10,000-square-foot multipurpose facility used for athletic, college, and community events.

Disabled Students: All of the campus is accessible. Facilities include wheelchair ramps, elevators, specially equipped restrooms, lowered drinking fountains, and lowered telephones.

Services: There is a reader service for the blind, and remedial math, reading, and writing. In addition, there are workshops in academic skills such as note taking, test taking, and study skills.

Campus Safety and Security: Measures include emergency notification system.

Programs of Study: St. Francis confers B.A. and B.S. degrees. Associates and master's degrees are also awarded. Bachelor's degrees are awarded in BIOLOGICAL SCIENCE (biology/biological science), BUSINESS (accounting and management science), COMMUNICATIONS AND THE ARTS (communications, English, and Spanish), COMPUTER AND PHYSICAL SCIENCE (chemistry, information sciences and systems, and mathematics), EDUCATION (elementary education, middle school education, physical education, and secondary education), HEALTH PROFESSIONS (health care administration, health science, medical laboratory technology, nursing, physician's assistant, and radiological science), SOCIAL SCIENCE (criminal justice, economics, history,

international studies, liberal arts/general studies, philosophy, political science/government, psychology, religion, social studies, and sociology). Biology, accounting, and psychology are the strongest academically. Management, communications, and psychology are the largest.

Required: The core curriculum varies according to the major, but all baccalaureate degree programs require courses in communications, english, fine arts, phys ed, history, philosophy, sociology, and science or math. A minimum 2.0 GPA and 128 credit hours are required to graduate.

Special: There are co-op programs in physical therapy, nursing, and computer science. Work-study with Methodist Hospital or the borough president's office, and there are preprofessional health programs with the State University of New York Health Science Center, Methodist Hospital, and St. Vincent's Catholic Medical Center. Study abroad in several countries, dual majors, pass/fail options, and credit for life experience are possible. There are 16 national honor societies and a freshman honors program.

Faculty/Classroom: 58% of faculty are male; 42% are female. All teach and do research. No introductory courses are taught by graduate students. The average class size in an introductory lecture is 25; in a laboratory is 19; and in a regular course is 20.

Admissions: 78% of the 2009-2010 applicants were accepted. The SAT scores for the 2009-2010 freshman class were: Critical Reading--66% below 500, 28% between 500 and 599, 5% between 600 and 700, and 1% above 700; Math--65% below 500, 30% between 500 and 599, 5% between 600 and 700, and % above 700.

Requirements: The SAT is required. In addition, applicants should graduate from an accredited secondary school or have a GED. An entrance essay is required, as well as the submission of SAT scores. AP and CLEP credits are accepted. Important factors in the admissions decision are advanced placement or honors courses, extracurricular activities record, and recommendations by school officials.

Procedure: Freshmen are admitted to all sessions. Entrance exams should be taken in spring of the junior year and fall of the senior year. There are deferred admissions and rolling admissions plans. Applications should be filed by April 1 for fall entry and November 1 for winter entry. The fall 2008 application fee was $35. Notification is sent on a rolling basis. Applications are accepted on-line.

Transfer: 127 transfer students enrolled in 2008-2009. A minimum 2.0 GPA is required for transfer students. Official transcripts from previous colleges and high school transcripts, or a graduation certificate, is also required. 30 of 128 credits required for the bachelor's degree must be completed at St. Francis.

Visiting: There are regularly scheduled orientations for prospective students, a student guided tour of the college, and meetings with faculty if desired. There are guides for informal visits and visitors may sit in on classes. To schedule a visit, contact the Office of Admissions at admissions@stfrancis.edu.

Financial Aid: In 2009-2010, 80% of all full-time freshmen and 55% of continuing full-time students received some form of financial aid. 56% of all full-time freshmen and 42% of continuing full-time students received need-based aid. The average freshmen award was $10,735, with $4,605 ($14,970 maximum) from need-based scholarships or need-based grants; $5,650 ($23,870 maximum) from need-based self-help aid (loans and jobs); $9,450 ($27,600 maximum) from non-need-based athletic scholarships; and $6,800 ($14,970 maximum) from other non-need-based awards and non-need-based scholarships. 5% of undergraduate students work part-time. Average annual earnings from campus work are $2100. The FAFSA, the state aid form, and the college's own financial statement are required. The priority date for freshman financial aid applications for fall entry is February 15.

International Students: There are 186 international students enrolled. The school actively recruits these students. They must take the TOEFL with a minimum score of 500 on the paper-based TOEFL (PBT) or 515 on the Internet-based version (iBT).

Computers: Wireless access is available. There are 158 PC workstations and 10 Kiosks available to students throughout the day. This includes the lab, library, academic enhancement, and psychology lab. The Internet is accessible to students on all machines, and there are wireless zones in many high traffic areas of the college. The campuswide network provides access to services such as Blackboard, Terriermail, and library resources that are accessible to students through the Internet from outside the college. All students may access the system. There are no time limits. The fee is $150.

Graduates: From July 1, 2008 to June 30, 2009, 368 bachelor's degrees were awarded. The most popular majors were business/marketing (18%), liberal arts (13%), and health professional & related sciences (12%). 20 companies recruited on campus in 2008-2009. In an average class, 1% graduate in 3 years or less, 31% graduate in 4 years or less, 51% graduate in 5 years or less, and 53% graduate in 6 years or less.

Admissions Contact: John McAuliffe, Director of Admissions. A campus DVD is available. E-Mail: *jmcauliffe@stfranciscollege.edu* Web: *www.stfranciscollege.edu*

SAINT JOHN FISHER COLLEGE B-3

Rochester, NY 14618

(585) 385-8064
(800) 444-4640; (585) 385-8386

Full-time: 1096 men, 1532 women	**Faculty:** 201
Part-time: 82 men, 122 women	**Ph.D.s:** 89%
Graduate: 346 men, 735 women	**Student/Faculty:** 13 to 1
Year: semesters, summer session	**Tuition:** $24,320
Application Deadline: rolling	**Room & Board:** $10,090
Freshman Class: 3440 applied, 2237 accepted, 558 enrolled	
SAT CR/M/W: 530/558/515	**ACT:** 24	**COMPETITIVE**

St. John Fisher College is an independent, liberal arts institution in the Catholic tradition of American higher education. Guided since its inception in 1948 by the educational philosophy of the Congregation of St. Basil, the college emphasizes liberal learning for students in traditional academic disciplines, as well as for those in more directly career-oriented fields. The college welcomes qualified students, faculty, and staff regardless of religious or cultural background. There are 4 undergraduate schools and 5 graduate schools. In addition to regional accreditation, Fisher has baccalaureate program accreditation with AACSB, ACS, CCNE, and NCATE. The library contains 211,901 volumes, 197,442 microform items, and 7908 audio/video tapes/CDs/DVDs, and subscribes to 33,852 periodicals including electronic. Computerized library services include interlibrary loans, database searching, and Internet access. Special learning facilities include a learning resource center, radio station, TV station, a multimedia center, "wet" and "dry" multidisciplinary science labs, animal labs, growth chambers, and a dance and fitness facility. The 154-acre campus is in a suburban area 6 miles southeast of Rochester. Including any residence halls, there are 24 buildings.

Student Life: 98% of undergraduates are from New York. Others are from 23 states and 5 foreign countries. 65% are from public schools. 85% are white. 52% are Catholic; 26% Protestant. The average age of freshmen is 18; all undergraduates, 21. 18% do not continue beyond their first year; 74% remain to graduate.

Housing: 1400 students can be accommodated in college housing, which includes single-sex and coed dorms. On-campus housing is available on a lottery system for upperclassmen. 52% of students live on campus; of those, 85% remain on campus on weekends. Upperclassmen may keep cars.

Activities: There are no fraternities or sororities. There are 70 groups on campus, including art, cheerleading, choir, chorale, chorus, Commuter Council, computers, dance, drama, ethnic, gay, honors, international, literary magazine, musical theater, newspaper, photography, political, professional, radio and TV, religious, Resident Student Association, social, social service, Student Activities Board, student government, Student Senate SGA, and yearbook. Popular campus events include Family Weekend, Senior Week, and TEDDI, a 24-hour dance marathon for charity.

Sports: There are 7 intercollegiate sports for men and 7 for women, and 5 intramural sports for men and 4 for women. Facilities include a 2100-seat stadium that is home to the football, soccer, and lacrosse teams; it is used by many of the college's intramural teams as well. There is also a baseball complex; other outdoor facilities include 4 tennis courts, 2 regulation-size grass practice fields, a softball complex, and a 9-hole golf course. The student life center includes a field house and features a 19,000-square-foot addition with a fitness center/weight room, training facilities, and team locker rooms. The college's basketball teams play at a gym located near the student life center.

Disabled Students: All of the campus is accessible. Facilities include wheelchair ramps, elevators, special parking, specially equipped rest rooms, special class scheduling, lowered drinking fountains, and lowered telephones. Accessible dorm rooms are available.

Services: Counseling and information services are available, as is tutoring in most subjects. There is a reader service for the blind. Math and writing centers provide help to students at all levels. Peer tutoring is available to all students in most undergraduate subject areas.

Campus Safety and Security: Measures include 24-hour foot and vehicle patrol, emergency notification system, and security escort services. There are shuttle buses, emergency telephones, and lighted pathways/sidewalks. Access to the residence halls is controlled either by locked entrance doors or the card access system. Residence halls are patrolled and monitored 24 hours a day by security officers or resident advisers. All other campus facilities are locked and unlocked according to established schedules.

Programs of Study: Fisher confers B.A. and B.S. degrees. Master's and doctoral degrees are also awarded. Bachelor's degrees are awarded in BIOLOGICAL SCIENCE (biology/biological science), BUSINESS (accounting, business administration and management, and sports management), COMMUNICATIONS AND THE ARTS (communications, English, French, and Spanish), COMPUTER AND PHYSICAL SCIENCE (chemistry, computer science, mathematics, physics, and science technology), EDUCATION (early childhood education, English education, foreign languages education, mathematics education, science education, secondary education, social studies education, and special education),

HEALTH PROFESSIONS (nursing), SOCIAL SCIENCE (American studies, anthropology, economics, history, interdisciplinary studies, international studies, philosophy, political science/government, psychology, religion, and sociology). Physical sciences are the strongest academically. Education, management, and nursing are the largest.

Required: To graduate, students must complete at least 120 credit hours, including at least 30 in the major, and maintain a 2.0 minimum GPA. The core curriculum consists of 15 courses that students must successfully complete to graduate; the core is composed of 2 tiers of study: Foundations courses and Perspectives courses. Freshmen must participate in one of the integrative learning communities.

Special: The college has cooperative programs and cross-registration with Rochester Area Colleges. The college offers internships in most majors, independent research in various majors, study abroad in 37 countries, work-study programs, accelerated degree programs in many areas, Washington semesters, dual and student-designed majors, and degrees in interdisciplinary studies or liberal studies. A 3-2 engineering degree is offered. Navy and Marine ROTC is available at the University of Rochester and Air Force and Army ROTC at the Rochester Institute of Technology. There are 10 national honor societies, a freshman honors program, and 13 departmental honors programs.

Faculty/Classroom: 42% of faculty are male; 58% are female. 82% teach undergraduates. No introductory courses are taught by graduate students. The average class size in an introductory lecture is 25; in a laboratory, 15; and in a regular course, 21.

Admissions: 65% of the 2009-2010 applicants were accepted. The SAT scores for the 2009-2010 freshman class were: Critical Reading--31% below 500, 53% between 500 and 599, 15% between 600 and 700, and 1% above 700; Math--19% below 500, 52% between 500 and 599, 28% between 600 and 700, and 2% above 700; Writing--42% below 500, 43% between 500 and 599, and 15% between 600 and 700. The ACT scores were 10% below 21, 38% between 21 and 23, 27% between 24 and 26, 19% between 27 and 28, and 5% above 28. 48% of the current freshmen were in the top fifth of their class; 81% were in the top two fifths. 5 freshmen graduated first in their class.

Requirements: The SAT or ACT is required. In addition, applicants must be graduates of an accredited secondary school. 16 academic credits are required, including 4 years each in English, history, and social studies, 3 each in math and science, and 2 in a foreign language. Interviews are recommended. AP and CLEP credits are accepted. Important factors in the admissions decision are advanced placement or honors courses, extracurricular activities record, and leadership record.

Procedure: Freshmen are admitted fall. There are early decision, deferred admissions and rolling admissions plans. Early decision applications should be filed by December 1; deadlines are rolling for regular applications. Application fee is $30. Notification of early decision is sent January 15; regular decision, December 1. Applications are accepted online.

Transfer: 287 transfer students enrolled in 2008-2009. Applicants must have a minimum GPA of 2.0 to be considered (mean GPA is 2.8). A high school transcript is required for students with fewer than 24 college credits. Interviews are recommended. 30 of 120 credits required for the bachelor's degree must be completed at Fisher.

Visiting: There are regularly scheduled orientations for prospective students, including a tour, an interview with a member of the admissions staff, meetings with faculty and coaches, and lunch on campus. There are guides for informal visits, and visitors may sit in on classes and stay overnight. To schedule a visit, contact the Freshman Admissions Office.

Financial Aid: In 2009-2010, 80% of all full-time freshmen and 81% of continuing full-time students received some form of financial aid. 80% of all full-time freshmen and 69% of continuing full-time students received need-based aid. The average freshman award was $20,822. Need-based scholarships or need-based grants averaged $14,893 ($34,000 maximum) and need-based self-help aid (loans and jobs) averaged $5452 ($34,000 maximum). 18% of undergraduate students work part-time. Average annual earnings from campus work are $879. The average financial indebtedness of the 2009 graduate was $30,281. The FAFSA is required. The priority date for freshman financial aid applications for fall entry is February 15.

International Students: There are 6 international students enrolled. They must take the TOEFL with a minimum score of 550 on the paper-based TOEFL (PBT) or 79-80 on the Internet-based version (iBT). They must also take the SAT or ACT.

Computers: Wireless access is available. Labs and classrooms have about 525 computers available to students when not in use by scheduled classes or events. All have a wide range of installed software. The Kearney Hall computer lab is available 24/7 during the academic year. Lab assistants are available to help those using the computing resources. There are numerous curriculum-specific labs, including nursing, computer science, and pharmacy. All dorm rooms have connections to the wired network. All students may access the system 24 hours. There are no time limits and no fees.

Graduates: From July 1, 2008 to June 30, 2009, 764 bachelor's degrees were awarded. The most popular majors were business management (26%), education (22%), and nursing (11%). In an average class, 2% graduate in 3 years or less, 63% graduate in 4 years or less, 73% graduate in 5 years or less, and 74% graduate in 6 years or less. 81 companies recruited on campus in 2008-2009. Of the 2008 graduating class, 35% were enrolled in graduate school within 6 months of graduation, and 92% were employed.

Admissions Contact: Stacy Ledermann, Director of Freshman Admissions. E-mail: *admissions@sjfc.edu* Web: *www.sjfc.edu*

SAINT JOHN'S UNIVERSITY   D-5
Queens, NY 11439   (718) 990-2000
                                    (888) 785-6467; (718) 990-2096

Full-time: 5437 men, 6387 women	**Faculty:** 610; I, av$
Part-time: 1162 men, 1822 women	**Ph.D.s:** 87%
Graduate: 2004 men, 3540 women	**Student/Faculty:** 19 to 1
Year: semesters, summer session	**Tuition:** $30,040
Application Deadline: open	**Room & Board:** $13,140
Freshman Class: 52,980 applied, 22,788 accepted, 3108 enrolled	
SAT CR/M: 520/540	**ACT:** required **COMPETITIVE**

Saint John's University, founded in 1870 by the Vincentian Fathers, is a private Roman Catholic institution offering programs in the arts and sciences, education, business, pharmacy and allied health professions, theology, and professional studies. There are 5 undergraduate schools and 7 graduate schools. In addition to regional accreditation, St. John's has baccalaureate program accreditation with AACSB, ACPE, NASAD, and TEAC. The 4 libraries contain 1.2 million volumes, 1.7 million microform items, and 11,202 audio/video tapes/CDs/DVDs, and subscribe to 45,196 periodicals including electronic. Computerized library services include interlibrary loans, database searching, Internet access, and laptop Internet portals. Special learning facilities include a learning resource center, art gallery, radio station, TV station, health education resource center, model pharmacy, speech and hearing clinic, instructional materials center, instructional media center, Institute of Asian Studies, and a writing center. The 105-acre campus is in a suburban area in a residential section of Queens. Including any residence halls, there are 30 buildings.

Student Life: 81% of undergraduates are from New York. Others are from 44 states, 83 foreign countries, and Canada. 64% are from public schools. 44% are foreign nationals; 43% white; 16% Asian American; 15% African American; 14% Hispanic. 51% are Catholic; 19% Muslim, Hindu, Buddhist, Greek Orthodox, Mormon, Russian Orthodox; 13% Protestant. The average age of freshmen is 18; all undergraduates, 20. 22% do not continue beyond their first year; 58% remain to graduate.

Housing: 4001 students can be accommodated in college housing, which includes coed dorms, on-campus apartments, and off-campus apartments. Theme housing is available. On-campus housing is available on a first-come, first-served basis, and is available on a lottery system for upperclassmen. 75% of students commute. All students may keep cars.

Activities: 6% of men belong to 5 local and 16 national fraternities; 7% of women belong to 9 local and 18 national sororities. There are 180 groups on campus, including art, cheerleading, choir, chorus, computers, dance, debate, drama, environmental, ethnic, film, honors, human rights, international, jazz band, literary magazine, musical theater, newspaper, pep band, photography, political, professional, radio and TV, religious, social, social service, student government, and yearbook. Popular campus events include International Night, Spring Fling, and Student Activities Fair.

Sports: There are 7 intercollegiate sports for men and 9 for women, and 13 intramural sports for men and 12 for women. Facilities include gyms, squash and tennis courts, weight and exercise rooms, baseball and softball diamonds, fields for football, lacrosse, and soccer, and basketball and racquetball courts.

Disabled Students: 95% of the campus is accessible. Facilities include wheelchair ramps, elevators, special parking, specially equipped restrooms, special class scheduling, lowered drinking fountains, and lowered telephones.

Services: Counseling and information services are available, as is tutoring in most subjects. There is a reader service for the blind, and remedial math, reading, and writing. Note-taking services, tape recorders, assistance in study skills, and a program for at-risk freshmen are available.

Campus Safety and Security: Measures include 24-hour foot and vehicle patrol, emergency notification system, and security escort services. There are shuttle buses, emergency telephones, lighted pathways/sidewalks, and a crime prevention awareness program.

Programs of Study: St. John's confers B.A., B.S., B.F.A., B.S.Ed., and B.S.Med.Tech. degrees. Associate, master's, and doctoral degrees are also awarded. Bachelor's degrees are awarded in BIOLOGICAL SCIENCE (biology/biological science, ecology, and toxicology), BUSINESS (accounting, banking and finance, business administration and management, business economics, funeral home services, hospitality management services, insurance and risk management, management science, marketing and distribution, and sports management), COMMUNICATIONS AND THE ARTS (advertising, communications, English, fine

arts, French, graphic design, illustration, Italian, journalism, languages, literature, photography, public relations, radio/television technology, Spanish, speech/debate/rhetoric, and telecommunications), COMPUTER AND PHYSICAL SCIENCE (actuarial science, chemistry, computer science, computer security and information assurance, information sciences and systems, mathematics, physical sciences, and physics), EDUCATION (bilingual/bicultural education, early childhood education, elementary education, English education, foreign languages education, mathematics education, middle school education, science education, secondary education, social studies education, and special education), ENGINEERING AND ENVIRONMENTAL DESIGN (environmental science and preengineering), HEALTH PROFESSIONS (health care administration, medical technology, pharmacy, physician's assistant, premedicine, radiological science, and speech pathology/audiology), SOCIAL SCIENCE (anthropology, Asian/Oriental studies, criminal justice, economics, history, human services, liberal arts/general studies, paralegal studies, philosophy, political science/government, prelaw, psychology, public administration, safety and security technology, social science, social studies, sociology, and theological studies). Pharmacy, biology, and psychology are the strongest academically and are the largest.

Required: To graduate, students must complete at least 126 credit hours, including core courses and distribution requirements, with a minimum GPA of 2.0 overall and in the major. Other requirements vary by program. Core courses include English, theology, philosophy, Discover NY, history, scientific inquiry, and speech. Distribution requirements include a second language, fine arts, language and culture, math, philosophy, theology, and social science.

Special: St. John's offers internships, cross-registration, study abroad in Europe, Central and South America, Australia, the Caribbean, Africa, and Asia, an accelerated degree program in many majors via early admissions and early admissions extension programs, B.A.-B.S. degrees, dual majors and combined degree programs, pass/fail options, and some credit for life, military, and work experience. There are cooperative programs in podiatry with NY College of Podiatric Medicine, engineering with Manhattan College, photography with the International Center of Photography, funeral service administration with the McAllister Institute, and optometry with SUNY College of Optometry. There is a 6-year doctor of pharmacy program for incoming freshmen. Other combined degree programs are possible. There are 17 national honor societies, a freshman honors program, and 11 departmental honors programs.

Faculty/Classroom: 57% of faculty are male; 43% are female. 87% teach undergraduates, 91% do research, and 78% do both. No introductory courses are taught by graduate students. The average class size in an introductory lecture is 25; in a laboratory, 22; and in a regular course, 24.

Admissions: 43% of the 2009-2010 applicants were accepted. The SAT scores for the 2009-2010 freshman class were: Critical Reading--33% below 500, 44% between 500 and 599, 20% between 600 and 700, and 3% above 700; Math--28% below 500, 41% between 500 and 599, 23% between 600 and 700, and 8% above 700. 43% of the current freshmen were in the top fifth of their class; 71% were in the top two fifths. 3 freshmen graduated first in their class.

Requirements: The SAT or ACT is required. Admissions decisions are made by committee and are based on several criteria, including standardized test scores, academic curriculum, and high school average. A GPA of 3.0 is required. AP and CLEP credits are accepted. Important factors in the admissions decision are advanced placement or honors courses, recommendations by school officials, and extracurricular activities record.

Procedure: Freshmen are admitted fall, spring, and summer. Entrance exams should be taken late in the junior year or early in the senior year. There are early admissions, deferred admissions, and rolling admissions plans. Application deadlines are open. The fall 2008 application fee was $50. Notification is sent on a rolling basis. Applications are accepted online (no fee). A waiting list is maintained.

Transfer: 490 transfer students enrolled in 2008-2009. Applicants must present official transcripts of high school and college work, as well as a list of courses in progress. If the student has been out of school a semester or more, a letter of explanation is also required. Admissions requirements for transfer students to the 6-year pharmacy program are stricter, and placement is limited. 33 of 126 credits required for the bachelor's degree must be completed at St. John's.

Visiting: There are regularly scheduled orientations for prospective students, including small group presentations and a tour of the campus. There are guides for informal visits and visitors may sit in on classes. To schedule a visit, contact the Office of Admission at *visit@stjohns.edu*.

Financial Aid: The FAFSA is required. The priority date for freshman financial aid applications for fall entry is February 1. The deadline for filing freshman financial aid applications for fall entry is March 1.

International Students: There are 576 international students enrolled. The school actively recruits these students. They must take the TOEFL with a minimum score of 500 on the paper-based TOEFL (PBT) or 61 on the Internet-based version (iBT) and the college's own test. They must also take the SAT or ACT, scoring 1000. This requirement may be waived for international students educated outside of the United States.

Computers: There are workstations for general use in classrooms, in the library, and in computer labs; there are 13,107 computers/terminals on campus for general student use. Students can also access the Internet (wired and wireless) from any location on campus. All students may access the system. There are no time limits and no fees. All students are required to have a personal computer.

Graduates: From July 1, 2008 to June 30, 2009, 2180 bachelor's degrees were awarded. The most popular majors were finance (8%), communication arts (7%), and criminal justice (7%). 250 companies recruited on campus in 2008-2009. In an average class, 1% graduate in 3 years or less, 38% graduate in 4 years or less, 49% graduate in 5 years or less, and 58% graduate in 6 years or less. Of the 2008 graduating class, 36% were enrolled in graduate school within 6 months of graduation, and 56% were employed.

Admissions Contact: Karen Vahey, Director.
E-mail: *admhelp@stjohns.edu* Web: *www.stjohns.edu*

SAINT JOSEPH'S COLLEGE, NEW YORK, BROOKLYN   D-5
CAMPUS

Brooklyn, NY 11205

(718) 636-6868
(866) AT ST JOE; (718) 636-8303

Full-time: 175 men, 560 women	Faculty: n/av
Part-time: 25 men, 65 women	Ph.Ds: n/av
Graduate: 20 men, 85 women	Student/Faculty: n/av
Year: semesters, summer session	Tuition: $14,900
Application Deadline: August 1	
Freshman Class: n/av	
SAT or ACT: required	**COMPETITIVE**

Saint Joseph's College, established in 1916, is a private, independent, multicampus, commuter institution offering undergraduate degrees in arts and sciences, child study, business, accounting, health professions, and nursing. There is a branch campus in Patchogue, Long Island. The figures in the above capsule and in this profile are approximate. There is 1 graduate school. In addition to regional accreditation, Saint Joseph's has baccalaureate program accreditation with NLN. The library contains 75,000 volumes, 4,341 microform items, and 4,504 audio/video tapes/CDs/DVDs, and subscribes to 434 periodicals including electronic. Computerized library services include interlibrary loans and database searching. The 3-acre campus is in an urban area 1 mile east of Manhattan. Including any residence halls, there are 5 buildings.

Student Life: 99% of undergraduates are from New York. Others are from 5 states, and Canada. 21% are from public schools. 45% are white; 37% African American; 12% Hispanic. The average age of freshmen is 18; all undergraduates, 27. 15% do not continue beyond their first year; 76% remain to graduate.

Housing: College-sponsored housing includes off-campus apartments. 98% of students commute. Alcohol is not permitted. All students may keep cars.

Activities: 15% of men belong to 1 local fraternity; 6% of women belong to 1 local sorority. There are 40 groups on campus, including art, cheerleading, chess, chorus, computers, dance, drama, ethnic, honors, jazz band, literary magazine, newspaper, political, professional, religious, social, social service, student government, and yearbook. Popular campus events include the annual dinner dance, Junior Class Night, and holiday party.

Sports: There are 4 intercollegiate sports for men and 5 for women, and 5 intramural sports for men and 5 for women. Facilities include a gym, a handball court, an outdoor mall, recreation rooms, and an exercise/weight room.

Disabled Students: 10% of the campus is accessible. Facilities include wheelchair ramps, elevators, and specially equipped restrooms.

Services: Counseling and information services are available, as is tutoring in most subjects. There is remedial writing.

Campus Safety and Security: Measures include emergency notification system, self-defense education, and security escort services. There are lighted pathways/sidewalks.

Programs of Study: Saint Joseph's confers B.A. and B.S. degrees. Master's degrees are also awarded. Bachelor's degrees are awarded in BIOLOGICAL SCIENCE (biology/biological science), BUSINESS (accounting, business administration and management, and organizational behavior), COMMUNICATIONS AND THE ARTS (English, Spanish, and speech/debate/rhetoric), COMPUTER AND PHYSICAL SCIENCE (chemistry, information sciences and systems, and mathematics), EDUCATION (early childhood education, elementary education, secondary education, and special education), HEALTH PROFESSIONS (community health work, health care administration, and nursing), SOCIAL SCIENCE (criminal justice, history, psychology, and social science). Child study, psychology, and speech are the largest.

Required: To graduate, students must complete a 51-credit core curriculum requirement consisting of 8 courses in humanities, 3 in social science and math/science, and 1 English composition course. The minimum GPA is 2.0. Students must earn 128 credits, with 30 to 36 credits in the major. Most majors require a thesis.

Special: The college offers internship programs in English, history, political science, psychology, sociology, speech, and business/accounting, and an interdisciplinary major in human relations. Adult students may pursue a general studies degree in which the college allows credit for life, military, and work experience. Cross-registration with Knowledge Workers Educational Alliance is possible. There are 5 national honor societies and a freshman honors program.

Faculty/Classroom: 44% of faculty are male; 56% are female. All teach undergraduates, and 10% do research. No introductory courses are taught by graduate students. The average class size in an introductory lecture is 16; in a laboratory is 11; and in a regular course is 12.

Requirements: The SAT or ACT is required, with a satisfactory score on the SAT. Applicants must graduate from an accredited secondary school or earn a GED. 16 Carnegie units are required, including 4 units of English and social studies, 3 of math, 2 of languages and science, and 3 elective units. Interviews are recommended. A GPA of 3.0 is required. AP and CLEP credits are accepted. Important factors in the admissions decision are advanced placement or honors courses, recommendations by school officials, and leadership record.

Procedure: Freshmen are admitted fall and spring. There are early decision, deferred admissions and rolling admissions plans. Applications should be filed by August 1 for fall entry and January 1 for spring entry, along with a $25 fee.

Transfer: 26 transfer students enrolled in a recent year. Transfer applicants must have a minimum GPA of 2.0. If fewer than 40 credits have been earned, the SAT or ACT is required with a satisfactory score on the SAT. 48 of 128 credits required for the bachelor's degree must be completed at Saint Joseph's.

Visiting: There are regularly scheduled orientations for prospective students, including meetings with faculty advisers and student-to-student sessions. There are guides for informal visits and visitors may sit in on classes. To schedule a visit, contact the Admissions Office.

Financial Aid: Saint Joseph's is a member of CSS. The FAFSA, the state aid form, and the college's own financial statement are required. Check with the school for current application deadlines.

International Students: They must take the TOEFL. They must also take the SAT or ACT.

Computers: All students may access the system. There are no time limits and no fees.

Admissions Contact: Theresa LaRocca Meyer, Director of Admissions. Web: *www.sjcny.edu*

SAINT JOSEPH'S COLLEGE, NEW YORK, SUFFOLK   E-5
CAMPUS

Patchogue, NY 11772

(631) 447-3219; (631) 447-1734

Full-time: 790 men, 2070 women	Faculty: IIB, av$
Part-time: 215 men, 685 women	Ph.Ds: 53%
Graduate: 70 men, 300 women	Student/Faculty: n/av
Year: 4-1-4, summer session	Tuition: $16,500
Application Deadline: see profile	
Freshman Class: n/av	
SAT: required	**COMPETITIVE**

Saint Joseph's College, established in 1916, is a private, independent, multicampus commuter institution offering a variety of undergraduate study options, including traditional liberal arts majors, special course offerings, and certificate, affiliated, and preprofessional programs. The school offers 12 Career Readiness Tracks. There is a campus in Brooklyn. Figures in the above capsule and this profile are approximate. There are 2 undergraduate schools and 2 graduate schools. In addition to regional accreditation, SJC has baccalaureate program accreditation with NLN. The library contains 120,000 volumes and subscribes to 400 periodicals including electronic. Computerized library services include database searching and Internet access. Special learning facilities include a learning resource center. The 25-acre campus is in a suburban area 60 miles east of New York City. There are 5 buildings.

Student Life: 99% of undergraduates are from New York. Others are from 13 states and 4 foreign countries. 85% are from public schools. 84% are white. The average age of freshmen is 18; all undergraduates, 20. 75% do not continue beyond their first year.

Housing: There are no residence halls. All students commute.

Activities: 1% of men belong to 1 local fraternity; 4% of women belong to 2 local sororities. There are 31 groups on campus, including cheerleading, chorus, computers, dance, drama, ethnic, jazz band, literary magazine, newspaper, political, religious, social, social service, and student government. Popular campus events include Club Fair, Make a Difference Day, and Spring Fling.

Sports: There are 6 intercollegiate sports for men and 8 for women. Facilities include a swimming pool, a fitness center, an aerobics studio, an indoor running track, and a competition-size basketball court.

Disabled Students: All of the campus is accessible. Facilities include wheelchair ramps, elevators, special parking, specially equipped rest rooms, and lowered drinking fountains.

Services: Counseling and information services are available, as is tutoring in most subjects.

Campus Safety and Security: Measures include 24-hour foot and vehicle patrol, emergency notification system, self-defense education, and security escort services. There are shuttle buses and lighted pathways/sidewalks. The school is monitored through closed-circuit screens.

Programs of Study: SJC confers B.A. and B.S. degrees. Master's degrees are also awarded. Bachelor's degrees are awarded in BIOLOGICAL SCIENCE (biology/biological science), BUSINESS (accounting, business administration and management, and recreation and leisure services), COMMUNICATIONS AND THE ARTS (English and speech/debate/rhetoric), COMPUTER AND PHYSICAL SCIENCE (information sciences and systems and mathematics), EDUCATION (secondary education), SOCIAL SCIENCE (child care/child and family studies, criminal justice, history, psychology, and social science). Child study, math/computer science, and business/accounting are the strongest academically. Child study and business/accounting are the largest.

Required: To graduate, students must complete a liberal arts core curriculum. A total of 128 credits is needed to graduate, with a minimum of 33 credits in the major. For education majors, a minimum GPA of 2.8 is required; for all other majors, 2.3.

Special: There is study abroad in approximately 10 countries, an interdisciplinary major in human relations, B.A.-B.S. degrees, and a dual major in child study (elementary and special education). There are 7 national honor societies and 6 departmental honors programs.

Faculty/Classroom: 42% of faculty are male; 58% are female. All teach undergraduates. No introductory courses are taught by graduate students. The average class size in an introductory lecture is 18; in a laboratory, 18; and in a regular course, 18.

Admissions: 2 freshmen graduated first in their class in a recent year.

Requirements: The SAT is required. In addition, high school transcripts, 2 letters of recommendation, a personal essay, and an interview are required. A GPA of 3.0 is required. AP and CLEP credits are accepted.

Procedure: Freshmen are admitted fall and spring. There is a rolling admissions plan. Application deadlines are open. The application fee is $25. Notification is sent on a rolling basis.

Transfer: 392 transfer students enrolled in a recent year. Child study and education majors need a 2.8 GPA; all others, 2.3. 48 of 128 credits required for the bachelor's degree must be completed at SJC.

Visiting: There are regularly scheduled orientations for prospective students, including open houses in fall and spring. There are guides for informal visits and visitors may sit in on classes. To schedule a visit, contact the Admissions Office.

Financial Aid: 5% of undergraduate students work part-time. The FAFSA and the college's own financial statement are required. Check with the school for current application deadlines.

International Students: There was 1 international student enrolled in a recent year. They must take the TOEFL with a minimum score of 550 on the paper-based TOEFL (PBT). They must also take the SAT or ACT, scoring 1000 on the SAT.

Computers: All students may access the system during school hours. There are no time limits and no fees.

Graduates: In a recent year, 901 bachelor's degrees were awarded. The most popular majors were education (20%), organizational management (6%), and business (5%).

Admissions Contact: Gigi Lamens, Director of Admissions.
E-mail: *suffolkas@sjcny.edu* Web: *www.sjcny.edu*

SAINT LAWRENCE UNIVERSITY C-2
Canton, NY 13617 (315) 229-5261
(800) 285-1856; (315) 229-5818

Full-time: 1030 men, 1244 women	**Faculty:** 166; IIB, +$
Part-time: 10 men, 11 women	**Ph.D.s:** 98%
Graduate: 33 men, 73 women	**Student/Faculty:** 14 to 1
Year: semesters, summer session	**Tuition:** $39,765
Application Deadline: February 1	**Room & Board:** $10,160
Freshman Class: 4715 applied, 1848 accepted, 580 enrolled	
SAT CR/M/W: 603/610/600	**HIGHLY COMPETITIVE**

St. Lawrence University, established in 1856, is a private liberal arts institution. There is 1 graduate school. The 2 libraries contain 601,778 volumes, 599,249 microform items, and 7129 audio/video tapes/CDs/DVDs, and subscribe to 49,321 periodicals including electronic. Computerized library services include interlibrary loans, database searching, and Internet access. Special learning facilities include a learning resource center, art gallery, radio station, and science field station. The 1000-acre campus is in a rural area 80 miles south of Ottawa, Canada. Including any residence halls, there are 30 buildings.

Student Life: 53% of undergraduates are from out of state, mostly the Northeast. Students are from 41 states, 46 foreign countries, and Canada. 67% are from public schools. 82% are white. The average age of freshmen is 18; all undergraduates, 20. 8% do not continue beyond their first year; 81% remain to graduate.

Housing: 2072 students can be accommodated in college housing, which includes coed dorms and on-campus apartments. In addition, there are special-interest houses, fraternity houses, sorority houses, and theme cottages, such as Habitat for Humanity. On-campus housing is guaranteed for all 4 years. 98% of students live on campus; of those, 90% remain on campus on weekends. All students may keep cars.

Activities: 4% of men belong to 2 national fraternities; 19% of women belong to 1 local and 3 national sororities. There are 100 groups on campus, including art, choir, chorus, computers, dance, drama, environmental, ethnic, forensics, gay, honors, international, jazz band, literary magazine, newspaper, orchestra, photography, political, professional, radio and TV, religious, social, social service, student government, and yearbook. Popular campus events include Moving-Up Day, 100th Night, and Candlelight Service.

Sports: There are 16 intercollegiate sports for men and 16 for women, and 11 intramural sports for men and 11 for women. Facilities include basketball, squash, and tennis courts, a swimming pool, and a 133-station fitness center. There are also 2 field houses, an arena, an artificial ice rink, an 18-hole golf course, riding stables, jogging and cross-country ski trails, indoor and outdoor competition tracks, and soccer, baseball, and softball fields.

Disabled Students: 75% of the campus is accessible. Facilities include wheelchair ramps, elevators, special parking, specially equipped restrooms, special class scheduling, lowered drinking fountains, and visual fire alarms.

Services: Counseling and information services are available, as is tutoring in every subject. There is a reader service for the blind. a writing center, and science and technology counseling.

Campus Safety and Security: Measures include 24-hour foot and vehicle patrol, emergency notification system, self-defense education, and security escort services. There are emergency telephones, lighted pathways/sidewalks, and student patrols.

Programs of Study: St. Lawrence confers B.A. and B.S. degrees. Master's degrees are also awarded. Bachelor's degrees are awarded in AGRICULTURE (conservation and regulation and environmental studies), BIOLOGICAL SCIENCE (biochemistry, biology/biological science, biophysics, and neurosciences), BUSINESS (international economics), COMMUNICATIONS AND THE ARTS (art, art history and appreciation, communications, creative writing, dramatic arts, English, fine arts, French, German, languages, modern language, music, Spanish, studio art, and visual and performing arts), COMPUTER AND PHYSICAL SCIENCE (chemistry, computer science, geology, mathematics, and physics), ENGINEERING AND ENVIRONMENTAL DESIGN (environmental science), SOCIAL SCIENCE (African studies, anthropology, Asian/Oriental studies, Canadian studies, economics, history, interdisciplinary studies, international studies, philosophy, political science/government, psychology, religion, and sociology). Psychology, economics, and government are the largest.

Required: To graduate, students must maintain a minimum GPA of 2.0 and complete 120 course hours, with 29 to 43 in the major. Freshmen must take a first-year program, a 2-semester team-taught course. Requirements also include 1 course in arts/expression, 1 in humanities, 1 in social science, 1 in math or foreign language, 2 in natural science/science studies, and 2 in diversity.

Special: Students may cross-register with the Associated Colleges of the St. Lawrence Valley. Internships are available through the sociology, psychology, and English departments and through a service learning program. Study-abroad in 15 countries and a Washington semester are offered. Dual majors and student-designed majors can be arranged. Students may earn 3-2 engineering degrees in conjunction with 7 engineering schools. Nondegree study and pass/fail options are available. An Adirondack semester is also offered. There are 20 national honor societies, including Phi Beta Kappa, and 17 departmental honors programs.

Faculty/Classroom: 55% of faculty are male; 45% are female. 99% teach undergraduates, and all do research. No introductory courses are taught by graduate students. The average class size in a regular course is 16.

Admissions: 39% of the 2009-2010 applicants were accepted. The SAT scores for the 2009-2010 freshman class were: Critical Reading--7% below 500, 35% between 500 and 599, 49% between 600 and 700, and 9% above 700; Math--5% below 500, 32% between 500 and 599, 54% between 600 and 700, and 9% above 700; Writing--5% below 500, 40% between 500 and 599, 48% between 600 and 700, and 6% above 700. 71% of the current freshmen were in the top fifth of their class; 92% were in the top two fifths. 13 freshmen graduated first in their class.

Requirements: Applicants must be graduates of an accredited high school. 16 or more academic credits are required, including 4 years of English and 3 years each of foreign languages, math, science, and social studies. Essays are required and interviews are recommended for all applicants. Submissions of standardized test scores is optional. AP credits are accepted. Important factors in the admissions decision are advanced placement or honors courses, extracurricular activities record, and recommendations by school officials.

Procedure: Freshmen are admitted fall and spring. Entrance exams should be taken during the spring of the junior year or the fall of the senior year. There are early decision and deferred admissions plans. Early decision applications should be filed by November 15 and January 15; regular applications, by February 1 for fall entry; and December 1 for spring entry, along with a $60 fee. Notification of early decision is sent December 15 and February 15; regular decision, March 30. 192 early decision candidates were accepted for the 2009-2010 class. 444 applicants were on the 2009 waiting list; 36 were admitted. Applications are accepted on-line.

Transfer: 24 transfer students enrolled in 2008-2009. The high school transcript and SAT scores will be evaluated, but college work is more important. High school and college recommendations are required. 16 of 120 credits required for the bachelor's degree must be completed at St. Lawrence.

Visiting: There are regularly scheduled orientations for prospective students, including interviews and tours. There are guides for informal visits, and visitors may sit in on classes and stay overnight. To schedule a visit, contact the Admissions Office.

Financial Aid: In 2009-2010, 85% of all full-time freshmen and 83% of continuing full-time students received some form of financial aid. 66% of all full-time students received need-based aid. The average freshman award was $36,029. Need-based scholarships or need-based grants averaged $27,822; need-based self-help aid (loans and jobs) averaged $4394; non-need-based athletic scholarships averaged $49,925; and other non-need-based awards and non-need-based scholarships averaged $11,344. 37% of undergraduate students work part-time. Average annual earnings from campus work are $1100. The average financial indebtedness of the 2009 graduate was $31,653. St. Lawrence is a member of CSS. The CSS/Profile, FAFSA, and the college's own financial statement are required. The deadline for filing freshman financial aid applications for fall entry is February 1.

International Students: There are 126 international students enrolled. The school actively recruits these students.

Computers: Wireless access is available throughout the campus. There are 660 public access computers. All students may access the system 24 hours per day. There are no time limits and no fees.

Graduates: From July 1, 2008 to June 30, 2009, 444 bachelor's degrees were awarded. The most popular majors were psychology (17%), economics (14%), and environmental studies (10%). 18 companies recruited on campus in 2008-2009. In an average class, 1% graduate in 3 years or less, 78% graduate in 4 years or less, 80% graduate in 5 years or less, and 81% graduate in 6 years or less. Of the 2008 graduating class, 24% were enrolled in graduate school within 6 months of graduation and 72% were employed.

Admissions Contact: Teresa Cowdrey, Vice President and Dean of Admissions and Financial Aid. E-mail: *admissions@stlawu.edu* Web: *www.stlawu.edu*

SAINT THOMAS AQUINAS COLLEGE D-5
Sparkill, NY 10976

(914) 398-4100
(800) 999-STAC; (914) 398-4224

Full-time: 1405 men and women	**Faculty:** IIB, +$
Part-time: 805 men and women	**Ph.Ds:** n/av
Graduate: 75 men, 125 women	**Student/Faculty:** n/av
Year: 4-1-4, summer session	**Tuition:** $20,000
Application Deadline: see profile	**Room & Board:** $10,000
Freshman Class: n/av	
SAT or ACT: required	**COMPETITIVE**

Saint Thomas Aquinas College, founded in 1952, is an independent liberal arts institution. Figures in above capsule and in this profile are approximate. There are 2 graduate schools. The library contains 102,943 volumes, 45,900 microform items, and subscribes to 108 periodicals including electronic. Computerized library services include interlibrary loans and database searching. Special learning facilities include a learning resource center, radio station, and TV station. The 43-acre campus is in a suburban area 15 miles north of New York City. Including any residence halls, there are 12 buildings.

Student Life: 75% of undergraduates are from New York. Others are from 6 states, 8 foreign countries, and Canada. 80% are from public schools. 84% are white. 62% are Catholic; 23% Protestant. The average age of freshmen is 18; all undergraduates, 23. 16% do not continue beyond their first year; 62% remain to graduate.

Housing: 450 students can be accommodated in college housing, which includes single-sex dorms and on-campus apartments. On-campus housing is guaranteed for all 4 years. 65% of students commute. Alcohol is not permitted. All students may keep cars.

Activities: There are no fraternities or sororities. There are 15 groups on campus, including cheerleading, chorus, computers, drama, honors, international, literary magazine, musical theater, newspaper, professional, radio and TV, religious, social service, student government, and yearbook. Popular campus events include trips to Broadway shows and Halloween and Christmas mixers.

Sports: There are 5 intercollegiate sports for men and 4 for women, and 6 intramural sports for men and 5 for women. Facilities include an auditorium, a 750-seat gym, a weight room, and basketball and tennis courts.

Disabled Students: 90% of the campus is accessible. Facilities include wheelchair ramps, elevators, special parking, specially equipped restrooms, special class scheduling, and lowered telephones.

Services: Counseling and information services are available, as is tutoring in most subjects. There is remedial math and writing.

Campus Safety and Security: Measures include 24-hour foot and vehicle patrol and security escort services. There are emergency telephones and lighted pathways/sidewalks.

Programs of Study: STAC confers B.A., B.S., and B.S.E. degrees. Associates and master's degrees are also awarded. Bachelor's degrees are awarded in BUSINESS (accounting, banking and finance, business administration and management, marketing/retailing/merchandising, and recreation and leisure services), COMMUNICATIONS AND THE ARTS (communications, English, fine arts, romance languages and literature, and Spanish), EDUCATION (art education, bilingual/bicultural education, elementary education, foreign languages education, science education, secondary education, and special education), ENGINEERING AND ENVIRONMENTAL DESIGN (commercial art), HEALTH PROFESSIONS (medical laboratory technology and premedicine), SOCIAL SCIENCE (criminal justice, history, philosophy, prelaw, psychology, religion, and social science). Education, business administration, and natural sciences are the strongest academically. Business administration is the largest.

Required: To graduate, all students must complete a total of 120 credit hours, with 36 to 54 in the major and a minimum GPA of 2.0. A core curriculum of 51 credits in liberal arts courses is required.

Special: The college offers cross-registration with Barry University and Aquinas College and internships in business, criminal justice, commercial design, recreation and leisure, and communications. Study abroad in Europe and Asia, a 3-2 engineering degree with George Washington University and Manhattan College, and in physical therapy with New York Medical College, and work-study programs are available. Nondegree study and pass/fail options are possible. There are 7 national honor societies, including Phi Beta Kappa, and a freshman honors program.

Faculty/Classroom: 55% of faculty are male; 45% are female. 99% teach undergraduates, 50% do research, and 50% do both. No introductory courses are taught by graduate students. The average class size in an introductory lecture is 35; in a laboratory is 15; and in a regular course is 20.

Requirements: The SAT or ACT is required. In addition, applicants must be graduates of an accredited secondary school or have a GED certificate. 16 Carnegie units are recommended, including 4 years of English, and social science, 2 years of math, foreign language, and science, including 2 years of lab science. A GPA of 2.2 is required. AP and CLEP credits are accepted. Important factors in the admissions decision are leadership record, extracurricular activities record, and advanced placement or honors courses.

Procedure: Freshmen are admitted fall and spring. Entrance exams should be taken by the spring of the junior year. There are early decision, early admissions, deferred admissions, and rolling admissions plans. Check with the school for current application deadlines. The fall 2009 application fee was $30. Notification is sent on a rolling basis. Applications are accepted on-line.

Transfer: Applicants must have a 2.0 GPA from the previous school. 30 of 120 credits required for the bachelor's degree must be completed at STAC.

Visiting: There are guides for informal visits; visitors may sit in on classes and stay overnight. To schedule a visit, contact the Admissions Office.

Financial Aid: STAC is a member of CSS. The FAFSA is required. Check with the school for current application deadlines.

International Students: The school actively recruits these students. They must take the TOEFL.

Computers: All students may access the system. There are no time limits. The fee is $100.

Admissions Contact: Tracey A. Howard-Ubelhoer, Director of Admissions. A campus DVD is available. E-Mail: *thoward@stac.edu* Web: *www.stac.edu*

SARAH LAWRENCE COLLEGE D-5
Bronxville, NY 10708

(914) 395-2510
(800) 888-2858; (914) 395-2515

Full-time: 325 men, 925 women	**Faculty:** IIB, ++$
Part-time: 15 men, 65 women	**Ph.Ds:** n/av
Graduate: 55 men, 310 women	**Student/Faculty:** n/av
Year: semesters	**Tuition:** $36,000
Application Deadline: see profile	**Room & Board:** $12,000
Freshman Class: n/av	**HIGHLY COMPETITIVE**

Sarah Lawrence College, established in 1926, is an independent institution conferring liberal arts degrees. The academic structure is based on the British don system. Students meet biweekly with professors in tutorials and are enrolled in small seminars. While there are no formal majors, students develop individual concentrations that are usually interdisciplinary. Figures in the above capsule and in this profile are approximate. There is 1 graduate school. The 3 libraries contain 282,676 volumes, 24,218 microform items, and 9,319 audio/video tapes/CDs/DVDs, and subscribe to 916 periodicals including electronic. Computerized library services include interlibrary loans, database searching, and Internet access. Special learning facilities include an art gallery, radio station, a slide library with 75,000 slides of art and architecture, early childhood center, electronic music studio; music library, student-run theater and student-run art gallery. The 41-acre campus is in a suburban area 15 miles north of midtown Manhattan. Including any residence halls, there are 50 buildings.

Student Life: 81% of undergraduates are from out of state, mostly the Middle Atlantic. Students are from 46 states, 25 foreign countries, and Canada. 65% are from public schools. 70% are white. The average age of freshmen is 18; all undergraduates, 20. 7% do not continue beyond their first year; 72% remain to graduate.

Housing: 965 students can be accommodated in college housing, which includes single-sex and coed dorms and on-campus apartments. In addition there is a French Interest House, the Perkins Art Co-op, and the Good Life House. On-campus housing is guaranteed for all 4 years. 87% of students live on campus; of those, 90% remain on campus on weekends. Upperclassmen may keep cars.

Activities: There are no fraternities or sororities. There are 30 groups on campus, including, art, choir, chorale, chorus, computers, dance, drama, ethnic, film, gay, human rights, international, jazz band, literary magazine, musical theater, newspaper, orchestra, philosophy, photography, poetry, political, radio and TV, religious, social, social service, student government, and yearbook. Popular campus events include Mayfair,.

Sports: There are 5 intercollegiate sports for men and 6 for women, and 9 intramural sports for men and 9 for women. Facilities include a sports center with a gym, a jogging track, a 6-lane swimming pool, a rowing tank, a multipurpose studio, and 3 squash courts; a fitness center and weight room; tennis courts; and a number of open fields and lawns. Off-campus, the college has the use of a boat house and stables.

Disabled Students: 50% of the campus is accessible. Facilities include wheelchair ramps, elevators, special parking, specially equipped restrooms, special class scheduling, lowered drinking fountains, and lowered telephones.

Services: Counseling and information services are available, as is tutoring in writing. There is a reader service for the blind.

Campus Safety and Security: Measures include 24-hour foot and vehicle patrol, self-defense education, and security escort services. There are shuttle buses, emergency telephones, and lighted pathways/sidewalks.

Programs of Study: Sarah Lawrence confers B.A. degrees. Master's degrees are also awarded. Bachelor's degrees are awarded in BIOLOGICAL SCIENCE (biology/biological science), COMMUNICATIONS AND THE ARTS (art history and appreciation, classics, creative writing, dance, dramatic arts, English, film arts, fine arts, French, German, Greek, Italian, Latin, literature, music, Russian, Spanish, and visual and performing arts), COMPUTER AND PHYSICAL SCIENCE (chemistry and mathematics), HEALTH PROFESSIONS (premedicine), SOCIAL SCIENCE (anthropology, Asian/Oriental studies, economics, history, liberal arts/general studies, philosophy, political science/government, psychology, religion, Russian and Slavic studies, sociology, and women's studies).

Required: To graduate, students must complete 120 credit hours and meet distribution requirements in 3 of 4 academic areas, including history and social sciences, creative and performing arts, natural science and math, and humanities. Students must fulfill a first-year studies requirement in one of 18 areas and meet a phys ed requirement. Students must also take 2 lecture courses, where the average class size is 40.

Special: Internships are available in a variety of fields, with the school offering proximity to New York City art galleries and agencies. Study abroad in many countries, work-study programs, dual concentrations, a 3-2 engineering degree with Columbia, and a general degree may be pursued. All concentrations are self-designed and can be combined.

Faculty/Classroom: 49% of faculty are male; 51% are female. All teach and do research. No introductory courses are taught by graduate students. The average class size in a regular course is 11.

Requirements: Important academic requirements are: secondary school record, teacher recommendation(s) and essay; class rank is considered. Nonacademic requirements include character and personality qualities; extracurricular activities, talent/ability, volunteer work, and work experience. Campus interview, alumnae relations, geographical residence, and minority status are considered. AP credits are accepted. Important factors in the admissions decision are recommendations by school officials, personality/intangible qualities, and extracurricular activities record.

Procedure: Freshmen are admitted in the fall. There are early decision, early admissions and deferred admissions plans. Early decision applications should be filed by November 15; regular applications, check with

the school for current application deadlines. The fall 2009 application fee was $50. Notification of early decision is sent December 15; regular decision, April 1. Applications are accepted on-line. A waiting list is maintained.

Transfer: Applicants must submit high school and college transcripts, and a statement of good standing from prior institution(s). A GPA of 3.0 is required and transfer applicants must have a minimum of 30 credits completed, or the equivalent of 2 semesters of full-time college work. Also required are a $50 application fee, Admission Information Form (in-house Form 1), essays, a graded academic paper, and 2 teacher/faculty evaluations. An interview is recommended, but not required. November 15 is the application deadline for spring entry. 60 of 120 credits required for the bachelor's degree must be completed at Sarah Lawrence.

Visiting: There are regularly scheduled orientations for prospective students, consisting of a full day of faculty and student panels, lectures, tours, and discussion with admissions officers, offered twice per year during the fall. There are guides for informal visits; visitors may sit in on classes and stay overnight. To schedule a visit, contact Linda Bloom, Receptionist, Admissions Office at slcadmit@slc.edu.

Financial Aid: Sarah Lawrence is a member of CSS. The CSS/Profile, FAFSA, and non-custodial parent statement are required. Check with the school for current application deadlines.

International Students: The school actively recruits these students. They must take the TOEFL, or SAT II: English as a second language test.

Computers: All students may access the system 24 hours a day. There are no time limits and no fees.

Admissions Contact: Dean of Admission E-Mail: *slcadmit@alc.edu* Web: *www.sarahlawrence.edu*

SCHOOL OF VISUAL ARTS D-5
New York, NY 10010-3994

(212) 592-2100
(800) 436-4204; (212) 592-2116

Full-time: 1480 men, 1735 women	Faculty: n/av
Part-time: 50 men, 70 women	Ph.D.s: n/av
Graduate: 175 men, 160 women	Student/Faculty: n/av
Year: semesters, summer session	Tuition: $24,000
Application Deadline: February 1	Room & Board: $12,500
Freshman Class: n/av	
SAT or ACT: required	SPECIAL

The School of Visual Arts, established in 1947, is a private college of art and design conferring undergraduate and graduate degrees in fine and commercial arts. The figures in the above capsule and in this profile are approximate. There is 1 graduate school. In addition to regional accreditation, SVA has baccalaureate program accreditation with FIDER and NASAD. The library contains 70,000 volumes, 1,070 microform items, and 3,168 audio/video tapes/CDs/DVDs, and subscribes to 307 periodicals including electronic. Computerized library services include database searching, Internet access, and laptop Internet portals. Special learning facilities include a learning resource center, art gallery, radio station, a design study center and archive, 5 student galleries, 3 media arts workshops, 3 film and 2 video studios, numerous editing facilities, animation studio with 3 pencil test facilities, digital audio room, tape transfer room, and multimedia facility with digital printing and editing systems. The campus is in an urban area in mid Manhattan. Including any residence halls, there are 14 buildings.

Student Life: 55% of undergraduates are from out of state, mostly the Middle Atlantic. Students are from 47 states, 45 foreign countries, and Canada. 53% are white; 13% Asian American; 13% foreign nationals. The average age of freshmen is 18; all undergraduates, 21. 16% do not continue beyond their first year; 66% remain to graduate.

Housing: 1150 students can be accommodated in college housing, which includes single-sex and coed dorms. On-campus housing is available on a first-come and first-served basis. 70% of students commute. Alcohol is not permitted. All students may keep cars.

Activities: There are no fraternities or sororities. There are 20 groups on campus, including art, drama, ethnic, film, gay, honors, international, literary magazine, photography, political, professional, radio and TV, religious, social, social service, student government, and yearbook. Popular campus events include an annual ski trip, and a Halloween party.

Sports: There is no sports program at SVA.

Disabled Students: All of the campus is accessible. Facilities include wheelchair ramps, elevators, specially equipped restrooms, special class scheduling, and lowered telephones.

Services: There is remedial reading and writing.

Campus Safety and Security: Measures include 24-hour foot and vehicle patrol. There are shuttle buses, emergency telephones, lighted pathways/sidewalks, and controlled access to dorms/residences.

Programs of Study: SVA confers B.F.A. degrees. Master's degrees are also awarded. Bachelor's degrees are awarded in COMMUNICATIONS AND THE ARTS (advertising, animation, film arts, fine arts, graphic design, illustration, photography, video, and visual effects), ENGINEER-

ING AND ENVIRONMENTAL DESIGN (computer graphics and interior design). Visual and critical studies; computer art; computer animation and special effects are the strongest academically. Graphic design; film/video and photography are the largest.

Required: To graduate, students must complete 120 credits, including at least 72 in the major, with a minimum GPA of 2.0. These credits must include 30 in humanities and sciences, 12 in art history, and 6 in electives. Students must complete 2 introductory courses in literature and writing and must pass a proficiency exam in the first semester. A thesis is required in most programs.

Special: SVA offers for-credit internships with more than 200 media-related, design, and advertising firms, including DC Comics, MTV, and Pentagram Design. A summer internship with Walt Disney Studios is possible for illustration/cartooning majors. There are a freshman honors program.

Faculty/Classroom: 64% of faculty are male; 36% are female. 86% teach undergraduates, and 12% do both. No introductory courses are taught by graduate students. The average class size in a regular course is 20.

Requirements: The SAT or ACT is required. In addition, applicants must graduate from an accredited secondary school or have a GED. A statement of intent is required of all students. A portfolio is also required. A personal interview and letters of recommendation are considered helpful. A GPA of 2.7 is required. AP and CLEP credits are accepted. Important factors in the admissions decision are personality/intangible qualities, extracurricular activities record, and evidence of special talent.

Procedure: Freshmen are admitted in the fall. There are early decision, deferred admissions and rolling admissions plans. Early decision applications should be filed by December 1; regular applications, by February 1 for fall entry. The fall 2009 application fee was $50. Notification of early decision is sent January 15. Applications are accepted on-line. 10 applicants were on a recent waiting list, 0 were accepted.

Transfer: 265 transfer students enrolled in a recent year. In a recenrt Year, College transcripts from all previously attended accredited colleges or universities, portfolio, admissions essay, high school transcripts are required for some, letters of recommendation are encouraged. 60 of 120 credits required for the bachelor's degree must be completed at SVA.

Visiting: There are regularly scheduled orientations for prospective students, including Saturday open house receptions and weekly tours. There are guides for informal visits. To schedule a visit, contact the Office of Admissions at admissions@sva.edu.

Financial Aid: In a recent year, 43% of all full-time freshmen and 40% of continuing full-time students received need-based aid. 7% of undergraduate students worked part-time. The average financial indebtedness of the 2009 graduate was $30,259. The FAFSA is required. Check with the school for current application deadlines.

International Students: There were 434 international students enrolled in a recent year. The school actively recruits these students. They must take the TOEFL and the college's own test, or earn a minimum score of 6 in all categories of the NYU English proficiency exam.

Computers: Wireless access is available. Every student is given a log-in id to the College's internal network, including Web-based e-mail account; computer network can be accessed from off-campus; SVA has over 700 PCs and Macs available for student use, including in the library, public areas on campus, and the writing resource center. All students may access the system. during normal operating hours of the library and the writing resource center. There are no time limits and no fees. It is strongly recommended that all students have a personal computer. A Intel based Mac is recommended.

Graduates: In a recent year, 631 bachelor's degrees were awarded. The most popular majors were graphic design (24%), photography (17%), and film and video (11%). 50 companies recruited on campus in 2008-2009. In an average class, 58% graduate in 4 years or less, 65% graduate in 5 years or less, and 66% graduate in 6 years or less. Of the 2008 graduating class, 6% were enrolled in graduate school within 6 months of graduation, and 76% were employed.

Admissions Contact: Adam Rogers, Director of Admissions. E-Mail: *admissions@sva.edu* Web: *www.schoolofvisualarts.edu*

SIENA COLLEGE   D-3

Loudonville, NY 12211-1462

(518) 783-2964
(888) AT SIENA; (518) 783-2436

Full-time: 1443 men, 1658 women	**Faculty:** 185; IIB, +$
Part-time: 80 men, 104 women	**Ph.Ds:** 89%
Graduate: 8 men, 12 women	**Student/Faculty:** 17 to 1
Year: semesters, summer session	**Tuition:** $25,285
Application Deadline: March 1	**Room & Board:** $9930
Freshman Class: 3889 accepted, 783 enrolled	
SAT CR/M: 559/583	**ACT:** 24 **VERY COMPETITIVE**

Siena College, founded in 1937, is a learning community advancing the ideals of a liberal arts education, rooted in its identity as a Franciscan and Catholic Institution. There are 3 undergraduate schools and 1 graduate school. In addition to regional accreditation, Siena has baccalaure-

ate program accreditation with AACSB and CSWE. The library contains 354,963 volumes, 27,720 microform items, and 11,051 audio/video tapes/CDs/DVDs, and subscribes to 23,688 periodicals including electronic. Computerized library services include interlibrary loans, database searching, Internet access, and laptop Internet portals. Special learning facilities include an art gallery, radio station, and the Hickey Financial Technology Center, which features real-time capital market trading room with stock ticker, data screens, workstations, and access to financial information sources and accounting labs. The 166-acre campus is in a suburban area 2 miles north of Albany. Including any residence halls, there are 28 buildings.

Student Life: 84% of undergraduates are from New York. Others are from 26 states, 6 foreign countries, and Canada. 81% are white. The average age of freshmen is 18; all undergraduates, 20. 11% do not continue beyond their first year; 80% remain to graduate.

Housing: 2480 students can be accommodated in college housing, which includes coed dorms, on-campus apartments, and off-campus apartments. In addition, there are special-interest houses. On-campus housing is guaranteed for the freshman year only and is available on a lottery system for upperclassmen. 76% of students live on campus; of those, 90% remain on campus on weekends. Upperclassmen may keep cars.

Activities: There are no fraternities or sororities. There are 70 groups on campus, including cheerleading, chorus, community service, computers, dance, debate, drama, ethnic, film, gay, honors, international, literary magazine, musical theater, newspaper, orchestra, pep band, political, professional, radio and TV, religious, social, social service, student government, and yearbook. Popular campus events include Charity Week, Sienafest, and Winter Weekend.

Sports: There are 7 intercollegiate sports for men and 1 for women, and 7 intramural sports for men and 7 for women. Facilities include an athletic complex with free weights, a training facility, an indoor track, an 8-lane, 25-meter pool, fitness equipment, life cycles, 4 multipurpose courts, 6 outdoor tennis courts, 5 outdoor fields, 2 squash courts, and racquetball courts.

Disabled Students: 90% of the campus is accessible. Facilities include wheelchair ramps, elevators, special parking, specially equipped restrooms, special class scheduling, special housing, and an office for students with disabilities that provides various resources.

Services: Counseling and information services are available, as is tutoring in most subjects. There is a reader service for the blind, and remedial math and writing. and a writing center that offers free one-to-one assistance.

Campus Safety and Security: Measures include 24-hour foot and vehicle patrol, emergency notification system, and security escort services. There are emergency telephones, lighted pathways/sidewalks, a card access system for residence halls, radio dispatch, and a 911 on-campus telephone system.

Programs of Study: Siena confers B.A., B.S., and B.B.A. degrees. Bachelor's degrees are awarded in BIOLOGICAL SCIENCE (biochemistry and biology/biological science), BUSINESS (accounting, banking and finance, business administration and management, and marketing management), COMMUNICATIONS AND THE ARTS (classics, English, French, Spanish, and visual and performing arts), COMPUTER AND PHYSICAL SCIENCE (actuarial science, chemistry, computer science, mathematics, and physics), ENGINEERING AND ENVIRONMENTAL DESIGN (environmental science), SOCIAL SCIENCE (American studies, economics, history, philosophy, political science/government, psychology, religion, social work, and sociology). Marketing/management, accounting, and biology are the largest.

Required: To graduate, students must earn 120 credits, including 30 to 39 depending on major, with at least a 2.0 GPA. At least a C-grade in every major field course used to satisfy the credit hour requirement of the major. The required core curriculum is 42 credits.

Special: The college has opportunities for cooperative programs in business, environmental science, engineering, medical education, social work, elementary education, and dentistry. Cross-registration with the Hudson-Mohawk Association is offered. Domestic and international internships, study abroad in 23 countries, a Washington semester, and work-study programs are available. The college offers dual majors in different divisions and a B.A.-B.S. degree in math, economics, and biology as well as a 3-2 engineering degree with Rensselaer Polytechnic Institute, Catholic University, Clarkson University, Manhattan College, SUNY Binghamton, and Western New England College. A 4-4 medical program with Albany Medical College is also offered. There are 15 national honor societies, a freshman honors program, and 4 departmental honors programs.

Faculty/Classroom: 63% of faculty are male; 37% are female. All teach undergraduates. No introductory courses are taught by graduate students. The average class size in an introductory lecture, 20, in a laboratory, 19, and in a regular course, 21.

Admissions: The SAT scores for the 2009-2010 freshman class were: Critical Reading--21% below 500, 48% between 500 and 599, 28% between 600 and 700, and 3% above 700; Math--13% below 500, 44%

between 500 and 599, 39% between 600 and 700, and 4% above 700; Writing--23% below 500, 48% between 500 and 599, 26% between 600 and 700, and 2% above 700. The ACT scores were 18% below 21, 28% between 21 and 23, 39% between 24 and 26, 7% between 27 and 28, and 7% above 28. 49% of the current freshmen were in the top fifth of their class; 82% were in the top two fifths.

Requirements: The SAT or ACT is required. In addition, applicants must be graduates of an accredited secondary school or have a GED. 13 academic credits are required, including 4 years of English, and 3 to 4 years each of history/social studies, math, and science, and a recommended 3 years of foreign language study. All applicants must submit an essay; an interview is recommended. AP and CLEP credits are accepted. Important factors in the admissions decision are advanced placement or honors courses, personality/intangible qualities, and extracurricular activities record.

Procedure: Freshmen are admitted fall and spring. Entrance exams should be taken during spring of the junior year or fall of the senior year. There are early decision, early admissions and deferred admissions plans. Early decision applications should be filed by December 1, regular applications should be filed by March 1 for fall entry, December 1 for spring entry, and January 1 for summer entry. The fall 2009 application fee was $50. Early decision applications should be filed by January 15; regular decision, March 15. Applications are accepted on-line. 341 applicants were on a recent waiting list, 25 were accepted.

Transfer: 225 transfer students enrolled in 2008-2009. Applicants must have a minimum 2.5 GPA. An interview is recommended. At least half of the major field requirements must be completed at Siena. 30 of 120 credits required for the bachelor's degree must be completed at Siena.

Visiting: There are regularly scheduled orientations for prospective students, Students may interview with an admissions counselor, tour campus, or attend a group information session. There are guides for informal visits; visitors may sit in on classes and stay overnight. To schedule a visit, contact the Admissions Office at admit@siena.edu.

Financial Aid: The FAFSA and the state aid form are required. The priority date for freshman financial aid applications for fall entry is February 15. Check with the school for current application deadlines.

International Students: There are 11 international students enrolled. They must take the TOEFL with a minimum score of 550 on the paper-based TOEFL (PBT) or 79 on the Internet-based version (iBT). They must also take the SAT or ACT.

Computers: Wireless access is available. All students have accounts established for them prior to arrival. The campus network is currently available in most residences, the student union, parts of the library, and in some classrooms. Students may access more than 123 PCs, Macs, and terminals in more than a dozen locations, some of which are open 24 hours a day. Every residential space includes a network connection. A wireless system is available in the student union, parts of the library, and in some classrooms. A total of 215 wired network connections are available. All students may access the system 24 hours per day. There are no time limits and no fees.

Graduates: From July 1, 2008 to June 30, 2009, 783 bachelor's degrees were awarded. The most popular majors were marketing/management (21%), accounting (13%), and psychology (11%). 700 companies recruited on campus in 2008-2009. In an average class, 1% graduate in 3 years or less, 70% graduate in 4 years or less, 76% graduate in 5 years or less, and 77% graduate in 6 years or less. Of the 2008 graduating class, 27% were enrolled in graduate school within 6 months of graduation, and 69% were employed.

Admissions Contact: Edward Jones, Assistant Vice President for Enrollment. E-Mail: *admit@siena.edu* Web: *www.siena.edu*

SKIDMORE COLLEGE D-3
Saratoga Springs, NY 12866-1632

(518) 580-5570
(800) 867-6007; (518) 580-5584

Full-time: 1060 men, 1555 women	**Faculty:** IIB, +$
Part-time: 60 men, 145 women	**Ph.D.s:** n/av
Graduate: 15 men, 45 women	**Student/Faculty:** n/av
Year: semesters, summer session	**Tuition:** $40,420
Application Deadline: January 15	**Room & Board:** $10,776
Freshman Class: n/av	
SAT or ACT: required	

Skidmore College, established in 1903, is an independent institution offering undergraduate programs in liberal arts and sciences, as well as preprofessional programs (business, social work, education, studio art, dance, and theater).The figures in the above capsule and in this profile are approximate. There is 1 graduate school. In addition to regional accreditation, Skidmore has baccalaureate program accreditation with CSWE and NASAD. The library contains 425,822 volumes, 13,567 microform items, and 14,592 audio/video tapes/CDs/DVDs, and subscribes to 4,718 periodicals including electronic. Computerized library services include interlibrary loans, database searching, and Internet access. Special learning facilities include a learning resource center, art gallery, radio station, TV station, an electronic music studio, music and art studios,

theater teaching facility, anthropology lab, and special biological habitats on campus. The 750-acre campus is in a small town 30 miles north of Albany. Including any residence halls, there are 49 buildings.

Student Life: 68% of undergraduates are from out of state, mostly the Northeast. Students are from 44 states, 41 foreign countries, and Canada. 63% are from public schools. 66% are white. The average age of freshmen is 18; all undergraduates, 20. 6% do not continue beyond their first year; 81% remain to graduate.

Housing: 1948 students can be accommodated in college housing, which includes single-sex and coed dorms and on-campus apartments. In addition, there is a gender neutral wing. On-campus housing is guaranteed for all 4 years and is available on a lottery system for upperclassmen. 85% of students live on campus; of those, 80% remain on campus on weekends. All students may keep cars.

Activities: There are no fraternities or sororities. There are 80 groups on campus, including art, band, chorale, chorus, computers, dance, debate, drama, environmental, ethnic, film, gay, honors, international, jazz band, literary magazine, musical theater, newspaper, opera, orchestra, photography, political, professional, radio and TV, religious, social, social service, student government, symphony, and yearbook. Popular campus events include Martin Luther King Week, Oktoberfest, and Spring Fling.

Sports: There are 9 intercollegiate sports for men and 10 for women, and 10 intramural sports for men. Facilities include a fitness center, an indoor swimming and diving pool, 2 gyms with 4 basketball courts, a weight room, fields for baseball and other sports, dance studios, cross-country ski trails, a riding center, courts for tennis, handball, racquetball, and squash, and an outdoor facility with a synthetic surface, a soccer/lacrosse field, an all-weather 400-meter track, lights, and permanent stands.

Disabled Students: 75% of the campus is accessible. Facilities include wheelchair ramps, elevators, special parking, specially equipped restrooms, lowered drinking fountains, and special housing.

Services: Counseling and information services are available, as is tutoring in most subjects. There is a reader service for the blind. Diagnostic services, note takers, and books on tape are also offered.

Campus Safety and Security: Measures include 24-hour foot and vehicle patrol, emergency notification system, and security escort services. There are shuttle buses, emergency telephones, lighted pathways/sidewalks, a special security alert system, rigorous fire response procedures, and a lock system on dorm entrances.

Programs of Study: Skidmore confers B.A. and B.S. degrees. Master's degrees are also awarded. Bachelor's degrees are awarded in AGRICULTURE (environmental studies), BIOLOGICAL SCIENCE (biochemistry, biology/biological science, and neurosciences), BUSINESS (business administration and management and business economics), COMMUNICATIONS AND THE ARTS (art, art history and appreciation, classics, dance, dramatic arts, English, French, German, music, and Spanish), COMPUTER AND PHYSICAL SCIENCE (chemistry, computer science, geology, mathematics, and physics), EDUCATION (elementary education), HEALTH PROFESSIONS (exercise science), SOCIAL SCIENCE (American studies, anthropology, Asian/Oriental studies, economics, French studies, history, international relations, liberal arts/general studies, philosophy, political science/government, psychology, religion, social science, social work, sociology, and women's studies). Business, English, and art are the largest.

Required: To graduate, students must complete 120 credits, including at least 24 at the 300 level, with a minimum GPA of 2.0 overall and in the major. B.A. candidates require 90 credits in the liberal arts to graduate; B.S. candidates require 60 credits. Students must fulfill all core curriculum, distribution, and major requirements.

Special: Skidmore offers cross-registration with the Hudson-Mohawk Consortium, individually designed internships, various study-abroad programs, a Washington semester in conjunction with American University, dual and student-designed majors, credit for life and experience, and pass/fail options, as well as a nondegree study program for senior citizens. There are cooperative programs in engineering with Dartmouth College and Clarkson University, and 4+1 M.B.A. programs with Clarkson and the Graduate College at Union University. There are 9 national honor societies, including Phi Beta Kappa, and a freshman honors program.

Faculty/Classroom: 44% of faculty are male; 56% are female. All teach undergraduates, all do research, and all teach and do research. No introductory courses are taught by graduate students. The average class size in a regular course is 17.

Requirements: The SAT or ACT is required. AP and CLEP credits are accepted. Important factors in the admissions decision are advanced placement or honors courses, recommendations by school officials, and evidence of special talent.

Procedure: Freshmen are admitted fall. Entrance exams should be taken by December of the senior year. There are early decision and deferred admissions plans. Early decision applications should be filed by November 15; regular applications, by January 15 for fall entry, along with a $60 fee. Notification of early decision is sent December 15; regular decision, April 1. Applications are accepted on-line. 1,584 applicants were on a recent waiting list, 59 were accepted.

Transfer: 36 transfer students enrolled in a recent year. Transfer students must have a GPA of 2.7 and must submit a high school transcript, all college transcripts, an essay or personal statement, test scores, and a statement of good standing from prior institutions. At least one professor recommendation from the current institution and a mid-term report are also required. 60 of 120 credits required for the bachelor's degree must be completed at Skidmore.

Visiting: There are regularly scheduled orientations for prospective students, including full-day open-house programs. There are guides for informal visits; visitors may sit in on classes and stay overnight. To schedule a visit, contact the Admissions Office at admissions@skidmore.edu.

Financial Aid: In a recent year, 43% of all full-time freshmen and 41% of continuing full-time students received some form of financial aid. 43% of all full-time freshmen and 41% of continuing full-time students received need-based aid. The average freshmen award was $32,960. 47% of undergraduate students worked part-time. Average annual earnings from campus work are $921. Skidmore is a member of CSS. The CSS/Profile and FAFSA are required. Check with the school for current application deadlines.

International Students: There were 78 international students enrolled in a recent year. The school actively recruits these students. They must take the TOEFL. They must also take the SAT or ACT.

Computers: Wireless access is available. Computers can be found in several public areas, the library, and labs. High speed connections are in all residential areas. All students may access the system. 24 hours per day. There are no time limits and no fees. It is strongly recommended that all students have a personal computer.

Graduates: In a recent year, 670 bachelor's degrees were awarded. The most popular majors were business (13%), psychology (8%), and English (8%). 420 companies recruited on campus in 2008-2009. In an average class, 78% graduate in 4 years or less, 81% graduate in 5 years or less, and 87% graduate in 6 years or less. Of the 2008 graduating class, 19% were enrolled in graduate school within 6 months of graduation, and 94% were employed.

Admissions Contact: Mary Lou Bates, Director of Admissions. A campus DVD is available. E-Mail: *admissions@skidmore.edu*
Web: *www.skidmore.edu*

STATE UNIVERSITY OF NEW YORK

The State University of New York, established in 1948, is a public system in New York. It is governed by a board of trustees, whose chief administrator is the chancellor. The primary goal of the system is teaching, research, and public service. The main priorities are to educate the largest number of people possible at the highest level, including educationally disadvantaged groups; the highest level; to provide students with enhanced educational skills and techniques; and to enhance the quality of life for all New Yorkers. Profiles of the 4-year campuses are included in this section.

STATE UNIVERSITY OF NEW YORK AT BINGHAMTON /BINGHAMTON UNIVERSITY   C-4

Binghamton, NY 13902-6000	**(607) 777-2171; (607) 777-4445**
Full-time: 5898 men, 5381 women	**Faculty:** 596; I, -$
Part-time: 251 men, 174 women	**Ph.D.s:** 91%
Graduate: 1558 men, 1449 women	**Student/Faculty:** 19 to 1
Year: semesters, summer session	**Tuition:** $6761 ($14,661)
Application Deadline: January 15	**Room & Board:** $10,614
Freshman Class: 29,062 applied, 9692 accepted, 2026 enrolled	
SAT CR/M: 630/660	**ACT:** 29
	HIGHLY COMPETITIVE+

Part of the State University of New York (SUNY) system, Bingham University was founded in 1946. The university offers programs in arts and sciences, education, nursing, management, engineering and applied science, and community and public affairs. There are 5 undergraduate schools and 1 graduate school. In addition to regional accreditation, Binghamton University has baccalaureate program accreditation with AACSB, ABET, CSWE, NASM, and TEAC. The 3 libraries contain 2.4 million volumes, 1.9 million microform items, and 125,656 audio/video tapes/CDs/DVDs, and subscribe to 81,959 periodicals including electronic. Computerized library services include interlibrary loans, database searching, Internet access, and laptop Internet portals. Special learning facilities include a learning resource center, art gallery, radio station, TV station, nature preserve, 4-climate greenhouse, performing arts center (5 theaters), art/dance studios, sculpture foundry, research centers, electron microscopy labs, geographic information systems core facility, public archeology facility, integrated electronics engineering center, institute for child development, and information commons. The 930-acre campus is in a suburban area 1 mile west of Binghamton. Including any residence halls, there are 107 buildings.

Student Life: 90% of undergraduates are from New York. Others are from 42 states, 69 foreign countries, and Canada. 87% are from public schools. 56% are white; 16% Asian American; 12% foreign nationals. 29% are Catholic; 24% claim no religious affiliation; 22% Jewish; 19% Protestant. The average age of freshmen is 18; all undergraduates, 21. 10% do not continue beyond their first year; 81% remain to graduate.

Housing: 6362 students can be accommodated in college housing, which includes coed dorms, on-campus apartments, off-campus apartments, and married student housing. In addition, there are special-interest houses, chemical- and smoke-free housing, and living-learning communities. On-campus housing is guaranteed for the freshman year only, is available on a first-come, first-served basis, and is available on a lottery system for upperclassmen. 61% of students live on campus; of those, 95% remain on campus on weekends. Upperclassmen may keep cars.

Activities: 9% of men belong to 1 local and 22 national fraternities; 11% of women belong to 23 national sororities. There are 296 groups on campus, including art, band, cheerleading, chess, choir, chorale, chorus, club sports/intramurals, computers, cultural, dance, debate, drama, environmental, ethnic, film, gay, honors, international, jazz band, literary magazine, musical theater, newspaper, opera, orchestra, pep band, photography, political, professional, radio and TV, religious, social, social service, special interest, student government, symphony, and yearbook. Popular campus events include China Night, Dawaii, and Spring Fling.

Sports: There are 11 intercollegiate sports for men and 10 for women, and 20 intramural sports for men and 18 for women. Facilities include a 5000-seat events center with basketball and tennis courts and a 200-meter track. 2 additional gyms are equipped with swimming pools, fitness center, all-purpose courts for basketball, volleyball, and other activities, and racquetball and squash courts, dance and karate studios. The campus has a 2500-seat soccer and lacrosse complex and separate facilities for baseball, softball, track and field, tennis, and cross-country. The campus also features a 190-acre nature preserve.

Disabled Students: 90% of the campus is accessible. Facilities include wheelchair ramps, elevators, special parking, specially equipped restrooms, lowered drinking fountains, lowered telephones, special housing, and a comprehensive array of services for students with physical, learning, or other disabilities.

Services: Counseling and information services are available, as is tutoring in most subjects. Walk-in tutoring is available Monday through Thursday. One-on-one and small-group tutoring are available 7 days per week.

Campus Safety and Security: Measures include 24-hour foot and vehicle patrol, emergency notification system, self-defense education, and security escort services. There are shuttle buses, emergency telephones, lighted pathways/sidewalks, controlled access to dorms/residences, police officers, monitored entrance to campus with proper identification between midnight and 5 A.M., and formal personal safety programs.

Programs of Study: Binghamton University confers B.A., B.S., and B.Mus. degrees. Master's and doctoral degrees are also awarded. Bachelor's degrees are awarded in BIOLOGICAL SCIENCE (biochemistry, biology/biological science, biophysics, cell biology, evolutionary biology, and molecular biology), BUSINESS (accounting, banking and finance, business administration and management, entrepreneurial studies, management information systems, management science, marketing management, operations management, and supply chain management), COMMUNICATIONS AND THE ARTS (Arabic, art, art history and appreciation, classics, comparative literature, creative writing, dance, dramatic arts, English, film arts, fine arts, French, German, Hebrew, Italian, Latin, linguistics, literature, music, music performance, Spanish, speech/debate/rhetoric, studio art, theater design, and visual and performing arts), COMPUTER AND PHYSICAL SCIENCE (actuarial science, applied physics, chemistry, computer science, environmental geology, geology, information sciences and systems, mathematics, and physics), ENGINEERING AND ENVIRONMENTAL DESIGN (bioengineering, computer engineering, electrical/electronics engineering, engineering, environmental science, industrial engineering, mechanical engineering, and systems engineering), HEALTH PROFESSIONS (nursing), SOCIAL SCIENCE (African American studies, anthropology, Asian/American studies, Caribbean studies, classical/ancient civilization, economics, geography, history, human development, interdisciplinary studies, international studies, Judaic studies, Latin American studies, medieval studies, philosophy, political science/government, psychobiology, psychology, and sociology). Management, political science, and biology are the strongest academically. Engineering, biology, and management are the largest.

Required: To graduate, all students must complete 124 to 130 credit hours, with 36 to 72 in the major and a minimum GPA of 2.0. General education requirements include courses in language and communication, global vision, science, aesthetic perspective, foreign language, humanities, math, social science, physical activity/wellness, and pluralism. Other requirements vary by school.

Special: The university offers innovative study through the individualized major program (student-designed majors), internships, independent study, study abroad in more than 100 countries, a Washington semester through American University, on- and off-campus work-study programs, and B.A.-B.S. degrees in 28 departments. There are also dual and inter-disciplinary majors such as philosophy, politics, and law and prehealth programs in medicine, denistry, optometry, veterinary medicine, podia-try, nutrition, physical and occupational therapy, and chiropractic. Early assurance programs guarantee graduate admission at partner SUNY schools. There are 23 national honor societies, including Phi Beta Kappa, a freshman honors program, and 32 departmental honors programs.

Faculty/Classroom: 57% of faculty are male; 43% are female. All teach and do research. Graduate students teach 6% of introductory courses. The average class size in an introductory lecture is 52; in a labo-ratory, 18; and in a regular course, 32.

Admissions: 33% of the 2009-2010 applicants were accepted. The SAT scores for the 2009-2010 freshman class were: Critical Reading--3% below 500, 29% between 500 and 599, 52% between 600 and 700; and 15% above 700; Math--15% between 500 and 599, 57% between 600 and 700, and 28% above 700. The ACT scores were 6% between 21 and 23, 19% between 24 and 26, 23% between 27 and 28, and 52% above 29. 78% of the current freshmen were in the top fifth of their class; 94% were in the top two fifths.

Requirements: The SAT or ACT is required. The ACT Optional Writ-ing test is also required. In addition, applicants must be graduates of an accredited secondary school or have a GED certificate and complete 16 academic credits. These include 4 units of English, 3 units of 1 foreign language or 2 units each of 2 foreign languages, 2 1/2 of math, and 2 each of science and social studies. Students may submit slides of art-work, request an audition for music, prepare a videotape for dance or theater, or share athletic achievements. An essay is required. AP and CLEP credits are accepted. Important factors in the admissions decision are advanced placement or honors courses, extracurricular activities re-cord, and evidence of special talent.

Procedure: Freshmen are admitted fall and spring. Entrance exams should be taken in the spring of the junior year or the fall of the senior year. There are deferred admissions and rolling admissions plans. Appli-cations should be filed by January 15 (priority date) for fall entry; No-vember 15 for spring entry, along with a $40 fee. Notification is sent on a rolling basis beginning April 1. Applications are accepted on-line. 735 applicants were on a recent waiting list, 45 were accepted.

Transfer: 1057 transfer students enrolled in 2008-2009. Applicants must submit college transcripts; students who wish to transfer after their first year of college must also submit their high school transcripts. 30 of 124 to 130 credits required for the bachelor's degree must be completed at Binghamton University.

Visiting: There are regularly scheduled orientations for prospective stu-dents, including an information session and a student-led tour of cam-pus. Visitors may sit in on classes. To schedule a visit, contact the Office of Undergraduate Admissions.

Financial Aid: In 2009-2010, 80% of all full-time freshmen and 87% of continuing full-time students received some form of financial aid. 60% of all full-time freshmen and 57% of continuing full-time students re-ceived need-based aid. The average freshmen award was $20,017. 8% of undergraduate students work part-time (not including work study). Average annual earnings from campus work are $1820. The average fi-nancial indebtedness of a 2008 graduate was $14,560. The FAFSA is re-quired. The deadline for filing freshman financial aid applications for fall entry is February 1.

International Students: There are 889 international students enrolled. The school actively recruits these students. They must take the TOEFL with a minimum score of 550 on the paper-based TOEFL (PBT) or 80 on the Internet-based version (iBT). The TOEFL replaces the SAT or ACT for nonnative speakers of English.

Computers: Wireless access is available. Every residence hall room has an ethernet port per resident. Wireless access is provided in all residential communities, throughout all academic buildings, in the Univesity Union and library, and in most outdoor spaces on the central campus. There are more than 1200 wireless access points. There are more than 620 computers in public computer rooms, classrooms, and labs, the largest of which is open nearly round-the-clock during the academic year. All students may access the system 24 hours per day. There are no time lim-its and no fees.

Graduates: From July 1, 2008 to June 30, 2009, 2742 bachelor's de-grees were awarded. The most popular majors were English (9%), man-agement (8%), and biology (8%). 873 companies recruited on campus in 2008-2009. In an average class, 3% graduate in 3 years or less, 70% graduate in 4 years or less, 80% graduate in 5 years or less, and 81% graduate in 6 years or less. Of the 2008 graduating class, 48% were en-rolled in graduate school within 6 months of graduation and 54% were employed.

Admissions Contact: Cheryl Brown, Director of Undergraduate Ad-missions. E-mail: *admit@binghamton.edu* Web: *www.binghamton.edu*

STATE UNIVERSITY OF NEW YORK AT FREDONIA   A-4

Fredonia, NY 14063

(716) 673-3251
(800) 252-1212; (716) 673-3249

Full-time: 2219 men, 2940 women	**Faculty:** 222; IIA, -$
Part-time: 98 men, 120 women	**Ph.D.s:** 81%
Graduate: 84 men, 296 women	**Student/Faculty:** 21 to 1
Year: semesters, summer session	**Tuition:** $6258 ($14,158)
Application Deadline: open	**Room & Board:** $9330
Freshman Class: 6632 applied, 3281 accepted, 1148 enrolled	
SAT CR/M: 550/560	**ACT:** 24 **VERY COMPETITIVE**

The State University of New York at Fredonia, established in 1826, is a public institution offering undergraduate programs in the arts and sci-ences, business and professional curricula, teacher preparation, and the fine and performing arts. There are 6 undergraduate schools and 1 grad-uate school. In addition to regional accreditation, Fredonia has bacca-laureate program accreditation with CSWE, NASAD, NASM, and NCATE. The library contains 391,121 volumes, 1.1 million microform items, and 26,574 audio/video tapes/CDs/DVDs, and subscribes to 1983 periodicals including electronic. Computerized library services include in-terlibrary loans, database searching, and Internet access. Special learning facilities include a learning resource center, art gallery, radio station, TV station, greenhouse, daycare center, speech clinic, and arts center. The 266-acre campus is in a small town 50 miles south of Buffalo and 45 miles north of Erie, Pennsylvania. Including any residence halls, there are 25 buildings.

Student Life: 97% of undergraduates are from New York. Others are from 17 states, 15 foreign countries, and Canada. 65% are from public schools. 92% are white. The average age of freshmen is 19; all under-graduates, 21. 16% do not continue beyond their first year; 62% remain to graduate.

Housing: 2621 students can be accommodated in college housing, which includes single-sex and coed dorms and on-campus apartments. In addition, there are special-interest houses, living space for fraternities and sororities in residence halls, houses for computer and athletics stu-dents, and quiet-hour centers. On-campus housing is guaranteed for all 4 years. 20% of students commute. All students may keep cars.

Activities: 8% of men belong to 4 national fraternities; 4% of women belong to 3 national sororities. There are 120 groups on campus, includ-ing art, band, cheerleading, choir, chorale, chorus, communications, computers, dance, drama, drill team, ethnic, gay, honors, international, jazz band, literary magazine, musical theater, opera, orchestra, pep band, photography, political, professional, religious, ski, social, social service, student government, and symphony. Popular campus events in-clude various Art Center presentations, Spring Fest, and Little Siblings Weekend.

Sports: There are 8 intercollegiate sports for men and 9 for women, and 15 intramural sports for men and 15 for women. Facilities include a basketball arena, an ice rink, a swimming pool, a gym, a weight room, dance studios, soccer fields, indoor and outdoor tracks, racquetball, ten-nis, and volleyball courts, and a soccer/lacrosse stadium.

Disabled Students: 85% of the campus is accessible. Facilities include wheelchair ramps, elevators, special parking, specially equipped rest rooms, special class scheduling, lowered drinking fountains, and lowered telephones.

Services: Counseling and information services are available, as is tutor-ing in most subjects. There is a reader service for the blind.

Campus Safety and Security: Measures include 24-hour foot and ve-hicle patrol, emergency notification system, self-defense education, and security escort services. There are shuttle buses, emergency telephones, lighted pathways/sidewalks, and card swipe access to residence halls.

Programs of Study: Fredonia confers B.A., B.F.A., B.S., B.S.Ed., and B.Mus. degrees. Master's degrees are also awarded. Bachelor's degrees are awarded in BIOLOGICAL SCIENCE (biochemistry and biology/biological science), BUSINESS (accounting, business administration and management, business economics, and sports management), COMMU-NICATIONS AND THE ARTS (audio technology, communications, dra-matic arts, English, fine arts, French, graphic design, media arts, music, and Spanish), COMPUTER AND PHYSICAL SCIENCE (chemistry, computer science, earth science, geology, mathematics, and physics), EDUCATION (early childhood education, elementary education, foreign languages education, middle school education, music education, science education, and secondary education), HEALTH PROFESSIONS (health care administration, medical laboratory technology, predentistry, pre-medicine, and speech pathology/audiology), SOCIAL SCIENCE (history, interdisciplinary studies, philosophy, political science/government, psy-chology, social work, and sociology). Business, communication, and ed-ucation are the largest.

Required: To graduate, students must complete 120 hours, including 36 to 90 or more in the major, with a 2.0 GPA. Students must take spe-cific courses in English and math and complete 36 hours of general edu-cation courses, including writing, statistical/quantitative abilities, oral communication, natural and social sciences, humanities, and arts.

Special: Cooperative programs are available with many other institutions. Students may cross-register with colleges in the Western New York Consortium. Fredonia offers a variety of internships, study-abroad programs in more than 50 countries, and a Washington semester. Accelerated degrees, a general studies degree, dual and student-designed majors, a 3-2 engineering degree program with 14 universities, nondegree study, and pass/fail grading options are available. There are 19 national honor societies, a freshman honors program, and 19 departmental honors programs.

Faculty/Classroom: 53% of faculty are male; 47% are female. All teach and do research. No introductory courses are taught by graduate students. The average class size in an introductory lecture is 35, in a laboratory, 16, and in a regular course, 20.

Admissions: 49% of the 2009-2010 applicants were accepted. The SAT scores for the 2009-2010 freshman class were: Critical Reading--30% below 500, 51% between 500 and 599, 18% between 600 and 700, and 1% above 700; Math--23% below 500, 53% between 500 and 599, 23% between 600 and 700, and 1& above 700. The ACT scores were 21% below 21, 35% between 21 and 23, 30% between 24 and 26, 8% between 27 and 28, and 6% above 28. 37% of the current freshmen were in the top fifth of their class; 74% were in the top two fifths. 10 freshmen graduated first in their class.

Requirements: The SAT or ACT is required, with a satisfactory score on the SAT or 20 on the ACT. Applicants must possess a high school diploma or have a GED. 16 academic credits are recommended, including 4 credits each in English and social studies and 3 each in math, science, and a foreign language. 4 years of math and science are encouraged. Essays are required. Where applicable, an audition or portfolio is required. A GPA of 2.5 is required. AP and CLEP credits are accepted: Important factors in the admissions decision are advanced placement or honors courses and recommendations by school officials.

Procedure: Freshmen are admitted fall and spring. Entrance exams should be taken during the spring of the junior year or fall of the senior year. There are early decision, deferred admissions and rolling admissions plans. Early decision applications should be filed by November 1; check with the school for current application deadlines. The application fee is $40. Notification of early decision is sent November 25; regular decision, December 15. Applications are accepted on-line.

Transfer: 455 transfer students enrolled in 2008-2009. Applicants should have a minimum GPA of 2.0. and appropriate academic course work to be considered. An interview is recommended. 45 of 120 credits required for the bachelor's degree must be completed at Fredonia.

Visiting: There are regularly scheduled orientations for prospective students, including various open house programs and information sessions and tours Monday through Friday, morning and afternoon, and Saturday tours once a month. Visitors may sit in on classes and stay overnight. To schedule a visit, contact the Office of Admissions.

Financial Aid: In 2009-2010, 83% of all full-time freshmen and 77% of continuing full-time students received some form of financial aid. 68% of all students received need-based aid. The average financial indebtedness of the 2009 graduate was $23,452. The FAFSA, the state aid form, and the Express TAP Application (ETA) are required. The priority date for freshman financial aid applications for fall entry is February 1.

International Students: There are 72 international students enrolled. The school actively recruits these students. They must take the TOEFL, with a minimum score of 500 on the paper-based TOEFL (PBT) or 62 on the Internet-based version (iBT), or the IELTS.

Computers: Wireless access is available. All students may access the system. There are no time limits and no fees. It is strongly recommended that all students have a personal computer.

Graduates: From July 1, 2008 to June 30, 2009, 1296 bachelor's degrees were awarded. The most popular majors were elementary education (17%), business administration (11%), and psychology (7%). 60 companies recruited on campus in 2008-2009. In an average class, 49% graduate in 4 years or less, 61% graduate in 5 years or less, and 63% graduate in 6 years or less.

Admissions Contact: Chris Dearth, Director of Admissions. E-Mail: *www.fredonia.edu* Web: *fredonia.edu*

STATE UNIVERSITY OF NEW YORK AT OSWEGO C-3

Oswego, NY 13126	(315) 312-2250; (315) 312-3260
Full-time: 3070 men, 3580 women	Faculty: IIA, -$
Part-time: 195 men, 280 women	Ph.Ds: n/av
Graduate: 345 men, 645 women	Student/Faculty: n/av
Year: semesters, summer session	Tuition: $6706 ($14,606)
Application Deadline: January 15	Room & Board: $9500
Freshman Class: n/av	
SAT or ACT: required	VERY COMPETITIVE

State University of New York at Oswego, founded in 1861, is a comprehensive institution offering more than 110 cooperative, preprofessional, and graduate programs in the arts and sciences, business, and education. The figures in the above capsule and in this profile are approximate. There are 3 undergraduate schools and 3 graduate schools. In ad-

dition to regional accreditation, Oswego has baccalaureate program accreditation with AACSB, NASM, and NCATE. The library contains 475,000 volumes, 2.1 million microform items, and 15,000 audio/video tapes/CDs/DVDs, and subscribes to 1,800 periodicals including electronic. Computerized library services include interlibrary loans, database searching, Internet access, and laptop Internet portals. Special learning facilities include a learning resource center, art gallery, planetarium, radio station, TV station, biological field station. The 696-acre campus is in a small town on the southeast shore of Lake Ontario, 35 miles northwest of Syracuse. Including any residence halls, there are 40 buildings.

Student Life: 97% of undergraduates are from New York. Others are from 26 states, 20 foreign countries, and Canada. 90% are from public schools. 88% are white. 42% are Catholic; 41% Protestant; 14% Jewish. The average age of freshmen is 18; all undergraduates, 21. 23% do not continue beyond their first year; 59% remain to graduate.

Housing: 4000 students can be accommodated in college housing, which includes coed dorms. In addition, there are resident hall living and learning communities, a freshmen-only building, and upperclassmen suites. On-campus housing is guaranteed for all 4 years. 58% of students live on campus; of those, 90% remain on campus on weekends. All students may keep cars.

Activities: 7% of men belong to 7 local and 10 national fraternities; 6% of women belong to 5 local and 7 national sororities. There are 135 groups on campus, including art, band, cheerleading, choir, chorale, chorus, computers, dance, drama, ethnic, gay, honors, international, jazz band, literary magazine, musical theater, newspaper, opera, orchestra, pep band, photography, political, professional, radio and TV, religious, social, social service, student government, and yearbook. Popular campus events include Honors Convocations and Quest, May Day, and College Open House.

Sports: There are 12 intercollegiate sports for men and 12 for women, and 25 intramural sports for men and 25 for women. Facilities include an ice hockey rink, a field house with an artificial-grass practice area, 18 tennis courts, an outdoor track, 3 soccer and 3 lacrosse fields, baseball and softball fields, numerous basketball courts, racquetball and squash courts, 2 indoor pools, and a diving well. The gym seats 3500. There are also 2 fitness centers and weight rooms, a cross-country ski lodge, and a martial arts/dance studio.

Disabled Students: 85% of the campus is accessible. Facilities include wheelchair ramps, elevators, special parking, specially equipped restrooms, special class scheduling, lowered drinking fountains, lowered telephones, special housing, and a student support group.

Services: Counseling and information services are available, as is tutoring in every subject. There is a reader service for the blind, and remedial math, reading, and writing. In addition, the Office of Disability Services provides general foundation support.

Campus Safety and Security: Measures include 24-hour foot and vehicle patrol, emergency notification system, self-defense education, and security escort services. There are shuttle buses, emergency telephones, lighted pathways/sidewalks, controlled access to dorms/residences, and an electronic device that locates students and alerts the police when pressed.

Programs of Study: Oswego confers B.A., B.S., and B.F.A. degrees. Master's degrees are also awarded. Bachelor's degrees are awarded in BIOLOGICAL SCIENCE (biochemistry, biology/biological science, and zoology), BUSINESS (accounting, banking and finance, business administration and management, human resources, international economics, management science, marketing/retailing/merchandising, and recreational facilities management), COMMUNICATIONS AND THE ARTS (art, broadcasting, communications, creative writing, dramatic arts, English, film arts, French, German, graphic design, journalism, linguistics, music, public relations, and Spanish), COMPUTER AND PHYSICAL SCIENCE (applied mathematics, atmospheric sciences and meteorology, chemistry, computer science, geochemistry, geology, information sciences and systems, mathematics, and physics), EDUCATION (agricultural education, business education, elementary education, foreign languages education, secondary education, teaching English as a second/foreign language (TESOL/TEFOL), trade and industrial education, and vocational education), ENGINEERING AND ENVIRONMENTAL DESIGN (technological management), SOCIAL SCIENCE (American studies, anthropology, cognitive science, criminal justice, economics, history, human development, international studies, philosophy, political science/government, psychology, sociology, and women's studies). Chemistry, computer science, and accounting are the strongest academically. Elementary/secondary education, business administration, and communication studies are the largest.

Required: To graduate, all students must complete 42 to 48 general education credits, including 6 in human diversity and 3 to 6 each in expository writing and math. Students must have a minimum 2.0 GPA and complete 122 total credit hours (127 hours for technology and vocational education students). The total number of hours in the major varies from 30 to 78.

Special: Oswego offers cross-registration with ACUSNY-Visiting Student Program. More than 1000 internships are available with business, social, cultural, and government agencies. The university also offers a Washington semester, study abroad in more than 40 programs, a 5-year accounting B.S./M.B.A. program, dual majors, B.A.-B.S. degrees in several sciences and a B.A.-B.F.A. in art, credit for military experience, non-degree study, and pass/fail options. A 3-2 engineering degree is offered with Clarkson University, SUNY at Binghamton, and Case Western Reserve University. A 3-4 degree in optometry with SUNY College of Optometry, a 3-2 degree in zoo technology with Santa Fe Community College and Niagara County Community College, and 2-2, 2-3, 3-3 and 4-3 degrees in health sciences with SUNY Health Sciences Center are also possible. There are 21 national honor societies, a freshman honors program, and 9 departmental honors programs.

Faculty/Classroom: 56% of faculty are male; 44% are female. 96% teach undergraduates. No introductory courses are taught by graduate students. The average class size in an introductory lecture is 40; in a laboratory is 15; and in a regular course is 24.

Requirements: The SAT or ACT is required. In addition, applicants must be graduates of an accredited secondary school or have a GED certificate. 18 academic credits are required, including 4 years each of English and social studies, 3 each of math and science, and 2 of a foreign language. An essay and interview are recommended. A GPA of 82.0 is required. AP and CLEP credits are accepted. Important factors in the admissions decision are advanced placement or honors courses, extracurricular activities record, and evidence of special talent.

Procedure: Freshmen are admitted fall and spring. Entrance exams should be taken during the spring of the junior year and fall of the senior year. There are early decision, early admissions, deferred admissions, and rolling admissions plans. Early decision applications should be filed by November 15; regular applications, by January 15 for fall entry and November 15 for spring entry, along with a $40 fee. Notification of early decision is sent December 15; regular decision, January 1. Applications are accepted on-line.

Transfer: 700 transfer students enrolled in a recent year. Applicants must submit official transcripts from previously attended colleges. Students with a minimum GPA of 2.3 are encouraged to apply. SUNY associate degree holders are given preference. Secondary school records may be required for 1-year transfers. 30 of 122 credits required for the bachelor's degree must be completed at Oswego.

Visiting: There are regularly scheduled orientations for prospective students, usually including a campus tour and a meeting/presentation with a counselor. There are guides for informal visits; visitors may sit in on classes and stay overnight. To schedule a visit, contact the Office of Admissions at (315) 312-2250.

Financial Aid: In a recent year, 82% of all full-time freshmen and 81% of continuing full-time students received some form of financial aid. 82% of all full-time freshmen and 81% of continuing full-time students received need-based aid. The average freshmen award was $7,132. 65% of undergraduate students worked part-time. Average annual earnings from campus work were $1500. The average financial indebtedness of the 2009 graduate was $18,606. Oswego is a member of CSS. The FAFSA and the state aid form are required. Check with the school for current application deadlines.

International Students: There were 80 international students enrolled in a recent year. The school actively recruits these students. They must take the TOEFL.

Computers: Wireless access is available. There are 11 open access labs and 40 departmental computer labs with more than 1000 computers available for student use. All residence halls are equipped with high speed Internet, and the library, the school of business, and several other academic buildings as well as all cafeterias have wireless Internet. The library is also accessible to all students through their Oswego accounts and offers rentals of laptop computers. All students may access the system anytime. There are no time limits and no fees. It is strongly recommended that all students have a personal computer. Students enrolled in School of Business majors must have a personal computer.

Graduates: In a recent year, 1505 bachelor's degrees were awarded. The most popular majors were education (25%), business (19%), and communications (12%). 150 companies recruited on campus in 2008-2009. In an average class, 32% graduate in 4 years or less, 54% graduate in 5 years or less, and 59% graduate in 6 years or less. Of the 2008 graduating class, 26% were enrolled in graduate school within 6 months of graduation, and 64% were employed.

Admissions Contact: Joseph F. Grant, Jr., Dean of Admissions. A campus DVD is available. E-Mail: *admiss@oswego.edu* Web: *www.oswego.edu*

STATE UNIVERSITY OF NEW YORK AT POTSDAM   C-2

Potsdam, NY 13676   (315) 267-2180; (315) 267-2163

Full-time: 1512 men, 2062 women	**Faculty:** 263; IIA, --$
Part-time: 69 men, 69 women	**Ph.D.s:** 77%
Graduate: 144 men, 418 women	**Student/Faculty:** 13 to 1
Year: semesters, summer session	**Tuition:** $6124 ($14,024)
Application Deadline: rolling	**Room & Board:** $9570

Freshman Class: 4525 applied, 2970 accepted, 841 enrolled
SAT CR/M: 515/520   **ACT:** 22   **COMPETITIVE**

The State University of New York at Potsdam, founded in 1816, joined the state university system in 1948. The school offers more than 40 undergraduate degree programs. There are 3 undergraduate schools and one graduate school. In addition to regional accreditation, SUNY Potsdam has baccalaureate program accreditation with NASM and NCATE. The 2 libraries contain 458,202 volumes, 768,676 microform items, and 20,455 audio/video tapes/CDs/DVDs, and subscribe to 20,000 periodicals including electronic. Computerized library services include interlibrary loans, database searching, Internet access, and laptop Internet portals. Special learning facilities include a learning resource center, art gallery, natural history museum, planetarium, radio station, electronic music composition lab, recording studios, and seismograph lab. The 240-acre campus is in a rural area 140 miles northeast of Syracuse. Including any residence halls, there are 55 buildings.

Student Life: 93% of undergraduates are from New York. Others are from 30 states, 22 foreign countries, and Canada. 75% are white. The average age of freshmen is 18; all undergraduates, 22. 23% do not continue beyond their first year; 77% remain to graduate.

Housing: 2763 students can be accommodated in college housing, which includes single-sex and coed dorms, on-campus apartments, and off-campus apartments. In addition, there are honors houses, special-interest houses, and First Year Experience, Substance Free, Study Intensive, Arts, International, and Transfer housing. On-campus housing is guaranteed for all 4 years. 57% of students live on campus; of those, 70% remain on campus on weekends. All students may keep cars.

Activities: 4% of men belong to 3 local fraternities and 1 national fraternity; 8% of women belong to 7 local and 2 national sororities. There are 100 groups on campus, including art, band, cheerleading, choir, chorale, chorus, computers, dance, drama, environmental, environmental awareness, ethnic, gay, honors, international, jazz band, literary magazine, musical threater, newspaper, opera, orchestra, pep band, photography, political, professional, radio and TV, social, social service, student government, and symphony. Popular campus events include Welcome Weekend Carnival, Spring Fest, and One Act Play Festival.

Sports: There are 7 intercollegiate sports for men and 9 for women, and 11 intramural sports for men and 11 for women. Facilities include a 2400-seat ice arena, an Olympic-size pool, a 3000-seat gym, indoor field house, indoor and outdoor tracks, racquetball, tennis, squash, handball, and basketball courts, a dance studio, softball field, an artificial turf stadium, in-line roller rink, recreational softball field, recreational soccer fields, outdoor basketball courts, indoor climbing wall, high ropes course, bouldering cave, and a fitness center with 38 cardio machines with personal viewing screens.

Disabled Students: 95% of the campus is accessible. Facilities include wheelchair ramps, elevators, special parking, specially equipped rest rooms, special class scheduling, lowered drinking fountains, lowered telephones, special housing, and electric doors.

Services: Counseling and information services are available, as is tutoring in most subjects. There is a reader service for the blind, math labs, and a writing center.

Campus Safety and Security: Measures include 24-hour foot and vehicle patrol, emergency notification system, and security escort services. There are emergency telephones, lighted pathways/sidewalks, controlled access to dorms/residences, educational programs, campus rescue squad, portable jump-start packs, vehicle lockouts, and parking management.

Programs of Study: SUNY Potsdam confers B.A., B.F.A., B.M., and B.S. degrees. Master's degrees are also awarded. Bachelor's degrees are awarded in AGRICULTURE (environmental studies), BIOLOGICAL SCIENCE (biochemistry and biology/biological science), BUSINESS (business administration and management and business economics), COMMUNICATIONS AND THE ARTS (communications, dance, dramatic arts, English, French, music, music business management, music performance, music theory and composition, Spanish, studio art, and visual and performing arts), COMPUTER AND PHYSICAL SCIENCE (chemistry, computer science, earth science, geology, mathematics, natural sciences, and physics), EDUCATION (early childhood education, elementary education, English education, foreign languages education, mathematics education, middle school education, music education, science education, secondary education, and social studies education), HEALTH PROFESSIONS (community health work), SOCIAL SCIENCE (anthropology, archeology, criminal justice, economics, history, interdisciplinary studies, philosophy, political science/government, psychology, sociology, and women's studies). Music, anthropology, and geology are the strongest academically. Music education, childhood education, and business administration are the largest.

Required: To graduate, students must earn 124 to 128 credit hours, with 30 to 33 in the major, and a minimum GPA of 2.0. General education requirements include 10 to 11 semester hours of freshman course work in verbal and quantitative skills, 21 of Modes of Inquiry in liberal arts, and 4 of phys ed, as well as 1 course each in written and oral communication above the freshman level, and demonstrated foreign language proficiency.

Special: Cross-registration is offered with Clarkson University, St. Lawrence University, and SUNY Canton. Political science internships in Albany, and many other internships are available. SUNY Postdam also offers work-study opportunities, a 3-2 engineering degree with Clarkson University, study abroad, 3-2 management and accounting degrees, student-designed majors, dual majors in interdisciplinary natural science, non-degree study, and pass/fail options. There are 17 national honor societies, a freshman honors program, and 6 departmental honors programs.

Faculty/Classroom: 52% of faculty are male; 47% are female. All teach undergraduates. No introductory courses are taught by graduate students.

Admissions: 66% of the 2009-2010 applicants were accepted. The SAT scores for the 2009-2010 freshman class were: Critical Reading--42% below 500, 43% between 500 and 599, 13% between 600 and 700, and 2 above 700; Math--40% below 500, 43% between 500 and 599, 16% between 600 and 700, and 1% above 700. The ACT scores were 47% below 21, 21% between 21 and 23, 25% between 24 and 26, 4% between 27 and 28, and 3% above 28. 17% of the current freshmen were in the top fifth of their class; 66% were in the top two fifths. There was 1 National Merit finalist. 6 freshmen graduated first in their class.

Requirements: The SAT or ACT and ACT Writing Test are recommended. In addition, applicants must be high school graduates in a college preparatory program or hold a GED. 4 years each of English and social studies, 3 years each of math, foreign language, and science, and 1 year of art or music recommended. An interview is recommended; an audition when appropriate is required. A GPA of 80.0 is required. AP and CLEP credits are accepted. Important factors in the admissions decision are advanced placement or honors courses, recommendations by school officials, and extracurricular activities record.

Procedure: Freshmen are admitted fall and spring. Entrance exams should be taken in the junior year or early senior year. There are early admissions, deferred admissions, and rolling admissions plans. Application deadlines are open. Application fee is $40. Notifications are sent October 1. Applications are accepted on-line.

Transfer: 318 transfer students enrolled in 2008-2009. Applicants must have earned 12 hours of college credit. Transfers with fewer than 24 credit hours must submit a high school transcript. 30 of 124 credits required for the bachelor's degree must be completed at SUNY Potsdam.

Visiting: There are regularly scheduled orientations for prospective students, including a full-day program prior to the start of classes and a tour of the campus. An online orientation is also available for transfer students. There are guides for informal visits and visitors may sit in on classes. To schedule a visit, contact the Admissions Office at (877) POTS-DAM.

Financial Aid: In 2009-2010, 84% of all full-time freshmen and 81% of continuing full-time students received some form of financial aid. 71% of all full-time freshmen and 66% of continuing full-time students received need-based aid. The average freshmen award was $15,271, with $14,764 ($17,111 maximum) from need-based scholarships or need-based grants; $21,970 ($8,303 maximum) from need-based self-help aid (loans and jobs); and $2,061 ($17,240 maximum) from other non-need-based awards and non-need-based scholarships. Average annual earnings from campus work are $1227. The average financial indebtedness of the 2009 graduate was $19,220. The FAFSA and the state aid form are required. The priority date for freshman financial aid applications for fall entry is March 1. The deadline for filing freshman financial aid applications for fall entry is May 1.

International Students: There are 137 international students enrolled. They must take the TOEFL with a minimum score of 550 on the paper-based TOEFL (PBT) or 79 on the Internet-based version (iBT), IELTS.

Computers: Wireless access is available. There are 690 PCs available on campus for student use. High speed connection is available in all dorm rooms. There are 80 wireless hot spots across campus for student use. All students may access the system 7 days a week, 24 hours per day. There are no time limits. The fee is $165 per semester.

Graduates: From July 1, 2008 to June 30, 2009, 661 bachelor's degrees were awarded. The most popular majors were music education (14%), childhood education (11%), and business administration (8%). 42 companies recruited on campus in 2008-2009. In an average class, 34% graduate in 4 years or less, 49% graduate in 5 years or less, and 51% graduate in 6 years or less. Of the 2008 graduating class, 49% were enrolled in graduate school within 6 months of graduation, and 42% were employed.

Admissions Contact: Thomas Nesbitt, Director of Admissions. E-Mail: *admissions@potsdam.edu* Web: *www.potsdam.edu*

STATE UNIVERSITY OF NEW YORK/COLLEGE AT BROCKPORT   B-3

Brockport, NY 14420   (585) 395-2751; (585) 395-5452

Full-time: 2718 men, 3537 women	**Faculty:** IIA, -$
Part-time: 266 men, 371 women	**Ph.D.s:** n/av
Graduate: 462 men, 843 women	**Student/Faculty:** n/av
Year: semesters, summer session	**Tuition:** $6108 ($14,008)
Application Deadline: open	**Room & Board:** $9200
Freshman Class: 8522 applied, 3571 accepted, 1038 enrolled	
SAT CR/M/W: 560/540/520	**ACT:** 24 **VERY COMPETITIVE**

The State University of New York/College at Brockport, established in 1835, is a comprehensive public liberal arts college offering 42 undergraduate, 27 graduate (masters level), and 18 teacher certificate programs. There are 5 undergraduate schools and 1 graduate school. In addition to regional accreditation, SUNY Brockport has baccalaureate program accreditation with AACSB, ABET, CSAB, CSWE, NCATE, and NRPA. The library contains 521,649 volumes, 2.1 million microform items, and 10,481 audio/video tapes/CDs/DVDs, and subscribes to 31,857 periodicals including electronic. Computerized library services include interlibrary loans, database searching, Internet access, and laptop Internet portals. Special learning facilities include a learning resource center, art gallery, planetarium, radio station, TV station, aquaculture ponds, weather information system, high-resolution germanium detector, research vessel on Lake Ontario, electron microscope, low-temperature physics lab, vacuum deposition lab, computational physics lab, 2 supercomputers, Doppler Radar system, hydrotherapy room, student learning center, academic computing center, theaters, and ultramodern dance facilities, including green room. The 454-acre campus is in a small town 16 miles west of Rochester. Including any residence halls, there are 68 buildings.

Student Life: 97% of undergraduates are from New York. Others are from 26 states, 25 foreign countries, and Canada. 87% are white. The average age of freshmen is 18; all undergraduates, 23. 16% do not continue beyond their first year; 84% remain to graduate.

Housing: 2800 students can be accommodated in college housing, which includes coed dorms and on-campus apartments. In addition, there are special-interest houses, special residence hall communities for first-year students, and international and academic excellence floors. On-campus housing is guaranteed for the freshman year only. 60% of students commute. All students may keep cars.

Activities: 1% of men belong to 4 national fraternities; 1% of women belong to 4 national sororities. There are 63 groups on campus, including art, business, cheerleading, chess, choir, chorus, computers, criminal justice, dance, drama, ethnic, film, gay, honors, international, jazz band, literary magazine, musical theater, newspaper, outdoors, photography, political, professional, radio and TV, religious, social, social service, and student government. Popular campus events include Brock the Port, Health Week, and Honors Convocation.

Sports: There are 11 intercollegiate sports for men and 12 for women, and 30 intramural sports for men and 30 for women. Facilities include field hockey, baseball, and softball fields, a soccer pitch, a swimming pool, 6 gyms, a gymnastics area, wrestling and weight rooms, handball, squash, tennis, and racquetball courts, an ice arena, and a Special Olympics stadium with a football field and track.

Disabled Students: 95% of the campus is accessible. Facilities include wheelchair ramps, elevators, special parking, specially equipped restrooms, special class scheduling, lowered drinking fountains, lowered telephones, and special housing.

Services: Counseling and information services are available, as is tutoring in some subjects, which vary from semester to semester. Study skills support is available to all students.

Campus Safety and Security: Measures include 24-hour foot and vehicle patrol and security escort services. There are shuttle buses, emergency telephones, lighted pathways/sidewalks, controlled access to dorms/residences, a community policing program, and bicycle patrols.

Programs of Study: SUNY Brockport confers B.A., B.S., B.F.A., and B.S.N. degrees. Master's degrees are also awarded. Bachelor's degrees are awarded in BIOLOGICAL SCIENCE (biology/biological science), BUSINESS (accounting, business administration and management, international business management, and recreation and leisure services), COMMUNICATIONS AND THE ARTS (communications, dance, dramatic arts, English, French, journalism, Spanish, and studio art), COMPUTER AND PHYSICAL SCIENCE (atmospheric sciences and meteorology, chemistry, computer science, earth science, geology, mathematics, and physics), EDUCATION (physical education), ENGINEERING AND ENVIRONMENTAL DESIGN (computational sciences and environmental science), HEALTH PROFESSIONS (health science, medical technology, and nursing), SOCIAL SCIENCE (African studies, African American studies, anthropology, criminal justice, history, interdisciplinary studies, international studies, philosophy, political science/government, psychology, social work, sociology, water resources, and women's studies). Business administration, physical education, and criminal justice are the largest.

Required: To graduate, students must complete a minimum of 120 credits, including 30 or more credits in the major, with a 2.0 GPA. The core curriculum includes the SUNY-wide general education requirements (1 course each in math, natural sciences, social sciences, American history, Western civilization, world (non-Western) civilization, humanities, the arts, foreign language, and basic communication). All students must take courses in contemporary issues, diversity, and perspectives on women and pass the appropriate competency exams. An academic planning seminar is required of entering freshmen.

Special: Co-op programs, internships in most majors, and work-study programs in education are available. Brockport offers cross-registration with Rochester area colleges, a Washington semester, study abroad in 16 countries, accelerated degree programs, and an interdisciplinary major in arts for children, emphasizing art, dance, music, and theater. Credit for military and work experience, nondegree study, and pass/fail grading options are available. An alternative general education program, Delta College, is an interdisciplinary program that emphasizes global issues and provides opportunities for work or study in other countries, as well as locally, regionally, and nationally. There are 24 national honor societies, a freshman honors program, and 3 departmental honors programs.

Faculty/Classroom: No introductory courses are taught by graduate students.

Admissions: 42% of the 2009-2010 applicants were accepted. The SAT scores for the 2009-2010 freshman class were: Critical Reading--15% below 500, 56% between 500 and 599, 28% between 600 and 700, and 1% above 700; Math--24% below 500, 57% between 500 and 599, 18% between 600 and 700, and 1% above 700; Writing--36% below 500, 49% between 500 and 599, 14% between 600 and 700, and 1% above 700. The ACT scores were 11% below 21, 38% between 21 and 23, 37% between 24 and 26, 11% between 27 and 28, and 4% above 28. 45% of the current freshmen were in the top fifth of their class; 85% were in the top two fifths.

Requirements: The SAT or ACT is required. SUNY Brockport seeks students who have demonstrated academic success and who show persistence. Applicants must have a high school diploma (preferably from the New York State Regents Program) or have completed a minimum of 18 academic units: 4 each in English and social studies, 4 in academic electives, and 3 each in math and science (1 with lab). An essay and letters of recommendation are encouraged. An audition is required for dance and theater applicants. A GPA of 85.0 is required. AP and CLEP credits are accepted. Important factors in the admissions decision are advanced placement or honors courses, leadership record, and extracurricular activities record.

Procedure: Freshmen are admitted fall and spring. Entrance exams should be taken during the spring of the junior year and fall of the senior year. There are deferred admissions and rolling admissions plans. Application deadlines are open. Application fee is $40. Notification is sent on a rolling basis. Applications are accepted on-line.

Transfer: 1297 transfer students enrolled in a recent year. applicants must have a minimum GPA of 2.25. Many departments specify prerequisite courses and a higher GPA. SUNY Brockport recommends that transfer applicants have an associate degree or 54 credit hours, with preference given to degree holders. 30 of 120 credits required for the bachelor's degree must be completed at SUNY Brockport.

Visiting: There are regularly scheduled orientations for prospective students, including daily admissions information presentations and campus tours. Visits may be arranged on selected Saturdays and holidays. There are guides for informal visits; visitors may sit in on classes and stay overnight. To schedule a visit, contact the Office of Undergraduate Admissions.

Financial Aid: In a recent year, 90% of all full-time freshmen and 84% of continuing full-time students received some form of financial aid. 66% of all full-time freshmen and 68% of continuing full-time students received need-based aid. The average freshman award was $9332. Need-based scholarships or need-based grants averaged $4138 ($12,573 maximum); need-based self-help aid (loans and jobs) averaged $4367 ($8125 maximum); and non-need-based awards and non-need-based scholarships averaged $3860 ($15,216 maximum). 71% of undergraduate students work part-time. Average annual earnings from campus work are $1303. The average financial indebtedness of a recent graduate was $22,489. SUNY Brockport is a member of CSS. The FAFSA is required. The deadline for filing freshman financial aid applications for fall entry is February 15.

International Students: There were 75 international students enrolled in a recent year. The school actively recruits these students. They must take the TOEFL with a minimum score of 530 on the paper-based TOEFL (PBT) or 71 on the Internet-based version (iBT) or take the MELAB. They must also take the SAT or ACT.

Computers: There are 650 PCs in public labs with full Internet access. The campus is wireless, including residence halls. All students may access the system 24 hours per day. There are no time limits. The fee is $234. It is strongly recommended that all students have a personal computer.

Graduates: In a recent year, 1682 bachelor's degrees were awarded. The most popular majors were business administration (15%), health

professions and related sciences (12%), and physical education (12%). 140 companies recruited on campus in 2008-2009. In an average class, 1% graduate in 3 years or less, 34% graduate in 4 years or less, 55% graduate in 5 years or less, and 60% graduate in 6 years or less. Of the 2008 graduating class, 30% were enrolled in graduate school within 6 months of graduation, and 81% were employed.

Admissions Contact: Bernard S. Valento, Director of Undergraduate Admissions. E-mail: *admit@brockport.edu* Web: *www.brockport.edu*

STATE UNIVERSITY OF NEW YORK/COLLEGE AT BUFFALO

A-3

Buffalo, NY 14222	**(716) 878-4017; (716) 878-6100**
Full-time: 3564 men, 5216 women	**Faculty:** 425; IIA, -$
Part-time: 491 men, 551 women	**Ph.D.s:** 84%
Graduate: 566 men, 1326 women	**Student/Faculty:** 21 to 1
Year: semesters, summer session	**Tuition:** $6007 ($13,907)
Application Deadline: open	**Room & Board:** $9726
Freshman Class: 11,132 applied, 4749 accepted, 1530 enrolled	
SAT CR/M: 480/490	**COMPETITIVE+**

The State University of New York/College at Buffalo, established in 1867, is a public institution conferring undergraduate liberal arts degrees. There are 4 undergraduate schools and 1 graduate school. In addition to regional accreditation, Buffalo State College has baccalaureate program accreditation with ABET, ACS, ADA, ASLA, CSWE, FIDER, IACBE, NASAD, NAST, and NCATE. The library contains 618,429 volumes, 1.0 million microform items, and 18,500 audio/video tapes/CDs/DVDs, and subscribes to 2948 periodicals including electronic. Computerized library services include interlibrary loans, database searching, and Internet access. Special learning facilities include a learning resource center, art gallery, planetarium, radio station, TV station, a speech, language, and hearing clinic, and a center for performing arts. The 115-acre campus is in an urban area in Buffalo. Including any residence halls, there are 38 buildings.

Student Life: 99% of undergraduates are from New York. Others are from 26 states, 20 foreign countries, and Canada. 85% are from public schools. 65% are white; 13% African American. The average age of freshmen is 19; all undergraduates, 25. 22% do not continue beyond their first year; 48% remain to graduate.

Housing: 2275 students can be accommodated in college housing, which includes coed dorms, on-campus apartments, married student housing, and an international student dorm. On-campus housing is available on a first-come, first-served basis. 77% of students commute. Alcohol is not permitted. Upperclassmen may keep cars.

Activities: 1% of men belong to 1 local fraternity and 9 national fraternities; 1% of women belong to 3 local and 7 national sororities. There are 75 groups on campus, including art, cheerleading, chess, choir, chorus, computers, dance, drama, ethnic, gay, honors, international, jazz band, literary magazine, musical theater, newspaper, orchestra, political, professional, radio and TV, religious, social, social service, and student government. Popular campus events include Commuter Daze, the Gathering, and Welcome Back Week.

Sports: There are 8 intercollegiate sports for men and 11 for women, and 24 intramural sports for men and 24 for women. Facilities include a gym, an indoor pool, a basketball/volleyball arena, an ice rink, a game field for football, soccer, and lacrosse, a 6-lane track, and a softball diamond.

Disabled Students: All of the campus is accessible. Facilities include wheelchair ramps, elevators, special parking, specially equipped restrooms, special class scheduling, lowered drinking fountains, lowered telephones, and special dorm accommodations.

Services: Counseling and information services are available, as is tutoring in every subject. There is a reader service for the blind, and remedial math, reading, and writing. Tutors for visually impaired and hearing impaired students are also available.

Campus Safety and Security: Measures include 24-hour foot and vehicle patrol, emergency notification system, self-defense education, and security escort services. There are shuttle buses, emergency telephones, lighted pathways/sidewalks, and community policing.

Programs of Study: Buffalo State College confers B.A., B.S., B.F.A., B.Mus., B.S.Ed., and B.Tech degrees. Master's degrees are also awarded. Bachelor's degrees are awarded in BIOLOGICAL SCIENCE (biology/biological science), BUSINESS (business administration and management and hospitality management services), COMMUNICATIONS AND THE ARTS (art, art history and appreciation, broadcasting, communications, design, dramatic arts, English, fine arts, French, journalism, music, painting, photography, printmaking, sculpture, and Spanish), COMPUTER AND PHYSICAL SCIENCE (chemistry, earth science, geology, information sciences and systems, mathematics, and physics), EDUCATION (art education, business education, elementary education, foreign languages education, industrial arts education, science education, secondary education, and special education), ENGINEERING AND ENVIRONMENTAL DESIGN (electrical/electronics engineering technology, industrial engineering technology, and mechanical engineering technology), HEALTH PROFESSIONS (health and speech pathology/audiology), SOCIAL SCIENCE (anthropology, criminal justice, dietetics, economics, geography, history, humanities, philosophy, political science/government, psychology, social work, sociology, and urban studies). Elementary education and exceptional education are the strongest academically. Elementary education, communication, and business are the largest.

Required: To graduate, students must complete a 60-hour general education requirement consisting of 42 core credits in applied science and education, arts, humanities, math and science, and social science and 18 hours of electives. Students must earn 123 credits with a minimum GPA of 2.0. The number of hours in the major varies.

Special: Students may cross-register with the Western New York Consortium and exchange with 160 campus members of the National Student Exchange. Internships, Washington and Albany semesters, study abroad in 7 countries, dual majors, and a general studies degree are offered. Students may earn 3-2 engineering degrees in association with Clarkson University, and the State University of New York centers at Buffalo and Binghamton. There is a cooperative program with the Fashion Institute of Technology. Credit for life, military, and work experience, nondegree study, and pass/fail grading options are available. There is a chapter of Phi Beta Kappa, a freshman honors program, and 13 departmental honors programs.

Faculty/Classroom: 51% of faculty are male; 49% are female. All teach undergraduates. No introductory courses are taught by graduate students. The average class size in an introductory lecture is 34; in a laboratory, 12; and in a regular course, 18.

Admissions: 43% of the 2009-2010 applicants were accepted. The SAT scores for the 2009-2010 freshman class were: Critical Reading--57% below 500, 36% between 500 and 599, 7% between 600 and 700, and 1% above 700; Math--51% below 500, 41% between 500 and 599, and 8% between 600 and 700. 22% of the current freshmen were in the top fifth of their class; 55% were in the top two fifths.

Requirements: The SAT is required. In addition, students must graduate from an accredited secondary school or have a GED. They must complete 4 years of English, 3 years each of math, science, and social studies, and 2 years of a foreign language. A portfolio is required for fine arts applicants. AP and CLEP credits are accepted. Important factors in the admissions decision are advanced placement or honors courses, evidence of special talent, and recommendations by school officials.

Procedure: Freshmen are admitted to all sessions. Entrance exams should be taken during the junior or senior years. There are early decision, early admissions, deferred admissions, and rolling admissions plans. Early decision applications should be filed by November 1 for fall entry; deadlines for regular applications are open. Application fee is $40. Notification of early decision is sent December 15; regular decision, on a rolling basis. 57 early decision candidates were accepted for the 2009-2010 class. Applications are accepted on-line.

Transfer: 1103 transfer students enrolled in 2008-2009. Transfer applicants must have a minimum GPA of 2.0. An associate degree is recommended, and a minimum of 15 credit hours must have been earned. 32 of 123 credits required for the bachelor's degree must be completed at Buffalo State College.

Visiting: There are regularly scheduled orientations for prospective students. There are guides for informal visits, and visitors may sit in on classes. To schedule a visit, contact the Admissions Office.

Financial Aid: In a recent year, 86% of all full-time freshmen and 80% of continuing full-time students received some form of financial aid. 71% of all full-time freshmen and 68% of continuing full-time students received need-based aid. Need-based scholarships or need-based grants averaged $4944; need-based self-help aid (loans and jobs) averaged $4534; and other non-need-based awards and non-need-based scholarships averaged $1978. The average financial indebtedness of a recent year's graduate was $17,657. Buffalo State College is a member of CSS. The FAFSA and TAP are required. The priority date for freshman financial aid applications for fall entry is March 1. The deadline for filing freshman financial aid applications for fall entry is May 1.

International Students: There are 77 international students enrolled. The school actively recruits these students. They must take the TOEFL with a minimum score of 500 on the paper-based TOEFL (PBT) or 65 on the Internet-based version (iBT). They must also take the SAT or ACT.

Computers: Wireless access is available. Students may use wireless access points in the library and the student union. All students may access the system during site hours. Dial-in access is available 24 hours per day. There are no time limits and no fees.

Graduates: From July 1, 2008 to June 30, 2009, 1768 bachelor's degrees were awarded. The most popular majors were elementary education (24%), business studies (13%), and social sciences (9%). In an average class, 1% graduate in 3 years or less, 21% graduate in 4 years or less, 42% graduate in 5 years or less, and 48% graduate in 6 years or less. 105 companies recruited on campus in 2008-2009. Of the 2008 graduating class, 24% were enrolled in graduate school within 6 months of graduation, and 75% were employed.

Admissions Contact: Carmella Thompson, Admissions Director. E-mail: *admissions@buffalostate.edu* Web: *www.buffalostate.edu*

STATE UNIVERSITY OF NEW YORK/COLLEGE AT CORTLAND   C-3

Cortland, NY 13045	(607) 753-4711; (607) 753-5998
Full-time: 2588 men, 3465 women	**Faculty:** 266; IIA, -$
Part-time: 102 men, 103 women	**Ph.D.s:** 84%
Graduate: 385 men, 679 women	**Student/Faculty:** 21 to 1
Year: semesters, summer session	**Room & Board:** $9790
Application Deadline:	
Freshman Class: 11968 applied, 4679 accepted, 1167 enrolled	
SAT or ACT: required	**COMPETITIVE**

The State University of New York College at Cortland, founded in 1868, is a public institution offering academic programs leading to baccalaureate and master's degrees in liberal arts and professional studies. There are 3 undergraduate schools and 3 graduate schools. In addition to regional accreditation, SUNY Cortland has baccalaureate program accreditation with CAHEA, NCATE, and NRPA. The library contains 421,640 volumes, 844,207 microform items, and 3,485 audio/video tapes/CDs/DVDs, and subscribes to 548 periodicals including electronic. Computerized library services include interlibrary loans and database searching. Special learning facilities include a learning resource center, art gallery, natural history museum, planetarium, radio station, TV station, a natural science museum, a greenhouse, a center for speech and hearing disorders, classrooms equipped with integrated technologies (multimedia enhanced instruction), and many specialized labs to support various program offerings. The 191-acre campus is in a small town 18 miles north of Ithaca and 29 miles south of Syracuse. Including any residence halls, there are 37 buildings.

Student Life: 98% of undergraduates are from New York. Students are from 8 states, and 2 foreign countries. 91% are from public schools. 89% are white. The average age of freshmen is 18; all undergraduates, 21. 26% do not continue beyond their first year; 53% remain to graduate.

Housing: 2775 students can be accommodated in college housing, which includes coed dorms and off-campus apartments. In addition, there are special-interest houses, fraternity houses, sorority houses, a wellness floor in a residence hall, a computer residence hall, quite residence halls, a residence for Americans majoring in international studies and/or studying abroad, a hall for students 21 years or older, and a leadership house. 55% of students live on campus. All students may keep cars.

Activities: 4% of men belong to 1 national fraternity; 9% of women belong to 1 local and 4 national sororities. There are 100 groups on campus, including art, band, cheerleading, chess, choir, chorale, chorus, computers, dance, drama, ethnic, film, gay, honors, international, jazz band, literary magazine, musical theater, newspaper, orchestra, political, professional, radio and TV, religious, social, social service, student government, symphony, and yearbook. Popular campus events include annual Cortland-Ithaca College football game, Winterfest, and Multicultural Festival.

Sports: There are 11 intercollegiate sports for men and 14 for women, and 55 intramural sports for men and 55 for women. Facilities include an outdoor multupurpose 8000-seat stadium complex, an Olympic-size pool, 3600- seat gym, ice arena, gymnastics arena, wrestling and weight romms, dance studio, handball/racquetball courts, squash courts, athletic training facility, fitness centers, free-swimming pool, track, baseball field, football/lacrosse/track field seating 4000, lighted soccer field, field house and 50 acres of athletic fields.

Disabled Students: 75% of the campus is accessible. Facilities include wheelchair ramps, elevators, special parking, specially equipped restrooms, special class scheduling, lowered drinking fountains, and lowered telephones.

Services: Counseling and information services are available, as is tutoring in some subjects. There is a reader service for the blind. There is a fully staffed Academic Support and Achievement Program for writing, math, study skills, and learning strategies. Specific course tutoring is available with peer tutors.

Campus Safety and Security: Measures include 24-hour foot and vehicle patrol, emergency notification system, self-defense education, and security escort services. There are shuttle buses, emergency telephones, lighted pathways/sidewalks, State University police maintain a web site with safety information and inks. University police also have a Silent Witness program for reporting crimes anonymously.

Programs of Study: SUNY Cortland confers B.A., B.S., and B.S.ED., B.F.A. degrees. Master's degrees are also awarded. Bachelor's degrees are awarded in BIOLOGICAL SCIENCE (biology/biological science), BUSINESS (management science and sports management), COMMUNICATIONS AND THE ARTS (art, communications, English, film arts, and musical theater), COMPUTER AND PHYSICAL SCIENCE (chemistry, geochemistry, geology, geophysics and seismology, mathematics, and physics), EDUCATION (athletic training, education services, foreign languages education, health education, middle school education, physical education, recreation education, and secondary education), ENGINEERING AND ENVIRONMENTAL DESIGN (environmental science), HEALTH PROFESSIONS (health science and speech pathology/audiology), SOCIAL SCIENCE (African American studies, anthropology, economics, geography, history, human services, international studies, philosophy, political science/government, psychology, and sociology). Biology, political science, and speech pathology/audiology are the strongest academically. Elementary education, phys ed, and communication studies are the largest.

Required: To graduate, undergraduates must complete 6 hours in English Composition, and at least 6 hours of writing-intensive courses, with 3 of those in the major. One course meeting the Quantitative Skills criteria must also be passed; 28 to 29 hours of courses in the General Education program must also be completed, with no more than 2 courses taken in any one of the 8 disciplines in the program. A major of 30 to 36 hours, with no more than 45 credits in discipline-specific courses must be completed. Completion of 90 credits of Liberal Arts and Science courses toward a B.A., 60 credits toward a B.S.E., or 75 credits toward a B.S. is required. A 2.0 GPA, both overall and in all minors and concentrations, must be maintained. Special requirements may be designated by each school of the College.

Special: Cortland offers cross-registration with Tompkins Cortland Communinty College and has cooperative programs with the State University of New York College of Environmental Science and Forestry, and Centers at Binghamton and Buffalo, and Cornell and Case Western Reserve Universities. Students may study abroad in 11 countries, and they may enroll in a Washington semester. Work-study programs are available. The college confers an individualized studies degree and allows dual majors. Students may pursue a 3-2 engineering degree in conjunction with Alfred, Case Western Reserve, and Clarkson Universities, and the State University of New York Centers at Binghamton, Buffalo, and Stony Brook. Cortland offers nondegree study opportunities. There are 19 national honor societies, including Phi Beta Kappa, a freshman honors program, and 5 departmental honors programs.

Faculty/Classroom: 53% of faculty are male; 48% are female. All teach undergraduates, 15% do research, and 15% do both. No introductory courses are taught by graduate students. The average class size in an introductory lecture is 38; in a laboratory is 26; and in a regular course is 22.

Admissions: 39% of the 2009-2010 applicants were accepted.

Requirements: The SAT or ACT is required. In addition, A\applicants must graduate from an accredited secondary school or have a GED. They must have earned 16 Carnegie units and 16 to 20 academic credits, including 4 units each in English and history or social studies and 2 (3 units preferred) each in math and science; the other 4 units must be taken in areas listed above or in a foreign language. Essays and recommendations are required, and in some cases auditions as well. Interviews are strongly recommended. AP and CLEP credits are accepted. Important factors in the admissions decision are advanced placement or honors courses, extracurricular activities record, and recommendations by school officials.

Procedure: Freshmen are admitted fall and spring. Entrance exams should be taken during the spring of the junior year or fall of the senior year. There are early decision, early admissions, deferred admissions, and rolling admissions plans. Early decision applications should be filed by November 15; check with the school for current application deadlines. The application fee is $40. Notification of early decision is sent December 15; regular decision, sent on a rolling basis. Applications are accepted on-line.

Transfer: 650 transfer students enrolled in 2008-2009. Applicants must have a minimum GPA of 2.5. Some programs are more competitive. Interviews are encouraged. 45 of 124 credits required for the bachelor's degree must be completed at SUNY Cortland.

Visiting: There are regularly scheduled orientations for prospective students, consisting of Autumn Preview Days for prospective students as well as Spring Open House for accepted students. There are guides for informal visits and visitors may sit in on classes. To schedule a visit, contact the Admissions Appointment Secretary at 607-753-4711.

Financial Aid: In 2009-2010, 61% of all full-time freshmen and 60% of continuing full-time students received some form of financial aid. 56% of all full-time freshmen and 54% of continuing full-time students received need-based aid. The average freshmen award was $6,977. The FAFSA, and NYS TAP application is required. The deadline for filing freshman financial aid applications for fall entry is April 1.

International Students: There are 29 international students enrolled. The school actively recruits these students. They must take the TOEFL, the SAT I or a General Certificate of Education is acceptable in lieu of the TOEFL. They must also take the SAT or ACT.

Computers: All students may access the system. 24 hours per day in some labs connected to the campus network. There are no time limits and no fees.

Graduates: From July 1, 2008 to June 30, 2009, 1354 bachelor's degrees were awarded. The most popular majors were elementaty education (14%), physical educaton (14%), and sports management (7%). In an average class, 58% graduate in 6 years or less.

Admissions Contact: Gradin Avery, Director of Admissions. A campus DVD is available. E-Mail: *admissions@cortland.edu*
Web: *www.cortland.edu*

STATE UNIVERSITY OF NEW YORK/COLLEGE AT GENESEO B-3

Geneseo, NY 14454	**(585) 245-5571; (585) 245-5550**
Full-time: 2301 men, 3093 women	**Faculty:** 251; IIA, -$
Part-time: 40 men, 60 women	**Ph.D.s:** 90%
Graduate: 26 men, 139 women	**Student/Faculty:** 21 to 1
Year: semesters, summer session	**Tuition:** $6326 ($14,226)
Application Deadline: January 1	**Room & Board:** $9550
Freshman Class: 10413 applied, 3630 accepted, 948 enrolled	
SAT CR/M: 670/670	**ACT:** 29 **MOST COMPETITIVE**

The State University of New York/College at Geneseo, founded in 1871, is a public institution offering liberal arts, business, and accounting programs, teaching certification, and training in communicative disorders and sciences. In addition to regional accreditation, Geneseo has baccalaureate program accreditation with AACSB and NCATE. The library contains 665,060 volumes, 848,654 microform items, and 25,474 audio/video tapes/CDs/DVDs, and subscribes to 62,691 periodicals including electronic. Computerized library services include interlibrary loans, database searching, Internet access, and laptop Internet portals. Special learning facilities include a learning resource center, art gallery, planetarium, radio station, TV station, and 4 theaters. The 220-acre campus is in a small town 30 miles south of Rochester. Including any residence halls, there are 54 buildings.

Student Life: 95% of undergraduates are from New York. Others are from 24 states, 44 foreign countries, and Canada. 79% are from public schools. 66% are white. 37% are Catholic; 16% claim no religious affiliation; 14% Protestant. The average age of freshmen is 18; all undergraduates, 20. 10% do not continue beyond their first year; 77% remain to graduate.

Housing: 3227 students can be accommodated in college housing, which includes coed dorms. In addition, there are special-interest houses. On-campus housing is guaranteed for all 4 years, is guaranteed for the freshman year only, and is available on a first-come, first-served basis. 55% of students live on campus. All students may keep cars.

Activities: 11% of men belong to 7 local fraternities and one national fraternity; 15% of women belong to 7 local and 5 national sororities. There are 187 groups on campus, including art, band, cheerleading, chess, choir, chorale, chorus, computers, dance, debate, drama, environmental, ethnic, gay, honors, international, jazz band, literary magazine, musical theater, newspaper, orchestra, pep band, political, professional, radio and TV, religious, social, social service, student government, and symphony. Popular campus events include Siblings Weekend, Blue & White Day, and Student Organization Expo.

Sports: There are 8 intercollegiate sports for men and 12 for women, and 14 intramural sports for men and 14 for women. Facilities include an ice arena, a swimming pool, 3 gyms, 3 squash and 8 tennis courts, an indoor jogging area, Nautilus and weight rooms, an outdoor track, and several playing fields. The largest auditorium/arena seats 3,000.

Disabled Students: 95% of the campus is accessible. Facilities include wheelchair ramps, elevators, special parking, specially equipped restrooms, special class scheduling, lowered drinking fountains, lowered telephones, and fire alarms for hearing-impaired students.

Services: Counseling and information services are available, as is tutoring in every subject. There is a reader service for the blind, and remedial math.

Campus Safety and Security: Measures include 24-hour foot and vehicle patrol, emergency notification system, self-defense education, and security escort services. There are shuttle buses, emergency telephones, lighted pathways/sidewalks, and controlled access to dorms/residences.

Programs of Study: Geneseo confers B.A., B.S., and B.S.Ed. degrees. Master's degrees are also awarded. Bachelor's degrees are awarded in BIOLOGICAL SCIENCE (biochemistry, biology/biological science, and biophysics), BUSINESS (accounting and business administration and management), COMMUNICATIONS AND THE ARTS (art history and appreciation, communications, comparative literature, English, French, music, musical theater, performing arts, Spanish, studio art, and theater design), COMPUTER AND PHYSICAL SCIENCE (applied physics, chemistry, computer science, geochemistry, geology, geophysics and seismology, mathematics, natural sciences, and physics), EDUCATION (early childhood education, elementary education, and special education), HEALTH PROFESSIONS (speech pathology/audiology), SOCIAL SCIENCE (African American studies, American studies, anthropology, economics, geography, history, international relations, philosophy, political science/government, psychology, and sociology). Education, biology, and business administration are the largest.

Required: To graduate, students must complete 120 credit hours with a minimum 2.0 GPA. The required core curriculum includes 2 courses each in humanities, fine arts, social sciences, and natural sciences and 1 course each in non-Western tradition, critical writing/reading, numeric and symbolic reasoning, U.S. history, and foreign language proficiency.

Special: The college offers a cooperative 3-2 engineering degree with Alfred, Case Western Reserve, Clarkson, Columbia, Penn State, and Syracuse Universities, SUNY at Binghamton and Buffalo, and the University of Rochester, as well as a 3-3 degree with Rochester Institute of Technology and Upstate Medical University. Cross-registration is available with the Rochester Area Colleges Consortium. Geneseo offers internships, study abroad, a Washington semester, dual majors, and work-study programs. There are 15 national honor societies, including Phi Beta Kappa, a freshman honors program, and 9 departmental honors programs.

Faculty/Classroom: 59% of faculty are male; 41% are female. All teach undergraduates. No introductory courses are taught by graduate students. The average class size in an introductory lecture is 31; in a laboratory is 17; and in a regular course is 28.

Admissions: 35% of the 2009-2010 applicants were accepted. The SAT scores for the 2009-2010 freshman class were: Critical Reading--1% below 500, 7% between 500 and 599, 64% between 600 and 700, and 28% above 700; Math-- 4% between 500 and 599, 75% between 600 and 700, and 22% above 700. The ACT scores were 1% between 21 and 23, 5% between 24 and 26, 37% between 27 and 28, and 58% above 28. 84% of the current freshmen were in the top fifth of their class; 98% were in the top two fifths. 36 freshmen graduated first in their class.

Requirements: The SAT or ACT is required. In addition, applicants must be graduates of an accredited secondary school or have a GED certificate. The academic program must have included 4 years each of English, math, science, and social studies and 3 years of a foreign language. An essay is required. A portfolio or audition for certain programs and an interview are recommended. AP and CLEP credits are accepted. Important factors in the admissions decision are advanced placement or honors courses, leadership record, and ability to finance college education.

Procedure: Freshmen are admitted fall and spring. Entrance exams should be taken during the spring of the junior year. There are early decision and deferred admissions plans. Early decision applications should be filed by November 15; regular applications, by January 1 for fall entry and October 1 for spring entry, along with a $40 fee. Notification of early decision is sent December 15; regular decision, March 1. 780 applicants were on the 2009 waiting list. Applications are accepted on-line.

Transfer: 569 transfer students enrolled in 2008-2009. Applicants must provide transcripts from all previously attended colleges. A minimum 3.0 GPA is required. Students with fewer than 24 credit hours must submit SAT or ACT scores. 30 of 120 credits required for the bachelor's degree must be completed at Geneseo.

Visiting: There are regularly scheduled orientations for prospective students, generally including a 90-minute campus tour and a 45-minute information session. Students may also elect to sit in on classes, visit faculty and coaches, or stay overnight. There are guides for informal visits, and visitors may sit in on classes and stay overnight. To schedule a visit, contact the Office of Admissions at (585) 245-5571.

Financial Aid: In 2009-2010, 72% of all full-time freshmen and 76% of continuing full-time students received some form of financial aid. 62% of all full-time freshmen and 65% of continuing full-time students received need-based aid. The average freshman award was $10,631, with $3,846 ($9,850 maximum) from need-based scholarships or need-based grants; $4,837 ($7,000 maximum) from need-based self-help aid (loans and jobs); and $2,164 ($6,000 maximum) from other non-need-based awards and non-need-based scholarships. 16% of undergraduate students work part-time. Average annual earnings from campus work are $2490. The average financial indebtedness of the 2009 graduate was $19,000. Geneseo is a member of CSS. The FAFSA is required. The deadline for filing freshman financial aid applications for fall entry is February 15.

International Students: There are 140 international students enrolled. The school actively recruits these students. They must take the TOEFL with a minimum score of 525 on the paper-based TOEFL (PBT) or 71 on the Internet-based version (iBT).

Computers: Geneseo provides almost 900 PCs for student use. Internet accessible PCs are provided in all academic buildings and residence halls. The college wireless network is partially present in all campus buildings, and full coverage is available in more than half of the buildings on campus. All students may access the system 24 hours a day. There are no time limits. The fee is $181. All students are required to have a personal computer.

Graduates: From July 1, 2008 to June 30, 2009, 1332 bachelor's degrees were awarded. The most popular majors were psychology (9%), biology (9%), and business administration (8%). 48 companies recruited on campus in 2008-2009. In an average class, 2% graduate in 3 years or less, 60% graduate in 4 years or less, 76% graduate in 5 years or less, and 77% graduate in 6 years or less. Of the 2008 graduating class, 41% were enrolled in graduate school within 6 months of graduation, and 49% were employed.

Admissions Contact: Kristine Shay, Director of Admissions. A campus DVD is available. E-Mail: *admissions@geneseo.edu* Web: *www.geneseo.edu*

STATE UNIVERSITY OF NEW YORK/COLLEGE AT OLD WESTBURY   D-5

Old Westbury, NY 11568-0210	**(516) 876-3073; (516) 876-3307**
Full-time: 1315 men, 1890 women	**Faculty:** 251; IIB, +$
Part-time: 254 men, 354 women	**Ph.D.s:** 83%
Graduate: 37 men, 47 women	**Student/Faculty:** 13 to 1
Year: semesters, summer session	**Tuition:** $5797 ($13,697)
Application Deadline: open	**Room & Board:** $9390
Freshman Class: 3610 applied, 1830 accepted, 414 enrolled	
SAT CR/M/W: 490/510/470	**ACT:** 21 **COMPETITIVE**

The State University of New York/College at Old Westbury, founded in 1965, is a public institution offering degree programs in the arts and sciences, business, education, fine arts, and health science. There are 3 undergraduate schools and 1 graduate school. In addition to regional accreditation, SUNY Old Westbury has baccalaureate program accreditation with NCATE. The library contains 195,254 volumes, 19,421 microform items, and 21,136 audio/video tapes/CDs/DVDs, and subscribes to 1642 periodicals including electronic. Computerized library services include interlibrary loans, database searching, Internet access, and laptop Internet portals. Special learning facilities include a learning resource center, art gallery, radio station, and TV studio. The 604-acre campus is in a suburban area 20 miles east of New York City. Including any residence halls, there are 22 buildings.

Student Life: 97% of undergraduates are from New York. Others are from 17 states and 32 foreign countries. 32% are white; 32% African American; 18% Hispanic. The average age of freshmen is 18; all undergraduates, 24. 25% do not continue beyond their first year; 35% remain to graduate.

Housing: 1500 students can be accommodated in college housing, which includes coed dorms. In addition, there are honors houses. On-campus housing is available on a first-come, first-served basis. Priority is given to out-of-town students. 74% of students commute. Alcohol is not permitted. All students may keep cars.

Activities: 1% of men belong to 6 national fraternities; 1% of women belong to 4 national sororities. There are 60 groups on campus, including art, cheerleading, choir, chorale, computers, dance, drama, ethnic, film, gay, honors, international, newspaper, photography, political, professional, radio and TV, religious, social, social service, and student government. Popular campus events include Welcome Back Festival, Wellness at Old Westbury, and Panther Pride Week.

Sports: There are 5 intercollegiate sports for men and 5 for women, and 7 intramural sports for men and 7 for women. Facilities include a 3000-seat gym, an auxiliary gym, a cross-country course, playing fields, a swimming pool, a fitness center, a weight room, jogging trails, a student union building, and courts for tennis, paddleball, handball, racquetball, and squash.

Disabled Students: 90% of the campus is accessible. Facilities include wheelchair ramps, elevators, special parking, specially equipped restrooms, special class scheduling, lowered drinking fountains, lowered telephones, and limited volunteer transportation.

Services: Counseling and information services are available, as is tutoring in most subjects. There is a reader service for the blind, and remedial math, reading, and writing.

Campus Safety and Security: Measures include 24-hour foot and vehicle patrol, emergency notification system, and security escort services. There are shuttle buses, emergency telephones, and lighted pathways/sidewalks. An officer patrols dormitories from 6 P.M. to 2 A.M.

Programs of Study: SUNY Old Westbury confers B.A., B.S., and B.P.S. degrees. Master's degrees are also awarded. Bachelor's degrees are awarded in BIOLOGICAL SCIENCE (biochemistry and biology/biological science), BUSINESS (accounting, banking and finance, business administration and management, labor studies, management information systems, and marketing/retailing/merchandising), COMMUNICATIONS AND THE ARTS (communications, media arts, Spanish, and visual and performing arts), COMPUTER AND PHYSICAL SCIENCE (chemistry, computer science, information sciences and systems, and mathematics), EDUCATION (bilingual/bicultural education, early childhood education, elementary education, foreign languages education, mathematics education, middle school education, science education, secondary education, social studies education, and special education), HEALTH PROFESSIONS (community health work and health), SOCIAL SCIENCE (American studies, criminology, economics, humanities, international studies, philosophy, political science/government, psychology, religion, and sociology). Teacher education, business, and psychology are the strongest academically and have the largest enrollments.

Required: To graduate, students must maintain a GPA of 2.0 to 3.0, depending on the major, in 120 or 128 semester credits (accounting and special education majors require 128 credits). General education requirements include courses in writing and reasoning skills, creative arts, ideas and ideology, cross-cultural perspectives, U.S. society and history, physical or life science, and foreign language. A senior project or capstone course is required, based on major.

Special: SUNY Old Westbury offers cross-registration with SUNY Empire State, Lirache, and colleges in Nassau and Suffolk counties, internships in teacher education, extensive study-abroad programs, a B.A.-B.S. in psychology, chemistry, industrial labor and relations, and sociology, dual majors, and a 3-2 engineering degree with SUNY at Stony Brook and SUNY Maritime College. Credit for military and life experience, nondegree study, and pass/fail options are available. There are 5 national honor societies, a freshman honors program, and 6 departmental honors programs.

Faculty/Classroom: 50% of faculty are male; 50% are female. All teach undergraduates, 12% do research, and 11% do both. No introductory courses are taught by graduate students. The average class size in an introductory lecture is 25; in a laboratory, 21; and in a regular course, 25.

Admissions: 51% of the 2009-2010 applicants were accepted. The SAT scores for the 2009-2010 freshman class were: Critical Reading--55% below 500, 40% between 500 and 599, and 5% between 600 and 700; Math--41% below 500, 52% between 500 and 599, 7% between 600 and 700, and 1% above 700; Writing--67% below 500, 30% between 500 and 599, and 3% between 600 and 700. The ACT scores were 39% below 21, 35% between 21 and 23, 16% between 24 and 26, 7% between 27 and 28, and 3% above 28.

Requirements: The SAT is required. In addition, applicants must be graduates of an accredited secondary school or have the GED. An essay, portfolio, and interview are also recommended. Students are evaluated according to qualifying categories of academic achievement, special knowledge and creative ability, paid work experience, and social or personal experience. AP and CLEP credits are accepted. Important factors in the admissions decision are leadership record, recommendations by school officials, and evidence of special talent.

Procedure: Freshmen are admitted fall and spring. There are early decision, deferred admissions, and rolling admissions plans. Application deadlines are open. Application fee is $40. Notification is sent on a rolling basis. Applications are accepted on-line.

Transfer: 1136 transfer students enrolled in a recent year. Applicants must submit official transcripts from all colleges attended. Those students with fewer than 24 college credits must also submit a high school transcript. The college requires a minimum overall GPA of 2.0. Specific academic majors may require a higher GPA. 48 of 120 to 128 credits required for the bachelor's degree must be completed at SUNY Old Westbury.

Visiting: There are regularly scheduled orientations for prospective students. There are guides for informal visits. To schedule a visit, contact Enrollment Services at (516) 876-3076.

Financial Aid: In 2009-2010, 69% of all full-time freshmen and 62% of continuing full-time students received some form of financial aid. 65% of all full-time freshmen and 57% of continuing full-time students received need-based aid. The average freshman award was $7207. Need-based scholarships or need-based grants averaged $6916, and need-based self-help aid (loans and jobs) averaged $2080. Average annual earnings from campus work are $902. The average financial indebtedness of the 2009 graduate was $15,901. The FAFSA, the IFAA (institutional application), and the previous year's household income are required. The deadline for filing freshman financial aid applications for fall entry is April 19.

International Students: There are 72 international students enrolled. The school actively recruits these students. They must take the TOEFL with a minimum score of 513 on the paper-based TOEFL (PBT) or 80 on the Internet-based version (iBT), and the college's own test.

Computers: Wireless access is available. The college supports a 2000-port network spanning the entire campus, including high-speed Internet access in dorm rooms. The wireless network is fully accessible in all academic buildings including the library, student union, and administrative building. There are roughly 450 public computers spread among 8 locations split between public access and departmental labs dedicated to specific disciplines. All students receive e-mail and computer accounts and have access to printers. All students may access the system daily. There are no time limits and no fees. It is strongly recommended that all students have a personal computer.

Graduates: From July 1, 2008 to June 30, 2009, 721 bachelor's degrees were awarded. The most popular majors were accounting (15%), psychology (11%), and childhood education (9%). 50 companies recruited on campus in 2008-2009.

Admissions Contact: Mary Marquez Bell, Vice President for Enrollment Services. A campus DVD is available.
E-mail: *enroll@oldwestbury.edu* Web: *www.oldwestbury.edu*

STATE UNIVERSITY OF NEW YORK/COLLEGE AT ONEONTA — D-3

Oneonta, NY 13820-4015

(607) 436-2524
(800) 786-9123; (607) 436-3074

Full-time: 2372 men, 3208 women	**Faculty:** 259; IIA, --$
Part-time: 63 men, 68 women	**Ph.D.s:** 84%
Graduate: 41 men, 141 women	**Student/Faculty:** 17 to 1
Year: semesters, summer session	**Tuition:** $6185 ($14,085)
Application Deadline: open	**Room & Board:** $8900
Freshman Class: 12688 applied, 4972 accepted, 1109 enrolled	
SAT CR/M: 551/579	**ACT:** 24 **VERY COMPETITIVE**

The State University of New York/College at Oneonta, founded in 1889, offers undergraduate and graduate programs in the arts and sciences with a campus-wide emphasis on educational technology, student engagement, diversity, and community service. There is 1 graduate school. In addition to regional accreditation, SUNY Oneonta has baccalaureate program accreditation with ADA, NASM, and NCATE. The library contains 25,850 volumes, 1.2 million microform items, and 26,942 audio/video tapes/CDs/DVDs, and subscribes to 25,553 periodicals including electronic. Computerized library services include interlibrary loans, database searching, Internet access, and laptop Internet portals. Special learning facilities include a learning resource center, art gallery, planetarium, radio station, TV station, observatory, science discovery center, community service center, college camp, children's center, and off-campus biological field station. The 250-acre campus is in a rural area 75 miles southwest of Albany and 55 miles northeast of Binghamton. Including any residence halls, there are 36 buildings.

Student Life: 95% of undergraduates are from New York. Others are from 8 states and 20 foreign countries. 81% are white. The average age of freshmen is 18; all undergraduates, 20. 18% do not continue beyond their first year; 60% remain to graduate.

Housing: 3049 students can be accommodated in college housing, which includes single-sex and coed dorms. In addition, there is freshman housing and special-interest groupings within residence halls. On-campus housing is guaranteed for the freshman year only, is available on a first-come, first-served basis, and is available on a lottery system for upperclassmen. 54% of students live on campus; of those, 60% remain on campus on weekends. Alcohol is not permitted. Upperclassmen may keep cars.

Activities: 2% of men belong to 3 national fraternities; 6% of women belong to 7 national sororities. There are 80 groups on campus, including academic, art, band, cheerleading, choir, chorale, chorus, computers, culture enrichment, dance, drama, environmental, ethnic, film, gay, honors, international, jazz band, musical theater, newspaper, orchestra, pep band, photography, political, professional, radio and TV, religious, social, social service, special interest, student government, and volunteer. Popular campus events include Exploration (campus orientation), Into the Streets (community service day), and OHFest (Main Street festival).

Sports: There are 10 intercollegiate sports for men and 11 for women, and 17 intramural sports for men and 17 for women. Facilities include a gym, a field house, dance studios, weight rooms, a pool, indoor racquetball courts, tennis courts, indoor and outdoor tracks, athletic fields, and a lighted all-weather field.

Disabled Students: 90% of the campus is accessible. Facilities include wheelchair ramps, elevators, special parking, specially equipped restrooms, special class scheduling, and lowered drinking fountains. All academic buildings and most residence halls are accessible.

Services: Counseling and information services are available, as is tutoring in most subjects. There is a reader service for the blind and remedial math, reading, and writing. Tutoring is also available in all introductory-level courses and most upper-level courses.

Campus Safety and Security: Measures include 24-hour foot and vehicle patrol, emergency notification system, self-defense education, and security escort services. There are shuttle buses, emergency telephones, lighted pathways/sidewalks, and controlled access to dorms/residences.

Programs of Study: SUNY Oneonta confers B.A. and B.S. degrees. Master's degrees are also awarded. Bachelor's degrees are awarded in BIOLOGICAL SCIENCE (biology/biological science), BUSINESS (accounting, business economics, and fashion merchandising), COMMUNICATIONS AND THE ARTS (art, communications, dramatic arts, English, fine arts, French, music, music business management, Spanish, and speech/debate/rhetoric), COMPUTER AND PHYSICAL SCIENCE (atmospheric sciences and meteorology, chemistry, computer science, earth science, geology, mathematics, physics, and statistics), EDUCATION (business education, elementary education, English education, foreign languages education, home economics education, mathematics education, science education, secondary education, and social science education), ENGINEERING AND ENVIRONMENTAL DESIGN (environmental science), HEALTH PROFESSIONS (predentistry and premedicine), SOCIAL SCIENCE (African studies, anthropology, child care/child and family studies, criminal justice, dietetics, economics, geography, gerontology, Hispanic American studies, history, home economics, interdisciplinary studies, international studies, philosophy, political science/government, prelaw, psychology, sociology, and water resources). Physical and natural sciences, business economics, and education are the strongest academically. Elementary education, music industry, and adolescent education are the largest.

Required: Students must complete 122 semester hours, with 30 to 36 hours in the major. A minimum GPA of 2.0 (2.5 for education majors) must be maintained. In addition, students must complete a 36-hour general education requirement including courses in math, natural sciences, social sciences, American history, Western civilization, humanities, the arts, foreign language, and basic communications. Students must also pass a writing exam.

Special: Oneonta offers limited cross-registration with Hartwick College, internships in most fields, study abroad in 400 countries, a Washington semester, work-study programs, and dual majors. A 3-2 engineering degree and other cooperative programs are offered. There are 14 national honor societies, a freshman honors program, and 10 departmental honors programs.

Faculty/Classroom: 54% of faculty are male; 46% are female. 99% teach undergraduates. No introductory courses are taught by graduate students. The average class size in an introductory lecture is 25; in a laboratory, 24; and in a regular course, 17.

Admissions: 39% of the 2009-2010 applicants were accepted. The SAT scores for the 2009-2010 freshman class were: Critical Reading--13% below 500, 66% between 500 and 599, 20% between 600 and 700, and 1% above 700; Math--5% below 500, 56% between 500 and 599, 37% between 600 and 700, and 2% above 700. The ACT scores were 5% below 21, 29% between 21 and 23, 34% between 24 and 26, 20% between 27 and 28, and 12% above 28. 51% of the current freshmen were in the top fifth of their class; 96% were in the top two fifths.

Requirements: The SAT or ACT is required. In addition, applicants should be graduates of an accredited secondary school and have 16 academic credits, including 4 years each of English and history and 8 years combined of foreign language, math, and science, with at least 2 years in each of these 3 broad areas. The GED is accepted. A GPA of 2.0 is required. AP and CLEP credits are accepted. Important factors in the admissions decision are advanced placement or honors courses, evidence of special talent, and leadership record.

Procedure: Freshmen are admitted fall and spring. Entrance exams should be taken in the spring of the junior year or the fall of the senior year. There are deferred admissions and rolling admissions plans. Application deadlines are open. The application fee is $40. Notifications are sent December 1. 354 applicants were on the 2009 waiting list; 2 were admitted. Applications are accepted on-line.

Transfer: 553 transfer students enrolled in 2008-2009. Official transcripts of all previous college work must be submitted. A minimum of 15 semester hours of transferable credit and a GPA of 2.0 (2.5 for education majors) are required. 45 of 122 credits required for the bachelor's degree must be completed at SUNY Oneonta.

Visiting: There are regularly scheduled orientations for prospective students, including 2 fall open houses, a summer open house, Friday and Saturday information sessions, and individual appointments. There are guides for informal visits, and visitors may sit in on classes and stay overnight. To schedule a visit, contact the Admissions Office.

Financial Aid: In 2009-2010, 54% of all full-time freshmen and 56% of continuing full-time students received some form of financial aid. 45% of all full-time freshmen and 46% of continuing full-time students received need-based aid. The average freshman award was $10,804. Need-based scholarships or need-based grants averaged $5131 ; need-based self-help aid (loans and jobs) averaged $3815; and other non-need-based awards and non-need-based scholarships averaged $1089. 36% of undergraduate students work part-time. Average annual earnings from campus work are $1003. The average financial indebtedness of the 2009 graduate was $12,527. The FAFSA and the state aid form are required. The priority date for freshman financial aid applications for fall entry is March 1. The deadline for filing freshman financial aid applications for fall entry is April 15.

International Students: There are 102 international students enrolled. The school actively recruits these students. They must take the TOEFL with a minimum score of 525 on the paper-based TOEFL (PBT) or 70 on the Internet-based version (iBT).

Computers: Wireless access is available. Wireless and high-speed connections are available campus-wide; more than 700 computers are available in general, departmental, and residence hall labs. There is free dial-up access for off-campus students. All students may access the system anytime. There are no time limits and no fees. It is strongly recommended that all students have a personal computer. A network-ready PC or Mac is recommended.

Graduates: From July 1, 2008 to June 30, 2009, 1356 bachelor's degrees were awarded. The most popular majors were education (18%), music industry (12%), and communications (12%). 45 companies recruited on campus in 2008-2009. In an average class, 1% graduate in 3 years or less, 43% graduate in 4 years or less, 58% graduate in 5 years or less, and 60% graduate in 6 years or less. Of the 2008 graduating

class, 49% were enrolled in graduate school within 6 months of graduation and 87% were employed.

Admissions Contact: Karen Brown, Director of Admissions.
E-mail: *admissions@oneonta.edu* Web: *www.oneonta.edu*

STATE UNIVERSITY OF NEW YORK/COLLEGE AT PLATTSBURGH   D-2

Plattsburgh, NY 12901-2681　　　　　　　　(518) 564-2040
　　　　　　　　　　　　　　　　(888) 673-0012; (518) 564-2045

Full-time: 2325 men, 2980 women	**Faculty:** IIA, -$
Part-time: 135 men, 210 women	**Ph.D.s:** n/av
Graduate: 185 men, 450 women	**Student/Faculty:** n/av
Year: semesters, summer session	**Tuition:** $5550 ($12,050)
Application Deadline: August 1	**Room & Board:** $9000
Freshman Class: n/av	
SAT or ACT: required	**COMPETITIVE**

The State University of New York/College at Plattsburgh, founded in 1889, is a public institution offering degree programs in the liberal arts and professional programs. The figures in the above capsule and in this profile are approximate. There are 3 undergraduate schools and 2 graduate schools. In addition to regional accreditation, Plattsburgh State has baccalaureate program accreditation with AACSB, ADA, ASLA, CSWE, and NLN. The library contains 299,556 volumes, 926,246 microform items, and 24,139 audio/video tapes/CDs/DVDs, and subscribes to 1,453 periodicals including electronic. Computerized library services include interlibrary loans, database searching, and Internet access. Special learning facilities include a learning resource center, art gallery, planetarium, radio station, TV station, an environmental science institute, a child care center, a research institute, a teacher resource center, a speech and hearing clinic, the Alzheimer's Disease Assistance Center, auditory research labs, a virtual reality simulator, and distance learning facilities. The 300-acre campus is in a suburban area 150 miles north of Albany, 25 miles west of Burlington, Vermont, and 65 miles south of Montreal, Can. Including any residence halls, there are 35 buildings.

Student Life: 89% of undergraduates are from New York. Others are from 32 states, 50 foreign countries, and Canada. 98% are from public schools. 72% are white. The average age of freshmen is 19; all undergraduates, 22. 22% do not continue beyond their first year; 55% remain to graduate.

Housing: 2991 students can be accommodated in college housing, which includes single-sex and coed dorms and on-campus apartments. In addition, there are special-interest houses, adult student halls/floors, wellness floors, a substance-free building, and vacation housing. On-campus housing is available on a first-come, first-served basis, and is available on a lottery system for upperclassmen. 52% of students commute. All students may keep cars.

Activities: 6% of men belong to 3 local and 4 national fraternities; 5% of women belong to 3 local and 4 national sororities. There are 118 groups on campus, including art, band, cheerleading, choir, chorale, chorus, computers, dance, drama, ethnic, film, gay, honors, international, jazz band, literary magazine, musical theater, newspaper, orchestra, photography, political, professional, radio and TV, religious, social, social service, student government, and symphony. Popular campus events include Canada Day, and Arts and Crafts Fair.

Sports: There are 8 intercollegiate sports for men and 9 for women, and 9 intramural sports for men and 9 for women. Facilities include a 3500-seat ice arena, a 1500-seat gym, an indoor track, soccer and volleyball areas, an indoor swimming pool, exercise and weight rooms, an aerobics studio, racquetball courts, lighted tennis courts, softball, lacrosse, and rugby fields, and a fitness center.

Disabled Students: 95% of the campus is accessible. Facilities include wheelchair ramps, elevators, special parking, specially equipped restrooms, special class scheduling, lowered drinking fountains, lowered telephones. curb cuts, and electronic doors.

Services: Counseling and information services are available, as is tutoring in every subject. There is a reader service for the blind, and remedial math, reading, and writing.

Campus Safety and Security: Measures include 24-hour foot and vehicle patrol, emergency notification system, self-defense education, and security escort services. There are shuttle buses, emergency telephones, lighted pathways/sidewalks, controlled access to dorms/residences , bicycle patrols, combination locks on student rooms, a computerized keyless entry system for residence hall access, door viewers, and basement and ground-level security windows in residence halls.

Programs of Study: Plattsburgh State confers B.A., B.S., B.F.A., and B.S.Ed. degrees. Master's degrees are also awarded. Bachelor's degrees are awarded in BIOLOGICAL SCIENCE (biochemistry, biology/biological science, cell biology, ecology, and nutrition), BUSINESS (accounting, business administration and management, business economics, entrepreneurial studies, hotel/motel and restaurant management, international business management, marketing/retailing/merchandising, and supply chain management), COMMUNICATIONS AND THE ARTS (art, communications, dramatic arts, English, French, journalism, music, public relations, and Spanish), COMPUTER AND PHYSICAL SCIENCE (chemistry, computer science, geology, mathematics, and physics), EDUCATION (education of the deaf and hearing impaired, elementary education, English education, mathematics education, science education, secondary education, social studies education, and special education), ENGINEERING AND ENVIRONMENTAL DESIGN (environmental science), HEALTH PROFESSIONS (cytotechnology, medical laboratory technology, and nursing), SOCIAL SCIENCE (anthropology, Canadian studies, child care/child and family studies, community services, criminal justice, dietetics, economics, geography, history, home economics, interdisciplinary studies, Latin American studies, philosophy, political science/government, psychology, social work, sociology, and women's studies). Cellular biochemistry, adolescence education (geology), and child and family service are the strongest academically. Psychology, education, and business are the largest.

Required: To graduate students must have a 2.0 GPA and complete at least 120 semester hours. Core curriculum courses total 41 to 46 credits. In addition, all students must demonstrate proficiency in writing by completion of English composition and an advanced writing requirement. Specific courses such as library research skills and computer science are offered. A comprehensive exam in some majors and a thesis in the upper-division honors program. Many majors require practicum and/or internship experience to complete a degree.

Special: The college offers cross-registration with Clinton Community College and Empire State College, internships, study abroad in 10 countries, cooperative programs in all majors, B.A.-B.S. degrees, dual and student-designed majors, an accelerated degree program in any major except nursing, and B.A./M.S.T. combined undergraduate and graduate programs. A 3-2 engineering degree is offered with SUNY Stony Brook and Binghamton, Clarkson, Syracuse, and McGill Universities, and the University of Vermont. There are 18 national honor societies and a freshman honors program.

Faculty/Classroom: 51% of faculty are male; 49% are female. All teach and do research. No introductory courses are taught by graduate students. The average class size in an introductory lecture is 27; in a laboratory is 14; and in a regular course is 21.

Requirements: The SAT or ACT is required. In addition, applicants must have at least 12 academic credits, including 4 years of English, 5 combined years of math and science, and 3 years of social studies. An essay, portfolio, audition, and interview may be recommended in some programs. The GED is accepted. Plattsburgh State requires applicants to be in the upper 50% of their class. A GPA of 78.0 is required. AP and CLEP credits are accepted. Important factors in the admissions decision are advanced placement or honors courses, recommendations by school officials, and leadership record.

Procedure: Freshmen are admitted fall and spring. Entrance exams should be taken during the second half of the junior year or the beginning of the senior year. There are early decision, early admissions, deferred admissions, and rolling admissions plans. Early decision applications should be filed by November 15; regular applications, by August 1 for fall entry and November 1 for spring entry. The fall 2009 application fee was $40. Notification of early decision is sent December 15; regular decision, January 15. Applications are accepted on-line. A waiting list is maintained.

Transfer: 578 transfer students enrolled in a recent year. Applicants must have a minimum 2.0 GPA. Most academic programs require a 2.5 GPA or better. 36 of 120 credits required for the bachelor's degree must be completed at Plattsburgh State.

Visiting: There are regularly scheduled orientations for prospective students, including a group, student-led tour, and either a group or individual interview. Special overnight events for accepted freshmen include meals with students and faculty, classroom visits, discussions with faculty, and special workshops. There are guides for informal visits; visitors may sit in on classes and stay overnight. To schedule a visit, contact the Admissions Office at admissions@plattsburgh.edu.

Financial Aid: In a recent year, 56% of all full-time freshmen and 49% of continuing full-time students received need-based aid. The average freshmen award was $9,694. 37% of undergraduate students worked part-time. Average annual earnings from campus work were $1650. The average financial indebtedness of the 2009 graduate was $21,855. The FAFSA, and In-state students must also file the TAP application. is required. Check with the school for current application deadlines.

International Students: There were 386 international students enrolled in a recent year. The school actively recruits these students. They must take the TOEFL with a minimum score of 540 on the paper-based TOEFL (PBT) or 76 on the Internet-based version (iBT).

Computers: All students may access the system. There are no time limits. The fee is $50 per semester. It is strongly recommended that all students have a personal computer. A Digital, IBM, Zenith, Dell or Mac is recommended.

Graduates: In a recent year, 1238 bachelor's degrees were awarded. The most popular majors were business/marketing (20%), education (12%), and psychology (8%). 120 companies recruited on campus in 2008-2009. In an average class, 1% graduate in 3 years or less, 30% graduate in 4 years or less, 52% graduate in 5 years or less, and 55% graduate in 6 years or less. Of the 2008 graduating class, 12% were enrolled in graduate school within 6 months of graduation, and 79% were employed.

Admissions Contact: Richard Higgins, Director of Admissions. E-Mail: *higginrj@splavb.cc.plattsburgh.edu* Web: *www.plattsburgh.edu*

STATE UNIVERSITY OF NEW YORK/COLLEGE AT PURCHASE
D-5

Purchase, NY 10577-1400   (914) 251-6306; (914) 251-6314

Full-time: 1603 men, 2006 women	**Faculty:** 144; IIB, av$
Part-time: 97 men, 124 women	**Ph.D.s:** 100%
Graduate: 53 men, 74 women	**Student/Faculty:** 25 to 1
Year: semesters, summer session	**Tuition:** $6681 ($14,581)
Application Deadline: August 15	**Room & Board:** $10,270
Freshman Class: n/av	
SAT or ACT: required	

COMPETITIVE

State University of New York/College at Purchase (also known as Purchase College SUNY), founded in 1967, is a public institution that offers programs in visual arts, music, acting, dance, film, theater/stage design technology, natural science, social science, and humanities. There is one graduate school. In addition to regional accreditation, Purchase College SUNY has baccalaureate program accreditation with NASAD and NASM. The library contains 241,984 volumes, 257,609 microform items, and 18,273 audio/video tapes/CDs/DVDs, and subscribes to 37,153 periodicals including electronic. Computerized library services include interlibrary loans, database searching, Internet access, and laptop Internet portals. Special learning facilities include a learning resource center, radio station, TV station, listening and viewing center, science and photography labs, music practice rooms and instruments, multitrack synthesizers, music composition labs, digital video editing labs, typesetting and computer graphics labs, experimental stage, a performing arts complex, an electron microscope, and the Children's Center. The 500-acre campus is in a suburban area 35 miles north of midtown Manhattan. Including any residence halls, there are 40 buildings.

Student Life: 80% of undergraduates are from New York. Others are from 43 states, 27 foreign countries, and Canada. 55% are white. The average age of freshmen is 18; all undergraduates, 22. 18% do not continue beyond their first year; 51% remain to graduate.

Housing: 2600 students can be accommodated in college housing, which includes single-sex and coed dorms and on-campus apartments. In addition, there are special-interest houses, transfer student units, nontraditional-aged student units, wellness halls, presidential scholars halls, sophomore communities, conservatory halls, and learning community halls. On-campus housing is guaranteed for the freshman year only and is available on a first-come, first-served basis. 67% of students live on campus; of those, 75% remain on campus on weekends. All students may keep cars.

Activities: There are no fraternities or sororities. There are more than 40 groups on campus, including art, band, cheerleading, choir, chorale, computers, dance, drama, environmental, ethnic, jazz band, literary magazine, opera, orchestra, photography, political, professional, religious, social, social service, student government, symphony, and visual arts. Popular campus events include Spring Concert, Alcohol Awareness Week, and film programs.

Sports: There are 7 intercollegiate sports for men and 6 for women, and 20 intramural sports for men and 20 for women. Facilities include a fitness center, 6-lane pool, aerobics studio, 3 basketball courts, 4 racquetball courts, 2 squash courts, 10 tennis courts, outdoor climbing wall, 5 soccer fields, baseball field, softball field, and 4-lane bowling alley.

Disabled Students: All of the campus is accessible. Facilities include wheelchair ramps, elevators, special parking, and specially equipped restrooms. There are note takers, extended test times, quiet rooms for tests, interpreters for the hearing impaired, readers for the visually impaired, a reading machine in the library, and special note-taking paper.

Services: Counseling and information services are available, as is tutoring in every subject. There is a reader service for the blind, and remedial math, reading, and writing. There are drop-in sessions for math and writing.

Campus Safety and Security: Measures include 24-hour foot and vehicle patrol and security escort services. There are emergency telephones and lighted pathways/sidewalks.

Programs of Study: Purchase College SUNY confers B.A., B.S., B.A.L.A., B.F.A., and Mus. B. degrees. Master's degrees are also awarded. Bachelor's degrees are awarded in BIOLOGICAL SCIENCE (biology/biological science), COMMUNICATIONS AND THE ARTS (art history and appreciation, creative writing, dance, dramatic arts, film arts, journalism, literature, music, theater design, and visual and performing arts), COMPUTER AND PHYSICAL SCIENCE (chemistry and mathematics), ENGINEERING AND ENVIRONMENTAL DESIGN (environmental science), SOCIAL SCIENCE (anthropology, economics, ethnic studies, history, liberal arts/general studies, philosophy, political science/government, psychology, sociology, and women's studies). Biology and journalism are the strongest academically. Visual arts, music, and liberal studies are the largest.

Required: A minimum 2.0 GPA is required with a minimum of 120 credits. Students majoring in the arts complete a minimum of 90 professional credits and the SUNY general education curriculum. Students majoring in the liberal arts and sciences complete the general education curriculum and major requirements and must complete a senior thesis.

Special: Purchase College offers cross-registration with Empire State colleges, internships with corporations, newspapers, and local agencies, and student-designed majors, dual majors, study abroad, work-study, nondegree study, and pass/fail options. There is also an arts conservatory program.

Faculty/Classroom: 54% of faculty are male; 46% are female. All teach undergraduates. No introductory courses are taught by graduate students. The average class size in an introductory lecture is 27; in a laboratory, 12; and in a regular course, 14.

Requirements: The SAT or ACT is required, with minimum required composite scores of 1100 on the SAT or 23 on the ACT. Applicants must be graduates of an accredited secondary school and have completed 16 academic credits and 16 Carnegie units, The GED is accepted. Visual arts students must submit an essay and portfolio and have an interview. Film students need an essay and an interview. Design technology students need a portfolio and an interview. Performing arts students must audition. A GPA of 2.0 is required. AP and CLEP credits are accepted. Important factors in the admissions decision are evidence of special talent, recommendations by school officials, and personality/intangible qualities.

Procedure: Freshmen are admitted fall and spring. Entrance exams should be taken by the fall of the senior year. There are early decision, early admissions, deferred admissions, and rolling admissions plans. Early decision applications should be filed by November 15; regular applications, by August 15 for fall entry and December 1 for spring entry, along with a $30 fee. Notification of early decision is sent December 15; regular decision, sent on a rolling basis. Applications are accepted on-line. A waiting list is maintained.

Transfer: Students transferring to the School of Arts (visual or performing arts) must pass an audition or portfolio review. Transfer credit is limited; students can contact the Office of Admission to get a preliminary credit evaluation. Students transferring to programs in liberal arts and sciences must have a minimum 2.0 G.P.A. if they have completed 30 or more semester hours; if they have fewer than 30 semester hours, the high school transcript is also reviewed. Liberal arts and science transfers can transfer a maximum of 90 semester hours from 4-year colleges and 75 semester hours from 2-year colleges. 30 of 120 credits required for the bachelor's degree must be completed at Purchase College SUNY.

Visiting: There are regularly scheduled orientations for prospective students, including group question and answer sessions followed by a tour of the campus. To schedule a visit, contact the Admissions Office.

Financial Aid: Purchase College SUNY is a member of CSS. The FAFSA is required. Check with the school for current deadlines.

International Students: The school actively recruits international students. They must take the TOEFL with a minimum score of 550 on the paper-based TOEFL (PBT) or 80 on the Internet-based version (iBT), or score 430 on the SAT: Verbal test, or take the IELTS.

Computers: There are no time limits. The fee is $150 per semester. It is strongly recommended that all students have a personal computer.

Admissions Contact: Dennis Craig, Vice President of Admissions. E-mail: *dennis.craig@purchase.edu* Web: *www.purchase.edu*

STATE UNIVERSITY OF NEW YORK/COLLEGE OF AGRICULTURE AND TECHNOLOGY AT COBLESKILL   D-3

Cobleskill, NY 12043

(518) 255-5525
(800) 295-8988; (518) 255-6769

Full-time: 1300 men, 1175 women	Faculty: III, av$
Part-time: 70 men, 70 women	Ph.D.s: n/av
Graduate: none	Student/Faculty: n/av
Year: semesters, summer session	Tuition: $6024 ($9814)
Application Deadline: August	Room & Board: $9460
Freshman Class: n/av	
SAT or ACT: recommended	COMPETITIVE

The State University of New York/College of Agriculture and Technology at Cobleskill, established in 1916, is a comprehensive public institution offering bachelors and associate degree and a certificate program. The figures in the above capsule and in this profile are approximate. The library contains 67,517 volumes, 32,165 microform items, and 4,462 audio/video tapes/CDs/DVDs, and subscribes to 22,228 periodicals including electronic. Computerized library services include interlibrary loans, database searching, Internet access, and laptop Internet portals. Special learning facilities include a learning resource center, art gallery, an arboretum, greenhouses, an equestrian center, dairy barns, fish hatchery, and a plant nursery. The 750-acre campus is in a rural area 35 miles south of Albany. Including any residence halls, there are 53 buildings.

Student Life: 90% of undergraduates are from New York. Others are from 15 states, and 15 foreign countries. 98% are from public schools. 73% are white. The average age of freshmen is 18; all undergraduates, 20. 26% do not continue beyond their first year; 52% remain to graduate.

Housing: 1890 students can be accommodated in college housing, which includes single-sex and coed dorms. In addition, there are special interest floors in residence halls. On-campus housing is guaranteed for the freshman year only, is available on a first-come, first-served basis, and is available on a lottery system for upperclassmen. 76% of students live on campus. Alcohol is not permitted. All students may keep cars.

Activities: There are no fraternities or sororities. There are 45 groups on campus, including cheerleading, choir, chorus, departmental, drama, environmental, ethnic, gay, honors, international, jazz band, musical theater, newspaper, photography, professional, radio and TV, religious, social, social service, and student government. Popular campus events include Alumni Weekend.

Sports: There are 10 intercollegiate sports for men and 10 for women, and 4 intramural sports for men and 4 for women. Facilities include indoor and outdoor basketball and tennis courts, playing fields, a gym, a fitness center, a swimming pool, bowling lanes, a field house, badminton, volleyball, and handball courts, archery and golf driving areas, a quarter-mile track, a ski center, and a fitness trail.

Disabled Students: 25% of the campus is accessible. Facilities include wheelchair ramps, elevators, special parking, specially equipped restrooms, special class scheduling, and special housing.

Services: Counseling and information services are available, as is tutoring in most subjects. There is a reader service for the blind, and remedial math, reading, and writing. There is also an academic support center.

Campus Safety and Security: Measures include 24-hour foot and vehicle patrol, self-defense education, and security escort services. There are emergency telephones, lighted pathways/sidewalks, and controlled access to dorms/residences.

Programs of Study: SUNY Cobleskill confers B.S., B.B.A., and B.T. degrees. Associates degrees are also awarded. Bachelor's degrees are awarded in AGRICULTURE (agricultural business management, agricultural mechanics, animal science, fishing and fisheries, plant science, and wildlife management), COMPUTER AND PHYSICAL SCIENCE (information sciences and systems), ENGINEERING AND ENVIRONMENTAL DESIGN (landscape architecture/design and technological management), SOCIAL SCIENCE (biopsychology and child care/child and family studies). Health science studies, fisheries and wildlife, and agricultural biotechnology are the strongest academically. Social science, animal science, and business administration are the largest.

Required: Degree requirements include completion of 126 credit hours. Students must maintain a minimum 2.0 GPA.

Special: The college sponsors internship programs and cross-registration is possible with the Hudson-Mohawk Area Consortium. Study abroad options are also available. There is 1 national honor society, a freshman honors program, and 1 departmental honors program.

Faculty/Classroom: 52% of faculty are male; 48% are female. All teach undergraduates, 10% do research, and 10% do both. No introductory courses are taught by graduate students. The average class size in an introductory lecture is 19; in a laboratory is 15; and in a regular course is 19.

Requirements: The SAT or ACT is recommended. In addition, applicants must have graduated from an accredited secondary school or earned a GED, and are encouraged to have completed college-preparatory courses. A GPA of 75.0 is required. AP and CLEP credits are accepted. Important factors in the admissions decision are advanced placement or honors courses, evidence of special talent, and leadership record.

Procedure: Freshmen are admitted fall and spring. There are early admissions, deferred admissions, and rolling admissions plans. Application deadlines are open. Application fee is $40. Applications are accepted on-line.

Transfer: 165 transfer students enrolled in a recent year. Applicants must have a minimum GPA of 2.0. 45 of 126 credits required for the bachelor's degree must be completed at SUNY Cobleskill.

Visiting: There are regularly scheduled orientations for prospective students. There are guides for informal visits; visitors may sit in on classes and stay overnight. To schedule a visit, contact the Office of Admissions at (518) 255-5528 or (800) 295-8988.

Financial Aid: In a recent year, 78% of all full-time freshmen and 69% of continuing full-time students received some form of financial aid. 60% of all full-time freshmen and 57% of continuing full-time students received need-based aid. The average freshmen award was $9,856, with $2,589 ($10,525 maximum) from need-based scholarships or need-based grants; $2,654 ($7,500 maximum) from need-based self-help aid (loans and jobs); and $954 ($2,500 maximum) from other non-need-based awards and non-need-based scholarships. 12% of undergraduate students worked part-time. Average annual earnings from campus work were $735. The average financial indebtedness of the 2009 graduate was $8,025. SUNY Cobleskill is a member of CSS. The FAFSA, the college's own financial statement, and EOP Financial eligibility form for EOP applicants only are required. Check with the school for current application deadlines.

International Students: There were 73 international students enrolled in a recent year. The school actively recruits these students. They must take the TOEFL with a minimum score of 500 on the paper-based TOEFL (PBT).

Computers: Wireless access is available. There are 270 college-owned computers for student use available in the library, residence halls, computer center, and open access labs. All resident halls are wired for high-speed Internet connections. Wireless capabilities are in various locations across campus. All students may access the system 24 hours a day/7 days a week (where wireless is in residence halls). There are no time limits. The fee is $270. It is strongly recommended that all students have a personal computer.

Graduates: In a recent year, 190 bachelor's degrees were awarded. The most popular majors were agriculture (48%), business/marketing (18%), and natural resources (12%). In an average class, 46% graduate in 3 years or less and 44% graduate in 4 years or less.

Admissions Contact: Chris Tacea, Interim Director of Admissions. E-Mail: *admissions@cobleskill.edu* Web: *www.cas..cobleskill.edu*

STATE UNIVERSITY OF NEW YORK/COLLEGE OF ENVIRONMENTAL SCIENCE AND FORESTRY   C-3

Syracuse, NY 13210-2779   (315) 470-6600; (315) 470-6933

Full-time: 909 men, 618 women	**Faculty:** 140; I, --$
Part-time: 303 men, 347 women	**Ph.D.s:** 96%
Graduate: 315 men, 314 women	**Student/Faculty:** 13 to 1
Year: semesters	**Tuition:** $5891 ($13,791)
Application Deadline: n/av	**Room & Board:** $12,460
Freshman Class: 1678 applied, 723 accepted, 284 enrolled	
SAT CR/M: 584/600	**ACT:** 25 **HIGHLY COMPETITIVE**

The SUNY College of Environmental Science and Forestry, founded in 1911, is the nation's oldest and largest college focused exclusively on the science, design, engineering, and management of our environment and natural resources. The college offers 21 undergraduate and 28 graduate degree programs, including 8 Ph.D. programs. Students also benefit from a special partnership with Syracuse University (SU) that provides access to courses, housing, and student organizations. There is one undergraduate school and one graduate school. In addition to regional accreditation, ESF has baccalaureate program accreditation with ABET, ASLA, and SAF. The library contains 135,305 volumes, 200,090 microform items, and 1,118 audio/video tapes/CDs/DVDs, and subscribes to 2,001 periodicals including electronic. Computerized library services include interlibrary loans, database searching, Internet access, and laptop Internet portals. Special learning facilities include a learning resource center, art gallery, natural history museum, radio station, and TV station. The 12-acre campus is in an urban area in Syracuse with 25,000 additional acres in New York State used for teaching and research. Including any residence halls, there are 7 buildings.

Student Life: 86% of undergraduates are from New York. Others are from 28 states and 6 foreign countries. 85% are from public schools. 85% are white. The average age of freshmen is 18; all undergraduates, 21. 22% do not continue beyond their first year; 65% remain to graduate.

Housing: 475 students can be accommodated in college housing, which includes single-sex and coed dorms, on-campus apartments, and off-campus apartments. In addition, there are special-interest houses, fraternity houses, sorority houses, and substance-free floors, quiet floors, and learning communities. On-campus housing is guaranteed for all 4 years and is available on a lottery system for upperclassmen. 3% of students commute. Alcohol is not permitted. Upperclassmen may keep cars.

Activities: 3% of men belong to 20 national fraternities; 3% of women belong to 20 national sororities. There are 300 groups on campus, including art, bagpipe, band, cheerleading, choir, chorale, chorus, computers, dance, debate, drama, environmental, ethnic, film, gay, honors, international, jazz band, literary magazine, marching band, musical theater, newspaper, orchestra, pep band, photography, political, professional, radio and TV, religious, social, social service, student government, symphony, and yearbook. Popular campus events include Earth Week, Awards Banquet, and December Soiree.

Sports: There are 4 intercollegiate sports for men and 3 for women, and 15 intramural sports for men and 15 for women. ESF has soccer, golf, cross-country, and woodsman's teams. Students can participate in all Syracuse University club teams, intramural sports, and recreational activities.

Disabled Students: 95% of the campus is accessible. Facilities include wheelchair ramps, elevators, special parking, specially equipped restrooms, lowered drinking fountains, lowered telephones, and special housing.

Services: Counseling and information services are available, as is tutoring in most subjects. There is a reader service for the blind.

Campus Safety and Security: Measures include 24-hour foot and vehicle patrol, emergency notification system, self-defense education, and security escort services. There are shuttle buses, emergency telephones, lighted pathways/sidewalks, and controlled access to dorms/residences.

Programs of Study: ESF confers B.S. and B.L.A. degrees. Associates, master's, and doctoral degrees are also awarded. Bachelor's degrees are awarded in AGRICULTURE (animal science, environmental studies, fishing and fisheries, forest engineering, forestry and related sciences, natural resource management, plant science, soil science, and wood science), BIOLOGICAL SCIENCE (biology/biological science, biotechnology, botany, ecology, entomology, environmental biology, microbiology, molecular biology, plant genetics, plant pathology, plant physiology, and wildlife biology), COMPUTER AND PHYSICAL SCIENCE (chemistry and polymer science), EDUCATION (environmental education and science education), ENGINEERING AND ENVIRONMENTAL DESIGN (chemical engineering, construction management, environmental design, environmental engineering, environmental science, landscape architecture/design, paper and pulp science, paper engineering, and survey and mapping technology), HEALTH PROFESSIONS (predentistry, premedicine, and prepharmacy), SOCIAL SCIENCE (prelaw). Engineering, chemistry, and biology are the strongest academically. Environmental and forest biology, landscape architecture, and environmental science are the largest.

Required: Students must complete 125 to 130 credit hours for the B.S. (160 for the B.L.A.), including 60 in the major, with a minimum 2.0 GPA. Courses in chemistry, English, math, and biology or physics are required.

Special: Cross-registration is offered with Syracuse University. Co-op programs, internships, and dual options in forest ecosystem science are available. Study abroad is available in landscape architecture and through Syracuse University. There is an honors program for outstanding students. There is 1 national honor society, a freshman honors program, and 8 departmental honors programs.

Faculty/Classroom: 72% of faculty are male; 28% are female. All teach and do research. No introductory courses are taught by graduate students. The average class size in a regular course is 25.

Admissions: 43% of the 2009-2010 applicants were accepted. The SAT scores for the 2009-2010 freshman class were: Critical Reading--7% below 500, 50% between 500 and 599, 37% between 600 and 700, and 6% above 700; Math--5% below 500, 44% between 500 and 599, 46% between 600 and 700, and 5% above 700. The ACT scores were 6% below 21, 29% between 21 and 23, 35% between 24 and 26, 21% between 27 and 28, and 9% above 28. 77% of the current freshmen were in the top fifth of their class; 96% were in the top two fifths. There was 1 National Merit finalist.

Requirements: The SAT or ACT is required. In addition, applicants are required to have a minimum of 3 years of math and science, including chemistry, in a college preparatory curriculum. A supplemental application form, essay and results of SAT or ACT exams are required. A campus visit, letters of recommendation, and a personal portfolio or resume are recommended. ESF requires applicants to be in the upper 50% of their class. A GPA of 85.0 is required. AP and CLEP credits are accepted. Important factors in the admissions decision are advanced placement or honors courses, leadership record, and extracurricular activities record.

Procedure: Freshmen are admitted fall and spring. Entrance exams should be taken by October of the senior year. There are early admissions, deferred admissions, and rolling admissions plans. Check with the school for current application deadlines. The application fee is $40. Notifications are sent March 1. Applications are accepted on-line. 70 applicants were on a recent waiting list, 20 were accepted.

Transfer: 226 transfer students enrolled in 2008-2009. Transfer requirements vary by major. Students must successfully complete prerequisite course work and must have a 2.5 or higher GPA to be considered. 24 of 125 credits required for the bachelor's degree must be completed at ESF.

Visiting: There are regularly scheduled orientations for prospective students, including a fall open house, which provides campus tours, faculty sessions, an activities fair, and student affairs presentations. There are guides for informal visits and visitors may sit in on classes. To schedule a visit, contact the Admissions Office at (315) 470-6600.

Financial Aid: In 2009-2010, 85% of all full-time freshmen and 85% of continuing full-time students received some form of financial aid. 80% of all full-time freshmen and 80% of continuing full-time students received need-based aid. The average freshmen award was $7,200, with $1,500 ($3,000 maximum) from need-based scholarships or need-based grants; $4,250 ($5,500 maximum) from need-based self-help aid (loans and jobs); and $4,500 ($6,000 maximum) from other non-need-based awards and non-need-based scholarships. 75% of undergraduate students work part-time. Average annual earnings from campus work are $1400. The average financial indebtedness of the 2009 graduate was $21,125. ESF is a member of CSS. The FAFSA is required. The priority date for freshman financial aid applications for fall entry is March 1.

International Students: There are 11 international students enrolled. They must take the TOEFL with a minimum score of 550 on the paper-based TOEFL (PBT) or 79 on the Internet-based version (iBT). They must also take the SAT or ACT.

Computers: All ESF students are provided e-mail addresses. All student housing has wireless and Internet access. Wireless is accessible at several locations on campus. The college has over 120 computers available in 4 computing labs for student use. All students may access the system any time. There are no time limits and no fees. Students enrolled in landscape architecture must have a personal computer.

Graduates: From July 1, 2008 to June 30, 2009, 286 bachelor's degrees were awarded. The most popular majors were environmental and forest biology (47%), environmental studies (20%), and landscape architecture (9%). 40 companies recruited on campus in 2008-2009. In an average class, 3% graduate in 3 years or less, 60% graduate in 4 years or less, 71% graduate in 5 years or less, and 72% graduate in 6 years or less. Of the 2008 graduating class, 16% were enrolled in graduate school within 6 months of graduation, and 61% were employed.

Admissions Contact: Susan H. Sanford, Director of Admissions and Inter-Institutional Relations. A campus DVD is available. E-Mail: *esfinfo@esf.edu* Web: *www.esf.edu*

STATE UNIVERSITY OF NEW YORK/COLLEGE OF TECHNOLOGY AT ALFRED   B-4

Alfred, NY 14802

(607) 587-4215
(800) 4-ALFRED; (607) 587-4299

Full-time: 2040 men, 1005 women	Faculty: III, -$
Part-time: 55 men, 220 women	Ph.D.s: n/av
Graduate: none	Student/Faculty: n/av
Year: semesters, summer session	Tuition: $6200 ($12,200)
Application Deadline: see pofile	Room & Board: $9000
Freshman Class: n/av	
SAT or ACT: required	COMPETITIVE

The State University of New York College of Technology at Alfred, founded in 1908, is a public institution conferring associate and bachelor's degrees. The figures in the above capsule and in this profile are approximate. There are 3 undergraduate schools. In addition to regional accreditation, Alfred State College has baccalaureate program accreditation with ABET. The 2 libraries contain 61,500 volumes, 8,148 audio/video tapes/CDs/DVDs, and subscribe to 5,500 periodicals including electronic. Computerized library services include interlibrary loans, database searching, Internet access, and laptop Internet portals. Special learning facilities include a learning resource center and radio station. The 150-acre campus is in a rural area 15 miles north of Pennsylvania, 75 miles south of Rochester, and 90 miles southeast of Buffalo. Including any residence halls, there are 49 buildings.

Student Life: 97% of undergraduates are from New York. Others are from 7 states, 12 foreign countries, and Canada. 89% are white. 34% are Catholic; 30% Protestant; 27% claim no religious affiliation. The average age of freshmen is 18; all undergraduates, 19. 52% remain to graduate.

Housing: College-sponsored housing includes coed dorms and on-campus apartments. In addition, there are honors houses, special-interest houses, wellness, computerized, and adult housing. On-campus housing is guaranteed for all 4 years. 70% of students live on campus; of those, 50% remain on campus on weekends. Alcohol is not permitted. All students may keep cars.

Activities: There are 3 local fraternities and 4 local sororities. There are 62 groups on campus including, band, cheerleading, chess, choir, chorale, chorus, computers, dance, drama, ethnic, gay, honors, international, jazz band, literary magazine, musical theater, newspaper, peer education network, pep band, professional, radio and TV, rescue and response team, social, social service, student government, and yearbook. Popular campus events include Family Weekend and Hot Dog Day.

Sports: There are 10 intercollegiate sports for men and 8 for women, and 26 intramural sports for men and 23 for women. Facilities include a fitness center/weight room, an indoor swimming pool, a wrestling room, a full gym, tennis courts, an outdoor track, baseball and softball fields, and practice fields.

Disabled Students: All of the campus is accessible. Facilities include wheelchair ramps, elevators, special parking, specially equipped restrooms, special class scheduling, lowered drinking fountains, lowered telephones, and special housing.

Services: Counseling and information services are available, as is tutoring in most subjects. There is a reader service for the blind, and remedial math, reading, and writing.

Campus Safety and Security: Measures include 24-hour foot and vehicle patrol, self-defense education, and security escort services. There are shuttle buses, emergency telephones, and lighted pathways/sidewalks.

Programs of Study: Alfred State College confers B.S., B.B.A., and B.T. degrees. Associates degrees are also awarded. Bachelor's degrees are awarded in BUSINESS (banking and finance), COMPUTER AND PHYSICAL SCIENCE (information sciences and systems), ENGINEER-

ING AND ENVIRONMENTAL DESIGN (architectural technology, computer technology, construction management, electrical/electronics engineering technology, electromechanical technology, manufacturing technology, mechanical engineering technology, survey and mapping technology, and technological management). Engineering Technology programs are the strongest academically and the largest.

Required: To graduate, candidates for a bachelor's degree must complete a total of 120 credits. A core sequence, including courses in math, physical sciences, and liberal studies, and a year-long senior technical project, are required. A phys ed course is also required.

Special: Cross-registration is offered with Alfred University, Houghton College, Rochester area colleges, and the Western New York Consortium. On-campus work-study programs are available, as are summer internships. There are 2 national honor societies, a freshman honors program, and 52 departmental honors programs.

Faculty/Classroom: 66% of faculty are male; 34% are female. All teach undergraduates. No introductory courses are taught by graduate students. The average class size in an introductory lecture is 40; in a laboratory is 20; and in a regular course is 20.

Requirements: The SAT or ACT is required. In addition, applicants must have graduated from an accredited secondary school or earned a GED. Specific course requirements vary by curriculum. A portfolio is required for applicants interested in computer art and design and Digital Media and Animation. AP and CLEP credits are accepted. Important factors in the admissions decision are parents or siblings attended your school, extracurricular activities record, and leadership record.

Procedure: Freshmen are admitted to all sessions. Entrance exams should be taken November 1 (rolling). There is a rolling admissions plan. Application deadlines are open. Application fee is $40. Notifications are sent November 1. Applications are accepted on-line. A waiting list is maintained.

Transfer: Transfer applicants must have a minimum 2.4 GPA. 30 of 120 credits required for the bachelor's degree must be completed at Alfred State College.

Visiting: There are regularly scheduled orientations for prospective students, including open houses during the fall and spring semesters. All aspects of the campus are open for visitation, and accepted students are invited to participate in an overnight visit. There are guides for informal visits; visitors may sit in on classes and stay overnight. To schedule a visit, contact the Admissions Office at 1-800-4-ALFRED.

Financial Aid: In a recent year, 80% of all full-time freshmen received some form of financial aid. 80% of all full-time freshmen and 80% of continuing full-time students received need-based aid. The average freshmen award was $8,000. 40% of undergraduate students worked part-time. Average annual earnings from campus work were $1000. The average financial indebtedness of the 2009 graduate was $6,000. The FAFSA is required. Check with the school for current application deadlines.

International Students: There were 30 international students enrolled in a recent year. They must take the TOEFL.

Computers: Wireless access is available. Alfred State maintains 4 proctored general access laboratories, open 24/7. All services on the campus network are available in the general access laboratories. Additional labs have more software programs available. All students may access the system. There are no time limits and no fees. All students are required to have a personal computer. Students enrolled in construction engineering technology, surveying engineering technology, technology must have a personal computer.

Admissions Contact: Deborah Goodrich, Associate Vice President for Enrollment Management. E-Mail: *admissions@alfredstate.edu* Web: *www.alfredstate.edu*

STATE UNIVERSITY OF NEW YORK/EMPIRE STATE COLLEGE   D-3

Saratoga Springs, NY 12866-4390   (518) 587-2100, ext. 2214
(800) 847-3000; (518) 580-9759

Full-time: 1559 men, 3317 women	Faculty: 149; IIB, -$
Part-time: 3823 men, 4700 women	Ph.D.s: 96%
Graduate: 388 men, 538 women	Student/Faculty: 33 to 1
Year: trimesters, summer session	Tuition: $5195 ($13,095)
Application Deadline: June 1	
Freshman Class: n/av	SPECIAL

Empire State College, founded in 1971, part of the State University of New York, offers degree programs in the arts and sciences through its statewide network of regional centers and units. It operates on a five-term calendar, with September, November, January, March, and May terms.The needs of adult learners are met through guided independent study, distance learning, study groups, cross-registration, and credit for lifelong learning. Computerized library services include interlibrary loans and database searching. Special learning facilities include a learning resource center and a technology building.

Student Life: 94% of undergraduates are from New York. Others are from 16 states, 10 foreign countries, and Canada. 61% are white; 13%

African American. The average age of freshmen is 29; all undergraduates, 36. 6% remain to graduate.

Housing: There are no residence halls. All students commute.

Activities: There are no fraternities or sororities. There are 2 groups on campus, a literary magazine and student government. Regional centers sponsor events and outside speakers throughout the year.

Sports: There is no sports program at Empire State College.

Disabled Students: 85% of the campus is accessible.

Programs of Study: Empire State College confers B.A., B.S., and B.P.S. degrees. Associates and master's degrees are also awarded. Bachelor's degrees are awarded in BUSINESS (business administration and management, labor studies, and management science), COMPUTER AND PHYSICAL SCIENCE (mathematics and science), EDUCATION (education), SOCIAL SCIENCE (community services, economics, history, human development, humanities and social science, interdisciplinary studies, liberal arts/general studies, and sociology). Business, management, and economics are the largest.

Required: Students must earn 128 credits, including 24 in their major and 30 credits that meet SUNY general education requirements, to graduate. Degree programs are customized and will vary in content.

Special: Empire State College offers cross-registration with numerous consortiums and institutions in New York State, internships in government, business, nonprofits, and academia, and study abroad in Greece, Lebanon, Czech Republic, Albania, and Dominican Republic. Accelerated degrees and dual and student-designed majors are possible in all programs. Nondegree study, credit for life, military, and work experience is possible.

Faculty/Classroom: 40% of faculty are male; 60% are female. 99% teach undergraduates, and 1% do both. No introductory courses are taught by graduate students.

Requirements: Applicants must be high school graduates, have a GED, or show ability to succeed at the college level. Empire State College also considers the ability of a learning location to meet individual needs. AP and CLEP credits are accepted. Important factors in the admissions decision are recommendations by school officials and personality/intangible qualities.

Procedure: Freshmen are admitted to all sessions. Entrance exams should be taken. There is a rolling admissions plan. Applications should be filed by June 1 for fall entry, November 1 for winter entry, January 1 for spring entry, and March 1 for summer entry. Applications are accepted on-line.

Transfer: 2309 transfer students enrolled in 2008-2009. Empire State College offers maximum flexibility to transfer applicants, who must provide official transcripts from previous colleges attended. 32 of 128 credits required for the bachelor's degree must be completed at Empire State College.

Visiting: There are regularly scheduled orientations for prospective students, by invitation, after students attend an information session. There are guides for informal visits. To schedule a visit, contact Melanie Kaiser at (518) 587-2100, ext. 2447.

Financial Aid: In 2009-2010, 50% of all full-time freshmen and 50% of continuing full-time students received some form of financial aid. 50% of all full-time freshmen and 50% of continuing full-time students received need-based aid. The average financial indebtedness of the 2009 graduate was $22,000. The FAFSA is required. Check with the school for current application deadlines.

International Students: There are 233 international students enrolled. They must take the TOEFL.

Computers: Students can access college resources and their student records via the college Web site. All students may access the system. 24 hours a day. There are no time limits and no fees. It is strongly recommended that all students have a personal computer.

Graduates: From July 1, 2008 to June 30, 2009, 2014 bachelor's degrees were awarded. The most popular majors were business, management, and economics (40%), community and human services (22%), and science, math, and technology (7%).

Admissions Contact: Jennifer D'Agostino, Director of Admissions. A campus DVD is available. E-Mail: *admissions@esc.edu* Web: *www.esc.edu*

STATE UNIVERSITY OF NEW YORK/INSTITUTE OF TECHNOLOGY   C-3

Utica, NY 13504

(315) 792-7500
1-866-2SUNYIT; (315) 792-7837

Full-time: 997 men, 549 women	Faculty: 78
Part-time: 197 men, 559 women	Ph.D.s: 76%
Graduate: 316 men, 279 women	Student/Faculty: 18 to 1
Year: semesters, summer session	Tuition: $6090 ($13,990)
Application Deadline: August 1	Room & Board: $8750
Freshman Class: 1770 applied, 678 accepted, 203 enrolled	
SAT CR/M: 500/550	ACT: 23 COMPETITIVE

The State University of New York/Institute of Technology, founded in 1966, is a public institution offering programs in technology and professional studies. There are 4 undergraduate schools and 4 graduate schools. In addition to regional accreditation, SUNYIT has baccalaureate program accreditation with AACSB and ABET. The library contains 200,730 volumes, 65,899 microform items, and 11,762 audio/video tapes/CDs/DVDs, and subscribes to 372 periodicals including electronic. Computerized library services include interlibrary loans, database searching, Internet access, and laptop Internet portals. Special learning facilities include a learning resource center, art gallery, radio station, and TV station. The 850-acre campus is in a suburban area at the western end of Mohawk Valley. Including any residence halls, there are 7 buildings.

Student Life: 98% of undergraduates are from New York. Others are from 11 states and 14 foreign countries. 85% are white. The average age of freshmen is 18; all undergraduates, 27. 30% do not continue beyond their first year; 50% remain to graduate.

Housing: 584 students can be accommodated in college housing, which includes coed dorms and special-interest houses. On-campus housing is guaranteed for the freshman year only, is available on a first-come, first-served basis, and is available on a lottery system for upperclassmen. Priority is given to out-of-town students. 80% of students commute. All students may keep cars.

Activities: There are no fraternities or sororities. There are 38 groups on campus, including computers, environmental, ethnic, international, jazz band, newspaper, professional, radio and TV, social, and student government. Popular campus events include Fall Fest Weekend, Diwali and Holi Festivals, and Apocalypse Week.

Sports: There are 7 intercollegiate sports for men and 7 for women, and 10 intramural sports for men and 10 for women. Facilities include indoor and outdoor facilities, fitness center, pool, fitness trail, outside fields, and a gym with indoor track.

Disabled Students: 99% of the campus is accessible. Facilities include wheelchair ramps, elevators, special parking, specially equipped restrooms, lowered drinking fountains, lowered telephones, and special housing.

Services: Counseling and information services are available, as is tutoring in most subjects. There is a reader service for the blind, and remedial math, reading, and writing.

Campus Safety and Security: Measures include 24-hour foot and vehicle patrol, emergency notification system, self-defense education, and security escort services. There are emergency telephones, lighted pathways/sidewalks, and emergency call boxes.

Programs of Study: SUNYIT confers B.A., B.S., B.B.A., and B.P.S. degrees. Master's degrees are also awarded. Bachelor's degrees are awarded in BUSINESS (accounting, banking and finance, and business administration and management), COMMUNICATIONS AND THE ARTS (communications technology and telecommunications), COMPUTER AND PHYSICAL SCIENCE (applied mathematics and computer science), ENGINEERING AND ENVIRONMENTAL DESIGN (civil engineering technology, computer technology, electrical/electronics engineering, electrical/electronics engineering technology, industrial engineering, and mechanical engineering technology), HEALTH PROFESSIONS (health, health care administration, and nursing), SOCIAL SCIENCE (criminal justice, liberal arts/general studies, psychology, and sociology). Engineering technology, computer science, and business are the largest.

Required: Students must meet general education requirements and complete 124 to 128 credit hours to graduate.

Special: SUNYIT offers cross-registration with the Mohawk Valley Consortium, internships, and work study. An accelerated degree program in nursing, telecommunications, and computer information science is possible, and there is a joint program in electrical engineering with Binghamton University. There are 2 national honor societies.

Faculty/Classroom: 66% of faculty are male; 34% are female. No introductory courses are taught by graduate students. The average class size in an introductory lecture is 24 and in a regular course, 18.

Admissions: 38% of the 2009-2010 applicants were accepted. The SAT scores for the 2009-2010 freshman class were: Critical Reading--44% below 500, 40% between 500 and 599, 15% between 600 and 700, and 1% above 700; Math--14% below 500, 60% between 500 and 599, 24% between 600 and 700, and 2% above 700. The ACT scores were 2% below 21, 45% between 21 and 23, 24% between 24 and 26,

3% between 27 and 28, and 8% above 28. 28% of the current freshmen were in the top fifth of their class; 62% were in the top two fifths. 1 freshman graduated first in the class.

Requirements: The SAT or ACT is required. In addition, test scores, essay, and supplemental application are required. A GPA of 3.2 is required. AP and CLEP credits are accepted. Important factors in the admissions decision are advanced placement or honors courses, evidence of special talent, and recommendations by school officials.

Procedure: Freshmen are admitted fall and spring. Entrance exams should be taken by April of year applicant intends to enroll. There are early admissions, deferred admissions, and rolling admissions plans. Application deadlines are open. Application fee is $40. Notifications are sent December 15. Applications are accepted on-line.

Transfer: 646 transfer students enrolled in 2008-2009. Transfer students generally must present a minimum cumulative GPA of 2.5 or better. Applicants presenting a GPA below 2.5 will be considered on an individual basis. 30 of 124 to 128 credits required for the bachelor's degree must be completed at SUNYIT.

Visiting: There are regularly scheduled orientations for prospective students. There are guides for informal visits; visitors may sit in on classes and stay overnight. To schedule a visit, contact the Admissions Office.

Financial Aid: In 2009-2010, 91% of all full-time freshmen and 87% of continuing full-time students received some form of financial aid. 72% of all full-time freshmen and 71% of continuing full-time students received need-based aid. Need-based scholarships or need-based grants averaged $6232 ($14,161 maximum); need-based self-help aid (loans and jobs) averaged $5463 ($9415 maximum); and non-need-based awards and non-need-based scholarships averaged $1884 ($6000 maximum). 7% of undergraduate students work part-time. Average annual earnings from campus work are $1298. The FAFSA and the state aid form are required. The priority date for freshman financial aid applications for fall entry is March 15.

International Students: The school actively recruits international students. They must take the TOEFL with a minimum score of 550 on the paper-based TOEFL (PBT) or 76 on the Internet-based version (iBT). First-time, full-time students must also take the SAT or ACT.

Computers: Wireless access is available. There are 120 computers across 8 labs with Internet access that all students may use. There are 290 PCs across 19 special purpose labs that are available to students of specific majors or enrolled in specific courses. 4 of those labs (70 PCs) are not networked by design. All students may access the system anytime. There are no time limits and no fees.

Graduates: From July 1, 2008 to June 30, 2009, 384 bachelor's degrees were awarded. The most popular majors were business administration (17%), nursing (14%), and computer science (13%). 72 companies recruited on campus in 2008-2009.

Admissions Contact: Jennifer Phelan-Ninh, Director of Admissions. E-mail: *admissions@sunyit.edu* Web: *www.sunyit.edu*

STATE UNIVERSITY OF NEW YORK/MARITIME COLLEGE
D-5

Throgs Neck, NY 10465

(718) 409-7221
(800) 642-1874; (718) 409-7465

Full-time: 1326 men, 137 women	**Faculty:** 69; IIA, -$
Part-time: 97 men, 15 women	**Ph.D.s:** 49%
Graduate: 151 men, 31 women	**Student/Faculty:** 21 to 1
Year: semesters, summer session	**Tuition:** $6090 ($13,990)
Application Deadline: open	**Room & Board:** $9930
Freshman Class: 1397 applied, 888 accepted, 356 enrolled	
SAT CR/M: 510/550	**ACT:** 22	**COMPETITIVE**

The Maritime College of the State University of New York, founded in 1874, is a public institution that prepares students for the U.S. Merchant Marine officers' license and for bachelor's degrees in engineering, naval architecture, marine environmental science, and marine transportation/business administration. In addition to regional accreditation, New York Maritime has baccalaureate program accreditation with ABET. The library contains 85,984 volumes, 28,400 microform items, and 774 audio/video tapes/CDs/DVDs, and subscribes to 38,735 periodicals including electronic. Computerized library services include interlibrary loans, database searching, and Internet access. Special learning facilities include a learning resource center, a 17,000-ton training ship, a tug, a barge, and a center for simulated marine operations, which contains bridge, radar, tanker, and oil spill response simulators. The 52-acre campus is in a suburban area on the Throgs Neck peninsula where Long Island Sound meets the East River. Including any residence halls, there are 31 buildings.

Student Life: 65% of undergraduates are from New York. Others are from 28 states, and 20 foreign countries. 70% are from public schools. 71% are white. The average age of freshmen is 19; all undergraduates, 21. 23% do not continue beyond their first year; 77% remain to graduate.

Housing: 1281 students can be accommodated in college housing, which includes single-sex and coed dorms. On-campus housing is guar-

anteed for all 4 years, is available on a first-come, first-served basis. 82% of students live on campus; of those; 25% remain on campus on weekends. Alcohol is not permitted. Upperclassmen may keep cars.

Activities: There are no fraternities or sororities. There are 30 groups on campus, including art, bagpipe, band, chorus, computers, drill team, ethnic, honors, international, jazz band, marching band, newspaper, pep band, photography, political, professional, religious, social, social service, and student government. Popular campus events include Thursdays in the TIV, Ring Dance, and Super Bowl Party.

Sports: There are 9 intercollegiate sports for men and 9 for women, and 6 intramural sports for men and 6 for women. Facilities include an athletic center containing a 2000-seat gym, a swimming pool, exercise and weight rooms, a rifle and pistol range, and 3 handball/racquetball and squash courts; a sailing center; and football, baseball, lacrosse, and soccer fields.

Disabled Students: 81% of the campus is accessible. Facilities include wheelchair ramps, elevators, special parking, and specially equipped rest rooms.

Services: Counseling and information services are available, as is tutoring in every subject.

Campus Safety and Security: Measures include 24-hour foot and vehicle patrol, emergency notification system, self-defense education, and security escort services. There are emergency telephones, lighted pathways/sidewalks, and controlled access to dorms/residences.

Programs of Study: New York Maritime confers B.S. and B.E. degrees. Associates and master's degrees are also awarded. Bachelor's degrees are awarded in BIOLOGICAL SCIENCE (marine science), BUSINESS (business administration and management and transportation management), COMPUTER AND PHYSICAL SCIENCE (atmospheric sciences and meteorology), ENGINEERING AND ENVIRONMENTAL DESIGN (electrical/electronics engineering, engineering, environmental science, marine engineering, maritime science, and naval architecture and marine engineering), SOCIAL SCIENCE (humanities). Marine operations, marine environmental science, and electrical engineering are the strongest academically. Marine transportation, marine engineering, and international transportation and trade are the largest.

Required: Bachelor's degree candidates must earn 126 to 181 credit hours, with a GPA of 2.0 and distribution requirements vary by the major. If pursuing the U.S. Merchant Marine officers' license, all students must spend 3 summer semesters at sea acquiring hands-on experience aboard the college's training vessel.

Special: The college offers co-op programs in engineering, an accelerated degree program in marine transportation/transportation management, and internships as cadet observers aboard commercial ships. There are 2 national honor societies, a freshman honors program, and 2 departmental honors programs.

Faculty/Classroom: 89% of faculty are male; 11% are female. 96% teach undergraduates, and 20% do both. No introductory courses are taught by graduate students. The average class size in an introductory lecture is 28; in a laboratory is 16; and in a regular course is 30.

Admissions: 64% of the 2009-2010 applicants were accepted. The SAT scores for the 2009-2010 freshman class were: Critical Reading--42% below 500, 45% between 500 and 599, 11% between 600 and 700, and 2% above 700; Math--20% below 500, 52% between 500 and 599, 26% between 600 and 700, and 2% above 700. The ACT scores were 35% below 21, 40% between 21 and 23, 16% between 24 and 26, 4% between 27 and 28, and 5% above 28. 19% of the current freshmen were in the top fifth of their class; 52% were in the top two fifths.

Requirements: The SAT is required. In addition, applicants must be high school graduates or hold a GED. 16 Carnegie units are required, including 4 years of English, 3 of math (4 are preferred), and 1 of physics or chemistry. An essay is required and an interview is recommended. A GPA of 80.0 is required. AP and CLEP credits are accepted. Important factors in the admissions decision are advanced placement or honors courses, extracurricular activities record, and leadership record.

Procedure: Freshmen are admitted fall and spring. Entrance exams should be taken during the junior or senior year. There are early decision, early admissions, deferred admissions, and rolling admissions plans. Early decision applications should be filed by November 15; check with the school for current application deadlines. The application fee is $40. Notification of early decision is sent December 15. Applications are accepted on-line.

Transfer: 77 transfer students enrolled in 2008-2009. Transfer students must have a 2.5 GPA.

Visiting: There are regularly scheduled orientations for prospective students, including a tour of the campus and facilities and meetings with faculty and students. There are guides for informal visits, visitors may sit in on classes, and stay overnight. To schedule a visit, contact the Admissions Office at admissions@sunymaritime.edu.

Financial Aid: In 2009-2010, 77% of all full-time freshmen and 80% of continuing full-time students received some form of financial aid. 44% of all full-time freshmen and 47% of continuing full-time students received need-based aid. The average financial indebtedness of the 2009 graduate was $17,345. The FAFSA and the college's own financial statement, and student and parent federal income tax returns are required. The priority date for freshman financial aid applications for fall entry is March 1. The deadline for filing freshman financial aid applications for fall entry is July 15.

International Students: There are 94 international students enrolled. The school actively recruits these students. They must take the TOEFL and the SAT or ACT.

Computers: Each student has access to 5 public computer labs within the science and engineering building, which is wireless. The library and fort classrooms are also wireless. All students may access the system from 8:30 A.M. to 11 P.M. The computer center stays open after 11 P.M. when there is sufficient demand. There are no time limits. The fee is $267 per year.

Graduates: From July 1, 2008 to June 30, 2009, 306 bachelor's degrees were awarded. The most popular majors were marine transportation (30%), international transportation and trade (18%), and naval architecture (9%). 22 companies recruited on campus in 2008-2009. In an average class, 31% graduate in 4 years or less, 47% graduate in 5 years or less, and 49% graduate in 6 years or less. Of the 2008 graduating class, 4% were enrolled in graduate school within 6 months of graduation, and 100% were employed.

Admissions Contact: Jonathan White, Dean of Admissions. A campus DVD is available. E-Mail: *sunymaritime.edu*
Web: *www.sunymaritime.edu*

STATE UNIVERSITY OF NEW YORK/UNIVERSITY AT ALBANY   D-3

Albany, NY 12222 (518) 442-5435; (518) 442-5383

Full-time: 6353 men, 5966 women	Faculty: 520; I, av$
Part-time: 417 men, 378 women	Ph.D.s: 95%
Graduate: 1896 men, 3010 women	Student/Faculty: 24 to 1
Year: semesters, summer session	Tuition: $6748 ($14,648)
Application Deadline: March 1	Room & Board: $10,238
Freshman Class: 20,249 applied, 10,442 accepted, 2333 enrolled	
SAT CR/M: 560/590	ACT: 25 VERY COMPETITIVE

The State University of New York/University at Albany, established in 1844, is a public institution conferring undergraduate and graduate degrees in humanities and fine arts, science and math, social and behavioral sciences, business, public policy, education, and social welfare. There are 8 undergraduate schools and 9 graduate schools. In addition to regional accreditation, University at Albany has baccalaureate program accreditation with AACSB, CSWE, and TEAC. The 3 libraries contain 2.2 million volumes, 2.9 million microform items, and 18,088 audio/video tapes/CDs/DVDs, and subscribe to 29,247 periodicals including electronic. Computerized library services include interlibrary loans, database searching, Internet access, and laptop Internet portals. Special learning facilities include a learning resource center, art gallery, radio station, linear accelerator, sophisticated weather data system, national lightning detection system, interactive media center, extensive art studios, state-of-the-art electronic library, and the Northeast Regional Forensic Institute (NERFI). The 560-acre campus is in a suburban area about 5 miles west of downtown Albany. Including any residence halls, there are 166 buildings.

Student Life: 95% of undergraduates are from New York. Others are from 38 states, 53 foreign countries, and Canada. 57% are white. The average age of freshmen is 18; all undergraduates, 21. 15% do not continue beyond their first year; 63% remain to graduate.

Housing: 7400 students can be accommodated in college housing, which includes coed dorms, on-campus apartments, and married student housing. In addition, there are honors houses, language houses, and special-interest houses. On-campus housing is available on a first-come, first-served basis and is available on a lottery system for upperclassmen. Priority is given to out-of-town students. 57% of students live on campus. Alcohol is not permitted. Upperclassmen may keep cars.

Activities: 2% of men belong to 11 national fraternities; 4% of women belong to 1 local and 16 national sororities. There are 200 groups on campus, including band, chamber singers, cheerleading, chess, chorale, computers, dance, debate, drama, electronic music ensemble, environmental, ethnic, film, gay, honors, international, jazz band, literary magazine, musical theater, newspaper, orchestra, pep band, percussion ensemble, photography, political, professional, radio and TV, religious, social, social service, student government, symphony, and yearbook. Popular campus events include outdoor concerts, Springtime Fountain Festival, and Clash of the Quads.

Sports: There are 8 intercollegiate sports for men and 11 for women, and 8 intramural sports for men and 8 for women. Facilities include a gym with an Olympic-size pool, an ancillary gym with a quarter-mile track, football, softball, soccer, and practice fields, an all-weather lacrosse field, and a 5000-seat recreation and convocation center.

Disabled Students: 99% of the campus is accessible. Facilities include wheelchair ramps, elevators, special parking, specially equipped restrooms, lowered drinking fountains, and lowered telephones. Disabled Student Services provides a broad range of personalized services to peo-

ple with disabilities, including preadmission information and accessible housing information.

Services: Counseling and information services are available, as is tutoring in most subjects. There is a reader service for the blind. The Excel program provides low-income and first-generation college students with a variety of mentoring, tutorial, and counseling services.

Campus Safety and Security: Measures include 24-hour foot and vehicle patrol, emergency notification system, self-defense education, and security escort services. There are shuttle buses, emergency telephones, and lighted pathways/sidewalks.

Programs of Study: University at Albany confers B.A. and B.S. degrees. Master's and doctoral degrees are also awarded. Bachelor's degrees are awarded in AGRICULTURE (environmental studies), BIOLOGICAL SCIENCE (biochemistry, biology/biological science, and molecular biology), BUSINESS (accounting and business administration and management), COMMUNICATIONS AND THE ARTS (art history and appreciation, Chinese, communications, dramatic arts, English, fine arts, French, Hebrew, Italian, Latin, linguistics, music, Russian, Spanish, and studio art), COMPUTER AND PHYSICAL SCIENCE (actuarial science, applied mathematics, atmospheric sciences and meteorology, chemistry, computer science, earth science, information sciences and systems, mathematics, and physics), ENGINEERING AND ENVIRONMENTAL DESIGN (materials engineering, materials science, and urban design), HEALTH PROFESSIONS (predentistry and premedicine), SOCIAL SCIENCE (African American studies, anthropology, Asian/Oriental studies, Caribbean studies, classical/ancient civilization, criminal justice, East Asian studies, Eastern European studies, economics, geography, Hispanic American studies, history, interdisciplinary studies, Latin American studies, medieval studies, philosophy, political science/government, prelaw, psychology, religion, Russian and Slavic studies, social work, sociology, and women's studies). Criminal justice, accounting, and public administration and policy are the strongest academically. Business, psychology, and communication and rhetoric are the largest.

Required: To graduate, students must complete a total of 120 credits with a 2.0 GPA in their major and minor, including 30 to 36 credits required in the major for a B.A. degree and 30 to 42 credits for a B.S. degree. B.A. degree candidates must complete 90 credits in liberal arts courses, and B.S. candidates must complete 60. The general education program at the University at Albany consists of a minimum of 30 credits of course work in the following areas: disciplinary perspectives, cultural and historical perspectives, and communication and reasoning competencies.

Special: Cross-registration is available with Rensselaer Polytechnic Institute, Albany Law School, and Union, Siena, and Russell Sage Colleges. Internships may be arranged with state government agencies and private organizations. Study abroad in many countries, a Washington semester, B.A.-B.S. degrees, and work-study programs are offered. Dual and student-designed majors, nondegree study, and pass/fail grading options are available. There are accelerated 5-year bachelor's/master's programs in 40 fields; most arts and sciences fields may be combined with an accelerated M.B.A. A 3-2 engineering degree with 1 of 4 institutions is also possible. There are 15 national honor societies, including Phi Beta Kappa, a freshman honors program, and 30 departmental honors programs.

Faculty/Classroom: 59% of faculty are male; 41% are female. 95% teach undergraduates, and 75% do research. Graduate students teach 15% of introductory courses. The average class size in an introductory lecture is 34; in a laboratory, 20; and in a regular course, 28.

Admissions: 52% of the 2009-2010 applicants were accepted. The SAT scores for the 2009-2010 freshman class were: Critical Reading--10% below 500, 60% between 500 and 599, 27% between 600 and 700, and 3% above 700; Math--4% below 500, 51% between 500 and 599, 41% between 600 and 700, and 4% above 700. The ACT scores were 1% below 21, 29% between 21 and 23, 39% between 24 and 26, 21% between 27 and 28, and 10% above 28. 48% of the current freshmen were in the top fifth of their class; 87% were in the top two fifths.

Requirements: The SAT or ACT is required. In addition, applicants must be graduates of an accredited secondary school or have a GED. 18 academic credits are required, including 2 to 3 units of math, 2 units of lab sciences, and 1 unit of foreign language study. AP and CLEP credits are accepted. Important factors in the admissions decision are advanced placement or honors courses, personality/intangible qualities, and leadership record.

Procedure: Freshmen are admitted fall, spring, and summer. Entrance exams should be taken by November of the senior year. There are early decision, deferred admissions, and rolling admissions plans. Early decision applications should be filed by November 15; regular applications, by March 1 for fall entry, December 1 for spring entry, and May 1 for summer entry, along with a $40 fee. Notification of early decision is sent January 1. Applications are accepted on-line. A waiting list is maintained.

Transfer: 1369 transfer students enrolled in 2008-2009. Admission to certain programs is competitive and based not only on a required GPA but also on completion of a certain set of prerequisite core courses. A grade average of B or better is required for applicants to the accounting, business administration, criminal justice, and social welfare programs. 30

of 120 credits required for the bachelor's degree must be completed at University at Albany.

Visiting: There are regularly scheduled orientations for prospective students, including a 2-day summer orientation session. There are guides for informal visits, and visitors may sit in on classes. To schedule a visit, contact the Undergraduate Admissions Office.

Financial Aid: In 2009-2010, 65% of all full-time freshmen and 62% of continuing full-time students received some form of financial aid. 54% of all full-time freshmen and 56% of continuing full-time students received need-based aid. The average freshman award was $9698. Need-based scholarships or need-based grants averaged $6331; need-based self-help aid (loans and jobs) averaged $4501; non-need-based athletic scholarships averaged $9764; and other non-need-based awards and non-need-based scholarships averaged $3445. 9% of undergraduate students work part-time. The FAFSA is required, and New York state residents should apply for TAP on-line at *http://www.tapweb.org*. The priority date for freshman financial aid applications for fall entry is March 15.

International Students: There are 356 international students enrolled. The school actively recruits these students. They must take the TOEFL with a minimum score of 550 on the paper-based TOEFL (PBT) or 79 on the Internet-based version (iBT). International students may submit SAT, ACT, or TOEFL results.

Computers: Wireless access is available. Wireless high-speed Internet connections are available in dorm rooms and in other select locations. Students without a wireless network interface card (NIC) can check one out at the circulation desk for use in the library. All students may access the system. There are no time limits and no fees.

Graduates: From July 1, 2008 to June 30, 2009, 2896 bachelor's degrees were awarded. The most popular majors were business (16%), psychology (12%), and communication and rhetoric (10%). 140 companies recruited on campus in 2008-2009. In an average class, 53% graduate in 4 years or less, 62% graduate in 5 years or less, and 63% graduate in 6 years or less. Of the 2008 graduating class, 51% were enrolled in graduate school within 6 months of graduation, and 43% were employed.

Admissions Contact: Robert Andrea, Director, Undergraduate Admissions. E-mail: *ugadmissions@albany.edu* Web: *www.albany.edu*

STATE UNIVERSITY OF NEW YORK/UNIVERSITY AT BUFFALO
(See University at Buffalo/State University of New York)

STATE UNIVERSITY OF NEW YORK/UNIVERSITY AT NEW PALTZ	D-4
New Paltz, NY 12561-2443	(845) 257-3200; (845) 257-3209
Full-time: 1690 men, 3585 women	Faculty: IIA, -$
Part-time: 295 men, 560 women	Ph.D.s: n/av
Graduate: 490 men, 940 women	Student/Faculty: n/av
Year: semesters, summer session	Tuition: $6010 ($13,910)
Application Deadline: April 1	Room & Board: $9000
Freshman Class: n/av	
SAT or ACT: required	COMPETITIVE

State University of New York/University at New Paltz, founded in 1828, is a public institution offering undergraduate and graduate programs in the liberal arts and sciences, business, education, engineering, fine and performing arts, and the health professions. The figures in the above capsule and in this profile are approximate. There are 5 undergraduate schools and 1 graduate school. In addition to regional accreditation, SUNY New Paltz has baccalaureate program accreditation with ABET, CSAB, NASAD, NASM, and NCATE. The library contains 499,048 volumes, 1.2 million microform items, and 4,030 audio/video tapes/CDs/DVDs, and subscribes to 32,361 periodicals including electronic. Computerized library services include interlibrary loans, database searching, Internet access, and laptop Internet portals. Special learning facilities include a learning resource center, planetarium, radio station, TV station, greenhouse, robotics lab, electron microscope facility, speech and hearing clinic, art museum, music therapy training facility, observatory, Fournier transform mass spectrometer, honors center, electronic media center, electronic classroom, and an IBM e-business virtual lab. The 216-acre campus is in a small town 100 miles north of New York City and 65 miles south of Albany. Including any residence halls, there are 53 buildings.

Student Life: 92% of undergraduates are from New York. Others are from 28 states, 48 foreign countries, and Canada. 90% are from public schools. 58% are white. The average age of freshmen is 18; all undergraduates, 20. 16% do not continue beyond their first year; 59% remain to graduate.

Housing: 2800 students can be accommodated in college housing, which includes coed dorms. In addition, there are special-interest houses. On-campus housing is guaranteed for the freshman year only, is available on a first-come, and first-served basis. Priority is given to out-

of-town students. 51% of students live on campus; of those, 90% remain on campus on weekends. Upperclassmen may keep cars.

Activities: 3% of men belong to 5 local and 5 national fraternities; 2% of women belong to 5 local and 8 national sororities. There are 136 groups on campus, including art, band, cheerleading, chess, choir, chorale, chorus, computers, dance, drama, ethnic, gay, honors, international, jazz band, literary magazine, musical theater, newspaper, orchestra, photography, political, professional, radio and TV, religious, social, social service, student government, and yearbook. Popular campus events include Spirit Weekend, New Paltz Summer Repertory Theater, and Rainbow Month.

Sports: There are 9 intercollegiate sports for men and 11 for women, and 12 intramural sports for men and 9 for women. Facilities include a gym with a swimming pool, numerous playing fields, a 35,000-square-foot air-supported structure for tennis, jogging, volleyball, and basketball, and 24 outdoor tennis courts.

Disabled Students: 90% of the campus is accessible. Facilities include wheelchair ramps, elevators, special parking, specially equipped restrooms, special class scheduling, lowered drinking fountains, lowered telephones, and special housing.

Services: Counseling and information services are available, as is tutoring in most subjects. There is a reader service for the blind, and remedial math, reading, and writing.

Campus Safety and Security: Measures include 24-hour foot and vehicle patrol, self-defense education, and security escort services. There are emergency telephones, lighted pathways/sidewalks, a bicycle patrol, locked residence halls, and a campus 911 system.

Programs of Study: SUNY New Paltz confers B.A., B.S., and B.F.A. degrees. Master's degrees are also awarded. Bachelor's degrees are awarded in BIOLOGICAL SCIENCE (biology/biological science), BUSINESS (accounting, banking and finance, business administration and management, international business management, and marketing/retailing/merchandising), COMMUNICATIONS AND THE ARTS (art history and appreciation, communications, dramatic arts, English, French, German, graphic design, journalism, metal/jewelry, music, painting, photography, sculpture, Spanish, speech/debate/rhetoric, studio art, theater design, and visual and performing arts), COMPUTER AND PHYSICAL SCIENCE (chemistry, computer science, environmental geology, geology, mathematics, and physics), EDUCATION (art education, early childhood education, elementary education, English education, foreign languages education, mathematics education, middle school education, science education, secondary education, and social studies education), ENGINEERING AND ENVIRONMENTAL DESIGN (computer engineering, electrical/electronics engineering, and woodworking), HEALTH PROFESSIONS (music therapy, nursing, and speech pathology/audiology), SOCIAL SCIENCE (African American studies, anthropology, Asian/Oriental studies, economics, geography, history, international relations, Latin American studies, liberal arts/general studies, philosophy, political science/government, psychology, social science, sociology, and women's studies). Business, computer science, and math are the strongest academically. Business, visual arts, and elementary education are the largest.

Required: To graduate, students must complete a minimum of 120 credits with a 2.0 GPA. The core curriculum of 16 to 17 credits includes courses in English composition, math and analytical skills, and modern world studies. The number of credits required in the major varies. Distribution requirements include courses in cultures and civilizations, American experience, social sciences, physical and biological sciences, foreign languages, and aesthetic expression, 1 writing-intensive course in the major, and 60 credits in upper-division courses. New York State Teacher Competency Exams are required of education majors. Engineering students must complete a senior project, and art majors must show their work in a senior exhibition.

Special: There is cross-registration with the Mid-Hudson Consortium of Colleges. The university offers co-op programs and internships in most majors, work-study programs on campus and at the Children's Center of New Paltz, and opportunities for student-designed or dual majors. Students may study abroad in 18 countries. A 3-2 advanced degree in environmental biology is offered with SUNY Environmental Science and Forestry. There are 7-year medical and optometry accelerated degree programs. B.A.-B.S. degrees are offered in liberal arts and science, education, business, science and, engineering, and fine and performing arts. There are 4 national honor societies, a freshman honors program, and 6 departmental honors programs.

Faculty/Classroom: 45% of faculty are male; 55% are female. 97% do both. Graduate students teach 1% of introductory courses. The average class size in an introductory lecture is 19; in a laboratory is 10; and in a regular course is 19.

Requirements: The SAT or ACT is required. In addition, 4 units each of English, and social studies, 3 to 4 units each of mathematics and science, including 2 units of lab science, and 2 to 4 units of foreign language are required. The GED is accepted but must be accompanied by a high school transcript and SAT or ACT scores. SUNY New Paltz requires applicants to be in the upper 50% of their class. A GPA of 3.0 is required. AP and CLEP credits are accepted. Important factors in the admissions decision are advanced placement or honors courses, recommendations by school officials, and evidence of special talent.

Procedure: Freshmen are admitted in the fall. Entrance exams should be taken before December 31. There are early admissions, deferred admissions, and rolling admissions plans. Applications should be filed by April 1 for fall entry. The fall 2009 application fee was $40. Notification is sent on a rolling basis. Applications are accepted on-line. A waiting list is maintained.

Transfer: 1011 transfer students enrolled in a recent year. To be considered, applicants must have maintained a minimum GPA of 2.75 in all previous college work at accredited institutions. Some programs require a higher GPA for consideration. 30 of 120 credits required for the bachelor's degree must be completed at SUNY New Paltz.

Visiting: There are regularly scheduled orientations for prospective students, including daily information sessions and campus tours. Visitors may sit in on classes. To schedule a visit, contact the Admissions Office.

Financial Aid: In a recent year, 70% of all full-time freshmen and 75% of continuing full-time students received some form of financial aid. 55% of all full-time freshmen and 75% of continuing full-time students received need-based aid. The average freshmen award was $5,500. 45% of undergraduate students worked part-time. Average annual earnings from campus work are $900. The average financial indebtedness of the 2009 graduate was $19,000. The FAFSA is required. Check with the school for current application deadlines.

International Students: There were 219 international students enrolled in a recent year. The school actively recruits these students. They must take the TOEFL with a minimum score of 550 on the paper-based TOEFL (PBT) or 80 on the Internet-based version (iBT), or take the SAT, or demonstrate English Proficiency. Conditional acceptance is available to both graduate and undergraduate students. Accepted students must take a placement test upon arrival at SUNY New Paltz. If the student is not yet proficient, he or she must take ESL courses until required proficiency is achieved.

Computers: Wireless access is available. All students may access the system 24 hours a day. There are no time limits and no fees. It is strongly recommended that all students have a personal computer.

Graduates: In recent year, 1592 bachelor's degrees were awarded. The most popular majors were education (21%), business and marketing (14%), and social science (11%). 135 companies recruited on campus in 2008-2009. In an average class, 36% graduate in 4 years or less, 59% graduate in 5 years or less, and 61% graduate in 6 years or less.

Admissions Contact: Kimberly Lavoie, Director of Freshman/ International Admissions. E-Mail: *admissions@newpaltz.edu* Web: *www.newpaltz.edu*

STATE UNIVERSITY OF NEW YORK/UNIVERSITY AT STONY BROOK
E-5

Stony Brook, NY 11794	**(631) 632-6868; 631) 632-9027**
Full-time: 7883 men, 7241 women	**Faculty:** 949; I, av$
Part-time: 578 men, 693 women	**Ph.D.s:** 98%
Graduate: 3510 men, 4787 women	**Student/Faculty:** 16 to 1
Year: semesters, summer session	**Tuition:** $6488 ($14,388)
Application Deadline: March 1	**Room & Board:** $9590
Freshman Class: 28587 applied, 11411 accepted, 2806 enrolled	
SAT CR/M/W: 580/630/580	**ACT:** 26 **HIGHLY COMPETITIVE**

Stony Brook University, founded in 1957, and part of the State University of New York, is a public institution offering degree programs in arts and sciences, engineering and applied sciences, business, journalism, marine sciences and environmental studies, nursing, health technology and management, and social work. Professional programs in medicine are offered at the graduate level. There are 9 undergraduate schools and 10 graduate schools. In addition to regional accreditation, Stony Brook University has baccalaureate program accreditation with ABET, ADA, APTA, CAAHEP, CAHEA, CSWE, and NLN. The 7 libraries contain 2.5 million volumes, 3.8 million microform items, and 52,872 audio/video tapes/CDs/DVDs, and subscribe to 64,803 periodicals including electronic. Computerized library services include interlibrary loans, database searching, and Internet access. Special learning facilities include a learning resource center, art gallery, radio station, TV station, The Museum of Long Island Natural Sciences, and the Fine Arts Center, which has an 1100-seat main theater, a 400-seat recital hall, and 3 experimental theaters. The 1450-acre campus is in a suburban area on Long Island, 60 miles from New York City. Including any residence halls, there are 200 buildings.

Student Life: 86% of undergraduates are from New York. Others are from 45 states, 99 foreign countries, and Canada. 89% are from public schools. 36% are white; 22% Asian American. 35% are Catholic; 26% Buddhist, Islamic, Mormon, Eastern Orthodox, Hindu, Baptist; 16% claim no religious affiliation; 15% Protestant. The average age of freshmen is 18; all undergraduates, 21. 11% do not continue beyond their first year; 66% remain to graduate.

Housing: 9903 students can be accommodated in college housing, which includes coed dorms, on-campus apartments, and married student housing. In addition, there are honors houses, special-interest houses, and a choice of undergraduate colleges that integrate academic experience with living environments. On-campus housing is guaranteed for all 4 years. 55% of students live on campus; of those, 65% remain on campus on weekends. Alcohol is not permitted. Upperclassmen may keep cars.

Activities: 2% of men belong to 1 local fraternity and 15 national fraternities; 2% of women belong to 2 local and 12 national sororities. There are 284 groups on campus, including band, cheerleading, choir, chorale, dance, drama, ethnic, film, gay, honors, international, jazz band, literary magazine, marching band, musical theater, newspaper, opera, orchestra, pep band, photography, political, professional, radio and TV, religious, social, and student government. Popular campus events include Fall Fest, Opening Week Activities, and Caribbean Weekend.

Sports: There are 10 intercollegiate sports for men and 10 for women, and 19 intramural sports for men and 19 for women. Facilities include an indoor sports complex housing a 4000-seat arena, an 1800-seat gym, a swimming pool, 6 squash and 8 racquetball courts, a dance studio, and exercise and universal gym rooms. Outdoor facilities include an 8100-seat stadium, a 500-seat softball facility, a 1000-seat baseball facility, 12 tennis courts, 2 multi-sport practice facilities, 2 recreationsl basketball and 4 handball courts, 2 recreational softball fields, and a multi-sport recreational area.

Disabled Students: 85% of the campus is accessible. Facilities include wheelchair ramps, elevators, special parking, specially equipped restrooms, special class scheduling, lowered drinking fountains, lowered telephones, special housing, and automatic door openers.

Services: There is a reader service for the blind, and remedial math and writing.

Campus Safety and Security: Measures include 24-hour foot and vehicle patrol, self-defense education, and security escort services. There are shuttle buses, emergency telephones, lighted pathways/sidewalks, a campus Crime Stoppers program, building access through use of cards, and controlled campus access after midnight.

Programs of Study: Stony Brook University confers B.A., B.S., and B.E. degrees. Master's and doctoral degrees are also awarded. Bachelor's degrees are awarded in AGRICULTURE (environmental studies), BIOLOGICAL SCIENCE (biochemistry, biology/biological science, ecology, and marine biology), BUSINESS (business administration and management), COMMUNICATIONS AND THE ARTS (art history and appreciation, comparative literature, dramatic arts, English, film arts, Germanic languages and literature, linguistics, music, Russian languages and literature, and studio art), COMPUTER AND PHYSICAL SCIENCE (applied mathematics, astronomy, atmospheric sciences and meteorology, chemistry, computer science, earth science, geology, information sciences and systems, mathematics, and physics), EDUCATION (athletic training), ENGINEERING AND ENVIRONMENTAL DESIGN (biomedical engineering, chemical engineering, computer engineering, electrical/ electronics engineering, engineering and applied science, engineering chemistry, environmental design, environmental science, mechanical engineering, and technological management), HEALTH PROFESSIONS (clinical science, cytotechnology, health science, nursing, occupational therapy, pharmacology, physical therapy, and respiratory therapy), SOCIAL SCIENCE (African studies, American studies, anthropology, Asian/ American studies, economics, ethnic studies, European studies, French studies, history, humanities, interdisciplinary studies, Italian studies, liberal arts/general studies, philosophy, political science/government, psychology, religion, social science, social work, sociology, Spanish studies, and women's studies). Biology, business management, and economics are the strongest academically. Psychology, history, and biochemistry are the largest.

Required: To graduate, students must have a minimum 2.0 GPA in 120 credit hours (B.A. and B.S.) or 128 (B.E.). The required number of hours in the major varies. At least 39 credits must be earned in upper-division courses. Students must take 14 to 16 courses to satisfy general education requirements in writing and quantitative reasoning skills, literary and philosophic analysis, exposure to the arts, disciplinary diversity, the interrelationship of science and society, and 3 culminating multicultural requirements. Arts and sciences majors must fulfill a foreign language requirement, unless completed through advanced high-school study. Other requirements vary by school.

Special: Cross-registration may be arranged through the Long Island Regional Advisory Council for Higher Education. The university offers a Washington semester and internships with a variety of government, legal, and social agencies, with hospitals and clinics, and in business and industry. The URECA Program allows undergraduates to work with faculty on research and creative projects. An accelerated degree program in nursing, dual majors, student-designed majors, a national student exchange program, and study abroad in 20 countries are available. Other academic opportunities include a scholars for medicine program, women in science, engineering program, and honors college. There are 6 national honor societies, including Phi Beta Kappa, a freshman honors program, and 30 departmental honors programs.

Faculty/Classroom: 62% of faculty are male; 38% are female. No introductory courses are taught by graduate students. The average class size in an introductory lecture is 46; in a laboratory is 21; and in a regular course is 45.

Admissions: 40% of the 2009-2010 applicants were accepted. The SAT scores for the 2009-2010 freshman class were: Critical Reading--17% below 500, 49% between 500 and 599, 38% between 600 and 700, and 5% above 700; Math--2% below 500, 25% between 500 and 599, 58% between 600 and 700, and 15% above 700; Writing--11% below 500, 46% between 500 and 599, 38% between 600 and 700, and 5% above 700. The ACT scores were 2% below 21, 12% between 21 and 23, 41% between 24 and 26, 21% between 27 and 28, and 24% above 28. 59% of the current freshmen were in the top fifth of their class; 86% were in the top two fifths. There were 2 National Merit finalists. 23 freshmen graduated first in their class.

Requirements: The SAT is required. In addition, applicants must be graduates of an accredited secondary school or have a GED certificate. 16 or 17 academic credits are required, including 4 years each of English and social studies, 3 or 4 of math, 3 of science (4 for engineering majors), and 2 or 3 of a foreign language. One letter of recommendation and supplemental application, including and essay, are required. 3 SAT Subject tests, an essay, and an interview are recommended. AP and CLEP credits are accepted. Important factors in the admissions decision are advanced placement or honors courses, extracurricular activities record, and evidence of special talent.

Procedure: Freshmen are admitted fall and spring. Entrance exams should be taken during the junior year or in the fall of the senior year. There are deferred admissions and rolling admissions plans. Applications should be filed by March 1 for fall entry and November 1 for spring entry. The fall 2009 application fee was $40. Notifications are sent March 1. 948 applicants were on the 2009 waiting list; 130 were admitted. Applications are accepted on-line.

Transfer: 1878 transfer students enrolled in 2008-2009. Applicants must have a minimum 2.5 GPA. An associate degree and an interview are recommended. Other requirements vary by program. Applicants who have earned fewer than 24 college credits must submit a high school transcript. 36 of 120 credits required for the bachelor's degree must be completed at Stony Brook University.

Visiting: There are regularly scheduled orientations for prospective students. There are guides for informal visits, and visitors may sit in on classes and stay overnight. To schedule a visit, contact the Admissions Office online at www.stonybrook.edu/ugadmissions.

Financial Aid: In 2009-2010, 74% of all full-time freshmen and 65% of continuing full-time students received some form of financial aid. 55% of all full-time freshmen and 53% of continuing full-time students received need-based aid. The average freshman award was $9,514, with $6,858 ($13,795 maximum) from need-based scholarships or need-based grants; $3,538 ($6,800 maximum) from need-based self-help aid (loans and jobs); $14,762 ($26,835 maximum) from non-need-based athletic scholarships; and $4,016 ($23,979 maximum) from other non-need-based awards and non-need-based scholarships. 13% of undergraduate students work part-time. Average annual earnings from campus work are $2208. The average financial indebtedness of the 2009 graduate was $17,524. Stony Brook University is a member of CSS. The FAFSA and the state aid form are required. The deadline for filing freshman financial aid applications for fall entry is March 1.

International Students: There are 1182 international students enrolled. They must take the TOEFL with a minimum score of 550 on the paper-based TOEFL (PBT) or 80 on the Internet-based version (iBT), and the SAT critical reading or the IELTS.

Computers: Wireless access is available. Network access is available in dorm rooms and lounges. All students may access the system 24 hours a day. There are no time limits and no fees.

Graduates: From July 1, 2008 to June 30, 2009, 3264 bachelor's degrees were awarded. The most popular majors were psychology (12%), biology (11%), and business management (9%). 455 companies recruited on campus in 2008-2009. In an average class, 44% graduate in 4 years or less, 62% graduate in 5 years or less, and 66% graduate in 6 years or less. Of the 2008 graduating class, 34% were enrolled in graduate school within 6 months of graduation, and 76% were employed.

Admissions Contact: Judith Burke-Berhanan E-Mail: enroll@stonybrook.edu Web: www.stonybrook.edu

SYRACUSE UNIVERSITY — C-3

Syracuse, NY 13244 (315) 443-3611

Full-time: 5255 men, 6476 women	Faculty: 911; I, -$
Part-time: 40 men, 25 women	Ph.Ds: 87%
Graduate: 2787 men, 3094 women	Student/Faculty: 14 to 1
Year: semesters, summer session	Tuition: $34,926
Application Deadline: January 1	Room & Board: $12,374
Freshman Class: 20951 applied, 12596 accepted, 3267 enrolled	
SAT or ACT: required	HIGHLY COMPETITIVE

Syracuse University, founded in 1870, is a private institution offering nearly 200 undergraduate programs in liberal arts, architecture, education, engineering and computer science, human ecology (including child and family studies, health and wellness, hospitality management, marriage and family therapy, nutrition sciences and dietetics, sport management, and social work); information management and technology; management; public communications; and visual and performing arts (including art, music, drama, and communication and rhetorical studies). SU is also noted for the quality of its internships, study abroad experiences, and partnerships. There are 9 undergraduate schools and 11 graduate schools. In addition to regional accreditation, Syracuse has baccalaureate program accreditation with ABET, ACEJMC, CSWE, FIDER, NAAB, NASAD, NASM, and NCATE. The 6 libraries contain 3.2 million volumes, 7.5 million microform items, and 1.1 million audio/video tapes/CDs/DVDs, and subscribe to 39,703 periodicals including electronic. Computerized library services include interlibrary loans, database searching, Internet access, and laptop Internet portals. Special learning facilities include a learning resource center, art gallery, radio station, TV station, the Global Collaboratory connecting students via satellite to sites all over the world, media laboratories for Web-based news reporting and broadcast journalism and a digital convergence center, the Syracuse Center of Excellence in Environmental and Energy Systems, a life sciences complex for interdisciplinary research and education, an advanced flight simulator for students in aerospace engineering, the Ballentine Investment Institute in the Whitman School of Management, an art building with studios and film, video, photo, and computer graphic labs, a technology center, a professional Equity theater, the Mary Ann Shaw Center for Public Service, a child development laboratory school, an audio laboratory, a writing center, a math clinic, and a speech, language, and hearing clinic. The 200-acre campus is in an urban area approximately 280 miles northwest of New York City. Including any residence halls, there are 232 buildings.

Student Life: 53% of undergraduates are from out of state, mostly the Northeast. Students are from 50 states, 62 foreign countries, and Canada. 75% are from public schools. 62% are white. 47% claim no religious affiliation; 23% Catholic; 14% Protestant; 12% Jewish. The average age of freshmen is 18; all undergraduates, 20. 9% do not continue beyond their first year; 82% remain to graduate.

Housing: 8075 students can be accommodated in college housing, which includes coed dorms, on-campus apartments, and married student housing. In addition, there are language houses, special-interest houses, and fraternity houses. There are single-sex floors and wings of residence halls. Learning communities and theme/interest housing are available. On-campus housing is guaranteed for freshmen and sophomores and is available on a lottery system for upperclassmen. 75% of students live on campus; of those, 85% remain on campus on weekends. Alcohol is not permitted. Upperclassmen may keep cars.

Activities: 16% of men belong to 29 national fraternities; 24% of women belong to 19 national sororities. There are 347 groups on campus, including art, band, cheerleading, chess, choir, chorale, chorus, computers, dance, debate, drama, environmental, ethnic, film, forensics, gay, honors, international, jazz band, literary magazine, marching band, musical theater, newspaper, orchestra, pep band, photography, political, professional, radio and TV, religious, social, social service, special interest, student government, symphony, and yearbook. Popular campus events include Block Party, Dance Works Annual Production, and First Year Players Annual Production.

Sports: There are 8 intercollegiate sports for men and 12 for women, and 12 intramural sports for men and 12 for women. Facilities include 4 gyms, 2 swimming pools, weight rooms, tennis courts, exercise rooms, a dance studio, courts for racquet sports, an indoor track, grass playing fields, multiple outdoor artificial turf fields, an outdoor track, a soccer stadium, and a softball stadium. There also are gymnasiums, fitness centers, and an ice skating pavilion. The multipurpose domed stadium seats 50,000 for football and 30,000 for basketball.

Disabled Students: 92% of the campus is accessible. Facilities include wheelchair ramps, elevators, special parking, specially equipped restrooms, special class scheduling, lowered drinking fountains, lowered telephones, and special housing.

Services: Counseling and information services are available, as is tutoring in most subjects. There is a reader service for the blind. Additional academic support services are available through programs in schools and colleges, individual departments and programs, and residence halls.

Campus Safety and Security: Measures include 24-hour foot and vehicle patrol, emergency notification system, self-defense education, and security escort services. There are shuttle buses, emergency telephones, lighted pathways/sidewalks, and controlled access to dorms/residences. Other services include a comprehensive crisis alert system, a blue light security system placed throughout campus with a direct link to the Department of Public Safety Communications Center in case of an emergency, and off-campus patrols in student rental neighborhoods.

Programs of Study: Syracuse confers B.A., B.S., B.Arch., B.F.A. B.I.D., B. Mus., and B.P.S. degrees. Associates, master's, and doctoral degrees are also awarded. Bachelor's degrees are awarded in BIOLOGICAL SCIENCE (biology/biological science and nutrition), BUSINESS (banking and finance, business administration and management, entrepreneurial studies, hospitality management services, marketing management, real estate, retailing, sports management, and supply chain management), COMMUNICATIONS AND THE ARTS (advertising, art, art history and appreciation, broadcasting, ceramic art and design, classics, communications, comparative literature, dramatic arts, English, English literature, fiber/textiles/weaving, film arts, fine arts, French, Germanic languages and literature, graphic design, Greek, illustration, industrial design, journalism, linguistics, media arts, metal/jewelry, modern language, music, music business management, music history and appreciation, music performance, music theory and composition, musical theater, painting, percussion, photography, piano/organ, printmaking, public relations, Russian, sculpture, Spanish, speech/debate/rhetoric, strings, telecommunications, theater design, theater management, video, voice, and winds), COMPUTER AND PHYSICAL SCIENCE (chemistry, computer science, geology, information sciences and systems, mathematics, physics, and statistics), EDUCATION (art education, early childhood education, education, elementary education, English education, mathematics education, middle school education, music education, physical education, science education, social studies education, and special education), ENGINEERING AND ENVIRONMENTAL DESIGN (aeronautical engineering, architecture, bioengineering, chemical engineering, civil engineering, computer engineering, computer graphics, electrical/electronics engineering, engineering physics, environmental engineering, interior design, and mechanical engineering), HEALTH PROFESSIONS (health science, predentistry, premedicine, preveterinary science, public health, and speech pathology/audiology), SOCIAL SCIENCE (African American studies, American studies, anthropology, child care/child and family studies, classical/ancient civilization, economics, European studies, fashion design and technology, food production/management/services, geography, history, international relations, Italian studies, Latin American studies, Middle Eastern studies, philosophy, political science/government, prelaw, psychology, religion, Russian and Slavic studies, social work, sociology, and women's studies). Architecture, public communications, and life sciences are the strongest academically. Psychology, architecture, and information management are the largest.

Required: A minimum of 120 credits with a minimum GPA of 2.0 is required to graduate. Because students are admitted directly to individual schools and colleges, academic requirements vary by college and major.

Special: SU students are encouraged to undertake internships both during the academic year and during summers in the Syracuse community and across the nation, both for credit and not for credit. Cooperative education programs are available in engineering. Study abroad is available in 7 university-operated centers and through other special programs, and a Washington semester is offered through the International Relations Program. Work-study programs, dual majors, and student-designed majors are available. There are 9 national honor societies, including Phi Beta Kappa, and an honors program open to all undergraduates.

Faculty/Classroom: 59% of faculty are male; 41% are female. No introductory courses are taught by graduate students. The average class size in a laboratory is 20 and in a regular course is 24.

Admissions: 60% of the 2009-2010 applicants were accepted. The SAT scores for the 2009-2010 freshman class were: Critical Reading--18% below 500, 47% between 500 and 599, 29% between 600 and 700, and 6% above 700; Math--12% below 500, 37% between 500 and 599, 41% between 600 and 700, and 10% above 700. 62% of the current freshmen were in the top fifth of their class; 89% were in the top two fifths.

Requirements: The SAT or ACT is required. The ACT Optional Writing test is also required. In addition, applicants should have a strong college preparatory record from an accredited secondary school or have a GED equivalent. Essays are required. A portfolio is required for art and architecture majors, and an audition is required for music and drama majors. A secondary school counselor evaluation, or 2 academic recommendations, and a high school transcript, are also required. AP credits are accepted. Important factors in the admissions decision are advanced placement or honors courses, evidence of special talent, and leadership record.

Procedure: Freshmen are admitted fall and spring. Entrance exams should be taken before January of the senior year for regular decision and before November of the senior year for early decision. There are early decision, early admissions and deferred admissions plans. Early decision applications should be filed by November 15; regular applications, by January 1 for fall entry and November 15 for spring entry. The fall 2009 application fee was $70. Notification of early decision is sent in December; regular decision, mid-March. Applications are accepted on-line. 1,150 applicants were on a recent waiting list, 504 were accepted.

Transfer: 318 transfer students enrolled in 2008-2009. Applicants must submit 2 academic recommendations from professors, official copies of college transcripts, a personal essay, and a descriptive statement about their college experience and their interest in SU; SAT or ACT scores and secondary school transcripts are required for applicants with fewer than 30 credit hours. A portfolio is required for art and architecture majors and an audition for music and drama majors. The number of credits that must be completed at Syracuse for the bachelor's degree varies by program.

Visiting: There are regularly scheduled orientations for prospective students, including information programs on admissions and financial aid, a campus and facilities tour, and personal interviews. There are guides for informal visits, and visitors may sit in on classes and stay overnight. To schedule a visit, contact the Office of Admissions at 315-443-3611.

Financial Aid: In 2009-2010, 80% of all full-time freshmen and 80% of continuing full-time students received some form of financial aid. 60% of all full-time freshmen and 60% of continuing full-time students received need-based aid. The average freshmen award was $32,500. 40% of undergraduate students work part-time. Average annual earnings from campus work are $2500. The average financial indebtedness of the 2009 graduate was $28,358. Syracuse is a member of CSS. The CSS/Profile and FAFSA are required. The deadline for filing freshman financial aid applications for fall entry is February 1.

International Students: There are 714 international students enrolled. The school actively recruits these students. They must take the TOEFL with a minimum score of 550 on the paper-based TOEFL (PBT) or 80 on the Internet-based version (iBT). They must also take the SAT or ACT.

Computers: High-speed wired and wireless Internet access is available in residence halls, academic/administrative buildings and adjacent grounds on campus. There are more than 3400 computers available in over 100 specified computer labs, computer teaching labs/classrooms and collaborative spaces, as well as in 172 technology classrooms. All students may access the system 24 hours per day. There are no time limits and no fees. It is strongly recommended that all students have a personal computer.

Graduates: From July 1, 2008 to June 30, 2009, 2670 bachelor's degrees were awarded. The most popular majors were business and marketing (21%), social sciences (13%), and visual and performing arts (12%). 230 companies recruited on campus in 2008-2009. In an average class, 70% graduate in 4 years or less, 79% graduate in 5 years or less, and 80% graduate in 6 years or less. Of the 2008 graduating class, 18% were enrolled in graduate school within 6 months of graduation, and 94% were employed.

Admissions Contact: Susan E. Donovan, Dean of Admissions. A campus DVD is available. E-Mail: *orange@syr.edu* Web: *www.syr.edu*

TOURO COLLEGE D-5

New York, NY 10010   (718) 252-7800, ext. 399; (718) 253-9455

Full-time: 2810 men, 5110 women	Faculty: n/av
Part-time: 910 men, 910 women	Ph.D.s: n/av
Graduate: 2285 men, 4580 women	Student/Faculty: n/av
Year: semesters, summer session	Tuition: $13,550
Application Deadline: open	Room & Board: $9600
Freshman Class: n/av	
SAT or ACT: recommended	COMPETITIVE

Touro College, founded in 1971, is a private institution offering undergraduate programs primarily through the Lander College of Liberal Arts and Sciences, the School of General Studies, and the School of Health Sciences. Campuses are in midtown Manhattan, Brooklyn, and Queens. The figures in the above capsule and in this profile are approximate. There are 6 undergraduate schools and 7 graduate schools. In addition to regional accreditation, has baccalaureate program accreditation with APTA and CAHEA. The 11 libraries contain 271,509 volumes, 14,100 microform items, and 4,054 audio/video tapes/CDs/DVDs, and subscribe to 3,163 periodicals including electronic. Computerized library services include interlibrary loans and database searching. Special learning facilities include a learning resource center. The campus is in an urban area. Including any residence halls, there are 12 buildings.

Student Life: 95% of undergraduates are from New York. Others are from 25 states, 30 foreign countries, and Canada. 27% do not continue beyond their first year; 47% remain to graduate.

Housing: 200 students can be accommodated in college housing, which includes single-sex dorms, on-campus apartments, and off-campus apartments. On-campus housing is available on a first-come and first-served basis. Priority is given to out-of-town students. Alcohol is not permitted. No one may keep cars.

Activities: There are no fraternities or sororities. There are 8 groups on campus, including computers, debate, literary magazine, newspaper, political, professional, religious, social, student government, and yearbook. Popular campus events include a student-sponsored lecture series and student-faculty social events.

Sports: Facilities include 1 baseball field, 2 tennis courts, and 2 basketball courts.

Disabled Students: All of the campus is accessible. Facilities include wheelchair ramps, elevators, specially equipped restrooms, lowered drinking fountains, and lowered telephones.

Services: Counseling and information services are available, as is tutoring in some subjects, accounting, math, English, and natural sciences There is remedial math, reading, and writing.

Campus Safety and Security: Measures include 24-hour foot and vehicle patrol.

Programs of Study: confers B.A., B.S., and B.P.S. degrees. Associates, master's, and doctoral degrees are also awarded. Bachelor's degrees are awarded in BIOLOGICAL SCIENCE (biology/biological science), BUSINESS (accounting, banking and finance, business administration and management, management science, and marketing/retailing/merchandising), COMMUNICATIONS AND THE ARTS (English, Hebrew, literature, and speech/debate/rhetoric), COMPUTER AND PHYSICAL SCIENCE (chemistry, computer science, mathematics, and physics), EDUCATION (elementary education and special education), HEALTH PROFESSIONS (occupational therapy, physical therapy, predentistry, and premedicine), SOCIAL SCIENCE (economics, history, human services, interdisciplinary studies, Judaic studies, liberal arts/general studies, philosophy, political science/government, prelaw, psychology, social science, and sociology). Business/accounting, education, and health sciences are the strongest academically. Psychology, education, and business are the largest.

Required: To graduate, all students must complete at least 120 credit hours (varies by major), with 30 to 70 in the major. A minimum 2.0 GPA is required, with 2.3 in the major. Specific disciplines include Judaic studies or ethnic studies. Required courses include English composition, history, literature, math, and social and natural sciences.

Special: The college offers cross-registration with the Fashion Institute of Technology, internships for juniors and seniors, study abroad in Israel, work-study programs, interdisciplinary majors, an accelerated degree program, credit for life, military, and work experience, pass/fail options, and dual majors. Early and/or preferential admission to professional programs is also possible. There are 2 national honor societies.

Faculty/Classroom: 60% of faculty are male; 40% are female. No introductory courses are taught by graduate students. The average class size in an introductory lecture is 16; in a laboratory is 12; and in a regular course is 15.

Requirements: The SAT or ACT is recommended. In addition, applicants must be graduates of an accredited secondary school with a satisfactory high school average. A satisfactory SAT score is recommended. A GPA of 3.2 is required. AP and CLEP credits are accepted. Important factors in the admissions decision are advanced placement or honors courses, recommendations by school officials, and extracurricular activities record.

Procedure: Freshmen are admitted fall, spring, and summer. Entrance exams should be taken in May of the junior year or fall of the senior year. There are early admissions, deferred admissions, and rolling admissions plans. Application deadlines are open. Application fee is $50.

Transfer: A 2.5 GPA is required. If the student has less than 60 credits, high school documentation is also required. 45 of 120 credits required for the bachelor's degree must be completed at Touro.

Visiting: There are regularly scheduled orientations for prospective students. There are guides for informal visits; visitors may sit in on classes and stay overnight. To schedule a visit, contact Steven Toplan.

Financial Aid: The CSS/Profile is required. Check with the school for current application deadlines.

International Students: They must take the TOEFL and the college's own test.

Computers: All students may access the system.

Admissions Contact: Steven Toplan, Director of Admissions. E-Mail: lasadmit@admin.touro.edu Web: www.touro.edu

UNION COLLEGE   D-3

Schenectady, NY 12308-2311   (518) 388-6112
                                    (888) 843-6688; (518) 388-6986

Full-time: 1110 men, 1047 women	**Faculty:** 213; IIB, +$
Part-time: 16 men, 21 women	**Ph.D.s:** 96%
Graduate: none	**Student/Faculty:** 10 to 1
Year: trimesters	**Tuition:** $50,439

Application Deadline: January 15
Freshman Class: 4829 applied, 1987 accepted, 520 enrolled
SAT CR/M/W: 630/660/630   **ACT:** 28

HIGHLY COMPETITIVE+

Union College, founded in 1795, is an independent liberal arts and engineering college. In addition to regional accreditation, Union has baccalaureate program accreditation with ABET. The library contains 634,183 volumes, 760,258 microform items, and 13,501 audio/video tapes/CDs/DVDs, and subscribes to 12,500 periodicals including electronic. Computerized library services include interlibrary loans, database searching, and Internet access. Special learning facilities include a radio station, a theater, a high-tech classroom, a lab center, a multimedia auditorium, a music center, and an art, science, and history gallery. The 12-acre campus is in an urban area 15 miles west of Albany. Including any residence halls, there are 100 buildings.

Student Life: 59% of undergraduates are from out of state, mostly the Northeast. Students are from 39 states, 35 foreign countries, and Canada. 74% are from public schools. 79% are white. The average age of freshmen is 19; all undergraduates, 20. 8% do not continue beyond their first year; 85% remain to graduate.

Housing: 1925 students can be accommodated in college housing, which includes single-sex and coed dorms and on-campus apartments. In addition, there are language houses, special-interest houses, fraternity houses, sorority houses, 12 theme houses that emphasize various community atmospheres, and a substance-free focused study option. On-campus housing is available on a lottery system for upperclassmen. 87% of students live on campus; of those, 80% remain on campus on weekends. Upperclassmen may keep cars.

Activities: 32% of men belong to 13 national fraternities; 31% of women belong to 6 national sororities. There are 100 groups on campus, including art, band, cheerleading, chess, choir, computers, dance, debate, drama, environmental, ethnic, gay, honors, international, jazz band, literary magazine, newspaper, orchestra, photography, political, professional, radio and TV, religious, social, social service, and student government. Popular campus events include Commencement, Party in the Garden, and Spring Fest.

Sports: There are 12 intercollegiate sports for men and 13 for women, and 11 intramural sports for men and 4 for women. Facilities include a field house for volleyball, recreational basketball, indoor track, and intramural activities; 2 synthetic grass fields for soccer, football, field hockey, lacrosse, intramurals, and recreation; a basketball/volleyball facility; an ice rink; a gym that includes a weight room, a fitness center, racquetball/squash courts, an aerobics room, and a swimming pool; 8 outdoor tennis courts; an outdoor basketball/street hockey court; and a boathouse and docks.

Disabled Students: 60% of the campus is accessible. Facilities include wheelchair ramps, elevators, special parking, specially equipped rest rooms, special class scheduling, lowered drinking fountains, lowered telephones, and special housing.

Services: Counseling and information services are available, as is tutoring in most subjects, including science and math. A writing center and a language center are available.

Campus Safety and Security: Measures include 24-hour foot and vehicle patrol, emergency notification system, self-defense education, and security escort services. There are shuttle buses, emergency telephones, lighted pathways/sidewalks, controlled access to dorms/residences, 24-hour locked residence halls, emergency medical assistance, awareness programs, a bicycle patrol, a trolley escort service, a shuttle van, and a security measures sheet.

Programs of Study: Union confers B.A. and B.S degrees. Bachelor's degrees are awarded in AGRICULTURE (environmental studies), BIOLOGICAL SCIENCE (biochemistry, biology/biological science, and neurosciences), COMMUNICATIONS AND THE ARTS (classics, English, fine arts, modern language, and studio art), COMPUTER AND PHYSICAL SCIENCE (astronomy, chemistry, computer science, geology, mathematics, physics, and science), ENGINEERING AND ENVIRONMENTAL DESIGN (bioengineering, computer engineering, electrical/electronics engineering, environmental science, and mechanical engineering), SOCIAL SCIENCE (American studies, anthropology, Asian/Oriental studies, Caribbean studies, economics, French studies, German area studies, history, humanities, interdisciplinary studies, liberal arts/general studies, philosophy, political science/government, psychology, religion, social science, sociology, Spanish studies, and women's studies). Chemistry, history, and political science are the strongest academically. Political science, psychology, and economics are the largest.

Required: Students must complete a minimum of 36 term courses (engineering may require up to 40) and requirements in the major field, degree program, or interdepartmental major, including the major field examination and/or thesis, as applicable, and attain a minimum GPA of 1.8 overall and 2.0 in the major (and 2.0 in the minor if a minor has been declared).

Special: Cross-registration is permitted with the Hudson Mohawk Consortium. Opportunities are provided for legislative internships in Albany and Washington, D.C., pass/fail options, B.A.-B.S. degrees, dual and student-designed majors, accelerated degree programs in law and medicine, and study abroad in 22 countries. There are 14 national honor societies, including Phi Beta Kappa, a freshman honors program, and 19 departmental honors programs.

Faculty/Classroom: 56% of faculty are male; 44% are female. All teach undergraduates, and 97% do reseach and teach. No introductory courses are taught by graduate students. The average class size in an introductory lecture is 20, in a laboratory, 13, and in a regular course, 16.

Admissions: 41% of the 2009-2010 applicants were accepted. The SAT scores for the 2009-2010 freshman class were: Critical Reading--2% below 500, 27% between 500 and 599, 58% between 600 and 700, and 13% above 700; Math-- 17% between 500 and 599, 55% between 600 and 700, and 28% above 700; Writing--2% below 500, 30% between 500 and 599, 52% between 600 and 700, and 16% above 700. The ACT scores were 6% between 21 and 23, 59% between 24 and 26, and 35% above 28. 77% of the current freshmen were in the top fifth of their class; 96% were in the top two fifths.

Requirements: Testing is optional except for combined programs. Applicants for the Leadership in Medicine and Law and Public Policy programs are required to submit the SAT and two SAT Subject tests. Graduation from an accredited secondary school is required. Applicants must submit a minimum of 16 full-year credits, distributed as follows: 4 years of English, 2 year of a foreign language, 2 1/2 to 3 1/2 years of math, 2 years each of science and social studies, and the remainder in college-preparatory courses. Engineering and math majors are expected to have completed additional math and science courses beyond the minimum requirements. An essay is also required, and an interview is recommended. AP credits are accepted. Important factors in the admissions decision are advanced placement or honors courses, recommendations by school officials, and extracurricular activities record.

Procedure: Freshmen are admitted fall. Entrance exams should be taken by January of the senior year (December for applicants to the Leadership in Medicine and Law and Public Policy programs). There are early decision and deferred admissions plan. Early decision applications should be filed by November 15; regular applications, by January 15 for fall entry, along with a $50 fee. Notification of early decision is sent December 15; regular decision, April 1. Applications are accepted on-line. 840 applicants were on a recent waiting list, 109 were accepted.

Transfer: 34 transfer students enrolled in 2008-2009. A 3.0 GPA and 1 full year of college academic work are required. Transfer students must study at Union for at least 2 years. 18 of 36 credits required for the bachelor's degree must be completed at Union.

Visiting: There are regularly scheduled orientations for prospective students, including interviews and a tour of the campus. There are guides for informal visits and visitors may sit in on classes. To schedule a visit, contact the Admissions Office.

Financial Aid: In 2009-2010, 69% of all full-time freshmen and 67% of continuing full-time students received some form of financial aid. 57% of all full-time freshmen and 52% of continuing full-time students received need-based aid. The average freshmen award was $30,400, with $4500 ($7300 maximum) from need-based self-help aid (loans and jobs) and $10,000 ($12,500 maximum) from other non-need-based awards and non-need-based scholarships. 45% of undergraduate students work part-time. Average annual earnings from campus work are $1350. The average financial indebtedness of the 2009 graduate was $24,739. Union is a member of CSS. The CSS/Profile, the FAFSA, and the Noncustodial Profile and the Business/Farm Supplement are required. The deadline for filing freshman financial aid applications for fall entry is February 1.

International Students: There are 73 international students enrolled. The school actively recruits these students. They must take the TOEFL with a minimum score of 600 on the paper-based TOEFL (PBT) or 90 on the Internet-based version (iBT). It is recommended that they also take the SAT or 2 SAT Subject tests or the ACT.

Computers: Wireless access is available. There are more than 1500 personal computers and workstations on campus, including in classrooms, labs, offices, and public spaces. The college's network goes to every building on campus, and there are more than 2100 network connections in residence halls. All residence halls have wireless networking available in public and study areas. In addition, the college's wireless network extends to all public/study areas on campus, all classrooms, the library, and all academic buildings. There are also 37 electronic classrooms and 3 general-use computer labs. All students may access the system. at any time. There are no time limits and no fees.

Graduates: From July 1, 2008 to June 30, 2009, 530 bachelor's degrees were awarded. The most popular majors were political science (11%), economics (9%), and English (8%). In an average class, 80% graduate in 4 years or less, 85% graduate in 5 years or less, and 86% graduate in 6 years or less. Of the 2008 graduating class, 28% were enrolled in graduate school within 6 months of graduation and 65% were employed.

Admissions Contact: Ann Fleming Brown, Director of Admission. A campus DVD is available. E-Mail: *admissions@union.edu* Web: *www.union.edu*

UNITED STATES MERCHANT MARINE ACADEMY   D-5

Kings Point, NY 11024-1699   (516) 773-5391
                                  (866) 546-4778; (516) 773-5390

Full-time: 810 men, 120 women	Faculty: n/av
Part-time: none	Ph.D.s: n/av
Graduate: none	Student/Faculty: n/av
Year: varies	Tuition: $4000
Application Deadline: March 1	
Freshman Class: n/av	
SAT or ACT: required	**HIGHLY COMPETITIVE**

The United States Merchant Marine Academy, founded in 1943, is a publicly supported institution offering maritime, military, and engineering programs for the purpose of training officers for the U.S. merchant marine, the maritime industry, and the armed forces. Students make no conventional tuition and room/board payments. Required fees for freshmen are approximately $7,020; costs in subsequent years are less. The figures in the above capsule and in this profile are approximate. In addition to regional accreditation, Kings Point has baccalaureate program ac-

creditation with ABET. The library contains 202,567 volumes, 19,341 microform items, and 3,722 audio/video tapes/CDs/DVDs, and subscribes to 964 periodicals including electronic. Computerized library services include interlibrary loans, database searching, Internet access, and laptop Internet portals. Special learning facilities include a learning resource center, planetarium, and a maritime museum. The 82-acre campus is in a suburban area 19 miles east of midtown New York City. Including any residence halls, there are 28 buildings.

Student Life: 90% of undergraduates are from out of state, mostly the Middle Atlantic. Students are from 50 states, and 5 foreign countries. 74% are from public schools. 89% are white. 49% are Protestant; 38% Catholic. The average age of freshmen is 19; all undergraduates, 21. 8% do not continue beyond their first year; 92% remain to graduate.

Housing: All students are accommodated in college housing, which includes coed dorms. On-campus housing is guaranteed for all 4 years. Alcohol is not permitted. Upperclassmen may keep cars.

Activities: There are no fraternities or sororities. There are 26 groups on campus, including band, choir, chorus, computers, debate, drill team, drum and bugle corps, ethnic, marching band, newspaper, pep band, professional, religious, and student government. Popular campus events include Ring Dance, Festival of Lights, and Battle Standard Dinner.

Sports: There are 14 intercollegiate sports for men and 5 for women, and 5 intramural sports for men. Facilities include a swimming pool and a football field.

Disabled Students: 5% of the campus is accessible. Facilities include wheelchair ramps, elevators, special parking, and specially equipped restrooms.

Services: Counseling and information services are available, as is tutoring in most subjects.

Campus Safety and Security: Measures include 24-hour foot and vehicle patrol and self-defense education. There are lighted pathways/sidewalks.

Programs of Study: Kings Point confers B.S. degrees. Master's degrees are also awarded. Bachelor's degrees are awarded in BUSINESS (logistics and transportation management), ENGINEERING AND ENVIRONMENTAL DESIGN (engineering, marine engineering, maritime science, naval architecture and marine engineering, and transportation technology). Marine engineering systems is the strongest academically. Logistics and intermodal transportation is the largest.

Required: To graduate, students must complete 160 credit hours with a 2.0 minimum GPA. The required core curriculum includes courses in math, science, English, humanities and history, naval science, phys ed, ship's medicine, and computer science. Students must spend 10 months during their combined sophomore and junior years at sea on U.S. flag merchant ships. All students must pass resident and sea project courses, the U.S. Coast Guard licensing exam and all required certificates, and the academy physical fitness test. Students must apply for and accept, if offered, a commission in the U.S. uniformed services.

Special: The college offers internships in the maritime industry and work-study programs with U.S. shipping companies.

Faculty/Classroom: 90% of faculty are male; 10% are female. All teach undergraduates. No introductory courses are taught by graduate students. The average class size in an introductory lecture is 18; in a laboratory is 16; and in a regular course is 17.

Requirements: The SAT or ACT is required. The ACT Optional Writing test is also required. In addition, candidates for admission to the academy must be nominated by a member of the U.S. Congress. They must be between the ages of 17 and 25, U.S. citizens (except by special arrangement), and in excellent physical condition. Applicants should be graduates of an accredited secondary school or have a GED equivalent. 18 academic credits are required, including 4 in English, 3 in math, 1 credit in physics or chemistry with a lab, and 10 in electives. An essay is required. AP credits are accepted. Important factors in the admissions decision are advanced placement or honors courses, leadership record, and extracurricular activities record.

Procedure: Freshmen are admitted in the fall. Entrance exams should be taken by the first test date of the year of entry. There are early decision and rolling admissions plans. Applications should be filed by March 1 for fall entry. Notifications are sent March 31. Applications are accepted on-line. A waiting list is maintained.

Transfer: All students must complete all 4 years of the Academy's program. 164 of 164 credits required for the bachelor's degree must be completed at Kings Point.

Visiting: There are guides for informal visits; visitors may sit in on classes and stay overnight. To schedule a visit, contact the Admissions Office.

Financial Aid: In a recent year, 33% of all full-time freshmen received some form of financial aid. 37% of all full-time freshmen received need-based aid. The average freshmen award was $5,442, with $2,375 ($4,050 maximum) from need-based scholarships or need-based grants; $5,334 ($8,000 maximum) from need-based self-help aid (loans and jobs); and $967 ($2,000 maximum) from other non-need-based awards and non-need-based scholarships. The average financial indebtedness of the 2009 graduate was $9,221. The FAFSA is required. Check with the school for current application deadlines.

International Students: There were 21 international students enrolled in a recent year. They must take the TOEFL with a minimum score of 533 on the paper-based TOEFL (PBT) or 73 on the Internet-based version (iBT). They must also take the SAT or ACT.

Computers: Wireless access is available. All students may access the system 24 hours per day. There are no time limits and no fees. All students are required to have a personal computer. A laptop computer is recommended.

Graduates: In a recent year, 210 bachelor's degrees were awarded. The most popular majors were logistics and intermodal transportation (34%), marine engineering systems (29%), and marine engineering and shipyard maintenance (15%). 70 companies recruited on campus in 2008-2009. In an average class, 45% graduate in 4 years or less, 27% graduate in 5 years or less, and 1% graduate in 6 years or less. Of the 2008 graduating class, 2% were enrolled in graduate school within 6 months of graduation, and 98% were employed.

Admissions Contact: CPT. Robert E. Johnson, Director of Admissions and Financial Aid. A campus DVD is available. E-Mail: *admissions@usmma.edu* Web: *www.usmma.edu*

UNITED STATES MILITARY ACADEMY   D-4

West Point, NY 10996   (845) 938-4041; (845) 938-8121

Full-time: 3535 men, 640 women	Faculty: n/av
Part-time: 0 men, 0 women	Ph.D.s: 39%
Graduate: none	Student/Faculty: n/av
Year: semesters, summer session	Tuition: see profile
Application Deadline: see profile	Room & Board: see profile
Freshman Class: n/av	
SAT or ACT: required	MOST COMPETITIVE

The United States Military Academy, founded in 1802, offers military, engineering, and comprehensive arts and sciences programs leading to a bachelor's degree and a commission as a second lieutenant in the U.S. Army, with a 5-year active duty service obligation. All students receive free tuition and room and board as well as an annual salary of $10,148. An initial deposit of $2900 is required. Figures in the above capsule are approximate. In addition to regional accreditation, West Point has baccalaureate program accreditation with ABET. The library contains 442,169 volumes, 748,443 microform items, and 12,378 audio/video tapes/CDs/DVDs, and subscribes to 1,963 periodicals including electronic. Computerized library services include interlibrary loans and database searching. Special learning facilities include a learning resource center, art gallery, radio station, TV station, and military museum. Cadets may conduct research in conjunction with the academic departments through the Operations Research Center, the Photonics Research Center, the Mechanical Engineering Research Center, and the Office of Artificial Intelligence, Analysis, and Evaluation. There is also a visiting artist program featuring painting, sculpture, and photography. The 16,080-acre campus is in a small town 56 miles north of New York City. Including any residence halls, there are 902 buildings.

Student Life: 92% of undergraduates are from out of state, mostly the Northeast. Students are from 50 states and 19 foreign countries. 81% are from public schools. 81% are white. 49% are Protestant; 33% Catholic; 15% claim no religious affiliation. The average age of freshmen is 18; all undergraduates, 20. 8% do not continue beyond their first year; 82% remain to graduate.

Housing: 4500 students can be accommodated in college housing. All cadets live in cadet barracks. On-campus housing is guaranteed for all 4 years. Upperclassmen may keep cars.

Activities: There are no fraternities or sororities. There are 105 groups on campus, including art, astronomy, bagpipe, band, cheerleading, chess, choir, chorale, chorus, computers, dance, debate, debate, drama, drill team, drum and bugle corps, ethnic, film, flying, forensics, honors, international, language, literary magazine, marching band, musical theater, newspaper, pep band, photography, professional, radio and TV, religious, social, social service, student government, and yearbook. Popular campus events include Ring Weekend and 100th Night for Seniors, 500th Night for Juniors, and Plebe-Parent Weekend for Freshmen.

Sports: There are 15 intercollegiate sports for men and 9 for women, and 18 intramural sports for men and 14 for women. Facilities include a 40,000-seat football stadium, baseball fields, a 2500-seat hockey rink, a 5000-seat basketball arena, a gymnasium with 5 gyms for squash, handball, tennis, and racquetball, 3 swimming pools, and workout areas, a field house, indoor/outdoor tracks, a golf course, a ski slope, and hunting, fishing, and boating facilities.

Disabled Students: Facilities include wheelchair ramps, elevators, special parking, specially equipped restrooms, lowered drinking fountains, and lowered telephones.

Services: Counseling and information services are available, as is tutoring in every subject. The Center for Enhanced Performance offers 2 courses that provide cadets an opportunity to learn and enhance reading, study, and mental skills.

Campus Safety and Security: Measures include 24-hour foot and vehicle patrol and self-defense education. There are shuttle buses and lighted pathways/sidewalks.

Programs of Study: West Point confers B.S. degrees. Bachelor's degrees are awarded in BIOLOGICAL SCIENCE (life science), BUSINESS (management science and operations research), COMMUNICATIONS AND THE ARTS (languages and literature), COMPUTER AND PHYSICAL SCIENCE (chemistry, computer science, mathematics, and physics), ENGINEERING AND ENVIRONMENTAL DESIGN (civil engineering, electrical/electronics engineering, engineering management, engineering physics, environmental engineering, mechanical engineering, military science, nuclear engineering, and systems engineering), SOCIAL SCIENCE (behavioral science, economics, geography, history, international studies, law, philosophy, and political science/government). Engineering, behavioral sciences, and history are the largest.

Required: All cadets must complete a core of 31 courses and 9 academic electives pertinent to their field of study. The major requires an additional 1 to 3 electives to the field. In addition, all cadets must complete 4 courses each in phys ed and military science and a senior thesis or design project in the major. A total of 140 credits, including 127 academic, 6 military, and 7 physical, with at least a C average, is required to graduate.

Special: Junior and senior cadets may participate in 3-week summer educational experiences, including Operations Crossroads Africa, research work in technical areas throughout the country, medical internships at Walter Reed Medical Center, workfellow positions with federal and Department of Defense agencies, language training in foreign countries, and study at other military and civilian institutions. There are 7 national honor societies, including Phi Beta Kappa, a freshman honors program, and 5 departmental honors programs.

Faculty/Classroom: 88% of faculty are male; 12% are female. 40% do research, and 40% do both. No introductory courses are taught by graduate students. The average class size in an introductory lecture is 15, in a laboratory, 15, and in a regular course, 15.

Requirements: The SAT or ACT is required. In addition, applicants must be qualified academically, physically, and medically. Candidates must be nominated for admission by members of the U.S. Congress or executive sources. West Point recommends that applicants have 4 years each of English and math, 2 years each of foreign language and lab science, such as chemistry and physics, and 1 year of U.S. history. Courses in geography, government, and economics are also suggested. An essay is required, and an interview is recommended. The GED is accepted. Applicants must be 17 to 22 years old, a U.S. citizen at the time of enrollment (except by agreement with another country), unmarried, and not pregnant or legally obligated to support children. AP credits are accepted. Important factors in the admissions decision are leadership record, extracurricular activities record, and recommendations by school officials.

Procedure: Freshmen are admitted summer. Entrance exams should be taken in the spring of the junior year and not later than the fall of the senior year. There are early decision, early admissions and rolling admissions plans. Check with the school for current application deadlines. A waiting list is maintained.

Transfer: All applicants must enter as freshmen. 140 of 140 credits required for the bachelor's degree must be completed at West Point.

Visiting: There are regularly scheduled orientations for prospective students. Candidates will be escorted by a cadet, attend class, have lunch with the Corps of Cadets, and talk with cadets about all phases of West Point life. There are guides for informal visits; visitors may sit in on classes and stay overnight. To schedule a visit, contact the Admissions Office.

Financial Aid: Check with the school for current application deadlines.

International Students: They must take the TOEFL. They must also take the SAT or ACT.

Computers: All students may access the system 24 hours daily. There are no time limits and no fees. All students are required to have a personal computer.

Admissions Contact: Colonel Michael L. Jones, Director of Admissions. A campus DVD is available. E-Mail: *admissions@usma.edu* Web: *www.usma.edu*

UNIVERSITY AT BUFFALO/STATE UNIVERSITY OF NEW YORK   A-3
State University of New York/University at Buffalo
Buffalo, NY 14214

(716) 645-6900
(888) UB-ADMIT; (716) 645-6411

Full-time: 9500 men, 8035 women	**Faculty:** I, av$
Part-time: 640 men, 625 women	**Ph.D.s:** n/av
Graduate: 4430 men, 4855 women	**Student/Faculty:** n/avn
Year: semesters, summer session	**Tuition:** $7013 ($14,913)
Application Deadline: see profile	**Room & Board:** $9000
Freshman Class: n/av	
SAT: required	**VERY COMPETITIVE+**

The University at Buffalo, State University of New York at Buffalo, established in 1846, is a public institution offering more than 300 bachelor's, master's, and doctoral degree programs. UB is a comprehensive research-extensive university and the largest in the 64-campus State University of New York system. The figures in the above capsule and in this profile are approximate. There are 8 undergraduate schools and 13 graduate schools. In addition to regional accreditation, UB has baccalaureate program accreditation with AACSB, ABET, ACPE, ADA, APTA, CSWE, NAAB, and NASAD. The 10 libraries contain 3.5 million volumes, 5.5 million microform items, and 200,600 audio/video tapes/CDs/DVDs, and subscribe to 37,500 periodicals including electronic. Computerized library services include interlibrary loans, database searching, Internet access, and laptop Internet portals. Special learning facilities include a learning resource center, art gallery, radio station, TV station, an earthquake engineering research center, an arts center, a bio-informatics and life sciences center, a document analysis and Recognition center, a concert hall, an anthropology research center, a computational research center, a poetry and rare books collection, a virtual site museum, center for engineering design and industrial innovation, an electronic poetry center, and a archeological center. The 1350-acre campus is in a suburban area 3 miles north of Buffalo. Including any residence halls, there are 226 buildings.

Student Life: 86% of undergraduates are from New York. Others are from 44 states, 87 foreign countries, and Canada. 67% are white; 11% foreign nationals. The average age of freshmen is 18; all undergraduates, 21. 13% do not continue beyond their first year; 63% remain to graduate.

Housing: 6947 students can be accommodated in college housing, which includes coed dorms, on-campus apartments, and married student housing. In addition, there are honors houses, special-interest houses, freshmen-only housing and cultural interest housing. On-campus housing is guaranteed for the freshman year only, is available on a first-come, first-served basis, and is available on a lottery system for upperclassmen. 64% of students commute. All students may keep cars.

Activities: There are 4 local and 21 national fraternities and 5 local and 16 national sororities. There are 300 groups on campus, including art, band, cheerleading, chess, choir, chorale, chorus, computers, dance, drama, ethnic, film, gay, honors, international, jazz band, literary magazine, marching band, musical theater, newspaper, orchestra, pep band, political, professional, radio and TV, religious, social, social service, student government, and symphony. Popular campus events include Homecoming, Family Weekend, and Fallfest.

Sports: There are 10 intercollegiate sports for men and 10 for women, and 13 intramural sports for men and 13 for women. Facilities include racquetball, squash, tennis, basketball, volleyball, badminton, and handball courts, baseball, soccer, hockey, and multipurpose fields, a football and track and field stadium, an indoor jogging track; an Olympic-size pool and diving well; a triple gym; weight training and wrestling rooms; dance studios; and a spinning room.

Disabled Students: 90% of the campus is accessible. Facilities include wheelchair ramps, elevators, special parking, specially equipped restrooms, special class scheduling, lowered drinking fountains, lowered telephones, and special housing.

Services: Counseling and information services are available, as is tutoring in most subjects. There is a reader service for the blind, and remedial math, reading, and writing. Peer tutoring and some computer-assisted instruction are also available.

Campus Safety and Security: Measures include 24-hour foot and vehicle patrol, emergency notification system, self-defense education, and security escort services. There are shuttle buses, emergency telephones, lighted pathways/sidewalks, controlled access to dorms/residences, an alarm system, routine patrols, student aides in residence halls, some security cameras, blue-light phones, and a university-wide safety committee.

Programs of Study: UB confers B.A., B.S., B.F.A., and Mus.B. degrees. Master's and doctoral degrees are also awarded. Bachelor's degrees are awarded in BIOLOGICAL SCIENCE (biochemistry, bioinformatics, biology/biological science, biophysics, and biotechnology), BUSINESS (business administration and management), COMMUNICATIONS AND THE ARTS (art history and appreciation, classics, communications, dance, English, film arts, fine arts, French, German, Italian, linguistics, media arts, music, music performance, musical theater, Spanish, studio art, and visual and performing arts), COMPUTER AND PHYSICAL SCIENCE (chemistry, computer science, geology, information sciences and systems, mathematics, and physics), ENGINEERING AND ENVIRONMENTAL DESIGN (aerospace studies, architecture, chemical engineering, civil engineering, computational sciences, computer engineering, electrical/electronics engineering, engineering physics, environmental design, environmental engineering, industrial engineering, and mechanical engineering), HEALTH PROFESSIONS (biomedical science, exercise science, medical technology, nuclear medical technology, nursing, occupational therapy, pharmaceutical science, pharmacology, pharmacy, physical therapy, and speech pathology/audiology), SOCIAL SCIENCE (African American studies, American studies, anthropology, Asian/Oriental studies, economics, geography, history, philosophy, political science/government, psychology, social science, sociology, and women's studies). Engineering, business administration, and psychology are the largest.

Required: To graduate, students must complete 120 semester hours with a minimum GPA of 2.0. General education requirements include writing skills, mathematical sciences, library skills, world civilizations, American pluralism, natural sciences, language, humanities, arts, social and behavioral sciences, and depth requirement. The total number of hours in the major varies.

Special: Students may cross-register with the Western New York Consortium. Internships are available, and students may study abroad in 29 countries. UB offers a Washington semester, work-study programs, accelerated degree programs, B.A.-B.S. degrees, dual, student-designed, and interdisciplinary majors, and credit for military experience. A 3-2 engineering degree can be pursued. Students may choose a successful/unsuccessful (S/U) grading option for selected courses. There is an early assurance of admission program to medical school for undergraduate sophomore students who possess a minimum approximate overall and science GPA of 3.75 and complete particular science courses. There are 39 national honor societies, including Phi Beta Kappa, a freshman honors program, and all departments have honors programs.

Faculty/Classroom: 63% of faculty are male; 37% are female. 80% teach undergraduates, all do research, and 80% do both. Graduate students teach 18% of introductory courses. The average class size in an introductory lecture is 53; in a laboratory is 26; and in a regular course is 37.

Requirements: The SAT is required. Freshmen are evaluated based on secondary school performance, strength of curriculum, standardized test scores, and, in some cases, a supplemental application. A high school diploma is required and the GED is accepted. Music applicants must audition. AP and CLEP credits are accepted. Important factors in the admissions decision are advanced placement or honors courses, recommendations by school officials, and evidence of special talent.

Procedure: Freshmen are admitted fall and spring. Entrance exams should be taken during the spring of the junior year or the fall of the senior year. There are early decision and rolling admissions plans. Early decision applications should be filed by November 1; check with the school for current application deadlines. The fall 2009 application fee was $40. Notification of early decision is sent December 15; regular decision, sent in February. Applications are accepted on-line. A waiting list is maintained.

Transfer: 1579 transfer students enrolled in in a recent year. Transfer applicants with fewer than 24 credit hours must supply high school transcripts, SAT and/or ACT test scores, and the previous college academic record. It is recommended that students present a strong record of college study, with a 2.5 GPA. Entry at junior level requires a higher GPA for some programs. Credit may be awarded for military experience and other nontraditional sources. 30 of 120 credits required for the bachelor's degree must be completed at UB.

Visiting: There are regularly scheduled orientations for prospective students, including the Visit UB program, in which visitors tour the campus and attend an information session to learn about application procedures, admissions criteria, housing, financial aid, and scholarship programs. The program is offered, with some exceptions, Monday through Friday year-round and on selected Saturdays during the academic year. Reservations are required. Visitors may sit in on classes. To schedule a visit, contact the Office of Admissions at http://admissions.buffalo.edu/visitubprogram.php.

Financial Aid: In a recent year, 98% of all full-time freshmen and 98% of continuing full-time students received some form of financial aid. 63% of all full-time freshmen and 69% of continuing full-time students received need-based aid. The average freshmen award was $3,019, with $6,623 from other forms of aid. The average financial indebtedness of the 2009 graduate was $18,000. The FAFSA is required. Check with the school for current application deadlines.

International Students: There were 1699 international students enrolled in a recent year. The school actively recruits these students. They must take the TOEFL with a minimum score of 550 on the paper-based TOEFL (PBT) or 79 on the Internet-based version (iBT). The SAT or ACT is strongly recommended.

Computers: Wireless access is available. Students have access to more than 2400 computers in labs that provides connectivity for mobile devices. Access to research networks, free mail, Microsoft productivity software for student PCs, and student web page hosting are provided. Many courses provide audio-or-video-streams of lectures which students can re-play on their portable devices. Learning spaces in the libraries and academic areas are equipped with technology to enable student group/team work and collaborative learning. A mobile campus initiative is underway to enable anywhere, anytime access to information and learning tools. All students may access the system any time. There are no time limits and no fees. It is strongly recommended that all students have a personal computer.

Graduates: In a recent year, 3939 bachelor's degrees were awarded. The most popular majors were business administration (19%), engineering (11%), and communications and psychology (10%). 240 companies recruited on campus in 2008-2009. In an average class, 1% graduate in 3 years or less, 40% graduate in 4 years or less, 57% graduate in 5 years or less, and 60% graduate in 6 years or less. Of the 2008 graduating class, 35% were enrolled in graduate school within 6 months of graduation, and 73% were employed.

Admissions Contact: Patricia Armstrong, Director of Admissions. E-Mail: *ubadmissions@buffalo.edu* Web: *www.buffalo.edu*

UNIVERSITY OF ROCHESTER B-3
Rochester, NY 14627-0251

(585) 275-3221
(888) 822-2256; (585) 461-4595

Full-time: 2568 men, 2625 women	**Faculty:** I, av$
Part-time: 47 men, 207 women	**Ph.D.s:** 88%
Graduate: 2259 men, 2270 women	**Student/Faculty:** n/av
Year: semesters, summer session	**Tuition:** $38,690
Application Deadline: January 1	**Room & Board:** $11,200
Freshman Class: 12111 applied, 4686 accepted, 1087 enrolled	
SAT CR/M/W: 650/680/650	**ACT:** 30 **MOST COMPETITIVE**

The University of Rochester, founded in 1850, is a private institution offering programs in the arts and sciences, engineering and applied science, nursing, medicine and dentistry, business administration, music, and education. There are 4 undergraduate schools and 7 graduate schools. In addition to regional accreditation, UR has baccalaureate program accreditation with AACSB, ABET, ACPE, ADA, NASM, NCATE, and NLNAC. The 15 libraries contain 3.7 million volumes, 5.1 million microform items, and 110,495 audio/video tapes/CDs/DVDs, and subscribe to 27,240 periodicals including electronic. Computerized library services include interlibrary loans, database searching, and Internet access. Special learning facilities include a learning resource center, radio station, labs for nuclear structure research and laser energetics, a center for visual science, the Strong Memorial Hospital, an art center, an observatory, an institute of optics, a center for electronic imaging systems, and the National Science Foundation Center for Photoinduced Charge Transfer. The 655-acre campus is in a suburban area 2 miles south of downtown Rochester. Including any residence halls, there are 159 buildings.

Student Life: 44% of undergraduates are from out of state, mostly the Middle Atlantic. Students are from 50 states, more than 50 foreign countries, and Canada. 75% are from public schools. 60% are white; 13% Asian American. 37% claim no religious affiliation; 19% Catholic; 13% Jewish. The average age of freshmen is 18; all undergraduates, 20. 4% do not continue beyond their first year; 88% remain to graduate.

Housing: 3629 students can be accommodated in college housing, which includes coed dorms, on-campus apartments, and married student housing. In addition, there are language houses, special-interest houses, and fraternity houses. On-campus housing is guaranteed for the freshman year only and is available on a lottery system for upperclassmen. 86% of students live on campus; of those, 90% remain on campus on weekends. Upperclassmen may keep cars.

Activities: 19% of men belong to 17 national fraternities; 20% of women belong to 13 national sororities. There are 220 groups on campus, including art, band, campus activities board, cheerleading, chess, choir, chorale, chorus, computers, dance, debate, drama, drill team, environmental, ethnic, film, gay, honors, international, jazz band, literary magazine, musical theater, newspaper, opera, orchestra, pep band, photography, political, professional, radio and TV, religious, social, social service, student government, symphony, and yearbook. Popular campus events include Dandelion Day, Yellowjacket Day, and Boar's Head Dinner.

Sports: There are 11 intercollegiate sports for men and 12 for women, and 7 intramural sports for men and 7 for women. Facilities include an 11,000-square-foot athletic center, a 5000-seat stadium, a field house, an ice rink, courts for handball, racquetball, squash, and tennis, an indoor track, a fitness center and weight room, a jogging path, and an aquatic center.

Disabled Students: 90% of the campus is accessible. Facilities include wheelchair ramps, elevators, special parking, specially equipped rest rooms, special class scheduling, lowered drinking fountains, lowered

telephones, and special housing. There is access to screened reading and adaptive software.

Services: Counseling and information services are available, as is tutoring in most subjects.

Campus Safety and Security: Measures include 24-hour foot and vehicle patrol, emergency notification system, self-defense education, and security escort services. There are shuttle buses, emergency telephones, lighted pathways/sidewalks, and controlled access to academic, administrative, and residential buildings.

Programs of Study: UR confers B.A., B.S., and B.M. degrees. Master's and doctoral degrees are also awarded. Bachelor's degrees are awarded in AGRICULTURE (environmental studies), BIOLOGICAL SCIENCE (biochemistry, biology/biological science, cell biology, ecology, microbiology, molecular biology, and neurosciences), BUSINESS (business economics), COMMUNICATIONS AND THE ARTS (American Sign Language, art history and appreciation, classics, comparative literature, English, film arts, French, German, Japanese, jazz, linguistics, media arts, music, music performance, music theory and composition, Russian, Spanish, and studio art), COMPUTER AND PHYSICAL SCIENCE (applied mathematics, astronomy, chemistry, computer science, geology, mathematics, optics, physics, and statistics), EDUCATION (music education), ENGINEERING AND ENVIRONMENTAL DESIGN (biomedical engineering, chemical engineering, electrical/electronics engineering, engineering and applied science, environmental science, geological engineering, and mechanical engineering), HEALTH PROFESSIONS (health, nursing, and public health), SOCIAL SCIENCE (African American studies, anthropology, archeology, cognitive science, economics, history, interdisciplinary studies, international relations, philosophy, political science/government, psychology, religion, Russian and Slavic studies, and women's studies). Biomedical engineering, optics, and political science are the strongest academically. Biology, economics, and engineering are the largest.

Required: Students focus on the humanities, social sciences, and natural sciences; 1 of the 3 areas will be their major, and they select a 3-course cluster in each of the other 2. A total of 128 credit hours with a minimum GPA of 2.0 is required to graduate. Additionally, all students satisfy a freshman writing requirement and take 2 upper-level courses in their major that are writing intensive.

Special: Cross-registration is offered with Rochester Area Colleges. Selective programs for exceptional undergraduates in medicine (REMS), business (REBS), engineering (GEAR), and education (GRADE) guarantee admission to professional or graduate school upon completion of the bachelor's degree. The Take Five Scholars Program allows students to stay tuition-free for a fifth year of study. Rochester offers 3-2 programs in business, engineering, human development, neuroscience, optics, physics and astronomy, and public health. Study abroad is possible in more than 30 countries. Internships, a Washington semester, B.A.-B.S. degrees, accelerated degree programs, dual and student-designed majors, nondegree study, and pass/fail options are available. There are 8 national honor societies, including Phi Beta Kappa, a freshman honors program, and 13 departmental honors programs.

Faculty/Classroom: 64% of faculty are male; 36% are female. No introductory courses are taught by graduate students. The average class size in an introductory lecture is 75; in a laboratory, 20; and in a regular course, 20.

Admissions: 39% of the 2009-2010 applicants were accepted. The SAT scores for the 2009-2010 freshman class were: Critical Reading--4% below 500, 26% between 500 and 599, 48% between 600 and 700, and 22% above 700; Math--2% below 500, 13% between 500 and 599, 48% between 600 and 700, and 37 above 700; Writing--3% below 500, 24% between 500 and 599, 52% between 600 and 700, and 21% above 700. The ACT scores were 2% between 21 and 23, 10% between 24 and 26, 19% between 27 and 28, and 69% above 28. 86% of the current freshmen were in the top fifth of their class; 99% were in the top two fifths. There were 21 National Merit finalists. 46 freshmen graduated first in their class.

Requirements: The SAT or ACT is required. In addition, applicants should be graduates of an accredited secondary school or have a GED equivalent. An essay or personal statement and recommendations are required. SAT Subject Tests and an interview are recommended. An audition is required for music majors. Applicants should complete the Common Application and the Rochester Supplement. AP credits are accepted. Important factors in the admissions decision are advanced placement or honors courses, personality/intangible qualities, and recommendations by school officials.

Procedure: Freshmen are admitted fall and spring. Entrance exams should be taken by December of the senior year. There are early decision and deferred admissions plan. Early decision applications should be filed by November 1; regular applications, by January 1 for fall entry and November 1 for spring entry, along with a $60 fee. Notification of early decision is sent December 15; regular decision, April 1. 300 early decision candidates were accepted for the 2009-2010 class. 1243 applicants were on the 2009 waiting list; 71 were admitted. Applications are accepted on-line.

Transfer: 89 transfer students enrolled in 2008-2009. The most important criterion is an applicant's college record. 64 of 128 credits required for the bachelor's degree must be completed at UR.

Visiting: There are regularly scheduled orientations for prospective students, including a group information session and a tour. There are guides for informal visits, and visitors may sit in on classes and stay overnight. To schedule a visit, contact the Office of Admissions.

Financial Aid: 60% of undergraduate students work part-time. Average annual earnings from campus work are $2500. UR is a member of CSS. The CSS/Profile, the FAFSA, and the state aid form are required. The deadline for filing freshman financial aid applications for fall entry is February 1.

International Students: There are 546 international students enrolled. The school actively recruits these students. They must take the TOEFL with a minimum score of 600 on the paper-based TOEFL (PBT) or 100 on the Internet-based version (iBT). They must also take the SAT or ACT.

Computers: Wireless access is available. There are 450 computers/terminals and 4,000 ports available on campus for general student use. High-speed Internet access is available in the residence halls. Wireless access is available in all academic areas. All students may access the system 24 hours daily. There are no time limits and no fees.

Graduates: From July 1, 2008 to June 30, 2009, 1253 bachelor's degrees were awarded. The most popular majors were biology/biological sciences (14%), psychology (9%), and engineering and economics (8%). In an average class, 74% graduate in 4 years or less, 82% graduate in 5 years or less, and 84% graduate in 6 years or less. More than 1000 companies recruited on campus in 2008-2009. Of the 2008 graduating class, 33% were enrolled in graduate school within 6 months of graduation, and 57% were employed.

Admissions Contact: Jonathan Burdick, Dean of Admissions and Financial Aid. A campus DVD is available.
E-mail: *admit@admissions.rochester.edu* Web: *www.rochester.edu*

UTICA COLLEGE   C-3
Utica, NY 13502-4892

	(315) 792-3006
	(800) 782-8884; (315) 792-3003
Full-time: 919 men, 1145 women	**Faculty:** IIB, -$
Part-time: 169 men, 304 women	**Ph.D.s:** n/av
Graduate: 251 men, 485 women	**Student/Faculty:** n/av
Year: semesters, summer session	**Tuition:** $27,284
Application Deadline: open	**Room & Board:** $10,850
Freshman Class: 2930 applied, 2297 accepted, 563 enrolled	
SAT or ACT: recommended	**COMPETITIVE**

Utica College, a private liberal arts institution founded by Syracuse University in 1946, confers the Syracuse University undergraduate degree and Utica College master's degrees. There is 1 graduate school. In addition to regional accreditation, UC has baccalaureate program accreditation with APTA and NLN. The library contains 178,804 volumes, 39,711 microform items, and 9868 audio/video tapes/CDs/DVDs, and subscribes to 2002 periodicals including electronic. Computerized library services include interlibrary loans, database searching, Internet access, and laptop Internet portals. Special learning facilities include a learning resource center, art gallery, radio station, TV station, and early childhood education lab. The 128-acre campus is in a suburban area 50 miles east of Syracuse. Including any residence halls, there are 18 buildings.

Student Life: 81% of undergraduates are from New York. Others are from 43 states, 19 foreign countries, and Canada. 80% are from public schools. 58% are white; 11% African American. The average age of freshmen is 18; all undergraduates, 23. 30% do not continue beyond their first year; 57% remain to graduate.

Housing: 1046 students can be accommodated in college housing, which includes single-sex and coed dorms. On-campus housing is guaranteed for all 4 years. 57% of students commute. All students may keep cars.

Activities: 1% of men belong to 2 local and 3 national fraternities; 1% of women belong to 2 local and 3 national sororities. There are 86 groups on campus, including art, band, cheerleading, choir, chorus, computers, dance, drama, ethnic, film, gay, honors, international, jazz band, literary magazine, musical theater, newspaper, pep band, photography, political, professional, radio and TV, religious, social, social service, and student government. Popular campus events include outdoor concerts, mock elections, and Winter Weekend.

Sports: There are 10 intercollegiate sports for men and 11 for women, and 28 intramural sports for men and 28 for women. Facilities include a 2200-seat gym, a competition-size swimming pool, tennis, racquetball, handball, and squash courts, a sauna, Nautilus and weight rooms, dance and aerobic rooms, playing fields, a stadium, and hockey facilities.

Disabled Students: 85% of the campus is accessible. Facilities include wheelchair ramps, elevators, special parking, specially equipped restrooms, and lowered drinking fountains.

Services: Counseling and information services are available, as is tutoring in most subjects. There is a reader service for the blind and remedial math, reading, and writing.

Campus Safety and Security: Measures include 24-hour foot and vehicle patrol, emergency notification system, and security escort services. There are shuttle buses, emergency telephones, and lighted pathways/sidewalks.

Programs of Study: UC confers B.A. and B.S. degrees. Master's and doctoral degrees are also awarded. Bachelor's degrees are awarded in BIOLOGICAL SCIENCE (biochemistry and biology/biological science), BUSINESS (accounting, business administration and management, business economics, and insurance and risk management), COMMUNICATIONS AND THE ARTS (communications, English, French, Hawaiian, journalism, public relations, and Spanish), COMPUTER AND PHYSICAL SCIENCE (chemistry, computer science, computer security and information assurance, geoscience, mathematics, and physics), ENGINEERING AND ENVIRONMENTAL DESIGN (construction management), HEALTH PROFESSIONS (nursing, occupational therapy, physical therapy, and recreation therapy), SOCIAL SCIENCE (child psychology/development, criminal justice, economics, gerontology, history, liberal arts/general studies, philosophy, political science/government, psychology, social studies, and sociology). Occupational therapy, psychology, and biology are the strongest academically. Management, psychology, and criminal justice/economic crime investigation are the largest.

Required: To graduate, students must complete a total of 120 to 128 hours with a minimum 2.0 GPA. They must complete a general education requirement including basic skills and distribution requirements.

Special: UC offers co-op programs, internships, work-study programs in all majors, accelerated degrees, dual majors, and cross-registration with Hamilton College and the Mohawk Valley Consortium. Study abroad may be arranged in 9 countries. There is a 3-2 engineering degree with Syracuse University. There are 5 national honor societies and a freshman honors program.

Faculty/Classroom: All faculty teach and do research. No introductory courses are taught by graduate students. The average class size in an introductory lecture is 23; in a laboratory is 11; and in a regular course, 17.

Admissions: 78% of the 2009-2010 applicants were accepted. The SAT scores for the 2009-2010 freshman class were: Critical Reading--70% below 500, 24% between 500 and 599, and 5% between 600 and 700; Math--64% below 500, 27% between 500 and 599, and 8% between 600 and 700; Writing--76% below 500, 20% between 500 and 599, and 4% between 600 and 700.

Requirements: The SAT or ACT and ACT Writing Test are recommended. Graduation from an accredited secondary school or satisfactory scores on the GED are required. Recommended high school courses include 4 years of English, 3 years each of math and social studies, and 2 years each of foreign language and science. An essay and an interview are also recommended. AP and CLEP credits are accepted. Important factors in the admissions decision are advanced placement or honors courses, extracurricular activities record, and leadership record.

Procedure: Freshmen are admitted fall and spring. Entrance exams should be taken during the junior year. There are deferred admissions and rolling admissions plans. Application deadlines are open. Application fee is $40. Notification is sent on a rolling basis. Applications are accepted on-line.

Transfer: 156 transfer students enrolled in fall 2009. Applicants must have a minimum GPA of 2.3. 30 of 128 credits required for the bachelor's degree must be completed at UC.

Visiting: There are regularly scheduled orientations for prospective students, including an interview, financial aid information, and a tour of the campus. There are guides for informal visits; visitors may sit in on classes and stay overnight. To schedule a visit, contact the Admissions Office.

Financial Aid: In 2009-2010, 90% of all full-time freshmen and 90% of continuing full-time students received some form of financial aid. 90% of all full-time freshmen and 90% of continuing full-time students received need-based aid. Need-based scholarships or need-based grants averaged $8635; and need-based self-help aid (loans and jobs) averaged $3958. The average financial indebtedness of the 2009 graduate was $22,317. UC is a member of CSS. The FAFSA is required. The deadline for filing freshman financial aid applications for fall entry is February 15.

International Students: There are 53 international students enrolled. The school actively recruits these students. They must take the TOEFL with a minimum score on the paper-based TOEFL (PBT) or on the Internet-based version (iBT), or take the Comprehensive English Language Test, IELTS, APIEL, or MELAB. The SAT is recommended if the student's primary language is English.

Computers: Wireless access is available. There are 410 workstations located in the library, the student center, and in computer labs. There are also 10 laptops available for use in the library only. Wireless access is available in the library and in all smart classrooms. 1 residence hall has wireless access. All students may access the system during posted hours. Time limits are imposed only during peak hours. The fee is $200.

Graduates: From July 1, 2008 to June 30, 2009, 432 bachelor's degrees were awarded. The most popular majors were health studies (22%), criminal justice (20%), and management/economics (14%). In an average class, 1% graduate in 3 years or less, 29% graduate in 4 years or less, 47% graduate in 5 years or less, and 49% graduate in 6 years or less.

Admissions Contact: Patrick Quinn, Vice President for Enrollment Management. E-mail: *admiss@utica.edu* Web: *www.utica.edu*

VASSAR COLLEGE   D-4
Poughkeepsie, NY 12604

	(845) 437-7300
	(800) 827-7270; (845) 437-7063
Full-time: 965 men, 1370 women	**Faculty:** IIB, +$
Part-time: 15 men, 40 women	**Ph.D.s:** 96%
Graduate: none	**Student/Faculty:** n/av
Year: semesters	**Tuition:** $41,930
Application Deadline: see profile	**Room & Board:** $9540
Freshman Class: n/av	
SAT or ACT: required	**MOST COMPETITIVE**

Vassar College, founded in 1861, is a private, independent college of the liberal arts and sciences. Figures in the above capsule are approximate. The 3 libraries contain 869,088 volumes, 611,076 microform items, and 23,590 audio/video tapes/CDs/DVDs, and subscribe to 4,001 periodicals including electronic. Computerized library services include interlibrary loans, database searching, Internet access, and laptop Internet portals. Special learning facilities include a learning resource center, art gallery, radio station, studio art building, geological museum, observatory, 3 theaters, concert hall, environmental field station, intercultural center, and research-oriented lab facilities for natural sciences. The 1000-acre campus is in a suburban area 75 miles north of New York City. Including any residence halls, there are 100 buildings.

Student Life: 74% of undergraduates are from out of state, mostly the Middle Atlantic. Students are from 50 states, 51 foreign countries, and Canada. 57% are from public schools. 74% are white. The average age of freshmen is 18; all undergraduates, 20. 4% do not continue beyond their first year; 89% remain to graduate.

Housing: 2305 students can be accommodated in college housing, which includes single-sex and coed dorms, on-campus apartments, off-campus apartments, and married student housing. There is 1 all-women residence hall and 1 cooperative living unit. On-campus housing is guaranteed for all 4 years. 98% of students live on campus; of those, 90% remain on campus on weekends. All students may keep cars.

Activities: There are no fraternities or sororities. There are 100 groups on campus, including art, band, chess, choir, chorale, chorus, computers, dance, debate, drama, ethnic, film, gay, honors, international, jazz band, literary magazine, newspaper, opera, orchestra, photography, political, radio and TV, religious, social, social service, student government, and yearbook. Popular campus events include Founders Day, spring and fall formals, and All Parents Weekend.

Sports: There are 12 intercollegiate sports for men and 13 for women, and 18 intramural sports for men and 18 for women. Facilities include a field house with a swimming pool, 5 indoor tennis courts, a weight and conditioning room, a gym with squash and racquetball courts and basketball facilities, a 9-hole golf course, 13 outdoor tennis courts, an all-weather track, 2 soccer fields, a baseball diamond, a rugby field, club and intramural fields, a competition basketball gym, a banked running track, and a 5000-square-foot exercise and fitness center.

Disabled Students: 50% of the campus is accessible. Facilities include wheelchair ramps, elevators, special parking, specially equipped restrooms, special class scheduling, and lowered drinking fountains. There is an Office of Disability and Support Services, signage in braille, and assisted listening devices.

Services: Counseling and information services are available, as is tutoring in most subjects. There is a reader service for the blind, and remedial math and writing.

Campus Safety and Security: Measures include 24-hour foot and vehicle patrol, self-defense education, and security escort services. There are shuttle buses, emergency telephones, and lighted pathways/sidewalks.

Programs of Study: Vassar confers B.A. degrees. Master's degrees are also awarded. Bachelor's degrees are awarded in AGRICULTURE (environmental studies), BIOLOGICAL SCIENCE (biochemistry, biology/biological science, and neurosciences), COMMUNICATIONS AND THE ARTS (art, Chinese, dramatic arts, English, film arts, Japanese, languages, media arts, and music), COMPUTER AND PHYSICAL SCIENCE (astronomy, chemistry, computer science, geology, mathematics, and physics), EDUCATION (foreign languages education), ENGINEERING AND ENVIRONMENTAL DESIGN (technology and public affairs), HEALTH PROFESSIONS (premedicine), SOCIAL SCIENCE (African studies, American studies, anthropology, Asian/Oriental studies, biopsychology, classical/ancient civilization, cognitive science, economics, geography, history, international studies, Judaic studies, Latin American studies, medieval studies, philosophy, political science/government, pre-

law, psychology, religion, social studies, sociology, Spanish studies, urban studies, Victorian studies, and women's studies). English, psychology, and political science are the largest.

Required: To graduate, students must have a total of 34 units equivalent to 120 credit hours, with a minimum GPA of 2.0. Of this total, no more than 17 units may be in a single field of concentration and 8 1/2 units must be outside the major field. Entering freshmen must take the freshman course. All students must meet the foreign language proficiency requirement and take a quantitative skills course before their third year. A thesis is required in most departments.

Special: The school offers fieldwork in social agencies and schools, dual majors, independent majors, student-designed majors, cross-registration with the College Consortium, and nonrecorded grade options. Vassar runs study-abroad programs in 7 countries and students also may study in other approved programs around the world. A 3-2 engineering degree with Dartmouth College is offered. There is a Phi Beta Kappa honors society.

Faculty/Classroom: 54% of faculty are male; 46% are female. All teach and do research. No introductory courses are taught by graduate students. The average class size in an introductory lecture is 21, in a laboratory, 7, and in a regular course, 16.

Requirements: The SAT is required. In addition, 2 SAT Subject tests, or the ACT, are required. Graduation from an accredited secondary school or satisfactory scores on the GED are required for admission. The high school program should typically include 4 years each of English, social studies, math, foreign language, and science. An essay and a writing sample are required. AP credits are accepted.

Procedure: Freshmen are admitted fall. Entrance exams should be taken as early as possible, but no later than December of the senior year. There are early decision and deferred admissions plans. Check with the school for current application deadlines. The application fee is $60. Applications are accepted on-line. A waiting list is maintained.

Transfer: Applicants must have a high level of achievement in both high school and college work. 17 of 34 credits required for the bachelor's degree must be completed at Vassar.

Visiting: There are regularly scheduled orientations for prospective students, including a campus tour, an information session, and a class visit when possible. There are guides for informal visits; visitors may sit in on classes and stay overnight. To schedule a visit, contact the Admissions Office.

Financial Aid: Vassar is a member of CSS. The CSS/Profile, FAFSA, FFS, and the college's own financial statement are required. Check with the school for current application deadlines.

International Students: The school actively recruits these students. They must take the TOEFL. They must also take the SAT or ACT.

Computers: Wireless access is available. All students may access the system, 24 hours per day. There are no time limits and no fees.

Admissions Contact: David Borus, Dean of Admission and Financial Aid. E-Mail: *admissions@vassar.edu* Web: *www.vassar.edu*

VAUGHN COLLEGE OF AERONAUTICS AND TECHNOLOGY   D-5
Flushing, NY 11369

Full-time: 740 men, 120 women	**(718) 429-6600; (718) 779-2231**
	Faculty: III, +$
Part-time: 255 men, 35 women	**Ph.D.s:** n/av
Graduate: none	**Student/Faculty:** n/av
Year: semesters, summer session	**Tuition:** $15,300
Application Deadline: open	
Freshman Class: n/av	
SAT: recommended	**SPECIAL**

The College of Aeronautics, founded in 1932, is a private aviation school offering undergraduate degrees in aeronautical engineering technology, computerized design/animated graphics, airport management, avionics, aviation maintenance, and aircraft operations. The figures in the above capsule and in this profile are approximate. In addition to regional accreditation, Vaughn has baccalaureate program accreditation with ABET. Computerized library services include interlibrary loans, database searching, and Internet access. Special learning facilities include a learning resource center, a flight simulator, nondestructive testing labs, and a 5000-square-foot hangar facility. The 6-acre campus is in an urban area at LaGuardia Airport, 4 miles east of Manhattan. Including any residence halls, there are 2 buildings.

Student Life: 95% of undergraduates are from New York. Others are from 9 states, 19 foreign countries, and Canada. 96% are from public schools. 35% are Hispanic; 19% African American; 17% white; 11% Asian American. The average age of freshmen is 21; all undergraduates, 23. 27% do not continue beyond their first year; 68% remain to graduate.

Housing: There are no residence halls. All students commute.

Activities: There are no fraternities or sororities. There are 6 groups on campus, including ethnic, professional, social, and student government. Popular campus events include Open House-Techno Expo, Winter Fest, and Spring Fest.

Sports: There are 3 intramural sports for men and 3 for women. Facilities include nearby areas for softball, flag football, weight lifting, and basketball.

Disabled Students: 95% of the campus is accessible. Facilities include wheelchair ramps, elevators, special parking, specially equipped restrooms, special class scheduling, lowered drinking fountains, and lowered telephones.

Services: Counseling and information services are available, as is tutoring in most subjects. There is remedial math, reading, and writing.

Campus Safety and Security: Measures include 24-hour foot and vehicle patrol.

Programs of Study: Vaughn confers B.S. degrees. Associates degrees are also awarded. Bachelor's degrees are awarded in ENGINEERING AND ENVIRONMENTAL DESIGN (aircraft mechanics, airline piloting and navigation, and aviation administration/management). Computerized design, flight operations, and aviation maintenance management are the strongest academically.

Required: All students must satisfy English, math, and science requirements and fulfill appropriate licensing requirements while maintaining a GPA of at least 2.0. Students with advanced credit must complete 30 credits in residency. A total of 134 credits is required to graduate.

Special: Work-study programs are available with Vaughn College and internships may be arranged through the career development office. B.A.-B.S. degrees are offered.

Faculty/Classroom: 90% of faculty are male; 10% are female. All teach undergraduates. No introductory courses are taught by graduate students. The average class size in an introductory lecture is 25; in a laboratory is 20; and in a regular course is 20.

Requirements: The SAT is recommended, with satisfactory scores. Applicants are required to have 3 years of math and 2 years each of English and science. An interview is also recommended. A GPA of 2.0 is required. AP credits are accepted. Important factors in the admissions decision are evidence of special talent, advanced placement or honors courses, and personality/intangible qualities.

Procedure: Freshmen are admitted fall and spring. There are early decision and rolling admissions plans. Early decision applications should be filed by November 1; regular applications, deadlines are open. The fall 2009 application fee was $40. Notification of early decision is sent December 15; regular decision, sent on a rolling basis.

Transfer: A minimum 2.0 GPA is required. 30 of 134 credits required for the bachelor's degree must be completed at Vaughn.

Visiting: There are regularly scheduled orientations for prospective students, scheduled prior to registration, which include a tour and academic advisement. There are guides for informal visits and visitors may sit in on classes. To schedule a visit, contact the Admissions Office at admitme.@vaughn.edu.

Financial Aid: The CSS/Profile, FAFSA, and the college's own financial statement are required. Check with the school for current application deadlines.

International Students: The school actively recruits these students. They must take the TOEFL and English Proficiency Certificate.

Computers: All students may access the system. There are no time limits and no fees.

Admissions Contact: Vincent Papandrea, Director of Admissions. E-Mail: *admitme@vaughn.edu* Web: *www.vaughn.edu*

WAGNER COLLEGE   D-5
Staten Island, NY 10301

(718) 390-3411
(800) 221-1010; (718) 390-3105

Full-time: 664 men, 1135 women	Faculty: 99; IIA, -$
Part-time: 19 men, 52 women	Ph.D.s: 88%
Graduate: 136 men, 259 women	Student/Faculty: 18 to 1
Year: semesters, summer session	Tuition: $32,580
Application Deadline: February 15	Room & Board: $9700
Freshman Class: 2842 applied, 1873 accepted, 519 enrolled	
SAT CR/M/W: 560/540/530	ACT: 25 VERY COMPETITIVE

Wagner College, founded in 1883, is a private liberal arts institution. There is 1 graduate school. In addition to regional accreditation, Wagner has baccalaureate program accreditation with ACBSP, NCATE, and NLN. The library contains 175,344 volumes, 219 microform items, and 3695 audio/video tapes/CDs/DVDs, and subscribes to 20,600 periodicals including electronic. Computerized library services include interlibrary loans, database searching, and Internet access. Special learning facilities include an art gallery, planetarium, and radio station. The 105-acre campus is in a suburban area 10 miles from Manhattan. Including any residence halls, there are 18 buildings.

Student Life: 51% of undergraduates are from out of state, mostly the Middle Atlantic. Others are from 43 states, 12 foreign countries, and Canada. 62% are from public schools. 84% are white. 69% claim no religious affiliation; 22% Catholic. The average age of freshmen is 18. 20% do not continue beyond their first year; 68% remain to graduate.

Housing: 1600 students can be accommodated in college housing, which includes coed dorms and off-campus apartments. In addition,

there are Greek floors, quiet floors, medical floors, and themed communities in dorms. 68% of students live on campus; of those, 70% remain on campus on weekends. Alcohol is not permitted. All students may keep cars.

Activities: 9% of men belong to 3 local and 2 national fraternities; 13% of women belong to 1 local and 3 national sororities. There are 62 groups on campus, including academic, art, band, cheerleading, chess, choir, chorale, computers, dance, debate, drama, environmental, ethnic, gay, honors, international, jazz band, literary magazine, musical threater, newspaper, opera, pep band, political, professional, religious, social, social service, student government, symphony, women's, and yearbook. Popular campus events include Songfest, Spring Fling Week, and Family Weekend.

Sports: There are 8 intercollegiate sports for men and 10 for women, and 8 intramural sports for men and 8 for women. Facilities include a football stadium, a gym, a fitness center, a track, and a basketball arena.

Disabled Students: 25% of the campus is accessible. Facilities include wheelchair ramps, elevators, special parking, specially equipped rest rooms, special class scheduling, and lowered drinking fountains.

Services: Counseling and information services are available, as is tutoring in every subject. There is a reader service for the blind, and remedial math, reading, and writing.

Campus Safety and Security: Measures include 24-hour foot and vehicle patrol, emergency notification system, and security escort services. There are shuttle buses, emergency telephones, lighted pathways/sidewalks, and ID card access into residence halls.

Programs of Study: Wagner confers B.A. and B.S. degrees. Master's degrees are also awarded. Bachelor's degrees are awarded in BIOLOGICAL SCIENCE (biology/biological science and microbiology), BUSINESS (accounting and business administration and management), COMMUNICATIONS AND THE ARTS (arts administration/management, dramatic arts, English, fine arts, and music), COMPUTER AND PHYSICAL SCIENCE (chemistry, computer science, mathematics, and physics), EDUCATION (elementary education, middle school education, and secondary education), HEALTH PROFESSIONS (nursing and physician's assistant), SOCIAL SCIENCE (anthropology, history, philosophy, political science/government, psychology, public administration, and sociology). Natural sciences and health professions is the strongest academically. Business, nursing, and psychology are the largest.

Required: To graduate, students must complete 36 units with 12 to 18 in the major and a minimum GPA of 2.0. All students must take courses in English, math, and multidisciplinary studies. In addition, students must fulfill distribution requirements in physical science, life science, math and computers, history, literature, philosophy and religion, foreign culture, aesthetics, and human behavior.

Special: Internships are required for business and English majors and are recommended for all majors. Students may earn B.A.-B.S. degrees in psychology. Student-designed and dual majors, credit for life experience, a Washington semester, nondegree study, and pass/fail options are available. Study abroad in 14 countries is possible. There are 11 national honor societies and a freshman honors program.

Faculty/Classroom: 53% of faculty are male; 47% are female. All teach undergraduates. No introductory courses are taught by graduate students. The average class size in an introductory lecture is 21; in a laboratory is 13; and in a regular course is 19.

Admissions: 66% of the 2009-2010 applicants were accepted. The SAT scores for the 2009-2010 freshman class were: Critical Reading--6% below 700, 41% between 600 and 700, 42% between 500 and 599, and 11% below 500; Math--7% below 500, 43% between 500 and 599, 43% between 600 and 700, and 7 above 700; Writing--13% below 500, 41% between 500 and 599, 40% between 600 and 700, and 6 above 700. The ACT scores were 5% below 21, 28% between 21 and 23, 42% between 24 and 26, 17% between 27 and 28, and 8% above 28. 35% of the current freshmen were in the top fifth of their class; 86% were in the top two fifths. In a recent year, 8 freshmen graduated first in their class and 94 were in the top 10% of their class.

Requirements: The SAT or ACT is required. In addition, graduation from an accredited secondary school is required, with 18 academic credits or Carnegie units, including 4 years of English, 3 years each of history and math, 2 years each of foreign language, science, and social studies, and 1 year each of art and music. An essay is required, and an interview is strongly recommended. Auditions are required for music and theater applicants. An interview is required for the Physician Assistant Program. A GPA of 3.0 is required. AP and CLEP credits are accepted. Important factors in the admissions decision are advanced placement or honors courses, recommendations by school officials, and extracurricular activities record.

Procedure: Freshmen are admitted fall and spring. Entrance exams should be taken by December of the senior year. There are early decision and deferred admissions plans. Early decision applications should be filed by December 1; regular applications, by February 15 for fall entry, along with a $50 fee. Notification of early decision is sent February 15; regular decision, March 1. Applications are accepted on-line. A waiting list is maintained.

Transfer: 66 transfer students enrolled in a recent year. Transfer students should have a minimum of 30 credit hours earned with a GPA of 2.5. Applicants must submit all college and high school transcripts, a letter of recommendation, and a personal statement. An interview is recommended. SAT or ACT scores taken within the past 5 years may be submitted. 9 of 36 credits required for the bachelor's degree must be completed at Wagner.

Visiting: There are regularly scheduled orientations for prospective students, including a presentation by the Admissions Office, a tour of the campus, and meetings with faculty and staff. There are guides for informal visits; visitors may sit in on classes and stay overnight. To schedule a visit, contact the Admissions Office.

Financial Aid: In 2009-2010, 92% of all full-time freshmen and 90% of continuing full-time students received some form of financial aid. 68% of all full-time freshmen and 57% of continuing full-time students received need-based aid. The average freshmen award was $21,102. 25% of undergraduate students work part-time. Average annual earnings from campus work are $800. The average financial indebtedness of the 2009 graduate was $36,988. Wagner is a member of CSS. The FAFSA, the state aid form, and the college's own financial statement are required. The priority date for freshman financial aid applications for fall entry is February 15.

International Students: There are 13 international students enrolled. The school actively recruits these students. They must take the TOEFL with a minimum score of 550 on the paper-based TOEFL (PBT) or 79 on the Internet-based version (iBT).

Computers: Wireless access is available. All students may access the system. There are no time limits and no fees. It is strongly recommended that all students have a personal computer.

Graduates: From July 1, 2008 to June 30, 2009, 475 bachelor's degrees were awarded. The most popular majors were business (21%), visual and performing arts (19%), and health professions (12%). In an average class, 62% graduate in 4 years or less, 67% graduate in 5 years or less, 68% graduate in 6 years or less. Of a recent graduating class, 20% were enrolled in graduate school within 6 months of graduation and 79% were employed.

Admissions Contact: Leigh-Ann Nowicki, Dean of Admissions. E-Mail: *admissions@wagner.edu* Web: *www.wagner.edu*

WEBB INSTITUTE   D-5
Glen Cove, NY 11542   (516) 671-2213; (516) 674-9838

Full-time: 65 men, 20 women	**Faculty:** n/av
Part-time: none	**Ph.D.s:** 50%
Graduate: none	**Student/Faculty:** n/av
Year: semesters	**Tuition:** $8500
Application Deadline: see profile	
Freshman Class: n/av	
SAT: required	**MOST COMPETITIVE**

Webb Institute, founded in 1889, is a private engineering school devoted to professional knowledge of ship construction, design, and motive power. All students receive 4-year, full-tuition scholarships. Figures in the above capsule are approximate. In addition to regional accreditation, Webb has baccalaureate program accreditation with ABET. The library contains 50,598 volumes, 1,633 microform items, and 1,851 audio/video tapes/CDs/DVDs, and subscribes to 267 periodicals including electronic. Computerized library services include interlibrary loans, database searching, and Internet access. The 26-acre campus is in a suburban area 24 miles east of New York City. Including any residence halls, there are 11 buildings.

Student Life: 76% of undergraduates are from out of state, mostly the Northeast. Students are from 22 states and 1 foreign country. 70% are from public schools. 96% are white. The average age of freshmen is 18; all undergraduates, 20. 4% do not continue beyond their first year; 73% remain to graduate.

Housing: 110 students can be accommodated in college housing, which includes single-sex dorms. On-campus housing is guaranteed for all 4 years. All students may keep cars.

Activities: There are no fraternities or sororities. Groups on campus include chorale, drama, orchestra, professional, social, student government, yachting, and yearbook. Popular campus events include Parents Day and Webbstock.

Sports: There are 6 intercollegiate sports for men and 6 for women, and 2 intramural sports for men and 2 for women. Facilities include a 60-seat gym, tennis courts, an athletic field, a boat house, and a beachfront dock.

Disabled Students: 90% of the campus is accessible. Facilities include elevators and special parking.

Services: Counseling and information services are available, as is tutoring in most subjects.

Campus Safety and Security: Measures include 24-hour foot and vehicle patrol. There are emergency telephones, lighted pathways/sidewalks, and student and professional security services.

Programs of Study: Webb confers B.S. degrees. Bachelor's degrees are awarded in ENGINEERING AND ENVIRONMENTAL DESIGN (naval architecture and marine engineering).

Required: The curriculum is prescribed, with all students taking the same courses in each of the 4 years. The Webb program has 4 practical 8-week paid work periods: freshman year, a helper mechanic in a shipyard; sophomore year, a cadet in the engine room of a ship; and junior and senior years, a draftsman or junior engineer in a design office. All students must complete a senior seminar, thesis, and technical reports, as well as make engineering inspection visits. A total of 146 credits with a minimum passing grade of 70% is required to graduate.

Special: All students are employed 2 months each year through co-op programs.

Faculty/Classroom: 100% of faculty are male. All teach undergraduates, and 40% do both. The average class size in an introductory lecture is 25, in a laboratory, 9, and in a regular course, 25.

Requirements: The SAT is required, with a minimum satisfactory score. Applicants should be graduates of an accredited secondary school with 16 academic credits completed, including 4 each in English and math, 2 each in history and science, 1 in foreign language, and 3 in electives. 3 SAT Subject tests in writing, math level I or II, and physics or chemistry are required, as is an interview. Candidates must be U.S. citizens. Webb requires applicants to be in the upper 20% of their class. A GPA of 3.2 is required. Important factors in the admissions decision are advanced placement or honors courses, evidence of special talent, and personality/intangible qualities.

Procedure: Freshmen are admitted fall. Entrance exams should be taken by January of the senior year. There is an early decision admissions plan. Check with the school for current application deadlines. The application fee is $25.

Transfer: Transfers must enter as freshmen. A 3.2 GPA is required. SAT scores and an interview are required. 146 of 146 credits required for the bachelor's degree must be completed at Webb.

Visiting: There are regularly scheduled orientations for prospective students, including a weekend open house in October. There are guides for informal visits; visitors may sit in on classes and stay overnight. To schedule a visit, contact the Associate Director of Admissions.

Financial Aid: The CSS/Profile and the college's own financial statement are required. Check with the school for current application deadlines.

Computers: Wireless access is available. The school provides laptops for all students. All students may access the system 24 hours per day.

Admissions Contact: Steven P Ostendorff, Director of Admissions. E-Mail: *admissions@webb-institute.edu* Web: *www.webb-institute.edu*

WELLS COLLEGE   C-3
Aurora, NY 13026   (315) 364-3264
                                  (800) 952-9355; (315) 364-3227

Full-time: 125 men, 415 women	**Faculty:** 48; IIB, av$
Part-time: 5 men, 15 women	**Ph.D.s:** 100%
Graduate: none	**Student/Faculty:** 11 to 1
Year: semesters	**Tuition:** $29680
Application Deadline: see profile	**Room & Board:** $9000
Freshman Class: n/av	
SAT or ACT: required	
	VERY COMPETITIVE

Wells College is a private liberal arts instituion, founded in 1868. Historically a women's college, it became coeducational in 2005. Figures in the above capsule are approximate. The library contains 218,002 volumes, 14,882 microform items, and 1,154 audio/video tapes/CDs/DVDs, and subscribes to 371 periodicals including electronic. Computerized library services include interlibrary loans, database searching, Internet access, and laptop Internet portals. Special learning facilities include a learning resource center, art gallery, radio station, and the Book Arts Center. The 365-acre campus is in a small town on Cayuga Lake, 30 miles north of Ithaca. Including any residence halls, there are 22 buildings.

Student Life: 67% of undergraduates are from New York. Others are from 32 states and 14 foreign countries. 93% are from public schools. 68% are white. The average age of freshmen is 18; all undergraduates, 20. 20% do not continue beyond their first year; 60% remain to graduate.

Housing: 450 students can be accommodated in college housing, which includes single-sex and coed dorms and off-campus apartments. In addition, there are special-interest houses and housing for nontraditional-age students. On-campus housing is guaranteed for all 4 years. 85% of students live on campus. All students may keep cars.

Activities: There are no fraternities or sororities. There are 42 groups on campus, including bell ringers, choir, chorale, communications, dance, drama, environmental, ethnic, forensics, gay, international, jazz band, literary magazine, newspaper, photography, political, professional, religious, social, social service, student government, WILL (Women In Lifelong Learning), and women's resource center. Popular campus events include the Odd-Even Basketball Game, Spring Weekend, and 100 Days for Seniors.

Sports: There are 5 intercollegiate sports for men and 7 for women, and 10 intramural sports for men and 10 for women. Facilities include a competition-size swimming pool, a gym, a fitness center with weight and cardio equipment, an athletic training room, 2 indoor tennis courts/practice space, a dance studio, a 9-hole golf course, 4 all-weather tennis courts, a skinned infield softball field, 2 game fields for soccer and lacrosse, a field hockey field, and a boat house and dock with canoes, kayaks, and sailboats.

Disabled Students: 51% of the campus is accessible. Facilities include wheelchair ramps, elevators, special parking, specially equipped restrooms, special class scheduling, lowered telephones, and special housing.

Services: Counseling and information services are available, as is tutoring in every subject. Assistance is provided on an individual, as-needed basis. Untimed and extended-time testing options are available.

Campus Safety and Security: Measures include 24-hour foot and vehicle patrol, self-defense education, and security escort services. There are shuttle buses, emergency telephones, and lighted pathways/sidewalks. All students must escort their guests on campus at all times; blue light phones are provided.

Programs of Study: Wells confers B.A. degrees. Bachelor's degrees are awarded in AGRICULTURE (environmental studies), BIOLOGICAL SCIENCE (biochemistry, biology/biological science, and molecular biology), BUSINESS (business administration and management), COMMUNICATIONS AND THE ARTS (dance, dramatic arts, English, fine arts, French, German, language arts, music, Spanish, and visual and performing arts), COMPUTER AND PHYSICAL SCIENCE (chemistry, computer science, mathematics, and physics), EDUCATION (elementary education), SOCIAL SCIENCE (American studies, anthropology, economics, ethics, politics, and social policy, history, international studies, philosophy, political science/government, psychology, public affairs, religion, sociology, and women's studies). Psychology, English, and biological and chemical sciences are the largest.

Required: To graduate, students must complete a total of 120 credit hours, including 33 to 63 in the major, with a minimum GPA of 2.0 overall and in the major. All students must complete 2 first-year experience courses, a comprehensive exam, 3 January intersession internships/courses, and a senior project/thesis. Distribution requirements include 4 courses in phys ed and wellness, 3 each in natural and social sciences and in arts and humanities, 2 in a foreign language, and 1 in formal reasoning.

Special: Wells offers cross-registration with Cornell University, Cayuga Community College, and Ithaca College, a Washington semester with American University, internships, and accelerated degree programs in all majors. Study abroad in 13 countries is permitted. A 3-2 engineering degree is available with Columbia, Clarkson, and Cornell Universities. Students may also earn 3-2 degrees in business and community health with the University of Rochester and a 3-4 degree in veterinary medicine with Cornell University. Student-designed majors and pass-fail options are available. Work-study, B.A.-B.S. degrees, and dual majors are also available. There are 2 national honor societies, including Phi Beta Kappa.

Faculty/Classroom: 44% of faculty are male; 56% are female. All teach undergraduates. No introductory courses are taught by graduate students. The average class size in an introductory lecture is 25, in a laboratory, 16, and in a regular course, 13.

Admissions: 3 freshmen graduated first in their class in a recent year.

Requirements: The SAT or ACT is required. In addition, graduation from an accredited secondary school should include 20 academic credits or Carnegie units. High school courses must include 4 years of English, 3 each of a foreign language and math, and 2 each of history and lab science. 2 teacher recommendations and an essay/personal statement are required, and an interview is strongly recommended. AP and CLEP credits are accepted. Important factors in the admissions decision are recommendations by school officials, extracurricular activities record, and advanced placement or honors courses.

Procedure: Freshmen are admitted fall. Entrance exams should be taken prior to application. There are early decision and deferred admissions plans. Check with the school for current application deadlines. The application fee is $40. Applications are accepted on-line.

Transfer: 56 transfer students enrolled in a recent year. Applicants must be in good standing at the institution last attended. A minimum GPA of 2.0 is required. Wells requires official college and high school transcripts, a personal statement, standardized test scores, and a recommendation from a professor. An interview is strongly recommended. 60 of 120 credits required for the bachelor's degree must be completed at Wells.

Visiting: There are regularly scheduled orientations for prospective students, including tours, interviews, class attendance, presentations, open houses, an overnight host program, and meetings with faculty and coaches. There are guides for informal visits; visitors may sit in on classes and stay overnight. To schedule a visit, contact the Admissions Office.

Financial Aid: In a recent year, 91% of all full-time freshmen and 88% of continuing full-time students received some form of financial aid. 71%

of all full-time freshmen and 76% of continuing full-time students received need-based aid. The average freshmen award was $18,505, with $13,645 ($21,320 maximum) from need-based scholarships or need-based grants; $4900 ($6600 maximum) from need-based self-help aid (loans and jobs); and $6850 ($10,500 maximum) from other non-need-based awards and non-need-based scholarships. 82% of undergraduate students work part-time. Average annual earnings from campus work are $1600. The average financial indebtedness of a recent graduate was $20,355. Wells is a member of CSS. The FAFSA is required. Early decision applicants must also submit the CSS Profile. Check with the school for current deadlines.

International Students: There were 14 international students enrolled in a recent year. The school actively recruits these students. They must take the TOEFL with a minimum score of 550 on the paper-based TOEFL (PBT) or 80 on the Internet-based version (iBT). They must also take the SAT or ACT.

Computers: All residence hall rooms have Internet connectivity. All students may access the system. It is strongly recommended that all students have a personal computer.

Graduates: In a recent year, 82 bachelor's degrees were awarded. The most popular majors were psychology (17%), English (10%), and sociology/anthropology (6%). In an average class, 2% graduate in 3 years or less, 60% graduate in 4 years or less, 61% graduate in 5 years or less, and 62% graduate in 6 years or less. Of a recent graduating class, 15% were enrolled in graduate school within 6 months of graduation and 37% were employed.

Admissions Contact: Susan Sloan, Director of Admissions. A campus DVD is available. E-Mail: *admissions@wells.edu* Web: *www.wells.edu*

YESHIVA UNIVERSITY   D-5

New York, NY 10033-3201	(212) 960-5277; (212) 960-0086
Full-time: 1305 men, 1010 women	**Faculty:** I, +$
Part-time: 40 men, 20 women	**Ph.D.s:** 79%
Graduate: 1300 men, 1700 women	**Student/Faculty:** n/av
Year: semesters, summer session	**Tuition:** $33,050
Application Deadline: see profile	**Room & Board:** $11,000
Freshman Class: n/av	
SAT or ACT: required	**VERY COMPETITIVE**

Yeshiva University, founded in 1886, is an independent liberal arts institution offering undergraduate programs through Yeshiva College, its undergraduate college for men, Stern College for Women, and Sy Syms School of Business. Figures in the above capsule are approximate. There are 7 graduate schools. In addition to regional accreditation, YU has baccalaureate program accreditation with CSWE. The 7 libraries contain 900,000 volumes, 759,000 microform items, and 980 audio/video tapes/CDs/DVDs, and subscribe to 7,790 periodicals including electronic. Computerized library services include interlibrary loans and database searching. Special learning facilities include an art gallery, radio station, and museum. The 26-acre campus is in an urban area.

Student Life: 44% of undergraduates are from out of state. Students are from 31 states, 16 foreign countries, and Canada. 14% are from public schools. The average age of freshmen is 17; all undergraduates, 19. 8% do not continue beyond their first year; 90% remain to graduate.

Housing: 1600 students can be accommodated in college housing, which includes single-sex dorms and off-campus apartments. On-campus housing is guaranteed for all 4 years. 85% of students live on campus. Alcohol is not permitted. All students may keep cars.

Activities: There are no fraternities or sororities. There are 70 groups on campus, including art, choir, computers, drama, honors, international, jazz band, literary magazine, musical theater, newspaper, political, professional, radio, religious, social service, special interest, student government, and yearbook. Popular campus events include holiday and dramatic presentations and Parents Day.

Sports: There are 8 intercollegiate sports for men and 2 for women, and 5 intramural sports for men and 4 for women. The athletic center at Yeshiva College houses a variety of facilities, including a 1000-seat gym.

Disabled Students: 95% of the campus is accessible. Facilities include wheelchair ramps and elevators.

Services: There is remedial reading and writing. There is also a writing center, which helps students with composition and verbal skills.

Campus Safety and Security: Measures include 24-hour foot and vehicle patrol and security escort services. There are shuttle buses, lighted pathways/sidewalks, ID cards, vulnerability surveys, fire drills, alarm systems, emergency telephone numbers, and transportation for routine and special events.

Programs of Study: YU confers B.A. and B.S. degrees. Associates degrees are also awarded. Bachelor's degrees are awarded in BIOLOGICAL SCIENCE (biology/biological science), BUSINESS (accounting, business administration and management, and marketing/retailing/merchandising), COMMUNICATIONS AND THE ARTS (classical languages, communications, English, French, Hebrew, music, and speech/debate/rhetoric), COMPUTER AND PHYSICAL SCIENCE (chemistry, computer science, and mathematics), ENGINEERING AND ENVIRONMENTAL DESIGN (preengineering), HEALTH PROFESSIONS (health science), SOCIAL SCIENCE (economics, history, philosophy, political science/government, psychology, religion, and sociology). The dual program of liberal arts and Jewish studies is the strongest academically. Accounting, psychology, and economics are the largest.

Required: To graduate, students must complete a total of 128 credit hours. Under the dual program, students pursue a liberal arts or business curriculum together with courses in Hebrew language, literature, and culture. Courses in Jewish learning are geared to the student's level of preparation.

Special: YU offers a 3-2 degree in occupational therapy with Columbia and New York Universities, a 3-4 degree in podiatry with the New York College of Podiatric Medicine, and a 3-2 or 4-2 degree in engineering with Columbia University. Stern College students may take courses in advertising, photography, and design at the Fashion Institute of Technology. Study-abroad programs may be arranged in Israel. The school offers independent study options and an optional pass/no credit system. There are 9 national honor societies and 20 departmental honors programs.

Faculty/Classroom: 73% of faculty are male; 27% are female. 58% teach undergraduates, 60% do research, and 28% do both. No introductory courses are taught by graduate students. The average class size in an introductory lecture is 38, in a laboratory, 15, and in a regular course, 18.

Requirements: The SAT or ACT is required. In addition, graduation from an accredited secondary school with 16 academic credits is required for admission. The GED is accepted under limited and specific circumstances. The SAT Subject test in Hebrew is recommended for placement purposes. An interview and an essay are required. A GPA of 3.3 is required. AP and CLEP credits are accepted. Important factors in the admissions decision are extracurricular activities record, personality/intangible qualities, and evidence of special talent.

Procedure: Freshmen are admitted to all sessions. There are early admissions, deferred admissions, and rolling admissions plans. Check with the school for current application deadlines. The application fee is $70. A waiting list is maintained.

Transfer: 95 of 128 credits required for the bachelor's degree must be completed at YU.

Visiting: YU holds open houses for high school students. There are guides for informal visits; visitors may sit in on classes and stay overnight. To schedule a visit, contact the Office of Admissions.

Financial Aid: YU is a member of CSS. The CSS/Profile and the college's own financial statement are required. Check with the school for current application deadlines.

International Students: The school actively recruits these students. They must take the TOEFL. They must also take the SAT or ACT.

Computers: All students may access the system 24 hours per day via modem or when buildings are open. There are no time limits and no fees.

Admissions Contact: Michael Kranzler, Director of Undergraduate Admissions. A campus DVD is available. E-Mail: *yuadmit@yu.edu* Web: *www.yu.edu*

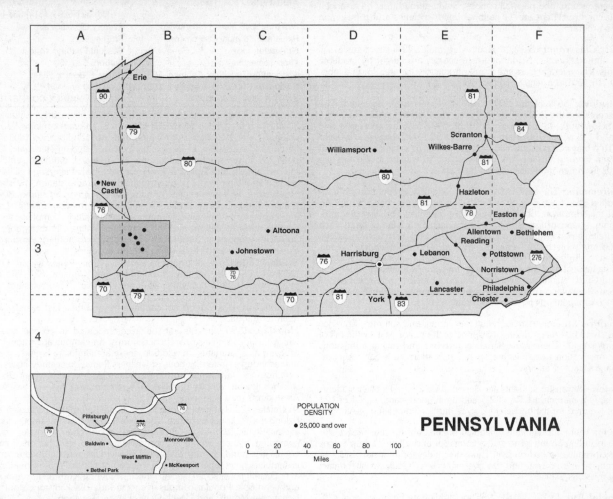

POPULATION
DENSITY

● 25,000 and over

PENNSYLVANIA

0   20   40   60   80   100
Miles

ALBRIGHT COLLEGE   E-3
Reading, PA 19612-5234

(610) 921-7512
(800) 252-1856; (610) 921-7294

Full-time: 725 men, 923 women	**Faculty:** 114; IIB, -$
Part-time: 21 women	**Ph.D.s:** 84%
Graduate: none	**Student/Faculty:** 14 to 1
Year: 4-1-4, summer session	**Tuition:** $28,884
Application Deadline: open	**Room & Board:** $8770
Freshman Class: 5565 applied, 3113 accepted, 541 enrolled	
SAT CR/M: 520/520	**COMPETITIVE**

Albright College, founded in 1856, is a private liberal arts institution affiliated with the United Methodist Church. There is 1 graduate school. Computerized library services include interlibrary loans, database searching, and Internet access. Special learning facilities include a learning resource center, art gallery, radio, station, a multicultural center, and centers for women and child development. The 118-acre campus is in a suburban area 55 miles west of Philadelphia. Including any residence halls, there are 47 buildings.

Student Life: 62% of undergraduates are from Pennsylvania. 73% are from public schools. The average age of freshmen is 18; all undergraduates, 22.

Housing: College-sponsored housing includes single-sex and coed dorms and on-campus apartments. In addition, there are honors houses and special-interest houses. On-campus housing is guaranteed for all 4 years. Upperclassmen may keep cars.

Activities: 16% of men belong to 4 national fraternities; 23% of women belong to 3 national sororities. There are 72 groups on campus, including band, cheerleading, chess, choir, chorus, computers, dance, debate, drama, environmental, ethnic, film, gay, honors, international, jazz band, literary magazine, musical theater, newspaper, pep band, photography, political, professional, radio and TV, religious, social, social service, and student government. Popular campus events include Greek Weekend and Spring Fever Weekend.

Sports: There are 10 intercollegiate sports for men and 10 for women. Facilities include a 5000-seat stadium, a 2000-seat gymnasium, baseball,

softball, and soccer fields, fitness center, weight room, indoor track, bowling alley, a swimming pool, and racquetball courts.

Disabled Students: 75% of the campus is accessible. Facilities include wheelchair ramps, elevators, special parking, specially equipped restrooms, and special class scheduling.

Services: Counseling and information services are available, as is tutoring in most subjects. There is a reader service for the blind. An academic learning center, a writing center, and an ESL program are available.

Campus Safety and Security: Measures include 24-hour foot and vehicle patrol, emergency notification system, self-defense education, and security escort services. There are shuttle buses, emergency telephones, lighted pathways/sidewalks, a Comprehensive Crisis Action Plan, and a bicycle patrol. All officers are CPR, AED, and first aid certified.

Programs of Study: Albright confers B.A. and B.S. degrees. Master's degrees are also awarded. Bachelor's degrees are awarded in BIOLOGICAL SCIENCE (biochemistry and biology/biological science), BUSINESS (accounting, business administration and management, and fashion merchandising), COMMUNICATIONS AND THE ARTS (art, communications, digital communications, dramatic arts, English, French, music business management, and Spanish), COMPUTER AND PHYSICAL SCIENCE (chemistry, computer science, information sciences and systems, mathematics, and physics), EDUCATION (elementary education, secondary education, and special education), ENGINEERING AND ENVIRONMENTAL DESIGN (environmental science), SOCIAL SCIENCE (American studies, child care/child and family studies, criminal justice, economics, history, Latin American studies, philosophy, political science/government, psychobiology, psychology, religion, sociology, textiles and clothing, and women's studies). Fashion and sociology are the largest.

Required: To graduate, students must complete 32 courses, including 13 to 14 in the major, with a minimum GPA of 2.0. All students take 1 interdisciplinary course, and they must fulfill the cultural experience requirement. General studies requirements include 11 to 15 courses in English composition, a foreign language, natural science, quantitative reasoning, social science, the arts, and humanities (literature, history, philosophy and religion).

Special: Co-op programs are available in forestry and environmental studies with Duke University. The school offers credit and noncredit internships, a Washington semester, an accelerated degree program for working adults, cross-registration, dual majors, student-designed majors, nondegree study, and pass/fail options. Study abroad may be arranged in any country. There are 11 national honor societies and a freshman honors program.

Faculty/Classroom: 51% of faculty are male; 49% are female. All teach undergraduates. No introductory courses are taught by graduate students. The average class size in an introductory lecture, 25, in a laboratory, 15, and in a regular course, 18.

Admissions: 56% of the 2009-2010 applicants were accepted. The SAT scores for the 2009-2010 freshman class were; Critical Reading--36% below 500, 45% between 500 and 599, 18% between 600 and 700, and 1 % above 700; Math--36% below 500, 47% between 500 and 599, 16% between 600 and 700, and 1% above 700. 41% of the current freshmen were in the top fifth of their class; 67% were in the top two fifths. 9 freshmen graduated first in their class.

Requirements: The SAT is required. In addition, graduation from an accredited secondary school or satisfactory scores on the GED are required for admission. Students must have a total of 16 Carnegie units, including 4 years of English, 3 in science, including 1 lab, 2 years each of a foreign language, math, and social studies, and 3 electives in college preparatory subjects. An essay is required, and an interview recommended. Submission of test scores is optional for admission. Students applying test optional must complete an on-campus admission interview. AP and CLEP credits are accepted. Important factors in the admissions decision are advanced placement or honors courses, leadership record, and recommendations by school officials.

Procedure: Freshmen are admitted fall, spring, and summer. Entrance exams should be taken during the spring of the junior year or the fall of the senior year. There are deferred admissions and rolling admissions plans. Application deadlines are open. Application fee is $25. Applications are accepted on-line.

Transfer: 48 transfer students enrolled in 2008-2009. Transfer students must have a minimum GPA of 2.5 and be in good standing. 64 of 128 credits required for the bachelor's degree must be completed at Albright.

Visiting: There are regularly scheduled orientations for prospective students, including an interview with a counselor and a tour of the campus with a currently enrolled student. There are guides for informal visits; visitors may sit in on classes and stay overnight. To schedule a visit, contact the Admissions Office.

Financial Aid: In 2009-2010, 96% of all full-time freshmen and 92% of continuing full-time students received some form of financial aid. 84% of all full-time freshmen and 83% of continuing full-time students received need-based aid. The average freshman award was $33,910. Need-based scholarships or need-based grants averaged $21,506 ($30,800 maximum); need-based self-help aid (loans and jobs) averaged $12,587; and other non-need-based awards and non-need-based scholarships averaged $13,389 ($20,000 maximum). 42% of undergraduate students work part-time. Average annual earnings from campus work are $1314. The average financial indebtedness of the 2009 graduate was $31,720. The FAFSA is required. The priority date for freshman financial aid applications for fall entry is March 1.

International Students: There are 124 international students enrolled. The school actively recruits these students. They must take the TOEFL or MELAB and the college's own test. They must also take the SAT and ACT.

Computers: Wireless access is available. There is a separate logical network, wired throughout the dorms, allowing students to attach a registered PC or MAC computing device to the Internet. Students may also register a wireless connection to the wireless LAN, which is available in all classrooms and in many public areas. There are more than 10 computer labs providing access to popular software such as MS-Office and the Internet. All students may access the system 24 hours/day, 7 days/week. There are no time limits and no fees. It is strongly recommended that all students have a personal computer.

Graduates: From July 1, 2008 to June 30, 2009, 334 bachelor's degrees were awarded. The most popular majors were business administration (13%), psychology (6%), and biology/biochemistry (6%). 68 companies recruited on campus in 2008-2009. In an average class, 1% graduate in 3 years or less, 52% graduate in 4 years or less, 61% graduate in 5 years or less, and 62% graduate in 6 years or less. Of the 2008 graduating class, 23% were enrolled in graduate school within 6 months of graduation, and 98% were employed.

Admissions Contact: Gregory E. Eichhorn, Vice President for Enrollment Management and Dean of Admissions. E-Mail: *albright@alb.edu* Web: *www.albright.edu*

ALLEGHENY COLLEGE
B-1
Meadville, PA 16335

(814) 332-4351
(800) 521-5293; (814) 337-0431

Full-time: 948 men, 1146 women	Faculty: 152; IIB, av$
Part-time: 15 men, 23 women	Ph.D.s: 93%
Graduate: none	Student/Faculty: 14 to 1
Year: semesters	Tuition: $33,560
Application Deadline: February 15	Room & Board: $8440
Freshman Class: 3916 applied, 2594 accepted, 580 enrolled	
SAT CR/M/W: 607/601/600	ACT: 26 HIGHLY COMPETITIVE

Allegheny College, founded in 1815, is a private liberal arts institution affiliated with the United Methodist Church. The library contains 935,113 volumes, 494,192 microform items, and 9,69 audio/video tapes/CDs/DVDs, and subscribes to 21,752 periodicals including electronic. Computerized library services include interlibrary loans, database searching, Internet access, and laptop Internet portals. Special learning facilities include a learning resource center, planetarium, radio station, TV station, observatory, 283-acre experimental research reserve, art studio, 80-acre protected forest, dance studio, Geographic Information Systems Learning Laboratory, language learning center, science complex, seismographic network station, and the Center for Political Participation. The 565-acre campus is in a suburban area 90 minutes north of Pittsburg. Including any residence halls, there are 36 buildings.

Student Life: 57% of undergraduates are from Pennsylvania. Others are from 47 states, 38 foreign countries, and Canada. 82% are from public schools. 88% are white. 35% are Catholic; 27% Protestant; 24% claim no religious affiliation. The average age of freshmen is 19; all undergraduates, 20. 12% do not continue beyond their first year; 73% remain to graduate.

Housing: 1590 students can be accommodated in college housing, which includes single-sex and coed dorms, on-campus apartments, and off-campus apartments. In addition, there are language houses, special-interest houses, fraternity houses, wellness floors, quiet study floors, and townhouses. On-campus housing is guaranteed for all 4 years. 78% of students live on campus; of those, 80% remain on campus on weekends. All students may keep cars.

Activities: 22% of men belong to 5 national fraternities; 33% of women belong to 5 national sororities. There are 113 groups on campus, including academic, art, band, cheerleading, chess, choir, chorale, chorus, computers, dance, drama, environmental, ethnic, gay, honors, international, jazz band, literary magazine, Model UN, musical theater, music ensembles, newspaper, orchestra, outdoor, political, professional, radio and TV, religious, social, social service, student government, symphony, and yearbook. Popular campus events include Black History Month, International Month, and Up til' Dawn Dance Marathon.

Sports: There are 10 intercollegiate sports for men and 11 for women, and 12 intramural sports for men and 12 for women. Facilities include a sports and fitness center that includes a training track, weight rooms, cardio machines, 4 multipurpose courts (volleyball, basketball, tennis, badminton, putting green, batting cage), a natatorium, a dance studio, 3 racquetball courts, an outdoor complex with a stadium, a cross-country course, 12 lighted tennis courts, a challenge course, and an 8-lane competition track. In addition, there are 80 wooded acres for mountain biking, hiking, and cross-country skiing.

Disabled Students: 35% of the campus is accessible. Facilities include wheelchair ramps, elevators, special parking, specially equipped restrooms, special class scheduling, lowered drinking fountains, and special housing. Reasonable accommodations are made for special needs.

Services: Counseling and information services are available, as is tutoring in some subjects. There is also help with study skills, a speech center, a learning center, note-taking scribe services, tape recorders, and books on tape.

Campus Safety and Security: Measures include 24-hour foot and vehicle patrol, emergency notification system, self-defense education, and security escort services. There are shuttle buses, emergency telephones, lighted pathways/sidewalks, controlled access to dorms/residences, TTY phones, emergency medical dispatching, and motorists' assistance.

Programs of Study: Allegheny confers B.A. and B.S. degrees. Bachelor's degrees are awarded in AGRICULTURE (environmental studies), BIOLOGICAL SCIENCE (biochemistry, biology/biological science, and neurosciences), COMMUNICATIONS AND THE ARTS (art, art history and appreciation, communications, dramatic arts, English, French, German, music, Spanish, and studio art), COMPUTER AND PHYSICAL SCIENCE (chemistry, computer science, environmental geology, geology, mathematics, physics, and software engineering), ENGINEERING AND ENVIRONMENTAL DESIGN (environmental science), SOCIAL SCIENCE (economics, history, international studies, philosophy, political science/government, psychology, religion, and women's studies). Physical and biological sciences, political science, and economics are the strongest academically. Biology, economics, and psychology are the largest.

Required: To graduate, students must complete 131 credit hours with a minimum GPA of 2.0 in both the major and minor. Between 36 and

64 hours are required in the major, including the junior seminar and senior research project. All students must fulfill liberal studies requirements of 8 credits each in arts and humanities, natural sciences, and social sciences. The liberal studies program extends through all 4 years. Additional required courses include freshman first seminar, freshman second seminar, a sophomore writing and speaking seminar, and academic planning seminars. All graduating seniors complete an independent research project. Most departments require an oral defense of the project.

Special: Allegheny offers a Washington semester, internships, dual majors, student-designed majors, study abroad in 14 countries, work study, and co-op programs. A 3-2 engineering degree is available with Case Western Reserve, Columbia, Duke, Pittsburgh, and Washington Universities. Accelerated programs, preprofessional programs, independent study, a marine biology study program, and an experiential learning term are also available. There are 15 national honor societies, including Phi Beta Kappa, and 18 departmental honors programs.

Faculty/Classroom: 56% of faculty are male; 44% are female. All teach and do research. The average class size in an introductory lecture is 22; in a laboratory, 18; and in a regular course, 19.

Admissions: 66% of the 2009-2010 applicants were accepted. The SAT scores for the 2009-2010 freshman class were: Critical Reading--8% below 500, 32% between 500 and 599, 46% between 600 and 700, and 14% above 700; Math--9% below 500, 33% between 500 and 599, 51% between 600 and 700, and 7% above 700; Writing--12% below 500, 38% between 500 and 599, 40% between 600 and 700, and 10% above 700. The ACT scores were 10% below 21, 22% between 21 and 23, 20% between 24 and 26, 17% between 27 and 28, and 31% above 28. 69% of the current freshmen were in the top fifth of their class; 92% were in the top two fifths. 25 freshmen graduated first in their class.

Requirements: The SAT or ACT is required. In addition, graduation from an accredited secondary school is required for admission. Students must have 16 Carnegie units, including 4 years of English, 3 years each of math, science, and social studies, and 2 years of a foreign language. An essay is required, and an interview is recommended. The GED is accepted. A college prep program and 2 letters of recommendation (1 from a guidance counselor, 1 from a teacher) are required. AP and CLEP credits are accepted.

Procedure: Freshmen are admitted fall and spring. Entrance exams should be taken by January of the senior year. There are early decision, early admissions, and deferred admissions plans. Early decision applications should be filed by November 15; regular applications, by February 15 for fall entry; and November 1 for spring entry, along with a $35 fee. Notification of early decision is sent December 15; regular decision, April 1. 61 early decision candidates were accepted for the 2009-2010 class. 327 applicants were on the 2009 waiting list; 6 were admitted. Applications are accepted on-line.

Transfer: 43 transfer students enrolled in 2008-2009. Transfer applicants must submit a transcript of all college courses, a high school transcript, standardized test scores, a statement of good standing from prior institutions, and a letter describing reasons for transfer, They must have a minimum GPA of 2.5, with 3.0 recommended. 64 of 128 credits required for the bachelor's degree must be completed at Allegheny.

Visiting: There are regularly scheduled orientations for prospective students, consisting of tours, panels, and presentations on academic programs, student life, admissions, and financial aid. There are guides for informal visits, visitors may sit in on classes, and stay overnight. To schedule a visit, contact the Office of Admissions.

Financial Aid: In 2009-2010, 99% of all full-time freshmen and 98% of continuing full-time students received some form of financial aid. 69% of all students received need-based aid. The average freshman award was $25,950. Need-based scholarships or need-based grants averaged $21,029 ($42,000 maximum); need-based self-help aid (loans and jobs) averaged $6590 ($8700 maximum); other non-need-based awards and non-need-based scholarships averaged $13,523 ($27,500 maximum); and other forms of aid, including tuition remission to students without regard to financial need, averaged $30,354 ($33,240 maximum). 59% of undergraduate students work part-time. Average annual earnings from campus work are $1315. The average financial indebtedness of the 2009 graduate was $20,771. The FAFSA is required. The priority date for freshman financial aid applications for fall entry is February 15.

International Students: There are 65 international students enrolled. The school actively recruits these students. They must take the TOEFL with a minimum score of 550 on the paper-based TOEFL (PBT) or 80 on the Internet-based version (iBT). They must also take the SAT or ACT.

Computers: Wireless access is available. 185 PCs are networked and available for students to use in the library, residence halls, the campus center, academic buildings, and computer services. The wireless system can accommodate approximately 500 simultaneous users. Wireless access is available in residence hall lounges and patios, the library, campus center, and food court area, plus there is 1 residence complex with total wireless capability. All students may access the system 24 hours per day. There are no time limits and no fees. It is strongly recommended that all students have a personal computer. An Intel/Windows model is recommended.

Graduates: From July 1, 2008 to June 30, 2009, 489 bachelor's degrees were awarded. The most popular majors were psychology (17%), biology (11%), and political science (9%). 21 companies recruited on campus in 2008-2009. Of the 2008 graduating class, 43% were enrolled in graduate school within 6 months of graduation and 51% were employed.

Admissions Contact: Jennifer Winge, Director of Admissions. E-Mail: *admissions@allegheny.edu* Web: *www.allegheny.edu/admissions/*

ALVERNIA COLLEGE — E-3

Reading, PA 19607
(610) 796-8220
(888) Alvernia; (610) 796-8336

Full-time: 500 men, 1000 women	Faculty: IIB, --$
Part-time: 120 men, 361 women	Ph.D.s: n/av
Graduate: 241 men, 498 women	Student/Faculty: 17 to 1
Year: semesters, summer session	Tuition: $23,028
Application Deadline: open	Room & Board: $7,299
Freshman Class: 922 applied, 699 accepted, 274 enrolled	COMPETITIVE

Alvernia College, established in 1958, is a Roman Catholic, liberal arts institution. Some figures in the above capsule and in this profile are approximate. There are no undergraduate schools and one graduate school. In addition to regional accreditation, Alvernia has baccalaureate program accreditation with APTA, CSWE, NCATE, and NLN. The library contains 86,647 volumes, 1,967 audio/video tapes/CDs/DVDs, and subscribes to 390 periodicals including electronic. Computerized library services include inter-library loans and database searching. The 85-acre campus is in a suburban area 3 miles southwest of Reading. Including any residence halls, there are 14 buildings.

Student Life: 88% of undergraduates are from Pennsylvania. Students are from 12 states, and 9 foreign countries. 76% are from public schools. 84% are white. 29% are Catholic; 19% claim no religious affiliation. The average age of freshmen is 19; all undergraduates, 24.

Housing: 500 students can be accommodated in college housing, which includes single-sex and coed dorms and on-campus apartments. In addition, there are honors houses. On-campus housing is guaranteed for the freshman year only, is available on a first-come, first-served basis. Priority is given to out-of-town students. 60% of students commute. Alcohol is not permitted. All students may keep cars.

Activities: There are no fraternities or sororities. There are 31 groups on campus, including cheerleading, chorus, computers, drama, ethnic, honors, international, literary magazine, newspaper, political, professional, religious, student government, and yearbook. Popular campus events include Christmas on Campus, Spring Fling, and Club Fair.

Sports: There are 6 intercollegiate sports for men and 8 for women, and 4 intramural sports for men and 2 for women. Facilities include a gym, a physical fitness and recreation center, playing fields, and outdoor tennis, basketball, and volleyball courts.

Disabled Students: 75% of the campus is accessible. Facilities include wheelchair ramps, elevators, special parking, specially equipped rest rooms, special class scheduling, lowered drinking fountains, lowered telephones, and special housing.

Services: Counseling and information services are available, as is tutoring in every subject. There is remedial math, reading, and writing. Facilities include a writing center and a math/science tutorial lab.

Campus Safety and Security: Measures include 24-hour foot and vehicle patrol and security escort services. There are emergency telephones, lighted pathways/sidewalks, and photo ID cards must be carried by students.

Programs of Study: Alvernia confers B.A., B.S., B.S.N., and B.S.W. degrees. Associates and master's degrees are also awarded. Bachelor's degrees are awarded in BIOLOGICAL SCIENCE (biochemistry and biology/biological science), BUSINESS (accounting, business administration and management, marketing and distribution, and sports management), COMMUNICATIONS AND THE ARTS (communications and English), COMPUTER AND PHYSICAL SCIENCE (chemistry, information sciences and systems, mathematics, and science), EDUCATION (athletic training, elementary education, and secondary education), HEALTH PROFESSIONS (nursing), SOCIAL SCIENCE (addiction studies, criminal justice, forensic studies, history, liberal arts/general studies, philosophy, political science/government, psychology, social studies, social work, and theological studies). Biology, chemistry, and occupational therapy are the strongest academically. Criminal justice, education, and forensic science are the largest.

Required: To graduate, all students must complete at least 123 credit hours with a minimum GPA of 2.0 overall and in the major (2.5 for elementary education and nursing majors). Requirements include 54 to 55 credits in a liberal arts core, consisting of theology and philosophy, social science, communications, literature, fine arts, math, and science. All students also must perform 40 clock hours of service to others before graduation, complete course work in college success skills and in human diversity, and demonstrate computer proficiency.

Special: The college offers co-op programs in business and sports management, internships, cross-registration with Kutztown University, Pennsylvania State University, Albright College, and Reading area community colleges; a Washington semester, dual and student-designed majors, and practicums in psychology, criminal justice, education, addiction studies, social work, athletic training, and occupational therapy. There are a freshman honors program.

Faculty/Classroom: 43% of faculty are male; 57% are female. All teach undergraduates. No introductory courses are taught by graduate students. The average class size in an introductory lecture is 21; in a laboratory is 15; and in a regular course is 18.

Admissions: 76% of the 2009-2010 applicants were accepted. 35% of the current freshmen were in the top fifth of their class; 53% were in the top two fifths.

Requirements: In addition, all applicants must be graduates of an accredited secondary school or have a GED certificate. They should have completed at least 16 academic units, including 4 in English and electives and 2 each in math, foreign language, science, and social studies. An interview is required for nursing applicants and strongly recommended for all others. A GPA of 2.0 is required. AP and CLEP credits are accepted. Important factors in the admissions decision are advanced placement or honors courses, recommendations by school officials, and extracurricular activities record.

Procedure: Freshmen are admitted fall and spring. Entrance exams should be taken in the spring of the junior year or fall of the senior year. There are deferred admissions and rolling admissions plans. Application deadlines are open. The fall 2008 application fee was $25. Notification is sent on a rolling basis. Applications are accepted on-line.

Transfer: 107 transfer students enrolled in 2008-2009. Applicants must have a college GPA of 2.0 or better. 45 of 123 credits required for the bachelor's degree must be completed at Alvernia.

Visiting: There are regularly scheduled orientations for prospective students, including faculty displays, lunch, tours of the campus, and the opportunity to interact with current students. There are guides for informal visits, visitors may sit in on classes, and stay overnight. To schedule a visit, contact the Admissions Office.

Financial Aid: In 2009-2010, 91% of all full-time freshmen and 91% of continuing full-time students received some form of financial aid. 84% of all full-time freshmen and 79% of continuing full-time students received need-based aid. The average freshmen award was $13,986. 80% of undergraduate students work part-time. Average annual earnings from campus work is $1000. The average financial indebtedness of the 2009 graduate was $6,749. Alvernia is a member of CSS. The FAFSA and the state aid form, and the noncustodial parent's statement, if applicable are required. Check with the school for current application deadlines.

International Students: They must take the TOEFL.

Computers: All students may access the system. Labs are open 17 hours per day, and the network is available 24 hours per day. There are no time limits and no fees. It is strongly recommended that all students have a personal computer. A a Pentium processor or equivalent is recommended.

Admissions Contact: Catherine Emery, Dean of Enrollment. E-Mail: admissions@alvernia.edu Web: www.alvernia.edu

ARCADIA UNIVERSITY   F-3
Glenside, PA 19038

(215) 572-2910
(877) ARCADIA; (215) 572-4049

Full-time: 480 men, 1270 women	Faculty: 103; IIA, av$
Part-time: 71 men, 136 women	Ph.D.s: 89%
Graduate: 353 men, 1095 women	Student/Faculty: 17 to 1
Year: semesters, summer session	Tuition: $27,440
Application Deadline: open	Room & Board: $9,300
Freshman Class: 2432 applied, 2056 accepted, 440 enrolled	
SAT: required	ACT: 25 COMPETITIVE+

Arcadia University, founded in 1853, is a private institution offering undergraduate and graduate programs in the fine arts, the sciences, business, education, and pre-professional fields. There are no undergraduate schools and one graduate school. In addition to regional accreditation, Arcadia has baccalaureate program accreditation with ACBSP, APTA, CAHEA, and NASAD. The library contains 148,271 volumes, 50,301 microform items, 3,236 audio/video tapes/CDs/DVDs, and subscribes to 7,832 periodicals including electronic. Computerized library services include inter-library loans, database searching, Internet access, and laptop Internet portals. Special learning facilities include a learning resource center, art gallery, radio station, observatory, theater, computer graphics and communication labs, and multimedia classrooms. The 76-acre campus is in a suburban area 10 miles north of Philadelphia. Including any residence halls, there are 21 buildings.

Student Life: 68% of undergraduates are from Pennsylvania. Students are from 24 states, and 12 foreign countries. 70% are from public schools. 70% are white. 77% claim no religious affiliation; 13% Catholic. The average age of freshmen is 18; all undergraduates, 22. 19% do not continue beyond their first year; 64% remain to graduate.

Housing: 1284 students can be accommodated in college housing, which includes single-sex and coed dorms, on-campus apartments, and off-campus apartments. There is a living and learning community in Grey Towers Castle. On-campus housing is guaranteed for all 4 years. 68% of students live on campus. Upperclassmen may keep cars.

Activities: There are no fraternities or sororities. There are 40 groups on campus, including art, cheerleading, choir, chorale, chorus, communications, computers, dance, drama, ethnic, gay, honors, international, literary magazine, musical theater, newspaper, photography, political, professional, radio and TV, religious, social, social service, student government, and yearbook. Popular campus events include Mr. Beaver contest, Woodstock Weekend, and International Festival.

Sports: There are 6 intercollegiate sports for men and 9 for women, and 5 intramural sports for men and 5 for women. Facilities include a softball field, outdoor tennis and basketball courts, field hockey and soccer/lacrosse fields, and an athletic and recreation center with a 1500-seat gym for basketball and volleyball, an indoor track, an indoor NCAA regulation swimming pool, an aerobics and dance studio, and fitness and training rooms.

Disabled Students: 70% of the campus is accessible. Facilities include wheelchair ramps, elevators, special parking, specially equipped rest rooms, special class scheduling, lowered drinking fountains, and lowered telephones.

Services: Counseling and information services are available, as is tutoring in every subject. There is a reader service for the blind, and remedial math, reading, and writing.

Campus Safety and Security: Measures include 24-hour foot and vehicle patrol, self-defense education, and security escort services. There are shuttle buses, emergency telephones, lighted pathways/sidewalks, alarmed doors, night receptionists, and card access to residence halls.

Programs of Study: confers B.A., B.S., and B.F.A. degrees. Master's and doctoral degrees are also awarded. Bachelor's degrees are awarded in BIOLOGICAL SCIENCE (biology/biological science), BUSINESS (accounting, banking and finance, business administration and management, international business management, marketing/retailing/merchandising, and personnel management), COMMUNICATIONS AND THE ARTS (art history and appreciation, communications, dramatic arts, English, fine arts, graphic design, illustration, photography, and theater design), COMPUTER AND PHYSICAL SCIENCE (chemistry, computer science, mathematics, and science), EDUCATION (art education, early childhood education, elementary education, music education, secondary education, and special education), ENGINEERING AND ENVIRONMENTAL DESIGN (engineering, environmental science, and interior design), HEALTH PROFESSIONS (art therapy, health care administration, predentistry, premedicine, preoptometry, and preveterinary science), SOCIAL SCIENCE (criminal justice, history, international studies, liberal arts/general studies, philosophy, political science/government, prelaw, psychobiology, psychology, and sociology). Biology, psychology, and math are the strongest academically. Fine arts, business, and education are the largest.

Required: Students must take English composition, math, 2 semesters each of a lab science, and a foreign language. They must also fulfill 24 credits of distribution requirements in the arts, humanities, and social sciences; core courses in American pluralism and non-Western cultures; and a final project or thesis. 128 credit hours are required to graduate, including 40 to 52 in the major, with a minimum GPA of 2.0.

Special: Internships are encouraged in all majors. There are study-abroad programs in 13 countries and co-op programs in business, computer science, chemistry, actuarial science, and accounting. There is a 3-2 engineering program with Columbia University and a 3-4 optometry program with Jefferson University, and a 3-4 optometry program with the Pennsylvania College of Optometry. Arcadia also offers a Washington semester, work-study, student-designed majors,. a dual major in chemistry and business, interdisciplinary majors in scientific illustration, credit by exam. There are 13 national honor societies and a freshman honors program.

Faculty/Classroom: 44% of faculty are male; 56% are female. All faculty does research. No introductory courses are taught by graduate students. The average class size in an introductory lecture is 28; in a laboratory is 20; and in a regular course is 16.

Admissions: 85% of the 2009-2010 applicants were accepted. 51% of the current freshmen were in the top fifth of their class; 86% were in the top two fifths. 4 freshmen graduated first in their class.

Requirements: The SAT is required.The ACT and ACT Writing Test are recommended. In addition, applicants must be graduates of an accredited secondary school or have a GED. A total of 16 academic credits is required, including 4 years of English, 3 each of math and social studies, and 2 each of a foreign language and science. An essay is required. All art and illustration majors (except art education) must submit a portfolio. AP and CLEP credits are accepted. Important factors in the admissions decision are advanced placement or honors courses, recommendations by school officials, and extracurricular activities record.

Procedure: Freshmen are admitted fall and spring. Entrance exams should be taken during orientation. There are early decision, early admissions, deferred admissions, and rolling admissions plans. Application deadlines are open. Application fee is $30. Notification of early decision is sent December 1; regular decision, sent on a rolling basis. Applications are accepted on-line.

Transfer: 167 transfer students enrolled in 2008-2009. Applicants must have a GPA of 2.5. Art majors must submit a portfolio. The SAT or the ACT is required if the student has earned less than 1 year of college credit. An interview is encouraged. 32 of 128 credits required for the bachelor's degree must be completed at Arcadia.

Visiting: There are regularly scheduled orientations for prospective students, including personal interviews Monday through Saturday, open houses, and opportunities to dine on campus and to meet with faculty, financial aid officers, and current students. There are guides for informal visits, visitors may sit in on classes, and stay overnight. To schedule a visit, contact the Office of Enrollment Management at admiss@arcadia.edu.

Financial Aid: In 2009-2010, 99% of all full-time freshmen and 94% of continuing full-time students received some form of financial aid. 77% of all full-time freshmen and % of continuing full-time students received need-based aid. 30% of undergraduate students work part-time. Average annual earnings from campus work are $709. The average financial indebtedness of the 2009 graduate was $31,923. The FAFSA and the college's own financial statement, and PHEAA, and parent and student tax returns are required. The priority date for freshman financial aid applications for fall entry is March 1.

International Students: There are 41 international students enrolled. The school actively recruits these students. They must take the TOEFL, ILET.

Computers: Wireless access is available. All students may access the system. There are no time limits and no fees.

Graduates: From July 1, 2008 to June 30, 2009, 381 bachelor's degrees were awarded. The most popular majors were business (15%), education (15%), and psychology (11%).

Admissions Contact: Office of Enrollment Management A campus DVD is available. E-Mail: admiss@arcadia.edu Web: www.arcadia.edu

BLOOMSBURG UNIVERSITY OF PENNSYLVANIA — E-2

Bloomsburg, PA 17815	(570) 389-4316; (570) 389-4741
Full-time: 3431 men, 4674 women	Faculty: 387; IIA, +$
Part-time: 188 men, 312 women	Ph.Ds: 92%
Graduate: 278 men, 629 women	Student/Faculty: 21 to 1
Year: semesters, summer session	Tuition: $7110 ($15,546)
Application Deadline: open	Room & Board: $6488
Freshman Class: 11,749 applied, 7473 accepted, 2040 enrolled	
SAT CR/M: 500/510	ACT: recommended
	COMPETITIVE

Bloomsburg University of Pennsylvania, founded in 1839, is a public institution offering undergraduate programs in the liberal arts, sciences, business, teacher education, technology, and health professions. There are 4 undergraduate schools and 1 graduate school. In addition to regional accreditation, BU has baccalaureate program accreditation with AACSB, ABET, CAAHEP, CCNE, CSWE, NASM, NAST, and NCATE. The library contains 489,636 volumes, 2.1 million microform items, and 13,502 audio/video tapes/CDs/DVDs, and subscribes to 1710 periodicals including electronic. Computerized library services include interlibrary loans, database searching, Internet access, and laptop Internet portals. Special learning facilities include a learning resource center, art gallery, radio station, and TV station. The 282-acre campus is in a small town 80 miles northeast of Harrisburg. Including any residence halls, there are 72 buildings.

Student Life: 89% of undergraduates are from Pennsylvania. Others are from 22 states, 23 foreign countries, and Canada. 88% are from public schools. 77% are white. The average age of freshmen is 18; all undergraduates, 21. 19% do not continue beyond their first year; 63% remain to graduate.

Housing: 3523 students can be accommodated in college housing, which includes coed dorms, on-campus apartments, and off-campus apartments. In addition, there are honors houses, special-interest houses, and living/learning communities in the residence halls. On-campus housing is guaranteed for the freshman year only and is available on a first-come, first-served basis. Alcohol is not permitted. All students may keep cars.

Activities: 7% of men belong to 3 local and 12 national fraternities; 9% of women belong to 5 local and 8 national sororities. There are 237 groups on campus, including art, band, cheerleading, chess, choir, chorale, chorus, computers, dance, drama, drill team, ethnic, film, forensics, gay, honors, international, jazz band, literary magazine, marching band, musical theater, newspaper, orchestra, pep band, political, professional, radio and TV, religious, social, social service, student government, and yearbook. Popular campus events include Renaissance Jamboree and Siblings and Children Weekend.

Sports: There are 9 intercollegiate sports for men and 9 for women, and 3 intramural sports for men and 3 for women. Facilities include a 5000-seat stadium, a gym, an athletic field, an indoor track, a 6-lane

PENNSYLVANIA 321

swimming pool, 9 practice fields, 18 Grasstex tennis courts, racquetball/handball courts, and a 57,000-square-foot recreation facility.

Disabled Students: Facilities include wheelchair ramps, elevators, special parking, specially equipped rest rooms, special class scheduling, lowered drinking fountains, and lowered telephones.

Services: Counseling and information services are available, as is tutoring in some subjects. There is a reader service for the blind, and remedial math, reading, and writing.

Campus Safety and Security: Measures include 24-hour foot and vehicle patrol, emergency notification system, self-defense education, and security escort services. There are shuttle buses, emergency telephones, lighted pathways/sidewalks, controlled access to dorms/residences, monitored surveillance cameras, and strict residence hall security.

Programs of Study: BU confers B.A., B.S., B.S.Ed., B.S.N., and B.S.W. degrees. Associate, master's, and doctoral degrees are also awarded. Bachelor's degrees are awarded in BIOLOGICAL SCIENCE (biology/biological science), BUSINESS (accounting, business administration and management, and business economics), COMMUNICATIONS AND THE ARTS (American Sign Language, art history and appreciation, communications, dramatic arts, English, French, German, music, Spanish, speech/debate/rhetoric, and studio art), COMPUTER AND PHYSICAL SCIENCE (chemistry, computer science, geoscience, mathematics, physics, and radiological technology), EDUCATION (business education, early childhood education, middle school education, secondary education, social studies education, and special education), ENGINEERING AND ENVIRONMENTAL DESIGN (electrical/electronics engineering), HEALTH PROFESSIONS (exercise science, health science, medical laboratory technology, nursing, and speech pathology/audiology), SOCIAL SCIENCE (anthropology, criminal justice, economics, geography, history, philosophy, political science/government, psychology, social work, and sociology). Elementary education, business administration, and special education are the largest.

Required: To graduate, students must complete 120 credit hours with a minimum GPA of 2.0. BU requires 12 semester hours each in humanities, social sciences, and natural sciences and math. There are specific course requirements in communication, quantitative/analytical reasoning, values, ethics, responsible decision making, and survival, fitness, and recreational skills.

Special: Internships for upperclassmen, study abroad in more than 11 countries, work-study programs, and dual majors are available. BU offers a 3-2 engineering degree with Pennsylvania State and Wilkes Universities. BU has partnered with Luzerne County Community College, Harrisburg Area Community College, and Lehigh Carbon Community College to provide a completion program in early childhood education. There is nondegree study, pass/fail options, and credit for life, military, and work experience. The school uses telecourses and interactive video. There are 9 national honor societies, a freshman honors program, and 15 departmental honors programs.

Faculty/Classroom: 53% of faculty are male; 47% are female. 87% teach undergraduates. No introductory courses are taught by graduate students. The average class size in a laboratory is 16; in a regular course, 31.

Admissions: 64% of the 2009-2010 applicants were accepted. The SAT scores for the 2009-2010 freshman class were: Critical Reading--49% below 500, 42% between 500 and 599, 8% between 600 and 700, and 1% above 700; Math--40% below 500, 46% between 500 and 599, 13% between 600 and 700, and 1% above 700. 28% of the current freshmen were in the top fifth of their class; 62% were in the top two fifths. 12 freshmen graduated first in their class.

Requirements: The SAT is required; the ACT is recommended. In addition, applicants must be graduates of an accredited secondary school. To be competitive, a student should also rank in the top 30% of the high school class with a B average. The GED is accepted. Applicants should complete 4 years each of English and social studies, 3 each of math and science, and 2 of a foreign language. An interview is recommended. AP and CLEP credits are accepted.

Procedure: Freshmen are admitted to all sessions. Entrance exams should be taken during the junior year. There are early decision, early admissions, deferred admissions, and rolling admissions plans. Early decision applications should be filed by November 15; for regular applications, deadlines are open for fall entry. Application fee is $30. Notification is sent on a rolling basis. 215 applicants were on the 2009 waiting list. Applications are accepted on-line.

Transfer: 568 transfer students enrolled in 2008-2009. Either the SAT or ACT is required from applicants who have completed fewer than 24 semester hours of college credits. An official secondary school transcript or a GED and official transcripts from any postsecondary schools attended are also required. Applicants must have a minimum GPA of 2.0 (2.5 or 2.8 for some majors) and be in good standing at the college last attended. Those who have completed 30 semester hours must select a major upon entering BU. 30 of 120 credits required for the bachelor's degree must be completed at BU.

Visiting: There are regularly scheduled orientations for prospective students, consisting of a general meeting with admissions staff, a question-

and-answer session, a campus tour, lunch, and meetings with academic faculty. There are guides for informal visits, and visitors may sit in on classes. To schedule a visit, contact the Admissions Office.

Financial Aid: In 2009-2010, 82% of all full-time freshmen and 80% of continuing full-time students received some form of financial aid. 62% of all full-time freshmen and 60% of continuing full-time students received need-based aid. The average freshman award was $11,880. Need-based scholarships or need-based grants averaged $6609; need-based self-help aid (loans and jobs) averaged $4122; non-need-based athletic scholarships averaged $2867; and other non-need-based awards and non-need-based scholarships averaged $2025. The average financial indebtedness of the 2009 graduate was $21,322. The FAFSA and PHEAA Aid Information Request (PAIR) are required. The priority date for freshman financial aid applications for fall entry is March 15.

International Students: There are 72 international students enrolled. They must take the TOEFL with a minimum score of 500 on the paper-based TOEFL (PBT).

Computers: Wireless access is available. The campuswide wireless network is installed in all major classroom buildings as well as in Andruss Library, the student services center, the student union, and Ben Franklin Hall. All students may access the system. There are no time limits and no fees.

Graduates: From July 1, 2008 to June 30, 2009, 1567 bachelor's degrees were awarded. The most popular majors were business administration (17%), elementary education (10%), and special education (6%). In an average class, 40% graduate in 4 years or less, 60% graduate in 5 years or less, and 63% graduate in 6 years or less. 39 companies recruited on campus in 2008-2009. Of the 2008 graduating class, 19% were enrolled in graduate school within 6 months of graduation, and 72% were employed.

Admissions Contact: Christopher Keller, Director of Admissions. E-mail: *buadmiss@bloomu.edu* Web: *www.bloomu.edu*

BRYN ATHYN COLLEGE OF THE NEW CHURCH | F-3

Bryn Athyn, PA 19009-0717	(267) 502-2511; (267) 502-2658
Full-time: 93 men, 88 women	**Faculty:** 25
Part-time: 1 man, 6 women	**Ph.D.s:** 56%
Graduate: 1 man, 7 women	**Student/Faculty:** 7 to 1
Year: trimesters	**Tuition:** $11,991
Application Deadline: February 1	**Room & Board:** $6300
Freshman Class: 227 applied, 208 accepted, 70 enrolled	
SAT CR/M/W: 540/530/540	**ACT:** 21	**COMPETITIVE**

Bryn Athyn College of the New Church, founded in 1877, is a private, independent, liberal arts institution affiliated with the General Church of the New Jerusalem. There is 1 graduate school. The 2 libraries contain 119,009 volumes, 3,459 microform items, and 1,769 audio/video tapes/CDs/DVDs. Computerized library services include interlibrary loans, database searching, and Internet access. Special learning facilities include a learning resource center, a museum, performing arts center,and archives. The 130-acre campus is in a suburban area 15 miles northeast of Philadelphia. Including any residence halls, there are 13 buildings.

Student Life: 63% of undergraduates are from Pennsylvania. Others are from 16 states, 12 foreign countries, and Canada. 24% are from public schools. 63% are white; 16% foreign nationals. 90% are General Church of the New Jerusalem. The average age of freshmen is 18; all undergraduates, 21. 26% do not continue beyond their first year; 31% remain to graduate.

Housing: 32 students can be accommodated in college housing, which includes single-sex dorms and off-campus apartments. On-campus housing is guaranteed for all 4 years. 71% of students live on campus; of those, all remain on campus on weekends. Alcohol is not permitted. All students may keep cars.

Activities: There are no fraternities or sororities. There are 18 groups on campus, including business, chorale, chorus, college games, communications, dance, drama, international, newspaper, outing club, psychology, social, social service, and student government. Popular campus events include charter day, service day, and alumni weekend.

Sports: There are 3 intercollegiate sports for men and 2 for women. Facilities include a 500-seat gym, an outdoor skating rink, tennis courts, 2 athletic fields, a fitness center, and a dance studio.

Disabled Students: 65% of the campus is accessible. Facilities include wheelchair ramps, elevators, special parking, and specially equipped rest rooms.

Services: Counseling and information services are available, as is tutoring in most subjects.

Campus Safety and Security: Measures include 24-hour foot and vehicle patrol. There are emergency telephones and lighted pathways/sidewalks.

Programs of Study: Bryn Athyn College confers B.A. and B.S. degrees. Associate and master's degrees are also awarded. Bachelor's degrees are awarded in BIOLOGICAL SCIENCE (biology/biological science), COMMUNICATIONS AND THE ARTS (English), EDUCATION (education), SOCIAL SCIENCE (history, interdisciplinary studies, and religion). Interdisciplinary studies, history, and education are the largest.

Required: To graduate, students must complete a total of 130 credit hours with a minimum GPA of 2.0 and must satisfy the Core Program. All students must take required courses in religion, writing, philosophy, and physical education. Some majors require a comprehensive project, exam, or thesis.

Special: Cross-registration is available with Holy Family University, co-op programs, internships, B.A.-B.S. degrees, student-designed majors, non-degree study, and study-abroad opportunities are also available.

Faculty/Classroom: 58% of faculty are male; 42% are female. All teach undergraduates, 24% do research, and 24% do both. No introductory courses are taught by graduate students. The average class size in a regular course is 8.

Admissions: 92% of the 2009-2010 applicants were accepted. The SAT scores for the 2009-2010 freshman class were: Critical Reading--28% below 500, 36% between 500 and 599, 27% between 600 and 700, and 9% above 700; Math--39% below 500, 34% between 500 and 599, 20% between 600 and 700, and 7% above 700; Writing--31% below 500, 40% between 500 and 599, 25% between 600 and 700, and 4% above 700. The ACT scores were 46% below 21, 38% between 21 and 23, 8% between 24 and 26, 8% between 27 and 28, and % above 28.

Requirements: The SAT or ACT is required. Applicants' SAT or ACT scores must reflect promise of success in college work. Applicants must be graduates of an accredited secondary school or achieve satisfactory scores on the GED. An interview is recommended. A GPA of 2.2 is required. AP and CLEP credits are accepted. Important factors in the admissions decision are recommendations by school officials, personality/intangible qualities, and advanced placement or honors courses.

Procedure: Freshmen are admitted fall, winter, and spring. Entrance exams should be taken by fall of senior year. There is a rolling admissions plan. Applications should be filed by February 1 for fall entry, October 1 for winter entry, and January 1 for spring entry. Notification is sent on a rolling basis. Applications are accepted on-line.

Transfer: 2 transfer students enrolled in 2008-2009. Transfer students must supply SAT or ACT scores, transcripts, course descriptions, and teacher, adviser, and employer recommendations. An interview is recommended. 60 of 130 credits required for the bachelor's degree must be completed at Bryn Athyn College.

Visiting: There are regularly scheduled orientations for prospective students, consisting of touring the campus, attending chapel, and visiting classes. There are guides for informal visits; visitors may sit in on classes and stay overnight. To schedule a visit, contact Jennifer Lindsay at (267) 502-2794.

Financial Aid: In 2009-2010, 75% of all full-time freshmen and 75% of continuing full-time students received some form of financial aid. 58% of all full-time freshmen and 58% of continuing full-time students received need-based aid. The average freshman award was $13,057. Need-based scholarships or need-based grants averaged $10,828 ($17,391 maximum); need-based self-help aid (loans and jobs) averaged $3,057($6,500 maximum); and other non-need based and non-need based scholarships averaged $3,495 ($19,927 maximum). 38% of undergraduate students work part-time. Average annual earnings from campus work are $3500. The average financial indebtedness of the 2009 graduate was $6,111. The FAFSA and the college's own financial statement are required. The deadline for filing freshman financial aid applications for fall entry is June 1.

International Students: There are 39 international students enrolled. They must take the TOEFL with a minimum score of 520 on the paper-based TOEFL (PBT) or 70 on the Internet-based version (iBT).

Computers: Wireless access is available. Students have wireless connections to the Internet and to the network anywhere on the main campus. Each residence hall room has two jacks, providing Internet and network access. In each residence hall there are 3 computers available 24 hours a day for residents. During library hours, students can access the 15 computers in the library's second floor lab and the 12 computers on the library's first floor. During normal school day hours, students can also access the 4 computers located in Pendleton Hall's student lounge. There is a portable lab of 16 laptops in the classrooms and there are 2 laptops in the education classroom. Students may also choose to participate in a laptop program, which loans them a laptop for the duration of their schooling, and becomes their personal computer with graduation. All students may access the system 24 hours a day. There are no time limits and no fees.

Graduates: From July 1, 2008 to June 30, 2009, 15 bachelor's degrees were awarded. The most popular majors were interdisciplinary studies (67%), history (20%), and education (7%). In an average class, 3% graduate in 3 years or less, 29% graduate in 4 years or less, 39% graduate in 5 years or less, and 39% graduate in 6 years or less. Of the 2008 graduating class, 9% were enrolled in graduate school within 6 months of graduation, and 73% were employed.

Admissions Contact: Jennifer Lindsay, Admissions Counselor. A campus DVD is available. E-Mail: *jennifer.lindsay@brynathyn.edu* Web: *www.brynathyn.edu*

BRYN MAWR COLLEGE

Bryn Mawr, PA 19010-2899

F-3

(610) 526-5152
(800) 262-1885; (610) 526-7471

Full-time: 1283 women	**Faculty:** 153; IIA, +$
Part-time: 24 women	**Ph.D.s:** 83%
Graduate: 99 men, 365 women	**Student/Faculty:** 8 to 1
Year: semesters, summer session	**Tuition:** $38,934
Application Deadline: January 15	**Room & Board:** $12,000
Freshman Class: 2276 applied, 1107 accepted, 362 enrolled	
SAT CR/M/W: 660/630/660	**ACT:** 28 **MOST COMPETITIVE**

Bryn Mawr College, founded in 1885, is an independent liberal arts institution, primarily for women. The Graduate School of Social Work and Research, the Graduate School of the Arts and Sciences, and the post-baccalaureate premedical programs are coed. There are 2 graduate schools. The 4 libraries contain 1.2 million volumes, 157,522 microform items, and 5652 audio/video tapes/CDs/DVDs, and subscribe to 1712 periodicals including electronic. Computerized library services include interlibrary loans, database searching, and Internet access. Special learning facilities include a learning resource center, art gallery, radio station, archeological museum, and language learning center with audio, video, and computer technology. The 136-acre campus is in a suburban area 11 miles west of Philadelphia. Including any residence halls, there are 57 buildings.

Student Life: 84% of undergraduates are from out of state, mostly the Middle Atlantic. Students are from 44 states, 44 foreign countries, and Canada. 64% are from public schools. 42% are white; 12% Asian American. The average age of freshmen is 18; all undergraduates, 20. 8% do not continue beyond their first year; 86% remain to graduate.

Housing: 1240 students can be accommodated in college housing, which includes single-sex and coed dorms. In addition, there are language houses, special-interest houses, an African American culture center that houses several students, and an environmental co-op house. On-campus housing is guaranteed for all 4 years. 95% of students live on campus; of those, 90% remain on campus on weekends. Upperclassmen may keep cars.

Activities: There are no fraternities or sororities. There are 100 groups on campus, including art, business, chess, choir, chorale, chorus, computers, dance, drama, environmental, ethnic, forensics, gay, Girl Scouts, honors, international, investing, literary magazine, media, Model UN, musical theater, orchestra, photography, political, professional, religious, social, social service, and student government. Popular campus events include May Day, Lantern Night, and Fall Frolic.

Sports: There are 12 intercollegiate sports for women, and 4 intramural sports for women. Facilities include 3 playing fields with access to an indoor track, a gym with an 8-lane pool and diving well, basketball, badminton, and volleyball courts, a gymnastics room and dance studio, a weight-training and fitness room, a 1000-seat auditorium, and a student center.

Disabled Students: Facilities include wheelchair ramps, elevators, special parking, specially equipped restrooms, special class scheduling, lowered drinking fountains, lowered telephones, and special housing.

Services: Counseling and information services are available, as is tutoring in every subject. There is a reader service for the blind.

Campus Safety and Security: Measures include 24-hour foot and vehicle patrol, emergency notification system, self-defense education, and security escort services. There are shuttle buses, emergency telephones, lighted pathways/sidewalks, controlled access to dorms/residences, a web page, bicycle registration, and personal safety education (road safety, car maintenance).

Programs of Study: Bryn Mawr confers A.B. degrees. Master's and doctoral degrees are also awarded. Bachelor's degrees are awarded in BIOLOGICAL SCIENCE (biology/biological science), COMMUNICATIONS AND THE ARTS (art history and appreciation, classical languages, classics, comparative literature, English, fine arts, French, German, Greek, Italian, Latin, linguistics, music, romance languages and literature, Russian, and Spanish), COMPUTER AND PHYSICAL SCIENCE (astronomy, chemistry, computer science, geology, mathematics, and physics), SOCIAL SCIENCE (anthropology, archeology, East Asian studies, economics, history, philosophy, political science/government, psychology, religion, sociology, and urban studies). English, psychology, and math are the largest.

Required: To graduate, students must complete 128 semester hours, with 40 to 60 in the major and a minimum GPA of 2.0. All students must complete 2 courses each in the social sciences, the humanities, and natural sciences or math, including 1 lab science. Additional required courses include 1 college seminar and 1 quantitative skills course. Students must be able to demonstrate proficiency in 1 foreign language.

Special: Students may cross-register with Haverford and Swarthmore Colleges and the University of Pennsylvania. Bryn Mawr sponsors more than 100 grants and internships for summer study in a wide range of disciplines and sponsors/cosponsors study abroad in 27 countries. Student-designed and dual majors are possible. Pass/fail options, work-study programs, a 3-2 degree in engineering with the California Institute of Tech-

nology, and a 3-2 degree in city and regional planning with the University of Pennsylvania are offered.

Faculty/Classroom: All faulty teach and do research. No introductory courses are taught by graduate students. The average class size in an introductory lecture is 25; in a laboratory, 15; and in a regular course, 16.

Admissions: 49% of the 2009-2010 applicants were accepted. The SAT scores for the 2009-2010 freshman class were: Critical Reading--2% below 500, 19% between 500 and 599, 51% between 600 and 700, and 28% above 700; Math--2% below 500, 29% between 500 and 599, 48% between 600 and 700, and 21% above 700; Writing--19% between 500 and 599, 50% between 600 and 700, and 31% above 700. The ACT scores were 2% below 21, 3% between 21 and 23, 24% between 24 and 26, 23% between 27 and 28, and 48% above 28. 80% of the current freshmen were in the top fifth of their class; 97% were in the top two fifths.

Requirements: The SAT is required. The ACT may be substituted for the SAT. Requirements for admission are 4 years of English, at least 3 years of math (2 of algebra and 1 of geometry), 3 years of a foreign language or 2 years of 2 languages, and 1 year each of science and history. Most applicants have taken at least 3 lab science courses and trigonometry. An essay is required. An interview is strongly recommended. AP credits are accepted. Important factors in the admissions decision are advanced placement or honors courses, evidence of special talent, and extracurricular activities record.

Procedure: Freshmen are admitted fall. Entrance exams should be taken in the spring of the junior year or the fall of the senior year. There are early decision and deferred admissions plans. Early decision applications should be filed by November 15; regular applications, by January 15 for fall entry, along with a $50 fee. Notification of early decision is sent December 15; regular decision, in April. 68 early decision candidates were accepted for the 2009-2010 class. 213 applicants were on the 2009 waiting list; 39 were admitted. Applications are accepted on-line.

Transfer: 7 transfer students enrolled in a recent year. Applicants for transfer must be in good academic standing at their current institutions. An official SAT score report or ACT score report, 2 professor recommendations, a school official's report, high school transcripts, college transcripts, and the Bryn Mawr Supplement to the College Application for Transfers must be submitted. 96 of 128 credits required for the bachelor's degree must be completed at Bryn Mawr.

Visiting: There are regularly scheduled orientations for prospective students, including student-guided campus tours, and interviews can be arranged. There are guides for informal visits, and visitors may sit in on classes and stay overnight. To schedule a visit, contact the Office of Admissions.

Financial Aid: In 2009-2010, 77% of all full-time freshmen and 58% of continuing full-time students received some form of financial aid. 69% of all full-time freshmen and 53% of continuing full-time students received need-based aid. The average freshman award was $36,562. Need-based scholarships or need-based grants averaged $33,108 ; need-based self-help aid (loans and jobs) averaged $4068; and other non-need-based awards and non-need-based scholarships averaged $5700. 74% of undergraduate students work part-time. Average annual earnings from campus work are $1500. The average financial indebtedness of the 2009 graduate was $20,156. Bryn Mawr is a member of CSS. The CSS/Profile, the FAFSA, the prior year's tax returns, the noncustodial parent statement, and the business/farm supplement are required. The deadline for filing freshman financial aid applications for fall entry is February 2.

International Students: There were 91 international students enrolled in a recent year. The school actively recruits these students. They must take the TOEFL, with a minimum score of 600 on the paper-based TOEFL (PBT) or 90 on the Internet-based version (iBT), or take the IELTS with a score of 7 or above. They must also take the SAT or ACT.

Computers: Wireless access is available. The libraries, campus center, computing center, some academic buildings, and many dorm living rooms have campus wireless networking. All public, academic, and residential buildings on campus are Ethernet wired to provide students with a connection to the campus network and the Internet. All students may access the system every day. There are no time limits and no fees.

Graduates: From July 1, 2008 to June 30, 2009, 331 bachelor's degrees were awarded. The most popular majors were English (11%), psychology (10%), and biology (8%). 175 companies recruited on campus in 2008-2009. In an average class, 1% graduate in 3 years or less, 79% graduate in 4 years or less, 82% graduate in 5 years or less, and 83% graduate in 6 years or less. Of a recent graduating class, 23% were enrolled in graduate school within 6 months of graduation and 62% were employed.

Admissions Contact: Jennifer Rickard, Dean of Admissions and Financial Aid. A campus DVD is available.
E-mail: *admissions@brynmawr.edu* Web: *www.brynmawr.edu*

BUCKNELL UNIVERSITY   D-2
Lewisburg, PA 17837   (570) 577-1101; (570) 577-3538

Full-time: 1719 men, 1804 women	Faculty: 345; IIA, +$
Part-time: 10 men, 10 women	Ph.D.s: 97%
Graduate: 46 men, 84 women	Student/Faculty: 10 to 1
Year: semesters, , summer session	Tuition: $40,816
Application Deadline: January 15	Room & Board: $9504
Freshman Class: 7572 applied, 2263 accepted, 920 enrolled	
SAT CR/M/W: 640/670/660	ACT: 29 MOST COMPETITIVE

Bucknell University, established in 1846, is a private independent institution offering undergraduate and graduate programs in arts, music, education, humanities, management, engineering, sciences, and social sciences. There are 2 undergraduate schools and one graduate school. In addition to regional accreditation, Bucknell has baccalaureate program accreditation with ABET, CSAB, and NASM. The library contains 818,837 volumes, 49,958 microform items, and 22,427 audio/video tapes/CDs/DVDs, and subscribes to 36,242 periodicals including electronic. Computerized library services include interlibrary loans, database searching, Internet access, and laptop Internet portals. Special learning facilities include a learning resource center, art gallery, radio station, an outdoor natural area, greenhouse, primate facility, observatory, photography lab, race and gender resource center, library resources training lab, electronic classroom, multimedia lab, conference center, performing arts center, and multicultural, writing, craft, and poetry centers, herbarium, and engineering structural test lab. The 450-acre campus is in a small town 75 miles north of Harrisburg. Including any residence halls, there are 123 buildings.

Student Life: 77% of undergraduates are from out of state, mostly the Middle Atlantic. Students are from 47 states, 52 foreign countries, and Canada. 67% are from public schools. 67% are white; 33% African American. 36% claim no religious affiliation; 27% Catholic; 25% Protestant. The average age of freshmen is 18; all undergraduates, 20. 6% do not continue beyond their first year; 90% remain to graduate.

Housing: 3058 students can be accommodated in college housing, which includes single-sex and coed dorms and on-campus apartments. In addition, there are special-interest houses, fraternity houses, substance-free housing and special interest housing. There are also 6 residential colleges for the first year (arts, environmental, humanities, global, science and technology, and social justice). On-campus housing is guaranteed for all 4 years and is available on a lottery system for upperclassmen. 87% of students live on campus; of those, 85% remain on campus on weekends. Upperclassmen may keep cars.

Activities: 42% of men belong to 12 national fraternities; 47% of women belong to 8 national sororities. There are 150 groups on campus, including and radio, art, band, cheerleading, chess, choir, chorale, chorus, computers, dance, drama, environmental, ethnic, forensics, gay, honors, international, jazz band, literary magazine, musical threater, newspaper, opera, orchestra, pep band, photography, political, professional, religious, social, social service, student government, symphony, and yearbook. Popular campus events include Celebration for the Arts, Chrysalis Ball, and Christmas Candlelight Service.

Sports: There are 13 intercollegiate sports for men and 14 for women, and 22 intramural sports for men and 21 for women. Facilities include an athletic and recreation center with an Olympic-size pool; a 16,000-sq.-foot fitness center; a 4,000-seat basketball arena; a 13,000-seat stadium with 8-lane track; hockey and lacrosse fields, baseball fields, and recreational fields for soccer, softball, and other activities; a field house with a 4-lane track, tennis, squash, and racquetball courts, climbing wall, and dance studio; an 18-hole golf course; and tennis courts.

Disabled Students: 70% of the campus is accessible. Facilities include wheelchair ramps, elevators, special parking, specially equipped rest rooms, special class scheduling, lowered drinking fountains, lowered telephones, special housing. Individual arrangements may be made with faculty for students with disabilities.

Services: Counseling and information services are available, as is tutoring in some subjects, biology, chemistry, physics, math, and writing across the curriculum.

Campus Safety and Security: Measures include 24-hour foot and vehicle patrol, emergency notification system, self-defense education, and security escort services. There are emergency telephones, lighted pathways/sidewalks, access controls for dorms/residences, campus safety alerts, and intrusion alarms in residence halls.

Programs of Study: Bucknell confers B.A., B.S., B.S.B.A., B.S.B.E., B.S.C.E., B.S.Ch.E., B.S.C.S.E., B.S.Ed., B.S.E.E., and B.Mus. degrees. Master's degrees are also awarded. Bachelor's degrees are awarded in AGRICULTURE (animal science), BIOLOGICAL SCIENCE (biochemistry, biology/biological science, cell biology, and neurosciences), BUSINESS (accounting and business administration and management), COMMUNICATIONS AND THE ARTS (art, art history and appreciation, classics, dramatic arts, English, fine arts, French, German, music, music history and appreciation, music performance, music theory and composition, Russian, Spanish, and visual and performing arts), COMPUTER AND PHYSICAL SCIENCE (chemistry, computer science, geology,

mathematics, physics, and quantitative methods), EDUCATION (early childhood education, education, educational statistics and research, elementary education, music education, and secondary education), ENGINEERING AND ENVIRONMENTAL DESIGN (biomedical engineering, chemical engineering, civil engineering, computer engineering, electrical/electronics engineering, engineering, environmental science, and mechanical engineering), SOCIAL SCIENCE (anthropology, East Asian studies, economics, geography, history, humanities, interdisciplinary studies, international relations, Latin American studies, philosophy, political science/government, psychology, religion, sociology, and women's studies). Humanities, biology, engineering, and English are the strongest academically. Biology, management, and mechanical engineering are the largest.

Required: Students devise a program in accordance with the College Core Curriculum and the University Writing Requirement. AP courses may count only for Disciplinary Perspectives courses without defined learning goals. Students enrolled in the College of Engineering have a common first semester and must complete Exploring Engineering (EG 100). A total of 32 courses (34 courses for engineering) and a minimum GPA of 2.0 are required to graduate.

Special: Bucknell offers internships, study abroad in more than 60 countries, a Washington semester, a 5-year B.A.-B.S. degree in arts and engineering, a 3-2 engineering degree, and dual and student-designed majors. An interdisciplinary major in animal behavior is offered through the biology and psychology departments. Nondegree study is possible, and a pass/fail grading option is offered in some courses. The Residential College program offers opportunities for an academic-residential mix and faculty-student collaborative learning. Undergraduate research opportunities are available in the humanities/social sciences and the sciences and engineering. There are 23 national honor societies, including Phi Beta Kappa, and 55 departmental honors programs.

Faculty/Classroom: 61% of faculty are male; 39% are female. All teach undergraduates, all do research, and all teach and do research. No introductory courses are taught by graduate students. The average class size in an introductory lecture is 19 and in a laboratory is 20.

Admissions: 30% of the 2009-2010 applicants were accepted. The SAT scores for the 2009-2010 freshman class were: Critical Reading--2% below 500, 21% between 500 and 599, 57% between 600 and 700, and 20 above 700; Math--2% below 500, 10% between 500 and 599, 54% between 600 and 700, and 34 above 700; Writing--3% below 500, 18% between 500 and 599, 54% between 600 and 700, and 25 above 700. The ACT scores were 1% below 21, 4% between 21 and 23, 15% between 24 and 26, 21% between 27 and 28, and 59% above 28. 80% of the current freshmen were in the top fifth of their class.

Requirements: The SAT or ACT is required. The ACT Optional Writing test is also required. In addition, applicants must graduate from an accredited secondary school or have a GED. 16 units must be earned, including 4 in English, 3 in math, and 2 each in history, science, social studies, and a foreign language. An essay is required, and an interview is recommended. Music applicants are required to audition. A portfolio is recommended for art applicants. AP and CLEP credits are accepted. Important factors in the admissions decision are advanced placement or honors courses, evidence of special talent, and extracurricular activities record.

Procedure: Freshmen are admitted fall. Entrance exams should be taken before January 1. There are early decision, deferred admissions plan. Early decision applications should be filed by November 15; regular applications, by January 15 for fall entry. The fall 2008 application fee was $60. Notification of early decision is sent December 15; regular decision, April 1. Applications are accepted on-line. 2073 applicants were on a recent waiting list, 23 were accepted.

Transfer: 24 transfer students enrolled in 2008-2009. Transfer students must have a minimum GPA of 2.5 in courses comparable to those offered at Bucknell. The SAT or ACT is required. A minimum of 16 credit hours must have been earned; 32 are recommended. Students are accepted on a space-available basis. An interview is recommended. 48 of 128 credits required for the bachelor's degree must be completed at Bucknell.

Visiting: There are regularly scheduled orientations for prospective students, including an open house for admitted students on the middle Saturday in April and fall visitation program for minority students, and open houses for prospective students in September and November. There are guides for informal visits and visitors may sit in on classes. To schedule a visit, contact the Admissions Office at (570) 577-1101.

Financial Aid: In 2009-2010, 59% of all full-time freshmen and 51% of continuing full-time students received some form of financial aid. 47% of all full-time freshmen and 46% of continuing full-time students received need-based aid. The average freshmen award was $26,900. 40% of undergraduate students work part-time. Average annual earnings from campus work are $1500. The average financial indebtedness of the 2009 graduate was $18,800. Bucknell is a member of CSS. The CSS/Profile and FAFSA, and noncustodial parent's statement are required. The deadline for filing freshman financial aid applications for fall entry is January 1.

International Students: There are 119 international students enrolled. The school actively recruits these students. They must take the TOEFL with a minimum score of 550 on the paper-based TOEFL (PBT) or 80 on the Internet-based version (iBT).

Computers: Wireless access is available. All spaces in academic, administrative, and co-curricular locations (such as lounges) in residence halls and most outdoor spaces are wireless. There are 970 student accessible PCs throughout campus, some of which are located in 42 labs and classrooms. All students may access the system. 24 hours per day, 7 days per week. There are no time limits and no fees. It is strongly recommended that all students have a personal computer.

Graduates: From July 1, 2008 to June 30, 2009, 865 bachelor's degrees were awarded. The most popular majors were economics (13%), management (9%), and English (6%). 397 companies recruited on campus in 2008-2009. In an average class, 87% graduate in 4 years or less, 90% graduate in 5 years or less, and 90% graduate in 6 years or less. Of the 2008 graduating class, 24% were enrolled in graduate school within 6 months of graduation, and 62% were employed.

Admissions Contact: Robert G. Springall, Dean of Admissions. A campus DVD is available. E-Mail: *admissions@bucknell.edu* Web: *www.bucknell.edu*

CABRINI COLLEGE   F-4
Radnor, PA 19087-3698

(610) 902-8552
(800) 848-1003; (610) 902-8508

Full-time: 510 men, 942 women	Faculty: 67
Part-time: 45 men, 57 women	Ph.D.s: 83%
Graduate: 438 men, 1522 women	Student/Faculty: 21 to 1
Year: semesters, summer session	Tuition: $31,030
Application Deadline: open	Room & Board: $11,400
Freshman Class: 2666 applied, 1988 accepted, 359 enrolled	
SAT CR/M: 477/470	COMPETITIVE

Cabrini College, founded in 1957, is a private liberal arts and professional institution founded by the Missionary Sisters of the Sacred Heart of Jesus, a Roman Catholic order. The college is known for its service learning emphasis. There is 1 graduate school. In addition to regional accreditation, Cabrini has baccalaureate program accreditation with CSWE. The library contains 163,901 volumes, and 2,619 audio/video tapes/CDs/DVDs, and subscribes to 43,038 periodicals including electronic. Computerized library services include interlibrary loans, database searching, Internet access, and laptop Internet portals. Special learning facilities include a learning resource center, radio station, a communications lab with a TV studio, a graphic design lab, a newsroom for the student newspaper, and a science education and technology building with biology, chemistry, and physics labs. There are also information science labs. The 112-acre campus is in a suburban area 20 miles west of Philadelphia. Including any residence halls, there are 23 buildings.

Student Life: 63% of undergraduates are from Pennsylvania. Others are from 21 states, and 19 foreign countries. 78% are white. 60% are Catholic; 14% Protestant. The average age of freshmen is 19; all undergraduates, 20. 34% do not continue beyond their first year; 52% remain to graduate.

Housing: 990 students can be accommodated in college housing, which includes single-sex and coed dorms, on-campus apartments, and off-campus apartments. In addition, there are honors houses and special-interest houses. On-campus housing is available on a first-come, first-served basis, and is available on a lottery system for upperclassmen. Priority is given to out-of-town students. 56% of students live on campus; of those, 56% remain on campus on weekends. Upperclassmen may keep cars.

Activities: There are no fraternities or sororities. There are 54 groups on campus, including cheerleading, choir, chorus, computers, dance, drama, ethnic, honors, international, literary magazine, musical theater, newspaper, photography, political, professional, radio and TV, religious, social, social service, and student government. Popular campus events include Cabrini Day, Yule Log, and Spring Fling.

Sports: There are 8 intercollegiate sports for men and 10 for women, and 11 intramural sports for men and 11 for women. Facilities include a weight room, a lighted artificial turf stadium with seating for 700, a 1500-seat gym, tennis courts, an Olympic-size pool, an indoor jogging track, squash courts, an aerobic dance studio, and a 100-yard auxiliary grass field.

Disabled Students: 90% of the campus is accessible. Facilities include wheelchair ramps, elevators, special parking, specially equipped restrooms, special class scheduling, lowered drinking fountains, lowered telephones, special housing, and special seating in some classrooms. Accommodations are made on an individual basis, with appropriate documentation.

Services: Counseling and information services are available, as is tutoring in most subjects. There is a reader service for the blind. Students may enroll in a study skills course or utilize individual tutoring to acquire learning skills.

Campus Safety and Security: Measures include 24-hour foot and vehicle patrol, self-defense education, and security escort services. There are shuttle buses, emergency telephones, and lighted pathways/sidewalks.

Programs of Study: Cabrini confers B.A., B.S., B.S.Ed., and B.S.W. degrees. Master's degrees are also awarded. Bachelor's degrees are awarded in BIOLOGICAL SCIENCE (biology/biological science), BUSINESS (accounting, banking and finance, business administration and management, human resources, and marketing/retailing/merchandising), COMMUNICATIONS AND THE ARTS (communications, English, French, graphic design, and Spanish), COMPUTER AND PHYSICAL SCIENCE (chemistry, information sciences and systems, and mathematics), EDUCATION (early childhood education, education, elementary education, and special education), HEALTH PROFESSIONS (sports medicine), SOCIAL SCIENCE (American studies, criminal justice, history, liberal arts/general studies, philosophy, political science/government, psychology, religion, social work, and sociology). Education, English, and communication are the strongest academically. Business, elementary education, and psychology are the largest.

Required: To graduate, students must complete a minimum of 123 credits with a minimum GPA of 2.0. All students must complete a core curriculum, which includes English, math, foreign language, information technology, an interdisciplinary seminar in self-understanding, and a junior seminar exploring the common good, which includes a community service project. Distribution requirements cover science, heritage, cultural diversity, values, the individual and society, contemporary issues, creativity, and religious studies. Most majors require a capstone experience, which can include an internship, student teaching, or a comprehensive project or paper. The average number of hours in the major is 45. A thesis is required in some majors.

Special: Cabrini offers cooperative programs, internships, study abroad, work-study programs, and cross-registration with Eastern University, Rosemont and Valley Forge Colleges, and other SEPCHE colleges and universities. Dual and student-designed majors and an accelerated degree program in organizational management are available. Credit by exam, credit for life/military/work experience, nondegree study, and pass/fail options are also offered. A Washington semester with the Washington Center for Internships and Academic Seminars is available. There are 18 national honor societies, a freshman honors program, and 11 departmental honors programs.

Faculty/Classroom: 42% of faculty are male; 58% are female. 65% teach undergraduates, and 61% do both. No introductory courses are taught by graduate students. The average class size in an introductory lecture, 18, in a laboratory, 15, and in a regular course, 17.

Admissions: 75% of the 2009-2010 applicants were accepted. The SAT scores for the 2009-2010 freshman class were: Critical Reading--63% below 500, 32% between 500 and 599, and 5% between 600 and 700; Math--65% below 500, 30% between 500 and 599, and 5% between 600 and 700. 20% of the current freshmen were in the top fifth of their class; 41% were in the top two fifths.

Requirements: The SAT is required. In addition, all students must be graduates of an accredited secondary school or have a GED. A minimum of 17 Carnegie units are required, consisting of 4 in English, 3 each in math, science, and social studies, 2 in a foreign language, and the rest in electives. An interview is recommended. A GPA of 2.0 is required. AP and CLEP credits are accepted. Important factors in the admissions decision are advanced placement or honors courses, extracurricular activities record, and leadership record.

Procedure: Freshmen are admitted to all sessions. Entrance exams should be taken before December of the senior year. There are early admissions, deferred admissions, and rolling admissions plans. Application deadlines are open. The fall 2009 application fee was $35. Notification is sent on a rolling basis. Applications are accepted on-line.

Transfer: 110 transfer students enrolled in a recent year. A minimum of 15 credit hours with at least a GPA of 2.2 overall is required; a 2.5 GPA is preferred. Some programs may have higher requirements. 45 of 123 credits required for the bachelor's degree must be completed at Cabrini.

Visiting: There are regularly scheduled orientations for prospective students, including fall orientation, held 3 to 5 days before classes begin, with students completing an electronic gateway prior to arriving. There are guides for informal visits; visitors may sit in on classes and stay overnight. To schedule a visit, contact the Admissions Office.

Financial Aid: In 2009-2010, 98% of all full-time freshmen and 97% of continuing full-time students received some form of financial aid. 78% of all full-time freshmen and 73% of continuing full-time students received need-based aid. The average freshman award was $23,154. Need-based scholarships or need-based grants averaged $9,521 ($28,470 maximum); need-based self-help aid (loans and jobs) averaged $4,439 ($7,500 maximum); and other non-need-based awards and non-need-based scholarships averaged $11,345 ($30,120 maximum). 15% of undergraduate students work part-time. Average annual earnings from campus work are $765. The average financial indebtedness of the 2009 graduate was $26,500. The FAFSA is required. The deadline for filing freshman financial aid applications for fall entry is April 1.

International Students: There are 23 international students enrolled. They must take the TOEFL with a minimum score of 500 on the paper-based TOEFL (PBT) or 173 on the Internet-based version (iBT) or take the MELAB, or successfully complete ESL if not from an English-speaking country. They must also take the SAT or ACT.

Computers: Wireless access is available. Every student receives a domain account and a campus e-mail address. With those accounts students can log in to any PC on campus and access the college's network. Students can access the Internet anywhere on campus, which is 90% wireless. All students may access the system 24 hours a day, 7 days a week. There are no time limits and no fees. It is strongly recommended that all students have a personal computer. A A Celeron at 600 MHz or a 1-GHz or faster Power Mac G4, or Dell is recommended.

Graduates: From July 1, 2008 to June 30, 2009, 385 bachelor's degrees were awarded. The most popular majors were English/communication (13%), special education (8%), and business (6%). 70 companies recruited on campus in 2008-2009. In an average class, 1% graduate in 3 years or less, 47% graduate in 4 years or less, 51% graduate in 5 years or less, and 52% graduate in 6 years or less. Of the 2008 graduating class, 22% were enrolled in graduate school within 6 months of graduation, and 84% were employed.

Admissions Contact: Douglas Swartz, Vice President for Enrollment Management. E-Mail: *admit@cabrini.edu* Web: *www.cabrini.edu*

CALIFORNIA UNIVERSITY OF PENNSYLVANIA   B-3

California, PA 15419-1394	(724) 938-4404; (724) 938-4564
Full-time: 2600 men, 2700 women	Faculty: 266; IIA, +$
Part-time: 249 men, 421 women	Ph.D.s: 55%
Graduate: 485 men, 756 women	Student/Faculty: 20 to 1
Year: semesters, summer session	Tuition: $6,700 ($9800)
Application Deadline: open	Room & Board: $7,788
Freshman Class: 3385 applied, 2633 accepted, 1285 enrolled	
SAT: required	ACT: 20 COMPETITIVE

California University of Pennsylvania, founded in 1852, is a state-supported institution offering degree programs in the arts and sciences, engineering, and education. There are 3 undergraduate schools and one graduate school. In addition to regional accreditation, the university has baccalaureate program accreditation with CSWE, NCATE, and NLN. The library contains 451,382 volumes, 830,298 microform items, 60,416 audio/video tapes/CDs/DVDs, and subscribes to 822 periodicals including electronic. Computerized library services include inter-library loans and database searching. Special learning facilities include a learning resource center, art gallery, natural history museum, radio station, and TV station. The 148-acre campus is in a small town 35 miles south of Pittsburgh. Including any residence halls, there are 38 buildings.

Student Life: 95% of undergraduates are from Pennsylvania. Students are from 35 states, 21 foreign countries, and Canada. 95% are from public schools. 93% are white. The average age of freshmen is 19; all undergraduates, 23. 25% do not continue beyond their first year; 50% remain to graduate.

Housing: 1467 students can be accommodated in college housing, which includes single-sex and coed dorms and off-campus apartments. In addition, there are honors houses, wellness, quiet. On-campus housing is available on a first-come, first-served basis, and is available on a lottery system for upperclassmen. 80% of students commute. Alcohol is not permitted. All students may keep cars.

Activities: 10% of men belong to 7 national fraternities; 6% of women belong to 7 national sororities. There are 78 groups on campus, including art, band, cheerleading, chess, choir, chorale, chorus, computers, dance, debate, drama, drill team, ethnic, forensics, honors, international, jazz band, literary magazine, marching band, musical theater, newspaper, pep band, professional, radio and TV, religious, student government, and yearbook.

Sports: There are 12 intercollegiate sports for men and 10 for women, and 13 intramural sports for men and 14 for women. Facilities include tennis and basketball courts, an all-weather track, a swimming pool, and a 4500-seat stadium.

Disabled Students: 95% of the campus is accessible. Facilities include wheelchair ramps, elevators, special parking, specially equipped rest rooms, special class scheduling, lowered drinking fountains, and lowered telephones.

Services: Counseling and information services are available, as is tutoring in most subjects. There is a reader service for the blind, and remedial math, reading, and writing.

Campus Safety and Security: Measures include 24-hour foot and vehicle patrol, self-defense education, and security escort services. There are shuttle buses and lighted pathways/sidewalks.

Programs of Study: The university confers B.A., B.S., B.S.Ed., and B.S.N. degrees. Associates and master's degrees are also awarded. Bachelor's degrees are awarded in BIOLOGICAL SCIENCE (biology/biological science), BUSINESS (accounting, business administration and management, management science, and sports management), COMMUNICATIONS AND THE ARTS (art, dramatic arts, English, French, graphic design, Spanish, and speech/debate/rhetoric), COMPUTER AND PHYSICAL SCIENCE (chemistry, geology, information sciences and systems, mathematics, physical sciences, and physics), EDUCATION (athletic training, early childhood education, education, elementary education, guidance education, reading education, school psychology, secondary education, and special education), ENGINEERING AND ENVIRONMENTAL DESIGN (commercial art, computer technology, electrical/electronics engineering technology, engineering technology, environmental science, and industrial engineering technology), HEALTH PROFESSIONS (medical laboratory technology, mental health/human services, nursing, and physical therapy assistant), SOCIAL SCIENCE (criminal justice, geography, gerontology, history, liberal arts/general studies, parks and recreation management, philosophy, political science/government, psychology, social science, and social work).

Required: Students must complete a minimum of 120 semester credits and must maintain a minimum GPA of 2.5 in teacher education curricula, 2.3 in the student's area of concentration, and 2.0 overall.

Special: Cooperative programs are available in all academic areas when eligibility requirements have been met. Opportunities are provided for internships, and an accelerated degree program in justice studies is also available. There are 25 national honor societies and a freshman honors program.

Faculty/Classroom: 58% of faculty are male; 42% are female. All teach undergraduates. No introductory courses are taught by graduate students. The average class size in an introductory lecture is 30; in a laboratory is 24; and in a regular course is 30.

Admissions: 78% of the 2009-2010 applicants were accepted. The ACT scores were 68% below 21, 21% between 21 and 23, 7% between 24 and 26, 3% between 27 and 28, and 1% above 28. 17% of the current freshmen were in the top fifth of their class; 44% were in the top two fifths. 3 freshmen graduated first in their class.

Requirements: The SAT is required. In addition, with a minimum composite score of 870 (400 verbal, 400 math); the ACT may be substituted, with a minimum score of 20. Graduation from an accredited secondary school is required; a GED will be accepted. Applicants should submit an academic record that includes 4 credits each in English and history, 3 each in math and academic electives, 2 in science, and 1 each in social studies and a foreign language. An essay and an interview are recommended. A GPA of 2.5 is required. AP and CLEP credits are accepted.

Procedure: Freshmen are admitted to all sessions. Entrance exams should be taken during the senior year. There is a rolling admissions plan. Application deadlines are open. Application fee is $25. Applications are accepted on-line.

Transfer: 619 transfer students enrolled in 2008-2009. Applicants must submit official transcripts from all previous colleges attended. If fewer than 30 transferable credits are submitted, applicants must also include a high school transcript and standardized test score. Grades of D are not transferable. 30 of 120 credits required for the bachelor's degree must be completed at the university.

Visiting: There are regularly scheduled orientations for prospective students. There are guides for informal visits, visitors may sit in on classes, and stay overnight. To schedule a visit, contact the Admissions Office.

Financial Aid: The FAFSA, and Pennsylvania State Grant and Federal Financial Aid Application is required. The priority date for freshman financial aid applications for fall entry is April 1. The deadline for filing freshman financial aid applications for fall entry is April 1.

International Students: There are 48 international students enrolled. They must take the TOEFL. They must also take the SAT. The SAT is recommended, with a minimum composite score of 800.

Computers: Wireless access is available. All students may access the system. There are no time limits and no fees.

Graduates: From July 1, 2008 to June 30, 2009, 983 bachelor's degrees were awarded. The most popular majors were education (21%), business (12%), and justice studies (8%). 62 companies recruited on campus in 2008-2009. In an average class, 21% graduate in 4 years or less, 43% graduate in 5 years or less, and 49% graduate in 6 years or less. Of the 2008 graduating class, 18% were enrolled in graduate school within 6 months of graduation, and 95% were employed.

Admissions Contact: William Edmonds, Director of Admissions. A campus DVD is available. E-Mail: *inquiry@cup.edu* Web: *www.cup.edu*

CARLOW UNIVERSITY
Pittsburgh, PA 15213

B-3

(412) 578-6059
(800) 333-CARLOW; (412) 578-6668

Full-time: 74 men, 1043 women	Faculty: 82; IIA, --$
Part-time: 124 men, 577 women	Ph.D.s: 72%
Graduate: 77 men, 707 women	Student/Faculty: 14 to 1
Year: semesters, summer session	Tuition: $ ($19,514)
Application Deadline: July 1	Room & Board: $8552
Freshman Class: 1205 applied, 743 accepted, 257 enrolled	
SAT CR/M/W: 480/470/475	ACT: 21	COMPETITIVE

Carlow University, founded in 1929, and the first women-centered, liberal arts university in Pennsylvania, prepares students for leadership and service in personal and professional life. There are 6 undergraduate schools and 5 graduate schools. In addition to regional accreditation, Carlow has baccalaureate program accreditation with CSWE. The library contains 133,864 volumes, 11,712 microform items, and 5,113 audio/video tapes/CDs/DVDs, and subscribes to 14,784 periodicals including electronic. Computerized library services include interlibrary loans, database searching, Internet access, and laptop Internet portals. Special learning facilities include a learning resource center, art gallery, greenhouse, communications lab, and cadaver lab. The 15-acre campus is in an urban area in the Oakland section of Pittsburgh. Including any residence halls, there are 14 buildings.

Student Life: 98% of undergraduates are from Pennsylvania. Others are from 11 states, and 7 foreign countries. 90% are from public schools. 56% are white; 14% African American. 43% are Catholic; 17% claim no religious affiliation. The average age of freshmen is 18; all undergraduates, 26. 31% do not continue beyond their first year; 47% remain to graduate.

Housing: 416 students can be accommodated in college housing, which includes single-sex dorms. On-campus housing is available on a first-come, first-served basis, and is available on a lottery system for upperclassmen. 76% of students commute. Alcohol is not permitted. All students may keep cars.

Activities: There are no fraternities or sororities. There are 23 groups on campus, including a campus activities board, students in the natural sciences, band, choir, chorale, chorus, communications, dance, drama, ethnic, honors, literary magazine, musical theater, newspaper, pep band, political, professional, social, social service, student education association, and student government. Popular campus events include Constitution Day, Halloween, and Spring Carnival.

Sports: There are 5 intercollegiate sports for women. Facilities include 2 fitness centers, a pool, and an aerobics room.

Disabled Students: 30% of the campus is accessible. Facilities include wheelchair ramps, elevators, special parking, specially equipped rest rooms, special class scheduling, lowered drinking fountains, lowered telephones, 6 power doors, and 1 doorbell.

Services: Counseling and information services are available, as is tutoring in most subjects. Professional tutoring is available for reading, writing, study skills, math, and sciences. Peer tutoring is available in other subject areas.

Campus Safety and Security: Measures include 24-hour foot and vehicle patrol, emergency notification system, self-defense education, and security escort services. There are emergency telephones, lighted pathways/sidewalks, and most doors on campus are secured electronically and require an ID badge to enter.

Programs of Study: Carlow confers B.A., B.S., B.S.N., and B.S.W. degrees. Master's and doctoral degrees are also awarded. Bachelor's degrees are awarded in BIOLOGICAL SCIENCE (biology/biological science), BUSINESS (accounting, business administration and management, business communications, and human resources), COMMUNICATIONS AND THE ARTS (art, art history and appreciation, communications, creative writing, English, media arts, Spanish, and technical and business writing), COMPUTER AND PHYSICAL SCIENCE (chemistry, information sciences and systems, and mathematics), EDUCATION (art education, early childhood education, elementary education, journalism education, middle school education, secondary education, and special education), HEALTH PROFESSIONS (art therapy, health care administration, nursing, and scientific/medical marketing), SOCIAL SCIENCE (forensic studies, history, liberal arts/general studies, philosophy, political science/government, psychology, public administration, social work, sociology, and theological studies). Nursing, creative writing, and education are the strongest academically. Nursing, psychology, and business management are the largest.

Required: A total of 120 credit hours (123 for nursing students), including 27 to 44 in the major, is required for the B.A. Appropriate credits must be earned in the core curriculum. An interdisciplinary course, English, service learning, and communication studies are also required. A minimum GPA of 2.0 is required. All students must demonstrate competence in writing, reading comprehension, and math, and must take basic skills courses in public speaking and research paper writing. All students undergo a comprehensive evaluation in their senior year.

Special: Carlow offers cross-registration to member institutions of the Pittsburgh Council for Higher Education, internships in all areas, and work-study. There are accelerated degree programs, and dual majors are possible in most majors, as are student-designed majors. There are 3-2 engineering programs with Carnegie Mellon University and a 3-2 biology/environmental science and management program with Duquesne University. Students can study abroad in all countries deemed by the government to be safe for travel. There are 4 national honor societies, a freshman honors program, and 31 departmental honors programs.

Faculty/Classroom: 24% of faculty are male; 76% are female. 79% teach undergraduates. No introductory courses are taught by graduate students. The average class size in an introductory lecture is 13; in a laboratory is 10; and in a regular course is 7.

Admissions: 62% of the 2009-2010 applicants were accepted. The SAT scores for the 2009-2010 freshman class were: Critical Reading--58% below 500, 32% between 500 and 599, 8% between 600 and 700, and 2% above 700; Math--65% below 500, 32% between 500 and 599, and 3% between 600 and 700; Writing--60% below 500, 30% between 500 and 599, 9% between 600 and 700, and 1% above 700. The ACT scores were 46% below 21, 32% between 21 and 23, 15% between 24 and 26, 3% between 27 and 28, and 4% above 28. 27% of the current freshmen were in the top fifth of their class; 60% were in the top two fifths.

Requirements: The SAT or ACT is required. In addition, The minimum scores depend on the major selected. Candidates must be graduates of an accredited secondary school. 18 Carnegie units are required, including 4 each in English and arts/humanities, 3 each in math and science, and 4 in electives. Applicants for nursing must have completed a minimum 4 units in English, 3 in social sciences, and 2 each in math (including algebra) and lab science (including chemistry), as required by the State Board of Nursing. The GED is accepted. An essay and/or interview are recommended. A GPA of 2.0 is required. AP and CLEP credits are accepted.

Procedure: Freshmen are admitted fall, spring, and summer. Entrance exams should be taken late in the junior year or early in the senior year. There are early admissions, deferred admissions, and rolling admissions plans. Applications should be filed by July 1 for fall entry and December 1 for spring entry, along with a $20 fee. Notification is sent on a rolling basis. Applications are accepted on-line. 5 applicants were on a recent waiting list, 5 were accepted.

Transfer: 273 transfer students enrolled in 2008-2009. Transfer students must have a minimum GPA of 2.0 and submit college transcripts. Certain programs have higher GPA requireements. An interview is also recommended. 32 of 120 credits (123 for nursiing) required for the bachelor's degree must be completed at Carlow.

Visiting: There are regularly scheduled orientations for prospective students, including a campus tour, information sessions on admission and financial aid, and interaction with faculty and students regarding academic and student life. There are guides for informal visits, visitors may sit in on classes, and stay overnight. To schedule a visit, contact the Admissions Office at 412-578-6059.

Financial Aid: In 2009-2010, all full-time freshmen received some form of financial aid. 86% of all full-time freshmen received need-based aid. The average freshmen award was $25,093, with $3,381 ($15,352 maximum) from need-based scholarships or need-based grants; $2,706 ($3,500 maximum) from need-based self-help aid (loans and jobs); $6,600 ($10,000 maximum) from non-need-based athletic scholarships; and $4,398 ($20,854 maximum) from other non-need-based awards and non-need-based scholarships. The average financial indebtedness of the 2009 graduate was $29,536. Carlow is a member of CSS. The FAFSA and verification worksheets and tax returns when applicable is required. The priority date for freshman financial aid applications for fall entry is April 1. The deadline for filing freshman financial aid applications for fall entry is rolling, until funds are exhausted.

International Students: There are 2 international students enrolled. They must take the TOEFL with a minimum score of 500 (550 for nursing) on the paper-based TOEFL (PBT) or 173 (213 for nursing) on the Internet-based version (iBT). In some cases, the SAT can replace the TOEFL; otherwise the SAT is recommended.

Computers: Wireless access is available. All students are required to access Carlow e-mail to communicate with the faculty, and they are required in many cases to use Blackboard for their classes. There are approximately 160 PCs in 8 computing labs. All students may access the system 24 hours a day, 7 days a week. There are no time limits and no fees. It is strongly recommended that all students have a personal computer.

Graduates: From July 1, 2008 to June 30, 2009, 350 bachelor's degrees were awarded. The most popular majors were nursing (30%), biology (10%), and elementary education (9%). 11 companies recruited on campus in 2008-2009. In an average class, 37% graduate in 4 years or less, 46% graduate in 5 years or less, and 47% graduate in 6 years or less. Of the 2008 graduating class, 36% were enrolled in graduate school within 6 months of graduation, and 61% were employed.

Admissions Contact: Susan Winstel, Director of Admissions. A campus DVD is available. E-Mail: *admissions@carlow.edu* Web: *www.carlow.edu*

CARNEGIE MELLON UNIVERSITY   B-3

Pittsburgh, PA 15213   (412) 268-2082; (412) 268-7838

Full-time: 3430 men, 2432 women	**Faculty:** I, +$
Part-time: 65 men, 36 women	**Ph.D.s:** 96%
Graduate: 3789 men, 1631 women	**Student/Faculty:** 7 to 1
Year: semesters, summer session	**Tuition:** $40,920
Application Deadline: see profile	**Room & Board:** $10,340
Freshman Class: 14,153 applied, 5132 accepted, 1423 enrolled	
SAT CR/M/W: 670/730/680	**ACT:** 31 **MOST COMPETITIVE**

Carnegie Mellon University, established in 1900, is a private nonsectarian institution offering undergraduate programs in liberal arts and science and technology. There are 6 undergraduate schools and 7 graduate schools. In addition to regional accreditation, Carnegie Mellon has baccalaureate program accreditation with AACSB, ABET, NAAB, NASAD, and NASM. The 4 libraries contain 1.1 million volumes, 1.1 million microform items, and 30,729 audio/video tapes/CDs/DVDs, and subscribe to 1955 periodicals including electronic. Computerized library services include interlibrary loans, database searching, Internet access, and laptop Internet portals. Special learning facilities include a learning resource center, art gallery, radio station, and TV station. The 145-acre campus is in a suburban area 4 miles from downtown Pittsburgh. Including any residence halls, there are 80 buildings.

Student Life: 81% of undergraduates are from out of state, mostly the Middle Atlantic. Students are from 49 states, 65 foreign countries, and Canada. 40% are white; 24% Asian American; 15% foreign nationals. The average age of freshmen is 18; all undergraduates, 20. 5% do not continue beyond their first year; 85% remain to graduate.

Housing: 3878 students can be accommodated in college housing, which includes single-sex and coed dorms, on-campus apartments, and off-campus apartments. In addition, there are honors houses, language houses, special-interest houses, fraternity houses, and sorority houses. On-campus housing is guaranteed for all 4 years. 64% of students live on campus. Alcohol is not permitted. Upperclassmen may keep cars.

Activities: 15% of men belong to 16 national fraternities; 10% of women belong to 7 national sororities. There are 225 groups on campus, including art, bagpipe, band, cheerleading, chess, choir, chorale, chorus, computers, debate, drama, ethnic, film, gay, honors, international, jazz band, literary magazine, marching band, musical theater, newspaper, opera, orchestra, pep band, photography, political, professional, radio and TV, religious, social, social service, student government, and symphony. Popular campus events include Spring Carnival, International Festival, and Watson Arts Festival.

Sports: There are 8 intercollegiate sports for men and 8 for women, and 38 intramural sports for men and 38 for women. Facilities include a gym, a football stadium with track, athletic fields, tennis and racquetball courts, and a pool.

Disabled Students: 98% of the campus is accessible. Facilities include wheelchair ramps, elevators, special parking, specially equipped restrooms, special class scheduling, lowered drinking fountains, and lowered telephones.

Services: Counseling and information services are available, as is tutoring in most subjects. There is a reader service for the blind.

Campus Safety and Security: Measures include 24-hour foot and vehicle patrol, emergency notification system, self-defense education, and security escort services. There are shuttle buses, emergency telephones, lighted pathways/sidewalks, and a SafeWalk Program.

Programs of Study: Carnegie Mellon confers B.A., B.S., B.A.H., B.Arch., B.F.A., and B.S.A. degrees. Master's and doctoral degrees are also awarded. Bachelor's degrees are awarded in BIOLOGICAL SCIENCE (biology/biological science), BUSINESS (business administration and management, business economics, and marketing/retailing/merchandising), COMMUNICATIONS AND THE ARTS (communications, design, dramatic arts, English, fine arts, French, German, journalism, languages, music, and Spanish), COMPUTER AND PHYSICAL SCIENCE (chemistry, computer programming, computer science, information sciences and systems, mathematics, physics, and statistics), EDUCATION (music education), ENGINEERING AND ENVIRONMENTAL DESIGN (chemical engineering, civil engineering, computer engineering, electrical/electronics engineering, engineering, and mechanical engineering), SOCIAL SCIENCE (economics, history, philosophy, political science/government, psychology, public administration, social science, and urban studies). Computer science, engineering, and business administration are the strongest academically. Engineering is the largest.

Required: To graduate, students must complete requirements in English, history, and computing skills, and they must have a GPA of 2.0. Distribution requirements, the number of credits needed to graduate, and the number of credits required in the major vary by college.

Special: Students may cross-register with other Pittsburgh Council of Higher Education institutions. Also available are internships, work-study

programs, study abroad in 49 countries, a Washington semester, accelerated degrees, B.A.-B.S. degrees, co-op programs, dual majors, and limited student-designed majors. There are 10 national honor societies, including Phi Beta Kappa, and a freshman honors program.

Faculty/Classroom: 72% of faculty are male; 28% are female. All teach and do research. No introductory courses are taught by graduate students.

Admissions: 36% of the 2009-2010 applicants were accepted. The SAT scores for the 2009-2010 freshman class were: Critical Reading--1% below 500, 14% between 500 and 599, 16% between 600 and 700, and 69% above 700; Math--1% below 500, 5% between 500 and 599, 28% between 600 and 700, and 66% above 700; Writing--1% below 500, 13% between 500 and 599, 47% between 600 and 700, and 39% above 700. The ACT scores were 2% below 21, 3% between 21 and 23, 6% between 24 and 26, 11% between 27 and 28, and 78% above 28. 88% of the current freshmen were in the top fifth of their class; 97% were in the top two fifths. 69 freshmen graduated first in their class.

Requirements: The SAT or ACT is required. SAT Subject tests are not required for drama, design, art, or music applicants. All other applicants must take appropriate tests, preferably by December but no later than January. Applicants must graduate from an accredited secondary school or have a GED. They must earn 16 Carnegie units and must have completed 4 years of English. Applicants to the Carnegie Institute of Technology and the Mellon College of Science must take 4 years of math and 1 year each of biology, chemistry, and physics. Essays are required, and interviews are recommended. Art and design applicants must submit a portfolio. Drama and music applicants must audition. AP credits are accepted.

Procedure: Freshmen are admitted in the fall. Entrance exams should be taken be received by Jan 1 (Dec 15 for College of Fine Arts). There are early decision, early admissions and deferred admissions plans. Check with the school for current application deadlines. The fall 2009 application fee was $70. Applications are accepted on-line. A waiting list is maintained.

Transfer: 47 transfer students enrolled in 2008-2009. Applicants must submit secondary school and college transcripts (including school catalogs with course descriptions so that Carnegie Mellon can evaluate transferable credits).

Visiting: There are regularly scheduled orientations for prospective students, including Saturday group sessions in September, October, November, and April. There are guides for informal visits, and visitors may sit in on classes and stay overnight. To schedule a visit, contact the Admissions Office.

Financial Aid: In 2009-2010, 76% of all full-time freshmen and 67% of continuing full-time students received some form of financial aid. 53% of all full-time freshmen and 47% of continuing full-time students received need-based aid. The average freshmen award was $28,678. 31% of undergraduate students work part-time. The average financial indebtedness of the 2009 graduate was $29,546. Carnegie Mellon is a member of CSS. The FAFSA and the college's own financial statement, and parent and student federal tax returns and W-2 forms are required. Check with the school for current application deadlines.

International Students: There are 933 international students enrolled. The school actively recruits these students. They must take the TOEFL with a minimum score of 600 on the paper-based TOEFL (PBT) or 100 on the Internet-based version (iBT) or take the MELAB. They must also take the SAT or ACT.

Computers: Wireless access is available. There are 444 computers in public clusters available to students. All students may access the system 24 hours per day. There are no time limits and no fees.

Graduates: From July 1, 2008 to June 30, 2009, 1349 bachelor's degrees were awarded. The most popular majors were computer science (11%), electrical and computer engineering (10%), and business administration (10%). In an average class, 82% graduate in 5 years or less and 85% graduate in 6 years or less. Of the 2008 graduating class, 33% were enrolled in graduate school within 6 months of graduation, and 83% were employed.

Admissions Contact: Michael Steidel, Director of Admissions. E-Mail: *undergraduate-admissions+@andrew.cmu.edu* Web: *www.cmu.edu*

CEDAR CREST COLLEGE   E-3

Allentown, PA 18104-6196   (610) 740-3780
                                        (800) 360-1222; (610) 606-4647

Full-time: 23 men, 944 women	**Faculty:** 91; IIB, -$
Part-time: 67 men, 651 women	**Ph.D.s:** 53%
Graduate: 19 men, 183 women	**Student/Faculty:** 11 to 1
Year: semesters, summer session	**Tuition:** $28,585
Application Deadline: open	**Room & Board:** $9321
Freshman Class: 1583 applied, 1004 accepted, 196 enrolled	
SAT CR/M/W: 529/520/512	**ACT:** 23 **COMPETITIVE+**

Cedar Crest College, founded in 1867, was one of the first women's colleges in the nation. Today it remains an independent, comprehensive liberal arts college for women that combines excellence in scholarship and undergraduate education with an extensive Lifelong Learning program and growing graduate programs that serve women and men in the surrounding region. There is 1 graduate school. Computerized library services include interlibrary loans, database searching, Internet access, and laptop Internet portals. Special learning facilities include a learning resource center, art gallery, radio station, an arboretum, theaters, and a sculpture garden. The 84-acre campus is in a suburban area 55 miles north of Philadelphia and 90 miles west of New York City. Including any residence halls, there are 20 buildings.

Student Life: 81% of undergraduates are from Pennsylvania. 95% are from public schools. 77% are white. 59% claim no religious affiliation; 17% Catholic. The average age of freshmen is 19; all undergraduates, 27. 21% do not continue beyond their first year; 55% remain to graduate.

Housing: 550 students can be accommodated in college housing, which includes single-sex dorms. Smoke-free floors and floors with limited visitation are available. On-campus housing is guaranteed for all 4 years. 69% of students commute. All students may keep cars.

Activities: There are no sororities. There are 51 groups on campus, including art, band, cheerleading, choir, chorus, computers, dance, drama, ethnic, forensics, gay, honors, international, literary magazine, musical theater, newspaper, political, professional, radio and TV, religious, social, social service, student government, and yearbook. Popular campus events include Student Faculty Frolic, Midnight Breakfast, and Ring Ceremony.

Sports: There are 8 intercollegiate sports and 4 intramural sports for women. Facilities include 5 tennis courts, softball, field hockey, soccer, and lacrosse fields, a cross-country course, a gym with basketball, volleyball, and badminton courts, dance and aerobics studios, weight training, and a fitness center.

Disabled Students: 35% of the campus is accessible. Facilities include wheelchair ramps, elevators, special parking, specially equipped restrooms, special class scheduling, lowered drinking fountains, and lowered telephones.

Services: Counseling and information services are available, as is tutoring in most subjects. There is remedial math and writing and a computer software skills program for underprepared students.

Campus Safety and Security: Measures include 24-hour foot and vehicle patrol, emergency notification system, self-defense education, and security escort services. There are emergency telephones and lighted pathways/sidewalks. Residence halls are equipped with fire/intrusion alarms, which are monitored 24 hours a day. A keyless access system is in place; exterior doors are locked 24 hours a day.

Programs of Study: Cedar Crest confers B.A. and B.S degrees. Master's degrees are also awarded. Bachelor's degrees are awarded in BIOLOGICAL SCIENCE (biochemistry, biology/biological science, environmental biology, genetics, neurosciences, and nutrition), BUSINESS (accounting, business administration and management, and marketing/retailing/merchandising), COMMUNICATIONS AND THE ARTS (art, communications, dance, dramatic arts, English, fine arts, and music), COMPUTER AND PHYSICAL SCIENCE (chemistry, information sciences and systems, mathematics, and science), EDUCATION (education and elementary education), HEALTH PROFESSIONS (nuclear medical technology and nursing), SOCIAL SCIENCE (criminal justice, history, industrial and organizational psychology, political science/government, psychology, and social work). Sciences and nursing are the strongest academically. Sciences, nursing, and psychology are the largest.

Required: To graduate, students must complete 120 credit hours (122 for nursing) with a minimum GPA of 2.0 (some majors have higher requirements). Distribution requirements include 7 credits in natural sciences; 6 each in writing, mathematics and logic, humanities, the arts, and social sciences; and 3 each in global studies and ethics. A major capstone experience is required.

Special: Cross-registration is available through the Lehigh Valley Association of Independent Colleges. Also available are internships, a Washington semester with American University, work-study programs, an accelerated degree program in business, and B.A.-B.S. degrees in math, biology, and psychology. Dual majors, student-designed majors, 3-2 engineering degrees with Georgia Institute of Technology and Washington University, pass/fail options, and credit for life, military, and work experience are offered. There are 15 national honor societies, a freshman honors program, and 1 departmental honors program.

Faculty/Classroom: 31% of faculty are male; 69% are female. All teach undergraduates. No introductory courses are taught by graduate students. The average class size in an introductory lecture is 20; in a laboratory, 13; and in a regular course, 14.

Admissions: 66% of the 2009-2010 applicants were accepted. The SAT scores for the 2009-2010 freshman class were: Critical Reading--33% below 500, 53% between 500 and 599, 13% between 600 and 700, and 1% above 700; Math--37% below 500, 50% between 500 and 599, and 13% between 600 and 700; Writing--39% below 500, 50% between 500 and 599, 9% between 600 and 700, and 2% above 700. The ACT scores were 25% below 21, 23% between 21 and 23, 28% between 24 and 26, 19% between 27 and 28, and 5% above 28. 50% of

the current freshmen were in the top fifth of their class; 72% were in the top two fifths. 2 freshmen graduated first in their class in a recent year.

Requirements: The SAT is required. In addition, applicants must be graduates of an accredited secondary school. The GED is accepted. Students should have completed 16 high school academic credits, including 4 years of English, 3 of math, 2 each of science, history, and foreign language, and 1 each of art, music, and social studies. An essay is required. Cedar Crest requires applicants to be in the upper 50% of their class. A GPA of 2.0 is required. AP and CLEP credits are accepted. Important factors in the admissions decision are advanced placement or honors courses, leadership record, and evidence of special talent.

Procedure: Freshmen are admitted fall and spring. Entrance exams should be taken in the junior year or early in the senior year. There are deferred admissions and rolling admissions plans. Application deadlines are open. Application fee is $30. Applications are accepted on-line.

Transfer: 134 transfer students enrolled in 2009-2010. Applicants should have a minimum college GPA of 2.0. An interview is recommended. 30 of 120 credits required for the bachelor's degree must be completed at Cedar Crest.

Visiting: There are regularly scheduled orientations for prospective students. There are guides for informal visits, and visitors may sit in on classes and stay overnight. To schedule a visit, contact the Admissions Office at admis@cedarcrest.edu.

Financial Aid: In 2009-2010, 98% of all full-time freshmen and 97% of continuing full-time students received some form of financial aid. 93% of all full-time freshmen and 90% of continuing full-time students received need-based aid. The average freshman award was $23,552. Need-based scholarships or need-based grants averaged $19,347; need-based self-help aid (loans and jobs) averaged $4663; and other non-need-based awards and non-need-based scholarships averaged $6146. 28% of undergraduate students work part-time. Average annual earnings from campus work are $2200. The average financial indebtedness of the 2009 graduate was $21,666. Cedar Crest is a member of CSS. The FAFSA, the state aid form, and the college's own financial statement are required. The priority date for freshman financial aid applications for fall entry is March 15. The deadline for filing freshman financial aid applications for fall entry is May 1.

International Students: There were 61 international students enrolled in a recent year. The school actively recruits these students. They must take the TOEFL with a minimum score of 550 on the paper-based TOEFL (PBT) or 61 on the Internet-based version (iBT).

Computers: Wireless access is available. Network access is available in all computer labs, residence halls, and the library. Wireless is available in all residence halls, common areas, the dining hall, and the library. There are 188 PCs available for general student use. All students may access the system. There are no time limits and no fees. It is strongly recommended that all students have a personal computer.

Graduates: From July 1, 2008 to June 30, 2009, 313 bachelor's degrees were awarded. The most popular majors were nursing (30%), psychology (12%), and elementary education (6%). In an average class, 45% graduate in 4 years or less, 52% graduate in 5 years or less, and 55% graduate in 6 years or less. 11 companies recruited on campus in 2008-2009. Of the 2008 graduating class, 7% were enrolled in graduate school within 6 months of graduation, and 70% were employed.

Admissions Contact: Kimberly C. Owens, Senior EVP Management and Student Affairs. A campus DVD is available.
E-mail: kowens@cedarcrest.edu Web: www.cedarcrest.edu

CHATHAM UNIVERSITY
Chatham College
B-3

Pittsburgh, PA 15232
(412) 365-1290
(800) 837-1290; (412) 365-1609

Full-time: 1 men, 594 women	**Faculty:** 55; IIA, --$
Part-time: 49 men, 231 women	**Ph.D.s:** 96%
Graduate: 175 men, 810 women	**Student/Faculty:** 11 to 1
Year: 4-1-4, summer session	**Tuition:** $26,116
Application Deadline: open	**Room & Board:** $7,892
Freshman Class: 600 applied, 453 accepted, 175 enrolled	
SAT CR/M: 530/510	**ACT:** 23 COMPETITIVE

Chatham University, formerly Chatham College and founded in 1869, is a private university offering undergraduate degree programs only to women in more than 30 liberal arts and pre-professional majors. Graduate degree programs in art and architecture, business, counseling psychology, health sciences and nursing, teaching, and writing and other continuing and professional studies programs are open to men as well as women. There are no undergraduate schools and 2 graduate schools. The library contains 89,382 volumes, 22,100 microform items, 1,144 audio/video tapes/CDs/DVDs, and subscribes to 361 periodicals including electronic. Computerized library services include inter-library loans, database searching, Internet access, and laptop Internet portals. Special learning facilities include a learning resource center, art gallery, theaters, a media center, and an arboretum. The 35-acre campus is in an urban area 5 miles east of downtown Pittsburgh. Including any residence halls, there are 33 buildings.

Student Life: 79% of undergraduates are from Pennsylvania. Students are from 32 states, 11 foreign countries, and Canada. 96% are from public schools. 65% are white; 11% African American. The average age of freshmen is 18; all undergraduates, 21. 28% do not continue beyond their first year; 53% remain to graduate.

Housing: 600 students can be accommodated in college housing, which includes single-sex dorms, on-campus apartments, and off-campus apartments. In addition, there are special-interest houses, and an intercultural residence hall. On-campus housing is available on a lottery system for upperclassmen. 61% of students live on campus; of those, 75% remain on campus on weekends. Upperclassmen may keep cars.

Activities: There are no fraternities or sororities. There are 28 groups on campus, including choir, dance, drama, environmental, ethnic, feminist, film, gay, honors, international, literary magazine, newspaper, photography, political, professional, religious, social service, and student government. Popular campus events include Fall Festival, Spring Fling, and Air Band Contest.

Sports: There are 9 intercollegiate sports for women, and 8 intramural sports for women. Facilities include an 8-lane swimming pool with 1-and 3-meter diving, a gym, a dance studio, squash courts, a climbing wall, a cardio-fitness center, and a field for both soccer and softball.

Disabled Students: 75% of the campus is accessible. Facilities include wheelchair ramps, elevators, special parking, specially equipped rest rooms, and special class scheduling.

Services: Counseling and information services are available, as is tutoring in every subject. There is a reader service for the blind, and remedial math, reading, and writing. One-on-one and group tutoring are available by both students and professional specialists, and there is also computer-aided tutoring and an organized study group.

Campus Safety and Security: Measures include 24-hour foot and vehicle patrol, emergency notification system, self-defense education, and security escort services. There are shuttle buses, emergency telephones, and lighted pathways/sidewalks.

Programs of Study: Chatham confers B.A., B.S., and B.S.W. degrees. Master's and doctoral degrees are also awarded. Bachelor's degrees are awarded in AGRICULTURE (environmental studies), BIOLOGICAL SCIENCE (biochemistry, bioinformatics, and biology/biological science), BUSINESS (accounting, business administration and management, international business management, management information systems, and marketing management), COMMUNICATIONS AND THE ARTS (art history and appreciation, arts administration/management, communications, dramatic arts, English, English literature, French, media arts, music, Spanish, and visual and performing arts), COMPUTER AND PHYSICAL SCIENCE (chemistry, computer science, mathematics, and physics), EDUCATION (education), ENGINEERING AND ENVIRONMENTAL DESIGN (environmental science), HEALTH PROFESSIONS (exercise science), SOCIAL SCIENCE (crosscultural studies, economics, forensic studies, history, interdisciplinary studies, international relations, political science/government, psychology, public affairs, social work, and women's studies). Biology, psychology, and English are the largest.

Required: To graduate, students must complete 120 credit hours, including a general education curriculum of 7 courses and a senior tutorial, with a minimum GPA of 2.0. Students must also demonstrate proficiencies in writing, math, and computer literacy.

Special: Chatham offers a study-abroad program in 7 countries, cross-registration with other Pittsburgh Council on Higher Education institutions, co-op programs in all majors, internships in the public and private sectors, and a Washington semester in conjunction with American University and the Public Leadership Education Network. Accelerated degree programs, work-study, combined B.A.-B.S. degrees, multidisciplinary majors, and dual and student-designed majors are available. There are 3-2 engineering degrees with Carnegie Mellon and Penn State Universities and the University of Pittsburgh, dual degree programs, and an accelerated Master's program with Carnegie Mellon's Heinz School. There are 7 national honor societies, including Phi Beta Kappa, a freshman honors program, and 100 departmental honors programs.

Faculty/Classroom: 32% of faculty are male; 68% are female. 57% teach undergraduates. No introductory courses are taught by graduate students. The average class size in an introductory lecture is 15; in a laboratory is 12; and in a regular course is 12.

Admissions: 76% of the 2009-2010 applicants were accepted. The SAT scores for the 2009-2010 freshman class were: Critical Reading--33% below 500, 46% between 500 and 599, 17% between 600 and 700, and 4 above 700; Math--44% below 500, 43% between 500 and 599, 13% between 600 and 700, and above 700.

Requirements: In addition, applicants who choose not to submit the SAT or ACT will be required instead to submit a graded writing sample and resume or list of curricular and co-curricular activities. Applicants will also have the option to submit a portfolio or special project or activity. These materials may also be applied toward Chatham's scholarship review process upon acceptance. AP and CLEP credits are accepted. Im-

portant factors in the admissions decision are recommendations by school officials, leadership record, and extracurricular activities record.

Procedure: Freshmen are admitted fall, winter, and spring. Entrance exams should be taken by fall of the senior year. There are deferred admissions and rolling admissions plans. Application deadlines are open. Application fee is $35. Notification is sent on a rolling basis. Applications are accepted on-line.

Transfer: 89 transfer students enrolled in 2008-2009. Applicants must present college transcripts 45 of 120 credits required for the bachelor's degree must be completed at Chatham.

Visiting: There are regularly scheduled orientations for prospective students, including campus tours, student and faculty panels, financial aid presentations, and athletic coach meetings. There are guides for informal visits, visitors may sit in on classes, and stay overnight. To schedule a visit, contact the Admissions Office.

Financial Aid: In 2009-2010, 100% of all full-time freshmen and 99% of continuing full-time students received some form of financial aid. 67% of all full-time freshmen and 72% of continuing full-time students received need-based aid. The average freshmen award was $18,771, with $4,937 ($17,000 maximum) from need-based scholarships or need-based grants; $7,380 ($8,825 maximum) from need-based self-help aid (loans and jobs); and $13,048 ($17,000 maximum) from other non-need-based awards and non-need-based scholarships. 33% of undergraduate students work part-time. Average annual earnings from campus work are $2200. The average financial indebtedness of the 2009 graduate was $21,013. The FAFSA is required. The deadline for filing freshman financial aid applications for fall entry is May 1.

International Students: There are 41 international students enrolled. The school actively recruits these students. They must take the TOEFL with a minimum score of 550 on the paper-based TOEFL (PBT) or 79 on the Internet-based version (iBT) or take the MELAB, or IELTS. The SAT is required if no TOEFL score is available.

Computers: All students may access the system. 24 hours per day from own or residence hall cluster computers. There are no time limits and no fees.

Graduates: From July 1, 2008 to June 30, 2009, 108 bachelor's degrees were awarded. The most popular majors were psychology (17%), biological/life sciences (11%), and English (8%). In an average class, 44% graduate in 4 years or less, 50% graduate in 5 years or less, and 53% graduate in 6 years or less. Of the 2008 graduating class, 29% were enrolled in graduate school within 6 months of graduation.

Admissions Contact: Michael Poll, Vice President of Admissions. E-Mail: *admissions@chatham.edu* Web: *www.chatham.edu*

CHESTNUT HILL COLLEGE F-3
Philadelphia, PA 19118-2693
(215) 248-7001
(800) 248-0052; (215) 248-7082

Full-time: 375 men, 776 women	**Faculty:** 62; IIA, --$
Part-time: 77 men, 252 women	**Ph.D.s:** 82%
Graduate: 182 men, 658 women	**Student/Faculty:** 19 to 1
Year: semesters, summer session	**Tuition:** $27,100
Application Deadline: open	**Room & Board:** $8690

Freshman Class: 2037 applied, 1844 accepted, 273 enrolled
SAT CR/M/W: 500/480/480   **ACT:** 19   **LESS COMPETITIVE**

Chestnut Hill College, founded in 1924, is a private, liberal arts institution affiliated with the Roman Catholic Church. In addition to the traditional program, CHC also offers an accelerated evening and weekend program for working adults. Courses in the accelerated program are offered in 6 8-week sessions per year, with 10 career-oriented majors. There are 2 undergraduate schools and one graduate school. The library contains 132,434 volumes, 219,532 microform items, and 2,462 audio/video tapes/CDs/DVDs, and subscribes to 1,296 periodicals including electronic. Computerized library services include interlibrary loans, database searching, Internet access, and laptop Internet portals. Special learning facilities include a learning resource center, art gallery, planetarium, TV station, rotating observatory, and technology center. The 75-acre campus is in a suburban area 25 miles northwest of downtown Philadelphia. Including any residence halls, there are 17 buildings.

Student Life: 75% of undergraduates are from Pennsylvania. Others are from 21 states, and 4 foreign countries. 47% are from public schools. 55% are white; 29% African American. 59% are Catholic; 26% claim no religious affiliation; 11% Protestant. The average age of freshmen is 18; all undergraduates, 24. 20% do not continue beyond their first year; 40% remain to graduate.

Housing: 578 students can be accommodated in college housing, which includes coed dorms. On-campus housing is available on a first-come and first-served basis. 65% of students live on campus; of those, 40% remain on campus on weekends. Alcohol is not permitted. Upperclassmen may keep cars.

Activities: There are no fraternities or sororities. There are 25 groups on campus, including chorale, chorus, computers, drama, environmental, ethnic, gay, honors, instrumental ensemble, international, literary magazine, musical theater, newspaper, orchestra, political, professional, radio and TV, religious, social, social service, and student government. Popular campus events include Empty Bowl Night, Intramural One-Act Play Night, and Christmas dance.

Sports: There are 6 intercollegiate sports for men and 8 for women, and 4 intramural sports for men and 4 for women. Facilities include a gym and an auxiliary gym, athletic training room, locker facilities, fitness room, indoor swimming pool, 8 tennis courts, playing fields for hockey, lacrosse, softball, and soccer, as well as neighboring public stables and country club golf course.

Disabled Students: 90% of the campus is accessible. Facilities include wheelchair ramps, elevators, special parking, specially equipped restrooms, a shower area in residence halls.

Services: Counseling and information services are available, as is tutoring in most subjects, There is a reader service for the blind, and remedial math and writing.

Campus Safety and Security: Measures include 24-hour foot and vehicle patrol and security escort services. There are lighted pathways/sidewalks, Doors are locked after 6 P.M. and on weekends and are monitored by cameras. Escorted shuttle cars to parking lots are available.

Programs of Study: CHC confers B.A., B.S., and B.M. degrees. Associate, master's, and doctoral degrees are also awarded. Bachelor's degrees are awarded in BIOLOGICAL SCIENCE (biochemistry, biology/biological science, and molecular biology), BUSINESS (accounting, business administration and management, business communications, human resources, and marketing/retailing/merchandising), COMMUNICATIONS AND THE ARTS (communications technology, English literature, French, music, and Spanish), COMPUTER AND PHYSICAL SCIENCE (chemistry, computer science, information sciences and systems, and mathematics), EDUCATION (early childhood education, elementary education, and music education), ENGINEERING AND ENVIRONMENTAL DESIGN (computer technology and environmental science), HEALTH PROFESSIONS (health care administration), SOCIAL SCIENCE (child care/child and family studies, criminal justice, forensic studies, history, human services, international studies, liberal arts/general studies, political science/government, psychology, and sociology). Biological/computer/physical sciences and humanities is the strongest academically. Business, human services, and education are the largest.

Required: To graduate, students must complete at least 120 credit hours with a general average of 2.0 overall and in the major. Course work must include 12 to 15 courses in the major, Introduction to the Liberal Arts, Interdisciplinary Global Studies Seminar, a writing course, 2 courses in religious studies, the College Experience; Career Connections, 2 1-credit courses in phys ed, courses in various ways of knowing, including historical (2 courses), literary (1), aesthetic (1), scientific (2 or 3), analytic (1), and interpreting human behavior (2), and a senior seminar and senior thesis. Proficiency must be demonstrated in math, computers, oral communication, and swimming. Students may choose from a wide variety of minors.

Special: Cross-registration is available with LaSalle University and at the 10 colleges in the Sisters of St. Joseph College Consortium Student Exchange Program. The college offers internships, study abroad in England, Spain, Italy, Austria, and France, work-study programs, B.A.-B.S. degrees, interdisciplinary majors, and dual and student-designed majors. Up to 6 credits may be given for life experience. Nondegree study and pass/fail options are available. The school offers unique career preparation programs in communications, international studies, environmental science, and international business. There are 6 national honor societies, a freshman honors program, and 14 departmental honors programs.

Faculty/Classroom: 41% of faculty are male; 59% are female. 73% teach undergraduates, 70% do research, and 55% do both. No introductory courses are taught by graduate students. The average class size in an introductory lecture is 25; in a laboratory is 15; and in a regular course is 15.

Admissions: 91% of the 2009-2010 applicants were accepted. The SAT scores for the 2009-2010 freshman class were: Critical Reading--49% below 500, 40% between 500 and 599, 8% between 600 and 700, and 2% above 700; Math--54% below 500, 34% between 500 and 599, 11% between 600 and 700, and 1% above 700; Writing--53% below 500, 37% between 500 and 599, 9% between 600 and 700, and 1% above 700. 23% of the current freshmen were in the top fifth of their class; 48% were in the top two fifths.

Requirements: The SAT or ACT is required. In addition, , with a satisfactory minimum composite score on the SAT. Applicants must be graduates of an accredited secondary school. 16 Carnegie units are required, with a recommended 4 units each of English, math, science, and social studies and 3 of foreign language. An interview is recommended for all students. An essay is required. A GPA of 2.0 is required. AP and CLEP credits are accepted. Important factors in the admissions decision are leadership record, extracurricular activities record, and advanced placement or honors courses.

Procedure: Freshmen are admitted fall and spring. Entrance exams should be taken early in the senior year. There are early admissions, deferred admissions, and rolling admissions plans. Application deadlines are open. Application fee is $35. Notification is sent on a rolling basis. Applications are accepted on-line.

Transfer: 76 transfer students enrolled in 2008-2009. Applicants must have a minimum GPA of 2.0; a 2.5 is recommended. 45 of 120 credits required for the bachelor's degree must be completed at CHC.

Visiting: There are regularly scheduled orientations for prospective students, including faculty/staff presentations and workshops on specific issues related to admissions (financial aid, curriculum, student life). There are guides for informal visits, visitors may sit in on classes, and stay overnight. To schedule a visit, contact the Admissions Office at (215) 248-7100.

Financial Aid: In 2009-2010, 79% of all full-time freshmen and 83% of continuing full-time students received some form of financial aid. % of all full-time freshmen and 90% of continuing full-time students received need-based aid. CHC is a member of CSS. The FAFSA is required. The deadline for filing freshman financial aid applications for fall entry is April 15.

International Students: There are 22 international students enrolled. The school actively recruits these students. They must take the TOEFL with a minimum score of 500 on the paper-based TOEFL (PBT). They must also take the SAT or ACT. The college also requires a complete set of academic credentials with English translations.

Computers: Wireless access is available. Students may access the Internet through PCs in the computer center (wired) or through wired connections in many classrooms or wirelessly in my locations, including residence halls. PCs are located in the computer center, classroom, labs, learning centers, and library. All students are provided with e-mail addresses and all are encouraged to have laptops. All students may access the system. There are no time limits and no fees.

Graduates: From July 1, 2008 to June 30, 2009, 235 bachelor's degrees were awarded. The most popular majors were human services (22%), criminal justice (15%), and psychology (14%). 25 companies recruited on campus in 2008-2009. In an average class, 40% graduate in 4 years or less, 42% graduate in 5 years or less, and 44% graduate in 6 years or less. Of the 2008 graduating class, 40% were enrolled in graduate school within 6 months of graduation, and 82% were employed.

Admissions Contact: Mark Osborn, Director of Admissions. A campus DVD is available. E-Mail: *chcapply@chc.edu* Web: *www.chc.edu*

CHEYNEY UNIVERSITY OF PENNSYLVANIA   F-4

Cheyney, PA 19319
(610) 399-2275
(800) 223-3608; (610) 399-2099

Full-time: none	Faculty: n/av
Part-time: 39 men, 67 women	Ph.D.s: 33%
Graduate: 51 men, 108 women	Student/Faculty: n/av
Year: semesters, summer session	Tuition: $6,412 ($14,269)
Application Deadline: May 30	Room & Board: $5,679
Freshman Class: n/av	
SAT or ACT: required	LESS COMPETITIVE

Cheyney University of Pennsylvania, founded in 1837, is a public, liberal arts institution offering programs in art, business, music, and teacher preparation. Cheyney University of Pennsylvania cherishes its legacy as the oldest historically black institution of higher education. There are 2 undergraduate schools and one graduate school. In addition to regional accreditation, Cheyney has baccalaureate program accreditation with NCATE. The library contains 290,000 volumes, 795,000 microform items, 1,451 audio/video tapes/CDs/DVDs, and subscribes to 485 periodicals including electronic. Computerized library services include Internet access. Special learning facilities include a planetarium, radio station, TV station, weather station, world cultures center, and theater arts center. The 275-acre campus is in a suburban area 24 miles west of Philadelphia. Including any residence halls, there are 33 buildings.

Student Life: 82% of undergraduates are from Pennsylvania. Students are from 21 states, and 6 foreign countries. 93% are African American. The average age of freshmen is 20; all undergraduates, 21. 43% do not continue beyond their first year; 33% remain to graduate.

Housing: 1273 students can be accommodated in college housing, which includes single-sex and coed dorms. In addition, there are honors houses. On-campus housing is available on a first-come and first-served basis. 76% of students live on campus. Alcohol is not permitted. All students may keep cars.

Activities: There are 30 groups on campus, including art, cheerleading, chess, choir, computers, drama, ethnic, honors, international, jazz band, newspaper, political, professional, radio and TV, religious, social, social service, and student government. Popular campus events include Founders Day Ball and Wade Wilson Football Classic.

Sports: There are 5 intercollegiate sports for men and 5 for women, and 3 intramural sports for men and 2 for women. Facilities include a track, tennis courts, outdoor and indoor basketball courts, a pool, a gym, and a weight room.

Disabled Students: 90% of the campus is accessible. Facilities include wheelchair ramps, elevators, special parking, specially equipped rest rooms, lowered drinking fountains, and lowered telephones.

Services: Counseling and information services are available, as is tutoring in most subjects. There is remedial math, reading, and writing. Both peers and professionals serve as tutors.

Campus Safety and Security: Measures include 24-hour foot and vehicle patrol. There are emergency telephones and lighted pathways/sidewalks.

Programs of Study: Cheyney confers B.A., B.S., and A.S., B.S. Ed. degrees. Associates and master's degrees are also awarded. Bachelor's degrees are awarded in BIOLOGICAL SCIENCE (biology/biological science), BUSINESS (business administration and management and hotel/motel and restaurant management), COMMUNICATIONS AND THE ARTS (communications, dramatic arts, English, and music), COMPUTER AND PHYSICAL SCIENCE (chemistry, computer science, mathematics, and science), EDUCATION (early childhood education, elementary education, home economics education, secondary education, and special education), HEALTH PROFESSIONS (medical laboratory technology), SOCIAL SCIENCE (clothing and textiles management/production/services, economics, geography, parks and recreation management, political science/government, psychology, and social science). Psychology, political science, and social relations are the strongest academically. Business administration and social relations is the largest.

Required: To graduate, students must complete at least 124 credit hours, with 30 in the major and a minimum GPA of 2.0. Distribution requirements include 6 credits each in communications, humanities, science, and social science, 4 in health and phys ed, and 3 in math.

Special: Students may participate in a co-op program and cross-register with West Chester University of Pennsylvania. Internships, study abroad, work-study programs, a chemistry-biology dual degree, non-degree study, pass/fail options, and credit for life, military, and work experience are available. There are 10 national honor societies, a freshman honors program, and 6 departmental honors programs.

Faculty/Classroom: 50% of faculty are male; 50% are female. 76% teach undergraduates. No introductory courses are taught by graduate students.

Requirements: The SAT or ACT is required. In addition, applicants must be graduates of an accredited secondary school or hold a GED. An interview is recommended. CLEP credits are accepted. Important factors in the admissions decision are ability to finance college education, extracurricular activities record, and geographical diversity.

Procedure: Freshmen are admitted fall and spring. Entrance exams should be taken during the junior or senior year. There are early decision, early admissions and rolling admissions plans. Early decision applications should be filed by November 30. Applications should be filed by May 30 for fall entry and November 15 for spring entry. The fall 2008 application fee was $20.

Transfer: 79 transfer students enrolled in 2008-2009. Applicants must have a C average from an accredited post-secondary institution; others may be admitted on probation. Students with fewer than 30 credits must submit a high school transcript. 30 of 124 credits required for the bachelor's degree must be completed at Cheyney.

Visiting: There are regularly scheduled orientations for prospective students. There are guides for informal visits and visitors may sit in on classes. To schedule a visit, contact the Office of Admissions at (800) Cheyney.

Financial Aid: In 2009-2010, 87% of all full-time freshmen and 90% of continuing full-time students received some form of financial aid. 85% of all full-time freshmen and 83% of continuing full-time students received need-based aid. Cheyney is a member of CSS. The FAFSA is required. The deadline for filing freshman financial aid applications for fall entry is April 15.

International Students: The school actively recruits these students. They must take the TOEFL.

Computers: Only authorized terminal operators may access the system. It is available for use 24 hours a day. There are no time limits and no fees.

Graduates: From July 1, 2008 to June 30, 2009, 138 bachelor's degrees were awarded. The most popular majors were social relations (42%), business administation (30%), and elementary education (26%).

Admissions Contact: Gemma Stemley, Director of Admission. A campus DVD is available. E-Mail: *gstemley@cheyney.edu* Web: *www.cheyney.edu*

CLARION UNIVERSITY OF PENNSYLVANIA   B-2

Clarion, PA 16214 (814) 393-2306; (814) 393-2030

Full-time: 2204 men, 3054 women	**Faculty:** IIA, +$
Part-time: 253 men, 712 women	**Ph.D.s:** 87%
Graduate: 245 men, 878 women	**Student/Faculty:** n/av
Year: semesters, , summer session	**Tuition:** $7380 ($13,038)
Application Deadline: open	**Room & Board:** $6390
Freshman Class: n/av	
SAT CR/M/W: 471/477/458	**COMPETITIVE**

Clarion University of Pennsylvania, founded in 1867, is a public institution and part of the Pennsylvania State System of Higher Education. There are 4 undergraduate schools and 4 graduate schools. In addition to regional accreditation, Clarion University has baccalaureate program accreditation with AACSB, NASAD, NASM, and NCATE. The 2 libraries contain 451,915 volumes, 1.5 million microform items, and 7756 audio/video tapes/CDs/DVDs, and subscribe to 23,536 periodicals including electronic. Computerized library services include interlibrary loans, database searching, Internet access, and laptop Internet portals. Special learning facilities include a learning resource center, art gallery, planetarium, radio station, and TV station. The 201-acre campus is in a small town 85 miles northeast of Pittsburgh. Including any residence halls, there are 54 buildings.

Student Life: 95% of undergraduates are from Pennsylvania. Others are from 35 states, 37 foreign countries, and Canada. 89% are from public schools. 92% are white. The average age of freshmen is 18; all undergraduates, 22. 30% do not continue beyond their first year; 50% remain to graduate.

Housing: 2255 students can be accommodated in college housing, which includes single-sex and coed dorms and off-campus apartments. 77% of students commute. Alcohol is not permitted. All students may keep cars.

Activities: 4% of men belong to 6 national fraternities; 7% of women belong to 8 national sororities. There are 150 groups on campus, including art, band, cheerleading, choir, chorus, computers, concert band, dance, debate, drama, ethnic, forensics, gay, honors, international, jazz band, literary magazine, marching band, musical theater, music ensembles, newspaper, orchestra, pep band, photography, political, professional, radio and TV, religious, rugby, skiing, social, social service, student government, and symphony. Popular campus events include Autumn Leaf Festival, Activities Day, and Martin Luther King Cultural Series.

Sports: There are 8 intercollegiate sports for men and 8 for women, and 50 intramural sports for men and 50 for women. Facilities include a 5000-seat stadium; a gym with a physical fitness center and recreational swimming; a natatorium; baseball, softball, soccer fields; a 48,000-square-foot recreation building with 3 full-size multipurpose courts, a 4-lane elevated track, and a 4800-square-foot weight room; tennis and basketball courts; sand volleyball pits; and an inline hockey rink.

Disabled Students: 98% of the campus is accessible. Facilities include wheelchair ramps, elevators, special parking, specially equipped rest rooms, special class scheduling, lowered drinking fountains, lowered telephones, and priority registration.

Services: Counseling and information services are available, as is tutoring in some subjects, including math, economics, accounting, biology, chemistry, physics, earth science, history, sociology, political science, psychology, and computer information sciences. There is a reader service for the blind, remedial math, reading, and writing, computer-assisted instruction, and a learning skills lab.

Campus Safety and Security: Measures include 24-hour foot and vehicle patrol, self-defense education, and security escort services. There are emergency telephones, lighted pathways/sidewalks, video surveillance cameras on campus, a bicycle patrol program, and a rape/aggressive defense program.

Programs of Study: Clarion University confers B.A., B.S., B.F.A., B.Mus., B.S.B.A., B.S.Ed., and B.S.N. degrees. Associate and master's degrees are also awarded. Bachelor's degrees are awarded in BIOLOGICAL SCIENCE (biology/biological science and molecular biology), BUSINESS (accounting, banking and finance, business administration and management, business economics, international business management, marketing/retailing/merchandising, and real estate), COMMUNICATIONS AND THE ARTS (art, communications, dramatic arts, English, French, Spanish, and speech/debate/rhetoric), COMPUTER AND PHYSICAL SCIENCE (chemistry, computer science, geology, information sciences and systems, mathematics, natural sciences, physics, and radiological technology), EDUCATION (athletic training, early childhood education, elementary education, foreign languages education, library science, music education, secondary education, and special education), ENGINEERING AND ENVIRONMENTAL DESIGN (environmental science and industrial administration/management), HEALTH PROFESSIONS (medical technology, nursing, rehabilitation therapy, and speech pathology/audiology), SOCIAL SCIENCE (anthropology, economics, history, liberal arts/general studies, philosophy, political science/government, psychology, social psychology, social science, and sociology). Education, mass media and journalism, and biology are the strongest academically. Elementary education, secondary education, and communication are the largest.

Required: To graduate, students must complete at least 120 credits, with a minimum GPA of 2.0 (2.8 for the College of Education and Human Services). Degree requirements include Writing II, completion of general education courses, including a mandated 12 credits in liberal education skills, 27 credits in liberal knowledge (9 credits each in physical and social sciences, social and behavioral sciences, and arts and humanities), and 3 credits in health and personal performance. Specific degree and class requirements vary by major.

Special: Clarion University has co-op programs in engineering with the University of Pittsburgh and Case Western Reserve University and in speech pathology and audiology with Gallaudet University and a cooperative M.S.L.S./J.D. degree with Widener University. Internships, study abroad, work-study programs, and dual and student-designed majors are also available. There are 15 national honor societies and a freshman honors program.

Faculty/Classroom: All teach undergraduates. No introductory courses are taught by graduate students.

Admissions: The SAT scores for the 2009-2010 freshman class were: Critical Reading--66% below 500, 27% between 500 and 599, and 7% between 600 and 700; Math--68% below 500, 30% between 500 and 599, and 8% between 600 and 700. 19% of the current freshmen were in the top fifth of their class; 48% were in the top two fifths.

Requirements: Applicants must be graduates of an accredited secondary school. The GED is accepted. Clarion University requires 4 years each of English and social studies and 3 years each of math and science and recommends 2 years of a foreign language. An essay and interview are recommended. A GPA of 2.0 is required. AP and CLEP credits are accepted. Important factors in the admissions decision are advanced placement or honors courses, evidence of special talent, and leadership record.

Procedure: Freshmen are admitted fall, spring, and summer. Entrance exams should be taken in the spring of the junior year or early fall of the senior year. There are deferred admissions and rolling admissions plans. Application deadlines are open. The application fee is $30. Applications are accepted on-line.

Transfer: 379 transfer students enrolled in 2008-2009. Applicants for transfer should have completed at least 6 college credit hours with a GPA of 2.8 for education and communication sciences and disorders majors, 2.5 for business majors, and 2.0 for other programs. An audition is required for music majors, and an interview and national test are required for nursing students. 45 of 120 credits required for the bachelor's degree must be completed at Clarion University.

Visiting: There are regularly scheduled orientations for prospective students, including 12 orientation sessions for new students, 6 in the spring and 6 in the summer. There are guides for informal visits and visitors may sit in on classes. To schedule a visit, contact the Admissions Office.

Financial Aid: In 2009-2010, 78% of all full-time freshmen and 75% of continuing full-time students received some form of financial aid. 77% of all full-time freshmen and 75% of continuing full-time students received need-based aid. The average freshman award was $7070. The FAFSA is required. The priority date for freshman financial aid applications for fall entry is April 1. The deadline for filing freshman financial aid applications for fall entry is May 1.

International Students: The school actively recruits these students. They must take the TOEFL.

Computers: Wireless access is available. There are 12 computer labs in various locations across the campus, including specially designated rooms in classroom buildings and the campus library. All students may access the system 24 hours a day. There are no time limits and no fees.

Graduates: From July 1, 2008 to June 30, 2009, 853 bachelor's degrees were awarded. The most popular majors were business/marketing (18%), education (16%), and health professions (12%). 100 companies recruited on campus in 2008-2009. In an average class, 25% graduate in 4 years or less, 45% graduate in 5 years or less, and 52% graduate in 6 years or less.

Admissions Contact: Admissions Officer. A campus DVD is available. E-mail: *admissions@clarion.edu* Web: *www.clarion.edu*

CURTIS INSTITUTE OF MUSIC   F-3

Philadelphia, PA 19103-6187   (215) 893-5262; (215) 893-9065

Full-time: 45 men, 85 women	**Faculty:** n/av
Part-time: 0 men, 0 women	**Ph.D.s:** n/av
Graduate: 10 men, 10 women	**Student/Faculty:** n/av
Year: varies	**Tuition:** n/av
Application Deadline: n/av	**Room & Board:** n/av
Freshman Class: n/av	
SAT: required	**SPECIAL**

Curtis Institute of Music, founded in 1924, is a private conservatory offering undergraduate, graduate, and professional programs in music. The institution serves an entirely commuter student body. All applicants are accepted on full-tuition scholarships. However, they must pay about

$700 in fees and provide all their living expenses. Figures given in the above capsule are approximate. There are no undergraduate schools and 2 graduate schools. In addition to regional accreditation, Curtis has baccalaureate program accreditation with NASM. The library contains 60,000 volumes, 100 microform items, 10,000 audio/video tapes/CDs/DVDs, and subscribes to 40 periodicals including electronic. Including any residence halls, there are 3 buildings.

Student Life: 92% of undergraduates are from out of state, mostly the Northeast. Students are from 30 states, 21 foreign countries, and Canada. 90% are from public schools. 62% are white. The average age of freshmen is 18. 2% do not continue beyond their first year; 98% remain to graduate.

Housing: There are no residence halls. All students commute.

Activities: There are no fraternities or sororities. Groups on campus include student government.

Sports: There is no sports program at Curtis.

Disabled Students: 1% of the campus is accessible. Facilities include elevators and specially equipped rest rooms.

Services: Counseling and information services are available. Tutoring is provided on an individual basis in every subject.

Campus Safety and Security: n/av

Programs of Study: Bachelor's degrees are awarded in COMMUNICATIONS AND THE ARTS (music).

Required: n/av

Special: n/av

Faculty/Classroom: No introductory courses are taught by graduate students.

Admissions: n/av

Requirements: The SAT is required. In addition, applicants must be graduates of an accredited secondary school or have earned a GED. Confidential letters of recommendation from 2 qualified musicians are required. Admission is based primarily on evidence of the applicant's special talent. An audition is required. AP and CLEP credits are accepted.

Procedure: Freshmen are admitted fall. Entrance exams should be taken by March of the senior year. Application deadlines are open.

Transfer: 97 of 131 credits required for the bachelor's degree must be completed at Curtis.

Visiting: n/av

Financial Aid: Curtis is a member of CSS. The CSS/Profile and the college's own financial statement are required. Check with the school for current application deadlines.

International Students: They must take the TOEFL. They must also take the SAT.

Computers: All students may access the system. There are no time limits and no fees.

Graduates: n/av

Admissions Contact: Judi L. Gattone, Director of Admissions. Web: *www.curtis.edu*

DE SALES UNIVERSITY   E-3

Center Valley, PA 18034-9568   (610) 282-1100, ext. 1475
                                          (877) 433-7253; (610) 282-0131

Full-time: 795 men, 934 women	**Faculty:** 104; IIA, --$
Part-time: none	**Ph.D.s:** 72%
Graduate: none	**Student/Faculty:** 17 to 1
Year: semesters, summer session	**Tuition:** $27,000
Application Deadline:	**Room & Board:** $9750
Freshman Class: 1998 applied, 1465 accepted, 378 enrolled	
SAT: required	**COMPETITIVE**

De Sales University, founded in 1964, is a private liberal arts institution affiliated with the Roman Catholic Church. In addition to regional accreditation, DSU has baccalaureate program accreditation with ACBSP and NLN. The library contains 161,314 volumes, 466,747 microform items, and 5720 audio/video tapes/CDs/DVDs, and subscribes to 9089 periodicals including electronic. Computerized library services include interlibrary loans, database searching, and Internet access. Special learning facilities include a learning resource center, radio station, TV station, 2 theaters, 2 dance studios, distant learning center, and science center. The 480-acre campus is in a suburban area 50 miles north of Philadelphia. Including any residence halls, there are 27 buildings.

Student Life: 66% of undergraduates are from Pennsylvania. Others are from 18 states and 2 foreign countries. 46% are from public schools. 88% are white. 67% are Catholic; 15% Protestant. The average age of freshmen is 18. 18% do not continue beyond their first year; 69% remain to graduate.

Housing: 1150 students can be accommodated in college housing, which includes single-sex dorms. In addition, there are special-interest houses. On-campus housing is guaranteed for all 4 years. 80% of students live on campus; of those, 60% remain on campus on weekends. All students may keep cars.

Activities: There are no fraternities; there is 1 local sorority. There are 31 groups on campus, including cheerleading, choir, chorale, chorus, computers, dance, debate, drama, ethnic, honors, international, literary magazine, musical theater, newspaper, pep band, political, professional, radio and TV, religious, social, social service, student government, and yearbook. Popular campus events include Act 1 Plays, annual lecture series, and Fall Fest.

Sports: There are 8 intercollegiate sports for men and 8 for women, and 8 intramural sports for men and 8 for women. There are facilities for soccer, baseball, softball, tennis, basketball, lacrosse, track, cross country, and volleyball and a sports and recreation facility featuring a fitness center, a student lounge, and multipurpose athletic courts.

Disabled Students: 98% of the campus is accessible. Facilities include wheelchair ramps, elevators, special parking, specially equipped restrooms, special class scheduling, lowered drinking fountains, and lowered telephones.

Services: Counseling and information services are available, as is tutoring in most subjects. There is a reader service for the blind and remedial reading and writing. The Academic Resource Center provides services (including tutoring) to all students.

Campus Safety and Security: Measures include 24-hour foot and vehicle patrol, emergency notification system, self-defense education, and security escort services. There are emergency telephones, lighted pathways/sidewalks, and 24-hour desk security in residence halls.

Programs of Study: DSU confers B.A., B.S., and B.S.N. degrees. Master's degrees are also awarded. Bachelor's degrees are awarded in BIOLOGICAL SCIENCE (biochemistry and biology/biological science), BUSINESS (accounting, banking and finance, business administration and management, electronic business, human resources, management information systems, marketing/retailing/merchandising, and sports management), COMMUNICATIONS AND THE ARTS (communications, dance, dramatic arts, English, film arts, performing arts, radio/television technology, and Spanish), COMPUTER AND PHYSICAL SCIENCE (chemistry, computer science, and mathematics), EDUCATION (elementary education), HEALTH PROFESSIONS (exercise science, nursing, pharmaceutical science, and physician's assistant), SOCIAL SCIENCE (criminal justice, family/consumer studies, history, liberal arts/general studies, philosophy, political science/government, psychology, and theological studies). Accounting, physician's assistant, and performing arts are the strongest academically. Nursing, performing and fine arts, and physician's assistant are the largest.

Required: For graduation, students must complete a minimum of 120 credit hours including a maximum of 48 in the major with a minimum GPA of 2.0 overall and in the major. Liberal arts distribution requirements consist of 12 to 16 courses including cultural literacy, modes of thinking, and Christian values and theology, as well as 3 units in phys ed. Internships are strongly encouraged for all majors.

Special: Students may cross-register with schools in the Lehigh Valley Association of Independent Colleges. Internships are strongly encouraged in all majors, and study abroad in 10 countries is possible. Dual majors, a Washington semester, pass/fail options, accelerated degree programs, and credit for life, military, and work experience are offered. There are 11 national honor societies and a freshman honors program.

Faculty/Classroom: 56% of faculty are male; 44% are female. All teach undergraduates and do research. No introductory courses are taught by graduate students. The average class size in an introductory lecture is 20; in a laboratory, 20; and in a regular course, 20.

Admissions: 73% of the 2009-2010 applicants were accepted. The SAT scores for the 2009-2010 freshman class were: Critical Reading--30% below 500, 44% between 500 and 599, 22% between 600 and 700, and 4% above 700; Math--30% below 500, 43% between 500 and 599, 24% between 600 and 700, and 3% above 700; Writing--31% below 500, 47% between 500 and 599, 18% between 600 and 700, and 4% above 700. 52% of freshmen were in the top 25% of their class; 77% were in the top 50%.

Requirements: The SAT is required. In addition, applicants must be graduates of an accredited secondary school. The GED is accepted. Applicants should have completed 17 college preparatory courses including 4 years each of English, history, and math, 3 years of science, and 2 years of foreign language. The school will accept an essay but strongly recommends an interview. For theater students, a performance appraisal is required. For dance students an audition is required. A GPA of 3.0 is required. AP and CLEP credits are accepted. Important factors in the admissions decision are advanced placement or honors courses, leadership record, and evidence of special talent.

Procedure: Freshmen are admitted fall and spring. Entrance exams should be taken during the junior or senior year. There are deferred admissions and rolling admissions plans. Application deadlines are open. Application fee is $30. Notification is sent on a rolling basis. Applications are accepted on-line.

Transfer: 68 transfer students enrolled in a recent year. Applicants for transfer should have completed a minimum of 24 college credit hours with a GPA of 2.5. An interview is recommended. 45 of 120 credits required for the bachelor's degree must be completed at DSU.

Visiting: There are regularly scheduled orientations for prospective students, including meetings with faculty advisers and social activities.

There are guides for informal visits; visitors may sit in on classes and stay overnight. To schedule a visit, contact the Enrollment Management Office at (610) 282-4443.

Financial Aid: In 2009-2010, 78% of all full-time freshmen and 74% of continuing full-time students received some form of financial aid. 77% of continuing full-time students received need-based aid. The average freshman award was $19,654. Need-based scholarships or need-based grants averaged $15,482; need-based self-help aid (loans and jobs) averaged $4896; and other non-need-based awards and non-need-based scholarships averaged $8464. 51% of undergraduate students work part-time. Average annual earnings from campus work are $733. The average financial indebtedness of the 2009 graduate was $18,700. DSU is a member of CSS. The FAFSA and the college's own financial statement are required. The deadline for filing freshman financial aid applications for fall entry is February 1.

International Students: There are 4 international students enrolled. The school actively recruits these students. They must take the TOEFL with a minimum score of 550 on the paper-based TOEFL (PBT) or 79 on the Internet-based version (iBT). The SAT is recommended but not required.

Computers: Wireless access is available. There is wireless access to the Internet in all residence hall rooms and all public places. There are special PC labs and approximately 150 PCs in Dooling Hall and the academic building, the library, and the university center. All students may access the system 24 hours a day from residence hall rooms, and 8 A.M. to 11 P.M. in public computing rooms. There are no time limits. The fee is $125 per semester. It is strongly recommended that all students have a personal computer.

Graduates: From July 1, 2008 to June 30, 2009, 518 bachelor's degrees were awarded. The most popular majors were business (26%), visual and performing arts (13%), and nursing (12%). 10 companies recruited on campus in 2008-2009. In an average class, 57% graduate in 4 years or less, 65% graduate in 5 years or less, and 67% graduate in 6 years or less. Of the 2008 graduating class, 6% were enrolled in graduate school within 6 months of graduation, and 76% were employed.

Admissions Contact: Mary Birkhead, Dean of Enrollment Management. E-mail: *admiss@desales.edu* Web: *www.desales.edu*

DELAWARE VALLEY COLLEGE   F-3
Doylestown, PA 18901-2697

(215) 489-2372
(800) 2-DEL-VAL; (215) 230-2968

Full-time: 700 men, 900 women	**Faculty:** 79; IIB, --$
Part-time: 209 men, 191 women	**Ph.D.s:** 62%
Graduate: 27 men, 43 women	**Student/Faculty:** 20 to 1
Year: semesters, summer session	**Tuition:** $22,000
Application Deadline: open	**Room & Board:** $8,130
Freshman Class: 1476 applied, 1164 accepted, 451 enrolled	
SAT: required	**ACT:** 22 **COMPETITIVE**

Delaware Valley College, founded in 1896, is a private institution offering undergraduate programs in specialized fields of agriculture, business administration, English, the sciences, math, criminal justice administration, and secondary education. The college also offers graduate programs in educational leadership, and in food and agribusiness. There are no undergraduate schools. The library contains 70,000 volumes, 162,914 microform items, and subscribes to 728 periodicals including electronic. Computerized library services include inter-library loans, database searching, Internet access, and laptop Internet portals. Special learning facilities include a learning resource center, radio station, TV station, a dairy science center, a livestock farm, horse facilities, an apiary, a small animal lab, a tissue culture lab, an arboretum, and greenhouses. The 550-acre campus is in a suburban area 20 miles north of Philadelphia. Including any residence halls, there are 36 buildings.

Student Life: 67% of undergraduates are from Pennsylvania. Students are from 22 states, 1 foreign countries, and Canada. 85% are from public schools. 80% are white. 35% are Catholic; 32% Protestant; 16% claim no religious affiliation; 14% Buddhist, Seventh-day Adventist, and others. The average age of freshmen is 18; all undergraduates, 21. 26% do not continue beyond their first year; 75% remain to graduate.

Housing: 960 students can be accommodated in college housing, which includes single-sex and coed dorms. In addition, there are honors houses. On-campus housing is available on a first-come, first-served basis, and is available on a lottery system for upperclassmen. 63% of students live on campus; of those, 65% remain on campus on weekends. Upperclassmen may keep cars.

Activities: 4% of men belong to 5 national fraternities; 5% of women belong to 3 national sororities. There are 40 groups on campus, including art, band, cheerleading, chess, choir, chorale, chorus, computers, dance, drama, ethnic, honors, international, literary magazine, newspaper, pep band, photography, professional, radio and TV, religious, social, social service, student government, and yearbook. Popular campus events include A-Day, Parents Day, and Family Weekend.

Sports: There are 8 intercollegiate sports for men and 7 for women, and 9 intramural sports for men and 9 for women. Facilities include 2 yms, tennis courts, outdoor playing courts and fields, a football stadium, a running track, a small lake, a video game room, picnic areas, nature walks, riding trails, and indoor and outdoor equine facilities.

Disabled Students: 85% of the campus is accessible. Facilities include wheelchair ramps, elevators, special parking, specially equipped rest rooms, special class scheduling, and lowered drinking fountains.

Services: Counseling and information services are available, as is tutoring in most subjects. There is a reader service for the blind, and remedial math, reading, and writing.

Campus Safety and Security: Measures include 24-hour foot and vehicle patrol, self-defense education, and security escort services. There are shuttle buses, emergency telephones, and lighted pathways/sidewalks.

Programs of Study: DVC confers B.A. and B.S. degrees. Associates and master's degrees are also awarded. Bachelor's degrees are awarded in AGRICULTURE (agronomy, animal science, dairy science, equine science, horticulture, and wildlife management), BIOLOGICAL SCIENCE (biology/biological science and zoology), BUSINESS (accounting, business administration and management, marketing/retailing/merchandising, and sports management), COMMUNICATIONS AND THE ARTS (English), COMPUTER AND PHYSICAL SCIENCE (chemistry and computer science), EDUCATION (secondary education), ENGINEERING AND ENVIRONMENTAL DESIGN (environmental science and food services technology), SOCIAL SCIENCE (criminal justice, food production/management/services, and food science). Physical and biological science and animal science is the strongest academically. Business administration and animal science is the largest.

Required: The bachelor's degree requires completion of at least 128 credits, including 48 in the major, with a minimum GPA of 2.0. The core curriculum consists of 48 credits of liberal arts courses, including cultural enrichment, phys ed, and an introduction to computers. Students must also fulfill employment program requirements.

Special: DVC offers a specialized methods and techniques program that enables students to learn lab techniques and gain experience in the practical aspects of their majors. There is a zoo science major that prepares students for careers in zoo management and animal conservation. There are co-op programs in all majors, dual majors, study abroad in England, internships, and work-study programs in a wide variety of employment and research settings. Cross-registration is available with Rutgers University and Middle Bucks Technical Institute. Non-degree study and pass/fail options are also available. There are 3 national honor societies, a freshman honors program, and 2 departmental honors programs.

Faculty/Classroom: 66% of faculty are male; 34% are female. All teach undergraduates. No introductory courses are taught by graduate students. The average class size in an introductory lecture is 24; in a laboratory is 21; and in a regular course is 20.

Admissions: 79% of the 2009-2010 applicants were accepted. The ACT scores were 38% below 21, 25% between 21 and 23, 25% between 24 and 26, 13% between 27 and 28, and % above 28. 25% of the current freshmen were in the top fifth of their class; 49% were in the top two fifths. 1 freshman graduated first in the class.

Requirements: The SAT or ACT is required. In addition, applicants must be graduates of accredited secondary schools or have earned a GED. The college requires 15 academic units, including 6 in electives, 3 in English, and 2 each in math, science, and social studies. An interview is recommended. DVC requires applicants to be in the upper 50% of their class. A GPA of 2.8 is required. AP and CLEP credits are accepted. Important factors in the admissions decision are leadership record, personality/intangible qualities, and extracurricular activities record.

Procedure: Freshmen are admitted fall and spring. Entrance exams should be taken in the junior or senior year. There are deferred admissions and rolling admissions plans. Application deadlines are open. Application fee is $35. Applications are accepted on-line.

Transfer: 109 transfer students enrolled in 2008-2009. Applicants must have a minimum GPA of 2.0 and must submit SAT scores. An interview is recommended. 60 of 130 credits required for the bachelor's degree must be completed at DVC.

Visiting: There are regularly scheduled orientations for prospective students, consisting of a student panel, meetings with department chairs, and general information sessions. There are guides for informal visits, visitors may sit in on classes, and stay overnight. To schedule a visit, contact the Admissions Department.

Financial Aid: In 2009-2010, 98% of all full-time freshmen and 94% of continuing full-time students received some form of financial aid. 78% of all full-time freshmen and 78% of continuing full-time students received need-based aid. The average freshmen award was $16,050. 20% of undergraduate students work part-time. Average annual earnings from campus work are $1600. The average financial indebtedness of the 2009 graduate was $17,760. The FAFSA is required. The deadline for filing freshman financial aid applications for fall entry is April 1.

International Students: There is 1 international student enrolled. International students must take the TOEFL. They must also take the SAT or ACT.

Computers: Wireless access is available. Wireless access is available in the library. All students may access the system. at designated times in the labs and 24 hours per day in most other areas. There are no time limits and no fees.

Graduates: From July 1, 2008 to June 30, 2009, 281 bachelor's degrees were awarded. The most popular majors were business administration (30%), animal science (22%), and ornamental horticulture (10%). 310 companies recruited on campus in 2008-2009. In an average class, 44% graduate in 4 years or less, 54% graduate in 5 years or less, and 57% graduate in 6 years or less. Of the 2008 graduating class, 24% were enrolled in graduate school within 6 months of graduation, and 80% were employed.

Admissions Contact: Stephen W. Zenko, Director of Admissions. A campus DVD is available. E-Mail: *admitme@devalcol.edu* Web: *www.devalcol.edu*

DEVRY UNIVERSITY/FORT WASHINGTON
Fort Washington, PA 19034-3204
F-3
(215) 591-5700
(866) 303-3879; (251) 591-5745

Full-time: 326 men, 113 women	**Faculty:** n/av
Part-time: 780 men, 176 women	**Ph.D.s:** n/av
Graduate: 72 men, 86 women	**Student/Faculty:** 10 to 1
Year: semesters, summer session	
Application Deadline: open	
Freshman Class: n/av	**LESS COMPETITIVE**

DeVry University/Fort Washington. 1 of 67 DeVry University locations in the United States and Canada, opened in 2002. It offers programs in business administration, computer engineering technology, computer information systems, electronics engineering technology, network and communications management, and technical management. There are no undergraduate schools. The library contains 4,211 volumes, and 618 audio/video tapes/CDs/DVDs, and subscribes to 68 periodicals including electronic. The campus 25 miles from downtown Philadelphia.

Student Life: 46% are white; 39% African American.

Housing: There are no residence halls. All students commute.

Activities: There are no fraternities or sororities.

Sports: There is no sports program.

Disabled Students: None of the campus is accessible.

Programs of Study: Associate and master's degrees are also awarded. Bachelor's degrees are awarded in BUSINESS (business administration and management), COMMUNICATIONS AND THE ARTS (telecommunications), COMPUTER AND PHYSICAL SCIENCE (information sciences and systems), ENGINEERING AND ENVIRONMENTAL DESIGN (computer engineering, electrical/electronics engineering technology, and technological management).

Required: To graduate, students must achieve a GPA of at least 2.0, complete 48 to 154 credit hours, and satisfactorily complete all curriculum requirements. Course requirements vary according to program. All first-semester students take course in business organization, computer applications, algebra, psychology, and student success strategies.

Special: Accelerated degree programs in computer information systems and technical management, co-op programs, and distance learning are available.

Faculty/Classroom: No introductory courses are taught by graduate students.

Requirements: In addition, admissions requirements include graduation from a secondary school; the GED is accepted. Applicants must pass the DeVry entrance exam or present satisfactory SAT I or ACT scores. An interview is required.

Procedure: Freshmen are admitted fall, spring, and summer. There are early admissions, deferred admissions, and rolling admissions plans. Application deadlines are open. Application fee is $50. Applications are accepted on-line.

Transfer: 138 transfer students enrolled in 2008-2009. Transfer students must have a minimum 2.0 G.P.A. 30 of 48 credits required for the bachelor's degree must be completed at DeVry.

Financial Aid: In 2009-2010, 74% of all full-time freshmen and 75% of continuing full-time students received some form of financial aid. 73% of all full-time freshmen and 73% of continuing full-time students received need-based aid. The average freshman award was $6,884. Need-based scholarships or need-based grants averaged $4,120 ; need-based self-help aid (loans and jobs) averaged $4,201; and other non-need-based awards and non-need-based scholarships averaged $8,122. The FAFSA is required. The deadline for filing freshman financial aid applications for fall entry is rolling.

International Students: They must take the TOEFL.

Graduates: The most popular majors were business/marketing (63%), computer and information sciences (28%), and engineering technologies (10%).

Admissions Contact: Director of Admissions E-Mail: *admissions@phi.devry.edu* Web: *www.devry.edu/fortwashington*

DICKINSON COLLEGE
D-3

Carlisle, PA 17013

(717) 245-1231
(800) 644-1773; (717) 245-1442

Full-time: 1025 men, 1315 women	**Faculty:** 193; IIB, +$
Part-time: 17 men, 19 women	**Ph.D.s:** 93%
Graduate: none	**Student/Faculty:** 12 to 1
Year: semesters, summer session	**Tuition:** $40,114
Application Deadline: February 1	**Room & Board:** $10,080
Freshman Class: 5026 applied, 2459 accepted, 582 enrolled	
SAT CR/M: 650/640	**ACT:** 28

HIGHLY COMPETITIVE+

Dickinson College, founded in 1783, is a private institution offering a liberal arts curriculum that includes international education and science. There are no undergraduate schools. The library contains 501,043 volumes, 168,649 microform items, 25,546 audio/video tapes/CDs/DVDs, and subscribes to 2,451 periodicals including electronic. Computerized library services include interlibrary loans, database searching, and Internet access. Special learning facilities include an art gallery, planetarium, radio station, fiber-optic and satellite telecommunications networks, a telescope observatory, and an archival collection. The 308-acre campus is in a suburban area about 20 miles west of Harrisburg, PA and 2 hours from Washington, D.C. Including any residence halls, there are 141 buildings.

Student Life: 75% of undergraduates are from out of state, mostly the Middle Atlantic. Students are from 44 states, and 41 foreign countries. 59% are from public schools. 77% are white. 30% are Protestant; 26% claim no religious affiliation; 25% Catholic. The average age of freshmen is 18; all undergraduates, 20. 8% do not continue beyond their first year; 82% remain to graduate.

Housing: 1999 students can be accommodated in college housing, which includes coed dorms and on-campus apartments. In addition, there are language houses, special-interest houses, fraternity houses, including arts, environmental, multicultural, and learning communities. On-campus housing is guaranteed for all 4 years. 94% of students live on campus; of those, 85% remain on campus on weekends. Upperclassmen may keep cars.

Activities: 13% of men belong to 5 national fraternities; 18% of women belong to 1 local and 5 national sororities. There are 112 groups on campus, including art, band, cheerleading, chess, choir, chorale, chorus, computers, dance, debate, drama, environmental, ethnic, film, gay, honors, international, jazz band, literary magazine, musical theater, newspaper, orchestra, photography, political, professional, radio and TV, religious, social, social service, student government, and symphony. Popular campus events include Amani (Black Arts) Festival, Multicultural Fair, and Public Affairs Symposium.

Sports: There are 11 intercollegiate sports for men and 12 for women, and 14 intramural sports for men and 11 for women. Facilities include an 8,000-square-foot fitness center with weight-training and 40 cardiorespiratory conditioning machines. The 38,600-square-foot Kline Center includes basketball, squash, racquetball, and handball courts. The gym area features a multipurpose polyurethane synthetic floor covering and includes an indoor 200-meter, 4-lane track with a hidden jump pit. There is a 25-yard competition swimming pool with separate diving well with seating for 350 spectators, tennis courts, a varsity football field, and lacrosse, baseball, and soccer fields. There is an outdoor track, jogging trails, and an indoor rock-climbing wall.

Disabled Students: 67% of the campus is accessible. Facilities include wheelchair ramps, elevators, special parking, specially equipped rest rooms, special class scheduling, lowered drinking fountains, lowered telephones, and special housing.

Services: Counseling and information services are available, as is tutoring in every subject, services are provided as necessary on a case-by-case basis. There is a reader service for the blind. There also is a writing center.

Campus Safety and Security: Measures include 24-hour foot and vehicle patrol, emergency notification system, self-defense education, and security escort services. There are shuttle buses, emergency telephones, lighted pathways/sidewalks, access controls for dorms/residences, electronic access to residence halls, and required electronic access for on campus administrative and academic buildings.

Programs of Study: Dickinson confers B.A. and B.S. degrees. Bachelor's degrees are awarded in BIOLOGICAL SCIENCE (biochemistry, biology/biological science, and neurosciences), BUSINESS (international business management), COMMUNICATIONS AND THE ARTS (classical languages, dance, dramatic arts, English, fine arts, French, German, Greek, Latin, music, Russian, and Spanish), COMPUTER AND PHYSICAL SCIENCE (chemistry, computer science, geology, mathematics, and physics), ENGINEERING AND ENVIRONMENTAL DESIGN (environmental science), HEALTH PROFESSIONS (environmental health science), SOCIAL SCIENCE (African studies, American studies, anthropology, archeology, classical/ancient civilization, East Asian studies, economics, history, international studies, Italian studies, Judaic studies, law, medieval studies, Middle Eastern studies, philosophy, political sci-

ence/government, psychology, public affairs, religion, sociology, and women's studies). International education/foreign languages, natural sciences, and preprofessional programs are the strongest academically. International business and management/international studies, political science, and psychology are the largest.

Required: To graduate, students must complete 32 courses with a minimum GPA of 2.0. The school requires 2 courses each in humanities, social sciences, and lab sciences. Also required are 3 courses of cross-cultural studies (including foreign language, comparative civilizations, and U.S. diversity), a first-year seminar, phys ed, and the completion of a major averaging 9 to 15 courses. Writing-intensive and quantitative reasoning courses are also required.

Special: Students may cross-register with Central Pennsylvania Consortium Colleges. 32 academic year or summer study-abroad programs are offered in 24 countries. A Washington semester, work-study, and accelerated degree programs are available, as are dual majors, student-designed majors, non-degree study, pass/fail options, and a 3-3 law degree with the Dickinson School of Law of Pennsylvania State University. There are 3-2 engineering degrees offered with Case Western Reserve University, Rensselaer Polytechnic Institute, and the University of Pennsylvania. Instruction in 12 languages is available. There is a certification program in Latin American studies. Through an articulation agreement with the University of East Anglia, graduates of Dickinson can pursue a M.A. in the Humanities, and through a direct admission agreement program can begin a MBA program with the Simon School of Business at the University of Rochester. There are 15 national honor societies, including Phi Beta Kappa, and 33 departmental honors programs.

Faculty/Classroom: 54% of faculty are male; 46% are female. All teach and do research. No introductory courses are taught by graduate students. The average class size in an introductory lecture is 35 and in a laboratory is 17.

Admissions: 49% of the 2009-2010 applicants were accepted. The SAT scores for the 2009-2010 freshman class were: Critical Reading--3% below 500, 22% between 500 and 599, 54% between 600 and 700, and 21% above 700; Math--4% below 500, 23% between 500 and 599, 57% between 600 and 700, and 16% above 700; Writing--4% below 500, 22% between 500 and 599, 52% between 600 and 700, and 22% above 700. The ACT scores were 1% below 21, 5% between 21 and 23, 23% between 24 and 26, 28% between 27 and 28, and 43% above 28. 63% of the current freshmen were in the top fifth of their class; 90% were in the top two fifths.

Requirements: In addition, the SAT and ACT Subject Tests are optional submissions. The GED is accepted. Applicants should have completed 16 academic credits, including 4 years of English, 3 each of math and science, 2 (preferably 3) of foreign language, 2 of social studies, and 2 additional courses drawn from the above areas. An essay is required, and an interview is recommended. AP credits are accepted. Important factors in the admissions decision are advanced placement or honors courses, extracurricular activities record, and recommendations by school officials.

Procedure: Freshmen are admitted fall. Entrance exams should be taken in the spring of the junior year or the fall of the senior year. There are early decision, early admissions and deferred admissions plans. Early decision applications should be filed by January 15; regular applications, by February 1 for fall entry. The fall 2008 application fee was $65. Notification of early decision is sent February 15; regular decision, March 31. Applications are accepted on-line. 297 applicants were on a recent waiting list, 65 were accepted.

Transfer: 15 transfer students enrolled in 2008-2009. Applicants for transfer must have at least a 2.0 cumulative GPA and must submit secondary school and college transcripts and 1 professor recommendation in addition to the standard application for admission. 64 of 128 credits required for the bachelor's degree must be completed at Dickinson.

Visiting: There are regularly scheduled orientations for prospective students, and student can participate in campus tours, individual interviews, group information sessions, class visits, overnight stays in residence halls, and open houses. There are guides for informal visits, visitors may sit in on classes, and stay overnight. To schedule a visit, contact the Admissions Office at (800) 644-1773.

Financial Aid: In 2009-2010, 64% of all full-time freshmen and 61% of continuing full-time students received some form of financial aid. 56% of all full-time freshmen and 51% of continuing full-time students received need-based aid. The average freshmen award was $32,037, with $29,286 ($52,884 maximum) from need-based scholarships or need-based grants; $5,723 ($7,700 maximum) from need-based self-help aid (loans and jobs); and $10,941 from other forms of aid. 47% of undergraduate students work part-time. Average annual earnings from campus work are $1218. The average financial indebtedness of the 2009 graduate was $23,224. Dickinson is a member of CSS. The CSS/Profile, FAFSA, and the state aid form, and noncustodial parent statement, and business farm supplement are required. The deadline for filing freshman financial aid applications for fall entry is February 1.

International Students: There are 145 international students enrolled. The school actively recruits these students. They must take the TOEFL with a minimum score of 573 on the paper-based TOEFL (PBT) or 89 on the Internet-based version (iBT).

Computers: Wireless access is available. The library hosts more than 100 computers equipped with the Microsoft Office suite and other applications, as well as laptop computers that may be borrowed by students. The campus has a range of computer labs with approximately 390 Windows and 271 Mac computers for student use. Laser printers are available. The campus is completely networked, and every student room has at least 1 Ethernet network connection. Students may access the Internet from any location on campus through wired Ethernet connections or through the wireless network in the Waider-Spahr Library, the Quarry, and the Holland Union Building. All students may access the system. There are no time limits and no fees.

Graduates: From July 1, 2008 to June 30, 2009, 576 bachelor's degrees were awarded. The most popular majors were international business and management (12%), political science (10%), and psychology (6%). 19 companies recruited on campus in 2008-2009. In an average class, 82% graduate in 4 years or less, 83% graduate in 5 years or less, and 84% graduate in 6 years or less. Of the 2008 graduating class, 37% were enrolled in graduate school within 6 months of graduation, and 67% were employed.

Admissions Contact: Stephanie Balmer, VP for Enrollment and Communication . A campus DVD is available. E-Mail: *admit@dickinson.edu* Web: *www.dickinson.edu*

DREXEL UNIVERSITY · F-3
Philadelphia, PA 19104

	(215) 895-2400
	(800) 2-DREXEL; (215) 895-5939
Full-time: 6244 men, 4573 women	Faculty: 729; I, -$
Part-time: 1209 men, 1458 women	Ph.D.s: 84%
Graduate: 3685 men, 5324 women	Student/Faculty: 15 to 1
Year: quarters, summer session	Tuition: $31,835
Application Deadline: March 1	Room & Board: $12,681
Freshman Class: 39,827 applied, 21,729 accepted, 2346 enrolled	
SAT CR/M/W: 580/620/580	VERY COMPETITIVE

Drexel University, established in 1891, is a private institution with undergraduate programs in business and administration, engineering, information studies, design arts, and arts and sciences. There are 9 undergraduate schools and 12 graduate schools. In addition to regional accreditation, Drexel has baccalaureate program accreditation with AACSB, ABET, ADA, APA, CSAB, FIDER, and NAAB. The 2 libraries contain 643,869 volumes, 18,070 microform items, and 3443 audio/video tapes/CDs/DVDs, and subscribe to 27,399 periodicals including electronic. Computerized library services include interlibrary loans, database searching, Internet access, and laptop Internet portals. Special learning facilities include a learning resource center, art gallery, radio station, and TV station. The 94-acre campus is in an urban area near the center of Philadelphia. Including any residence halls, there are 98 buildings.

Student Life: 51% of undergraduates are from out of state, mostly the Middle Atlantic. Students are from 50 states, 134 foreign countries, and Canada. 57% are white; 12% Asian American. The average age of freshmen is 18; all undergraduates, 23. 14% do not continue beyond their first year; 62% remain to graduate.

Housing: 4100 students can be accommodated in college housing, which includes coed dorms, on-campus apartments, and off-campus apartments. In addition, there are fraternity houses, sorority houses, honors floors in residence halls, and international student housing. On-campus housing is guaranteed for the freshman year only, is available on a first-come, first-served basis, and is available on a lottery system for upperclassmen. 66% of students commute. All students may keep cars.

Activities: 9% of men belong to 14 national fraternities; 8% of women belong to 10 national sororities. There are 180 groups on campus, including art, band, cheerleading, chess, choir, chorus, computers, dance, drama, environmental, ethnic, film, forensics, gay, honors, international, jazz band, literary magazine, musical theater, newspaper, orchestra, pep band, photography, political, professional, radio and TV, religious, social, social service, and student government. Popular campus events include an ongoing program of musical, cultural, and art events.

Sports: There are 8 intercollegiate sports for men and 8 for women, and 7 intramural sports for men and 7 for women. Facilities include an athletic center with 3 gyms, 5 squash courts, a 25-yard swimming pool, a diving well, 4 exercise rooms, and 1 wrestling room; a recreation center with 2 gyms, 2 floors of fitness (18,000 square feet), 2 exercise studios, 2 squash courts, a climbing wall, and an indoor track; and an armory with 3 multipurpose courts.

Disabled Students: 98% of the campus is accessible. Facilities include wheelchair ramps, elevators, special parking, specially equipped restrooms, special class scheduling, lowered drinking fountains, and special housing.

Services: Counseling and information services are available, as is tutoring in most subjects. There is remedial math, reading, and writing and a resident tutor program.

Campus Safety and Security: Measures include 24-hour foot and vehicle patrol, emergency notification system, self-defense education, and security escort services. There are shuttle buses, emergency telephones, lighted pathways/sidewalks, controlled access to dorms/residences, and residential and commuter safety and security programs.

Programs of Study: Drexel confers B.A., B.S., and B.Arch. degrees. Master's and doctoral degrees are also awarded. Bachelor's degrees are awarded in BIOLOGICAL SCIENCE (biology/biological science and nutrition), BUSINESS (business administration and management, fashion merchandising, hotel/motel and restaurant management, and marketing/retailing/merchandising), COMMUNICATIONS AND THE ARTS (communications, creative writing, design, film arts, graphic design, literature, music, photography, and video), COMPUTER AND PHYSICAL SCIENCE (chemistry, computer science, digital arts/technology, information sciences and systems, mathematics, physics, and science), EDUCATION (education), ENGINEERING AND ENVIRONMENTAL DESIGN (architectural engineering, architecture, biomedical engineering, chemical engineering, civil engineering, computer engineering, construction management, electrical/electronics engineering, environmental engineering, environmental science, interior design, materials engineering, and mechanical engineering), HEALTH PROFESSIONS (predentistry and premedicine), SOCIAL SCIENCE (fashion design and technology, food production/management/services, history, international studies, political science/government, prelaw, psychology, and sociology). Engineering, business, and design arts are the strongest academically. Business, mechanical engineering, and biological sciences are the largest.

Required: To graduate, students must complete 180 to 192 term credits with a minimum GPA of 2.0 and must earn the number of Drexel Co-op Units determined by the major. There are requirements in math, computer literacy, English, lab science, humanities, and history.

Special: The Drexel Plan of Cooperative Education enables students to alternate periods of full-time classroom studies and full-time employment with university-approved employers. Participation in cooperative education is mandatory for most students. Cross-registration is available with Indiana University of Pennsylvania and Lincoln University. Drexel also offers study abroad, internships, accelerated degrees, 3-3 engineering degrees, dual majors, nondegree study, and credit/no credit options. There is 1 national honor society, a freshman honors program, and 3 departmental honors programs.

Faculty/Classroom: 56% of faculty are male; 44% are female. 72% teach undergraduates, 38% do research, and 24% do both. Graduate students teach 6% of introductory courses. The average class size in an introductory lecture is 28; in a laboratory, 22; and in a regular course, 24.

Admissions: 55% of the 2009-2010 applicants were accepted. The SAT scores for the 2009-2010 freshman class were: Critical Reading--9% below 500, 47% between 500 and 599, 38% between 600 and 700, and 6% above 700; Math--3% below 500, 32% between 500 and 599, 53% between 600 and 700, and 12% above 700; Writing--12% below 500, 46% between 500 and 599, 36% between 600 and 700, and 6% above 700. 54% of the current freshmen were in the top fifth of their class; 83% were in the top two fifths.

Requirements: The SAT or ACT is required; the SAT I is preferred. In addition, applicants must be graduates of an accredited secondary school. The GED is accepted. An interview is recommended. A GPA of 2.0 is required. AP and CLEP credits are accepted. Important factors in the admissions decision are advanced placement or honors courses, evidence of special talent, and recommendations by school officials.

Procedure: Freshmen are admitted fall. There are deferred admissions and rolling admissions plans. Applications should be filed by March 1 for fall entry, along with a $75 fee (no fee for on-line applications). Notification is sent on a rolling basis. 3849 applicants were on the 2009 waiting list; 924 were admitted. Applications are accepted on-line.

Transfer: Applicants must have a minimum GPA of 2.5. Other requirements vary among the individual colleges within the university. 45 of 180 to 192 term credits required for the bachelor's degree must be completed at Drexel.

Visiting: There are regularly scheduled orientations for prospective students, consisting of a 2-day program for new freshmen and their parents in late July. There are guides for informal visits, and visitors may sit in on classes and stay overnight. To schedule a visit, contact the Admissions Office.

Financial Aid: The FAFSA is required. The deadline for filing freshman financial aid applications for fall entry is February 15.

International Students: There are 850 international students enrolled. The school actively recruits these students. They must take the TOEFL with a minimum score of 550 on the paper-based TOEFL (PBT) or 79 on the Internet-based version (iBT), or take the IELTS.

Computers: Wireless access is available. Drexel provides both wireless and wired Internet and Internet2 access across the entire campus, including all residence halls and classrooms. The campus network includes more than 24,000 active Gigabit Ethernet connections of which about 2500 are available for "plug and play" use. The wireless network Dragonfly connects more than 8000 devices, including laptops, game consoles, and mobile phones. All students may access the system 24 hours a day. There are no time limits and no fees. All students are required to have a personal computer.

Graduates: From July 1, 2008 to June 30, 2009, 2728 bachelor's degrees were awarded. The most popular majors were business administration (23%), engineering (21%), and health professions (19%). In an average class, 62% graduate in 6 years or less. 459 companies recruited on campus in 2008-2009. Of the 2008 graduating class, 16% were enrolled in graduate school within 6 months of graduation, and 69% were employed.

Admissions Contact: Director of Admissions. A campus DVD is available. E-mail: *enroll@drexel.edu* Web: *www.drexel.edu*

DUQUESNE UNIVERSITY
B-3

Pittsburgh, PA 15282-0201

(412) 396-6222
(800) 456-0590; (412) 396-5644

Full-time: 2406 men, 3142 women	**Faculty:** 435; IIA, +$
Part-time: 105 men, 117 women	**Ph.D.s:** 85%
Graduate: 1811 men, 2692 women	**Student/Faculty:** 13 to 1
Year: semesters, summer session	**Tuition:** $26,468
Application Deadline: July 1	**Room & Board:** $9200
Freshman Class: 6626 applied, 5054 accepted, 1432 enrolled	
SAT CR/M/W: 559/568/553	**ACT:** 25 **VERY COMPETITIVE**

Duquesne University, founded in 1878 by the Spiritan Congregation, is a private Roman Catholic institution offering programs in liberal arts, natural and environmental sciences, nursing, health sciences, pharmacy, business, music, teacher preparation, preprofessional training, law, and leadership and professional development. There are 9 undergraduate schools and 10 graduate schools. In addition to regional accreditation, Duquesne has baccalaureate program accreditation with AACSB, ACPE, NASM, and NCATE. The library contains 715,518 volumes, 292,871 microform items, and 31,060 audio/video tapes/CDs/DVDs, and subscribes to 0 periodicals including electronic. Computerized library services include interlibrary loans, database searching, Internet access, and laptop Internet portals. Special learning facilities include a learning resource center, art gallery, radio station, TV station, and 160 multimedia-enhanced teaching facilities. The 49-acre campus is in an urban area on a private, self-contained campus in the center of Pittsburgh. Including any residence halls, there are 31 buildings.

Student Life: 78% of undergraduates are from Pennsylvania. Others are from 39 states, 43 foreign countries, and Canada. 84% are white. 53% are Catholic; 27% claim no religious affiliation. The average age of freshmen is 18; all undergraduates, 20. 13% do not continue beyond their first year; 72% remain to graduate.

Housing: 3538 students can be accommodated in college housing, which includes single-sex and coed dorms and on-campus apartments. In addition, there are honors houses, special-interest houses, fraternity and sorority wings, international wings, and club wings. On-campus housing is guaranteed for the freshman year only, is available on a first-come, first-served basis, and is available on a lottery system for upperclassmen. 58% of students live on campus; of those, 70% remain on campus on weekends. Upperclassmen may keep cars.

Activities: 14% of men belong to 1 local and 9 national fraternities; 20% of women belong to 7 national sororities. There are 160 groups on campus, including art, band, cheerleading, chess, choir, chorale, chorus, computers, dance, debate, drama, drill team, environmental, ethnic, film, forensics, gay, honors, international, jazz band, literary magazine, musical theater, newspaper, opera, orchestra, pep band, photography, political, professional, radio and TV, religious, social, social programming, social service, student government, symphony, and yearbook. Popular campus events include Carnival, Bluffstock Music Festival, and International Night.

Sports: There are 10 intercollegiate sports for men and 10 for women, and 9 intramural sports for men and 27 for women. Facilities include an athletic center, a swimming pool, football, soccer, lacrosse, and baseball fields, an intramural field with an all-weather track, a weight room and exercise facilities, and volleyball, tennis, and basketball courts.

Disabled Students: 95% of the campus is accessible. Facilities include wheelchair ramps, elevators, special parking, specially equipped restrooms, special class scheduling, lowered drinking fountains, lowered telephones, special housing, and special assistive technology in the Gumberg Library for certain disabilities, including the visually impaired.

Services: Counseling and information services are available, as is tutoring in every subject. There is a reader service for the blind, and remedial math, reading, and writing.

Campus Safety and Security: Measures include 24-hour foot and vehicle patrol, emergency notification system, self-defense education, and security escort services. There are shuttle buses, emergency telephones, lighted pathways/sidewalks,and controlled access to dorms/residences. There are security cameras throughout campus that monitor exterior areas 24 hours a day.

Programs of Study: Duquesne confers B.A., B.S., B.M., B.S.A.T., B.S.B.A., B.S.Ed., B.S.H.M.S., B.S.H.S., B.S.N., and B.S.P.S. degrees.

Master's and doctoral degrees are also awarded. Bachelor's degrees are awarded in BIOLOGICAL SCIENCE (biochemistry and biology/biological science), BUSINESS (accounting, banking and finance, business administration and management, business communications, business economics, business law, entrepreneurial studies, international business management, investments and securities, management information systems, management science, marketing/retailing/merchandising, nonprofit/public organization management, organizational leadership and management, sports marketing, and supply chain management), COMMUNICATIONS AND THE ARTS (advertising, art history and appreciation, classical languages, communications, dramatic arts, English, Greek (classical), journalism, Latin, literature, media arts, modern language, multimedia, music performance, music technology, Spanish, and speech/debate/rhetoric), COMPUTER AND PHYSICAL SCIENCE (chemistry, computer science, computer security and information assurance, mathematics, physics, and web technology), EDUCATION (athletic training, early childhood education, education, elementary education, English education, foreign languages education, mathematics education, music education, secondary education, and special education), ENGINEERING AND ENVIRONMENTAL DESIGN (environmental science), HEALTH PROFESSIONS (health care administration, music therapy, nursing, occupational therapy, pharmaceutical science, physical therapy, physician's assistant, premedicine, and speech pathology/audiology), SOCIAL SCIENCE (classical/ancient civilization, criminal justice, economics, history, international relations, liberal arts/general studies, philosophy, political science/government, prelaw, psychology, sociology, and theological studies). Pharmacy, nursing, and psychology are the largest.

Required: To graduate, students are required to complete at least 120 credit hours, including a specified number in the major (varies by program), with a minimum 2.0 GPA. General requirements vary by department, but there is a 34 credit liberal arts core curriculum.

Special: The university offers cross-registration through the Pittsburgh Council on Higher Education, internships, study abroad in 26 countries, and a Washington semester. Also available are B.A.-B.S. degrees, accelerated degree programs, dual and student-designed majors, a 3-2 engineering program with Case Western Reserve University and University of Pittsburgh, a 3-3 law degree and a 3-2 business degree, pass/fail options, and credit for life, military, and work experience. There are 22 national honor societies, a freshman honors program, and all departments have honors programs.

Faculty/Classroom: 59% of faculty are male; 41% are female. 94% teach undergraduates. No introductory courses are taught by graduate students. The average class size in an introductory lecture, 32, in a laboratory, 25, and in a regular course, 26.

Admissions: 76% of the 2009-2010 applicants were accepted. The SAT scores for the 2009-2010 freshman class were: Critical Reading--16% below 500, 56% between 500 and 599, 26% between 600 and 700, and 2% above 700; Math--15% below 500, 50% between 500 and 599, 32% between 600 and 700, and 3% above 700; Writing--19% below 500, 53% between 500 and 599, 26% between 600 and 700, and 2% above 700. The ACT scores were 3% below 21, 27% between 21 and 23, 35% between 24 and 26, 19% between 27 and 28, and 16% above 28. 46% of the current freshmen were in the top fifth of their class; 79% were in the top two fifths. 28 freshmen graduated first in their class.

Requirements: The SAT or ACT is required. The ACT Optional Writing test is also required. In addition, students should have either a high school diploma or the GED. Applicants are required to have 16 academic credits, including 4 each in English and academic electives, and 8 combined in social studies, language, math, and science. An audition is required for music majors. An essay is required, and an interview is recommended. A GPA of 3.0 is required. AP and CLEP credits are accepted.

Procedure: Freshmen are admitted to all sessions. Entrance exams should be taken during the spring of the junior year or the fall of the senior year. There are early decision, early admissions, deferred admissions, and rolling admissions plans. Early decision applications should be filed by November 1; regular applications, by July 1 for fall entry, December 1 for spring entry, and April 1 for summer entry, along with a $50 fee. Notification of early decision is sent December 15; regular decision, sent on a rolling basis. Applications are accepted on-line.

Transfer: 189 transfer students enrolled in 2008-2009. Applicants must submit complete high school and college transcripts. Students should have a minimum GPA of 2.5 for the university, but some schools require a higher average. A minimum of 12 credits earned is required, and an interview is recommended. 30 of 120 credits required for the bachelor's degree must be completed at Duquesne.

Visiting: There are regularly scheduled orientations for prospective students, consisting of a campus tour and individual interviews with counselors and professors. There are guides for informal visits and visitors may sit in on classes. To schedule a visit, contact the Office of Admissions at (412) 396-5001.

Financial Aid: In 2009-2010, 100% of all full-time freshmen and 96% of continuing full-time students received some form of financial aid. 67% of all full-time freshmen and 67% of continuing full-time students received need-based aid. The average freshmen award was $24,945, with $16,252 ($21,632 maximum) from need-based scholarships or need-based grants; $10,124 ($34,735 maximum) from need-based self-help aid (loans and jobs); $15,113 ($42,940 maximum) from non-need-based athletic scholarships; and $7,168 ($24,356 maximum) from other non-need-based awards and non-need-based scholarships. The FAFSA and the college's own financial statement are required. The deadline for filing freshman financial aid applications for fall entry is May 1.

International Students: There are 139 international students enrolled. The school actively recruits these students. They must take the TOEFL or MELAB.

Computers: Wireless access is available. The campus is covered by a 7,000-node Ethernet network, a wireless network, and more than 850 computers in computer labs. All students may access the system. There are no time limits and no fees. It is strongly recommended that all students have a personal computer. A Dell or Apple is recommended.

Graduates: From July 1, 2008 to June 30, 2009, 1201 bachelor's degrees were awarded. The most popular majors were liberal arts (29%), business (23%), and nursing (10%). 139 companies recruited on campus in 2008-2009. In an average class, 62% graduate in 4 years or less, 71% graduate in 5 years or less, and 72% graduate in 6 years or less. Of the 2008 graduating class, 21% were enrolled in graduate school within 6 months of graduation, and 63% were employed.

Admissions Contact: Paul-James Cukanna, Associate Vice President of Enrollment Management and Director of Admissions. A campus DVD is available. E-Mail: admissions@duq.edu Web: www.duq.edu

EAST STROUDSBURG UNIVERSITY OF PENNSYLVANIA — F-2

East Stroudsburg, PA 18301
(570) 422-3833
(877) 230-5547; (570) 422-3933

Full-time: 2689 men, 3148 women	**Faculty:** 301; IIA, av$
Part-time: 230 men, 324 women	**Ph.D.s:** 75%
Graduate: 340 men, 845 women	**Student/Faculty:** 18 to 1
Year: semesters, summer session	**Tuition:** $7394 ($15,830)
Application Deadline: April 1	**Room & Board:** $6418
Freshman Class: 6959 applied, 4814 accepted, 1358 enrolled	
SAT CR/M/W: 480/490/480	**COMPETITIVE**

East Stroudsburg University of Pennsylvania, founded in 1893, is a part of the Pennsylvania State System of Higher Education and offers programs in arts and science, health science and human performance, education, business management, and economics. There are 4 undergraduate schools and 1 graduate school. In addition to regional accreditation, East Stroudsburg has baccalaureate program accreditation with NCATE, NLN, and NRPA. The library contains 559,231 volumes, 1.4 million microform items, and 12,471 audio/video tapes/CDs/DVDs, and subscribes to 28,670 periodicals including electronic. Computerized library services include interlibrary loans, database searching, and Internet access. Special learning facilities include a learning resource center, art gallery, planetarium, radio station, an observatory, a wildlife museum and greenhouse, and a working restaurant. The 256-acre campus is in a small town 75 miles west of New York City and 85 miles northeast of Philadelphia. Including any residence halls, there are 66 buildings.

Student Life: 74% of undergraduates are from Pennsylvania. Others are from 27 states, 27 foreign countries, and Canada. 75% are white. The average age of freshmen is 18; all undergraduates, 21. 22% do not continue beyond their first year; 59% remain to graduate.

Housing: 2100 students can be accommodated in college housing, which includes coed dorms and on-campus apartments. In addition, there are honors floors. On-campus housing is guaranteed for all 4 years. 62% of students commute. Alcohol is not permitted. Upperclassmen may keep cars.

Activities: 4% of men belong to 5 national fraternities; 5% of women belong to 1 local and 4 national sororities. There are 100 groups on campus, including art, band, cheerleading, chess, choir, chorus, computers, dance, drama, ethnic, gay, honors, international, jazz band, literary magazine, marching band, musical theater, newspaper, orchestra, pep band, photography, political, professional, radio and TV, religious, social, social service, student government, and symphony. Popular campus events include concerts, Spring Music Festival, and international celebrations.

Sports: There are 10 intercollegiate sports for men and 12 for women, and 10 intramural sports for men and 10 for women. Facilities include a 6000-seat stadium, a 2600-seat gym, a second gym, 10 athletic fields, 12 outdoor tennis courts, 1 indoor tennis court, a swimming pool, indoor and outdoor tracks, a wrestling room, and weight rooms. In addition, the recreation center includes a 4-court arena for basketball, volleyball, and tennis, an elevated track, a boxing zone, a fitness center, 3 racquetball courts, and 1 outdoor multipurpose recreation field.

Disabled Students: 98% of the campus is accessible. Facilities include wheelchair ramps, elevators, special parking, specially equipped restrooms, special class scheduling, lowered drinking fountains, and lowered telephones.

Services: Counseling and information services are available, as is tutoring in every subject. There is remedial math, reading, and writing.

Campus Safety and Security: Measures include 24-hour foot and vehicle patrol, emergency notification system, self-defense education, and security escort services. There are shuttle buses, emergency telephones, lighted pathways/sidewalks, controlled access to dorms/residences, and controlled building access.

Programs of Study: East Stroudsburg confers B.A. and B.S. degrees. Master's degrees are also awarded. Bachelor's degrees are awarded in BIOLOGICAL SCIENCE (biochemistry, biology/biological science, and marine science), BUSINESS (business administration and management and hotel/motel and restaurant management), COMMUNICATIONS AND THE ARTS (art, communications, dramatic arts, English, fine arts, French, media arts, music, and Spanish), COMPUTER AND PHYSICAL SCIENCE (chemistry, computer science, earth science, mathematics, physical sciences, and science), EDUCATION (early childhood education, elementary education, foreign languages education, health education, secondary education, and special education), ENGINEERING AND ENVIRONMENTAL DESIGN (environmental science), HEALTH PROFESSIONS (medical laboratory technology, nursing, premedicine, and speech pathology/audiology), SOCIAL SCIENCE (economics, geography, history, parks and recreation management, philosophy, physical fitness/movement, political science/government, psychology, social studies, and sociology). Biological sciences, business management, and physical education are the largest.

Required: All students must maintain a GPA of at least 2.0 while taking at least 120 semester hours, including 27 to 83 hours in the major. General education courses total 50 credits, with English composition (3 credits) and phys ed (2 credits) required courses. Distribution requirements include 15 hours each in arts and letters, science, and social science.

Special: Internships are offered in most programs, as are dual majors. Also offered are an accelerated degree program in law, B.A.-B.S. degrees, 3-2 engineering degrees with Pennsylvania State University or the University of Pittsburgh, and a transfer program in podiatry. Nondegree study, study abroad, and cross-registration through the National Student Exchange are possible. There are 23 national honor societies, a freshman honors program, and all departments have honors programs.

Faculty/Classroom: 51% of faculty are male; 49% are female. All teach undergraduates. No introductory courses are taught by graduate students. The average class size in an introductory lecture, 40, in a laboratory ,20, and in a regular course, 25.

Admissions: 69% of the 2009-2010 applicants were accepted. The SAT scores for the 2009-2010 freshman class were: Critical Reading--61% below 500, 34% between 500 and 599, and 5% between 600 and 700; Math--52% below 500, 38% between 500 and 599, and 9% between 600 and 700; Writing--62% below 500, 34% between 500 and 599, 4% between 600 and 700, and 1% above 700. 20% of the current freshmen were in the top fifth of their class; 33% were in the top two fifths. 2 freshmen graduated first in their class.

Requirements: The SAT is required. In addition, applicants must be graduates of an accredited secondary school. The GED is accepted. AP and CLEP credits are accepted. Important factors in the admissions decision are advanced placement or honors courses, evidence of special talent, and leadership record.

Procedure: Freshmen are admitted fall and spring. There is a rolling admissions plan. Applications should be filed by April 1 for fall entry and November 15 for spring entry. The fall 2009 application fee was $35. Notifications are sent December 1. 48 applicants were on the 2009 waiting list; 48 were admitted. Applications are accepted on-line.

Transfer: 578 transfer students enrolled in 2008-2009. Transfer students must have a 2.0 GPA earned over at least 24 credit hours. 32 of 120 credits required for the bachelor's degree must be completed at East Stroudsburg.

Visiting: There are regularly scheduled orientations for prospective students. There are guides for informal visits and visitors may sit in on classes. To schedule a visit, contact the Admissions Office at (877) 230-5547.

Financial Aid: In a recent year, 52% of all full-time freshmen and 54% of continuing full-time students received some form of financial aid. The average freshman award was $3890. Need-based scholarships and need-based grants averaged $3367 ($3438 maximum); need-based self-help aid (loans and jobs) averaged $4536 ($6011 maximum; non-need-based athletic scholarships averaged $2511(maximum); and other non-need-based awards and non-need-based scholarships averaged $7552 ($7828 maximum). 8% of undergraduates work part time. Average annual earnings from campus work were $2145. The average financial indebtedness of the 2007 graduate was $16,857.East Stroudsburg is a member of CSS. The FAFSA is required. Check with the school for current application deadlines.

International Students: There are 47 international students enrolled. They must take the TOEFL with a minimum score of 550 on the paper-based TOEFL (PBT) or 79 on the Internet-based version (iBT).

Computers: Wireless access is available. There are 223 computers available to students. Students are assigned network accounts in order to use a computer in 1 of the 23 labs on campus, which all have Internet access. All residence halls have wired or wireless Internet access. All students may access the system. Most computers are available 8 A.M. to 10 P.M., with some available on weekends. There are no time limits and no fees. A Lenovo is recommended.

Graduates: From July 1, 2008 to June 30, 2009, 1274 bachelor's degrees were awarded. The most popular majors were business management (10%), elementary education (7%), and sociology (6%). In an average class, 36% graduate in 4 years or less, 55% graduate in 5 years or less, and 59% graduate in 6 years or less.

Admissions Contact: Jeff Jones, Director, Admissions Office. E-Mail: *undergrads@esu.edu* Web: *www4.esu.edu*

EASTERN UNIVERSITY
F-3

St. Davids, PA 19087-3696
(610) 341-5967
(800) 452-0996; (610) 341-1723

Full-time: 525 men, 1035 women	Faculty: 64; IIA, --$
Part-time: 125 men, 235 women	Ph.D.s: 75%
Graduate: 330 men, 540 women	Student/Faculty: 24 to 1
Year: semesters, summer session	Tuition: $21,350
Application Deadline:	Room & Board: $7,225
Freshman Class: n/av	
SAT or ACT: required	COMPETITIVE

Eastern University, founded in 1932, is a private liberal arts institution affiliated with the American Baptist Church. Enrollment and faculty information in the above capsule is approximate. There are no undergraduate schools and one graduate school. In addition to regional accreditation, Eastern has baccalaureate program accreditation with CSWE and NLN. The 2 libraries contain 131,000 volumes, 716,396 microform items, 13,242 audio/video tapes/CDs/DVDs, and subscribe to 1,079 periodicals including electronic. Computerized library services include inter-library loans and database searching. Special learning facilities include a planetarium, and a radio station. The 106-acre campus is in a small town 20 miles northwest of Philadelphia. Including any residence halls, there are 23 buildings.

Student Life: 60% of undergraduates are from Pennsylvania. Students are from 38 states, 26 foreign countries, and Canada. 72% are from public schools. 81% are white; 14% African American. 68% are Assembly of God, Christian, Evangelical, Mennonite, Pentecostal; 13% claim no religious affiliation; 11% Catholic. The average age of freshmen is 19; all undergraduates, 27. 28% do not continue beyond their first year; 55% remain to graduate.

Housing: 840 students can be accommodated in college housing, which includes single-sex and coed dorms and on-campus apartments. On-campus housing is guaranteed for all 4 years. 53% of students commute. Alcohol is not permitted. All students may keep cars.

Activities: There are no fraternities or sororities. There are 70 groups on campus, including band, cheerleading, choir, chorale, chorus, communications, computers, dance, drama, drill team, ethnic, honors, international, jazz band, literary magazine, musical theater, newspaper, orchestra, pep band, political, professional, radio and TV, religious, social, social service, student government, and yearbook. Popular campus events include President's Christmas Party, Spring Banquet, and World Culture Day.

Sports: There are 5 intercollegiate sports for men and 7 for women, and 3 intramural sports for men and 3 for women. Facilities include a gym, a soccer pitch, a baseball/field hockey/softball field, a weight room, an outdoor track, 4 tennis courts, a health fitness trail, an outdoor pool, and basketball/volleyball courts.

Disabled Students: 75% of the campus is accessible. Facilities include wheelchair ramps, elevators, special parking, specially equipped rest rooms, special class scheduling, lowered drinking fountains, lowered telephones, and special housing.

Services: Counseling and information services are available, as is tutoring in every subject. There is a reader service for the blind, and remedial math, reading, and writing. and a summer skills workshop

Campus Safety and Security: Measures include 24-hour foot and vehicle patrol, self-defense education, and security escort services. There are shuttle buses, emergency telephones, and lighted pathways/sidewalks.

Programs of Study: Eastern confers B.A., B.S., B.S.N., and B.S.W. degrees. Associates and master's degrees are also awarded. Bachelor's degrees are awarded in AGRICULTURE (environmental studies), BIOLOGICAL SCIENCE (biochemistry and biology/biological science), BUSINESS (accounting, business administration and management, management information systems, and marketing/retailing/merchandising), COMMUNICATIONS AND THE ARTS (art history and appreciation, communications, dance, English literature, French, music, Spanish, and studio art), COMPUTER AND PHYSICAL SCIENCE (astronomy, chemistry, and mathematics), EDUCATION (elementary education, English education, secondary education, and special education), ENGINEERING AND ENVIRONMENTAL DESIGN (city/community/regional planning), HEALTH PROFESSIONS (health care administration and health science), SOCIAL SCIENCE (biblical studies, history,

missions, political science/government, psychology, social work, sociology, theological studies, urban studies, and youth ministry). Biblical/theological studies and English literature is the strongest academically. Youth ministries and elementary education is the largest.

Required: To graduate, all students must complete at least 127 credit hours with a minimum 2.0 GPA. The required hours in the major vary. Students must take courses in the Old and New Testament, humanities, social sciences, non-Western heritage, natural sciences, college writing, Living and Learning in Community, Heritage of Western Thought and Civilization, Science Technology and Values, and Justice in a Pluralistic Society and complete a capstone.

Special: The college offers cross-registration with Cabrini and Rosemont Colleges, Valley Forge Military Academy, and Villanova University, internships, a Washington semester in the American studies program, and student-designed majors. Also available are accelerated degree programs in organizational management and management of information systems, credit for experience, non-degree study, and pass/fail options. There is a different calendar for the organizational management program. There are 10 national honor societies, a freshman honors program, and 1 departmental honors program.

Faculty/Classroom: 54% of faculty are male; 46% are female. 83% teach undergraduates. No introductory courses are taught by graduate students. The average class size in an introductory lecture is 45; in a laboratory is 14; and in a regular course is 14.

Admissions: n/av

Requirements: The SAT or ACT is required. A GPA of 2.0 is required. AP and CLEP credits are accepted.

Procedure: Freshmen are admitted to all sessions. Entrance exams should be taken as early as possible. There are early admissions, deferred admissions, and rolling admissions plans. Check with the school for current application deadlines. The fall 2008 application fee was $25. Applications are accepted on-line.

Transfer: Applicants should have a 2.0 GPA with more than 24 credits, and a 2.5 GPA with fewer than 24 credits. Candidates must be in good standing at their previous institution. 32 of 127 credits required for the bachelor's degree must be completed at Eastern.

Visiting: There are regularly scheduled orientations for prospective students, including a preview of academics, student life, and athletics. There are guides for informal visits, visitors may sit in on classes, and stay overnight. To schedule a visit, contact the Admissions Office.

Financial Aid: In 2009-2010, 95% of all full-time freshmen received some form of financial aid. 95% of all full-time freshmen received need-based aid. Eastern is a member of CSS. The FAFSA and the college's own financial statement, and income tax forms are required. Check with the school for current application deadlines.

International Students: The school actively recruits these students. They must take the TOEFL.

Computers: All students may access the system. There are no time limits and no fees. It is strongly recommended that all students have a personal computer.

Graduates: n/av

Admissions Contact: David Urban/Jim Henderson, Executive Director of Enrollment Management. E-Mail: *ugadm@eastern.edu* Web: *www.eastern.edu*

EDINBORO UNIVERSITY OF PENNSYLVANIA
B-1

Edinboro, PA 16444
(814) 732-2761
(888) 8GO-BORO; (814) 732-2420

Full-time: 2451 men, 3144 women	Faculty: IIA, av$
Part-time: 323 men, 494 women	Ph.D.s: n/av
Graduate: 351 men, 923 women	Student/Faculty: n/av
Year: semesters, summer session	Tuition: $6,484 ($9,067)
Application Deadline:	Room & Board: $5,718
Freshman Class: 3612 applied, 2944 accepted, 1252 enrolled	
SAT CR/M/W: 460/450/440	ACT: 18 COMPETITIVE

Edinboro University of Pennsylvania, founded in 1857, is a public institution and a member of the Pennsylvania State System of Higher Education. The university offers programs in fine and liberal arts, business, engineering, health science, and teacher preparation. There are 3 undergraduate schools and one graduate school. In addition to regional accreditation, EUP has baccalaureate program accreditation with ACBSP, ADA, CSWE, NASAD, NASM, NCATE, and NLN. The library contains 491,849 volumes, 1.4 million microform items, 12,718 audio/video tapes/CDs/DVDs, and subscribes to 1,362 periodicals including electronic. Computerized library services include inter-library loans, database searching, Internet access, and laptop Internet portals. Special learning facilities include an art gallery, planetarium, radio station, TV station, a newspaper. The 585-acre campus is in a small town 18 miles south of Erie. Including any residence halls, there are 41 buildings.

Student Life: 74% of undergraduates are from Pennsylvania. Students are from 33 states, 34 foreign countries, and Canada. 88% are white. The average age of freshmen is 19; all undergraduates, 23. 31% do not continue beyond their first year; 48% remain to graduate.

Housing: 1900 students can be accommodated in college housing, which includes single-sex and coed dorms. In addition, there are honors houses, special-interest houses, floors by academic major, quiet floors, and nonsmoking residence halls. On-campus housing is guaranteed for the freshman year only, is available on a first-come, and first-served basis. 72% of students commute. Alcohol is not permitted. All students may keep cars.

Activities: There are 141 groups on campus, including art, bagpipe, band, cheerleading, chess, choir, chorale, chorus, communications, computers, dance, debate, drama, drill team, ethnic, film, forensics, gay, honors, international, literary magazine, marching band, musical theater, newspaper, opera, orchestra, pep band, photography, political, professional, radio and TV, religious, social, social service, student government, and symphony. Popular campus events include Moving in Day/Ice Cream Social, Academic Festival, and Snowfest.

Sports: There are 6 intercollegiate sports for men and 8 for women, and 12 intramural sports for men and 12 for women. Facilities include a field house, a stadium, 6 tennis courts, 4 gyms, a swimming pool, 3 racquetball courts, 2 aerobics rooms, an indoor and outdoor track, a fitness center, men's and women's locker rooms, an athletic training office, a wrestling room, saunas, steam rooms, a weight room, a combative sport room, an outdoor ropes course, a softball field, multiple outdoor sport fields, an outdoor recreation office, and a climbing wall.

Disabled Students: 97% of the campus is accessible. Facilities include wheelchair ramps, elevators, special parking, specially equipped rest rooms, special class scheduling, lowered drinking fountains, lowered telephones, special housing.

Services: Counseling and information services are available, as is tutoring in most subjects. There is a reader service for the blind, and remedial math, reading, and writing. Academic aides are available as are services in the academic support library.

Campus Safety and Security: Measures include 24-hour foot and vehicle patrol and self-defense education. There are emergency telephones, lighted pathways/sidewalks, There are 14 commissioned police officers and optional engraving of personal property.

Programs of Study: EUP confers B.A., B.S., B.F.A., B.S.A.E., B.S.Ed., B.S.H.P.E., and B.S.N. degrees. Associates and master's degrees are also awarded. Bachelor's degrees are awarded in BIOLOGICAL SCIENCE (biochemistry, biology/biological science, and nutrition), BUSINESS (accounting, banking and finance, business administration and management, marketing management, and sports management), COMMUNICATIONS AND THE ARTS (advertising, applied art, art, art history and appreciation, broadcasting, ceramic art and design, communications, creative writing, dramatic arts, drawing, English, English literature, fiber/textiles/weaving, film arts, fine arts, German, graphic design, journalism, media arts, metal/jewelry, music, painting, photography, printmaking, sculpture, Spanish, and speech/debate/rhetoric), COMPUTER AND PHYSICAL SCIENCE (chemistry, computer science, earth science, geology, information sciences and systems, mathematics, natural sciences, and physics), EDUCATION (art education, early childhood education, elementary education, English education, foreign languages education, health education, mathematics education, middle school education, music education, physical education, science education, secondary education, social studies education, and special education), ENGINEERING AND ENVIRONMENTAL DESIGN (engineering physics, environmental science, manufacturing technology, and woodworking), HEALTH PROFESSIONS (medical laboratory technology, nuclear medical technology, nursing, predentistry, premedicine, preveterinary science, public health, and speech pathology/audiology), SOCIAL SCIENCE (anthropology, counseling/psychology, criminal justice, economics, forensic studies, geography, history, humanities, Latin American studies, liberal arts/general studies, philosophy, political science/government, prelaw, psychology, social science, social work, sociology, and women's studies). Applied media arts, business administration, and education are the largest.

Required: To graduate, students must complete a minimum of 120 semester hours with a minimum GPA of 2.0. General education requirements include 48 hours of courses, consisting of a 21-semester-hour core with 3 hours each in artistic expression, world civilizations, American civilizations, human behavior, cultural diversity and social pluralism, ethics, and science and technology and a 12-hour distribution with 9 hours in English and math skills and 3 hours of health and phys ed.

Special: The university offers cooperative programs in engineering, prelaw, pre-pharmacy, and osteopathic medicine, and cross-registration through the Pennsylvania State System of Higher Education and the Marine Science Consortium at Wallops Island, Virginia, and with Mercyhurst College and Gannon University. A Harrisburg semester, internships in most majors, a general studies program, student-designed majors, dual majors in education, a 3-2 engineering degree, study abroad in more than 10 countries, and non-degree study are also offered. Students may select pass/fail options and receive credit for life, military, and work experience. There are 10 national honor societies, a freshman honors program, and 9 departmental honors programs.

Faculty/Classroom: 55% of faculty are male; 45% are female. 92% teach undergraduates. No introductory courses are taught by graduate students. The average class size in an introductory lecture is 30.

Admissions: 82% of the 2009-2010 applicants were accepted. The SAT scores for the 2009-2010 freshman class were: Critical Reading-- 64% below 500, 28% between 500 and 599, 6% between 600 and 700, and 2 above 700; Math--66% below 500, 26% between 500 and 599, 6% between 600 and 700, and 2 above 700; Writing--74% below 500, 22% between 500 and 599, 3% between 600 and 700, and 1 above 700. The ACT scores were 43% below 21, 51% between 21 and 23, 6% between 24 and 26, % between 27 and 28, and % above 28. 5 freshmen graduated first in their class.

Requirements: The SAT or ACT is required. In addition, candidates for admission should be graduates of an accredited secondary school or the equivalent. The GED is accepted. A GPA of 2.0 is recommended. A portfolio is recommended for art students, and an audition is required for music students. An interview is recommended for all. Admissions decisions are based upon the academic major requested, high school curriculum, grades, GPA, class rank, SAT or ACT scores, and leadership and extracurricular activities record. AP and CLEP credits are accepted. Important factors in the admissions decision are advanced placement or honors courses, extracurricular activities record, and personality/ intangible qualities.

Procedure: Freshmen are admitted to all sessions. Entrance exams should be taken in the junior year or early in the senior year. There are early admissions, deferred admissions, and rolling admissions plans. Application deadlines are open. Application fee is $30. Applications are accepted on-line.

Transfer: 434 transfer students enrolled in 2008-2009. Applicants should have a 2.0 GPA and must submit transcripts from previous institutions. An interview is recommended. 30 of 120 credits required for the bachelor's degree must be completed at EUP.

Visiting: There are regularly scheduled orientations for prospective students, including admissions, financial aid, and academic affairs presentations followed by campus tours. There are guides for informal visits, visitors may sit in on classes, and stay overnight. To schedule a visit, contact the Admissions Office.

Financial Aid: In 2009-2010, 96% of all full-time freshmen and 98% of continuing full-time students received some form of financial aid. 92% of all full-time freshmen and 92% of continuing full-time students received need-based aid. The average freshmen award was $6,069. 11% of undergraduate students work part-time. Average annual earnings from campus work are $2146. The average financial indebtedness of the 2009 graduate was $16,119. The FAFSA is required. The priority date for freshman financial aid applications for fall entry is March 15. The deadline for filing freshman financial aid applications for fall entry is May 1.

International Students: There are 60 international students enrolled. The school actively recruits these students. They must take the TOEFL with a minimum score of 500 on the paper-based TOEFL (PBT).

Computers: Wireless access is available. Access to network resources can be obtained in lounges, dining areas, and some outdoor areas. All students automatically receive a network account and e-mail account when they register. There are 9 general-access computer labs, 13 instructional labs, and 32 computer classrooms. All students may access the system, although lab hours vary. There are no time limits and no fees.

Graduates: From July 1, 2008 to June 30, 2009, 1097 bachelor's degrees were awarded. The most popular majors were education (30%), criminal justice (7%), and applied media arts (6%). In an average class, 23% graduate in 4 years or less, 44% graduate in 5 years or less, and 50% graduate in 6 years or less.

Admissions Contact: Admissions Office E-Mail: *eup_admissions@edinboro.edu* Web: *www.edinboro.edu*

ELIZABETHTOWN COLLEGE D-3

Elizabethtown, PA 17022   (717) 361-1400; (717) 361-1365

Full-time: 686 men, 1200 women	**Faculty:** 123
Part-time: 158 men, 278 women	**Ph.D.s:** 99%
Graduate: 5 men, 40 women	**Student/Faculty:** 15 to 1
Year: semesters, summer session	**Tuition:** $31,800
Application Deadline: open	**Room & Board:** $8150
Freshman Class: 3323 applied, 2488 accepted, 568 enrolled	
SAT CR/M: 560/580	**ACT:** 24 **VERY COMPETITIVE**

Elizabethtown College, founded in 1899, is a private college founded by members of the Church of the Brethren. It offers nearly 50 majors and 70 minors with concentrations in the arts, sciences, humanities, and professional programs, and a master's program in occupational therapy. In addition to regional accreditation, E-town has baccalaureate program accreditation with ABET, ACBSP, CSWE, and NASM. The library contains 260,037 volumes, 23,614 microform items, and 4,474 audio/video tapes/CDs/DVDs, and subscribes to 40,003 periodicals including electronic. Computerized library services include interlibrary loans, database searching, Internet access, and laptop Internet portals. Special learning facilities include a learning resource center, art gallery, radio station, TV station, and the Young Center for Anabaptist and Pietist Studies, a nationally unique academic research facility. The 201-acre campus is in a small town 10 minutes from Hershey and 25 minutes from Lancaster and Harrisburg. Including any residence halls, there are 26 buildings.

Student Life: 71% of undergraduates are from Pennsylvania. Others are from 28 states, 18 foreign countries, and Canada. 83% are from public schools. 91% are white. 28% are Protestant; 22% Catholic. The average age of freshmen is 18; all undergraduates, 20. 17% do not continue beyond their first year; 70% remain to graduate.

Housing: 1490 students can be accommodated in college housing, which includes single-sex and coed dorms and on-campus apartments. In addition, there are honors houses, special-interest houses, substance free and quiet study. On-campus housing is guaranteed for all 4 years. 83% of students live on campus; of those, 70% remain on campus on weekends. All students may keep cars.

Activities: There are no fraternities or sororities. There are 76 groups on campus, including learning communities, residential, academic, art, band, cheerleading, choir, chorale, chorus, computers, dance, drama, environmental, ethnic, forensics, gay, honors, international, jazz band, literary magazine, musical theater, newspaper, orchestra, photography, political, professional, radio and TV, religious, social, social service, student government, and yearbook. Popular campus events include Thank God It's Spring, Into the Streets, and Super S.W.E.E.T. Weekends.

Sports: There are 10 intercollegiate sports for men and 10 for women, and 9 intramural sports for men and 9 for women. Facilities include a 6-lane swimming pool, weight training rooms, a 2,200-seat soccer complex, a 2,400-seat gym, a track and field complex, racquetball and tennis courts, basketball and sand volleyball courts, a fitness center, and baseball, softball, lacrosse, and field hockey fields.

Disabled Students: 75% of the campus is accessible. Facilities include wheelchair ramps, elevators, special parking, specially equipped rest rooms, special class scheduling, lowered drinking fountains, and lowered telephones.

Services: Counseling and information services are available, as is tutoring in most subjects. There is a reader service for the blind, and remedial math, reading, and writing. Workshops and individual help with study skills as well as assistive technology is also available.

Campus Safety and Security: Measures include 24-hour foot and vehicle patrol, emergency notification system, self-defense education, and security escort services. There are emergency telephones, lighted pathways/sidewalks, and a crime prevention program.

Programs of Study: E-town confers B.A., B.S., and B.M. degrees. Associates and master's degrees are also awarded. Bachelor's degrees are awarded in AGRICULTURE (forestry and related sciences), BIOLOGICAL SCIENCE (biochemistry, biology/biological science, and biotechnology), BUSINESS (accounting, business administration and management, business economics, business systems analysis, entrepreneurial studies, international business management, and marketing management), COMMUNICATIONS AND THE ARTS (art, communications, dramatic arts, English, English literature, French, German, Japanese, modern language, music, and Spanish), COMPUTER AND PHYSICAL SCIENCE (actuarial science, chemistry, computer science, information sciences and systems, mathematics, and physics), EDUCATION (early childhood education, elementary education, English education, mathematics education, music education, science education, secondary education, and social studies education), ENGINEERING AND ENVIRONMENTAL DESIGN (computer engineering, engineering, environmental science, industrial engineering, and preengineering), HEALTH PROFESSIONS (allied health, music therapy, occupational therapy, and premedicine), SOCIAL SCIENCE (criminal justice, economics, history, philosophy, political science/government, psychology, religion, social studies, social work, and sociology). Business administration, communications, and elementary education are the largest.

Required: The core curriculum includes a first-year seminar and a colloquium, and courses in math, language, creative expression, western cultural heritage, non-western cultural heritage, the natural and social sciences, and humanities. Distribution requirements include 40 hours in 8 areas of understanding. Students must complete 125 credit hours and maintain a GPA of 2.0 overall and in their major.

Special: Students can participate in short-term, semester-long, and year-long study-abroad experiences in 18 different locations worldwide. Also available are work-study programs, internships, a Washington semester, accelerated degrees, and dual majors, including sociology and anthropology. There is a 3-2 engineering degree with Pennsylvania State University; a 3-3 allied health degree and a 3-3 physical therapy degree with Thomas Jefferson University, Widener University, and the University of Maryland/Baltimore County; and a 3-2 forestry or environmental management degree with Duke University. There are 19 national honor societies, a freshman honors program, and 100 departmental honors programs.

Faculty/Classroom: 58% of faculty are male; 42% are female. All teach and do research. No introductory courses are taught by graduate students. The average class size in an introductory lecture is 22; in a laboratory is 14; and in a regular course is 16.

Admissions: 75% of the 2009-2010 applicants were accepted. The SAT scores for the 2009-2010 freshman class were: Critical Reading--19% below 500, 50% between 500 and 599, 27% between 600 and 700, and 4 above 700; Math--18% below 500, 40% between 500 and 599, 37% between 600 and 700, and 5 above 700. The ACT scores were 29% below 21, 21% between 21 and 23, 23% between 24 and 26, 12% between 27 and 28, and 15% above 28. 54% of the current freshmen were in the top fifth of their class; 85% were in the top two fifths. 11 freshmen graduated first in their class.

Requirements: The SAT or ACT is required. Recommended composite scores for the SAT range from 1030 to 1230; for the ACT, 21 to 27. Applicants must be graduates of an accredited secondary school or have earned a GED. The college encourages completion of 18 academic credits, based on 4 years of English, 3 of math, 2 each of lab science, social studies, and consecutive foreign language, and 5 additional college preparatory units. An audition is required for music majors and an interview is required for occupational therapy majors. AP and CLEP credits are accepted. Important factors in the admissions decision are advanced placement or honors courses, recommendations by school officials, and extracurricular activities record.

Procedure: Freshmen are admitted to all sessions. Entrance exams should be taken in spring of the junior year or fall of the senior year. There are deferred admissions and rolling admissions plans. Application deadlines are open. Application fee is $30. Applications are accepted on-line. 80 applicants were on a recent waiting list, 0 were accepted.

Transfer: 24 transfer students enrolled in 2008-2009. Applicants should present a minimum GPA of 3.0 in at least 15 credit hours earned from a community college, or 2.5 from a 4-year institution. 30 of 125 credits required for the bachelor's degree must be completed at E-town.

Visiting: There are regularly scheduled orientations for prospective students, including 5 open houses and weekday appointments throughout the year. Special academic department days are also hosted. There are guides for informal visits, visitors may sit in on classes, and stay overnight. To schedule a visit, contact the Admissions Office at (717) 361-1400.

Financial Aid: In 2009-2010, 99% of all full-time freshmen and 96% of continuing full-time students received some form of financial aid. 74% of all full-time freshmen and 73% of continuing full-time students received need-based aid. The average freshmen award was $23,278, with $19,243 ($32,020 maximum) from need-based scholarships or need-based grants and $4,926 ($8,000 maximum) from need-based self-help aid (loans and jobs). All undergraduate students work part-time. Average annual earnings from campus work are $1109. E-town is a member of CSS. The FAFSA, the college's own financial statement, and family federal tax returns are required. The deadline for filing freshman financial aid applications for fall entry is March 15.

International Students: There are 48 international students enrolled. The school actively recruits these students. They must take the TOEFL with a minimum score of 525 on the paper-based TOEFL (PBT) or 75 on the Internet-based version (iBT).

Computers: All students are provided with Internet access and e-mail service. PCs are available in computer centers and labs, residence halls, the library, and the student center. There are open, wired network connections in the library, computer labs, and elsewhere on campus. All of the college-owned and college-operated housing units are wired for high-speed Internet access. Some areas of the campus have wireless access. All students may access the system. any time. There are no time limits and no fees. It is strongly recommended that all students have a personal computer.

Graduates: From July 1, 2008 to June 30, 2009, 520 bachelor's degrees were awarded. The most popular majors were business (29%), education (12%), and communications (10%). 60 companies recruited on campus in 2008-2009. In an average class, 70% graduate in 4 years or less, 73% graduate in 5 years or less, and 73% graduate in 6 years or less. Of the 2008 graduating class, 20% were enrolled in graduate school within 6 months of graduation.

Admissions Contact: Paul Cramer, Vice President for Enrollment. E-Mail: *admissions@etown.edu* Web: *www.etown.edu*

FRANKLIN AND MARSHALL COLLEGE
Lancaster, PA 17604-3003

E-3

(717) 291-3953
(877) 678-9111; (717) 291-4389

Full-time: 1043 men, 1016 women	Faculty: 184; IIB, +$
Part-time: 21 men, 24 women	Ph.D.s: 97%
Graduate: none	Student/Faculty: 11 to 1
Year: semesters, summer session	Tuition: $36,480
Application Deadline: February 1	Room & Board: $9,174
Freshman Class: 5018 applied, 1873 accepted, 570 enrolled	
SAT CR/M: 641/654	MOST COMPETITIVE

Franklin and Marshall College, founded in 1787, is a private liberal arts institution. There are no undergraduate schools. The 2 libraries contain 436,822 volumes, 230,755 microform items, 9,982 audio/video tapes/CDs/DVDs, and subscribe to 2,980 periodicals including electronic.

Computerized library services include inter-library loans, database searching, and Internet access. Special learning facilities include an art gallery, natural history museum, planetarium, radio station, TV station, academic technology services, advanced language lab, writing center, and student newspaper. The 209-acre campus is in a suburban area 60 miles west of Philadelphia. Including any residence halls, there are 45 buildings.

Student Life: 69% of undergraduates are from out of state, mostly the Middle Atlantic. Students are from 40 states, 47 foreign countries, and Canada. 57% are from public schools. 72% are white. 43% claim no religious affiliation; 21% Catholic; 18% Protestant. The average age of freshmen is 18; all undergraduates, 20. 9% do not continue beyond their first year; 82% remain to graduate.

Housing: 1570 students can be accommodated in college housing, which includes single-sex and coed dorms, on-campus apartments, and off-campus apartments. In addition, there are language houses, special-interest houses, including a French house, an arts house, an international living center, and a community outreach house. On-campus housing is guaranteed for the freshman year only and is available on a lottery system for upperclassmen. 80% of students live on campus. Upperclassmen may keep cars.

Activities: 26% of men belong to 7 national fraternities; 12% of women belong to 3 national sororities. There are 120 groups on campus, including (a student-run club/restaurant), and Ben's Underground, art, band, cheerleading, chess, choir, chorale, chorus, communications, computers, dance, debate, drama, environmental, ethnic, film, forensics, gay, honors, international, jazz band, literary magazine, musical theater, newspaper, opera, orchestra, photography, political, professional, radio and TV, religious, social, social service, student government, symphony, and yearbook. Popular campus events include Spring Arts Weekend, Freshman Feast, and Senior Surprise.

Sports: There are 13 intercollegiate sports for men and 13 for women, and 12 intramural sports for men and 12 for women. Facilities include a 3000-seat gym, 4 squash courts, a wrestling room, 54 acres of playing fields, a 400-meter all-weather track, a wellness/aerobic center, a strength training center, and tennis courts. A sports center features a fitness center, 5 multipurpose courts, 2 jogging tracks, and an Olympic-size pool.

Disabled Students: 80% of the campus is accessible. Facilities include wheelchair ramps, elevators, special parking, specially equipped rest rooms, special class scheduling, lowered drinking fountains, lowered telephones, and special housing.

Services: Counseling and information services are available, as is tutoring in every subject.

Campus Safety and Security: Measures include 24-hour foot and vehicle patrol, emergency notification system, self-defense education, and security escort services. There are shuttle buses, emergency telephones, lighted pathways/sidewalks, and regular fire safety drills are held in residence halls and academic buildings and residence hall access requires a fob.

Programs of Study: F & M confers B.A. degrees. Bachelor's degrees are awarded in AGRICULTURE (environmental studies), BIOLOGICAL SCIENCE (biochemistry, biology/biological science, and neurosciences), BUSINESS (business administration and management), COMMUNICATIONS AND THE ARTS (art history and appreciation, classics, dramatic arts, English, fine arts, French, German, Greek, Latin, music, Spanish, and studio art), COMPUTER AND PHYSICAL SCIENCE (astronomy, astrophysics, chemistry, geology, mathematics, and physics), ENGINEERING AND ENVIRONMENTAL DESIGN (environmental science), SOCIAL SCIENCE (African studies, American studies, anthropology, economics, history, interdisciplinary studies, philosophy, political science/government, psychology, religion, and sociology). Chemistry, geosciences, and psychology are the strongest academically. Government, business, organizations and society are the largest.

Required: General education requirements proceed from 2 foundations courses and a distribution requirement to an upper-level coherent exploration and a major. Students must take at least 1 course in arts, humanities, social science, non-Western cultures, and 1 natural science (including a lab) and a second lab course or natural science in perspective course. 3 semesters of language study are required. Students must also satisfy the writing proficiency requirement. The bachelor's degree requires completion of 32 courses, including a minimum of 8 in the major, with a minimum GPA of 2.0.

Special: There is a 3-2 degree program in forestry and environmental studies with Duke University as well as 3-2 degree programs in engineering with the Pennsylvania State University College of Engineering, Columbia University, Rensselaer Polytechnic Institute, Case Western Reserve, and Washington University at St. Louis. Cross-registration is possible with the Lancaster Theological Seminary, the Central Pennsylvania Consortium, and Millersville University allows students to study at nearby Dickinson College or Gettysburg College. Students may also study architecture and urban planning at Columbia University, studio art at the School of Visual Arts in New York City, theater in Connecticut, oceanography in Massachusetts, and American studies at American University. There are study-abroad programs in England, France, Germany,

Greece, Italy, Denmark, India, Japan, and other countries. There are internships for credit, joint majors, many minors, dual majors, student-designed majors, independent study, interdisciplinary studies, optional first-year seminars, collaborative projects, pass/fail options, and non-degree study. There are 12 national honor societies and including Phi Beta Kappa.

Faculty/Classroom: 65% of faculty are male; 35% are female. All teach undergraduates, and all teach and do research. No introductory courses are taught by graduate students. The average class size in an introductory lecture is 23; in a laboratory is 19; and in a regular course is 19.

Admissions: 37% of the 2009-2010 applicants were accepted. The SAT scores for the 2009-2010 freshman class were: Critical Reading--% below 500, 23% between 500 and 599, 55% between 600 and 700, and 22 above 700; Math--1% below 500, 13% between 500 and 599, 63% between 600 and 700, and 23 above 700. 83% of the current freshmen were in the top fifth of their class; 96% were in the top two fifths.

Requirements: In addition, standardized tests are optional for students; if this option is selected, 2 recent graded writing samples are required. Applicants must be graduates of accredited secondary schools. Recommended college preparatory study includes 4 years each of English and math, 3 or 4 of foreign language, 3 each of lab science and history/social studies, and 1 or 2 courses in art or music. All students must also submit their high school transcripts, recommendations from a teacher and a counselor, and a personal essay. An interview is recommended. AP and CLEP credits are accepted. Important factors in the admissions decision are advanced placement or honors courses, recommendations by school officials, and extracurricular activities record.

Procedure: Freshmen are admitted fall and spring. Entrance exams should be taken by December of the senior year. There early decision, deferred admissions plan. Early decision applications should be filed by November 15; regular applications, by February 1 for fall entry, along with a $50 fee. Notification of early decision is sent December 15; regular decision, April 1. Applications are accepted on-line. 511 applicants were on a recent waiting list, 52 were accepted.

Transfer: 27 transfer students enrolled in 2008-2009. Applicants must present a minimum of 4 course credits (16 semester hours) completed at an accredited college. An interview, SAT or ACT scores, college and secondary school transcripts, a dean's form, recommendations from 2 professors, and a letter explaining the reason for transfer are also required. 16 of 32 credits required for the bachelor's degree must be completed at F & M.

Visiting: There are regularly scheduled orientations for prospective students, including a campus tour, an interview, and a class visit. There are guides for informal visits and visitors may sit in on classes. To schedule a visit, contact the Admission Office at (877) 678-9111.

Financial Aid: In 2009-2010, 69% of all full-time freshmen and 70% of continuing full-time students received some form of financial aid. 45% of all full-time freshmen and 41% of continuing full-time students received need-based aid. The average freshmen award was $19,861. 44% of undergraduate students work part-time. The average financial indebtedness of the 2009 graduate was $24,752. F & M is a member of CSS. The CSS/Profile, FAFSA, and the college's own financial statement, and If applicable, the business/farm supplement and noncustodial parents statement are required. are required. The deadline for filing freshman financial aid applications for fall entry is February 1.

International Students: There are 159 international students enrolled. The school actively recruits these students. They must take the TOEFL. They must also take the SAT or ACT.

Computers: Wireless access is available. All students may access the system. 24 hours a day, 7 days a week. There are no time limits and no fees. It is strongly recommended that all students have a personal computer. An Apple is recommended.

Graduates: From July 1, 2008 to June 30, 2009, 466 bachelor's degrees were awarded. The most popular majors were government (14%), business/organizations/society (14%), and English (6%). 26 companies recruited on campus in 2008-2009. In an average class, 79% graduate in 4 years or less, 79% graduate in 5 years or less, and 84% graduate in 6 years or less. Of the 2008 graduating class, 25% were enrolled in graduate school within 6 months of graduation, and 75% were employed.

Admissions Contact: Sara Harberson, Vice President for Enrollment Management and Dean of Admissions. A campus DVD is available. E-Mail: admission@fandm.edu Web: www.fandm.edu

GANNON UNIVERSITY   B-1
Erie, PA 16541

(814) 871-7240
(800) GANNON U; (814) 871-5803

Full-time: 1024 men, 1420 women	Faculty: 170; IIA, --$
Part-time: 207 men, 327 women	Ph.D.s: 71%
Graduate: 530 men, 730 women	Student/Faculty: 14 to 1
Year: semesters, summer session	Tuition: $23,574
Application Deadline: open	Room & Board: $9330
Freshman Class: 3019 applied, 2527 accepted, 660 enrolled	
SAT CR/M/W: 500/520/500	ACT: 22	COMPETITIVE

Gannon University, founded in 1925, is a private liberal arts and teaching-oriented university affiliated with the Roman Catholic Church. There are 3 undergraduate schools and 1 graduate school. In addition to regional accreditation, Gannon has baccalaureate program accreditation with ABET, ACBSP, ADA, APTA, and CSWE. The library contains 263,600 volumes, 193,078 microform items, and 3,911 audio/video tapes/CDs/DVDs, and subscribes to 39,737 periodicals including electronic. Computerized library services include interlibrary loans, database searching, Internet access, and laptop Internet portals. Special learning facilities include a learning resource center, art gallery, radio station, and an Environaut - vessel used for research on Lake Erie. The 13-acre campus is in an urban area 128 miles north of Pittsburgh, 99 miles east of Cleveland, and 106 miles southwest of Buffalo. Including any residence halls, there are 46 buildings.

Student Life: 75% of undergraduates are from Pennsylvania. Students are from 25 states, 13 foreign countries, and Canada. 84% are from public schools. 84% are white. 51% are Catholic; 21% Protestant. The average age of freshmen is 18; all undergraduates, 20. 18% do not continue beyond their first year; 64% remain to graduate.

Housing: 1245 students can be accommodated in college housing, which includes coed dorms and on-campus apartments. On-campus housing is guaranteed for the freshman year only and is available on a lottery system for upperclassmen. Priority is given to out-of-town students. 51% of students commute. Upperclassmen may keep cars. Alcohol is permitted, if over 21.

Activities: 10% of men belong to 5 national fraternities; 11% of women belong to 5 national sororities. There are 77 groups on campus, including activities programming, cheerleading, chorus, computers, dance, drama, environmental, ethnic, honors, international, literary magazine, musical theater, newspaper, pep band, political, professional, radio station, religious, residence union, social, social service, student government, and yearbook. Popular campus events include Family Weekend, Distinguished Speaker Series, and Springtopia.

Sports: There are 9 intercollegiate sports for men and 9 for women, and 20 intramural sports for men and 20 for women. Facilities include indoor basketball, tennis and soccer courts, running track, 6 regulation racquetball courts, a pool, fitness rooms, and a 16,000 sq.ft. multipurpose athletic field that includes 5 NCAA regulation fields that seats up to 2500 people. There is also a 3000 seat basketball and volleyball venue.

Disabled Students: 75% of the campus is accessible. Facilities include wheelchair ramps, elevators, special parking, specially equipped restrooms, special class scheduling, lowered drinking fountains, lowered telephones, special housing, special, and drop-off points.

Services: Counseling and information services are available, as is tutoring in most subjects. There is a reader service for the blind, and remedial math and writing. There are math, writing, and advising centers.

Campus Safety and Security: Measures include 24-hour foot and vehicle patrol, emergency notification system, and security escort services. There are emergency telephones, lighted pathways/sidewalks, and security cameras in buildings.

Programs of Study: Gannon confers B.A., B.S., B.S.E.E., B.S.M.E., and B.S.N. degrees. Associate, master's, and doctoral degrees are also awarded. Bachelor's degrees are awarded in BIOLOGICAL SCIENCE (bioinformatics, biology/biological science, biotechnology, and nutrition), BUSINESS (accounting, banking and finance, business administration and management, funeral home services, insurance and risk management, international business management, management information systems, marketing/retailing/merchandising, and sports management), COMMUNICATIONS AND THE ARTS (advertising, communications, dramatic arts, English, journalism, and languages), COMPUTER AND PHYSICAL SCIENCE (chemistry, computer science, mathematics, science, and software engineering), EDUCATION (early childhood education, elementary education, foreign languages education, secondary education, and special education), ENGINEERING AND ENVIRONMENTAL DESIGN (electrical/electronics engineering, environmental engineering, environmental science, and mechanical engineering), HEALTH PROFESSIONS (medical technology, nursing, occupational therapy, physical therapy, physician's assistant, predentistry, premedicine, preoptometry, preosteopathy, prepharmacy, prepodiatry, preveterinary science, respiratory therapy, and sports medicine), SOCIAL SCIENCE (criminal justice, history, international studies, liberal arts/general studies, paralegal studies, philosophy, political science/

government, prelaw, psychology, social work, and theological studies). Preprofessional, physicians assistant, and nursing are the strongest academically. Nursing, physician's assistant, sports and exercise are the largest.

Required: Students must complete at least 128 hours of academic work. Each academic program has specific course requirements. Students must have a cumulative GPA of at least 2.0 overall and in the area of concentration.

Special: The university offers study abroad in more than 5 countries, co-op programs, dual majors, summer internships, Washington semesters, pass/fail options, work-study programs, a general studies program, accelerated degree programs in law, optometry, podiatry, medical veterinary, and pharmacy, a 3-2 chemical engineering degree with the Universities of Akron and Pittsburgh and non-degree study. The B.S. in mortuary science program consists of 3 years of study at Gannon with degree completion at a school of mortuary science. There are 14 national honor societies, a freshman honors program, and 10 departmental honors programs.

Faculty/Classroom: 57% of faculty are male; 43% are female. Graduate students teach 2% of introductory courses. The average class size in an introductory lecture, 22, in a laboratory, 16, and in a regular course, 18.

Admissions: 84% of the 2009-2010 applicants were accepted. The SAT scores for the 2009-2010 freshman class were: Critical Reading--48% below 500, 40% between 500 and 599, 11% between 600 and 700, and 2% above 700; Math--40% below 500, 37% between 500 and 599, 21% between 600 and 700, and 2% above 700; Writing--48% below 500, 36% between 500 and 599, 13% between 600 and 700, and 1% above 700. The ACT scores were 36% below 21, 21% between 21 and 23, 19% between 24 and 26, 14% between 27 and 28, and 9% above 28. 40% of the current freshmen were in the top fifth of their class; 63% were in the top two fifths. 26 freshmen graduated first in their class.

Requirements: The SAT or ACT is required. The ACT Optional Writing test is also required. In addition, candidates should have completed 16 academic units including 4 in English and 12 in social sciences, foreign languages, math, and science, depending on the degree sought. Specific courses in math and science are required for some majors in health sciences and engineering. AP and CLEP credits are accepted. Important factors in the admissions decision are advanced placement or honors courses, leadership record, and recommendations by school officials.

Procedure: Freshmen are admitted fall, spring, and summer. Entrance exams should be taken at the end of the junior year or the beginning of the senior year. There are deferred admissions and rolling admissions plans. Application deadlines are open. Application fee is $25. Notification is sent on a rolling basis. 25 applicants were on the 2009 waiting list; 25 were admitted. Applications are accepted on-line.

Transfer: 102 transfer students enrolled in 2008-2009. Transfer students should be in good standing at their previous institution with at least a 2.0 GPA. They must submit a college clearance from the college most recently attended and all transcripts. A high school transcript is required from transfer students with fewer than 30 credits. Several health science programs are not designed to accommodate transfers. 30 of 128 credits required for the bachelor's degree must be completed at Gannon.

Visiting: There are regularly scheduled orientations for prospective students, consisting of open houses for prospective students in the fall and spring. Students may meet with faculty, tour the campus, and sit in on a variety of presentations. There are guides for informal visits; visitors may sit in on classes and stay overnight. To schedule a visit, contact Nancy Kulhanek, Campus Visit at 1 (800) 426-6668.

Financial Aid: In 2009-2010, 99% of all full-time freshmen and 97% of continuing full-time students received some form of financial aid. 89% of all full-time freshmen and 85% of continuing full-time students received need-based aid. The average freshman award was $15,584. Need-based scholarships or need-based grants averaged $16,853; need-based self-help aid (loans and jobs) averaged $4,245; non-need based athletic scholarships averaged $9,514; and other non-need based awards and non-need based scholarships averaged $10,043. 24% of undergraduate students work part-time. Average annual earnings from campus work are $1846. The average financial indebtedness of the 2009 graduate was $20,808. Gannon is a member of CSS. The FAFSA and the college's own financial statement are required. The priority date for freshman financial aid applications for fall entry is March 15.

International Students: There are 57 international students enrolled. The school actively recruits these students. They must take the TOEFL with a minimum score of 500 on the paper-based TOEFL (PBT) or 61 on the Internet-based version (iBT). They must also take the SAT or ACT.

Computers: Wireless access is available. Gannon University provides more than 175 Pentium II - Pentium IV computers in 8 labs. Each computer has Microsoft Office (Word, Excel, Access, PowerPoint), Web-based e-mail and Microsoft Internet Explorer. Each lab also has a network laser printer. Gannon also provides 4 Desktop Publishing Workstations configured with a scanner, Photoshop, Acrobat, MS Publisher an MS FrontPage. Residence halls and campus apartments have connections to the Gannon Network. These connections give students direct access to the Internet, e-mail, and Nash Library online resources. All students may access the system 24 hours a day. There are no time limits and no fees. Students enrolled in Radiologic Sciences must have a personal computer. A Tablet PC is recommended.

Graduates: From July 1, 2008 to June 30, 2009, 454 bachelor's degrees were awarded. The most popular majors were nursing (12%), biology (11%), and business administration (5%). 6 companies recruited on campus in 2008-2009. In an average class, 50% graduate in 4 years or less, 63% graduate in 5 years or less, and 64% graduate in 6 years or less. Of the 2008 graduating class, 41% were enrolled in graduate school within 6 months of graduation, and 58% were employed.

Admissions Contact: Patricia Maughn, Coordinator, Admissions Inquiries. E-Mail: *admissions@gannon.edu* Web: *www.gannon.edu*

GENEVA COLLEGE   A-3
Beaver Falls, PA 15010

	(724) 847-6500
	(800) 847-8255; (724) 847-6776
Full-time: 605 men, 730 women	**Faculty:** 75; IIB, -$
Part-time: 30 men, 30 women	**Ph.D.s:** 76%
Graduate: 122 men, 182 women	**Student/Faculty:** 18 to 1
Year: semesters, summer session	**Tuition:** $20,900
Application Deadline: open	**Room & Board:** $6,380
Freshman Class: n/av	
SAT or ACT: required	**COMPETITIVE**

Geneva College, founded in 1848, is a private institution affiliated with the Reformed Presbyterian Church of North America. The college offers undergraduate programs in the arts and sciences, business, education, health science, biblical and religious studies, engineering, and pre-professional training. In addition to the above figures, there are 440 non-traditional undergraduates. There are no undergraduate schools. In addition to regional accreditation, Geneva has baccalaureate program accreditation with ABET and ACBSP. The library contains 167,206 volumes, 198,624 micro-form items, 12,901 audio/video tapes/CDs/DVDs, and subscribes to 879 periodicals including electronic. Computerized library services include inter-library loans, database searching, and Internet access. Special learning facilities include a radio station, TV station, an observatory. The 50-acre campus is in a small town 35 miles northwest of Pittsburgh. Including any residence halls, there are 30 buildings.

Student Life: 73% of undergraduates are from Pennsylvania. Students are from 37 states, 19 foreign countries, and Canada. 87% are from public schools. 91% are white. 89% are Protestant. The average age of freshmen is 19; all undergraduates, 26. 23% do not continue beyond their first year; 55% remain to graduate.

Housing: 994 students can be accommodated in college housing, which includes single-sex dorms, on-campus apartments, off-campus apartment, and a Discipleship House for those interested in structural growth opportunities. On-campus housing is guaranteed for all 4 years. 73% of students live on campus; of those, 70% remain on campus on weekends. Alcohol is not permitted. Upperclassmen may keep cars.

Activities: There are no fraternities or sororities. There are 50 groups on campus, including and radio, band, cheerleading, chess, choir, chorale, chorus, computers, drama, ethnic, forensics, honors, international, literary magazine, marching band, newspaper, photography, political, professional, religious, social, social service, student government, and yearbook. Popular campus events include International Day, Fall Fest, and The Big Event.

Sports: There are 6 intercollegiate sports for men and 5 for women, and 6 intramural sports for men and 5 for women. Facilities include a 5600-seat stadium, a field house, a 3200-seat gym, a practice gym, a track, athletic fields, racquetball and tennis courts, weight training rooms, and the Merriman Athletic Soccer/ Track Complex.

Disabled Students: 90% of the campus is accessible. Facilities include wheelchair ramps, elevators, special parking, specially equipped rest rooms, special class scheduling, lowered drinking fountains, and lowered telephones.

Services: Counseling and information services are available, as is tutoring in most subjects. There is remedial math, reading, and writing.

Campus Safety and Security: Measures include security escort services. There are emergency telephones, lighted pathways/sidewalks, an off-duty city policemen on campus from 4:30 P.M. to 7 A.M. daily, and a full-time Director of Campus Security.

Programs of Study: Geneva confers B.A., B.S., B.S.B.A., B.S.E., and B.S.Ed. degrees. Associates and master's degrees are also awarded. Bachelor's degrees are awarded in BIOLOGICAL SCIENCE (biology/biological science), BUSINESS (accounting and business administration and management), COMMUNICATIONS AND THE ARTS (applied music, broadcasting, communications, creative writing, English, music, music business management, Spanish, and speech/debate/rhetoric), COMPUTER AND PHYSICAL SCIENCE (applied mathematics, chemistry, computer science, and physics), EDUCATION (elementary education, mathematics education, and music education), ENGINEERING AND

ENVIRONMENTAL DESIGN (aviation administration/management, chemical engineering, and engineering), HEALTH PROFESSIONS (speech pathology/audiology), SOCIAL SCIENCE (biblical studies, counseling/psychology, history, human services, interdisciplinary studies, ministries, philosophy, political science/government, psychology, and sociology). Engineering, business administration, and education are the strongest academically. Elementary education, business administration, and psychology are the largest.

Required: The core curriculum includes 12 hours of humanities, 9 each of biblical studies and social science, 8 to 10 of natural science, 6 of communications, 2 of phys ed, and the 1-hour Freshman Experience course. Students must also fulfill a chapel requirement per semester. To graduate, students must complete 126 to 138 semester hours, including those required for a major, with a minimum GPA of 2.0 in the major.

Special: Cross-registration is offered in conjunction with Pennsylvania State University/Beaver Campus and Community College of Beaver County. There is a 3-1 degree program in cardiovascular technology, and an accelerated degree programs in human resources and community ministry. Off-campus study includes programs at the Philadelphia Center for Urban Theological Studies, a Washington semester, a summer program at AuSable, Institute of Environmental Studies in Michigan, art studies in Pittsburgh, CCCU music program in Martha's Vineyard, film studies in Los Angeles, and study abroad in Costa Rica, Egypt, China, England, Russia, and Israel. Geneva also offers internships, independent study, and credit by proficiency exam. Non-degree study is available through adult education programs. There are 2 national honor societies, a freshman honors program, and 1 departmental honors programs.

Faculty/Classroom: 76% of faculty are male; 24% are female. 95% teach undergraduates. No introductory courses are taught by graduate students. The average class size in an introductory lecture is 135; in a laboratory is 22; and in a regular course is 20.

Admissions: There were 3 National Merit finalists. 10 freshmen graduated first in their class.

Requirements: The SAT or ACT is required. In addition, applicants must be graduates of an accredited secondary school or have earned a GED. Geneva requires 16 academic units, based on 4 each of English and electives, 3 of social studies, 2 each of math and foreign language, and 1 of science. An essay is required and an interview is recommended. A GPA of 2.5 is required. AP and CLEP credits are accepted. Important factors in the admissions decision are recommendations by school officials, advanced placement or honors courses, and leadership record.

Procedure: Freshmen are admitted to all sessions. Entrance exams should be taken during the junior or senior year. There are deferred admissions and rolling admissions plans. Application deadlines are open. Application fee is $25. Notification is sent on a rolling basis. Applications are accepted on-line.

Transfer: 96 transfer students enrolled in 2008-2009. Applicants must have a GPA of 2.0, must complete 48 semester hours at Geneva, including 15 in a chosen major, have a high school diploma or GED, and take the SAT I/ACT if less than 3 years out of high school. Letters of recommendation are required. 48 of 126 credits required for the bachelor's degree must be completed at Geneva.

Visiting: There are regularly scheduled orientations for prospective students, including class visits, a campus tour, meetings with faculty, admissions, and financial aid counselors, and meetings with coaches. There are guides for informal visits, visitors may sit in on classes, and stay overnight. To schedule a visit, contact Victoria Chapoloko, Campus Visit Coordinator at (724) 847-6501.

Financial Aid: In 2009-2010, 90% of all full-time freshmen and 90% of continuing full-time students received some form of financial aid. 70% of all full-time freshmen and 70% of continuing full-time students received need-based aid. The average freshmen award was $13,785, with $10,241 ($22,000 maximum) from need-based scholarships or need-based grants; $4,212 ($5,625 maximum) from need-based self-help aid (loans and jobs); and $2,542 ($14,980 maximum) from non-need-based athletic scholarships. 75% of undergraduate students work part-time. Average annual earnings from campus work are $1000. The average financial indebtedness of the 2009 graduate was $20,000. Geneva is a member of CSS. The FAFSA is required. The priority date for freshman financial aid applications for fall entry is March 15. The deadline for filing freshman financial aid applications for fall entry is April 15.

International Students: There are 18 international students enrolled. The school actively recruits these students. They must take the TOEFL and the college's own test.

Computers: All students may access the system. There are no time limits. The fee is $100 per semester.

Graduates: From July 1, 2008 to June 30, 2009, 454 bachelor's degrees were awarded. The most popular majors were business and marketing (40%), philosophy/religion/theology (14%), and education (12%). In an average class, 1% graduate in 3 years or less, 42% graduate in 4 years or less, 55% graduate in 5 years or less, and 56% graduate in 6 years or less.

Admissions Contact: Director of Admissions A campus DVD is available. E-Mail: *admissions@geneva.edu* Web: *www.geneva.edu*

GETTYSBURG COLLEGE | D-4

Gettysburg, PA 17325-1484

(717) 337-6100
(800) 431-0803; (717) 337-6145

Full-time: 1172 men, 1297 women	**Faculty:** IIB, +$
Part-time: 12 men, 16 women	**Ph.D.s:** 95%
Graduate: none	**Student/Faculty:** n/av
Year: semesters	**Tuition:** $35,990
Application Deadline: February 1	**Room & Board:** $8,630
Freshman Class: 6126 applied, 2180 accepted, 695 enrolled	
SAT or ACT: required	**HIGHLY COMPETITIVE**

Gettysburg College, founded in 1832, is a nationally ranked college offering programs in the liberal arts and sciences. There are no undergraduate schools. The library contains 484,357 volumes, 75,067 microform items, 21,128 audio/video tapes/CDs/DVDs, and subscribes to 23,208 periodicals including electronic. Computerized library services include inter-library loans, database searching, Internet access, and laptop Internet portals. Special learning facilities include an art gallery, planetarium, radio station, TV station, electron microscopes, spectrometers, an optics lab, plasma physics lab, greenhouse, observatory, child study lab, fine and performing arts facilities, and a challenge course. The 200-acre campus is in a suburban area 30 miles south of Harrisburg, 55 miles from Baltimore, MD, and 80 miles from Washington, D.C. Including any residence halls, there are 63 buildings.

Student Life: 74% of undergraduates are from out of state, mostly the Middle Atlantic. Students are from 40 states, 35 foreign countries, and Canada. 70% are from public schools. 86% are white. 34% are Protestant; 30% Catholic. The average age of freshmen is 18; all undergraduates, 20. 10% do not continue beyond their first year; 80% remain to graduate.

Housing: 2220 students can be accommodated in college housing, which includes single-sex and coed dorms, on-campus apartments, and off-campus apartments. In addition, there are honors houses, language houses, special-interest houses, and fraternity houses. On-campus housing is guaranteed for all 4 years. All students may keep cars.

Activities: 40% of men belong to 10 national fraternities; 26% of women belong to 6 national sororities. There are 120 groups on campus, including dance ensemble, outdoor recreation program, student activities council, art, band, cheerleading, choir, chorale, chorus, communications, computers, dance, drama, ethnic, film, gay, honors, international, jazz band, literary magazine, marching band, musical theater, newspaper, opera, orchestra, pep band, photography, political, professional, radio and TV, religious, social, social service, student government, and symphony. Popular campus events include Holiday Concert, all-campus picnics, and Family Weekend.

Sports: There are 12 intercollegiate sports for men and 12 for women. Facilities include basketball courts, indoor and outdoor tennis courts, a pool, several tracks and fields, 2 outdoor turf fields, a field house, fitness and weight rooms, and an athletic complex.

Disabled Students: 90% of the campus is accessible. Facilities include wheelchair ramps, elevators, special parking, specially equipped rest rooms, special class scheduling, lowered drinking fountains, and special housing.

Services: Counseling and information services are available, as is tutoring in most subjects.

Campus Safety and Security: Measures include 24-hour foot and vehicle patrol, emergency notification system, self-defense education, and security escort services. There are emergency telephones and lighted pathways/sidewalks.

Programs of Study: Gettysburg confers B.A., B.S., and B.M. (Performance) and B.S. (Music Education) degrees. Bachelor's degrees are awarded in BIOLOGICAL SCIENCE (biochemistry and biology/biological science), BUSINESS (business administration and management), COMMUNICATIONS AND THE ARTS (art history and appreciation, classics, dramatic arts, English, French, German, Greek, Latin, music, Spanish, and studio art), COMPUTER AND PHYSICAL SCIENCE (chemistry, computer science, mathematics, and physics), EDUCATION (elementary education, foreign languages education, music education, science education, and secondary education), ENGINEERING AND ENVIRONMENTAL DESIGN (environmental science), HEALTH PROFESSIONS (health science, predentistry, and premedicine), SOCIAL SCIENCE (anthropology, economics, history, international relations, Japanese studies, philosophy, political science/government, prelaw, psychology, religion, sociology, and women's studies). The sciences, psychology, and history are the strongest academically. Management, political science, and psychology are the largest.

Required: All students must complete 32 courses including a concentration in a major field of study culminating with a capstone experience; 1 course each in humanities, social studies, reasoning, composition, diversity: non-western culture; diversity: domestic and conceptual; science, technology, and society; 2 courses in natural sciences and 4 courses in a foreign language. The minimum GPA is 2.0.

Special: The college offers cross-registration with the Central Pennsylvania Consortium, and an extensive study-abroad program and has spe-

cial centers worldwide. There are summer internships and a Washington semester with American University. Cross-registration is possible with members of the Central Pennsylvania Consortium. There is a United Nations semester at Drew University, and a 3-2 engineering program with Columbia University, Rensselaer Polytechnic, and Washington University in St. Louis. There are also joint programs in optometry with the Pennsylvania College of Optometry, and forestry and environmental studies with Duke University. The college also offers double majors, student-designed majors, and B.A.-B.S. degrees in biology, chemistry, physics, biochemistry, and molecular biology, environmental studies and health and exercise sciences. Education certification is also available. There are 16 national honor societies, including Phi Beta Kappa.

Faculty/Classroom: 56% of faculty are male; 44% are female. All teach and do research. No introductory courses are taught by graduate students. The average class size in an introductory lecture is 19; in a laboratory is 15; and in a regular course is 18.

Admissions: 36% of the 2009-2010 applicants were accepted. The SAT scores for the 2009-2010 freshman class were: Critical Reading--% below 500, 18% between 500 and 599, 63% between 600 and 700, and 19 above 700; Math--% below 500, 25% between 500 and 599, 65% between 600 and 700, and 10 above 700. 81% of the current freshmen were in the top fifth of their class; 99% were in the top two fifths.

Requirements: The SAT or ACT is required. In addition, an essay is required. Art students can submit a portfolio, and music students must audition. An interview and SAT Subject tests are recommended. A GPA of 3.0 is required. AP credits are accepted. Important factors in the admissions decision are evidence of special talent, recommendations by school officials, and advanced placement or honors courses.

Procedure: Freshmen are admitted fall and spring. Entrance exams should be taken by the January testing date of the senior year. There are early decision and deferred admissions plan. Early decision applications should be filed by November 15; regular applications, by February 1 for fall entry, along with a $55 fee. Notifications are sent April 1. Applications are accepted on-line. A waiting list is maintained.

Transfer: 25 transfer students enrolled in 2008-2009. Transfer applicants must have a GPA of at least 2.5. An interview is recommended. The high school record, test scores, and a Dean's transfer recommendation form are also considered. 16 of 32 credits required for the bachelor's degree must be completed at Gettysburg.

Visiting: There are regularly scheduled orientations for prospective students, including interviews, tours, day and overnight visits, open houses, and group sessions. There are guides for informal visits and visitors may sit in on classes. To schedule a visit, contact the Admissions Office at (800) 431-0803.

Financial Aid: In 2009-2010, 52% of all full-time freshmen and 63% of continuing full-time students received some form of financial aid. 51% of all full-time freshmen and 55% of continuing full-time students received need-based aid. The average freshmen award was $24,487. 46% of undergraduate students work part-time. Average annual earnings from campus work are $1500. The average financial indebtedness of the 2009 graduate was $21,810. Gettysburg is a member of CSS. The CSS/Profile and FAFSA are required. The deadline for filing freshman financial aid applications for fall entry is February 15.

International Students: There are 44 international students enrolled. The school actively recruits these students. They must take the TOEFL. They must also take the SAT or ACT.

Computers: Wireless access is available. All students may access the system. 24 hours a day. There are no time limits and no fees. It is strongly recommended that all students have a personal computer. A discounted laptop purchase program is offered.

Graduates: From July 1, 2008 to June 30, 2009, 648 bachelor's degrees were awarded. The most popular majors were management (17%), political science (9%), and history (8%). 160 companies recruited on campus in 2008-2009. In an average class, 77% graduate in 4 years or less, 80% graduate in 5 years or less, and 81% graduate in 6 years or less. Of the 2008 graduating class, 18% were enrolled in graduate school within 6 months of graduation, and 78% were employed.

Admissions Contact: Gail Sweezey, Director of Admissions. E-Mail: *admiss@gettysburg.edu* Web: *www.gettysburg.edu*

GROVE CITY COLLEGE | B-2

Grove City, PA 16127-2104

(724) 458-2100; (724) 458-3395

Full-time: 1257 men, 1242 women	**Faculty:** 128
Part-time: 20 men, 11 women	**Ph.D.s:** 92%
Graduate: none	**Student/Faculty:** 20 to 1
Year: semesters	**Tuition:** $12,590
Application Deadline: February 1	**Room & Board:** $6824
Freshman Class: 1761 applied, 1123 accepted, 633 enrolled	
SAT CR/M: 630/629	**ACT:** 28
	HIGHLY COMPETITIVE+

Grove City College, founded in 1876, is a private, liberal arts and science Christian college that is committed to providing rigorous academics within a Christian environment at an amazing value. There are 2 undergraduate schools. In addition to regional accreditation, Grove City has baccalaureate program accreditation with ABET. The library contains 135,100 volumes, 117,862 microform items, and 2,905 audio/video tapes/CDs/DVDs, and subscribes to 36,992 periodicals including electronic. Computerized library services include interlibrary loans, database searching, Internet access, and laptop Internet portals. Special learning facilities include an art gallery, radio station, TV station, and research grade observatory. The 150-acre campus is in a small town 60 miles north of Pittsburgh. Including any residence halls, there are 30 buildings.

Student Life: 53% of undergraduates are from out of state, mostly the Northeast. Students are from 43 states, 9 foreign countries, and Canada. 69% are from public schools. 94% are white.68% are Protestant; 26% claim no religious affiliation. The average age of freshmen is 18; all undergraduates, 20. 7% do not continue beyond their first year; 93% remain to graduate.

Housing: 2305 students can be accommodated in college housing, which includes single-sex dorms and on-campus apartments. On-campus housing is guaranteed for all 4 years and is available on a lottery system for upperclassmen. 93% of students live on campus; of those, 90% remain on campus on weekends. Alcohol is not permitted. Upperclassmen may keep cars.

Activities: 15% of men belong to 10 local fraternities; 24% of women belong to 8 local sororities. There are more than 130 groups on campus, including art, band, cheerleading, choir, chorale, chorus, computers, dance, debate, drama, drill team, ethnic, film, forensics, honors, international, jazz band, literary magazine, marching band, musical theater, newspaper, opera, orchestra, pep band, photography, political, professional, radio and TV, religious, social, social service, student government, symphony, and yearbook. Popular campus events include Parents Weekend, Christmas Candlelight Service, and President's Gala.

Sports: There are 9 intercollegiate sports for men and 10 for women, and 11 intramural sports for men and 12 for women. Facilities include a field house, a recreation building that includes 2 indoor pools, an indoor running track, 4 basketball, volleyball, or tennis courts, 3 racquetball courts, bowling lanes, and 2 fitness room, 10 outdoor tennis courts, a football stadium with an all-weather track, baseball, soccer, and softball fields, and 3 intramural fields.

Disabled Students: All of the campus is accessible. Facilities include wheelchair ramps, elevators, special parking, specially equipped restrooms, special class scheduling, lowered drinking fountains, lowered telephones, and special housing. The college's hillside location presents some difficulty for the seriously disabled.

Services: Counseling and information services are available, as is tutoring in most subjects. A student tutoring program is available for a small fee.

Campus Safety and Security: Measures include 24-hour foot and vehicle patrol, emergency notification system, self-defense education, and security escort services. There are emergency telephones, lighted pathways/sidewalks, and an emergency response program is in place, which includes a public warning siren and cell phone text message system.

Programs of Study: Grove City confers B.A., B.S., B.Mus., B.S.E.E., and B.S.M.E. degrees. Bachelor's degrees are awarded in BIOLOGICAL SCIENCE (biochemistry and biology/biological science), BUSINESS (accounting, banking and finance, business administration and management, entrepreneurial studies, international business management, management information systems, and marketing/retailing/merchandising), COMMUNICATIONS AND THE ARTS (communications, English, French, music, music business management, music performance, and Spanish), COMPUTER AND PHYSICAL SCIENCE (chemistry, computer science, mathematics, and physics), EDUCATION (elementary education, music education, science education, and secondary education), ENGINEERING AND ENVIRONMENTAL DESIGN (electrical/electronics engineering, industrial administration/management, and mechanical engineering), HEALTH PROFESSIONS (predentistry and premedicine), SOCIAL SCIENCE (economics, history, philosophy, political science/government, prelaw, psychology, religion, and religious music). Engineering, computer science, and premedicine are the strongest academically. Mechanical engineering, biology, and English are the largest.

Required: Students are required to complete a minimum of 128 credit hours (130 for engineering students). All students must complete the 40-46-semester-hour general education curriculum, which includes 18 hours of humanities, 8 of natural science, and 3 of science faith, and technology and 3 each of social science, and quantitative and logical reasoning. Specific courses required include 4 chapel credits, 2 hours of phys ed, and 2 years demonstrated proficiency in a foreign language. A minimum GPA of 2.0 is required.

Special: The college offers study abroad, accelerated and double major degrees, summer internships, student-designed interdisciplinary majors, and a Washington semester. There are 9 national honor societies.

Faculty/Classroom: 74% of faculty are male; 26% are female. All teach undergraduates, and 40% do both. No introductory courses are taught by graduate students. The average class size in an introductory lecture, 35, in a laboratory, 20, and in a regular course, 25.

Admissions: 64% of the 2009-2010 applicants were accepted. The SAT scores for the 2009-2010 freshman class were: Critical Reading--1% below 500, 27% between 500 and 599, 44% between 600 and 700, and 21% above 700; Math--2% below 500, 27% between 500 and 599, 53% between 600 and 700, and 18% above 700. The ACT scores were 2% below 21, 10% between 21 and 23, 22% between 24 and 26, 25% between 27 and 28, and 41% above 28. 77% of the current freshmen were in the top fifth of their class; 93% were in the top two fifths. There were 21 National Merit finalists. 57 freshmen graduated first in their class.

Requirements: The SAT or ACT is required. In addition, the academic or college preparatory course is highly recommended, including 4 units each of English, history, math, science, and a foreign language. An essay is required of all applicants, and an audition is required of music students. An interview is highly recommended. AP and CLEP credits are accepted. Important factors in the admissions decision are advanced placement or honors courses, personality/intangible qualities, and extracurricular activities record.

Procedure: Freshmen are admitted fall and spring. Entrance exams should be taken in the spring of the junior year or the fall of the senior year. There are early admissions and deferred admissions plans. Early decision applications should be filed by November 15; regular applications should be filed by February 1 for fall entry and December 15 for spring entry, along with a $50 fee. Notification of early decision is sent December 15; regular notifications, March 15. 331 early decision candidates were accepted for the 2008-2009 class. 176 applicants were on the 2009 waiting list; 61 were admitted. Applications are accepted on-line.

Transfer: 34 transfer students enrolled in 2008-2009. Applicants should have a minimum 2.0 GPA. Either the SAT or the ACT is required as well as 2 letters of recommendation, official high and college transcripts, essays and an interview is highly recommended. 64 of 128 credits required for the bachelor's degree must be completed at Grove City.

Visiting: There are regularly scheduled orientations for prospective students, consisting of daily interviews and tours, 2 high school visitation days in the fall, and visitation day in the spring. There are science, engineering, math, and computer open houses. There are guides for informal visits; visitors may sit in on classes and stay overnight. To schedule a visit, contact the Admissions Office at 724-458-2100.

Financial Aid: In 2009-2010, 43% of all full-time freshmen and 38% of continuing full-time students received some form of financial aid. 43% of all full-time freshmen and 38% of continuing full-time students received need-based aid. The average freshman award was $6,024. Need-based scholarships or need-based grants averaged $6,024. 40% of undergraduate students work part-time. Average annual earnings from campus work are $1000. The average financial indebtedness of the 2009 graduate was $24,895. The the the college's own financial statement is required. The deadline for filing freshman financial aid applications for fall entry is April 15.

International Students: There are 14 international students enrolled. They must take the TOEFL with a minimum score of 550 on the paper-based TOEFL (PBT) or 79 on the Internet-based version (iBT). If the TOEFL is not available, either the SAT or the ACT is required.

Computers: Wireless access is available. All students are provided a tablet PC and have access to the network via their residence hall rooms and wireless areas on campus. All students may access the system any time. There are no time limits and no fees. All students are required to have a personal computer. All freshmen receive an HP Tablet PC.

Graduates: From July 1, 2008 to June 30, 2009, 563 bachelor's degrees were awarded. The most popular majors were English (7%), elementary education (7%), and history (6%). 216 companies recruited on campus in 2008-2009. In an average class, 2% graduate in 3 years or less, 78% graduate in 4 years or less, 83% graduate in 5 years or less, and 83% graduate in 6 years or less. Of the 2008 graduating class, 21% were enrolled in graduate school within 6 months of graduation, and 92% were employed.

Admissions Contact: Jeffrey C. Mincey, Director of Admissions. E-Mail: *admissions@gcc.edu* Web: *www.gcc.edu*

GWYNEDD-MERCY COLLEGE   F-4
Gwynedd Valley, PA 19437   (215) 641-5510
(800) DIAL-GMC; (215) 641-5556

Full-time: 416 men, 1077 women	**Faculty:** 69; IIB, -$
Part-time: 165 men, 538 women	**Ph.D.s:** 63%
Graduate: 113 men, 320 women	**Student/Faculty:** 22 to 1
Year: semesters, summer session	**Tuition:** $24,230
Application Deadline: see profile	**Room & Board:** $9330
Freshman Class: 2043 applied, 1219 accepted, 229 enrolled	
SAT CR/M: 490/490	**COMPETITIVE**

Gwynedd-Mercy College, founded in 1948, is a private institution affiliated with the Roman Catholic Church and offering degree programs in the arts and sciences, business, education, and health fields. There are 5 undergraduate schools and 2 graduate schools. In addition to regional accreditation, Gwynedd-Mercy has baccalaureate program accreditation with NLN. The library contains 104,899 volumes, and 11,775 audio/video tapes/CDs/DVDs. Computerized library services include interlibrary loans, database searching, Internet access, and laptop Internet portals. Special learning facilities include a learning resource center, a lab school for education majors. The 170-acre campus is in a suburban area 20 miles northwest of Philadelphia. Including any residence halls, there are 21 buildings.

Student Life: 92% of undergraduates are from Pennsylvania. Others are from 14 states, and 38 foreign countries. 59% are from public schools. 69% are white; 20% African American. 54% are Catholic; 13% Protestant. The average age of freshmen is 25; all undergraduates, 28. 24% do not continue beyond their first year; 69% remain to graduate.

Housing: 550 students can be accommodated in college housing, which includes coed dorms. On-campus housing is available on a first-come and first-served basis. 72% of students commute. Alcohol is not permitted. All students may keep cars.

Activities: There are no fraternities or sororities. There are 21 groups on campus, including choir, chorus, drama, ethnic, honors, international, literary magazine, newspaper, professional, religious, social, social service, and student government. Popular campus events include Fall Fest, Carol Night, and International Night.

Sports: There are 6 intercollegiate sports for men and 7 for women. Facilities include a recreation center housing men's and women's basketball, women's volleyball, a walking track, indoor racquetball courts, a weight room, team locker rooms, and a sauna. Outdoor facilities include soccer, baseball, softball, and field hockey fields.

Disabled Students: 75% of the campus is accessible. Facilities include wheelchair ramps, elevators, special parking, specially equipped restrooms, and special class scheduling.

Services: Counseling and information services are available, as is tutoring in most subjects. There is remedial math, reading, and writing. Tutoring is made available in conjunction with student needs.

Campus Safety and Security: Measures include 24-hour foot and vehicle patrol, emergency notification system, and security escort services. There are shuttle buses, emergency telephones, and lighted pathways/sidewalks.

Programs of Study: Gwynedd-Mercy confers B.A., B.S., and B.H.S. degrees. Associate and master's degrees are also awarded. Bachelor's degrees are awarded in BIOLOGICAL SCIENCE (biology/biological science), BUSINESS (accounting, banking and finance, business administration and management, human resources, international business management, management science, marketing and distribution, and sports management), COMMUNICATIONS AND THE ARTS (communications, English, and public relations), COMPUTER AND PHYSICAL SCIENCE (computer science, information sciences and systems, mathematics, natural sciences, and radiological technology), EDUCATION (business education, elementary education, mathematics education, science education, secondary education, social studies education, and special education), HEALTH PROFESSIONS (clinical science, health care administration, medical laboratory technology, medical technology, nursing, radiation therapy, and respiratory therapy), SOCIAL SCIENCE (criminal justice, gerontology, history, human services, psychology, social work, and sociology). Nursing, biology, and medical technology are the strongest academically. Nursing, business, and education are the largest.

Required: All students must complete at least 125 credit hours, including 60 in the major, with a minimum GPA of 2.0. (Some programs require a higher GPA.) General education courses cover language, literature and fine arts, behavioral and social sciences, humanities, and natural science. Specific courses in English composition, literature, philosophy, and religious studies are required.

Special: The college offers co-op programs in computer science, business administration, and accounting, as well as internships, dual majors, accelerated degree programs, B.A.-B.S. degrees, and pass/fail options. Cross-registration is offered with South Eastern Pennsylvania Consortium for Higher Education. All programs require or have the option for hands-on experience. There is a 3-1 program in medical technology available wherein the last year is a hospital rotation. There are 4 national honor societies, a freshman honors program, and 1 departmental honors program.

Faculty/Classroom: 29% of faculty are male; 71% are female. 92% teach undergraduates. No introductory courses are taught by graduate students. The average class size in an introductory lecture, 24, in a laboratory, 15, and in a regular course, 17.

Admissions: 60% of the 2009-2010 applicants were accepted. The SAT scores for the 2009-2010 freshman class were: Critical Reading--48% below 500, 41% between 500 and 599, 10% between 600 and 700, and 1% above 700; Math--56% below 500, 36% between 500 and 599, 7% between 600 and 700, and 1% above 700. 18% of the current freshmen were in the top fifth of their class; 42% were in the top two fifths.

Requirements: The SAT is required. In addition, candidates for admission must be graduates of accredited secondary schools and have completed 16 academic credits/Carnegie units, including 4 credits in English, 3 each in math, science, and college preparatory electives, 2 in a foreign language, and 1 in history. The GED is accepted. An interview is recom-

mended for all candidates and is required for some programs. A GPA of 2.0 is required. AP and CLEP credits are accepted. Important factors in the admissions decision are advanced placement or honors courses, parents or siblings attended your school, and recommendations by alumni.

Procedure: Freshmen are admitted fall and spring. Entrance exams should be taken in the spring of the junior year or the fall of the senior year. There are deferred admissions and rolling admissions plans. Check with the school for current application deadlines. The application fee is $25. Applications are accepted on-line.

Transfer: 198 transfer students enrolled in 2008-2009. Neither the SAT nor the ACT is required for transfer students out of high school for 2 or more years. A minimum GPA of 2.0 is necessary; some programs require a higher GPA. An interview is recommended. 45 of 125 credits required for the bachelor's degree must be completed at Gwynedd-Mercy.

Visiting: There are regularly scheduled orientations for prospective students, consisting of open houses with formal presentations and campus tours, and class days with class visitations and campus tours. There are guides for informal visits; visitors may sit in on classes and stay overnight. To schedule a visit, contact the Admissions Office.

Financial Aid: In 2009-2010, 73% of all full-time freshmen and 74% of continuing full-time students received some form of financial aid. 72% of all full-time freshmen and 73% of continuing full-time students received need-based aid. The average freshman award was $14,349. The average financial indebtedness of the 2009 graduate was $20,636. The FAFSA and the college's own financial statement, and federal income tax returns are required. The priority date for freshman financial aid applications for fall entry is March 1. The deadline for filing freshman financial aid applications for fall entry is March 15.

International Students: There are 47 international students enrolled. They must take the TOEFL with a minimum score of 525 on the paper-based TOEFL (PBT), or score 88 on the MTELP.

Computers: Wireless access is available. All students may access the system 65 hours a week.

Graduates: From July 1, 2008 to June 30, 2009, 358 bachelor's degrees were awarded. The most popular majors were business administration (34%), nursing (21%), and education (15%). In an average class, 1% graduate in 3 years or less, 50% graduate in 4 years or less, 67% graduate in 5 years or less, and 69% graduate in 6 years or less.

Admissions Contact: Michelle Diehl, Director of Undergraduate Admissions. E-Mail: *admissions@gmc.edu* Web: *www.gmc.edu*

HAVERFORD COLLEGE   E-4

Haverford, PA 19041-1392	**(610) 896-1350; (610) 896-1338**
Full-time: 538 men, 652 women	**Faculty:** 121; IIB, +$
Part-time: none	**Ph.D.s:** 97%
Graduate: none	**Student/Faculty:** 10 to 1
Year: semesters	**Tuition:** $39,085
Application Deadline: January 15	**Room & Board:** $11,890
Freshman Class: 3403 applied, 862 accepted, 323 enrolled	
SAT CR/M/W: 710/690/700	**ACT:** required
	MOST COMPETITIVE

Haverford College, founded in 1833, is a private liberal arts college. The 4 libraries contain 595,855 volumes, 6,752 microform items, and 14,727 audio/video tapes/CDs/DVDs, and subscribe to 6,246 periodicals including electronic. Computerized library services include interlibrary loans, database searching, Internet access, and laptop Internet portals. Special learning facilities include an art gallery, radio station, observatory, and arboretum. The 200-acre campus is in a suburban area 10 miles west of Philadelphia. Including any residence halls, there are 72 buildings.

Student Life: 86% of undergraduates are from out of state, mostly the Middle Atlantic. Students are from 44 states, 35 foreign countries, and Canada. 57% are from public schools. 68% are white. The average age of freshmen is 18; all undergraduates, 20. 2% do not continue beyond their first year; 98% remain to graduate.

Housing: 1190 students can be accommodated in college housing, which includes single-sex and coed dorms and on-campus apartments. In addition, there are language houses, special-interest houses, and Haverford students may live at Bryn Mawr College through a dorm exchange program. On-campus housing is guaranteed for all 4 years. 99% of students live on campus; of those, 90% remain on campus on weekends. Upperclassmen may keep cars.

Activities: There are no fraternities or sororities. There are 170 groups on campus, including chess, chorale, computers, dance, debate, drama, environmental, ethnic, film, gay, international, jazz band, literary magazine, musical theater, newspaper, orchestra, photography, political, radio and TV, religious, social, social service, and student government. Popular campus events include Haverfest, Snowball, and Haverford vs. Swarthmore athletic events.

Sports: There are 10 intercollegiate sports for men and 12 for women, and 3 intramural sports for men and 3 for women. Facilities include a 10,000-square-foot gym with a 1200-seat arena, 3 practice basketball/volleyball/badminton courts, and a multipurpose room used primarily for aerobics, dance, and martial arts. There is a fencing salle and 5 international squash courts, a conference room, and a 7,200-square foot fitness center. The alumni field house has a 4-lane, 200-meter track plus 2 long jump pits and high jump and pole vault pits. The field house also contains a batting cage and a "playing field" for sports such as field hockey, lacrosse, soccer, and baseball/softball. The infield can be used for tennis (4 courts) and recreational and intramural basketball (4 courts).

Disabled Students: 60% of the campus is accessible. Facilities include wheelchair ramps, elevators, special parking, specially equipped restrooms, special class scheduling, lowered drinking fountains, lowered telephones, and reasonable accommodations.

Services: Counseling and information services are available, as is tutoring in every subject. There is a reader service for the blind.

Campus Safety and Security: Measures include 24-hour foot and vehicle patrol, emergency notification system, self-defense education, and security escort services. There are shuttle buses, emergency telephones, lighted pathways/sidewalks, controlled access to dorms/residences, and a fire safety program.

Programs of Study: Haverford confers B.A. and B.S. degrees. Bachelor's degrees are awarded in BIOLOGICAL SCIENCE (biology/biological science), COMMUNICATIONS AND THE ARTS (art history and appreciation, classics, comparative literature, English, fine arts, French, German, Greek, Italian, Latin, linguistics, music, romance languages and literature, Russian, Spanish, and visual and performing arts), COMPUTER AND PHYSICAL SCIENCE (astronomy, chemistry, computer science, geology, information sciences and systems, mathematics, and physics), SOCIAL SCIENCE (anthropology, archeology, East Asian studies, economics, history, interdisciplinary studies, liberal arts/general studies, philosophy, political science/government, psychology, religion, sociology, and urban studies). Natural and physical sciences, English, and history are the strongest academically. Biology, political science, and economics are the largest.

Required: All students must take a minimum of 32 course credits, including freshman writing and 3 courses each in social science, natural science, and the humanities. Students must also take 3 semesters of phys ed and demonstrate proficiency in a foreign language. Students must take a minimum of 6 courses in the major and 6 in related fields. Each major includes a capstone experience.

Special: Haverford offers internship programs, cross-registration with Bryn Mawr and Swarthmore Colleges, study abroad in 35 countries, dual majors, and student-designed majors. Pass/fail options are limited to 4 in 4 years. There is 1 national honor society, Phi Beta Kappa, and 28 departmental honors programs.

Faculty/Classroom: 53% of faculty are male; 47% are female. All teach undergraduates. The average class size in an introductory lecture is 30.

Admissions: 25% of the 2009-2010 applicants were accepted. The SAT scores for the 2009-2010 freshman class were: Critical Reading--7% between 500 and 599, 40% between 600 and 700, and 53% above 700; Math--11% between 500 and 599, 47% between 600 and 700, and 41% above 700; Writing--6% between 500 and 599, 45% between 600 and 700, and 49% above 700. 98% of the current freshmen were in the top fifth of their class; all were in the top two fifths.

Requirements: First-year applicants must take the SAT (all 3 tests, including Writing) or the ACT and 2 SAT subject tests before the deadline for the decision plan chosen. Candidates for admission must be graduates of an accredited secondary school and have taken 4 courses in English, 3 each in a foreign language and math, 2 in social studies, and 1 in science. The GED is accepted. An essay is required, and an interview is recommended. AP credits are accepted. Important factors in the admissions decision are advanced placement or honors courses, leadership record, and recommendations by school officials.

Procedure: Freshmen are admitted in the fall. Entrance exams should be taken by January 15. There are early decision, early admissions and deferred admissions plans. Early decision applications should be filed by November 15; regular applications, by January 15 for fall entry, along with a $60 fee. Notification of early decision is sent December 15; regular decision, April 15. Applications are accepted on-line. 311 applicants were on a recent waiting list, 13 were accepted.

Transfer: 7 transfer students enrolled in 2008-2009. Transfer students must be able to enter the sophomore or junior class. Admission depends mainly on the strength of college grades. A minimum GPA of 3.0 is necessary and the SAT is recommended. The equivalent of 1 year of courses must have been earned. A liberal arts curriculum is also recommended. 64 of 128 credits required for the bachelor's degree must be completed at Haverford.

Visiting: There are guides for informal visits, visitors may sit in on classes, and stay overnight. To schedule a visit, contact the Admissions Office at (610) 896-1350.

Financial Aid: In 2009-2010, 48% of all full-time freshmen and 48% of continuing full-time students received some form of financial aid. 45% of all full-time freshmen and 44% of continuing full-time students received need-based aid. The average freshman award was $33,575. The average financial indebtedness of the 2009 graduate was $16,500. Haverford is a member of CSS. The CSS/Profile and FAFSA are re-

quired. The deadline for filing freshman financial aid applications for fall entry is January 31.

International Students: There are 70 international students enrolled. The school actively recruits these students. They must take the TOEFL with a minimum score of 600 on the paper-based TOEFL (PBT) or 100 on the Internet-based version (iBT). Haverford also requires the SAT (all 3 tests, including Writing) or the ACT plus 2 SAT subject tests.

Computers: Wireless access is available. All students may access the system. There are no time limits and no fees.

Graduates: From July 1, 2008 to June 30, 2009, 307 bachelor's degrees were awarded. The most popular majors were biology (13%), political science (12%), and economics (11%). In an average class, 91% graduate in 4 years or less and 92% graduate in 6 years or less. 101 companies recruited on campus in a recent year. Of the 2008 graduating class, 17% were enrolled in graduate school within 6 months of graduation, and 54% were employed.

Admissions Contact: Jess Lord, Director of Admission. A campus DVD is available. E-mail: *admitme@haverford.edu* Web: *www.haverford.edu*

HOLY FAMILY UNIVERSITY F-3

Philadelphia, PA 19114
(215) 637-3050
(800) 637-1191; (215) 281-1022

Full-time: 325 men, 1060 women	Faculty: 75; IIB, -$
Part-time: 153 men, 533 women	Ph.D.s: 69%
Graduate: 215 men, 908 women	Student/Faculty: 18 to 1
Year: semesters, summer session	Tuition: $20,300
Application Deadline: open	Room & Board: $8,000
Freshman Class: n/av	
SAT or ACT: required	COMPETITIVE

Holy Family College, established in 1954 and affiliated with the Roman Catholic Church, is a private, nonresidential institution with a liberal arts core. There are no undergraduate schools and 3 graduate schools. In addition to regional accreditation, Holy Family has baccalaureate program accreditation with AACSB and NLN. The library contains 101,392 volumes, 8,588 microform items, 2,975 audio/video tapes/CDs/DVDs, and subscribes to 709 periodicals including electronic. Computerized library services include inter-library loans and database searching. Special learning facilities include a learning resource center, and writing resource center. The 46-acre campus is in a suburban area within city limits. Including any residence halls, there are 8 buildings.

Student Life: 90% of undergraduates are from Pennsylvania. Students are from 7 states, and 17 foreign countries. 24% are from public schools. 92% are white. 78% are Catholic. The average age of freshmen is 18; all undergraduates, 21. 18% do not continue beyond their first year; 65% remain to graduate.

Housing: There are no residence halls. All students commute.

Activities: There are no fraternities or sororities. There are 62 groups on campus, including cheerleading, drama, honors, international, literary magazine, newspaper, professional, religious, social service, student government, and yearbook. Popular campus events include Buddy Day, Christmas Rose, and Spring Fling.

Sports: There are 3 intercollegiate sports for men and 4 for women, and 5 intramural sports for men and 5 for women. Facilities include a gym, a weight room, racquetball courts, and soccer and softball fields.

Disabled Students: All of the campus is accessible. Facilities include wheelchair ramps, elevators, special parking, specially equipped rest rooms, lowered drinking fountains, and lowered telephones.

Services: Counseling and information services are available, as is tutoring in some subjects, writing, reading, and math.

Campus Safety and Security: Measures include 24-hour foot and vehicle patrol and security escort services. There are emergency telephones and lighted pathways/sidewalks.

Programs of Study: Holy Family confers B.A., B.S., and B.S.N. degrees. Associates and master's degrees are also awarded. Bachelor's degrees are awarded in BIOLOGICAL SCIENCE (biochemistry and biology/biological science), BUSINESS (accounting, business administration and management, and marketing/retailing/merchandising), COMMUNICATIONS AND THE ARTS (art, English, French, and Spanish), COMPUTER AND PHYSICAL SCIENCE (chemistry, information sciences and systems, and mathematics), EDUCATION (early childhood education, elementary education, foreign languages education, science education, secondary education, and special education), HEALTH PROFESSIONS (medical laboratory technology, nursing, and premedicine), SOCIAL SCIENCE (criminal justice, economics, history, humanities, prelaw, psychology, religion, social work, and sociology). Nursing, elementary education, and accounting are the strongest academically. Nursing, education, and business are the largest.

Required: Students must complete 120 to 130 semester hours, including at least 30 in the major, with a minimum GPA of 2.0. Nursing, medical technology, and education majors must maintain a GPA of 2.5. Specific discipline requirements include English, science, math, philosophy, religious studies, social studies, humanities, and foreign language. A core curriculum of communication, quantification, philosophy, humanities, social science, natural sciences, senior ethics, and religious studies must be fulfilled. All majors require satisfactory performance on a comprehensive exam.

Special: Opportunities are provided for study abroad, co-op programs in 23 majors with more than 200 companies, a B.A.-B.S. degree, an accelerated degree program, independent study, credit by exam, non-degree study, and pass/fail options. Students may pursue dual majors in business and French or Spanish, international business and French or Spanish, and elementary and special education. There are 10 national honor societies, a freshman honors program, and 2 departmental honors programs.

Faculty/Classroom: 44% of faculty are male; 56% are female. No introductory courses are taught by graduate students. The average class size in an introductory lecture is 20; in a laboratory is 17; and in a regular course is 21.

Admissions: n/av
Requirements: The SAT or ACT is required. In addition, graduation from an accredited secondary school is required, or a GED is accepted. Applicants must submit 16 academic credits, including 4 courses in English, 3 each in history and math, 2 each in foreign language and science, 1 in social studies, and the remainder in academic electives. Holy Family requires applicants to be in the upper 40% of their class. A GPA of 2.5 is required. AP and CLEP credits are accepted.

Procedure: Freshmen are admitted to all sessions. Entrance exams should be taken by October or November of the senior year. There are early decision, deferred admissions and rolling admissions plans. Application deadlines are open. Application fee is $25. Notification is sent on a rolling basis. Applications are accepted on-line.

Transfer: 172 transfer students enrolled in 2008-2009. Applicants must submit official transcripts from all previous colleges. Grades of D are not transferable. A maximum of 75 credits will be accepted for transfer. 45 of 120 credits required for the bachelor's degree must be completed at Holy Family.

Visiting: There are regularly scheduled orientations for prospective students. There are guides for informal visits, visitors may sit in on classes, and stay overnight. To schedule a visit, contact the Office of Admissions at admissions@holyfamily.edu.

Financial Aid: In 2009-2010, 85% of all full-time freshmen and 85% of continuing full-time students received some form of financial aid. 85% of all full-time freshmen and 85% of continuing full-time students received need-based aid. 105% of undergraduate students work part-time. Average annual earnings from campus work are $400. The average financial indebtedness of the 2009 graduate was $17,125. Holy Family is a member of CSS. The FAFSA is required. The deadline for filing freshman financial aid applications for fall entry is May 1.

International Students: They must take the TOEFL.

Computers: All students may access the system. 6 days a week (7-day remote Internet access for subscribers). There are no time limits and no fees.

Graduates: n/av
Admissions Contact: Lauren Campbell, Director of Undergraduate Admissions. E-Mail: admissions@holyfamily.edu
Web: www.holyfamily.edu

IMMACULATA UNIVERSITY

IMMACULATA UNIVERSITY	**E-4**
Immaculata, PA 19345	(610) 647-4400, ext. 3015
	(877) IC-TODAY; (610) 640-0836
Full-time: 250 men, 750 women	**Faculty:** IIA, --$
Part-time: 390 men, 1475 women	**Ph.D.s:** n/av
Graduate: 260 men, 860 women	**Student/Faculty:** 10 to 1
Year: semesters, summer session	**Tuition:** $26,540
Application Deadline: see profile	**Room & Board:** $10,920
Freshman Class: n/av	
SAT: required	**COMPETITIVE**

Immaculata University, founded in 1920, is a private Catholic, primarily women's liberal arts and career preparation college. There is 1 undergraduate schools and 1 graduate school. Enrollment figures in the above capsule and figures in this profile are approximate. In addition to regional accreditation, Immaculata has baccalaureate program accreditation with ADA, AHEA, NASM, and NLN. The library contains 130,000 volumes, 1373 microform items, and 1500 audio/video tapes/CDs/DVDs, and subscribes to 760 periodicals including electronic. Computerized library services include interlibrary loans, database searching, and Internet access. Special learning facilities include a learning resource center and language labs. The 400-acre campus is in a suburban area 20 miles west of Philadelphia. Including any residence halls, there are 13 buildings.

Student Life: 69% of undergraduates are from Pennsylvania. 38% are from public schools. 75% are white. 76% are Catholic; 16% Protestant. The average age of freshmen is 18; all undergraduates, 19. 30% do not continue beyond their first year; 55% remain to graduate.

Housing: 380 students can be accommodated in college housing, which includes single-sex and coed dorms and on-campus apartments.

On-campus housing is guaranteed for all 4 years. 71% of students live on campus. Alcohol is not permitted. All students may keep cars.

Activities: There are no fraternities or sororities. There are 32 groups on campus, including art, choir, chorale, chorus, computers, dance, debate, drama, ethnic, honors, international, literary magazine, musical theater, newspaper, orchestra, photography, political, professional, religious, social, social service, and student government. Popular campus events include Rose Arbor Dinner, class proms, and Friday's Pub.

Sports: There are 6 intercollegiate sports for women, and 10 intramural sports for women. Facilities include tennis courts, a full gym, a handball gym, an Olympic-size swimming pool, hockey and softball fields, and a weight room.

Disabled Students: All of the campus is accessible. Facilities include wheelchair ramps, elevators, special parking, specially equipped restrooms, special class scheduling, lowered drinking fountains, lowered telephones, and special housing.

Services: Counseling and information services are available, as is tutoring in most subjects. There is a reader service for the blind, and remedial math, reading, and writing.

Campus Safety and Security: Measures include 24-hour foot and vehicle patrol, self-defense education, and security escort services. There are emergency telephones and lighted pathways/sidewalks.

Programs of Study: Immaculata confers B.A., B.S., B.Mus., and B.S.N. degrees. Associates, master's, and doctoral degrees are also awarded. Bachelor's degrees are awarded in BIOLOGICAL SCIENCE (biochemistry and biology/biological science), BUSINESS (accounting, banking and finance, business administration and management, and fashion merchandising), COMMUNICATIONS AND THE ARTS (English, French, music, and Spanish), COMPUTER AND PHYSICAL SCIENCE (information sciences and systems and mathematics), EDUCATION (early childhood education, elementary education, foreign languages education, home economics education, middle school education, music education, science education, and secondary education), HEALTH PROFESSIONS (music therapy, nursing, and premedicine), SOCIAL SCIENCE (dietetics, economics, experimental psychology, food science, history, international relations, prelaw, psychology, social science, sociology, and theological studies). Premedicine, education, and dietetics are the strongest academically. Education, business, and music therapy are the largest.

Required: To graduate, all students must complete 54 credits in liberal arts, including distribution requirements in humanities, social sciences, and sciences. Students must take a minimum of 126 credits, including 36 to 52 in the major. 2 credits of phys ed are also required. The college requires a minimum GPA of 2.0. A thesis, which is the outcome of a required senior seminar, is also required. Internships are required for dietetics, music therapy, and education.

Special: All majors offer opportunities for internships, and most require them. Students may study abroad in 6 countries. The university offers dual-majors, 3 accelerated degree programs in organization dynamics, human resource management, and nursing, and nondegree study and pass/fail options. There are 16 national honor societies, including Phi Beta Kappa, a freshman honors program, and 13 departmental honors programs.

Faculty/Classroom: 40% of faculty are male; 60% are female. 92% teach undergraduates, and 4% teach and do research. No introductory courses are taught by graduate students.

Requirements: The SAT is required. In addition, candidates for admission should be graduates of an accredited secondary school with a minimum of 16 academic credits including 4 in English, 2 each in a foreign language, math, science, and social studies, 1 in history, and 3 more in college preparatory courses. The GED is accepted. An audition is required for music students, and an essay and an interview are recommended for all. A GPA of 2.0 is required. AP and CLEP credits are accepted. Important factors in the admissions decision are advanced placement or honors courses, recommendations by school officials, and extracurricular activities record.

Procedure: Freshmen are admitted fall and spring. Entrance exams should be taken in the spring of the junior year. There are deferred admissions and rolling admissions plans. Check with the school for current application deadlines. The application fee is $35. Applications are accepted on-line.

Transfer: 32 transfer students enrolled in a recent year. In addition to high school credentials, transfer applicants must present college transcripts. Courses in which the student has achieved a C or better are accepted if they are comparable to Immaculata's courses. A minimum satisfactory score on the SAT is required, as is an interview. Students must have a minimum GPA of 2.0. 64 of 126 credits required for the bachelor's degree must be completed at Immaculata.

Visiting: There are regularly scheduled orientations for prospective students, including an open house and class visit. There are guides for informal visits, and visitors may stay overnight. To schedule a visit, contact the Office of Admissions at (610) 647-4400, ext. 3015.

Financial Aid: In a recent year, 81% of all full-time freshmen and 68% of continuing full-time students received some form of financial aid. 74%

of all full-time freshmen and 61% of continuing full-time students received need-based aid. The average freshmen award was $16,122. Immaculata is a member of CSS. The FAFSA is required. Check with the school for current deadlines.

International Students: The school actively recruits these students. They must take the TOEFL with a minimum score of 550 on the paper-based TOEFL (PBT). They must also take the SAT or ACT.

Computers: All students may access the system. There are no time limits and no fees.

Graduates: In a recent year, 437 bachelor's degrees were awarded. The most popular majors were health professions (43%), business/marketing (38%), and psychology (2%). In an average class, 52% graduate in 4 years or less, 55% graduate in 5 years or less, and 55% graduate in 6 years or less.

Admissions Contact: Sarah Fox, Assistant Director of Admissions. A campus DVD is available. E-Mail: *admiss@immaculata.edu* Web: *www.immaculata.edu*

INDIANA UNIVERSITY OF PENNSYLVANIA   B-3

Indiana, PA 15705   (724) 357-2230; (800) 442-6830

Full-time: 4960 men, 6401 women	**Faculty:** 611; I, --$
Part-time: 447 men, 483 women	**Ph.Ds:** 91%
Graduate: 983 men, 1364 women	**Student/Faculty:** 19 to 1
Year: semesters, summer session	**Tuition:** $7209 ($15,645)
Application Deadline: open	**Room & Board:** $8558
Freshman Class: 11669 applied, 7041 accepted, 3008 enrolled	
SAT CR/M/W: 480/490/480	**COMPETITIVE**

Indiana University of Pennsylvania, founded in 1875, is a public member of the Pennsylvania State System of Higher Education offering programs in liberal and fine arts, business, preengineering, health science, military science, teacher preparation, basic and applied science, social science and humanities, criminology, and safety science. There are 7 undergraduate schools and 1 graduate school. In addition to regional accreditation, IUP has baccalaureate program accreditation with AACSB, ABET, ADA, CAHEA, NASM, and NCATE. The library contains 877,928 volumes, 2.4 million microform items, and 57,691 audio/video tapes/CDs/DVDs, and subscribes to 21,245 periodicals including electronic. Computerized library services include interlibrary loans, database searching, Internet access, and laptop Internet portals. Special learning facilities include a learning resource center, art gallery, planetarium, radio station, and TV station. The 374-acre campus is in a small town 50 miles northeast of Pittsburgh. Including any residence halls, there are 63 buildings.

Student Life: 54% of undergraduates are from Pennsylvania. Others are from 46 states, 72 foreign countries, and Canada. 78% are white; 11% African American. The average age of freshmen is 18; all undergraduates, 21. 26% do not continue beyond their first year; 51% remain to graduate.

Housing: 3980 students can be accommodated in college housing, which includes single-sex and coed dorms and on-campus apartments. In addition, there are honors houses, 24-hour intensified study floors, substance-free housing, academic specialty housing, and an international house. On-campus housing is guaranteed for the freshman year only and is available on a lottery system for upperclassmen. 67% of students commute. Alcohol is not permitted. All students may keep cars.

Activities: 9% of men belong to 18 national fraternities; 8% of women belong to 13 national sororities. There are 210 groups on campus, including art, band, cheerleading, choir, chorale, chorus, computers, dance, drama, drill team, environmental, ethnic, film, gay, honors, international, jazz band, marching band, musical theater, newspaper, orchestra, pep band, political, professional, radio and TV, religious, social, social service, student government, and symphony. Popular campus events include International Day, Pantiellenic Recruitment, and Student Life Fair.

Sports: There are 8 intercollegiate sports for men and 11 for women, and 14 intramural sports for men and 14 for women. Facilities include a 6500-seat stadium, 2 swimming pools, a fitness/bike trail, 2 softball fields, 2 baseball fields and courts for tennis, badminton, 6 handball/racquetball courts, 6 basketball courts, a rugby field, an outdoor track, 2 soccer fields, 2 grass practice fields, 8 volleyball courts, a sailing base, a frisbee course, 2 fishing ponds, an archery range, a simulated golf range, and 3 fitness centers.

Disabled Students: 98% of the campus is accessible. Facilities include wheelchair ramps, elevators, special parking, specially equipped restrooms, special class scheduling, lowered drinking fountains, and lowered telephones.

Services: Counseling and information services are available, as is tutoring in some subjects. There is a reader service for the blind, and remedial math, reading, and writing.

Campus Safety and Security: Measures include 24-hour foot and vehicle patrol, emergency notification system, self-defense education, and security escort services. There are shuttle buses, emergency telephones,

lighted pathways/sidewalks, controlled access to dorms/residences, bicycle registration, operation ID, and a crime tip hotline.

Programs of Study: IUP confers B.A., B.S., B.F.A., and B.S.Ed. degrees. Associates, master's, and doctoral degrees are also awarded. Bachelor's degrees are awarded in BIOLOGICAL SCIENCE (biochemistry, biology/biological science, cell biology, and molecular biology), BUSINESS (accounting, banking and finance, business administration and management, business law, business systems analysis, entrepreneurial studies, fashion merchandising, hotel/motel and restaurant management, human resources, international business management, management information systems, and marketing/retailing/merchandising), COMMUNICATIONS AND THE ARTS (art, art history and appreciation, communications, dramatic arts, English, fine arts, French, German, journalism, media arts, music, music history and appreciation, music performance, music theory and composition, Russian, Spanish, and studio art), COMPUTER AND PHYSICAL SCIENCE (applied mathematics, applied physics, chemistry, computer programming, computer science, computer security and information assurance, geology, geoscience, mathematics, natural sciences, and physics), EDUCATION (art education, business education, early childhood education, education of the deaf and hearing impaired, education of the mentally handicapped, education of the physically handicapped, elementary education, English education, foreign languages education, mathematics education, music education, nutrition education, physical education, science education, social science education, special education, sports studies, and vocational education), ENGINEERING AND ENVIRONMENTAL DESIGN (city/community/regional planning and interior design), HEALTH PROFESSIONS (clinical science, environmental health science, medical technology, nuclear medical technology, nursing, premedicine, rehabilitation therapy, respiratory therapy, and speech pathology/audiology), SOCIAL SCIENCE (anthropology, applied psychology, Asian/Oriental studies, child care/child and family studies, consumer services, criminology, dietetics, economics, family/consumer studies, food production/management/services, food science, geography, history, international studies, philosophy, political science/government, prelaw, psychology, religion, safety and security technology, social science, and sociology). Nursing, criminology, and psychology are the largest.

Required: All candidates for graduation must complete approximately 120 credits, including 48 credits in the liberal studies core. The total number of hours and the minimum GPA vary with the major.

Special: IUP offers co-op programs, cross-registration through the National Student Exchange Consortium, a 3-2 engineering degree with the University of Pittsburgh and Drexel University, and a B.A.-B.S. degree. Internships and dual and student-designed majors are available. Students may study abroad in 28 countries. Also available are work-study programs, a Washington semester, an accelerated degree program, and credit for military experience. There are 21 national honor societies and a freshman honors program.

Faculty/Classroom: 51% of faculty are male; 49% are female. No introductory courses are taught by graduate students. The average class size in an introductory lecture, 43, in a laboratory, 16, and in a regular course, 25.

Admissions: 60% of the 2009-2010 applicants were accepted. The SAT scores for the 2009-2010 freshman class were: Critical Reading--59% below 500, 36% between 500 and 599, 7% between 600 and 700, and 1% above 700; Math--53% below 500, 38% between 500 and 599, and 8% between 600 and 700; Writing--57% below 500, 36% between 500 and 599, 6% between 600 and 700, and 1% above 700. 19% of the current freshmen were in the top fifth of their class; 48% were in the top two fifths. 4 freshmen graduated first in their class.

Requirements: The SAT is required. In addition, candidates for admission should be graduates of an accredited secondary school. There are no specific course requirements. Art majors must have a portfolio and music majors must audition. AP and CLEP credits are accepted. Important factors in the admissions decision are advanced placement or honors courses, extracurricular activities record, and evidence of special talent.

Procedure: Freshmen are admitted fall and spring. Entrance exams should be taken by December of the preceding year. There are deferred admissions and rolling admissions plans. Application deadlines are open. The fall 2008 application fee was $35. Notification is sent on a rolling basis. Applications are accepted on-line.

Transfer: 601 transfer students enrolled in 2008-2009. Transfer students must have a minimum GPA of 2.0 for all subjects (2.5 for education students). 45 of 120 credits required for the bachelor's degree must be completed at IUP.

Visiting: There are regularly scheduled orientations for prospective students. There are guides for informal visits and visitors may sit in on classes. To schedule a visit, contact the Admissions Office at admission_inquiry@iup.edu.

Financial Aid: In 2009-2010, 68% of all full-time freshmen and 66% of continuing full-time students received some form of financial aid. 47% of all full-time freshmen and 46% of continuing full-time students received need-based aid. The average freshman award was $10,032. 18% of undergraduate students work part-time. Average annual earnings from campus work are $1500. The FAFSA and Pennsylvania State Grant form are required. The priority date for freshman financial aid applications for fall entry is April 15.

International Students: There are 242 international students enrolled. The school actively recruits these students. They must take the TOEFL.

Computers: Wireless access is available. Students have access to the network in nearly all areas of campus, with half of classrooms wireless accessible. The most used areas are library, student union, and residence halls. There is virtual access to many services on campus such as dining service menu, advising, financial aid, applying for admission, and registering for classes. All students may access the system 24 hours a day, 7 days a week. A Dell is recommended.

Graduates: From July 1, 2008 to June 30, 2009, 2079 bachelor's degrees were awarded. The most popular majors were criminology (8%), elementary education (6%), and communication media (5%). 129 companies recruited on campus in 2008-2009. In an average class, 31% graduate in 5 years or less and 51% graduate in 6 years or less.

Admissions Contact: Rhonda Luckey, Interim VP for Student Affairs. A campus DVD is available. Web: *www.iup.edu/admissions*

JUNIATA COLLEGE
C-3

Huntingdon, PA 16652

(814) 641-3420
(877) JUNIATA; (814) 641-3100

Full-time: 611 men, 788 women	**Faculty:** 102; IIB, av$
Part-time: 32 men, 37 women	**Ph.D.s:** 94%
Graduate: none	**Student/Faculty:** 14 to 1
Year: semesters, summer session	**Tuition:** $32,820
Application Deadline: March 15	**Room & Board:** $8980
Freshman Class: 1964 applied, 1410 accepted, 366 enrolled	
SAT CR/M: 590/600	**ACT:** 26 HIGHLY COMPETITIVE

Juniata College, founded in 1876, is an independent liberal arts college. In addition to regional accreditation, Juniata has baccalaureate program accreditation with CSWE. The library contains 350,000 volumes, 400 microform items, and 2,100 audio/video tapes/CDs/DVDs, and subscribes to 1,000 periodicals including electronic. Computerized library services include interlibrary loans, database searching, Internet access, and laptop Internet portals. Special learning facilities include a learning resource center, art gallery, radio station, an observatory, an environmental studies field station, a nature preserve, an early childhood education center, and a ceramics studio with an Anagama kiln. The 110-acre campus is in a small town 31 miles south of State College, in the heart of rural Pennsylvania. Including any residence halls, there are 43 buildings.

Student Life: 64% of undergraduates are from Pennsylvania. Others are from 37 states, and 32 foreign countries. 92% are from public schools. 86% are white. 60% are Protestant; 29% Catholic. The average age of freshmen is 18; all undergraduates, 20. 14% do not continue beyond their first year; 85% remain to graduate.

Housing: 1210 students can be accommodated in college housing, which includes single-sex and coed dorms, on-campus apartments, and off-campus apartments. In addition, there are special-interest houses and international housing. On-campus housing is guaranteed for all 4 years. 82% of students live on campus; of those, 75% remain on campus on weekends. All students may keep cars.

Activities: There are no fraternities or sororities. There are 92 groups on campus, including art, band, cheerleading, chess, choir, chorale, chorus, computers, dance, debate, drama, environmental, ethnic, forensics, gay, honors, international, jazz band, literary magazine, Model UN, musical theater, newspaper, orchestra, outing, photography, political, professional, radio and TV, religious, social, social service, student government, and symphony. Popular campus events include Mountain Day, Christmas Madrigal Dinner, and Mr. Juniata.

Sports: There are 9 intercollegiate sports for men and 10 for women, and 4 intramural sports for men and 4 for women. Facilities include 2 gyms, a swimming pool, a fitness center, 4 racquetball courts, a multipurpose room, a varsity football field and stadium, baseball, soccer, softball, and hockey fields, an outdoor running track, 7 tennis courts, and 1 outdoor basketball court.

Disabled Students: 75% of the campus is accessible. Facilities include wheelchair ramps, elevators, special parking, specially equipped restrooms, and lowered drinking fountains.

Services: Counseling and information services are available, as is tutoring in most subjects. There is a reader service for the blind. Juniata also offers courses and workshops in study, reading, and writing skills.

Campus Safety and Security: Measures include 24-hour foot and vehicle patrol, emergency notification system, self-defense education, and security escort services. There are emergency telephones, awareness programs, fire safety training, weather alerts, terror alerts, an emergency operation plan, a firearms storage vault, vehicle lockout service, identification processing, and evacuation mapping.

Programs of Study: Juniata confers B.A. and B.S. degrees. Bachelor's degrees are awarded in AGRICULTURE (environmental studies), BIOLOGICAL SCIENCE (biochemistry, biology/biological science, botany, ecology, marine science, microbiology, molecular biology, and zoology), BUSINESS (accounting, banking and finance, business administration and management, human resources, international business management, and marketing/retailing/merchandising), COMMUNICATIONS AND THE ARTS (art history and appreciation, communications, digital communications, dramatic arts, English, French, German, Russian, Spanish, and studio art), COMPUTER AND PHYSICAL SCIENCE (chemistry, computer science, earth science, geology, information sciences and systems, mathematics, and physics), EDUCATION (early childhood education, elementary education, English education, foreign languages education, mathematics education, museum studies, science education, secondary education, social studies education, and special education), ENGINEERING AND ENVIRONMENTAL DESIGN (engineering physics and environmental science), HEALTH PROFESSIONS (chiropractic, physician's assistant, preallied health, predentistry, premedicine, preoptometry, prepharmacy, prepodiatry, and preveterinary science), SOCIAL SCIENCE (anthropology, criminal justice, economics, history, international studies, peace studies, philosophy, political science/government, prelaw, psychology, public administration, social work, sociology, and theological studies). Biology, chemistry, and psychology are the strongest academically. Biology, business, and education are the largest.

Required: Students are required to complete a minimum of 120 credit hours, including courses in fine arts, international studies, social sciences, humanities, and natural sciences, as well as 4 communications-based courses, 2 cultural analysis courses, a math and statistics course, and the college writing seminar. The total number of hours required for the program of emphasis varies from 45 to 60; majors do not exist as such, and students must develop a program of emphasis and complete it to obtain their degree. Students must have a minimum GPA of 2.0.

Special: Juniata offers cooperative programs in marine science, cytogenetics, cytotechnology, marine biology, biotechnology, nursing, medical technology, diagnostic imaging, occupational and physical therapy, dentistry, medicine, optometry, and podiatry. Internships, study abroad in 19 countries, Washington and Philadelphia semesters, and nondegree study are also offered. There are 3-2 engineering degrees with Columbia, Clarkson, Washington, and Pennsylvania State Universities, a 3-3 law program with Duquesne University, and various preprofessional programs, including optometry, chiropractic, medicine, dentistry, pharmacy, physician assistant, and podiatry. With the assistance of faculty advisers, most students design their own majors to meet their individual goals. There are 16 national honor societies, a freshman honors program, and 16 departmental honors programs.

Faculty/Classroom: 53% of faculty are male; 47% are female. All teach undergraduates. No introductory courses are taught by graduate students. The average class size in an introductory lecture, 16, in a laboratory, 14, and in a regular course, 16.

Admissions: 72% of the 2009-2010 applicants were accepted. The SAT scores for the 2009-2010 freshman class were: Critical Reading--9% below 500, 44% between 500 and 599, 33% between 600 and 700, and 15% above 700; Math--7% below 500, 40% between 500 and 599, 41% between 600 and 700, and 12% above 700. 66% of the current freshmen were in the top fifth of their class; 92% were in the top two fifths. There were 4 National Merit finalists. 8 freshmen graduated first in their class.

Requirements: The SAT or ACT is recommended. In addition, candidates for admission should be graduates of an accredited secondary school and have completed 16 academic credits, including 4 in English, 2 in a foreign language, and a combination of 10 in math, social studies, and lab science. The GED is accepted, and home schoolers are encouraged to apply. An essay is required, and an interview is recommended. A GPA of 3.0 is required. AP credits are accepted. Important factors in the admissions decision are advanced placement or honors courses, leadership record, and recommendations by school officials.

Procedure: Freshmen are admitted fall and spring. Entrance exams should be taken by the January test date of the year of admission for fall entry. There are early decision, early admissions, deferred admissions, and rolling admissions plans. Early decision applications should be filed by December 1; regular applications, by March 15 for fall entry and December 1 for spring entry, along with a $30 fee. Notification of early decision is sent December 31; regular decision, sent on a rolling basis. Applications are accepted on-line. 87 applicants were on a recent waiting list, 4 were accepted.

Transfer: 20 transfer students enrolled in 2008-2009. A GPA of 2.5 is required. Applicants must submit a high school transcript, a college transcript, and an essay. SAT scores are required of some students. 30 of 120 credits required for the bachelor's degree must be completed at Juniata.

Visiting: There are regularly scheduled orientations for prospective students, including a campus tour, interviews, attend classes, meet with faculty, coaches, and, members of the financial planning staff. There are guides for informal visits; visitors may sit in on classes and stay overnight. To schedule a visit, contact Pam Zilch, Campus Visit Coordinator at (814) 641-3428.

Financial Aid: In 2009-2010, all full-time freshmen and all of continuing full-time students received some form of financial aid. 72% of all full-time freshmen and 71% of continuing full-time students received need-based aid. The average freshmen award was $26,119, with $13,609 ($38,030 maximum) from need-based scholarships or need-based grants and $5,226 ($6,000 maximum) from need-based self-help aid (loans and jobs). 51% of undergraduate students work part-time. Average annual earnings from campus work are $811. The average financial indebtedness of the 2009 graduate was $23,618. The FAFSA is required. The priority date for freshman financial aid applications for fall entry is March 1. The deadline for filing freshman financial aid applications for fall entry is May 1.

International Students: There are 126 international students enrolled. The school actively recruits these students. They must take the TOEFL with a minimum score of 550 on the paper-based TOEFL (PBT).

Computers: Wireless access is available. 5 major public computing areas provide students access to PC-based word processing, spreadsheet, presentations, statistics, and database software in addition to e-mail and Internet access. All classrooms are equipped with technology. In addition, the campus includes a network and telecommunications lab, an on-demand education resource and collaboration center, a foreign language/education lab, a graphics processing center, a telelearning and teleconferencing classroom, a computer imaging studio, a cybercafe, and the technology Solutions Center (digital video production). All students may access the system. There are no time limits and no fees. It is strongly recommended that all students have a personal computer. A Dell or Apple is recommended.

Graduates: From July 1, 2008 to June 30, 2009, 332 bachelor's degrees were awarded. The most popular majors were biology/prehealth (20%), business/accounting (12%), and education (8%). 70 companies recruited on campus in 2008-2009. In an average class, 70% graduate in 4 years or less, 70% graduate in 5 years or less, and 80% graduate in 6 years or less. Of the 2008 graduating class, 27% were enrolled in graduate school within 6 months of graduation, and 45% were employed.

Admissions Contact: Office of Enrollment E-Mail: *admissions@juniata.edu* Web: *www.juniata.edu*

KEYSTONE COLLEGE
E-4

La Plume, PA 18440

(570) 945-8111
(877) 4COLLEGE; (570) 945-7916

Full-time: 558 men, 720 women	**Faculty:** n/av
Part-time: 99 men, 264 women	**Ph.D.s:** 20%
Graduate: 12 men, 38 women	**Student/Faculty:** n/av
Year: semesters, summer session	**Tuition:** $19,920
Application Deadline: July 1	**Room & Board:** $8760
Freshman Class: 778 applied, 739 accepted, 336 enrolled	
SAT CRM/W: 445/440/445	**ACT:** 17 **LESS COMPETITIVE**

Keystone College, founded in 1868, is a private co-ed, residential, and culturally diverse institution. There are no undergraduate schools. The library contains 45,967 volumes, 29,352 microform items, and 2243 audio/video tapes/CDs/DVDs, and subscribes to 10,918 periodicals including electronic. Computerized library services include interlibrary loans, database searching, Internet access, and laptop Internet portals. Special learning facilities include a learning resource center, art gallery, radio station, and observatory. The 270-acre campus is in a rural area 15 miles north of Scranton and 40 miles south of Binghamton, New York. Including any residence halls, there are 29 buildings.

Student Life: 89% of undergraduates are from Pennsylvania. Others are from 18 states and 9 foreign countries. 68% are white. The average age of freshmen is 18; all undergraduates, 24. 39% do not continue beyond their first year; 36% remain to graduate.

Housing: 404 students can be accommodated in college housing, which includes single-sex and coed dorms. In addition, there are single rooms for upperclassmen. On-campus housing is guaranteed for all 4 years. 77% of students commute. Alcohol is not permitted. All students may keep cars.

Activities: There are no fraternities or sororities. There are 19 groups on campus, including art, cheerleading, dance, drama, environmental, ethnic, film, forensics, gay, honors, international, literary magazine, newspaper, photography, professional, professional chefs, radio and TV, religious, Rotaract, ski/snowboarding, social service, student government, wrestling, and yearbook. Popular campus events include Winterfest, Spring Fling, and Independence Day.

Sports: There are 7 intercollegiate sports for men and 8 for women, and 5 intramural sports for men and 5 for women. Facilities include an athletic center,(basketball court, weight room, cardio fitness room), tennis courts, playing fields, and a trail system.

Disabled Students: 90% of the campus is accessible. Facilities include wheelchair ramps, elevators, special parking, specially equipped restrooms, special class scheduling, lowered drinking fountains, lowered telephones, and special housing.

Services: Counseling and information services are available, as is tutoring in every subject. There is remedial reading and writing. A writing

center is available and there are some services for those with learning disabilities.

Campus Safety and Security: Measures include 24-hour foot and vehicle patrol, emergency notification system, and security escort services. There are shuttle buses, emergency telephones, and lighted pathways/sidewalks.

Programs of Study: Keystone confers B.A. and B.S. degrees.Associates degrees are also awarded. Bachelor's degrees are awarded in AGRICULTURE (natural resource management), BIOLOGICAL SCIENCE (biology/biological science), BUSINESS (accounting, business administration and management, organizational leadership and management, and sports management), COMMUNICATIONS AND THE ARTS (communications and visual and performing arts), COMPUTER AND PHYSICAL SCIENCE (information sciences and systems and natural sciences), EDUCATION (art education, early childhood education, elementary education, mathematics education, and social studies education), ENGINEERING AND ENVIRONMENTAL DESIGN (environmental science), SOCIAL SCIENCE (criminal justice, forensic studies, psychology, and social science). Visual art, environmental resource management, and natural sciences are the strongest academically. Education is the largest.

Required: To graduate, students must complete 120 to 130 credit hours and maintain a GPA of 2.0. The required core curriculum includes courses in interdisciplinary studies, math, English, speech, computer, and fitness. Distribution requirements and total credit hours vary with the major.

Special: Keystone offers co-op programs in all majors, as well as paid and unpaid internships. Study abroad is available in 14 countries and dependent on major interest or program. The Weekender program accommodates the needs of busy adult students and operates on a trimester basis. There is 1 national honor society and a freshman honors program.

Faculty/Classroom: 45% of faculty are male; 55% are female. All teach undergraduates. No introductory courses are taught by graduate students. The average class size in an introductory lecture, 15, in a laboratory, 11, and in a regular course, 15.

Admissions: 95% of the 2009-2010 applicants were accepted. The SAT scores for the 2009-2010 freshman class were: Critical Reading--80% below 500, 19% between 500 and 599, 1% between 600 and 700, and 1% above 700; Math--79% below 500, 18% between 500 and 599, 4% between 600 and 700. Writing--82% below 500, 16% between 500 and 599, 1% between 600 and 700, and 1% above 700. The ACT scores were 86% below 21, 6% between 21 and 23, and 8% above 28. 14% of the current freshmen were in the top fifth of their class; 40% were in the top two fifths.

Requirements: The SAT is required. The ACT Optional Writing test is also required. An interview is recommended for all. An art portfolio is required for all students whose intended major is art or art education. SAT or ACT scores are required (will accept either). A GPA of 2.0 is required. AP and CLEP credits are accepted. Important factors in the admissions decision are extracurricular activities record, leadership record, and advanced placement or honors courses.

Procedure: Freshmen are admitted fall, spring, and summer. Entrance exams should be taken in the spring of the junior year or early fall of the senior year. There are early admissions, deferred admissions, and rolling admissions plans. Applications should be filed by July 1 for fall entry and December 15 for spring entry, along with a $30 fee. Applications are accepted on-line.

Transfer: 140 transfer students enrolled in 2008-2009. Applicants with more than 12 academic college credits must have a minimum GPA of 2.0. Official transcripts from all colleges attended and a letter of recommendation is required. 45 of 120 to 130 credits required for the bachelor's degree must be completed at Keystone.

Visiting: There are regularly scheduled orientations for prospective students, consisting of 7 open houses and 3 visitation days. There are guides for informal visits, visitors may sit in on classes, and stay overnight. To schedule a visit, contact the Admissions Office.

Financial Aid: In 2009-2010, 94% of all full-time freshmen and 93% of continuing full-time students received some form of financial aid. 89% of all students received some form of need-based aid. 15% of undergraduate students work part-time. Average annual earnings from campus work are $1450. The average financial indebtedness of the 2009 graduate was $21,000. Keystone is a member of CSS. The FAFSA and the state aid form are required. The priority date for freshman financial aid applications for fall entry is April. The deadline for filing freshman financial aid applications for fall entry is May 1.

International Students: There are 13 international students enrolled. They must take the TOEFL with a minimum score of 550 on the paper-based TOEFL (PBT) or 80 on the Internet-based version (iBT) or take the MELAB and the college's own test.

Computers: Wireless access is available. All students are provided with a network sign-on as well as an e-mail address. Most of the campus, including the residence halls, is wireless. All residence halls have Internet access in the student rooms. Computer labs are located throughout the campus for student use. All students may access the system. There are no time limits and no fees.

Graduates: From July 1, 2008 to June 30, 2009, 251 bachelor's degrees were awarded. The most popular majors were business (18%), education (13%), and criminal justice (12%). 20 companies recruited on campus in 2008-2009. Of the 2008 graduating class, 17% were enrolled in graduate school within 6 months of graduation, and 76% were employed.

Admissions Contact: Sarah S. Keating, Vice President for Enrollment/Director of Admissions. E-Mail: *admissions@keystone.edu* Web: *www.keystone.edu*

KING'S COLLEGE   E-2

Wilkes Barre, PA 18711   (570) 208-5858
                                                    (888) 546-4772; (570) 208-5971

Full-time: 1014 men, 952 women	**Faculty:** 124; IIB, av$
Part-time: 132 men, 198 women	**Ph.D.s:** 85%
Graduate: 69 men, 280 women	**Student/Faculty:** 16 to 1
Year: semesters, summer session	**Tuition:** $25,644
Application Deadline: open	**Room & Board:** $9838
Freshman Class: 2172 applied, 1690 accepted, 496 enrolled	
SAT CR/M: 513/519	**COMPETITIVE**

King's College, founded in 1946, is a private institution affiliated with the Roman Catholic Church. The college offers 35 undergraduate majors plus master's degree programs in health care administration, education with a concentration in reading, and curriculum and instruction. A 5-year physician assistant program is also offered. There is 1 graduate school. In addition to regional accreditation, King's has baccalaureate program accreditation with AACSB. The library contains 180,042 volumes, 579,427 microform items, and 3,103 audio/video tapes/CDs/DVDs, and subscribes to 14,675 periodicals including electronic. Computerized library services include interlibrary loans, database searching, Internet access, and laptop Internet portals. Special learning facilities include a learning resource center, art gallery, radio station, a TV studio. The 48-acre campus is in an urban area in northeastern Pennsylvania 19 miles south of Scranton. Including any residence halls, there are 29 buildings.

Student Life: 72% of undergraduates are from Pennsylvania. Others are from 20 states, 4 foreign countries, and Canada. 78% are from public schools. 82% are white. 58% are Catholic; 16% Protestant. The average age of freshmen is 18; all undergraduates, 19. 19% do not continue beyond their first year; 70% remain to graduate.

Housing: 1068 students can be accommodated in college housing, which includes single-sex and coed dorms and on-campus apartments. On-campus housing is guaranteed for all 4 years. 52% of students live on campus; of those, 80% remain on campus on weekends. Alcohol is not permitted. All students may keep cars.

Activities: There are no fraternities or sororities. There are 50 groups on campus, including art, cheerleading, choir, chorale, chorus, computers, dance, debate, drama, ethnic, film, honors, international, jazz band, literary magazine, musical theater, newspaper, pep band, photography, political, professional, radio and TV, religious, social, social service, student government, and yearbook. Popular campus events include All College Ball, Student Activities Fair, and Spring Fling.

Sports: There are 10 intercollegiate sports for men and 9 for women, and 6 intramural sports for men and 6 for women. Facilities include a phys ed center, outdoor basketball courts, a fitness center, a wrestling room, racquetball courts, a swimming pool, a multipurpose area, a 3200-seat gym, a free weight area, an outdoor athletic complex with a field house, a field hockey field, a football stadium, and baseball, softball, and soccer fields.

Disabled Students: 99% of the campus is accessible. Facilities include wheelchair ramps, elevators, special parking, specially equipped restrooms, special class scheduling, lowered drinking fountains, lowered telephones, and special housing.

Services: Counseling and information services are available, as is tutoring in every subject. The academic skills center provides a writing center, learning skills workshops, a tutoring program, and learning disability services.

Campus Safety and Security: Measures include 24-hour foot and vehicle patrol, emergency notification system, self-defense education, and security escort services. There are shuttle buses, emergency telephones, and lighted pathways/sidewalks.

Programs of Study: King's confers B.A. and B.S. degrees. Associates and master's degrees are also awarded. Bachelor's degrees are awarded in AGRICULTURE (environmental studies), BIOLOGICAL SCIENCE (biology/biological science and neurosciences), BUSINESS (accounting, banking and finance, business administration and management, international business management, marketing/retailing/merchandising, and personnel management), COMMUNICATIONS AND THE ARTS (communications, dramatic arts, English, French, and Spanish), COMPUTER AND PHYSICAL SCIENCE (chemistry, computer science, information sciences and systems, mathematics, and science), EDUCATION (early childhood education, elementary education, foreign languages education, middle school education, science education, secondary education,

and special education), HEALTH PROFESSIONS (medical laboratory technology, physician's assistant, predentistry, premedicine, and sports medicine), SOCIAL SCIENCE (criminal justice, economics, history, philosophy, political science/government, prelaw, psychology, sociology, and theological studies). Accounting, English, and biology are the strongest academically. Business administration, elementary education, and accounting are the largest.

Required: All students must earn a minimum of 120 credits and maintain a GPA of 2.0. The core requirements represent between 52 and 59 credits. The major comprises a maximum of 60 credits, of which up to 40 can be specified in the major department, with the balance designated for related fields.

Special: A co-op program in special education and cross-registration with Wilkes University and College Misericordia are offered. The Experiential Learning Program provides internship opportunities in all majors with a variety of employers. King's also offers study-abroad through an agreement with Webster University and John Cabot University, a Washington semester, study-abroad programs in 12 countries, an accelerated degree program in health-care administration, B.A.-B.S. degrees in psychology, dual majors, credit for life experience, and pass/fail options on a few courses. Student-designed majors are available through the King's honors program. There are 11 national honor societies and a freshman honors program.

Faculty/Classroom: 60% of faculty are male; 40% are female. All teach undergraduates. No introductory courses are taught by graduate students. The average class size in an introductory lecture is 20; in a laboratory is 13; and in a regular course is 18.

Admissions: 78% of the 2009-2010 applicants were accepted. The SAT scores for the 2009-2010 freshman class were: Critical Reading--43% below 500, 46% between 500 and 599, and 10% between 600 and 700; Math--41% below 500, 45% between 500 and 599, 13% between 600 and 700, and 1% above 700; Writing--49% below 500, 41% between 500 and 599, and 10% between 600 and 700. 33% of the current freshmen were in the top fifth of their class; 61% were in the top two fifths.

Requirements: The SAT is recommended. In addition, King's requires 16 academic credits, although 24 are recommended, including 4 in English, 3 each in science, math, and social studies, and 2 in foreign language. A GPA of 2.0 is required. AP and CLEP credits are accepted.

Procedure: Freshmen are admitted fall, spring, and summer. Entrance exams should be taken so that scores are received by April 1. There are deferred admissions and rolling admissions plans. Application deadlines are open. Application fee is $30. Notification is sent on a rolling basis. Applications are accepted on-line.

Transfer: 86 transfer students enrolled in 2008-2009. Applicants must present a minimum GPA of 2.0 to 3.0. Students must have earned at least 12 credit hours at another college. An interview is recommended. 60 of 120 credits required for the bachelor's degree must be completed at King's.

Visiting: There are regularly scheduled orientations for prospective students, consisting of admissions interviews, financial aid presentations, faculty one-on-one meetings, and campus tours. There are guides for informal visits; visitors may sit in on classes and stay overnight. To schedule a visit, contact the Admissions Office at 1 (888) KINGS-PA.

Financial Aid: In 2009-2010, 99% of all full-time freshmen and 99% of continuing full-time students received some form of financial aid. 86% of all full-time freshmen and 80% of continuing full-time students received need-based aid. The average freshman award was $20,209. Need-based scholarships or need-based grants averaged $13,487 ($29,528 maximum); need-based self-help aid (loans and jobs) averaged $4,700 ($7,500 maximum); and other non-need-based awards and non-need-based scholarships averaged $9,864 ($25,644 maximum). 26% of undergraduate students work part-time. Average annual earnings from campus work are $1200. The average financial indebtedness of the 2009 graduate was $30,843. King's is a member of CSS. The FAFSA and the college's own financial statement are required. The priority date for freshman financial aid applications for fall entry is February 15.

International Students: There are 6 international students enrolled. The school actively recruits these students. They must take the TOEFL with a minimum score of 530 on the paper-based TOEFL (PBT) or 71 on the Internet-based version (iBT). They must also take the SAT or ACT.

Computers: Wireless access is available. Internet and e-mail access is available to each student from residence hall rooms via networked, high-speed, dedicated data ports. Wireless networking is also available in most areas of the campus and at the college's athletic facilities. All students may access the system. One 24-hour networked public lab exists as well as 18 other networked labs. There are no time limits and no fees.

Graduates: From July 1, 2008 to June 30, 2009, 438 bachelor's degrees were awarded. The most popular majors were business administration (13%), elementary education (11%), and accounting (11%). 33 companies recruited on campus in 2008-2009. In an average class, 62% graduate in 4 years or less, 69% graduate in 5 years or less, and 71%

graduate in 6 years or less. Of the 2008 graduating class, 27% were enrolled in graduate school within 6 months of graduation, and 67% were employed.

Admissions Contact: Michelle Lawrence-Schmude, Director of Admissions. A campus DVD is available. E-Mail: *admissions@kings.edu* Web: *www.kings.edu*

KUTZTOWN UNIVERSITY OF PENNSYLVANIA   E-3

Kutztown, PA 19530   **(610) 683-4060; (610) 683-1375**

Full-time: 3781 men, 4953 women	**Faculty:** 425; IIA, av$
Part-time: 250 men, 630 women	**Ph.D.s:** 84%
Graduate: 289 men, 731 women	**Student/Faculty:** 21 to 1
Year: semesters, summer session	**Tuition:** $7397 ($15,833)
Application Deadline: open	**Room & Board:** $7698
Freshman Class: 9494 applied, 6285 accepted, 1986 enrolled	
SAT CR/M/W: 489/490/477	**ACT:** 20 **COMPETITIVE**

Kutztown University of Pennsylvania, founded in 1866, is a public institution within the Pennsylvania State System of Higher Education. The university offers undergraduate programs in the arts and sciences, business, education, and visual and performing arts. There are 4 undergraduate schools and 1 graduate school. In addition to regional accreditation, KU has baccalaureate program accreditation with CSWE, NASAD, NASM, NCATE, and NLN. The library contains 555,934 volumes, 1.3 million microform items, and 15,953 audio/video tapes/CDs/DVDs, and subscribes to 48,603 periodicals including electronic. Computerized library services include interlibrary loans, database searching, and Internet access. Special learning facilities include a learning resource center, art gallery, planetarium, radio station, TV station, women's center, cartography lab, and German Cultural Heritage Center. The 326-acre campus is in a small town 90 miles north of Philadelphia, midway between Reading and Allentown. Including any residence halls, there are 68 buildings.

Student Life: 90% of undergraduates are from Pennsylvania. Others are from 23 states, 45 foreign countries, and Canada. 86% are white. The average age of freshmen is 18; all undergraduates, 21. 22% do not continue beyond their first year; 51% remain to graduate.

Housing: 4400 students can be accommodated in college housing, which includes single-sex and coed dorms and on-campus apartments. In addition, there are honors houses and special-interest houses. On-campus housing is guaranteed for the freshman year only and is available on a first-come, first-served basis. 50% of students commute. Alcohol is not permitted. Upperclassmen may keep cars.

Activities: 1% of men belong to 8 national fraternities; 2% of women belong to 9 national sororities. There are 202 groups on campus, including art, band, cheerleading, chess, choir, chorus, computers, dance, debate, drama, environmental, ethnic, film, gay, honors, international, jazz band, literary magazine, marching band, musical theater, newspaper, orchestra, photography, political, professional, programming board, radio and TV, recreational sports, religious, social, social service, student government, symphony, and yearbook. Popular campus events include Bearfest, Performing Diversity, and Five Days of Justice.

Sports: There are 7 intercollegiate sports for men and 13 for women, and 13 intramural sports for men and 13 for women. Facilities include a 5600-seat stadium and outdoor track, a 55,000-sq-ft field house and 200-meter indoor track, a swimming pool, 7 outdoor tennis courts, a 3400-seat arena, athletic fields, a street hockey rink, basketball courts, a rifle range, a fitness center, a free-weight room, and a 64,000-sq-ft student recreation center with fitness center/weight room, 2 fitness studios, 2 racquetball courts, indoor rock climbing wall, a .1 mile suspended jogging track, and locker rooms with Jacuzzis.

Disabled Students: 90% of the campus is accessible. Facilities include wheelchair ramps, elevators, special parking, specially equipped restrooms, special class scheduling, and lowered drinking fountains. All programs are accessible to students with disabilities.

Services: Counseling and information services are available, as is tutoring in most subjects. There is a reader service for the blind, and remedial math, reading, and writing.

Campus Safety and Security: Measures include 24-hour foot and vehicle patrol, emergency notification system, self-defense education, and security escort services. There are shuttle buses, emergency telephones, lighted pathways/sidewalks, a bike patrol, crime prevention programs, automatic fire protection systems, door alarms, safety screens, and student monitors in the dorms.

Programs of Study: KU confers B.A., B.S., B.F.A., B.S.B.A, B.S.Ed., B.S.N., and B.S.W. degrees. Master's degrees are also awarded. Bachelor's degrees are awarded in BIOLOGICAL SCIENCE (biochemistry, biology/biological science, ecology, marine science, microbiology, and molecular biology), BUSINESS (accounting, banking and finance, business administration and management, business economics, international business management, marketing/retailing/merchandising, and recreation and leisure services), COMMUNICATIONS AND THE ARTS (ceramic art and design, crafts, dramatic arts, drawing, English, fiber/textiles/weaving, fine arts, French, German, graphic design, illustration, literature, music, musical theater, painting, photography, printmaking,

sculpture, Spanish, speech/debate/rhetoric, studio art, telecommunications, and visual and performing arts), COMPUTER AND PHYSICAL SCIENCE (chemistry, computer science, environmental geology, geology, information sciences and systems, mathematics, physics, and software engineering), EDUCATION (art education, early childhood education, education of the mentally handicapped, education of the physically handicapped, education of the visually handicapped, elementary education, English education, foreign languages education, library science, mathematics education, psychology education, science education, secondary education, social science education, social studies education, special education, and speech correction), ENGINEERING AND ENVIRONMENTAL DESIGN (environmental science and preengineering), HEALTH PROFESSIONS (medical laboratory technology, medical technology, nursing, predentistry, premedicine, and speech pathology/audiology), SOCIAL SCIENCE (anthropology, clinical psychology, counseling/psychology, criminal justice, geography, history, industrial and organizational psychology, liberal arts/general studies, paralegal studies, philosophy, philosophy and religion, political science/government, psychology, public administration, social work, and sociology). Physical science and math are the strongest academically. Business administration, criminal justice, and nursing are the largest.

Required: General education requirements vary by program, but all students must take phys ed or introduction to dance, speech, and English composition. Distribution requirements also include courses in humanities, social sciences, natural sciences, and math. To graduate, students must complete at least 120 semester hours, including 33 to 80 in a major field, with a minimum GPA of 2.0. Students in the College of Liberal Arts and Sciences must take a comprehensive exam.

Special: Students may study abroad in 11 countries. There is a 3-2 engineering degree program with Pennsylvania State University and cross-registration with area colleges. KU also offers internships, student-designed majors, dual majors, and a general studies degree. Nondegree study is possible. There are 15 national honor societies, a freshman honors program, and 30 departmental honors programs.

Faculty/Classroom: 53% of faculty are male; 47% are female. 90% teach undergraduates. No introductory courses are taught by graduate students. The average class size in an introductory lecture is 35; in a laboratory, 16; and in a regular course, 18.

Admissions: 66% of the 2009-2010 applicants were accepted. The SAT scores for the 2009-2010 freshman class were: Critical Reading--58% below 500, 35% between 500 and 599, 6% between 600 and 700, and 1% above 700; Math--56% below 500, 35% between 500 and 599, 8% between 600 and 700, and 1% above 700; Writing--62% below 500, 33% between 500 and 599, and 5% between 600 and 700. The ACT scores were 61% below 21, 37% between 21 and 23, 10% between 24 and 26, 1% between 27 and 28, and 1% above 28. 16% of the current freshmen were in the top fifth of their class; 45% were in the top two fifths.

Requirements: The SAT or ACT is required. The ACT Optional Writing test is also required. In addition, applicants must be graduates of accredited secondary schools or have earned a GED. Recommended Carnegie units include 4 each of English, social studies, science, and math and 2 to 4 of foreign language. SAT Subject tests in biology/chemistry are required for medical technology. Portfolios or auditions are required for art or music majors. A GPA of 2.0 is required. AP and CLEP credits are accepted.

Procedure: Freshmen are admitted fall and spring. Entrance exams should be taken no later than fall of the senior year. There are deferred admissions and rolling admissions plans. Application deadlines are open. The fall 2009 application fee was $35. Notification is sent on a rolling basis. Applications are accepted on-line.

Transfer: 696 transfer students enrolled in 2008-2009. Applicants must present a GPA of 2.0 (3.0 for education) and official transcripts from all colleges and secondary schools previously attended. Students transferring fewer than 12 credit hours must also submit the SAT or ACT scores. 30 of 120 credits required for the bachelor's degree must be completed at KU.

Visiting: There are regularly scheduled orientations for prospective students, consisting of daily visits, including group tours. There is a comprehensive summer orientation program for enrolling students. There are guides for informal visits, and visitors may sit in on classes. To schedule a visit, contact the Admissions Office.

Financial Aid: In 2009-2010, 65% of all full-time freshmen and 61% of continuing full-time students received some form of financial aid. 59% of all full-time freshmen and 56% of continuing full-time students received need-based aid. The average freshman award was $6,713. Need-based scholarships or need-based grants averaged $4766 ($8857 maximum); need-based self-help aid (loans and jobs) averaged $3285 ($7500 maximum); non-need-based athletic scholarships averaged $2133 ($13,600 maximum); and other non-need-based awards and non-need-based scholarships averaged $1872 ($7358 maximum). 70% of undergraduate students work part-time. Average annual earnings from campus work are $1490. The average financial indebtedness of the 2009 graduate was $20,707. The FAFSA is required. The deadline for filing freshman financial aid applications for fall entry is February 15.

International Students: There are 63 international students enrolled. They must take the TOEFL with a minimum score of 550 on the paper-based TOEFL (PBT) or 79 on the Internet-based version (iBT).

Computers: The campus is wireless with 30 student-accessible computer labs containing nearly 500 PCs/Macs. All residence halls are wired for Internet and campus network access. All students may access the system. There are no time limits and no fees.

Graduates: From July 1, 2008 to June 30, 2009, 1738 bachelor's degrees were awarded. The most popular majors were business administration/management (7%), buisness administration/marketing (6%), and psychology (5%). 26 companies recruited on campus in 2008-2009. In an average class, 33% graduate in 4 years or less, 49% graduate in 5 years or less, and 51% graduate in 6 years or less. Of the 2008 graduating class, 19% were enrolled in graduate school within 6 months of graduation, and 57% were employed.

Admissions Contact: William Stahler, Director of Admissions. E-mail: *admissions@kutztown.edu* Web: *www.kutztown.edu*

LA ROCHE COLLEGE   B-3

Pittsburgh, PA 15237   **(412) 536-1275**
                                  (800) 838-4LRC; (412) 847-1820

Full-time: 377 men, 607 women	**Faculty:** 63
Part-time: 65 men, 181 women	**Ph.D.s:** 76%
Graduate: 28 men, 98 women	**Student/Faculty:** 16 to 1
Year: semesters, summer session	**Tuition:** $21,638
Application Deadline: open	**Room & Board:** $8756
Freshman Class: 859 applied, 580 accepted, 190 enrolled	
SAT CR/M/W: 440/440/460	**ACT:** 20	**COMPETITIVE**

La Roche College, founded in 1963, is a private Catholic institution offering undergraduate programs in arts and sciences, business, graphic and interior design, health science, nursing, professional training, and religious studies. There are 2 undergraduate schools and 3 graduate schools. In addition to regional accreditation, La Roche has baccalaureate program accreditation with ACBSP, FIDER, NASAD, and NLN. The library contains 110,756 volumes, 35,105 microform items, and 1006 audio/video tapes/CDs/DVDs, and subscribes to 7900 periodicals including electronic. Computerized library services include interlibrary loans, database searching, Internet access, and laptop Internet portals. Special learning facilities include a learning resource center, art gallery, radio station, and interior and graphic design studios. The 43-acre campus is in a suburban area 10 miles north of Pittsburgh. Including any residence halls, there are 11 buildings.

Student Life: 93% of undergraduates are from Pennsylvania. Others are from 15 states, 38 foreign countries, and Canada. 67% are white. 47% claim no religious affiliation; 34% Catholic; 16% Protestant. The average age of freshmen is 18; all undergraduates, 24. 40% do not continue beyond their first year; 59% remain to graduate.

Housing: 493 students can be accommodated in college housing, which includes coed dorms. On-campus housing is guaranteed for all 4 years. 63% of students commute. Alcohol is not permitted. All students may keep cars.

Activities: There are no fraternities or sororities. There are 42 groups on campus, including art, cheerleading, chorus, computers, dance, drama, environmental, ethnic, honors, international, literary magazine, newspaper, photography, political, professional, radio and TV, religious, social, social service, and student government. Popular campus events include Battle of the Bands, the Gateway Clipper Cruise, and Freak Week (a week-long competition among residence halls).

Sports: There are 5 intercollegiate sports for men and 6 for women, and 10 intramural sports for men and 9 for women. Facilities include soccer, softball, and baseball fields, tennis courts, hiking trails, a fitness/sports center that houses a gym, racquetball courts, an indoor track, an aerobics room, and a weight room, and a nearby county park with tennis courts and a swimming pool.

Disabled Students: 80% of the campus is accessible. Facilities include wheelchair ramps, elevators, special parking, specially equipped restrooms, special class scheduling, lowered drinking fountains, lowered telephones, and special housing.

Services: Counseling and information services are available, as is tutoring in every subject. There is a reader service for the blind, and remedial math and writing.

Campus Safety and Security: Measures include 24-hour foot and vehicle patrol, emergency notification system, and security escort services. There are shuttle buses, emergency telephones, lighted pathways/sidewalks, an intercom security system, and residence halls that are locked 24 hours a day.

Programs of Study: La Roche confers B.A., B.S., B.S.I.D., and B.S.N. degrees. Associate and master's degrees are also awarded. Bachelor's degrees are awarded in BIOLOGICAL SCIENCE (biology/biological science), BUSINESS (accounting, banking and finance, business administration and management, institutional management, international business management, marketing management, and real estate), COMMUNICATIONS AND THE ARTS (communications, creative writing, dance, English, graphic design, and Spanish), COMPUTER AND PHYSICAL SCIENCE (chemistry, computer science, information sciences and systems, and mathematics), EDUCATION (elementary education and English education), ENGINEERING AND ENVIRONMENTAL DESIGN (interior design), HEALTH PROFESSIONS (nursing, radiograph medical technology, and respiratory therapy), SOCIAL SCIENCE (criminal justice, history, human services, international relations, liberal arts/general studies, psychology, religion, religious education, safety and security technology, and sociology). Graphic design, interior design, and professional writing are the strongest academically. Design areas, elementary education, and psychology are the largest.

Required: 12 credits in basic skills areas, including math and computer applications, and 12 credits in liberal arts areas, including history, science, religion or philosophy, aesthetics, literature, and social and cultural systems are required. Also, a 6-credit sequence of 2 interdisciplinary courses that emphasizes the concepts of community, the individual, and global perspectives is required. A minimum of 120 credit hours and a GPA of 2.0 are requirements for graduation, as is a senior seminar in most majors. Some majors require a higher GPA and slightly more credit hours.

Special: There is cross-registration with members of the Pittsburgh Council of Higher Education. Internships, for which students may receive up to 6 credits, are available for juniors and seniors with numerous employers in the Pittsburgh area. La Roche also offers study abroad in 13 countries, a Washington semester, dual majors, credit for life experience, directed research, honors programs, independent study, and pass/fail options. Accelerated degrees may be earned in management, criminal justice, and nursing. A 3-2 engineering degree with the University of Pittsburgh is possible, as are cooperative programs in athletic training, physician's assistant, physical therapy, speech/language pathology, and occupational therapy with Duquesne University. There is a freshman honors program.

Faculty/Classroom: 49% of faculty are male; 51% are female. 95% teach undergraduates. No introductory courses are taught by graduate students. The average class size in an introductory lecture is 25; in a laboratory is 12; and in a regular course is 15.

Admissions: 68% of the 2009-2010 applicants were accepted. The SAT scores for the 2009-2010 freshman class were: Critical Reading--75% below 500, 21% between 500 and 599, and 4% between 600 and 700; Math--75% below 500, 21% between 500 and 599, 7% between 600 and 700, and 1% above 700; Writing--64% below 500, 31% between 500 and 599, and 5% between 600 and 700. The ACT scores were 59% below 21, 26% between 21 and 23, and 15% between 24 and 26. 21% of the current freshmen were in the top fifth of their class; 42% were in the top two fifths.

Requirements: The SAT or ACT is required. In addition, applicants must be graduates of accredited secondary schools or have earned a GED. An interview is recommended for all applicants. At least 2 letters of recommendation are required. A GPA of 2.0 is required. AP and CLEP credits are accepted. Important factors in the admissions decision are advanced placement or honors courses, personality/intangible qualities, and recommendations by school officials.

Procedure: Freshmen are admitted to all sessions. Entrance exams should be taken by the fall of the senior year. There is a rolling admissions plan. Application deadlines are open. Application fee is $50. Applications are accepted on-line.

Transfer: 171 transfer students enrolled in 2008-2009. Transfer design students must submit all post-secondary trancripts, have a 2.0 GPA, and may be required to submit a portfolio. 30 of 120 credits required for the bachelor's degree must be completed at La Roche.

Visiting: There are regularly scheduled orientations for prospective students, including an overnight stay, information and interactive sessions, class attendance, and meeting with faculty. There are also 1-day visits on Saturday. There are guides for informal visits, and visitors may sit in on classes and stay overnight. To schedule a visit, contact the Admissions Office at admissions@laroche.edu.

Financial Aid: In 2009-2010, 95% of all full-time freshmen and 94% of continuing full-time students received some form of financial aid. 60% of all full-time freshmen and 59% of continuing full-time students received need-based aid. The average freshman award was $8,460, with $6,468 ($10,000 maximum) from other non-need-based awards and non-need-based scholarships. 15% of undergraduate students work part-time. Average annual earnings from campus work are $900. The average financial indebtedness of the 2009 graduate was $18,750. La Roche is a member of CSS. The FAFSA and the college's own financial statement are required. The priority date for freshman financial aid applications for fall entry is May 1. The deadline for filing freshman financial aid applications for fall entry is May 1.

International Students: There are 124 international students enrolled. The school actively recruits these students. They must take the TOEFL, or, if their native language is English, they must take the SAT or ACT.

Computers: Wireless access is available. All students may access the system. There are no time limits and no fees. Students enrolled in graphic design, interior design, and communication must have a personal computer. A IBM ThinkPads and Apple PowerBooks are recommended.

Graduates: From July 1, 2008 to June 30, 2009, 265 bachelor's degrees were awarded. The most popular majors were business (24%), elementary education (12%), and graphic design (10%). In an average class, 2% graduate in 3 years or less and 58% graduate in 4 years or less.

Admissions Contact: David McFarland, Director of Admissions. A campus DVD is available. E-Mail: *admissions@laroche.edu* Web: *www.laroche.edu*

LA SALLE UNIVERSITY   F-3
Philadelphia, PA 19141-1199

(215) 951-1500
(800) 328-1910; (215) 951-1656

Full-time: 3359 men and women	**Faculty:** IIA, +$
Part-time: 1314 men and women	**Ph.D.s:** 90%
Graduate: 1900 men and women	**Student/Faculty:** 14 to 1
Year: semesters, summer session	**Tuition:** $33,500
Application Deadline: see profile	**Room & Board:** $11,230
Freshman Class: n/av	
SAT: required	**ACT:** recommended
	COMPETITIVE

La Salle University, founded in 1863, is a private institution conducted under the auspices of the Christian Brothers of the Roman Catholic Church. The university offers undergraduate and graduate programs in the arts and sciences, business, education, fine arts, religious studies, and nursing. There are 4 undergraduate schools and 14 graduate schools. Figures in this profile are approximate. In addition to regional accreditation, La Salle has baccalaureate program accreditation with AACSB, CSWE, and NLN. The library contains 370,000 volumes, 265,000 microform items, and 10,000 audio/video tapes/CDs/DVDs, and subscribes to 7450 periodicals including electronic. Computerized library services include interlibrary loans, database searching, Internet access, and laptop Internet portals. Special learning facilities include a learning resource center, art gallery, radio station, and TV station. The 130-acre campus is in an urban area 8 miles northwest of Center City, Philadelphia. Including any residence halls, there are 54 buildings.

Student Life: 56% of undergraduates are from Pennsylvania. Others are from 45 states and 35 foreign countries. 50% are from public schools. 77% are white; 46% Hispanic; 12% African American. 81% are Catholic; 11% Protestant. The average age of freshmen is 19; all undergraduates, 21. 17% do not continue beyond their first year; 75% remain to graduate.

Housing: 2114 students can be accommodated in college housing, which includes single-sex and coed dorms and on-campus apartments. In addition, there are honors houses. On-campus housing is guaranteed for all 4 years. 61% of students live on campus; of those, 70% remain on campus on weekends. Upperclassmen may keep cars.

Activities: 14% of men belong to 1 local and 5 national fraternities; 14% of women belong to 1 local and 34 national sororities. There are 105 groups on campus, including art, band, cheerleading, choir, chorus, computers, dance, drama, drill team, environmental, ethnic, forensics, gay, honors, international, jazz band, literary magazine, musical theater, orchestra, pep band, photography, political, professional, religious, social, social service, student government, and yearbook. Popular campus events include Oktoberfest and Diplomat-in-Residence Program.

Sports: There are 11 intercollegiate sports for men and 12 for women, and 14 intramural sports for men and 14 for women. Facilities include a fitness center, a 4000-seat arena, a 6000-seat lighted stadium and track, swimming pool, wrestling rooms, sauna, and basketball, volleyball, tennis, and squash courts.

Disabled Students: 95% of the campus is accessible. Facilities include wheelchair ramps, elevators, special parking, specially equipped restrooms, special class scheduling, and lowered drinking fountains.

Services: Counseling and information services are available, as is tutoring in most subjects. A writing center is also available.

Campus Safety and Security: Measures include 24-hour foot and vehicle patrol, emergency notification system, and security escort services. There are shuttle buses, emergency telephones, lighted pathways/sidewalks, and magnetic card access to residence facilities.

Programs of Study: La Salle confers B.A., B.S., B.S.N., and B.S.W. degrees. Associates, master's, and doctoral degrees are also awarded. Bachelor's degrees are awarded in BIOLOGICAL SCIENCE (biochemistry, biology/biological science, and nutrition), BUSINESS (accounting, banking and finance, business administration and management, international economics, management information systems, marketing/retailing/merchandising, and organizational behavior), COMMUNICATIONS AND THE ARTS (classical languages, communications, English, fine arts, French, German, Italian, multimedia, music, Russian, and Spanish), COMPUTER AND PHYSICAL SCIENCE (chemistry, computer science, geology, information sciences and systems, mathematics, and science), EDUCATION (elementary education, foreign languages education, science education, secondary education, social studies education, and special education), ENGINEERING AND ENVIRONMENTAL DESIGN (computer graphics and environmental science), HEALTH PROFES-

SIONS (nursing, preallied health, predentistry, premedicine, and speech pathology/audiology), SOCIAL SCIENCE (criminal justice, economics, history, philosophy, political science/government, prelaw, psychology, public administration, religion, social work, and sociology). English, accounting, and education are the strongest academically. Communication, education, and nursing are the largest.

Required: Students take courses in writing, computer science, religion, philosophy, history, literature, math, the natural sciences, the social sciences, and information technology. The core curriculum is distinguished by 2 requirements: the "double," a thematically linked pair of courses taught by 2 facility partners from different disciplines, and the "metro," a year-long program of cocurricular activities conducted by a faculty member and designed to help students take advantage of the resources of the City of Philadelphia.

Special: Cross-registration is offered in conjunction with Chestnut Hill College, and there is a 2-2 program in allied health with Thomas Jefferson University. La Salle also offers study abroad, co-op programs in business and computer science, work-study programs, internships in most majors, dual majors, an honors program for gifted students, and pass/fail options. An E-Commerce Institute has been created to educate all students about this business tool. An integrated science, business, and technology program is offered. There are 14 national honor societies and a freshman honors program.

Faculty/Classroom: 52% of faculty are male; 48% are female. 83% teach undergraduates, and 60% do research. No introductory courses are taught by graduate students. The average class size in an introductory lecture is 23; in a laboratory, 14; and in a regular course, 19.

Requirements: The SAT is required. The ACT is recommended. The SAT Subject test in math is also recommended. In addition, applicants must be graduates of accredited secondary schools or have earned a GED. La Salle requires 16 academic units, based on 4 years of English, 3 of math, 2 of foreign language, and 1 of history, with the remaining 5 units in academic electives; science and math majors must have an additional one-half unit of math. An essay is required, and an interview is recommended. AP and CLEP credits are accepted. Important factors in the admissions decision are advanced placement or honors courses, leadership record, and recommendations by school officials.

Procedure: Freshmen are admitted fall and spring. Entrance exams should be taken before January of the senior year. There are early admissions, deferred admissions, and rolling admissions plans. Check with the school for current application deadlines and fee. Applications are accepted on-line.

Transfer: 196 transfer students enrolled in a recent year. Transfer applicants should have a minimum cumulative GPA of 2.5. Nursing applicants should have at least a 3.0. 50 of 120 credits required for the bachelor's degree must be completed at La Salle.

Visiting: There are regularly scheduled orientations for prospective students, including campus tours 5 Saturdays throughout the fall, 1 Saturday during the winter, and 3 Saturdays during the spring. There are guides for informal visits; visitors may sit in on classes and stay overnight. To schedule a visit, contact the Office of Undergraduate Admissions at (215) 951-1500.

Financial Aid: In a recent year, 97% of all full-time freshmen and 88% of continuing full-time students received some form of financial aid. 77% of all full-time freshmen and 67% of continuing full-time students received need-based aid. The average freshmen award was $17,858, with $15,939 ($38,210 maximum) from need-based scholarships or need-based grants; $3867 ($7500 maximum) from need-based self-help aid (loans and jobs); and $10,447 ($40,960 maximum) from non-need-based athletic scholarships. 15% of undergraduate students work part-time. Average annual earnings from campus work are $1800. The average financial indebtedness of a recent graduate was $35,613. The FAFSA is required. Check with the school for current deadlines.

International Students: There were 75 international students enrolled in a recent year. The school actively recruits these students. They must take the TOEFL with a minimum score of 500 on the paper-based TOEFL (PBT).

Computers: A wireless network extends through evey academic building and most nonresidence campus areas, as well as some residence halls. There are student PC labs and classrooms, as well as PCs in common areas and lounges. Student help-desk support is available from 8 A.M. until 11 P.M., supplemented by on-line support. The university's web portal includes innovative applications, as well as the customary on-line registration, financial aid information, grades, and so on. All students may access the system 8 A.M. to 11 P.M. weekdays, 9 A.M. to 7 P.M. Saturdays, and noon to 11 P.M. Sundays. There are no time limits and no fees. It is strongly recommended that all students have a personal computer. A Lenovo ThinkPad is recommended.

Graduates: In a recent year, 927 bachelor's degrees were awarded. The most popular majors were nursing (24%), communication (10%), and education (7%). 198 companies recruited on campus in a recent year. In an average class, 64% graduate in 4 years or less, 73% graduate in 5 years or less, and 75% graduate in 6 years or less. Of a recent graduating class, 18% were enrolled in graduate school within 6 months of graduation, and 91% were employed.

Admissions Contact: Robert Voss, Dean of Admissions and Financial Aid. E-Mail: *admiss@lasalle.edu* Web: *www.lasalle.edu*

LAFAYETTE COLLEGE   F-3

Easton, PA 18042   **(610) 330-5100; (610) 330-5355**

Full-time: 1226 men, 1123 women	**Faculty:** 208; IIB, ++$
Part-time: 28 men, 26 women	**Ph.D.s:** 100%
Graduate: none	**Student/Faculty:** 11 to 1
Year: semesters, summer session	**Tuition:** $38,490
Application Deadline: January 1	**Room & Board:** $11,799
Freshman Class: n/av	
SAT CR/M/W: 620/660/630	**ACT:** 28 **MOST COMPETITIVE**

Lafayette College, founded in 1826 is a highly selective, private institution emphasizing the liberal arts, sciences, and engineering. There are no undergraduate schools. In addition to regional accreditation, Lafayette has baccalaureate program accreditation with ABET. The 2 libraries contain 510,000 volumes, 120,000 microform items, and subscribe to 2,600 periodicals including electronic. Computerized library services include interlibrary loans and database searching. Special learning facilities include a learning resource center, art gallery, radio station, geological museum, foreign languages lab, and calculus lab. The 342-acre campus is in a suburban area 70 miles west of New York City. Including any residence halls, there are 65 buildings.

Student Life: 76% of undergraduates are from out of state, mostly the Middle Atlantic. Students are from 40 states, 46 foreign countries, and Canada. 70% are from public schools. 78% are white. 29% are Catholic; 27% claim no religious affiliation; 22% Protestant; 14% Jewish. The average age of freshmen is 18; all undergraduates, 20. 5% do not continue beyond their first year; 90% remain to graduate.

Housing: 2100 students can be accommodated in college housing, which includes single-sex and coed dorms, on-campus apartments, and off-campus apartments. In addition, there are honors houses, special-interest houses, fraternity houses, sorority houses, diversity-oriented houses, arts houses, a black cultural center, and language and special-interest floors. On-campus housing is guaranteed for all 4 years. 98% of students live on campus; of those, 95% remain on campus on weekends. Upperclassmen may keep cars.

Activities: 26% of men belong to 8 national fraternities; 45% of women belong to 6 national sororities. There are 250 groups on campus, including AIDS awareness, art, band, cheerleading, chess, choir, chorale, chorus, computers, dance, debate, drama, environmental, ethnic, film, forensics, gay, honors, international, jazz band, literary magazine, musical theater, newspaper, orchestra, pep band, photography, political, professional, radio and TV, religious, social, social service, and student government. Popular campus events include All College Day, Earth Day, and International Extravaganza.

Sports: There are 11 intercollegiate sports for men and 11 for women, and 22 intramural sports for men and 22 for women. Facilities include an 14,000-seat stadium, a sports center containing a 3500-seat gym, a field house, a varsity house, a natatorium, fitness center, 2 exercise rooms, weight training room, an outdoor track, an indoor track, a climbing wall, 6 racquet courts, and 3 multipurpose courts. In addition, there is a 230-acre athletic complex for lacrosse, field hockey, soccer, and baseball.

Disabled Students: 95% of the campus is accessible. Facilities include wheelchair ramps, elevators, special parking, specially equipped restrooms, special class scheduling, lowered drinking fountains, and lowered telephones.

Services: Counseling and information services are available, as is tutoring in most subjects, most 100-level and many 200-level classes.

Campus Safety and Security: Measures include 24-hour foot and vehicle patrol, emergency notification system, self-defense education, and security escort services. There are shuttle buses, emergency telephones, lighted pathways/sidewalks, controlled access to dorms/residences, advisers in all residence halls, and residence hall lock down from 8 P.M. to 7 A.M.

Programs of Study: Lafayette confers A.B., B.S., and B.S.Eng. degrees. Bachelor's degrees are awarded in BIOLOGICAL SCIENCE (biochemistry, biology/biological science, and neurosciences), BUSINESS (business economics and international economics), COMMUNICATIONS AND THE ARTS (art, English, French, German, music, and Spanish), COMPUTER AND PHYSICAL SCIENCE (chemistry, computer science, geology, mathematics, and physics), ENGINEERING AND ENVIRONMENTAL DESIGN (chemical engineering, civil engineering, electrical/electronics engineering, engineering, and mechanical engineering), SOCIAL SCIENCE (African studies, American studies, anthropology, Asian/Oriental studies, economics, history, interdisciplinary studies, international relations, philosophy, political science/government, prelaw, psychology, religion, Russian and Slavic studies, and sociology). Engineering, psychology, and English are the strongest academically. Economics, business, and engineering are the largest.

Required: To graduate, students must maintain a GPA of 2.0, and take a minimum of 32 to 38 courses. The common course of study, designed to build a background in the liberal arts and sciences is taken in the first 2 years, which includes interdisciplinary seminars, 3 courses in humanities/social science, 2 in natural science, and 1 each in college writing and math/computer science/philosophy. Students must fulfill a foreign culture requirement, and A.B. and B.S. majors must take 2 upper-level writing courses.

Special: Cross-registration is available through the Lehigh Valley Association of Independent Colleges, internships in all academic departments, study abroad in 3 countries as well as through other individually arranged plans, a Washington semester at American University, and work-study programs with area employers are possible. An accelerated degree plan in all majors, dual and student-designed majors, 5-year dual-degree programs, and pass/fail options in any nonmajor subject also are available. There are 12 national honor societies, including Phi Beta Kappa, and 24 departmental honors programs.

Faculty/Classroom: 65% of faculty are male; 35% are female. All teach and do research. No introductory courses are taught by graduate students. The average class size in a laboratory is 12 and in a regular course is 17.

Admissions: The SAT scores for the 2009-2010 freshman class were: Critical Reading--4% below 500, 33% between 500 and 599, 49% between 600 and 700, and 14% above 700; Math--1% below 500, 20% between 500 and 599, 50% between 600 and 700, and 28% above 700; Writing--4% below 500, 28% between 500 and 599, 50% between 600 and 700, and 19% above 700.

Requirements: The SAT or ACT is required. The ACT Optional Writing test is also required. In addition, applicants should have taken 4 years of English, 3 of math (4 for science or engineering majors), 2 each of a foreign language and lab science (with physics and chemistry for science or engineering students), and at least an additional 5 units in academic subjects. An essay is required and an interview recommended. Evaluations from the secondary school counselor and a teacher are required. The GED is accepted. AP credits are accepted. Important factors in the admissions decision are advanced placement or honors courses, evidence of special talent, and personality/intangible qualities.

Procedure: Freshmen are admitted fall. Entrance exams should be taken by January of the senior year. There are early decision and deferred admissions plans. Early decision applications should be filed by January 1. Applications should be filed by January 1 for fall entry, along with a $60 fee. Notifications are sent in March. Applications are accepted online. 1449 applicants were on a recent waiting list, 80 were accepted.

Transfer: 214 transfer students enrolled in 2008-2009. Acceptance usually depends on college-level performance and achievements. An interview is required if the student lives within 200 miles of the college. No minimum GPA is required, and neither the SAT nor the ACT is needed. The number of credit hours required varies with the program, but usually enough for freshman status with advanced standing is needed. 16 of 32 credits required for the bachelor's degree must be completed at Lafayette.

Visiting: There are regularly scheduled orientations for prospective students. Student visits include student/faculty panel discussions, tours, and departmental open houses. There are guides for informal visits, visitors may sit in on classes, and stay overnight. To schedule a visit, contact the Admissions Office at admissions@lafayette.edu.

Financial Aid: In 2009-2010, 42% of all full-time freshmen and 46% of continuing full-time students received some form of financial aid. 41% of all full-time freshmen and 45% of continuing full-time students received need-based aid. The average freshmen award was $31,097. 22% of undergraduate students work part-time. Average annual earnings from campus work are $2600. The average financial indebtedness of the 2009 graduate was $20,745. The CSS/Profile, FAFSA, and the college's own financial statement, and the Business/Farm supplement, and Divorce/Separation parent statement (if applicable) are required. are required. The deadline for filing freshman financial aid applications for fall entry is February 15.

International Students: There are 159 international students enrolled. The school actively recruits these students. They must take the TOEFL and the Comprehensive English Language Test. They must also take the SAT or ACT.

Computers: Wireless access is available. All students may access the system. 24 hours per day. There are no time limits and no fees.

Graduates: From July 1, 2008 to June 30, 2009, 573 bachelor's degrees were awarded. The most popular majors were engineering (16%), psychology (8%), and english (7%). 83 companies recruited on campus in 2008-2009. In an average class, 1% graduate in 3 years or less, 86% graduate in 4 years or less, 89% graduate in 5 years or less, and 90% graduate in 6 years or less. Of the 2008 graduating class, 24% were enrolled in graduate school within 6 months of graduation, and 65% were employed.

Admissions Contact: Carol Rowlands, Director of Admissions. A campus DVD is available. E-Mail: *rowlandc@lafayette.edu* Web: *www.lafayette.edu*

LEBANON VALLEY COLLEGE — E-3
Annville, PA 17003-1400
(717) 867-6181
(866) LVC-4ADM; (717) 867-6026

Full-time: 699 men, 883 women	Faculty: 100; IIB, av$
Part-time: 63 men, 102 women	Ph.Ds: 88%
Graduate: 126 men, 172 women	Student/Faculty: 16 to 1
Year: semesters, , summer session	Tuition: n/av
Application Deadline:	Room & Board: $8,080
Freshman Class: 1698 applied, 1368 accepted, 378 enrolled	
SAT CR/M/W: 540/560/530	ACT: 22 COMPETITIVE

Founded in 1866, Lebanon Valley College is a private institution that offers 34 major fields of study, where students can develop their own individualized major. LVC offers graduate programs in physical therapy, business, music education, and science education. There are no undergraduate schools. In addition to regional accreditation, LVC has baccalaureate program accreditation with NASM. The library contains 203,335 volumes, 15,485 microform items, 17,827 audio/video tapes/CDs/DVDs, and subscribes to 792 periodicals including electronic. Computerized library services include interlibrary loans, database searching, Internet access, and laptop Internet portals. Special learning facilities include a learning resource center, art gallery, and a radio station. The 340-acre campus is in a small town 6 miles east of Hershey, PA. Including any residence halls, there are 53 buildings.

Student Life: 80% of undergraduates are from Pennsylvania. Students are from 23 states, 3 foreign countries, and Canada. 94% are from public schools. 92% are white. The average age of freshmen is 18; all undergraduates, 20. 14% do not continue beyond their first year; 71% remain to graduate.

Housing: 1292 students can be accommodated in college housing, which includes single-sex and coed dorms and on-campus apartments. In addition, there are special-interest houses. On-campus housing is guaranteed for all 4 years. 74% of students live on campus; of those, 60% remain on campus on weekends. All students may keep cars.

Activities: 9% of men belong to 2 local and 2 national fraternities; 9% of women belong to 1 local and 3 national sororities. There are 85 groups on campus, including music ensembles, art, band, cheerleading, choir, chorus, concert band, drama, ethnic, gay, honors, international, jazz band, literary magazine, marching band, musical threater, newspaper, orchestra, political, professional, radio and TV, religious, social, social service, student government, and symphony. Popular campus events include Christmas at the Valley, Valley Festival, and Dutchmen Day.

Sports: There are 12 intercollegiate sports for men and 11 for women, and 12 intramural sports for men and 12 for women. Facilities include a 3000-seat stadium, a sports center, more than 60 acres of athletic fields, indoor and outdoor tracks, a 1660 seat gym, playing courts for basketball, handball, squash, and tennis, a 500-seat baseball grandstand, and a football field.

Disabled Students: 80% of the campus is accessible. Facilities include wheelchair ramps, elevators, special parking, specially equipped rest rooms, special class scheduling, lowered drinking fountains, lowered telephones, and special housing.

Services: Counseling and information services are available, as is tutoring in every subject. There is a reader service for the blind.

Campus Safety and Security: Measures include 24-hour foot and vehicle patrol, self-defense education, and security escort services. There are emergency telephones and lighted pathways/sidewalks.

Programs of Study: LVC confers B.A., B.S., B.M., B.S.Ch., and B.S.Med.Tech. degrees. Associates, master's, and doctoral degrees are also awarded. Bachelor's degrees are awarded in BIOLOGICAL SCIENCE (biochemistry and biology/biological science), BUSINESS (accounting and business administration and management), COMMUNICATIONS AND THE ARTS (art, audio technology, communications technology, English, French, German, music, music business management, and Spanish), COMPUTER AND PHYSICAL SCIENCE (actuarial science, chemistry, computer science, mathematics, and physics), EDUCATION (early childhood education, elementary education, music education, and special education), HEALTH PROFESSIONS (health, health care administration, and medical laboratory technology), SOCIAL SCIENCE (American studies, criminal justice, economics, history, philosophy, political science/government, psychobiology, psychology, religion, and sociology). Actuarial science, natural sciences, and education are the strongest academically. Education, business, and natural sciences are the largest.

Required: The general education program consists of course work in these areas: communications, liberal studies, foreign studies, social diversity studies, and disciplinary perspectives. Students are required to complete 3 writing process courses, and be proficient in computer applications and modes of information access and retrieval. To graduate, students must complete at least 120 credit hours, 2 units of phys ed, and the requirements for the major with a minimum cumulative GPA of 2.0.

Special: Study abroad opportunities are available in Argentina, Australia, England, France, Italy, Germany, Greece, Sweden, Spain, the Netherlands, and New Zealand. There are also 2 off-campus domestic programs in Philadelphia and Washingtgon, D.C. There are 3-2 degree programs in engineering with Penn State University and Case Western Reserve, and in forestry with Duke University. There is also a 2-2 degree program in allied health sciences with Thomas Jefferson University. LVC offers internships in a number of areas. There are 6 national honor societies and 11 departmental honors programs.

Faculty/Classroom: 63% of faculty are male; 37% are female. 90% teach undergraduates. No introductory courses are taught by graduate students. The average class size in an introductory lecture is 23; in a laboratory is 14; and in a regular course is 19.

Admissions: 81% of the 2009-2010 applicants were accepted. The SAT scores for the 2009-2010 freshman class were: Critical Reading--31% below 500, 48% between 500 and 599, 19% between 600 and 700, and 3 above 700; Math--24% below 500, 41% between 500 and 599, 32% between 600 and 700, and 4 above 700; Writing--36% below 500, 43% between 500 and 599, 20% between 600 and 700, and 1 above 700. The ACT scores were 35% below 21, 23% between 21 and 23, 28% between 24 and 26, 8% between 27 and 28, and 6% above 28. 54% of the current freshmen were in the top fifth of their class; 75% were in the top two fifths. 9 freshmen graduated first in their class.

Requirements: The SAT is required. The ACT Optional Writing test is also required. In addition, applicants must be graduates of an accredited secondary school or have earned a GED. LVC requires 16 academic units or 16 Carnegie units, including 4 in English, 2 each in math and foreign language, and 1 each in science and social studies. An interview is recommended. Students applying as music majors must audition. AP and CLEP credits are accepted. Important factors in the admissions decision are advanced placement or honors courses, leadership record, and personality/intangible qualities.

Procedure: Freshmen are admitted fall and spring. Entrance exams should be taken optional. There is a rolling admissions plan. Application deadlines are open. Application fee is $30. Notifications are sent October 15. Applications are accepted on-line.

Transfer: 49 transfer students enrolled in 2008-2009. Requirements for transfer applicants include a minimum GPA of 2.0, SAT scores, and an interview. 30 of 120 credits required for the bachelor's degree must be completed at LVC.

Visiting: There are regularly scheduled orientations for prospective students, and visiting students can take tours, and schedule interviews and meetings with professors. There are guides for informal visits and visitors may sit in on classes. To schedule a visit, contact Susan Jones, Director of Admission at 1(866) LVC-4ADM.

Financial Aid: In 2009-2010, 99% of all full-time freshmen and 98% of continuing full-time students received some form of financial aid. 85% of all full-time freshmen and 80% of continuing full-time students received need-based aid. The average freshmen award was $24,801, with $20,015 ($22,945 maximum) from need-based scholarships or need-based grants; $5,597 ($9,250 maximum) from need-based self-help aid (loans and jobs); and $12,684 ($29,780 maximum) from other non-need-based awards and non-need-based scholarships. 48% of undergraduate students work part-time. Average annual earnings from campus work are $1071. The average financial indebtedness of the 2009 graduate was $27,319. LVC is a member of CSS. The FAFSA and the college's own financial statement are required. The priority date for freshman financial aid applications for fall entry is March 1.

International Students: There are 9 international students enrolled. They must take the TOEFL with a minimum score of 550 on the paper-based TOEFL (PBT) or 80 on the Internet-based version (iBT).

Computers: Wireless access is available. Students may use the network and other computer facilities for academic or other purposes. There are about 200 PC's for student use in the library, academic buildings, and student center. Wireless internet access is available throughout campus including the residence halls. All students may access the system. There are no time limits. The fee is $225.

Graduates: From July 1, 2008 to June 30, 2009, 424 bachelor's degrees were awarded. The most popular majors were education (17%), business administration (14%), and social science (11%). 65 companies recruited on campus in 2008-2009. In an average class, 68% graduate in 4 years or less, 75% graduate in 5 years or less, and 76% graduate in 6 years or less. Of the 2008 graduating class, 26% were enrolled in graduate school within 6 months of graduation, and 82% were employed.

Admissions Contact: Susan Jones, Director of Admission. E-Mail: admission@lvc.edu Web: www.lvc.edu

LEHIGH UNIVERSITY — F-3

Bethlehem, PA 18015   (610) 758-3100; (610) 758-4361

Full-time: 2790 men, 1956 women	**Faculty:** 432; I, av$
Part-time: 31 men, 15 women	**Ph.Ds:** 99%
Graduate: 1164 men, 1023 women	**Student/Faculty:** 10 to 1
Year: semesters, summer session	**Tuition:** $38,630
Application Deadline: January 1	**Room & Board:** $10,200
Freshman Class: 11170 applied, 3662 accepted, 1193 enrolled	
SAT CR/M/W: 630/670/630	**ACT:** required
	MOST COMPETITIVE

Lehigh University, founded in 1865, is a private research university offering both undergraduate and graduate programs in liberal arts, sciences, business, education, and engineering. Our students experience interesting, independent research, and work closely with faculty who offer their time and attention on hands-on projects, internships, and innovative studies. There are 3 undergraduate schools and 4 graduate schools. In addition to regional accreditation, Lehigh has baccalaureate program accreditation with AACSB, ABET, and NCATE. The 2 libraries contain 1.2 million volumes, 1.7 million microform items, and 21,500 audio/video tapes/CDs/DVDs, and subscribe to 0 periodicals including electronic. Computerized library services include interlibrary loans, database searching, Internet access, and laptop Internet portals. Special learning facilities include a learning resource center, art gallery, radio station, TV station, special collections/rare book reading room, digital media studio, financial services lab, and international multimedia resource center. The 1600-acre campus is in a suburban area 50 miles north of Philadelphia and 75 miles southwest of New York City. Including any residence halls, there are 153 buildings.

Student Life: 75% of undergraduates are from out of state, mostly the Middle Atlantic. Students are from 49 states, 51 foreign countries, and Canada. 70% are white. The average age of freshmen is 18; all undergraduates, 20. 6% do not continue beyond their first year; 86% remain to graduate.

Housing: 2508 students can be accommodated in college housing, which includes coed dorms, on-campus apartments, and married student housing. In addition, there are special-interest houses, fraternity houses, sorority houses, substance free housing, UMOJA house, and an ROTC house. On-campus housing is guaranteed for the freshman year only, is available on a first-come, first-served basis, and is available on a lottery system for upperclassmen. 68% of students live on campus; of those, 80% remain on campus on weekends. Upperclassmen may keep cars.

Activities: 38% of men belong to 21 national fraternities; 39% of women belong to 9 national sororities. There are 200 groups on campus, including art, band, cheerleading, chess, choir, chorale, chorus, computers, dance, drama, environmental, ethnic, gay, honors, international, jazz band, literary magazine, marching band, musical theater, newspaper, orchestra, pep band, photography, political, professional, radio and TV, religious, social, social service, student government, symphony, and yearbook. Popular campus events include Greek Week, Spring Fest, and South Side Alive.

Sports: There are 11 intercollegiate sports for men and 12 for women, and 14 intramural sports for men and 14 for women. Facilities include a 16,000-seat stadium, a 6500-seat arena, a gym, a champion cross-country course, a field house with basketball and tennis courts, swimming pools, a track, indoor squash and racquetball courts, playing fields including astro-turf for field hockey, football, lacrosse, and soccer, weight rooms, a fitness center, climbing wall, and an indoor tennis center.

Disabled Students: 35% of the campus is accessible. Facilities include wheelchair ramps, elevators, special parking, specially equipped restrooms, special class scheduling, lowered drinking fountains, and lowered telephones.

Services: Counseling and information services are available, as is tutoring in most subjects, calculus, physics, English, accounting, finance, and economics. There is a reader service for the blind. Tutoring is available upon request. Also, there are special programs for students with learning disabilities and English as a Second Language.

Campus Safety and Security: Measures include 24-hour foot and vehicle patrol, emergency notification system, self-defense education, and security escort services. There are shuttle buses, emergency telephones, lighted pathways/sidewalks, controlled access to dorms/residences, and a LU-alert text messaging system.

Programs of Study: Lehigh confers B.A., B.S., B.S.B.A., and B.S.E. degrees. Master's and doctoral degrees are also awarded. Bachelor's degrees are awarded in AGRICULTURE (environmental studies), BIOLOGICAL SCIENCE (biochemistry, biology/biological science, ecology, life science, and molecular biology), BUSINESS (accounting, banking and finance, business administration and management, business economics, business systems analysis, marketing/retailing/merchandising, and supply chain management), COMMUNICATIONS AND THE ARTS (art, art history and appreciation, classics, design, dramatic arts, English, French, German, journalism, music, music history and appreciation, music theory and composition, Spanish, and theater management), COMPUTER AND PHYSICAL SCIENCE (applied science, astronomy, astro-physics, chemistry, computer science, geology, information sciences and systems, mathematics, physics, science technology, and statistics), ENGINEERING AND ENVIRONMENTAL DESIGN (architectural history, architecture, bioengineering, chemical engineering, civil engineering, computer engineering, construction engineering, electrical/electronics engineering, engineering, engineering mechanics, engineering physics, environmental engineering, environmental science, industrial engineering, materials engineering, and mechanical engineering), HEALTH PROFESSIONS (predentistry, premedicine, and preoptometry), SOCIAL SCIENCE (African studies, American studies, anthropology, Asian/Oriental studies, behavioral science, classical/ancient civilization, cognitive science, economics, history, international relations, philosophy, political science/government, psychology, religion, sociology, and women's studies). Finance, mechanical engineering, and psychology are the largest.

Required: Graduation requirements vary by degree sought, but all students must complete 2 semesters of English, at least 30 credits in the chosen major, and a minimum of 121 credit hours. Students must also maintain a minimum GPA of 2.0.

Special: Lehigh offers many interdisciplinary programs including Integrated Product Development, Computer Science and Business, Integrated Business and Engineering, Integrated Degree in Engineering, Arts and Sciences, Global Citizenship, Lehigh Earth Observatory, and South Mountain College, Lehighüs residential academic program. The university offers co-op programs, cross-registration with the Lehigh Valley Association of Independent Colleges, many combinations of dual majors, study abroad programs in 40 countries, internships, a Washington semester, work-study, a 7-year BA/MD program with Drexel University College of Medicine, and a 7-year BA/OD program with SUNY Optometry. There are 18 national honor societies, including Phi Beta Kappa, and a freshman honors program.

Faculty/Classroom: 67% of faculty are male; 33% are female. All teach and do research. No introductory courses are taught by graduate students. The average class size in an introductory lecture is 39 and in a regular course is 27.

Admissions: 33% of the 2009-2010 applicants were accepted. The SAT scores for the 2009-2010 freshman class were: Critical Reading--4% below 500, 25% between 500 and 599, 55% between 600 and 700, and 16% above 700; Math--1% below 500, 12% between 500 and 599, 54% between 600 and 700, and 33% above 700; Writing--5% below 500, 27% between 500 and 599, 53% between 600 and 700, and 16% above 700. 99% of the current freshmen were in the top fifth of their class; 100% were in the top two fifths. 1 freshman graduated first in the class.

Requirements: The SAT or ACT is required. The ACT Optional Writing test is also required. In addition, candidates for admission should have completed 4 years of English, 3 years of math and electives, and 2 years each of a foreign language, science, and social science. Most students present 4 years each of science, math, and English. An on-campus interview is recommended. AP credits are accepted. Important factors in the admissions decision are advanced placement or honors courses, evidence of special talent, and leadership record.

Procedure: Freshmen are admitted fall and spring. Entrance exams should be taken by the January test date. There is a early decision admissions plan. Early decision applications should be filed by November 15; regular applications, by January 1 for fall entry and November 15 for spring entry, along with a $70 fee. Notification of early decision is sent December 15; regular decision, April 1. Applications are accepted online. 1160 applicants were on a recent waiting list, 43 were accepted.

Transfer: 49 transfer students enrolled in 2008-2009. Transfer candidates should have a minimum GPA of 3.25 and submit high school and college transcripts, an essay, and a statement of good standing from previous institutions. 30 of 121 credits required for the bachelor's degree must be completed at Lehigh.

Visiting: There are regularly scheduled orientations for prospective students, Including group information sessions and tours scheduled Monday through Friday, and some Saturdays, as well as special events and open houses. There are guides for informal visits, visitors may sit in on classes, and stay overnight. To schedule a visit, contact the Office of Admissions at (610) 758-3100.

Financial Aid: In 2009-2010, 44% of all full-time freshmen and 45% of continuing full-time students received some form of financial aid. 45% of all full-time freshmen and 44% of continuing full-time students received need-based aid. The average freshmen award was $32,081, with $4,605 ($7,200 maximum) from need-based self-help aid (loans and jobs); $30,506 ($48,530 maximum) from non-need-based athletic scholarships; and $10,139 ($38,330 maximum) from other non-need-based awards and non-need-based scholarships. 26% of undergraduate students work part-time. Average annual earnings from campus work are $2337. The average financial indebtedness of the 2009 graduate was $31,123. Lehigh is a member of CSS. The CSS/Profile, FAFSA, and the college's own financial statement, and noncustodial profile, and business/farm supplement are required. The deadline for filing freshman financial aid applications for fall entry is February 15.

International Students: There are 182 international students enrolled. The school actively recruits these students. They must take the TOEFL with a minimum score of 570 on the paper-based TOEFL (PBT) or 90 on the Internet-based version (iBT). They must also take the SAT or ACT.

Computers: Wireless access is available. All students may access the system 24 hours per day, 7 days per week. There are no time limits and no fees.

Graduates: From July 1, 2008 to June 30, 2009, 1202 bachelor's degrees were awarded. The most popular majors were business/marketing (31%), engineering (26%), and social sciences (6%). 243 companies recruited on campus in 2008-2009. In an average class, 1% graduate in 3 years or less, 76% graduate in 4 years or less, 85% graduate in 5 years or less, and 86% graduate in 6 years or less. Of the 2008 graduating class, 31% were enrolled in graduate school within 6 months of graduation, and 60% were employed.

Admissions Contact: J. Bruce Gardiner, Director of Admissions. E-Mail: *admissions@lehigh.edu* Web: *www.lehigh.edu*

LINCOLN UNIVERSITY

E-4

Lincoln University, PA 19352

(484) 365-7206
(800) 790-0191; (484) 365-7209

Full-time: 750 men, 1115 women	**Faculty:** IIA, -$
Part-time: 20 men, 25 women	**Ph.Ds:** n/av
Graduate: 180 men, 365 women	**Student/Faculty:** 18 to 1
Year: semesters, summer session	**Tuition:** $7938 ($12,282)
Application Deadline: open	**Room & Board:** $7768
Freshman Class: n/av	
SAT or ACT: required	**COMPETITIVE+**

Lincoln University, founded in 1854, is a public institution offering programs in liberal arts and teacher preparation. There are 3 undergraduate schools and 1 graduate school. Enrollment figures in the above capsule and figures in this profile are approximate. The library contains 189,350 volumes, 212,000 microform items, and 2700 audio/video tapes/CDs/DVDs. Computerized library services include interlibrary loans and database searching. Special learning facilities include an art gallery, radio station, and TV station. The 422-acre campus is in a rural area 45 miles southwest of Philadelphia. Including any residence halls, there are 38 buildings.

Student Life: 57% of undergraduates are from out of state, mostly the Northeast. Students are from 26 states and 23 foreign countries. 94% are African American. The average age of freshmen is 18; all undergraduates, 19. 34% do not continue beyond their first year; 44% remain to graduate.

Housing: 1768 students can be accommodated in college housing, which includes single-sex and coed dorms and on-campus apartments. On-campus housing is guaranteed for the freshman year only and is available on a first-come, first-served basis. 96% of students live on campus; of those, 80% remain on campus on weekends. Upperclassmen may keep cars.

Activities: 5% of men belong to 4 national fraternities; 5% of women belong to 4 national sororities. There are 90 groups on campus, including art, band, cheerleading, choir, chorale, computers, dance, drama, drill team, honors, international, jazz band, newspaper, pep band, political, radio and TV, religious, social, social service, and student government. Popular campus events include lectures and recitals, Black History Month, and convocations.

Sports: There are 7 intercollegiate sports for men and 8 for women, and 2 intramural sports for men and 2 for women. Facilities include a 2000-seat gym, softball and track fields, a fitness trail, a swimming pool, big screen TV, games, table tennis, a pool table, and a bowling alley.

Disabled Students: The campus is accessible. Facilities include wheelchair ramps, elevators, special parking, and specially equipped restrooms.

Services: Counseling and information services are available, as is tutoring in every subject. There is remedial math, reading, and writing.

Campus Safety and Security: Measures include 24-hour foot and vehicle patrol, self-defense education, and security escort services. There are shuttle buses, emergency telephones, and lighted pathways/sidewalks.

Programs of Study: Lincoln confers B.A. and B.S. degrees. Master's degrees are also awarded. Bachelor's degrees are awarded in BIOLOGICAL SCIENCE (biology/biological science), BUSINESS (accounting, banking and finance, and business administration and management), COMMUNICATIONS AND THE ARTS (communications, English, French, journalism, music, Spanish, and studio art), COMPUTER AND PHYSICAL SCIENCE (actuarial science, chemistry, computer science, mathematics, physics, and science), EDUCATION (early childhood education, elementary education, English education, mathematics education, music education, physical education, secondary education, and special education), ENGINEERING AND ENVIRONMENTAL DESIGN (environmental science and preengineering), HEALTH PROFESSIONS (health science and recreation therapy), SOCIAL SCIENCE (anthropology, criminal justice, economics, history, human services, industrial and organizational psychology, international relations, liberal arts/general studies, philosophy, political science/government, psychobiology, psychology, religion, and sociology). Physics, chemistry, and biology are the strongest academically. Business administration, elementary education, and criminal justice are the largest.

Required: Required courses include 8 in the humanities, 3 each in the social and natural sciences, 2 to 4 in foreign language, 2 each in phys ed, writing emphasis, speaking emphasis, critical thinking, and university seminar, and 1 in computer applications. Students must take Integrative Themes in the Liberal Arts, pass a writing proficiency exam, and participate in the Major Field Achievement Assessment. For graduation, a total of 120 semester hours is required, including 60 in the major, with a GPA of 2.0.

Special: Lincoln offers co-op programs, internships, study abroad in 18 countries, work-study, and pass/fail options. 3-2 engineering degrees are offered with 7 other universities and institutes. Accelerated degree programs, B.A.-B.S. degrees, and dual majors are possible. There are 7 national honor societies, a freshman honors program, and 3 departmental honors programs.

Faculty/Classroom: 65% of faculty are male; 35% are female. 81% teach undergraduates. No introductory courses are taught by graduate students.

Requirements: The SAT or ACT is required. In addition, applicants should complete 21 credit hours, including 4 credits in English, 3 each in math, science, social studies, 2 in art, and 1 in phys ed. The GED is accepted. An essay and an interview are required. Lincoln requires applicants to be in the upper 50% of their class. A GPA of 2.0 is required. AP and CLEP credits are accepted. Important factors in the admissions decision are advanced placement or honors courses, evidence of special talent, and leadership record.

Procedure: Freshmen are admitted fall and spring. Entrance exams should be taken prior to admission. There is a rolling admissions plan. Application deadlines are open. The application fee is $20. Notification is sent on a rolling basis. Applications are accepted on-line.

Transfer: 43 transfer students enrolled in a recent year. Applicants must have completed at least 12 semester hours, be in good standing at all previously attended institutions, and submit official transcripts. 60 of 120 credits required for the bachelor's degree must be completed at Lincoln.

Visiting: There are regularly scheduled orientations for prospective students. There are guides for informal visits; visitors may sit in on classes and stay overnight. To schedule a visit, contact the Director of Admissions.

Financial Aid: In a recent year, 96% of all full-time freshmen and 90% of continuing full-time students received some form of financial aid. 88% of all full-time freshmen and 94% of continuing full-time students received need-based aid. The average freshmen award was $15,894, with $5777 ($13,560 maximum) from need-based scholarships or need-based grants; $6405 ($12,500 maximum) from need-based self-help aid (loans and jobs); and $9239 ($22,500 maximum) from other non-need-based awards and non-need-based scholarships. 24% of undergraduate students work part-time. Average annual earnings from campus work are $4200. The average financial indebtedness of a recent graduate was $28,582. The FAFSA and PHEAA are required. Check with the school for current deadlines.

International Students: There were 57 international students enrolled in a recent year. The school actively recruits these students. They must take the TOEFL with a minimum score of 550 on the paper-based TOEFL (PBT) or 80 on the Internet-based version (iBT). They must also take the ACT or SAT, scoring 850.

Computers: Wireless access is available. Computer labs and free e-mail accounts are available. All students may access the system. There are no time limits and no fees.

Graduates: In a recent year, 229 bachelor's degrees were awarded. The most popular majors were criminal justice (10%), communication (8%), and elementary education (8%). 48 companies recruited on campus in a recent year. In an average class, 1% graduate in 3 years or less, 27% graduate in 4 years or less, 40% graduate in 5 years or less, and 43% graduate in 6 years or less.

Admissions Contact: Germel Eaton-Clarke, Interim Director of Admissions. E-Mail: *admiss@lincoln.edu* Web: *www.lincoln.edu*

LOCK HAVEN UNIVERSITY OF PENNSYLVANIA   D-2
Lock Haven, PA 17745   (570) 484-2027
(800) 233-8978; (570) 484-2201

Full-time: 2040 men, 2629 women	**Faculty:** 248; IIB, av$
Part-time: 116 men, 259 women	**Ph.D.s:** 78%
Graduate: 83 men, 202 women	**Student/Faculty:** 19 to 1
Year: semesters, summer session	**Tuition:** $7201 ($13,637)
Application Deadline: open	**Room & Board:** $7736
Freshman Class: 4449 applied, 3438 accepted, 488 enrolled	
SAT CR/M/W: 465/473/453	**ACT:** 19 **LESS COMPETITIVE**

Lock Haven University, established in 1870, is a public institution offering undergraduate degrees in arts and sciences, education, and human services. The university maintains a branch campus in Clearfield. There are 2 undergraduate schools and 1 graduate school. In addition to regional accreditation, LHU has baccalaureate program accreditation with ABET, CSWE, NCATE, NLN, and NRPA. Computerized library services include interlibrary loans, database searching, Internet access, and laptop Internet portals. Special learning facilities include a learning resource center, art gallery, planetarium, radio station, TV station, primate and human performance labs, and cadaver dissection lab. The 135-acre campus is in a rural area 30 miles west of Williamsport.

Student Life: 90% of undergraduates are from Pennsylvania. 87% are white. The average age of freshmen is 18; all undergraduates, 21. 30% do not continue beyond their first year; 51% remain to graduate.

Housing: 1650 students can be accommodated in college housing, which includes single-sex and coed dorms and off-campus apartments. On-campus housing is guaranteed for the freshman year only and is available on a lottery system for upperclassmen. 62% of students commute. Alcohol is not permitted. All students may keep cars.

Activities: 3% of men belong to 6 national fraternities; 4% of women belong to 4 national sororities. There are 100 groups on campus, including art, band, cheerleading, chess, choir, chorale, chorus, computers, dance, drama, environmental, ethnic, film, forensics, gay, honors, international, jazz band, literary magazine, marching band, musical threater, newspaper, orchestra, pep band, photography, political, professional, radio and TV, religious, social, social service, student government, symphony, and yearbook. Popular campus events include Family Day, Alcohol Awareness Week, and Spring Carnival.

Sports: There are 7 intercollegiate sports for men and 9 for women. Facilities include a 5000-seat stadium containing a football field and an all-weather track, a 2500-seat field house with a wrestling room, a recreation facility, a gym used for intramurals and weight training, and a gym that houses a swimming pool.

Disabled Students: 95% of the campus is accessible. Facilities include wheelchair ramps, elevators, special parking, specially equipped rest rooms, special class scheduling, lowered drinking fountains, lowered telephones, and special housing.

Services: Counseling and information services are available, as is tutoring in most subjects. There is a reader service for the blind and remedial math, reading, and writing. There are also writing and math centers.

Campus Safety and Security: Measures include 24-hour foot and vehicle patrol, emergency notification system, and security escort services. There are shuttle buses, emergency telephones, and lighted pathways/sidewalks.

Programs of Study: LHU confers B.A., B.S., B.F.A., and B.S.Ed. degrees. Associates and master's degrees are also awarded. Bachelor's degrees are awarded in BIOLOGICAL SCIENCE (biology/biological science and environmental biology), BUSINESS (business administration and management), COMMUNICATIONS AND THE ARTS (communications, English, fine arts, French, German, journalism, music, Spanish, and speech/debate/rhetoric), COMPUTER AND PHYSICAL SCIENCE (chemistry, computer science, earth science, geology, information sciences and systems, mathematics, and physics), EDUCATION (early childhood education, elementary education, foreign languages education, physical education, science education, secondary education, and special education), HEALTH PROFESSIONS (health science and medical laboratory technology), SOCIAL SCIENCE (criminal justice, economics, geography, history, humanities and social science, international studies, Latin American studies, liberal arts/general studies, paralegal studies, philosophy, political science/government, psychology, social science, social work, and sociology). Health science and biological sciences are the strongest academically. Education, health science, and recreation are the largest.

Required: To graduate, students must complete 60 hours of general education, including 12 in humanities and in social and behavioral sciences, 9 in skills core, 6 in science, 3 in wellness core, and the rest in electives. A total of 120 credit hours is required, including 61 to 68 in the major, with a minimum GPA of 2.0.

Special: There are cooperative programs in music education and engineering, including a 3-2 engineering degree with Pennsylvania State University. Lock Haven also offers study-abroad programs in more than 20 countries, a dual major in education, work-study options, an accelerated degree program for honor students, a student-designed general studies major, and internships, which are required in some majors. Pass/fail grading options are limited to 1 course outside the major per semester, not to exceed 12 credit hours. There are 11 national honor societies and a freshman honors program.

Faculty/Classroom: 54% of faculty are male; 46% are female. All teach undergraduates. No introductory courses are taught by graduate students. The average class size in an introductory lecture is 32 and in a regular course is 25.

Admissions: 77% of the 2009-2010 applicants were accepted. The SAT scores for the 2009-2010 freshman class were: Critical Reading--67% below 500, 25% between 500 and 599, and 5% between 600 and 700; Math--65% below 500, 28% between 500 and 599, and 7% between 600 and 700; Writing--71% below 500, 24% between 500 and 599, and 4% between 600 and 700. The ACT scores were 38% below 21, 49% between 21 and 23, 12% between 24 and 26, and 30% between 27 and 28. 18% of the current freshmen were in the top fifth of their class; 47% were in the top two-fifths.

Requirements: The SAT is required. In addition, applicants must graduate from an accredited secondary school or have a GED. 16 academic credits are required, and a college preparatory course is recommended. AP and CLEP credits are accepted. Important factors in the admissions decision are evidence of special talent and extracurricular activities record.

Procedure: Freshmen are admitted to all sessions. Entrance exams should be taken during the spring of the junior year or the fall of the senior year. There are deferred admissions and rolling admissions plans. Application deadlines are open. Application fee is $25. Applications are accepted on-line.

Transfer: 192 transfer students enrolled in a recent year. Priority is given to applicants who have completed 24 or more transferable credits. A minimum GPA of 2.0 is required. 30 of 120 credits required for the bachelor's degree must be completed at LHU.

Visiting: There are regularly scheduled orientations for prospective students, consisting of an introduction to the administration, sessions with faculty, and an information arena/departmental showcase; small group visits are also scheduled. There are guides for informal visits and visitors may sit in on classes. To schedule a visit, contact the Admissions Office at (570) 484-2027 or (800) 332-8900.

Financial Aid: The FAFSA and PHEAA is required. Check with the school for current application deadlines.

International Students: There were 111 international students enrolled in a recent year. The school actively recruits these students. They must take the TOEFL.

Computers: Wireless access is available. All students may access the system. There are no time limits and no fees. All students are required to have a personal computer.

Graduates: In a recent year, 761 bachelor's degrees were awarded. The most popular majors were parks and recreation (18%), education (16%), and health professional (10%). In an average class, 31% graduate in 4 years or less, 48% graduate in 5 years or less, and 51% graduate in 6 years or less. Of a recent graduating class, 13% were enrolled in graduate school within 6 months of graduation, and 82% were employed.

Admissions Contact: Stephen Lees, Director of Admissions. A campus DVD is available. E-Mail: *admissions@lhup.edu* Web: *www.lhup.edu*

LYCOMING COLLEGE   D-2
Williamsport, PA 17701-5192   (570) 321-4026
(800) 345-3920; (570) 321-4317

Full-time: 642 men, 705 women	**Faculty:** 82; IIB, -$
Part-time: 10 men, 16 women	**Ph.D.s:** 92%
Graduate: none	**Student/Faculty:** 16 to 1
Year: semesters, summer session	**Tuition:** $29,894
Application Deadline: April 1	**Room & Board:** $8134
Freshman Class: 1913 applied, 1297 accepted, 386 enrolled	
SAT CR/M/W: 521/530/512	**ACT:** 22 **COMPETITIVE**

Lycoming College, established in 1812, is a private, residential, liberal arts institution affiliated with the United Methodist Church. In addition to regional accreditation, Lycoming has baccalaureate program accreditation with AACSB. The library contains 205,859 volumes, 182,960 microform items, and 707 audio/video tapes/CDs/DVDs, and subscribes to 3,356 periodicals including electronic. Computerized library services include interlibrary loans, database searching, Internet access, and laptop Internet portals. Special learning facilities include a learning resource center, art gallery, planetarium, radio station, and TV station. The 35-acre campus is in a small town in north central Pennsylvania. Including any residence halls, there are 25 buildings.

Student Life: 67% of undergraduates are from Pennsylvania. Others are from 32 states, 7 foreign countries, and Canada. 81% are from public schools. 87% are white. 27% are Protestant; 23% Catholic. The average age of freshmen is 18; all undergraduates, 20. 20% do not continue beyond their first year; 71% remain to graduate.

Housing: 1240 students can be accommodated in college housing, which includes single-sex and coed dorms, on-campus apartments, and off-campus apartments. In addition, there are language houses, special-interest houses, and nonsmoking, intensive study, and Greek floors. On-campus housing is guaranteed for all 4 years. 85% of students live on campus; of those, 67% remain on campus on weekends. All students may keep cars.

Activities: 18% of men belong to 5 national fraternities; 25% of women belong to 3 local and 2 national sororities. There are 83 groups on campus, including art, band, cheerleading, choir, chorus, computers, dance, drama, environmental, ethnic, film, gay, honors, international, jazz band, literary magazine, musical theater, newspaper, pep band, photography, political, professional, radio and TV, religious, social, social service, student government, and yearbook. Popular campus events include Campus Carnival, Annual Christmas Candlelight Service, and Choir Concert.

Sports: There are 9 intercollegiate sports for men and 8 for women, and 6 intramural sports for men and 6 for women. Facilities include an outdoor softball, football, soccer, and lacrosse complex, indoor basketball courts, weight and exercise rooms, indoor pool, and intramural fields.

Disabled Students: 85% of the campus is accessible. Facilities include wheelchair ramps, elevators, special parking, specially equipped restrooms, special class scheduling, lowered drinking fountains, lowered telephones, and special housing.

Services: Counseling and information services are available, as is tutoring in every subject. There is remedial math, reading, and writing.

Campus Safety and Security: Measures include 24-hour foot and vehicle patrol, emergency notification system, self-defense education, and security escort services. There are emergency telephones and lighted pathways/sidewalks.

Programs of Study: Lycoming confers B.A. and B.S. degrees. Bachelor's degrees are awarded in BIOLOGICAL SCIENCE (biology/biological science), BUSINESS (accounting and business administration and management), COMMUNICATIONS AND THE ARTS (art, art history and appreciation, communications, creative writing, digital communications, dramatic arts, English, French, German, literature, music, Spanish, and studio art), COMPUTER AND PHYSICAL SCIENCE (astronomy, chemistry, mathematics, and physics), SOCIAL SCIENCE (anthropology, archeology, criminal justice, economics, history, international studies, philosophy, political science/government, psychology, religion, and sociology). Archeology, chemistry, and physics are the strongest academically. Business, psychology, and biology are the largest.

Required: To graduate, students must complete 128 credits with a minimum GPA of 2.0. Distribution requirements include 4 courses in humanities and 2 each in English, foreign language, math, fine arts, natural science, social science, and cultural diversity. Students must also complete 2 semesters of phys ed, wellness, or community service. Several majors offer a capstone course for which a major research paper or project is completed.

Special: Cooperative programs are available with the Ohio and Pennsylvania Colleges of Podiatric Medicine, Pennsylvania College of Optometry, and Penn State and Duke Universities. Cross-registration is available with the Pennsylvania College of Technology. More than 200 internships, including teacher programs, study abroad in 7 countries, and a Washington semester at American University are available. Lycoming offers work-study programs, dual and student-designed majors, and an accelerated degree program in conjunction with the college's Scholar Program in optometry, podiatric medicine, and dentistry. Non-degree study and pass/fail grading options are available. There are 23 national honor societies, a freshman honors program, and 35 departmental honors programs.

Faculty/Classroom: 62% of faculty are male; 38% are female. All teach undergraduates. No introductory courses are taught by graduate students. The average class size in an introductory lecture, 25, in a laboratory, 15, and in a regular course, 18.

Admissions: 68% of the 2009-2010 applicants were accepted. The SAT scores for the 2009-2010 freshman class were: Critical Reading--38% below 500, 42% between 500 and 599, 18% between 600 and 700, and 1% above 700; Math--34% below 500, 47% between 500 and 599, 16% between 600 and 700, and 2% above 700; Writing--44% below 500, 37% between 500 and 599, 16% between 600 and 700, and 1% above 700. The ACT scores were 36% below 21, 28% between 21 and 23, 18% between 24 and 26, 7% between 27 and 28, and 1% above 28. 37% of the current freshmen were in the top fifth of their class; 65% were in the top two fifths. 8 freshmen graduated first in their class.

Requirements: The SAT or ACT is required. In addition, applicants must graduate from an accredited secondary school or have a GED. They must have earned 16 academic units including a minimum of 4 years of English, 3 each of math and social studies, and 2 each of lab science, a foreign language, and academic electives. 2 personal letters of recommendation are requested. Admissions interview is recommended. Portfolios and auditions may be required for students seeking scholarships in the arts. A GPA of 2.3 is required. AP and CLEP credits are accepted. Important factors in the admissions decision are advanced placement or honors courses, leadership record, and evidence of special talent.

Procedure: Freshmen are admitted fall and spring. Entrance exams should be taken during the junior year or by January of the senior year. There are early admissions, deferred admissions, and rolling admissions plans. Applications should be filed by April 1 for fall entry and December 1 for spring entry, along with a $35 fee. Notification is sent on a rolling basis. Applications are accepted on-line.

Transfer: 60 transfer students enrolled in 2008-2009. Applicants must submit appropriate transcripts and have a minimum GPA of 2.0 in transferable courses. Students who have completed 24 transferable semester hours are not required to submit SAT or ACT results. 32 of 128 credits required for the bachelor's degree must be completed at Lycoming.

Visiting: There are regularly scheduled orientations for prospective students, consisting of a student-guided tour of campus and an interview with an admissions counselor. Meetings with professors and coaches and attending a class are possible upon request. There are guides for informal visits; visitors may sit in on classes and stay overnight. To schedule a visit, contact the Admissions House at (800) 345-3920, ext. 4026.

Financial Aid: In 2009-2010, 98% of all full-time freshmen and 97% of continuing full-time students received some form of financial aid. 89% of all full-time freshmen and 85% of continuing full-time students received need-based aid. The average freshman award was $24,693. Need-based scholarships or need-based grants averaged $20,667 ($28,000 maximum); need-based self-help aid (loans and jobs) averaged $5,995 ($7,500 maximum); and other non-need based awards and non-need based scholarships averaged $15,993 ($25,200 maximum). 29% of undergraduate students work part-time. Average annual earnings from campus work are $793. The average financial indebtedness of the 2009 graduate was $29,478. Lycoming is a member of CSS. The FAFSA and the college's own financial statement are required. The priority date for freshman financial aid applications for fall entry is March 1. The deadline for filing freshman financial aid applications for fall entry is April 15.

International Students: There are 18 international students enrolled. They must take the TOEFL. They must also take the SAT or ACT. This requirement may be waived, however.

Computers: Wireless access is available. All students may access the system 24 hours a day. There are no time limits and no fees. It is strongly recommended that all students have a personal computer.

Graduates: From July 1, 2008 to June 30, 2009, 281 bachelor's degrees were awarded. The most popular majors were psychology (14%), business (13%), and biology (12%). 25 companies recruited on campus in 2008-2009. In an average class, 2% graduate in 3 years or less, 63% graduate in 4 years or less, and 71% graduate in 5 years or less. Of the 2008 graduating class, 22% were enrolled in graduate school within 6 months of graduation, and 95% were employed.

Admissions Contact: James Spencer, Dean of Admissions and Financial Aid. E-Mail: *admissions@lycoming.edu* Web: *www.lycoming.edu*

MANSFIELD UNIVERSITY
Mansfield, PA 16933

D-1

(570) 662-4243
(800) 577-6826; (570) 662-4121

Full-time: 1169 men, 1669 women	**Faculty:** 156; IIB, +$
Part-time: 71 men, 159 women	**Ph.D.s:** 86%
Graduate: 78 men, 423 women	**Student/Faculty:** 18 to 1
Year: semesters, summer session	**Tuition:** $7746 ($15,802)
Application Deadline: open	**Room & Board:** $6722
Freshman Class: 2800 applied, 2108 accepted, 717 enrolled	
SAT CR/M/W: 480/480/460	**ACT:** required **COMPETITIVE**

Mansfield University, founded in 1857, is a public university that is part of the Pennsylvania State System of Higher Education. It offers programs in professional studies and the arts and sciences. There is 1 undergraduate school and 1 graduate school. In addition to regional accreditation, Mansfield has baccalaureate program accreditation with CSWE, NASM, NCATE, and NLN. The library contains 249,874 volumes, 841,548 microform items, and 30,875 audio/video tapes/CDs/DVDs, and subscribes to 650 periodicals including electronic. Computerized library services include interlibrary loans, database searching, and Internet access. Special learning facilities include a learning resource center, art gallery, natural history museum, planetarium, radio station, TV station, and high-tech lecture lab. The 175-acre campus is in a rural area 28 miles south of Corning/Elmira, New York, and 58 miles north of Williamsport. Including any residence halls, there are 42 buildings.

Student Life: 77% of undergraduates are from Pennsylvania. Others are from 35 states, 20 foreign countries, and Canada. 80% are white. The average age of freshmen is 18; all undergraduates, 22. 26% do not continue beyond their first year; 48% remain to graduate.

Housing: 1721 students can be accommodated in college housing, which includes coed dorms. In addition, there are special-interest houses, wellness floors, 24-hour quiet floors, and honors floors in residence halls, plus one freshmen-only residence hall. On-campus housing is guaranteed for all 4 years. 50% of students commute. Alcohol is not permitted. All students may keep cars.

Activities: 7% of men belong to 4 national fraternities; 6% of women belong to 4 national sororities. There are 122 groups on campus, including art, band, cheerleading, choir, chorale, chorus, computers, dance, debate, drama, environmental, ethnic, film, forensics, gay, honors, international, jazz band, literary magazine, marching band, musical theater, newspaper, orchestra, pep band, photography, political, professional, radio and TV, religious, social, social service, student government, and symphony. Popular campus events include Fabulous 1890s Weekend.

Sports: There are 6 intercollegiate sports for men and 7 for women, and 16 intramural sports for men and 16 for women. Facilities include a track, a recreation center, a 4000-seat stadium, a 1500-seat indoor gym, a 1200-seat auditorium, football, baseball, and hockey fields, and a fitness center.

Disabled Students: 80% of the campus is accessible. Facilities include wheelchair ramps, elevators, special parking, specially equipped restrooms, special class scheduling, lowered drinking fountains, lowered telephones, and a wheelchair lift.

Services: Counseling and information services are available, as is tutoring in most subjects. There is a reader service for the blind, and remedial math, reading, and writing.

Campus Safety and Security: Measures include 24-hour foot and vehicle patrol, emergency notification system, self-defense education, and security escort services. There are shuttle buses, emergency telephones, and lighted pathways/sidewalks.

Programs of Study: Mansfield confers B.A., B.S., B.M., B.S.E., B.S.N., and B.S.W. degrees. Associate and master's degrees are also awarded. Bachelor's degrees are awarded in AGRICULTURE (fishing and fisheries), BIOLOGICAL SCIENCE (biochemistry, biology/biological science, and molecular biology), BUSINESS (business administration and management, business economics, international business management, personnel management, and tourism), COMMUNICATIONS AND THE ARTS (art history and appreciation, broadcasting, English, French, German, graphic design, journalism, music, music business management, music performance, public relations, and Spanish), COMPUTER AND PHYSICAL SCIENCE (chemistry, computer science, information sciences and systems, mathematics, and physics), EDUCATION (art education, early childhood education, education of the exceptional child, elementary education, English education, foreign languages education, mathematics education, music education, science education, secondary education, social studies education, and special education), ENGINEERING AND ENVIRONMENTAL DESIGN (city/community/regional planning, environmental science, and preengineering), HEALTH PROFESSIONS (medical technology and nursing), SOCIAL SCIENCE (anthropology, criminal justice, dietetics, economics, geography, history, international studies, liberal arts/general studies, philosophy, political science/government, prelaw, psychology, social work, and sociology). Music, physical sciences, and social sciences are the strongest academically. Education, music, and social sciences are the largest.

Required: To graduate, students must complete 120 credit hours with a 2.0 GPA in core courses, distribution requirements, general education electives, and major requirements. Some degrees require a higher GPA.

Special: There are co-op programs in preengineering and medical technology. Stidents may study abroad in France, Russia, Canada, Australia, Spain, and Germany. There is a 3-2 engineering program with Penn State University. The university also offers work-study, dual majors, a liberal studies degree, credit by exam, credit for military experience, nondegree study, and pass/fail options. There are 6 national honor societies, including Phi Beta Kappa, and a freshman honors program.

Faculty/Classroom: 48% of faculty are male; 52% are female. All teach undergraduates. No introductory courses are taught by graduate students. The average class size in an introductory lecture is 32; in a laboratory, 19; and in a regular course, 30.

Admissions: 75% of the 2009-2010 applicants were accepted. The SAT scores for the 2009-2010 freshman class were: Critical Reading--59% below 500, 32% between 500 and 599, 8% between 600 and 700, and 1% above 700; Math--61% below 500, 30% between 500 and 599, 8% between 600 and 700, and 1 above 700; Writing--66% below 500, 31% between 500 and 599, 3% between 600 and 700, and 1% above 700. 26% of the current freshmen were in the top fifth of their class; 53% were in the top two fifths. 6 freshmen graduated first in their class.

Requirements: The SAT or ACT is required, with a satisfactory SAT score or a minimum ACT score of 19. A GED is accepted. Applicants should prepare with 4 credits of English and history, 3 each of math, science, and social studies, 2 of foreign language, and 6 of additional academic electives. Art students must submit a portfolio; music students must audition. Mansfield requires applicants to be in the upper 60% of their class. A GPA of 2.0 is required. AP and CLEP credits are accepted. Important factors in the admissions decision are advanced placement or honors courses, evidence of special talent, and leadership record.

Procedure: Freshmen are admitted fall and spring. Entrance exams should be taken by the junior or senior year of high school. There are early admissions, deferred admissions, and rolling admissions plans.

Check with the school for current application deadlines. The application fee is $25. Notification is sent on a rolling basis. Applications are accepted on-line.

Transfer: 263 transfer students enrolled in 2008-2009. Applicants must have a GPA of at least 2.0 and must submit all college transcripts. 32 of 120 credits required for the bachelor's degree must be completed at Mansfield.

Visiting: There are regularly scheduled orientations for prospective students. There are guides for informal visits, and visitors may sit in on classes. To schedule a visit, contact the Admissions Office.

Financial Aid: In 2009-2010, 91% of all full-time freshmen and 74% of continuing full-time students received some form of financial aid. 55% of all full-time freshmen and 55% of continuing full-time students received need-based aid. The average freshman award was $10,082. Need-based scholarships or need-based grants averaged $4051; need-based self-help aid (loans and jobs) averaged $2805; non-need-based athletic scholarships averaged $1630; and other non-need-based awards and non-need-based scholarships averaged $1534. 28% of undergraduate students work part-time. Average annual earnings from campus work are $1200. The average financial indebtedness of the 2009 graduate was $22,821. Mansfield is a member of CSS. The FAFSA and the college's own financial statement are required. The priority date for freshman financial aid applications for fall entry is March 15.

International Students: There are 41 international students enrolled. The school actively recruits these students. They must take the TOEFL with a minimum score of 500 on the paper-based TOEFL (PBT) or 61 on the Internet-based version (iBT).

Computers: Wireless access is available. All students may access the system. There are no time limits and no fees.

Graduates: From July 1, 2008 to June 30, 2009, 549 bachelor's degrees were awarded. The most popular majors were education (13%), psychology (11%), and business (9%). In an average class, 2% graduate in 3 years or less, 30% graduate in 4 years or less, 47% graduate in 5 years or less, and 49% graduate in 6 years or less.

Admissions Contact: Brian D. Barden, Director, Enrollment Services. E-mail: *admissns@mansfield.edu* Web: *www.mansfield.edu*

MARYWOOD UNIVERSITY E-2
Scranton, PA 18509-1598
(570) 348-6234
(866) 279-9663; (570) 961-4763

Full-time: 616 men, 1437 women	**Faculty:** IIA, -$
Part-time: 49 men, 82 women	**Ph.Ds:** 85%
Graduate: 264 men, 1023 women	**Student/Faculty:** n/av
Year: semesters, summer session	**Tuition:** $26,270
Application Deadline: open	**Room & Board:** $11,498
Freshman Class: 1923 applied, 1392 accepted, 473 enrolled	
SAT CR/M/W: 520/520/520	**ACT:** 22	**COMPETITIVE**

Marywood University, founded in 1915, is an independent comprehensive Catholic institution committed to the integration of liberal arts and professional studies in the context of ethical and religious values. Marywood offers more than 60 undergraduate programs. There are 4 undergraduate schools and 4 graduate schools. In addition to regional accreditation, Marywood has baccalaureate program accreditation with ACBSP, ADA, CSWE, NASAD, NASM, NCATE, and NLN. The library contains 223,500 volumes, 378,148 microform items, and 22,566 audio/video tapes/CDs/DVDs, and subscribes to 17,923 periodicals including electronic. Computerized library services include interlibrary loans, database searching, Internet access, and laptop Internet portals. Special learning facilities include a learning resource center, art gallery, radio station, TV station, assistive technology labs, communication disorders clinic, on-campus preschool and day care center, psychology/education research lab, science multimedia lab, human performance lab, videoconferencing classroom, culinary labs, graphic design lab, and studio arts center, including 3 art museums. The 115-acre campus is in a suburban area 120 miles west of New York City and 115 miles north of Philadelphia. Including any residence halls, there are 30 buildings.

Student Life: 73% of undergraduates are from Pennsylvania. Others are from 21 states and 14 foreign countries. 78% are from public schools. 85% are white. 58% are Catholic; 14% Protestant. The average age of freshmen is 18; all undergraduates, 21. 16% do not continue beyond their first year; 69% remain to graduate.

Housing: 985 students can be accommodated in college housing, which includes single-sex and coed dorms and on-campus apartments. In addition, there are honors houses, a community service residence, and an American-international student wing. On-campus housing is guaranteed for all 4 years. 55% of students commute. Alcohol is not permitted. All students may keep cars.

Activities: There are no fraternities; 4% of women belong to 1 local sorority. There are 53 groups on campus, including volunteer, art, band, cheerleading, choir, chorus, commuter, computers, dance, drama, environmental, ethnic, film, gay, honors, international, jazz band, literary magazine, musical theater, newspaper, orchestra, photography, political, professional, radio and TV, religious, social, social service, student government, symphony, and yearbook. Popular campus events include Family Weekend, Spring Fling, and Midnight Madness.

Sports: There are 6 intercollegiate sports for men and 8 for women, and 28 intramural sports for men and 28 for women. Facilities include the Center for Athletics and Wellness includes a fitness center, a climbing wall, an elevated running track, a dance/aerobic studio, an arena to showcase Pacer sports, and high-tech athletic training areas. Another center houses a 25-meter indoor swimming pool and racquetball courts. Outdoor facilities 3 grass fields and 1 multipurpose turf field, a sand volleyball court, and basketball courts.

Disabled Students: 98% of the campus is accessible. Facilities include wheelchair ramps, elevators, special parking, specially equipped restrooms, special class scheduling, lowered drinking fountains, lowered telephones, and special housing.

Services: Counseling and information services are available, as is tutoring in every subject. There is a reader service for the blind and remedial math, reading, and writing. Remedial study skills and nonremedial tutoring, oral tests, note taking, tutors, tape recorders for physically challenged students, and interpreters for students with hearing impairments are available. There is a summer tutoring program, online tutoring, and several tutoring centers.

Campus Safety and Security: Measures include 24-hour foot and vehicle patrol, emergency notification system, self-defense education, and security escort services. There are emergency telephones, lighted pathways/sidewalks, night security in dorms, card access to dorm floors, and transportation on request.

Programs of Study: Marywood confers B.A., B.S., B.B.A., B.F.A., B.M., B.S.N., and B.S.W. degrees. Master's and doctoral degrees are also awarded. Bachelor's degrees are awarded in BIOLOGICAL SCIENCE (biology/biological science and biotechnology), BUSINESS (accounting, banking and finance, business administration and management, hospitality management services, international business management, marketing/retailing/merchandising, and retailing), COMMUNICATIONS AND THE ARTS (advertising, arts administration/management, broadcasting, ceramic art and design, communications, digital communications, dramatic arts, English, French, graphic design, illustration, music business management, music performance, musical theater, painting, photography, sculpture, Spanish, studio art, and theater management), COMPUTER AND PHYSICAL SCIENCE (information sciences and systems, mathematics, and science), EDUCATION (art education, athletic training, dance education, early childhood education, education of the deaf and hearing impaired, elementary education, English education, foreign languages education, mathematics education, music education, physical education, science education, secondary education, social science education, special education, and teaching English as a second/foreign language (TESOL/TEFOL)), ENGINEERING AND ENVIRONMENTAL DESIGN (architecture, aviation administration/management, environmental design, environmental science, and interior design), HEALTH PROFESSIONS (art therapy, health care administration, health science, medical technology, music therapy, nursing, premedicine, preosteopathy, and speech pathology/audiology), SOCIAL SCIENCE (clinical psychology, criminal justice, dietetics, family/consumer studies, gerontology, history, industrial and organizational psychology, philosophy, physical fitness/movement, political science/government, prelaw, psychology, religion, social science, social work, and sociology). Art, business, and science are the strongest academically.

Required: To graduate, students must complete a liberal arts core requirement consisting of religious studies, philosophy, math, science, psychology, history, social science, world literature, foreign language, and fine arts. Additional course requirements include speech, writing, and phys ed. Students must have a GPA of 2.0, with 2.33 in the major, although some programs require a higher GPA. A minimum of 126 credits must be earned, 60 of which must be taken at Marywood. Half of the major credits, the total of which varies by major, must be taken at Marywood.

Special: Marywood offers cross-registration with the University of Scranton, internships, study abroad, accelerated degree programs in dietetics and social work, dual majors, and student-designed majors. Students may earn credit for life, military, and work experience. There are 23 national honor societies, a freshman honors program, and 18 departmental honors programs.

Faculty/Classroom: 44% of faculty are male; 56% are female. No introductory courses are taught by graduate students. The average class size in an introductory lecture is 21; in a laboratory, 16; and in a regular course, 19.

Admissions: 72% of the 2009-2010 applicants were accepted. The SAT scores for the 2009-2010 freshman class were: Critical Reading--35% below 500, 48% between 500 and 599, 16% between 600 and 700, and 1% above 700; Math--37% below 500, 47% between 500 and 599, 14% between 600 and 700, and 2% above 700. 45% of the current freshmen were in the top fifth of their class; 75% were in the top two fifths. 5 freshmen graduated first in their class.

Requirements: The SAT is required. The ACT is recommended. In addition, applicants are expected to be graduates of an accredited secondary school or have the GED. A minimum of 16 academic credits is re-

quired, including 4 in English, 3 each in social studies and science (1 as lab), and 2 in math. A letter of support is required in selected majors, as is a portfolio or an audition where appropriate. A personal interview is strongly recommended. A GPA of 2.5 is required. AP and CLEP credits are accepted. Important factors in the admissions decision are advanced placement or honors courses, extracurricular activities record, and leadership record.

Procedure: Freshmen are admitted to all sessions. Entrance exams should be taken in the junior year or the senior year before February 1. There are early admissions, deferred admissions, and rolling admissions plans. Application deadlines are open. The fall 2009 application fee was $35. Applications are accepted on-line.

Transfer: 162 transfer students enrolled in 2008-2009. SAT or ACT scores are required of transfer applicants who have earned fewer than 12 college credits; both secondary school and college transcripts are required. Transfer students are required to have earned a minimum GPA of 2.5 at the college most recently attended (3.0 minimum for some majors). A grade of C is the minimum requirement for transfer of academic credit. The SAT is required for nursing transfer students. 46 credits required for the bachelor's degree must be completed at Marywood.

Visiting: There are regularly scheduled orientations for prospective students, including a campus tour, meetings with an admissions counselor and financial aid counselor, an appointment with an academic advisor, and a full summer orientation program for first-year students. There are guides for informal visits, and visitors may sit in on classes and stay overnight. To schedule a visit, contact the Office of University Admissions.

Financial Aid: In 2009-2010, the average freshman award was $27,131. Need-based scholarships or need-based grants averaged $18,572 ($39,223 maximum); need-based self-help aid (loans and jobs) averaged $11,188 ($37,760 maximum); and other non-need-based awards and non-need-based scholarships averaged $18,798 ($34,519 maximum). 40% of undergraduate students work part-time. Average annual earnings from campus work are $2000. The FAFSA and the college's own financial statement are required. The priority date for freshman financial aid applications for fall entry is February 15.

International Students: The school actively recruits these students. They must take the TOEFL, with a minimum score of 530 on the paper-based TOEFL (PBT) or 71 on the Internet-based version (iBT), or the IELTS. They must also take the SAT or ACT. for applicants whose native language is English.

Computers: Wireless access is available. The library offers 18 wireless laptops for sign-out. Wireless access is available in nearly all major buildings. More than 600 students own computers and are connected to the campus network in their dorm rooms. All students may access the system 24 hours per day. There are no time limits and no fees. It is strongly recommended that all students have a personal computer.

Graduates: From July 1, 2008 to June 30, 2009, 400 bachelor's degrees were awarded. The most popular majors were health professions and related sciences (22%), education (18%), and visual and performing arts (17%). In an average class, 51% graduate in 4 years or less, 59% graduate in 5 years or less, and 69% graduate in 6 years or less. Of the 2008 graduating class, 30% were enrolled in graduate school within 6 months of graduation and 61% were employed.

Admissions Contact: Christian DiGregorio, Director of University Admissions. A campus DVD is available.
E-mail: *yourfuture@marywood.edu* Web: *www.marywood.edu*

MERCYHURST COLLEGE   B-1
Erie, PA 16546   (814) 824-3125
                                    (800) 825-1926; (814) 824-2071

Full-time: 1350 men, 1950 women	**Faculty:** IIB, --$
Part-time: 120 men, 325 women	**Ph.Ds:** n/av
Graduate: 140 men, 140 women	**Student/Faculty:** n/av
Year: varies, summer session	**Tuition:** $16,346
Application Deadline: open	**Room & Board:** $9195
Freshman Class: n/av	
SAT or ACT: required	**COMPETITIVE**

Mercyhurst College, established in 1926, is a private, nonprofit institution affiliated with the Roman Catholic Church. The college offers undergraduate degrees in the arts, business, health science, liberal arts, religious studies, and teacher preparation as well as a degree-directed program for the learning disabled. There is 1 undergraduate school and 1 graduate school. Enrollment figures in the above capsule and figures in this profile are approximate. In addition to regional accreditation, Mercyhurst has baccalaureate program accreditation with ADA and CSWE. The library contains 165,644 volumes, 50,631 microform items, and 9309 audio/video tapes/CDs/DVDs, and subscribes to 848 periodicals including electronic. Computerized library services include interlibrary loans and database searching. Special learning facilities include a learning resource center, art gallery, planetarium, radio station, TV station, northwestern Pennsylvania historical archives, and archeological institute. The 88-acre campus is in a suburban area within Erie. Including any residence halls, there are 44 buildings.

Student Life: 60% of undergraduates are from Pennsylvania. Others are from 37 states, 14 foreign countries, and Canada. 76% are from public schools. 91% are white. 53% are Catholic; 21% Protestant; 18% claim no religious affiliation. The average age of freshmen is 18; all undergraduates, 26. 20% do not continue beyond their first year; 62% remain to graduate.

Housing: 1718 students can be accommodated in college housing, which includes single-sex and coed dorms, on-campus apartments, and married student housing. On-campus housing is guaranteed for all 4 years. 65% of students live on campus; of those, 91% remain on campus on weekends. Upperclassmen may keep cars.

Activities: There are no fraternities or sororities. There are 49 groups on campus, including art, band, cheerleading, choir, chorus, communications, computers, dance, debate, drama, ethnic, film, gay, honors, international, jazz band, literary magazine, musical theater, newspaper, opera, orchestra, pep band, photography, political, professional, radio and TV, religious, social, social service, and student government. Popular campus events include Activities Day and winter and spring formals.

Sports: There are 13 intercollegiate sports for men and 12 for women, and 9 intramural sports for men and 9 for women. Facilities include indoor crew tanks, football, field hockey, lacrosse, and soccer fields, an ice hockey rink/arena, Nautilus facilities, a free-weight room, a baseball/softball complex, a training room, and a basketball arena.

Disabled Students: 90% of the campus is accessible. Facilities include wheelchair ramps, elevators, special parking, specially equipped restrooms, and lowered drinking fountains.

Services: Counseling and information services are available, as is tutoring in every subject. There is remedial math, reading, and writing.

Campus Safety and Security: Measures include 24-hour foot and vehicle patrol and self-defense education. There are shuttle buses, emergency telephones, lighted pathways/sidewalks, and a 24-hour security camera surveillance system.

Programs of Study: Mercyhurst confers B.A., B.S., and B.M. degrees. Associates and master's degrees are also awarded. Bachelor's degrees are awarded in BIOLOGICAL SCIENCE (biochemistry and biology/biological science), BUSINESS (accounting, banking and finance, business administration and management, fashion merchandising, hotel/motel and restaurant management, insurance and risk management, management information systems, and marketing/retailing/merchandising), COMMUNICATIONS AND THE ARTS (advertising, broadcasting, communications, dance, English, graphic design, journalism, languages, music, musical theater, public relations, and studio art), COMPUTER AND PHYSICAL SCIENCE (chemistry, earth science, geology, mathematics, web services, and web technology), EDUCATION (art education, athletic training, business education, early childhood education, elementary education, home economics education, mathematics education, music education, science education, secondary education, social science education, and special education), ENGINEERING AND ENVIRONMENTAL DESIGN (environmental science and interior design), HEALTH PROFESSIONS (art therapy, medical laboratory technology, predentistry, premedicine, preosteopathy, prepharmacy, preveterinary science, and sports medicine), SOCIAL SCIENCE (anthropology, archeology, criminal justice, family/consumer studies, forensic studies, history, philosophy, political science/government, prelaw, psychology, religion, religious education, social work, and sociology). Archeology/anthropology, intelligence studies, and sports medicine are the strongest academically. Business, education, and sports medicine are the largest.

Required: To graduate, students must complete the core curriculum, which includes English, math, science, religion, philosophy, history, and a computer course. Distribution requirements include American history, cultural appreciation, human behavior, and ethics. A minimum GPA of 2.0 is required, with a 2.5 in the major, and a minimum total of 123 credit hours. The number of credit hours in the major varies, with a minimum of 30. A thesis is necessary for history and English majors.

Special: Mercyhurst offers cross-registration with Gannon University, internships in all majors through the co-op office, and study abroad in London and Dublin. Dual and student-designed majors, credit for life, military, or work experience, nondegree study, work-study, and a pass/fail grading option are also available. There are 7 national honor societies, a freshman honors program, and 4 departmental honors programs.

Faculty/Classroom: 57% of faculty are male; 43% are female. All teach undergraduates, and 30% do research. No introductory courses are taught by graduate students. The average class size in an introductory lecture is 35; in a laboratory, 12; and in a regular course, 25.

Requirements: The SAT or ACT is required. In addition, applicants must graduate from an accredited secondary school or have a GED. 16 academic credits are required, including 4 years of English, 3 each of math and social studies, and 2 each of history, science, and a foreign language. Interviews are recommended. Art applicants must submit portfolios; auditions are required of music and dance applicants. Mercyhurst requires applicants to be in the upper 50% of their class. A GPA of 2.8 is required. AP and CLEP credits are accepted. Important factors in the admissions decision are recommendations by alumni, evidence of special talent, and personality/intangible qualities.

Procedure: Freshmen are admitted to all sessions. Entrance exams should be taken during the spring of the junior year. There are deferred admissions and rolling admissions plans. Application deadlines are open. Application fee is $30. Notification is sent on a rolling basis. Applications are accepted on-line.

Transfer: 90 transfer students enrolled in a recent year. A minimum GPA of 2.0 on previous college work is required. 45 of 123 credits required for the bachelor's degree must be completed at Mercyhurst.

Visiting: There are regularly scheduled orientations for prospective students, including tours, class visits, faculty meetings, and interviews with financial aid and admissions counselors. There are guides for informal visits, and visitors may stay overnight. To schedule a visit, contact the Admissions Office.

Financial Aid: The FAFSA is required. Check with the school for current deadlines.

International Students: The school actively recruits these students. They must take the TOEFL and also take the SAT or ACT.

Computers: The campus is 90% wireless, and there are labs in the library and the student union. Access is available for all students in residence halls. All students may access the system 24 hours a day, 7 days a week. There are no time limits. There is a fee.

Admissions Contact: Christopher Coons, Director of Admissions. A campus DVD is available. E-Mail: ccoons@mercyhurst.edu Web: www.mercyhurst.edu

MESSIAH COLLEGE   D-3
Grantham, PA 17027

(717) 691-6000
(800) 233-4220; (717) 796-5374

Full-time: 1025 men, 1750 women	Faculty: IIB, -$
Part-time: 25 men, 35 women	Ph.Ds: n/av
Graduate: none	Student/Faculty: 16 to 1
Year: semesters, summer session	Tuition: $26,700
Application Deadline: open	Room & Board: $7490
Freshman Class: n/av	
SAT or ACT: required	VERY COMPETITIVE

Messiah College, founded in 1909, is a private Christian college of the liberal and applied arts and sciences. The college is committed to the evangelical spirit rooted in the Anabaptist, Pietist, and Wesleyan traditions. There are 5 undergraduate schools. Enrollment figures in the above capsule and figures in this profile are approximate. In addition to regional accreditation, Messiah has baccalaureate program accreditation with ABET, ADA, CSWE, NASAD, and NASM. The library contains 297,257 volumes, 119,622 microform items, and 20,519 audio/video tapes/CDs/DVDs, and subscribes to 27,958 periodicals including electronic. Computerized library services include interlibrary loans, database searching, and Internet access. Special learning facilities include a learning resource center, art gallery, natural history museum, and radio station. The 471-acre campus is in a small town 12 miles southwest of Harrisburg. Including any residence halls, there are 52 buildings.

Student Life: 54% of undergraduates are from Pennsylvania. Others are from 37 states, 23 foreign countries, and Canada. 75% are from public schools. 91% are white. 98% are Protestant. The average age of freshmen is 18; all undergraduates, 20. 14% do not continue beyond their first year; 75% remain to graduate.

Housing: 2383 students can be accommodated in college housing, which includes single-sex and coed dorms, on-campus apartments, and off-campus apartments. In addition, there are special-interest houses. On-campus housing is guaranteed for all 4 years. 85% of students live on campus; of those, 70% remain on campus on weekends. Alcohol is not permitted. All students may keep cars.

Activities: There are no fraternities or sororities. There are 63 groups on campus, including art, band, cheerleading, choir, chorale, chorus, dance, drama, environmental, ethnic, film, honors, international, jazz band, literary magazine, musical theater, newspaper, orchestra, pep band, political, professional, radio and TV, religious, social, social service, student government, symphony, and yearbook. Popular campus events include cultural series, traveling music ensembles, and theater productions.

Sports: There are 10 intercollegiate sports for men and 10 for women, and 10 intramural sports for men and 10 for women. Facilities include indoor and outdoor tracks, a pool with separate diving well, wrestling and gymnastics areas, a weight room, numerous playing fields, and courts for racquetball, basketball, and tennis. The campus center provides additional recreational facilities.

Disabled Students: 80% of the campus is accessible. Facilities include wheelchair ramps, elevators, special parking, specially equipped restrooms, special class scheduling, and lowered drinking fountains.

Services: Counseling and information services are available, as is tutoring in most subjects. There is a reader service for the blind, and remedial math, reading, and writing. There is supplemental instruction for "high-risk" courses and a math help room.

Campus Safety and Security: Measures include 24-hour foot and vehicle patrol, emergency notification system, self-defense education, and security escort services. There are emergency telephones and lighted pathways/sidewalks.

Programs of Study: Messiah confers B.A., B.S., B.S.E., B.S.N., and B.S.W degrees. Bachelor's degrees are awarded in AGRICULTURE (environmental studies), BIOLOGICAL SCIENCE (biochemistry, biology/biological science, and nutrition), BUSINESS (accounting, business administration and management, entrepreneurial studies, international business management, management information systems, marketing/retailing/merchandising, personnel management, and sports management), COMMUNICATIONS AND THE ARTS (art history and appreciation, arts administration/management, broadcasting, communications, dramatic arts, English, French, German, journalism, music, Spanish, and studio art), COMPUTER AND PHYSICAL SCIENCE (chemistry, computer science, mathematics, and physics), EDUCATION (art education, athletic training, early childhood education, elementary education, English education, environmental education, foreign languages education, mathematics education, music education, physical education, recreation education, science education, and social studies education), ENGINEERING AND ENVIRONMENTAL DESIGN (engineering and environmental science), HEALTH PROFESSIONS (exercise science and nursing), SOCIAL SCIENCE (biopsychology, criminal justice, dietetics, economics, family/consumer studies, history, human development, humanities, interdisciplinary studies, ministries, philosophy, political science/government, psychology, social work, sociology, Spanish studies, and theological studies). Nursing, elementary education, and biology are the largest.

Required: All students must complete at least 126 credits with a minimum GPA of 2.0. The last 30 credits must be taken at Messiah College and a minimum of 12 credits must be in the major. For general education requirements, students must take 9 credits each in Christian faith, math, natural sciences, humanities and arts, and languages and cultures; 6 credits each in Christian faith, social sciences and history, and interdisciplinary studies; 3 credits in first-year seminar, oral communications, a writing enrichment course, 3 credits from ethics, world views or pluralism, and contemporary society; and 2 courses health/phys ed.

Special: Students may cross-register at Temple University in Philadelphia. Off-campus study is available through Brethren Colleges Abroad, at Jerusalem University College at Oxford University, in Thailand, and through Latin American, Central American, Middle East, and Russian studies programs, among others. Off-campus options within the United States include the American and Urban Studies programs, the AuSable Institute of Environmental Studies, Los Angeles Film Studies, Oregon Extension, and others. Students may also spend a semester or a year at any of 12 other Christian Consortium colleges in a student exchange program. Numerous internships, practicums, and ministry opportunities are available. There are 7 national honor societies, a freshman honors program, and 17 departmental honors programs.

Faculty/Classroom: 63% of faculty are male; 37% are female. All teach undergraduates. No introductory courses are taught by graduate students. The average class size in an introductory lecture is 27; in a laboratory, 18; and in a regular course, 24.

Requirements: The SAT or ACT is required for some programs. Applicants graduating in the top 20% of their class have a scoreless option that requires an interview. Applicants must have graduated from an accredited high school or the equivalent. Secondary preparation of students who enroll usually includes 4 units in English, 3 or 4 in math, 3 each in natural science, social studies, and foreign languages, and 4 in academic electives. Students who enroll are usually in the top one third of their class and have a B average or better. A campus visit with an interview/information session is recommended. Potential music majors must audition. AP and CLEP credits are accepted. Important factors in the admissions decision are leadership record, recommendations by school officials, and advanced placement or honors courses.

Procedure: Freshmen are admitted fall and spring. Entrance exams should be taken in the spring of the junior year. There is a rolling admissions plan. Application deadlines are open. Application fee is $30. Notification is sent on a rolling basis. Applications are accepted on-line ($20 fee waived if received prior to November 15). A waiting list is maintained.

Transfer: 91 transfer students enrolled in a recent year. Transfer applicants should have earned a 2.5 GPA in at least 30 college credits. The college prefers that applicants also have composite SAT or ACT scores and that they seek a campus visit. Students with fewer than 30 credits in college should submit a high school transcript as well. 30 of 126 credits required for the bachelor's degree must be completed at Messiah.

Visiting: There are regularly scheduled orientations for prospective students, including a campus tour, academic and career advising, and a financial aid information session. There are guides for informal visits; visitors may sit in on classes and stay overnight. To schedule a visit, contact Ellen Shaffer at *eshaffer@messiah.edu*.

Financial Aid: In a recent year, 99% of all full-time freshmen and 96% of continuing full-time students received some form of financial aid. 71% of all full-time freshmen and 68% of continuing full-time students received need-based aid. The average freshmen award was $19,433. 58% of undergraduate students work part-time. Average annual earnings

from campus work are $1898. The average financial indebtedness of a recent graduate was $33,283. Messiah is a member of CSS. The FAFSA is required. Check with the school for current deadlines.

International Students: There were 59 international students enrolled in a recent year. The school actively recruits these students. They must take the TOEFL and also take the SAT or ACT.

Computers: Wireless access is available. All students may access the system 24 hours a day. There are no time limits and no fees.

Graduates: In a recent year, 668 bachelor's degrees were awarded. The most popular majors were nursing (7%), elementary education (7%), and English (5%). In an average class, 71% graduate in 4 years or less and 75% graduate in 5 years or less. Of a recent graduating class, 17% were enrolled in graduate school within 6 months of graduation, and 80% were employed.

Admissions Contact: John Chopka, Vice President of Enrollment Management. A campus DVD is available. E-Mail: *admiss@messiah.edu* Web: *www.messiah.edu*

MILLERSVILLE UNIVERSITY OF PENNSYLVANIA E-4

Millersville, PA 17551-0302 (717) 872-3371; (717) 871-2147

Full-time: 2901 men, 3788 women	Faculty: 305; IIA, +$
Part-time: 321 men, 349 women	Ph.D.s: 95%
Graduate: 264 men, 804 women	Student/Faculty: 22 to 1
Year: 4-1-4, summer session	Tuition: $7147 ($15,583)
Application Deadline: open	Room & Board: $7766
Freshman Class: 7241 applied, 3849 accepted, 1333 enrolled	
SAT CR/M/W: 520/540/510	COMPETITIVE

Millersville University, founded as Lancaster County Normal School in 1855, is a public institution offering undergraduate and graduate programs in liberal arts and sciences and education. There are 3 undergraduate schools and 1 graduate school. In addition to regional accreditation, Millersville has baccalaureate program accreditation with ABET, ACBSP, CSAB, CSWE, NASAD, NASM, NCATE, and NLN. The library contains 603,224 volumes, 551,089 microform items, and 5,909 audio/video tapes/CDs/DVDs, and subscribes to 16,712 periodicals including electronic. Computerized library services include interlibrary loans, database searching, Internet access, and laptop Internet portals. Special learning facilities include a learning resource center, art gallery, radio station, TV station, foreign language lab, weather station, and teleconferencing center. The 250-acre campus is in a small town 5 miles west of Lancaster. Including any residence halls, there are 83 buildings.

Student Life: 95% of undergraduates are from Pennsylvania. Others are from 20 states, 53 foreign countries, and Canada. 80% are white. The average age of freshmen is 19; all undergraduates, 21. 19% do not continue beyond their first year; 62% remain to graduate.

Housing: 2284 students can be accommodated in college housing, which includes coed dorms, on-campus apartments, and off-campus apartments. In addition, there are honors houses, center for service learning and leadership, international student house, and freshman resident hall. On-campus housing is guaranteed for the freshman year only, is available on a first-come, first-served basis, and is available on a lottery system for upperclassmen. 70% of students commute. Alcohol is not permitted. Upperclassmen may keep cars.

Activities: 4% of men belong to 9 national fraternities; 5% of women belong to 2 local and 8 national sororities. There are 120 groups on campus, including art, band, cheerleading, choir, chorus, dance, drama, ethnic, film, gay, honors, international, jazz band, literary magazine, marching band, musical theater, newspaper, orchestra, pep band, political, professional, radio and TV, religious, social, social service, student government, and symphony. Popular campus events include Organizational Outbreak, Superfest, and Wellness Week.

Sports: There are 9 intercollegiate sports for men and 11 for women, and 14 intramural sports for men and 14 for women. Facilities include a football stadium, 2 pools, 2 gyms, 2 fitness centers, a dance studio, a ropes course, wrestling and weight rooms, basketball, volleyball, tennis, and badminton courts, and indoor running track.

Disabled Students: 85% of the campus is accessible. Facilities include wheelchair ramps, elevators, special parking, specially equipped restrooms, special class scheduling, lowered drinking fountains, lowered telephones, and special housing.

Services: Counseling and information services are available, as is tutoring in most subjects. There is a reader service for the blind, and remedial math and writing. Every effort is made to tailor a tutoring program to individual needs. Note takers, interpreters, and some physical aids/ other specialized equipment are provided, as available.

Campus Safety and Security: Measures include 24-hour foot and vehicle patrol, emergency notification system, self-defense education, and security escort services. There are shuttle buses, emergency telephones, lighted pathways/sidewalks, timely warning messages sent via e-mail and text messages, and regularly scheduled crime awareness programs.

Programs of Study: Millersville confers B.A., B.S., B.F.A., B.S.Ed., and B.S.N. degrees. Associate and master's degrees are also awarded. Bachelor's degrees are awarded in BIOLOGICAL SCIENCE (biology/

biological science), BUSINESS (business administration and management), COMMUNICATIONS AND THE ARTS (art, communications, English, French, German, music, and Spanish), COMPUTER AND PHYSICAL SCIENCE (atmospheric sciences and meteorology, chemistry, computer science, earth science, geology, mathematics, oceanography, and physics), EDUCATION (art education, elementary education, music education, social studies education, special education, and technical education), ENGINEERING AND ENVIRONMENTAL DESIGN (industrial engineering technology and occupational safety and health), HEALTH PROFESSIONS (nursing), SOCIAL SCIENCE (anthropology, economics, geography, history, international studies, philosophy, political science/government, psychology, social work, and sociology). Elementary education and special education are the strongest academically. Early childhood education, language and literacy education, and business administration are the largest.

Required: All students must complete at least 120 hours, demonstrating proficiency in mathematics and English and maintaining a minimum 2.0 GPA. Students must complete the general education program and complete specific courses in physical education and fundamentals of speech

Special: Numerous co-op and internship programs, including student teaching opportunities, are available. Millersville has exchange agreements with Franklin and Marshall College, Lancaster Theological Seminary, and Wallops Island Consortium, as well as 3-2 chemical and physical engineering programs with Pennsylvania State University and the University of Southern California. Study abroad is offered in Australia, Germany, England, Japan, Scotland, Chile, Spain, France, Northern Ireland, and South Africa. Dual majors and accelerated degrees are possible in most disciplines. There are 11 national honor societies, a freshman honors program, and 15 departmental honors programs.

Faculty/Classroom: 51% of faculty are male; 49% are female. All teach undergraduates. No introductory courses are taught by graduate students. The average class size in an introductory lecture, 25, in a laboratory, 35, and in a regular course, 24.

Admissions: 53% of the 2009-2010 applicants were accepted. The SAT scores for the 2009-2010 freshman class were: Critical Reading--33% below 500, 49% between 500 and 599, 17% between 600 and 700, and 1% above 700; Math--28% below 500, 49% between 500 and 599, 22% between 600 and 700, and 1% above 700; Writing--40% below 500, 46% between 500 and 599, 13% between 600 and 700, and 1% above 700. 51% of the current freshmen were in the top fifth of their class; 66% were in the top two fifths.

Requirements: The SAT is required, the ACT is accepted. Applicants must hold a high school diploma or GED. The distribution of high school course units include: 4 units of English, 3 units each in math, science, and social studies, and 2 units of history. Auditions are required for the dance and theater programs. Millersville requires applicants to be in the upper 40% of their class. A GPA of 2.0 is required. AP and CLEP credits are accepted. Important factors in the admissions decision are evidence of special talent, recommendations by school officials, and leadership record.

Procedure: Freshmen are admitted to all sessions. Entrance exams should be taken in the spring of the junior year. There are deferred admissions and rolling admissions plans. Application deadlines are open. The fall 2009 application fee was $50. Notification is sent on a rolling basis. Applications are accepted on-line. 862 applicants were on a recent waiting list, 65 were accepted.

Transfer: 504 transfer students enrolled in 2008-2009. All applicants must submit college transcripts and a statement of good standing from prior institution(s). Preference is given to students with 30 or more transferable credits with a 2.5 GPA or higher. Preference is given to graduates of in-state community colleges or transfers from other Pennsylvania State of Higher Education schools. Applicants must have at least a 2.0 college GPA. 30 of 120 credits required for the bachelor's degree must be completed at Millersville.

Visiting: There are regularly scheduled orientations for prospective students, including tours of art/humanities facilities, athletic facilities, science and social science facilities, and student service facilities. There are guides for informal visits and visitors may sit in on classes. To schedule a visit, contact Welcome Center Coordinator at (717) 872-3371.

Financial Aid: In 2009-2009, 82% of all full-time freshmen and 73% of continuing full-time students received some form of financial aid. 57% of all full-time freshmen and 51% of continuing full-time students received need-based aid. The average freshman award was $10,157. Need-based scholarships or need-based grants averaged $2,828 ($20,617 maximum); need-based self-help aid (loans and jobs) averaged $6,045 ($31,644 maximum); non-need based athletic scholarships averaged $57 ($13,000 maximum); and other non-need based awards and non-need based scholarships averaged $1,284 ($21,825 maximum). 25% of undergraduate students work part-time. Average annual earnings from campus work are $1496. The average financial indebtedness of the 2009 graduate was $22,408. The FAFSA is required. The deadline for filing freshman financial aid applications for fall entry is March 15.

International Students: There are 40 international students enrolled. The school actively recruits these students. They must take the TOEFL with a minimum score of 500 on the paper-based TOEFL (PBT) or 65 on the Internet-based version (iBT). They must also take the SAT.

Computers: Wireless access is available. All students have access to their supplied services: the my'Ville Portal, Marauder e-mail, and Banner Max. As appropriate, students have access to the Blackboard instructional support system and specialized labs/software/systems used for specific academic programs. In addition to full Internet access (wired and wireless)for their personally owned computers, students have access to to 15 general-purpose labs equipped with a mix of Windows and Macintosh computers. All students may access the system 24 hours, 7 days a week. There are no time limits and no fees. It is strongly recommended that all students have a personal computer.

Graduates: From July 1, 2008 to June 30, 2009, 1427 bachelor's degrees were awarded. The most popular majors were elementary education (17%), business administration (14%), and psychology (9%). 75 companies recruited on campus in 2008-2009. In an average class, 37% graduate in 4 years or less, 57% graduate in 5 years or less, and 62% graduate in 6 years or less.

Admissions Contact: Douglas Zander, Provost for Enrollment Management. E-Mail: *admissions@millersville.edu* Web: *www.millersville.edu/~admit/*

MISERICORDIA UNIVERSITY
College Misericordia
B-2

Dallas, PA 18612

(570) 674-6400
(866) 262-6363; (570) 675-2441

Full-time: 534 men, 1131 women	Faculty: 94; IIB, -$
Part-time: 161 men, 542 women	Ph.D.s: 79%
Graduate: 108 men, 260 women	Student/Faculty: 17 to 1
Year: semesters, , summer session	Tuition: $24,050
Application Deadline:	Room & Board: $10,050
Freshman Class: 1289 applied, 1060 accepted, 371 enrolled	
SAT CR/M: 500/510	ACT: 22 COMPETITIVE

Misericordia University, founded in 1924 by the Sisters of Mercy, is a private liberal arts institution affiliated with the Roman Catholic Church and offers professional programs in health-related fields. There are 3 undergraduate schools and one graduate school. In addition to regional accreditation, has baccalaureate program accreditation with ASLA, CAHEA, CSWE, and NLN. The library contains 79,503 volumes, 7,821 microform items, and 3,479 audio/video tapes/CDs/DVDs, and subscribes to 355 periodicals including electronic. Computerized library services include interlibrary loans, database searching, Internet access, and laptop Internet portals. Special learning facilities include a learning resource center, art gallery, radio station, and TV station. The 120-acre campus is in a suburban area 9 miles north of Wilkes-Barre. Including any residence halls, there are 16 buildings.

Student Life: 79% of undergraduates are from Pennsylvania. Others are from 19 states, 1 foreign countries, and Canada. 86% are from public schools. 95% are white. 59% are Catholic; 26% Protestant. The average age of freshmen is 18; all undergraduates, 25. 15% do not continue beyond their first year.

Housing: 850 students can be accommodated in college housing, which includes coed dorms. In addition, there are special-interest houses. On-campus housing is guaranteed for the freshman year only, is available on a first-come, first-served basis, and is available on a lottery system for upperclassmen. 52% of students live on campus; of those, 50% remain on campus on weekends. Upperclassmen may keep cars.

Activities: There are no fraternities or sororities. There are 23 groups on campus, including , cheerleading, choir, chorale, chorus, drama, ethnic, honors, international, literary magazine, musical threater, newspaper, political, professional, radio and TV, religious, social service, and student government. Popular campus events include Winter Snowball dance.

Sports: There are 9 intercollegiate sports for men and 11 for women, and 14 intramural sports for men and 14 for women. Facilities include the sports and health center, a 7800-square-foot multipurpose facility with a competitive wood floor, 3 cross courts, a synthetic surfaced indoor running track, and a 6-lane NCAA competitive pool with observation deck, and the athletic complex and field, a 23-acre facility for field hockey, soccer, lacrosse, and track. A 6-lane synthetic track encircles the field.

Disabled Students: 95% of the campus is accessible. Facilities include wheelchair ramps, elevators, special parking, specially equipped rest rooms, special class scheduling, and lowered drinking fountains.

Services: Counseling and information services are available, as is tutoring in most subjects. There is a reader service for the blind, and remedial math and reading. Services for students with disabilities are provided through the Alternative Learners Program.

Campus Safety and Security: Measures include 24-hour foot and vehicle patrol, emergency notification system, and security escort services. There are emergency telephones, lighted pathways/sidewalks, and access controls for dorms/residences.

Programs of Study: confers B.A., B.S., B.S.N., and B.S.W. degrees. Master's and doctoral degrees are also awarded. Bachelor's degrees are awarded in BIOLOGICAL SCIENCE (biochemistry and biology/biological science), BUSINESS (accounting, business administration and management, marketing/retailing/merchandising, and sports management), COMMUNICATIONS AND THE ARTS (communications and English), COMPUTER AND PHYSICAL SCIENCE (chemistry, computer science, information sciences and systems, and mathematics), EDUCATION (elementary education and special education), HEALTH PROFESSIONS (medical laboratory technology, nursing, occupational therapy, physical therapy, radiograph medical technology, and speech therapy), SOCIAL SCIENCE (history, interdisciplinary studies, liberal arts/general studies, philosophy, psychology, and social work). Occupational therapy and physical therapy is the strongest academically. Nursing, physical and occupational therapy, and elementary education are the largest.

Required: To graduate, students must earn a minimum of 120 credits with at least 60 credits in the major. The required 48-credit core curriculum includes courses in behavioral science, English literature, fine arts, history, math, philosophy, religious studies, and natural science. Two courses must be writing intensive. A minimum GPA of 2.0 is required.

Special: Students may cross-register with King's College and Wilkes University. The college offers internships in all majors, work-study programs, study abroad, an accelerated degree program in business and nursing for adult students, student-designed majors, and dual majors in elementary and special education, and math and computer science. Credit may be granted for life, military, and work experience. Nondegree study is also available. The college offers an alternative learner's project, which accepts a limited number of learning disabled students each year. There are 5 national honor societies, a freshman honors program, and 1 departmental honors program.

Faculty/Classroom: 46% of faculty are male; 54% are female. 98% teach undergraduates, and 10% do both. No introductory courses are taught by graduate students. The average class size in an introductory lecture is 22; in a laboratory is 14; and in a regular course is 19.

Admissions: 82% of the 2009-2010 applicants were accepted. The SAT scores for the 2009-2010 freshman class were: Critical Reading--42% below 500, 48% between 500 and 599, 9% between 600 and 700, and 1 above 700; Math--42% below 500, 44% between 500 and 599, 17% between 600 and 700, and 1 above 700. The ACT scores were 30% below 21, 30% between 21 and 23, 30% between 24 and 26, 10% between 27 and 28, and 0% above 28. 41% of the current freshmen were in the top fifth of their class; 69% were in the top two fifths. 3 freshmen graduated first in their class.

Requirements: The SAT is required. In addition, applicants must graduate from an accredited secondary school or have a GED. 16 Carnegie units must be earned, and students must complete 3 years each in English, math, history, and science, and 2 to 3 years in social studies. requires applicants to be in the upper 50% of their class. A GPA of 2.0 is required. AP and CLEP credits are accepted. Important factors in the admissions decision are advanced placement or honors courses, leadership record, and personality/intangible qualities.

Procedure: Freshmen are admitted fall and spring. Entrance exams should be taken during the junior year. There are deferred admissions and rolling admissions plans. Application deadlines are open. Application fee is $25. Applications are accepted on-line. 50 applicants were on a recent waiting list.

Transfer: 173 transfer students enrolled in 2008-2009. Applicants must have a minimum GPA of 2.0. Requirements may be higher for selected majors. 30 of 120 credits required for the bachelor's degree must be completed at .

Visiting: There are regularly scheduled orientations for prospective students, including meetings with admissions and financial aid counselors, a tour of the campus, and optional meetings with faculty and coaches. There are guides for informal visits, visitors may sit in on classes, and stay overnight. To schedule a visit, contact the Admissions Office at (570) 675-4449.

Financial Aid: In 2009-2010, 99% of all full-time freshmen and 98% of continuing full-time students received some form of financial aid. 78% of all full-time freshmen and 75% of continuing full-time students received need-based aid. The average freshmen award was $22,832, with $5,359 ($22,850 maximum) from need-based scholarships or need-based grants; $2,385 ($5,500 maximum) from need-based self-help aid (loans and jobs); $7,650 ($30,350 maximum) from other non-need-based awards and non-need-based scholarships; and $7,438 from other forms of aid. 14% of undergraduate students work part-time. Average annual earnings from campus work are $1479. The average financial indebtedness of the 2009 graduate was $26,151. is a member of CSS. The FAFSA and the college's own financial statement are required. The priority date for freshman financial aid applications for fall entry is March 1. The deadline for filing freshman financial aid applications for fall entry is May 1.

International Students: There are 2 international students enrolled. The school actively recruits these students. They must take the TOEFL with a minimum score of 550 on the paper-based TOEFL (PBT) or 80 on the Internet-based version (iBT).

Computers: Wireless access is available. The College has 4 open computer labs with 50 computers and 3 teaching labs, in addition to 20 PCs in the residence halls. Wireless laptops are loaned to students through the library. The student center is wireless. All students may access the system. There are no time limits and no fees.

Graduates: From July 1, 2008 to June 30, 2009, 410 bachelor's degrees were awarded. The most popular majors were nursing (21%), business (14%), and elementary education (8%). In an average class, 58% graduate in 4 years or less, 67% graduate in 5 years or less, and 68% graduate in 6 years or less. Of the 2008 graduating class, 15% were enrolled in graduate school within 6 months of graduation, and 93% were employed.

Admissions Contact: Glenn Bozinski, Director of Admissions. E-Mail: *admiss@misericordia.edu* Web: *www.misericordia.edu*

MOORE COLLEGE OF ART AND DESIGN   F-3
Philadelphia, PA 19103   (215) 568-4515, ext. 1105
                (800) 523-2025, ext. 1105; (215) 568-8017

Full-time: 450 women	**Faculty:** n/av
Part-time: 100 women	**Ph.D.s:** n/av
Graduate: 100 women	**Student/Faculty:** 14 to 1
Year: semesters, summer session	**Tuition:** $29,240
Application Deadline: open	**Room & Board:** $10,930
Freshman Class: n/av	
SAT: recommended	**SPECIAL**

Moore College of Art and Design, founded in 1844, is a private (not for profit) professional and fine arts college for women. There is 1 undergraduate school and 1 graduate school. Enrollment figures in the above capsule and figures in this profile are approximate. In addition to regional accreditation, Moore has baccalaureate program accreditation with FIDER and NASAD. The library contains 34,000 volumes and subscribes to 250 periodicals including electronic. Computerized library services include interlibrary loans, database searching, and Internet access. Special learning facilities include 2 art galleries. The 4-acre campus is in an urban area in Philadelphia. Including any residence halls, there are 4 buildings.

Student Life: 61% of undergraduates are from Pennsylvania. Others are from 29 states and 7 foreign countries. 60% are from public schools. 77% are white. The average age of freshmen is 19; all undergraduates, 23. 15% do not continue beyond their first year; 55% remain to graduate.

Housing: 194 students can be accommodated in college housing, which includes dorms and off-campus apartments. On-campus housing is guaranteed for all 4 years. 70% of students commute. Alcohol is not permitted. All students may keep cars.

Activities: There are no fraternities or sororities. There are 10 groups on campus, including computers, environmental action, ethnic, film, gay, international, newspaper, professional, social service, student government, and yearbook. Popular campus events include Spring Fling.

Sports: There is no sports program at Moore. Facilities include a fitness center with a weight room.

Disabled Students: All of the campus is accessible. Facilities include wheelchair ramps, elevators, special parking, specially equipped restrooms, lowered drinking fountains, and lowered telephones.

Services: Counseling and information services are available, as is tutoring in most subjects. English as a second language is offered.

Campus Safety and Security: Measures include 24-hour foot and vehicle patrol, self-defense education, and security escort services. There are shuttle buses, emergency telephones, and lighted pathways/sidewalks.

Programs of Study: Moore confers B.F.A. degrees. Master's degrees are also awarded. Bachelor's degrees are awarded in COMMUNICATIONS AND THE ARTS (fine arts, graphic design, illustration, painting, and sculpture), EDUCATION (art education), ENGINEERING AND ENVIRONMENTAL DESIGN (interior design), SOCIAL SCIENCE (fashion design and technology). Interior design is the strongest academically. Graphic design is the largest.

Required: All students take 36 credits in basic arts, including design, drawing, color, and art history, and a liberal arts core in history, humanities, and social science. A total of 125.5 to 137 credits, with a 2.0 minimum GPA, is required for graduation. A thesis is required in some programs.

Special: Moore has long-established cooperative relationships with various employers who provide training to supplement academic studies in all majors. Dual majors, nondegree study, study abroad, and continuing education programs are offered.

Faculty/Classroom: 38% of faculty are male; 62% are female. All teach undergraduates. No introductory courses are taught by graduate students. The average class size in an introductory lecture is 20 and in a regular course, 10.

Requirements: The SAT is recommended. In addition, applicants should be graduates of accredited high schools or the equivalent, having taken 4 years of English and 2 years each of social studies, science, and math. At least 2 years of art study are also recommended. The most important part of the application is the portfolio of 8 to 12 original pieces, 6 of which should be drawings from observation. In addition, Moore strongly recommends a personal interview. A GPA of 2.5 is required. AP and CLEP credits are accepted. Important factors in the admissions decision are evidence of special talent, personality/intangible qualities, and extracurricular activities record.

Procedure: Freshmen are admitted fall and spring. There are early admissions, deferred admissions, and rolling admissions plans. Application deadlines are open. Check with the school for current application fee. Notification is sent on a rolling basis.

Transfer: Transfer applicants from non-art programs must meet freshman admission requirements. Others must submit a portfolio for review. Applicants should have at least a 2.0 GPA in previous college work and submit satisfactory SAT scores. A personal interview is required. 50 of 126 credits required for the bachelor's degree must be completed at Moore.

Visiting: There are regularly scheduled orientations for prospective students, including an open house in November. There are guides for informal visits; visitors may sit in on classes and stay overnight. To schedule a visit, contact the Admissions Office.

Financial Aid: Moore is a member of CSS. The CSS/Profile and the college's own financial statement are required. Check with the school for current deadlines.

International Students: The school actively recruits these students. They must take the TOEFL.

Computers: There are no time limits and no fees.

Admissions Contact: Heeseung Lee, Director of Admissions and Enrollment Management. E-Mail: *admiss@moore.edu*
Web: *www.moore.edu*

MORAVIAN COLLEGE   F-3
Bethlehem, PA 18018

	(610) 861-1320
	(800) 441-3191; (610) 625-7930
Full-time: 663 men, 870 women	**Faculty:** IIB, av$
Part-time: 60 men, 135 women	**Ph.D.s:** n/av
Graduate: 45 men, 90 women	**Student/Faculty:** 11 to 1
Year: semesters, summer session	**Tuition:** $31,250
Application Deadline: see profile	**Room & Board:** $8728
Freshman Class: n/av	
SAT or ACT: required	**VERY COMPETITIVE**

Moravian College, established in 1742, is a private, liberal arts institution affiliated with the Moravian Church. There are 2 undergraduate schools and 1 graduate school. Enrollment figures in the above capsule and figures in this profile are approximate. In addition to regional accreditation, Moravian has baccalaureate program accreditation with CAHEA and NASM. The library contains 263,000 volumes, 11,000 microform items, and 5385 audio/video tapes/CDs/DVDs, and subscribes to 15,415 periodicals including electronic. Computerized library services include interlibrary loans, database searching, and Internet access. Special learning facilities include a learning resource center, art gallery, and radio station. The 80-acre campus is in a suburban area 60 miles north of Philadelphia and 90 miles west of New York City. Including any residence halls, there are 127 buildings.

Student Life: 63% of undergraduates are from Pennsylvania. Others are from 20 states and 15 foreign countries. 79% are from public schools. 90% are white. 40% are Catholic; 27% Protestant; 12% claim no religious affiliation. The average age of freshmen is 18; all undergraduates, 20. 14% do not continue beyond their first year; 75% remain to graduate.

Housing: 1093 students can be accommodated in college housing, which includes single-sex and coed dorms and on-campus apartments. In addition, there are special-interest houses, fraternity houses, and sorority houses. On-campus housing is guaranteed for all 4 years. 71% of students live on campus; of those, 65% remain on campus on weekends. Upperclassmen may keep cars.

Activities: 10% of men belong to 1 local and 2 national fraternities; 22% of women belong to 4 national sororities. There are 77 groups on campus, including alumni, art, band, cheerleading, choir, chorale, chorus, communications, computers, dance, debate, drama, environmental, ethnic, gay, honors, international, jazz band, literary magazine, marching band, newspaper, orchestra, outdoor recreation, pep band, photography, political, professional, radio, religious, social, social service, and student government. Popular campus events include arts and lecture series, Christmas vesper services, and Mardi Gras dance.

Sports: There are 10 intercollegiate sports for men and 10 for women, and 11 intramural sports for men and 11 for women. Facilities include a 1200-seat gym, football, soccer, field hockey, and lacrosse fields, baseball and softball diamonds, indoor and all-weather tracks, indoor and outdoor tennis courts, a field house, a fitness room, an aerobics and dance studio, and 4 multipurpose courts.

Disabled Students: Facilities include wheelchair ramps, elevators, special parking, specially equipped restrooms, special class scheduling, lowered drinking fountains, lowered telephones, and special housing.

Services: Counseling and information services are available, as is tutoring in most subjects. There is a reader service for the blind, peer assistance, and a writing center.

Campus Safety and Security: Measures include 24-hour foot and vehicle patrol, emergency notification system, self-defense education, and security escort services. There are shuttle buses, emergency telephones, lighted pathways/sidewalks, and an ongoing crime prevention program supervised by a crime prevention officer.

Programs of Study: Moravian confers B.A., B.S., and B.Mus. degrees. Master's degrees are also awarded. Bachelor's degrees are awarded in BIOLOGICAL SCIENCE (biochemistry, biology/biological science, and neurosciences), BUSINESS (accounting, business administration and management, business economics, and international business management), COMMUNICATIONS AND THE ARTS (art history and appreciation, classics, dramatic arts, English, French, German, graphic design, music, Spanish, and studio art), COMPUTER AND PHYSICAL SCIENCE (chemistry, computer science, mathematics, and physics), EDUCATION (art education, elementary education, music education, and secondary education), HEALTH PROFESSIONS (nursing), SOCIAL SCIENCE (criminal justice, economics, German area studies, history, philosophy, political science/government, psychology, religion, social science, and sociology). Physics, chemistry, and computer science are the strongest academically. Psychology, management, and sociology are the largest.

Required: To graduate, students must complete a Learning in Common curriculum, which includes courses in writing, quantitative reasoning, historical studies, ultimate questions, cultural values and global issues, natural sciences, a foreign language, social sciences, aesthetic expression, literature, moral life, and phys ed. They must maintain a minimum GPA of 2.0 and complete 32 courses equivalent to 128 credits. The number of hours required in the major varies.

Special: The college offers 3-2 engineering degrees in conjunction with Washington University and a 4-1 engineering program with Lehigh University. Moravian also offers cooperative programs in allied health, natural resource management, and geology with Lehigh, Duke, and Thomas Jefferson Universities. Cross-registration is available with Lehigh and DeSales Universities and Lafayette, Muhlenberg, and Cedar Crest Colleges. Internships, study abroad in many countries, a Washington semester, and student-designed majors may be pursued. There are 17 national honor societies and 30 departmental honors programs.

Faculty/Classroom: 51% of faculty are male; 49% are female. All teach and do research. No introductory courses are taught by graduate students. The average class size in an introductory lecture is 19; in a laboratory, 15; and in a regular course, 17.

Requirements: The SAT or ACT is required. In addition, applicants must graduate from an accredited secondary school or have a GED. Moravian requires 16 Carnegie units, based on 4 years each of English and social science, 3 to 4 of math, and 2 each of lab science, a foreign language, and electives. Essays are required and interviews are recommended. For music students, auditions are required; for art students, portfolios are required. AP and CLEP credits are accepted. Important factors in the admissions decision are advanced placement or honors courses, recommendations by school officials, and leadership record.

Procedure: Freshmen are admitted fall and spring. Entrance exams should be taken with enough time to submit scores by the application deadline. There are early decision and deferred admissions plans. Early decision applications should be filed by February 1; check with the school for current application deadlines and fee. Notification of early decision is sent December 15. Applications are accepted on-line. 221 applicants were on a recent waiting list, 30 were accepted.

Transfer: 107 transfer students enrolled in a recent year. Applicants must have a minimum GPA of 3.0 and are required to submit recommendations, secondary and postsecondary transcripts, and standardized test scores. 32 of 128 credits required for the bachelor's degree must be completed at Moravian.

Visiting: There are regularly scheduled orientations for prospective students, including information sessions, tours and interviews with admissions staff. There are guides for informal visits; visitors may sit in on classes and stay overnight. To schedule a visit, contact the Office of Admission.

Financial Aid: In a recent year, 95% of all full-time freshmen and 93% of continuing full-time students received some form of financial aid. 72% of all full-time freshmen and 73% of continuing full-time students received need-based aid. The average freshmen award was $23,728. 43% of undergraduate students work part-time. Average annual earnings from campus work are $675. Moravian is a member of CSS. The CSS/Profile and FAFSA are required. Check with the school for current deadlines.

International Students: There were 18 international students enrolled in a recent year. The school actively recruits these students. They must take the TOEFL with a minimum score of 550 on the paper-based TOE-

FL (PBT) or 80 on the Internet-based version (iBT). The SAT or ACT is preferred for all students and required if the student's first language is English.

Computers: Wireless access is available in all academic buildings and common areas. All students may access the system 24 hours per day. There are no time limits and no fees.

Graduates: In a recent year, 378 bachelor's degrees were awarded. The most popular majors were management (16%), psychology (12%), and sociology (11%). 14 companies recruited on campus in a recent year. In an average class, 2% graduate in 3 years or less, 70% graduate in 4 years or less, 74% graduate in 5 years or less, and 75% graduate in 6 years or less. Of a recent graduating class, 21% were enrolled in graduate school within 6 months of graduation, and 67% were employed.

Admissions Contact: James P. Mackin, Director of Admission. E-Mail: *admissions@moravian.edu* Web: *www.moravian.edu*

MOUNT ALOYSIUS COLLEGE   C-3
Cresson, PA 16630

	(814) 886-6383
	(888) 823-2220; (814) 886-6441
Full-time: 330 men, 820 women	Faculty: n/av
Part-time: 85 men, 250 women	Ph.D.s: n/av
Graduate: 15 men, 45 women	Student/Faculty: 19 to 1
Year: semesters, summer session	Tuition: $19,080
Application Deadline: open	Room & Board: $8060
Freshman Class: n/av	
SAT or ACT: required	LESS COMPETITIVE

Mount Aloysius, established 1853 by the Sisters of Mercy, is a private, liberal arts college affiliated with the Roman Catholic Church. There is 1 undergraduate schools. Enrollment figures in the above capsule and figures in this profile are approximate. In addition to regional accreditation, MAC has baccalaureate program accreditation with APTA and NLN. The library contains 77,186 volumes, 4680 microform items, and 2431 audio/video tapes/CDs/DVDs, and subscribes to 275 periodicals including electronic. Computerized library services include interlibrary loans and database searching. Special learning facilities include a learning resource center and art gallery. The 165-acre campus is in a small town located in the southern Allegheny Mountains between Altoona and Johnstown. Including any residence halls, there are 8 buildings.

Student Life: 96% of undergraduates are from Pennsylvania. Others are from 20 states, 15 foreign countries, and Canada. 94% are white. 43% are Catholic; 13% Protestant. The average age of freshmen is 21; all undergraduates, 27. 28% do not continue beyond their first year; 67% remain to graduate.

Housing: 237 students can be accommodated in college housing, which includes single-sex and coed dorms and rooms for hearing-impaired students. On-campus housing is guaranteed for all 4 years. 85% of students commute. Alcohol is not permitted. All students may keep cars.

Activities: There are no fraternities or sororities. There are 30 groups on campus, including art, cheerleading, chorale, chorus, community service, computers, drama, ethnic, honors, musical theater, newspaper, photography, professional, religious, social, social service, student government, and yearbook. Popular campus events include Madrigal Dinner, Heritage Days, and Christmas at the Mount.

Sports: There are 5 intercollegiate sports for men and 5 for women, and 13 intramural sports for men and 12 for women. Facilities include an 1800-seat health and physical fitness center with 3 basketball courts, 2 tennis courts, a volleyball court, a weight-and-exercise room equipped with a sauna, and 2 locker rooms.

Disabled Students: 95% of the campus is accessible. Facilities include wheelchair ramps, elevators, special parking, specially equipped restrooms, lowered drinking fountains, lowered telephones, and special housing.

Services: Counseling and information services are available, as is tutoring in every subject. There is remedial math, reading, and writing.

Campus Safety and Security: Measures include 24-hour foot and vehicle patrol and security escort services. There are emergency telephones and lighted pathways/sidewalks.

Programs of Study: MAC confers B.A. and B.S. degrees. Associates and master's degrees are also awarded. Bachelor's degrees are awarded in BUSINESS (accounting and business administration and management), COMMUNICATIONS AND THE ARTS (English), COMPUTER AND PHYSICAL SCIENCE (information sciences and systems and science), EDUCATION (elementary education), HEALTH PROFESSIONS (medical laboratory technology, nursing, and occupational therapy), SOCIAL SCIENCE (criminology, history, interpreter for the deaf, prelaw, and psychology). Nursing, prelaw, and criminology are the strongest academically. Nursing, criminology, and elementary education are the largest.

Required: Baccalaureate-level students are required during their final semester of study to complete 2 3-credit courses designed to integrate and synthesize scientific, behavioral, and moral concepts. Students in al-

lied health programs must complete an approved clinical experience. Courses in research writing and speech are required. A total of 120 credits is required with an overall 2.0 GPA, including a C average in all core courses.

Special: The Professional Studies curriculum provides a student-designed course of study with an emphasis in behavior and social science, humanities, math/science/computer science, or prelaw. B.A.-B.S. degrees are offered as are internships in nursing, business, criminology, and student teaching. Dual majors are possible in elementary education/early childhood education. There are 3 national honor societies, a freshman honors program, and 1 departmental honors program.

Faculty/Classroom: 37% of faculty are male; 63% are female. All teach and do research. No introductory courses are taught by graduate students. The average class size in an introductory lecture is 17; in a laboratory, 12; and in a regular course, 17.

Admissions: 77% of the 2009-2010 applicants were accepted. The ACT scores were 84% below 21, 15% between 21 and 23, 1%

Requirements: The SAT or ACT is required. In addition, applicants must graduate from an accredited high school or have the GED. A placement test and any necessary developmental studies classes may need to be taken. Science classes and an interview are required of some allied health programs. A GPA of 2.5 is required. AP and CLEP credits are accepted. Important factors in the admissions decision are recommendations by school officials, advanced placement or honors courses, and leadership record.

Procedure: Freshmen are admitted fall and spring. Entrance exams should be taken as early as possible. There is a rolling admissions plan. Application deadlines are open. Check with the school for current application fee. Notification is sent on a rolling basis. Applications are accepted on-line.

Transfer: Transfer students must have a 2.0 GPA. Only courses with a C or better will be considered for transfer; all other requirements are the same as for freshmen. 30 of 120 credits required for the bachelor's degree must be completed at MAC.

Visiting: There are regularly scheduled orientations for prospective students, including 3 daily sessions. There are guides for informal visits; visitors may sit in on classes and stay overnight. To schedule a visit, contact the Admissions Office.

Financial Aid: MAC is a member of CSS. The FAFSA is required. Check with the school for current deadlines.

International Students: The school actively recruits these students. They must take the TOEFL. They must also take the SAT or ACT and the New Jersey Basic Skills Test.

Computers: Wireless access is available. All students may access the system from 8 A.M. to 10 P.M. There are no time limits and no fees.

Admissions Contact: Francis Crouse Jr., Dean of Enrollment Management. E-Mail: *admissions@mtaloy.edu* Web: *www.mtaloy.edu*

MUHLENBERG COLLEGE   E-3
Allentown, PA 18104

	(484) 664-3200; (484) 664-3234
Full-time: 1001 men, 1351 women	Faculty: 166; IIB, av$
Part-time: 79 men, 86 women	Ph.D.s: 87%
Graduate: none	Student/Faculty: 14 to 1
Year: semesters, summer session	Tuition: $36,990
Application Deadline: February 15	Room & Board: $8440
Freshman Class: 4110 applied, 2002 accepted, 577 enrolled	
SAT CR/M/W: 610/610/610	ACT: 20 HIGHLY COMPETITIVE

Muhlenberg College, established in 1848, is a private liberal arts institution affiliated with the Lutheran Church. The library contains 233,410 volumes, 138,090 microform items, and 16,519 audio/video tapes/CDs/DVDs, and subscribes to 24,894 periodicals including electronic. Computerized library services include interlibrary loans, database searching, Internet access, and laptop Internet portals. Special learning facilities include a learning resource center, art gallery, natural history museum, radio station, TV station, and 2 environmental field stations. The 82-acre campus is in a suburban area 50 miles north of Philadelphia and 90 miles west of New York City. Including any residence halls, there are 91 buildings.

Student Life: 71% of undergraduates are from out of state, mostly the Middle Atlantic. Students are from 34 states, 5 foreign countries, and Canada. 73% are from public schools. 91% are white. 31% are Catholic; 31% Jewish; 18% claim no religious affiliation; 12% Protestant. The average age of freshmen is 18; all undergraduates, 21. 8% do not continue beyond their first year; 85% remain to graduate.

Housing: 1996 students can be accommodated in college housing, which includes single-sex and coed dorms, on-campus apartments, and off-campus apartments. In addition, there are language houses, special-interest houses, fraternity houses, and college-owned houses in the surrounding community. On-campus housing is guaranteed for all 4 years. 92% of students live on campus; of those, 80% remain on campus on weekends. Upperclassmen may keep cars.

Activities: 14% of men belong to 4 national fraternities; 17% of women belong to 4 national sororities. There are 126 groups on campus, including art, band, cheerleading, chess, choir, chorale, chorus, computers, dance, drama, environmental, ethnic, film, gay, honors, human rights, international, jazz band, literary magazine, musical theater, newspaper, opera, orchestra, pep band, photography, political, professional, radio and TV, religious, social, social service, step team, student government, and yearbook. Popular campus events include Spring Fling Weekend, Candlelight Carols, and Jefferson Field Day.

Sports: There are 11 intercollegiate sports for men and 11 for women, and 13 intramural sports for men and 13 for women. Facilities include a sports center, which contains a 6-lane swimming pool, racquetball and squash courts, and wrestling and weight-training rooms; a multipurpose field house with indoor tennis courts, a running track, basketball and tennis courts, and a large aerobic fitness center and weight room; outdoor volleyball courts; and a football/lacrosse/field hockey stadium.

Disabled Students: 95% of the campus is accessible. Facilities include wheelchair ramps, elevators, special parking, specially equipped rest rooms, special class scheduling, lowered drinking fountains, lowered telephones, and special housing.

Services: Counseling and information services are available, as is tutoring in every subject. There is a reader service for the blind. There is also a writing center.

Campus Safety and Security: Measures include 24-hour foot and vehicle patrol, self-defense education, and security escort services. There are shuttle buses, emergency telephones, and lighted pathways/sidewalks.

Programs of Study: Berg confers B.A. and B.S. degrees. Associates degrees are also awarded. Bachelor's degrees are awarded in BIOLOGICAL SCIENCE (biochemistry, biology/biological science, and neurosciences), BUSINESS (accounting, banking and finance, and business administration and management), COMMUNICATIONS AND THE ARTS (art, communications, dance, dramatic arts, English, film arts, French, German, music, and Spanish), COMPUTER AND PHYSICAL SCIENCE (chemistry, computer science, mathematics, natural sciences, physical sciences, and physics), ENGINEERING AND ENVIRONMENTAL DESIGN (environmental science), SOCIAL SCIENCE (American studies, anthropology, economics, German area studies, history, international studies, philosophy, political science/government, psychology, religion, Russian and Slavic studies, and sociology). Biology, theater, and psychology are the strongest academically. Biology, business administration, and communication are the largest.

Required: To graduate, students must complete requirements in literature and the arts, religion or philosophy, human behavior and social institutions, historical studies, physical and life sciences, and other cultures. They must have a minimum GPA of 2.0 in a total of 34 course units, with 9 to 14 units in the major. All students must take 1 quarter of phys ed, including a wellness course, and freshman and senior seminars.

Special: Students may cross-register with Lehigh, Lafayette, Cedar Crest, Moravian, and Allentown Colleges. Internships, work-study programs, B.A.-B.S. degrees, study abroad in Asia, Australia, Latin America, Russia, and Europe, and a Washington semester are available. Dual majors and student-designed majors may be pursued. A 3-2 engineering degree is available in cooperation with Columbia and Washington Universities, a 4-4 assured admission medical program with Drexel University College of Medicine, a 3-4 dental program with the University of Pennsylvania, and a 3-2 forestry degreewith Duke University. An army ROTC program is also available. Nondegree study and a pass/fail grading option are also offered. There are 14 national honor societies, including Phi Beta Kappa, a freshman honors program, and 8 departmental honors programs.

Faculty/Classroom: 53% of faculty are male; 47% are female. All teach undergraduates, and 84% teach and do research. No introductory courses are taught by graduate students. The average class size in an introductory lecture is 35, in a laboratory, 19, and in a regular course, 21.

Admissions: 49% of the 2009-2010 applicants were accepted. The SAT scores for the 2009-2010 freshman class were: Critical Reading--9% below 500, 34% between 500 and 599, 45% between 600 and 700, and 13% above 700; Math--8% below 500, 35% between 500 and 599, 48% between 600 and 700, and 10% above 700; Writing--7% below 500, 35% between 500 and 599, 42% between 600 and 700, and 15% above 700. The ACT scores were 2% below 21, 8% between 21 and 23, 33% between 24 and 26, 33% between 27 and 28, and 23% above 28. 84% of the current freshmen were in the top fifth of their class; 96% were in the top two fifths. 4 freshmen graduated first in their class in a recent year.

Requirements: Applicants must graduate from an accredited secondary school or have a GED. 16 Carnegie units are required, with 4 courses in English, 3 in math, and 2 each in history, science, and a foreign language. All students must submit essays. Interviews are recommended and are required for those who do not submit SAT scores. AP and CLEP credits are accepted. Important factors in the admissions decision are evidence of special talent, leadership record, and advanced placement or honors courses.

Procedure: Freshmen are admitted fall and spring. Entrance exams should be taken during the spring of the junior year or fall of the senior year. There are early decision, deferred admissions plan. Early decision

applications should be filed by February 1; regular applications should be filed by February 15 for fall entry, along with a $50 fee. Notification of early decision is sent on a rolling basis; and sent March 15. Applications are accepted on-line. 354 applicants were on a recent waiting list, 21 were accepted.

Transfer: 12 transfer students enrolled in a recent year. A minimum college GPA of 2.5 and an interview are required. 17 of 34 credits required for the bachelor's degree must be completed at Berg.

Visiting: There are regularly scheduled orientations for prospective students, consisting of a tour of the campus and a personal interview. There are 2 open houses in the fall and 1 in the spring. There are guides for informal visits; visitors may sit in on classes and stay overnight. To schedule a visit, contact Bonnie Reabold or Alyssa Rabenold at (484) 664-3202.

Financial Aid: In a recent year, 72% of all full-time freshmen and 74% of continuing full-time students received some form of financial aid. 34% of all full-time freshmen and 38% of continuing full-time students received need-based aid. The average freshmen award was $21,653, with $19,426 ($35,580 maximum) from need-based scholarships or need-based grants; $4960 ($7800 maximum) from need-based self-help aid (loans and jobs); and $8319 ($21,500 maximum) from other non-need-based awards and non-need-based scholarships. 41% of undergraduate students work part-time. Average annual earnings from campus work are $1128. The average financial indebtedness of a recent graduate was $20,668. Berg is a member of CSS. The CSS/Profile, FAFSA, the college's own financial statement, and parent and student tax returns and W-2 forms are required. The deadline for filing freshman financial aid applications for fall entry is February 15.

International Students: There were 5 international students enrolled in a recent year. The school actively recruits these students. They must take the TOEFL with a minimum score of 550 on the paper-based TOEFL (PBT).

Computers: Wireless access is available. There are student computers throughout campus and in residence halls. All students may access the system 24 hours a day. There are no time limits and no fees. It is strongly recommended that all students have a personal computer.

Graduates: In a recent year, 542 bachelor's degrees were awarded. The most popular majors were business (14%), psychology (11%), and media and communication (9%). 74 companies recruited on campus in a recent year. Of a recent graduating class, 35% were enrolled in graduate school within 6 months of graduation and 62% were employed.

Admissions Contact: Christopher Hooker-Haring, Dean, Admissions. E-Mail: *admissions@muhlenberg.edu* Web: *www.muhlenberg.edu*

NEUMANN COLLEGE
E-4

Aston, PA 19014-1298

(610) 558-5616
(800) 9NEUMAN; (610) 558-5652

Full-time: 720 men, 1292 women	**Faculty:** 85; IIB, --$
Part-time: 150 men, 339 women	**Ph.D.s:** 63%
Graduate: 191 men, 407 women	**Student/Faculty:** 24 to 1
Year: semesters, summer session	**Tuition:** $21,360
Application Deadline: open	**Room & Board:** $9718
Freshman Class: 2358 applied, 2213 accepted, 520 enrolled	
SAT: required	**LESS COMPETITIVE**

Neumann University, formerly Neumann College and founded in 1965 by the Sisters of St. Francis, is a private liberal arts institution affiliated with the Roman Catholic Church. There 5 graduate schools. In addition to regional accreditation, Neumann has baccalaureate program accreditation with ACBSP, CAHEA, CAPTE, and NLN. The library contains 90,000 volumes, 99,758 microform items, and 36,562 audio/video tapes/CDs/DVDs, and subscribes to 700 periodicals including electronic. Computerized library services include interlibrary loans, database searching, and Internet access. Special learning facilities include a learning resource center, radio station, and a learning assistance center. The 50-acre campus is in a suburban area 15 miles southwest of Philadelphia. Including any residence halls, there are 6 buildings.

Student Life: 68% of undergraduates are from Pennsylvania. Others are from 24 states, 8 foreign countries, and Canada. 35% are from public schools. 58% are white; 13% African American. 56% are Catholic; 30% Protestant; 11% claim no religious affiliation. The average age of freshmen is 18; all undergraduates, 20. 26% do not continue beyond their first year; 55% remain to graduate.

Housing: 800 students can be accommodated in college housing, which includes coed dorms and off-campus apartments. On-campus housing is available on a first-come, first-served basis. Priority is given to out-of-town students. 60% of students commute. Alcohol is not permitted. All students may keep cars.

Activities: There are no fraternities or sororities. There are 17 groups on campus, including cheerleading, choir, chorus, dance, drama, ethnic, honors, literary magazine, newspaper, photography, political, professional, radio and TV, religious, social, social service, and student government. Popular campus events include dinner dances, Spring Fling, and charity fund-raising.

Sports: There are 8 intercollegiate sports for men and 9 for women, and 6 intramural sports for men and 6 for women. Facilities include a 350-seat gym, weight and fitness rooms, tennis courts, baseball and softball fields, an ice hockey rink, video games, and a theater.

Disabled Students: All of the campus is accessible. Facilities include wheelchair ramps, elevators, special parking, specially equipped restrooms, and special class scheduling.

Services: Counseling and information services are available, as is tutoring in every subject. There is a reader service for the blind, and remedial math, reading, and writing.

Campus Safety and Security: Measures include 24-hour foot and vehicle patrol, emergency notification system, self-defense education, and security escort services. There are shuttle buses, emergency telephones, and lighted pathways/sidewalks.

Programs of Study: Neumann confers B.A. and B.S. degrees. Associate, master's, and doctoral degrees are also awarded. Bachelor's degrees are awarded in AGRICULTURE (environmental studies), BIOLOGICAL SCIENCE (biology/biological science), BUSINESS (accounting, business administration and management, international business management, marketing and distribution, and sports management), COMMUNICATIONS AND THE ARTS (communications, digital communications, English, and performing arts), COMPUTER AND PHYSICAL SCIENCE (computer science), EDUCATION (athletic training, early childhood education, and elementary education), HEALTH PROFESSIONS (nursing), SOCIAL SCIENCE (criminal justice, liberal arts/general studies, political science/government, and psychology). Biology, nursing, and elementary education are the strongest academically. Nursing, elementary education, and liberal studies are the largest.

Required: To graduate, all students must complete 120 to 130 credits, including 44 credits of core requirements, with 30 to 50 in the major. A minimum 2.0 GPA is required.

Special: The college offers co-op programs in all majors, study abroad in England, Italy, Spain, and France, internships, work-study programs, dual majors, and a general studies degree. Credit for life, work, and military experience, nondegree study, an accelerated degree program in liberal studies, and pass/fail options are available. There are 4 national honor societies, a freshman honors program, and 1 departmental honors program.

Faculty/Classroom: 40% of faculty are male; 60% are female. 96% teach undergraduates, and 15% both teach and do research. No introductory courses are taught by graduate students. The average class size in an introductory lecture is 26; in a laboratory, 18; and in a regular course, 19.

Admissions: 94% of the 2009-2010 applicants were accepted. 30% of the current freshmen were in the top fifth of their class; 90% were in the top two fifths.

Requirements: The SAT is required. In addition, applicants must be graduates of an accredited secondary school or have a GED. High school courses must include 4 years of English and 2 years each of a foreign language, history, and science. An interview is recommended. A GPA of 2.0 is required. AP and CLEP credits are accepted. An important factor in the admissions decision is recommendations by school officials.

Procedure: Freshmen are admitted fall and spring. Entrance exams should be taken by December of the senior year. There are deferred admissions and rolling admissions plans. Application deadlines are open. Application fee is $35. Applications are accepted on-line.

Transfer: 68 transfer students enrolled in a recent year. Applicants should submit transcripts from all institutions attended. 30 of 120 to 130 credits required for the bachelor's degree must be completed at Neumann.

Visiting: There are regularly scheduled orientations for prospective students, including class visits and informal meetings with faculty. There are guides for informal visits, and visitors may sit in on classes. To schedule a visit, contact the Admissions Office.

Financial Aid: In 2009-2010, 95% of all full-time freshmen and 90% of continuing full-time students received some form of financial aid. 90% of all full-time students received need-based aid. The average freshman award was $18,000. Need-based scholarships or need-based grants averaged $15,000 ($18,000 maximum) and need-based self-help aid (loans and jobs) averaged $5,000 ($7,000 maximum). 90% of undergraduate students work part-time. Average annual earnings from campus work are $1600. The average financial indebtedness of the 2009 graduate was $40,000. The FAFSA is required. The deadline for filing freshman financial aid applications for fall entry is March 15.

International Students: There are 55 international students enrolled. They must take the TOEFL with a minimum score of 550 on the paper-based TOEFL (PBT) or 70 on the Internet-based version (iBT). They must also take the SAT.

Computers: Wireless access is available. Every student has access to the college's network. Dorms have Internet cable connections. All students may access the system at any time. There are no time limits and no fees. It is strongly recommended that all students have a personal computer.

Graduates: From July 1, 2008 to June 30, 2009, 464 bachelor's degrees were awarded. The most popular majors were liberal studies (30%), nursing (14%), and elementary education (13%). In an average class, 40% graduate in 4 years or less, 50% graduate in 5 years or less, and 55% graduate in 6 years or less. 55 companies recruited on campus in 2008-2009. Of the 2008 graduating class, 20% were enrolled in graduate school within 6 months of graduation, and 95% were employed.

Admissions Contact: Christina Rufo, Director of Admissions. E-mail: *neumann@neumann.edu* Web: *www.neumann.edu*

PEIRCE COLLEGE — F-3
Philadelphia, PA 19102
(215) 670-9214
(888) 467-3472; (888) 467-3472

Full-time: 200 men, 600 women	**Faculty:** n/av
Part-time: 320 men, 845 women	**Ph.D.s:** n/av
Graduate: none	**Student/Faculty:** 27 to 1
Year: see profile, summer session	**Tuition:** $14,850
Application Deadline: open	**Room & Board:** n/app
Freshman Class: n/av	

NONCOMPETITIVE

Peirce College, founded in 1865, is a private specialized institution providing practical curricula to primarily working adults. Peirce offers accelerated bachelor's and associate degree programs in business administration, information technology, and paralegal studies, utilizing 3 interchangeable delivery formats: on campus, in Center City Philadelphia; on site at corporate and community locations throughout the region; and on=line through web-based distance learning. There is 1 undergraduate school. Enrollment figures in the above capsule and figures in this profile are approximate. In addition to regional accreditation, Peirce has baccalaureate program accreditation with ACBSP. The library contains 30,000 volumes and subscribes to 25,000 periodicals including electronic. Computerized library services include interlibrary loans, database searching, and Internet access. Special learning facilities include a learning resource center, the Walker Center for Academic Excellence. The 1-acre campus is in an urban area in the Center City Business District. There are 2 buildings.

Student Life: 80% of undergraduates are from Pennsylvania. Others are from 40 states, 30 foreign countries, and Canada. 50% are African American; 31% white. The average age of freshmen is 31; all undergraduates, 33. 7% do not continue beyond their first year; 53% remain to graduate.

Housing: There are no residence halls. All students commute.

Activities: There are no fraternities or sororities. There are 3 groups on campus, including honors and professional. Popular campus events include Student Leadership Retreat, Welcome Back Day, and Annual Awards Induction Ceremony.

Sports: There is no sports program at Peirce.

Disabled Students: All of the campus is accessible. Facilities include wheelchair ramps, elevators, specially equipped restrooms, special class scheduling, lowered drinking fountains, and lowered telephones.

Services: Counseling and information services are available, as is tutoring in most subjects. There is a reader service for the blind, and remedial math, reading, and writing.

Campus Safety and Security: Measures include 24-hour foot and vehicle patrol and security escort services. There are emergency telephones, lighted pathways/sidewalks, and security cameras throughout the campus.

Programs of Study: Peirce confers B.S. degrees. Associates degrees are also awarded. Bachelor's degrees are awarded in BUSINESS (accounting, business administration and management, business law, entrepreneurial studies, human resources, management information systems, marketing management, and real estate), COMPUTER AND PHYSICAL SCIENCE (computer management, computer programming, and information sciences and systems), ENGINEERING AND ENVIRONMENTAL DESIGN (computer technology), SOCIAL SCIENCE (paralegal studies). Paralegal studies is the strongest academically. Business administration is the largest.

Required: To graduate, all students must complete 121 credit hours, including a core curriculum, and maintain a minimum cumulative GPA of 2.0.

Special: The college offers accelerated degrees and co-op programs in most major programs of study. There are 2 national honor societies.

Faculty/Classroom: 62% of faculty are male; 38% are female. All teach undergraduates. No introductory courses are taught by graduate students. The average class size in an introductory lecture is 19 and in a regular course, 18.

Requirements: Applicants for a degree program must submit an official transcript documenting high school graduation or a copy of the GED or state equivalency diploma and scores. AP and CLEP credits are accepted.

Procedure: Freshmen are admitted to all sessions. Entrance exams are offered continuously. There are deferred admissions and rolling admissions plans. Application deadlines are open. Application fee is $50. Notification is sent on a rolling basis. Applications are accepted on-line.

Transfer: Transcripts from other colleges attended must be submitted. 31 of 121 credits required for the bachelor's degree must be completed at Peirce.

Visiting: There are regularly scheduled orientations for prospective students, including a campus tour and a meeting with an adviser. There are guides for informal visits, and visitors may sit in on classes. To schedule a visit, contact Enrollment Services.

Financial Aid: The FAFSA and the college's own financial statement are required. Check with the school for current deadlines.

International Students: The school actively recruits these students.

Computers: Wireless access is available. Over 230 computers are available for student use on campus in classrooms, labs, and the library. Students may access electronic courseware, e-mail, the Internet, and library databases. Students can register for courses and pay bills on-line. Through electronic courseware, they can participate in lectures, student organizations, and discussions. They can also view grades and communicate with classmates and instructors. Wireless connectivity is available in the library and labs. All students may access the system. There are no time limits and no fees. All students are required to have a personal computer.

Admissions Contact: Admissions, Enrollment Representative. E-Mail: *info@peirce.edu* Web: *www.peirce.edu*

PENN STATE ERIE/THE BEHREND COLLEGE
Erie, PA 16563

B-1

(814) 898-6100
(866) 374-3378; (814) 898-6044

Full-time: 2175 men, 1075 women	Faculty: n/av
Part-time: 150 men, 75 women	Ph.D.s: n/av
Graduate: 100 men, 60 women	Student/Faculty: 16 to 1
Year: semesters, summer session	Tuition: $12,750 ($19,078)
Application Deadline: open	Room & Board: $8820
Freshman Class: n/av	
SAT or ACT: required	COMPETITIVE

Penn State Erie The Behrend College, founded in 1948, offers 26 baccalaureate programs as well as the first 2 years of most Penn State University Park baccalaureate programs. It offers courses in business, humanities, social sciences, science, engineering technology, and engineering. There are 4 undergraduate schools and 2 graduate schools. Enrollment figures in the above capsule and figures in this profile are approximate. In addition to regional accreditation, Penn State Erie has baccalaureate program accreditation with AACSB and ABET. The library contains 100,000 volumes, 75,190 microform items, and 351 audio/video tapes/CDs/DVDs, and subscribes to 700 periodicals including electronic. Computerized library services include interlibrary loans, database searching, Internet access, and laptop Internet portals. Special learning facilities include a learning resource center, radio station, engineering workstation labs, media labs, and observatory. The 725-acre campus is in a suburban area 5 miles east of Erie. Including any residence halls, there are 42 buildings.

Student Life: 92% of undergraduates are from Pennsylvania. Others are from 32 states, 23 foreign countries, and Canada. 79% are white; 14% foreign nationals. The average age of freshmen is 18; all undergraduates, 22. 9% do not continue beyond their first year; 61% remain to graduate.

Housing: 1650 students can be accommodated in college housing, which includes single-sex and coed dorms and on-campus apartments. In addition, there are honors houses, special-interest houses, and freshman interest groups housing. On-campus housing is guaranteed for the freshman year only, is available on a first-come, first-served basis, and is available on a lottery system for upperclassmen. 53% of students commute. Alcohol is not permitted. All students may keep cars.

Activities: 5% of men belong to 3 national fraternities; 16% of women belong to 3 national sororities. There are 80 groups on campus, including band, cheerleading, chess, choir, computers, dance, drama, ethnic, gay, honors, international, jazz band, literary magazine, newspaper, pep band, political, professional, radio and TV, religious, social, social service, student government, and yearbook. Popular campus events include a speaker series and Black Cultural Awareness Month.

Sports: There are 10 intercollegiate sports for men and 11 for women, and 18 intramural sports for men and 18 for women. Facilities include an athletic center with an indoor track and an 8-lane pool, tennis courts, a weight room, a fitness trail, basketball courts, and baseball, softball, and soccer fields.

Disabled Students: 90% of the campus is accessible. Facilities include wheelchair ramps, elevators, special parking, specially equipped restrooms, special class scheduling, lowered drinking fountains, and lowered telephones.

Services: Counseling and information services are available, as is tutoring in every subject. There is a reader service for the blind, and remedial math, reading, and writing.

Campus Safety and Security: Measures include 24-hour foot and vehicle patrol, self-defense education, and security escort services. There are emergency telephones and lighted pathways/sidewalks.

Programs of Study: Penn State Erie confers B.A., B.S., and B.F.A. degrees. Associates and master's degrees are also awarded. Bachelor's degrees are awarded in BIOLOGICAL SCIENCE (biology/biological science), BUSINESS (accounting, banking and finance, business administration and management, business economics, management information systems, and marketing management), COMMUNICATIONS AND THE ARTS (communications and English), COMPUTER AND PHYSICAL SCIENCE (chemistry, computer science, mathematics, physics, and science), ENGINEERING AND ENVIRONMENTAL DESIGN (computer engineering, engineering, engineering technology, mechanical engineering technology, and plastics technology), SOCIAL SCIENCE (economics, history, political science/government, and psychology). Management information systems, psychology, and math are the strongest academically. Engineering, business, and psychology are the largest.

Required: All baccalaureate degree candidates must take 46 general education credits, including 27 in arts, humanities, natural science, and social and behavioral sciences including a cultural diversity course, 15 in quantification and communication skills including a writing intensive course, and 3 in health, phys ed, and freshman seminar. All students must complete a minimum of 120 credit hours with a minimum GPA of 2.0. Further requirements vary by degree program.

Special: Internships, study abroad in 14 countries, work-study programs, and accelerated degree programs are available. In addition, a B.A.-B.S. degree in psychology, a 3-2 engineering degree with Edinboro University, dual majors, a general studies degree, and student-designed majors in business and general arts and sciences are offered. Nondegree study and up to 12 credits of pass/fail options are possible. There are 4 national honor societies and a freshman honors program.

Faculty/Classroom: 70% of faculty are male; 30% are female. All teach and do research. No introductory courses are taught by graduate students. The average class size in an introductory lecture is 35; in a laboratory, 18; and in a regular course, 29.

Requirements: The SAT or ACT is required. In addition, candidates for admission must have 15 academic credits or 15 Carnegie units, including 5 in social studies, 4 in English, 3 each in math and science, and 2 in foreign language. The GED is accepted. AP and CLEP credits are accepted.

Procedure: Freshmen are admitted to all sessions. Entrance exams should be taken during the junior year. There are deferred admissions and rolling admissions plans. Application deadlines are open. Application fee is $50. Notification is sent on a rolling basis. Applications are accepted on-line.

Transfer: Transfer candidates need a minimum GPA of 2.4, good academic standing, and 18 or more credits from a regionally accredited institution at the college level. 36 of 120 credits required for the bachelor's degree must be completed at Penn State Erie.

Visiting: There are regularly scheduled orientations for prospective students, including meetings with a counselor and faculty, a campus tour, and a class visit. There are guides for informal visits; visitors may sit in on classes and stay overnight. To schedule a visit, contact the Admissions Office.

Financial Aid: The FAFSA is required. Check with the school for current deadlines.

International Students: The school actively recruits these students. They must take the TOEFL.

Computers: Wireless access is available. All students may access the system any time by modem or network. There are no time limits and no fees. It is strongly recommended that all students have a personal computer.

Admissions Contact: Mary-Ellen Madigan, Director of Admissions. E-Mail: *behrend.admissions@psu.edu* Web: *www.pserie.psu.edu*

PENN STATE UNIVERSITY/ALTOONA
Altoona, PA 16601

(814) 949-5466; (800) 848-9843

Full-time: 1950 men, 1800 women	Faculty: n/av
Part-time: 110 men, 1775 women	Ph.D.s: n/av
Graduate: 2 men, 3 women	Student/Faculty: 31 to 1
Year: semesters, summer session	Tuition: $12,750 ($19,078)
Application Deadline: open	
Freshman Class: n/av	
SAT or ACT: required	COMPETITIVE

Penn State Altoona, founded in 1939, offers 18 baccalaureate degree programs, 8 associate degrees, and 19 minors. There are 17 undergraduate schools and 1 graduate school. Enrollment figures in the above capsule and figures in this profile are approximate. In addition to regional accreditation, Penn State Altoona has baccalaureate program accreditation with ABET, NASAD, NCATE, and NRPA. The library contains 90,000 audio/video tapes/CDs/DVDs, and subscribes to 500 periodicals including electronic. Computerized library services include interlibrary loans, database searching, Internet access, and laptop Internet portals. Special learning facilities include a learning resource center, art gallery, Pic-Tel teleconferencing, 5 state-of-the-art engineering labs, and CAD/CAM computer lab facilities. The 150-acre campus is in a suburban area. Including any residence halls, there are 33 buildings.

Student Life: 85% of undergraduates are from Pennsylvania. Others are from 28 states, 20 foreign countries, and Canada. 84% are white. The average age of freshmen is 18; all undergraduates, 22. 12% do not continue beyond their first year; 65% remain to graduate.

Housing: 900 students can be accommodated in college housing, which includes single-sex and coed dorms. In addition, there are honors houses, special-interest houses, and alcohol-free and substance-free housing. On-campus housing is available on a first-come, first-served basis and is available on a lottery system for upperclassmen. 78% of students commute. Alcohol is not permitted. All students may keep cars.

Activities: There are 5 local fraternities and 2 local sororities. There are 70 groups on campus, including cheerleading, choir, communications, dance, drama, ethnic, gay, honors, horticulture, international, jazz band, literary magazine, martial arts, newspaper, pep band, political, professional, religious, social, social service, STEP team, student government, and yearbook. Popular campus events include Distinguished Speaker Series, Hoops Hysteria, and Black History and Women's History Month events.

Sports: There are 6 intercollegiate sports for men and 6 for women. Facilities include a large gym, an indoor pool, racquetball courts, a weight room, a fitness loft, tennis courts, an outdoor track, sand volleyball courts, and baseball, softball, and soccer fields.

Disabled Students: 95% of the campus is accessible. Facilities include wheelchair ramps, elevators, special parking, specially equipped restrooms, special class scheduling, lowered drinking fountains, and lowered telephones.

Services: Counseling and information services are available, as is tutoring in most subjects. There is remedial math, reading, and writing.

Campus Safety and Security: Measures include 24-hour foot and vehicle patrol, emergency notification system, self-defense education, and security escort services. There are shuttle buses, emergency telephones, and lighted pathways/sidewalks.

Programs of Study: Penn State Altoona confers B.A. and B.S. degrees. Associates and master's degrees are also awarded. Bachelor's degrees are awarded in AGRICULTURE (environmental studies), BIOLOGICAL SCIENCE (biology/biological science), BUSINESS (business administration and management), COMMUNICATIONS AND THE ARTS (communications, English, and visual and performing arts), COMPUTER AND PHYSICAL SCIENCE (mathematics and science), EDUCATION (elementary education), ENGINEERING AND ENVIRONMENTAL DESIGN (electromechanical technology), HEALTH PROFESSIONS (nursing), SOCIAL SCIENCE (criminal justice, history, human development, and liberal arts/general studies). Engineering and education are the strongest academically. Business, criminal justice, and elementary education are the largest.

Required: To graduate, students must complete a minimum of 120 credit hours with a minimum GPA of 2.0. They must complete 46 general education credits, including 27 in arts, humanities, natural science, and social and behavioral sciences and 15 in quantification and communication skills.

Special: Internships, study abroad in 5 countries, work-study programs, B.A.-B.S. degrees, accelerated degree programs, and dual and student-designed majors are available. There is an integrative arts major, which allows students to pursue interest across artistic boundaries. There is a chapter of Phi Beta Kappa and a freshman honors program.

Faculty/Classroom: No introductory courses are taught by graduate students. The average class size in an introductory lecture is 50; in a laboratory, 24; and in a regular course, 28.

Requirements: The SAT or ACT is required. In addition, applicants should have 15 academic or Carnegie units, including 4 in English, 3 each in math, science, and social studies, and 2 in foreign language (required for some majors). The GED is accepted. AP and CLEP credits are accepted.

Procedure: Freshmen are admitted to all sessions. Entrance exams should be taken during the junior year. There are deferred admissions and rolling admissions plans. Application deadlines are open, but applications should be submitted by November 30. The application fee is $50. Notification is sent on a rolling basis. Applications are accepted online.

Transfer: 100 transfer students enrolled in a recent year. High school and college transcripts are required, as is good academic standing. The minimum GPA varies by major. 36 of 120 credits required for the bachelor's degree must be completed at Penn State Altoona.

Visiting: There are regularly scheduled orientations for prospective students, including campus tours and meetings with academic counselors and faculty. There are guides for informal visits; visitors may sit in on classes and stay overnight. To schedule a visit, contact the Admissions Office.

Financial Aid: Some academic scholarships require a specific application, which varies according to the college/major. Check with the school for current deadlines.

International Students: There were 8 international students enrolled in a recent year. The school actively recruits these students. They must take the TOEFL and also take the SAT or ACT.

Computers: Wireless access is available. All students may access the system. There are no time limits and no fees. It is strongly recommended that all students have a personal computer.

Graduates: In a recent year, 350 bachelor's degrees were awarded. The most popular majors were business (15%), criminal justice (14%), and elementary education (13%). In an average class, 38% graduate in 4 years or less, 64% graduate in 5 years or less, and 65% graduate in 6 years or less.

Admissions Contact: Richard Shaffer, Director of Admissions. A campus DVD is available. E-Mail: *rks8@psu.edu* Web: *www.aa.psu.edu*

PENN STATE UNIVERSITY/UNIVERSITY PARK CAMPUS   C-3

University Park, PA 16802	(814) 865-5471; (814) 863-7590
Full-time: 20484 men, 17001 women	Faculty: I, -$
Part-time: 694 men, 451 women	Ph.D.s: 75%
Graduate: 3596 men, 2959 women	Student/Faculty: n/av
Year: semesters, summer session	Tuition: $14,416 ($25,946)
Application Deadline: November 30	Room & Board: $8170
Freshman Class: 40714 applied, 21017 accepted, 6560 enrolled	
SAT CR/M/W: 580/620/590	ACT: required
	VERY COMPETITIVE

Penn State University/University Park Campus, founded in 1855, is a public institution that is the oldest and largest of 24 campuses in the Penn State system. The university offers undergraduate and graduate degrees in agricultural sciences, arts and architecture, business, earth and mineral sciences, education, engineering, health and human development, liberal arts, science, communications, and information sciences and technology. Penn State also offers graduate and first professional degrees in medicine and law. There are 15 undergraduate schools and one graduate school. In addition to regional accreditation, Penn State has baccalaureate program accreditation with AACSB, ABET, ACEJMC, APTA, ASLA, CSAB, NAAB, NASAD, NASM, NCATE, NLN, and SAF. The 14 libraries contain 5.2 million volumes, 5.4 million microform items, and 178,672 audio/video tapes/CDs/DVDs, and subscribe to 68,876 periodicals including electronic. Computerized library services include interlibrary loans, database searching, Internet access, and laptop Internet portals. Special learning facilities include a learning resource center, art gallery, planetarium, radio station, TV station, 5 major museums at University Park house, significant research and educational collections in the fields of agriculture, anthropology, entomology, earth and mineral sciences, and the fine arts. The 7264-acre campus is in a suburban area 90 miles west of Harrisburg, PA. Including any residence halls, there are 933 buildings.

Student Life: 71% of undergraduates are from Pennsylvania. Students are from 50 states, and Canada. 74% are white. The average age of freshmen is 18; all undergraduates, 20. 7% do not continue beyond their first year; 93% remain to graduate.

Housing: 13664 students can be accommodated in college housing, which includes single-sex and coed dorms, on-campus apartments, and married student housing. In addition, there are honors houses, language houses, special-interest houses, fraternity houses, and sorority houses. On-campus housing is guaranteed for all 4 years. 64% of students commute. Upperclassmen may keep cars.

Activities: 13% of men belong to 57 national fraternities; 11% of women belong to 33 national sororities. There are 735 groups on campus, including art, band, cheerleading, chess, choir, chorale, chorus, computers, dance, debate, drama, drill team, environmental, ethnic, film, forensics, gay, honors, international, jazz band, literary magazine, marching band, musical theater, newspaper, opera, orchestra, pep band, photography, political, professional, radio and TV, religious, social, social service, student government, symphony, and yearbook. Popular campus events include Late Night Penn State, Dance Marathon, and Penn State football.

Sports: There are 15 intercollegiate sports for men and 14 for women, and 18 intramural sports for men and 18 for women. Facilities include a 107,282-seat football stadium, a baseball field with seating for 6000, a 15,000-seat basketball center, 2 golf courses, an ice skating pavilion, an indoor track/multipurpose field, an outdoor track, a soccer field with seating for 5000, indoor and outdoor swimming pools, bowling lanes, a tennis center, 4 fitness facilities, Shaver's Creek Environmental Center, Stone Valley Recreation Center (fishing, swimming, canoeing, sailing, and kayaking), a rifle range, and facilities for gymnastics, volleyball, field hockey, lacrosse, fencing, and wrestling.

Disabled Students: 95% of the campus is accessible. Facilities include wheelchair ramps, elevators, special parking, specially equipped restrooms, special class scheduling, lowered drinking fountains, lowered telephones, and special housing.

Services: Counseling and information services are available, as is tutoring in most subjects. There is a reader service for the blind, and remedial math, reading, and writing.

Campus Safety and Security: Measures include 24-hour foot and vehicle patrol, emergency notification system, self-defense education, and security escort services. There are shuttle buses, emergency telephones, lighted pathways/sidewalks, and controlled access to dorms/residences.

Programs of Study: Penn State confers B.A., B.S., B.A.E, B.Arch., B.Des., B.Eled. B.F.A., B.Hum., B.L.A., B.M., B.M.A., B.M.E., B.Ph., and B.Sosc. degrees. Associates, master's, and doctoral degrees are also awarded. Bachelor's degrees are awarded in AGRICULTURE (agricultural business management, agriculture, agronomy, animal science, forestry production and processing, forestry and related sciences, horticulture, natural resource management, and soil science), BIOLOGICAL SCIENCE (biochemistry, biology/biological science, biotechnology, ecology, microbiology, and nutrition), BUSINESS (accounting, banking and finance, business administration and management, hotel/motel and restaurant management, labor studies, management information systems, marketing/retailing/merchandising, and organizational behavior), COMMUNICATIONS AND THE ARTS (advertising, art, art history and appreciation, broadcasting, classics, communications, comparative literature, dramatic arts, English, film arts, French, German, graphic design, Italian, Japanese, journalism, music, music performance, Russian, Spanish, speech/debate/rhetoric, theater design, and visual and performing arts), COMPUTER AND PHYSICAL SCIENCE (actuarial science, astronomy, atmospheric sciences and meteorology, chemistry, computer science, earth science, geoscience, information sciences and systems, mathematics, physical sciences, physics, science, and statistics), EDUCATION (agricultural education, art education, elementary education, foreign languages education, health education, music education, secondary education, and special education), ENGINEERING AND ENVIRONMENTAL DESIGN (aeronautical engineering, agricultural engineering, architectural engineering, architecture, biomedical engineering, chemical engineering, civil engineering, computer engineering, electrical/electronics engineering, engineering, environmental science, industrial engineering, landscape architecture/design, materials science, mechanical engineering, mining and mineral engineering, nuclear engineering, and petroleum/natural gas engineering), HEALTH PROFESSIONS (biomedical science, exercise science, health care administration, nursing, premedicine, rehabilitation therapy, and speech pathology/audiology), SOCIAL SCIENCE (African American studies, American studies, anthropology, archeology, criminal justice, East Asian studies, economics, food science, geography, history, human development, international relations, Judaic studies, Latin American studies, liberal arts/general studies, medieval studies, parks and recreation management, philosophy, physical fitness/movement, political science/government, psychology, religion, sociology, and women's studies). Engineering, liberal arts, and business are the largest.

Required: The typical baccalaureate Penn State academic program requires the completion of between 120 and 130 credits. The General Education requirements are common to all degree programs and compose about one third of the course work (45 credits). All students must also complete a Writing-Across-The-Curriculum course (3 credits), a first-year seminar (1 credit), United States Culture (3 credits), and International Cultures (3 credits) as part of their degree program.

Special: Co-op programs, internships, study-abroad in more than 45 countries, and work-study programs are available. Dual majors and student-designed majors are possible. Accelerated degree programs, a Washington semester, and a 3-2 engineering degree are also offered. There are 34 national honor societies, including Phi Beta Kappa, and a freshman honors program.

Faculty/Classroom: 65% of faculty are male; 35% are female. No introductory courses are taught by graduate students.

Admissions: 52% of the 2009-2010 applicants were accepted. The SAT scores for the 2009-2010 freshman class were: Critical Reading-- 13% below 500, 44% between 500 and 599, 36% between 600 and 700, and 7% above 700; Math--8% below 500, 30% between 500 and 599, 47% between 600 and 700, and 15% above 700; Writing--11% below 500, 40% between 500 and 599, 41% between 600 and 700, and 8% above 700. The ACT scores were 25% below 21, 32% between 21 and 23, 23% between 24 and 26, 10% between 27 and 28, and 10% above 28.

Requirements: The SAT or ACT is required. In addition, applicants may submit an SAT or ACT scores. Admissions decisions for first-year students are made on the basis of several combined factors. Approximately two thirds of the decision for each student is based upon the high school GPA. The remaining one third of the decision is based on the factors, which may include standardized critical reading and math test scores, class rank, personal statement, and activities list. Weighted average or class rank for students who have taken AP/Honors courses are considered. AP and CLEP credits are accepted.

Procedure: Freshmen are admitted fall, spring, and summer. Entrance exams should be taken in the junior year. There are early admissions, deferred admissions, and rolling admissions plans. Applications should be filed by November 30 for fall entry, along with a $50 fee. Notification is sent on a rolling basis. Applications are accepted on-line. 1456 applicants were on a recent waiting list, 1455 were accepted.

Transfer: 398 transfer students enrolled in 2008-2009. Each academic college has its own criteria for transfer admission. See http://admissions.psu.edu/academics/majors/requirements/transfer. Transfer

applicants need a minimum GPA of 2.0 and good academic standing. 36 of 120 credits required for the bachelor's degree must be completed at Penn State.

Visiting: There are regularly scheduled orientations for prospective students. There are guides for informal visits, visitors may sit in on classes, and stay overnight. To schedule a visit, contact Penn State Undergraduate Admissions at (814) 865-4700.

Financial Aid: The average financial indebtedness of the 2009 graduate was $28,680. The FAFSA is required. The deadline for filing freshman financial aid applications for fall entry is February 15.

International Students: There are 1663 international students enrolled. They must take the TOEFL with a minimum score of 550 on the paper-based TOEFL (PBT) or 80 on the Internet-based version (iBT). Students whose native language is English or if U.S. citizen or permanent resident must submit SAT or ACT scores; others submit TOEFL.

Computers: Wireless access is available. There are more than 50 computer labs and classrooms with about 2400 computers on the University Park campus. There are more than 1000 mobile computing ports that provide users with workstations and peripherals for Windows, Mac, and Unix platforms. The labs are equipped with printers and scanners, as well as more specialized hardware such as digital cameras and CD burners. All students may access the system. 24 hours a day, every day. There are no time limits. There is a fee. It is strongly recommended that all students have a personal computer. Students enrolled in The College of Education has a new notebook computer requirement for the Elementary must have a personal computer.

Graduates: From July 1, 2008 to June 30, 2009, 9692 bachelor's degrees were awarded. The most popular majors were business (18%), engineering (13%), and communications (9%). 1515 companies recruited on campus in 2008-2009. In an average class, 63% graduate in 4 years or less, 83% graduate in 5 years or less, and 85% graduate in 6 years or less. Of the 2008 graduating class, 22% were enrolled in graduate school within 6 months of graduation, and 64% were employed.

Admissions Contact: Anne Rohrbach, Executive Director of Admissions. E-Mail: *admissions@psu.edu* Web: *www.psu.edu*

PENNSYLVANIA COLLEGE OF TECHNOLOGY   D-2

Williamsport, PA 17701
(570) 327-4761
(800) 367-9222; (570) 321-5551

Full-time: 3748 men, 1721 women	**Faculty:** 297
Part-time: 390 men, 550 women	**Ph.D s:** 21%
Graduate: none	**Student/Faculty:** 18 to 1
Year: semesters, summer session	**Tuition:** $12,480 ($15,630)
Application Deadline: July 1	**Room & Board:** $8050
Freshman Class: 2501 applied, 2501 accepted, 1090 enrolled	
SAT or ACT: required	**NONCOMPETITIVE**

Pennsylvania College of Technology, founded in 1989, is a public technical college affiliated with Pennsylvania State University. There are 9 undergraduate schools. The library contains 111,065 volumes, 15,137 microform items, and 14,413 audio/video tapes/CDs/DVDs, and subscribes to 19,262 periodicals including electronic. Computerized library services include interlibrary loans, database searching, Internet access, and laptop Internet portals. Special learning facilities include a learning resource center, art gallery, radio station, restaurant and dental hygiene clinic that are open to the public, and the Penn College Children's Learning Center. The 124-acre campus is in an urban area 65 miles east of State College and 80 miles west of Wilkes Barre. Including any residence halls, there are 27 buildings.

Student Life: 89% of undergraduates are from Pennsylvania. Others are from 39 states and 15 foreign countries. 92% are white. The average age of freshmen is 19; all undergraduates, 20.

Housing: 1500 students can be accommodated in college housing, which includes single-sex and coed on-campus apartments. On-campus housing is available on a first-come, first-served basis. 78% of students commute. Alcohol is not permitted. All students may keep cars.

Activities: There are 4 local fraternities and 2 local sororities. There are 49 groups on campus, including computers, dance, environmental, ethnic, gay, honors, international, professional, radio, religious, social, social service, student government, and yearbook. Popular campus events include a cultural series, Spring Fling Week, and Penn Environment Week.

Sports: There are 9 intercollegiate sports for men and 9 for women, and 35 intramural sports for men and 35 for women. Facilities include a fitness center, a field house, a gym, a soccer field, 5 tennis courts, a sand volleyball court, an outdoor basketball court, and an intramural field.

Disabled Students: All of the campus is accessible. Facilities include wheelchair ramps, elevators, special parking, specially equipped restrooms, lowered drinking fountains, and lowered telephones.

Services: Counseling and information services are available, as is tutoring in some subjects, which is provided on request if tutors are available. There is a reader service for the blind, and remedial math, reading, and writing. Services for hearing-impaired students, adaptive equipment, and note takers are available. Also available is Smarthinking (on-line tutoring)

Campus Safety and Security: Measures include 24-hour foot and vehicle patrol, emergency notification system, self-defense education, and security escort services. There are shuttle buses, emergency telephones, lighted pathways/sidewalks, and controlled access to dorms/residences. Each residence hall complex is surrounded by an 8-foot fence with gates. The gates and all residence hall building doors are secured from 10 P.M. to 5 A.M. each day, and a uniformed police officer works at each complex from 9 P.M. to 5 A.M. each day. Identifications are checked from 10 P.M. to 5 A.M.

Programs of Study: Penn College confers B.S. and B.S.N. degrees. Associate degrees are also awarded. Bachelor's degrees are awarded in BUSINESS (accounting, business administration and management, management information systems, marketing and distribution, and marketing management), COMMUNICATIONS AND THE ARTS (graphic design), COMPUTER AND PHYSICAL SCIENCE (information sciences and systems), ENGINEERING AND ENVIRONMENTAL DESIGN (aircraft mechanics, automotive technology, civil engineering technology, computer engineering, construction management, construction technology, drafting and design, electrical/electronics engineering technology, graphic arts technology, manufacturing engineering, mechanical design technology, mechanical engineering technology, plastics engineering, technological management, and welding engineering), HEALTH PROFESSIONS (dental hygiene, health, health science, medical records administration/services, mental health/human services, nursing, occupational therapy, physician's assistant, and radiograph medical technology), SOCIAL SCIENCE (culinary arts and paralegal studies). Information technology, construction management, and electronics technology are the largest.

Required: To graduate, students must complete at least 120 credits with a minimum GPA of 2.0 overall and in the major. The core curriculum consists of 18 to 21 credits in humanities, social science, art, and foreign language, 9 in communications, 7 in science, 6 in math, 2 in health and fitness, and a course in computer information.

Special: Penn College offers cooperative and internship programs, cross-registration with Lycoming College and Penn State, dual and student-designed majors, and credit by exam and for work and/or life experience. There is a chapter of Phi Beta Kappa.

Faculty/Classroom: All teach undergraduates. No introductory courses are taught by graduate students. The average class size in a regular course is 18.

Admissions: All of the 2009-2010 applicants were accepted.

Requirements: The SAT or ACT is required. In addition, applicants must have a high school diploma or GED and must take the college's placement exams. Other admissions criteria vary by program. AP and CLEP credits are accepted.

Procedure: Freshmen are admitted to all sessions. Entrance exams should be taken prior to scheduling classes. There are early decision, early admissions, deferred admissions, and rolling admissions plans. Applications should be filed by July 1 for fall entry, along with a $50 fee. Notification is sent on a rolling basis. 48 applicants were on the 2009 waiting list; all were admitted. Applications are accepted on-line.

Transfer: 744 transfer students enrolled in 2008-2009. Transfer procedures vary with each degree program. Courses are evaluated for transfer equivalency. 36 of the final 60 credits required for the bachelor's degree must be completed at Penn College.

Visiting: There are regularly scheduled orientations for prospective students, including registration, a multimedia presentation, admission and financial aid sessions, a question-and-answer period, a tour of campus facilities, and a reception. There are guides for informal visits, and visitors may sit in on classes. To schedule a visit, contact the Office of Admissions.

Financial Aid: In 2009-2010, 78% of all full-time freshmen and 78% of continuing full-time students received some form of financial aid. 78% of all full-time freshmen and 78% of continuing full-time students received need-based aid. The average freshman award was $14,061. 1% of undergraduate students work part-time. Average annual earnings from campus work are $1364. The average financial indebtedness of the 2009 graduate was $26,877. The FAFSA and the college's own financial statement are required. The priority date for freshman financial aid applications for fall entry is April 1.

International Students: There are 21 international students enrolled. They must take the TOEFL with a minimum score of 500 on the paper-based TOEFL (PBT) or 61 on the Internet-based version (iBT).

Computers: Wireless access is available. There are 50 computer labs with more than 1500 PCs all networked with a 100 Mbps Internet connection. 80% of campus inside spaces have wireless coverage. All students may access the system. There are no time limits and no fees. Students enrolled in information technology and physician's assistant programs must have a personal computer.

Graduates: From July 1, 2008 to June 30, 2009, 568 bachelor's degrees were awarded. The most popular majors were nursing (5%), automotive technology (3%), and building construction technology (3%). In

an average class, 12% graduate in 3 years or less, 24% graduate in 4 years or less, 9% graduate in 5 years or less, and 1% graduate in 6 years or less. Of the 2008 graduating class, 65% were employed within 6 months of graduation.

Admissions Contact: Dennis Correll, Director of Admissions.
E-mail: *admissions@pct.edu* Web: *www.pct.edu*

PENNSYLVANIA STATE SYSTEM OF HIGHER EDUCATION

The Pennsylvania State System of Higher Education, established in 1983, is a public system in Pennsylvania. It is governed by a board of governors, whose chief administrator is the chancellor. The primary goal of the system is to provide high-quality liberal arts education at an affordable cost with a central mission of teaching and service. The main priorities are capital facilities matters of maintenance and funding, social equity, and tuition stabilization through appropriate funding. Profiles of the 4-year campuses are included in this section.

PHILADELPHIA BIBLICAL UNIVERSITY   F-3
Langhorne, PA 19047-2990   (215) 752-5800
                                    (800) 366-0049; (215) 702-4248

Full-time: 444 men, 533 women	**Faculty:** IIB, --$
Part-time: 42 men, 25 women	**Ph.D.s:** n/av
Graduate: 125 men, 149 women	**Student/Faculty:** n/av
Year: semesters, summer session	**Tuition:** $19,797
Application Deadline: open	**Room & Board:** $8050
Freshman Class: 465 applied, 356 accepted, 195 enrolled	
SAT or ACT: required	**LESS COMPETITIVE**

Philadelphia Biblical University, founded in 1913, is a private institution offering instruction in the Scriptures and liberal arts and professional theory. There are 7 undergraduate schools and 4 graduate schools. In addition to regional accreditation, PBU has baccalaureate program accreditation with CSWE, NASM, and NCATE. The library contains 127,711 volumes, 63,827 microform items, and 9237 audio/video tapes/CDs/DVDs, and subscribes to 10,161 periodicals including electronic. Computerized library services include interlibrary loans, database searching, Internet access, and laptop Internet portals. Special learning facilities include a learning resource center. The 115-acre campus is in a suburban area 30 miles north of Philadelphia. Including any residence halls, there are 25 buildings.

Student Life: 65% of undergraduates are from Pennsylvania. Others are from 41 states, 18 foreign countries, and Canada. 60% are from public schools. 76% are white; 13% African American. 96% are Protestant. The average age of freshmen is 18; all undergraduates, 23.

Housing: 666 students can be accommodated in college housing, which includes single-sex dorms, on-campus apartments, and married student housing. On-campus housing is guaranteed for all 4 years. 64% of students live on campus. Alcohol is not permitted. All students may keep cars.

Activities: There are no fraternities or sororities. There are 21 groups on campus, including art, band, cheerleading, choir, chorale, chorus, computers, drama, ethnic, honors, international, musical theater, newspaper, opera, orchestra, professional, religious, social, student government, and symphony. Popular campus events include Late Skates, Christmas and Valentine socials, and Spring Formal.

Sports: There are 6 intercollegiate sports for men and 6 for women, and 4 intramural sports for men and 4 for women. Facilities include a gym, a baseball diamond, soccer, hockey, and softball fields, a sand volleyball court, 4 tennis courts, a fitness circuit, and a weight room.

Disabled Students: All of the campus is accessible. Facilities include wheelchair ramps, elevators, special parking, specially equipped restrooms, lowered drinking fountains, and special housing.

Services: Counseling and information services are available, as is tutoring in most subjects. The AIMS Program provides academic support for freshmen who need it.

Campus Safety and Security: Measures include 24-hour foot and vehicle patrol, emergency notification system, and security escort services. There are shuttle buses, emergency telephones, and lighted pathways/sidewalks.

Programs of Study: PBU confers B.S., B.Mus., B.S.B.A., B.S.Ed., and B.S.W. degrees. Master's degrees are also awarded. Bachelor's degrees are awarded in BUSINESS (business administration and management), COMMUNICATIONS AND THE ARTS (music), EDUCATION (education), SOCIAL SCIENCE (biblical studies and social work). Bible is the strongest academically. Teacher education and Bible are the largest.

Required: Students must complete 51 credits in Bible, 48 in general education, and 27 in professional studies. A total of 126 credits, with a minimum GPA of 2.0, is required. 3 credits in phys ed must be taken. The number of hours in the major varies: 57 in Bible, 80 in music, 43 in social work, and 47 in education. All matriculating baccalaureate students major in Bible and receive a B.S. in Bible degree. About 48% of those students are enrolled in dual degree programs and receive the B.S. in Bible degree plus a degree in their professional area.

Special: PBU offers co-op programs in accounting, computer and microcomputer applications, and office administration; cross-registration with Bucks County Community College; various church ministries, education, social work, and music internships; and study abroad in Israel. An accelerated degree program in Biblical leadership is offered. There are dual majors in social work, music, education, and business administration. Student-designed interdisciplinary majors are possible. There is 1 national honor society and a freshman honors program.

Faculty/Classroom: 66% of faculty are male; 34% are female. 87% teach undergraduates. No introductory courses are taught by graduate students. The average class size in an introductory lecture is 25; in a laboratory, 9; and in a regular course, 20.

Admissions: 77% of the 2009-2010 applicants were accepted.

Requirements: The SAT or ACT is required, with satisfactory scores. A high school diploma or the GED is needed. An essay and a pastor's reference are required. A GPA of 2.0 is also required. AP and CLEP credits are accepted. Important factors in the admissions decision are advanced placement or honors courses, personality/intangible qualities, and leadership record.

Procedure: Freshmen are admitted fall and spring. Entrance exams should be taken in the junior or senior year of high school. There are early admissions, deferred admissions, and rolling admissions plans. Application deadlines are open. The application fee is $25. Notification is sent on a rolling basis. Applications are accepted on-line.

Transfer: 90 transfer students enrolled in 2008-2009. Transfers must submit an application, a pastor's reference, college transcripts, and a health form. SAT scores and high school transcripts are required if the student has fewer than 60 college credit hours. 60 of 126 credits required for the bachelor's degree must be completed at PBU.

Visiting: There are regularly scheduled orientations for prospective students, including chapel, class visits, a meal in the dining room, and an interview with a counselor. There are guides for informal visits, and visitors may sit in on classes and stay overnight. To schedule a visit, contact the Admissions Department at (215) 702-4235.

Financial Aid: In 2009-2010, 84% of all full-time freshmen and 83% of continuing full-time students received some form of financial aid. 69% of all full-time freshmen and 78% of continuing full-time students received need-based aid. The average freshman award was $13,544. Need-based scholarships or need-based grants averaged $10,419; need-based self-help aid (loans and jobs) averaged $3968; and other non-need-based awards and non-need-based scholarships averaged $5681. 55% of undergraduate students work part-time. Average annual earnings from campus work are $1750. The average financial indebtedness of the 2009 graduate was $28,214. The FAFSA is required. Check with the school for current application deadlines.

International Students: There were 17 international students enrolled in a recent year. They must take the TOEFL with a minimum score of 520 on the paper-based TOEFL (PBT) or 68 on the Internet-based version (iBT).

Computers: Wireless access is available. All students may access the system. There are no time limits and no fees. It is strongly recommended that all students have a personal computer.

Graduates: From July 1, 2008 to June 30, 2009, 307 bachelor's degrees were awarded. The most popular majors were philosophy and religious studies (70%), education (12%), and public administration/social services (9%). Of a recent graduating class, 38% were enrolled in graduate school within 6 months of graduation and 87% were employed.

Admissions Contact: Lisa Yoder, Director of Admissions. A campus DVD is available. E-mail: admissions@pbu.edu Web: www.pbu.edu

PHILADELPHIA UNIVERSITY   F-3

Philadelphia, PA 19144-5497   **(215) 951-2700**
(800) 951-7287; (215) 951-2907

Full-time: 886 men, 1789 women	Faculty: 110; IIA, av$
Part-time: 64 men, 153 women	Ph.D.s: 83%
Graduate: 211 men, 390 women	Student/Faculty: 24 to 1
Year: semesters, summer session	Tuition: $27,428
Application Deadline: open	Room & Board: $9182
Freshman Class: 3800 applied, 2707 accepted, 717 enrolled	
SAT or ACT: required	COMPETITIVE

Philadelphia University, founded in 1884, is a private institution offering preprofessional programs in architecture, design, business, sciences, textiles, fashion, and health. There are 6 undergraduate schools and 1 graduate school. In addition to regional accreditation, Phila. U. has baccalaureate program accreditation with ABET, FIDER, NAAB, and NASAD. The library contains 109,235 volumes, 125,000 microform items, and 50,630 audio/video tapes/CDs/DVDs, and subscribes to 1,011 periodicals including electronic. Computerized library services include interlibrary loans and database searching. Special learning facilities include a learning resource center, art gallery, and a design center. The 100-acre campus is in a suburban area 10 minutes west of metropolitan Philadelphia. Including any residence halls, there are 56 buildings.

Student Life: 52% of undergraduates are from Pennsylvania. Others are from 37 states, 24 foreign countries, and Canada. 65% are from public schools. 72% are white. 18% claim no religious affiliation The average age of freshmen is 23; all undergraduates, 20. 20% do not continue beyond their first year; 56% remain to graduate.

Housing: 1265 students can be accommodated in college housing, which includes single-sex and coed dorms, on-campus apartments, and off-campus apartments. In addition, there are town houses. On-campus housing is guaranteed for the freshman year only, is available on a first-come, first-served basis, and is available on a lottery system for upperclassmen. Priority is given to out-of-town students. 51% of students commute. Upperclassmen may keep cars.

Activities: 1% of men belong to 1 national fraternity; 1% of women belong to 1 national sorority. There are 30 groups on campus, including cheerleading, choir, dance, drama, ethnic, gay, honors, international, newspaper, professional, religious, social, social service, and student government. Popular campus events include annual fashion show and design competition, Welcome Week, and Spring Weekend.

Sports: There are 6 intercollegiate sports for men and 8 for women, and 13 intramural sports for men and 13 for women. Facilities include 2 gyms, a fitness center, 6 tennis courts, 3 athletic fields, and a student center recreation room.

Disabled Students: 85% of the campus is accessible. Facilities include wheelchair ramps, elevators, special parking, specially equipped restrooms, special class scheduling, lowered drinking fountains, and lowered telephones.

Services: Counseling and information services are available, as is tutoring in every subject. There is a reader service for the blind, and remedial math, reading, and writing, study skills workshops, course-related workshops, math review sessions, writing review sessions, time management and stress reduction workshops.

Campus Safety and Security: Measures include 24-hour foot and vehicle patrol, self-defense education, and security escort services. There are shuttle buses, emergency telephones, and lighted pathways/sidewalks.

Programs of Study: Phila. U. confers B.S. and B.Arch. degrees. Associate, master's, and doctoral degrees are also awarded. Bachelor's degrees are awarded in BIOLOGICAL SCIENCE (biochemistry and biology/biological science), BUSINESS (accounting, banking and finance, fashion merchandising, international business management, management information systems, management science, and marketing/retailing/merchandising), COMMUNICATIONS AND THE ARTS (graphic design and industrial design), COMPUTER AND PHYSICAL SCIENCE (chemistry, digital arts/technology, and science and management), ENGINEERING AND ENVIRONMENTAL DESIGN (architecture, engineering, environmental science, industrial engineering, interior design, landscape architecture/design, textile engineering, and textile technology), HEALTH PROFESSIONS (physician's assistant and premedicine), SOCIAL SCIENCE (biopsychology, fashion design and technology, and psychology). Physician's assistant, architecture, and engineering are the strongest academically. Architecture, fashion merchandising, and fashion design are the largest.

Required: All students are required to complete 60-credit residency with courses in math, science, social science, computer literacy, English, history, and the humanities. A total of 121 to 146 credits is required with an overall GPA of 2.0

Special: Internships in all academic majors, study abroad, a dual major in international business, an accelerated business administration degree program, and an integrated major in business and science are available. There is a freshman honors program.

Faculty/Classroom: 58% of faculty are male; 42% are female. All teach undergraduates, and 50% do both. No introductory courses are taught by graduate students. The average class size in an introductory lecture, 25, in a laboratory, 14, and in a regular course, 17.

Admissions: 71% of the 2009-2010 applicants were accepted. 31% of the current freshmen were in the top fifth of their class; 65% were in the top two fifths.

Requirements: The SAT or ACT is required. In addition, applicants should be high school graduates or have earned the GED. Recommended secondary preparation includes 4 years each of English and history, 3 years of math which must include algebra II and geometry, and 3 years of science and 2 years of social studies, and 1 year of history. Potential science majors are strongly urged to take 4 years of math and science. A GPA of 2.5 is required. AP and CLEP credits are accepted. Important factors in the admissions decision are evidence of special talent, extracurricular activities record, and leadership record.

Procedure: Freshmen are admitted fall and spring. There are deferred admissions and rolling admissions plans. Application deadlines are open. Application fee is $40. Notifications are sent November 1. Applications are accepted on-line.

Transfer: 95 transfer students enrolled in 2008-2009. A 2.5 GPA is usually required, and previously attended college transcripts. An interview is recommended. 60 of 121 credits required for the bachelor's degree must be completed at Phila. U..

Visiting: There are regularly scheduled orientations for prospective students, including an interview and a campus tour. There are guides for informal visits; visitors may sit in on classes and stay overnight. To schedule a visit, contact the Admissions Office at Patricia Coleman.

Financial Aid: In 2009-2010, at least 78% of all full-time freshmen and 71% of continuing full-time students received some form of financial aid. At least 78% of all full-time freshmen and 69% of continuing full-time students received need-based aid. The average freshman award was $22,240. Need-based scholarships or need-based grants averaged $16,233; need-based self-help aid (loans and jobs) averaged $5,326. Institutional awards averaged $6,542. 28% of undergraduate students work part-time. Average annual earnings from campus work are $1067. The average financial indebtedness of the 2009 graduate was $18,714. The FAFSA is required. Check with the school for current application deadlines.

International Students: There are 14 international students enrolled. The school actively recruits these students. They must take the TOEFL with a minimum score of 500 on the paper-based TOEFL (PBT). They must also take an English placement test.

Computers: Wireless access is available. There are more than 250 PCs available in general purpose labs, specific labs, all facilities on campus, and in the library. All students may access the system 7 days a week. There are no time limits and no fees. It is strongly recommended that all students have a personal computer.

Graduates: From July 1, 2008 to June 30, 2009, 561 bachelor's degrees were awarded. The most popular majors were business/marketing (41%), visual and performing arts (24%), and architecture (18%). 70 companies recruited on campus in 2008-2009. In an average class, 43% graduate in 4 years or less, 58% graduate in 5 years or less, and 60% graduate in 6 years or less. Of the 2008 graduating class, 19% were enrolled in graduate school within 6 months of graduation, and 71% were employed.

Admissions Contact: Christine Greb, Director of Admissions. E-Mail: *admissions@philau.edu* Web: *www.philau.edu*

POINT PARK UNIVERSITY   B-3

Pittsburgh, PA 15222   (412) 392-3430; (412) 392-3902

Full-time: 1023 men, 1579 women	**Faculty:** ; IIA, -$
Part-time: 329 men, 476 women	**Ph.D.s:** 62%
Graduate: 258 men, 321 women	**Student/Faculty:** n/av
Year: semesters, summer session	**Tuition:** $21,334
Application Deadline: open	**Room & Board:** $9020
Freshman Class: 3089 applied, 2235 accepted, 530 enrolled	
SAT CR/M/W: 521/502/516	**ACT:** 22 COMPETITIVE

Point Park University, founded in 1960, is an independent institution offering programs in liberal arts, business, engineering technology, natural and health science, communication, and the performing arts. There are 4 undergraduate schools and 4 graduate schools. In addition to regional accreditation, Point Park has baccalaureate program accreditation with ABET. The library contains 119,000 volumes, 17,478 microform items, and 3563 audio/video tapes/CDs/DVDs, and subscribes to 39,000 periodicals including electronic. Computerized library services include interlibrary loans, database searching, Internet access, and laptop Internet portals. Special learning facilities include a learning resource center, art gallery, radio station, TV station, theaters, dance studios, and digital film-editing suites. The campus is in an urban area in downtown Pittsburgh. Including any residence halls, there are 15 buildings.

Student Life: 83% of undergraduates are from Pennsylvania. Others are from 44 states, 35 foreign countries, and Canada. 76% are white; 20% African American. The average age of freshmen is 18; all undergraduates, 24. 23% do not continue beyond their first year; 53% remain to graduate.

Housing: 942 students can be accommodated in college housing, which includes single-sex and coed dorms and on-campus apartments. In addition, there are living and learning communities. On-campus housing is guaranteed for all 4 years. 75% of students commute. Upperclassmen may keep cars.

Activities: There are no fraternities or sororities. There are 18 groups on campus, including choir, chorale, computers, dance, drama, ethnic, film, gay, honors, international, literary magazine, musical theater, newspaper, photography, political, professional, radio and TV, religious, social, social service, and student government. Popular campus events include Snowball (Christmas) Dance, Spring Fling (spring dance), and dance and theater productions.

Sports: There are 5 intercollegiate sports for men and 6 for women, and 8 intramural sports for men and 8 for women. Facilities include a recreation center and a 130-seat auditorium.

Disabled Students: 90% of the campus is accessible. Facilities include wheelchair ramps, elevators, specially equipped rest rooms, special class scheduling, lowered drinking fountains, lowered telephones, and special housing.

Services: Counseling and information services are available, as is tutoring in some subjects. Learning-disabled services are available on a case-

by-case basis. There is a reader service for the blind and remedial math, reading, and writing.

Campus Safety and Security: Measures include 24-hour foot and vehicle patrol, emergency notification system, self-defense education, and security escort services. There are shuttle buses, emergency telephones, and lighted pathways/sidewalks.

Programs of Study: Point Park confers B.A., B.S., and B.F.A. degrees. Associates and master's degrees are also awarded. Bachelor's degrees are awarded in BIOLOGICAL SCIENCE (biology/biological science and biotechnology), BUSINESS (accounting, business administration and management, funeral home services, human resources, management science, and sports management), COMMUNICATIONS AND THE ARTS (advertising, applied art, arts administration/management, broadcasting, communications, dance, dramatic arts, English, film arts, journalism, media arts, photography, and video), COMPUTER AND PHYSICAL SCIENCE (computer science, digital arts/technology, and information sciences and systems), EDUCATION (dance education, drama education, early childhood education, elementary education, and secondary education), ENGINEERING AND ENVIRONMENTAL DESIGN (civil engineering technology, electrical/electronics engineering technology, engineering management, environmental science, mechanical engineering technology, and systems engineering), HEALTH PROFESSIONS (health care administration and respiratory therapy), SOCIAL SCIENCE (behavioral science, criminal justice, history, international studies, law enforcement and corrections, liberal arts/general studies, paralegal studies, political science/government, psychology, and public administration). Accelerated business, dance, and theater are the largest.

Required: All majors leading to a baccalaureate degree require a minimum of 120 credits. Most programs require 42 core curriculum credits, with at least 30 completed in residence. A 2.0 GPA is required.

Special: Cross-registration is available through the Pittsburgh Council on Higher Education. The university offers internships, study abroad, work study, dual and student-designed majors, credit by exam and for life/military/work experience, and nondegree study. Capstone programs are available for students with associate degrees. Accelerated degree programs are available. There are 2 national honor societies and a freshman honors program.

Faculty/Classroom: 61% of faculty are male; 39% are female. No introductory courses are taught by graduate students.

Admissions: 72% of the 2009-2010 applicants were accepted. The SAT scores for the 2009-2010 freshman class were: Critical Reading--37% below 500, 47% between 500 and 599, 14% between 600 and 700, and 2% above 700; Math--48% below 500, 37% between 500 and 599, 14% between 600 and 700, and 1% above 700; Writing--41% below 500, 42% between 500 and 599, 15% between 600 and 700, and 2% above 700. The ACT scores were 35% below 21, 34% between 21 and 23, 22% between 24 and 26, 5% between 27 and 28, and 4% above 28.

Requirements: The SAT or ACT is required. In addition, students should have completed 12 academic credits or 16 Carnegie units consisting of 4 in English, 3 in history, science, and math, and 2 years of foreign language. The GED is accepted. Theater and dance students must audition, and an interview is requested for all candidates. A GPA of 2.0 is required. AP and CLEP credits are accepted. Important factors in the admissions decision are advanced placement or honors courses, evidence of special talent, and personality/intangible qualities.

Procedure: Freshmen are admitted to all sessions. Entrance exams should be taken in the junior or senior year. There are deferred admissions and rolling admissions plans. Application deadlines are open. Application fee is $40. Notification is sent on a rolling basis. Applications are accepted on-line with no application fee.

Transfer: 553 transfer students enrolled in 2008-2009. Applicants must have completed 12 credit hours with at least a 2.0 GPA. The SAT or ACT and an interview are recommended. 30 of 120 credits required for the bachelor's degree must be completed at Point Park.

Visiting: There are regularly scheduled orientations for prospective students. There are guides for informal visits and visitors may sit in on classes. To schedule a visit, contact the Office of Admissions.

Financial Aid: In 2009-2010, 99% of all full-time freshmen and 92% of continuing full-time students received some form of financial aid. 82% of continuing full-time students received need-based aid. The average freshmen award was $21,338, with $4,440 ($13,720 maximum) from need-based scholarships or need-based grants; $7,912 ($12,500 maximum) from need-based self-help aid (loans and jobs); $6,405 ($21,334 maximum) from non-need-based athletic scholarships; and $6,553 ($17,000 maximum) from other non-need-based awards and non-need-based scholarships. 21% of undergraduate students work part-time. Average annual earnings from campus work are $2330. The average financial indebtedness of the 2009 graduate was $19,860. The FAFSA is required. The priority date for freshman financial aid applications for fall entry is April 15. The deadline for filing freshman financial aid applications for fall entry is December 1.

International Students: The school actively recruits these students. They must take the TOEFL with a minimum score of 500 on the paper-based TOEFL (PBT) or 61 on the Internet-based version (iBT). Students may also satisfy the university's English language proficiency requirements by completing level 112 of the university's ELS program and also take the TWE, scoring 4. Students whose native language is English may submit SAT scores.

Computers: Wireless access is available. All students may access the system 7 days a week; lab hours vary by facility. There are no time limits and no fees.

Graduates: From July 1, 2008 to June 30, 2009, 673 bachelor's degrees were awarded. The most popular majors were business (accelerated) (15%), criminal justice (9%), and theater arts (7%). In an average class, 53% graduate in 6 years or less.

Admissions Contact: Joell Minford, Full-Time Admissions. A campus DVD is available. E-Mail: enroll@pointpark.edu
Web: www.pointpark.edu

ROBERT MORRIS UNIVERSITY
B-3
Moon Township, PA 15108-1189

(800) 762-0097
(412) 397-2425

Full-time: 1753 men, 1353 women	**Faculty:** 177; IIA, av$
Part-time: 265 men, 286 women	**Ph.D.s:** 81%
Graduate: 500 men, 626 women	**Student/Faculty:** 18 to 1
Year: semesters, summer session	**Tuition:** $20,560
Application Deadline: July 1	**Room & Board:** $10,370
Freshman Class: 3775 applied, 3460 accepted, 722 enrolled	
SAT CR/M/W: 499/510/480	**ACT:** 21 **LESS COMPETITIVE**

Robert Morris University, founded in 1921, is a private institution offering 334 undergraduate degree programs and 17 master's and doctoral degree programs. There are 5 undergraduate schools and 5 graduate schools. In addition to regional accreditation, RMU has baccalaureate program accreditation with AACSB, ABET, and TEAC. The 2 libraries contain 125,121 volumes, 325,289 microform items, and 34,471 audio/video tapes/CDs/DVDs, and subscribe to 766 periodicals including electronic. Computerized library services include interlibrary loans, database searching, and Internet access. Special learning facilities include a learning resource center, art gallery, radio station, TV station, and manufacturing lab for engineering and other students. The 230-acre campus is in a suburban area 17 miles southwest of downtown Pittsburgh. Including any residence halls, there are 25 buildings.

Student Life: 86% of undergraduates are from Pennsylvania. Others are from 34 states, 33 foreign countries, and Canada. 90% are from public schools. 80% are white. 41% are Catholic; 35% Protestant. The average age of freshmen is 18; all undergraduates, 23. 21% do not continue beyond their first year; 58% remain to graduate.

Housing: 1320 students can be accommodated in college housing, which includes single-sex and coed dorms and on-campus apartments. On-campus housing is available on a first-come, first-served basis. 67% of students commute. Alcohol is not permitted. All students may keep cars.

Activities: 3% of men belong to 4 national fraternities; 4% of women belong to 3 national sororities. There are 95 groups on campus, including band, cheerleading, choir, computers, drama, ethnic, film, gay, honors, international, literary magazine, marching band, musical theater, newspaper, pep band, photography, political, professional, radio and TV, religious, social, social service, and student government. Popular campus events include Snow Ball and Spring Fest.

Sports: There are 10 intercollegiate sports for men and 13 for women, and 15 intramural sports for men and 15 for women. Facilities include a field house, gym, health club, and 11 athletic fields. The sports center (4 miles away) has 2 hockey rinks, golf dome, batting cages, health club, and an 8-lane track.

Disabled Students: 75% of the campus is accessible. Facilities include wheelchair ramps, elevators, special parking, specially equipped restrooms, special class scheduling, lowered drinking fountains, and lowered telephones.

Services: Counseling and information services are available, as is tutoring in most subjects. There is a reader service for the blind, and remedial math, reading, and writing.

Campus Safety and Security: Measures include 24-hour foot and vehicle patrol, emergency notification system, and security escort services. There are shuttle buses, emergency telephones, and lighted pathways/sidewalks.

Programs of Study: RMU confers B.A., B.S., B.F.A., B.S.B.A., and B.S.N. degrees. Master's and doctoral degrees are also awarded. Bachelor's degrees are awarded in BIOLOGICAL SCIENCE (biology/biological science), BUSINESS (accounting, banking and finance, business administration and management, hospitality management services, marketing/retailing/merchandising, organizational behavior, and sports management), COMMUNICATIONS AND THE ARTS (communications, English, and media arts), COMPUTER AND PHYSICAL SCIENCE (actuarial science, information sciences and systems, and mathematics), EDUCATION (business education and elementary education), ENGINEERING AND ENVIRONMENTAL DESIGN (engineering, environ-

mental science, and manufacturing engineering), HEALTH PROFESSIONS (health care administration, nuclear medical technology, and nursing), SOCIAL SCIENCE (applied psychology, economics, and social science). Actuarial science and engineering are the strongest academically. Accounting, management, and communication are the largest.

Required: All candidates must complete 126 to 135 credit hours, including 24 to 31 in the major, with a 2.0 GPA overall and a 2.5 in the major. A core curriculum varies with each major and consists of humanities, communication skills, social sciences, computing, and math. All students must demonstrate competency in computer software applications.

Special: The university offers internship programs in all majors, cross-registration with the 9 colleges of the Pittsburgh Council of Higher Education, work-study programs, study abroad in 12 countries, and nondegree study. Credit by exam and pass/fail options are available. There are 9 national honor societies, a freshman honors program, and 1 departmental honors program.

Faculty/Classroom: 63% of faculty are male; 37% are female. All teach undergraduates, 80% do research, and 80% do both. No introductory courses are taught by graduate students. The average class size in an introductory lecture is 23; in a laboratory, 12; and in a regular course, 23.

Admissions: 92% of the 2009-2010 applicants were accepted. The SAT scores for the 2009-2010 freshman class were: Critical Reading--50% below 500, 40% between 500 and 599, 9% between 600 and 700, and 1% above 700; Math--42% below 500, 36% between 500 and 599, 19% between 600 and 700, and 3% above 700; Writing--53% below 500, 37% between 500 and 599, 9% between 600 and 700, and 1% above 700. The ACT scores were 40% below 21, 30% between 21 and 23, 19% between 24 and 26, 7% between 27 and 28, and 4% above 28. 24% of the current freshmen were in the top fifth of their class; 57% were in the top two fifths. 3 freshmen graduated first in their class.

Requirements: The SAT is required. In addition, applicants should be graduates of an accredited secondary school or hold a GED diploma. They must have completed 16 Carnegie units, including 4 in English, 3 each in math and social studies, 2 in science, and 1 in history. An interview is required for some and recommended for all others. A GPA of 2.0 is required. AP and CLEP credits are accepted. Important factors in the admissions decision are advanced placement or honors courses, leadership record, and personality/intangible qualities.

Procedure: Freshmen are admitted both fall and spring. Entrance exams should be taken by fall or late winter of the senior year. There are deferred admissions and rolling admissions plans. Applications should be filed by July 1 for fall entry and December 1 for spring entry, along with a $30 fee. Notification is sent on a rolling basis. Applications are accepted on-line.

Transfer: 378 transfer students enrolled in 2008-2009. Students must have a minimum 2.0 GPA in nondevelopmental academic courses. Those with fewer than 30 earned credits must also submit an official high school transcript and test results of the SAT or ACT. An interview is recommended. 30 of 126 to 135 credits required for the bachelor's degree must be completed at RMU.

Visiting: There are regularly scheduled orientations for prospective students, consisting of placement testing, orientation, and academic advising. There are guides for informal visits; visitors may sit in on classes and stay overnight. To schedule a visit, contact the Enrollment Office at (412) 397-5200.

Financial Aid: In 2009-2010, 80% of all full-time freshmen and 77% of continuing full-time students received some form of financial aid. 79% of all full-time freshmen and 73% of continuing full-time students received need-based aid. The average freshman award was $18,482. Need-based scholarships or need-based grants averaged $13,211; need-based self-help aid (loans and jobs) averaged $6182; and non-need-based athletic scholarships averaged $14,950. All undergraduate students work part-time. The average financial indebtedness of the 2009 graduate was $35,055. RMU is a member of CSS. The FAFSA and PHEAA is required. The deadline for filing freshman financial aid applications for fall entry is May 1.

International Students: There are 97 international students enrolled. The school actively recruits these students. They must take the TOEFL with a minimum score of 500 on the paper-based TOEFL (PBT) or 61 on the Internet-based version (iBT).

Computers: Wireless access is available. Computer labs with a total of 300 PCs are provided in several classroom buildings as well as in the library and residence halls. Dorm rooms are wired for high-speed Internet access, and wireless nodes are provided in several campus locations. All students may access the system. There are no time limits and no fees.

Graduates: From July 1, 2008 to June 30, 2009, 865 bachelor's degrees were awarded. The most popular majors were management (14%), accounting (12%), and marketing (11%). 140 companies recruited on campus in 2008-2009. In an average class, 34% graduate in 4 years or less, 53% graduate in 5 years or less, and 58% graduate in 6 years or less. Of the 2008 graduating class, 5% were enrolled in graduate school within 6 months of graduation, and 87% were employed.

Admissions Contact: Kellie Laurenzi, Dean of Admissions. A campus DVD is available. E-mail: *enrollmentoffice@rmu.edu* Web: *www.rmu.edu*

ROSEMONT COLLEGE F-4

Rosemont, PA 19010-1699

(610) 527-0200
(800) 331-0708; (610) 520-4399

Full-time: 82 men, 352 women	**Faculty:** 29
Part-time: 27 men, 95 women	**Ph.Ds:** 91%
Graduate: 90 men, 314 women	**Student/Faculty:** 15 to 1
Year: semesters	**Tuition:** $26,250
Application Deadline: open	**Room & Board:** $10,580
Freshman Class: 1104 applied, 595 accepted, 177 enrolled	
SAT CR/M/W: 450/440/440	**ACT:** 21 **COMPETITIVE**

Rosemont College, founded in 1921, is an independent liberal arts and sciences college affiliated with the Roman Catholic Church. Accelerated degree and graduate programs are offered in the School of Graduate and Professional Studies. There is 1 graduate school. The library contains 165,000 volumes, 24,981 microform items, and 3000 audio/video tapes/CDs/DVDs, and subscribes to 1660 periodicals including electronic. Computerized library services include interlibrary loans, database searching, Internet access, and laptop Internet portals. Special learning facilities include a learning resource center and art gallery. The 56-acre campus is in a suburban area 11 miles west of Philadelphia. Including any residence halls, there are 15 buildings.

Student Life: 72% of undergraduates are from Pennsylvania. Others are from 15 states and 9 foreign countries. 46% are African American; 32% white. 60% are Catholic; 17% Protestant; 15% Muslim, Quaker, and not indicated. The average age of freshmen is 18; all undergraduates, 23. 8% do not continue beyond their first year; 72% remain to graduate.

Housing: 293 students can be accommodated in college housing, which includes single-sex and coed dorms. In addition, there are special-interest houses. On-campus housing is guaranteed for all 4 years. 68% of students live on campus; of those, 60% remain on campus on weekends. All students may keep cars.

Activities: There are no fraternities or sororities. There are more than 20 groups on campus, including art, band, choir, chorus, dance, drama, ethnic, gay, honors, international, jazz band, literary magazine, marching band, musical theater, newspaper, orchestra, photography, political, professional, religious, social service, student government, symphony, and yearbook. Popular campus events include Oktoberfest, Founders Day, and International/Multi-Cultural Festival.

Sports: There are 5 intercollegiate sports for men and 7 for women. Facilities include hockey and softball fields, tennis courts, treadmills, weight equipment, a 500-seat auditorium, and indoor basketball, badminton, and volleyball courts.

Disabled Students: 20% of the campus is accessible. Facilities include wheelchair ramps, elevators, special parking, specially equipped restrooms, special class scheduling, lowered drinking fountains, and lowered telephones.

Services: Counseling and information services are available, as is tutoring in every subject. There is a writing and learning resource center.

Campus Safety and Security: Measures include 24-hour foot and vehicle patrol, emergency notification system, self-defense education, and security escort services. There are shuttle buses, emergency telephones, lighted pathways/sidewalks, and electronically operated residence hall entrances activated by security cards.

Programs of Study: Rosemont confers B.A., B.S., and B.F.A. degrees. Master's degrees are also awarded. Bachelor's degrees are awarded in BIOLOGICAL SCIENCE (biochemistry and biology/biological science), BUSINESS (accounting and business administration and management), COMMUNICATIONS AND THE ARTS (communications, English, fine arts, French, German, and Spanish), COMPUTER AND PHYSICAL SCIENCE (chemistry and mathematics), EDUCATION (art education, foreign languages education, and secondary education), ENGINEERING AND ENVIRONMENTAL DESIGN (environmental science), HEALTH PROFESSIONS (predentistry and premedicine), SOCIAL SCIENCE (economics, history, humanities, Italian studies, liberal arts/general studies, philosophy, political science/government, prelaw, psychology, religion, social science, sociology, and women's studies). Psychology, English literature, and studio art are the largest.

Required: A new general education curriculum was initiated in the fall 2009 semester. The new core curriculum includes the First Year Connections Seminar and courses in ethics, multicultural and gender studies, global awareness, foreign language, sustainability, and creative expression. Senior Capstone is required for most majors. Each student is required to complete an experiential learning component as a requirement for graduation from the Undergraduate College. Among the experiential components, a student can choose internships, service learning, undergraduate research, and study-abroad opportunities.

Special: Cross-registration opportunities are available with Villanova, Arcadia, Eastern, Holy Family, Immaculata, and Neumann Universities;

Cabrini, Gwynedd-Mercy, and Chestnut Hill Colleges; and the Art Institute International Exchange Program. There is a joint admission program with Temple University School of Dentistry and Drexel University College of Medicine. Internships, study abroad, a Washington semester, dual and student-designed majors, and accelerated degree programs are also available. There are 6 national honor societies.

Faculty/Classroom: 34% of faculty are male; 66% are female. All teach undergraduates, and 70% both teach and do research. No introductory courses are taught by graduate students. The average class size in an introductory lecture is 20; in a laboratory, 10; and in a regular course, 12.

Admissions: 54% of the 2009-2010 applicants were accepted. The SAT scores for the 2009-2010 freshman class were: Critical Reading--71% below 500, 21% between 500 and 599, and 8% between 600 and 700; Math--77% below 500, 18% between 500 and 599, and 5% between 600 and 700; Writing--73% below 500, 20% between 500 and 599, and 7% between 600 and 700.

Requirements: The SAT or ACT is required. The GED is accepted. Applicants must complete 16 academic units, including 4 in English and 2 each in foreign language, history, math, and science. An interview is recommended. A GPA of 2.0 is required. AP and CLEP credits are accepted. Important factors in the admissions decision are advanced placement or honors courses, leadership record, and recommendations by school officials.

Procedure: Freshmen are admitted fall and spring. Entrance exams should be taken before January of the senior year. There are deferred admissions and rolling admissions plans. Application deadlines are open. Application fee is $35. Notification is sent on a rolling basis. Applications are accepted on-line.

Transfer: 44 transfer students enrolled in 2008-2009. Transfer applicants should submit transcripts from each college attended, a letter of good standing from the dean at the last college attended, and catalogs from the colleges from which the student wishes to transfer credits. Students with fewer than 30 credits are required to submit high school transcripts and SAT scores. The minimum GPA is 2.0. An associate degree and interview are recommended. 36 of 120 credits required for the bachelor's degree must be completed at Rosemont.

Visiting: There are regularly scheduled orientations for prospective students, including a campus tour and meetings with financial aid advisers, faculty, and student life representatives. There are guides for informal visits, and visitors may sit in on classes and stay overnight. To schedule a visit, contact the Admissions Office at (610) 526-2966.

Financial Aid: In 2009-2010, 99% of all full-time freshmen and 95% of continuing full-time students received some form of financial aid. 93% of all full-time freshmen and 86% of continuing full-time students received need-based aid. The average freshman award was $25,744. Need-based scholarships or need-based grants averaged $22,462 ($36,530 maximum) and need-based self-help aid (loans and jobs) averaged $3562 ($11,000 maximum). 27% of undergraduate students work part-time. Average annual earnings from campus work are $805. The average financial indebtedness of the 2009 graduate was $18,943. The FAFSA is required. The priority date for freshman financial aid applications for fall entry is February 15. The deadline for filing freshman financial aid applications for fall entry is March 15.

International Students: There are 4 international students enrolled. The school actively recruits these students. They must take the TOEFL with a minimum score of 500 on the paper-based TOEFL (PBT) or 61 on the Internet-based version (iBT). They must also take the SAT or ACT.

Computers: Wireless access is available. All students may access the system. There are no time limits and no fees.

Graduates: From July 1, 2008 to June 30, 2009, 144 bachelor's degrees were awarded. The most popular majors were psychology (23%), English literature (15%), and accounting/business (13%). In an average class, 74% graduate in 4 years or less and 77% graduate in 5 years or less. 18 companies recruited on campus in 2008-2009. Of the 2008 graduating class, 20% were enrolled in graduate school within 6 months of graduation, and 60% were employed.

Admissions Contact: Chuck Walz, Vice President for Enrollment Management. A campus DVD is available.
E-mail: *admissions@rosemont.edu* Web: *www.rosemont.edu*

SAINT FRANCIS UNIVERSITY   C-3

Loretto, PA 15940   (814) 472-3100
(866) 342-5738; (814) 472-3335

Full-time: 500 men, 680 women	**Faculty:** n/av
Part-time: 50 men, 130 women	**Ph.D.s:** n/av
Graduate: 200 men, 310 women	**Student/Faculty:** 13 to 1
Year: semesters, summer session	**Tuition:** $25,554
Application Deadline: June 1	**Room & Board:** $9148
Freshman Class: n/av	
SAT or ACT: required	**LESS COMPETITIVE**

Saint Francis University, founded in 1847, is a private Franciscan institution affiliated with the Roman Catholic Church. It offers programs in business, education, humanities, sciences, social science, and preprofessional programs. There is 1 undergraduate schools and 7 graduate schools. Enrollment figures in the above capsule and figures in this profile are approximate. In addition to regional accreditation, Saint Francis has baccalaureate program accreditation with APTA, CAHEA, and CSWE. The library contains 117,870 volumes, 7648 microform items, and 2701 audio/video tapes/CDs/DVDs, and subscribes to 7293 periodicals including electronic. Computerized library services include interlibrary loans, database searching, and Internet access. Special learning facilities include a learning resource center, art gallery, radio station, TV station, classroom satellite hookup, art studio, wireless technology lab, and computer assurance lab. The 600-acre campus is in a rural area 85 miles east of Pittsburgh. Including any residence halls, there are 23 buildings.

Student Life: 77% of undergraduates are from Pennsylvania. Others are from 27 states, 6 foreign countries, and Canada. 66% are from public schools. 85% are white; 11% African American. 55% are Catholic; 40% Protestant. The average age of freshmen is 19; all undergraduates, 21. 21% do not continue beyond their first year; 62% remain to graduate.

Housing: 983 students can be accommodated in college housing, which includes single-sex dorms, on-campus apartments, off-campus apartments, married student housing, and intensive study floors. On-campus housing is guaranteed for all 4 years. 56% of students live on campus; of those, 20% remain on campus on weekends. Alcohol is not permitted. Upperclassmen may keep cars.

Activities: 1% of men belong to 1 national fraternity; 2% of women belong to 1 local and 2 national sororities. There are 54 groups on campus, including academic, art, cheerleading, choir, computers, drama, ethnic, honors, international, literary magazine, newspaper, pep band, photography, political, professional, radio and TV, religious, social, social service, student government, theater production, and yearbook. Popular campus events include Days of Reflection, Winter Weekend, and Christmas Mass.

Sports: There are 9 intercollegiate sports for men and 12 for women, and 8 intramural sports for men and 8 for women. Facilities include an athletic center with a 6-lane swimming pool, 3 racquetball courts, a suspended running track, a weight room, a 3500-seat basketball arena, and a multipurpose gym. Outdoor facilities include recreational areas and game fields, jogging/walking trails, 9-hole golf course, a lake, and beach volleyball pits.

Disabled Students: Facilities include wheelchair ramps, elevators, special parking, specially equipped restrooms, lowered drinking fountains, lowered telephones, and special housing.

Services: Counseling and information services are available, as is tutoring in most subjects. There is remedial math, reading, and writing.

Campus Safety and Security: Measures include 24-hour foot and vehicle patrol, self-defense education, and security escort services. There are emergency telephones, lighted pathways/sidewalks, and a certified police force.

Programs of Study: Saint Francis confers B.A., B.S., B.S.N., and B.S.W. degrees. Master's degrees are also awarded. Bachelor's degrees are awarded in BIOLOGICAL SCIENCE (biology/biological science), BUSINESS (accounting, management information systems, and management science), COMMUNICATIONS AND THE ARTS (communications, English, French, modern language, and Spanish), COMPUTER AND PHYSICAL SCIENCE (chemistry, computer science, and mathematics), EDUCATION (elementary education and secondary education), HEALTH PROFESSIONS (medical laboratory technology, nursing, occupational therapy, physical therapy, and physician's assistant), SOCIAL SCIENCE (criminal justice, economics, history, international studies, philosophy, political science/government, psychology, public administration, religion, social work, and sociology). Business, occupational therapy, and chemistry are the strongest academically. Business, physician's assistant, and education are the largest.

Required: Students must complete 128 credits, with at least 36 in the major, while maintaining a 2.0 GPA. The core curriculum, totaling 58 credits, includes writing, public speaking, fine arts, foreign language, history, philosophy, religious studies (with required service component), psychology, sociology, political science, and economics. A word processing and research workshop is required in the freshman year. In addition to a comprehensive exam in the major, an English proficiency exam must be taken in the junior year.

Special: The university offers internships, co-op programs, study abroad in 10 countries, a Washington semester, work-study programs, and nondegree study. Student-designed majors and 3-2 engineering degrees with Pennsylvania State and Clarkson Universities and the University of Pittsburgh are available. There is a dual major available in international business/modern languages. Credit by exam and pass/fail options are also offered. There are 11 national honor societies, a freshman honors program, and 10 departmental honors programs.

Faculty/Classroom: 56% of faculty are male; 44% are female. 99% teach undergraduates and 50% also do research. No introductory courses are taught by graduate students. The average class size in an introductory lecture is 23; in a laboratory, 16; and in a regular course, 19.

Requirements: The SAT or ACT is required. In addition, Applicants must be graduates of an accredited secondary school or have earned a GED certificate. All applicants must have completed 16 Carnegie units, consisting of 4 years of English, 2 each of math and social science, 1 lab science, and 7 academic electives. Applicants to biology and allied health majors need an additional unit of science. Chemistry, computer science, engineering, and math applicants need 4 math units and 2 science units. Physical therapy applicants must have 4 units of math and 4 of science. AP and CLEP credits are accepted. Important factors in the admissions decision are advanced placement or honors courses, extracurricular activities record, and recommendations by school officials.

Procedure: Freshmen are admitted to all sessions. Entrance exams should be taken in spring of the junior year and fall of the senior year. There are deferred admissions and rolling admissions plans. Applications should be filed by June 1 for fall entry. Applicantions to physician's assistant, physical therapy, and occupational therapy programs should be filed by January 15. The application fee is $30. Notification is sent on a rolling basis. Applications are accepted on-line.

Transfer: Applicants must have a minimum GPA of 2.0 for consideration, 2.5 for nursing majors, and 2.75 for physician's assistant majors. 64 of 128 credits required for the bachelor's degree must be completed at Saint Francis.

Visiting: There are regularly scheduled orientations for prospective students, including an interview by financial aid and admission staff, tour, meeting with faculty, and attending class. There are guides for informal visits; visitors may sit in on classes and stay overnight. To schedule a visit, contact the Admissions Office.

Financial Aid: The FAFSA and the college's own financial statement are required. Check with the school for current deadlines.

International Students: The school actively recruits these students. They must take the TOEFL and also take the SAT or ACT.

Computers: All students may access the system. There are no time limits and no fees. All students are required to have a personal computer. A laptop is provided by the university.

Admissions Contact: Evan Lipp, Dean for Enrollment Management. E-Mail: *admissions@francis.edu* Web: *www.francis.edu*

SAINT JOSEPH'S UNIVERSITY   F-3

Philadelphia, PA 19131   (610) 660-1300
(888) BE-A-HAWK; (610) 660-1314

Full-time: 2215 men, 2312 women	**Faculty:** 284; IIA, +$
Part-time: 375 men, 502 women	**Ph.D.s:** 98%
Graduate: 1211 men, 1723 women	**Student/Faculty:** 16 to 1
Year: semesters, summer session	**Tuition:** $34,090
Application Deadline: February 1	**Room & Board:** $11,575
Freshman Class: 6520 applied, 5370 accepted, 1189 enrolled	
SAT CR/M: 550/570	**ACT:** 23 **VERY COMPETITIVE**

Saint Joseph's University, founded in 1851, is a Catholic, private college affiliated with the Jesuit order. It offers undergraduate programs in arts and sciences and business administration. There are 3 undergraduate schools and 2 graduate schools. In addition to regional accreditation, Saint Joseph's has baccalaureate program accreditation with AACSB. The 2 libraries contain 355,000 volumes, 868,000 microform items, and 5,100 audio/video tapes/CDs/DVDs, and subscribe to 29,000 periodicals including electronic. Computerized library services include interlibrary loans, database searching, and Internet access. Special learning facilities include a learning resource center, art gallery, radio station, instructional media center, foreign language labs, Mandeville Hall, Wall Street Trading Room, and Claver Honors House. The 103-acre campus is in a suburban area on the western edge of Philadelphia and eastern Montgomery County. Including any residence halls, there are 75 buildings.

Student Life: 52% of undergraduates are from Pennsylvania. Others are from 38 states, 38 foreign countries, and Canada. 49% are from public schools. 81% are white. 72% are Catholic; 17% other Christian, non-Christian and non-Jewish. The average age of freshmen is 18; all undergraduates, 20. 12% do not continue beyond their first year; 80% remain to graduate.

Housing: 2385 students can be accommodated in college housing, which includes single-sex and coed dorms, on-campus apartments, and off-campus apartments. In addition, there are honors houses, special-interest houses, and special interest floors. On-campus housing is available on a lottery system for upperclassmen. 59% of students live on campus. Upperclassmen may keep cars.

Activities: 8% of men belong to 4 national fraternities; 11% of women belong to 4 national sororities. There are 100 groups on campus, including art, cheerleading, choir, chorale, dance, debate, drama, ethnic, forensics, gay, honors, international, jazz band, literary magazine, musical theater, newspaper, pep band, political, professional, radio, religious, social, social service, and student government. Popular campus events include Hand in Hand, Up 'Til Dawn, and Intercultural Week.

Sports: There are 9 intercollegiate sports for men and 9 for women. Facilities include a recreation complex consisting of a field house, a 4-court area, convertible for basketball, tennis, and volleyball, an indoor, 4-lane, 220-yard practice running track, a 25-meter, 8-lane indoor pool with a 300-seat observation area, 4 racquetball/handball courts, and saunas. Outside the complex, there is a 400-meter, 6-lane Balsam track and an All Pro field. Adjacent to the field are 4 tennis courts.

Disabled Students: 85% of the campus is accessible. Facilities include wheelchair ramps, elevators, special parking, specially equipped restrooms, special class scheduling, lowered drinking fountains, lowered telephones special housing, automatic eye doors, curb cuts, a specially equipped van for wheelchairs, a pool lift, and a bell system at major road crossings.

Services: Counseling and information services are available, as is tutoring in most subjects. There is a reader service for the blind. In addition to tutoring, there are study and life skills workshops, supplemental instruction, a writing center, and other educational support services to help students.

Campus Safety and Security: Measures include 24-hour foot and vehicle patrol, emergency notification system, self-defense education, and security escort services. There are shuttle buses, emergency telephones, lighted pathways/sidewalks, and a bicycle patrol.

Programs of Study: Saint Joseph's confers B.A., B.S., and B.B.A. degrees. Associate, master's, and doctoral degrees are also awarded. Bachelor's degrees are awarded in BIOLOGICAL SCIENCE (biology/biological science), BUSINESS (accounting, banking and finance, business administration and management, international business management, management information systems, and marketing/retailing/merchandising), COMMUNICATIONS AND THE ARTS (English, fine arts, French, German, Latin, and Spanish), COMPUTER AND PHYSICAL SCIENCE (actuarial science, chemistry, computer science, information sciences and systems, mathematics, and physics), EDUCATION (elementary education, secondary education, and special education), ENGINEERING AND ENVIRONMENTAL DESIGN (environmental science), HEALTH PROFESSIONS (health care administration), SOCIAL SCIENCE (criminal justice, economics, European studies, French studies, history, international relations, philosophy, political science/government, psychology, public administration, sociology, and theological studies). Biology and accounting are the strongest academically. Marketing, finance, and biology are the largest.

Required: All students must take general education courses in English, theology, philosophy, and history. Distribution requirements include courses in social/behavioral sciences, theology, foreign language at the intermediate level, math, natural sciences, and philosophy. A minimum of 120 credit hours is required for graduation.

Special: The university offers internships, a Washington semester, advanced 5-year degrees in international marketing, psychology, and education, dual majors, minor concentrations, and study abroad in 16 countries. There are co-op programs for students majoring in accounting, finance, marketing, pharmaceutical marketing, decision/system sciences, management, food marketing, and international business and an interdisciplinary major in health services. There are 17 national honor societies, including Phi Beta Kappa, and a freshman honors program.

Faculty/Classroom: 61% of faculty are male; 39% are female. 80% teach undergraduates. No introductory courses are taught by graduate students. The average class size in an introductory lecture, 29, in a laboratory, 15 and in a regular course, 26.

Admissions: 82% of the 2009-2010 applicants were accepted. The SAT scores for the 2009-2010 freshman class were: Critical Reading--19% below 500, 54% between 500 and 599, 24% between 600 and 700, and 3% above 700; Math--17% below 500, 48% between 500 and 599, 31% between 600 and 700, and 4% above 700; Writing--16% below 500, 55% between 500 and 599, 26% between 600 and 700, and 3% above 700. The ACT scores were 16% below 21, 34% between 21 and 23, 28% between 24 and 26, 11% between 27 and 28, and 11% above 28.

Requirements: The SAT or ACT is required. In addition, careful consideration is given to the applicant's GPA, the rigor of the high school record, the application essay, counselor or teacher recommendations, and character/personal qualities. Other factors include class rank, ACT/SAT scores, volunteer work, work experience, and alumni connections. A GPA of 3.0 is required. AP credits are accepted. Important factors in the admissions decision are advanced placement or honors courses, extracurricular activities record, and leadership record.

Procedure: Freshmen are admitted fall and spring. Entrance exams should be taken in the spring of the junior year and/or the fall of the senior year. There are early action and deferred admissions plans. Early action applications should be filed by November 15; regular applications should be filed by February 1 for fall entry, along with a $60 fee. Notifications are sent for early action by December 25; for regular decision by March 15. 234 applicants were on the 2009 waiting list, 114 were admitted. Applications are accepted on-line.

Transfer: 67 transfer students enrolled in 2008-2009. Transfer applicants must have a GPA of at least 2.5 and must submit former test scores and high school and college transcripts. 60 of 120 credits required for the bachelor's degree must be completed at Saint Joseph's.

Visiting: There are regularly scheduled orientations for prospective students, consisting of open houses, tours, and information sessions. There are guides for informal visits and visitors may sit in on classes. To schedule a visit, contact the Admissions Office at 888-BE-A-HAWK.

Financial Aid: Saint Joseph's is a member of CSS. The FAFSA is required. Check with the school for current application deadlines.

International Students: There are 91 international students enrolled. The school actively recruits these students. They must take the TOEFL with a minimum score of 550 on the paper-based TOEFL (PBT) or 79 on the Internet-based version (iBT). They must also take the SAT or ACT, scoring at least 450 on Critical Reading.

Computers: Wireless access is available. There are more than 80 technologically equipped classrooms, 60 computer lab/learning spaces, 15 classrooms with built in TV/VCR and DVD players, and 5 video-conferencing rooms. All university-owned housing is connected to the campus voice and data networks. In total, there are more than 7000 network connections points in classrooms, labs, offices, and residence halls. All students may access the system. There are no time limits and no fees. It is strongly recommended that all students have a personal computer. Students enrolled in Laptops for business school and psychology majors must have a personal computer. A Lenovo Thinkpad (business school); Apple (psychology majors) is recommended.

Graduates: From July 1, 2008 to June 30, 2009, 1108 bachelor's degrees were awarded. The most popular majors were marketing (15%), finance (10%), and accounting (8%). 760 companies recruited on campus in 2008-2009. In an average class, 71% graduate in 4 years or less, 76% graduate in 5 years or less, and 78% graduate in 6 years or less. Of the 2008 graduating class, 23% were enrolled in graduate school within 6 months of graduation, and 63% were employed.

Admissions Contact: Maureen Mathis, Executive Director of Undergraduate Admissions. A campus DVD is available. E-Mail: admit@sju.edu Web: www.sju.edu

SAINT VINCENT COLLEGE

B-2

Latrobe, PA 15650

(724) 537-4540
(800) SVC-5549; (724) 532-5069

Full-time: 800 men, 800 women	**Faculty:** IIB, -$
Part-time: 50 men, 50 women	**Ph.D.s:** n/av
Graduate: 90 men, 130 women	**Student/Faculty:** 18 to 1
Year: semesters, summer session	**Tuition:** $25,350
Application Deadline: see profile	**Room & Board:** $8082
Freshman Class: n/av	
SAT or ACT: required	**VERY COMPETITIVE**

Saint Vincent College, founded in 1846, is a private Catholic college of liberal arts and sciences sponsored by the Benedictine monks. There are 4 undergraduate schools and 3 graduate schools. Enrollment figures in the above capsule and figures in this profile are approximate. In addition to regional accreditation, Saint Vincent has baccalaureate program accreditation with ACBSP. The library contains 278,561 volumes, 91,144 microform items, and 5482 audio/video tapes/CDs/DVDs, and subscribes to 2500 periodicals including electronic. Computerized library services include interlibrary loans, database searching, and Internet access. Special learning facilities include a learning resource center, art gallery, planetarium, radio station, TV station, observatory, radio telescope, and small-business development center. The 200-acre campus is in a suburban area 35 miles east of Pittsburgh. Including any residence halls, there are 22 buildings.

Student Life: 87% of undergraduates are from Pennsylvania. Others are from 24 states, 15 foreign countries, and Canada. 76% are from public schools. 93% are white. 60% are Catholic; 21% Protestant; 18% unknown/no preference. The average age of freshmen is 18; all undergraduates, 21. 16% do not continue beyond their first year; 70% remain to graduate.

Housing: 1283 students can be accommodated in college housing, which includes coed dorms and on-campus apartments. On-campus housing is guaranteed for the freshman year only, is available on a first-come, first-served basis, and is available on a lottery system for upperclassmen. 75% of students live on campus; of those, 70% remain on campus on weekends. All students may keep cars.

Activities: There are no fraternities or sororities. There are 63 groups on campus, including art, band, cheerleading, choir, chorale, chorus, dance, drama, environmental, ethnic, honors, international, literary magazine, musical theater, newspaper, pep band, political, professional, radio and TV, religious, social, social service, student government, and yearbook. Popular campus events include Founder's Day, the Threshold Lecture Series, and Pittsburgh Steelers training camp.

Sports: There are 10 intercollegiate sports for men and 10 for women, and 9 intramural sports for men and 9 for women. Facilities include a 2400-seat gym, a 1050-seat grandstand, basketball and volleyball facilities, a weight and exercise room, an indoor pool, tennis courts, baseball, soccer, and football fields, a 999-seat auditorium/arena, and a student union and game room area.

Disabled Students: 95% of the campus is accessible. Facilities include wheelchair ramps, elevators, special parking, specially equipped restrooms, lowered drinking fountains, and special housing.

Services: Counseling and information services are available, as is tutoring in most subjects. The Opportunity Office provides individual counseling and a study skills class for first-year students.

Campus Safety and Security: Measures include 24-hour foot and vehicle patrol, emergency notification system, and security escort services. There are emergency telephones and lighted pathways/sidewalks.

Programs of Study: Saint Vincent confers B.A. and B.S. degrees. Master's degrees are also awarded. Bachelor's degrees are awarded in BIOLOGICAL SCIENCE (biochemistry, bioinformatics, and biology/biological science), BUSINESS (accounting, banking and finance, business administration and management, international business management, and marketing/retailing/merchandising), COMMUNICATIONS AND THE ARTS (art, art history and appreciation, arts administration/management, communications, English, fine arts, French, music, music performance, Spanish, studio art, and visual and performing arts), COMPUTER AND PHYSICAL SCIENCE (chemistry, computer science, information sciences and systems, mathematics, and physics), EDUCATION (art education, business education, elementary education, psychology education, and science education), ENGINEERING AND ENVIRONMENTAL DESIGN (environmental science), HEALTH PROFESSIONS (occupational therapy, physical therapy, physician's assistant, predentistry, premedicine, prepharmacy, and preveterinary science), SOCIAL SCIENCE (anthropology, economics, history, liberal arts/general studies, philosophy, political science/government, prelaw, psychology, public affairs, religious education, sociology, and theological studies). Biology, economics, and psychology are the strongest academically. Biology, psychology, and history are the largest.

Required: To graduate, students must complete 124 credit hours with a minimum GPA of 2.0. All students are required to take Language and Rhetoric, Exploring Religious Meaning, and Philosophy I. The core curriculum includes 9 hours each of social science, theology, and English, 8 of natural sciences, 6 hours each of history, philosophy, and foreign language, and 3 of math. Total number of hours in major varies depending on the program. All majors require a culminating activity, such as a thesis, research project, or capstone course/seminar.

Special: There is cross-registration with Seton Hill University, co-op programs, internships, study abroad in Europe and Asia, a Washington semester, a work-study program, dual majors, a general studies degree, credit by exam and for life/military/work experience, nondegree study, and pass/fail options. There is an accelerated degree engineering program and a 3-2 engineering option with Boston University, Pennsylvania state university, the University of Pittsburgh, and the Catholic University of America. The college offers teacher certificate programs in early childhood, elementary, and secondary education. There are 11 national honor societies, a freshman honors program, and 100 departmental honors programs.

Faculty/Classroom: 68% of faculty are male; 32% are female. All teach and do research. No introductory courses are taught by graduate students. The average class size in an introductory lecture is 24; in a laboratory, 17; and in a regular course, 20.

Requirements: The SAT or ACT is required. In addition, applicants must complete 15 academic credits, including 4 of English, 3 each of social studies and math, 2 of foreign language, and 1 of a lab science. Art students must submit a portfolio, and music and theater students must audition. An essay is required. A GED is accepted. A GPA of 3.2 is required. AP and CLEP credits are accepted. Important factors in the admissions decision are advanced placement or honors courses, evidence of special talent, and recommendations by school officials.

Procedure: Freshmen are admitted fall and spring. Entrance exams should be taken at the end of the junior year or the beginning of the senior year. There are early admissions, deferred admissions, and rolling admissions plans. Check with the school for current application deadlines. The application fee is $25. Applications are accepted on-line. 213 applicants were on a recent waiting list, 54 were accepted.

Transfer: 57 transfer students enrolled in a recent year. Transfer applicants must submit transcripts from postsecondary schools attended and a catalog describing courses taken, plus secondary school transcript(s). 34 of 124 credits required for the bachelor's degree must be completed at Saint Vincent.

Visiting: There are regularly scheduled orientations for prospective students, consisting of a general information session, an informal meeting with faculty, and campus tours. There are guides for informal visits; visitors may sit in on classes and stay overnight. To schedule a visit, contact the Admission and Financial Aid Office.

Financial Aid: In a recent year, 97% of all full-time freshmen and 93% of continuing full-time students received some form of financial aid. 79% of all full-time freshmen and 74% of continuing full-time students received need-based aid. The average freshmen award was $19,319, with $5533 ($15,500 maximum) from need-based scholarships or need-based grants; $3787 ($7800 maximum) from need-based self-help aid (loans and jobs); and $8890 ($31,356 maximum) from other non-need-based awards and non-need-based scholarships. 44% of undergraduate students work part-time. Average annual earnings from campus work are $1895. The average financial indebtedness of a recent graduate was $20,548. The FAFSA is required. Check with the school for current deadlines.

International Students: There were 21 international students enrolled in a recent year. They must take the TOEFL with a minimum score of 550 on the paper-based TOEFL (PBT). They must also take the SAT or ACT.

Computers: Wireless access is available. There are 286 public PCs in many locations on campus, network connections in all residence hall rooms, and wireless access in many campus locations, including the student center. All students may access the system during computer lab hours and 24 hours from dorm rooms. There are no time limits and no fees.

Graduates: In a recent year, 331 bachelor's degrees were awarded. The most popular majors were history (10%), psychology (9%), and biology (7%). 140 companies recruited on campus in a recent year. In an average class, 1% graduate in 3 years or less, 64% graduate in 4 years or less, 68% graduate in 5 years or less, and 70% graduate in 6 years or less. Of a recent graduating class, 23% were enrolled in graduate school within 6 months of graduation, and 53% were employed.

Admissions Contact: Admission and Financial Aid Office. A campus DVD is available. E-Mail: admission@stvincent.edu Web: www.stvincent.edu

SETON HILL UNIVERSITY   B-4
Greensburg, PA 15601-1599   (724) 838-4255
(800) 826-6234; (724) 830-1294

Full-time: 530 men, 851 women	**Faculty:** 68; IIB, -$
Part-time: 60 men, 131 women	**Ph.D.s:** 88%
Graduate: 98 men, 306 women	**Student/Faculty:** 20 to 1
Year: 4-1-4, summer session	**Tuition:** $26,622
Application Deadline: open	**Room & Board:** $8550
Freshman Class: 1728 applied, 1143 accepted, 299 enrolled	
SAT or ACT: recommended	**COMPETITIVE**

Seton Hill University, founded in 1883, is a private university affiliated with the Roman Catholic Church and offers programs in liberal arts and career preparation. There is 1 graduate school. In addition to regional accreditation, Seton Hill has baccalaureate program accreditation with ADA, CSWE, and NASM. The library contains 123,538 volumes, 5403 microform items, and 6684 audio/video tapes/CDs/DVDs, and subscribes to 423 periodicals including electronic. Computerized library services include interlibrary loans, database searching, and Internet access. Special learning facilities include an art gallery, a TV station, a nursery school that functions as laboratory school for education students, a performing arts center, a visual arts center, and a technology wing. The 200-acre campus is in a small town 35 miles east of Pittsburgh. Including any residence halls, there are 19 buildings.

Student Life: 79% of undergraduates are from Pennsylvania. Others are from 32 states, 16 foreign countries, and Canada. 80% are white. The average age of freshmen is 18; all undergraduates, 21. 19% do not continue beyond their first year; 64% remain to graduate.

Housing: 750 students can be accommodated in college housing, which includes single-sex and coed dorms. On-campus housing is guaranteed for all 4 years. 69% of students live on campus. Alcohol is not permitted. All students may keep cars.

Activities: There are no fraternities or sororities. There are 40 groups on campus, including art, bagpipe, band, cheerleading, choir, chorale, chorus, dance, drama, entrepreneurial, environmental, ethnic, gay, honors, international, jazz band, literary magazine, marching band, musical theater, newspaper, orchestra, pep band, political, professional, religious, social, social service, student government, and symphony. Popular campus events include Christmas on the Hill, Family Weekend, and President's Reception.

Sports: There are 10 intercollegiate sports for men and 12 for women. Facilities include 2 gyms, 1 with a seating capacity of 1200, a fitness center, an aerobics room, a swimming pool, a field house with weight and training rooms, 3 natural grass playing fields, and a football stadium.

Disabled Students: 95% of the campus is accessible. Facilities include wheelchair ramps, elevators, special parking, specially equipped restrooms, special class scheduling, lowered drinking fountains, and lowered telephones.

Services: Counseling and information services are available, as is tutoring in most subjects. There is a reader service for the blind and remedial math and writing.

Campus Safety and Security: Measures include 24-hour foot and vehicle patrol, emergency notification system, self-defense education, and security escort services. There are shuttle buses, emergency telephones, and lighted pathways/sidewalks.

Programs of Study: Seton Hill confers B.A., B.S., B.F.A., B.Mus., B.S.Med.Tech., and B.S.W. degrees. Master's degrees are also awarded. Bachelor's degrees are awarded in BIOLOGICAL SCIENCE (biochemistry and biology/biological science), BUSINESS (accounting, business administration and management, business economics, entrepreneurial studies, human resources, international business management, management information systems, marketing/retailing/merchandising, personnel management, sports management, and tourism), COMMUNICATIONS AND THE ARTS (art history and appreciation, arts administration/management, communications, creative writing, dramatic arts, English, fine arts, graphic design, journalism, music, musical theater, performing arts, Spanish, studio art, theater design, and theater management), COMPUTER AND PHYSICAL SCIENCE (actuarial science, chemistry, computer science, mathematics, and physics), EDUCATION (art education, early childhood education, elementary education, English education, foreign languages education, home economics education, mathematics education, music education, science education, secondary education, social science education, and special education), ENGINEERING AND ENVIRONMENTAL DESIGN (engineering), HEALTH PROFESSIONS (art therapy, medical laboratory technology, music therapy, pharmacy, physician's assistant, predentistry, premedicine, preosteopathy, and preveterinary science), SOCIAL SCIENCE (child care/child and family studies, criminal justice, dietetics, economics, family/consumer resource management, family/consumer studies, food production/management/services, forensic studies, history, human services, international studies, liberal arts/general studies, political science/government, prelaw, psychology, religion, religious music, social work, and sociology). Sciences, education, and fine arts are the strongest academically. Psychology, art, and business are the largest.

Required: The core corriculum requires 6 credits in Western cultures, 6 credits in writing, and 3 each in theology, philosophy/senior seminar, math, computer science, science, college-level foreign language, U.S. cultures, non-Western cultures, and artistic expression. A total of 120 credit hours with a minimum GPA of 2.0 is required for graduation.

Special: There are cooperative programs in all majors and cross-registration with St. Vincent College, the University of Pittsburgh at Greensburg, and Westmoreland County Community College. Internships are encouraged. Seton Hill offers study abroad, a Washington semester, work-study, dual and student-designed majors, accelerated degree programs, a 3-2 engineering program with Pennsylvania State University and Georgia Institute of Technology, a 2-2 nursing program with Catholic University of America, a 3-2 or 3-1 medical technology program with area hospitals, credit by exam and for life/military/work experience, nondegree study, and pass/fail options. There are 5 national honor societies and a freshman honors program.

Faculty/Classroom: 40% of faculty are male; 60% are female. 87% teach undergraduates, and 60% do research. No introductory courses are taught by graduate students. The average class size in an introductory lecture is 25; in a laboratory, 16; and in a regular course, 17.

Admissions: 66% of the 2009-2010 applicants were accepted.

Requirements: The SAT or ACT is recommended. 2 graded writing samples are accepted in place of SAT or ACT scores. A total of 15 Carnegie units is required, including 4 each of English and electives, 2 each of math, social studies, and foreign language, and 1 of a lab science. Art students must submit a portfolio; music and theater students must audition. An interview is recommended. The GED is accepted with supporting recommendations. A GPA of 2.5 is required. AP and CLEP credits are accepted. Important factors in the admissions decision are advanced placement or honors courses, evidence of special talent, and leadership record.

Procedure: Freshmen are admitted fall and spring. Entrance exams should be taken in spring of the junior year or fall of the senior year. There are deferred admissions and rolling admissions plans. Application deadlines are open. The application fee is $35. Notification is sent on a rolling basis. Applications are accepted on-line.

Transfer: 99 transfer students enrolled in a recent year. Applicants must submit college transcripts and have a GPA of at least 2.0. An interview is recommended, as are supporting letters. 48 of 120 credits required for the bachelor's degree must be completed at Seton Hill.

Visiting: There are regularly scheduled orientations for prospective students, consisting of an introduction, an address by the president or dean, an open reception with faculty, a financial aid session, a student panel, and a campus tour. There are guides for informal visits, and visitors may sit in on classes and stay overnight. To schedule a visit, contact Campus Visit Coordinator at (724) 838-4255.

Financial Aid: In a recent year, 95% of all full-time freshmen and 82% of continuing full-time students received some form of financial aid. 94% of all full-time freshmen and 81% of continuing full-time students received need-based aid. The average freshman award was $21,878. Need-based scholarships or need-based grants averaged $17,293 ($20,500 maximum); need-based self-help aid (loans and jobs) averaged $5542 ($9861 maximum); non-need-based athletic scholarships averaged $9177 ($28,900 maximum); and other non-need-based awards and non-need-based scholarships averaged $4423 ($28,900 maximum). 60% of undergraduate students work part-time. Average annual earnings from campus work are $1300. The average financial indebtedness of the 2009 graduate was $26,872. The FAFSA and the college's own financial statement are required. The priority date for freshman financial aid applications for fall entry is April 30. The deadline for filing freshman financial aid applications for fall entry is August 1.

International Students: There are 26 international students enrolled. The school actively recruits these students. They must take the TOEFL with a minimum score of 550 on the paper-based TOEFL (PBT) or 79 on the Internet-based version (iBT).

Computers: Wireless access is available. All classrooms, labs, offices, and dorm rooms have Internet access. There are approximately 600 university-owned computers used daily on campus. The Management/Student Information System and the Course Management System as well as all e-mail accounts are accessible from off campus via Internet. All students may access the system 24 hours per day. There are no time limits and no fees.

Graduates: From July 1, 2008 to June 30, 2009, 272 bachelor's degrees were awarded. The most popular majors were business (23%), physician's assistant (7%), and art (4%). 51 companies recruited on campus in 2008-2009. In an average class, 2% graduate in 3 years or less, 50% graduate in 4 years or less, 54% graduate in 5 years or less, and 59% graduate in 6 years or less. Of a recent graduating class, 31% were enrolled in graduate school within 6 months of graduation and 92% were employed.

Admissions Contact: Sherri Bett, Director of Admissions. A campus DVD is available. E-mail: *admit@setonhill.edu*
Web: *www.setonhill.edu*

SHIPPENSBURG UNIVERSITY OF PENNSYLVANIA C-4

Shippensburg, PA 17257-2299   (717) 477-1231; (717) 477-4016

Full-time: 3157 men, 3479 women	**Faculty:** 312; IIA, av$
Part-time: 123 men, 183 women	**Ph.D.s:** 93%
Graduate: 410 men, 901 women	**Student/Faculty:** 21 to 1
Year: semesters, summer session	**Tuition:** $7444 ($15,880)
Application Deadline:	**Room & Board:** $6698
Freshman Class: 7001 applied, 5008 accepted, 1679 enrolled	
SAT CR/M/W: 500/520/490	**ACT:** 20 **COMPETITIVE**

Shippensburg University, founded in 1871, is a public university that is part of the Pennsylvania State System of Higher Education, offering undergraduate and graduate degree programs in the College of Arts and Sciences, College of Business, and College of Education and Human Services. There are 4 undergraduate schools and 1 graduate school. In addition to regional accreditation, Ship has baccalaureate program accreditation with AACSB, ABET, CSWE, and NCATE. The library contains 439,254 volumes, 1.3 million microform items, and 72,831 audio/video tapes/CDs/DVDs, and subscribes to 1,062 periodicals including electronic. Computerized library services include interlibrary loans, database searching, Internet access, and laptop Internet portals. Special learning facilities include a learning resource center, art gallery, planetarium, radio station, TV station, a closed-circuit television, fashion archives center, vertebrate museum, women's center, on-campus elementary school, electron microscope, greenhouse, and herbarium. The 200-acre campus is in a rural area 40 miles southwest of Harrisburg. Including any residence halls, there are 50 buildings.

Student Life: 94% of undergraduates are from Pennsylvania. Others are from 18 states, 10 foreign countries, and Canada. 88% are from public schools. 82% are white. The average age of freshmen is 18; all undergraduates, 21. 28% do not continue beyond their first year; 63% remain to graduate.

Housing: 2643 students can be accommodated in college housing, which includes single-sex and coed dorms, on-campus apartments, and off-campus apartments. In addition, there is a designated "quiet" hall and a scholars hall. On-campus housing is guaranteed for the freshman year only. 63% of students commute. Alcohol is not permitted. All students may keep cars.

Activities: 6% of men belong to 12 national fraternities; 8% of women belong to 15 national sororities. There are 200 groups on campus, including activities program board, art, band, big brother/big sister, cheerleading, choir, chorale, chorus, computers, dance, debate, drama, environmental, ethnic, gay, honors, international, jazz band, literary magazine, marching band, musical theater, newspaper, orchestra, pep band, photography, political, professional, radio and TV, religious, ROTC ranger challenge team, social, social service, student government, vet's, and yearbook. Popular campus events include planetarium shows, Senior Olympics, and Summer Music Festival.

Sports: There are 8 intercollegiate sports for men and 10 for women, and 8 intramural sports for men and 8 for women. Facilities include a

7700-seat stadium for football and track-and-field events and complexes for varsity baseball, softball, and tennis. There is a 450-seat stadium with an artificial turf surface for soccer, field hockey, and lacrosse. Basketball, volleyball, and wrestling competitions are conducted within a 2700-seat facility, with swimming facilities. Outdoor recreational facilities include a 12-acre sports complex. Students also have access to a 64,000-square-foot recreational building.

Disabled Students: 91% of the campus is accessible. Facilities include wheelchair ramps, elevators, special parking, specially equipped restrooms, special class scheduling, lowered drinking fountains, and lowered telephones.

Services: Counseling and information services are available, as is tutoring in most subjects, most general education courses and writing. Individual meetings with learning specialists are available to students interested in developing more efficient learning strategies and group study.

Campus Safety and Security: Measures include 24-hour foot and vehicle patrol, emergency notification system, self-defense education, and security escort services. There are shuttle buses, emergency telephones, and lighted pathways/sidewalks. Residence halls are equipped with an automatic heat/smoke detection sprinkler system monitored 24 hours a day by police. A strobe light unit notifies students who are hearing impaired. Residence hall doors are locked 24 hours a day. There are digital cameras at the main entrance to residence halls, computer labs, and other buildings, as well as many exterior cameras covering parking lots and other campus areas. A text emergency message system was also recently implemented.

Programs of Study: Ship confers B.A., B.S., B.S.B.A., B.S.Ed., and B.S.W. degrees. Master's degrees are also awarded. Bachelor's degrees are awarded in BIOLOGICAL SCIENCE (biology/biological science), BUSINESS (accounting, banking and finance, management information systems, management science, marketing management, and supply chain management), COMMUNICATIONS AND THE ARTS (art, communications, English, French, journalism, Spanish, and speech/debate/rhetoric), COMPUTER AND PHYSICAL SCIENCE (applied physics, chemistry, computer science, earth science, geoenvironmental studies, mathematics, and physics), EDUCATION (art education, business education, elementary education, English education, foreign languages education, mathematics education, middle school education, science education, secondary education, and social studies education), ENGINEERING AND ENVIRONMENTAL DESIGN (environmental science), HEALTH PROFESSIONS (exercise science and health care administration), SOCIAL SCIENCE (criminal justice, early childhood studies, economics, geography, history, interdisciplinary studies, political science/government, psychology, public administration, social work, and sociology). Elementary education, criminal justice, and psychology are the largest.

Required: General education courses include English composition, oral communications, math, and history, as well as courses in logic and numbers for rational thinking; linguistic, literary, artistic, and cultural traditions; lab science; biological and physical science; political, economic, and geographic sciences; and social and behavioral sciences. The core curriculum varies for degree programs. Most degree programs require 120 credit hours, with 22 to 30 hours in the major, and a 2.0 minimum GPA for graduation.

Special: The university offers internships, an accelerated degree program, study abroad in 21 countries and a 3-2 engineering degree with Pennsylvania State University and the University of Maryland. Students have the option of taking courses for a semester at one of the 13 other schools in the Pennsylvania State System of Higher Education. There is also a Visiting Student Program with Wilson College and with the Fashion Institute of Technology of New York City. As a member of the Marine Science Consortium, the university also offers opportunities for field and laboratory studies in marine science at Wallops Island, Virginia. There are 23 national honor societies, a freshman honors program, and 1 departmental honors program.

Faculty/Classroom: 55% of faculty are male; 45% are female. 95% teach undergraduates, and 34% do both. No introductory courses are taught by graduate students. The average class size in an introductory lecture, 33, in a laboratory, 17, and in a regular course, 28.

Admissions: 72% of the 2009-2010 applicants were accepted. The SAT scores for the 2009-2010 freshman class were: Critical Reading--45% below 500, 43% between 500 and 599, 11% between 600 and 700, and 1% above 700; Math--38% below 500, 47% between 500 and 599, 14% between 600 and 700, and 1% above 700; Writing--53% below 500, 40% between 500 and 599, and 7% between 600 and 700. The ACT scores were 50% below 21, 31% between 21 and 23, 14% between 24 and 26, and 5% between 27 and 28. 25% of the current freshmen were in the top fifth of their class; 59% were in the top two fifths. 7 freshmen graduated first in their class.

Requirements: The SAT is required. In addition, applicants are urged to pursue a typical college preparatory program, which should include 4 units of English, 3 social sciences, 3 math, 3 lab science, and 3 foreign language. A GED is accepted. AP and CLEP credits are accepted. Important factors in the admissions decision are advanced placement or honors courses, recommendations by school officials, and evidence of special talent.

Procedure: Freshmen are admitted fall and spring. Entrance exams should be taken in the junior year and senior year. There are early admissions, deferred admissions, and rolling admissions plans. Application deadlines are open. The fall 2008 application fee was $30. Notification is sent on a rolling basis. Applications are accepted on-line.

Transfer: 548 transfer students enrolled in 2008-2009. Applicants must provide high school and college transcripts and SAT or ACT scores if they have fewer than 30 college credits. 45 of 120 credits required for the bachelor's degree must be completed at Ship.

Visiting: There are regularly scheduled orientations for prospective students, including daily academic group meetings, campus tours, and 5 weekend open house programs per year. There are guides for informal visits and visitors may sit in on classes. To schedule a visit, contact the Admissions Office.

Financial Aid: In 2009-2010, 85% of all full-time freshmen and 78% of continuing full-time students received some form of financial aid. 61% of all full-time freshmen and 53% of continuing full-time students received need-based aid. The average freshmen award was $9,277, with $6,115 ($16,122 maximum) from need-based scholarships or need-based grants; $5,764 ($21,670 maximum) from need-based self-help aid (loans and jobs); $2,113 ($14,722 maximum) from non-need-based athletic scholarships; and $6,783 ($25,500 maximum) from other non-need-based awards and non-need-based scholarships. 5% of undergraduate students work part-time. Average annual earnings from campus work are $1135. The average financial indebtedness of the 2009 graduate was $21,163. Ship is a member of CSS. The FAFSA and PHEAA are required. The deadline for filing freshman financial aid applications for fall entry is May 1.

International Students: There are 19 international students enrolled. They must take the TOEFL with a minimum score of 550 on the paper-based TOEFL (PBT) or 80 on the Internet-based version (iBT). Students whose native language is English must submit SAT scores instead of TOEFL. They must also take the SAT or ACT.

Computers: Wireless access is available. Students may use their PCs to access the campus network from residence halls using both wired and wireless connectivity. Additionally, wireless is available in common areas and academic classrooms throughout the campus. Public and department-specific computer classrooms and labs allow students access to the campus network. All students may access the system 24 hours a day. There are no time limits and no fees. It is strongly recommended that all students have a personal computer.

Graduates: From July 1, 2008 to June 30, 2009, 1284 bachelor's degrees were awarded. The most popular majors were elementary education (14%), psychology (8%), and marketing (8%). 84 companies recruited on campus in 2008-2009. In an average class, 45% graduate in 4 years or less, 60% graduate in 5 years or less, and 63% graduate in 6 years or less.

Admissions Contact: Thomas Speakman, Enrollment Services. A campus DVD is available. E-Mail: *admiss@ship.edu* Web: *www.ship.edu*

SLIPPERY ROCK UNIVERSITY OF PENNSYLVANIA   B-2

Slippery Rock, PA 16057

(724) 738-2015
(800) 929-4778; (724) 738-2913

Full-time: 2860 men, 3565 women	Faculty: IIA, av$
Part-time: 225 men, 415 women	Ph.D.s: n/av
Graduate: 235 men, 510 women	Student/Faculty: 18 to 1
Year: semesters, summer session	Tuition: $7600 ($13,500)
Application Deadline: see profile	Room & Board: $8700
Freshman Class: n/av	
SAT: required	ACT: recommended
	LESS COMPETITIVE

Slippery Rock University of Pennsylvania, founded in 1889, is a public institution that is part of the Pennsylvania State System of Higher Education. It offers programs in business, information, social sciences, education, health, environment, science, humanities, and fine and performing arts. There are 4 undergraduate schools and 1 graduate school. Enrollment figures in the above capsule and figures in this profile are approximate. In addition to regional accreditation, The Rock has baccalaureate program accreditation with ACBSP, APTA, CSWE, NASAD, NASM, NCATE, NLN, and NRPA. The library contains 502,974 volumes, 1.5 million microform items, and 22,707 audio/video tapes/CDs/DVDs, and subscribes to 1300 periodicals including electronic. Computerized library services include interlibrary loans, database searching, and Internet access. Special learning facilities include a learning resource center, art gallery, natural history museum, planetarium, radio station, and TV station. The 600-acre campus is in a small town 50 miles north of Pittsburgh. Including any residence halls, there are 60 buildings.

Student Life: 96% of undergraduates are from Pennsylvania. Others are from 35 states, 47 foreign countries, and Canada. 70% are from public schools. 87% are white. The average age of freshmen is 18; all undergraduates, 22. 22% do not continue beyond their first year; 49% remain to graduate.

Housing: 2810 students can be accommodated in college housing, which includes single-sex and coed dorms, on-campus apartments, off-campus apartments, and married student housing. In addition, there are honors houses, language houses, special-interest houses, fraternity houses, and sorority houses. On-campus housing is guaranteed for the freshman year only and is available on a first-come, first-served basis. 62% of students commute. Alcohol is not permitted. All students may keep cars.

Activities: 7% of men belong to 11 national fraternities; 6% of women belong to 9 national sororities. There are 100 groups on campus, including art, band, cheerleading, chess, choir, chorale, chorus, communications, computers, dance, drama, ethnic, film, gay, honors, international, jazz band, literary magazine, marching band, musical theater, newspaper, orchestra, pep band, photography, political, professional, radio and TV, religious, social, social service, student government, symphony, and yearbook. Popular campus events include Spring Weekend.

Sports: There are 12 intercollegiate sports for men and 12 for women, and 7 intramural sports for men and 7 for women. Facilities include a field house, a gym, and a fitness center. The campus stadium seats 10,000, the indoor gym seats 3000, and the largest auditorium/arena seats 1000.

Disabled Students: 80% of the campus is accessible. Facilities include wheelchair ramps, elevators, special parking, specially equipped restrooms, special class scheduling, lowered drinking fountains, lowered telephones, and special housing.

Services: Counseling and information services are available, as is tutoring in about 60 introductory-level general liberal studies courses. There is a reader service for the blind, and remedial math and writing.

Campus Safety and Security: Measures include 24-hour foot and vehicle patrol, self-defense education, and security escort services. There are shuttle buses, emergency telephones, and lighted pathways/sidewalks. The university maintains its own police department, with officers having the same powers as municipal police.

Programs of Study: The Rock confers B.A., B.S., B.F.A., B.Mus., B.Mus.Ed., B.S.B.A., B.S.Ed., and B.S.N. degrees. Master's and doctoral degrees are also awarded. Bachelor's degrees are awarded in BIOLOGICAL SCIENCE (biology/biological science), BUSINESS (accounting, business administration and management, international business management, and marketing/retailing/merchandising), COMMUNICATIONS AND THE ARTS (communications, dance, English, fine arts, French, German, music, and Spanish), COMPUTER AND PHYSICAL SCIENCE (chemistry, computer science, earth science, geology, information sciences and systems, mathematics, and physics), EDUCATION (early childhood education, elementary education, foreign languages education, health education, music education, science education, secondary education, and special education), HEALTH PROFESSIONS (community health work, medical laboratory technology, and nursing), SOCIAL SCIENCE (anthropology, economics, geography, history, parks and recreation management, philosophy, political science/government, psychology, public administration, social science, social work, and sociology). Business, education, and health science areas are the largest.

Required: B.A. students must demonstrate proficiency in a foreign language, and all must complete 42 to 53 credits in a 7-part liberal studies program, including basic competencies, arts, cultural diversity/global perspective, human institutions, science and math, natural experience, and modern age. Specific requirements include public speaking, college writing, algebra, and phys ed. A minimum of 120 credit hours, with at least 30 in the major, is required for graduation.

Special: Study abroad is available in 16 countries. Internships are offered in most majors, and international internships are available in Scotland and England. There is a 3-2 engineering program with Pennsylvania State University. The dual major is an option, and credit is given for military experience. Pass/fail options also are available. There are 26 national honor societies, a freshman honors program, and 33 departmental honors programs.

Faculty/Classroom: 53% of faculty are male; 47% are female. All teach undergraduates. No introductory courses are taught by graduate students. The average class size in an introductory lecture is 33; in a laboratory, 20; and in a regular course, 25.

Requirements: The SAT is required. The ACT is recommended. In addition, students should graduate from an accredited secondary school or have a GED. A total of 16 academic credits is required. The recommended college preparatory program includes 4 years of English and social studies, 3 each of science and math, and 2 of a foreign language. An interview is recommended. AP and CLEP credits are accepted. Important factors in the admissions decision are advanced placement or honors courses, extracurricular activities record, and evidence of special talent.

Procedure: Freshmen are admitted fall, spring, and summer. Entrance exams should be taken in the junior year or fall of the senior year. There are deferred admissions and rolling admissions plans. Check with the school for current application deadlines and fee. Notification is sent on a rolling basis. Applications are accepted on-line. A waiting list is maintained.

Transfer: Applicants should have completed at least 24 credit hours with a GPA of 2.5. The SAT or ACT, as well as an interview, are recommended. 36 of 120 credits required for the bachelor's degree must be completed at The Rock.

Visiting: There are regularly scheduled orientations for prospective students, including a meeting with faculty, an information fair, and a campus tour. There are guides for informal visits; visitors may sit in on classes and stay overnight. To schedule a visit, contact the Admissions Office.

Financial Aid: The Rock is a member of CSS. The FAFSA is required. Check with the school for current deadlines.

International Students: The school actively recruits these students. They must take the TOEFL.

Computers: All students may access the system. The mainframe system is accessible 24 hours a day. Campus terminal and PC labs are generally open more than 100 hours per week. There are no time limits and no fees.

Admissions Contact: Jim Barrett, Director of Admissions. A campus DVD is available. E-Mail: *asktherock@sru.edu* Web: *www.sru.edu*

SUSQUEHANNA UNIVERSITY
D-3
Selinsgrove, PA 17870-1001

(570) 372-4260
(800) 326-9672; (570) 372-2722

Full-time: 910 men, 1050 women	**Faculty:** IIB, av$
Part-time: 10 men, 5 women	**Ph.D.s:** n/av
Graduate: none	**Student/Faculty:** 16 to 1
Year: semesters, summer session	**Tuition:** $34,070
Application Deadline: see profile	**Room & Board:** $9230
Freshman Class: n/av	
SAT or ACT: required	**VERY COMPETITIVE**

Susquehanna University, founded in 1858, is an independent, selective, residential institution affiliated with the Lutheran Church. It offers programs through schools of arts, humanities and communications, natural and social sciences, and business. There are 3 undergraduate schools. Enrollment figures in the above capsule and figures in this profile are approximate. In addition to regional accreditation, SU has baccalaureate program accreditation with AACSB and NASM. The library contains 341,020 volumes, 126,067 microform items, and 8681 audio/video tapes/CDs/DVDs, and subscribes to 16,480 periodicals including electronic. Computerized library services include interlibrary loans, database searching, Internet access, and laptop Internet portals. Special learning facilities include a learning resource center, radio station, multimedia classrooms, video studios, a campuswide telecommunications network, satellite dishes and distribution system for foreign-language broadcasts, video conferencing facility, ecological field station and observatory, child development center, and electronic music lab. The 220-acre campus is in a small town 50 miles north of Harrisburg. Including any residence halls, there are 52 buildings.

Student Life: 57% of undergraduates are from Pennsylvania. Others are from 31 states, 10 foreign countries, and Canada. 82% are from public schools. 91% are white. 46% are Protestant; 35% Catholic; 14% claim no religious affiliation. The average age of freshmen is 18; all undergraduates, 20. 17% do not continue beyond their first year; 80% remain to graduate.

Housing: 1513 students can be accommodated in college housing, which includes coed dorms, on-campus apartments, and off-campus apartments. In addition, there are honors houses, special-interest houses, fraternity houses, sorority houses, and multicultural and international houses. Volunteer project groups may reside in former private homes adjacent to the university with suite-type accommodations. On-campus housing is guaranteed for all 4 years. 77% of students live on campus; of those, 85% remain on campus on weekends. All students may keep cars.

Activities: 20% of men belong to 6 national fraternities; 25% of women belong to 6 national sororities. There are 129 groups on campus, including academic, art, athletic, band, cheerleading, chess, choir, chorale, chorus, computers, dance, drama, environmental, ethnic, film, gay, honors, international, jazz band, literary magazine, musical theater, newspaper, opera, orchestra, outdoors, pep band, photography, political, professional, radio and TV, religious, social, social service, student government, volunteer, women's, and yearbook. Popular campus events include Thanksgiving Dinner, Spring Weekend, and Candlelight Christmas Service.

Sports: There are 11 intercollegiate sports for men and 12 for women, and 10 intramural sports for men and 10 for women. Facilities include a field house with indoor track, tennis, and basketball courts, football stadium and track, soccer, baseball, lacrosse, rugby, and hockey fields, basketball and tennis courts, a swimming pool, racquetball courts, a weight training room, fitness center, and a sauna.

Disabled Students: 80% of the campus is accessible. Facilities include wheelchair ramps, elevators, special parking, specially equipped restrooms, special class scheduling, lowered drinking fountains, and lowered telephones.

Services: Counseling and information services are available, as is tutoring in writing, math, foreign languages, and study skills. Academic departments also provide tutoring.

Campus Safety and Security: Measures include 24-hour foot and vehicle patrol, emergency notification system, self-defense education, and security escort services. There are emergency telephones, lighted pathways/sidewalks, controlled access to dorms/residences, and closed-circuit TV cameras in common exterior areas on campus.

Programs of Study: SU confers B.A., B.S., and B.M. degrees. Associates degrees are also awarded. Bachelor's degrees are awarded in BIOLOGICAL SCIENCE (biochemistry, biology/biological science, and ecology), BUSINESS (accounting and business administration and management), COMMUNICATIONS AND THE ARTS (art history and appreciation, communications, English, French, German, graphic design, music, music performance, Spanish, studio art, and visual and performing arts), COMPUTER AND PHYSICAL SCIENCE (chemistry, computer science, earth science, information sciences and systems, mathematics, and physics), EDUCATION (early childhood education, elementary education, and music education), ENGINEERING AND ENVIRONMENTAL DESIGN (environmental science), SOCIAL SCIENCE (economics, history, international studies, liberal arts/general studies, philosophy, political science/government, psychology, religion, and sociology). Biology, chemistry, and graphic design are the strongest academically. Business, elementary education, and creative writing are the largest.

Required: All students must complete a 4-part core curriculum of about 40 semester hours: personal development, intellectual skills, perspectives on the world, and a capstone course. To fulfill the personal development requirement, first-year students complete a 2-semester-hour course intended to aid students' transition to college life. To fulfill the instinctual skills and perspectives on the world requirements, students complete a variety of courses in foreign language, mathematics/logic, critical thinking/writing, academic skills, history, fine arts, literature, society and the individual, science and technology, and religion/philosophy. The capstone requirement is normally completed in the students senior year. 32 to 48 semester hours are required for most departmental majors. The remainder of a 130-hour minimum required total to graduate is completed as electives. A minimum GPA of 2.0 is required to graduate.

Special: There is cross-registration with Bucknell University. Internships are offered in almost all majors and study abroad is available on 6 continents. The School of Business offers a semester in London for junior business majors. 2-week study seminars in Australia are available, as is a Boston semester, a Washington semester, a United Nations semester, and a work-and-study semester through the Philadelphia Center. The university offers dual and student-designed majors, work-study programs, credit by examination, nondegree study, and pass/fail options. The B.A.-B.S. degree is available in several majors, and there is a 3-2 program in forestry with Duke University, a 2-2 program in allied health with Thomas Jefferson University, and a 3-2 program in dentistry with Temple University. Highly motivated students have the option of earning their baccalaureate degree in 3 years. There are 19 national honor societies, a freshman honors program, and 16 departmental honors programs.

Faculty/Classroom: 60% of faculty are male; 40% are female. All teach and do research. No introductory courses are taught by graduate students. The average class size in an introductory lecture is 22; in a laboratory, 14; and in a regular course, 18.

Requirements: The SAT or ACT is required. The ACT Optional Writing test is also required. Students with a cumulative class rank in the top 20% in a strong college preparatory program have the option of submitting either the SAT, ACT, or 2 graded writing samples. Students should be graduates of an accredited high school. Preparation should include 4 years of English and math, 3 to 4 years of science, and 2 to 3 years each of social studies and foreign language. In addition, 1 unit of art or music is recommended. An essay is required, as are, for relevant fields, a music audition or writing portfolio. An interview is strongly recommended. A GPA of 3.0 is required. AP and CLEP credits are accepted. Important factors in the admissions decision are advanced placement or honors courses, evidence of special talent, and recommendations by school officials.

Procedure: Freshmen are admitted fall and spring. Entrance exams should be taken by January of the senior year. There are early decision, deferred admissions and rolling admissions plans. Early decision applications should be filed by November 15; check with the school for current application deadlines. The application fee is $35. Notification of early decision is sent December 1. Applications are accepted on-line. 68 applicants were on a recent waiting list, 14 were accepted.

Transfer: 30 transfer students enrolled in a recent year. Applicants must submit high school and college transcripts, test scores, and a recommendation from a dean. An interview is strongly recommended. A music audition or writing portfolio is required for relevant fields. 65 of 130 credits required for the bachelor's degree must be completed at SU.

Visiting: There are regularly scheduled orientations for prospective students, including special visiting days for prospective students and their parents held in the spring and fall, which consist of sessions with faculty, admissions, financial aid, and placement staff and tours of the campus. There are guides for informal visits; visitors may sit in on classes and stay overnight. To schedule a visit, contact the Office of Admissions.

Financial Aid: In a recent year, 96% of all full-time freshmen and 96% of continuing full-time students received some form of financial aid. 66% of all full-time freshmen and 63% of continuing full-time students received need-based aid. 51% of undergraduate students work part-time. Average annual earnings from campus work are $839. SU is a member of CSS. The CSS/Profile, FAFSA, and prior year federal tax return for parents and students are required. Check with the school for current deadlines.

International Students: There were 15 international students enrolled in a recent year. The school actively recruits these students. They must take the TOEFL.

Computers: Wireless access is available. All students from their resident hall rooms have access to a high-speed broadband network connection that allows unrestricted access to the Internet. Students also have access to wireless Internet throughout most of the nonresidential campus buildings. More than 300 public computer labs and kiosks are available to students around the campus. Off-campus students have access to the same wireless and labs. All students may access the system 24 hours a day. There are no time limits and no fees. It is strongly recommended that all students have a personal computer.

Graduates: In a recent year, 441 bachelor's degrees were awarded. The most popular majors were business/marketing (25%), communications (14%), and education (12%). 82 companies recruited on campus in a recent year. In an average class, 79% graduate in 4 years or less, 81% graduate in 5 years or less, and 82% graduate in 6 years or less. Of a recent graduating class, 24% were enrolled in graduate school within 6 months of graduation, and 72% were employed.

Admissions Contact: Chris Markle, Director of Admissions. E-Mail: suadmiss@susqu.edu Web: www.susqu.edu

SWARTHMORE COLLEGE   F-4
Swarthmore, PA 19081-1397

(610) 328-8300
(800) 667-3110; (610) 328-8580

Full-time: 727 men, 783 women	**Faculty:** 175; IIB, ++$
Part-time: 3 men, 12 women	**Ph.D.s:** 100%
Graduate: none	**Student/Faculty:** 9 to 1
Year: semesters	**Tuition:** $37,860
Application Deadline: January 2	**Room & Board:** $11,740
Freshman Class: 5575 applied, 969 accepted, 394 enrolled	
SAT CR/M/W: 720/720/720	**ACT:** 32 **MOST COMPETITIVE**

Swarthmore College, established in 1864, is a private, nonprofit institution offering undergraduate courses in liberal arts and engineering. In addition to regional accreditation, Swarthmore has baccalaureate program accreditation with ABET. The 7 libraries contain 842,722 volumes, 142,530 microform items, and 28,048 audio/video tapes/CDs/DVDs, and subscribe to 16,142 periodicals including electronic. Computerized library services include interlibrary loans, database searching, Internet access, and laptop Internet portals. Special learning facilities include an art gallery, a radio station, a LEED-certified integrated science center with an observatory and robotics and solar energy labs, specialty libraries for the study of classical Jewish texts, the Friends Historical Library and Peace Collection, and the Lang Center for Civic and Social Responsibility. The 399-acre campus is in a suburban area 11 miles southwest of Philadelphia, approximately 20 minutes by commuter rail. Including any residence halls, there are 56 buildings.

Student Life: 87% of undergraduates are from out of state, mostly the Middle Atlantic. Students are from 50 states, 34 foreign countries, and Canada. 59% are from public schools. 45% are white; 16% Asian American; 11% Hispanic. The average age of freshmen is 18; all undergraduates, 20. 2% do not continue beyond their first year; 93% remain to graduate.

Housing: 1366 students can be accommodated in college housing, which includes single-sex and coed dorms. On-campus housing is guaranteed for all 4 years. 95% of students live on campus. Upperclassmen may keep cars.

Activities: 12% of men belong to 1 local and 1 national fraternity. There are no sororities. There are 100 groups on campus, including a cappella, art, band, chess, choir, chorus, club sports, computers, dance, debate, drama, drama board, environmental, ethnic, film, gay, honors, international, jazz band, literary magazine, musical theater, newspaper, orchestra, photography, political, radio and TV, religious, social, social service, student government, and yearbook. Popular campus events include Crum Regatta, McCabe Mile race, and Midnight Breakfast before finals.

Sports: There are 10 intercollegiate sports for men and 12 for women, and 7 intramural sports for men and 7 for women. Facilities include a lighted stadium, a 400-meter durometer track, a synthetic grass playing field, a fitness center and indoor tennis courts, a fitness center with aerobic and Medx equipment, a professionally staffed sports medicine facility with 3 full-time trainers, and wooded hiking trails.

Disabled Students: 85% of the campus is accessible. Facilities include wheelchair ramps, elevators, special parking, specially equipped restrooms, special class scheduling, lowered drinking fountains, lowered telephones, and special housing.

Services: Counseling and information services are available, as is tutoring in most subjects. There is a reader service for the blind. The campus writing center, Student Academic Mentors, and Science and Math Associates provide academic support to students.

Campus Safety and Security: Measures include 24-hour foot and vehicle patrol, emergency notification system, and security escort services. There are shuttle buses, emergency telephones, and lighted pathways/sidewalks.

Programs of Study: Swarthmore confers B.A. and B.S. degrees. Bachelor's degrees are awarded in BIOLOGICAL SCIENCE (biochemistry and biology/biological science), COMMUNICATIONS AND THE ARTS (art, art history and appreciation, Chinese, classics, comparative literature, dance, dramatic arts, English literature, film arts, French, German, Greek, Japanese, Latin, linguistics, literature, music, Russian, and Spanish), COMPUTER AND PHYSICAL SCIENCE (astronomy, astrophysics, chemical physics, chemistry, computer science, mathematics, and physics), EDUCATION (education), ENGINEERING AND ENVIRONMENTAL DESIGN (engineering), SOCIAL SCIENCE (anthropology, Asian/Oriental studies, classical/ancient civilization, economics, gender studies, German area studies, history, medieval studies, philosophy, political science/government, psychobiology, psychology, religion, and sociology). Economics, biology, and political science are the largest.

Required: To graduate, students must complete 3 courses in each of 3 divisions consisting of humanities, natural sciences and engineering, and social sciences. Concurrent with distribution and/or major requirements, there is a requirement of 3 writing courses and a science lab. Students must demonstrate foreign language competency and fulfill a phys ed requirement including a swimming test. Each major has a culminating experience, which may be a thesis, project, or comprehensive exam.

Special: Students may cross-register with Haverford and Bryn Mawr Colleges and the University of Pennsylvania. They may study abroad in their country of choice. Dual and student-designed majors and a B.A.-B.S. degree in engineering are available. Swarthmore's honors program features small groups of students working closely with faculty and peers, with an emphasis on independent learning and a final exam by outside scholars. There are 3 national honor societies, including Phi Beta Kappa, and 24 departmental honors programs.

Faculty/Classroom: 59% of faculty are male; 41% are female. All teach and do research. The average class size in an introductory lecture is 22; in a laboratory, 12; and in a regular course, 15.

Admissions: 17% of the 2009-2010 applicants were accepted. The SAT scores for the 2009-2010 freshman class were: Critical Reading--1% below 500, 7% between 500 and 599, 25% between 600 and 700, and 67% above 700; Math--5% between 500 and 599, 33% between 600 and 700, and 61% above 700; Writing--4% between 500 and 599, 30% between 600 and 700, and 65% above 700. The ACT scores were 2% between 21 and 23, 7% between 24 and 26, 10% between 27 and 28, and 81% above 28. 97% of the current freshmen were in the top fifth of their class; 100% were in the top two fifths. 46 freshmen graduated first in their class.

Requirements: Applicants are required to submit scores for either the SAT and any 2 SAT Subject tests, the ACT with Writing, or the SAT and the ACT. Swarthmore does not require a specific high school curriculum but recommends the inclusion of 4 years of English, 3 years each of math, the sciences, and history and social studies, the study of 1 or 2 foreign languages, and course work in art and music. 2 essays are required, and interviews are recommended. AP credits are accepted.

Procedure: Freshmen are admitted fall. Entrance exams should be taken in spring of the junior year or fall of the senior year. There are early decison and deferred admissions plans. Early decision applications should be filed by November 15; regular applications, by January 2 for fall entry. The fall 2009 application fee was $60. Notification of early decision is sent December 15; regular decision, April 1. Applications are accepted on-line. A waiting list is maintained.

Transfer: 25 transfer students enrolled in 2008-2009. Applicants for transfer must present both secondary and college transcripts and an official statement of good standing from the tertiary institution. 16 of 32 credits required for the bachelor's degree must be completed at Swarthmore.

Visiting: There are regularly scheduled orientations for prospective students, including tours, information sessions, and interviews. There are guides for informal visits, and visitors may sit in on classes and stay overnight. To schedule a visit, contact the Admissions Office.

Financial Aid: In 2009-2010, 54% of all full-time freshmen and 49% of continuing full-time students received some form of financial aid, including need-based aid. The average freshman award was $36,008. 81% of undergraduate students work part-time. Average annual earnings

from campus work are $1483. Swarthmore is a member of CSS. The CSS/Profile, FAFSA, the state aid form, the college's own financial statement, tax returns, W-2 statements, and year-end paycheck stubs are required. The deadline for filing freshman financial aid applications for fall entry is February 15.

International Students: There are 99 international students enrolled. The school actively recruits these students. They must submit scores for either the SAT and any 2 SAT Subject tests, the ACT with Writing, or the SAT and ACT.

Computers: There are more than 250 PCs and Macs available for student use in libraries, dorms, and classrooms. Course materials and academic software are available on-line for many courses. The Media Center may be used for audio, video, and graphics projects, and wireless networking is available in all campus buildings and most outdoor spaces. All students may access the system. There are no time limits and no fees.

Graduates: From July 1, 2008 to June 30, 2009, 394 bachelor's degrees were awarded. The most popular majors were economics (14%), biology (9%), and political science (8%). 63 companies recruited on campus in 2008-2009. In an average class, 1% graduate in 3 years or less, 91% graduate in 4 years or less, 92% graduate in 5 years or less, and 93% graduate in 6 years or less.

Admissions Contact: James L. Bock, Dean of Admissions and Financial Aid. A campus DVD is available.
E-mail: *admissions@swarthmore.edu* Web: *www.swarthmore.edu*

TEMPLE UNIVERSITY   F-3

Philadelphia, PA 19122-1803   (215) 204-8556; (888) 340-2222

Full-time: 11,301 men, 12,811 women	**Faculty:** 1278; I, -$
Part-time: 1378 men, 1555 women	**Ph.D.s:** 76%
Graduate: 4270 men, 5190 women	**Student/Faculty:** 19 to 1
Year: semesters, summer session	**Tuition:** $11,764 ($21,044)
Application Deadline: March 1	**Room & Board:** $9198
Freshman Class: 23,584 applied, 15,626 accepted, 7104 enrolled	
SAT CR/M/W: 549/561/549	**ACT:** 22 **VERY COMPETITIVE**

Temple University, founded in 1888, is part of the Commonwealth System of Higher Education in Pennsylvania. It offers programs in the liberal arts and science and technology, health professions, education, engineering, art, business and management, communications and theater, architecture, landscape architecture and horticulture, music and dance, and social administration. Temple has 6 other campuses, including 1 in Rome and 1 in Tokyo. There are 17 undergraduate schools and 16 graduate schools. In addition to regional accreditation, Temple has baccalaureate program accreditation with AACSB, ABET, ACEJMC, ACPE, APTA, CAHEA, CAHIM, CAHME, CEPH, CSWE, NAAB, NASAD, NASM, NASSM, NATA, NRPA, and TEAC. The 11 libraries contain 3.2 million volumes, 3.3 million microform items, and 34,438 audio/video tapes/CDs/DVDs, and subscribe to 60,586 periodicals including electronic. Computerized library services include interlibrary loans, database searching, Internet access, and laptop Internet portals. Special learning facilities include a learning resource center, art gallery, planetarium, radio station, TV station, dance lab theater, media learning center for the study of critical languages, and multimedia lab for teacher education in music. The 330-acre campus is in an urban area approximately 1.5 miles from downtown Philadelphia. Including any residence halls, there are 142 buildings.

Student Life: 75% of undergraduates are from Pennsylvania. Others are from 46 states, 100 foreign countries, and Canada. 76% are from public schools. 58% are white; 16% African American. The average age of freshmen is 18; all undergraduates, 21. 12% do not continue beyond their first year; 67% remain to graduate.

Housing: 5106 students can be accommodated in college housing, which includes coed dorms, on-campus apartments, and off-campus apartments. In addition, there are honors houses, special-interest houses, and living-learning communities. On-campus housing is guaranteed for the freshman year only. 81% of students commute. Alcohol is not permitted. All students may keep cars.

Activities: 4% of men belong to 21 local fraternities; 3% of women belong to 14 local sororities. There are 270 groups on campus, including art, band, cheerleading, chess, choir, chorus, computers, dance, drama, drill team, ethnic, film, honors, international, jazz band, literary magazine, marching band, musical theater, newspaper, orchestra, pep band, photography, political, professional, radio and TV, religious, social, social service, and student government. Popular campus events include Film Series at the Reel, Free Food and Fun Fridays, and Spring Fling.

Sports: There are 11 intercollegiate sports for men and 13 for women, and 5 intramural sports for men and 3 for women. 68% of students participate. Facilities include fitness areas with free weight and cardiovascular equipment, circuit training area, stretch abs/back area, tread wall, 4 racquetball courts, a group fitness room, martial arts/aerobic room, indoor walking/jogging track, and 4 indoor multipurpose courts. There are also 2 large playing fields, a 6-lane, 1/4 mile track with synthetic surface, sand volleyball court, outdoor basketball, volleyball, and tennis courts, outdoor in-line skating, and 2 Olympic-size swimming pools.

Procedure: Freshmen are admitted fall and spring. Entrance exams should be taken by November of the senior year. There are early admissions and deferred admissions plans. Early decision applications should be filed by November 1 and regular applications by January 15 for fall entry and November 1 for spring entry, along with a $55 fee. Notifications are sent March 15. Applications are accepted on-line. 1173 applicants were on a recent waiting list, 146 were accepted.

Transfer: 606 transfer students enrolled in 2008-2009. Successful transfer students generally have a GPA of 2.75 to 3.0 in credited courses and meet the same entrance requirements as freshmen. Considerations include the college and high school records, the major indicated, and availability of space at UVM. 30 of 122 credits required for the bachelor's degree must be completed at UVM.

Visiting: There are regularly scheduled orientations for prospective students, consisting of information sessions and tours most weekdays and many Saturdays year round. Visitors may sit in on classes. To schedule a visit, contact the Admissions Office at 802-656-3370.

Financial Aid: In a recent year, 83% of all full-time freshmen and 73% of continuing full-time students received some form of financial aid. 57% of all full-time freshmen and 55% of continuing full-time students received need-based aid. The average freshman award was $18,611. Need-based scholarships or need-based grants averaged $11,723 ($34,100 maximum); need-based self-help aid (loans and jobs) averaged $6,269 ($14,325 maximum); non-need-based athletic scholarships averaged $19,602 (maximum $30,109); other non-need-based awards and non-need-based scholarships averaged $3,652 ($31,107 maximum). The average financial indebtedness of the 2009 graduate was $25,079. The FAFSA is required. Check with the school for current application deadlines.

International Students: There were 47 international students enrolled in a recent year. They must take the TOEFL or ELPT. They must also take the SAT or ACT.

Computers: Wireless access is available. All students may access the system at any time. There are no time limits and no fees. Students enrolled in business majors must have a personal computer. A IBM, Mac, or Dell is recommended.

Graduates: From July 1, 2008 to June 30, 2009, 2215 bachelor's degrees were awarded. The most popular majors were business (10%), psychology (8%), and political science (7%). 170 companies recruited on campus in 2008-2009. In an average class, 55% graduate in 4 years or less, 69% graduate in 5 years or less, and 71% graduate in 6 years or less. Of the 2008 graduating class, 16% were enrolled in graduate school within 6 months of graduation, and 70% were employed.

Admissions Contact: Dr. Beth A. Wiser, Director of Admission. E-Mail: admissions@uvm.edu Web: www.uvm.edu

VERMONT STATE COLLEGES

The Vermont State Colleges, established in 1962, is a public system in Vermont. It is governed by a board of trustees, whose chief administrator is chancellor. The primary goal of the system is teaching. The main priorities are to insure that all Vermonters have access to higher education and continuous learning opportunities, and to provide educational programs that are affordable, high quality, student centered and accessible to maintain the quality of cultural, social, and economic life in Vermont. The total enrollment in a recent year of all 5 campuses was 9040; there were 280 faculty members. Altogether there are 60 baccalaureate, and 5 master's programs offered in the Vermont State Colleges. Profiles of the 4-year campuses are included in this section.

VERMONT TECHNICAL COLLEGE
Randolph Center, VT 05061   **(802) 728-1000**

Full-time: 655 men, 380 women	Faculty: III, --$
Part-time: 165 men, 160 women	Ph.D.s: 54%
Graduate: none	Student/Faculty: n/av
Year: semesters	Tuition: $12,000 ($21,000)
Application Deadline: open	Room & Board: $7800
Freshman Class: n/av	
SAT or ACT: required	**COMPETITIVE**

Vermont Technical College, founded in 1910, is one of the 5 institutions in the Vermont State Colleges System and is the state's only public technical college. Figures in the above capsule and this profile are approximate. In addition to regional accreditation, VTC has baccalaureate program accreditation with ABET. The library contains 59,480 volumes, 5920 microform items, and 4122 audio/video tapes/CDs/DVDs, and subscribes to 348 periodicals including electronic. Computerized library services include interlibrary loans, database searching, and Internet access. Special learning facilities include a learning resource center, radio station, and Vermont Interactive Television. The 544-acre campus is in a rural area Randolph Center. Including any residence halls, there are 19 buildings.

Student Life: 60% of undergraduates are from Vermont. Others are from 12 states and 2 foreign countries. 90% are from public schools.

94% are white. The average age of freshmen is 25; all undergraduates, 26. 25% do not continue beyond their first year; 55% remain to graduate.

Housing: 550 students can be accommodated in college housing, which includes single-sex and coed dorms. On-campus housing is guaranteed for all 4 years. 60% of students commute. All students may keep cars.

Activities: There are no fraternities or sororities. Groups on campus include chess, computers, drama, ethnic, gay, international, photography, professional, radio and TV, religious, social, social service, and student government. Popular campus events include Harvest Days, Winter Carnival, and Spring Fling.

Sports: There are 6 intercollegiate sports for men and 5 for women, and 21 intramural sports for men and 21 for women. Facilities include a double-court gym, 2 racquetball courts, a 6-lane 25-yard pool, a fitness center, outdoor soccer, baseball, and softball fields, trails for cross-country skiing, and a downhill ski run.

Disabled Students: All of the campus is accessible. Facilities include wheelchair ramps, elevators, special parking, specially equipped rest rooms, special class scheduling, lowered drinking fountains, and lowered telephones.

Services: Counseling and information services are available, as is tutoring in every subject.

Campus Safety and Security: Measures include 24-hour foot and vehicle patrol, self-defense education, and security escort services. There are emergency telephones and lighted pathways/sidewalks.

Programs of Study: VTC confers B.S. degrees. Associates degrees are also awarded. Bachelor's degrees are awarded in COMPUTER AND PHYSICAL SCIENCE (information sciences and systems and software engineering), EDUCATION (business education), ENGINEERING AND ENVIRONMENTAL DESIGN (architectural engineering, computer engineering, and electromechanical technology). Electromechanical engineering technology are the strongest academically. Architectural engineering technology and business are the largest.

Required: To graduate, students must complete 120 to 130 credit hours with a minimum GPA of 2.0. Required courses include those in English, technical communications, math, and computer.

Special: Cross-registration, internships, work-study programs, and dual majors are offered. There are 2 national honor societies, a freshman honors program, and 2 departmental honors programs.

Faculty/Classroom: 58% of faculty are male; 42% are female. All teach undergraduates. The average class size in an introductory lecture is 28; in a laboratory, 16; and in a regular course, 32.

Requirements: The SAT or ACT is required. AP and CLEP credits are accepted.

Procedure: Freshmen are admitted fall and spring. There is a rolling admissions plan. Application deadlines are open. The application fee is $38. Applications are accepted on-line. A waiting list is maintained.

Transfer: 251 transfer students enrolled in a recent year. Transcripts are required from all colleges attended. 50 of 120 credits required for the bachelor's degree must be completed at VTC.

Visiting: There are regularly scheduled orientations for prospective students. There are guides for informal visits, and visitors may sit in on classes and stay overnight. To schedule a visit, contact Admissions.

Financial Aid: The FAFSA is required. Check with the school for current application deadlines.

International Students: They must take the TOEFL. They must also take the SAT or ACT and the college's own entrance exam.

Computers: All students may access the system. There are no time limits and no fees. It is strongly recommended that all students have a personal computer.

Admissions Contact: Office of Admissions.
E-mail: admissions@vtc.edu Web: www.vtc.edu

WOODBURY INSTITUTE OF CHAMPLAIN COLLEGE IN BURLINGTON
Woodbury College
Montpelier, VT 05602   **(802) 229-0516**
(800) 639-6039; (802) 229-2141

Full-time: 15 men, 80 women	Faculty: n/av
Part-time: 10 men, 30 women	Ph.D.s: 75%
Graduate: 5 men, 10 women	Student/Faculty: n/av
Year: semesters	Tuition: $27,200
Application Deadline: open	
Freshman Class: n/av	**LESS COMPETITIVE**

Woodbury Institute of Champlain College, formerly Woodbury College, was established in 1975 and offers adult-focused, career-oriented programs in legal and paralegal studies, mediation/conflict management, and prevention and community development. Figures in the above capsule and this profile are approximate. There is 1 undergraduate school. The library contains 17,000 volumes and subscribes to 20,000 periodicals including electronic. Computerized library services include interlibrary loans and database searching. The 8-acre campus is in a small town 1 1/2 miles north of the Center of Montpelier and the Vermont state government district. There is 1 building.

Student Life: 97% of undergraduates are from Vermont. Others are from 3 states and 1 foreign country. 96% are white. The average age of freshmen is 35; all undergraduates, 35. 15% do not continue beyond their first year; 85% remain to graduate.

Housing: College-sponsored housing consists of dorms and on-campus apartments.

Activities: There are no fraternities or sororities. Popular campus events include town meetings and community luncheons.

Sports: There is no sports program at Woodbury.

Disabled Students: Facilities include wheelchair ramps, elevators, special parking, and specially equipped rest rooms.

Services: Counseling and information services are available, as is tutoring in most subjects.

Programs of Study: Woodbury confers B.S. degrees. Associate degrees are also awarded. Bachelor's degrees are awarded in SOCIAL SCIENCE (community services, human services, interdisciplinary studies, law, and paralegal studies). Paralegal and mediation and applied conflict studies are the largest.

Required: Each student must demonstrate satisfactory competency in core courses and program requirements. A total of 120 credit hours must be completed, with 48 in the major.

Special: Internships are required for all undergraduate students. A student-designed major in interdisciplinary studies is possible. Certificate programs are offered.

Faculty/Classroom: 39% of faculty are male; 61% are female. All teach undergraduates. No introductory courses are taught by graduate students. The average class size in an introductory lecture is 12; in a laboratory, 12; and in a regular course, 12.

Requirements: Students must submit a completed application, a high school diploma or GED, and an essay. An interview is optional. AP and CLEP credits are accepted. Important factors in the admissions decision are personality/intangible qualities, recommendations by alumni, and recommendations by school officials.

Procedure: Freshmen are admitted to all sessions. There are deferred admissions and rolling admissions plans. Application deadlines are open. The fall 2009 application fee was $30. Notification is sent on a rolling basis. Applications are accepted on-line.

Transfer: Requirements are the same as for incoming freshmen, including high school transcripts, and an essay. 45 of 120 credits required for the bachelor's degree must be completed at Woodbury.

Visiting: There are regularly scheduled orientations for prospective students, including an introductory meeting, a school philosophy presentation, a financial aid discussion, a free class, a meal, and a Q&A session. There are guides for informal visits and visitors may stay overnight. To schedule a visit, contact Admissions.

Financial Aid: In a recent year, 83% of all full-time freshmen and 87% of continuing full-time students received some form of financial aid. 75% of all full-time freshmen and 81% of continuing full-time students received need-based aid. The average freshman award was $10,110. The FAFSA and the college's own financial statement are required. Check with the school for current application deadlines.

Computers: All students may access the system.

Admissions Contact: Admissions Director. E-Mail: *admission@champlain.edu* Web: *www.champlain.edu*

INDEX